P9-AOU-446
DA912
.N48

University of Winnipeg, 515 Portage Ave., Winnipeg, MB. R3B 2E9 Canada

A NEW HISTORY OF IRELAND

UNDER THE AUSPICES OF THE
ROYAL IRISH ACADEMY

III

EARLY MODERN IRELAND
1534–1691

A NEW HISTORY OF IRELAND

UNDER THE AUSPICES OF THE ROYAL IRISH ACADEMY

Vol. I	Prehistoric and early medieval Ireland
Vol. II	Medieval Ireland (1169–1534)
Vol. III	Early modern Ireland (1534–1691)
Vol. IV	Eighteenth-century Ireland (1691–1800)
Vol. V	Ireland under the union, I (1801–70)
Vol. VI	Ireland under the union, II (1870–1921)
Vol. VII	Ireland since 1921
Vol. VIII	Chronology, maps, and other reference matter
Vol. IX	General bibliography, illustrations, and other reference matter

A NEW HISTORY OF IRELAND

EDITED BY

T. W. MOODY F. X. MARTIN
F. J. BYRNE

III

EARLY MODERN IRELAND
1534–1691

OXFORD
AT THE CLARENDON PRESS

Oxford University Press, Walton Street, Oxford OX2 6DP

OXFORD LONDON GLASGOW
NEW YORK TORONTO MELBOURNE WELLINGTON
IBADAN NAIROBI DAR ES SALAAM LUSAKA CAPE TOWN
KUALA LUMPUR SINGAPORE JAKARTA HONG KONG TOKYO
DELHI BOMBAY CALCUTTA MADRAS KARACHI

ISBN 0 19 821739 0

© *Oxford University Press 1976*
on behalf of the editors and contributors

First published 1976
Reprinted, with corrections 1978

All rights reserved. No part of this publication may be reproduced, stored in a retrieval system, or transmitted, in any form or by any means, electronic, mechanical, photocopying, recording, or otherwise, without the prior permission of Oxford University Press

Printed in Great Britain
at the University Press, Oxford
by Vivian Ridler
Printer to the University

PREFACE

THIS is the first volume to be published of a cooperative history of Ireland in nine volumes, under the auspices of the Royal Irish Academy. The idea of such a history was initiated in 1962, a plan was drawn up in 1968, and the work is being carried out in accordance with that plan as expanded and amended. A full account of the project as a whole will appear in volume I.

That volume III is appearing first is due to factors beyond our control: several scholars who originally engaged to write important sections of volumes I and II withdrew—some of them very late in the day—and had to be replaced. Progress has also been retarded by illness and overwork. But we are confident that volumes I and II will be ready for the printer before the end of 1976; volumes IV–VII should therefore appear in their proper order. Of the two reference volumes (VIII and IX) the first is due to be published in 1977; it includes a chronology, maps, and succession lists, referable to the entire history. The second reference volume will appear last; some of its components will be addenda and corrigenda that can be compiled only when all the rest of the history is in print. These two volumes will together form a companion to the whole work.

This history, though the work of many scholars, has been conceived as a unity, based on a detailed plan for the nine volumes as a whole. Each contributor has had complete freedom to treat in his own way the part of the history assigned to him, while each has worked within an agreed general framework and according to a specification and conditions accepted by all. Though each volume has been designed to cover an identifiable period of Irish history, the work is not a series of isolated volumes but a harvesting of the best contemporary scholarship available for each period up to the end of 1974. Each volume, whatever its own date of publication, will broadly reflect the stage of advance in historical research attained by that date. But in the years over which the production of our nine volumes will necessarily be spread, new research may call for revision of statements written by contributors or radically affect assessments they have made. In such cases we will, wherever possible, facilitate contributors in taking such new work into account.

In accordance with the specification for this history, the text, in so far as it deals with well-established facts and accepted views, is not footnoted. But sources and authorities are cited where a contributor is drawing upon recent or unpublished research, of his own or of other scholars, or where he is writing about matters that are the subject of controversy among scholars, or generally where he considers that there is particular reason for referring to the source or the historiography of a statement in the text. References are given for all quoted passages.

In all such matters as the use of capitals, punctuation, italics, dates, numerals, quotations, and footnote references, our standard practice is that prescribed in *Irish Historical Studies; rules for contributors* (2nd revised edition, by T. W. Moody, 1975). On points of English usage we have been guided by *The complete plain words* of Sir Ernest Gowers (revised edition, by Sir Bruce Fraser, 1973). On the spelling of English proper names we have used as our standard of reference the *Dictionary of national biography*.

The spelling of Irish proper names presents a special problem. For place-names we follow the anglicised spelling of the current ordnance survey maps (except that we use Connacht, not Connaught). For personal and family names two modes of spelling, one Gaelic Irish, the other anglicised Irish, were in use during the period covered by this volume. To have prescribed either exclusively would have been insensitive and unhistorical. Instead we left it to contributors to use either mode, so long as they did so consistently for the same persons. Where a contributor uses the Irish form of a name well known in English, but virtually unrecognisable to readers without a knowledge of Irish (for example Séathrun Céitinn, for Geoffrey Keating), we have added the English form in brackets. We have also accepted certain well-established hybrid forms, such as Turlough Luineach O'Neill. We have generally followed the spelling of Irish and anglicised forms of names in Dr Edward MacLysaght's *A guide to Irish surnames* (2nd edition, Dublin, 1965).

For the indexing of Irish names beginning with O, Mac, Mc, Ní, Nic, we carefully considered the advantages of entering them according to the basic element in the name and not according to the prefix (Mac Aonghusa under A, O'Brien under B, Nic Chárthaigh under C). We decided against this, in some ways attractive, plan because, owing to the coexistence of English and Irish forms of the same names, it would create practical difficulties for users of the index quite out of proportion to its logical advantages (for example Magennis would be entered under M, but the same name in its Irish form, Mac Aonghusa, under A; similarly with Maguire under M, and Mag Uidhir under U). We have used the English forms of all names as primary entries, but have included cross-references from their Irish forms; we intend to publish in volume IX a concordance of proper names in Irish and in English.

The maps included in this volume are related immediately to particular points in the text, as distinct from maps in volume VIII that relate to the period of the present volume but form part of a series designed for general reference. The illustrations are intended not for embellishment but to serve as documentary additions to the text.

The bibliography, on a standard plan for the whole history, is intended both as a conspectus of the materials on which this volume is based, and also as a guide to further study of early modern Ireland. Sources and works relating to more than two volumes of this history are not as a rule included in the bibliographies to individual volumes, but will be included in the general bibliography to be published in volume IX.

This history is planned to integrate all major aspects of the life of society in Ireland with the general course of Irish history, in so far as existing scholarship permits. It is therefore necessary to point out that the treatment of certain topics for the period covered by the present volume is included in specialist chapters in other volumes: visual arts to 1603 by Edwin Rae in volume II, and from 1603 by Anne Crookshank in volume IV; music from the early seventeenth century by Brian Boydell, and legal developments from 1603 by Geoffrey Hand in volume IV. The economic history of Ireland before 1660 is a largely unworked field, but we have been able to include a survey of the economy from 1600 to 1660, and economic trends of the sixteenth century are indicated in earlier chapters, especially I and V.

In launching this enterprise, which we think we can without immodesty describe as unprecedented in the historiography of Ireland, we are happy to acknowledge the indispensable help we have received since 1968 from the government of Ireland, without whose annual grant, given without any restrictions whatever, our project could not have been carried into effect. We recall with gratitude the friendly and understanding relations we have had with successive ministers for education—Dr Patrick Hillery, Mr George Colley, the late Donough O'Malley, and Messrs Brian Lenihan, Patrick Faulkner, and Richard Burke. We are much indebted to Dr John Mulcahy of New York, for a munificent donation, associated with the names of his parents, the late Patrick Mulcahy, formerly town clerk of Dungarvan, and his wife Agnes, which enabled us to expand the range of this work by employing young scholars to carry out research that we could not otherwise have had available. We thank the many good friends of our undertaking who in various ways have supported us from its early stages, especially Dr C. S. Andrews and Dr Tarlach Ó Raifeartaigh. We are grateful also to the Royal Irish Academy, under whose auspices our project has flourished, and to past and present officers of that venerable body, especially the late Vincent Barry, Rev. Professor J. R. McConnell, Dr Liam O'Sullivan, Dr Joseph Raftery, Professor David Greene, Dr Thomas Walsh, and Professor Patrick Lynch.

Among many libraries and repositories of manuscripts to which we are indebted we wish specially to record our appreciation of the kindness and help we have received from the staffs of the National Library of Ireland and of the library of Trinity College, Dublin. Our special thanks are due to the library, administrative, and secretarial staff of the Royal Irish Academy. We have pleasure in acknowledging the invaluable services of Liam O'Sullivan, our first secretary (1968–73), and of his successor, Richard Hawkins, our present secretary; and also the distinguished work of our devoted typist, Margaret Dominica Morgan. From Gerald Simms and Margaret Moody we have received inestimable help in the reading and checking of all the proofs.

T. W. Moody
F. X. Martin
F. J. Byrne

October 1975

Since this preface was written we have to record the death, on 27 November 1975, of one of our contributors, Gerard Anthony Hayes-McCoy, whom, both as a man and a scholar, we held in great respect and affection, and whose early death we mourn.

T. W. M.
F. X. M.
F. J. B.

December 1975

CONTENTS

VI THE IRISH ECONOMY, 1600–60 by Aidan Clarke

VII PACIFICATION, PLANTATION, AND THE CATHOLIC QUESTION, 1603–23 by Aidan Clarke, with R. Dudley Edwards

XIX THE WAR OF THE TWO KINGS, 1685–91

by J. G. Simms

XX THE IRISH LANGUAGE IN THE EARLY MODERN PERIOD

by Brian Ó Cuív

CONTRIBUTORS

John Harwood Andrews	M.A. (Dubl., Cantab.), M. Litt. (Dubl.), Ph.D. (Lond.); fellow, and lecturer in geography, Trinity College, Dublin
Alan Joseph Bliss	B.A. (Lond.), M.A., B. Litt. (Oxon.); M.R.I.A.; professor of Old and Middle English, University College, Dublin
Robin Alan Butlin	B.A., M.A. (Liv.); senior lecturer in geography, Queen Mary College, University of London
Aidan Clarke	M.A., Ph.D. (Dubl.); fellow, and lecturer in modern history, Trinity College, Dublin
Patrick Joseph Corish	M.A. (N.U.I.), D.D. (Maynooth); M.R.I.A.; professor of modern history, St Patrick's College, Maynooth
Louis Michael Cullen	M.A. (N.U.I.), Ph.D. (Lond.); fellow, and associate professor of modern history, Trinity College, Dublin
Michael Dolley	B.A. (Lond.); F.S.A.; F.R. Hist. Soc.; M.R.I.A.; professor of historical numismatics, Queen's University, Belfast
Robert Dudley Edwards	M.A., D. Litt. (N.U.I.). Ph.D. (Lond.); F.R. Hist. Soc.; M.R.I.A.; professor of modern Irish history, University College, Dublin
Gerard Anthony Hayes-McCoy	M.A., Ph.D. (Edin.), D. Litt. (N.U.I.), B. Comm., H. Dip. Ed.; M.R.I.A.; professor of history, University College, Galway (1958–75; died 27 Nov. 1975)
Benignus Millett	B.A. (N.U.I.), Dr Hist. Eccles. (Pontifical Gregorian University); superior of Franciscan House of Studies, Killiney, County Dublin
Theodore William Moody	B.A. (Q.U.B.), M.A. (Dubl.), Ph.D. (Lond.), Hon. D. Lit. (Q.U.B.); F.R. Hist. Soc.; M.R.I.A.; senior fellow, and professor of modern history, Trinity College, Dublin
Kenneth William Nicholls	Lecturer in Irish history, University College, Cork

Brian Ó Cuív	M.A., D. Litt. (N.U.I.); M.R.I.A.; senior professor, School of Celtic Studies, Dublin Institute for Advanced Studies
David Beers Quinn	M.A., D. Lit. (Q.U.B.), Ph.D. (Lond.), Hon. D. Litt. (Newfoundland and N.U.U.); F.R. Hist. Soc.; M.R.I.A.; Andrew Geddes and John Rankin professor of modern history, University of Liverpool
John Joseph Silke	M.A., Ph.D. (N.U.I.); archivist, Pontifical Irish College, Rome
John Gerald Simms	M.A. (Dubl., Oxon.), Ph.D. (Dubl.); M.R.I.A.; fellow emeritus, Trinity College, Dublin

The maps have been drawn by Martha Lyons, under the direction of Mary Davies, B.A., cartographical adviser to this history, from material supplied by contributors, by Mrs Davies, author of map 4, and by Robert John Hunter, M.A., M.Litt., lecturer in history, The New University of Ulster, joint author of map 5.

The index is the work of Alison Moffat Quinn, M.A., registered indexer of the Society of Indexers.

MAPS

ILLUSTRATIONS

The originals of these illustrations were made available through the courtesy of the following, and are published by their permission: the Board of Trinity College, Dublin, plates 1, 5, 6, 7; the National Library of Ireland, plates 3, 4, 8, 9, 10, 12; Professor Brian Ó Cuív, plate 13; the Franciscan House of Studies, Killiney, plate 14. Plate 11 is taken from a print formerly in the possession of the late W. S. Ferguson, of Foyle College, Derry.

ABBREVIATIONS

Abbreviations used in footnotes and bibliography are listed below. They consist of (a) the relevant items from the list in *Irish Historical Studies*, supplement I (Jan. 1968) and (b) abbreviations, on the same model, for sources and works not included in the *Irish Historical Studies* list.

A.F.M.	*Annala rioghachta Eireann: Annals of the kingdom of Ireland by the Four Masters from the earliest period to the year 1616*, ed. and trans. John O'Donovan (7 vols, Dublin, 1851; reprint, New York, 1966)
A.L.C.	*The Annals of Loch Cé: a chronicle of Irish affairs, 1014–1690*, ed. W. M. Hennessy (2 vols, London, 1871; reflex facsimile, I.M.C., Dublin, 1939)
A.U.	*Annála Uladh, Annals of Ulster; otherwise Annála Senait, Annals of Senat: a chronicle of Irish affairs, 431–1131, 1155–1541*, ed. W. M. Hennessy and B. MacCarthy (4 vols, Dublin, 1887–1901)
Acts & ordinances, interregnum	*Acts and ordinances of the interregnum, 1642–1660*, ed. C. H. Firth and R. S. Rait (3 vols, London, 1911)
Acts privy council, 1542–7 [etc.]	*Acts of the privy council of England, 1542–1547* [etc.] (London, 1890–)
Acts privy council, Ire., 1556–71	'Acts of the privy council in Ireland, 1556–1571', ed. J. T. Gilbert, in *H.M.C. rep. 15*, app.III (London, 1897)
Advertisements for Ire.	*Advertisements for Ireland, being a description of . . . Ireland in the reign of James I*, ed. George O'Brien (R.S.A.I., Dublin, 1923)
Alen's reg.	*Calendar of Archbishop Alen's register, c. 1172–1534; prepared and edited from the original in the registry of the united dioceses of Dublin and Glendalough and Kildare*, ed. Charles MacNeill; index by Liam Price (R.S.A.I., Dublin, 1950)
Amer. Phil. Soc. Proc.	*Proceedings of the American Philosophical Society* (Philadelphia, 1838–)
Amer. Phil. Soc. Trans.	*Transactions of the American Philosophical Society* (6 vols, Philadelphia, 1769–1809; new series, 1818–)
Anal. Hib.	*Analecta Hibernica, including the reports of the Irish Manuscripts Commission* (Dublin, 1930–)
Anc. rec. Dublin	*Calendar of ancient records of Dublin, in the possession of the municipal corporation*, ed. Sir J. T. Gilbert and Lady Gilbert (19 vols, Dublin, 1889–1944)

Ann. Conn.	*Annála Connacht*, . . . (*A.D. 1224–1544*), ed. A. Martin Freeman (Dublin Institute for Advanced Studies, 1944)
Archiv. Hib.	*Archivium Hibernicum: or Irish historical records* (Catholic Record Society of Ireland, Maynooth, 1912–)
B.M.	Library of the British Museum (now British Library)
B.M. cat. Ir. MSS	S. H. O'Grady and Robin Flower, *Catalogue of Irish manuscripts in the British Museum* (2 vols, London, 1926)
Bagwell, *Stuarts*	Richard Bagwell, *Ireland under the Stuarts* . . . (3 vols, London, 1909–16; reprint, 1963)
Bagwell, *Tudors*	Richard Bagwell, *Ireland under the Tudors* . . . (3 vols, London, 1885–90; reprint, 1963)
Beckett, *Mod. Ire.*	J. C. Beckett, *The making of modern Ireland, 1603–1923* (London, 1966)
Belfast Natur. Hist. Soc. Proc.	*Proceedings and Reports of the Belfast Natural History and Philosophical Society* (Belfast, 1873–)
Bk Fen.	*The Book of Fenagh*, ed. W. M. Hennessy and D. H. Kelly (Dublin, 1875; reflex facsimile, I.M.C., Dublin, 1939)
Bk Fen., supp.	*Book of Fenagh, supplementary volume*, ed. R. A. S. Macalister (I.M.C., Dublin, 1939)
Bks survey & dist., Roscommon [etc.]	*Books of survey and distribution: being abstracts of various surveys and instruments of title*, vol. i: *county of Roscommon* [etc.], prepared for publication . . . by Robert C. Simington (I.M.C., Dublin, 1944–)
Bodl.	Bodleian Library, Oxford
Bottigheimer, *Eng. money & Ir. land*	Karl Bottigheimer, *English money and Irish land: the 'adventurers' in the Cromwellian settlement of Ireland* (Oxford, 1971)
Butler, *Confiscation*	W. F. T. Butler, *Confiscation in Irish history* (Dublin, 1917)
Butler, *Gleanings*	W. F. T. Butler, *Gleanings from Irish history* (London, 1925)
Butler Soc. Jn.	*Journal of the Butler Society* ([Kilkenny], 1968–)
Cal. Carew MSS	*Calendar of the Carew manuscripts preserved in the archiepiscopal library at Lambeth, 1515–74* [etc.] (6 vols, London, 1867–73)
Cal. pat. rolls Ire., Hen. VIII–Eliz.	*Calendar of patent and close rolls of chancery in Ireland, Henry VIII to 18th Elizabeth*, ed. James Morrin (Dublin, 1861)
Cal. pat. rolls Ire., Eliz.	*Calendar of patent and close rolls of chancery in Ireland Elizabeth, 19 year to end of reign*, ed. James Morrin (Dublin, 1862)

Cal. pat. rolls Ire., Jas I	*Irish patent rolls of James I: facsimile of the Irish record commissioners' calendar prepared prior to 1830*, with foreword by M. C. Griffith (I.M.C., Dublin, 1966)
Cal. S.P. dom., 1547–80 [etc.]	*Calendar of state papers, domestic series, 1547–1580* [etc.] (London, 1856–)
Cal. S.P. Ire., 1509–73 [etc.]	*Calendar of the state papers relating to Ireland, 1509–1573* [etc.] (24 vols, London, 1860–1911)
Cal. treas. bks, 1660–67 [etc.]	*Calendar of treasury books, 1660–1667* [etc.] (London, 1904–)
Camb. mod. hist.	*Cambridge modern history* (13 vols+atlas, Cambridge, 1902–12)
Campion, 'Hist. Ire.', ed. Ware	Edmund Campion, 'A historie of Ireland written in the year 1571' in *Ancient Irish histories: the works of Spencer, Campion, Hanmer and Marleburrough* (2 vols, Dublin, 1809; first printed, ed. James Ware, Dublin, 1633)
Campion. *Hist. Ire.*, ed. Vossen	Edmund Campion, *Two bokes of the histories of Ireland*, . . . ed. A. F. Vossen (Assen, Netherlands, 1963)
Carte, *Ormond*	Thomas Carte, *History of the life of James, first duke of Ormonde* (2nd ed., 6 vols, Oxford, 1851)
Celtic Soc. misc.	*Miscellany of the Celtic Society*, ed. John O'Donovan (Dublin, 1849)
Celtica	*Celtica* (Dublin, 1950–)
Census Ire., 1659	*A census of Ireland circa 1659, with supplementary material from the poll money ordinances (1660–61)*, ed. Séamus Pender (I.M.C., Dublin, 1939)
Civil Survey	*The Civil Survey*, A.D. *1654–56*, ed. R. C. Simington, (I.M.C., 10 vols, Dublin, 1931–61)
Clarendon corr.	*The correspondence of Henry Hyde, earl of Clarendon, and of his brother, Laurence Hyde, earl of Rochester*, ed. S. W. Singer (2 vols, London, 1828)
Clarendon, *State letters*	*The state letters of Henry, earl of Clarendon, lord lieutenant of Ireland . . . and his lordship's diary for the years 1687, 1688, 1689 and 1690 . . .* (2 vols, Oxford, 1765)
Clarke, *Old English*	Aidan Clarke, *The Old English in Ireland, 1625–42* (London, 1966)
Clogher Rec.	*Clogher Record* ([Monaghan], 1953–)
Collect. Hib.	*Collectanea Hibernica: sources for Irish history* (Dublin, 1958–)
Comment. Rinucc.	Richard O'Ferrall and Robert O'Connell, *Commentarius Rinuccinianus, de sedis apostolicae legatione ad foederatos Hiberniae catholicos per annos 1645–9*, ed. Rev. Stanislaus Kavanagh (I.M.C., 6 vols, Dublin, 1932–49)
Commons' jn. Ire.	*Journals of the house of commons of the kingdom of Ireland . . .* (1613–1791, 28 vols, Dublin, 1753–91;

	reprinted and continued, 1613–1800, 19 vols, Dublin, 1796–1800)
Comp. bk Conn.	*The compossicion booke of Conought*, ed. A. M. Freeman (I.M.C., Dublin, 1936)
Connell, *Population*	K. H. Connell, *The population of Ireland, 1750–1845* (Oxford, 1950)
Corish, *Ir. catholicism*	Patrick J. Corish (ed.), *A history of Irish catholicism* (26 fascicles, Dublin and Melbourne, 1967–)
Cork Hist. Soc. Jn.	*Journal of the Cork Historical and Archaeological Society* (Cork, 1892–)
Council bk Cork	*The council book of Cork*, ed. Richard Caulfield (Guildford, 1876)
Council bk Kinsale	*The council book of Kinsale*, ed. Richard Caulfield (Guildford, 1879)
Council bks Waterford	*Council books of the corporation of Waterford, 1662–1700 . . .*, ed. Séamus Pender (I.M.C., Dublin, 1964)
Council bk Youghal	*The council book of Youghal*, ed. Richard Caulfield (Guildford, 1878)
Cromwell, *Writings*	*The writings and speeches of Oliver Cromwell*, ed. W. C. Abbott (4 vols, Camb., Mass., 1937–47)
Cullen, *Anglo-Ir. trade*	L. M. Cullen, *Anglo-Irish trade, 1660–1800* (Manchester, 1968)
Cullen, *Econ. hist. Ire. since 1660*	L. M. Cullen, *An economic history of Ireland since 1660* (London, 1972)
Curtis, *Ire.*	Edmund Curtis, *History of Ireland* (London, 1936; 6th ed. 1950; subsequent reprints)
Danish force in Ire.	*The Danish force in Ireland, 1690–1691*, ed. Kevin Danaher and J. G. Simms (I.M.C., Dublin, 1962)
Davies, *Prose works*	*The complete prose works of Sir John Davies*, ed. A. B. Grosart (3 vols, London, 1869–76)
Desid. cur. Hib.	*Desiderata curiosa Hibernica, or a select collection of state papers*, ed. [John Lodge] (2 vols, Dublin, 1732)
Description of Ire., 1598	*The description of Ireland . . . in anno 1598*, ed. Edmund Hogan (Dublin and London, 1878)
Docwra, *Narration*	Henry Docwra, 'A narration of the services done by the army ymployed to Lough-Foyle . . .' in *Celtic Soc. misc.*
Downshire MSS	*Report on the manuscripts of the marquess of Downshire, preserved at Easthampstead Park, Berkshire* (H.M.C., 4 vols, London, 1924–40)
Dunlop, *Commonwealth*	*Ireland under the commonwealth: being a selection of documents relating to the government of Ireland, 1651–9*, ed. Robert Dunlop (2 vols, Manchester, 1913)
E.H.R.	*English Historical Review* (London, 1886–)
Econ. Hist.	*Economic History; or supplement of the Economic Journal* (London, 1926–)

Econ. Hist. Rev.	*Economic History Review* (London, 1927–)
Economica	*Economica: issued terminally by the London School of Economics and Political Science* (London, 1921–)
Edwards, *Church & state*	R. Dudley Edwards, *Church and state in Tudor Ireland* (Dublin, 1935)
Egmont MSS	*Report on the manuscripts of the earl of Egmont* (H.M.C., 2 vols, London, 1905–9)
Éigse	*Éigse: a journal of Irish studies* (Dublin, 1939–)
Eng. hist. docs	*English historical documents*, general editor David C. Douglas (12 vols, London, 1955–)
Evans, *Ir. folkways*	E. Estyn Evans, *Irish folkways* (2nd ed., London 1957)
Extents Ir. mon. possessions	*Extents of Irish monastic possessions, 1540–1541, from manuscripts in the Public Record Office, London*, ed. Newport B. White (I.M.C., Dublin, 1943)
Facs. nat. MSS Ire.	*Facsimiles of the national manuscripts of Ireland*, ed. J. T. Gilbert (4 vols, Dublin, 1874–84)
Falkiner, *Illustrations*	C. Litton Falkiner, *Illustrations of Irish history and topography, mainly of the seventeenth century* (London, 1904)
Father Luke Wadding	*Father Luke Wadding: commemorative volume*, ed. Franciscan Fathers, Dún Mhuire, Killiney (Dublin, 1957)
Féil-sgríbhinn Eóin Mhic Néill	*Féil-sgríbhinn Eóin Mhic Néill; essays and studies presented to Professor Eóin MacNeill on the occasion of his seventieth birthday*, ed. Rev. John Ryan (Dublin, 1940)
Fiants Ire., Hen. VIII	'Calendar to fiants of the reign of Henry VIII . . .' [etc.] in *P.R.I. rep. D.K. 7–22* (Dublin, 1875–90)
Gadelica	*Gadelica: a journal of modern Irish studies*, ed. T. F. O'Rahilly (Dublin, 1912–13)
Galvia	*Galvia: irisleabhar Chumann Seandáluíochta is Staire na Gaillimhe* ([Galway], [1954]–)
Galway Arch. Soc. Jn.	*Journal of the Galway Archaeological and Historical Society* (Galway, 1900–)
Gardiner, *Eng.*	S. R. Gardiner, *History of England from the accession of James I to the outbreak of the civil war, 1603–1642* (10 vols, London, 1863–81; new ed., 10 vols, 1883–4; later eds)
Geneal. Office	Genealogical Office, Dublin Castle
Gent. Mag.	*The Gentleman's Magazine* (303 vols and subsequent unnumbered issues, London, 1731–1922)
Gilbert, *Contemp hist., 1641–52*	J. T. Gilbert (ed.), *A contemporary history of affairs in Ireland, from* A.D. *1641 to 1652 . . .* (Irish Archaeological Society, 3 vols, Dublin, 1879)
Gilbert, *Ir. confed.*	J. T. Gilbert (ed.), *History of the Irish confederation and the war in Ireland, 1641–3 . . .* (7 vols, Dublin, 1882–91)

Gilbert, *Jacobite narr.*	J. T. Gilbert (ed.), *A Jacobite narrative of the war in Ireland, 1688–1691* (Dublin, 1892; reprint, with introduction by J. G. Simms, Shannon, 1971)
Gwynn, *Med. province Armagh*	Aubrey Gwynn, *The medieval province of Armagh, 1470–1545* (Dundalk, 1946)
H.M.C. rep. 1 [etc.]	*Historical Manuscripts Commission, first* [etc.] *report* (London, 1870–)
Hardiman, *Galway*	James Hardiman, *History of the town and county of Galway* (Dublin, 1820; reprint, Galway, 1926, 1958)
Hastings MSS	*Report on the manuscripts of the late Reginald Rawdon Hastings, esq.* (H.M.C., 4 vols, London, 1928–47)
Hayes-McCoy, *Ir. battles*	G. A. Hayes-McCoy, *Irish battles* (London, 1969)
Hayes-McCoy, *Scots mercenary forces*	G. A. Hayes-McCoy, *Scots mercenary forces in Ireland (1565–1603)* . . . (Dublin, 1937)
Herbert corresp.	*Herbert correspondence: the sixteenth and seventeenth century letters of the Herberts of Chirbury, Powis Castle and Dolguog, formerly at Powis Castle in Montgomeryshire*, ed. W. J. Smith (Cardiff: University of Wales Press; Dublin: I.M.C., 1965)
Hist. Studies	*Historical Studies: papers read before the Irish Conference of Historians* (i–vii, London, 1958–69; viii, Dublin, 1971; ix, Belfast, 1974; in progress)
Hill, *MacDonnells of Antrim*	George Hill, *An historical account of the MacDonnells of Antrim* . . . (Belfast, 1873)
Hill, *Plantation*	George Hill, *An historical account of the plantation in Ulster . . . 1608–20* (Belfast, 1877; reprint, Shannon, 1970)
Holinshed, *Chronicles* (1577 ed.) [etc.]	Raphael Holinshed, *The . . . chronicles of England, Scotlande and Irelande . . .* (London, 1577; ed. John Hooker and others, 3 vols, 1587; ed. Henry Ellis, 6 vols, 1807–8)
Hore, *Wexford town*	P. H. Hore, *History of the town and county of Wexford* (6 vols, London, 1900–11)
Hore & Graves, *Southern & eastern counties*	H. F. Hore and J. Graves (ed.), *The social state of the southern and eastern counties of Ireland in the sixteenth century* . . . (Annuary of the Royal Historical and Archaeological Association of Ireland for 1868–9)
Hyde, *Lit. hist. Ire.*	Douglas Hyde, *A literary history of Ireland from earliest times to the present day* (London, 1899; reissue, with introduction by Brian Ó Cuív, London, 1967)
I.B.L.	*The Irish Book Lover* (Dublin, 1909–57, 32 vols)
I.C.H.S. Bull.	*Bulletin of the Irish Committee of Historical Sciences* (typescript, Dublin, 1939–)

I.E.R.	*Irish Ecclesiastical Record* (171 vols, Dublin, 1864–1968)
I.H.R. Bull.	*Bulletin of the Institute of Historical Research* (London, 1923–)
I.H.S.	*Irish Historical Studies: the joint journal of the Irish Historical Society and the Ulster Society for Irish Historical Studies* (Dublin, 1938–)
I.M.C.	Irish Manuscripts Commission, Dublin
Ibernia Ignat.	*Ibernia Ignatiana*, ed. Edmund Hogan (Dublin, 1880)
Inchiquin MSS	*The Inchiquin manuscripts*, ed. John Ainsworth (I.M.C., Dublin, 1961)
Ir. Arch. Soc. misc.	*The miscellany of the Irish Archaeological Society*, i (Dublin, 1846; no subsequent volumes)
Ir. Cath. Hist. Comm. Proc.	*Proceedings of the Irish Catholic Historical Committee* (Dublin, 1955–)
Ir. Geneal.	*The Irish Genealogist: official organ of the Irish Genealogical Research Society* (London, 1937–)
Ir. Geography	*Irish Geography* (Bulletin of the Geographical Society of Ireland) . . . (Dublin, 1944–)
Ir. geog. studies	*Irish geographical studies in honour of E. Estyn Evans*, ed. Nicholas Stephens and R. E. Glasscock (Belfast, 1970)
Ir. Jurist	*The Irish Jurist*, N.S. (Dublin, 1966–)
Ir. Monthly	*Irish Monthly Magazine* [later entitled *Irish Monthly*] (London and Dublin, 1873–1954)
Ir. Sword	*Irish Sword: the journal of the Military History Society of Ireland* (Dublin, [1949]–)
Ir. texts	*Irish texts*, ed. J. Fraser, P. Grosjean, and J. G. O'Keeffe (fascs 1–5, London, 1931–4)
Ir. Texts Soc.	Irish Texts Society
Ir. Theol. Quart.	*Irish Theological Quarterly* (17 vols, Dublin, 1906–22; Maynooth, 1951–)
Jn. Ecc. Hist.	*Journal of Ecclesiastical History* (London, 1950–)
Kearney, *Strafford in Ireland*	H. F. Kearney, *Strafford in Ireland, 1633–41: a study in absolutism* (Manchester, 1959; reprint, 1961)
Kerry Arch. Soc. Jn.	*Journal of the Kerry Archaeological and Historical Society* ([Tralee], 1968–)
Kildare Arch. Soc. Jn.	*Journal of the County Kildare Archaeological Society* (Dublin, 1891–)
King's Inns cat. Ir. MSS	Pádraig de Brún, *Catalogue of Irish manuscripts in King's Inns Library, Dublin* (Dublin Institute for Advanced Studies, 1972)
L. & P. Hen. VIII, 1509–13 [etc.]	*Letters and papers, foreign and domestic, Henry VIII* (21 vols, London, 1862–1932)
L. & P. Ir. reb., 1642–6	*Letters and papers relating to the Irish rebellion between 1642–46*, ed. James Hogan (I.M.C., Dublin, 1936)

Liber primus Kilkenn.	*Kilkenny city records; Liber primus Kilkenniensis*, ed. Charles McNeill (I.M.C., Dublin, 1931)
Lismore papers	*Lismore papers, by Richard Boyle, earl of Cork* [1566–1643], ed. A. B. Grosart (10 vols, London, 1886–8)
Longfield, *Anglo-Ir. trade*	A. K. Longfield, *Anglo-Irish trade in the sixteenth century* (London, 1929)
Lords' jn. Ire.	*Journal of the house of lords* [*of Ireland*], 1634–1800 (8 vols, Dublin, 1779–1800)
Lr Cl. Aodha Buidhe	*Leabhar Cloinne Aodha Buidhe*, ed. Tadhg Ó Donnchadha (I.M.C., Dublin, 1931)
Lynch, *De praesulibus Hib.*	John Lynch, *De praesulibus Hiberniae potissimis catholicae religionis in Hibernia, serendae, propagandae, et conservandae authoribus*, ed. J. F. O'Doherty (I.M.C., 2 vols, Dublin, 1944)
McCracken, *Ir. woods*	Eileen McCracken, *The Irish woods since Tudor times* (Newton Abbot, 1971)
MacLysaght, *Ir. life after Cromwell*	Edward MacLysaght, *Irish life in the seventeenth century: after Cromwell* (2nd edition, Cork, 1950)
Maxwell, *Sources, 1509–1610*	Constantia Maxwell (ed.), *Irish history from contemporary sources, 1509–1610* (London, 1923)
Med. studies presented to A. Gwynn	*Medieval studies presented to Aubrey Gwynn, S.J.*, ed. J. A. Watt, J. B. Morrall, and F. X. Martin (Dublin, 1961)
Medium Aevum	*Medium Aevum* (Oxford, 1932–)
Millett, *Ir. Franciscans*	Benignus Millett, *The Irish Franciscans, 1651–1655* (Rome, 1964)
Moody, *Londonderry plantation*	T. W. Moody, *The Londonderry plantation, 1609–41: the city of London and the plantation in Ulster* (Belfast, 1939)
Moody & Martin, *Ir. hist.*	T. W. Moody and F. X. Martin (ed.), *The course of Irish history* (Cork and New York, 1967)
Moryson, *Itinerary*	Fynes Moryson, *An Itinerary* . . . (4 vols, Glasgow, 1907–8; first published in 1617)
N.L.I.	National Library of Ireland
N.L.I. cat. Ir. MSS	Nessa Ní Shéaghdha, *Catalogue of Irish manuscripts in the National Library of Ireland* (2 fasc., Dublin Institute for Advanced Studies, 1961–7)
N.S.	New series; or, in dating, New Style
N. Munster Antiq. Jn.	*North Munster Antiquarian Journal* (Limerick, 1936–)
Négoc. d'Avaux en Irl.	*Négociations de M. le Comte d'Avaux en Irlande 1689–90* [London, 1844], reflex facsimile, with introduction by James Hogan (I.M.C., Dublin, 1934)
New Camb. mod. hist.	*The new Cambridge modern history* (13 vols+atlas, Cambridge, 1957–70)
Nicholls, *Gaelic Ire.*	K. W. Nicholls, *Gaelic and gaelicised Ireland in the middle ages* (Dublin and London, 1972)

O'Brien, *Econ. hist. Ire. 17th cent.*	George O'Brien, *The economic history of Ireland in the seventeenth century* (Dublin, 1919)
Ó Bruadair, *Poems*	*Duanaire Dháibhidh Uí Bhruadair: the poems of David Ó Bruadair*, ed. J. C. MacErlean (Ir. Texts Soc., 3 pts, London, 1910, 1911, 1917)
Ó Cianáin, *Flight*	Tadhg Ó Cianáin, *The flight of the earls*, ed. Paul Walsh (Dublin, 1916)
Ó Clérigh, *Aodh Ruadh O Domhnaill*	*The life of Aodh Ruadh O Domhnaill transcribed from the Book of Lughaidh Ó Clérigh*, ed. Paul Walsh (Ir. Texts Soc., 2 pts, Dublin, 1948, 1957)
Ó Cuív, *Seven centuries*	Brian Ó Cuív (ed.), *Seven centuries of Irish learning, 1000–1700* ([Dublin], 1961; reprint 1971)
O'Donovan, *Econ. hist.*	John O'Donovan, *The economic history of livestock in Ireland* (Cork, 1940)
O'Flaherty, *West Connaught*	Roderick O'Flaherty, *A chorographical description of West or h-Iar Connaught, written A.D. 1684*, ed. James Hardiman (Irish Archaeological Society, Dublin, 1846)
Ó Huiginn, *Poems*	*The bardic poems [1550–91] of Tadhg Dall Ó Huiginn*, ed. Eleanor Knott (Ir. Texts Soc., 2 pts, Dublin, 1922, 1926)
Ormond deeds, 1172–1350 [etc.]	*Calendar of Ormond deeds, 1172–1350* [etc.], ed. Edmund Curtis (I.M.C., 6 vols, Dublin, 1932–43)
Ormonde MSS	*Calendar of the manuscripts of the marquess of Ormonde, preserved at Kilkenny Castle* (H.M.C., 11 vols, London, 1895–1920: vol. i, *H.M.C. rep. 14*, app. vii (1895), vol. ii (1899), index to vols i and ii (1909); new series, vols i–viii (1902–20))
Orrery papers	*Calendar of the Orrery papers*, ed. Edward MacLysaght (I.M.C., Dublin, 1941)
Orrery, *State letters*	*A collection of the state letters of the . . . first earl of Orrery*, ed. Thomas Morrice (2 vols, Dublin, 1743)
O'Sullivan, *Cork*	William O'Sullivan, *The economic history of Cork city . . . to the act of union* (Cork, 1937)
O'Sullivan Beare, *Hist. cath. Ibern.*	*Historiae catholicae Iberniae compendium*, ed. Matthew Kelly (Dublin, 1850; first published, Lisbon, 1621)
O'Sullivan Beare, *Ire. under Eliz.*	*Ireland under Elizabeth . . . being a portion of The history of catholic Ireland, by Don Philip O'Sullivan Bear*, trans. M. J. Byrne (Dublin, 1903)
O'Sullivan Beare, *Zoilomastix*, ed. O'Donnell	*Selections from the Zoilomastix of O'Sullivan Beare*, ed. T. J. O'Donnell (I.M.C., Dublin, 1960)
P.R.I. rep. D.K. 1 [etc.]	*First* [etc.] *report of the deputy keeper of the public records in Ireland* (Dublin, 1869–)
P.R.O.	Public Record Office of England
P.R.O.I.	Public Record Office of Ireland
Past	*The Past: the organ of the Ui Ceinnsealaigh Historical Society* (Wexford, 1920–)

Past & Present	*Past and Present* . . . (London, 1952–)
Perrot, *Chron. Ire., 1584–1608*	James Perrot, *The chronicles of Ireland, 1584–1608*, ed. Herbert Wood (I.M.C., Dublin, 1933)
Petty, *Econ. writings*	*The economic writings of Sir William Petty* . . . , ed. C. H. Hull (2 vols, Cambridge, 1899)
Petty papers	*The Petty papers: some unpublished writings of Sir William Petty*, ed. marquis of Lansdowne (2 vols, London, 1927)
Petty 'Political anatomy', ed. Hull, i	William Petty, 'The political anatomy of Ireland [1672]' in Petty, *Econ. writings*, i
Petty, 'Treatise of Ire.', ed. Hull, ii	William Petty, 'A treatise of Ireland, 1687' in Petty, *Econ. writings*, ii
Phillips, *Ch. of Ire.*	W. A. Phillips (ed.), *History of the Church of Ireland* (3 vols, London, 1933–4)
Prendergast, *Cromwellian settlement*	J. P. Prendergast, *The Cromwellian settlement of Ireland* (2nd edition, Dublin, 1870; reprint, 1922)
Quinn, *Elizabethans & Irish*	D. B. Quinn, *The Elizabethans and the Irish* (Ithaca, New York, 1966)
R.I.A. cat. Ir. MSS	T. F. O'Rahilly and others, *Catalogue of Irish manuscripts in the Royal Irish Academy* (Dublin, 1926–)
R.I.A. Proc.	*Proceedings of the Royal Irish Academy* (Dublin, 1836–)
R.I.A. Trans.	*Transactions of the Royal Irish Academy* (33 vols, Dublin, 1786–1907)
R.S.A.I.	Royal Society of Antiquaries of Ireland, Dublin
R.S.A.I. Jn.	*Journal of the Royal Society of Antiquaries of Ireland* (Dublin, 1850–)
R. Soc. Notes & Records	*Notes and Records of the Royal Society of London* (London, 1938–)
R. Soc. Phil. Trans.	*Philosophical Transactions of the Royal Society of London* (London, 1665–)
Reid, *Presb. ch. in Ire.*	J. S. Reid, *History of the presbyterian church in Ireland*, ed. W. D. Killen (3 vols, Belfast, 1867)
Richardson & Sayles, *Ir. parl. in middle ages*	H. G. Richardson and G. O. Sayles, *The Irish parliament in the middle ages* (Philadelphia, 1952; reissue, 1964)
Scot. Hist. Rev.	*Scottish Historical Review* (25 vols, Glasgow, 1903–28, 1947–)
S.P. Hen. VIII	*State papers, Henry VIII* (11 vols, London, 1830–52)
Shirley, *Ch. in Ire., 1547–57*	E. P. Shirley (ed.), *Original letters and papers in illustration of the history of the church in Ireland during the reigns of Edward VI, Mary & Elizabeth* (London, 1851)
Sidney letters	*Letters and memorials of state . . . written and collected by Sir Henry Sidney . . . , Sir Philip Sidney and his brother Sir Robert Sidney* . . ., ed. Arthur Collins (2 vols, London, 1746)

Sidney S.P.	*Sidney state papers, 1565–70*, ed. Tomás Ó Laidhin (I.M.C., Dublin, 1962)
Smith, *Cork*	Charles Smith, *Antient and present state of the city and county of Cork* . . . (Dublin, 1750)
Smith, *Waterford*	Charles Smith, *Antient and present state of the city and county of Waterford* . . . (Dublin, 1746; 2nd ed., 1774)
Spanish knights	*Spanish knights of Irish origin: documents from continental archives*, ed. Micheline Walsh (I.M.C., 3 vols, Dublin, 1960, 1965, 1970)
Spenser, *View*, ed. Renwick (1970)	Edmund Spenser, *A view of the present state of Ireland*, ed. W. L. Renwick (Oxford, 1970)
Spicil. Ossor.	*Spicilegium Ossoriense: being a collection of original letters and papers illustrative of the history of the Irish church from the reformation to the year 1800* ed. P. F. Moran (3 vols, Dublin, 1874–84)
Stanihurst, 'Description of Ire.' in Holinshed, *Chronicles* (1577 ed.) [etc.]	Richard Stanihurst, 'A treatise containing a plain and perfect description of Ireland . . . ' in Holinshed, *Chronicles* (1577 ed.) [etc.]
Stat. Ire.	*The statutes at large passed in the parliaments held in Ireland* . . . (1310–1761, 8 vols, Dublin, 1765; 1310–1800, 20 vols, Dublin, 1786–1801)
Stat. Ire., 1–12 Edw. IV	*Statute rolls of the parliament of Ireland, 1st to the 12th years of the reign of King Edward IV*, ed. H. F. Berry (Dublin, 1914)
Stat. Ire., 12–22 Edw. IV	*Statute rolls of the parliament of Ireland, 12th and 13th to the 21st and 22nd years of the reign of King Edward IV*, ed. James F. Morrissey (Dublin, 1939)
Stat. Ire., Hen. VII & VIII	'The bills and statutes of the Irish parliaments of Henry VII and Henry VIII', ed. D. B. Quinn, in *Anal. Hib.*, no. 10 (1941)
Steele, *Tudor & Stuart proclam.*	R. Steele (ed.), *Tudor and Stuart proclamations 1485–1714* (2 vols, Oxford, 1910)
Strafford, *Letters*	*The earl of Strafforde's letters and despatches*, ed. William Knowler (2 vols, London, 1799)
Strafford MSS	Strafford MSS in Sheffield Central Library
Studia Celt.	*Studia Celtica* (Cardiff, 1966–)
Studia Hib.	*Studia Hibernica* (Dublin, 1961–)
Studies	*Studies: an Irish quarterly review* (Dublin, 1912–)
Swift, *Corr.*	*The correspondence of Jonathan Swift*, ed. Harold Williams (5 vols, Oxford, 1963–5)
Swift, *Prose works*	*The prose works of Jonathan Swift*, ed. Herbert Davis (14 vols, Oxford, 1939–68)
T.C.D.	Library of Trinity College, Dublin
Theiner, *Vetera mon.*	A. Theiner, *Vetera monumenta Hibernorum et Scotorum* (Rome, 1864)
Thurloe, *S.P.*	*A collection of state papers of John Thurloe* . . . , ed. Thomas Birch (7 vols, London, 1742)

U.J.A.	*Ulster Journal of Archaeology* (Belfast, 3 series: 1853–62, 9 vols; 1895–1911, 17 vols; 1938–)
Ulster maps c. 1600	*Ulster and other Irish maps c. 1600*, ed. G. A. Hayes-McCoy (I.M.C., Dublin, 1964)
Wadding papers	*Wadding papers, 1614–38*, ed. Brendan Jennings (I.M.C., Dublin, 1953)
Walsh, *Ir. chiefs*	Paul Walsh, *Irish chiefs and leaders*, ed. Colm Ó Lochlainn (Dublin, 1960)
Walsh, *Ir. men of learning*	Paul Walsh, *Irish men of learning*, ed. Colm Ó Lochlainn (Dublin, 1947)
Waterford Arch. Soc. Jn.	*Journal of the Waterford and South-East of Ireland Archaeological Society* (19 vols, Waterford, 1894–1920)
Webb, *Ir. biog.*	Alfred Webb, *A compendium of Irish biography* (Dublin, 1878)
Wild geese in Spanish Flanders	*Wild geese in Spanish Flanders, 1582–1700: documents relating chiefly to Irish regiments, from the Archives Générales du Royaume, Brussels, and other sources*, ed. Brendan Jennings (I.M.C., Dublin, 1964)

NOTE ON DATING

DURING the period 1582–1700 the Old Style, or Julian, calendar, used in Ireland and in England, was ten days behind the New Style, or Gregorian, calendar, introduced by Pope Gregory XIII in 1582 and adopted by most continental countries. Moreover, the beginning of the year Old Style generally used in England and Ireland was Lady Day, or 25 March, but in New Style dating as used on the Continent it was 1 January.

In this volume dating is according to Old Style for the day and the month, but according to New Style for the year. Thus, the death of Queen Elizabeth I, which occurred on 24 March 1602 Old Style, or 3 April 1603 New Style, is here dated 24 March 1603. Where an event in continental history is mentioned, New Style dating is generally used, followed by 'N.S.' in brackets. Thus the death of Richelieu is given as 4 December 1642 (N.S.).

INTRODUCTION

Early modern Ireland

T. W. MOODY

THE period covered by the present volume saw the effective conquest of all Ireland by the English state. The medieval conquest that had begun with the Anglo-Norman invasion of 1169 had never been complete. It had established an English colony and an English administration on Irish soil, and the claim of the English crown to lordship over the whole island. But after more than three and a half centuries the actual authority of the crown in Ireland was slight, and real power was largely in the hands of local magnates, Anglo-Irish and Gaelic. All this was decisively changed between 1534 and 1691.

Before 1534, apart from spasmodic and short-lived interventions from London, earls of Kildare had ruled Dublin for three-quarters of a century as deputies of the English king. The English lordship of Ireland, centred at Dublin, had nominal authority over the whole island, but its actual authority was largely restricted to the Pale, an area abutting on the coast between Dundalk and Dublin and extending inland for some twenty to forty miles.[1] This was the heartland of the medieval English colony and the one region that habitually felt the action of the Dublin government. Outside the Pale, only the independent towns—principally Waterford, Cork, Limerick, and Galway—and the royal fortress of Carrickfergus, remained centres of English civilisation and allegiance. The Palesmen as a body regarded themselves as pre-eminently the 'king's subjects', who looked to a royal conquest of the island to deliver them from the anarchy and oppression they suffered at the hands both of their and the king's 'Irish enemies' (the Gaelic Irish) and of the Anglo-Irish feudal magnates—the 'king's English rebels'.[2] Beyond the Pale and its outliers political power was shared between Anglo-Irish and Gaelic lordships, which had acquired exemption from, or had usurped, or did not recognise, the royal authority, but formed two independent power-systems which in varying degrees had interacted on each other both politically and culturally. Among the Anglo-Irish the Fitzgeralds of Kildare had emerged as the greatest dynastic family of the medieval colony, connected by marriage and political alliances with the leading families of both the Anglo-Irish and the Gaelic worlds, controlling the royal administration at

[1] See map 1. [2] *S.P. Hen. VIII*, ii, 1–31.

Dublin, and invested by the English crown with a shadowy, but not insignificant, authority over all Ireland. But, drawn in opposite directions by their contradictory roles as deputies of an English king and as independent Irish princes, they were unable to resolve their dualism and to create a single polity in which the native Irish and the colonists would have their due place. The weakness of their position was demonstrated by the unsuccessful rebellion in 1534 of Thomas Fitzgerald ('Silken Thomas'), which put an end to their era and opened an era of direct rule that was to last till 1921.

King Henry VIII, in resuming the direct government of his Irish lordship in 1534 (he exchanged his title of 'lord', for that of 'king', of Ireland in 1541), committed the English monarchy to a task that proved, unlike previous Tudor interventions in Ireland, to be an unlimited liability. The Tudor conquest was a complex, piecemeal, and spasmodic movement, a series of responses to immediate circumstances rather than the execution of any coherent plan; and the political conflict was rendered all the more intractable and bitter because, under Henry VIII, it became inextricably involved in religious schism. Rebellions, both of Gaelic Irish and Anglo-Irish, were repeatedly crushed; great Anglo-Irish palatinates were extinguished; and in certain areas—in Leix and Offaly and in Munster—the lands of defeated rebels were confiscated and 'planted', or colonised with loyal subjects under state direction and control.[1] But conciliation alternated with coercion: over extensive areas, and especially in Connacht, land titles were resettled by peaceful arrangement between the crown and the occupying people. It was not till the last decade of Queen Elizabeth's reign that the decisive struggle for sovereignty was fought. The rebellion of Hugh O'Neill, the supremely able Gaelic lord of Tyrone, who had built up a confederacy that combined Gaelic and gaelicised lords over a wide area, confronted the English crown with the most formidable challenge it had ever had to face in Ireland. In meeting it successfully, at a time when she was involved in war with Spain, Elizabeth had to strain her resources to the limit.

The failure of O'Neill's rebellion was a defeat not only for the Gaelic order but also for the catholic religion, which had been a bond of unity among his supporters. The English reformation in its successive phases was introduced into Ireland from 1534, not as the outcome of any popular reaction against papal authority, or of any spontaneous movement of religious reform, but as an inevitable consequence of ecclesiastical changes in Tudor England; '*cuius regio, eius religio*'. The English, episcopal, protestant church was generally rejected by the old colonial stock in Ireland no less than by the Gaelic Irish, but after 1603 it was able to consolidate its position as the church established by law, the church of the new English colony that the Tudor advance had brought in its train. On the other hand, the catholic church continued to function in defiance of the law, and, though the church

[1] See map 2.

of the great majority, had to pay the price of its defiance in the proscription of its clergy and their jurisdiction, the confiscation of its property, and the suppression of its religious orders. From 1534 bishops were appointed by the crown wherever it was able to assert its authority, and by 1605 all dioceses had royally appointed bishops. The catholic response to this was a sustained and largely successful effort to maintain in most dioceses a succession of papally appointed bishops or vicars apostolic, despite the loss of their temporalities and of the cathedrals and parish churches of their sees. In the struggle of the catholics to maintain their outlawed church, Ireland became a battle-ground of the European counter-reformation, with the regular clergy leading the fight against protestantism and fostering popular allegiance to Rome. Resistance to English authority became inseparable from the cause of the counter-reformation in Ireland, and the rebellions of the latter part of Elizabeth's reign took on the character of religious wars, for which the Irish leaders constantly sought to enlist the help of catholic powers on the Continent. The intervention of Spain highlighted the danger of a disaffected Ireland serving as a back-door for a foreign attack on England. The defeat of O'Neill and his confederates was thus a defeat for Spanish designs on England as well as a victory for the protestant cause.

The Tudor conquest meant the reduction of the whole island, for the first time, to English authority. The independence of the great lordships, both Gaelic and Anglo-Irish, was finally destroyed, and the social structure of Gaelic and gaelicised Ireland undermined. But this political and military subjection of both the 'king's Irish enemies' and the 'king's English rebels' was not matched by confiscation of their land. There were extensive forfeitures of land between 1534 and 1603, but even so the Tudor conquest left the great bulk of Irish soil in the hands of catholic owners, that is, of Anglo-Irish and Gaelic Irish. O'Neill's submission to King James I at Mellifont in 1603 did not involve any general forfeiture by the defeated rebels. The Tudor conquest was more concerned with the assertion of sovereignty than with expropriation.

The 'treaty of Mellifont' left O'Neill and his Ulster associates in a highly unstable situation. On the one hand they found it difficult to adapt themselves to their new status of landlords deprived of their traditional authority over their former followers, and on the other their difficulties were exploited by English officials and adventurers who had hoped for a wholesale confiscation of their lands. In September 1607 O'Neill, O'Donnell, and other Ulster lords extricated themselves from a position they felt to be critical by a secret withdrawal abroad. This enigmatic 'flight of the earls', followed by the revolt of Sir Cahir O'Doherty of Inishowen, offered the government a unique opportunity for reversing its policy of maintaining the Gaelic aristocracy of Ulster as English-style proprietors. Instead, in total disregard of the rights of the native occupiers generally, the greater part of the soil of six counties was confiscated and assigned to English and Scottish 'undertakers', to the city of London (whose participation is commemorated in the name Londonderry), to servitors (army officers who had served the crown in Ireland), and to selected natives.[1] The area affected was far larger than that of the Munster and of the Leix–Offaly plantations, the plantation scheme far more systematic and thorough, and its execution far more successful. This plantation, together with an influx, from 1603 onwards, of private adventurers, both Scottish and English, into Antrim and Down, effected a revolutionary transfer of land from catholic to protestant ownership in Ulster, created a strong British colony in a province hitherto a Gaelic stronghold, and thus decisively augmented the new colonial and protestant element that the Tudor conquest had introduced into Ireland since 1534.

The tradition of loyalty to the English crown was now shared between this 'New English' protestant element (*Nua Ghaill*[2]) and the descendants of the medieval English colony who, though refusing to become protestant, had remained firm in their allegiance to the crown. The term 'Old English' (*Sean Ghaill*[2]) was current in the seventeenth century to describe this loyalist element, and is so used by historians. It is also used by some writers on the sixteenth century to describe the loyalist element both before and after the reformation, and by others as synonymous with the sixteenth-century term 'Anglo-Irish' ('Anglo-Hiberni'[3] or 'English-Irish'[4]) to describe the old colonial stock in general. These different uses of the same term present no serious difficulty provided that the Old English of the seventeenth century are seen not as exclusively composed of people of English descent but as constituting a political interest or party, catholic in its religious identity but distinct in its political outlook from the Gaelic Irish (*Gaedhil*) or 'Old Irish'. Thus, for example, in the 1640s one of the Old English leaders was Donogh MacCarthy, Lord Muskerry, who came of distinguished Gaelic lineage. Conversely one of the most notable of the New English leaders in the 1640s was the marquis of Ormond, whose ancestry went back to the beginnings of the Anglo-Norman invasion. The Old English after 1603 were catholics who expected to share with the New English in the benefits of the Tudor conquest. In particular they expected to play a full part in public affairs. Their efforts to maintain a working compromise between their temporal allegiance to a protestant king and their spiritual allegiance to the pope had some success down to 1641. But their constitutional and social position deterioriated. Though Charles I, involved in disputes with his

[1] See map 5.

[2] Geoffrey Keating, *Foras feasa ar Éirinn* (completed about 1634), ed. David Comyn and P. S. Dinneen (Ir. Texts Soc., 4 vols, 1902–14), i, 2–3.

[3] Richard Stanihurst, *De rebus in Hibernia gestis* (Antwerp, 1584), p. 30; Philip O'Sullivan Beare, *Zoilomastix* (written in 1625), ed. O'Donnell, pp 61–3.

[4] Fynes Moryson, *Itinerary* (1617), in Faulkiner, *Illustrations*, p. 250.

English parliament and in wars with Spain and France, made temporary concessions to them in return for cash payments, neither he nor his servants in the administration of Ireland really trusted them, or fully accepted the distinction they consistently tried to demonstrate between themselves and the Old Irish. Their loyalty was still more suspect to the English parliament, and to the New English, who insisted that only protestants were entitled to full rights of citizenship. Confronted with increasing danger to their liberties as catholics, to their standing in parliament, and to their landed property, they were ultimately driven into making common cause, in the rebellion of 1641, with the Old Irish, whose allegiance to Rome they shared but from whom they had been separated by age-long traditions of political and cultural hostility, and by conflicting attitudes towards the church reforms required by the council of Trent.

The 1641 rebellion was primarily a movement of the Old Irish of Ulster to overthrow the plantation and restore catholicism. The Ulster colony, though it had developed slowly, had become strongly entrenched—a protestant community, comprising all social classes, whose preponderant element was Scottish in origin, presbyterian in religion, and therefore at loggerheads with the established church. The Ulster rebellion was preceded by a revolt of presbyterian Scotland in 1638—which produced sympathetic vibrations among the Scots in Ulster—against the religious policy of Charles I. The king was compelled to turn for help to the English parliament, which exploited the emergency to demand constitutional innovations amounting to a transfer of sovereignty from king to parliament. The Old Irish leaders were quick to realise the new threat to catholic interests that the victory of an English puritan parliament would entail; and in taking up arms against the English government of Ireland they professed to be acting with the king's authority. The Old English of the Pale, left defenceless against the rebels by the Dublin government, followed the Old Irish into rebellion, but only after obtaining from them a public avowal of their loyalty to the crown. Thus emerged the idea of a united catholic Ireland, fighting for its liberties against English power while declaring its allegiance to the English king. The idea, crystallised in the motto of the 'confederate catholics'—'*pro deo, pro rege, pro patria Hibernia unanimis*', took shape in a provisional government and a representative assembly at Kilkenny, in whose name armies were maintained and civil authority exercised over extensive areas.

But the idea was mocked by the reality of chronic and paralysing divisions between Old English and Old Irish, the former eager to reach a moderate settlement with Charles I as soon as possible, the latter, led by Owen Roe O'Neill and supported by a papal nuncio, Archbishop Rinuccini, demanding complete freedom for their church and the restoration of their former lands in Ulster. The Old English showed less than no enthusiasm for the special interests of their Old Irish allies; what they aimed at was a restored kingdom of Ireland under Charles I, but ruled by themselves as a catholic landed aristocracy, entrenched in a parliament having the sole power of making laws for Ireland. The forces engaged in the defence of the *status quo* were even more divided: the king's army, which, under the marquis of Ormond (Charles I's lord lieutenant from 1643 to 1649), generally maintained an uneasy truce with the confederate catholics, was confronted after the outbreak of the English civil war in 1642 by a parliamentary army; an army sent from Scotland to the help of the Scottish colony in Ulster took its own line and limited its activities to that region, but generally supported the parliamentary forces. The situation remained confused and unstable till after the final defeat of Charles I and the replacement of the monarchy in 1649 by a puritan commonwealth, maintained by an army in which Oliver Cromwell was the ruling power. His first major task was the reconquest of Ireland. This was achieved by his unprecedented offensive of 1649–50, which, as followed up by his successors in Ireland during the next two years, put an end to nearly ten years of anarchy and reduced all the warring elements to submission. There followed the most catastrophic land-confiscation and social upheaval in Irish history, involving the expropriation of catholic landowners, both Old English and Old Irish, on a vast scale, the transplantation to Connacht of most of those who survived, and an influx of English landowners and settlers to augment the New English element. This Cromwellian confiscation was substantially confirmed after the restoration of the monarchy in 1660. But the catholic Irish were not yet finally crushed.

The attempt of King James II to restore catholicism in England, and his consequent expulsion from his English throne in the revolution of 1688, caused him to put himself at the head of a catholic counter-revolution in Ireland, a movement led by the Old English who again combined with the Old Irish in an alliance weakened by conflicts of interest similar to those that had divided the confederate catholics in the 1640s. Again, as in 1641, the catholic Irish identified their cause with the English monarchy, but in 1689–91 their final effort to overthrow the New English domination took the paradoxical form of a war in which each side was led by a king of England—the catholics by James II, king by hereditary right, the protestants by William III, king by act of parliament. The victory of Williamites over Jacobites, symbolised in protestant tradition by the siege of Derry (1689) and the battle of the Boyne (1690) and embodied in the treaty of Limerick in 1691, reestablished English power more firmly than ever on a basis of protestant supremacy and catholic subjugation. A new confiscation reduced still further the area of land remaining in catholic ownership, and completed the ruin of the Old English as a distinctive and influential element in Irish life. The New English finally consolidated their position as the beneficiaries of the modern English conquest. It was from this element, typified in the late sixteenth and early seventeenth centuries by Richard Boyle, who became earl of Cork, and in Cromwellian Ireland by Sir William Petty, ancestor of the Lansdowne family, that the bulk of the landowners of Ireland thenceforth derived their titles.

The polarisation of Irish life on a denominational basis was one of the crucial changes of the seventeenth century. The line of cleavage between catholics and protestants was still somewhat blurred at the end of the sixteenth century, but with the rebellion of 1641 it became sharply and irrevocably drawn. Though anti-catholic legislation did not attain its full development till after 1691, long before then the catholic laity were experiencing the consequences of their recusancy in their exclusion from public office and in restrictions on the practice of their religion. While the state made provision for education in the context of the established church, education acceptable to catholics became increasingly difficult to obtain at home; from about the mid-sixteenth century, catholics who could do so sent their sons, generally those destined for the priesthood, to catholic colleges abroad. This resort of catholic students to the Continent became a settled habit, giving rise from about 1590 to the founding of Irish colleges in Spain, France, the Low Countries, Italy, and elsewhere, which served as training centres for the work of the counter-reformation in Ireland; and Irish catholic scholars thus educated earned distinction in the European world of letters of the seventeenth century exceeding that of any Irish protestant scholar except James Ussher. Ussher was one of the first students to attend the new university, Trinity College, Dublin, founded by the crown in 1592 for the education of students 'in the liberal arts and in the cultivation of virtue and religion'. The religion was that of the protestant established church, and it was hoped that the new foundation would counteract the tendency of Irish students 'to get learning in foreign universities, whereby they have been infected with popery and other ill qualities and so become evil subjects'.[1] But though Trinity College did for a time attract some catholic students, it had no significant effect on the catholic exodus to continental seminaries. On the other hand, by its early success as a home of learning and a base for the supply of an educated clergy for the service of the established church, it fulfilled a primary aim of its founders.

The religious cleavage is exemplified in a special way in the history of the Irish parliament, a colonial institution modelled on the parliament of England, and traditionally dominated by the Anglo-Irish lords and gentry. During the late fifteenth century the Irish parliament had been blatantly exploited by overmighty subjects such as Kildare, acting in the king's name against the king's interests. This was made legally impossible for the future by a system of royal control, introduced in 1495 during an interval of direct rule under Sir Edward Poynings. 'Poynings' law' provided that no parliament

[1] Constantia Maxwell, *A history of Trinity College, Dublin, 1591–1892* (Dublin, 1940), pp 5–6.

could legally meet until licence had been obtained from the king, and that all measures to be submitted to parliament must first be approved both by the king's deputy and his council in Ireland and by the king and his council in England. Parliament could thereafter be summoned only with the approval of the king, and could legislate only in accordance with proposals previously approved both by the Irish executive and the king. The act was regarded by the 'loyal' Anglo-Irish as a safeguard against disloyal lord deputies; and in the new era of English, and necessarily loyal, lord deputies that began in 1534, it was defended by the Anglo-Irish against an executive that repeatedly attempted to have it suspended or repealed in order to rush unpopular measures through parliament. This situation was especially characteristic of the later parliaments of Elizabeth's reign, when religious and constitutional grievances combined to produce a strong Anglo-Irish opposition to the crown in the house of commons. The ecclesiastical revolution of the sixteenth century did not exclude catholics from parliament, which itself had enacted the revolutionary legislation, but the Anglo-Irish gradually found themselves, as catholics, in a losing competition with the protestant New English. In Elizabeth's reign they still formed the majority in the house of commons, stubbornly defending what they claimed to be their constitutional rights, including the Poynings' law system, against the executive, and opposing any extension of anti-catholic legislation. In the first parliament to meet after the completion of the Tudor conquest, that of 1613–15, the issue between Old English and New English was dramatically defined.

An extensive body of new legislation, including more stringent measures against catholicism, was contemplated by the government, which made elaborate preparations to ensure a protestant majority in both houses. Many new parliamentary boroughs, especially in Ulster, were created for the purpose, and all of them returned protestant members. The counties, which were now for the first time all represented, returned a strong catholic majority, the protestant minority being mainly from the counties of Ulster. The result of the general election of 1613 was 132 protestants to 100 catholics, 63 of the former and only one of the latter being returned by Ulster constituencies. The protestant members were all New English, and over 80 of the catholic members were Old English. The Irish parliament, like that of England, represented the propertied classes, not the general population; but, even so, the distribution of seats as between catholics and protestants in 1613 was unfair to the catholics, and they reacted against it so clamorously that the crown felt obliged to make concessions. The elections in 13 constituencies were disallowed, and the protestant majority was so reduced that the government had to abandon all its contentious proposals.

This was the limit of parliamentary success for the catholics. Under the strong and ruthless government of Wentworth (1633–40), bent on extracting a maximum of advantage for the king from the Irish situation, parliament was turned into a mere instrument of government policy; protestants were played off against catholics, and the catholics found that Poynings' law, far from serving as a protective mechanism, could be used by a tough and resourceful executive as an effective means of controlling parliament. In the reaction that followed the attack on Wentworth by the English parliament (November 1640), catholic and protestant members joined in an unsuccessful effort to revive the earlier interpretation of the Poynings' law system before the outbreak of rebellion in 1641 involved the withdrawal of the Old English from parliament. They endeavoured to carry over their parliamentary tradition to the Kilkenny assembly, but the eventual defeat of the confederate catholics left them politically in the wilderness. Typical of these Old English was the lawyer, Patrick Darcy, who as a member of the house of commons delivered, in June 1641 (before the rebellion), a weighty statement of the claim of the Irish parliament to be the sole legislative authority for Ireland. His argument was adopted as fundamental doctrine by the Old English, and was printed at Waterford in 1643 by the printer to the confederate catholics, of whose supreme council Darcy had become a leading member.

Under the Cromwellian regime Ireland was merged constitutionally in a single commonwealth with England and Scotland, and had representatives, all protestant, in the Westminster parliament. But this parliamentary union did not strike root, and the Irish parliament was reconstituted under Charles II at the restoration. Though catholics were not debarred by law from being members, only one catholic was returned to the house of commons, and he did not take his seat. From 1661 onwards, except in 1689, the house of commons was exclusively, and the house of lords almost entirely, a protestant assembly, dominated by the New English. Having secured a land settlement highly favourable to the occupying Cromwellians, and having agreed to a settlement of the permanent revenues highly favourable to the crown, parliament was kept in abeyance from 1666 to 1692, apart from James II's revolutionary assembly of 1689. The short-lived reappearance of the Old English on the parliamentary scene in that year, when, in the parliament—almost entirely catholic in composition—irregularly summoned by James II, they had a large majority over the Old Irish, served to write their historical epitaph. They secured James's assent to a bill declaring that the parliament of England had no right to legislate for Ireland, as it had egregiously done since 1642, but could not induce him to agree to the repeal of Poynings' law. They hoped to reestablish the catholic church, but all that James would accept was equal religious liberty for all Christian churches. They repealed the restoration land-settlement, and, while not restoring lands confiscated from catholics before 1642, threatened all protestant landowners with expropriation by a wide-ranging act of attainder. All these intentions were quickly nullified by the victory of the Williamites. Parliament reemerged in 1692, its colonial identity more strongly marked than ever, as a preserve of the protestants, who, in return for their ascendancy in Ireland, had to submit to its subordination both to the crown and to the parliament of England.

Though the conflicts of the sixteenth and seventeenth centuries involved great suffering and devastation, the early modern age was far from being one of unrelieved violence and economic ruin. The mainly subsistence and relatively primitive agricultural economy of the sixteenth century was succeeded by a more progressive and diversified economy in which industrial production and external trade played an increasing part, though at the end of the seventeenth century the economy was still overwhelmingly pastoral, with livestock products greatly exceeding all other exports in value. The seventeenth century in Ireland, despite the catastrophic changes that it witnessed, was a time of relative peace: the public violence of the century was crowded into two short intervals—1641–53 and 1689–91—between two periods of rapid economic recovery. In each of these periods the influx of new colonists from England and Scotland brought new energies and capital to bear on the economy and stimulated its growth. Despite the destruction in the intervals of violence and despite emigration, the population appears to have doubled between 1600 and 1713 (from 1·4 to 2·8 millions), which indicates a high growth-rate by contemporary European standards.[1] The most populous and prosperous regions were those in which the colonial culture was strongest and where tillage was a distinctive part of the farming pattern, as in the counties of the former Pale, while the opposite extreme was exemplified by west Connacht. The most striking population change came about in Ulster, which in the early seventeenth century was the province least inhabited and least developed economically. The Ulster colony grew slowly to 1641 and suffered heavy losses during the rebellion and the ensuing wars, but was quick to recover and was strongly reinforced by fresh waves of immigration from Scotland, especially in the 1680s. Towards the end of the century Ulster was regarded as the most thickly populated and the most economically progressive of the four provinces, and it was certainly the most British. Here, as elsewhere, there were marked local contrasts between the improving conditions of colonists well established in the fertile lowlands, and the impoverished farming of native Irish squeezed out into the hills and bogs; and the socio-economic profile of Ireland in general was broadly paralleled by the contrasts between Antrim, Down, and Armagh on the one hand and western Ulster on the other.[2]

Urban development was a feature of seventeenth-century Ireland; of its 117 municipal corporations in 1692, about two-thirds (80) had been created since 1603.[3] The largest proportionate increases were in Ulster (from 2 to 29

[1] See ch. XV. [2] See ch. XVIII. [3] See map 13.

boroughs) and in Connacht (from 2 to 10). Many of the new boroughs were incorporated in the early years of the century for the purpose of ensuring the return of protestant burgesses to the house of commons, and many failed to justify in economic terms the municipal privileges conferred on them by their charters. This was particularly true of the Ulster towns, most of which remained very small and underdeveloped, the largest of them, Derry, having only about 2,000 inhabitants by the end of the century. The greatest expansion took place in some of the older towns—most notably Dublin, Cork, Waterford, and Limerick—and in the latter half of the century. Dublin in 1685, with between 50,000 and 60,000 inhabitants, was not only by far the largest city in Ireland but was the second city of the British empire.[1]

English economic policy towards Ireland, as it took shape during the seventeenth century, was characterised not so much by malevolence to Ireland as by overriding concern for English interests. Where Irish and English interests conflicted there was no question but that the former must be sacrificed. This applied in a crucial way to wool and the woollen industry, which had a central place in the English economy and was also a principal element in Ireland's export trade. English policy was directed to protecting home supplies of wool for the English clothing trade, to ensuring such outside supplies as were needed by that trade, and to minimising the export of raw wool from Ireland to England's continental competitors. This did not prevent the growth of large and valuable exports of wool and coarse woollen products from Ireland, mainly to England, but also to the Continent. The other comparable export, live cattle, was largely destroyed by English legislation of 1663, 1667, and 1681, passed in response to cattle-breeding (as distinct from cattle-fattening) interests in England. The injury thus caused to the Irish economy was compensated by a remarkable expansion in the export, not so much of beef, as has generally been believed, as of butter, especially to France. In the transatlantic trade, under the mercantile system developed after 1650 Ireland was at first treated on the same footing as England in relation to the English colonies in America. This was altered by acts of 1663 and 1671 which required that trade between Ireland and these colonies must be conducted through England. But an exception was made in favour of the direct export of provisions, horses, and servants from Ireland, which proved more advantageous to the Irish economy than the prohibition of direct importation of colonial goods proved disadvantageous. The colonial product mainly imported was tobacco from Virginia, the consumption of which was relatively large and continued to increase after its direct shipment to Ireland was prohibited.

While Ireland as a whole made impressive economic advances during the seventeenth century, the benefits were far from being evenly shared by the various elements that made up Ireland's population. Since land was the

[1] See ch. XVII, XVIII.

source of nearly all the wealth of the country the principal beneficiaries were the landowners. At the opening of the seventeenth century the great bulk of the land was owned by catholics, of both Gaelic and Anglo-Irish stock, the rest being in the hands of New English. The deterioration in the economic position of the catholics during the century is reflected in the shrinkage of the area of land owned by them. By 1641, as a result largely of the Ulster confiscations, their share had fallen to 59 per cent, divided in roughly equal shares between Gaelic Irish and Old English; after the Cromwellian and the restoration land-settlements only 22 per cent remained in catholic hands, and by 1703 only 14 per cent.[1] Between 1641 and 1703 the proportion of land in protestant ownership had thus risen from 41 to 86 per cent. By the end of the century protestants, who amounted to not much more than one-quarter of the whole population, were distinctively the landowning class, and catholics, who were nearly three-quarters of the population, were as distinctively the tenant class. This was the general pattern in most of Ireland. But in Ulster, where there was a concentration of protestants comprising all social classes, a large proportion of the tenants were protestant; and in Connacht many of the landlords were catholic.

The change in the distribution of landownership as between catholics and protestants was one dimension of a vast social upheaval; another was the destruction of the native Irish system of landholding based on ownership by extended family groups and on the rights of local lords to dues and services from their followers and subjects. The system had infinite variety and complexity; landless men and labourers formed an important element in it, along with landowners and free tenants, great and small; but its most distinctive feature was that, in contrast with English primogeniture, inheritance was normally divided among sons (not necessarily legitimate according to canon, or English common, law), or, failing sons, among the male next-of-kin. While ultimate ownership lay with the family group, ownership in effect was widely dispersed, and there was a large body of small gentry. All this was transformed by the advance of the English centralised state which, both by negotiated settlements with Gaelic lords and, still more, by direct conquest and confiscation, replaced a Gaelic with an English land-system throughout Ireland. A relatively simple structure emerged in which a high proportion of all the land was owned by a small number of great landowners, and occupied by a large mass of tenants, mostly of small holdings but comprising a wide range of social and economic conditions. This was to remain the basic structure of rural Ireland till the agrarian revolution of the late nineteenth century.

The destruction of the Gaelic land-system was part of a revolution that destroyed the political, and much of the social, structure of Gaelic Ireland.

[1] See map 10.

The breaking-up after 1603 of that aristocratic society, in which the professional learned classes and their schools of traditional learning had a privileged place, deprived hereditary poets, historians, lawyers, and medical men of their patrons and left them at the mercy of a new and unsympathetic social order. In so far as Gaelic popular culture survived the shocks of the seventeenth century, it did so mainly in social customs—marriage patterns, house types, agricultural practices, sports and pastimes; in the prestige of the priest, the poet, the scholar, the storyteller, and the harper; in oral tradition; and, most distinctively, in the Irish language. While English was the speech of the Old English and of the New English, and became increasingly the speech of Leinster, Irish continued throughout the seventeenth century to be spoken by the majority of the catholic population in the other three provinces. On its intellectual side, despite the monastic dissolutions and the decline of the schools of traditional learning, Gaelic culture produced in the seventeenth century a rich and varied literature that ranged from the Annals of the Four Masters to the work of one of the greatest of Irish poets, David Ó Bruadair (d. 1698). This literary output in Irish was paralleled by a no less remarkable flowering of literature in Latin by writers both of Gaelic and of Old English stock. Some of these latinists wrote in Ireland, but increasingly they came to be based on centres of Irish learning on the Continent. Their preoccupation with the controversies of the counter-reformation age and the fact that their innumerable volumes issued from printing-houses widely dispersed over the Continent are an expression of Ireland's new involvement in the intellectual life of Europe.[1]

The activity of Irish scholars on the Continent was an aspect of a larger and many-sided movement of Irish catholic emigration, as characteristic of early modern Ireland as the immigration of new, protestant settlers. Students went to the Continent for general education and training for the priesthood, and many remained. Clergy found shelter there from persecution and during times of crisis, as in the commonwealth period, large numbers were forcibly banished there or to America. Others went abroad to prepare Irish students in continental seminaries to take part in the counter-reformation at home, or to ensure communications between the bishops and clergy in Ireland and the papacy, or to act as diplomatic agents of Irish leaders of rebellion in quest of foreign support. Professional laymen and merchants sought opportunities abroad denied to them at home; and a stream of mixed humanity, ranging from nobles and gentry to plain soldiers, largely the victims of rebellion and war, intermittently trickled or poured out of Ireland to seek hospitality, social recognition, employment, or mere survival in most countries of western Europe. Irish exiles became a familiar element in most European capitals, and at many European courts. Irish soldiers fought in the armies of nearly every European state from Sweden to Spain, from the Low

[1] See ch. XXI, XXII.

Countries to Austria; Irish regiments formed in the service of Spain, France, and the Netherlands established an identity under officers drawn from many famous Irish families, and earned a high reputation in the wars of the seventeenth century. Long before the culminating exodus of Irish soldiers—'the wild geese'—that followed the treaty of Limerick, soldiering had become the recognised occupation of the great majority of Irish emigrants to the Continent. Whatever their destinations and their occupations, the emigrants took with them the values and traditions of their homeland, including an incurable tendency to quarrel among themselves. Thus the controversies of the confederate period between Old Irish and Old English were reproduced on the Continent in unbridled polemics conducted in Latin by rival groups of clergy.[1]

Of the two elements in Irish catholicism, the Old English seemed in the early years of the seventeenth century to be a potential bridge between the cultures of the Gael and of the English. But English policy weakened, alienated, and eventually eliminated the Old English as a political and social force and established the New English as a protestant ascendancy. The bulk of the Old English who remained in Ireland eventually became merged culturally with the Old Irish, while a minority, mainly those who survived as landowners, adopted the culture of the New English. The cultural cleavage between Gaelic Ireland and Anglo-Ireland was thus irremediably widened. At the end of the seventeenth century the former, mainly Irish-speaking and wholly catholic, was strongest on the lower levels of society and in the infertile regions of the western seaboard. Rural, archaic, and economically backward, stamped with defeat and loss of its leaders, it was nevertheless proud of its ancient lineage and the cultural heritage preserved in its literature and its oral tradition, as sustained and popularised by its poets and storytellers. Highly localised, it was also highly conscious of its Irish identity; and through a long process of emigration it had acquired many links with catholic Europe, to which it looked for sympathy and support. The Irish diaspora of the early modern period gave a new dimension to Irish culture: in the seventeenth century the Irish on the Continent supplied the most outstanding spokesmen of Irish national claims, the greatest conservators of Irish learning, nearly all the confederate commanders in the wars of 1641–52, and the principal examples of social and commercial success achieved by catholic Irishmen during the century. The other Ireland, English-speaking and overwhelmingly protestant, was both urban and rural. In general the Ireland of the landowning and moneyed interests, it was strongest in Dublin, in the area of the former Pale, and in Ulster, where it included a large body of tenant farmers and industrial workers. Its culture, largely a transplant from England and Scotland, had taken root in a soil prepared for it by the Old English whom the New English displaced.

[1] See ch. XXII, XXIII.

Dynamic, acquisitive, progressive, and self-confident, this culture was reflected in economic expansion, in town life, in domestic architecture, urban and rural, in literary and scientific interests, and in political and social institutions. It was still a colonial rather than an Irish culture, but it had acquired a sense of continuity with the Irish past that found expression in a selective interest in Irish history: thus the claim of the medieval Irish parliament to legislative independence found an echo in the convention parliament of 1660, which, though dominated by the Cromwellians, declared that Ireland had a centuries-old right to be governed by a parliament of its own. By the end of the seventeenth century the New English colony could boast of a substantial and increasing output of writings, historical, religious, scientific, and political, but together they did not amount to an Anglo-Irish literature. The problem of corporate identity was all the more difficult for the colony because it included the Ulster Scots, who maintained close connections with their presbyterian brethren in Scotland and who in the 1640s regarded themselves simply as part of the Scottish nation residing in Ireland.

There was, of course, no complete separation between the two cultures. They coexisted in varying strengths and interacted on each other in varying degrees over most of the country. The cleavage was sharpest and most permanent in the colonised areas of Ulster, and was probably most blurred in Leinster and the inland towns generally. On the highest level of scholarship there was mutual respect and understanding between writers identified with New English, Old English, and Old Irish traditions, but generally and increasingly the New English looked upon the catholic Irish as belonging to an out-of-date and inferior, if not degenerate, culture. The catholic Irish reactions to this attitude ranged from scorn, denunciation, and defiance to passive resistance, submission, and sycophancy. Aspiring Irish peasants who aped the manners and speech of their English-speaking landlords were satirised in an Irish tract of the later seventeenth century, *Páirlimint Chloinne Tomáis*, which expresses the anger of a professional scholar at the destruction of the social fabric that had given his profession status and security.

The spirit of the age and the character of Irish history in the sixteenth and seventeenth centuries favoured new developments in Irish historiography;[1] and during this period the output, both published and unpublished, of Irish history, in close association with descriptive and expository writing about Ireland, was an integral part of the historical process itself. Historiography in the form of annals and genealogies had a long-established and distinguished place in Gaelic culture, which it continued to hold until well into the seventeenth century.[2] Four important series of Annals marked the end of a long

[1] See bibliography, § III B 1 and 3, IV D 9, for full particulars of all works referred to in this and succeeding paragraphs.

[2] See ch. xx.

tradition: the Annals of Ulster, extending from 431 to 1541; the Annals of Loch Cé, from 1014 to 1590; the Annals of Connacht, from 1224 to 1544; and the Annals of the Four Masters, from the earliest times to 1616. The last of these, which became the best known, was compiled by the Franciscan, Michael O'Clery, and his lay associates near the ancient friary of Donegal in 1632–6, as the Gaelic world of which they were the last of the traditional chroniclers was breaking up before their eyes. As they approached their own times these latest Annals showed an increasing tendency to depart from the traditional form of mere chronology in favour of narrative. A contemporary of the Four Masters, Geoffrey Keating, a secular priest of Tipperary, wrote his 'Foras feasa ar Éirinn' (completed *c.* 1634) entirely in narrative. It was a pioneer attempt to assemble all that its learned author could discover from manuscript sources and from tradition about his country's early history and mythology down to the Anglo-Norman invasion. Though the body of the work is a mixture of fact and legend, it has a long critical introduction in which Keating castigates previous writers, especially Giraldus Cambrensis and Richard Stanihurst, for statements about both the Gaelic Irish and the Anglo-Irish that he alleges to be false and defamatory. Keating's 'Basis of knowledge about Ireland' deals with the country as a whole; and whereas the annalists tended to be artificial and archaic, Keating wrote a highly readable, and at the same time classical, prose. His book became a standard text, which was frequently copied and widely read. Two other narrative works of the early seventeenth century in Irish were important contributions to contemporary history: a detailed account of the travels of O'Neill, O'Donnell, and others, beginning with their 'flight' from Lough Swilly and ending with their arrival in Rome (1607–8), by a professional historian who accompanied them, Tadhg Ó Cianáin; and a life of Hugh Roe O'Donnell from 1587 to 1602, by Lughaidh O'Clery (*c.* 1616), which was one of the sources used by the Four Masters.

The tradition of genealogical writing was conspicuously exemplified by Duald MacFirbis (1585–1670), member of a family of Lackan, County Sligo, renowned for many generations as hereditary historians, who devoted his long life to genealogical writing, and to the collecting, transcribing, and translating of Irish manuscripts. A great book of genealogies that he compiled at Galway in 1645–50 is a comprehensive work of reference for all the principal Gaelic families of Ireland. He was the last of his line, and the last great master of his art, though Gaelic genealogies continued to be compiled till the early years of the eighteenth century.

The transition from annals to historical narratives occurred sooner in works written in English, though the annalistic form continued in English writing till beyond the middle of the seventeenth century. From about 1570 historical accounts and descriptions of existing conditions (the two generally went together) were being produced that reflect the curiosity of the Elizabethans about an Ireland struggling to resist the advance of English power. Edmund Campion, a brilliant young scholar from Oxford, who was attracted to Ireland in 1569 by a project for setting up a university in Dublin and who was to earn notoriety and martyrdom (1581) as a Jesuit missionary in England; John Hooker *alias* Vowell, writer and editor, and chamberlain of Exeter; Edmund Spenser and Sir John Davies, poets and officials of the Irish government; Fynes Moryson, fellow of Peterhouse, traveller, and secretary to Lord Deputy Mountjoy (1600–03); Thomas Stafford, soldier and secretary to Sir George Carew as lord president of Munster (1600–03); Sir James Perrot, M.P. for Haverfordwest, illegitimate son of one Irish lord deputy (Sir John Perrot), and brother-in-law of another (Sir Arthur Chichester) through whom he obtained a military command at Newry (1608–10)—these were outstanding examples of newcomers to Ireland who as writers expressed New English attitudes, especially in their sense of the barbarity of Gaelic culture and the necessity for English conquest. On the other hand, a pupil of Campion's at Oxford, Richard Stanihurst, whose family had long roots in Dublin, though typically Old English in his contemptuous attitude to the Irish language, shows some sympathetic insight into Gaelic culture and institutions; even so, he is included by Keating, himself of Anglo-Irish stock, with Giraldus Cambrensis and the 'new foreigners' whom Keating denounces as traducers both of the Gaels and of the 'old foreigners'.

Campion compiled a jejune chronicle down to about 1500, from which point onwards he, Stanihurst, and Hooker between them carried the story down to 1586 in lively and overlapping narratives. Stanihurst also wrote a description of Ireland, published in 1577, a history of the Anglo-Norman invasion of Ireland, *De rebus in Hibernia gestis* (1584), and a life of St Patrick. Moryson and Stafford provide a detailed account of the final years of the war with Hugh O'Neill. Perrot, who drew on government records and recollections of leading actors in the events he describes, continued 'the chronicle of Ireland' from 1584, where 'the last writer' (presumably Hooker) left it, to 1600, and ended inconclusively with some notes on 1604–8. Spenser's 'View of the present state of Ireland' (1596) and Davies's *Discovery of the true causes why Ireland was never entirely subdued . . . until the beginning of his majesty's happy reign* (1612) are both books on a high level of conceptual thinking and contemporary observation. Spenser had a poet's eye not only for the beauty of the Irish countryside but also for its indigenous population and their distinctive way of life, though he advocated the policy of forcible anglicisation and justified the savagery of English military operations. The optimistic Davies, writing after the Tudor conquest, analysed the causes of chronic disturbance in Ireland with considerable knowledge and insight, claimed that they had now for the first time been removed, and predicted for Ireland a peaceful and prosperous future under the strong and even-handed government of James I and his successors.

While Keating was at pains to distinguish between Gaelic Irish and Old English on the one hand and New English on the other, most catholic historians of the age, generally writing in Latin, were preoccupied with the catholic–protestant antithesis. Peter Lombard (catholic archbishop of Armagh, 1601–25) wrote in 1600, at Rome, an account of Hugh O'Neill's rebellion seen as a war for the catholic religion. His *De regno Hiberniae commentarius* was intended to enlist the support of Pope Clement VIII on O'Neill's side. Don Philip O'Sullivan Beare, exiled member of a once-powerful Gaelic family of County Cork, published at Lisbon in 1621 his *Historiae catholicae Iberniae compendium*, which, after a survey of Irish history to 1588, describes the religious conflicts of the later Elizabethan period in the light of information received from his father and other contemporaries. The *Analecta sacra nova et mira de rebus catholicorum in Hibernia . . . gestis* (Cologne, 1616–19), of David Rothe (bishop of Ossory, 1618–50), records the sufferings of catholics at the hands of the state, giving pre-eminence to the lives of three martyred prelates, Richard Creagh (archbishop of Armagh, 1564–85), Dermot O'Hurley (archbishop of Cashel, 1581–4), and Cornelius O'Devany (bishop of Down and Connor, 1582–1612). There was no counterpart to such historiography on the side of the established church. The catholic reaction under Mary produced no protestant martyrs, but one of the Edwardian reformers whose position was quickly made untenable by Mary's accession, the English John Bale, wrote a revealing account of his tribulations as protestant bishop of Ossory in 1553.

A remarkable initiative in the study of early Irish history was taken by a group of Franciscans at the Irish college of St Anthony's, Louvain (founded in 1606). Hugh Ward, John Colgan, Michael O'Clery (all three from Donegal), and others formed an ambitious plan to discover, collect, present, and use the surviving source-materials for Irish ecclesiastical history, and through their efforts a wealth of manuscripts from many parts of Europe was assembled at Louvain. The scheme was never completed, but it did result in a number of valuable Latin publications, most notable among them the *Acta sanctorum . . . Hiberniae* (Louvain, 1645) and the *Triadis thaumaturgae . . . acta* (Louvain, 1647), both edited by Colgan and setting a new standard in Irish hagiography. The much more famous Annals of the Four Masters was in a sense a by-product of the Louvain project, being a development of Michael O'Clery's collecting work in Ireland.

Two protestant scholars, both graduates of Trinity College, were also engaged in similar fundamental research—James Ussher (archbishop of Armagh, 1625–56) and Sir James Ware (1594–1666), auditor general of Ireland. Ussher, a polymath of European fame, with a prodigious mastery of biblical and patristic learning, laid the foundations of an anglican view of Irish history. Ware wrote pioneer works of reference on the bishops (to 1665) and on the writers of Ireland (the latter a proto-bibliography), annals for the period 1485–1558, and a study of Irish antiquities—all in Latin and all remarkably free from sectarian animus. Ussher had friendly contacts with leading Irish catholic scholars at home and on the Continent, and Ware, who was interested in materials in the Irish language, employed Duald MacFirbis to transcribe and translate Irish texts for him. His voluminous manuscripts, now principally in the British Library and the Bodleian, are an invaluable collection of extracts from sources, for many of which the originals are no longer extant. The erudite John Lynch, for many years catholic archdeacon of Tuam, described Ware as 'vir clarissimus' and relied largely on his *De praesulibus Hiberniae* (1665) for a history of the Irish bishops that he wrote under the same title in 1672. While acknowledging his indebtedness to Ware, Lynch supplements him by evidence from Gaelic and Roman sources, and instead of following Ware's protestant succession of bishops after 1534 replaces it with a catholic succession.

Lynch was one of many Irish historians of the age who felt called upon to denounce Giraldus Cambrensis, the twelfth-century Norman-Welsh writer, whose 'Topographia Hibernica' and 'Expugnatio Hibernica', primary sources for the Anglo-Norman invasion of Ireland, were published by the English chronicler, William Camden, in 1602. He was the 'poisoned spring whence all other writers who hate Ireland imbibe their envenomed calumnies',[1] prominent among these others being Richard Stanihurst, whose *De rebus in Hibernia gestis* drew heavily on Giraldus. To refute the alleged calumnies was not so much a matter of correcting historical errors as of vindicating Ireland's good name in the eyes of continental scholars. An extreme attempt to do this was Philip O'Sullivan Beare's 'Zoilomastix' ('a whip for the detractor') written in Latin in 1625. A laboured and tedious diatribe, it nevertheless contains valuable descriptive matter. The anti-English and anti-protestant prejudice that permeates it is well illustrated by its author's comment on the term 'Anglo-Ibernici' (Anglo-Irish), which, he says, was invented by Stanihurst. Repenting of having used it himself he condemns it as no more applicable to Irishmen than 'Lutheran-Irish' or 'Puritan-Irish' or 'Atheist-Irish' would be.[2]

The rebellion of 1641 and the ensuing wars gave new stimulus to polemical history and a new emphasis to the distinctions between Old Irish, Old English, and New English. The 'Aphorismical discovery of treasonable faction' is a strongly partisan account of the confederate period by a writer who identified himself with Owen Roe O'Neill, the Old Irish leader. A narrative in Irish on the fighting in Ulster and Leinster during 1641–7, written from the same standpoint, was probably the work of a Franciscan, Turlough O'Mellon, who appears to have been chaplain to Sir Phelim

[1] John Lynch, *Cambrensis eversus* (1662), quoted by T. J. O'Donnell in his learned and invaluable introduction to O'Sullivan Beare, *Zoilomastix.*

[2] *Zoilomastix*, pp 61–3; cf. above, p. xlii.

O'Neill. The voluminous 'Commentarius Rinuccinianus', written in 1661–6, is a monumental effort by two Capuchins, Richard O'Ferrall and Robert O'Connell, to vindicate, largely by means of documentary evidence, the conduct of Rinuccini, who, as papal nuncio (1645–9) to the confederate catholics, had identified himself with the cause of the Old Irish. An Old English interpretation of the confederate period, set against a broad background of Irish history, is contained in two works by the erudite John Lynch, *Cambrensis eversus* ([St Malo], 1662) and *Alithinologia* (St Malo, 1664, 1667). Lynch had been forced into exile by the Cromwellian conquest, but remained an unshakeable advocate of the Old English position, condemned the rising of 1641, and was strongly critical of Rinuccini. A much less disinterested defender of the Old English was Richard Bellings, secretary to the confederate supreme council, who had studied law at Lincoln's Inn and added a sixth book to Sir Philip Sidney's *Arcadia*. Bellings's narrative of affairs in Ireland, 1641–9, is persuasively slanted in favour of Ormond, Charles I's viceroy, through whose influence Bellings had recovered part of his estates after the restoration.

On the new English side, Sir John Temple, master of the rolls in Ireland (1640–3) and eldest son of a provost of Trinity College, published in 1646 an inflammatory history of the 1641 rebellion, which was widely accepted among protestants as an authoritative source for the massacres of 1641. Another, less successful, work of the same kind, by Edmund Borlase, son of the Sir John Borlase who was lord justice in 1640–3, was published in 1680. It was partly cribbed from an unpublished 'History of the rebellion and civil wars in Ireland', by Edward Hyde (1609–74), earl of Clarendon, the moderate English royalist who had been friend and adviser to Charles I in 1641–5 and lord chancellor of England under Charles II. His account of the English rebellion is the most valuable single narrative of the period 1640–60 by a contemporary, and one of the historical masterpieces of the seventeenth century. His treatment of events in Ireland during the same period is much less well informed, and is largely concerned with defending the conduct of Ormond against attacks by Nicholas French, catholic bishop of Ferns, a leading member of the Kilkenny assembly.

The most distinctive contributions to our knowledge of Ireland made by the New English in the later seventeenth century were not in the field of history but in that of contemporary description and analysis. Continuing a tradition that reached back to the Elizabethans, but in a scientific spirit characteristic of their own age, Sir William Petty and William Molyneux explored the geographical, economic, and social state of the country, and left on record a wealth of precise information and intelligent commentary. Petty, an acquisitive adventurer and a practical genius of phenomenal range and versatility, established a scientific cartography of Ireland with his Down Survey maps. He wrote a general account of the Irish economy and social structure (1672), laid the foundation of a statistical study of the country, and produced its first comprehensive atlas (*Hiberniae delineatio*, 1685). Molyneux, secretary, and one of the founders, with Petty, of the Dublin Philosophical Society (1683), organised a cooperative survey of twenty-two counties in 1682–3, which produced an extensive collection of detailed local information. Unlike previous surveys such as Petty's, made to give effect to schemes of confiscation, Molyneux's was the first of its kind in Ireland to be undertaken in the interests of knowledge for its own sake.

Associated with Molyneux was Roderick O'Flaherty, a Gaelic scholar and a landowner impoverished by the Cromwellian confiscation. A friend of John Lynch and pupil of Duald MacFirbis, he devoted his great though wayward learning not, as might have been expected, to polemic against the New English, but to the study of Irish history and antiquities and to the defence of Old Irish loyalty to the Stuart monarchy. His 'Chorographical description of West or h-Iar Connaught', written in 1684, was a contribution to Molyneux's scheme; and his *Ogygia, seu rerum Hibernicarum chronologia*, published in London in 1685, extends to his own day, and carries a dedication to the duke of York, soon to become King James II.

The final convulsion of the seventeenth century, resulting from the English revolution of 1688, produced a further crop of polemic and of contemporary history. On the Jacobite side the conflict was recounted from an Old English standpoint in 'A light to the blind' (probably by Nicholas Plunkett of Dunsoghly, member of a landowning family of County Dublin),[1] and from that of the Old Irish in 'Macariae excidium, or the destruction of Cyprus', an allegorical history by Charles O'Kelly, lord of the manor of Screen, County Galway, who fought as an officer in James II's forces. The Williamite interpretation is represented by *The state of the protestants in Ireland under the late King James's government*, by William King, bishop of Derry; and by two narratives by George Story, an English clergyman who served as chaplain in the Williamite army, was present at the battle of the Boyne, and later became dean of Connor. King's book is actively partisan and does less than justice to James II; Story's *Impartial history* endeavours to be fair and is an indispensable source for events of the war period.

A New English view of Irish history was written shortly before the Jacobite war by Sir Richard Cox, recorder of Kinsale, who took part in the war and eventually became lord chancellor. His *Hibernica Anglicana, or the history of Ireland from the conquest thereof by the English to this present time* (London, 1689–90), is mainly important for the documents it contains and for its avowed intention of showing 'that the Irish did continue in their barbarity, poverty, and ignorance until the English conquest, and that all the improvements themselves and their country received . . . is to be ascribed to the

[1] See J. G. Simms's introduction to the reprint (Shannon, 1971) of Gilbert's edition, entitled *A Jacobite narrative of the war in Ireland*, . . . (Dublin, 1892).

English government'. Cox was the spokesman of the protestants of the established church. The dissenting element within protestantism, which had grown up since the early years of the century and was composed overwhelmingly of Ulster-Scottish presbyterians, found its historian in a contemporary of Cox, Patrick Adair, who came to Ulster from Scotland as a minister in 1646 and from then till his death in 1694 was deeply involved both in the religious life and in the politics of presbyterianism. His 'True narrative of the rise and progress of the presbyterian church in Ireland', which carries the story down to 1670, records the sufferings of Ulster presbyterians at the hands not only of the catholics, but also of the ascendant protestants. The antagonism between episcopalians and presbyterians assumed a special form in rival claims about the defence of Derry in 1689. An account of the great siege by the anglican clergyman, George Walker, who was governor of the city, was challenged by a presbyterian minister, John Mackenzie. He claimed that Walker was unfair to the presbyterians who like himself had shared in the defence; and thus began a vicious sectarian controversy that was to echo down to the present century. Of the new dissenting sects introduced from England during the commonwealth period, the early history of the quakers, or Religious Society of Friends, is reflected in the journal of their leading member in Ireland, William Edmundson (1627–1712), which casts light not only on the religious life but also on the society and politics of the latter half of the seventeenth century.

This historiography we have been considering has a twofold significance—as a contribution to Irish history and as historical evidence for the age that produced it. As history, it was frankly tendentious: in conformity with the accepted values of the times, it sought to vindicate or to condemn as much as to inform and explain. In so far as it relates to early and medieval Ireland, there is little of it that is indispensable to modern scholarship except the Irish annals and genealogies, works by Colgan, Ussher, Ware, and Lynch, and material in Keating's history and elsewhere derived from sources that have not survived. But most of the historical writing of the early modern period relates to that period itself, and it is here that its value as history chiefly lies. The Irish annalists and genealogists; Lughaidh O'Clery, Tadhg Ó Cianáin, and the author of 'O'Mellon's journal'; Campion, Stanihurst, Hooker, and Perrot; Spenser and Davies; Stafford and Moryson; Lombard, O'Sullivan Beare, and Rothe; Ware; O'Ferrall, O'Connell, the author of the 'Aphorismical discovery', and Bellings; Lynch and O'Flaherty; the author of 'A light to the blind' and O'Kelly; King and Story; Cox; Adair, Walker and Mackenzie, and Edmundson—all contain information about early modern Ireland, and much documentary material, not otherwise available. In the works of such writers history proper merges with contemporary history and contemporary description. But whether they are writing about the immediate, the recent, or the remote past, and whatever their scholarly merit, the historians of the period reveal their own age, and in doing so are on common ground with its scientific observers.

Seventeenth-century Europe saw the beginnings of modern historical scholarship, with its insistence on the critical use of primary sources. A shining example was the work of the Bollandists, the group of Belgian Jesuits, who in 1643 published the first volumes of their gigantic undertaking the *Acta sanctorum* (still in progress), with which the scheme of the Irish Franciscans at Louvain had much in common. Ussher and Ware, Colgan and Lynch, and many of the Irish scholars on the Continent such as Luke Wadding, the historian of the Franciscan order, may be regarded as contributors to the new historiography. It was not till the nineteenth century that Irish scholars of similar calibre—Petrie, O'Donovan, O'Curry, Todd, Reeves, and others—were to resume work on the foundations thus laid.

From a review of the early modern period as a whole certain major themes emerge: the continuing and progressively successful effort of the English state to assert its authority over the whole island; the struggle, progressively unsuccessful, of the Gaelic Irish to defend their own political and social order and their own culture; the forcible introduction, by English authority, of the protestant reformation, producing a bitter and irremediable division between the religion of the state in Ireland and that of the great majority of its subjects; the massive and unshakeable adherence of Irish catholics to the papal authority, and the consequent tendency of the state to identify catholicism with treason; the new involvement of the catholic Irish in the counter-reformation and the intervention of Spain in Irish rebellions; the reanimation and reformation of religious life within the catholic body under the combined impact of persecution and the counter-reformation; the rise of a new British and protestant colony, endowed with land confiscated from catholics, and supplying decisive stimulus to economic growth; the development of the state church as the church of the New English establishment, with a puritan-oriented theology and clergy educated in the new university, Trinity College, Dublin; the rise of the presbyterian church and other dissenting bodies within the new British colony, and the tensions resulting from their relationship of civil inferiority to the protestants of the established church; the excruciating dilemma of the Old English, torn between their catholicism and their ancient tradition of loyalty to the English crown; the two unsuccessful attempts of the Old English and the Old Irish in combination to overthrow or to halt the advance of the New English; and the rise of the concept of a catholic Irish nation, embracing Old English and Old Irish, and aspiring to an independent parliamentary constitution under the English crown; and the emigration of catholic Irish to the Continent and to America.

The concept of a catholic nation took shape in the catholic confederacy of 1642–9 and found its fullest expression in the Jacobite war, with Patrick

Sarsfield as its hero-figure and the 'flight of the wild geese' as the penalty of defeat. But the distinction between the Old Irish and the Old English remained scarcely less evident than that between both and the New English. Each of these three elements preserved its own identity and its own view of Irish history. Even after the disasters of 1689–91, the Old English author of 'A light to the blind' could write:

The just interest of the crown of England is only preserved in Ireland by maintaining in a high state the true conquerors of that kingdom, who by their blood annexed the Irish crown to the English diadem. . . . Those victors, being catholics, landed from England in Ireland under the happy fortune of Henry the Second. . . . Their posterity have continued in the like gallantry and loyalty even to this day, propping the true kings of England, at the hazard of their lives and fortunes, while the upstart protestants have of late years endeavoured to cast down those crowned heads, and actually prevailed.[1]

While Old English attitudes provide clues to the history of early modern Ireland, English policy provides the key. Viewed from England, Ireland was a strategic risk, and a pawn in the English political game: the great conflicts of sixteenth-century Ireland were inseparable from English strategic interests and ecclesiastical changes, and the major crises of the seventeenth century were precipitated by revolutionary situations in England. Shaping and reinforcing these connections was the fact that Ireland had become a new field for the expansive and acquisitive energies of the English; and the attitudes of the new English colonists towards the old inhabitants of Ireland were those of the English state. Belief in the necessity for, and the justification of, English conquest and confiscation were held just as firmly by Spenser and Davies, Temple and Borlase, Petty, King, Cox, and Adair as by Cromwell, who characterised the rebellion of 1641 as an unprovoked massacre of innocent protestants and an outrageous attack on the legitimate authority of England by Irish papists, instigated by wicked and bloodthirsty priests. The levellers in the New Model army who objected to taking part in the reconquest of Ireland in 1649 generally did so because of their grievances as soldiers, not through any understanding of the nature of the Irish struggle. But there were one or two astonishing exceptions. One of the leveller leaders, William Walwyn, among other views obnoxious to fellow puritans, is reported to have asserted

that the sending over forces to Ireland is for nothing else but to make way by the blood of the army to enlarge their [the commonwealth government's] territories of power and tyranny; that it is an unlawful war, a cruel and bloody work to go to destroy the Irish natives for their consciences and to drive them from their proper natural and native rights;[2] . . . that the cause of the Irish natives in seeking their

[1] Gilbert, *Jacobite narr.*, p. 5.

[2] Extracted from *Walwins wiles* (London, 1649), an anti-Walwyn pamphlet reprinted in *The leveller tracts, 1647–53*, ed. William Haller and Godfrey Davies (Gloucester, Mass., 1964), pp 288–9.

just freedoms, immunities and liberties is the very same with our cause here, in endeavouring our own rescue and freedom from the power of oppressors.[1]

A long time was to pass before the idea was again voiced by an Englishman that Irish resistance to English conquest was a natural right, and the common cause of men fighting for liberty in England no less than in Ireland.

The period 1534–1691 in Irish history, though an age of economic advance and intellectual activity, was above all an age of disruption. Prolonged and fundamental conflict over sovereignty, land, religion, and culture produced changes more catastrophic and far-reaching than anything Ireland had experienced since the Anglo-Norman invasion of the twelfth century, or was to experience again till the great famine, the land war, and the struggle for national independence.

[1] Ibid., p. 310; 'is' has been substituted in the quotation for 'was' in the original, which appears at this point to be using indirect speech.

CHAPTER I

Ireland in 1534

D. B. QUINN AND K. W. NICHOLLS

IRELAND in 1534 was considerably more than a geographical expression and much less than a political entity.[1] To Henry VIII the lordship of Ireland was, like the kingdom of France, part of his inheritance, but one that was not under his effective control. He made several strenuous efforts to expand his Calais bridgehead, but no systematic attempt to conquer France as a whole; similarly, in Ireland, he had tried several times to make his authority over the Pale bridgehead more effective, but had not persisted. In contrast to France there was in Ireland no single competing authority. The gradation in English influence and authority over the island was a subtle one: only at the borders of a very few major Irish lordships could it be said to have ended, and even there some nominal recognition of English overlordship was conceded from time to time. The concept of Ireland as a political entity, apart from the English lordship, seems to have been weak, though the cultural unity of the Gaelic (and gaelicised) areas, expressed in the similarity in social and cultural institutions over the greater part of the island, was very real.

The year 1534 stands out in retrospect as a parting of the medieval ways in Ireland, and as, perhaps, the beginning of her early modern history. The installation in this year of an English-manned and militarily based administration in Dublin, and the initiation of the attempt to conciliate or conquer the Irish lordship (or to do both together) by a Tudor king, involved, we can see, the beginnings of the decline of the Irish social and cultural system, however protracted this process was to be. In the end Ireland was to prove impossible to assimilate and more difficult to conquer than could have been predicted in 1534, but our knowledge of the subsequent history of Ireland should not blind us to the fact that the political and military intervention of the Tudor state in Ireland could be seen for a long time after 1534 as one that was potentially temporary rather than inevitably permanent. The expectation that Ireland might revert at some time to indirect rather than direct English rule, and that the autonomy of the Dublin administration should in some measure be restored, is likely to have underlain the thoughts and actions of a generation or more of both Old English and Irish after 1534.

[1] See map 1, below; and maps 43–7, vol. viii.

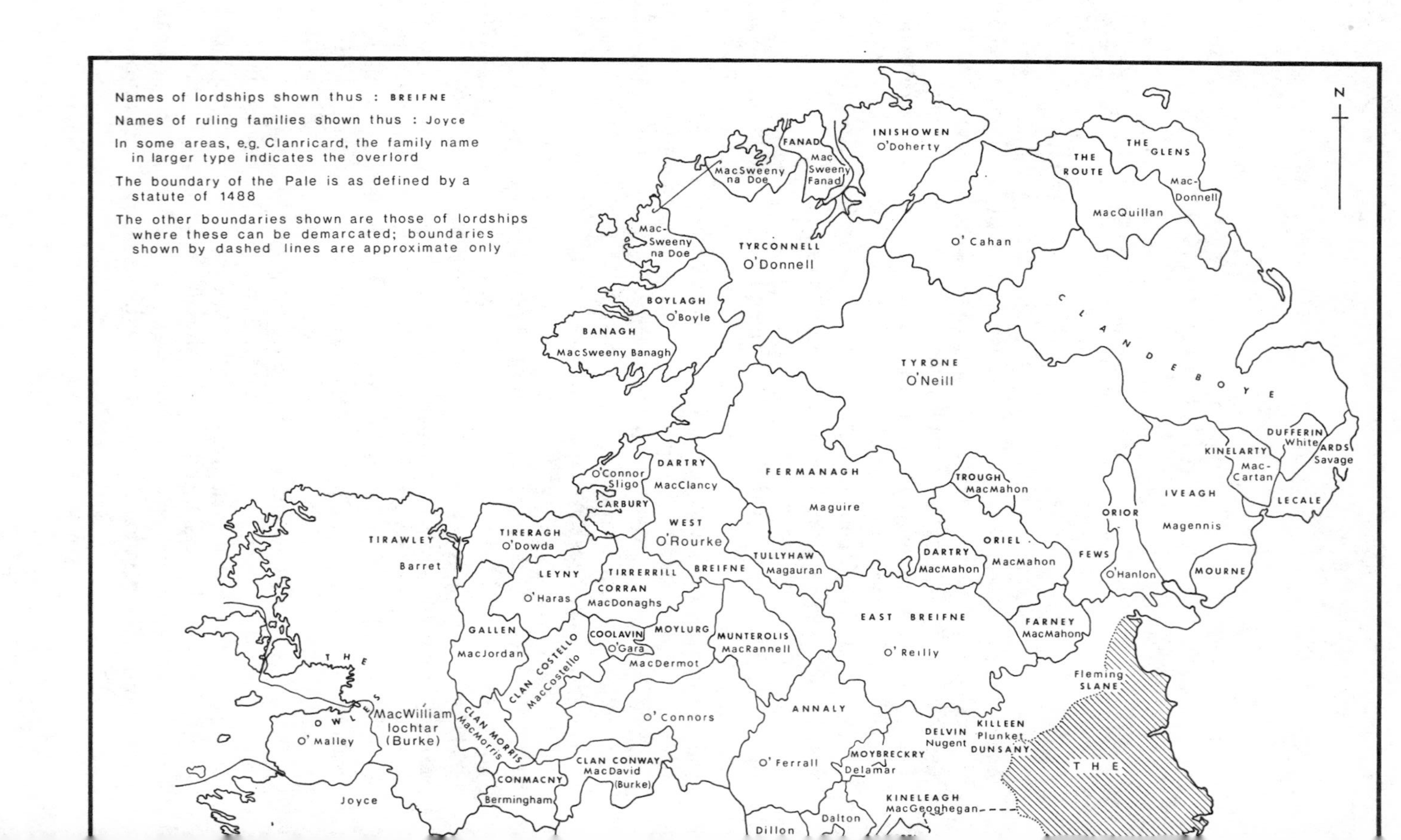

Names of lordships shown thus : BREIFNE
Names of ruling families shown thus : Joyce
In some areas, e.g. Clanricard, the family name in larger type indicates the overlord
The boundary of the Pale is as defined by a statute of 1488
The other boundaries shown are those of lordships where these can be demarcated; boundaries shown by dashed lines are approximate only
N
INISHOWEN
O'Doherty
FANAD
MacSweeny Fanad
MacSweeny na Doe
Mac-Sweeny na Doe
TYRCONNELL
O'Donnell
BOYLAGH
O'Boyle
BANAGH
MacSweeny Banagh
THE ROUTE
THE GLENS
MacQuillan
Mac-Donnell
O'Cahan
CLANDEBOYE
TYRONE
O'Neill
DUFFERIN
White
ARDS
Savage
KINELARTY
Mac-Cartan
LECALE
IVEAGH
Magennis
MOURNE
ORIOR
O'Hanlon
FEWS
TROUGH
MacMahon
ORIEL
MacMahon
DARTRY
MacMahon
FARNEY
MacMahon
FERMANAGH
Maguire
O'Connor Sligo
CARBURY
DARTRY
MacClancy
WEST BREIFNE
O'Rourke
TULLYHAW
Magauran
EAST BREIFNE
O'Reilly
TIRERAGH
O'Dowda
LEYNY
O'Haras
TIRRERRILL
CORRAN
MacDonaghs
COOLAVIN
O'Gara
MOYLURG
MacDermot
MUNTEROLIS
MacRannell
GALLEN
MacJordan
CLAN COSTELLO
MacCostello
TIRAWLEY
Barret
THE OWLS
O'Malley
MacWilliam Iochtar (Burke)
Joyce
CLAN MORRIS
MacMorris
CONMACNY
Bermingham
CLAN CONWAY
MacDavid (Burke)
O'Connors
ANNALY
O'Ferrall
Dillon
Dalton
MOYBRECKRY
Delamar
DELVIN
Nugent
KILLEEN
Plunket
DUNSANY
KINELEAGH
MacGeoghegan
Fleming
SLANE
THE

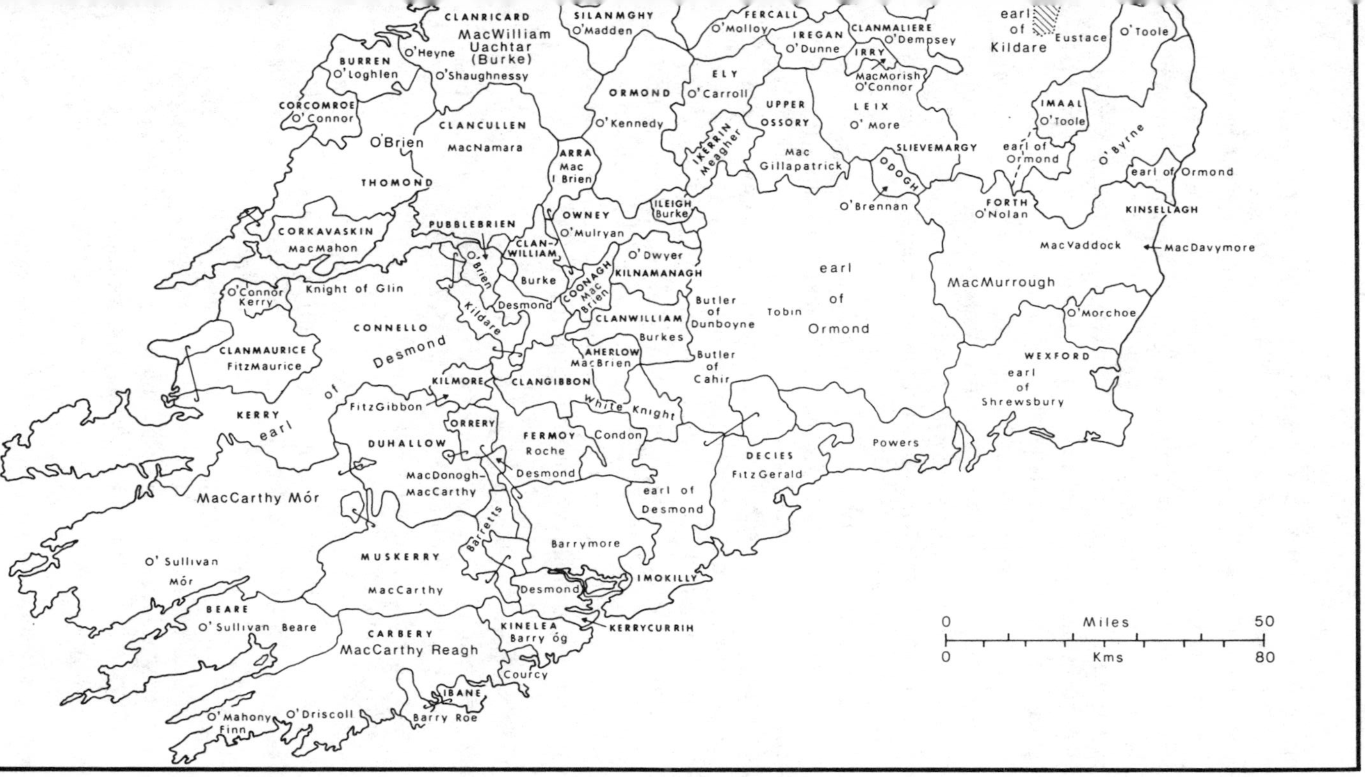

Map I LORDSHIPS, *c.* 1534, by K. W. Nicholls

The nature of Gaelic society and its exceptional capacity for assimilating outside institutions and influences—and individuals—made it very resilient and capable of responding flexibly to external and internal stresses; it also made it highly vulnerable to attack from an England where state power had become highly concentrated and therefore capable of imposing governmental structures on Ireland, with the legal criteria and beliefs which went with them, however novel or alien they were to Irish practice. The conflict between the two societies had been present since the initial conquest, but, with the consolidation of state power in England and its transformation under the impact of renaissance and reformation Europe, the polarisation between them had become complete. This polarisation was not new in 1534; adumbrated under Henry VII, with the Poynings administration, and, under Henry VIII, with the Surrey and Skeffington interventions, it was to dominate Ireland after 1534.

The state of Ireland in the early sixteenth century was not a happy one. Though our evidence is far from adequate for the detailed examination of specific areas, it would appear that from at least 1500 onwards there was a growing violence, a spreading anarchy in Irish society, with signs in a number of areas of an increasing and general economic breakdown. Lands appear to have been falling increasingly into waste; it is probable that the population was declining; and the amount and intensity of local war appear to have been steadily increasing. This is especially evident in the ecclesiastical sphere where a number of the old-established ecclesiastical settlements, monastic and secular, were being wasted and deserted in the first half of the sixteenth century;[1] the decay revealed in many areas in the returns of monastic lands in 1540–41[2] was not new. Border areas too, both between the major Irish lordships and between Old English lordships and their Irish neighbours, were increasingly becoming empty. This state of affairs is best documented for the borders of the Pale, but it also appears to have been a characteristic of many of the purely Irish areas.

In opening a survey of Ireland in 1534 it is best to start at Dublin. Besides being an administrative centre and a considerable port, Dublin was the focus for that substantial part of the eastern lowlands—the 'English Pale' in its wider, more popular, significance—which was firmly under the control of the government and where the landowning class remained Anglo-Norman in culture as well as in descent. That their tenantry, a more dense and settled population than was usual in Ireland, was largely of Gaelic origin did not prevent the structure of society in this region, the 'obedient shires', from being basically English. Dublin and its suburbs—including the privileged

[1] See e.g. the accounts of Ardagh and Clonmacnoise in 1517, in Theiner, *Vetera mon.*, pp 518, 521.

[2] *Extents Ir. mon. possessions*; Brendan Bradshaw, *The dissolution of the religious orders in Ireland under Henry VIII* (Cambridge, 1974), pp 8–38.

ecclesiastical liberties—possessed a number of important religious houses, and something like half the area of County Dublin was owned by the church.[1] Drogheda, situated in a commanding position at the mouth of the Boyne, on the borders of Meath and Louth, may have been a more important commercial port than Dublin. The manor of Termonfeckin near Drogheda was the usual residence of the archbishops of Armagh, to whom, as Englishmen or Palesmen, residence in Armagh itself, among the Irishry of the north, would have had few attractions. The county of Louth—still sometimes known by its older name of Uriel—suffered considerably from Irish raids and invasions, although to obviate them it paid 'black rent' to both O'Neill and MacMahon.[2] At its northern end, Dundalk, almost on the frontier, was a port and trading centre of some importance, while Carlingford was at this period in decline. Inland in both Meath and Louth there were also a number of walled towns, such as Ardee, Navan, and Athboy, where urban life continued to flourish. Trim was the county town of Meath and an administrative centre, although its great castle had been allowed to fall into neglect; it possessed a number of religious houses, including the abbey of St Mary whose wonder-working image of the Blessed Virgin drew pilgrims from the Gaelic regions as well as the Pale. Kells, almost on the O'Reilly frontier, had close ties with the Irishry; its abbey of St Mary was almost always ruled by a Gaelic abbot from Breifne. It was the centre for a considerable marcher area, where such families as the rapidly expanding Nugents (headed by the baron of Delvin), the Betaghs, and those branches of the Plunketts who dwelt on the frontier formed to some degree a buffer between the Pale and the O'Reillys and O'Ferralls, with whom they frequently intermarried. Further south, the other Old English of western Meath—to be shired as the county of Westmeath in 1543—had progressed even further along the same path; beyond them, and outside the sphere of Dublin control, were the gaelicised lordships of the Dillons, Daltons, Tyrrells, and Delamares, practising succession by tanistry and gavelkind, who should be classed as gaelicised lords rather than English marchers. Mullingar, almost on the frontier, was an important market town under the control of its lords, the Petit family.

County Kildare had by 1534 become an autonomous liberty belonging to the earl of Kildare and for many purposes outside the control of Dublin, but

[1] A. J. Otway-Ruthven, 'The medieval church lands of County Dublin' in *Med. studies presented to A. Gwynn*, pp 54–73 and map at end; see also Colmcille Ó Conbhui, 'The lands of St Mary's abbey, Dublin' in *R.I.A. Proc.*, lxii, sect. C (1962), pp 21–84 and map.

[2] The county of Louth paid £40 to O'Neill (*S.P. Hen. VIII*, ii, 9); for MacMahon's tribute, see S. Ó Dufaigh, 'Cíos Mhic Mhathghamhna' in *Clogher Rec.*, iv (1960–62), pp 125–38. 'Black rent' can be considered either as a subsidy paid by the settled districts of the Pale to assist their Gaelic neighbours in maintaining peace on the borders, or as an exaction paid by them under the threat of Irish raids if they did not. Certain 'black rents' were paid by the Dublin exchequer, others by the county communities. In a wider significance 'black rent' translates various Gaelic terms (*cion dubh*, *dubhdholadh*, etc.) used to denote any tribute exacted without legal right or the consent of the payer.

many of its Anglo-Norman gentry, such as Suttons and Aylmers, were strongly Old English in sentiment and hostile to the Geraldines.[1] The Berminghams of Carbury, in the north-west of County Kildare, had been 'English rebels' since 1367 and their territory, known in Irish as Clann Fheorais, lay entirely within the Gaelic polity. The county of Carlow consisted for practical purposes of a narrow strip along the northern border of the present county, but extending east to include the very extensive lands of the Cistercian abbey of Baltinglass, still under Anglo-Norman control; the county was under Kildare domination and its sheriffdom a hereditary perquisite of the local family of Wall.[2] On the state of the town of Carlow itself there is no information.

The city of Dublin was not only a focus for Old English authority and external trade but was the centre of a system of coastal contacts, both commercial and political, along the eastern seaboard. It maintained contact not only with the major port of Drogheda but with others of lesser importance, and even with the Bann salmon fishery to the north, and this coastal connection was a vital factor in preserving English influence beyond the limits of the Pale. To the south, Wicklow, Arklow, and Wexford were likewise within the orbit of Dublin's coastal contacts, extending its influence into the mainly Irish area of Wicklow and north Wexford, and linking up at Wexford with the south-eastern coastal system. Dublin had a significant cross-channel trade with England, especially through the port of Chester, but was increasingly involved, as the century went on, with both Beaumaris and Liverpool. Its position as a coastal and internal redistributor of external products and collector of domestic produce was unrivalled except by Waterford.

Once we enter the foothills of the Leinster mountain chain, a few miles south of Dublin, Old English influence thins out and soon disappears. The manorial villages of County Dublin to the north and west of the chain, such as Tallaght, Saggart, and—most remote—Ballymore Eustace,[3] were subject to continual harassment by the Irish, while in the south-east of the county—including what is now the north-easternmost corner of County Wicklow—the marcher lineages of the Walshes, Harolds, and Archbolds[4] were hardly under the control of the government until well into the sixteenth century. The north-western part of County Wicklow was more or less a no-man's

[1] D. B. Quinn, 'Anglo-Irish local government, 1485–1534' in *I.H.S.*, i, no. 4 (Sept. 1939), pp 377–81; see David Sutton's complaints against Kildare in 1537 (Hore & Graves, *Southern & eastern counties*, pp 155–66).

[2] Hubert Gallwey, *The Wall family in Ireland* (Naas, 1970), pp 34, 45–8.

[3] Since 1836 in County Kildare.

[4] In the fourteenth century the Harolds and Archbolds, at least, had been English rebels, and were classed with the O'Byrnes (Otway-Ruthven, *Med. Ire.*, p. 277). The Harolds had celebrated Richard II's first visit to Ireland by ravaging County Dublin in alliance with the O'Byrnes and O'Tooles (Geneal. Office, MS 192, p. 405). In the fifteenth century they seem to have been on better terms with the administration, but cf. *Stat. Ire., 1–12 Edw. IV*, pp 666–9.

land until the eighth earl of Kildare bought out surviving but nominal medieval land-titles, apparently from the Dunboyne Butlers, to give to his sons by his second marriage. Most of the present Wicklow belonged to the O'Tooles and O'Byrnes, both notably hostile to Dublin and addicted to raiding the neighbouring County Kildare as well. The O'Tooles occupied the mountainous centre of the county, Imaal to the west of the watershed and Fercullen (Powerscourt) and Ferter (Castlekevin) to the east; these lands also had figured in Kildare's speculation on behalf of his younger sons.[1] To the east of the O'Tooles the O'Byrnes occupied a very lengthy territory stretching along the sea coast from Delgany to Annareilly, a little north of Arklow, and thence inland as far as the south-western extremity of the present county. It was thus enfolded on the south by the territories of the MacMurroughs.

The MacMurroughs, nominal kings of Leinster, whose surname was Kavanagh, ruled a large area comprising most of County Carlow and the northern two-thirds of County Wexford, with some adjacent districts. For a century or so before 1525 they controlled Arklow, where there was a small trading port and borough. Within this large area—'Low Leinster', as it was sometimes called in contemporary records—which included some of the most heavily forested country in Ireland, were many sub-lordships. Until well into the sixteenth century the MacMurroughs received substantial payments of 'black rent' both from the Dublin exchequer and from the liberty of Wexford;[2] and, controlling the road between Carlow and Kilkenny by their possession of the Barrow valley, they could render communications between Dublin and the southern districts that still recognised English authority difficult or even impossible.

The southern portion of the present County Wexford formed the palatinate or liberty of Wexford, in the hands of the earl of Shrewsbury, an absentee. Along its northern border was another no-man's-land, the title to the larger part of which had been acquired by the eighth earl of Kildare, who thereupon took it over from the Irish occupants.[3] The town of Wexford was not directly subject to the authority of Shrewsbury's officials but was an autonomous unit. It was Ireland's most important fishing port and market for fish in the fifteenth and early sixteenth centuries. Many small fishing vessels of local and English ownership based themselves there, and the trade in fish led to very close contacts with Bristol. A timber trade too was significant and was to develop further during the later sixteenth century. The administration of the Wexford liberty was usually in the hands of local families; manorial courts were maintained and land was conveyed by

[1] Lord Walter FitzGerald, 'The manor and castle of Powerscourt . . . in the sixteenth century' in *Kildare Arch. Soc. Jn.*, vi (1909–11), pp 127–39; *Alen's register*, p. 162.

[2] *S.P. Hen. VIII*, ii, 9. The payments were 80 marks and £40 respectively.

[3] Kildare Rental Book (B.M., Harl. MS 3756), ff 85v–6, and list of deeds formerly in the possession of the duke of Leinster, compiled by John T. Gilbert, in N.L.I., MS 10, 203 (4).

copy of court roll. Shrewsbury assumed that English law was still being administered and, though he remained an absentee, occasionally sent a few soldiers to maintain his authority.[1]

Waterford harbour was a focus for settlement and commerce, which is the geographical key to much of the south midlands, its three rivers, the Barrow, Suir, and Nore, providing unparalleled opportunities for penetration by water. It was thus an exceptionally important city, commanding an interior trade network in which New Ross on the Barrow, Kilkenny and Thomastown on the Nore, and Carrick and Clonmel on the Suir all played a considerable part.[2] It was a principal outlet for Irish commerce in hides and cloth both to England and Europe and the main source of continental and English products for a large part of Ireland. Its merchants had many personal connections in French ports, as well as across the Irish Sea in Bristol; they traded with Spain, Portugal, and the Atlantic islands. Waterford had also interests in deep-sea fisheries and was probably the first Irish port to send vessels to the Newfoundland Banks. The most consciously English of the southern port towns, it sought to preserve itself from contamination by the surrounding Gaelic influences, and maintained a long struggle with its immediate neighbours, the semi-gaelicised Powers.

Inland from Waterford lay the great, mainly lowland, area controlled by the Butler earls of Ormond or, during the period when the earls were absentees, by their local kinsmen acting as their representatives. Kilkenny was in theory an ordinary county subject to the Dublin administration; Tipperary was an Ormond liberty, but during the fifteenth century the earl seems to have claimed liberty rights in Kilkenny as well. Statutes issued by the 'White Earl' in 1434 declared that the counties of Kilkenny and Tipperary 'should be one country under one rule or under one lordship' and provided for the government of Tipperary, Kilkenny, and their crosses as a single unit.[3] Kilkenny was effectively resumed into the hands of the crown after 1534. In this area a mixture of English and Gaelic ('brehon') law was administered, the criminal law—codified in the ordinances issued at Kilcash by James Butler in 1474[4]—being entirely Irish and based on the principles

[1] *L. & P. Hen. VIII*, ii, 430, no. 3852; for County Wexford, Hore, *Wexford*, is exceptionally valuable, but unfortunately unfinished. Part of the remainder was published in *Past*, i (1920), pp 62–106; ii (1921), pp 38–99; iii (1925), pp 1–40. For the liberty in 1537, see Hore & Graves, *Southern & eastern counties*, pp 1–66.

[2] For Waterford see 'Archives of the municipal corporation of Waterford', ed. John T. Gilbert, in *H.M.C. rep. 10*, app. v, pp 265–339 (see also *H.M.C. rep. 1*, app., pp 131–2, which contains the invaluable series of town statutes from 1365 to 1525); R. H. Ryland, *History of Waterford* (London, 1824); Smith, *Waterford*, and *Waterford Arch. Soc. Jn.*, 1894–1920. The Bristol customs records in the P.R.O. are of exceptional value, and some significant material is in *Cal. Carew MSS* (*Book of Howth*), pp 470–76. For the dispute between Waterford and New Ross over the prisage of wine claimed by the former throughout the estuary of the three rivers, see *Ormond deeds, 1413–1509*, pp 290–96.

[3] B.M., Add. MS 4797, f. 123ᵛ.

[4] N.L.I., MS 2551, f. 2ᵛ.

of compensation and collective responsibility, while the land law was still essentially feudal and the government of the towns remained English in character. A substantial number of major boroughs, of which Kilkenny was the most important, formed significant nuclei of English influence and centres of resistance to gaelicisation.[1] The whole area enjoyed a substantial period of prosperity in the early sixteenth century, in spite of the disorder on the frontiers and of that caused by the feuds of the rival Butler houses, especially that between those of Cahir and Dunboyne, in County Tipperary.

Northern and much of central Tipperary was in the hands of various local Irish lords, who paid some sort of tribute to the earl of Ormond and recognised him as their overlord. Quite independent were the O'Carrolls of Ely—who levied black rent from County Kilkenny[2]—and the MacGillapatricks, two redoubtable foes on the northern frontier of the Butler lordship. The MacGillapatricks' country of Upper Ossory was nominally within County Kilkenny, as Ely O'Carroll was nominally inside County Tipperary. Both these families, technically within the Butler sphere of influence, were bitterly hostile to the earls of Ormond whenever they attempted to interfere in their affairs, and so tended to side with Kildare in his disputes with Ormond.

The eastern part of County Waterford formed the Power or 'Poeryn' country, ruled by the Powers of Curraghmore as hereditary sheriffs of the county, an office they exercised from 1425 at least and retained in spite of an Irish statute of 1476 granting it to the citizens of Waterford. At that date Richard Power—'an enemy to God and a great rebel to the king'—had occupied the shrievalty for twenty years.[3] The hostility between the citizens and the Powers was perpetual and deeply established, and a similar hostility existed between the latter and their western neighbours, the Fitzgeralds of the Decies, whose territory extended from Kilmacthomas to the Blackwater. The lords of the Decies were a branch of the house of Desmond, founded by the younger brother of that earl who had been executed at Drogheda in 1468, and were usually at feud with the heads of the family, maintaining their independence by alliance with the Butlers. Within the Decies, Dungarvan—a moderately important port—was in theory a royal outpost, but in practice was disputed between Desmond and Decies. Youghal was at the mouth of

[1] For the area in general see C. A. Empey, 'The Butler lordship' in *Butler Soc. Jn.*, 3 (1970–71), pp 174–87, and Hore & Graves, *Southern & eastern counties*, pp 77–136, 221–57. For Kilkenny, see *Liber primus Kilkenn.* (1931; trans. by A. J. Otway-Ruthven, Kilkenny [1961]); there are important articles in early numbers of the *Journal of the Kilkenny and South-East of Ireland Archaeological Society* (afterwards *R.S.A.I. Jn.*) and much material in *Ormond deeds*. For Clonmel, see W. P. Burke, *History of Clonmel* (Waterford, 1907).

[2] *S.P. Hen. VIII*, ii, p. 9.

[3] Hore & Graves, *Southern & eastern counties*, pp 177–220, esp. p. 184 (where 'untyll Maghyn', misunderstood by the editors, means of course 'unto the Mahon [river]'); *Stat. Ire., 12–22 Edw. IV*, pp 558–63.

the significant Blackwater river system, famous for its salmon and later for its timber. Dominated by the earls of Desmond, it was a fairly important town and port. Its trade with France was appreciable and it was also in close contact with Bristol.[1]

Cork itself, though we have comparatively little information on it relative to its importance at this period, was a rich, if small, city with a number of wealthy families. Like Waterford, it had continued to obtain its charters through the English, rather than the Irish, chancery, in order to emphasise its direct links with the crown. Its trade with Flanders, western France, and the Iberian peninsula appears to have been appreciable, and it was in close trading contact with Bristol, and even with London. It acted as a collecting centre for a wide area in the interior and along the coast, mainly to the west rather than the east.[2] Cork harbour, a magnificent natural port with many anchorages, was closely linked with Kinsale and its harbour. Kinsale was to some extent a sub-collecting centre for Cork, as well as having a trade of its own with England and the Continent. The most important economic feature on this coast was the fishery, which attracted many foreign fishing vessels during the season, as well as employing local boats. The foreigners needed local facilities to land and dry their nets and catches, and at Baltimore in the territory of O'Driscoll, a vassal of MacCarthy Reagh, there was an important fishing port and haven whose dues brought in large revenues to its lords.[3] Kinsale and the west Cork coast came increasingly in the later sixteenth century within the purview of the high court of admiralty in London, and English ships engaged in privateering and piracy developed a substantial prize mart on this coast.[4] The O'Driscolls, already mentioned, were noted as pirates.[5]

The districts from Youghal to Cork harbour and on the western shore of the latter were in the hands of the elder Desmond line, but much land was held by independent Old English lords. The Courceys still used the title of Lord Courcey; the alleged viscountcies claimed by the Roches (Viscount Fermoy) and the Barrys (Viscount Buttevant) had no legal basis, though they came to be recognised by the crown. Barrys and Roches, like other great Old English families in County Cork, were highly gaelicised, employ-

[1] There are only a few sources of information for this period in *Council bk Youghal*; see also the deeds calendared by Richard Caulfield in *Gent. Mag.*, Aug. 1864, pp 191–4. Youghal appears with moderate frequency in the Bristol customs accounts.

[2] There is nothing for this period in *Council bk Cork*, but scraps appear in Smith, *Cork*, and there are some incidental references in the *Cork Hist. Soc. Jn.* (1892 ff). William O'Sullivan in *Econ. hist. Cork city* uses some of the extant customs accounts for Bristol. See also the wills (later, however, than this period) and deeds calendared by Richard Caulfield, 'Wills and inventories, Cork' in *Gent. Mag.*, 1861, May, pp 530–32; July, pp 33–7; Sept., pp 257–62; Nov., pp 501–5; 1862, Jan., pp 28–31; Feb., pp 165–8; Apr., pp 439–44; June, pp 710–14; Sept., pp 299–302; 'Original documents relating to the county and city of Cork', ibid., Nov., pp 559–62; 1865; Mar., pp 316–28; Apr., pp 449–52; June, pp 719–22; Aug., pp 176–80.

[3] *Celtic Soc. misc.*, pp 103–5.

[4] For Kinsale see *Council bk Kinsale*, and appendices.

[5] *Celtic Soc. misc.*, pp 93–8.

ing brehons and patronising bardic poetry (e.g. that contained in the Book of Fermoy written for the Roche family in the fifteenth and sixteenth centuries).

Western County Cork is physically divided into three sectors with an east–west axis, drained by the rivers Blackwater, Lee, and Bandon, and ruled, respectively, by three MacCarthy lords: MacDonagh Carthy of Duhallow in the north-west, MacCarthy of Muskerry in the Lee valley immediately to the west of Cork itself, and MacCarthy Reagh of Carbery in the south-west.[1] MacCarthy Reagh, who paid tribute to the earls of Desmond, though with what regularity we cannot say, had under him not only many lesser Gaelic lords but also the gaelicised Barry Roes of Ibane to whom belonged the two peninsulas west of Timoleague. Within Carbery there was an urban presence in the walled episcopal town of Rosscarbery, which in 1517 had 200 houses.[2] The MacCarthys of Muskerry were, for Gaelic lords, rather exceptional. They traced their possession of Muskerry proper, the district around Macroom, to a grant by Edward III;[3] during the fifteenth century they had expanded eastwards at the expense of their English neighbours—from whom they took Cloghroe and Blarney—and southward at the expense of the O'Mahonys. They were hereditary enemies, as was MacCarthy Reagh, of the earls of Desmond, and for this reason sought alliance with the earls of Ormond.[4] In 1524 the battle of Mourne Abbey arose from an attempt by Desmond finally to break the power of Muskerry, but the earl was heavily defeated owing to the defection of some of his own relatives, including the uncle who was to be his successor.

MacCarthy Mór was the Irish king of Desmond and ruled the territory corresponding roughly to the southern half of County Kerry. Under him were the two O'Sullivans, O'Sullivan Mór and O'Sullivan Beare,[5] the latter an important maritime lord who drew a large revenue from the fishing and trading vessels which made use of his harbours at Bearehaven and Bantry, and passed on a share of it to his overlord.[6] MacCarthy Mór also laid claim to suzerainty over the MacCarthys of Duhallow and Muskerry, though it is unlikely that he was able to interfere to any great extent in their affairs.[7]

The border between Desmond and MacCarthy power in Kerry ran

[1] For the MacCarthy lords and their country see Butler, *Gleanings*, passim. His account of Muskerry must be read with caution; he was not aware of the grant of 1353 nor fully apprised of the role of the Lombard family as victims of Muskerry expansion. His genealogies are inaccurate. See also Nicholls, *Gaelic Ire.*, pp 160–63.

[2] Theiner, *Vetera mon.*, p. 529.

[3] A. J. Otway-Ruthven, 'Ireland in the 1350s: Sir Thomas de Rokeby and his successors' in *R.S.A.I. Jn.*, xcvii (1967), p. 51.

[4] e.g. *Ormond deeds, 1413–1509*, no. 319. For similar approaches by MacCarthy Reagh, see *Ormond deeds, 1509–47*, no. 16 (1).

[5] The greater part of O'Sullivan Beare's territory is now in County Cork.

[6] Butler, *Gleanings*, pp 38–9, 40; see letter of protection for an English merchant from Donal MacCarthy, prince of Desmond, and Dermot O'Sullivan, 20 June 1461 (Exeter City R.O., D. 1235).

[7] Butler, *Gleanings*, passim.

roughly along the river Maine, and Kerry was a palatine liberty of the earl's, in which he had two great castles at Tralee and Castleisland; but his immediate power also extended over much of County Limerick, where he had strong castles at Newcastle and Askeaton in the west and at Lough Gur and Knockany in the east. In Kerry, Dingle had a merchant population and a municipal organisation, together with ships, and a trade with Bristol and Bordeaux.[1] Fish again formed the nucleus of her commerce. Northern Kerry, known as Clanmaurice, was in the hands of the Fitzmaurice family, lords of Lixnaw, kinsmen of the Desmonds, with whom their relations were often troubled. Treaties of 1421 and 1540 attempted to define the relations between them.[2]

As a city Limerick at this time may have been as extensive and with as large a population as Cork, though we have very few municipal documents on it, and it does not appear to any extent in the English customs accounts. It tapped the very extensive Shannon valley and also the rich agricultural and grazing land to the south. It had important salmon fisheries of its own on the Shannon. Like Galway, it had extensive links with the Iberian peninsula, and had a number of large seagoing vessels. It had municipal links with Cork and was also inclined to maintain a few direct links with the crown in England. Inland, Kilmallock was a considerable town; Adare may also have had the rudiments of an urban organisation and was an important ecclesiastical centre, with three friaries. It was one of a group of County Limerick manors which belonged to the earls of Kildare and which formed a basis for their influence in this area. On the borders of Counties Limerick and Tipperary were the Burkes of Clanwilliam. After 1466 the local lords of this area, the Burkes and the MacBriens of Coonagh and Aherlow, appear to have fallen under the overlordship of the O'Briens of Thomond, who occupied directly the district of Onaght in County Tipperary and exercised some sort of authority in this area until they surrendered their rights to the crown in 1542.[3] The O'Briens, having formerly been enemies of the city of Limerick, seem to have developed a working arrangement with it at a later date and after 1456 drew a tribute from it, as they also did from County Limerick, or rather its eastern portion.[4] The O'Briens of Thomond were thus, on occasion, able to play an active part in the affairs of Limerick and Tipperary. An exiled branch of the family had settled in the barony of Pubblebrien, to the south-west of the city of Limerick, with which they seem to have been on bad terms.

[1] Cf. e.g. Jacques Bernard, *Navires & gens de mer à Bordeaux* (Paris, 1968), i, 217.

[2] K. W. Nicholls, 'The Fitzmaurices of Kerry' in *Kerry Arch. Soc. Jn.*, iii (1970), pp 23–42; *Ormond deeds, 1509–47*, pp 203–5.

[3] *S.P. Hen. VIII*, iii, 363, 465. Cf. *Ormond deeds, 1509–47*, no. 93, where 'Castell Coure' is Knockacurra near Bansha, County Tipperary.

[4] 'Annals of Ireland from 1443 to 1465' in *Ir. Arch. Soc. Misc.*, i (1846), pp 258–9; *S.P. Hen. VIII*, ii, 9; iii, 363.

Thomond, the present County Clare, was an O'Brien preserve. The kingdom of Thomond was one of the most coherent Irish lordships of this period, with a more definite political organisation than most, though not much detail survives to indicate precisely how it operated. Effective geographical unity, apart from its eastern bridgehead, provides one reason for this: another was its relative isolation from English influence for a substantial period. Its lesser Irish lords were very much under the control of the O'Briens. The northern frontier of Thomond marked the southern boundary of the Upper MacWilliams, or the MacWilliams of Clanricard, as the ruling de Burgo or Burke family had come to be called when it took on an Irish colouring. Although they were neighbours of the equally powerful O'Briens, the Upper MacWilliams were, curiously enough, not their enemies but their allies. The centre of the MacWilliams' power was Loughrea, formerly the centre of the de Burgo lordship of Connacht. From the fourteenth century the family and territory had been gaelicised to a far greater degree than any of the Norman lordships of Munster, but nevertheless they, or some of their Burke vassals such as the MacHuberts, continued to provide a nominal sheriff of Connacht. Their vassals also included the Gaelic O'Heynes and O'Shaughnessys. Inside their territory they had an Old English enclave in the trading town of Athenry,[1] with which they were on good terms and whose ecclesiastical foundations they patronised: they had some claim, or made some, to the customs of the port of Galway.[2]

Galway itself was another of the independent English towns, probably the most completely detached from the care of either the Dublin or the London administrations, although Kildare had intervened in 1504 to save it from being taken over fully by MacWilliam, and cases concerning it were heard from time to time in English courts, even by the king's council. The law used in the town—and in other towns of the west as well—was the civil (Roman) law and not the common law, and its contacts with the Iberian peninsula, both with Portugal and with Andalusia in particular, were strong. It was a port of call on the fifteenth-century route of the Bristol ships to Iceland, and they probably carried Irish goods to that far northern European colony.[3] Direct commerce with Spain and Portugal was considerable. The riches of St Nicholas's church and the town friaries, and their embellishment in the fifteenth century, as well as the size and magnificence of the town houses and castles of its merchants, all indicate that the late fifteenth and early sixteenth centuries were for it a period of prosperity. Its merchants traded through Connacht and had effective control over most of the coastal commerce of the west and north-west from the mouth of the

[1] Athenry had its own port at Stradbally, in Clanricard territory (*Cal. pat. rolls, 1401–5*, p. 134).

[2] See *A.L.C.*, ii, 342 (misunderstood by the translator; *cóiceid na Gaillimhe* means 'the cocket [customs duty] of Galway'); Hardiman, *Galway*, p. 82; *Cal. Carew MSS, 1515–74*, p. 204.

[3] See D. B. Quinn, *England and the discovery of America, 1481–1620* (London, 1974), pp 49, 52–3, 71.

Shannon as far as Donegal.[1] After 1500 Athenry's decline meant that a number of her merchant families migrated to Galway where several became prominent; in 1543 the two towns made an agreement by which each conceded burgess privileges to townsmen of the other.[2]

Northwards from Galway along the western coast the territory was entirely Irish. The lands of the O'Flahertys—Iar Connacht—included all the rough areas west of Lough Corrib.[3] North of Iar Connacht again we find the O'Malleys, but they were subject, at least nominally, to the other major Burke family, the Lower MacWilliams, while the O'Flahertys were completely independent. The nucleus of the authority of the Lower MacWilliams lay to the east of Lough Mask, at Ballinrobe; their territory covered most of the present County Mayo. The two MacWilliams were hereditary rivals, and all the other lords of Connacht, Gaelic or Norman, tended to depend on one or the other.

The very extensive O'Kelly territory lay in the east of County Galway and the south of County Roscommon, extending from Athenry to Athlone; that of the O'Maddens to the south of them again in east County Galway. Both these were Gaelic lords who had lost their territories to the Normans but had reoccupied them in the fourteenth century; both were hereditary enemies of the Upper MacWilliams of Clanricard and allies of the Lower MacWilliams. Both, during the sixteenth century, suffered penetration by the lords of Clanricard, who secured possession of castles (such as Portumna) and lands in their countries.[4] Weakened by internal contentions, the O'Kelly lordship was virtually divided by the early sixteenth century into eastern and western halves.[5] In central Roscommon the old royal house of O'Connor survived in the two rival lines of O'Connor Donn (the brown) and O'Connor Roe (the red). O'Connor Roe was a hereditary ally of the Lower MacWilliams and O'Connor Donn of the Upper, and the fortunes of the two branches—whose territories were inextricably intermingled—tended to rise and fall with the fortunes of the rival Burke houses. To the north of the O'Connors were the powerful MacDermots of Moylurg.

In northern Connacht the influence of the Lower MacWilliams had been declining for half a century before 1534 in favour of that of their erstwhile allies, but now bitter enemies, the O'Donnells. Both powers claimed control over the third branch of the O'Connors, the O'Connors of Sligo, and over other lords in that neighbourhood. The port of Sligo was of some importance

[1] Galway has a reasonably good, though old, history by James Hardiman (Dublin, 1820). Original materials can be found in John T. Gilbert, ed., 'Archives of the town of Galway' in *H.M.C., rep. 10*, app. v, pp 380–520, and the documents printed by Hardiman in the appendices to his edition of O'Flaherty, *West Connaught*, and in *Ir. Arch Soc. misc.*, i (1846), pp 44–90; also Martin J. Blake, *Blake family records, 1300 to 1600* (London, 1902).

[2] *H.M.C., rep. 10*, app. v, pp 388–9, 407; *Acts privy council, Ire., 1556–71*, p. 278.

[3] See O'Flaherty, *West Connaught*, and Hardiman, *Galway*, passim.

[4] See e.g. *S.P. Hen. VIII*, iii, 361.

[5] See the forthcoming *Survey of Irish lordships: I Uí Maine and Síl Anmchadha* by K. W. Nicholls, to be published by the I.M.C.

and had a highly regarded export trade in herrings.[1] Though it had its merchants, notably the great Gaelic merchant family of O'Crean,[2] it is unlikely that it had any form of municipal organisation. Its customs duties (cocket) were a valuable source of revenue, enjoyed at different times by O'Connor and O'Donnell, according to which had possession of the castle of Sligo.

Tyrconnell, the present county of Donegal, was the lordship of the O'Donnells, whose strong position in the late fifteenth and early sixteenth century was partly due to the continuity of two successive lords who between them exercised effective authority for the greater part of eighty years. The O'Donnells retained a considerable degree of loyalty from their subjects, such as the MacSweeneys, who provided galloglass for many other parts of Ireland as well as Tyrconnell, and they could also rely on mercenary Scottish troops whom they seem to have been the first to introduce on a seasonal basis, anticipating the 'new Scots' of the later sixteenth century. They drew a considerable revenue from the herring fisheries of Arranmore.[3] They were both well entrenched in their own territories and accustomed to raid and inflict extensive damage on Counties Sligo and Mayo; during the fifteenth century we find them conducting raids into the southern part of County Galway and into Westmeath and Longford, even appearing on one occasion at Limerick. They appear to have been a ruthless family with a greater drive and a stronger sense of political direction than the great majority of Irish lords. The fact that an O'Donnell paid a visit to Rome early in the sixteenth century may give an indication that they had at least some feeling of contact with the European states system. They also sought relations with the king of Scots and were in relatively frequent touch by messenger with the English court. Along with the earls of Desmond, we might say that they alone had any understanding of, and interest in, that international setting of which most of Ireland was unregarding.

The O'Neills of Tyrone were the traditional kings of the north. Their power was centred on the castle of Dungannon[4] in eastern Tyrone, but they also controlled, immediately or through their vassals, the present counties of Londonderry and Armagh, as well as exercising a vague overlordship over a much wider area, including much of County Antrim, parts of County Down, and Counties Cavan and Fermanagh. The tribute of the Inishowen peninsula, the lordship of O'Doherty, was continually in dispute between them and the O'Donnells, as were the border lands further to the south on both banks of the Foyle, Cinéal Moen. With their strong position in central Ulster, the O'Neills had the military advantage of the interior movement. They were

[1] E. M. Carus-Wilson, *Medieval merchant venturers* (London, 1967), pp 17, 21; Carus-Wilson, *The overseas trade of Bristol in the later middle ages* (Bristol, 1937), p. 107.

[2] For the O'Creans see *A.U.*, iii, 482, 572–4; *A.L.C.*, ii, 512; *Cal. pat. rolls Ire., Jas I*, p. 20.

[3] *S.P. Hen. VIII*, iii, 481. In 1561 O'Donnell is described as the 'best lord of fish in Ireland and he exchangeth fish always with foreign merchants for wine' (*Cal. Carew MSS, 1515–74*, p. 308).

[4] See plate 3.

baulked in attempts to expand westwards by the compact physical and political unity of Tyrconnell. A significant feature in Tyrone politics was the existence in the north-west of a sept of O'Neills allied to the O'Donnells and at enmity with their own chief; this role was played successively by several different branches, finally by the sons of Art Óg (*d.* 1519). To the south of their main territories was the wide glacis of the broken drumlin country which offered them means of penetrating into the Pale and of ambushing counter-raiding parties, and which contributed to their substantial influence in north-central Ireland.[1] The O'Neills of the Fews in the south of County Armagh were a branch of the Tyrone line, immediate neighbours of the English Pale upon which they had substantially encroached in the neighbourhood of Dundalk. To their east the O'Hanlons, also vassals of O'Neill, were in close relationship with the earls of Kildare; they had ceded Omeath on the Louth frontier to the eighth earl in 1508.[2] The city of Armagh and the surrounding lands were ruled by the archbishop or his representatives and occupied by those who held under him. The archbishops carried on an interminable struggle against the encroachments of the O'Neills on their lands and tenants.[3] In the north, Derry was an important ecclesiastical centre near the mouth of the river Foyle, with its valuable salmon fisheries, and Lough Foyle drew some trading ships whose customs brought revenue to O'Neill. The larger part of the modern county of Londonderry was ruled by O'Cahan, a powerful vassal of O'Neill. O'Cahan appears to have levied a toll from the important Bann salmon fishery, which was normally leased by the crown to English fishing interests, frequently those of the city of Chester. The fishery itself produced some revenue for the Dublin government, and illustrates the interdependence of the coastal areas in a manner which ignored or transcended political divisions.[4]

Oriel, the modern County Monaghan, was the lordship of the MacMahons, as Fermanagh was of the Maguires. Oriel was a strong and coherent state whose relationship with the O'Neills had been one of alliance rather than of subjection, but after the death of Ross MacMahon in 1513 the usual disputes arising from the proliferation of the ruling house led to the baronies of Dartry and Farney becoming lordships virtually independent of the ruling MacMahon at Monaghan. The ninth earl of Kildare had cessed his galloglass on the country.[5] The MacMahons, as has been noted, had in the fifteenth century levied a heavy black rent on the county of Louth. This may have lapsed by the sixteenth century,[6] but by that time the lords of Farney had

[1] See vol. ii, map illustrating the autonomy of the north-west.

[2] N.L.I., MS 10, 203 (4), referring to a deed formerly in the possession of the duke of Leinster.

[3] Gwynn, *Med. province Armagh*, pp 265–7; Katharine Simms, 'The archbishops of Armagh and the O'Neills, 1347–1471' in *I.H.S.*, xix, no. 73 (Mar. 1974), pp 38–55.

[4] D. B. Quinn, *Ulster, 1460–1550* ([Belfast], 1935), pp 12–14 (reprinted from *Belfast Natur. Hist. Soc. Proc.*, *1933–4* (1935)).

[5] *Cal. Carew MSS*, *1515–74*, p. 264.

[6] It is not mentioned in the list of black rents paid to the Irish in *S.P. Hen. VIII*, ii, 9.

encroached upon Louth by occupying the border manor of Stonetown, which they retained until late in the century.[1] The history of Fermanagh is known to us in exceptional detail through the existence of a local chronicle forming the later part of the Annals of Ulster. Fermanagh was a prosperous and well-settled land, whose natural geographical basis was the east–west waterway provided by Lough Erne, though this could, on occasion, form a strategic route for invaders into the heart of the country.[2] Its relations with its neighbours seem to have been exceptionally peaceful, but in the early sixteenth century it passed through a period of weakness of which O'Donnell took advantage to assert his control over the country, levying tribute and even for a time annexing a portion outright.[3] On the borders of Fermanagh, Tyrone, and Tyrconnell was situated the place in Ireland best known to contemporary Europeans: Lough Derg with the Purgatory of St Patrick which drew pilgrims from overseas and had soon recovered from its suppression by papal order in 1497.[4]

The larger part of northern Antrim formed the territory of the Route, the lordship of the MacQuillans, whose ancestors had come into Ireland in the thirteenth century as mercenaries to the de Burgo earls of Ulster. A powerful family in the fifteenth century, they declined very rapidly in the sixteenth, at least partly through Scottish intrusions by the MacDonnells of the Glens. The Glens, the area extending roughly from Ballycastle to Glenarm, was a Scottish enclave in the hands of the MacDonalds of Kintyre and Islay, who had originally begun to settle in this area about 1400. It served as a base for Scottish infiltration into the neighbouring regions. In south County Antrim and northern County Down was the extensive territory of the O'Neills of Clandeboye (Clann Aodha Buidhe), descendants of Hugh the Yellow (died 1283), who seem to owe the origins of their power to the support and assistance of the MacDonalds of the Isles against the main branch of the O'Neills, and who had displaced not only the Norman settlers in the area but also its original Gaelic families. West of the Bann, Clandeboye extended to include the wild forested area of Glenconkeyne and Killeightragh in the south-east of County Londonderry, the original lands of their ancestor Hugh the Yellow. By 1534 the lordship of the O'Neills of Clandeboye, a major power through the preceding century, was showing signs of imminent dissolution.

Carrickfergus and its hinterland survived as a remnant of the older English settlement. It had strong trading links with both Scotland and Dublin, and acted as the main distributing centre for local products and imports in the north of Ireland. The town, which had a moderately strong

[1] *Anal. Hib.*, no. 24 (1967), p. 168; cf. *Fiants Ire.*, *Eliz.*, no. 1751.

[2] As for O'Donnell in 1541 (*Ann. Conn.*, 1541, 8, 9).

[3] So we understand *Ann. Conn.*, 1542, 19. In 1514 O'Neill had recognised O'Donnell's claim to suzerainty over Fermanagh (ibid., 1514, 13).

[4] Gwynn, *Med. province Armagh*, pp 172–5.

merchant class, was the seat of a small English garrison, which it required for its independent survival since it was frequently attacked by O'Neill of Clandeboye. It was burnt on more than one occasion and was rescued on others by the earl of Kildare, who several times cleared the O'Neills from the castle at the Belfast ford of the Lagan. Carrickfergus castle, accessible by sea, was one of the strongest in Ireland.[1]

South of Clandeboye the Magennises occupied the south-west part of the modern County Down. In the early sixteenth century they were a growingly important house, who were penetrating by more or less legal means into the remnant of the earldom of Ulster along the Down coast. The Savages of the Ards held the southern part of that peninsula; though largely gaelicised, they still retained the nominal seneschalship of Ulster. Downpatrick, with important ecclesiastical foundations, was a sizeable town; Ardglass was well enclosed by its 'new work' and defended by several strong castles; it had some export trade with Scotland and Dublin and, like Carrickfergus, was visited by Breton fishing-vessels, since an important herring fishery existed off-shore. The earls of Kildare had attempted to revive this small and rather ghostly remnant of the earldom of Ulster, the eighth earl receiving grants of land from Henry VII and buying the estates—including Ardglass—of the extinct Dartas family, and the ninth earl being given more land by Henry VIII.[2] Immediately to the north was the lordship of Dufferin, belonging to the White family, who in the fifteenth century had played an important part in Ulster and had—with the Savages—provided seneschals for the declining earldom.

In the north midlands the two principal Irish powers were the ruling families of O'Rourke and O'Reilly, lords respectively of west and east Breifne. The O'Rourke territory corresponded roughly to modern Leitrim and that of O'Reilly to County Cavan. The O'Reillys seem to have had a highly developed lordship, and one chief, Owen, who died in 1449, is said to have given a code of laws to his country.[3] They were in close contact, sometimes peaceful, sometimes warlike, with the English Pale. Within their country, the sixteenth century saw their capital, Cavan, become a trading town, owing perhaps to the Gaelic merchant family of MacBrady, whose members traded within the Pale.[4] While both O'Reillys and O'Rourkes were of considerable political importance, the O'Reillys, being much nearer neighbours of the Pale, figure more prominently in the records, and the political orientation of the O'Rourkes, besides, was directed more towards their northern and western neighbours than to the east. The trade of their country must largely have passed through Sligo. Breifne was historically part

[1] Quinn, *Ulster, 1460–1550*, pp 14–17.

[2] Ibid., p. 6; K. W. Nicholls, 'The descendants of Margaret Dartas' in *Ir. Geneal.*, iv (1968–72), pp 392–3.

[3] James Carney (ed.), *A genealogical history of the O'Reillys* (Cavan, 1959), pp 19–20.

[4] There was a market at Cavan by 1480 (*Stat. Ire., 12–22 Edw. IV*, p. 818).

of the kingdom of Connacht, however, and it is only in the late fifteenth century that we begin to find a northern orientation among the O'Reillys.

Annaly, the present County Longford, since the death in 1509 of William O'Ferrall, bishop of Ardagh as well as secular lord of the country, had been divided into the two lordships of O'Ferrall Bane in the north-east and O'Ferrall Boy in the south-west. The episcopal 'city' of Ardagh had been laid in ruins in the time of Bishop William.[1] The eighth and ninth earls of Kildare had considerable authority in Annaly, which the eighth earl had laid under contribution for his galloglass.[2]

To the south and east of Annaly, in the western frontier of Meath, were a number of small lordships of Anglo-Norman origin which had become completely gaelicised—those of the Dillons, Daltons, and Delamares—and south of them others of purely Gaelic origin. Economically the whole region was noted for its eel fisheries, which centred on Athlone. The Dillons had been hereditary constables of Athlone castle, on the west bank of the Shannon, until ejected by their Connacht neighbours, the O'Kellys, in 1455, and they managed to recover it for short periods in later years. The O'Melaghlins, the remnant of the ancient kingly house of Meath, were very much in decline at this period, but with their vassals, the MacCoghlans, still held a considerable territory. To their south and east were two important Gaelic lordships, Fercall and Kineleagh, territories respectively of the O'Molloys and the MacGeoghegans. The O'Molloys held a large area, strong because of its extensive oak woods and bogs. There, in an island castle in Lough Coura (now drained), in the centre of modern County Offaly, Brian O'Connor of Offaly had his most secure retreat. The MacGeoghegans, through producing in the fourteenth and fifteenth centuries a series of able leaders who had laid the nearby marcher areas under contribution and kept at bay their powerful neighbours, the O'Connors of Offaly, had enjoyed greater prestige than the extent of their territory would seem to have justified; they retained it in the sixteenth century. Kildare influence was strong in Kineleagh, where the earls had obtained extensive concessions of land from the MacGeoghegans, whom they nevertheless retained as tenants.[3] East of Kineleagh the Tyrrells of Fertullagh were almost, if not quite, as gaelicised as Dillons and Delamares.

The eastern part of modern County Offaly with the north-east corner of Leix was the old territory of Offaly, ruled by the O'Connors. Throughout the fifteenth and early sixteenth centuries they received a large annual payment of black rent from County Meath, which they were otherwise accustomed to ravage. Of all the Irish lords the O'Connors exercised the greatest influence

[1] Theiner, *Vetera mon.*, p. 521.

[2] *Cal. Carew MSS, 1515–74*, p. 264.

[3] Kildare rental in *R.S.A.I. Jn.*, vii, 126–9. *H.M.C.*, *rep.* 9, pt 2, app., p. 277. For the MacGeoghegans see Walsh, *Irish chiefs*, pp 226–69.

on the English Pale. Their relationship with the earls of Kildare was shifting and ambiguous. The latter claimed to be rightful lords of O'Connor territory; conversely, when the earls of Kildare were at a low ebb in the first half of the fifteenth century, the O'Connors had occupied a number of their border castles and lands in Kildare, notably Rathangan, the O'Connor centre before the Norman conquest. Along the southern frontier of the O'Connors were three vassal lordships, those of the O'Dunnes of Iregan, the O'Dempseys of Clanmaliere—with a tradition of English alliance—and that branch of the O'Connors known as the MacMorishes of Irry. In this area the earls of Kildare had recovered possession of the important castles and manors of Lea and Moret, so that their influence here was much stronger than in Offaly proper. Most of eastern County Leix belonged to the O'More lordship. Like the O'Connors, the O'Mores were hereditary enemies of the adjacent English areas and especially of County Kildare. They gave much trouble to the eighth and ninth earls, who claimed by old titles many lands in their country.

And here our circuit of Ireland ends. It has shown, we hope, how difficult it is to generalise about the distribution of territorial power and influence in the Ireland of the early sixteenth century. For every clearly defined sphere of authority there were others where power was divided between rival Irish groups or where Old English and Irish customs and people were hopelessly intermingled; or, indeed, where the process of gaelicisation had gone far to blur or eliminate the barriers between Irish and English law and custom. The greater Irish lordships, like the greatest Old English ones, were substantial and formidable powers, inside the macrocosm of the island. But there was much weakness among the competing authorities and more disorder was creeping over the island as stronger authorities split into weaker ones, and, on the other hand, a few strong powers came to strengthen themselves by more systematic devastation of their neighbours. Yet inside this variety there was prosperity and even beauty being created: some of the finest church buildings and the most attractive ornament since the Norman conquest belong to this period.[1]

The institutions of government to which we must now turn were no more uniform than the topographical and political divisions. Though, once more, Dublin is the logical starting-point, it must be clearly understood that the Dublin administration was the effective government of only a very limited part of Ireland, and that its effectiveness varied in many different parts where it operated in greater or lesser degree. At the same time it should be recognised that the machinery of government located in Dublin was elaborate and so designed that, in theory at least, it could comprehend the whole of the

[1] See E. C. Rae in vol. ii.

island. Modelled closely on that of medieval England, it had remained structurally unchanged since the early fourteenth century, and contained a number of institutions and offices which by 1534 were purely nominal. It continued to be a focus for the careers of a number of gentry and bourgeois families, mainly lawyers and financial officials, some drawn from Dublin, a number from the old-established families of the four counties of Dublin, Meath, Louth, and Kildare, a very few from other Old English groups outside the Pale, and a few Englishmen who held posts to which they had been appointed by the crown or on account of their tenure of ecclesiastical office. These latter categories were to expand and to achieve a dominant position immediately after 1534, and retained a predominance in administration, though not necessarily in the courts, thereafter.

The chief governor, normally resident in Dublin castle, was the representative of the king of England as lord of Ireland. Normally he was the deputy to the lieutenant, who was often a royal prince when the title was not subsumed in that of the crown. During the seventy-four years before 1534, the effective office in Dublin had been held for only some nine years by men of English birth; and for nearly half that term the office had been in the hands of three members of the house of Kildare, the seventh, eighth, and ninth earls, and longest and most continuously by the Great Earl, the limits of whose office-holding, though there were interruptions, extended from 1478 to his death in 1513. During the deputy's absence from Ireland or at his death, his functions were exercised by a temporary official, the lord justice (or in earlier terminology 'justiciar'), who was appointed by methods that altered from time to time but normally involved action by the council.

The king's council in Ireland was, for working purposes of government, an official or 'privy' council, consisting of the great officers of state. At the head of these were the chancellor and the chief justice of king's bench (sometimes called 'chief place'). Theoretically, after 1496, both of these were appointed directly by the king; in practice they might form part of the Old English entourage of the chief governor for the time being. The office of chancellor was a temporary one, but the judges held office for life. The remaining judges, from the courts of king's bench, common bench, and exchequer, might be appointed to the council and removed from it by the chief governor, but, having security of tenure as judges, had some degree of independence from him in practice. The chief governor, however, was normally able to dominate the official council, though he might have to contend with opposition and with the sending of complaints against him to the king. Besides the working council there was what is sometimes described as the common council; the official council afforced with local magnates, chosen either on a traditional basis or according to the wishes of the chief governor. This council was necessary to give force to certain administrative decisions. Finally there was the great council, representing much the same groups as parliament, though normally drawn only from the English Pale; it too was needed to implement certain decisions such as the calling of a general hosting, but its function had become largely nominal, though it had more freedom in its proceedings than a parliament could have after the passage of Poynings' law in 1494–5.

Parliament itself was intended to comprise (*a*) lords, spiritual and temporal, (*b*) representatives of the shires and boroughs, and (*c*) representatives of the lower clergy, through their proctors, from the whole of the king's lordship of Ireland. In practice, lords spiritual and temporal from a wide area were eligible to attend, though only a few from outside the Pale normally did so; proctors of the lesser clergy appeared from such dioceses as were *inter Anglicos*, though again the number of those from outside the Pale was small. Of the commons also, most representatives were from the counties of the Pale, but there were some from the counties and towns of Kilkenny, Wexford, and Waterford, though few would normally appear. Sessions were usually held at Dublin or Drogheda, but they might be and were held elsewhere from time to time. In accordance with Poynings' law the bills that came before parliament after 1494 had their origin in the official council and had to have prior authorisation in England before being placed before parliament, but their scope was fairly wide and their impact was not confined to the Pale alone. They covered alterations in the law, the regulation of administrative matters, the imposition of certain taxes, and the satisfaction of individual or corporate grievances by private acts. The laws passed by parliament were enforced by the judges on circuit and, in theory at least, in all corporate towns, but it is difficult to establish how effective they were before 1534 outside the Pale.

The Dublin administration contained a relatively elaborate exchequer system. The treasurership was largely a nominal office, the vice-treasurer being the effective officer as the executive head of the exchequer of receipt. Under the Kildare deputyship, however, the vice-treasurer had usually been brushed aside, and the receiver general, who was very much the earl's personal financial officer, took his place. The older system was revived in 1520. Whoever managed the finances, the effectiveness of the Dublin administration largely depended on his ability to pay official salaries and the cost of implementing decisions made by the council and courts. The revenues consisted of receipts from royal lands, many of them in the hands of the earls of Kildare; the profits of justice, which were not large; feudal incidents, which rarely found their way into the exchequer; the important customs and poundage, which came into the treasury from a few ports only, as elsewhere they had been assigned or alienated; a tax on the land and other income of absentees; and—most significant—a subsidy granted intermittently for periods of years by parliament. Only a few isolated items of revenue reached Dublin from outside the Pale, though a certain amount was raised and assigned to pay fees of local royal officials or to maintain the walls of outlying municipalities. The amount of revenue at the disposal of a chief governor largely determined the level and range of his activities. Even when the expenses of the day-to-day administration were covered, a chief governor from England depended almost wholly for his effectiveness on subsidies from English revenues or from personal funds he brought with him, while an Old English deputy had to find the resources with which alone he could govern effectively from his own estates or clients.

The common-law courts were very similar to those of their English model. Courts of king's bench (chief place) and common bench were not unlike their English counterparts, as was the court of exchequer, which, under its chief and second barons, was perhaps the most active of the three. The records do not survive which would establish this clearly, but it is probable that, by 1534, their procedures were somewhat archaic by English standards, though a certain number of the Old English legal families sent their sons to the inns of court so as to keep moderately up to date. There are occasional references in Ireland to an equitable jurisdiction vested in the chancellor, such as had already come into existence in England by the early fifteenth century, and we find references in parliament rolls to legal matters being referred to the chancellor for settlement,[1] but only after the fall of Kildare does the equitable jurisdiction seem to have achieved an importance equal to that which it enjoyed in England. Records of decrees of the Irish chancery began in 1534, so that it would seem that by then the lord chancellor and his officials were in close touch with the developments of the chancellor's equitable jurisdiction in England.

Of local courts within the Pale we know little. The sheriff's 'tourn' in the baronies—equivalent to the English hundreds—was still taking place in the latter part of the sixteenth century.[2] The commonplace book of Christopher Cusack, sheriff of Meath in 1511,[3] shows him undertaking a number of administrative duties: overseeing the appointment of, and apparently supervising, the collectors of subsidies, continuing to undertake various military responsibilities, and also exercising a certain amount of jurisdiction in virtue of his office. It might seem that he was acting more like the thirteenth-century English sheriff than his Tudor contemporary. The main contact between the central and local jurisdictions came through the judges on circuit. When the chief governor was weak the assizes might be confined to the Pale alone, but when he was able to act effectively outside the Pale he took the judges with him on his progresses and administered the king's justice extensively throughout the midlands and the south of Ireland.

[1] Richardson & Sayles, *Ir. parl. in middle ages*, 2nd ed., pp 215–19; *Christ Church deeds*, nos 326, 378.

[2] *Cal. Carew MSS, 1575–88*, p. 422.

[3] T.C.D., MS E3. 33.

Special resident justices were appointed from time to time for Counties Kilkenny and Waterford, and special commissions to hold assizes over a wide area from Kilkenny to Limerick and Cork were issued on occasion.[1]

When we come to deal with more narrowly local jurisdiction our knowledge is limited. Some local courts within the Pale continued to function actively: those of the archbishop of Dublin, for example, in the liberty of the cross (lands under ecclesiastical jurisdiction exempted from the operation of the common-law courts in certain respects) of Dublin (St Sepulchre's), which dealt not only in minor pleas but in capital criminal matters.[2] The creation of a liberty in County Kildare about 1500 detached that county from the normal processes of common-law jurisdiction and put them instead in the hands of Kildare's own officials.[3] The towns naturally continued to exercise the rights of jurisdiction conferred by their charters. Justices of the peace were regularly appointed within the Pale and in some other English areas, but we know almost nothing about such changes as may have taken place in their functions since the fourteenth century.

Outside the Pale, there were major liberty jurisdictions in Wexford, Tipperary, and Kerry, with their own officials and procedures. Though we know a little of what went on in Clonmel, and have a few hints about the Wexford jurisdiction, no documents from Desmond's administration at Tralee for this time have survived. The local jurisdictions exercised by the outlying towns were wide and there was little recourse from them to the royal courts in Dublin, though this recourse was not impeded if petitioners wished to resort to it. Customs officials were appointed for the ports inside the Pale, and they operated as far north as Carrickfergus. The major ports in the south-east, south, and west had customs officers, but they were usually their own rather than the king's, since in most such towns royal customs had been granted to the municipalities for murage (building or repairing the town walls) and other purposes. The earl of Ormond had the right to collect prisage (or butlerage), a tax on imported wines, which was a perquisite of his hereditary office of king's butler. It did not always prove possible for him to enforce the right even in Dublin and Drogheda, let alone the more distant port towns, and it was late into the sixteenth century before it could be enforced in Galway, where the town's claim to exemption had been upheld by the English council in 1526.[4]

It is difficult in any study of jurisdiction and revenue in the English lordship in this period to distinguish between shadow and substance. Theoreti-

[1] See Quinn, 'Anglo-Irish local government' in *I.H.S.*, i, no. 4 (Sept. 1939), pp 358–9.

[2] For a later date see the *Court book of the liberty of St Sepulchre*, ed. Herbert Wood (Dublin, 1930).

[3] See above, pp 5–6.

[4] Hardiman, *Galway*, pp 78, 82 n. v, 91–2, 92 n.; *Cal. pat. rolls, Ire., Eliz.*, ii, 7, 101–2; *Cal. S.P. Ire., 1575–84*, pp 535–6; *Ormond deeds, 1509–47*, no. 181, *1547–84*, nos 85, 244–5, 319; P.R.O.I., salved chancery pleadings, A 254, B 254, C 127–9, D 15, etc.

cally the king's writ ran anywhere in the island where it was not excluded by legally recognised liberties, and the judges could similarly go anywhere on circuit. Writs were issued to peers, convocations, sheriffs, and mayors to send members to parliament when in fact this had not been done for many years. Lists of sheriffs who were supposed to appear in the exchequer with their proffers—many of whom like the sheriff of Connacht may not have done so for a century or more—were regularly entered on the memoranda rolls. Writs were issued for the collection of subsidies where none had for long been effectively levied. Yet it is significant that the exchequer officials knew the names of the sheriffs and had some dealings with them even if they did not appear; and it might be that some unexpected official would put in an appearance in Dublin or a small payment of subsidy from an unexpected quarter appear in the treasurer's books. The potential range of the effectiveness of the Dublin administration was as great as its actual operation was narrowly limited.

Once we turn from the residual English administration to Gaelic and gaelicised Ireland, it will be clear from our circuit of Ireland in 1534 that we have to deal with a large number of usually small and more or less independent political units or 'lordships' whose number was increasing rather than diminishing as some of the larger—such as the O'Ferrall lordship of Annaly—split into fractions between contending candidates for rule. The degree of independence of these units varied widely and was subject to frequent changes, but all of their lords sought the greatest possible degree of autonomous action, while few if any of them were exempt on occasion from the interference of a neighbour who, even if only temporarily, was more powerful.[1] Geographically, the nature of these units varied between region and region. In the purely Gaelic areas of the north and west the lordships were in general solid blocks of territory, while in the Anglo-Norman regions and, most of all, in those marcher areas such as Westmeath and the Tipperary–Limerick border which had been fought over by various powers during a long period, they were often territorially very discontinuous and discrete; a notable example was in the mingling of the 'eastern fractions' of Muskerry with the Barretts' lordship to the west of Cork. Division of an originally united lordship could have the same effect; the extremely intermingled territories of O'Connor Donn and O'Connor Roe—where the sub-lordship of the O'Beirns was divided between the two overlords although subject to a single lord of its own—were the consequence of a division which had left each line in the possession of those areas whose inhabitants supported it. Internally, the Irish lordship had little of the political organisation of

[1] For these units see Nicholls, *Gaelic Ire.*, pp 21 ff; for a contemporary view (1515), *S.P. Hen. VIII*, ii, 1–8.

a 'state'; its administrative system—if such a term is deserved—was personalised and undeveloped, and its political stability, in most cases, under perpetual attack from the proliferating members of the ruling lineage. This proliferation of the ruling lines, combined with the defective mechanisms of elective succession—the system referred to by contemporary English writers as 'tanistry'—constituted the most serious weakness of Gaelic polity, leading to endless factional dissensions within the lordships.

Every territory had an official brehon (judge) or brehons appointed by the lord, whose primary function was trying cases affecting his interests or those of the territory as a whole. Although crimes were matters for composition between the injured party and the offender, the lord was entitled to fines for offences such as theft and bloodshed, while in cases of homicide he received the larger proportion of the *éraic* or blood-price. In theory, a brehon award was an arbitration which could be made only by the consent of both parties, but in cases which touched himself the lord could be expected to compel a recalcitrant defendant to submit to it. In other cases the plaintiff would himself seek to force the defendant to resort to arbitration by seizing on his property—or that of his kindred—as a pledge, a practice greatly disapproved by the English administration in Ireland and afterwards forbidden by statute.[1] In general, outside the great palatine liberties of the earls of Ormond and Desmond, which possessed an administrative hierarchy surviving from the early medieval period, the comparable institutions in the Irish lordships were of a most rudimentary kind. The lords possessed stewards or collectors—often, as one would expect, a hereditary office in certain families—to levy their rents or tributes, and a very important and universal official was the marshal (*marasgal*) whose duty was to arrange the actual apportionment for the support of troops and their quartering on the country. The apprehension of malefactors, the collection of fines, and the execution of the lord's orders in general were the functions of the household kern (kernety: *ceithearn tighe*).[2] It is sometimes difficult to know whether the term kern is being used of this force or of a purely military body, though of course we can be certain that the kernety were employed as light troops in time of war and indeed it would not have been possible to draw a line between their internal police functions and the repelling of outside invaders. The offices of marshal and of captain of the kernety were also often hereditary. Great lords such as Ormond and Desmond would have constables in their various castles, and these would have had some other administrative functions, and most great lords in the sixteenth century would have a permanent hereditary constable commanding a standing body of galloglass.[3] It seems to have been the rule for

[1] For a brief summary of late medieval Irish law and legal process see K. W. Nicholls, 'Gaelic society and economy', above, vol. ii, and *Gaelic Ire.*, pp 44, 67.

[2] For references see, e.g., Hore & Graves, *Southern & eastern counties*, p. 266.

[3] See below, pp 31–2.

the inhabitants of a territory, or those of some standing (*maithe*), to assemble twice a year, at Mayday and All Souls—the terms of the Irish year—at some traditional meeting-place, always a hill, to transact any political business that might require their presence.[1] In the Desmond liberty of Kerry all the freeholders of the county were required to be present at the great sessions of the county which were held once a year at Tralee, and to bring with them not only provisions sufficient for the earl and his retinue but also women to cook the provisions.[2]

Outside the area described as being under the control of the Dublin government there is only limited evidence that the common law continued to function. Thus in Kilkenny and in Tipperary judgements of Irish brehons employed by the earls of Ormond for this purpose were a usual part of legal practice, and an amalgam of Irish and English law, in which compensation for crime was the normal practice, prevailed. Special justices and judges on circuit appear to have dealt with a limited range of cases only. The lawyers in the Pale were trained mostly by apprenticeship in legal families in Dublin. Outside Dublin there is little evidence of an organised legal training. Throughout both the Gaelic area and the march, as well as in the independent towns of the south and west, the civil law seems to have exerted a strong influence. It was, of course, studied along with canon law by the ecclesiastical lawyers who operated in the church courts and whose field was not restricted in these areas by the existence of an effectual secular jurisdiction. There is evidence that the brehons were often well informed in Roman law, and although we cannot say whether it was actually taught in the same schools as the brehon law, it seems likely that it was. These schools were kept by prominent brehon families. We know little about clerical education throughout most of the country. There are constant references to persons who were studying civil and canon law, not in a university—as a result of repressive legislation the flow of Irish students to Oxford seems to have dried up after about 1400—but according to the custom of the country.[3] This presumably means the sort of schools referred to by Campion in the late sixteenth century,[4] where boys and young men learned the Institutes of Justinian by rote.

It is not possible to draw a line between secular and clerical education. The common factor of a literate upbringing led to a close connection between the clergy in the Gaelic areas and the Irish learned families, the brehons,

[1] *Ir. Arch. Soc. Misc.*, i, 192–3; Nicholls, *Gaelic Ire.*, pp 30–1.

[2] S. M. Hussey, *Desmond survey of County Kerry* (privately printed, Tralee, 1923; repr. *Kerryman*, Aug.–Oct. 1927).

[3] Canice Mooney, 'The church in Gaelic Ireland' in Corish, *Ir. catholicism*, ii, ch. 5, pp 21–7; Nicholls, *Gaelic Ire.*, pp 98–9.

[4] *Hist. Ire.*, ed. Vossen, p. 24; cf. *A.U.*, iii, 108–9.

chroniclers, poets, and others, and a large proportion of the members of these families adopted the clerical profession. The poets or bards, who made their living by eulogising the Gaelic chiefs and gaelicised lords, also maintained schools at which members of bardic families learnt the intricate metres of medieval Irish verse. Besides their position as eulogists, they were feared for their satires and lampoons, which were believed to have magical powers that could bring misfortune or even death to the person satirised; and we find them for this reason invoked as sureties for the performance of treaties. Their wealth and influence is perhaps the most surprising survival of an archaic institution in Irish society of the later middle ages.[1] Another literate class were the coarb and erenagh families, the hereditary tenants of church lands who were to be found throughout the northern and western regions and who in the Gaelic system enjoyed a quasi-clerical status.

From literacy to language is a natural step. It is difficult to give an exact picture of the comparative status of the two vernaculars in the Ireland of 1534, but broadly speaking it could be said that English was the language of the Pale, of the liberty of Wexford—except its borders—and of the towns everywhere, and Irish that of the rest of the country. As to the knowledge and use of English in the Irish-speaking parts, when Lord Leonard Grey toured Munster in 1535 he found that most of the magnates—including Lord Barry, a youth of 17 or 18, and old Sir John of Desmond, in his seventies—could speak 'very good English'; on the other hand, the lord of the Decies, Garret MacShane, was 'a man that can speak never a word of English', so that the ability was not universal among the Munster lords.[2] In Connacht we find the same inconsistency; in 1540 the prior of Roscommon could speak good English,[3] but a contemporary tells us that Roland de Burgo, a cousin of the first earl of Clanricard who became bishop of Clonfert in 1534 and had a long and prominent career, could neither speak nor understand it.[4] We cannot say how widely Irish was understood in the Pale—probably pretty extensively—but the merchants of the southern and western towns must have known it well because of their commercial dealings with the surrounding countryside, and it is possible that the position of English in the towns themselves was coming under pressure. A Waterford city statute of 1492–3 decreed that no dweller in the city or suburbs, whether freeman or stranger, 'shall enpleade nor defende in Yrish tonge ayenste ony man in the court, but . . . shall have a man that can spek English to declare his matier, excepte one party be of the countre; then every such dueller shal be att liberte to speke Yrish'.[5] In 1523 the town council of Galway found it necessary to decree that no one who could not speak English should be

[1] See Brian Ó Cuív (ed.), *Seven centuries of Irish learning, 1000–1700* ([Dublin], 1961, repr. 1971); Nicholls, *Gaelic Ire.*, pp 79–84.

[2] *S.P. Hen. VIII*, iii, 282, 284–5.

[3] *Cal. Carew MSS, 1515–74*, p. 169.

[4] *Acts privy council Ire., 1556–71*, p. 226.

[5] *H.M.C. rep. 10*, app. v, p. 323.

made a freeman.[1] Hibernian English was allied to the dialects of the west of England, and still retained at this date, and later, some archaic dialectal features.[2]

The articulation of ecclesiastical institutions had not changed by 1534. The traditional divisions of the church, *inter Anglicos* and *inter Hibernicos*, had been maintained. Cardinal Wolsey had made an attempt to assert his legatine authority over Ireland; he had been repelled by the dioceses *inter Anglicos* and ignored by those *inter Hibernicos*. As has already been shown, ecclesiastics, secular and regular, took part in parliament, in jurisdiction, and, in fact also, in the implementation of the secular laws under which they served. Monastic institutions, rather than cathedrals or parish churches, or even castles, were the most prominent features of the man-made landscape. Not only had a number of the older abbeys been extended and refurnished in recent years, though others had gone into decay, but a number of extensive friaries had recently been built, especially in the western half of the country and under the auspices of Irish lords.[3] On the other hand, a number of cathedrals and many parish churches were in decline or even in ruins.[4] The secular clergy had in general a poor reputation for attention to their duties; the regular clergy of the older orders were absorbed to a considerable degree in lay pursuits; the mendicant friars alone were said to preach and minister effectively to the common people.

In the Irish church, as in secular matters, a sharp distinction must be drawn between conditions in the Pale and in such cities as Waterford, where the state of the church approximated to that of England, and those in the remainder of the country. There the church differed widely in both organisation and actual condition from the English norm, being both more archaic and regional on the one hand and more in line with general European conditions on the other. As the statute of provisors was a dead letter outside the area effectively controlled by the government, a large proportion of the benefices—and all the important ones, bishoprics, deaneries, and abbacies—were filled by papal nominees. The poverty of Irish benefices—so great that in most cases those provided were excused payment of the usual fees[5]—and the fact that a large part of the revenues, according to the Irish custom, were collected in the form of entertainment had prevented the abuse, common elsewhere in Europe, of the appointment of Italian absentees; but a perhaps greater abuse had arisen towards the close of the fifteenth century in the

[1] Ibid., p. 400.

[2] Angus McIntosh and M. L. Samuels, 'Prolegomena to a study of medieval Anglo-Irish' in *Medium Aevum*, xxxvii (1968), pp 1–11; see below, ch. XXI.

[3] For the Gaelic church in general see Canice Mooney, 'The church in Gaelic Ireland' in Corish, *Ir. catholicism*, ii, ch. 5; Bradshaw, *Dissolution of the religious orders*, pp 8–38.

[4] See, e.g., Theiner, *Vetera mon.*, pp 518, 521 (but cf., for a different picture, ibid., p. 529); *Archiv. Hib.*, xiii (1947), pp 24–9.

[5] Mooney, op. cit., p. 17; *S.P. Hen. VIII*, ii, 102–4.

appointment of scions of great families who had no intention of actually taking orders, but who continued to live and conduct themselves as laymen. This, and the growing secularisation of the clergy themselves, led at the close of the medieval period to a loss of the traditional immunity which had been enjoyed in Gaelic Ireland by the church and its possessions, both from secular exactions and in war. The evil effects of the system of provisions mentioned above would seem to have been worst in Connacht and Thomond and to have been least prevalent in Gaelic Ulster, where the old ecclesiastical polity seems to have survived intact and where almost all the benefices remained in the hands of members of the hereditary clerical families.

As the majority of the Irish clergy were at least technically illegitimate, either as the sons of clerics themselves or because their parents were within the wide degrees of consanguinity and affinity within which marriage was forbidden by medieval canon law—and cousin marriage remained the norm in Gaelic Ireland throughout the later middle ages as in the pre-Norman period—they needed papal dispensations to hold their benefices,[1] a fact which encouraged their close contacts with Rome and which was closely tied up with the system of papal provision to benefices. This close connection between the Irish and Rome, and the attitude to which it led—for in Ireland, in contradiction to the position in England, the papacy and the curia must have been regarded as friendly bestowers of favours, not as avaricious extorters of money—were perhaps significant factors in the failure of both the Henrician schism and the subsequent reformation to win over the country.

The older religious orders, such as the Cistercians, Augustinian Canons, and Premonstratensians, became in the later middle ages even more laicised than the secular clergy; the continued appointment by papal provision of commendatory abbots and priors, secular clerics, or laymen of great families with a mere pretence to minor orders, had destroyed the whole basis of conventual life in the houses of these orders outside a few abbeys of the Pale, where alone the Cistercian habit, for example, was still worn.[2]

Outside the structure of the organised church, the actual religious life of later medieval Ireland has been little studied. The cult of the Irish saints, for instance, presents a wide field which has been little explored. It would seem that their cult, while important, was largely motivated towards secular ends, and it has been remarked that they scarcely figure in the devotional poetry of the period. Individual instances of piety and asceticism were frequent, and provide a striking contrast with the laicisation of the official church, to which only the mendicant orders of friars were an exception.[3] The latter, who were

[1] *S.P. Hen. VIII*, ii, 102–4; iii, 104.

[2] Otway-Ruthven, *Med. Ire.*, pp 102 ff; Nicholls, *Gaelic Ire.*, pp 106–9.

[3] For the friars see F. X. Martin, 'The Irish friars and the Observant movement in the fifteenth century' in *Ir. Cath. Hist. Comm. Proc. 1960* (1961), pp 10–16, and the references there cited.

still in 1534 experiencing the upsurge which had led to the Observant movement and to the founding of numerous friaries during the century and a half before 1510, could be said to be the only section of the Irish church that maintained the normal standards of contemporary European religious life, and it is natural, therefore, that from them the strongest opposition to the reformation in Ireland should have come.

Ireland in 1534 was a land of constant war, yet by contemporary standards its military techniques were rather out of date and inefficient. In the English Pale the military needs were still partly met by the old feudal 'rising-out', and when scutage was said to run it had to be proclaimed formally through an afforced council. Money compositions could be exacted, carts acquired for transport, and purveyance levied for the maintenance of the troops. The Irish system was much the same, but more extreme in all respects. In all the Irish and marcher regions the general rising-out, by which all able-bodied men were required to serve at the lord's command (only clerics, brehons, bards, and chroniclers—men of letters—being exempt), operated, but in spite of the fines imposed for non-attendance, a lord might find that whole sections of his subjects disobeyed his summons because of their political opposition to him. In addition, great lords would have the services of a permanent standing body of galloglass, quartered on their territory, while lesser lords would hire galloglass at need.

The galloglass were in origin mercenary Highland Scots soldiers who came into Ireland in the second half of the thirteenth and the early part of the fourteenth century. From Ulster, where they first appeared, they had moved into Connacht by the middle of the fourteenth century. One galloglass house, the MacSweeneys, established themselves with territorial power under the O'Donnells in County Donegal, and branches of that lineage migrated at intervals right down the west coast of Ireland first into Connacht and then in the late fifteenth century into Munster and made settlements there. The MacDonalds from the Scottish isles migrated at an early date through Ulster, where one branch remained to act as constables to the O'Neills, into Connacht, and from Connacht a branch of them came to Leinster to serve the earls of Kildare.[1] In the sixteenth century—and perhaps somewhat earlier[2]—one finds new Scots coming in, such as Campbells, but these do not seem to have made any permanent settlements. The typical galloglass, although they were normally styled *Scotici* (Scots), were in fact, so far as their captains were concerned, derived from families only remotely of Scottish origin, and many of the members of the ranks were of pure Irish descent. After 1534 the crown quite normally hired galloglass, but

[1] There is no work so far on the movements of the galloglass lineages. See, however, for the MacSweeneys, Paul Walsh, *Leabhar Chlainne Suibhne* (Dublin, 1920).

[2] Note two MacLeans slain while apparently in service with a MacRannell, 1486 (*A.U.*, iii, 304).

there is not much record of that being done in the campaigns waged under English deputies before 1534, and in fact what seems to have happened is that the crown took over the Kildare galloglass into its own service. In general, certain families of galloglass tended to identify their interests with certain factions among the Irish; the MacDonnell and MacDowell galloglass were identified in Connacht with the faction headed by the Lower MacWilliam, and the MacSweeneys with that headed by the Upper MacWilliam. Similarly, in Munster, the MacSweeneys tended to take service with the O'Briens, Butlers, and other various enemies of the earls of Desmond, whose own galloglass were the MacSheehys, a family of MacDonnell connections. The galloglass were heavily-armed soldiers each of whose fighting men was normally accompanied by an armour-bearer and a boy. They were always equipped with helmets and long mail-coats, and their standard weapon was a heavy battle-axe with a six-foot handle, though they also used other weapons. They received high wages and served under very restricted conditions as to the times of their service, being hired for three-month periods. They were quartered on the country, and their pay and maintenance must have represented a very heavy burden for the areas on which they were cessed and billeted.[1]

The lighter Irish troops were the kern, footmen without armour and carrying light weapons. The term kern (*ceithearn*) is a collective meaning simply 'troop' and has no primary specialised meaning: the 'household kern' (kernety), as has been explained above,[2] were a kind of police in the service of the lord who were certainly also employed as light troops in time of war. The majority of the kern, however, were recruited only for campaigns, and it is probable that the greater part of the rising-out were automatically classed as kern. Only the more well-to-do among the natives would have provided horsemen. The Irish horseman was not a very efficient soldier by the standards of the time; as he rode without stirrups, he was incapable of carrying through a sustained charge, since he carried his javelin over his head.[3] For this reason the showing of the horseman in general throughout the century in conflict with English troops was very poor. In the Pale the horsemen were more heavily armed, using stirrups and heavy lances.

During the greater part of this period, the earls of Kildare employed infantrymen with firearms and had a small artillery train. The city of Dublin had had guns since the fourteenth century. But in general medieval weapons were still employed on both sides, and the extensive use of firearms only really began after 1534.[4]

[1] See Nicholls, *Gaelic Ire.*, pp 87–90.

[2] Above, p. 26.

[3] For the horsemen's equipment see Nicholls, *Gaelic Ire.*, p. 85; and Liam Price (ed.), 'Armed forces of the Irish chiefs in the early 16th century' in *R.S.A.I. Jn.*, lxii (1932), pp 206–7 (this document is misdated by the editor; it in fact belongs to the 1480s).

[4] G. A. Hayes-McCoy, 'The early history of guns in Ireland' in *Galway Arch. Soc. Jn.*, xviii (1938–9), pp 43–65.

The cattle raids between rival Irish lords had often the aspect of a traditional sport or prowess-proving exercise, though their destructive effect on the economy must not be minimised. Yet the increasing use of firearms was rendering war an increasingly serious and destructive undertaking. War appears to have increased in its incidence and range in the quarter-century before 1534. The precise causes of this increase and its specific effects on Irish and Old English society are still almost unknown.

It is not, on the available evidence, clear how far it is possible to compare the nature of the agricultural economy of England and that of the anglicised parts of Ireland. Conditions in the Pale could perhaps be compared to those in the northern border counties of England, even if there were some significant differences in emphasis in respect of livestock and tillage. Along the coast from Dalkey to Dundalk, and in the Liffey and Boyne valleys, there was considerable stability in the Old English families and estates. The economy was basically a manorial one in an increasing state of dissolution; as in England, substantial yeoman farmers had largely replaced peasant smallholders. This was true also of church lands in the eastern midlands, and of parts of the liberty of Wexford. Tenancy was generally by copyhold or lease, though an increasing number of these tenants were of Irish stock; a few Irish serfs (betaghs) survived on ecclesiastical and possibly on temporal lands. On the other hand a large part of the Pale was influenced to some considerable extent by its proximity to the march; having heavier military responsibilities of a local character it had less stability, was liable to raids, particularly cattle raids,[1] and might have its harvests interfered with, while the cultural infiltration from the Irish side was considerable. It was said of Sir William Darcy early in the century that he was almost the only man who still wore gown and doublet and rode in the English fashion—i.e. with a saddle—in the western part of Meath,[2] and it is probable that besides social customs and the use of the Irish language, Irish tenures and the leasing of land to Irish tenants were increasing in the border areas.

The Ormond territories and some others in which similar conditions prevailed, such as the western parts of County Kildare and perhaps parts of Wexford, represented a transitional area between the English ways of the Pale and those of the purely gaelicised areas. There, as has been observed, the English legal system was no longer operating; judgements were being given by brehons on the Irish principle of composition for crimes. Again, the lords cessed their troops upon the country. But, on the other hand, this country was not completely gaelicised and the remnants of a manorial system still survived, although between the middle of the fifteenth century and the middle of the sixteenth we find a change in the method of tenure affecting

[1] See plate 2. [2] *Ormond deeds, 1509–47*, p. 357.

the actual cultivators. Fixed rents for small plots of land were being replaced by a system in which the landlord took a share of the crop, usually a quarter or a third, but if the landlord provided half the seed, then half. The exact implications of this change are not clear, but it is tempting to see it as a response to increasing insecurity. Apart from some of the smaller semi-, or wholly, agricultural borough communities, there is no evidence for survival of a manorial system in the Desmond territories or under the smaller Norman lords of Munster, though again the lack of records does not permit certainty on this point.

It might therefore be said that in the English areas there was a market economy, a normal profit-and-loss system of trading in agricultural produce, hides, wool, and certain types of cloth, and that all the towns were active markets. There was nothing very exceptional about the character of the economy in the Pale, compared with other parts of western Europe, except for the absence of any really extensive domestic manufacture, though there was a considerable amount of spinning and weaving of both wool and linen. There is also evidence of the finishing of substantial quantities of English cloth. The problem as regards the rest of Ireland is that the evidence does not appear to be adequate to determine to what extent a market economy operated. There was, however, a considerable export trade in hides, linen, and coarse cloths such as friezes, as well as other products such as sheep-skins, furs, tallow, and butter. Trade often tended to be monopolised by the various lords of territories, who frequently issued ordinances by which they granted to a single merchant the monopoly of trading within their territory, no doubt in return for financial concessions made to themselves.[1]

In the purely Gaelic and completely gaelicised areas, conditions were quite exceptional by European standards: the population was small, and settlement was of a scattered and largely impermanent nature. The economy was by and large a pastoral one, and although there was a considerable amount of cultivation, it seems to have been to a great extent on a shifting or 'long-fallow' basis, the land being tilled for two or three years successively and then left to lie waste for ten years or more.[2] This low intensity of land utilisation was reflected in the Irish system of landholding and was in turn influenced by the latter, which militated against any intensive exploitation of the land or the making of enclosures, buildings, or other improvements.

Land was owned corporately by agnatic descent groups ('septs', in contemporary English terminology), the descendants of a not-so-distant common male ancestor. The lands of the sept would normally be held by its individual members under a system of periodic redistribution, sometimes only annual, from Mayday to Mayday, but often for a longer term. The

[1] Nicholls, *Gaelic Ire.*, pp 39–40; Hore & Graves, *Southern & eastern counties*, pp 164, 188, 245–6; cf. *Anal. Hib.*, no. 10 (1941), p. 140.

[2] For the Gaelic economy in general see Nicholls, 'Gaelic society and economy', above, vol. ii.

customs varied from region to region. In most areas the youngest co-heir made the division of the land and the senior took first choice, but in some parts the senior or chief of the sept both made the division and took the first choice, a system which tended to concentrate landownership in these districts in the hands of the chiefs. The co-heirs, however, could make a permanent partition at any time if they so agreed, and in this case the lands set out to each member would in future be divided only among his own descendants. The same was the case with lands individually acquired by any member of the sept. This was the 'custom in nature of gavelkind' of English writers. Irish land was normally burdened with heavy exactions in kind by the lord of the district, and by custom, if the heirs were unable to meet these charges, they might surrender the land to the use and occupancy of the lord, while remaining theoretically entitled to it if they chose to return and take up possession. Theoretical ownership and actual possession of land were thus often distinct. The conveyance of land was normally by pledge or mortgage, the owners surrendering it in return for a payment in kind or money and being entitled to recover it on repayment, though the conditions for redemption were usually onerous and often virtually impossible of fulfilment.[1] There was a constant transfer of land in this way from declining families to rising and expanding ones, usually the ruling houses of the various territories.

Although the pastoral economy was general to both English and Irish areas, it was of much greater importance in the latter, where much land of good quality must have been normally in use for pasturage, as well as the indifferent land, hills, mountain slopes, and woods. The great herds of cattle and horses possessed by the lords and other persons of importance, together with their herdsmen and guards and the dependants who accompanied them, were called by the collective term *caoruigheachta* (anglicised as 'creaghts'). The word could also, on occasion, denote the human personnel alone. These herds represented a highly mobile form of economic resource, which could be easily moved, in case of trouble, from one district to another and which could, if necessary, follow the army in time of war. The Ulster creaghts, especially, occur in this context late into the seventeenth century. The general Gaelic custom allowed the herds to be grazed freely over unused or unoccupied lands, a rule which in the Irish conditions of the time permitted a wide range of movement and allowed the creaghts, at least in some areas, to follow an itinerant way of life. This wandering of the herds over waste grounds is not always to be clearly distinguished from transhumance or 'booleying', a purely seasonal movement of the cattle, with their human attendants, to summer pastures in the high mountains.[2] In each case the people who accompanied the cattle lived in temporary huts at each halting-place or grazing-place.[3]

[1] Ibid.; *Gaelic Ire.*, pp 56–67; *Anal. Hib.*, no. 26 (1970), pp 105–29.

[2] Cf. Spenser, quoted below, p. 152.

[3] Nicholls, above, vol. ii.

It is doubtful to what extent the Gaelic and gaelicised areas could be said to have possessed a peasantry in the European sense. Tenants seem to have been either persons of some substance, who could negotiate with their landlords on fairly equal terms, and, more importantly, protect themselves, their stock, and dependants against raids, or—more usually—mere share-cropping labourers, completely dependent on their landlords for stock and without any substance of their own. The information on this bottom stratum of the population is very scanty, but, quite apart from the creaghts, they seem to have wandered from place to place and master to master to a surprising degree, though the Irish lords claimed that their subjects, and not only the humble ones, were bound to remain in their lordships. This claim has been misinterpreted as implying the general existence of a servile class bound to the soil.[1]

Sixteenth-century Ireland still possessed a very considerable extent of woodland,[2] though extensive grazing must have been limiting natural regeneration, and it is noteworthy that in the later part of the century English writers note a lack of good timber in many areas, the woods, although extensive, being low and scrubby. The Pale was already almost treeless. The south-east, however, produced good oak timber, and a considerable export trade in shipbuilding timber to England and Scotland was flourishing from the south-eastern ports—Wexford, Wicklow, and Arklow—in the second half of the century, and, as it is referred to at Arklow in 1525,[3] it was probably already well established by that date. Besides timber, the woods also produced furs such as squirrel and marten skins, as well as the goshawks for which Ireland was noted at the period. More troublesome inhabitants of the woods were the wolves which were still numerous and whose skins appear in the Bristol trade.

Irish trade as a whole during this period has not been studied comprehensively, though trade with England has been surveyed in outline, and the records of that with Bristol and Chester, the major ports in this connection, are substantial.[4] It would be difficult to decide as between fish and hides which was the more significant product of Irish land and waters. There is no doubt that Irish salmon were extensively fished and actively exported from all the main ports and estuaries, from the Bann, Dublin, Wexford, New Ross, Waterford, Youghal, Limerick, and Galway. The herring of Wexford, Sligo,

[1] Nicholls, *Gaelic Ire.*, pp 68–70. The wording of the proclamation of 1605, printed in M. J. Bonn, *Die englische Kolonisation in Irland* (Stuttgart and Berlin, 1906), i, 394–7, is quite unambiguous as to the rights claimed by the lords being jurisdictional ones.

[2] McCracken, *Ir. woods*, is unfortunately unreliable for the earlier part of the period covered.

[3] *Ormond deeds, 1509–47*, p. 104.

[4] See K. P. Wilson (ed.), *Chester customs accounts, 1301–1566* (Liverpool, 1969); Carus-Wilson, *Overseas trade of Bristol*, and *Medieval merchant venturers*; Longfield, *Anglo-Ir. trade*.

and Ardglass occupied many Irish fishermen and attracted both English and French fishermen and English merchants. The rhyme

Herring of Sligo and salmon of Bann
Has made in Bristol many a rich man

may not scan very well but it emphasises the importance of these two fisheries. The larger food fishes of the continental shelf, haddock and cod in particular, were especially important off the south coast, attracting many foreign fishing vessels, whose seasonal commerce, as well as the drying of fish on shore, was significant for the Irish economy. Cowhides and calfskins were what made Ireland, especially Munster, well known throughout the Continent, a particularly important customer being Castile. Sheepskins and lambskins were also of considerable importance, though probably mainly in the English trade. With them can be classed furs from wolf and fox, squirrel and marten, the last-named a valuable fur. Textiles were also significant staples; woollen cloths—rug, frieze, kersey, and blanket, all coarsely woven fabrics—especially when made up into the Irish mantle, were known all over western Europe and the western Mediterranean, though the mantle was expensive and somewhat of a luxury product. Irish linen cloth was also well known, but it is difficult to estimate how its export would compare quantitatively with the very great annual exports of the Low Countries at this time; it may not have been very large.

The south-coast ports tended to trade largely with the Continent, those of the east mainly with England and Scotland. Bristol ships not only traded directly with many Irish ports but also played an active part in the transit trade,[1] picking up Irish products on their way from Bristol to France, Spain, Portugal, or the Mediterranean, and returning to Ireland on their way home to Bristol with Mediterranean, Iberian, and French produce. The western Irish ports did not in general own ships of their own, as did Waterford and Wexford.

Wine was probably the principal Irish import. It was obtained direct from France and Spain, but it also reached eastern Ireland in some quantity by way of English ports. Salt was needed for the fishery, as well as for domestic use, and was extensively imported by all the fishing ports from Wexford to Sligo. Some of it came direct from France, Spain, and Portugal in foreign ships, possibly more came through the agency of Bristol vessels, which carried considerable quantities of bay salt from Brittany. The third major import was iron. Much English cloth reached Ireland, a substantial amount of it undressed (*pannus sine grano*), and with it materials, soap and dyes, with which to prepare it. Metal goods and pottery too were extensively imported. Wheat, rye, and oats came to Bristol in some quantity from Wexford. Beans went extensively from the Severn valley to Ireland. Broadly, though

[1] Carus-Wilson, *Medieval merchant venturers*, p. 21.

there were exceptions, Ireland exported raw materials and imported manufactured or luxury products.[1]

In the present state of Irish historical studies such a broad survey as this is bound to be somewhat superficial in a number of respects. A great deal of research on many localities in Ireland at this time requires to be done before generalisations can hope to be precise. Social and economic inquiry into many aspects of Irish life has scarcely begun; records may be scarce or non-existent, especially in these areas, but much more can yet be clearly established. While on some aspects of the Irish scene it is possible to write with a reasonable degree of authority, there are many others where general statements still have much of the character of more or less well-informed guesswork. It is with these qualifications that this survey should be read.

[1] Longfield, *Anglo-Ir. trade*, especially pp 213–19, and further particulars of customs accounts in P.R.O.

University of Winnipeg, 515 Portage Ave., Winnipeg, MB. R3B 2E9 Canada

CHAPTER II

The royal supremacy and ecclesiastical revolution, 1534–47

G. A. HAYES-MCCOY

THE fact that the population of the island was made up of two elements, Gaelic Irish and Old English, was the central feature of Irish life throughout the sixteenth century. From the time of the statutes of Kilkenny in the fourteenth century to the reign of Henry VIII, English policy had, in effect, sought to maintain this duality. The policy had not altogether succeeded in staying the process of integration. The Gaelic Irish and the English by blood continued to intermingle. At the topmost level, the Fitzgeralds of Kildare and Desmond intermarried with the ruling families of their Gaelic neighbours. Lower in the scale, the Old English of the northern Pale were sufficiently associated with the Gaelic people of Tyrone to develop the closest business relations with them. The Old English town of Galway sought to restrain the convivialities within its walls of the Irish inhabitants of the surrounding countryside, but not to shut them out; indeed the existence of Galway depended on trade with its predominantly Gaelic hinterland, and there were men of Gaelic name even among the town's craftsmen. Despite statutory proscription, intermarriage of persons of what contemporaries called the 'two nations' must, all over the country, have been widespread. Still, a 'wild Irishman' was distinguishable from one of the king's established subjects in the reign of Henry VIII, and for long after. His speech, his personal appearance and clothing, and, if there were occasion to probe beneath the surface, his concept of society were different. He was, most notably, a product of the countryside. Galway and Athenry were still the only towns in Connacht, Carrickfergus the only town in Ulster.

The two elements had learnt to live side by side, however uneasily in places; their systems had fused, for the ordinary occasions of everyday life, in the border areas; but the consequences of the failure of the Anglo-Normans to complete their conquest and of the success of Gaelic Ireland in preserving its own institutions, and with them its own civilisation, were everywhere manifest. Two cultures were evident. The Palesmen, the townsmen, and, in the Old English lordships, at least the members of the ruling families still remembered their English origin. Their Irish neighbours carried forward their own traditions from the past. As the sixteenth century progressed, however, the expansion to Ireland of the structure of the English state, the ethos of which was so different from that of the Gaelic and gaelicised communities, promoted friction between Irish and Old English. It determined too the political, and much of the social, development of Ireland as a whole. This expansion may be traced through an initial phase of experiment, already initiated before 1534 and extending well into the reign of Elizabeth I, in which the English government sought the means to control Ireland without a major bureaucratic or military involvement in its affairs, followed by a second phase in which the necessity of thorough conquest came, not without reluctance because of its difficulty and expense, to be accepted.

The year 1534 proved to be a turning-point in Irish history because the events that occurred then brought on a demonstration of English power such as Ireland had not previously experienced, and because the forceful effort to manage Irish affairs that was then made, although it was from time to time to be relaxed, was not subsequently abandoned. 'Silken Thomas', Lord Offaly, the son of the ninth earl of Kildare, and the chief governor in his father's absence in London, rebelled in June. Enraged at the treatment of his father, whom he mistakenly believed to have been executed, Thomas renounced his allegiance to King Henry VIII, enlisted support in the Pale and its hinterland, and, overawing the citizens, laid siege to Dublin castle. The revolt showed that the Palesmen, who were certainly not all as hotheaded as their leader, were widely dissatisfied with Tudor rule, but the rebels, opposed by, among others, Piers Butler, earl of Ossory, failed either to intimidate Dublin or to take the castle, and support for Silken Thomas had already declined when Sir William Skeffington, accompanied by troops, returned to Ireland as deputy in October. The rebellion collapsed when Skeffington took Maynooth castle, the Fitzgerald stronghold, in March 1535. The bombardment and assault of Maynooth and the summary execution of its defenders provided a demonstration of power and a presage of the further use of force which stirred all Ireland.

We can see now that the disturbance of mind was proportionate to the importance of the event, for the ruin of the Fitzgeralds foreshadowed something that Ireland had not previously experienced, the effective exercise of centralised authority. From the reinstatement of Skeffington as deputy in 1534, no Irishman was directly to represent the Tudor monarchy in Ireland. This in itself was significant. More significant still was the consolidation in Dublin of the English bureaucracy. England, since 1496, had experimented with the exertion of a continuing influence on the Irish council. This could be done only by ensuring that the council contained some members who could be relied upon to further the king's affairs, and this, in the circumstances, meant Englishmen. When the earls of Kildare were deputies, the members of the council and the Dublin government officials had largely been Palesmen, many of whom were the creatures of the deputies. Affairs as a whole had been conducted in an Irish atmosphere. Despite efforts to ensure that the chancellor, the chief justice of the king's bench, and, on occasion, other members of the council were English, it had proved difficult to maintain a consistent balance of English and Old English members. The earl of Kildare had sometimes been given his head even in regard to the key posts. But, starting with the appointment of the Englishman John Alen, archbishop of Dublin, as chancellor in 1528, men of a different character, Englishmen whose only interest in Ireland was an official one, came to the fore. Prominent among them in the years following 1534 were Sir John Alen, who was perhaps a relative of the archbishop and who was chancellor from 1538, and Sir William Brabazon, the vice-treasurer. Both were Englishmen and both served until the middle years of the century. Under them and under their successors were minor officials, also Englishmen, of the same class. Some were self-seekers, but in the main they were painstaking civil servants who kept the king and their fellows in England supplied with regular reports of Irish affairs. They helped to guide and sometimes even to displace the deputies and they laboured, in an age which saw the beginnings of professional diplomacy, to control Ireland in the English interest.

There had been earlier indications that a stronger line would be pursued in Irish affairs. The opinion declared in the earl of Surrey's prophetic statement that 'this land shall never be brought to good order and due subjection but only by conquest'[1] was widely shared in government circles. But lack of money prevented a conquest from being attempted, particularly at a time when the showy pursuit of power had involved Henry in vast continental enterprises and had emptied the treasury that his father had filled, a treasury intended not for dissipation but for use as the surest resource of a dynasty that might still have to struggle for its existence. Henry had accepted the position, and had advised Surrey to use 'sober ways, politic drifts, and amiable persuasions' rather than 'rigorous dealing', but he had said too that if gentleness did not avail he would not hesitate to use force.[2] The fact that the king and his council had produced such a statement of Irish policy shows how deeply Irish affairs had been pondered. Alternative courses of action had been weighed against the possibilities, in view of the shortage of money, of implementing them, and the resulting decisions were not, as so many earlier decisions had been, defeatist, or even pessimistic. Although Henry VIII's Irish proposals involved conciliation rather than coercion, they made up a positive policy. Furthermore, they laid down a programme for Ireland as a whole, not just a series of defensive measures designed to safeguard the area of the Pale.

[1] *S.P. Hen. VIII*, ii, 73. [2] Ibid., pp 53–7.

The disturbed condition, during the reign of Henry VIII, of that part of Ireland which was 'subject unto the king's laws' was the consequence of the inability of the king's representatives to impose and maintain order. W. F. T. Butler remarked many years ago that the major defect in the institutional systems of the Ireland that lay outside the Pale was 'want of power'.[1] But a deficiency of power was noticeable throughout the whole island. There was such a deficiency in the territories of the 'king's Irish enemies', each of whom had 'imperial jurisdiction within his room'[2] but was permanently weakened by the succession struggles that were part of the Gaelic system. There was a similar lack of power in the Old English lordships. The marches of the Pale, the frontier of English and Irish law, suffered the consequences of a complete absence of settled authority. The Palesmen inveighed against extortions which were the inevitable result of perennial, and perennially inadequate, attempts to suppress the chronic warfare of the border. They suffered the confusion and uncertainty caused by frequent changes of deputies and cried out as poor subjects at the failure of the king to defend them. Ireland was unsettled because of long-standing organisational defects, and a want of effective power was apparent at all levels, from the remotest and smallest of the Irish lordships to the Dublin administration. The Tudor monarchs, who had already had to deal with a not dissimilar situation in England, were eventually to fill the vacuum.

Henry and his father, long before 1534, had established a stable England. Henry VII had set the pattern of Tudor government: efficient, tightly controlled, popular because it was effective and because it so notably fulfilled the requirements of the time. On his succession, his son inherited a flourishing concern. But the first two Tudors were still on the defensive. Henry VII had won the crown on the battlefield, and both he and his son had rival claimants, real or imaginary, to contend with. Each was conscious of the necessity of watchfulness. Each, as the royal watchers of more ruthless days felt forced to do, insured himself by liquidating possible opponents. The father judicially murdered the earl of Warwick, whom Lambert Simnel had impersonated, in 1499. The son removed the earl of Suffolk in 1513 and the duke of Buckingham in 1521. And Henry VIII, widening the scope of his defences to protect the state as well as the dynasty, watched and removed his counsellors as well.

It followed from this that the management that Ireland too would experience would be designed to increase the security of 'this realm of England' which, according to the English act for the restraint of appeals to Rome of 1533, was 'an empire governed by one supreme head and king unto whom a body politic be bounden and ought to bear, next to God, a natural and humble obedience'.[3] The 'body politic' that owed obedience to Henry extended, in the minds of the king and his advisers, to the lordship of Ireland.

[1] Butler, *Gleanings*, p. xiv. [2] *S.P. Hen. VIII*, ii, 1. [3] 24 Hen. VIII, c. 12.

By the 1530s, Henry had shown that he could liquidate Irish as well as English opponents, the motive of the Irish liquidation being to save the English interest in Ireland, as he and his father had saved England, from overmighty subjects, and thus further to strengthen himself. The opponents removed, the process of salvation was continued.

Maynooth having fallen, Silken Thomas surrendered in August 1535. He was sent to England, where he was eventually executed, together with five of his uncles, in 1537. But the Kildare name did not suffer an immediate eclipse. The remnant of the supporters of the Fitzgeralds protected Gerald, the son of the ninth earl by his second wife, Lady Elizabeth Grey, and the half brother of Silken Thomas. The king was anxious to have this boy brought to England, where his mother, his younger brother, and his three sisters already were. But the friends of his house were successful in their efforts to keep him out of the king's grasp. The Kildare practice of intermarriage with the Gaelic, as well as the English, nobility meant that Gerald, in the alarms and excursions which attended him during the five years that followed, had relations on both sides, among the Irish who sheltered him and the English who sought to secure him. Lord Leonard Grey, who became deputy in 1536, after Skeffington's death at the end of the previous year, was the boy's uncle. Gerald's relations were most numerous, however, beyond the Pale, and beyond the reach of the state's malevolence. He was shuttled about through the four provinces until 1540, when, having more than once inspired his well-wishers with thoughts of a Kildare restoration and having as frequently alarmed the Dublin administration, he was sent to France, and eventually to Italy.

Grey, like Skeffington, was a martial figure, and his movements, even though the motives which inspired some of them were suspect at the time and are still obscure, show that Irish conditions imposed upon the new type of deputy the same general course of action that had been found blameworthy in the old. Grey too undertook, and was eventually condemned for, warlike expeditions throughout Ireland, some of which are distinctly reminiscent of those of the great earl of Kildare. This procedure was begun, for the new dispensation, by Skeffington, who, in the autumn of 1535, had used the small force with which he had defeated Silken Thomas to take Dungarvan castle, County Waterford, and to transfer its custody from the Fitzgeralds of Desmond to Piers Butler, the grantee of 1528.[1] After Skeffington's death, Grey, with the same force and with the assistance of the Butlers, upon whom Skeffington had, by instruction, also relied, continued the late deputy's work in Munster. The borders of the Pale had been quieted by the surrender at the beginning of the year of O'Connor of Offaly and O'Byrne of Wicklow. Chief Justice Aylmer and Sir John Alen said that 'Irishmen were never in such fear as they be at this instant time',[2] but the Desmond Fitzgeralds and the

[1] See above, vol. ii. [2] *S.P. Hen. VIII*, ii, 295.

O'Briens of Thomond were still agitated by the movements of young Gerald Fitzgerald. Gerald was then in the custody of the latter and was soon to be moved southward to County Cork to the care of his aunt, Eleanor, the widow of MacCarthy Reagh and the prime mover in the alliances that were formed to assist him.

Using the artillery which the Kildares and Skeffington had already shown to be so effective and the little army of seven hundred irregularly paid men of which he had been marshal in Skeffington's time and which now overawed all the king's opponents, Grey campaigned in Limerick against the O'Briens and their supporters in the summer of 1536. He destroyed the crossing-place from Thomond to Tipperary at O'Brien's Bridge on the Shannon. Although his operations meant no more than temporary local adjustments in a district interminably distracted by contentious Fitzgeralds, Butlers, and O'Briens, Grey, in conducting them, demonstrated, if not the king's continuing authority, at least his power. He campaigned again in 1537, when he repeated the lesson of Maynooth by taking Dangan castle in Offaly and regaining possession for the crown of Athlone castle. The deputy showed great energy and skill in moving his cannon through a countryside where transport was very difficult. He invaded Offaly and Carlow again in 1538, and, still intent on the old task of clearing the border of the Pale, attacked the MacMahons in Farney. He made two longer journeys, one in 1538, when he went as far as Galway and was greeted by the mayor and town council (proudly flaunting, so far afield, their scarlet robes of office), and one in the following year through Munster. He reached Dungannon in the course of operations against Conn Bacach O'Neill in 1540, and plunged into the mountain fastness of Glenmalure in pursuit of the O'Byrnes. Such ubiquity of the king's forces was portentous. Grey remarked more than once in the course of his movements that 'there never was deputy with carts' in the remote places which he traversed.[1]

The efforts of local lords to maintain, or to extend, their independence by furthering the claims of Gerald Fitzgerald came to a head in 1539. Rumour credited Conn O'Neill, Manus O'Donnell—who had by this time married Eleanor MacCarthy and with whom young Gerald had now sought refuge—the Wicklowmen and the malcontents of Desmond, Thomond, and the midlands with the intention of cooperating in Ireland with the king's continental enemies, the emperor, Charles V, and Francis I of France, and with James V, king of Scots. It was said that the Gaelic lords of Ulster proposed to invade the Pale and to proclaim O'Neill king of Ireland at Tara. The sequel suggests that what the Ulstermen planned was no more than a glorified raid on the Pale, perhaps with a vague intention 'to elevate and fortify the Geraldine sect'.[2]

Royal commissioners, led by Sir Anthony St Leger, had been sent to

[1] *S.P. Hen. VIII*, ii, 351. [2] Ibid., iii, 175.

Ireland in 1537. They were charged primarily with the investigation of the revenue, the reduction of public expenditure, and the eradication of peculation (for the replacement of the earls of Kildare by an extension of the English bureaucracy was already proving expensive), but they were also required to manage the parliament which was then in being and to gather general information concerning Irish affairs. The commissioners returned to England with their report in April 1538, leaving tension behind them. To add to the difficulties of the Irish administration, feeling was mounting against Grey. The deputy would have found it difficult enough to implement with his slender resources the forceful policy that the occasion seemed to require. The fact that he was related to the fallen, but still not prostrate, Geraldines made it easy for his enemies to accuse him of dragging his feet. On the other hand, he was charged with having made useless and expensive journeys into areas beyond the marches of the Pale. One result of St Leger's visit was the reduction, by half, of the strength of the standing force, which was fixed at 340 men. Grey was irascible. He quarrelled in turn with Skeffington, Brabazon, Archbishop Browne of Dublin, and other members of the Dublin council, and with Piers Butler, earl of Ossory until 1539, when his claim to the earldom of Ormond was finally made good. Lord James Butler, pursuing a household feud, saw in Grey 'the earl of Kildare born again'.[1]

Grey's campaigns of 1539 and the early weeks of 1540 were his most ambitious ventures. He went as far as Armagh in May 1539 in an unsuccessful attempt, as he himself explained it, to get O'Neill and O'Donnell, who were momentarily allied, to give up Gerald Fitzgerald. O'Neill, accompanied by Maguire, O'Rourke, Magennis, and other Ulster lords, and possibly by O'Donnell, invaded the Pale in August. They burnt Navan and Ardee, destroyed the ripening corn and carried off great numbers of cattle. The deputy reacted at once. He pursued the raiders with the Dublin and Drogheda trained bands, some of the Palesmen, and less than two hundred of the king's soldiers, surprised them at dawn at Bellahoe, south of Carrickmacross, and completely defeated them (August 1539). Grey was in Munster in November, where he took steps to set up the new earl of Desmond, James Fitzgerald, a royal nominee who was destined for a brief career. Then, in February 1540, this restless man again entered Ulster, advanced with a small force to Dungannon and spoiled the heart of the Tyrone lordship. O'Neill once more evaded him. Grey, on the other hand, was summoned to London to face the long list of treasonable charges that had been made against him. His fate, in that century of ruthless monarchs and self-abasing subjects, was typical. He was tried, pleaded guilty, and was executed (June 1541), but not before the real architect of Henry's administrative greatness and Grey's fellow in casting himself, self-accused, on the royal mercy, Thomas Cromwell, had preceded him to the scaffold.

[1] *L. & P. Hen. VIII, 1538*, pt 1, p. 453 (20 June 1538).

The successor to the deputyship was St Leger, the commissioner of 1537, who assumed responsibility for the government of Ireland in July 1540. St Leger commenced operations in traditional fashion by harassing the Kavanaghs, the O'Mores, and O'Connors in still another effort to quieten the marches of the Pale. Then, as Grey had done, he cast his net wider. He went to Munster to settle the affairs of Desmond, where the royal nominee to the earldom had been murdered, and received the submission of James FitzJohn Fitzgerald, who was then acknowledged as earl. Like Grey, St Leger boasted of having gone where no deputy had been before. That these journeys into the interior, when they were made by English viceroys, were something more than a mere showing of the St George flag of England soon became apparent. O'Neill and O'Donnell were reconciled to the state. So were the O'Briens. MacWilliam Burke of Clanricard, the greatest lord in Connacht, wrote apologetically to the king to explain that his family had been 'brought to Irish and disobedient rule' by association with 'those Irish, sometime rebels' who were his neighbours.[1] On the whole, the closing months of 1540 and the early months of 1541 were a period of submission and reconciliation. The formulas of submission may have covered a multitude of reservations, the motives of those who acknowledged the sovereignty of the king may have been opportunist and even naïve, as when O'Neill advised Henry not to trouble himself with Ulster, but the political climate was clearly changing. Henry had proposed, even before the overthrow of the Fitzgeralds of Kildare, to require the Irish parliament to accept the fact that Ireland was a conquered country and that the crown was, in consequence, entitled to dispose of Irish land. The programme was interrupted by the rebellion of Silken Thomas, and it was thought wise, fearing an extension of the revolt, to play down the intention of interfering with the ownership of land, but the martial activities of Skeffington, Grey, and St Leger, following the fall of Maynooth, greatly improved the king's position. The tiny force of troops that these men had at their disposal and the effective use that they made of it tipped the balance of power, an interesting exposition of the weakness, for all the threat that it had been to the Pale, of Irish recalcitrance. Henry was now seen to be a ruler, and his Irish representatives were seen to be men of power by the Old English lords, the citizens of Cork, Galway, and the other towns and the Irish lords who had for so long lived a life of their own, and had exercised a sovereignty of their own, far beyond the marches of the Pale. It remained, at this juncture, formally to assert the sovereignty of the king in Ireland and further to extend the process of submission to him.

The assertion of sovereignty was accomplished by the parliament St Leger summoned in 1541, which enacted on 18 June 'that the king's highness, his

[1] *S.P. Hen. VIII*, iii, 290.

heirs and successors, kings of England, be always kings of this land of Ireland.'[1] The wording of the act made it clear that the innovation was one in name only. Hitherto the monarch, although his Irish title had been 'lord of this land', had held in Ireland 'all manner kingly jurisdiction', and he and his progenitors 'were, and of right ought to be, kings of Ireland, and so to be reputed, taken, named, and called'. 'For lack of naming' of the sovereignty of their ruler, however, the Irish had not been as obedient to Henry and his predecessors 'as they of right and according to their allegiance and bounden duties ought to have been'.

St Leger, in reporting the proceedings of parliament to the king, made much of the occasion, and indeed it was of the utmost significance. Thirty-five lords spiritual and temporal were present, including MacGillapatrick, the Irish baron of Upper Ossory. Representatives of the Old English of the Leinster and Munster counties and of the cities and boroughs sat in the commons. Several Irish lords were in attendance, although they did not sit as members; they included Cahir MacArt Kavanagh, O'Reilly, O'Neill of Clandeboye, Kedagh O'More, and representatives of O'Brien. Dublin, according to St Leger, was *en fête*. Guns were fired, wine flowed, bonfires blazed. The act was read to a congregation of 2,000 after a solemn mass in St Patrick's. Not the least interesting feature of the parliamentary proceedings was the translation of the act into Irish.[2]

The promotion of the obedience of the Irish was not the only motive that prompted Henry to assume the royal title. The real source of sovereignty was still uncertain. Although the statute claimed that, before its enactment, Henry had been, in fact if not in name, the king of Ireland, there were many lords outside the area of English rule who claimed a local sovereignty of their own; some indeed would continue to do so. Furthermore, the possibility of the disposal of an Irish crown by Irishmen, and not by Englishmen, was a live issue. Edward Bruce, the opponent of England, had been crowned king of Ireland by 'the Gaels of Ireland' in 1316, however ineffectual the ceremony may have been. It was said that the Ulstermen who were suspected of conspiracy in 1540 proposed to acknowledge James V of Scotland as their overlord. O'Neill—in the minds of some English informants—was to be crowned king at Tara in 1539. As events of the later sixteenth century were to show, the formal assumption of the crown by Henry VIII was not to prevent the Irish from offering it to the continental enemies of England.

There was a still further consideration, which was given prominence at the time, although it passed unmentioned in the act, and which has been well remembered. As the chancellor, Sir John Alen, noted in 1537, it was generally believed in Ireland that the 'regal estate' of the island rested in the papacy and that the lordship enjoyed by the kings of England was 'but a governance

[1] 33 Hen. VIII, c. 1 (*Stat. Ire., Hen. VII & VIII*, p. 176).
[2] *S.P. Hen. VIII*, iii, 304–5.

under the obedience of the same'.[1] That the king's advisers took this claim seriously is shown by the fact that grounds of title other than the papal grant were advanced, fanciful claims spun from imaginary happenings of extreme antiquity and exaggerated claims based on submissions to Henry II and Richard II. In this context, the declaration of 1541 was a logical consequence of Henry's breach with Rome, which had extended, with all its civil as well as religious implications, to Ireland by 1536.[2] Henry's decision that his title should be that of king was thus an obvious pre-emptive stroke, a stroke of policy that was indeed essential if he was to retain the initiative in Ireland. In causing the declaration to be made by the Irish parliament, Henry ensured for it the widest Irish backing that he could command. He now had a new kingdom, although he had still to make good the alleged conquest of it.

St Leger continued to implement the policy of persuasion that had been initiated by Surrey and pushed brusquely forward by Grey. Grey had been accused of failure to ensure that the promises of submission made to him in the course of his frequent journeys would in fact be performed. St Leger was more thorough. Starting with the marches of the Pale, he soon dug more deeply; within twelve months of his assumption of the deputyship he had shown himself in Cork, Limerick, and Cavan; by 1544 he had secured the formal submission of more than thirty of the lords, Irish and Old English. These submissions were of a far greater significance than those procured by Grey, although Grey's work, and Skeffington's, had been their prelude. They introduced what has come to be called 'the policy of surrender and regrant', a phrase that records a central feature of the submissions, a surrender by the lords of what they claimed to be their lands, followed by a grant made with the intention that these lands should be held for the future by titles valid in English law. St Leger bridled the great lords, some only for the moment, but others permanently. His greatest successes were in the west, where the O'Briens and Burkes had reigned as 'chief captains', rendering obedience to 'no other temporal person'. Murrough O'Brien, having surrendered, was received into favour and was created earl of Thomond in 1543. His nephew, the tanist of the O'Brien lordship, became baron of Ibracken, with right of succession to the earldom. Ulick MacWilliam Burke was made earl of Clanricard. All three were formally received in England and were subjected, at the centre of Henry's dominion, to the immediate influence of the royal power.

These, after initial friction, were to prove stable settlements. In general, the O'Briens, who had pursued their own interest in north Munster up to the eve of their submission, and the Galway Burkes, who, although they now claimed to remember their descent 'of English blood', had been no less independent, stood by their new allegiance. The O'Briens, following the rising power, proved to be the Campbells of Gaelic Ireland. This Burke–

[1] *S.P. Hen. VIII*, ii, 480. [2] See below, pp 56–7.

O'Brien enclave, in the present counties of Galway and Clare, was to act later in the century as a wedge between the two centres of intransigence, west Munster and Ulster. By thus initiating the pacification of the western hinterland, St Leger ensured the success of the subsequent drive to subdue the midlands, and in this way lessened the threat to the Pale. His settlements bestowed advantages on those who submitted and, by creating vested interests, promised durability.

The king prescribed in 1541 that, in the implementation of policy, Irishmen should be divided into two categories: those whose territories were close to the Pale and who lay, in consequence, 'upon the danger of our power', and those who were more remote and could not so easily be coerced. A firm line should be taken with the first group, but 'extreme demands' should be avoided by the deputy in his dealings with the others, lest, if the yoke galled them, 'they should revolt to their former beastliness'. All, proximate and remote, should be made aware by 'good and discreet persuasions' that the lands which they held were really the king's and that, if they acknowledged this and lived 'in civility', the king would protect them. All were to become the king's 'true subjects, obedient to his laws, forsaking their Irish laws, habits, and customs'.[1]

St Leger must everywhere have suited his approach to the local conditions. He prevailed on the Old English of Cork and their Irish neighbours the MacCarthys and O'Sullivan Beare to accept the king's peace when he made a wider settlement with the new earl of Desmond. 'The winning of the earl of Desmond was the winning of the rest of Munster with small charges', said the lord chancellor, Sir Thomas Cusack, in 1553.[2] The Magennises of Iveagh, O'More of Leix, O'Kelly of Hy Many (Uí Mhaine), O'Rourke of Leitrim, and many more submitted to him. Where possible, he ensured that those who surrendered and agreed to hold their lands of the crown would be liable for the payment of rent charges, and he provided for further revenue by arranging that grantees should hold by knight service, thereby making them liable for the payments incident to wardships and liveries. St Leger's greatest catch, or so it appeared, was on the periphery, where he made settlements with O'Donnell and O'Neill. Manus O'Donnell, whose house usually sought to keep on good terms with Dublin, bound himself to what was in reality a treaty (6 August 1541). He recognised the king as his liege lord, agreed to receive and hold his lands from him, promised to attend parliament and to appear at hostings, and undertook to serve the king at his own expense. In return, the deputy and council promised to assist O'Donnell against all who sought to injure him or to invade his country.

Conn O'Neill's surrender was less spontaneous. He refused at first to meet the deputy, who then incited O'Neill's neighbours, including O'Donnell, to attack Tyrone in August 1541. After St Leger had raided Tyrone

[1] *S.P. Hen. VIII*, iii, 348. [2] *Cal. Carew MSS*, *1515–74*, p. 245.

in the following winter O'Neill submitted (28 December 1541). He undertook—and this, if it was to hold good, was the final reality of submission, since it meant the denial of one system and the acceptance of another—utterly to forsake the name of O'Neill; he 'refused his name and state', which he acknowledged himself to have 'usurped', or, as the Irish annalists said, he obeyed the king's injunction 'that he should not be called O'Neill any longer'. In return, having gone to England as the first O'Neill ever to have done so, and having prostrated himself before the king, he was created earl of Tyrone.[1]

The surrenders followed a confrontation of two different systems of organisation, the centralised system of England and the localised Irish system of family rule, based on a different law and a different scheme of land holding, and confused in the sixteenth century by contentions bred of its own inadequacies. We know that the English had not, in Henry VIII's time, sought to understand the Gaelic system and that, through ignorance and arrogance, they decried it. But we do not know, and are never likely to know, what the Irish lords thought of the arguments used to establish the king's title to land, or what future they visualised for the hasty wedding, in which they acquiesced, of the two systems. Force was certainly—after Maynooth and Dangan—in the air, although, save in the case of O'Neill, the deputy made no notable use of force; for one thing, his military strength was very limited. It seems true that the lords thought that they had gained rather than lost. The Four Masters' statement that 'the sovereignty of every Gaelic lord was lowered' by the submissions to Henry VIII had the benefit of seventy years' experience and the evidence of the downfall of the Gaelic system to justify it.[2]

Only the topmost stratum of society was involved. Power in the Gaelic communities was rigidly confined to the aristocracy: 'the lord', as Lughaidh O'Clery said, 'is more powerful than his people'.[3] The fact that it was only the big men who mattered was well known to the English officials, despite their professed concern for the common folk. Sir John Alen had said in 1536 that the Irish might be made good subjects, 'the heads being subdued'.[4] The widespread changes that, in later years, followed the confiscation of land were to affect a great part of the population, but, in the 1540s, the effect of the surrender of O'Neill, O'Donnell, and the other 'heads' cannot have been noticeable outside the narrow circles of their immediate relations. It was here that the advantages of a law of succession based on primogeniture and a legally established (if English law must prevail) control of landed property were apparent. Ability to add the lands of suppressed monasteries to estates and to secure a proportion of the first fruits of church benefices, as the crown

[1] *Cal. Carew MSS, 1515–74*, pp 189, 199. *Cal. pat. rolls, Ire., Hen. VIII–Eliz.*, p. 85.

[2] *A.F.M.*, v, 1477 (1542).

[3] Ó Clérigh, *Aodh Ruadh O Domhnaill*, i, 52.

[4] *S.P. Hen. VIII*, ii, 373.

had recommended 'for the better alluring of those of the remote parts', were advantages too. And St Leger's diplomacy disposed of some immediately obvious disadvantages, as when provision was made in Thomond for the tanist as well as for O'Brien. On the whole, Henry's settlement was made in the spirit of the instruction that had been given to Surrey when he was lord lieutenant; Surrey was told that if he found some of the Irish laws to be 'good and reasonable' he might approve of them, 'and the rigour of our laws, if they shall think them too hard, [might] be mitigated and brought to such moderation as they may conveniently live under the same'.[1]

Although Henry's policy did not fulfil one part of its purpose, since it did not bring the Irish revenue 'to such a mass as may defend the state there', it was, in the king's lifetime, an apparent success. The inducement of the Irish lords to surrender to the king was a stroke of policy, a *démarche* designed to meet the needs of the moment. But it had far-reaching implications. It represented a reversal of English thought, since it was now contemplated that the Gaelic part of the Irish population would be received as subjects. Henry's policy was thus, from whichever side it is viewed, revolutionary. Its results were to colour the whole subsequent history of the century. In fact, after two generations of violent reaction, the surrender of the Irish lords was to bring about what it set out to accomplish, the absorption of the Gaelic world into the English world.

In 1537 parliament declared that diversity of language, dress, and manners caused the population of the island to appear 'as it were of sundry sorts, or rather of sundry countries, where indeed they be wholly together one body', and required both the Gaelic Irish and Old English to speak English and to wear clothing of the English fashion.[2] The new concern for uniformity, which meant the imposition on the Irish as a whole of a language that few could speak and an alteration of the habits and customs of the majority, found expression again in the terms of surrender. Conn O'Neill bound himself and his heirs to speak 'to their knowledge the English language', and undertook as well, on behalf of the people of Tyrone, to see that English dress was worn, to adopt the English agricultural system, and to build houses of the same pattern as the houses of the English countryside—that is, to change, as far as could be done by human effort, the whole appearance and economy of his lordship in the interest of a politically-motivated uniformity. Efforts to extend the use of English and to cause the Irish to abandon their distinctive costume and their methods of land appropriation, tillage, and crop management continued to be made under Henry's successors. Associated with them, and prompted by the same motive of anglicisation, was the long series of proscriptive measures that was adopted with a view to the elimination of the brehons, bards, senachies, rhymers, harpers, gamesters, and others, the learned and professional classes and the purveyors of conviviality,

[1] Ibid., p. 53. [2] 28 Hen. VIII, c. 15 (*Stat. Ire.*, I (1765), pp 119–27).

who promoted culture, interpreted the law, and kindled the vital social spark in Gaelic life. The numerous members of these classes were looked upon by the English as idle and seditious persons, the disreputable fringe of a fabric that seemed essentially barbarous.

The Irish–Old English dichotomy was reflected in the organisation of the church. Although there is no evidence of a rigid segregation of the churchmen of the two elements of the population, cultural difference and the differences in civil life of the Irish and those of the Old English districts that had not been extensively gaelicised made a uniformity of ecclesiastical organisation—such a uniformity as existed in England—impossible. This was to have a marked significance in retarding the progress of the religious reform that Henry VIII sought to introduce in 1536.

The Irish church was not wealthy in the English sense. The institutional system of the Irish lordships provided for the temporalities of both secular and regular clergy by appropriations of land and contributions of livestock and farm produce, but there is no indication that this ensured wealth for the church in the Irish areas. Its temporal possessions were, in fact, greatest in the richer parts of the island, the east and south, where English influence was greatest. The great monasteries were, almost without exception, in those parts of Ireland that, in the beginning, had been overrun and settled by the Normans. Of more than thirty Cistercian houses, only three—those at Assaroe, Clare Island, and Corcomroe—were in Irish areas. The same was true of all the older orders. Even the newer ones, the ubiquitous mendicants or 'poor friars beggars' of the Dominican, Franciscan, Carmelite, and Augustinian orders who were the most widespread of the regular clergy, had more houses in the Pale, the towns, and the Old English lordships of the south and west than they had in Ulster, the Gaelic areas in Connacht and west Munster, and the isolated Gaelic pockets in other parts of Ireland.[1]

In general, Rome supported the efforts of the English monarchy to mould the Irish church in accordance with the necessities of the moment, as the monarchy saw them. The papacy backed English policy rather than Irish resistance to it. When dioceses fell vacant, the king, acting on the advice of the deputy and council, recommended those whom he thought most suitable for appointment to them; when appointments were made by papal provision, the wishes of the state were usually acceded to. Henry VIII, until his divorce proceedings began, was the most loyal of the European monarchs in his support of the papacy, and the papacy responded by supporting him. Of the archbishoprics, Armagh and Dublin, the key posts, were filled by Englishmen who might be relied on to carry out the royal policy. Henry

[1] Distribution is shown in *Map of monastic Ireland* (Ordnance Survey, Dublin, 2nd ed., 1965); see vol. viii, maps 32–4.

nominated George Cromer for Armagh in 1521 and John Alen for Dublin in 1528. The Butler interest prevailed in Cashel. Tuam showed a succession of Gaelic names until 1537, when Christopher Bodkin was transferred to the archdiocese from Kilmacduagh by the king's authority. Bishops appointed to the Leinster dioceses and to the less remote dioceses in Munster and Connacht were acceptable to the government; many were, in effect, nominees of the king, like Edward Staples, who was appointed to Meath in 1529. Vacancies in Ulster were filled by papal provision, the opinions of deans and chapters and the wishes of the territorial magnates having, no doubt, received due consideration. When the succession to Raphoe was in dispute in 1538, one whom Henry would have thought a complete outsider, James V of Scotland, sought to intervene by writing to Pope Paul III—another outsider, following the breach with Rome—in favour of one of the contestants.[1]

In these appointments, and in appointments to the minor benefices as well, a continual struggle between spiritual and material considerations was evident. Pressure of the king and of the local lords, who frequently sought preferment for members of their own families, led to papal concessions, since no appointee could function without an assured possession of the temporalities which these laymen could, in varying degree, control. The state conceded to reality by proportioning its interest in appointments to the extent of its authority. And the unsettled condition of the country occasioned by the raids on the Pale and the frequent outbreaks of violence which marked contested successions in the lay sphere and disputes arising from conflicting claims to lordship seriously affected the welfare of the church. The result was a weakly organised church which had, up to Henry's reign, done little to shape the course of Irish affairs.

Evidence of the condition of the clergy at the dramatic moment when Tudor management was extended to the church is slight. What there is indicates disunity, an unhealthy preoccupation with material concerns, an addiction to simony, and possibly a general deficiency in learning. A decision of a provincial synod, held in Dublin in 1513, that candidates for the priesthood should be examined, and that only those who were fit for their work should be accepted, suggests an episcopal effort to remedy a defect, but it also indicates that the defect existed. The bishops and parochial clergy as a whole are said to have been wanting in spiritual fire and to have been extortionate, the church buildings to have been in poor condition in the Irish districts and not much better in the Pale. Neglect of duty, irregularity of life, even an addiction to violence are further charges. 'The noble folk of Ireland' are blamed for oppressing 'the prelates of the church of Christ' and for spoiling them 'of their possessions and liberties'.[2] Allegations of this kind, made by witnesses at least some of whom were not disinterested and all of whom saw Ireland from the Pale, are doubtless exaggerated. Many may be

[1] *Anal. Hib.*, no. 12 (1943), pp 179–81. [2] *S.P. Hen. VIII*, ii, 1–31.

traceable to difficulties of collecting church revenues in an unsettled country. The modern inquirer is troubled not so much by the fact that the evidence is one-sided—there is little on which an estimate of the condition of the Irish part of the church may be founded—as that it is meagre. In view of the momentous events that were about to occur, and of the danger of prejudice of which these events and their consequences are still the occasion, some pitfalls are probably unavoidable. We might well think that the Irish church lacked an independent leadership since there is little evidence to suggest that it had any leadership at all, and we might feel that some part of our lack of information is due to this deficiency. Yet how can we explain the ultimate reaction to Henry's innovations save on the basis of the existence of a leadership that was very competent indeed?

Henry's interest in the church was no doubt sincere, but his interest in the world—his world—was greater. His quarrel with the church was a conflict of organisation. It involved an opposition of the king's will to what Sir Thomas More called 'the consent of all Christendom for more than a thousand years'. The king was supported in his own country by a people whom he may have intimidated, but by a people too among whom anti-clericalism was widespread and nationalism, which meant loyalty to the king, was more widespread still. The breach with Rome, which made Henry a schismatic and made his headship of the church of England a reality, was complete by 1534. By that date Henry had discarded his wife Catherine and had married Anne Boleyn, who had borne him the future Queen Elizabeth. He had cowed the clergy by threatening them with the statute of praemunire—and Wolsey's case had demonstrated how quickly such a threat could become a charge of treason. Supported by parliament, the king had stopped the flow of revenue from England to the papacy, had abolished the system of appeals to the papal court, and had established a complete control of the episcopate. In 1535 Thomas Cromwell, the successor to the pliant Wolsey and the obdurate More, began as vicar general his successful assault on the monasteries. The administrative part of the ecclesiastical revolution was soon complete.

It was in these circumstances that Henry took in hand the reformation of the Irish church. Ireland showed no such anti-clericalism as England or Luther's Germany did. Struggles occurred between ambitious lords and some of the few wealthy churchmen, who, like the lords, were landed proprietors. The Palesmen must have thought clerics in the Gaelic areas inferior to their own. But no strain is evident between a dissatisfied commons, urban or rural, and the clergy. The days of great monastic building were long past, but, as evidence of a continued and popular extension of the church, at least in some areas, new monasteries were still being founded by the mendicant orders. The Dominicans built additions to their convent in Galway after 1488; the Augustinians built a new friary in the same town in

1508. As many as twenty Franciscan monasteries appear to have been founded in the period 1478–1530, most of them in Irish districts. Some trace of the new doctrines and new concepts of church organisation which had already spread from Germany through central and northern Europe may be suggested by Archbishop Browne's condemnation of sacramentaries in Dublin in 1536.[1] But if there was religious dissatisfaction it was slight. The reform, when it was attempted, did not come in response to popular demand. It came from above, and, most notably, from outside.

Henry's concern was to bring the Irish ecclesiastical system into conformity with that of England. The first rush of the English reform had been dependent on the king's sovereignty; it involved a conflict of the rival authorities of the papacy and the crown, and Henry, because he was sovereign lord in his own kingdom, was the victor. The extension of the schism to Ireland had the same implication. Indeed the question of sovereignty received in Ireland an added significance, since the reality of Henry's temporal authority in the island was still in question. Thus, from the beginning of the reformation in Ireland, religion and politics were bound together. Henry's claim had, to all appearances, been established in England. It was essential that the same claim should be made and should be established in Ireland. From that viewpoint, the royal headship of the church was a part of absolutism and resistance to it was, in the last resort, seen by the state not as a matter of conscience but as treason. The revolt of Silken Thomas thus provided a practical demonstration of the need for a speedy religious settlement. Before any step had been taken to extend to Ireland Henry's own revolt against the church, other than an instruction to the viceroy Skeffington requiring him to oppose the papal authority and to summon parliament to enact the Irish counterpart of the English reform, the Geraldine rebels had proclaimed that they were in arms in support of the papacy against the schismatic king. In fact, despite his own statement to the contrary, religious grievance can scarcely have been among Thomas Fitzgerald's major reasons for his action. But, whatever its basis, the king must have looked upon his statement as dangerous.

The Irish reformation, like the implementation of Henry's civil policy, was managed by the loyal servants of the crown. The English-born bishops, the officials of the Dublin bureaucracy, and a few ambitious members of the Old English community like Piers Butler, earl of Ossory and afterwards of Ormond, and his son all played their part. So did those effective agents at the opening stage, Sir Anthony St Leger and his fellow commissioners who were sent to Ireland in 1537 to see to the enforcement of the king's wishes. The parliament which Lord Deputy Grey had summoned to meet in May 1536 had been prorogued many times before the commissioners arrived in Dublin in September 1537. The commons were drawn only from the Pale,

[1] *S.P. Hen. VIII*, ii, 512.

the towns, and the Old English districts in Leinster and Munster, that is, the shired area from which 'the English of blood or English of birth' could return representatives. As Sir John Davies was to say when he was speaker in the parliament of 1613, the state did not hold the Irish—he meant the Gaelic Irish—'fit to be trusted with the counsel of the realm'.[1] Much care was taken by persons of influence like the earl of Ossory to make sure that the right burgesses and knights of the shire were returned. Indeed, as was later to transpire, and as was not uncommon in England at the time, the law was broken by the return of some members who were disqualified by non-residence from representing the shires or boroughs for which they were chosen. The result was a house of commons that was believed to be 'marvellous good for the king's causes'. The atmosphere changed when the full programme of legislation was unfolded and it was seen to affect the material interests of the members, but the state had nothing to regret in the Irish parliament's attitude to the revolutionary claims of the king.

The bureaucracy proposed the legislation, and the king's possession of the initiative was further ensured, not only by the provision of Poynings' law that required that bills for consideration should already have been certified under the great seal of England, but by the administration's ability to have Poynings' law suspended—as was done during the lifetime of the parliament—when circumstances required it.[2] The king and his counsellors, chief of whom now was Cromwell, manager of the English reform, had, during the year preceding the assembly of parliament, carefully debated the drafting of a series of bills that would bring the church in Ireland into line with the church in England. This proposed legislation had originated with the Irish council, but it was given the requisite form in London, if not under the eye of the king at the hands of those who knew the king's wishes.

The reception by the Irish parliament of the ecclesiastical part of the proposals has, in view of the paucity of the evidence and, much more, in view of the sequel, given rise to considerable debate among modern historians. What happened afterwards has blinded many inquirers to what happened at the time. Yet the course of events seems clear enough.[3] Within a fortnight or so of the assembly of parliament in Dublin in May 1536, it had been enacted that King Henry was 'the only supreme head in earth of the whole church of Ireland'. The king's unilateral solution of the long-drawn-out divorce controversy had been adopted for Ireland, as it had already been adopted for England, by a declaration that the succession to the crown lay in the progeny of Anne Boleyn and that the king's marriage to Catherine of

[1] Davies, *Prose works*, ii, 228.

[2] R. Dudley Edwards and T. W. Moody, 'The history of Poynings' law: part I, 1494–1615' in *I.H.S.*, ii, no. 8 (Sept. 1941), pp 415–24.

[3] See R. Dudley Edwards, 'The Irish reformation parliament of Henry VIII, 1536–7' in *Hist. Studies*, vi (1968), pp 59–84; and Brendan Bradshaw, 'The opposition to the ecclesiastical legislation in the Irish reformation parliament' in *I.H.S.*, xvi, no. 63 (Mar. 1969), pp 285–303.

Aragon was invalid; it would be necessary to repeal the enactment regarding the succession because of the downfall of Anne, and the same parliament would, in a later session, do so by providing for the succession of the children of Jane Seymour. Furthermore, it had been enacted that it was high treason to say that the king was a heretic, a schismatic, or a usurper; Henry's supremacy in the administration of the Irish church had been established by an act of appeals, which made the royal chancery, and not the Roman curia, the final court of appeal in ecclesiastical causes; and parliament had done what it could to cut off the revenue derived by the papacy from Ireland by an act of first fruits which required benefice holders to pay the income of their first year of appointment to the king.[1]

This legislation, which formally broke the connection of the Irish church with Rome, was revolutionary. The sanctions provided to prevent transgression of the law were explicit. Acceptance of the provisions of the act of succession, which gave the title of supreme head of the Church of England and Ireland to Henry, was required under oath. In short, the alignment of Ireland on the king's side in the dispute with Rome was, according to the letter of the law, placed beyond doubt, and transgression of the law implied treason.

What private opinions and mental reservations the members, including the lords spiritual or bishops and abbots who were in the majority in the upper house, may have had, was, as far as the reality of the legislation was concerned, immaterial. The passage of the ecclesiastical bills provoked but slight opposition. The lords and commons, it appears, readily acquiesced. Only the proctors of the lower clergy, who formed a body of their own that had no counterpart in the English parliament, protested. As Brabazon, the vice-treasurer, reported to Cromwell while the first session was still in progress, 'the proctors of the spirituality somewhat do stick in divers of these acts, and loth they are that the king's grace should be the supreme head of the church'.[2] That was all. The position of the proctors in the hierarchy of parliament was unsettled, or at least, as what happened later shows, disputable. They were anxious, according to their function, to express themselves in regard to ecclesiastical matters, and posterity, committed to taking sides by the course of history in the intervening centuries and fastening with relief on what looks like a definite stand made at the beginning, has applauded their intransigence; they have been called heroic. But the proctors' reservations in regard to the supreme headship did not affect the government programme. The fact remains that, at the very outset, parliament passed the required acts. Well might the Irish council bear testimony to 'the loving mind of the commons in this parliament toward the king'.[3] Well might the

[1] These enactments were: 28 Hen. VIII, cc 2, 5, 7, 8, 10.
[2] *S.P. Hen. VIII*, ii, 316.
[3] Ibid., p. 318.

king, as he did afterwards, thank both the lords and commons. Henry had had an easy victory.

The rest was anti-climax, although wishful moderns, convinced that the counter-revolution must have begun at the beginning, have seen the later sessions of Grey's parliament as a long-drawn-out struggle, the resistance offered by an unwilling assembly to the king's ecclesiastical innovations. Parliament met while the passions of the Geraldine revolt were still hot and while the lesson of Maynooth still rang in the public ear. The fact that the supporters of the Geraldines were numerous must have accounted for some of the care taken in the choice of members, and some part of the spirit of loyalty to the crown that inspired the parliamentary proceedings may have been the result of a determination to avoid incurring suspicion of adherence to what seemed the beaten side. The first act passed was not an ecclesiastical one, or one touching the succession, but an act of attainder of the ninth earl of Kildare and the chief accomplices of his son, and of forfeiture of their lands.[1]

The state of the country once more dictated procedure at the end of May 1536. When the most important part of the proposed legislation had been enacted, parliament was prorogued and Grey set off on the journey to south Leinster and Munster that culminated in his campaign against the O'Briens and Fitzgeralds of Desmond. Parliament became peripatetic and accompanied the deputy and his troops. Sessions, which if they had no other result must have served to bolster Grey's, and Henry's, stock in the hinterland of the Pale, were held in Kilkenny, Cashel, and Limerick. Little business was transacted, however, and it was not until September, when parliament reassembled in Dublin, that the programme of legislation was resumed.

This time, the king's business was not so easily transacted. The commons stiffened when their pockets were touched. They refused to pass a bill that sought to impose a tax on incomes, a bill proposing to arrogate a customs levy to the crown, and a bill 'for the suppression of certain monasteries'. Their rally in support of the monks has been taken as evidence of their real feelings in the struggle between king and pope. The suggestion is that, perhaps because they had had time for second thoughts during the summer, perhaps because circumstances had altered in some way that is unknown to us, the commons decided to make a stand in matters of religion and, by obstruction, to resist an attempt to give practical expression to the royal supremacy which they had already conceded. But it is not at all clear that the newly discovered intransigence was motivated by religion. It seems rather to have been a new phase of the old struggle of the colony to resist what they felt was exploitation at the hands of the administration, the newly-arrived English by birth.

Parliament was again prorogued and two representatives of the commons were sent to London to explain their opposition to the bills. Their

[1] 28 Hen. VIII, c. 1.

fellow members had reassembled before their return, but, opposition being once more manifest, meetings were adjourned to the following May. The long adjournment made the administration's position no better. When parliament reassembled, the clerical proctors claimed that no ecclesiastical measure could be passed without their approval. They had not, as far as we know, pushed their opposition to the supremacy bill in the first session to the extent of claiming a right to veto it. Why this constitutional question should have arisen when it did is not clear, unless we are to accept the suggestion that it was the result of a filibuster staged by the bishops.[1] Its ventilation can have occurred only in regard to taxation, or to the proposed suppression of monasteries. At all events, deadlock was reached when the lords spiritual backed the lower clergy and the summer session of parliament again broke up before the desired enactments had been secured. This time Grey and Brabazon blamed the bishops, saying that the opposition of the proctors was a 'crafty cast devised betwixt their masters the bishops and them'.[2]

Meanwhile, however, the reins were tightened. Throughout the reformation, and as the circumstances of autocratic government and the hierarchical arrangement of society demanded, the crown based its administrative control of the church on a control of the bishops. This practice was very evident in Ireland, where the fact that the archdioceses of Armagh and Dublin and some of the bishoprics of the Pale were already influenced by the English state was of vital importance for the success of the new departure. George Cromer, who had been nominated for Armagh by the king and appointed by the pope and who had been removed from the chancellorship after a short term of office in 1534, played, apparently because of illness, no prominent part in affairs, but George Browne, archbishop of Dublin, and Edward Staples, bishop of Meath, did. Staples's was a papal provision, again on the king's nomination, but Browne, a protégé of Cromwell's and the former English provincial of the Augustinians, was consecrated for Dublin without papal sanction. The first session of Grey's parliament was over and Henry's supremacy had been legally established before Browne's arrival in Ireland. The archbishop was conditioned by his earlier support of the king's claim in England to play a prominent role in the implementation of ecclesiastical policy in his new country, yet both he and Staples needed reminders before they became fully cooperative. They had clearly done less than was expected of them to handle the recalcitrants in the upper house. Henry wrote forcefully to Browne at the end of July 1537 accusing him of negligence in providing for 'the instruction of our people there in the word of God' and of having failed 'to stand us in any stead for the furtherance of our affairs'. Browne was told to 'reform' himself and was warned that, if he failed to appreciate the king's 'gentle advertisement', Henry, who had placed him in

[1] Bradshaw, as above, pp 298–9. [2] *S.P. Hen. VIII*, ii, 439.

office, would remove him. Staples was addressed in the same terms.[1] Browne was thoroughly cowed. He hoped that 'the ground should open' and swallow him up if he failed 'in rebuking the papistical power' or in the advancement of the king's affairs.[2] He and Staples were, after 1537, to be among the chief exponents of the new order. The king wrote also to the lords and commons requiring their conformity. Furthermore, he instructed Sir Anthony St Leger, Paulet, Moyle, and Berners, the four recipients of the special commission of 31 July 1537, to assume responsibility for the passage of the controversial legislation through parliament. Grey and the Irish council were required to assist the commissioners, who had authority to appear in parliament and to issue a solemn warning that if the members continued to resist the king's wishes they would do so at their peril.

Parliament met again in October 1537. By this time the administration had conciliated the commons. The customs legislation was dropped and the new taxation was confined to the clergy. Duly informed of the king's chagrin by the commissioners and mollified by the state's modification of its proposals for taxation, the members were now more cooperative. Their cooperation in ecclesiastical matters extended to the permanent exclusion from parliament of the clerical proctors, the only members who had at the beginning opposed what would soon be opposed by the majority of the Old English, the royal supremacy over the church. Parliament agreed to the dissolution of thirteen monasteries. It passed an act denying papal authority in Ireland and prescribed that office holders must take an oath acknowledging the royal supremacy, and a further act declaring that the crown, and not the papacy, would thenceforward issue ecclesiastical licences and dispensations. When the assembly was dissolved in December legal effect had been given to the constitution of a state church that was independent of Rome.

What was the reason for this certainly not unwilling acceptance of the reorganisation of the church, a reorganisation that was soon to split Irishmen irreconcilably? Clearly, parliament acted as it did because it was composed of men who regarded themselves as English subjects and who accepted the sovereignty of the king. Such men would, we presume, take the wording of the act of supremacy literally:

> Like as the king's majesty justly and rightfully is and ought to be supreme head of the church of England, and so is recognised by the clergy, and authorised by an act of parliament made and established in the said realm: so in like manner of wise, forasmuch as this land of Ireland is depending and belonging justly and rightfully to the imperial crown of England, for increase of virtue in Christ's religion within the said land of Ireland, and to repress and extirp all errors, heresies, and other enormities and abuses heretofore used in the same: be it enacted by authority of this present parliament, that the king our sovereign lord, his heirs and successors,

[1] *S.P. Hen. VIII*, ii, 465; *L. & P. Hen. VIII*, *1537*, pt 2, p. 153.
[2] *S.P. Hen. VIII*, ii, 513–14.

kings of the said realm of England and lords of this said land of Ireland, shall be accepted, taken, and reputed the only supreme head in earth of the whole church of Ireland.

The members of the Irish parliament and that part of the Irish population which they represented did, in fact, depend upon England. The English connection was their lifeline, and their acceptance of the Henrician revolution was a consequence of their position as a colony bordering on a hostile, or potentially hostile, people. As yet, the English reformation had no doctrinal implications. When the acts of Grey's parliament were passed the reform was a matter of reorganisation, and it may have been widely seen as no more than the consequence of a jurisdictional dispute. In England only More and Fisher stood out against the royal supremacy. Apparently they had no real fellows in Ireland.

We should note too the king's anxiety to proceed constitutionally in his new venture. Parliamentary acceptance of the new ecclesiastical dispensation was believed to be essential. When, in the last decade of his reign, Henry sought to extend his sovereignty to embrace the whole island and, reversing the procedure of earlier times, to receive the Irish as well as the Old English as subjects, the incidence of the law, including the ecclesiastical legislation, was extended accordingly. Theoretically—in line with the fiction that the Irish parliament was what its name implied—from the time of the passage of the acts of 1536, Henry was the supreme head of the Irish church in its entirety, outside as well as inside the Pale and the other English districts. He and his successors on the throne were prudent enough to recognise that Gaelic Ireland required special treatment, but the position of the church as established by parliament was not departed from. The breach with Rome admitted of no compromise.

Steps were taken from 1538 onwards to implement the new legislation, but the changes made were, save for the suppression of the monasteries, gradual. The reformation was, in a very real sense, and once the royal supremacy had been accepted, exploratory. Administratively, the primary concern of the state was with the bishops and the monasteries—with the bishops because they were the leaders of the clergy, the spiritual lords who exercised local control, and with the monasteries because they were the preserve of regular orders which were subject to an outside authority and which, as such, continued to acknowledge the supremacy of the pope. Added reasons for the state's interest in the monastic houses were that, from the viewpoint of the reformers, they could be dispensed with and, as institutions some of which were wealthy, they were a potential source of revenue.

Henry's control of the episcopate, if largely dictated by necessity, was sanctioned by contemporary procedure. It was facilitated by the theory of the age, which regarded obedience to the civil power as a requirement of society. Catholics and reformers alike, as the breach in the church widened, were to preach the doctrine of obedience to territorial rulers. The Irish bishops who were already the king's nominees presented the least difficulty. Browne and Staples, particularly after their receipt of the royal reprimands, were cooperative. So was Richard Nangle of Clonfert, although he was soon ousted by the papal nominee de Burgo, who secured the see because he was supported by the local magnate, Burke of Clanricard; the fact that the king ultimately recognised de Burgo shows his unwillingness to provoke a conflict, which he had little chance of winning, with a local lord whom in any event he had hopes of out-manœuvring in the material sphere. The state also enjoyed some measure of cooperation from Butler, the archbishop of Cashel, and from Baron of Ossory, Nugent of Kilmore, Comyn of Waterford, Bodkin of Kilmacduagh, and Quin of Limerick. Cromer of Armagh remained aloof, but his later suspension by Rome suggests that his withdrawal from the forefront of affairs was not prejudicial to the king. Henry's treatment of the remaining Irish bishops with whom his administration came in contact was in keeping with his civil policy of 'amiable persuasions'. He was, in general, content with the most nominal conformity. In order to secure this, he accepted the surrender of the papal bulls of bishops who owed their sees to papal provision and, in return, secured them legally in their dioceses by royal grant. Such surrenders were apparently understood by Rome to be no more than the formal gestures that had always been made by bishops prior to the receipt of the temporalities of their sees from their temporal lord the king. They were not, whatever the king's hopes may have been, looked upon as an abandonment of Rome.

Henry continued to fill with canonically consecrated appointees such vacancies in the episcopate as arose within his sphere of effective authority; beyond that, and beyond his efforts to secure the surrender of bulls, his policy was one of non-interference with the existing incumbents of sees. The papacy took a much stronger line. Rome ignored the king's new appointments, regarded the sees to which they were made as vacant and provided bishops of its own. Thus began what ultimately developed into the parallel systems of an illegal catholic episcopate and a legal reformed one. The state church was, in the last decade of Henry's reign, largely an unreal establishment, an establishment the unreality of which mounted territorially as the distance from Dublin increased. Gaelic Ireland and the territories of the semi-independent Old English lords were almost totally unaffected by the breach; their clergy and laity remained in communion with the Roman church. But the principle of royal ecclesiastical patronage, which was not, until the time of the breach, rejected by the Roman curia, now became all-important. State appointment to the episcopacy became the mainstay of the reformed church, and as the English state extended its control over Ireland the strength of the new ecclesiastical establishment, resting on a reformed episcopate, was increased proportionately.

The monasteries, at least those within the English sphere, went down easily. In their suppression the state had, because confiscation and the reallocation of land were involved, a secular support that was lacking in regard to other aspects of the ecclesiastical revolution. The priory of the Augustinian canonesses at Grane, County Carlow, was suppressed as early as 1535; we who know that the servants of the state were to figure prominently among the beneficiaries when the monastic lands as a whole came to be shared out may consider it symbolic that the grantee of the canonesses' land was Leonard Grey, the lord deputy. Parliament sanctioned the suppression of monasteries in the Pale and the south-east, the Cistercian houses of Bective, Baltinglass, Duiske, Dunbrody, and Tintern among them, in 1537. The king 'having resolved to resume into his hands all the monasteries and religious houses for their better reformation', commissioners were appointed in 1539 to receive voluntary submissions and 'to apprehend and punish such as adhere to the usurped authority of the Romish pontiff and contumaciously refuse to surrender their houses'.[1] By the end of the year, and without any sign of active resistance, monastic life had ceased in the greater part of Leinster. By the end of the reign, some 130 Irish monasteries had been suppressed.[2]

Petitions for the preservation of some houses on the ground that they were of material value to society because of the hospitality they offered to travellers 'in default of common inns, which are not in this land', as the deputy and council—who were among the petitioners—said, or that they contained schools where the English language was taught, went unheeded. Houses in the Pale in which 'young men and childer, both gentlemen childer and other, both of man kind and woman kind, be brought up in virtue, learning, and in the English tongue and behaviour' were, notwithstanding this, closed.[3] Some of the monks received secular benefices and some of the houses were converted into parochial churches. The monastic lands, which were forfeited to the state, were granted, subject to rent charges, to prominent laymen, or sold, according to the king's wish, 'to men of honesty and good disposition to civility'.[4] The plate, jewels, and principal ornaments of the houses became the property of the crown.

The members of at least thirty-nine houses of monks and six of nuns received 'competent pensions to maintain them during their lives', or until they were preferred to benefices. Payments, some of which were still being made in Queen Elizabeth's reign, were charged on the landed property of the suppressed houses. Records of them provide almost the only evidence which

[1] *Cal. pat. rolls, Ire., Hen. VIII–Eliz.*, p. 55.

[2] Details of the suppression of the monasteries are given in Edwards, *Church & state*, pp 68–73; and in Brendan Bradshaw, *The dissolution of the religious orders in Ireland under Henry VIII* (Cambridge, 1974), especially pp 70–77, 110–25. See map of the dissolution in vol. viii.

[3] *S.P. Hen. VIII*, iii, 130.

[4] Ibid., pp 295–6.

we have of the monks and nuns as individuals.[1] They show that, even in houses in Dublin, there were some religious whose names were Gaelic, but monks and nuns of Old English surname were in the vast majority in Counties Dublin, Meath, Westmeath, Louth, Kildare, and Kilkenny. Only in the monasteries of Counties Tipperary and Longford, which were closed in Henry VIII's reign and for which details of pensions survive, did Gaelic names predominate. Not all the members of the suppressed houses received pensions. None of the mendicants seem to have done so.[2] Since the inmates of the older houses seem to have been few in number their displacement may have been a relatively minor upheaval, and may have been unremarked outside the localities in which it took place. But the eviction of the mendicants, who, almost certainly, were much more numerous, soon provoked a reaction. They were entirely dispossessed, were in continuous touch with the people, and were in touch too with an international ecclesiastical opinion that was quick to identify the action of the state in Ireland as part of the contemporary heresy.

The positive side of the reform—the efforts made to remove abuses and to provide, under the new establishment, for religious ministration to the people—made a slow beginning. It was easier to legislate than to secure observance of the law, to destroy than to reconstruct. In the Pale and in places where the Dublin government had authority, images that were the objects of pilgrimage or of ostentatious veneration were, from 1539 forward, removed or broken up. This was an extension to Ireland of the process enjoined for England in the 'New injunctions'[3] by which Cromwell had sought to regulate religious observance in the previous year. As time went on and the line came to be drawn between catholicism and protestantism, the Irish majority was to see image-breaking as vindictiveness, the fruit of the pride, vainglory, avarice, and lust which the annalists allege were the causes of the reformation,[4] but there is no reason to regard its beginnings in this light. The humanists had decried the thoughtless importunity of, as the reformers now phrased it, 'blessings and good things . . . of this or that saint or image'.[5]

It is extremely difficult to assess the changes at parochial level or to measure the reaction of priests and people to a reformation that was so obviously, and so narrowly, contrived. The atmosphere during the closing years of Henry's reign must, for those who were concerned, have been one of foreboding, perhaps even of expectancy, rather than dissension. How far concernment extended is unknown. Apart from the establishment of the

[1] Details of pensions are in *Fiants Ire., Hen. VIII* (*P.R.I. rep. D.K.* 7, pp 27–110). For pensions paid in reign of Elizabeth I—*Anal. Hib.*, no. 1 (1930), p. 70. For 'rewards' given to heads of houses—Charles McNeill, 'Accounts of sums realised by sales of chattels of some suppressed Irish monasteries' in *R.S.A.I. Jn.*, lii (1922), p. 12.

[2] Save one Franciscan, who was blind (*Cal. pat. rolls, Ire., Hen. VIII–Eliz.*, p. 66).

[3] See Edwards, *Church & state*, p. 22.

[4] *A.F.M.*, v, 1445 (1537).

[5] See Edwards, *Church & state*, p. 59.

king's headship of the church, the efforts that were made to place the episcopacy under royal control, the initiation of a dissolution of the monasteries, and the vague abjuration of the papacy by the lords who formally accepted Henry as their sovereign there was little change. In Ireland, as in England, dogma remained unchanged. Archbishop Browne, exhorted to do so, as we have seen, by the king, sought to implement a series of directions and interpretations which paralleled that contained for England in the 'Ten articles' and the 'Injunctions to the clergy' of 1536, the 'Institution of a Christian man' of 1537, and the 'New injunctions' of 1538. Browne's statement, which was ordered in 1538 to be read at Sunday masses, was 'The form of the beads'.[1] This merely recited provisions of the old dogma and explained the ecclesiastical legislation. It contained nothing that could have disturbed those who heard it read save an attack on the papacy, although this was sufficient, on Browne's showing, to cause resentment among the Dublin clergy. The crucial difference between the new and the old was the royal supremacy. Religion had, said Browne, been blotted out of Irishmen's hearts by 'that monster, the bishop of Rome and his adherents'.[2] Acceptance of the royal supremacy required, from the beginning, this denigration of the papacy, and it was on this head that resistance first became manifest.

Browne found, or sensed, even in Dublin, a widespread reluctance to abandon the papacy. The great majority of the Dublin clergy was, he said, uncooperative. No efforts on his part, neither 'gentle exhortation' nor 'evangelical instruction', neither threats nor 'oaths of them solemnly taken', could persuade them to preach as he wished; instead, in his absence, they did their best to hinder him and to 'pluck back' among the people the results of what he himself had done.[3] At best, as time went by, only the outward conformity of the secular clergy of the Pale was secured.

The first realistic steps to extend conformity to the new order beyond the sees of Dublin and Meath were taken at the beginning of 1539. They clearly associated the ecclesiastical reorganisation with the civil power. Alen, the chancellor, Aylmer, Brabazon, the vice-treasurer, and Cowley, the solicitor general, were accompanied to Kilkenny, Carlow, Wexford, Waterford, and Clonmel by Browne. The archbishop, who appeared as an official rather than an evangelist, sought by preaching and by exhorting the local clergy to conformity to give a spiritual tone to the proceedings of the civilians. Apparently his text was unvaried: the necessity to accept the royal supremacy. A commission was received in February by Alen, Brabazon, who was among the most cooperative of the Dublin administration, and Browne empowering them to deputise for Cromwell in his capacity as vicar general. The commissioners were to provide for ecclesiastical appeals which had formerly been made to Rome. Again, the letter of the law outran its performance. There was little hope of stopping the gaps, and although the royal commissioners

[1] *S.P. Hen. VIII*, ii, 564. [2] Ibid., p. 569. [3] Ibid., ii, 539; iii, 6.

of 1537 had already sought at local level in south Leinster to prevent appeals to the curia, communication with Rome remained, for the country at large, unimpaired. The human failings of the reformers served to obstruct progress. Browne, whose zeal in any event slackened after the fall of his patron Cromwell, quarrelled with his neighbour, Staples of Meath. Neither side, the king's or the pope's, produced a recognisable leader, and the influences that were to condition the outcome operated without obvious direction in the background. 'An evil and erroneous opinion', said a Wexford informant in 1538, was held 'of the king's most noble grace and of all those that, under his majesty, be the setters forth of the true word of God.'[1]

No firm line was taken, or could be taken. Subscription to the oath of supremacy, although it was occasionally required, as by Grey of the Limerick corporation in 1538, was not made compulsory for office holders. Nothing was done to improve the moral tone of the clergy, to renovate churches, or to ensure a functioning pastorate; indeed, in the areas where the reformation had brought about changes, confusion must have been widespread and religion must have suffered a decline. Clerical celibacy, which was never uniformly observed in Ireland, but which was now required by the new administration of the church in England, was not enforced. Browne and others of the reformers were married men. Where efforts were made by the appointment of suitable incumbents to extend the new order outside the Pale, the project was foredoomed to failure by the requirement that the appointees should preach only in English. The Irish were said in 1542 to be for the most part ignorant of true religion and—it seemed to be the same thing—disobedient to the king 'for lack of preaching'.[2]

Inevitably, resistance to the new measures assumed a political complexion. An informant who sent news of happenings in O'Donnell's country in 1539, when efforts were being made to enlist support for 'the Geraldine sect', wrote:

> The friars and priests of all the Irishry do preach daily that every man ought, for the salvation of his soul, [to] fight and make war against our sovereign lord the king's majesty and if any of them die in the quarrel, his soul, that so shall be dead, shall go to heaven as the souls of SS Peter, Paul, and others, which suffered death and martyrdom for God's sake.[3]

No doubt such language was used on occasion in all districts outside the Pale, and perhaps, *sotto voce*, even in Dublin, but the extent to which immediate considerations prevailed over matters of principle was shown by the reception which met the first of the Jesuits to come to Ireland in 1542.

These were a Picard and a Spaniard, two of the earliest members of the newly formed Society of Jesus. They came on the advice of Robert Wauchop, the Scotsman who had been appointed by the papacy to administer the see of Armagh during Cromer's suspension, and they were

[1] *S.P. Hen. VIII*, ii, 561. [2] Ibid., iii, 431. [3] Ibid., p. 141.

instructed for their mission by Ignatius de Loyola. They bore letters of introduction, including one to Conn O'Neill from James V of Scotland. The pope, Paul III, had also written to O'Neill (whom he called a champion 'of the catholic faith') in response to a letter in which O'Neill had informed him of the manner in which Ireland was 'cruelly ravaged by the present king'. But the arrival of the Jesuits proved inopportune for O'Neill and the other Ulster lords, who had some weeks previously surrendered to Sir Anthony St Leger and were now in no mood to resist the king. The Jesuits, who spent little more than a month in Ulster and were received by none of the lords, returned to the Continent, as they had come from it, by way of Scotland. They made some contact with the people, but Ireland did not impress them. They thought the Irish barbarous, and their church, which as they saw it can scarcely have been affected by Henry's changes, ill-regulated. An Ireland that was content to let its own situations ripen was, not for the first or last time, incomprehensible to the foreigner.

The closing years of Henry VIII's reign were peaceful, if, for the English government in Ireland, poverty-stricken, and, for the Dublin officials, acrimonious. The surrenders of the lords had been effected at little cost, but the land grants that accompanied them brought in little revenue. An annual English subvention of £5,000 was required to help pay expenses. The standing force, which had been increased under St Leger, was reduced again to 500 men, although the soldiers' pay remained still in arrears. The king's administration was strongly established, but differences of opinion between St Leger and his council and the officials impaired its efficiency. St Leger quarrelled with Alen and Walter Cowley, the solicitor general, and with James Butler, the new earl of Ormond. Tentative arrangements were made for circuit courts in Munster and for an extension of the county organisation beyond the Pale; the setting up of a system of presidencies to promote the establishment of the English order in Munster, Connacht, and Ulster was discussed; but a great part of this programme remained unaccomplished fifty years later. For the moment, the council's time was spent in argument between the advocates of conciliation, St Leger and Sir Thomas Cusack, and the supporters of more forceful policies.

That Henry's Irish policy as a whole had brought about great changes is shown by two happenings of his later years. When England was at war with France and Scotland in 1544 and 1545 Irish soldiers were recruited for the king's service in France in the campaign of the siege of Boulogne and in Scotland in the earl of Hertford's invasion. These men, drawn both from Irish and Old English areas, were, in the modern period, the first of a long line of Irishmen to serve the English monarchy outside Ireland.[1] When St

[1] List of names in *Facs. nat. MSS Ire.*, iii, plate lxxvi. See D. G. White, 'Henry VIII's Irish kerne in France and Scotland, 1544–1545' in *Ir. Sword*, iii (no. 13, Winter 1958), pp 213–25.

Leger was preparing to go to England in 1546 to defend himself—as it happened with success—against those who had spoken against him in Ireland, he summoned the Irish lords, including the earls of Desmond, Thomond, and Tyrone, and arranged with them to keep the peace in his absence. Hitherto, it was remarked, the Munster Fitzgeralds, O'Briens, and O'Neills 'would not be brought under subjection with 10,000 men'. Now their lords had come in on receipt of the deputy's letters. Cusack, who was soon to be made chancellor, could claim that Ireland 'was never in so good case, nor nothing like, for honest obedience'.[1]

[1] *S.P. Hen. VIII*, iii, 563.

CHAPTER III

Conciliation, coercion, and the protestant reformation, 1547–71

G. A. HAYES-McCOY

THE brief reign of Edward VI served to emphasise the greatness of his father and grandfather. Those who acted successively as regents, Somerset and Northumberland, might have plunged a state less solidly constituted than the England of Henry VII and Henry VIII into a recurrence of the civil wars of the previous century. As it was, England survived social unrest (which twice culminated in rebellion), avoided financial chaos, and roundly defeated the Scots in another of the long series of wars undertaken to establish English control of the whole island of Britain. The Tudor dynasty survived an ominous minority and the state church assumed a quality of protestantism that was to frustrate the efforts of Mary Tudor, the next monarch, to reestablish a lasting communion with Rome. The middle years of the century were crucial for an England which, weathering them, was to achieve greatness under Elizabeth.

For Ireland, Edward's reign began, in the post-Henrician context, the alternation of conciliation and coercion that was to become, as time went on, a settled pattern of her relationship with England. Sir Anthony St Leger was continued in office under Edward. This, his first term as deputy, terminated in 1548. He was reappointed in August 1550, but was recalled the following year. He was appointed for a third time in October 1553, following Mary's coronation, but in fulfilment of the late king's intention to reemploy him. He remained conciliatory throughout, and while he was in office Ireland was, in general, subject to Henry's policy of 'amiable persuasions'.

But, in the intervals of St Leger's government, there were two other deputies, Sir Edward Bellingham and Sir James Croft, both soldiers and each more aggressive than St Leger. As the state alternated between the uses of persuasion and force, the king's Irish representative was selected to suit the policy of the moment. There were, of course, as in Henry's time, reasons other than theoretical and personal for these changes. When England was at war, as she was with Scotland in 1547–8 and with Scotland's ally France until 1550, an unsettled Ireland was dangerous, and necessity dictated firm rule. When the payment of soldiers had emptied the treasury milder counsels prevailed. Differences in outlook of the Old English and English-born members of the Dublin council—such as Sir Thomas Cusack on the one side and the vice-treasurer, Sir William Brabazon, on the other—and fluctuations in the degree of influence that these men could, from time to time, exert were further causes of policy changes. The chief purpose of the administration remained, however, the strengthening of the defences of the Pale and the maintenance of the *status quo* in the Old English lordships. Bellingham and Croft found it necessary to conduct more extensive hostilities than were implied in Henry's settlement, but few further attempts were made, or could, in the circumstances of Edward VI's reign, be made, to extend the king's sovereignty in outlying areas.

St Leger's view of the conduct of Irish affairs was accorded a diminishing respect by Somerset's government, and Bellingham, a member of the privy council, was sent to Ireland as captain-general of the forces in the summer of 1547. He brought reinforcements, and St Leger was instructed to defer to him in military matters. Operations were restricted to the south midlands, where the O'Connors of Offaly were strongly opposed, and a fortification, named Fort Governor, was erected on the site of Dangan castle. This planting of a garrison in a recently subdued Irish area was a new venture, but one that was frequently to be repeated, with varied results, as the century advanced. The Offaly fort was intended to protect the Pale, but its construction, and that of other posts like it, committed the state to the use of a far greater measure of sustained force than was expected.

The opposition group in the council, led, apparently, by Brabazon, developed an active lobby against St Leger in the winter of 1547–8. They accused him of being 'more favourable to Irishmen than to the king's subjects', and said that his policy of conciliating the Irish lords was endangering the security of the state.[1] They were listened to in London. Protector Somerset's council recalled St Leger and made Bellingham deputy in April 1548. A fresh display of force followed in the midlands, where Bellingham strengthened Fort Governor and began to build a new stronghold, appropriately named Fort Protector, in O'More's country of Leix. Athlone also was garrisoned. These three posts were to remain in the hands of the government, and although much fighting was still to be done in the midlands, and the Old English areas of Kildare and Meath still saw raiders, the old days of terror in the western part of the Pale were already over.

Further south, Bellingham repeated his practice in Leix and Offaly by garrisoning Leighlinbridge on the river Barrow, to quiet the Kavanaghs. He lacked both power and opportunity to do much outside Leinster, although he installed the Staffordshire family of Bagenal, later to be of such consequence in Ulster, at Newry. He admonished, but could not interfere with, the earl of

[1] See D. G. White, 'The reign of Edward VI in Ireland: some political, social and economic aspects' in *I.H.S.*, xiv, no. 55 (Mar. 1965), pp 197–211.

Thomond, saying that 'whatsoever he be that shall, with manifest invasion, enter, burn and destroy the king's people, I will no more suffer it than to have my heart torn out of my body'.[1] The Old English lords were, however, occupied by their domestic affairs. Bellingham bickered with the widow of the ninth earl of Ormond, whose son, a minor, was safely in England, and for a moment shared the state's fear that she might give rise to a dynasty more dangerous than that of the Fitzgeralds of Kildare by marrying the heir of the earl of Desmond. Ulick Burke, the recently created earl of Clanricard, died in 1544, and, although his son and heir, Richard, succeeded him and was to have his loyalty to the crown commemorated in his appellation Sassanach (English), south Connacht was upset by the ensuing squabbles of rival Burkes.

Bellingham left Ireland in 1549, at the time of Somerset's eclipse by the earl of Warwick (soon to be created duke of Northumberland), and died shortly after. The Irish council elected justices, one of whom was Brabazon, to manage affairs until a new deputy was appointed. The new deputy was, again, St Leger; this time he held his place and exercised his moderating influence for less than a year. Sir John Alen, the new deputy's opponent, was deprived of the chancellorship and Cusack, St Leger's supporter, was elevated in Alen's place. St Leger had little opportunity to shape the course of affairs. England and France were now at peace, but the fear of French interference in Ireland persisted. There were constant rumours of the passage of messages between the Ulster lords, the O'Connors of Offaly, and the French court, one English informant claiming that 'the whole nobility of Ireland' had 'conspired to rid themselves from the yoke of England', fearing that, unless they bestirred themselves to do so, they would all, in the long run, be treated as the O'Connors and O'Mores were being treated.[2] There is no doubt that this, if it envisaged French intervention or concerted action on the part of the lords, was greatly exaggerated, but it was sufficient to alert Northumberland's council. It was also an accurate forecast of the treatment that the Irish lords would eventually suffer. Once again it was felt that Ireland needed the presence of a soldier. Sir James Croft was sent from England to inspect the harbours and possible defences of the Munster coast, the place of landfall of interlopers from the Continent.

The other area that seemed open to invasion, this time from Scotland, was east Ulster. The greatest man in Ulster, although he was now old, was Conn Bacach O'Neill, recently ennobled as earl of Tyrone. As was soon to be disclosed, Henry's attempt to integrate the Irish lords into the English system of nobility, and thus to dispose of their local sovereignty, was to have far different results in Ulster from those achieved in other parts of Ireland.[3]

1 A. G. Richey, *A short history of the Irish people* (Dublin, 1887), p. 393.
2 Sir John Mason to the privy council, 14 June 1550; cited in Bagwell, *Tudors*, i, 348.
3 See below, pp 79–83.

Conn, the great O'Neill, lord of Tyrone and overlord, according to the claim of his house, of the lords of Ulster, had many children. At least three of his partners, Alison Fitzgerald, daughter of the eighth earl of Kildare, and the daughters of O'Neill of Clandeboye and of O'Byrne, were married to him. Each helped to increase his family, and he had six or more children less legitimately. If the English influence had not penetrated to Ulster when it did, the succession to the lordship would, no doubt, on Conn's death, have worked itself out in the usual manner: a dispute, a struggle, and a settlement, either enforced by the strongest or luckiest of the claimants or brought about by exhaustion. But Conn's ennoblement, the institution of the barony of Dungannon at the same time as the earldom of Tyrone, required that Conn should be succeeded not by him who had been tanist but by the baron, that is, by the one whom Conn had nominated as his eldest son. Although the English were at pains later to show that, according to English law, they were within their rights in doing so, it was a misfortune for them to have picked, or to have assented to Conn's choice of, Matthew, one of the illegitimates, for the barony. If Shane, who claimed to be Conn's eldest legitimate son and who appears to have been the tanist, had been picked, the result might have been far different. The succession, whether it was to the lordship or to the earldom of Tyrone, or both, brought on a direct conflict of the Gaelic and English institutional systems, something that neither Henry VIII nor St Leger would have welcomed.

Meanwhile, Conn O'Neill came under suspicion of carrying on a treasonable correspondence with the king of France, and the lordship of Tyrone, where his prospective successors gathered strength, remained disturbed. Further north, in these years of the Scots reaction to the 'English wooing', the continued infiltration of west Highlanders into Antrim gave cause for disquiet. The MacDonalds and their followers who crossed to Ireland in the disturbed reign of James V of Scotland were pursuing their own interest in the area of the fifteenth-century Bisset inheritance, but the English in Ireland saw their activities in the wider context of a possible Franco-Scottish invasion that would receive the assistance of Gaelic Ulster. Croft was accordingly ordered to survey the harbours of east Ulster as well as Munster.

In the spring of 1551, before Croft had completed his work in the south, St Leger was again recalled and Croft was elevated to the deputyship. Reinforced by a thousand soldiers, he soon overreached himself. He mustered his forces in Carrickfergus and, supported by shipping, proposed to raid Rathlin Island, a stronghold of the Scots under James MacDonald of Dunyveg. The deputy failed either to come to grips with them or to interfere with their occupation of the Glens of Antrim, or indeed their movement westward into the Route or southward towards Carrickfergus. He attempted, from the English foothold on the periphery, to oversee the affairs of Ulster by receiving the Ulster lords, including Tyrone, O'Donnell, Maguire, and O'Neill of Clandeboye, and by listening to their complaints. He garrisoned Carrickfergus and Armagh, but the only other efforts he could make towards the perpetuation of his slight settlement were to charge Matthew, the baron of Dungannon, and Sir Nicholas Bagenal to do what they could to keep the peace in Tyrone, that is, to oppose Shane, and to entice the earl to Dublin, where he was detained for over a year.

The Tudor attempt to settle Ireland proceeded uneasily. The state still had hope of attaining its end by conciliation, but the military resources of the deputies were steadily increased, and, although the power of the administration was as yet quite inadequate for a military conquest, the use of force to secure short-term objectives was becoming more and more attractive. Expense mounted as the position hardened. Public finance and the economy in general were seriously affected by a debasement of the coinage which was imposed in both countries, but which had worse results in Ireland than in England.[1] Prices rose, trade suffered, and, instead of the hoped-for advance towards a position in which an anglicised Ireland would pay for itself, the administration of the country cost the crown infinitely more than it had ever done before. The fact that the king was a minor led to the widespread mismanagement of the machine of state that his two predecessors had so laboriously constructed; most notably, English government in Ireland lacked the leadership that it had been given by Henry VIII.

The chancellor Cusack might claim in 1553 that justices of the peace rode their circuits even in Kerry, that the Munster lords, Irish and Old English, remained each in his own country 'without hindrance of other', that Leinster was 'in meetly good stay', Connacht at peace, and Ulster, following Croft's arrangements, on the way to reform, but his optimistic forecast that soon sheriffs would function everywhere to 'put back their Irish laws and election of captains' and that a new English Ireland would be the result was unwarranted.[2] The tranquillity he reported depended on promises to keep order by employing galloglass in the king's name and on a string of garrisons that were easier to place than to maintain. The remodelling of that part of the Irish church of which the administration had control, to keep it in line with changes taking place in England, went uneasily forward. In England, the first cautious doctrinal changes promoted a confusion in which the protestant voices were the louder. The pace quickened under Northumberland. Secular control of the hierarchy was tightened. The new communion service of 1548 replaced the mass. Surviving images were removed, and parliament, which authorised the new service-book, the Book of Common Prayer, together with its revision of 1552, established an authorised form of worship with penalties for non-observance. In these crucial years, as crucial

[1] See below, ch. XVI.

[2] *Cal. Carew MSS, 1515–74*, pp 235–47.

for religious development as for civil stability, the anglican church, under the primate, Cranmer, moved steadily in the direction that the continental reformers had indicated as being not only desirable but inevitable for those who had broken with Rome.

The counterpart of this development in Ireland, where confusion was greater and change slower, and where no parliament was summoned to maintain the Henrician appearance of public support, served more than ever to identify the reform with the wishes of the Dublin Englishmen. The protectorate council does not seem to have considered that Ireland required special treatment. English ecclesiastical legislation was simply applied to Ireland, and, although no question of constitutionality seems to have arisen, confusion certainly followed: thus John Bale, when he was consecrated bishop of Ossory in 1553, held out for the use of the formulary of the second prayer-book, which had been authorised by the English parliament in the previous year, in opposition to the Irish clergy and laity, who held that the use of that book, with its more advanced protestant content, was not mandatory in Ireland. The small official group, acting, it would seem, as much out of loyalty to the state as on conviction, made an effort to follow England. They had got no further by the end of the reign than the formal acceptance of the first prayer-book and—although this, since it denied transubstantiation, was crucial—the substitution in a few places of the communion service for the mass.

Although Bellingham was more positive in religious matters than St Leger, there is evidence that mass was still being celebrated in Dublin, with apparent official approval, throughout most of 1548. Before the end of that year, however, Bishop Staples of Meath had denied that the mass was a sacrifice. Bellingham supported him in the ensuing controversy, but the primate, George Dowdall, who had been appointed archbishop of Armagh by Henry VIII, did not.

The laymen continued to set the pace. Thus the deputy and council, prior to a formal visit to Kilkenny in 1549, ordered the burghers to assemble the local clergy, clearly with the intention of admonishing them regarding traffic with the Roman court and, in all probability, in the hope of proscribing the celebration of mass. When St Leger succeeded Bellingham in the following year, he was ordered to establish the new service and to see that 'the liturgy and prayers of the church' were made available and were recited in English. Although he was more cautious than Bellingham, St Leger still tried to further the state's wishes. He ordered by proclamation that catholic ceremonies should cease and warned Dowdall not to continue the celebration of mass. But, to the annoyance of Browne, archbishop of Dublin, he refrained from coercion. Croft received the same instructions as St Leger, and tried, in his movements through Munster, to enforce the use of the prayer-book. He found the bishops 'blind and obstinate' however, and asked that 'some learned men' should be sent from England to help him.[1] Dowdall gave up, in Croft's time, his struggle to avoid the mounting protestantism and left Ireland.

The only episcopal appointment of an active reformer was that of Bale to Ossory, and he, on his own showing, was roundly opposed by clergy and laity when he tried to enforce the use of the second prayer-book in Kilkenny. The less active and less vehement Staples met similar opposition. There is plenty of evidence of outward conformity in successive deputies' dealings with the lords and townsmen in the south and west; and even the Ulster lords professed conformity. But everywhere beyond the view of the reformers mass was still said and the primacy of Rome was acknowledged. The continued adherence of Gaelic Ireland to the papacy was regarded as evidence that the lords, particularly the lords of Ulster, sought a French invasion.

The succession of Mary in July 1553 brought to the throne a princess who was determined that the state church of England should return to communion with Rome. The mass was restored almost at once, and, although the English parliament refused to permit the queen to abandon the title of supreme head of the church, as it refused to contemplate the restoration of church lands, reunion with the papacy had been effected by 1554. Much of Mary's subsequent tribulation flowed from this facile success, for, with Henry's second daughter Elizabeth, whose birth had ensured the breach with Rome, very present and very much in line for succession, the only real hope of a continued catholic future lay in a fruitful royal marriage. When the queen's consort proved to be Philip of Spain, Mary was estranged from her subjects.

Mary's religious beliefs were well known before her accession, and it was expected in Ireland that she would undo Edward's changes. Bishop Bale said that, within little more than a month of her proclamation in London, the citizens of Kilkenny had resumed 'the whole papism . . . without either statute or yet proclamation'. Bale, as an extremist, may have exaggerated, but there is no reason to doubt the enthusiasm, as he reports it, of the Kilkenny people:

> They rung all the bells . . . they flung up their caps to the battlement of the great temple [St Canice's cathedral], with smilings and laughings most dissolutely . . . they brought forth their copes, candlesticks, holy water stock, cross, and censers, they mustered forth in general procession most gorgeously, all the town over, with *Sancta Maria, ora pro nobis* and the rest of the Latin litany.[2]

Official confirmation of the intention to reestablish the old order in the church followed. St Leger, whose final term as deputy began in October 1553, was instructed to bring the Irish church back to the state in which it

[1] *Cal. S.P., Ire., 1509–73*, p. 124.
[2] 'The vocation of John Bale' in *Harleian Miscellany*, vi (1745), pp 416–17.

had been under Henry VIII, that is, to discontinue the Edwardian service and to restore the mass. The queen appointed to vacant sees. Those of the Irish bishops, including Browne and Staples, and other clergy who were married men were ejected. When Lord Fitzwalter, afterwards created earl of Sussex, replaced St Leger as deputy in 1556 he was ordered to promote 'the true catholic faith and religion now by God's great goodness and special grace recovered in our realms of England and Ireland'.[1] The Irish parliament that met in the following year repeated the English enactment by which the kingdom was reconciled to Rome, although, in Ireland as in England, lands that had been taken from the church were not restored. Thus the schism was ended and the papal connection reestablished. None of the Dublin councillors was dismissed, just as, in the following years of the bloody persecution of protestants in England, there were no Irish burnings.

Lord Deputy Sussex, backed by another newcomer, Sir Henry Sidney, who came to Ireland with him as vice-treasurer, undertook warlike journeys into the interior in 1556 and 1557. None of them produced lasting results. The mere march of a thousand men was not enough to alter the future of an Irish lordship. Yet the government, if it was to function at all, was committed to such demonstrations. It proved impossible to reduce the strength, or the expense, of the forces of the crown; a thousand strong at the beginning of the reign, they were two thousand at the end.

Beyond the range of Sussex's power to interfere with them, the lords fought their own battles. Following the death in 1553 of Donough O'Brien, second earl of Thomond (the former tanist who had been created baron of Ibracken), the dead man's son and the dead man's brother fought to decide whether the settlement should be maintained. The former, who was eventually successful, wanted to be an earl, the latter wanted to put the clock back and be O'Brien. In the north, Shane O'Neill, who had already been spurned in the Tyrone settlement, had, while the earl still lived, begun, as Sidney says, to behave like a 'monstrous monarchal tyrant of all Ulster'. He wanted not only to be O'Neill, lord of Tyrone, but to be king, in the Gaelic sense, of Ulster. His ambition would, in due course, be opposed by the state, the Antrim Scots, and the O'Donnells. Meanwhile, the O'Donnells were involved in a conflict of their own. Manus, the old lord of Tyrconnell, had been deposed, and his sons, Calvagh and Hugh, disputed the succession. Shane, taking advantage of the disturbance, encamped with his forces near Strabane in 1557 and attempted to enforce control of Tyrconnell. Calvagh O'Donnell surprised and routed him.

The government's fear of Scots and French interference in Irish affairs was revived in 1557, when Mary declared war on France. Sidney, who was

[1] *Cal. Carew MSS, 1515–74*, p. 252.

lord justice in the winter in which England lost Calais, feared that the Highland leader James MacDonald would invade Ulster and would receive help even in the Pale, where, as he said, the people groaned under the exactions of the queen's soldiers. Sorley Boy, James's brother, was reported to have 'said plainly that Englishmen had no right to Ireland'.[1] The queen

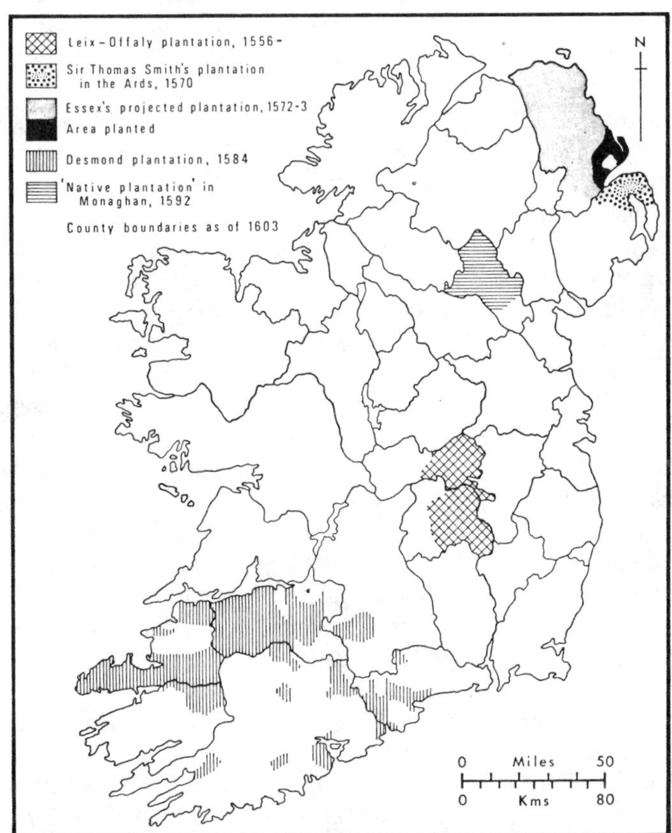

Map 2 TUDOR PLANTATIONS, by K. W. Nicholls

wrote in March 1558 to the lords, encouraging them to keep the peace and to help the deputy.

One settlement that was made by Mary's government had a bleak sequel, but was the forerunner of a new departure in the English management of Ireland. This was the confiscation and attempted plantation of Leix and Offaly, an effort to extend the Pale so as to include the area the inhabitants of which had been the greatest scourge of the Palesmen. By Edward's time,

[1] H. F. Hore, 'The Ulster state papers' in *U.J.A.*, ser. 1, vii (1859), p. 49. See George Hill, *MacDonnells of Antrim*, p. 122.

the course of events had begun to suggest to some Englishmen and Palesmen that Henry VIII's Irish policy might not, after all, produce the required result. At best, conciliation backed by a modicum of force was bound to be a slow process. Was it wise, in view of the temptation that an unsettled Ireland presented to the enemies of England, to wait so long? Was it in the best interest of the Pale to make friends with wild Irishmen? Of the lords who had submitted to Henry, none had, so far, shown themselves to be active or enthusiastic reformers. Some were suspected of back-sliding. All had obviously served, or were serving, their own ends first.

There had always been those who, regardless of consequences or expense, had advocated more forceful measures, and such men were, as we have seen, increasingly listened to since Henry's time. There were those too who thought that a search should be made for a better course of action than raiding and spoliation. Total clearance of the native population and its replacement by a more docile people had been considered. But the deputy and council believed in 1540 that it would be impossible to furnish Ireland as a whole with 'new inhabitants', since no prince could spare so many people from his own country; genocide, as well as being 'a marvellous sumptuous charge', would result only in a void. The council recommended therefore that, while the submission of those Irishmen who had 'not heinously offended' should be accepted, the 'principals' should be hunted down and garrisons should be planted 'in every quarter' to keep the country in subjection.[1] Many garrisons had been established by 1557, but the only certainty of provisioning them lay in transporting what was necessary from the Pale, thus adding to the expense. It was felt therefore, and this was true particularly in regard to Forts Governor and Protector, that the planting of colonies of settlers from England and the Pale—sturdy agricultural communities that would establish and defend their own economy—in the vicinity of garrisons would cheapen their maintenance and add to their security. This was the genesis of the midland plantation.

The formal settlement of Leix and Offaly was 'in good towardness' in the reign of Edward VI. The process was expedited in that of Mary. The government's purpose was to establish that the entire territory of the O'Connors, O'Mores, O'Dempseys, and others was crown property, and that, the existing proprietors having rebelled against the king, the area was at the disposal of the monarchy for a fresh allocation. A difficulty arose from the fact that, since the region had not been shired, local juries could not be empanelled to find the title of the crown. This Gordian knot was cut in 1557 by the Irish parliament, which enacted that Leix should become Queen's County and Offaly King's County, that the whole territory should be confiscated, and that the English system of local organisation and law enforcement should be established. Forts Protector and Governor were renamed

[1] *S.P. Hen. VIII*, iii, 176.

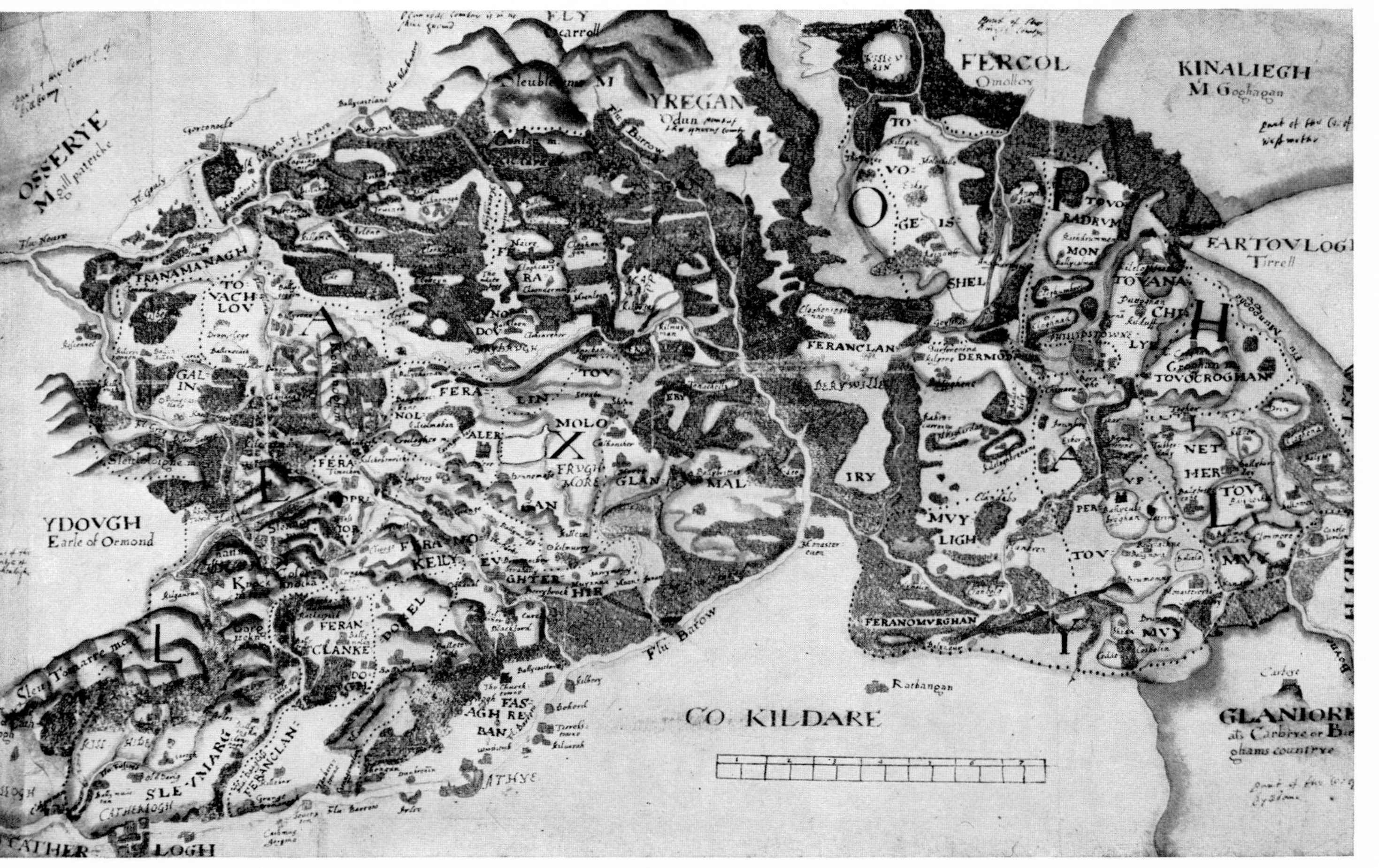

Plate 1. LEIX AND OFFALY, *c.* 1565 (T.C.D., MS 1209, no. 9); size of original 21″ × 13″

Plate 2. CATTLE-RAID, from John Derricke, *The image of Irelande* (London, 1581)

Maryborough and Philipstown with the intention that they should become the nuclei of towns.[1]

This confiscation had to some extent been anticipated by Bellingham and Croft, who had placed English settlers in the area. The removal of the Gaelic landholders into narrow confines comprising but a third of their former territories was now authorised. The remaining two-thirds was allocated for plantation, following grants in fee farm, by 'Englishmen born in England or Ireland'. Although many of the Irish were expelled and many new tenants were introduced to replace them, the enterprise had only a limited success. Pressure on the Pale was certainly reduced, communications between Dublin, the Ormond lordship, and, eventually, south Munster were made more secure, but these results were achieved only by concentrating the attention of 'the races and offspring of the native inhabitors' on the local targets of the forts and settlers. The efforts of the dispossessed to eject the newcomers did not cease until the end of the century. Nor was the settlement a financial success. Sidney said in 1575 that the English tenants were to be pitied and that 'the revenue of both the countries countervails not the twentieth part of the charge, so that the purchase of that plot is, and hath been, very dear'.[2]

Two Irish questions remained unanswered when Elizabeth came to the throne in 1558: was the surrender of Conn O'Neill absolute, and who, when Conn died, would succeed to the new earldom of Tyrone? Conn died in 1559, Matthew, his successor designate, having predeceased him in 1558. No second earl was to appear until 1585, when Hugh, Matthew's second son, received a grant of the earldom. The grant was delayed because the O'Neills wanted to interpret it in their own way. They were not unwilling to be earls, provided they might retain their sovereignty as O'Neills. It did not finally emerge until Hugh O'Neill left Ireland in 1607 that this was impossible, and that the reality of Conn's surrender could not be avoided. Gaelic Ireland was to live meanwhile, uneasily and under mounting pressure from a hostile England, on borrowed time.

The managers of English affairs in Ireland in the opening years of the new reign were the earl of Sussex (who was lord deputy until the summer of 1560 and was then elevated to the lieutenancy), Sir Henry Sidney (who served as lord justice when Sussex was absent from time to time in England in 1558 and 1559), and another newcomer, Sir William Fitzwilliam, lord justice at intervals in 1560 and 1561. It was a time of dangerous uncertainty for England. The queen had yet to win the acclaim of her later years. The question of her successor, which was for long to be a question of whether or not she should marry, hung over her from the start. The further question of the religious future of England demanded immediate attention.

[1] See plate 1.

[2] *Sidney letters*, i, 83.

The year of Elizabeth's accession was that also in which Mary, queen of Scots, married the dauphin of France. Mary was Elizabeth's most likely successor, and if Elizabeth were to die, as she very nearly did in 1562, catholic France, with a grip on Scotland, might, for a time at least, engulf England. Strict catholicism regarded Elizabeth as illegitimate, and therefore incapable of ruling, and France had proclaimed Mary Stuart queen of England on Mary Tudor's death. Since Philip II of Spain had not abandoned hope of continuing to direct England, the country, on the verge of bankruptcy following the mismanagement of the last two reigns, might well become the scene not only of civil war but of international strife.

All this necessarily coloured England's relations with Ireland, and added, in the queen's early years, to the reasons for a concentration of attention on Ulster. While Ulster lay outside the control of Dublin it was open at two levels to penetration from Scotland: the conflict of central Scottish and local authority in the west Highlands promoted the infiltration of the MacDonalds into Antrim; the alliance of the Scottish crown with France threatened to extend to Ulster the danger of an encirclement of England by her continental enemies. Shane O'Neill was thus something more than a mere hindrance to the working-out of the settlement which had been made with his father. It was suspected that he and the earls of Desmond and Kildare were intriguing with the French. Kildare was the boy of Silken Thomas's time who, having returned from the Continent, had by now been restored to his earldom.[1] It was known that Shane, as the years went by and his power grew, was involved in Scots politics. He corresponded not only with the earl of Argyle, the most powerful man in the west, but with Queen Mary. The pressure on Elizabeth was lightened by the peace of Câteau Cambrésis (1559) and the treaty of Edinburgh (1560). Still, the return of Mary to Scotland in 1561, following the death of her first husband, and the English involvement in the religious war in France left ample material for strife.

Both Elizabeth and Shane O'Neill sought to control Ulster, outside which Shane had no ambition. At first, when the queen was beset with difficulties, the advisability of jettisoning Matthew and his line and making Shane the earl was considered. Shane, who claimed both the new earldom and the old lordship of Tyrone, agreed, when Sidney visited him, to abide by the queen's decision. Then, when Elizabeth's position became easier, a policy of supporting Brian, the young baron of Dungannon, was entertained. Finally, by 1561, two alternatives were weighed. The first was to summon Shane to England and, after the queen had seen him and the influence of English surroundings had had time to work, to seek to bind him to the state. The second was to overcome him in Ireland, an expedient that would have denied the strange rivals their mutual inspection.

Sussex, who clearly disliked Shane as much as Shane disliked him, ex-

[1] See above, p. 43.

hausted the resources of violence in 1561. That he did so at a time when negotiations were being carried on with a view to bringing Shane to England was not considered amiss. Cynicism is a perennial weed. Efforts were made to isolate Shane by stirring up the O'Donnells and O'Reillys against him and by encouraging the Campbells and MacDonalds to deny him assistance from Scotland. Sussex placed a garrison in Armagh cathedral, raided MacMahon's country in Monaghan and carried off great numbers of cattle, but the English were novices in the warfare of the north, where the terrain fought for the Ulstermen. Surprised by Shane's men in difficult country, the rearguard of their marching column fled ignominiously.

Sussex was taught two further lessons in that year: that a warlike expedition had to be mounted each time supplies ran out in a distant garrison like Armagh and that one might march across Ulster without injuring Shane. For Sussex, who went as far as Lough Foyle in September, the year's campaigns were a failure. Shane, who kept out of his way, drew a distinction between the queen's agent and the queen. He said that Sussex had invaded his country without cause and had prevented his going to England to submit in person. It seems that both Shane and his cousin the earl of Kildare, having for the moment given up hope of Spanish or French assistance in a struggle against the queen, were now prepared to try what friendship with Elizabeth might offer. Shane's hand as a negotiator was strengthened by the failure of an attempt which Sussex made to have him poisoned. The queen, whom Sussex had made privy to his barbarity, expressed the wish 'rather to recover our subject, submitting himself, by mercy than by extremity', and Shane, having first made sure of a pardon, a safe-conduct, and the payment of his expenses by the crown, went to London in December 1561.[1]

The dramatic confrontation of Elizabeth and long catechising of Shane and his advisers by Sir William Cecil, the prolonged sojourn of the Ulster group in London—all this had strangely little result. Shane came and went; it has been said that he was lucky to get away, but he was in fact safer in England, where he was removed from his own dangerous realities, than he had been, or would be, in Ireland. His ability to compromise was restricted to his relations with the English; on his own ground his goal was the risky one of power, with no half measures.

Shane had argued his case cogently. He and his counsellors were by no means the wild men or the figures of fun that, when passions mounted, they were to become in English legend.[2] Although he scarcely strengthened his own claim by doing so, Shane denied that his father's patent was valid. He said that Conn had held his place only with the consent of the lords and inhabitants of Tyrone, and had enjoyed no heritable estate. Nothing had

[1] See James Hogan, 'Shane O'Neill comes to the court of Elizabeth' in Séamus Pender (ed.), *Essays and studies presented to Professor Tadhg Ua Donnchadha* (*Torna*) (Cork, 1947), pp 154–70.

[2] As related by Campion, 'Hist. Ire.', ed. Ware, i, 189–90.

been done at Conn's ennoblement to alter this. No letters patent could take effect without inquisition, and no inquisition had been held, or could have been held, in Tyrone, since Tyrone was not a shire. Cecil and Sussex, who was present for the interrogation, could answer this only by saying that the crown held 'in the Irishry' by conquest. Might, even if it had not yet been exercised, was right. Shane said that the progeny of the baron of Dungannon could have no claim in Tyrone, since Matthew was not an O'Neill, and that even if he, Shane, did not exist there were a hundred of the name of O'Neill who would resist Matthew's sons' pretensions. As for his own claim to lordship, he had been chosen in the Gaelic manner by the people of Tyrone as 'the most ablest and the worthiest of the headmen', that is, he was the member of his *derbhfine* who had been made O'Neill.[1]

Matthew's eldest son and Shane's rival, Brian, was killed in Ulster in Shane's absence (April 1562), but the second son, the eleven-year-old Hugh, was then in England, where Sir Henry Sidney had brought him, probably in 1559.[2] In the end, the crown made no decision regarding the earldom. The fact of Shane's authority was recognised, although it was only very generally defined. Shane claimed to rule not only in Tyrone but in Maguire's country of Fermanagh, MacMahon's of Monaghan, O'Hanlon's of south Armagh, the countries of Magennis, MacCartan, the Savages and the Dufferins in Down, and O'Cahan's country in the present County Londonderry—that is, from Strangford Lough to the Erne and from the Pale to the Foyle. This area comprised practically all of Ulster save the O'Donnell country of Tyrconnell, and Antrim, where indeed Shane said that the Scots were intruders in Clandeboye and the Route, territories rightfully his. It was an area that included much of the old earldom of Ulster, the rights of which were, ominously, vested in the crown. Shane said that the lords of Ulster were his *uirríoghtha* (sub-kings). *Ceart Uí Néill*, a statement of 'the customary right and lordship of O'Neill over the province of Ulster', as these demands stood in the sixteenth century, provides all that is known to have survived of the Gaelic documentation of Shane's claim.[3] This manuscript gives details of the military service and other contributions that, as the O'Neills had for long held, were due to them from most of the lordships mentioned by Shane. In it the O'Neills also recorded claims on O'Donnell and O'Reilly. Shane told Cecil that his rights over both of these were in dispute, and Sussex had already tried to stir up both of them against him. Sidney saw Shane as a Lucifer in pride when he 'took upon him the name of O'Neill, with the whole superiority, rule and governance of all the lords

[1] Articles to be answered by Shane O'Neill, 7 Feb. 1562; cited in *Bagwell*, Tudors, ii, 36.

[2] See J. K. Graham, 'The birth-date of Hugh O'Neill, second earl of Tyrone' in *I.H.S.*, i, no. 1 (Mar. 1938), pp 58–9; Sean O'Faolain, *The great O'Neill* (London, 1942), pp 36, 282.

[3] Printed from R.I.A. MS 24 P 33 in *Lr Cl. Aodha Buidhe*, pp 41–7; English translation by Myles Dillon in *Studia Celt.*, i (1966), pp 1–18. See Éamon Ó Doibhlín, 'Ceart Uí Néill' in *Seanchas Ard Mhacha*, v (1970), pp 324–58.

and captains of Ulster'.[1] As Shane himself pointed out, he was merely asserting the traditional claims of his dynasty. His successors, Turlough Luineach and Hugh, were to do the same.

Shane was confirmed as 'captain' of Tyrone, O'Cahan's country and part of Antrim, with a reservation regarding the rights of Hugh, baron of Dungannon, and with a provision that he should not levy exactions elsewhere. The matters that he disputed with O'Donnell and O'Reilly were remitted to an arbitration that was never awarded. The English garrison was to remain in Armagh. This, indeed, save for Shane's acknowledgement of the queen's overlordship and the guarantee that, in settling his own claims, he would keep Ulster occupied pending a better opportunity for further intervention, was, from the English viewpoint, the only practical result of the settlement, and Armagh was not for long to remain English.

Outside Ulster, the early years of Elizabeth's reign passed, for Ireland, peacefully. England was preoccupied with her own uncertainties, and the mission of Sussex, the justices, and the council was to mollify Ormond, Desmond, and the volatile Kildare, to perform the impossible by reducing expenses, and to keep Ireland quiet. Parliament was assembled briefly in January 1560 to establish the queen's title to her dead sister's succession and, with indecent haste, to undo the Marian ecclesiastical legislation. The tide had turned again. Elizabeth's English parliament of 1559, which made her supreme governor in spiritual matters and restored in a modified form the prayer-book of 1552, had reestablished a protestant church of England. Lacking Mary's conviction and compelled to decide between a catholicism and a protestantism that were by now sharply divided, Elizabeth took a popular line, one that was largely dictated by a national resentment of papal supremacy. The Irish parliament proved cooperative, the changes made by Henry VIII and Edward VI were reaffirmed, and, as far as the law extended through the island and could extend into men's minds, the pope and his organisation were again cast off.

There were hopes of an improvement in trade, still largely an export trade in hides, woolfells and woollen mantles, tallow and fish, with an inward trickle of iron, wine, salt, and such exotic commodities as spices, when the coinage, which had been further depreciated under Mary, was reformed. The economy was still primitive, and would long remain so. The island was under-populated, and there must have been large areas, particularly in the Irish districts, and over and above the vast expanses of woodland and boggy country, that were not permanently occupied. There was plenty of room for the seasonal movement of cattle from winter to summer pasturage, plenty of space for the wandering existence of creaghts, which the English believed, erroneously, to be a form of nomadism.[2] The Palesmen

[1] The phrase is from the act of attainder of Shane O'Neill: 11 Eliz., c. 1 (*Stat. Ire.*, p. 322). Sidney's reference to Shane is in *Cal. S.P. Ire., 1509–73*, p. 289.

[2] See above, p. 35.

still considered themselves oppressed by the burdens, in particular those arising from the billeting of troops, that were placed upon them by the administration. They resented having, as they said, to pay the whole of the greatly increased expenses of government, and their resentment sharpened the squabbles that continued to mark the Irish council's deliberations. Coyne and livery, the debased form of the Gaelic system of billeting and maintaining mercenaries which, as early as the fourteenth century, had overflowed into the Old English areas, was still practised, despite continued legal proscription, and was still the chief prop of the local independence of the lords. Shane O'Neill could claim in 1561 that his country was better governed than the Pale. He advanced as proof of this that 300 farmers had abandoned their livelihood in the Pale and had gone to Tyrone to accept the Gaelic way of life and become his clients. Tongue in cheek, he remarked that it was 'a very evil sign that men shall forsake the Pale and come and dwell among wild savage people'.[1] Sidney, who visited Tyrone shortly before that, went far to bear him out; he said that Tyrone was prosperous and had a greater population than any Irish country. All that the administration could do to extend the English version of civilisation was to push forward, against fierce opposition, the settlement of crown tenants in Leix and Offaly.

Shane O'Neill, who completely overshadowed the tanist, Turlough Luineach, and the supporters of the late Matthew's sons, did not remain quiet for long. Inevitably, since he sought to enforce what the O'Neills claimed to be their rights, he was surrounded by enemies, of whom the most powerful were the O'Donnells and the Antrim Scots. The O'Donnells, who not only opposed Shane's claim to exercise control over them but advanced a counter-claim of their own to paramountcy in Ulster,[2] had defeated Shane in 1557. Yet Shane still overawed Tyrconnell, and, raiding southward, practised coercion on the inhabitants of Maguire and O'Reilly's countries. He undertook the militarisation of his lordship by arming the churls, the workers in the fields, who had not hitherto been involved, in Tyrone or any other Gaelic community, in the struggles of their betters, the small ruling class. Shane 'furnished all the peasants and husbandmen of his country with armour and weapons, and trained them up in the knowledge of the wars', said the English, adding the significant statement that he was 'the first that ever so did of an Irishman'.[3]

Those whom Shane oppressed, Maguire, MacMahon, and O'Reilly, appealed to the queen for assistance against him. Their appeal was fruitless. Shane, inviolate in his own country, refused to meet Sussex, and the viceroy, who, as his best effort, penetrated momentarily and ineffectually to Dungannon and Clogher in 1563, was hard put to it to maintain the garrison in

[1] P.R.O., S.P. 63/3, p. 14.

[2] See Colm Ó Lochlainn, 'Ó Domhnaill's claim for military service' in *Ir. Sword*, v (1961), pp 117–18.

[3] John Hooker in Holinshed, *Chronicles*, ii, 113.

Armagh. The earls of Kildare and Ormond were sent to reason with Shane, but to no end. According to Shane, another attempt was made to poison him. In the autumn of 1563, following representations made by the ever-conciliatory Sir Thomas Cusack, the queen accepted the inevitable and again made peace with Shane. He was acknowledged as O'Neill, although this clearly meant much less to the crown than it did to him. His claim to the earldom was said still to be the subject of examination, and, a final blow to Sussex, it was agreed to withdraw the Armagh garrison. So far, the crown had gained nothing from Shane, either in peace or war. In keeping with his boast that Ulster was his, he attacked and defeated the Scots at Glenshesk in north Antrim in May 1565, thus doing what the English had been unable to do.

If the deficiency that the Irish lords suffered was a lack of power, it could be made good only by the attainment of more power. Authority, in Ulster, in Ireland as a whole, and in the last resort in England, depended on leadership, willingly accepted or enjoined, and backed by force. By 'challenging superiority' over the lords of Ulster, the O'Neills of the sixteenth century attempted a course of action which, in other countries, had led to, or was eventually to lead to, national union. Their tragedy, and perhaps the tragedy of Ireland, was that their attempt was made too late.

Shane O'Neill was toppled by the O'Donnells, not by the English. Sussex's period of office ended in 1565, when Sir Henry Sidney succeeded him. Sidney, who, as we have seen, already knew Ireland well, and who moved in that part of the court circle that followed Lord Robert Dudley (the queen's favourite, who was Sidney's brother-in-law and who had just been made earl of Leicester), was then lord president of Wales. Returning to Dublin in 1566, when he found the administration rent by bitter wrangling over disputed muster figures, peculation, and all the personal accusations that marked inability to curb mounting public expense, Sidney brought an active mind and a forceful personality to the management of the queen's affairs. He advised that Shane should be opposed and that Calvagh O'Donnell, whom Shane had earlier held prisoner, should be restored in Tyrconnell. The queen's first hope was that Sidney might reform Shane, but she abandoned this and had come by March 1566 to consider how this 'cankred dangerous rebel' might be 'utterly extirped'.[1]

Shane wrote to the French court in 1566 asking for an army to help him to expel the English. Knowing this, Sidney said that Ulster in French hands would be a far greater threat to England than the now lost Calais had been to France. Shane burnt Armagh cathedral, fearing English attempts to re-occupy it as a military post, and continued his intrigues with the Scots court and the earl of Argyle. Sidney marched north in the autumn, the season when he could live off the harvest and destroy what his men could not eat. His intention was to restore Calvagh and to harass Shane, whom he thought able

[1] *Sidney S.P.*, p. 18.

to bring 5,000 men into the field. He was assisted by the first large-scale amphibious operation of the reign, a type of movement often to be repeated by the sea-conscious English. Edward Randolph, lieutenant of the ordnance, brought a thousand men by sea from Bristol to Lough Foyle, where he met Sidney in September and subsequently fortified himself at Derry. Thereafter, Sidney made a triumphal progress to Tyrconnell, where Calvagh was reinstated, and returned to Dublin by Boyle and Athlone. Once again, the lords and people through whose territories the deputy had advanced unopposed were impressed by the power of the crown. Once again, Shane O'Neill carefully avoided the queen's representative. But Shane resented the violation of Ulster. He attacked Randolph in November, and although still another characteristic of the Irish wars was demonstrated, the impotence of the Irish against fieldworks defended with firearms, Randolph was killed. The garrison sickened, and when their powder blew up in the following April the survivors were forced to evacuate Derry and to withdraw to Carrickfergus. The north was still beyond the sphere of effective English control.

Shane made his last throw in May 1567. Calvagh O'Donnell had died a few weeks after his reinstatement and his brother Hugh had been made O'Donnell. Shane moved against Hugh, crossed the river Swilly at Farsetmore, near Letterkenny, was attacked suddenly by the O'Donnells and was utterly defeated (8 May). He himself escaped his overthrow, crossed Tyrone, and threw himself into the hands of the Scots at Cushendun. Much intermarried and with much in common, the Highland Scots and the Irish had in general, outside Shane's power structure, got on well. But, unless much is hidden from us, it must seem madness in Shane that, following Glenshesk, he should have put himself at their mercy now. Their hostile reaction seems predictable, although it must totally have surprised Shane; and, following a quarrel, they cut him to pieces (2 June). The Carrickfergus English, who were negotiating for the service of the Scots against Shane, secured his head. It went pickled in a barrel to Dublin, and, to show that the last word was the queen's, was impaled on a spike on the wall of the castle.

That Shane had scarcely been a major obstacle to English rule in Ireland, whatever the implications were, was shown by the slight effect his removal had on affairs as a whole. His death was of small consequence outside Ulster. Within Ulster, the crown gained little by it; a favourable settlement still eluded the queen. So far, although Elizabeth's officials had spent a great deal of money in Ireland, they had little to show for their outlay. Munster, indeed, witnessed in these years the Old English version of the isolated power struggle of the north, a struggle between the old rivals, the houses of Desmond and Ormond. Gerald, the fourteenth earl of Desmond, was, after detention in England, allowed back to Ireland in 1564 in the hope that his presence would reduce strife on the border of the two earldoms and would promote order in Munster, as it had been hoped the return of Shane O'Neill would do in Ulster. The queen's government was, in both instances, over-sanguine.

Successive earls of Desmond, whose authority extended in varying shades of actuality from Dungarvan to Kerry and from Limerick to Cork, who overawed the MacCarthys and O'Sullivans, and on whom the towns of Cork, Kinsale, and Youghal were dependent for protection, had maintained themselves largely by aggression. Restored to his own country, this earl showed no inclination to break with tradition. He interfered in the neighbouring lordship of the O'Briens in the struggle that was then proceeding between the new order of the earl of Thomond and the old order of a tanist whose future the changes had imperilled. By championing the tanist, Desmond showed a preference for the old Ireland. The earl of Clanricard, whose interest lay rather in an Ireland reformed, backed the earl of Thomond. But Desmond's real concern was to vindicate the claims of his house against the queen's kinsman, Black Tom Butler, the tenth earl of Ormond. As the ruling families of the south had in this instance followed the Ulster pattern of the intermarriage of hereditary enemies, although such things seem to have meant little in Ireland, Black Tom was the son of Desmond's wife by her first marriage. The Fitzgerald–Butler dispute over what could be got from the income of lands to which both houses laid claim had already wasted wide areas in Limerick, Tipperary, and Kilkenny. When the earl of Desmond attempted in 1565 to distrain for what he claimed were his dues in the Decies in west Waterford—a territory that a Fitzgerald collateral claimed to hold from the crown—the earl of Ormond mustered his forces against him and a fight ensued between their private armies at Affane, near the river Blackwater below Lismore. Desmond was defeated and captured by the Butlers.

It was impossible for a reforming government to ignore this assumption by nominal loyalists of a right to settle a family dispute by an appeal to arms. The earls were summoned to London, where their clash was exacerbated by the fact that Sussex, the enemy of the queen's favourite Leicester, supported Ormond, while Leicester's brother-in-law, Sidney, spoke up for Desmond, thus linking an Irish quarrel with a court intrigue. Both Irish earls incurred the royal disfavour, although the queen, who was always to like Black Tom, brought up as he had been in the inner court circle, showed clearly that she thought Desmond the more blameworthy of the two. They agreed to abide by the queen's orders. This Ormond did, although Sidney still irked him, but Desmond eventually did not.

Sidney found in the course of a lengthy sojourn in Munster and Connacht in 1567 that, in the earl's continued absence, Ormond's brothers carried on the affairs of the palatinate of Tipperary in their own interest and with a high hand, that the earls of Thomond and Desmond—Desmond having come home again—were ungovernable, and that, although the earl of Clanricard was 'of great humbleness', his sons, the so-called Mac an Iarlas (sons of the earl), were the very opposite. They had so upset their own and the surrounding territories that Galway was more like 'a town of war, frontiering upon an enemy, than a civil town in a country under the sovereign'. Sidney thought that the unruly lords could never be brought to heel or the lower orders be protected or encouraged to live peaceably unless, as had already been proposed, local agents of the crown, Englishmen with authority and means to enforce English law, were established in Munster and Connacht.[1] Something more than a wishful reliance on such weak members as the local magnates, men who were either unwilling or unable to act as reformers, was required. Cecil, who was indebted to Sidney for much of his Irish information, said that Elizabeth, although entitled queen of Ireland, did not hold the Irish crown 'in deed'.[2]

Ulster seemed quiet only because the Dublin administration knew little of what went on there. South Connacht was in turmoil because of the succession dispute of the Mac an Iarla half-brothers, Ulick and John, sons of Richard Sassanach, second earl of Clanricard. Thomond, where the earl was opposed by his uncle, was in like case. The original earls of Clanricard and Thomond had, unfortunately for the English, died shortly after their English ennoblement. The transition from pseudo-Gaelic or pure Gaelic rule to the English system was thus, in neither lordship, managed by a vigorous, able, and long-lived appointee. In Clanricard, the promiscuous marital relations of the Burkes, together with a plenitude of offspring, added to the confusion. In both lordships, those who considered that Gaelic institutions were preferable, or gave them a better chance of furthering their own ends, resisted change. But, outside Ulster, the queen's government experienced most resistance in Munster.

Change, in the south as elsewhere, was gradual. Although the earl of Desmond had made a bad impression in London and Dublin and was little calculated to prove cooperative, he was not removed from the territory of his earldom until the spring of 1567, and even then his removal was not final. The trouble was that, until the system of lordship had been replaced by an extension of the royal administration, the lord's presence in office was essential. His removal left a vacuum; hence the Gaelic dictum, 'a lordship without a lord is a dead lordship'. The state, as a practical concession, accepted this when it recognised the rulership of Irish lords while at the same time denying the validity of Irish institutions. The continued absence of a lord was even worse than a disputed succession, since it promoted an anarchic fragmentation of authority. Yet much time went by, much friction and frustration were experienced and a great fund of resentment of the

[1] *Cal. S.P. Ire., 1509–73*, p. 330.
[2] Ibid., p. 336.

state's efforts was built up before the administration could resolve to make a clean sweep of existing institutions, feudal as well as Gaelic, or was able to do so. Adjudged to have damaged the conformist Ormond to the amount of £20,000, the nonconformist Desmond was sent as a prisoner to London at the end of 1567. He remained there until 1573, when, having sworn loyalty to the queen, and having surrendered his palatine rights to her, he was restored in person to his earldom. Meanwhile, Munster revolted.

The immediate occasion of the revolt was the failure of the administration, in the simultaneous absence of the two earls, to make adequate provision for the management of the province. But the bones of contention were many. Jealous of their own authority, the local lords suspected the intentions of the government. Rumours of the impending institution of what emerged as the presidential system, rumours coloured by the detention of Desmond, suggested to the Fitzgeralds that the entire Geraldine lordship, the historic power-structure on which, since the Norman invasion, so much of Munster depended, was about to be undermined. Land titles were clearly at risk. The appearance on the Irish scene of the first of the Elizabethan adventurers, whose numbers were to increase as the century progressed and to whom Old English and Gaelic Irish were alike exploitable, was noted with alarm. Of these, the Devon man, Sir Peter Carew, secured the backing of the Irish council in 1568 for a claim, based on his alleged descent from the Norman invader, Robert Fitzstephen, to lands in Meath and Carlow and seemed likely to secure legal backing for a still more fantastic demand, disturbing alike to the Geraldines and Irish lords, in respect of lands in Kerry, Cork, and Waterford. Sir Warham St Leger, the former deputy's grandson, and Richard Grenville of the *Revenge* secured lands on Cork harbour, and a group which included the future explorer, Humphrey Gilbert, proposed to build a town on the west Cork coast and to exploit the fishery. The advent of these products of Tudor enterprise and arrogance, at a time when the crown set the tone of English aspirations by reviving such claims as those of the earldom of Ulster, was disquieting alike to the Fitzgeralds, Butlers, and MacCarthys. It drove Butlers and Fitzgeralds to make for the moment a common cause. Ormond's brother, Sir Edmund Butler, was the proprietor of some of the lands that Carew claimed in Carlow. When Butler rebelled in 1569 it was, he said, with the intention of making war not against the queen, but 'against those that banish [*sic*] Ireland and mean conquest'.[1]

These were material considerations. The Munster revolt was also an ideological struggle. No general effort had yet been made to ensure religious conformity, although the establishment in 1564 of an Irish court of high commission with power to enforce reform was a formal step in that direction.[2] The state church made little real progress in the first decade of the queen's reign. It had an official life in the Pale, south Leinster, and the Munster

[1] P.R.O., S.P. 63/29, p. 24.

[2] *Cal. pat. rolls Ire., Hen. VIII–Eliz.*, pp 489–90.

towns; but, hampered from the beginning by a shortage of functioning clergy and by its identification with a state system that provoked increasing opposition, it had little else. At best, the queen's servants, including a few bishops such as Adam Loftus, archbishop of Dublin, and Hugh Brady, bishop of Meath, enforced the law in matters of religion when it was possible to do so. Ireland remained catholic. And catholic Ireland showed signs that it would not remain quiescent.

The real leader in Munster in the earl of Desmond's absence was James Fitzmaurice Fitzgerald, the earl's cousin. Fitzmaurice claimed that the earl had appointed him as his deputy, and his position was strengthened in 1568 when a gathering of the Fitzgeralds and their supporters acknowledged him as their captain. Disregarding admonitions from Dublin, Fitzmaurice strove to assert his authority over the Fitzgerald collaterals in Kerry and elsewhere. While the old order, which rested ultimately on the traditional force of the MacSheehy galloglass and other Desmond retainers, was thus being maintained in the earldom, strife was evident in the adjoining areas. The earl of Ormond's three brothers showed a fractiousness of their own, and MacCarthy Mór, although he had recently been created earl of Clancare, plundered the territories of his neighbours with the help of his own MacSwiney galloglass. By 1569, led by Fitzmaurice, the greater part of Munster was in revolt against Sidney's authority. Ormond's brothers joined Fitzmaurice and MacCarthy; Cork, Kinsale, and Youghal were threatened; Kilmallock was attacked; and an uncoordinated warfare of spoliation and incendiarism spread to Limerick and Waterford. Vexed by the dangerous projects of Carew and his fellows, distrustful of the lord deputy, and momentarily released from the restraint which their hereditary leaders might have exercised over them, the old ruling families of Munster struck out inadequately.

Fitzmaurice consistently sounded a new religious note. He said that the queen was trying to force the Irish 'to forsake the catholic faith by God unto his church given and by the see of Rome hitherto prescribed to all Christian men'[1] and, then and later, sought to rationalise the motives of resistance to the state's authority and to transform the struggle into a crusade. He was, in this, well abreast of contemporary European opinion. The hope, which had for long been entertained in continental catholic circles, that Elizabeth might be reconciled to the papacy had been, by now, all but abandoned. Archbishop Richard Creagh, the papal primate, and the Jesuit David Wolfe, the papal representative in Ireland, were both prisoners in Dublin castle, and the Geraldine Maurice Fitzgibbon, the papal appointee to the archbishopric of Cashel, was, at Fitzmaurice's instance, a suitor at the court of Philip II of Spain for material assistance for Irish catholicism. Fitzgibbon revived an

[1] P.R.O., S.P. 63/29, p. 8. See the Irish appeal to Philip II, 1569: *Spicil. Ossor.*, i, 59–61; and D. A. Binchy, 'An Irish ambassador at the Spanish court, 1569–74' in *Studies*, x (1921), p. 365.

appeal that had been made in 1559 for the establishment in Ireland of a ruler of Philip's choice, one who would save the country from heresy. A zealous tridentine catholic, Fitzmaurice made himself, no doubt with the approval of many of his followers, the first lay exponent of the counter-reformation in Ireland.

Sidney soon showed that, in an appeal to arms, he was the stronger. Munster had been aroused, but only to the extent of a few thousand men, the retainers of individual lords. Fitzmaurice might try to use religion as a catalyst to make a common cause of local grievances, but the Munster confederacy remained brittle, its components individuals whose ambitions had been frustrated, its violence a shower of stones cast at the monolith of the state. The decisive factor was the return of Black Tom, earl of Ormond, in August 1569. The Butlers were disturbed by the rumour that Leicester, Ormond's foe, was to marry the queen and that Sidney, who rode about with the ragged-staff device of Leicester on his pennon, would become king of Ireland; but they surrendered. Sidney went south with 600 men in July. Four hundred more who had come by sea from England joined him in Munster. Desmond, where the disaffected allowed themselves to be cornered in castles, was not Ulster, and the rebellion withered before Sidney's show of force. Thomas Roe Fitzgerald, Desmond's half-brother, surrendered, as did Rory MacSheehy, constable of the Desmond galloglass. Hitherto, although Fitzmaurice still held out, this might have been thought a sufficient acknowledgement of defeat, but by now the tone of Irish warfare had changed. Humphrey Gilbert, given the title of colonel, was ordered to complete the pacification of Munster. He did so with a new ruthlessness that made death the wages of revolt. Only Fitzmaurice, who retired into the wooded wilderness of the glen of Aherlow, escaped him. Ormond, his quarrel with Sidney patched up in 1570, now, and for the remainder of his long life, cooperated fully. He helped to pacify the O'Briens, although the earl of Thomond, in a last desperate effort before he too acknowledged that the initiative in planning the future of Ireland was the queen's, fled to France to seek assistance from a potential enemy of England.

The instructions that Sidney received on his appointment as deputy in 1565 disclosed the crown's intention, following earlier recommendations, to establish a regional organ of government in the south, and probably in the west. The council of the north in England, and the council of the marches of Wales had served the Tudors well, and, as the need arose to consolidate the progress that was being slowly made by the Dublin government, there was every reason to follow the English precedents in Ireland. Although there was a clear case for the immediate establishment of a body with executive and administrative power in Munster, where the independent actions and claims to palatine jurisdiction of the earls of Desmond and Ormond were an obstacle to strong government, and where the danger of continental interference was greatest, no effective appointments were, despite pressure from Sidney, made until 1571, when Sir John Perrot took up office as president of Munster. Perrot, who acted under the control of the deputy and council, was assisted by justices and a provincial council, and was given a military force. He was required to act in accordance with the common law, but had wide power to use martial law where necessary, and to prosecute rebels.[1] Sir Edward Fitton had already been appointed in a similar capacity for Connacht.

Perrot began operations in the spring of 1571 and, taking up again Gilbert's work of marching, skirmishing, and the seizure of castles, reduced Desmond to uneasy quietness. Fitzmaurice gathered strength from time to time and even burned Kilmallock, but he submitted to Perrot in January 1572. For such as he, the issue of the papal bull *Regnans in excelsis* in February 1570 must have been most encouraging. Catholicism had adopted a hard line. Elizabeth, the 'pretended queen', was excommunicated. Catholics might no longer attend services of the state church; it might indeed be held that they were in duty bound to resist the civil power. On the other hand, the government, which had been disinclined to antagonise the Irish majority by forcing the pace in religious matters, came to regard catholicism as treason. Fitzmaurice, accepting what was for him the inevitable, fled to France in 1575.

Meanwhile, Fitton made slow progress in Galway and Thomond, the only parts of his presidency in which he could operate with any effect. He found the earl of Clanricard professedly loyal, but, because his real wish was the old independence, doubtfully cooperative. The earl of Thomond was, before his departure for France, hostile. Clanricard and his sons, the Mac an Iarlas, were alternately imprisoned and released, Athlone suffered spoliation at the hands of the sons, and the landed proprietors of south Connacht as a whole were antagonised by Fitton's attempts to substitute a liability to support the queen's forces for the old system of private retainers. It was clear by the end of 1572 that only the earl could rule in south Connacht, and that, until the power of the state was increased, he would prefer to do so on his own terms.

The parliament that Sidney summoned in January 1569 was used to promote the policy of conquest. It also brought out the first evidence of parliamentary opposition to the methods employed to make conquest a reality. Still representative only of that part of the island where English control or influence were manifest, its membership was greater than before, much of the increase being made up, to match the current domination of the Irish administration by Englishmen, by English newcomers. The commons divided at once into a court party and an opposition which was composed of the Pale gentry and some of the representatives of the towns, and which had as its first leader the prospective rebel, Ormond's brother Sir Edmund

[1] Perrot's instructions are in *Sidney letters*, i, 48.

Butler. This was scarcely ominous and far from being openly disloyal, but the opposition still made it necessary for Sidney to tighten the reins of management, and its existence precluded haste in the introduction of further religious changes.

An act involving the retrospective attainder of Shane O'Neill drew attention to the major obstacle to English rule, the sovereignty of the Irish lords. The statement that 'the name of O'Neill, in the judgements of the uncivil people of this realm, doth carry in itself so great a sovereignty as they suppose that all the lords and people of Ulster should rather live in servitude to that name than in subjection to the crown of England' went, as Shane's career had indicated and as subsequent events were to bear out, to the heart of the matter. The act enjoined that the name of O'Neill, in the sense that it was used to indicate sovereignty in Ulster, together with all authority claimed 'as in right of that name', should be 'utterly abolished and extinct for ever'.[1] Although the O'Neills were specified, a clear warning was here sounded for every lord, whether he was Old English or Irish, that there could be but one sovereignty in Ireland.

Sidney's parliament must have been a disappointment to him. He had not expected that the legislative programme he proposed would meet with such obstruction, and certainly not that the sessions would drag on to 1571.[2] Although the steps taken to establish governmental control in Munster must have done much to neutralise parliamentary opposition, and although parliament dutifully attainted the Munster rebels in 1570, a series of measures that sought to centralise authority was passed with obvious reluctance. These measures included bills to secure the abolition of those 'captainries' that had not been established by patent, to provide that five principal men in each shire should be held responsible for the actions of the rest, and to curtail coyne and livery. The state had not been consistent in its attitude to coyne and livery, having itself used the system which it condemned to maintain forces for the crown, and having gone so far in recent years as to employ MacDonnell galloglass in Leinster on a semi-permanent basis. Now that the luxury of a repentance for these expediencies could be had, if Ireland was prepared to pay for it with a rent to the crown of 13*s.* 4*d.* a ploughland, it was natural that the magnates should wonder whether the old system as managed by themselves was not better than a new one which might be mismanaged to their disadvantage. Steps were taken to increase revenue by renewing the parliamentary subsidy and taxing overseas trade, and areas that had been brought under some semblance of control were shired, but the Irish institutional system was not remodelled. Sidney's handling of Irish affairs had progressed beyond mere expediency, but not beyond compromise.

[1] 11 Eliz., c. 1.

[2] For the parliament see V. W. Treadwell, 'The Irish parliament of 1569–71' in *R.I.A. Proc.*, lxv (1966–7), sect. C, pp 55–89.

CHAPTER IV

The completion of the Tudor conquest and the advance of the counter-reformation, 1571–1603

G. A. HAYES-MCCOY

THE growth of English power disclosed fresh opportunities for the queen's government to extend its control of Irish affairs. It served also to draw attention to a major obstacle: the fact that the Gaelic and gaelicised social and institutional conditions, and the Irish economy over the greater part of the island, favoured the opponents of change. The lack of commodities 'which are in England everywhere',[1] but which, in Ireland, could be obtained by the queen's forces only in the Pale and the few other districts which to the English eye were settled, made it difficult and costly to provide supplies for outlying garrisons, such as those at Armagh and the midland forts. The civil reformation as a whole depended on the government's ability not only to pay but to feed its troops, and so, despite the great strides that had been made since Henry VIII's time, the English conquest was still a matter of painful progress from east to west. Such peripheral places as Carrickfergus and Newry were maintained only because they could, when necessary, be supplied by sea. Although the whole English presence in Ireland was dependent on an exploitation of the opportunities created by sea power, the English having, as Lord Mountjoy was later to put it, 'the commodity of the sea' to supply them,[2] yet, as the Derry attempts had shown, there was a limit to what could be done to further the conquest by the mere use of shipping. Many parts of the interior, including those in which the measure of the government's power was the extent of the goodwill of the local lords, remained to be penetrated. Even where penetration had been effected, a transformation of the economy based on a complete alteration of the system of land holding, if not of land usage as well, was necessary before English law could be enforced, an acceptance of English rule could be established, and revenue might be produced.

[1] 'A letter sent by I.B.' (concerning Smith's project, 1571) in Hill, *MacDonnells of Antrim*, p. 413.
[2] Moryson, *Itinerary*, ii, 392.

It was in these circumstances that a new generation of Englishmen came to examine afresh the possibility of accelerating the conquest by the development of new English colonies in Ireland. The queen, Sir William Cecil, and the policy makers saw this as a ready method of pushing their advantage in a situation in which the initiative was already theirs. Englishmen, their spirit at once adventurous and practical, recognised the possibility of gain. They had no doubt that the Irish organisation of society was inferior to their own and they could, in reflective moments, convince themselves that they had a mission to amend it. They were aware that the existence of the Irish system of independent local control was an obstacle to attempts to remodel Ireland. They saw too that, in the management of Irish affairs, Englishmen were the ones to trust. It followed that the presence in Ireland of a sufficient number of their compatriots was England's surest resource. But if these men were soldiers, set to dragoon and garrison conquered areas, they would have to be paid and fed, and England's resources were still limited. The alternative was citizen soldiers, sturdy English colonists who would bring with them their own way of life, would guard in arms their newly acquired property, and would, in due course, leaven the mass of the wayward native population. Policy and profit might thus, with a little effort, be combined.

When the introduction of colonists had been tried in Leix and Offaly, the Irish administration had played the part of entrepreneur. It was obvious, ten years later, that this was expensive. Private enterprise, to which the Elizabethans, urged forward by social and economic change in their own country, had shown themselves so much inclined, promised the same, or perhaps even better, results at a cut price. Lord Deputy Sidney, for one, thought so. He advocated, in the years following 1566, the establishment in the hinterland of Carrickfergus of a colony which would be organised not as that in the midlands had been, but 'at sundry men's charges, without exhausting of the prince's particular purse'.[1] Both Cecil and the queen grasped at the possibility of enlisting the profit-seeking motive on a common-stock basis to make Ireland more manageable at less cost. So shone the illusory light.

The removal of Shane O'Neill seemed to clear the way for an enterprise such as Sidney advocated. The project, as well as providing for a northward extension of the Pale, promised the erection of a barrier against Scots interlopers. The queen's title to the land, resting on the succession of the crown to the earldom of Ulster, was understood by the Ulstermen, although they did not accept that Elizabeth, in exercising what she believed to be her rights, could make a reallocation in favour of outsiders of lands which they and their ancestors had occupied for centuries.

The state received various private proposals for the planting of colonies in Ulster. Measures were taken to implement two of them. The first was the

[1] Sidney as quoted in D. B. Quinn, 'Sir Thomas Smith (1513–77) and the beginnings of English colonial theory' in *Amer. Phil. Soc. Proc.*, lxxxix, no. 4 (1945), p. 544.

proposal put forward by the many-sided Sir Thomas Smith, classical scholar, public-office holder, and projector in the ripe spirit of the renaissance. Smith and his son secured a grant in 1571 of a vast area stretching around the coast of Belfast Lough from the Ards peninsula to Lough Neagh, that is to say, the lordship of the O'Neills of Clandeboye. This the Smiths and a band of fellow adventurers were to conquer at their own expense. They were to drive out the upper class of the inhabitants, including the clients who, although they leased land and stock from the O'Neills, might even in normal circumstances elect to go elsewhere, but they were to retain the churls under their rule. These last were to provide the labour force for the English colony which it was proposed to establish and the eventual productivity of which would reimburse, or make the fortunes of, the entrepreneurs. The Smiths were to hold as tenants of the earldom, that is, of the crown. But they assembled a far from sufficient force to make a beginning in the Ards. They landed, a hundred strong, at Strangford Lough in August 1572. Brian MacPhelim O'Neill of Clandeboye, who claimed, with the gaelicised Norman family of Savage, possession of the Ards, reacted vehemently. He had fought against Shane O'Neill and was subsequently an opponent of Turlough Luineach, Shane's successor. Brian was called 'a true subject', and much of the safety of Carrickfergus depended on his being kept on the queen's side. Now, it seemed, he was being deliberately provoked to take up arms against Englishmen. The Smith project failed miserably. The younger Smith, the active leader of the colony, was killed by an Irishman 'of his own household'. Those of his comrades who survived him were swept out of Comber by Brian MacPhelim's followers, and, although Sir Thomas exerted himself to reinforce them, their enterprise had collapsed by 1574.

Meanwhile, the second and more elaborate of the Ulster projects had got under way. This was a scheme in pursuance of which Walter Devereux, earl of Essex since 1572, received a grant of almost the whole of Antrim save the immediate surroundings of Carrickfergus. It was proposed to make good the possession of this area by the exertions of 1,200 soldiers, to be furnished equally by the queen and Essex, and to divide it between the earl and several gentlemen adventurers, with reservations of certain areas for the crown. The rights of the O'Neills, MacDonnells, MacQuillans, and their adherents, the existing landholders or claimants, were totally disregarded. Essex assured the queen that he would not imbrue his hands with more of their blood 'than the necessity of the cause requireth'.[1] In the end, he was no more successful than the Smiths. His activities, rounded off as they were by two acts of savagery, presented the new order in a most unattractive light and did much to stiffen Irish resistance. Some at least of the advocates of these Ulster projects proposed an enslavement of the great mass of the inhabitants,

[1] W. B. Devereux, *Lives of the Devereux earls of Essex* (1853), i, 32; *Cal. Carew MSS, 1515–74*, pp 439–41.

although this was a matter that did not, because of the failure of the schemes, arise. But the fact that such a proposal could have been entertained showed that when, after centuries of preoccupation with their own affairs, the English confronted the Gaelic Irish, they considered them, out of hand and apparently as a matter of course, to be inferior to themselves and even, in the last resort, expendable.

Save for forays in the hinterland and fruitless marches into the interior in 1573–5, Essex's colonists never got far from Carrickfergus. They were opposed by the Irish and the Scots. Brian MacPhelim O'Neill surrendered to Essex, was later proclaimed a traitor, and surrendered again in 1574. The colonists received little local assistance in an area the inhabitants of which were far from united, their most consistent supporter being Hugh O'Neill, baron of Dungannon. Hugh's movements in this early part of his career, following his return from England in 1568, are uncertain, his motives a matter for speculation. He opposed Turlough Luineach, the lord of Tyrone, who, for his part, did all that he could to oppose Essex. It is said that Hugh O'Neill did this of necessity, with an eye to the main chance. At any rate, he stuck close to the English.

Essex was continually at the mercy of circumstance. The queen's Ulster policy was inconsistent, Essex's soldiers poor fellows, his gentlemen associates ill cast in the role of *conquistadores*. Essex's relations with the Dublin administration were for ever awry; indeed friction with the queen's representative's unsteady machine of government was ingrained in the earl's semi-independent enterprise, and in that of the Smiths before him. The cooperation of Sir William Fitzwilliam, lord deputy following Sidney's departure in 1571, which the queen enjoined, was scarcely ensured by Fitzwilliam's knowledge that it was proposed, with so much to be done elsewhere, that the Ulster venture should receive priority treatment and that the office of deputy should be given to Essex. And the Irish victims of the exercise made their own use of their opponents' confusion of authority. They were, they said, 'no rebels'. They sought only to defend 'their own lands and goods'. They suggested that if the struggle really were the queen's war, Fitzwilliam, and not Essex, would have been appointed to lead it.[1] Essex was, to strengthen his hand, made governor of Ulster. Moving his base from Carrickfergus to the Pale, he sought a meeting with Turlough Luineach at the river Blackwater. But he found Turlough as coy as Sussex had found Shane O'Neill. No meeting occurred. The earl then crossed southern Tyrone to Lifford, received supplies from ships which had come to the Foyle from Carrickfergus, met O'Donnell, and tentatively conferred with him. Hugh O'Donnell, to whom Essex restored Lifford castle, which the late Calvagh's son Conn had held as his own, undertook, perhaps cynically, to oppose Turlough Luineach when the queen did. Essex burnt

[1] *Cal. S.P. Ire., 1509–73*, p. 530.

Turlough's corn, but Fitzwilliam was rightly sceptical of the value of the expedition.

Then followed Essex's essays in frightfulness. Brian MacPhelim of Clandebôye and a party which he had assembled to hold a parley at Belfast in October 1574 were attacked without warning by an English force. Two hundred were killed. Brian, his wife, and his brother were taken to Dublin, where they were executed. This, the Irish annalists were soon to say, 'was a sufficient cause of hatred and disgust [of the English] to the Irish'.[1] A massacre of more than 500 Scots on Rathlin Island, which took place in July 1575, was the last act in Essex's abortive attempt at colonisation. It too failed in its purpose, for Rathlin, which, as a staging post on the way to and from the south Hebrides, was described as 'the greatest enemy that Ireland hath . . ., the only succour of the Scots',[2] proved impossible to retain.

The government gained nothing in Ulster in these years. Essex built a bridge across the Blackwater north of Armagh in 1575 in the hope of opening such a passage into the heart of the province as Sidney had opened into Connacht by building the bridge of Athlone eight years earlier, but the O'Neills were still disputing the crossing of the Blackwater with the advancing forces of the crown at the end of the century. Turlough Luineach O'Neill, following his marriage to Agnes Campbell, the widow of James MacDonald, in 1569, posed a problem for the English. He had submitted to Sidney in 1567, professing willingness to renounce the name of O'Neill, that is, to accept the conditions of Shane's forfeiture, but his continuance in independence and his Scottish marriage suggested ominous possibilities. Scotland was in ferment, following the deposition of Queen Mary and her detention in England, and the earl of Argyle, who was Mary's supporter and was as powerful in the west Highlands as the O'Neills were in Ulster, was Agnes Campbell's brother. Retrospection may suggest that Queen Elizabeth had, in reality, little to fear from any of these peripheral figures, whose outlook was, in each case, bounded by a limited self-interest, but their Gaelic world was little known to an arrogant, but still apprehensive, England, and uncertainty bred suspicion. Fitzwilliam believed that Turlough had 3,000 Scots mercenaries in his service after his marriage, and English fears were heightened by the fact that O'Donnell too had married a Scot, Agnes's daughter, Finola. Agnes greatly impressed Sidney when Turlough, 'eaten out' by his mercenaries, again submitted in 1575, and, with her ability to discern where the main chance lay, she probably restrained rather than incited her vacillating husband. Apprehension concerning the possible outcome of Scots–Irish intrigue did not subside until the execution of Queen Mary in 1587.

The year 1575 marked a lull in the affairs of Ulster. The government had,

[1] *A.F.M.*, v, 1679 (1574).
[2] P.R.O., S.P. 63/28, p. 10.

for the moment, gained its point, which was to restrain Turlough from attempting to exercise authority over his neighbours, the O'Neill 'urraghs' (sub-chiefs), and from bringing in undue forces of Scots mercenaries to help him to do so. But those who bore arms in Ulster, the Irish lords and their followers, the Scots who came in the spring of each year seeking hire, or seeking to consolidate themselves in Antrim, the English who marched up from the Pale and burnt the corn—all, the occasional passages of pure savagery apart, merely went through the motions of violence. No one was as yet powerful enough to fight for and to enforce a lasting settlement. Essex most notably underestimated the force necessary to subdue Ulster. At any rate, the possibility for the English of making headway in that province vanished for the moment in 1575 when, in the interest of economy, a third of the queen's force in Ireland was disbanded.

Munster and Connacht, where the Dublin administration was well on the way to total commitment in the struggle between the crown and independent local authority, demanded more of Fitzwilliam's attention, and that of Sidney, following his return as deputy in 1575, than Ulster. The institution of the presidencies did not immediately transform the south and west. The presidents were intrusive, their resources were limited, and, dependent as they were on the support of the deputy and council, their fortunes were conditioned by the play of personalities. Fitton got on badly with Fitzwilliam, both when he was president of Connacht and later when he became vice-treasurer. Perrot, the president of Munster, thought that Essex was bent on discrediting him. Both Fitton and Perrot were irascible. The scheme of local administration that the presidents sought to implement ran counter in Connacht to the ambitions of the earl of Clanricard and in Munster to those of the earl of Desmond. In general, the local lords, great and small, opposed the presidents, and, since the state was not yet strong enough to dispense with whatever assistance the lords were willing to give, the presidencies suffered, in their early years, from the extemporaneous nature of government policy. This was particularly noticeable in Munster, where Perrot continued his vigorous career of law enforcement and the discouragement of Gaelic institutions. The fourteenth earl of Desmond was, contrary to Perrot's advice, permitted to return to Ireland in 1573. Required to remain for the moment in 'easy restraint' in Dublin, he soon decamped to his earldom and, treating his followers to the symbolism of an appearance in the proscribed Irish dress, created the impression that he was about to retract the promises on condition of which his long imprisonment in London had been terminated: that is, to keep the peace, to accept the reformed church, and not to interfere in the affairs of his neighbours. It had been hoped that Desmond would help Perrot. But the earl was the victim of the transition that he had been sent home to assist. Within a decade, circumstances had forced him to demonstrate the irreconcilability of an earldom such as his and the Tudor machine.

Sir Henry Sidney, whose final period of office in Ireland extended from 1575 to 1578, was, in one sense, before his time. Articulate, competent, energetic, more far-seeing and imaginative than any other representative of the queen, and as well connected at court as was possible in that age of uncertainty, Sidney did much to advance the cause of England in Ireland. But his position was a false one. He was expected to govern a country a great part of which could not, in the English sense, be governed until its conquest had been completed. Furthermore, he was expected to curtail expenses. In his time, when visions of frugal colonisation were still entertained, nobody realised, or was willing to admit, that a complete conquest was impossible without unprecedented expenditure. Sidney, whose bent was administration and not conquest, seemed fated to be frustrated. Perrot and Fitton were absent at the same time from their presidencies, which meant that much of Sidney's effort in his last years in office was directed to the performance of duties of which he had earlier hoped the establishment of the presidencies would relieve him. The earl of Desmond, in particular, profited by Perrot's absence. He did what he could to rehabilitate himself and was soon making progresses through his dominion, conferring with his neighbours and recovering castles of which Perrot's efforts had deprived him. Sir William Cecil, Lord Burghley since 1571, did his best to woo Desmond in 1574. He sent messengers, one of whom was the earl of Essex, to ask him what mark he shot at. But Desmond was wary. He professed loyalty to the queen, although he was reported to have said that, for the future, Irish and not English law would be administered in his territory. Induced to go to Dublin on safe conduct to confer with the council, he alleged ill-treatment. His bluff was, however, easily called. Spurred on by the queen, who said that Desmond was a rebel and must be treated as such, Fitzwilliam bestirred himself for the last time before his replacement by Sidney. Ormond assisted him and Desmond's castle of Derrinlaur near Clonmel was taken in August 1574. The defenders were executed. This sufficed, for both sides. Desmond submitted, although nothing was done to bind him for the future.

Fitzwilliam, whose administration was considered costly, had always claimed that lack of money made such superficial government as this inevitable. He had accepted the inevitability, and although rumour spoke of a widespread conspiracy, involving Desmond and Turlough Luineach, against the English power in Ireland, a conspiracy which threatened Spanish, or perhaps French, intervention in the catholic interest, he had, in effect, left Ireland to the local lords. Now Sidney was expected to show more activity, to produce more favourable results—and to spend less.

He was certainly active. By the summer of 1576 he had moved on a mission of inquiry, conciliation, and administrative settlement through east Ulster, the Pale and south Leinster, Munster and south Connacht. The cumulative effect of his demonstration at local level of the working of authoritative government was considerable. For one thing, his execution of malefactors, men who would have lived to make a different atonement for their misdeeds if they had been tried according to Irish law, left no possibility of apathy.

Sidney found the northern frontier of the Pale and, beyond it, Armagh, parts of Down, and the surroundings of Newry and Carrickfergus—the places where a penetration of Irish territory had been attempted—much wasted. Raiding from beyond the frontier had declined, but the billeting and movement of soldiers had impoverished the community. Kildare, Carlow, and most of south Leinster were still intermittently lawless. The settlements in King's and Queen's counties, where Rory Óg O'More, claiming the lordship of Leix, was openly hostile until his death in 1578, were declining and the revenue they produced was slight.

Sidney's visits to Waterford, Cork, Limerick, and Galway were the occasions of scenes that are reminiscent of the surrenders to Henry VIII. He was met with obsequiousness and promises. The earls of Desmond, Thomond, and Clancare, the less prominent local lords, including 'many of the ruined relics of the ancient English inhabitants', several bishops, and some of the MacSwiney captains of galloglass came to him to Cork. Galway, where Sidney spent three weeks, attracted a similar gathering of notables, Irish and Old English, ecclesiastical and lay, some of them, as he claimed, crying 'for English government'.[1] He completed the shiring of Connacht, which Fitton had already put in hand, and, basing his division on a tentative survey, made the new County Galway from the area of Clanricard's paramountcy, County Mayo from the dominion of MacWilliam Burke and his neighbours, and Counties Sligo and Roscommon from the lordships of the two branches of the O'Connor family. Sheriffs were appointed in Clare and Mayo. Following the accepted pattern of the recognition for the moment of local realities, MacWilliam, O'Flaherty of Iar Connacht, and O'Connor Sligo were made seneschals of what had been their lordships.

A discordant note, indicating that promises were not performance, was struck by Clanricard's sons, the Mac an Iarla half-brothers, who had been irreconcilable since the 1560s. Brought by Sidney as prisoners to Dublin, they soon escaped, and, recrossing the Shannon and emulating Desmond by exchanging their English garments for Irish clothes, reverted to violence. Their actions proved to Sidney that their father's professions of allegiance were no substitute for a strict presidential control. The deputy returned at once to the west, where Clanricard acknowledged his sons' treason and besought the queen's pardon. The earl was later imprisoned. Sidney

[1] *Sidney letters*, i, 105–6. See Sidney's 'Memoir of government in Ireland' in *U.J.A.*, series 1, iii (1855), pp 33–44, 85–99, 336–57; v (1857), pp 299–315; viii (1860), pp 179–95.

settled Sir William Drury in office as president of Munster at Limerick, and then, going again to Galway, placed Sir Nicholas Malby as military governor of Connacht. These men, both of them soldiers, used violence to combat what the state called lawlessness, but what retrospection shows us to have been the inevitable reaction of vested interests to an enforced change in the pattern of society. Drury struck at the galloglass and the lords' retainers in Munster, men who represented the organised violence that was the sanction of local independence; in Connacht, Malby, in opposing the Mac an Iarla brothers and the turbulent Burkes of Mayo, set himself also to combat a new enemy of the crown, the Scots mercenaries.

These latter were Scots from the western Highlands and islands, men with the same background as the original galloglass and the would-be settlers in Antrim. Driven to seek an outlet for their activities in Ireland by political and economic pressure, and apparently by a rising population in their homeland, they sought to push their chances of seasonal mercenary employment southward into Connacht, and even north Munster. They came in large numbers, and were drawn to troubled areas by a system of communications that the English could not interrupt. Together with the established galloglass, they made possible from the 1550s to the 1580s much of the warlike activity of the Connacht lords. Malby said that they were 'the only hope that any evil-disposed Irishry have to sustain them in their enterprises'.[1]

Burning houses and corn, sparing 'neither old nor young', and executing those who sought to defend castles against him, Malby had quieted southern Connacht by 1578. To the Irish and Old English, he and Drury were unattractive outsiders, arrogant and ruthless men whose system threatened a wide spectrum of the existing society, from the learned class, the jurists, poets, and musicians to the men of war. Suspect of the same sadism as that shown by Humphrey Gilbert, who had 'killed man, woman, and child' and had terrorised Munster by exhibiting to the people 'the heads of their dead fathers, brothers, children, kinsfolk and friends',[2] Malby and Drury were seen by the Gaelic and gaelicised feudal aristocrats as 'English churls', part of a nation against which Irish antagonism mounted steadily. The provincial governors were looked at askance too, because their proposed reformation threatened to increase the burdens of the landholders as a whole. Malby and Drury both sought to abolish the Irish system of exactions, and hoped to establish instead a uniform land tax which would increase the revenue of the state and help to pay for the queen's soldiers. The question for Connacht and Munstermen was whether this proposal, apart

[1] *Cal. Carew MSS, 1575–88*, p. 272. See P.R.O., S.P. 63/126, p. 17; Hayes-McCoy, *Scots mercenary forces*, pp 12–14, 109–14, and A. McKerral, 'West Highland mercenaries in Ireland' in *Scot. Hist. Rev.*, xxx (1951), pp 1–14.

[2] Thomas Churchyard, *A generall rehearsal of warres* . . . (London, 1579).

from its other disadvantages, would cost them more than they would have to pay if their institutions remained unaltered.[1]

The question of revenue naturally disturbed the country as a whole. Sidney knew that it was impossible to govern Ireland without the support of an army, payment for which made by far the greatest call on the public purse. He chafed continually under the queen's dissatisfaction at the army's rising cost and made every effort to oblige Ireland to contribute to the support of the forces which, in the English interest, were keeping her in order. The result was a struggle which must have embittered his last years. The Palesmen, no less than the Munster and Connacht landholders, objected to being made responsible for the expense of the army, but whereas, in the south and west, the objection was to the overthrow of a whole institutional system, in the Pale it was a matter of consent to be taxed. The government held that a fixed contribution in lieu of cess, or the charge levied for the upkeep of soldiers, was a customary payment and that the royal prerogative, as exercised by Sidney, was a sufficient warrant for its imposition. The Palesmen claimed that taxation could be levied only by parliament and that fair prices for food for the army, which they were willing to supply, should be fixed by the same body. In their view, the cess, by which provisions were taken up 'at mean and low prices' not only for the army but for the deputy's household, was no better than the coyne and livery that successive statutes had proscribed. The quarrel, which was settled for the moment by compromise in 1579, showed again the mounting aversion of the Irish-born to English bureaucracy. Government had to proceed with caution lest the universal distaste for the cess might drive the Munster and Connacht lords to make a common cause of their grievances and, upsetting precedent, combine against it.

Sir William Gerrard, who was appointed chancellor in 1576, saw English policy as 'by little and little to stretch the Pale further', to the eventual end of shaping a submissive and revenue-producing Ireland.[2] Everywhere resisted by the lords, the operation was to prove more difficult in Munster than in Connacht, and most difficult of all in Ulster. In Munster, violence escalated. Drury executed hundreds of malefactors, some after sentence in the courts, others by martial law. He and Desmond were soon at loggerheads. Sidney, who left Ireland in 1578 under a cloud of official disapproval because what he had done had cost a great deal of money, had been able to keep the earl of Desmond quiet. On his departure, a new element, the increasing probability of continental intervention in the catholic interest, combined with local unrest to bring about an explosion.

The 1570s, years of international catholic intrigue in favour of Mary Stuart,

[1] Bagwell, *Tudors*, ii, 182–3. See P.R.O., S.P. 63/30, p. 56.
[2] *Cal. Carew MSS, 1575–88*, p. 70.

witnessed renewed efforts to deploy the forces of the counter-reformation in Ireland. These efforts were made largely by the leader of the earlier revolt, the earl of Desmond's cousin James Fitzmaurice Fitzgerald, and by a group of Irish ecclesiastics of whom Maurice Fitzgibbon, papal archbishop of Cashel, was the most active. They were almost entirely frustrated by the dictates of international politics, as the catholic monarchs, Philip II of Spain and the kings and queen-mother of France, saw them. Spain, in particular, was alive to the fact that intervention in Ireland would injure England. It was accepted too that the Irish, since they had resisted protestantism, had a claim for help on religious grounds. Yet Philip, with the revolt in the Netherlands to quell, was not convinced that his best interest lay in a conflict which might drive Elizabeth into alliance with his rivals, the French. The French, on the other hand, had troubles enough at home, and did not wish to add to them by promoting an Anglo-Spanish alliance. England might be provoked, but not lightly attacked. Ireland, then as always, was peripheral. The archbishop of Cashel and Fitzmaurice, after his flight to the Continent in 1575, shuttled about between France and Spain in a sustained but fruitless effort to secure assistance. They made much of Irish religious grievances and exaggerated the support against England they were likely to receive in Ireland. The papacy alone sought to aid them, but Gregory XIII's attempt to do so in 1578 ended in fiasco. Thomas Stukeley, who had served under Sidney in Ireland but was now behaving as an adventurer in the Mediterranean countries, commanded a papal expeditionary force which was designed for Ireland but was deflected to Africa. Fitzmaurice eventually secured the small residue of Stukeley's motley band, and, financed by the church and making use of the Hispano-Irish communications that were already well established by traders and sea rovers, brought it to Kerry in the summer of 1579.

Fitzmaurice was a leader who miscalculated his chances. That he had a potential following was shown by the course of events subsequent to his arrival, but the organisation of the revolt he contemplated was not—what revolutionary's is?—as easy as he supposed. His own fortuitous removal certainly upset everything, but he had ranged against him, and his successors in action had ranged against them, the organised power of England, an overwhelming obstacle to their puny efforts. Against this he and they opposed what they could drum up in an unsettled Ireland, seeking to make positive revolt out of negative discontent, and seeking too to involve a cautious Europe in a probably unrewarding struggle, on their own terms. Real religious persecution was still a long way off in Ireland. Trent had strengthened the determination of the international church to oppose protestantism, even in Ireland, but the English were hated for their interference before they were opposed as reformers and most Irishmen of influence were content to confine their opposition to resentment. Even Fitzmaurice, although we must look upon his concern for the church as genuine, was a Fitzgerald dynast to whom the transition to an English-ordered Munster was as much a challenge as a threat.

The promoters of the crusade changed their ground as they reassessed their chances, or perhaps as their assessments of their audiences' reactions suggested. They had sought in 1570 to induce King Philip to make Don John of Austria king of Ireland (sixteenth-century Irish leaders more than once behaved as though, despite parliament's action in 1541, the crown of Ireland was theirs to bestow), saying 'if we had a king like other nations none would venture to attack us'.[1] Now, following the arrival of Fitzmaurice, they invited the Irish lords to join in their struggle, not against 'the legitimate sceptre and honourable throne of England', but against 'Elizabeth, the pretensed queen of England', a 'she-tyrant' who had 'deservedly lost her royal power by refusing to listen to Christ in the person of his vicar', the pope.[2] Fitzmaurice, with whom came the papal commissary Dr Nicholas Sanders, 'the supporting pillar of the catholic faith', said that he had been appointed general of the catholic force by the pope, but that he intended to act on the advice of the Irish lords, 'whom he took in great part for his betters'. He fought for the restoration of the rights of the old church 'which the heretics have impiously taken away'. If any of those to whom his proclamations were addressed failed to combat heresy, 'it is they who rob Ireland of peace, and not us'.[3] Emotive language, and so perhaps suspect, but at least those who used it, of all who disapproved of the Tudor changes, put opposition to Elizabeth to the test of action.

Fitzmaurice's arrival (17 July 1579) at Smerwick, where he constructed a fortified camp, was the first of a series of events that furthered the English cause by destroying the Desmond lordship. It was also the first flourish of an ideological opposition to things English that was eventually to make impossible the continuance of English rule. Fitzmaurice communicated at once with the earl of Desmond, without whose support his hopes must wither, saying that he longed 'to see us all one'.[4] The newcomers were no more than 700 strong, but they brought arms and money. Drury, lord justice since Sidney's departure, mustered against them by land, as did Sir Humphrey Gilbert by sea. Fitzmaurice sought help from the earl of Kildare, the Munster lords, Turlough Luineach, O'Donnell, and O'Rourke, and, declaring that he and his followers were 'defending our country' and that

1 Irish lords (including Fitzmaurice) to archbishop of Cashel, 4 May 1570 (Arch. Gen. de Simancas, L. 8336, 27).

2 For the extreme catholic attitude to Elizabeth, see statement presented to Philip II of Spain by the archbishop of Cashel in 1571 (*Spicil. Ossor.*, i, 59).

3 Fitzmaurice's declarations are printed in *R.S.A.I. Jn.*, v (1858–9), pp 364–9. *Cal. S.P. Ire., 1574–85*, pp 172–3; *Cal. Carew MSS, 1515–74*, pp 397–400 (mistakenly dated 1569).

4 Ibid., pp 397–400. See P.R.O., S.P. 63/67, pp 32, 33; *Cal. S.P. Ire., 1574–85*, p. 183.

he could pay those who assisted him, tried to enlist mercenaries in Connacht and Ulster.[1]

The enchantment was broken in a month. Fitzmaurice was killed in a chance encounter with the Limerick Burkes (18 August) and the revolt, inevitably, degenerated to the dreary viciousness of a war of extermination. Henry Davells, sent by Drury to confirm Desmond in his allegiance, was murdered by the earl's brother, Sir John of Desmond, who assumed leadership in Fitzmaurice's place. Drury, with whom the earl of Desmond had half-heartedly cooperated, died at the end of September, and Sir Nicholas Malby, fresh from Connacht and reinforced from England, was made temporary governor of Munster. Malby showed his mettle by beating a force of 2,000 men led under Fitzmaurice's papal banner, a new symbol in Irish warfare, by John of Desmond and his half-brother, James, at Monasternenagh, County Limerick, on 3 October, the only considerable engagement of the struggle. Sir William Pelham, a newcomer to Ireland, succeeded Drury as lord justice, and Sir John Perrot, returning to the scene of his earlier exploits, in an age when Englishmen of action were expected to perform as well on sea as on land, was commissioned to patrol the coast so as to forbid the entry of further foreigners. The revolt was for the moment confined to Munster. Turlough Luineach O'Neill, whose horizon was as circumscribed as ever, did nothing to assist it.

Pope or queen? Which of them the earl of Desmond would back was a matter of critical importance—for the ideological protagonists, for the queen's representatives, Pelham, Malby, and the earl of Ormond, who succeeded Malby as general in Munster after Drury's death, and, not least, for Desmond himself. If it had been possible, Desmond would, in all probability, have remained on the fence. Showing no strong religious feelings, he neither trusted, nor was trusted by, the government; his best effort was a shambling support, at first of the state, later of the rebellion. His carping aloofness—like Shane O'Neill's, like Turlough Luineach's—was typically Irish, perhaps because circumstances left the sixteenth-century Irish lords no other role to play. It must have galled him that he was at the mercy of minor figures, such as Drury and Malby, while other minor figures, such as Fitzmaurice and his own brothers, called the pace. Pelham cut the knot by proclaiming him a traitor (2 November).

Following Ormond's arrival, the struggle in Munster took on much of the flavour of the hereditary Butler–Fitzgerald feud. Desmond, who received widespread sympathy but far less active support, abandoned his castles and took to the fields, the deep woods, and the hills. Now fully committed, although he was to make more than one effort to surrender on terms, he pillaged Youghal, where he pulled down the royal arms from the wall of the courthouse and had them trodden underfoot. He said that his struggle was

[1] Letters in *Facs. nat. MSS Ire.*, iv, plate xiv.

to defend the catholic faith and to oppose Englishmen who 'go about to overrun our country and make it their own'.[1] But his opponents, driving westward to Dingle, swept off great herds of cattle, burnt the ripening harvest of 1580, and, in a starving countryside, received the submission of the MacCarthys, O'Sullivans, O'Callaghans, and MacDonoghs. Further submissions followed, and, Malby having resumed his work in Connacht, where he dragooned the Mayo Burkes, resistance was beaten down in the south and west when, unexpectedly, the pope's banner was raised again by James Eustace, Viscount Baltinglass, in Leinster. Baltinglass was another Fitzmaurice, although a more fortunate one, since he was to escape for the moment with his life. A dynamic catholic in a Pale that was by his time fixed in its catholicism but, like the queen, was wary of provoking religious strife, he told Ormond that 'a woman uncapax of all holy orders' could not be supreme governor of the church and that, if it was the queen's wish to administer justice, it was time she began, since Ireland had witnessed 'more oppressing of poor subjects under pretence of justice' in her reign than ever before.[2] He had been in touch with the Desmond rebels since the beginning of 1580, and he joined his neighbour Fiach MacHugh O'Byrne in arms in July and tried to induce the earl of Kildare to make common cause with him. The Leinster revolt had its only success in a rough area where the formal forces of the crown were always at a disadvantage. The new lord deputy, Arthur, Baron Grey of Wilton, a headstrong puritan whom his secretary, the poet Edmund Spenser, was later to defend, was defeated in Glenmalure in August, although the queen's army had been heavily reinforced.

'There was', said Spenser, 'no part free from the contagion, but all conspired in one to cast off their subjection to the crown of England'.[3] Yet the success in Wicklow had but a minimal effect. As was to be shown again and again before the century closed, England, provided that she held on to her gains in accessible places, used her shipping to supply and reinforce her outposts and to protect the coast, and relied on her superior power to redress temporary reverses, could write off losses in the Irish areas. Desmond's followers continued to desert him, and his half-brother James was taken and hanged. The disturbances in Ulster, where the baron of Dungannon's stock still dropped, Connacht, where the Mayo Burkes still carried on their succession struggle, and the midlands, where the O'Connors still refused to be reconciled to expropriation, were all local. Every lord had his own horizon.

Sanders, who remained with Desmond until his death in 1581, kept up communications with Spain and Rome, but when help came to the Munster rebels in September it proved to be little more than a filibustering expedition. San Giuseppe, who brought 600 men to Fitzmaurice's old camp, the Golden

[1] Richard Cox, *Hibernia Anglicana*, i (1689), p. 361.
[2] *Cal. Carew MSS*, *1575–88*, p. 289.
[3] Spenser, *View*, ed. Renwick (1970), p. 19.

Fort at Smerwick, could be disowned by Spain and the pope, although the English saw him as a real danger and took immediate steps to destroy him. It was a weakness in any small invading force that it could not, like Desmond and the warlike Irish lords, lose itself in the countryside when it chose to do so, but must remain a sitting target. The weakness was exploited by Grey, who, accompanied by Ormond, beset the Golden Fort by land and sea, and battered it with his guns. Desmond having made no apparent attempt to relieve them, San Giuseppe's Italians and Spaniards surrendered. Grey sent in 'certain bands' which 'straight fell to execution'. The entire force was slain. Grey, to whom as a protestant zealot the pope's flag, which the invaders showed, was as a red rag to a bull, was frowned on for his severity by many of his English contemporaries, but not by the queen.[1]

Massacres such as that at Smerwick were distinctly an English innovation; the Irish of the time, milder, less tightly bound to the letter, would have called the capacity to perpetrate them an English characteristic. Bringing war to the homesteads of the people in as widespread and ruthless a manner as was done in Munster in the years before 1583, when the last embers of the Desmond revolt were stamped out, was an innovation too. Grey, the advocate of 'fear and not dandling', a 'bloody man [who] regarded not the life of [the queen's] subjects, no more than dogs',[2] would doubtless have subscribed to General Sherman's determination to finish his particular war by making it 'terrible beyond endurance'.

Although the government, with its ever-expanding forces, had the upper hand in Munster from the beginning, the men who led the troops were faced with a difficulty in their attempts to run the earl of Desmond to earth. Ormond, the lord general, was accused of unwillingness, or inability, to bring things to a head. The queen, anxious as always to curtail expense, decided that a general pardon should be granted to all save the leaders, although Grey said that this would mean leaving 'the Irish to tumble to their own sensual government', since each would, ambivalently, demand protection yet remain 'upon his keeping', or, in other words, would maintain his right to be a traitor.[3] In such circumstances, the ultimate destruction of which Spenser is the classic chronicler—'in short space there were none almost left and a most populous and plentiful country suddenly left void of man or beast'[4]—was inevitable, and it was inevitable too that Spenser and his contemporaries should have held the Irish, and not the English, res-

[1] For the controversy regarding the terms of surrender see Alfred O'Rahilly, *The massacre at Smerwick, 1580* (Cork, 1938). For the defence of the fort see J. Hagan (ed.), 'Miscellanea Vaticano-Hibernica (1572–85)' in *Archiv. Hib.*, vii (1918–21), pp 272, 282.

[2] Spenser, *View*, p. 106, reporting contemporary opinion. See N. P. Canny, 'The ideology of English colonization: from Ireland to America' in *William and Mary Quarterly*, series 3, xxx (1973), pp 581–3. Spenser, who was Grey's private secretary, idealises the lord deputy as Sir Artegall in *The faerie queene*, book v: 'The legend of Artegall, or of justice.'

[3] P.R.O., S.P. 63/82, p. 54; 63/83, p. 16.

[4] Spenser, *View*, p. 104.

ponsible for it. The earl of Desmond and his die-hards were stalked like vermin. The slaughter of the earl in Kerry in the winter of 1583 closed, says Bagwell, the medieval history of Munster.[1] Malby used the same drastic methods in Connacht. He chased the Scots out of the province and patched up peace in Mayo and Galway: in Mayo, by recognising the former tanist Richard an Iarainn as MacWilliam, and in Galway, where the earl of Clanricard died in 1582, by hanging one of the Mac an Iarla brothers and making a temporary division of the Burke lands between the other two.

By the time of Grey's recall in August 1582, famine raged even in the Pale and the towns. But it was the Irish, not the new English bureaucracy, who suffered from the effects of waste and exhaustion and from impositions of the soldiery, which, in wartime, far exceeded the burden of cess. The state's efforts were rewarded. The forward policy of Sidney and his successors had by now overcome the opposition of the lords in Munster and Connacht, and it was possible to proceed in earnest with the settlement. Munster, the richer province of the two and the one that, because it was more open to continental invasion, required closer attention, presented a notable opportunity, following the attainder of the late earl of Desmond and his associates in 1586, for complete reformation. This, after elaborate planning, was attempted. Meanwhile, Connacht was dealt with.

The system whereby land, the source of wealth, was owned and used in the Irish and gaelicised areas formed the basis of local independence. The destruction of this independence west of the Shannon was one of the two main objectives aimed at by the government in the settlement negotiated with the Connacht lords in 1585. The other objective was fiscal. Sir Henry Docwra, who helped to establish the settlement, said later that its purpose was

> to take away the greatness of the Irish lords . . . that the inferior subject might be freed from their Irish customs, cuttings and unreasonable exactions, and by knowing what was their own . . . be drawn to depend ever after upon the state, and not on those Irish lords or gentlemen: which also might not only much avail her majesty in time of any stirs or revolts, by drawing the common people from following the great chief lords, but also bring a more certainer yearly rent or revenue into her majesty's coffers.[2]

The landowning class that emerged soon came to view the settlement in another light, if indeed the Connachtmen had not been led from the beginning to set too high a value on the advantages that would accrue from acceptance of the state's proposals; they may well have done so, since the queen had proposed an agreement 'whereby our prerogatives may be known and their rights and titles reduced from the uncertainty wherein it [*sic*]

[1] Bagwell, *Tudors*, iii, 114. [2] Docwra, *Narration*, p. 190.

stood to continue certain for ever hereafter'.[1] The next generation was to argue against Lord Deputy Wentworth, who took a different view, that what was done in 1585 had given their fathers security of title.

The settlement or composition of Connacht, the culmination of the efforts of Sidney and Fitton to improve on a haphazard cess, was the result of work carried out in the late summer of 1585 by commissioners who were authorised to call before them the nobility, chiefs and lords of the province and 'in lieu of the uncertain cess accustomed to be borne to us for the marshal government of that country and of the uncertain cutting and spendings of the lords . . . to compound . . . for a charge and a rent certain to us upon every quarter or quantity of land'.[1] Some of the commissioners were local men, Irish and Old English, but the project was carried through, with the help of the Dublin bureaucrats, by a new lord deputy and a new chief commissioner, or governor, of Connacht. These were the former president of Munster, Sir John Perrot, and Sir Richard Bingham, who was sent to succeed Malby. Malby, having 'placed all Connacht under bondage',[2] had died in the previous year. The composition involved a progression of the commissioners through the province, the empanelling of the principal inhabitants to determine the extent and occupancy of the major holdings in each area, and the entry into indentures, whereby the subscribers undertook to pay a yearly rent to the crown of ten shillings a quarter for usable land, to appear at hostings with an agreed number of men, and to abolish Irish jurisdictions and the system of land and stock allocation that was part of them. Although the tenor of the composition was the same in all areas, special provisions indicate that the state accepted the fact that it was stronger, and more likely to be able to enforce its will, in some parts than in others. Some of the followers both of Ulick Burke, the new earl of Clanricard, and of MacWilliam of Mayo were separately provided for, thus weakening these magnates. Sir Brian O'Rourke, on the other hand, was accepted as the overlord of Leitrim, and, save for a provision for the lives of the existing 'petty lords and captains' who came next in the Gaelic social order above 'the meaner sort of the freeholders', his territory does not appear to have been greatly fragmented.

Much work still remains to be done before we can see clearly how the composition affected the Connachtmen as a whole, of all social classes, but it is at least clear that the great lords were empowered to retain for themselves substantial revenues, derived from land left free of the composition rent, although the state, by curtailing and defining the lords' power, gained its end, which was to prevent their chronic struggle for more power. The sanction of force, which had been so well demonstrated, was no doubt present in the minds of all, and subsequent events were to show that many were dissatisfied; but, on the whole, the composition, speedily made and in some

[1] Text of commission in *Comp. bk Conn.*, p. 4.

[2] *A.L.C.*, ii, 459.

areas incomplete in its coverage, was a success. It created vested interests which operated to consolidate English control. Fiscally, the composition produced a situation in which the province began to pay for itself.

The Munster settlement was, in contrast, tardy; unlike Connacht, Munster had suffered a violent upheaval, and time was needed to organise the new departure which, from the viewpoint of the state as beneficiary of the Fitzgerald collapse, the occasion demanded. Meanwhile, the new lord deputy became involved, with no more success than his predecessors, in the affairs of Ulster. Perrot had large ideas. He saw that, although the Irish lords had never acted together against the crown, their affairs were interrelated, and that disturbance in one area caused trouble in another. In fact, since the lords were now being subjected to a common pressure, the state's efforts invited a common resistance, and, as the pressure increased with the ever-increasing penetration of the interior, the danger of concerted opposition grew progressively greater. The situation required a continued vigilance, which, Perrot thought, could best be maintained by an expansion of the panacea that Sussex had suggested in 1562, encastellation and bridge-building. Perrot proposed a series of garrisoned posts strategically placed throughout the island, and the construction of further bridges on the model of that of Athlone to establish communications between them.

Munster quieted, Perrot saw danger in Ulster, and for the same reasons, that it sheltered local independence and was open to the intervention of outsiders. His plan for the reformation of Ireland called for garrisons at Coleraine, Lifford, and Ballyshannon; he believed that these would prevent the Scots from overrunning north-east Ulster, upsetting the province by supplying mercenary assistance to the lords, and infiltrating, for the same purpose and with the same result, into Connacht. Turlough Luineach's relatively quiet, but still, for the state, ominous, continuance in power in Tyrone was clearly dependent on the great number of Scots mercenaries he retained. Scotland, which Elizabeth's England still strove to dominate, was, in Perrot's mind, the prime enemy, and when the Scots became unusually active in Ulster in 1584 and 1585 he reacted forcefully. The Scots activity had two motives. The MacLeans of Mull and the surrounding isles were the kinsfolk of some of Shane O'Neill's sons, one of whom invoked their aid with a view to securing the succession to Turlough. The MacDonalds of Islay and Kintyre continued to push their chances in north Antrim and the Route. All diversified these activities by mercenary service. Perrot took and garrisoned Dunluce castle in north Antrim, which, it was said, was held for James VI king of Scots. But the Scots, easily reinforced across the North Channel, combined against the English, and Sorley Boy MacDonnell recovered Dunluce before the end of 1585. Suggestions that the young king of Scots was involved in plotting to upset Elizabeth in Ireland evaporated on the conclusion of the treaty of Berwick between England and Scotland in 1586. Angus MacDonnell was confirmed in possession of the Glens of Antrim, Sorley received the Route, and the queen reprimanded Perrot for 'such rash unadvised journeys' as his Ulster expeditions. In Connacht, Bingham, who used martial law to expedite acceptance of the composition, performed what was called 'the only piece of service, next to Smerwick, that hath been done in this land in many years'.[1] This was the massacre at Ardnaree on the river Moy of 2,000 Scots, fighting men, women, and children, led by Angus MacDonnell's brother Donald, who sought to enter service with the dissatisfied Mayo Burkes (22 September 1586).

Ulster was little affected by Perrot's proceedings, but one significant step was taken. Hugh, baron of Dungannon, who had helped Perrot in Antrim, was advanced in the peerage. He became the second earl of Tyrone. Hitherto, he had lived largely on his wits; now he was given, as far as the crown could give them, 'larger territories than any other earl of Ireland'.[2] These included the south-eastern part of Tyrone, for which the new earl was to pay rent to Turlough, and a great part of County Armagh. A reservation of land was, however, made for the fort on the Blackwater. Hugh O'Neill's persistent pursuit of preferment at English hands and his struggle to establish himself among the people of Tyrone had borne fruit in his favour.

Perrot summoned the last of the three Irish parliaments of the reign in 1585. Parliament, which was of secondary importance in the scheme of government, was still a small assembly. The membership of the two houses of the 1585 body, counted together, was little more than a hundred, although this, following increases in the county and borough membership in the commons to keep pace with the territorial extension of English authority, was an advance on the membership of Sidney's parliament of 1569. The commons were, as far as possible and as a matter of course, screened in advance by the administration. A few of them bore Gaelic names, and, as before, many Irish lords, clad in English garments 'which they embraced like fetters', were invited to attend as observers. Turlough Luineach was present, and Earl Hugh took his seat in the upper house along with the Irish earls of Thomond and Clancare and the baron of Upper Ossory. A new formality marked the opening proceedings, and the initiative and driving force remained throughout in the hands of the deputy and the Englishmen, although the Old English, who formed the mass of the assembly, soon showed themselves to be barely cooperative.[3]

Parliament distrusted the administration. A bill proposing the substitution of a land tax for the hated cess was argued through the two parliamentary

[1] *Cal. S.P. Ire., 1586–8*, p. 162.

[2] Proclamation of 1595 against the earl (*Cal. Carew MSS, 1589–1600*, p. 111).

[3] List of members in *Tracts relating to Ireland* (Ir. Arch. Soc.), ii (Dublin, 1843), pp 134–8; E. C. S., *The government of Ireland under Sir John Perrot, 1584–8* (London, 1626), pp 58–60; T. W. Moody, 'The Irish parliament under Elizabeth and James I' in *R.I.A. Proc.*, xlv, sect. C (1939–40), pp 41–81.

sessions and finally abandoned, the state being later forced to abolish the cess and compound instead for an annual payment of £2,100 from Leinster. Religion was another stumbling-block. Hitherto the queen and her advisers had been content to overlook the 'wilful obstinate separation' of the Irish subjects from the state church because they feared that undue severity in regard to religion would increase civil resistance. It was more important that the queen should rule Ireland than that Ireland should abandon the pope. But that climate soon changed. Despite the rebellion of the Netherlands, Philip of Spain had grown stronger. He had made a truce with the Turks and gained Portugal. Allied with the catholic league in France, he might soon control the French channel coast, and, relying on his growing maritime strength, might escalate the cold war into an invasion of England. The 1580s were years of crisis for Elizabeth. In that decade the ideological struggle of protestant and catholic reached the simplification of an equation in which all catholics were traitors, and the still considerable body of English catholics was persecuted accordingly. This hardened attitude was reflected in Ireland, not by attempts to strengthen the established church, which was left to struggle against impossible odds, or, as Spenser suggested, to cherish its 'warm nests' at the expense of God's harvest, but by a pursuit of catholic churchmen as dangerous traitors. Archbishop Dermot O'Hurley, the successor in the see of Cashel of Maurice Fitzgibbon, was tortured 'to gain his knowledge of all foreign practices against her majesty's states'.[1] He was executed for treason in 1584. But their number, which was clearly demonstrated in the proceedings of Perrot's parliament, saved the Irish catholics from the worst cruelties suffered by their co-religionists in England. Perrot was forced to admit the impossibility of coercing the majority into conformity, and to drop government proposals for penal legislation against recusancy. Significantly, no further parliament was summoned during the reign. Later assemblies, if there had been such, might have proved even less cooperative.

The retrospective condemnation of the late earl of Desmond was, however, another matter. Ormond haggled over the fate of lands in Tipperary that were in dispute between Butlers and Fitzgeralds, but parliament made no demur to the attainder of the earl of Desmond and his chief supporters, nor to the vesting of their lands, without inquisition, in the crown. The confiscation had been anticipated by Elizabeth and her advisers. A hasty survey, made in 1584, had shown the dispeopled state of parts of Munster, and the decision had already been taken to seize this golden opportunity of substituting English for Irish inhabitants. Despite the ill success of the earlier ventures, the English mind was still full of the possibilities of colonisation.

The Munster plantation, carefully planned if less successfully executed, was,

[1] *Cal. S.P. Ire., 1574–85*, p. 482.

by contemporary European standards, a major movement of population.[1] As it was continued in the early years of the next century, it added a new and, in terms of wealth and the possession of political power, important element to the Irish population. In all its circumstances—the creation and taking advantage of opportunity, the utilisation of the resources of state, the disregard of the natives—it epitomised the Tudor achievement in Ireland.

The plan of the plantation, to which the queen gave her assent in 1586, was laid by the government in London. Burghley and other court circle enthusiasts, again taking advantage of private enterprise, appealed to the element that had earlier supported Smith and Essex, largely to west country and channel coast magnates. They did so, however, on a much larger scale, and, this time, they made a more determined effort to retain control. Still, they were dogged by the inadequacies of the machine of state. It was one thing to divide up on paper the quarter-million acres of usable land that was supposedly available, granting great areas called seignories to the chosen undertakers and providing for the occupancy of the land by English-born tenants, but it was beyond the power of London to secure a settlement of the colonists on the ground. Many of the English already in Ireland proved lukewarm supporters of the scheme, and Perrot gave little help. So much time elapsed before the first of the planters arrived in Munster that very many of the former occupants had reestablished themselves, either by their success in vindicating their legal claims, although the state favoured the undertakers in the many disputes that arose, or simply by squatting. The new arrivals found that Munster was not a wilderness. It was certainly wasted, but it was already populated, and although the existing inhabitants could be and were enlisted as subtenants and thus helped to initiate the project, their presence, their counter-claims, and their resentment made for confusion, and would soon promote strife.[2]

Little progress had been made by 1588, when the long-drawn-out initial work was complete, but, two years later, a total settler population of at least 3,000 had been fitted in on scattered estates among the Irish and Old English landholders who had survived the upheaval. By 1598, when disaster befell them, there may have been in all 12,000 colonists, men, women, and children, in Munster. These were engaged in arable farming and grazing. They had begun what became a profitable trade in timber for barrel staves, shipbuilding, and other uses, and they paid quit-rents to the crown of £2,000 a year and upwards. The area intended for the colony had been considerably reduced by successful local counter-claims and there were fewer arrivals from England than had been expected, but society in the former Desmond lordship was quite altered by the new element. Formerly,

[1] See D. B. Quinn, 'The Munster plantation: problems and opportunities' in *Cork Hist. Soc. Jn.*, lxxi (1966), pp 19–40.

[2] Robert Dunlop, 'The plantation of Munster, 1584–1589' in *E.H.R.*, iii (1888), pp 250–69.

to draw attention to but one result of the enterprise, the great galloglass family of the MacSheehys, who played a prominent part in the rebellion, had owned perhaps 10,000 acres in County Limerick. Their land was now held by foreign landlords who supported, not the Fitzgeralds, but the presidential system.[1] Munster, like Connacht after the composition, would not be the same again.

Although the Irish impact of the Spanish armada of 1588 was slight, it served to demonstrate what the government had by that date accomplished and what still remained to be done. Perrot's administration had, in the years before that, received frequent reports of an impending Spanish invasion. The armada had no Irish mission and those of the Spaniards who succeeded in landing on the west coast after the failure of their projected invasion of England were castaways and not invaders, but it was significant that they were succoured nowhere save in north Connacht and Ulster. The veteran Sir William Fitzwilliam, who returned to Ireland to succeed Perrot as deputy, proved as wary of Ulster as Perrot had been, and the government, at this time, felt its first suspicion of the earl of Tyrone.

The salient feature of the last decade of the century was the resistance shown by Gaelic Ireland to the completion of the Tudor conquest. That the state would continue its efforts until the sovereignty of the crown had been everywhere established and that the Irish lords would abandon their authority with reluctance were, by that date, alike predictable, but it was not foreseen, after the settlement of Connacht and Munster, that the Gaelic order would prove so difficult to overcome, or that its attempted supersession in Ulster would provoke such a disturbance as it did in other parts of the island.

Its authority newly asserted in the west and south, and, in consequence, its control of Irish affairs tighter than it had been before, the government, following the Tyrone settlement between the new earl and Turlough Luineach, could, it appeared, look to the steady progress of its designs in the north. The threat from Scotland was reduced. Although the plantation schemes had failed in Ulster east of the Bann, the fact that power was uneasily shared by many lords in that area favoured the prospect of an ultimate English penetration from Carrickfergus and Newry. At the other side of the province, the O'Donnell lordship was, to outside appearance, far from stable. The succession to Hugh O'Donnell, lord of Tyrconnell since 1566, would, it appeared, be contested by at least four rival claimants. The O'Donnell claim to overlordship in north Connacht had, it was hoped, been negatived by the composition of 1585, and the government, two years later, had weakened Tyrconnell still further by the seizure of O'Donnell's son, Hugh Roe, and his addition to the stock of hostages held as state prisoners in Dublin castle.

[1] Hayes-McCoy, *Scots mercenary forces*, p. 67.

On the southern border of Ulster, MacMahon's lordship of Monaghan and Maguire's lordship of Fermanagh were both infiltrated by the new authority. Fitzwilliam sought, on the death of Rory MacMahon in August 1589, to have Monaghan divided among the principal MacMahons. Foiled in this, the deputy acknowledged Hugh Roe MacMahon as Rory's successor. When Hugh proved less than cooperative, however, Fitzwilliam arrested him, had him tried, and—startling everybody—saw to his execution. He then effected his original purpose by securing local agreement in 1591 for the division of the lordship on the Connacht pattern. The attempt to subvert the authority of the Maguires in Fermanagh followed the succession of Hugh Maguire to his father Cuchonnacht in 1589. Nominally tributary to Turlough Luineach, the Maguires, who did not impress the English as being a warlike family, had, since the middle of the century, been subjected to intermittent pressure by the O'Donnells. Fitzwilliam tried to substitute the queen for the two would-be overlords, O'Neill and O'Donnell, by establishing a sheriff in Fermanagh. His attempt proved premature. The man chosen to be sheriff, Captain Humphrey Willis, exasperated both the O'Donnells and Maguires by his high-handed actions and was soon forced out of Ulster.

Still, the reduction of Ulster seemed destined to follow the Connacht pattern. Much depended on the continued loyalty to the crown of the new earl of Tyrone. If he were to disappoint the state however, he could not, it seemed, be worse than Shane O'Neill had been, nor could his overthrow prove more difficult than that of the earl of Desmond. The English assessment allowed neither for the reanimation, at the eleventh hour, of Gaelic Ireland, nor for the vigour of the last effort to consolidate Ulster under the rule of the house of Tyrone.

Things looked different from the Irish viewpoint; how different we are unable to say, since the surviving evidence permits but slight insight into any Gaelic Irishman's mind. The outlook was certainly unpromising enough to provoke an increasingly hostile reaction to what must by now have been recognised as the settled methods of the government. Sir Richard Bingham's administration of Connacht showed what the Ulstermen would have to put up with if sheriffs and the paraphernalia of English law enforcement were admitted into the north. The O'Connors of Sligo, the O'Flahertys of Iar Connacht, and the Mayo Burkes, backed by the MacDonnell galloglass, whose livelihood was now doomed, accused Bingham of failure to honour his word, of irregularly dispossessing men of their land, and of a misuse of martial law. Fitzwilliam's government failed to resolve the dispute. Bingham operated the composition and produced revenue, and, since that was what mattered, London supported him. Local feeling was of secondary importance.

But that part of Ulster society which, proud of its institutions and averse to change, influenced opinion in the north was deeply, and, as far as the queen's government was concerned, ominously, affected. For these Ulstermen, the catalogue of English outrage had grown long with the years. The English had tried to poison Shane O'Neill. They had massacred the Scots in Rathlin and at Ardnaree. They had broken faith on occasions innumerable; most of the charges on this head were susceptible of different interpretations, but the killing of Brian MacPhelim of Clandeboye has remained simply an act of treachery. The English had used trickery to seize Hugh Roe O'Donnell. They had, Ulster said, murdered MacMahon and Brian O'Rourke, lord of Leitrim; the latter, who had helped the Spanish castaways in 1588 and had later permitted an effigy of Queen Elizabeth to be made and publicly insulted, was handed over by James VI of Scotland to the queen and was hanged at Tyburn. Rankling for years in the Ulster mind, this evidence of English duplicity bred distrust, fear, and, finally, hatred of the officers of the queen. No more, perhaps, than the inevitable by-product of any central power's effort to establish its supremacy, and matched by some, although not nearly as many, black passages on the Irish side, the state's ruthlessness widened the breach between the English *Herrenvolk* and the less positive, but still unyielding, Irish.

The final stage of the struggle for Ulster had its beginning in Maguire's country. English pressure was exerted, inevitably, from the south-east and south-west, from the Pale and Connacht, the one the original bridgehead of English power, the other the area success in which might hopefully be reinforced to bring the whole west coast and its hinterland under the state's control.

Tyrone, where Turlough Luineach, the earl, and the sons of Shane O'Neill were rivals for power, appeared to the English in 1590 to be no more stable and no less susceptible to control by the state than Tyrconnell. The earl claimed at that time to be no more than 'her highness's lieutenant under the deputy'. Three years later, however, the Ulster lords, the earl included, showed the insubstantiality of English hopes for the future of the province. In the interval, Hugh Roe escaped from Dublin castle, regained Tyrconnell, and, his father retiring from public life, was inaugurated as O'Donnell. Turlough Luineach resigned in 1593 and the earl became, in effect, the ruler of Tyrone. When Turlough died in September 1595 he became O'Neill.

The earl was, at best, a speculative investment for the English. His early associations with Englishmen had, to all appearance, conditioned him to be a supporter of the state, and his position in Ulster depended initially on the state's backing. Only the state could, however, attain power in Ulster outside the existing institutional system. Therefore the earl, who sought power at all stages of his career, was forced by his ambition to move upward, not as the queen's servant but as a Gaelic dynast. He had to make his way where he lived. Accordingly, while maintaining his connections with the Leicester–Sidney interest of his London days, while assisting Essex, Perrot, and Fitzwilliam and supporting the government's efforts in Desmond, he consolidated his position where his real interest lay, and where his rivals operated.

His inheritance, augmented by his settlement with Turlough, whose own territorial location was at Strabane, at the other end of the lordship, established the earl at Dungannon, which, with Tullaghoge, the place of inauguration, lying to the northward, had been the centre of O'Neill power since the fourteenth century. In that area he controlled the *lucht tighe Uí Néill*, which the English called the 'lotie' or 'household or demesne land of the Oneales'.[1] Gradually, he won the support of the hereditary Tyrone galloglass family, the MacDonnells of Knockinclohy, and of the east Tyrone lords, the O'Hagans, O'Quinns, MacCanns, O'Devlins, and others. This provided him with a much more realistic basis of power than Turlough Luineach's Scots mercenaries. It meant that the earl, to add to his new dignity in the peerage, was in effective control in the Gaelic sense of the more important part of the O'Neill lordship. When his persistence was rewarded in 1595 by the succession to Turlough, it meant also that, whatever he was in blood, the O'Neills and their supporters had accepted him as a member of the royal house, and had preferred him as a ruler to Turlough and Agnes Campbell's son Art, to the MacShanes, and to all other claimants. He became the greatest of the Irish lords, and the historic O'Neill claim to the overlordship of Ulster was, at the moment when the crown was about to make an issue of sovereignty in the north, his to exploit.

When this man decided to oppose the crown seems impossible to determine. His acceptance of the O'Neillship, although it suggests his belief that the old order could be continued in central Ulster, was not necessarily a declaration of war against the queen. He said that if he had not accepted it someone else would, and this was true. Local sovereignty in Tyrone and subjection to the crown were scarcely compatible, but transition condones anomaly; the earl was to maintain himself, quietly if ambiguously, a potential sovereign to the Ulstermen but a peer of the realm to the English, for some years, and the evidence indicates that he thought it not impossible to continue the practice indefinitely.

Since the Maguires, O'Donnells, and O'Neills were interrelated, the developing confederacy of the Ulster lords has the quality of a family compact. Hugh Maguire, the earl's son-in-law, mounted, in 1593, a preemptive campaign against the English officials who, with the obvious intention of implementing his father's surrender of 1585, were threatening to surround and displace him. Maguire claimed later that he had been forced into rebellion by these men. Events soon showed that he had the support of his cousin O'Donnell. As time passed, the English came to believe that it was the earl, who was much the senior of these young men, who goaded them on.

[1] So called in Richard Bartlett's map of 1603 (P.R.O., MPF 36). See *Ulster maps c. 1600*, xiii, 8, and Éamon Ó Doibhlin, *Domhnach Mór* (Omagh, 1969), pp 43–62.

For the moment, however, the earl gave ineffectual assistance to the queen by negotiating with Maguire and O'Donnell, and, since no settlement was possible while the government remained determined to have its way, by assisting the marshal, Sir Henry Bagenal, to overawe Fermanagh in October 1593. In the following February the English captured Enniskillen castle, a place of major importance in the event of further aggression against Tyrone, and an addition to the already garrisoned posts of Carrickfergus, Newry, Blackwater fort, and Monaghan. O'Donnell, Maguire, O'Rourke, and the MacMahons, threatened alike with an unpalatable reorganisation, all sought, in the following years, to remove the queen's soldiers from their front. So, encouraged by his dislike of Bagenal, did the earl. As had been shown elsewhere in Ireland and was now to be demonstrated in Ulster, the government's difficulty lay not in planting such garrisons in remote places, but in maintaining them. Enniskillen was, in the circumstances, untenable and was retaken by Maguire in May 1595.[1]

The earl of Tyrone's connivance at what was called the treasonable conduct of his neighbours was shown more clearly in 1595, when his brother Cormac, leading a force of Tyrone men, assisted Maguire. Whether he seemed to help his neighbours or the state, however, the earl consistently sought to increase his own strength. The government had authorised him to maintain an armed peace-keeping force within the area of his jurisdiction. He took advantage of this to resume Shane O'Neill's scheme for the militarisation of his lordship. He bought arms, ammunition, and equipment in the western Scottish Lowlands, and, in cooperation with O'Donnell, sent agents to the west Highlands to seek mercenary forces. The Irish council noted in December 1594 that the other Ulster lords had been 'drawn to his party', and that 'her majesty's best urraghs'—the Gaelic phrase is significant—had been forced out by the earl's efforts to establish his own paramountcy.[2] At this stage, in conferences with commissioners appointed by the government and in a statement to the earl of Ormond, Tyrone, acting again the part affected by Shane, alleged that his ambiguous conduct was the consequence of Fitzwilliam's and Bagenal's antipathy to him. If the queen and Burghley had been content to agree to give him the exclusive administration of Ulster as a separate government, the earl might, for the moment at least, have remained cooperative.

The real struggle began in 1595. In February, Tyrone sent his brother Art to attack, capture, and later destroy the fort and bridge that the earl of Essex had built at the river Blackwater, thus removing, although he had helped Essex to establish it, a post that had become as obnoxious to him as the Armagh garrison had been to Shane. Six months earlier, Tyrone had gained a point in what had by then become a game of bluff by appearing unexpectedly in Dublin on the day following Fitzwilliam's departure for

[1] See map 3. [2] *Cal. S.P. Ire., 1592–6*, p. 284.

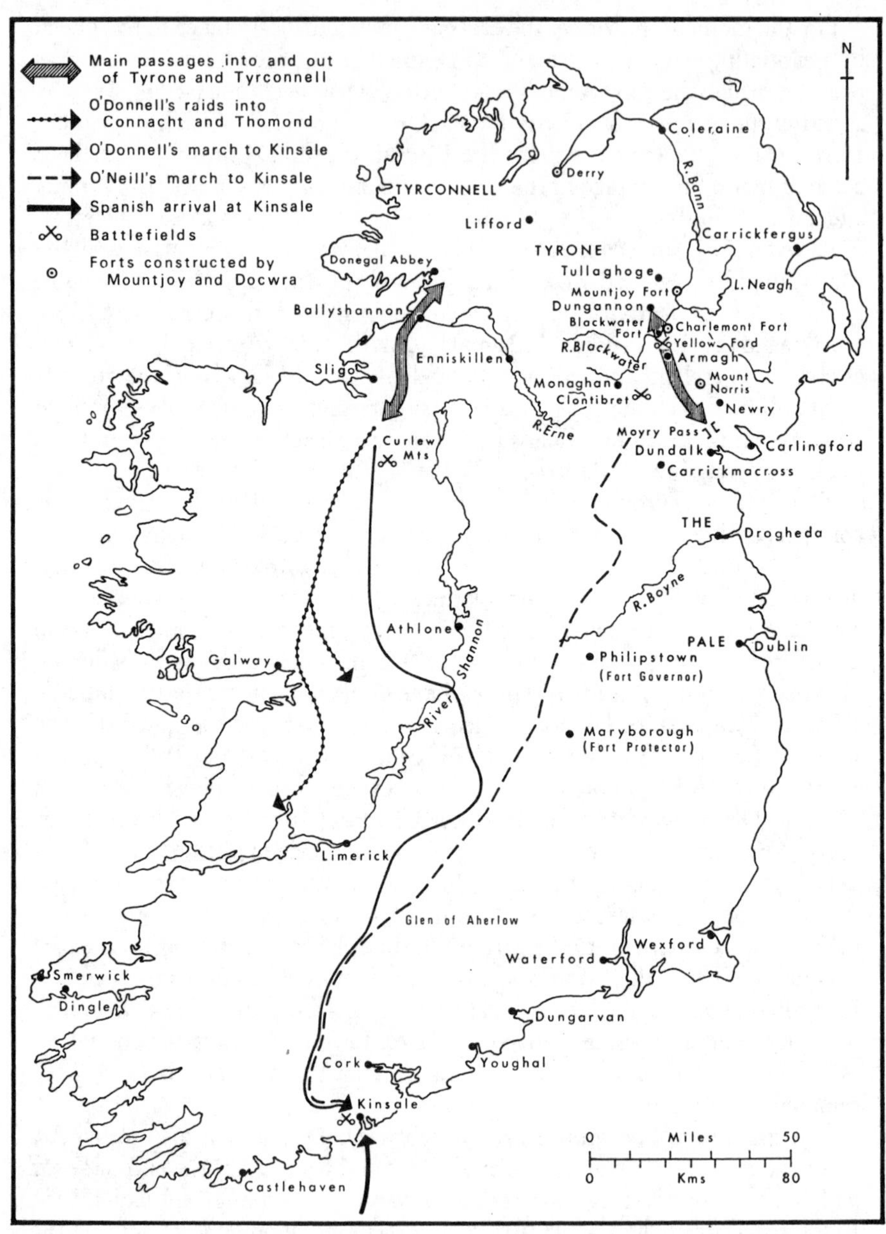

Map 3 HUGH O'NEILL'S REBELLION, 1593–1603, by G. A. Hayes-McCoy

England. Sir William Russell, to whom Fitzwilliam handed over the sword of state, was too much of a newcomer to rally the council against so obsequious a suppliant as Tyrone. Promising to mend his ways, and, in particular, to eject the Scots mercenaries and use his influence to cause his rebellious neighbours to submit, the earl was, to the queen's chagrin, permitted to return to Ulster. The O'Neill name, although it seemed blown upon, still inspired respect. By the summer of 1595, following the earl's attack at Clontibret on a large force under Bagenal that had been sent to bring supplies to Monaghan, it struck awe. In this, Tyrone's first personal confrontation with the state, the earl was reported to have said that 'it should be seen whether the queen or they should be masters of the field and owners of Ulster'.[1] Bagenal escaped, although he was severely mauled. In what was to become O'Donnell's sphere of operations in the struggle for Ulster which had now so plainly begun, Sligo was lost to the state, and O'Donnell was soon more powerful than Bingham in north Connacht. The position on the west coast was, in fact, reversed. The hope of Bingham and others had been, prior to this, that Sligo might be used to secure the occupation of Ballyshannon, the gateway to Tyrconnell. Thenceforward, the state was on the defensive in Connacht.

The earl of Tyrone was proclaimed a traitor in June. He had lost face, and was now called, in reversal of the crown's earlier view, 'the son of one Matthew . . . a bastard son of Conn O'Neill'.[2] Russell, flourishing the proclamation, but wary, since Clontibret, of the earl's military capacity, showed force by advancing to the Blackwater. The crown forces had been augmented by men withdrawn from service against the Spaniards in Brittany and by one of the periodic and widely unpopular levies of manpower which, made throughout the English shires, must have done much to rouse public opinion against Ireland. The aggressive potential of the state was further increased by the appointment of Sir John Norris, who had earlier been seconded from the presidency of Munster and was now fresh from success in Brittany, to act as military commander. The strength of the army had risen by the end of 1595 to 7,000 men, yet nothing had been done to chasten Ulster. Armagh was garrisoned, but it immediately became a liability, since another Clontibret was risked every time the garrison ran out of supplies.

Evidence of the earl's complicity in a widespread rebellion increased as his and his accomplices' ability to deny entry to Ulster to the queen's servants became more manifest. The government was aware by 1595 that the Ulster lords were in communication with Philip II of Spain with a view to securing his support against Elizabeth. Their efforts had begun in 1593, when a group of Ulster and Connacht ecclesiastics had associated themselves with O'Donnell and Maguire in an approach, through the Irish political exiles then in Spain, to the Spanish crown. They sought military assistance.

[1] Perrot, *Chron. Ire., 1584–1608*, p. 93.

[2] *Cal. Carew MSS, 1589–1600*, p. 111.

The earl joined in the request, probably early in 1595. Communications were interrupted, and Philip, preoccupied with his struggles against the Dutch and English in the Netherlands and Brittany and his intermittent hostilities with the changeable French, proved non-committal. But the Ulstermen, more likely to be heard now that the earl was seen to have joined them, redoubled their efforts. The earl and O'Donnell, some of whose letters were intercepted by the English, asked for 3,000 men.[1]

The pattern that the Ulster struggle was to follow for the next six years was now set. The earl of Tyrone was the accepted leader of a group of lords some of whose ancestors had been the traditional enemies of the O'Neills. He was engaged in a defensive struggle the primary aim of which was the preservation of the existing order within Ulster. The Spanish assistance for which he and his colleagues had called would, obviously, not be forthcoming for the narrow purpose of maintaining the local paramountcy of a group of leading families. Accordingly, or, it may well be, because their immediate ambition left room for wider and perhaps more idealistic aspirations, the Ulstermen represented their cause as an Irish one. They spoke of their grievances as those of 'the whole Irish nobility', and, in 1595, they offered the crown of Ireland to Philip if he would deliver them from their English oppressors.[2] As well as this, they claimed to be the champions of the old church in its contest with protestantism. But their determination to resist the hitherto all-powerful state and to seek Spanish assistance in doing so was tempered by the prospect of a change which might for them be an improvement in the English attitude to Ireland following the death of the ageing queen and suggested the necessity for caution and delay. They could not, as they awaited developments, afford to risk defeat, since it would inevitably cause defection from their association. In these circumstances, the Ulstermen were to seek in the years to come to hold on to their part of Ireland by the exercise of policy and force. They were to be assisted in doing this by the nature of a terrain that gave their forces every advantage over the armies of the queen, by the skill of the earl in organisation and diplomacy, and by the English reluctance to incur increased expense by having recourse to extremities before it was absolutely necessary to do so.

For Ulster, 1596 was a year of manœuvre. The earl, apparently to gain time, had begun negotiations with Norris in the previous year. Norris favoured compromise, because, lacking a field force, he believed he had no alternative. The government, anxious to save money and still hoping to intimidate or outmanœuvre the rebels, continued the discussion. The Ulstermen held out for liberty of conscience, or at least for immunity from harass-

[1] See J. J. Silke, 'The Irish appeal of 1593 to Spain' in *I.E.R.*, series 5, xcii (1959), pp 279–90, 362–71.

[2] *Cal. Carew MSS, 1589–1600*, pp 122–3; *Cal. S.P. Ire., 1592–6*, pp 406–7, 409–10.

ment for their clergy. They asked that their transgressions of the royal authority should be pardoned, that, in effect, the state structure should be swept back in Ulster to Newry and Carrickfergus, and that O'Donnell's claims in Connacht should be acknowledged, which would have upset the composition. The queen was for long unwilling to reinstate Tyrone in his earldom, or to admit that he had any authority over his neighbours. She wished him, in one of the lapses from realism that her parsimony from time to time occasioned, to be economically opposed. Ultimately, but far from conclusively, he was pardoned in May 1596, having agreed to break off his negotiations with Spain and to abandon his efforts to establish his authority east of the Bann. His status elsewhere in Ulster was left vague. His colleagues, O'Donnell having tried meanwhile, with local assistance, to reconstitute the Irish lordships in north Connacht, were similarly pardoned.

In fact, the likelihood of Spanish intervention increased in 1596, the year in which the English sacked Cadiz. Messengers from Philip II arrived in Ulster, bringing arms and ammunition to O'Donnell and conferring, in May and again later, with the earl. Their chief, Alonso Cobos, viewed the west coast with the intention of recommending a landing-place. The Spaniards favoured Limerick, O'Neill and O'Donnell Galway. As was to be confirmed in 1601, and as indeed military and political necessity dictated, both the Irish and Spaniards understood that, when the revolt was intensified, and defence gave place to aggression, action must occur outside Ulster. Two expeditions, one destined for Ireland and one for the south-west coast of England, set sail in October, but both were overwhelmed by storms and their survivors were forced back to Spain.

In this period, which the English were to remember as one of 'deluding parlies', Tyrone and his associates, adopting the role of champions of 'Christ's catholic religion', called on 'the gentlemen of Munster' to join the Ulster confederacy and to 'make war with us'.[1] The commencement of attacks on the Munster settlers showed that the call was heard. Reaction to the methods that had, in recent years, been used by Bingham and others and mounting exasperation at the overbearing demands of the state's augmented military force tempted many, of whom the most notable was Fiach MacHugh O'Byrne of Wicklow, to rebel.

Two newcomers, both with experience of continental warfare, Thomas, Lord Burgh, who replaced Russell as deputy, and Sir Conyers Clifford, who succeeded Bingham in Connacht, brought on a brief renewal of hostilities in 1597. Burgh, convinced that the Ulstermen had only to be faced to be overcome, sought to invade the north by an advance on his own part through Armagh and a simultaneous movement by Clifford towards Ballyshannon. They forced their way across the Blackwater and Erne, but neither of them could overcome mounting opposition and go further. Before he died of

[1] *Cal. Carew MSS, 1589–1600*, p. 179.

typhus at Newry in October, Burgh made a disposition that was to embarrass the crown in the following year. He dug and garrisoned a field fortification—the Portmore of the Irish and the Blackwater fort of the English—to cover the ford of the Blackwater close to the site of Essex's former bridge. The earl of Tyrone promptly blockaded it.

Burgh was the first viceroy to have died in office for sixty-two years. His death and that of Sir John Norris, which occurred some weeks earlier, placed civil and military authority in Ireland in the hands of a committee, with the inevitable consequences of indecision and procrastination. Burgh was not replaced until 1599, when the queen's favourite, the second earl of Essex, was appointed lord lieutenant. Meanwhile, Archbishop Loftus and Chief Justice Gardiner acted as justices, and the military command was given to the elderly, although by no means inactive, Ormond, arrangements which must have suited Tyrone. The two earls met in December. Tyrone submitted to Ormond, with another promise of reformation, but no abatement of his demands. A truce followed.

By the summer, when the period of truce came to an end, the problems of the northern rebellion were narrowed to the single question of what was to be done about Blackwater fort, which was closely beset by Tyrone and the garrison of which was starving. Any attempt to relieve the fort was certain to be contested and could be made only by a large force, which, on its approach and return, must cross ground favourable to the use of the tactics of controlled attack of which the Ulstermen had shown themselves to be masters. The risk of disaster was great, and, in the long debate of the matter which took place, Ormond and the council inclined towards cutting their losses and writing off Burgh's 'scurvy fort of Blackwater'. But they feared the inevitable consequence of the queen's wrath. The impasse was resolved by the arrival of reinforcements, and by an offer of the marshal, Sir Henry Bagenal, to lead a relief expedition. A marching force of over 4,000 men was mustered: old soldiers of the Irish warfare, many of them Irishmen, men brought back from the struggle against the Spaniards in Picardy, and raw recruits from England. Ormond, who had much experience of the Irish methods of fighting, avoided the obvious duty of going himself and permitted Bagenal, despite his lack of military training and his earlier shortcomings, to assume command. The result was disaster. The earl, O'Donnell, and Maguire attacked Bagenal on the march at the Yellow Ford, between Armagh and the Blackwater, on 14 August, and defeated him with a loss in killed, wounded, and missing of nearly half his force.[1] Bagenal was killed. The survivors got back to Armagh, whence they made their way out of Ulster—a broken army that had lost the greater part of its guns and equipment and all its credit. The earl, to whom Blackwater fort was surrendered, did not seek to make his victory one of annihilation. He may have been

[1] See Hayes-McCoy, *Ir. battles*, pp 106–31.

unable to do so because he had exhausted his stock of gunpowder, or he may have held his hand to keep his options in the way of further negotiation open. In any event, the bloody and unforgettable battles of Irish history were reserved for the next century.

Hitherto, the government's control of an efficient, if usually small, army had been sufficient to quell Irish resistance. Now even a large army was inadequate. Why was this? Although much more was involved, the basic reason for the earl's ability to achieve victory was that he operated in Ulster, an area that was, for the Dublin administration, remote and relatively inaccessible. Added to the fact that so much of the Ulster terrain suited the Irish method of fighting was the equally important fact that the earl and his allies were able, as the years went by, to organise themselves for war within an enclave free from English interference and capable of supporting their efforts. The wealth in cattle, corn, fish, and other produce of Tyrone, Tyrconnell, Fermanagh, and Monaghan, measured by the ability of these areas to feed fighting men, is shown by the events of the years following 1593 to have been very considerable. 'Ill inhabited as it was, with no industry and most part wasted', the earl could raise £80,000 a year in Ulster. Indeed it was said that Tyrone and Tyrconnell had never been so rich, and had never before produced so much food, as they did in the war years.[1]

The Ulster lords, each of whom had, apparently, absolute control of the resources of his own lordship, employed 'bonaghts', or native mercenary soldiers, during the war. These, together with the traditional fighting men supplied by the 'rising-out' of their people, and, when they could get them, the established mercenaries of the galloglass and migrant Scots, furnished them with large forces. It was estimated that the lords had 2,000 bonaghts in 1594 and from 4,000 to 6,000, regularly enlisted by proclamation outside the churches on Sundays and formed in companies like the English infantry, in later years. These men had, for the most part, good weapons of contemporary types, collected in Ireland, smuggled in from Scotland and even England, and supplied by Spain: muskets, calivers, and pikes, as well as the older axes, javelins, and bows. 'Even the farmers, ploughmen, swineherds, shepherds, and very boys' had learnt the use of firearms. They were 'infinitely belaboured with training in all parts of Ulster', and were, the English admitted, 'in discipline and weapons . . . little inferior, in body and courage equal, if not superior, to us'. Their instructors were the queen's captains of the years of the earl's loyalty, a few Spaniards, some Irishmen who had served in the Netherlands, and a stream of Irish deserters from the English army.[2]

The war was said to cost the earl £500 a day when he had all his forces assembled in 1598. Although this cannot mean that coin circulated freely in

[1] *Cal. S.P. Ire.*, *1596–7*, p. 408; Moryson, *Itinerary*, iii, 201.

[2] See Hayes-McCoy, 'The army of Ulster, 1593–1601' in *Ir. Sword*, i (1949–53), pp 105–17.

Ulster, it argues the existence of a buoyant economy. A barter of such produce as cattle, hides, tallow, sheepskins, grain, and yarn for weapons, managed by the 'grey merchants', or itinerant traders, must ordinarily have satisfied requirements within Ireland, although there were occasions when the rebels did trade their produce for cash. Gunpowder, imported from Scotland, and on at least one occasion from Danzig, must, in general, have been paid for in cash, or perhaps by valuables, like the wrought silver work that O'Donnell sent to the Hebrides in 1595 to pay for mercenaries. The government claimed that Ulster sold its produce elsewhere in Ireland and used the money obtained for it, some of it money sent from England to pay the troops, to trade with the Continent for arms, ammunition, and other commodities. Although the Ulstermen owned no large vessels, foreign craft entered their havens freely, and they were never cut off from Europe.

Military organisation for which there is no earlier Irish parallel, combined action that, save for minor defections, kept the Ulster lords together almost to the end, and, above all, the unique qualities of the earl—these were factors that made this last struggle of the old Gaelic Ireland the greatest single obstacle to the completion of the Tudor conquest. The earl was, of course, the mainspring of the revolt. The earlier collapse of the houses of Kildare and Desmond enhanced, in the Irish context, the sovereignty of the O'Neills, and the earl, as cautious as he was arrogant, skilful, and determined, proved himself to be the greatest of his name. He retained the support not only of O'Donnell, his traditionally hostile neighbour, but also of Maguire, whose allegiance had long been in dispute between O'Neill and O'Donnell. The earl's forces, skilfully handled on ground that he and his allies could choose—since his enemy's conduct of operations meant that all the earlier actions of the war followed attempts to relieve isolated garrisons in what for the English was the wilderness—were, until 1601, a match for the soldiers of the queen.

On the other hand, the queen's Irish administration showed, until the end of the century, a conspicuous lack of leadership in coping with the new problems that faced it. The Dublin government was unable simultaneously to deal with the earl and the outstanding problems of the recently settled areas of Munster and Connacht. Basically, the difficulty was one of finance, although there was a problem of organisation as well, since the civil and military leaders were frequently at loggerheads. London kept a tight grip on finance, and, with army expense mounting, there was never enough money to go round. The Ulster raids, together with the expense of convoying supplies to the garrisons, were said to have cost £300,000 by 1597. Later expenditure was far greater. The fact that there was nothing positive to show for this outlay left the queen and her advisers, not always intelligent outsiders where Ireland was concerned, dissatisfied with the way in which the Irish government was being carried on. This was so although London, by leaving the Dublin administration leaderless after Burgh's death, was itself largely to blame for the obvious shortcomings.

The Dublin interregnum ended in April 1599, when Robert Devereux, second earl of Essex, arrived to take up office as lord lieutenant. Much was expected of this popular hero of the Cadiz operation, who came to Ireland saying 'By God, I will beat Tyrone in the field',[1] and who was given the largest army that, in a reign notable for its overseas expeditions, had yet been sent out from England. Most of his troops were raw recruits, but there were over 16,000 of them. The complexities of Ireland were too much for Essex, however, and too much at this stage for the queen's government, which allowed its chosen general to begin operations with no clear conception either on its part or his of what form the operations would take. A single forceful authority was certainly needed to oppose Tyrone, and to reactivate the conquest. But, even when the state's share of responsibility for what followed is accepted, Essex, an indifferent soldier, must be said to have fallen short of the requirement.[2]

The fate of Burgh and Bagenal had shown the difficulty of mounting an attack on rebellious Ulster from the south. The possibility of lessening this difficulty by effecting a landing on the northern coast, preferably in Lough Foyle, which marked the dividing line between the earl's command and O'Donnell's, had for long been apparent to a state that had considerable experience of amphibious operations. The Irish council recorded its unanimous opinion shortly before Bagenal's defeat that 'a special force . . . [should] be sent out of England by sea directly to Lough Foyle'.[3] There is evidence that Essex too advocated 'landing on his [Tyrone's] back at Loughfoile',[4] but if this was high on his list of priorities in 1599 no provision was made for it when the forces allotted to him were sent to Ireland. The disposition of force, if not indeed the direct wish of the queen and her English advisers, confined Essex's prospective action against Ulster to a repetition of Burgh's.

Essex spent twenty-one ineffectual weeks in Ireland. In the interval between the battle of the Yellow Ford and his arrival, a growing adherence to the emotive cause of Tyrone and the Ulstermen brought about a virtual collapse of the state's authority in Connacht, Munster, and parts of Leinster. Tyrone invited the Munster lords to look forward to a time when 'this island of Ireland shall be at our direction and counsel', and he told Ormond that 'they that are joined with me fight for the catholic religion and liberties of our country'.[5] O'Donnell's will prevailed in the greater part of Connacht,

[1] John Harington, *Nugae antiquae* (ed. Thomas Park), ii (1804), p. 29.

[2] Essex is defended in L. W. Henry, 'The earl of Essex and Ireland, 1599' in *I.H.R. Bull.*, xxxii (1959), pp 1–23. See also the same writer's 'Contemporary sources for Essex's lieutenancy in Ireland' in *I.H.S.*, xi, no. 41 (Mar. 1958), pp 8–17.

[3] *Cal. S.P. Ire., 1598–9*, p. 140.

[4] Henry, 'The earl of Essex and Ireland, 1599', loc. cit., p. 3.

[5] *Cal. S.P. Ire., 1599–1600*, pp 208–9.

although the earl of Thomond, after a struggle, vindicated his authority in Clare. The supporters of the state were overrun in the midlands, as were the scattered settlers in Munster. Cork, Waterford, Limerick, and Youghal, which in common with the other towns were not threatened, became each a place of refuge for the surrounding countryside. Tyrone, who sent bonaghts to aid the disaffected in the province, was increasingly respected in Munster, and it was with his sponsorship that James Fitzthomas Fitzgerald, nephew of the earl of Desmond who was killed in 1583, sought, despite the confiscation of the earldom, to set himself up as the new earl. Fitzthomas, whom the English called the *súgán* (or straw rope) earl, claimed that the queen's servants were not content to have the 'lands and livings' of such as he, but now wanted their lives.[1] Ormond, his command of the forces reduced to guarding his own lordship, did what he could to keep Tipperary and Kilkenny quiet, but some even of his own family were in revolt.

In this crisis Essex proved strikingly out of place. Reflecting the wishes of a cautious council, and perhaps deciding that his resources were not as great as they appeared, he opted for the easier task of subduing disaffection in Leinster, and eventually in Munster, and postponed the confrontation with Tyrone. But his march as far west as Askeaton was a 'progress' after the fashion of more than half a century before. The queen stigmatised it as such. He took a few castles, provisioned the midland forts, reinforced the troops of the Munster presidency, and perhaps raised doubts in the Munstermen's minds of the advisability of supporting Tyrone, but he did little more.

The queen's soldiers suffered shameful reverses during the summer, in Wicklow, Louth, Kildare, and Roscommon. Although Essex was present on none of these occasions and bore no responsibility for what happened, Tyrone's success confused, if it did not intimidate, him. His officers, being asked for their advice—a demonstration of their leader's indecision, if it was not, as the queen suspected, an attempt to show that he had the backing of the army in a deeper plot—recommended inaction; they said that there was no hope of establishing a post on Lough Foyle and that, such had been the wastage of the army, Tyrone could not be confronted at the Blackwater with much hope of success. Astounded, the queen peremptorily ordered Essex to move northward. Essex declared fatuously that 'we will, on one side or the other, end the war',[2] and moved from Dublin with 4,000 men. He scarcely emerged from the Pale. Tyrone confronted him south of Carrickmacross, surprised him into a parley and conversed privately with him for the greater part of an hour. The result was an agreed cessation of hostilities, which, again, suited Tyrone's Fabian policy, and, in regard to the English opinion of Essex, promoted an ambiguity that was to contribute to his downfall. When Essex was tried for treason in 1601 it was alleged that Tyrone had incited him 'to stand for himself', promising that, if he did so, 'he would

[1] *Cal. S.P. Ire., 1598–9*, p. 288.

[2] Devereux, *Lives of the Devereux*, ii, 56.

join with him'.[1] This suggests that Tyrone tried to take advantage of the differences that had arisen in the English court between a conservative group, led by Burghley's son and successor Sir Robert Cecil, and a group of opportunists, of whom Essex, the last surviving favourite, was the foremost. Whether or not Tyrone had assisted the process, Essex was corrupted by ambition—or driven desperate by a realisation of failure—when, on 24 September, he deserted his post and rushed to London in an unavailing effort to try his blandishments on the queen.

The advantage appeared to lie with the earl of Tyrone when Essex's successor, Charles Blount, Lord Mountjoy, arrived in February 1600. Tyrone and his associates continued to press for Spanish aid, and the earl sought papal recognition of the Irish war as a catholic crusade, believing that this would encourage the Leinster and Munster lords to support him. European politics had entered a new phase since the peace of Vervins and the death of Philip II of Spain in 1598. Philip III, whose half-sister, the archduchess Isabel, had a claim to the much canvassed succession to Elizabeth, was as yet unconvinced of the advisability of attacking England through Ireland. Still, he encouraged Tyrone to persevere in his resistance, sent him arms and ammunition, and did nothing to damp the hope that he would, by dispatching a military expedition, perform what his father had led the Ulstermen to expect. Tyrone, profiting by the uncertainty that Essex had aroused, made what looked like a royal progress in Munster in the winter of 1599–1600; it was at this time that the English alleged that his real ambition was 'to wear a crown'. He reached the Cork coast, where he surveyed Kinsale among other places, received many assurances of support, chastised some who had aroused his ire, and everywhere stressed the religious aspect of his struggle. None opposed him, although the death in a chance encounter outside Cork of his staunch adherent Hugh Maguire was a heavy blow.

The arrival of Mountjoy was climacteric. He was a new kind of deputy, at once a soldier and an administrator. His purpose was the destruction of Tyrone's sovereignty. His method in the accomplishment of this task, the urgency of which was heightened in what must be the queen's declining years by the abiding Spanish threat, was the unspectacular but difficult one of doing what the English experience of many years had suggested, but what none of his predecessors had had the capacity to accomplish. He aimed to stabilise the presidency in Munster, to maintain pressure on Tyrone and his supporters at all seasons, to reduce them by the ruthless destruction of their economic resources, to secure the permanent establishment of garrisons in Ulster, and to utilise English sea-power to the full extent in support of land operations. Each of these expedients had been separately tried; Mountjoy was to try them together.

[1] G. P. V. Akrigg, *Shakespeare and the earl of Southampton* (London, 1968), p. 92.

The earl of Tyrone's grip on Munster was soon broken by Sir George Carew (cousin of the land speculator Sir Peter Carew), who accompanied Mountjoy to Ireland as the new president of the province. Backed by a reinforcement of over 3,000 men and adopting the methods which had already been used to put down the Desmond rebellion, Carew scattered and quickly overcame Tyrone's bonaghts and the *súgán* earl's supporters. He neutralised Florence MacCarthy, who was potentially the greatest Irish lord in Munster, but who ruined his chances by trying to play with both sides. Munster, where communications were easy, supplies procurable, and the support of the towns assured, was, for a determined executant of the state policy, a different proposition from Ulster. Carew's work had indeed been largely performed twenty years earlier by men like Gilbert and Drury. Fitzgerald support of the *súgán* earl was never enthusiastic, and, although James Fitzgerald, son of the rebel earl, was given no more than a derisory welcome when he was sent from England to act as a counterpoise to his cousin, Tyrone's nominee was chased into the glen of Aherlow, the great Munster wilderness, and eventually captured in May 1601. Sent to the Tower, he died there seven years later.

Ulster was, of course, Mountjoy's real problem. He was ready to deal with it by May 1600, when the greatest combined operation of the century in Ireland was accomplished, the long-threatened landing of a force in Lough Foyle and the movement northward of a second force which was intended to draw the attention of the earl of Tyrone away from the landing. Sir Henry Docwra, who had been given command of the 4,000 men ordered to Lough Foyle, sailed from Carrickfergus, and, after an uneventful passage, disembarked his force and dug himself in amid the ruins at Derry.[1] This time the English were to hold on there. They were indeed little opposed, the Irish being as incapable of interfering with water-borne military traffic as they were of assaulting fortifications. Docwra, who had served with Malby in Connacht, was cautious. He underestimated neither the difficulty of survival in isolation nor the danger of surprise should he make a premature attempt to march inland. Consequently, he remained at Derry during the summer and autumn. His food soon ran short and his men fell sick, but he represented the state, and, as always, the state attracted support from the discontented. Sir Arthur O'Neill, Turlough Luineach's son, and Niall Garbh O'Donnell, Calvagh's grandson and cousin of Hugh, the reigning O'Donnell—the one a pretender in Tyrone and the other, although he had been trusted by Hugh, a pretender in Tyrconnell—came in to him, to be followed early in 1601 by some of the O'Dohertys of Inishowen. Docwra made his first significant move in October, when, having been reinforced by sea, he sent Niall Garbh to take Lifford.

Mountjoy's move northward to cover Docwra's landing brought him his

[1] Details in Docwra, *Narration*, and in Cyril Falls, *Elizabeth's Irish wars* (London, 1950), p. 262.

first experience of action against Tyrone. It must have confirmed him in a resolution to match his tactics with Docwra's and not to run risks. The earl was now strong enough to oppose an invasion of Ulster, not at the Blackwater, but at the Moyry pass. Mountjoy did not attempt to go beyond Newry, and he returned at once, not by the pass but by the safer passage through Carlingford. His purpose was served, although the operation had the flavour of a moral victory for the earl. Tyrone and O'Donnell were still confident, as was shown by O'Donnell leaving Docwra behind him and raiding as far away as south Galway and Clare. The territories of the earls of Thomond and Clanricard were wasted—a touch of Tyrone's Munster practice of the chastisement of those who were unwilling to join the Ulster confederacy, and perhaps an attempt to dispose of potential obstacles in anticipation of a Spanish landing.

Spoliation was, of course, an established procedure in Irish warfare, and its incidence had, as we have seen, increased as the Elizabethan struggle progressed, but it was left for Mountjoy and his lieutenants coldly and deliberately to close their minds to the consequences for non-combatants and to use the total destruction of material resources as an instrument of policy and a weapon of war. 'When the plough and breeding of cattle shall cease', said a government informant in 1600, 'then will the rebellion end'. Docwra agreed: 'the strength of this war consisteth in the men'; their maintenance depended on cattle and corn; therefore 'all our counsels' should be directed to the destruction of these commodities.[1] Mountjoy told the privy council that he knew of no means other than famine to overcome the Irish rebels. The result of Mountjoy's destruction of the harvests, driving off and slaughter of cattle, and burning of houses was, according to English evidence, horrible in the extreme. His secretary, Moryson, records that 'the common sort of the rebels were driven to unspeakable extremities, beyond the record of most histories that ever I did read'.[2] Locked in a fight to the finish, neither side relaxed. Mountjoy, who filled the intervals of his northern journeys by raids on the troublesome areas in Leinster, found, hidden behind boggy land west of the fort of Philipstown, a prosperous territory. 'It is incredible', he said, 'in so barbarous a country how well the ground was manured, how orderly their fields were fenced, their towns inhabited, and every highway and path so well beaten'. His were the first troops to enter the area, and, by burning the houses and cutting the ripening corn with their swords, they brought savagery with them: 'the wheat that we destroyed was valued at above ten thousand pounds, being almost the only means for them to live', but being too 'the chief treasure wherewith they do entertain their bonaghts'.[3]

Although, as the crisis approached, the earl held out grimly, he was

[1] *Cal. S.P. Ire., 1600*, pp 178, 194–8.

[2] Moryson, *Itinerary*, iii, 282.

[3] *Cal. S.P. Ire., 1600*, p. 338.

greatly reduced. Short of money and food, threatened from the north by Docwra and the south by Mountjoy, suffering desertion from his ranks and cut off from a Munster that had all but abandoned him, he could not, if he was to keep the struggle alive, afford to give up much more ground. This explains his determined resistance to Mountjoy in the Moyry pass in October 1600, when he was reported to have said that if the English got through it was 'farewell Ulster and all the north'. Everything, as both he and Mountjoy knew, now depended on the speedy arrival of Spanish assistance. The earl and O'Donnell had, by the end of 1600, made little real progress in Rome, where Peter Lombard of Waterford was their agent, or in Spain, where Edmund MacDonnell, dean of Armagh, represented them. Pope Clement VIII, who was in any event antagonistic to Philip III, feared that the Leinster and Munster catholics might, if they were seen to back Tyrone, provoke the queen to substitute persecution for the mild treatment of their recusancy that policy had so far suggested. The pope accordingly withheld a whole-hearted support of the Ulster cause.[1] Philip was deterred from positive action by doubts regarding the succession to Elizabeth, for which James VI of Scotland was still the best-placed candidate, and by the dragging progress of the Anglo-Spanish peace negotiations. A Spanish messenger, Martín de la Cerdá, accompanied by the Franciscan Mateo de Oviedo, papal archbishop of Dublin since the previous year, brought a thousand more infantry firearms, with equipment and ammunition, to Tyrconnell in April 1600. Although the earl and O'Donnell represented their situation as desperate, they agreed, in the hope that a Spanish force would have arrived by then, to hold out until the end of the year. Catholic Ireland, which presented possibilities of increased trade with Spain and of providing a counterblast to Elizabeth's assistance of the Spanish rebels in the Netherlands, seemed an obvious theatre for Spanish intervention, and Philip soon warmed to the project. Thus, in circumstances which, however, changed inexorably for the worse for the Ulstermen, Spain took the first steps in the autumn of 1600 to organise shipping and troops for an Irish expedition, although it was soon seen that nothing could be ready before the following year. Further Spanish messengers, bringing more arms and money, came to Teelin, County Donegal, in December. They still avoided committing their king to the Ulster leaders, but at least they gave them what they had lacked in Ireland since Mountjoy's arrival, encouragement. Once more, Tyrone and O'Donnell agreed to hold out, this time until July 1601, and they repeated an earlier recommendation that if the Spanish force was to be a large one it should land in Munster, preferably at Cork.

The discussion regarding the landing-place was soon to be exacerbated. If and when the Spaniards came, the Irish struggle would, in military terms, cease to be defensive. The earl and his associates must, in alliance with the

[1] See J. J. Silke, *Kinsale* (Liverpool, 1970), pp 83–4.

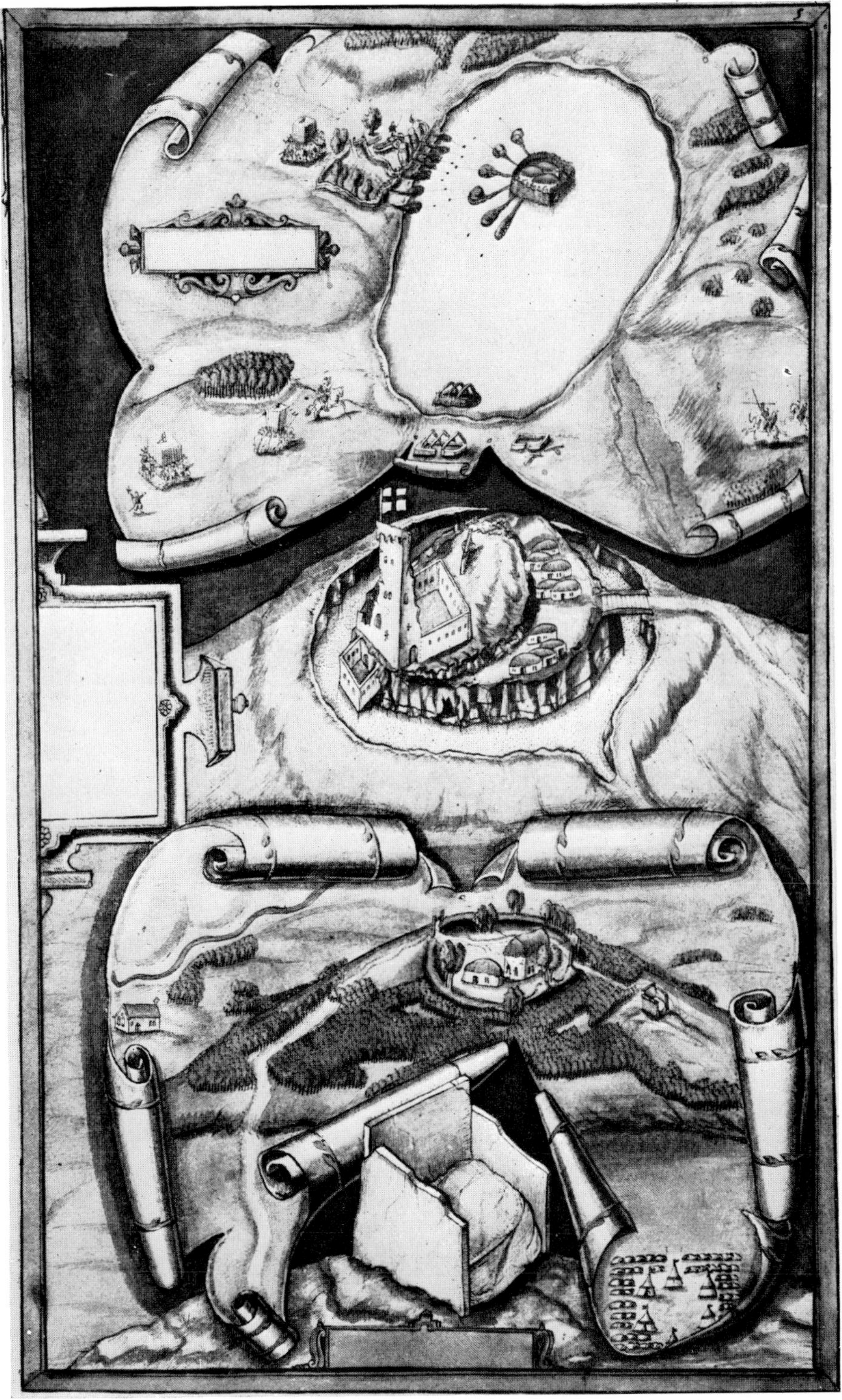

Plate 3. DUNGANNON (centre of plate), TULLAGHOGE (foot), AND A CRANNOG (top), by Richard Bartlett (*Ulster maps c. 1600*, facing p. 10); size of original 16″ × 10″. Dungannon was O'Neill's principal house, Tullaghoge his inauguration place. A crannog was a lake-fortress.

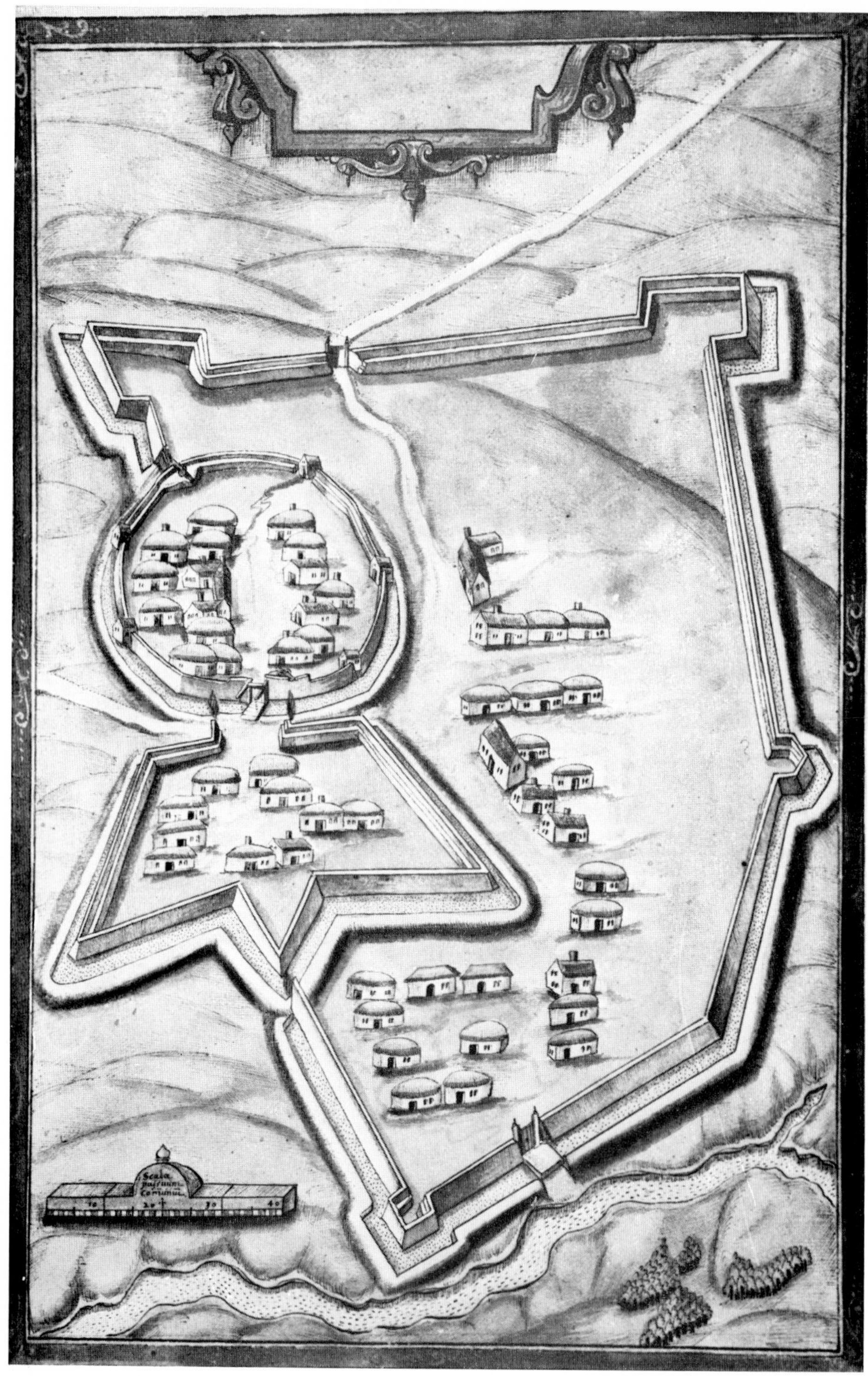

Plate 4. MOUNT NORRIS, CO. ARMAGH, by Richard Bartlett (*Ulster maps c. 1600*, facing p. 14); size of original $15\frac{1}{2}'' \times 11''$

Spaniards, pass over to the attack. This meant that the theatre of war would lie outside Ulster, something that the feeding of a Spanish force would at any rate make necessary. These things being so, where should the Spaniards land? Tyrone's own choice was, apparently, Drogheda, where he could most readily and effectively join them. But the Spaniards were concerned to pick a place which, allowing for wind, weather, and the queen's ships, they could most easily reach and continue to use. This ruled out the east coast. Munster, all considered, was seen to be best. Thanks to Carew, however, the possibility of Munster support either for Ulstermen or Spaniards receded after the summer of 1600. By the beginning of 1601, therefore, the proposed strength of the Spaniards had, because of the rising strength of the English, become a determining factor; Tyrone and O'Donnell's advice was that an expedition of 6,000 men should make for the Munster coast, 4,000 for the mouth of the Shannon, 2,000 for Donegal bay. If the Spaniards were few, they should land where the Ulstermen could join them at once.

Well aware of the progress of the Spanish preparations, and aware too of the probability that an invasion would occur in the south, Mountjoy was careful in 1601 not to involve himself too deeply in Ulster. Tyrone was surrounded. The new Blackwater fort, almost within sight of Dungannon, was closely supported by new garrisons to the south. Sir Arthur Chichester, who was based on the old stronghold of Carrickfergus, had overrun Clandeboye and was poised to cross Lough Neagh. To the north-west, Docwra and Niall Garbh taxed O'Donnell to the utmost in the Foyle valley; intent on the original objective of cutting Connacht off from Ulster by taking Ballyshannon, they occupied Donegal abbey in August. As the suspense mounted, all were aware that another push could upset the earl and his confederates. England, her expenditure at its height, was committed to the speedy completion of the conquest. Ireland as a whole was affected by the tremendous efforts that the war entailed; trade was interrupted, or artificially stimulated by the necessity of maintaining supplies, and, within reach of the numerous garrisons, tillage was wasted and the crops and herds, the wealth and life of the country, were destroyed.

In these circumstances, and following the treaty of Lyons, which, since it made peace between France and Savoy, released troops that it might otherwise have been necessary for Philip to have retained at home, the long-awaited Spaniards arrived. The question of where to land vexed them to the end. After lengthy argument in Spain, Juan del Águila, who was appointed to command the troops and who wanted to land in Tyrconnell, was forced to give way to Oviedo, who claimed to know the minds of the Irish leaders and who clung to what he remembered from 1600 as their wish, that the disembarkation should be in Munster. Changed conditions in Munster and the mistaken belief that Cork and Waterford had been fortified had meanwhile led the Ulstermen to substitute Limerick or north of it for their earlier plan; a last-minute effort to communicate again with them proved abortive. The Spanish force, which was less than 4,500 strong, obeyed orders and made for the Cork coast. About 3,500 of the troops landed unopposed at Kinsale on 21 September and the days following.[1]

Mountjoy's reaction was immediate. By the end of October, stripping them even from the Ulster forts, although not from Docwra, who still had an active role to play, Mountjoy had almost 7,000 men in Cork. Resistance to the invasion, which he clearly identified as the real threat, justified the taking of risks in the north. The Spaniards were soon shut into Kinsale, supplies and reinforcements were urgently bespoken from England, and by the beginning of November operations had begun for the reduction of the town. Munster was disturbed only by the marching of English troops.

The response of the earl and of O'Donnell to the belated fulfilment of their hopes may appear, in contrast to the deputy's movements, dilatory, but the new aspect of affairs posed a bigger problem for them than for Mountjoy. Realising as they did that most of the Munster lords who were left would be unable or unwilling to assist them, Tyrone and O'Donnell's first move, as far as we know, was to request Águila to embark afresh and to come at least as far as Sligo to meet them. This would have involved their remaining in Ulster for the time, and it probably explains some part of their delay. Furthermore, the Ulstermen were now so closely beset, and this applied particularly to O'Donnell, whose lordship was dangerously penetrated, that it could be disastrous for them to leave their area, that is, unless the result of their doing so were to be victory in the south. Their decision could not therefore be taken quickly. Indeed, the Irish march to Kinsale was a heroic movement which argued, even at this eleventh hour, a high degree of control and organisational power on the part of Tyrone and O'Donnell, and which is without parallel in Gaelic history.

O'Donnell marched southward through Connacht to the neighbourhood of Roscrea in the first week of November. Sidestepping Sir George Carew, whom Mountjoy detached from Kinsale to oppose his progress, he passed through County Limerick and reached Bandon. The earl of Tyrone delayed to raid the Pale—obviously in the hope of relieving the pressure on Águila, but without doing so—and then followed O'Donnell. Their united force was about 5,500 strong when they moved down the Bandon river valley to take up a position behind Mountjoy's army of investment. They were soon joined by some 500 Munstermen and less than 200 Spaniards, stragglers from Águila's forces who had put in at Castlehaven.

The Irish and Spaniards thus came into proximity with each other in unpromising circumstances, with no prospect of effecting a junction save in the midst of battle. Although Águila had defended himself well and was still full of fight, he was closely shut in, and his supplies were failing. The

[1] Silke, *Kinsale*, pp 108–22; Cyril Falls, *Mountjoy: Elizabethan general* (1955), pp 164–8.

English too were largely cut off between the Irish and the town, and were losing heavily through sickness. Of the three forces, Mountjoy's was the one which must have been most anxious to fight, and which could least afford to be unwary. Both sides had, at last, been forced to stake everything on an engagement that allowed room neither for manœuvre nor retraction.

Contrary to the promise given by their performance over the years, the Irish were the first to commit themselves. They moved forward early on the morning of 24 December, found the English on the alert, hesitated, withdrew with the object of improving their position, and then proceeded clumsily to deploy. Leaving the greater part of his force to watch the Spaniards and taking advantage of the fact that he could, for the first time in the struggle against the earl, use his superior cavalry strength to effect, Mountjoy charged the largest of Tyrone's three infantry divisions and broke it. The battle was over in a very short time, and the Irish, who showed that they were unable to adapt themselves to action in formation, were scattered with heavy loss. Águila took no part in the battle, apparently because the Irish did not reach the place appointed for a meeting with the Spaniards, and he surrendered to Mountjoy nine days later.

The war was won at Kinsale, the battle which marked the failure of the Spanish effort, the collapse of the Ulster resistance, the completion of the Tudor conquest, and the eclipse of Gaelic Ireland—although not the eclipse of the earl of Tyrone. O'Donnell went to Spain, where he died within a few months. The earl returned to Ulster, where he was still to suffer much, although much less than many lesser enemies of the state.

Mountjoy's first care, although the Spanish threat soon paled, was to provide against a further attempt at invasion. Forts were built in 1602 at Castle Park in Kinsale, Haulbowline in Cork harbour, and at Galway. In the summer, Mountjoy, assisted by Docwra, began the final harrying of Ulster. He was unopposed, the earl having burnt Dungannon and fled to the woods of Glenconkeyne and Killeightragh. To show that the real significance of his victory over the Ulstermen lay in the abolition of a sovereignty which conflicted with the queen's, he 'broke down the chair wherein the O'Neills were wont to be created' at Tullaghoge.[1] His men, as usual, cut down and burnt the corn. The harvest time was at hand, but they 'found everywhere men dead of famine', and were told that there had been, since the beginning of the summer, 'above three thousand starved in Tyrone'.

The earl sought to open negotiations with Mountjoy within weeks of his defeat at Kinsale. The result, a year later, was a settlement, following which 'that damnable rebel Tyrone [was] brought to England, courteously favoured,

[1] Moryson, *Itinerary*, iii, 205. See Hayes-McCoy, 'The making of an O'Neill' in *U.J.A.*, series 3, xxxiii (1970), pp 89–94.

honoured and well liked'.[1] Although there was no doubt of Tyrone's having been forced to surrender, the consequences seemed so little hurtful to him that four years of the reign of James I, Elizabeth's successor, were to elapse before it was made clear, and that by the earl himself, that it was not he who had won.

No servant of the state had ever been quite sure how the queen wished the earl to be treated. Consequently, Mountjoy proceeded cautiously. Information was conveyed to the earl that, if he were to be allowed terms, the state would insist on his disclaiming both 'the name of O'Neill' and all authority outside Tyrone, that is, over the urraghs, would require that sheriffs be established and garrisons maintained within his lordship, and would demand that he renounce dependence on the king of Spain.[2] The queen seemed intransigent, hence the relentless prosecution of military operations throughout 1602, when it was known that the earl still refused to accept garrisons and claimed that any attempt to curtail his authority would be an infringement of his patent of 1585. The queen did not authorise Mountjoy to negotiate until February 1603, and then only on the understanding that the earl could petition only for himself and 'his own natural followers in Tyrone'. When the earl submitted at Mellifont in March, Mountjoy knew that Elizabeth had died six days earlier, but Tyrone did not. Tyrone agreed to the general terms of the previous year, but Mountjoy, rendered pliable by his belief that it was vital to effect a settlement before Tyrone realised that the queen was dead, allowed two important concessions: recognition of the earl as the absolute owner of his lordship and retention by him of authority over his chief urragh, O'Cahan.[3]

The new king, who had been well posted through the years in the affairs of an Ulster that had loomed large in the Scottish scene, and with whom Tyrone had communicated in the past, accepted Mountjoy's arrangement. When Mountjoy, now elevated to the lord lieutenancy and soon to be created earl of Devonshire, left Ireland in May, the earl of Tyrone went with him, to be well received and formally pardoned by the king. It must strike us as strange that 'the author of so much trouble'[4] escaped attainder, and no less astonishing that a pardoned rebel was allowed to uphold, and could have upheld so successfully, the terms of his own grant of nobility. Even though Mountjoy may have gained the earl's submission by concealing it, the queen's death, with all the manœuvring for position in respect of the new monarch that it involved, was clearly a happening of which the earl, even in his reduced circumstances, could take advantage.

The English, who condemned the Irish lords as tyrants, proclaimed that,

[1] Harington, *Nugae antiquae*, i, 340.

[2] *Cal. Carew MSS, 1601–3*, pp 212–14.

[3] See N. P. Canny, 'The treaty of Mellifont and the reorganisation of Ulster, 1603' in *Ir. Sword*, ix (1969–70), pp 249–62.

[4] Thomas Gainsford, *The true exemplary and remarkable history of the earl of Tyrone* (1619), p. 39.

on the conclusion of the rebellion, the Irish at large were 'the free, natural, and immediate subjects of his majesty, and [were] not to be reputed or called the natives or natural followers of any other lord or chieftain whatsoever'.[1] Their immediate settlement in Ulster, however, had the effect of increasing rather than diminishing the local authority, although not the political power, of the earl of Tyrone and of Rory, the brother of the late O'Donnell, who was created earl of Tyrconnell in 1603. These two were given more than Gaelic law had allowed them, although there were individual Irishmen who had aspired to as much: the sole ownership, under the crown, of their lordships. Once again, as in Henry VIII's time, and despite all that had happened in the meantime, the state, advised by Mountjoy, placed its trust in the new Irish nobles and contented itself with having 'one assured in Tyrconnell and another in Tyrone'.[2] The intention of organising Ulster as a presidency was abandoned, no doubt because the earl of Tyrone, if he himself were not made president, would have made a presidency unworkable. As was soon to appear, it was a brittle settlement, and one that did not match the conquest that had been effected.

Sixteenth-century Ireland, 'dismembered on account of religion'[3] and further upset by the political, administrative, and social changes that culminated in the overthrow of local authority in Ulster, suffered a suspension of much of its intellectual life. The century witnessed little artistic or literary achievement, and no notable architectural development. Organised education was, almost everywhere, and throughout most of the century, at the mercy of the requirements of state. The schools of the Pale and the towns were, in the early years, conducted by the church, while the task of pedagogy was shared in the Irish and gaelicised areas by the clergy and the bards, legists and other learned elements of the older society. Since the government, in its efforts to control Ireland, clashed with the church and the Gaelic institutions, the schools, clerical and lay, suffered.

The dissolution of the monasteries in Ireland, as in England and Scotland, closed many schools. The resulting vacuum, particularly in the towns, was soon filled in the neighbouring countries by the opening of new schools. There were vigorous universities both in England and Scotland, and the intention of promoting education which was part of the spirit of the reformation ensured, despite financial difficulties, a continuance, indeed an improvement, of organised learning. The case was different in Ireland. Although new schools were opened during the century, particularly in its last quarter, when several good lay schools flourished in the towns, and although the

[1] Proclamation of Lord Deputy Chichester, 11 Mar. 1605 (P.R.O., S.P. 63/217, p. 16), printed in M. J. Bonn, *Die englische Kolonisation in Irland*, i (Stuttgart and Berlin, 1906), pp 394–7; Steele, *Tudor & Stuart proclam.*, ii, 167.

[2] *Cal. S.P. Ire., 1603–6*, p. 24.

[3] *Cal. Carew MSS, 1575–88*, p. 289.

deficiency of a university was belatedly supplied, friction and apathy were, in regard to education, more characteristic of Ireland than of the neighbouring kingdoms. Proselytism and attempts to preserve the old religion were prime factors in Irish education, and the catholic–protestant cleavage, together with the intention of making all Irishmen subjects of the crown, soon disturbed the instruction of youth.

It was not the intention of the state, in dissolving the monasteries, to leave Ireland without schools. Quite the contrary. The Irish parliament sought, as early as 1537, to establish parish schools,[1] and when this effort was unproductive a commission was set up in 1563 to inquire into Irish education and to examine proposals for the institution of a university. Sir Henry Sidney and his fellow commissioners found that, if progress was to be made in the reformation of religion and the anglicisation of the country, the state must undertake educational control. The result was an act passed by Sidney's parliament in 1570 which provided for the setting up of grammar schools, the instruction to be given in which was to be subject to the approval of the establishment.[2] Passage of the act was delayed by a dispute that arose between Sidney and the reformed bishops regarding the administration of the schools; an extension of the same dispute, exacerbated by an exchange of personalities between Lord Deputy Perrot and Adam Loftus, archbishop of Dublin, but basically the consequence of a widespread difference of opinion as to which should have priority, education or the cure of souls, delayed the foundation of a university for years.

Meanwhile, the struggle to score religious advantage from the monopolisation of schools was under way. When Edmund Campion, a recognised scholar, soon to be martyred for his catholicism, came to Dublin in 1569, he was regarded as a man likely to secure a post in the proposed university. Similarly, more than ten years later, schools taught by Peter White in Waterford and Alexander Lynch in Galway were clearly catholic rather than protestant institutions, yet they were not seriously interfered with for being so. But the onset of the repression of catholicism in England, following the rising in the north and the excommunication of the queen, led the Irish administration to adopt a stricter attitude to a recusancy which increased in obstinacy with the growing success of the counter-reformation. Schools opened in the Munster towns in the 1560s by Jesuits, led by Fr David Wolfe, had been closed by government order by the 1580s, and, although the state obviously found it difficult to operate the legislation, schools which were officially recognised as protestant were opened in Cork, Limerick, and Waterford within a decade or so of the passage of the 1570 act. The increasing wariness of Old English catholics led, however, to much confusion. Bishop Lyon of Cork and Ross found in 1596 that the queen's 'style and title' had

[1] 28 Hen. VIII, c. 15; see *S.P. Hen. VIII*, ii, 452, 458.

[2] 12 Eliz., c. 1; see *Cal. Carew MSS, 1515–74*, p. 359 and *Cal. S.P. Ire., 1509–73*, p. 400.

been torn out of the grammars in all the schools in his diocese, 'although they came new from the merchants' shops', and that, even more significantly, parents who were willing to have their children taught English objected to their being instructed as members of the reformed church.[1] Catholics would acknowledge Elizabeth as queen, but not as head of the church. It was said in 1589 that, although schoolmasters were not permitted to teach in England until they had been licensed to do so by the bishops, 'in Ireland schoolmasters may teach what they list, and children should be sent as far as from Dublin to Achonry to him that can best nurse them up in popery and bring them in contempt of her majesty's government'.[2]

The migration to the Continent of catholic students who wished to continue their studies for the priesthood had started by this time, as it had started in England. Evidence of the earlier schooling of these boys shows that there was no lack of catholic primary schoolmasters in their own country, some of whom avoided the attentions of the state by leading a peripatetic existence.[3] Part of the government's interest in promoting the foundation of an Irish university was a consequence of the belief, recorded in 1579 by the queen when she imaginatively proposed Clonfert by the 'river of Shein' [Shannon] as the site of the new institution, that these 'runagates' would return 'freight with superstition and treason' as instruments 'to stir up our subjects to undutifulness and rebellion'.[4] Although places other than Clonfert, including Drogheda, Trim, Armagh, and Limerick, were proposed, there was never a doubt that the location of the university would be in Dublin, where it was eventually established by royal charter in 1592. Loftus was satisfied when proposals, made at intervals from Henry VIII's time forward, that St Patrick's cathedral should be dissolved and the university founded on its site were not implemented, and when 'his church was not turned into Perrot's college'.[5] He became the first provost of the new institution, which, incorporated in 1592 as 'the College of the Holy and Undivided Trinity, near Dublin', was opened for students in 1594. Described in its charter as the 'mother of a university' and presumably intended to lead to a university with constituent colleges, on the Oxford and Cambridge model, the new college was invested with all the powers of a university from the beginning. It was strongly influenced by Trinity College, Cambridge, the protestant stronghold from which it took its name and much of its academic arrangements. The site—that of the dissolved Augustinian monastery of All Hallows—had been granted, and a considerable part of the original funds subscribed, by the city of Dublin.[6] This circumstance and

[1] *Cal. S.P. Ire., 1596–7*, pp 13–20.

[2] P.R.O., S.P. 63/144, p. 35.

[3] Details in lists of students entering at Salamanca college in D. J. O'Doherty, 'Students of the Irish College, Salamanca' in *Archiv. Hib.*, ii (1913), pp 1–36; iii (1914), pp 87–112.

[4] O'Flaherty, *West Connaught*, p. 306.

[5] *Cal. S.P. Ire., 1574–85*, p. 579.

[6] J. W. Stubbs, *History of the University of Dublin* (Dublin, 1889); William Urwick, *The early history of Trinity College, Dublin, 1591–1660* (London, 1891); J. P. Mahaffy, *An epoch in Irish*

the fact that contributions of money for the support of the foundation came, in the early years, from other parts of Ireland showed that it was felt to be worthy of Irish assistance. However, the delayed institution of what was to be the only Irish university for two and a half centuries to come meant that, unlike the older English and Scottish universities, it was a product of the reformation, and not a catholic university which had been reformed. This coloured it in Irish eyes. Although there were catholics among its students, particularly in its earlier years, it was a protestant foundation, indeed a pillar of the state church, and catholic controversialists regarded it as a place 'in which the Irish youth shall be taught heresy by English teachers'.[1] Loftus looked upon the college as 'a means of civilising the nation', and its charter declared its object to be 'the study of the liberal arts' and 'the cultivation of virtue and religion'. It was the product of its place and time, and was for long to retain the dual character which was imposed upon it: not only the service of scholarship but the maintenance of a division of minds.

On the collapse of the Ulster rebellion in 1603, the meaning of all that had been done by England to secure control of Ireland became apparent. The long series of efforts to provide for the extension of the system of the Pale throughout Leinster, to force the rule of English law on the south and west, and to rescue the towns from isolation amid Gaelic and gaelicised rural communities now bore fruit. The pattern was completed by the reduction of Ulster. Not only was local lordship everywhere abolished as a basis of power, and the exclusive sovereignty of the crown everywhere vindicated, but, for the first time in Irish history, all the inhabitants of the island were made subject to the authority of one government. The establishment of this single authority in place of the warring sovereignties of the past was seminal, and it brought Ireland into line with western European development. But it was no less pregnant with consequence that the century of struggle had decided that the authority was to be an English one. The earl of Tyrone and his associates were said to have sought, at one stage, a government of Ireland by Irishmen, under the English crown.[2] The settlement of Ireland to which James I was heir showed this to be as Utopian a concept as the earl's demand that the church of Ireland should 'be wholly governed by the pope'.

After almost a century of forceful management, Ireland was controlled rather than pacified. Despite the ferocity of the warfare, the country was not utterly wasted. There was no widespread shortage of cattle or corn, and

history: Trinity College, Dublin, 1591–1660 (London, 1903); Constantia Maxwell, *A history of Trinity College, Dublin, 1591–1892* (Dublin, 1946).

[1] *Ibernia Ignat.*, p. 37.

[2] *Cal. S.P. Ire., 1599–1600*, pp 279–80.

although the foreign trade of Dublin had fallen almost to nothing by the end of the queen's reign, this was more the result of the state's debasement of the coinage in a futile attempt to curb the expenses of the war than evidence of an economic decline. The abnormal conditions of the turn of the century led to a sharp increase in prices, but trade was soon renewed in the ports and the export of timber and barrel staves from Wexford, Waterford, and Youghal and of beef from Cork were fresh developments that marked the initiation of a period of recovery. A country, great parts of which were still rich and capable of development, naturally grew in prosperity as it became more peaceful, but a lasting peace under the crown was inhibited by irreconcilabilities. The happenings of the queen's reign served to confirm the English in their belief that they were superior to the Irish, and the Irish in their dislike of the English—an unpromising point of departure for the millennium to which Sir John Davies, the Irish attorney general, looked forward, when the Irish 'in tongue and heart and every way else [would] become English, so as there will be no difference or distinction but the Irish Sea betwixt us'.[1] The poor progress of the state's effort to impose a reformation on the Irish church merely underlined the differences between the two peoples. Most ominous for the future was the fact that, in the Ireland whose conquest had been completed by the Tudors, there was no room for the existence of an Irish interest at government level.

[1] Davies, 'Discovery' in Morley, *Ire. under Eliz. & Jas I*, pp 335–6.

CHAPTER V

Land and people, *c.* 1600

R. A. BUTLIN

IRELAND at the beginning of the seventeenth century was still perceived by Englishmen as a colony on the western periphery of Europe—an island lying, as Campion had described it thirty years before, 'aloofe in the weast ocean'.[1] Notwithstanding the rapid decline and transformation of the authority of the Gaelic chiefs, large areas of the country were still characterised by a way of life totally alien to the experience of English observers, which had much more in common with the 'pastoralist' regions of the Atlantic periphery of north-western Europe than with the essentially 'lowland' cultures of south and south-eastern England and the great basins and plains of continental western Europe. The cultural, social, economic, and religious *mores* of Ireland were so far removed from those of the English that they were partly used as justification for a policy of attempted 'civilisation' and anglicisation aimed at decreasing political instability and negativing the use of Ireland as a strategic base for an attack on England, notably by Spain.

Much of the evidence for the geographical character of Ireland at this time derives from the observations of English visitors, and it is often difficult, therefore, to distinguish between the 'real' Ireland and Ireland as viewed through the perceptual lenses of statesmen, soldiers, officials, settlers, and curious observers, few of whom were able to give objective accounts of their experiences. In the sense that political decisions were often made on the basis of incomplete or even fictitious or mythical notions of geography, Ireland as perceived at this time is an interesting topic,[2] but contemporary accounts must be balanced by the realities of life and landscape which in large measure survived the ephemeral and relatively ineffective attempts at reform and change.

Appraisals of the physiography, vegetation, and climate of Ireland at this time tended to relate to the conduct of military campaigns. Woods, bog, and mountain 'fastnesses' were seen by the military as extensive havens of refuge for outlaws and rebels, and accounts of their size were thus prone to

[1] Campion, *Hist. Ire.*, ed. Vossen, p. [7].
[2] Extensively treated in Quinn, *Elizabethans & Irish.*

exaggeration and contradiction. This is suggested in Moryson's 'Description of Ireland':

Ulster and the western parts of Munster yield vast woods in which the rebels, cutting up trees and casting them on heaps, used to stop the passages, and therein, as also upon fenny and boggy places, to fight with the English. But I confess myself to have been deceived in the common fame that all Ireland is woody, having found in my long journey from Armagh to Kinsale few or no woods by the way excepting the great wood of Ophalia [Offaly] and some low shrubby places which they call 'glins'.[1]

A 'Discourse of Ireland', *c.* 1599, also speaks of the woods being 'over greate and thick serving for a covert unto rebells and theeves'.[2] Dimmok believed that there was plenty of woodland, except in Leinster, and this view concurs with Campion's observation that although in Cambrensis's time there was much woodland, 'nowe the Englishe Pale is to naked'.[3]

The most recent and authoritative work on the woodlands of Ireland shows that the main woodland areas lay to the north-west of Lough Neagh, in the Erne basin, along the Shannon, in the river valleys of the west and south, and on the eastern slopes of the Wicklow and Wexford hills, with 'smaller but significant areas . . . in eastern County Down, in the Glens of Antrim, in the Sperrin valleys, on the western coast of Lough Swilly, on the western coast of Donegal and in north Sligo and south Galway'.[4] The dominant species of trees in the Irish woods were deciduous hardwoods—oak, ash, hazel, holly, alder, willow, and birch. Oak and ash were dominant in the more fertile lowlands and river valleys and regions of boulder clay, including the drumlin belt. Alder and willow were common in areas of poor drainage, notably south of Lough Neagh. Among the large oak forests were those of Mountreivelin,[5] Killeightragh, and Glenconkeyne west and north of Lough Neagh, the valleys of Cork and Kerry, the woods of Coillaughrim[6] on the Wexford–Carlow border, the woods of Shillelagh on the borders of Wicklow and Wexford, and parts of the Shannon valley. Areas with low densities of woodland included the bogs and lowlands of the central plain, the higher mountains, and the areas which had experienced extensive woodland clearance, notably the Pale, though extensive woods remained in Offaly and Leix, north-west Kildare, and on the periphery of the boglands. Woodland covered about one-eighth of the country at the beginning of the seventeenth century, but was gradually being cleared for fuel, for timber

[1] Moryson, *Itinerary*, iv, 195. For Offaly see plate 1.

[2] D. B. Quinn (ed.), '"A discourse of Ireland" (*circa* 1599): a sidelight on English colonial policy' in *R.I.A. Proc.*, xlvii, sect. C, no. 3 (1942), p. 160.

[3] Campion, *Hist. Ire.*, ed. Vossen, p. [15].

[4] McCracken, *Ir. woods*, p. 35; see map 4.

[5] A corruption of 'Muinterdoibhilen' (Hogan, *Onomasticon*, p. 547); rendered 'Monterneavlin' in *Civil Survey*, iii, 248 (editorial note).

[6] The original ordnance survey of Wexford shows 'Killoughrum forest' 5 miles W.N.W. of Enniscorthy (editorial note).

Map 4 IRELAND, *c*. 1600, by K. M. Davies

Woodlands, *c*. 1600 after Eileen McCracken, *Ir. woods*; bogs (as of 1907) simplified from the Geological Survey of Ireland's map showing the distribution of peat bogs and coalfields (1920); county boundaries after K. W. Nicholls (see vol. viii, map 45).

used in building and for making barrel staves and implements, for charcoal (used in iron-making), and for strategic purposes.

The widespread existence of both upland and lowland peat bogs is noted by contemporaries, especially in the context of military strategy, and a common complaint of English soldiers was that 'the woods and bogs are a great hindrance to us and help to the rebels',[1] the latter being able, with only a handful of men, to engage in 'ambushcados' and, when necessary, escape with ease. The economic potential of the lowland bogs was not yet realised, though careful observers noted their use in summer, when the water table was low, for pasturing cattle. Then, as now, the principal areas of bog, both of raised and blanket types, were the areas of high rainfall, with the raised bogs mainly east of the Shannon and the blanket bogs in the uplands and lowlands of the west and on some of the eastern mountains, notably parts of the Leinster chain.

The extensive mountains and uplands, particularly of Ulster, Connacht, and Munster, also served as zones of refuge and as important summer grazing grounds. The central highlands of the Inishowen peninsula, for example, were 'all high and waste mountain, good for feeding of cows in the summer only, but all waste, desolate and uninhabited'.[2] The Wicklow and Dublin mountains, sometimes referred to as the 'Irish mountains', housed 'mountain rebels' who posed a constant threat to the inhabitants of Dublin and the Pale. The 'countries' of Muskerry, Carbery, Duhallow, and Desmond were 'in nature exceeding strong', because of 'the multitude of huge mountains in the same',[3] and were therefore hardly affected by the military campaigns in Munster, and acted as regions of refuge for the 'rebels'.

The rivers and lakes of Ireland are referred to in contemporary literature most frequently in the context of the obstacles which they posed to inland communication and the protection which they afforded to the 'rebels'. Some of them were notoriously difficult to ford at times of high rainfall. Names of rivers are rarely given, though the Shannon is recognised as an important river, from the point of view both of acting as a boundary and as a communications artery. The larger inland lakes, like Lough Erne and Lough Neagh, are also mentioned.

Evidence for the weather and climate of early seventeenth-century Ireland is scarce and subjective, and often refers to extreme rather than average conditions. Sir Oliver Lambert's complaint, in the month of June, that 'there has been so much rain that the bogs and mountains are too wet and the rivers too high for me to drive the enemy out of the Curlews',[4] is repeated in Sir George Fenton's remark: 'in all the time of my service in this land I have not seen so tempestuous weather so long together'.[5] There was clear

[1] *Cal. S.P. Ire.*, *1601–3*, p. 253.
[2] Ibid., *1600–01*, p. 94.
[3] *Cal. Carew MSS*, *1589–1600*, p. 427.
[4] *Cal. S.P. Ire.*, *1601–3*, p. 421.
[5] Ibid., *1600–01*, p. 139.

recognition of general climatic variations—that Ulster had higher rainfall than Munster, for example—but there is insufficient evidence on which to base any comparative study of the climate and weather *c.* 1600 with that of the present day. Fynes Moryson, in 1600, described Ireland as being 'open to winds and floods of rain', and observed

> the winter's cold to be far more mild than it is in England, so as the Irish pastures are more green . . . but that in summer, by reason of the cloudy air and watery soil, the heat of the sun hath not such power to ripen corn and fruits, so as their harvest is much later than in England.[1]

Although harvests may have been later in places, the evidence suggests that they appear to have been good harvests. A common cause for complaint was the tempestuousness of the Irish Sea:

> Our mariners observe the sailing into Ireland to be more dangerous, not only because many tides meeting make the sea apt to swell upon any storm, but especially because they ever find the coast of Ireland covered with mists.[2]

Though there were many natural 'waste' areas in Ireland at this time, there were some such areas that were not the product of the activities of nature, for the Irish landscape in 1600 contained plentiful evidence of devastation and decay, and the accounts in the state papers and other sources leave little doubt as to the cause—the incessant military campaigns and guerrilla warfare conducted between English and Irish, and the minor internecine conflicts between indigenous factions. A scorched-earth policy was a dominant and consistent feature of the military campaigns. Lord Mountjoy, writing in 1600 of an incursion into the Wicklow mountains, described how he had 'spoiled and ransacked the countries of Ranelagh and Cosshay, swept away the most part of their [the rebels'] cattle and goods, burnt all their corn and almost all their houses, leaving them little or nothing that might relieve them'.[3] From the camp at the Blackwater in 1601 he wrote:

> We have spoiled here good store of corn already . . . We mean to spoil it all, God willing, ere we go hence, and then cannot he [Tyrone] keep any men this winter. And we find by experience that it is the only sound course to ruin this rebellion.[4]

Tyrone's retaliations took a similar form. Viscount Buttevant in November 1600 had to send to England for corn and provisions for himself and his tenants, 'whose corn and haggards, with most of their cattle, the traitor Tyrone this last summer altogether burned, foraged, and spoiled'.[5] Louth, Meath, and Westmeath in particular seem to have suffered from the constant movement of armies, though none of the border regions of the Pale appears to have escaped the attentions of hostile Irish neighbours. That the Pale itself

[1] Moryson, *Itinerary*, iv, 192.

[2] Ibid., p. 191.

[3] *Cal. S.P. Ire., 1600–01*, p. 178. Ranelagh is the Glenmalure country, Cosshay or Cosha the country around the Derry river between Aughrim and Shillelagh (Liam Price, *The place-names of Co. Wicklow*, pt I (Dublin, 1945), pp 25–6; pt II (1946), pp 80–81) (editorial note).

[4] *Cal. S.P. Ire., 1600–01* p. 442.

[5] Ibid., p. 22.

had also been affected by English armies is evidenced in complaints that English soldiers had

> not much [less] consumed, impoverished, and annoyed the Pale than the traitors. The horse companies, in their passing through the same . . . crossing the country to and fro, wasting with their lingering journeys the inhabitants' corn excessively with their horses, and their goods with their extortion.[1]

Many areas had been wholly devastated, and towns and villages and castles burned and ruined. Ulster, the main objective of the Essex and Mountjoy campaigns, was said to be a desert, and towns such as Armagh and Downpatrick had been more than once devastated. Fynes Moryson described Armagh as 'the metropolitan city of the whole island', but in the time of the rebellion as 'altogether ruinated'.[2] Downpatrick was also 'at this time a ruined town'.[2] Large areas of Connacht had been wasted in the closing years of the sixteenth century: in 1598 County Galway was

> in a manner unpeopled by reason of the spoyles committed in the last rebellion, partlie by the rebell and partlie by the souldier, and the great famine that followed thereupon, which hath so wasted this countie that scarce the hundereth men or hous is to be found now that was several years ago.[3]

County Roscommon was also 'all wasted',[4] and many of the towns of Galway were in decay, notably Athenry which was 'all ruined save the wall'.[5] The process of subjugation of Munster had been completed, and that of Ulster was soon to follow the Irish disaster at Kinsale in 1601. Ireland was thus still in a state of flux, and the landscape of both towns and countryside bore the scars of intensive military campaigns.

The size of the population at this time must have been fairly static, in spite of immigration, for the effects of warfare, devastation, and plague, together with high natural birth rates and death rates, must have kept the population only at replacement level. In the absence of any reliable population figures, the total population at this time can only be conjectured as being less than one million. At a rough guess, the rural population density for *c.* 1600 was probably less than 20 per square mile—very low indeed when compared with the present-day figure of *c.* 100 per square mile. In practice, however, rural densities of population must have differed widely, with relatively high densities in the coastlands, plains, and valleys of Leinster and Munster, and in the more favoured parts of Ulster and Connacht, though all provinces contained large areas of mountain, hill, and bogland which were largely devoid of population except, in some cases, in summer. There is evidence of underpopulation of rural areas in Elizabethan times, for many parts of the country had suffered famine, largely as a result of devastation during the military campaigns and local wars, though bad summers sometimes had a

[1] *Cal. Carew MSS, 1589–1600*, p. 261. [2] Moryson, *Itinerary*, iv, 190.
[3] *Description of Ire. 1598*, pp 138–9. [4] Ibid., p. 150. [5] Ibid., p. 131.

similar effect. The Gaelic system known to the English as 'gavelkind' was held by English observers to be conducive to overpopulation, and was made illegal in 1606, though its practice does not seem to have been as widespread as was sometimes thought. High densities of population existed in the larger towns, though even in Dublin overcrowding did not take place until much later in the seventeenth century.

The population of Ireland derived from three main stocks: Irish, English, and Scots. The Gaelic population, still the great majority, practised a way of life that had its roots in prehistory. The descendants of the Norman English were most numerous in the larger towns and cities, where they formed an oligarchy, and in the feudalised areas of Leinster and Munster, and in very limited parts of Ulster and Connacht. In parts of Munster and Connacht, however, there had been much fusion with the Irish, and the allegiance of Anglo-Norman lords had declined. A third element was of Scottish descent, and included both those who had migrated to the Glens of Antrim in the sixteenth century, and the itinerant mercenaries or heavily armed professional fighting men—'galloglass'[1]—originally of Scottish origin. The regions in which the Gaelic way of life was maintained until the end of the sixteenth century were generally the north and west: Ulster, parts of Connacht, south and west Leinster, west Meath, and south-west Munster. The influence of this difference of origin on the society and economy of Ireland in the sixteenth century was strong, and dictated the geographical pattern of military activity and 'colonial' policy. The military campaigns in Elizabethan times were first waged against the Anglo-Norman lords of Munster and Leinster and then against the Gaelic chiefs of Ulster, with Anglo-Norman authority in the west largely modified by the 'composition of Connacht'.

A striking aspect of the population geography of Ireland at this time was the amount of migration and movement. This included the constant movement of English military forces and their Irish opponents, the latter including many galloglass; the seasonal movement of the Gaelic pastoralists to the high summer pasture on the mountains; the influx of new settlers to the plantation areas, albeit only for short periods of time; and the movement of administrators and officials into, about, and from the country.

Notwithstanding the catholicism of the majority of the population, many of the abbeys and monasteries had been dissolved and their lands confiscated, and many had been totally destroyed during the military campaigns.

Two basic and apparently contrasting traditions influenced the rural landscape and economy of Ireland at this time: the pastoral tradition of the Atlantic fringes of north-western Europe and the tillage-based tradition of the European lowlands. The former was epitomised by the life and landscape

[1] Cf. above, pp 31–2.

of much of the north and west of Ireland, where native tradition still held its own, and the latter by the customs and traditions of the settlers in the Pale and the regions of Leinster and Munster that had been settled by the Anglo-Normans and their descendants. The pastoral economy of the 'Atlantic ends' of Europe, which had evolved since neolithic times, was characterised by distinctive house-types, a general (but not exclusive) emphasis on cattle and sheep-rearing, with seasonal summer usage of hill and mountain pastures, tillage on a relatively small scale, absence of an urban framework, and highly complex forms of land tenure and social structure. The contrasting 'lowland' economy was characterised by greater emphasis on tillage and a more 'sedentary' form of agriculture, village forms of settlement, a higher density of towns and therefore of markets, and a dominance of feudal land tenures and social structures. There were, however, in reality considerable variations in and departures from these 'models' of contrasting rural economies in terms both of their functional characteristics and their spatial distribution, particularly in regions where the two sets of cultural and economic traditions had been intermingled since the time of the Norman settlements.

Within the rural landscape as a whole, one of the contrasts apparent from contemporary descriptions was that between unenclosed or 'champion' land and enclosed land. General accounts give the impression of few enclosures, with the exception of parts of the east and south, and in areas around the larger cities. County Kilkenny was described in 1598 as having 'the most show of civilitie of any other of the border counties, in respect of the fayre seats of houses, the number of castles and the Inglysh manner of inclosure of their grounds'.[1] Fynes Moryson, in Leix in 1600, states that 'it seemed incredible, that by so barbarous inhabitants, the ground should be so well manured, the fields so orderly fenced . . .'[2] The country in the immediate vicinity of Dublin was probably enclosed at this time, and also parts of south Wexford. In apparent contrast were the champion areas. In 1585 Wallop had written that 'in verie few places of Ireland have they any enclosures',[3] and in 1623 the writer of *Advertisements for Ireland* was to write that 'their fields lie open and unclosed'.[4] Tipperary was described as 'a fair champion way',[5] and the Inishowen peninsula 'after the fashion of the country, lies all open, without any manner enclosures'.[6] The country between Trim, Mullingar, and Athlone was all 'champion, whereof the greatest part lay waste'.[7] 'The Liffer' (Lifford) was 'seated in the richest soil of all the north, the country about it champaign'.[6]

Such observations of apparent contrasts in landscape may well be

[1] *Description of Ire., 1598*, p. 65.
[2] Moryson, *Itinerary*, ii, 330.
[3] Cited in F. H. A. Aalen, 'Enclosures in eastern Ireland' in *Ir. Geography*, v, no. 2 (1965), p. 32.
[4] *Advertisements for Ire.*, p. 33.
[5] *Cal. Carew MSS, 1589–1600*, p. 306.
[6] *Cal. S.P. Ire., 1600–01*, p. 94.
[7] Moryson, *Itinerary*, ii, 352.

misleading. The term 'champion' certainly meant to English observers country lacking in conspicuous and obtrusive hedgerows, but this does not necessarily mean that all the land was open and common. Most of the mountains, hills, and uplands were definitely unenclosed, but in some of the lowland areas fields were undoubtedly surrounded and enclosed by such unobtrusive features as low banks, shallow ditches, and wattle fences, which would go unnoticed to the inexperienced eye more used to substantial hedgerows as means of enclosure. There were temporary enclosures to keep livestock off grazing crops: 'where wood is plentiful they hedge in all their corn with stakes and bushes and pull them down in winter and burn them';[1] and the fenced fields that Moryson saw in Leix were probably of the same type. In some cases, the boundaries of properties may have consisted of rows of stones, streams, or turf walls.

The perception of enclosures by alien observers was conditioned to some extent by views of their role in military strategy and attempts at 'anglicisation'. The lack of conspicuous enclosures and hedgerows was a source of irritation to the soldiers, who felt that the movement of the enemy was thus facilitated (though some English writers felt that an open countryside facilitated the movement of their own army), and to administrators and officials who felt that without enclosed fields a stable rural existence for the Irish could not be achieved. One writer thus complained that 'the want of good enclosures is a great help to the rebels, who suddenly raid for cattle and drive them off . . . The Irish churls are not acquainted with this nor any other good English husbandry.'[2]

The existence over large areas of Ireland of a rural landscape not dominated by large hedgerows and fences does not necessarily indicate the ubiquitous occurrence of types of farming based on open or common fields, though there is evidence that various types of open field existed. Medieval evidence for the large baronial estates of the south and east indicates large open tilled fields, subject to three-course rotations, and subdivided into strips, though the classic so-called 'three-field' system does not seem to have been conspicuous. Some survivals of open fields occurred on the archbishop of Dublin's estates as late as the eighteenth century, and there is evidence for large-scale arable cultivation in open fields in parts of south Tipperary in the early seventeenth century.[3] The lowlands of Leinster and Munster were noted for their corn, and it is in these regions that one would expect large-scale arable cultivation to occur. In Connacht and Ulster, in contrast, arable cultivation was on a much smaller scale, though in favoured areas substantial quantities of cereals were grown. The basis of cultivation here seems to

[1] *Advertisements for Ire.*, p. 33. [2] *Cal. S.P. Ire.*, *1601–3*, pp 252–3.

[3] Ingeborg Leister, *Das Werden der Agrarlandschaft in der Grafschaft Tipperary* (*Irland*) (Marburg, 1963).

have been the relatively small open field, often cultivated in common by joint tenants or kin groups, divided into parcels or strips, with the strips of each farmer located in different places within the field. The strips in the open field in some cases were periodically reallocated by ballot. Not all the land in the north and west, however, was held and cultivated in this way: almost certainly there were also compact holdings owned and cultivated by individuals. The general contrast between 'highland' Ireland and the south and east is essentially one of scale of cultivation, for early seventeenth-century surveys show that the amounts of arable land in many settlements of the west in particular were quite small, the total sometimes being less than fifty acres. The denominations of land measurement varied widely, and it is often difficult to assess the area under any particular form of land use. Units commonly used included quarters, trines, cartrons, gneeves, ploughlands, balliboes, gallons, pottles, pints, polls, carves, carucates, stangs, and various kinds of acre, though there was no fixed relationship between the larger and smaller units—for example between the Irish acre and the quarter—and it is also difficult to distinguish the use of these terms as units of assessment from their use as units of measurement.

The methods by which arable land was cultivated varied. In the stony soils of parts of the west of Ireland, land was dug by spades. In other regions ploughing was used. The horse was the dominant means of plough traction and seems to have replaced in the colony, but not in Gaelic Ireland, the oxen mentioned in medieval documents. 'Ploughing by the tail' (the attaching of horses to ploughs by the hairs of their tails) was still practised, including the use of 'the labour of five several persons to every plough and their team of . . . five or six horses were placed all in front, having neither cords, chains nor lines whereby to draw, but every horse by his own tail'.[1] Such methods were used in the west and north, and were associated with a light plough. Heavier ploughs were in use elsewhere. The land was intensively manured and frequently ploughed into ridges, on which the seeds were sown, but there is little evidence of the ridge and furrow topography so characteristic of the heavy clay soils of midland England. The amount of arable land in any given community could be increased, or tired land replaced, by the improvement of pasture land—a right recognised in some of the urban charters and land grants of the period. Common wasteland at Ballinraghter in County Waterford, for example, could be ploughed up for the payment to the lord of the manor of eightpence for every acre ploughed.[2]

The crops cultivated were oats, barley, wheat, rye, and some legumes, with oats more important in the north and west and wheat in the areas of lower rainfall. On Inishowen, 'the commodities this whole island affordeth is only flax, oats and barley; wheat, rye or peas it hath none'.[3] The

[1] Cited in Quinn, *Elizabethans & Irish*, p. 78.
[2] *Cal. pat. rolls Ire., Eliz.*, p. 325
[3] *Cal. S.P. Ire., 1600–01*, p. 94.

organisation of labour for cultivation and harvesting of crops was achieved by a variety of means, ranging from the concerted activities of small groups, often linked by kin, to the large-scale services obligatory under feudal systems. An example of the latter is given in an early seventeenth-century charter for Carlow:

Each of the tenants and cottagers shall weed, in the demesne, corn yearly for three days and reap the corn in autumn for three days; and one woman out of every house in the town shall bind the sheaves of corn in autumn, for one day in each year . . . each of them [the tenants] having a draught horse . . . shall draw the sheaves of corn out of the fields to the area of the castle, for three days yearly . . . ; the tenants shall plow, with their nine plows, in the demesne lands, viz: for the sowing of wheat, three days, and of oats, three days, in each year; and shall carry, with nine wagons, the sheaves of corn for sale, at the fairs or markets yearly held in the town.[1]

The Irish practice of burning grain from the crop standing in the field, or from the straw, receives frequent mention. Arable land, in many instances, formed only a small part of the land of a community and was an ingredient in a complex system of land use, in which land of different quality was employed for different purposes. Arable land, meadowland, and lowland and upland pastures played complementary roles within each micro-economic unit or system. Thus, livestock could be fed on the stubble of fields after the crops had been harvested, but while crops were growing they would be confined to areas of common pasture, and, in summer, in some regions, to more distant pastures. Common lowland pastures in Ireland were normally stinted, because of their relatively small areas and the need to control the number of cattle grazing on them. The full-grown cow was the basic unit, termed variously *collop* or *sum*, and this was converted into livestock equivalents for other type of stock. Urban charters frequently contain reference to the rights of grazing cattle and of gathering turf and fuel which could be exercised on near-by commons.

The pasture lands nearest the settlement were linked with transhumance or 'booleying', that is of taking the cattle to more extensive distant pastures during the summer. The most common venue was the hill and mountain pasture, but movement also took place to pastures on lowland bogs which dried out in the summer. The practice of transhumance received much attention from English observers and was generally condemned as barbarous. Spenser's Irenaeus says:

There is one use amongst them, to keep their cattle and to live themselves the most part of the year in bollies, pasturing upon the mountain and waste wild places, and removing still to fresh land as they have depastured the former days [*sic*].[2]

Booleying was condemned on the ground that it provided hiding-places for

[1] *Cal. pat. rolls Ire., Eliz.*, p. 515.

[2] Spenser, *View*, ed. Renwick (1970), p. 49.

outlaws and malcontents, and stolen cattle, and as conducive to laziness and licentiousness. The booleys were the settlements on the summer pastures where the young people would live in turf or wickerwork huts while tending the cattle, usually from May to autumn. Milk was made into butter and cheese, and ultimately taken back to the home settlement for storage. Land was sometimes cultivated near the booley. Cattle were often brought at night into an enclosure. Definite linkages existed between the lowland areas of the parent settlements and the summer pastures, and settlements exercised strong proprietorial rights over them. These rhythmic seasonal movements were very much part of the Atlantic pastoral tradition, and particularly characteristic of most mountain areas of Ulster, Connacht, and west Munster.

There can be no doubt of the continuing importance of cattle and other animals in the Irish rural economy at this time. In practice, that economy was mixed in character, and just as the picture given of a society of 'nomadic pastoralists' in the remoter areas must be tempered by recognition of the fact that tillage was an important adjunct, so it must be recognised that cattle-rearing on a large scale was not confined to the non-anglicised parts of the country. The statistics, albeit exaggerated in many cases, are impressive. One of Tyrone's excursions into Louth produced a prey 'estimated as 2,000 cows, 1,000 garrauds [garrans, or small horses], 4,000 sheep and swine'.[1] The garrison at Derry, in a raid on Inch island, claimed to have brought away 2,000 sheep, 200 garrans, 250 cows.[2] On Inishowen, 'the cattle that feed most upon it are cows, horses, sheep and swine, of every of which sort there was wonderful plenty'.[2] In 1598 it was estimated that the earl of Tyrone had not less than 120,000 milch cows in Tyrone, with 'three times more of barren kine besides other cattle'.[3] In some regions there were large numbers of horses, and 'where they are not compelled to eat up their stud mares ... they have great breeds of horses, which are a very great commodity'.[4] The large numbers of cattle, sheep, horses, and pigs are indisputable, though in many cases they cannot have been of very good quality. The existence of extensive herds of animals made them vulnerable to stealing, both as military action and by the time-honoured practice of cattle-raiding,[5] and necessitated protective measures, including the use of enclosures for night-time protection, the herding of the animals into bogs and woods, and the employment of herdsmen. In addition to human enemies and wolves, the climate in winter could pose severe problems in some areas, which could be countered only by keeping them in dwelling-houses and feeding them with straw and hay, though these may not have been available in Gaelic areas, where straw was burned and not much hay made.

The dependence of the people on milk and milk products or 'whitemeats' is constantly noted by contemporary observers. The continuation of the rebellion

[1] *Cal. S.P. Ire., 1601–3*, p. 135. [2] Ibid., *1600–01*, p. 94. [3] Ibid., *1598–9*, pp 384–5. [4] Ibid., *1601–3*, p. 251. [5] See plate 2.

in the summer of 1600 was attributed to the fact that the Irish 'were living upon the milk and butter of their kine grazing on the mountains and in fastnesses'.[1] Milk, curds, cheese, and butter were extremely important items in the Irish diet, but meat was also a significant item.

The ways in which land was held were exceedingly complex and varied, but a crude distinction may perhaps be made between areas where Gaelic and Norman modes of tenure prevailed. In the Gaelic and gaelicised regions the periodic redistribution of land under the native systems of partible and collective inheritance (the 'custom in nature of gavelkind', as it is called by English writers)[2] tended to discourage the erection of permanent buildings or even fences, and was a primary reason for the general rarity of enclosed fields which has been already referred to. The actual systems of partition varied from district to district; in some areas care was taken to secure an equal and impartial division between the various co-heirs entitled to share, while in others—such as parts of Munster and Ulster—the lord could set out shares to his kinsmen more or less at his own will, and keep the largest and best portion for himself. In some areas, again, the lands were redistributed anew every year, but in most places a fresh division took place only after the death of a co-heir. Continued subdivision over several generations could result in the fragmentation of a large property into very small holdings, a process usually followed by one of reconsolidation by purchase or mortgage in the hands of a single rich or powerful individual. Actual cultivation of the lands might be undertaken by the landowners themselves with the aid of dependent or hired labourers or might be carried on by tenants, holding either by a fixed contractual rent or on a share-cropping basis. Letting for the 'fourth sheaf', by which the tenants paid the landlord a fourth of the crop, along with various other exactions and duties in kind, was usual in the Gaelic areas in this period. In the Gaelic and gaelicised Norman areas there must have been little practical difference, in economic terms, between the position of the free landowner burdened with various exactions by his lord or chief and that of the tenant-at-will, but the difference became a vital one after the imposition of English law. The difficulties experienced in determining the precise status under English law of the occupiers of Irish land were especially prominent in Munster in the aftermath of the Desmond rebellion.[3]

By the late sixteenth century the various medieval forms of manorial tenures in the Anglo-Norman areas had been replaced by or reduced to two main systems; the leasing of 'farms' for fixed rents, usually for twenty-one years, and letting on a share-cropping basis, here usually the 'third sheaf' or

[1] *Cal. S.P. Ire., 1600*, p. 244.

[2] See Nicholls, 'Gaelic society and economy', above, vol. ii; 'Some documents on Irish law and custom in the 16th century' in *Anal. Hib.* no. 26 (1970), pp 105–29; *Gaelic Ire.*, pp 57–67.

[3] Nicholls, 'Gaelic society and economy', as above.

even half the crop, rather than the 'fourth sheaf' already referred to as usual in the Gaelic and more gaelicised regions. The tenants might be either single individuals of substance or groups of smaller tenants, though there is seldom information as to whether the latter would have cultivated their lands jointly or have subdivided among themselves. Subletting was common. In the counties of the Pale fairly large farms, held and cultivated by substantial tenants, seem to have been usual. The small manorial freeholds and copyholds had by this date been largely consolidated in the hands of fairly large proprietors, though this consolidation of proprietorship was not always or necessarily accompanied by physical consolidation of the actual holdings themselves. In the case of letting for a third or half the crop the landlord provided a corresponding share of the seed; in 1610 'the ancient usage' of County Wexford was that the landlord provided half the seed and received half the crop (after deduction of the reapers' wages and of the customary payment to the smith), the tenants being bound not only to provide the labour for cultivation but also to reap, bind, rick, cart, and thresh the landlord's share of the crop.[1] Different forms of tenancy could coexist even on the same estate. In 1607 Lord Tulleophelim's lands in County Carlow were set on various systems; the demesne lands were set for the 'fourth sheaf', along with customary labour services and renders in pigs, sheep, hens, and butter; the outlying townlands either for money rents alone, for money rents accompanied by labour services and customary payments in kind, or for the 'third sheaf'.[2] Such labour services and customary renders were commonly reserved on leases in some areas, such as County Kilkenny.

The patterns of rural settlement associated with such highly complex rural societies and tenurial systems appear to have varied widely. It is difficult to distinguish between areas of strongly clustered settlement forms and areas of isolated or more dispersed settlement, for most parts of the country seem to have had a variety of forms, representing in some instances a strong continuity with the past linked to new settlement forms. The terminology of contemporary commentators is less than helpful, for reference is made to villages, hamlets, and 'towns' without their connotation always being made clear. Nucleated settlements certainly existed, some in the vicinity of forts. At Lifford, in Donegal, there were 'some eighty houses set in a plain green upon the river side, and compassed with an old ditch'.[3] Near Armagh, Sir Henry Danvers was sent in 1601 'to burn some twenty fair timber houses';[4] in the same year Tyrone spoiled twenty-two villages in Meath,[5] and Sir Henry Power, in a campaign in Offaly, burned a 'town and houses in the woods'.[6] Moryson wrote:

For other Irish dwellings, it may be said of them as Caesar said of the old

[1] Nicholls, *Gaelic Ire.*, p. 116.
[2] N.L.I., MS 2506, f. 33.
[3] *Cal. S.P. Ire.*, *1600–01*, p. 93.
[4] Moryson, *Itinerary*, ii, 415.
[5] *Cal. S.P. Ire.*, *1601–3*, p. 135.
[6] Ibid., *1600–01*, p. 227.

Britons' houses. They call it a town when they have compassed a skirt of wood with trees cut down, whither they may retire themselves and their cattle.[1]

In 1599 the earl of Essex refers to resistance 'at a village on our right hand, seated on the skirt of a great wood, and flanked on two sides with two groves of underwood'.[2] At Nislerath in Louth, near a castle and bawn, were 'many thatched houses to lodge our men in'.[3] Part of Inishowen was 'so full of poor Irish houses, as it seems all in a manner but one town'.[4]

In contrast to these villages and hamlets were the tall square castles or tower houses both of Old English and Irish lords, constituting in many cases a form of dispersed settlement. Mostly built of stone in the later medieval period, they seem to be the outcome of a desire for greater ostentation of living style, and were very numerous. In some cases they had separate or conjoined halls which were the living quarters. Moryson says that 'commonly they have a spatious hall joyning to the castle, and built of timber and clay, wherein they eat with their family'.[5] Some also had a great bawn or enclosure in which the cattle could be kept at night: 'the cattle are brought at evening within the bawns of castles where they stand or lie all night in a dirty yard'.[6] Isolated dwellings were also characteristic of some of the areas settled early under the scheme for the plantation in Munster, but such dispersal rendered the new settlers highly vulnerable to attack: a report in 1597 states that

where divers Englishmen have been lately murdered and spoiled, by reason they have so singled their dwellings that they lie open to the malefactor without ability of defence or mutual succour . . . all English inhabitants should be drawn into a near neighbourhood of twenty households at the least; . . . and none not inhabiting in a castle to be suffered to dwell out of such neighbourhood.[7]

In addition to the settlement types described above, there were also survivals of ancient dispersed settlement forms, notably raths and crannogs, some of which continued in use at this time. Maps produced by Bartlett, Mountjoy's cartographer, show examples of both. At Monaghan, for example, there was a 'gentleman's residence' in a crannog: the chief dwelling-place of MacMahon, the lord of the district, was protected by a wattle palisade within which was a bawn and a house.[8] Earthen enclosures (*cinn áite*) were also used by some settlers, for example in Roscommon. Crannogs were very common in Ulster[9] and Connacht. At Tullaghoge, in the heartland of the

[1] Cited in Quinn, *Elizabethans & Irish*, p. 74.
[2] *Cal. Carew MSS*, *1589–1600*, p. 309.
[3] *Cal. S.P. Ire.*, *1599–1600*, p. 146.
[4] Ibid., *1600–01*, p. 94.
[5] Cited by C. Ó Danachair, 'Representation of houses on some Irish maps of *c.* 1600' in G. Jenkins (ed.), *Studies in folk life* (London, 1969), p. 96.
[6] Cited in Quinn, *Elizabethans & Irish*, p. 74.
[7] *Cal. Carew MSS*, *1589–1600*, p. 208.
[8] *Ulster maps*, *c. 1600*, p. 9; see also Ó Danachair, loc. cit., p. 96.
[9] See, for example, plate 3.

O'Neills, there was a rath with houses inside.[1] The degree of settlement dispersal varied regionally, but there are references to dispersed houses in the south and west, and in pre-plantation Ulster 'living dispersedly' was regarded by the English as the hallmark of the native Irish, though the exact connotations of the term are not clear.

The mode of construction and type of building materials used for rural dwellings varied. Apart from its use in the construction of castles, stone was rarely used. Far more common was the use of timber, clay, turf sods, and tree boughs as basic construction materials, and these were often covered with turf, straw, and wattles. Wattling was common, and there were several different types. Roofs were frequently thatched, with corn straw in many cases, though there are examples of tiled roofs. Decoration of walls took the form of lime-washing (whitewashing). There were chimneys and windows in the more substantial dwellings. The ground plans could be elliptical, round, rectangular, or square, indicating the intermixture of heterogeneous cultural influences. There are many examples of the varying combinations of styles and materials. At Mountnorris, some fifty-four houses were shown on a map of *c.* 1600, thirty-six of which had an 'Irish' type of elliptical ground plan. They were all thatched, and seven had chimneys. Most of the others were 'English' style cottages with tiled gable roofs, and some had chimneys.[2] At Armagh, where Camden described 'a few small wattled cottages',[2] there were six small thatched buildings, oval or elliptical in plan, with plastered wattle and whitewashed walls.[2] These appear similar to the 'beehive' dwellings shown on other Elizabethan maps, at Carrickfergus, for example.[3] The walls of these dwellings were rounded or sub-rectangular, because of the fragility of the building material.

The towns in Elizabethan Ireland were few in number, for the wave of town development in the north had yet to come. The principal towns were the seaport towns located on sites which for the most part had first been chosen by the Norsemen. Without exception, all the larger towns were sited in sheltered situations at the head of estuaries or bays which facilitated the vital external links with Britain, and also with France and Spain. In a sense, the urban system of Ireland at this time formed part of an imperial system, based on England, in that it comprised

> a series of local networks of interconnected coastal points bound together into oceanic trunk lines to the home base . . . with various holdings providing military and logistic support. In geographical form it was fragmentary, shallow in continental penetration, irregular in its territorial political hierarchy, and unstable in territorial pattern over any considerable period of time.[4]

[1] Plate 3; Ó Danachair, loc. cit., p. 96. [2] Plate 4.
[3] G. Camblin, *The town in Ulster* (Belfast, 1951), frontispiece.
[4] D. W. Meinig, 'A macrogeography of western imperialism: some morphologies of moving

The tenuous nature of the links between these port towns and England had, however, produced a high degree of political autonomy which was deemed by some to be detrimental to the colonial interest. Such a feeling was expressed by Sir George Carew in a letter advising the privy council in November 1600 to 'be sparing in any such grant [to enlarge the powers of the Munster towns], for the people are sufficiently insolent, stubborn and proud already, and the increasing of their franchises will increase ill humours in them'.[1] Nevertheless the towns had acted as bastions of loyalty during times of rebellion, and some of them had suffered considerably as a result. In 1600 the ecclesiastical city of Armagh was in a ruinous condition; Galway was greatly 'decayed'. Athenry was described by Sir Henry Sidney as 'the most woeful spectacle that I ever looked on in any of the queen's dominions',[2] for it had been totally burned. Kilmallock had also been burned, but was recovering rapidly.

Towns were most numerous in Leinster and Munster—provinces long settled by peoples with strong urban traditions. The principal city was Dublin, 'the royal city of Ireland, its most notable mart and chief seat of justice, defended with strong walls, adorned with beautiful buildings and well peopled with inhabitants'.[3] There were navigational difficulties in Dublin Bay—'the only fault of this city is that it is less frequented of merchant estrangers because of the bare [barred] haven'[4]—occasioned by the bar and the location of the port area at Ringsend, but, these notwithstanding, Dublin was an extremely important centre of administration and a very large market. Its port hinterland included the whole of Leinster and parts of Ulster. In aspect Dublin was still a medieval town, the greater part of it located within the walls, of which Dublin castle marked the south-eastern limit. Speed's map of 1610, which shows Dublin largely as it was in Elizabethan times (though with some post-1603 detail), suggests that there had been very little development outside the walls, apart from some suburbs to the south and the newly founded Trinity College to the east.[5] The city of Waterford had been described in 1577 as

> properly builded, and very well compact, somewhat close by reason of their thick buildings and narrow streets. The haven is passing good, by which the citizens through the increase of foreign traffic in short space attaign to abundance of wealth.[6]

Unlike Dublin it had an excellent harbour, and the quays could be approached by large vessels at all states of the tide. It had strong trading links with

frontiers of political control' in Fay Gale and Graham H. Lawton (ed.), *Settlement and encounter* (Melbourne, 1969), pp 222–3.

[1] *Cal. Carew MSS*, *1589–1600*, p. 472.

[2] Ibid., p. lxxvii.

[3] William Camden, *Britannia*, ed. R. Gough (London, 1789), iii, 549.

[4] Stanihurst, 'Description of Ire.' in Holinshed (1807–8 ed.), vi, 21.

[5] See plate 5.

[6] Ibid., p. 29.

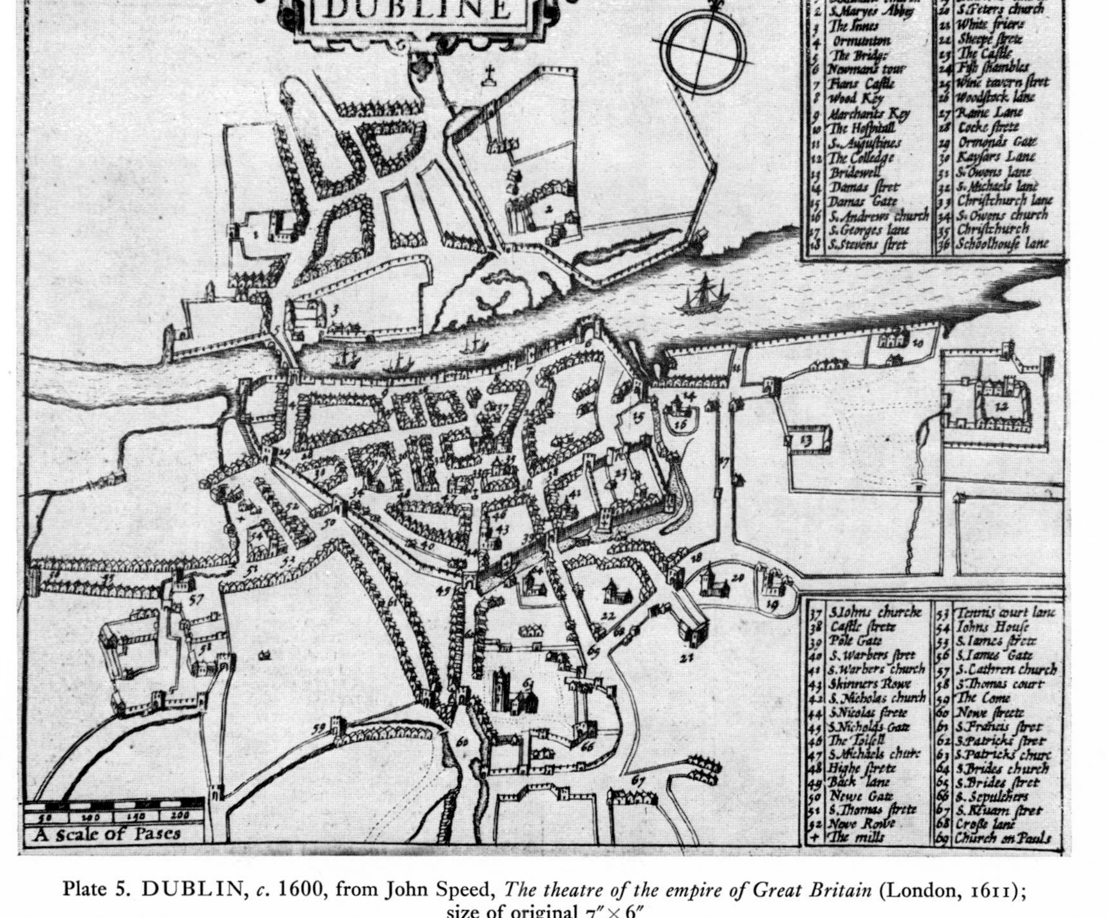

Plate 5. DUBLIN, *c.* 1600, from John Speed, *The theatre of the empire of Great Britain* (London, 1611); size of original 7″ × 6″

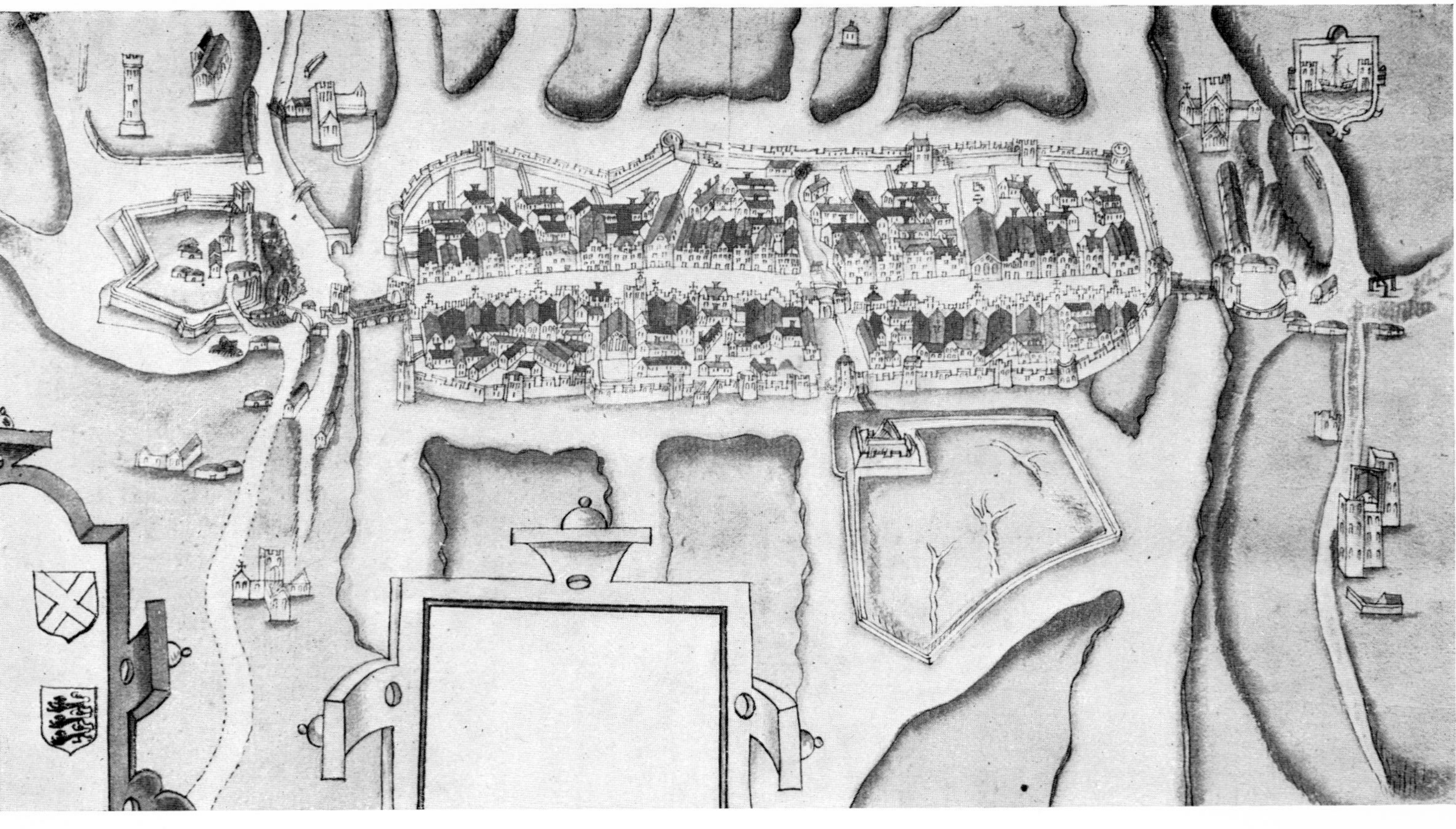

Plate 6. CORK, *c.* 1601 (T.C.D., MS 1209, no. 46); size of original 19″ × 10″

south-west England, Spain, and France: 'there belongeth more ships to the citties of Waterford and Wexford than to all Ireland besides'.[1] Limerick was an important city, the second or third largest in Ireland at the time. It had the considerable geographical advantage of a location on the Shannon estuary—'the very main sea is three score miles distant from the town, and yet the river is so navigable as a ship of 200 tons may sail to the quay of the city'[1]—but had suffered economically from the conflicts in Munster, and its prosperity had declined. Cork had suffered in a similar way, though 'happily planted on the sea' with a 'haven royal',[1] but appears to have made a rapid recovery.[2] Both Cork and Limerick occupied islands: Cork, on an island or alluvial flat in the river Lee, was oval in shape, and accessible only by bridges;[3] the 'English town' at Limerick was sited on the King's Island. Both were heavily fortified. Galway had developed as the main city of Connacht, and by virtue of its remoteness from other cities and royal authority had become almost autonomous. Increasing attempts to pacify and subjugate the west and to anticipate attacks via the west coast led to an increase in the city's fortifications. The merchants were 'rich, and great adventurers at sea'[4] and the town 'exceeding fayre and well built', partly in Spanish style on account of the substantial trading links with Spain.[5]

The smaller port towns included Wexford, Youghal, Dundalk, Drogheda, and New Ross. Wexford, with a sheltered harbour formed by the estuary of the river Slaney, was an important fishing port. Youghal, still largely within its medieval walls, had been much damaged by warfare in the later sixteenth century, but was in a prosperous condition at the turn of the century, being a significant trading and fishing port. A temporary boost in its fortune had come from its function as a port for the new plantation settlements in Munster. Its main links were with the ports of south-west England, and its main exports were timber and wool. The main imports included grain, wine, salt, cloth, hardware, and hops.[6]

Drogheda had in 1577 been 'accounted the best town in Ireland, and truly not far behind some of the cities',[7] and on account of the increasing success of military campaigns against Ulster in the late sixteenth century enjoyed an expansion of function and increase in prosperity. Trading links were with Chester. New Ross, which 'seems to have been in ancient time a town of great port',[7] had apparently declined in prosperity, but was still strongly fortified.

There were very few large inland towns. Kilkenny was one of these: 'the chief of the towns within land, memorable for the civility of its inhabitants'.[8]

[1] Ibid., p. 30. [2] Beckett, *Mod. Ire.*, p. 31. [3] See plate 6.

[4] *Cal. Carew MSS*, *1603–24*, p. 295. [5] *Description of Ire.*, *1598*, p. 131.

[6] A. R. Orme, 'Youghal, County Cork—growth, decay, resurgence' in *Ir. Geography*, v, no. 3 (1966), p. 131.

[7] Stanihurst, 'Description of Ire.' in Holinshed, vi, 30.

[8] Moryson, *Itinerary*, iv, 187–8.

Within the settled areas of the Pale and its borderlands there was a network of small towns, many of them walled, some of which had suffered extreme vicissitudes of fortune. Typical of the small market towns were Athboy, Kells, Trim, Dunboyne, and Navan in Meath; Mullingar in Westmeath; Thomastown, Callan, Inistioge, and Gowran in Kilkenny; Kildare, Kilcullen, Naas, Leixlip, and Maynooth in Kildare; and Swords and Lusk in Dublin.

There were very few towns in Ulster, apart from such older garrison towns as Newry and Carrickfergus, and such ecclesiastical settlements as Armagh, Derry, and Downpatrick. Newry had developed around a Norman castle and Cistercian abbey, and in the late sixteenth century had been described by Sir Henry Sidney as 'well planted with inhabitants and increased in beauty and building'.[1] Armagh and Downpatrick had been badly plundered, and both were in a ruinous state at this time. Contemporary plans of Carrickfergus show it as a walled town, though it may not have been fully walled with stone until after 1600, with both castellated dwellings and 'beehive' cottages inside the walled area, only a small part of which was actually built on.[2] Carrickfergus was an important port. Derry, an ancient monastic settlement associated with St Columba, had been marked out since the middle of the sixteenth century as a place that ought to be occupied and held for the crown. But apart from a short-lived attempt in 1566–7 nothing was done till 1600, when, at a critical point in the war against O'Neill, Sir Henry Docwra succeeded in planting a garrison at Derry. This contributed to the defeat of O'Neill and prepared the way for the far-reaching enterprise of the city of London which, ten years later, was to give the place a new name, Londonderry.[3]

Urban densities thus varied widely, but there were similarities in the urban morphology and character of many of the towns. Common features were town walls and fortifications. In Elizabethan Ireland there were over forty walled towns, their fortifications having been constructed to withstand prolonged as well as sudden attacks. The port towns frequently had quays guarded by moles and small castles, as at Carrickfergus. The walls themselves were often of substantial proportions; those of Dublin, Wexford, Limerick, Cork, and Galway appear to have been extremely thick, and constant efforts were made to maintain and improve their efficiency. The walls ran between towers and castles, and massive gates allowed passage into the towns. The continued existence of walled towns at this time is a clear testimony to the general state of insecurity. In Cork, where the walls were ten feet thick in places and fifty feet high, the gates were continually guarded because of 'evil neighbours, the Irish outlaws'.[4] The necessity for

[1] Camblin, *The town in Ulster*, p. 12. [2] Ibid., frontispiece, p. 12; pl. 1.

[3] Moody, *Londonderry plantation*, pp 51–6, 62–78; and see above, pp 130–31.

[4] Stanihurst, 'Description of Ire.' in Holinshed, vi, 30.

vigilance is clearly demonstrated by the fate of such places as Athenry and Mullingar.

Within the walls of the towns the streets appear to have been narrow and dark: Waterford was described as having 'thick buildings and narrow streets',[1] and surviving street patterns in Kilkenny, New Ross, Wexford, and Limerick preserve this image. The long narrow building-blocks, frequently associated with curving streets, reflect in many cases the influence of physical site on Norman town planning. Buildings varied in construction. According to Fynes Moryson,

> the houses of the Irish cities, as Cork, Galway and Limerick (the fairest of them for building) are of unwrought free stone or flint, or unpolished stones, built some two stories high, and covered with tile. The houses of Dublin and Waterford are for the most part of timber, clay and plaster.[2]

Dingle, in 1598, comprised one main street with gates at each end to open and close in time of war. The houses were 'strong built, [with] thick walls, and narrow windows, like unto castles'.[3] The use of stone and brick was increasing in Dublin at this time, and replacing the Tudor cage-work houses.[4] A castellated tower-house type of dwelling was quite common. An interesting feature is the presence, in some towns, of thatched cottages of varying styles. They are particularly conspicuous in the north; at Newry, in a plan of 1570, a number of small beehive dwellings are shown, notably on the northern side of 'the Bayse town' in an unfortified area.[5] Similar dwellings are shown on maps of Armagh.[6] Not all of the thatched dwellings were of the 'Irish' type; some were obviously imitations of English styles, and were probably used to house soldiers. They were a great fire risk:

> In the heart of the best walled towns, cities, and boroughs there stand many poor cottages of straw, chaff and clay to the eyesore of the whole town . . . . These late years, fire hath wasted many houses in most towns there, which I take proceeds from the number of thatched houses there in the walled towns.[7]

The wealthier and more important inhabitants lived in the centre of the cities—a pattern maintained in Dublin, for example, until the late seventeenth century—and there is little evidence of 'extra-mural' suburban development on a large scale, though there were some such suburbs in Dublin and Cork.

The older towns of Ireland at this time had a broad functional basis: they acted as centres of administration and defence, and as market towns, and many of them were also port towns. The right to hold markets and fairs was written into successive charters, and the monopolistic trading-rights of the burgesses and inhabitants were jealously guarded, and improved wherever

[1] Ibid., p. 28.
[2] Moryson, *Itinerary*, iii, 498.
[3] *Description of Ire., 1598*, p. 189.
[4] Beckett, *Mod. Ire.*, p. 30.
[5] Camblin, *The town in Ulster*, p. 14.
[6] *Ulster maps, c. 1600*, pp 5–6.
[7] *Advertisements for Ire.*, p. 36.

possible. A problem that constantly perturbed English visitors was the reluctance of the Irish to bring their cattle and produce to the towns for sale, which was considered to be conducive to lawlessness. The association of towns with a 'civilised' existence had influenced, and continued to influence, English attempts to establish a more comprehensive urban network in Ireland.

Attempts at plantation in the sixteenth century in Leix and Offaly and in Munster had in part initiated the development of a new type of town. In 1556 the territories of Leix and Offaly were shired and named Queen's and King's Counties, and the small forts at Daingean and Fort Leix renamed Philipstown and Maryborough. In 1567 they were made market towns and in 1569 given borough status, sending representatives to the parliament, but this process was the result of unrealistic and over-optimistic thinking, in the sense that the two new 'towns' remained little more than fortified garrisons, though they did provide bases for future urbanisation in an unurbanised region. Attempts to effect a major colonisation of Munster were largely thwarted by mismanagement and native opposition, and the development of new or redeveloped towns awaited the entrepreneurial skill of Richard Boyle in the early years of the seventeenth century. The major wave of urbanisation, under the Ulster plantation, had yet to come.

The communications system of Ireland at this time was poor. The port towns could maintain communication by sea, but inland communication, notably by road, was notoriously bad, necessitating the use of sea and river routes. Sir George Carew, writing in 1600, says that he had to retain a crompster [galley] 'to waft victual from Corke to Gallwaye'.[1] The 'river of Lough Erne' was also 'convenient'[2] for transporting victuals. Victuals for the armies in Ulster were transported by sea. Inland, there can have been very few roads, and journeys on horseback through the 'straits', passes, and fastnesses were fraught with dangers, both from the enemy and from the elements. Bridges were rare, and rivers often had to be forded. In 1601 parts of the south-west were described thus: 'all these countries are sunken with bogs and woods [and] the passages are very strait passes and fords up to [the] saddle skirts in sundry places within a mile'.[3] After seven days of continuous rain during one period in the summer of 1600, the fords near Armagh and Newry were totally impassable.[4] Spenser's Irenaeus says that 'in all straits and narrow passages, as between two bogs, or through any deep ford, or under any mountain side, there should be some little fortilage, or wooden castle set' for the protection of travellers. Similarly he suggested that bridges should be built upon all rivers, and all the fords 'marred and spilt' to give easier control of movement.[5]

[1] *Cal. Carew MSS*, *1589–1600*, p. 403. [2] Ibid., p. 199. [3] Ibid., p. 368.
[4] *Cal. S.P. Ire.*, *1600–01*, p. 29. [5] Spenser, *View*, ed. Renwick (1970), p. 164.

There is no evidence of attempts at improvement of inland communications, and it appears that the network used was that inherited from earlier times. Even in 1623 the complaint was made that 'the ways are not passable as being not smooth nor repaired, not yet much frequented by carriers, wainmen and the like industrious men here so common'.[1] Inns were rare—a contrast to England at this time, where they were frequent along the major thoroughfares and facilitated the movement of men and goods over long distances. The rivers of Ireland were extensively used for the transportation of goods, notably timber, though their navigation was hindered by fords, various natural obstructions, and 'weirs and other bars there overthwart the waters by private men for catching of the fish'.[2]

The most common vehicle for road or land transport was probably the wheel-less slide-car, better adapted to the physical conditions, notably of the bog roads, than the heavier two-wheeled cart. The low-backed block-wheel car was also in use, though mainly in the urban areas.[3]

The external communications network of Ireland was more extensive and relatively efficient, befitting an island situation. In addition to the major port towns, there was a host of smaller ports engaged in various trading activities with ports in England, Scotland, Wales, France, and Spain. A sixteenth-century survey lists seventy 'havens' in Ireland, including Strangford Lough, 'a "real haven" wherein there is thought to be an island for every day of the year', Ardglass, 'a crib for small boats', Dundrum, 'for small boats and barks for timber', Dundalk, 'a shole bay', and Malahide, 'a bar haven'.[4]

One feature that constantly figures in contemporary accounts is the use of the small ports of the north and west for trade between the 'rebels' and the Scots and French. There was 'frequent trade' into Strangford Lough 'of Scottish barques with munition, cloth, wine, and *aqua vitae*, often supplying the rebel',[5] and similar trade into Lough Foyle, where 'some of the Scottish galleys trading with those parts bring victuals and other necessaries to the rebels'.[6]

The major towns of England and Wales involved in trade with Ireland were naturally the ports of the west and south-west, notably Liverpool, Chester, Milford, Carmarthen, Gloucester, Cardiff, Bristol, Barnstaple, and many smaller south-western ports, including Bridgwater, Minehead, Dartmouth, Exeter, Fowey, Plymouth, Poole, Ilfracombe, Penzance, and Helford.[7] There was little trade with the eastern ports of England, or with London. Trade with Spain and France, which had formerly been extensive, had declined.

[1] *Advertisements for Ire.*, p. 33. [2] Ibid., p. 34.

[3] Evans, *Ir. folkways*, pp 165, 174; A. T. Lucas, 'Cattle in ancient and medieval Irish society' in *O'Connell School Union Record, 1937–58* (1958).

[4] *Cal. S.P. Ire., 1601–3*, pp 676–7. [5] Ibid., p. 505.

[6] *Cal. Carew MSS, 1589–1600*, p. 375.

[7] Ada Longfield, 'Anglo-Irish trade in the sixteenth century as illustrated by the English customs accounts and port books' in *R.I.A. Proc.*, xxxvi, sect. C, no. 17 (1924), p. 321.

The major exports from Ireland were fish, hides, wool, linen and linen yarn, timber, wax, and tallow. The abundant fish stocks in the seas and rivers of Ireland constantly figure in contemporary accounts:

The rivers or lakes of fresh water, as the same be many, even so do they minister abondance of fish and of salmons above all other greatest plentye. Upon the sea coastes is such abondance of fish for every season that many nations make their repaire thither for fish namely herrings, codde . . .[1]

Lough Swilly 'hath an excellent good herring fishing for two months in the latter end of summer, and it is full of good oysters', and the rivers running into it were full of salmon.[2] Strangford Lough 'and all the coast from Strangford to Howth is so plentiful all the year round with cod and ling that a whole army might be victualled from the fishings there'.[3] Oyster fisheries were widespread.[4] Salmon, herrings, and hake were the major fish exported, with ling, haddock, and cod less important. Quantities of salt fish were also exported.

As becoming a country where cattle and a variety of wild animals were common, hides were also a major export. They included those of the marten, cattle, sheep, kid, rabbit, deer, fawn, otter, wolf, and fox.[5] Wool and woollen cloths and clothes were also significant. The wool produced in Ireland was generally of a coarse variety, 'but where their breede . . . is maintained they prove well and their wooles in such places be staple enough and of their courser sortes are made rugges the best in the world'.[6] Such rugs, together with cloaks or mantles, flannel, and blankets were exported in large quantities to England.

The export of linen and linen yarn had been restricted in the sixteenth century both by statute and by the effects of warfare, particularly in the south, but both items were exported from the ports of the east and north coasts. The 'rebels' of the north, for example, were known to have 'a great commodity of yarn which formerly they have traded into England but now they reserve it to exchange for munition'.[7]

Large quantities of timber were exported in the forms of semi-processed timber and a variety of staves, including pipe staves, hogshead and barrel staves, and wainscot staves. The major producing and exporting region was south Munster, from which timber was shipped to England, France, the Low Countries, the Mediterranean, and the Canary Islands. Timber was also shipped to Scotland.

The principal imports were salt, coal, iron, wine, and a host of 'luxury'

[1] Quinn (ed.), 'A discourse of Ireland', p. 160.

[2] *Cal. S.P. Ire.*, *1600–01*, p. 94.

[3] Ibid., *1601–3*, p. 317.

[4] A. E. J. Went, 'Historical notes on the oyster fisheries of Ireland' in *R.I.A. Proc.*, lxii, sect. C, no. 7 (1962), pp 195–223.

[5] Longfield, 'Anglo-Irish trade', p. 323.

[6] Quinn (ed.), 'A discourse of Ireland', p. 324.

[7] *Cal. S.P. Ire.*, *1601–3*, p. 251.

commodities. Salt was used, *inter alia*, for processing and preserving fish and hides, and was imported from Spain, France, and England. Coal came mainly from South Wales, and iron from Spain and England. Wine from France and Spain was imported directly and indirectly via England. The import of 'provisions' was extensive.

Piracy and smuggling were significant features of Irish maritime activity, the former being the more prominent in contemporary accounts. It was urged that 'galleys should be built and sent over to Ireland to keep the sea coasts from the O'Malleys and other rebels. These live by robbing poor fishermen and others that pass in small vessels.'[1] In 1600 Sir George Carew refers to the presence of English galleys having 'freed these coasts of Irish pirates, and cleared the Shannon of the traitors' galleys, wherein they begin to abound, being now grown very perfect seamen'.[2]

Manufactured or processed goods contributed little to Ireland's exports for the simple reason that industry was very poorly developed. Much of the substantial raw material available was exported for processing elsewhere, and industrial activity was extremely limited. The basis of domestic industry was wool.

> Their wool is coarse, and merchants may not export it, forbidden by a law made on behalf of the poor, that they may be nourished by making it into cloth, namely rugs (whereof the best are made at Waterford) and mantles generally worn by men and women and exported in great quantity.[3]

In spite of statutory limitation on the export of wool, it was in fact exported, often by smuggling, and it may be that lack of supplies hindered the full development of a woollen industry, but it seems that the production of woollen cloths and goods was increasing. It was to receive further stimulus from the efforts of planters such as Boyle in Munster. Linen goods and linen yarn also were produced and used in domestic industry, but the wars of the late sixteenth century seem to have had the effect of limiting the growing of flax and production of linen and yarn in the areas around Carlingford, Drogheda, Dundalk, and Dublin, though some twenty years later the author of *Advertisements for Ireland* could point to a revival: 'neither can any man deny but that the quantity of yarn there since that time hath much increased by the continuance of peace'.[4]

The woodlands of Ireland were extensively exploited and formed the basis for a variety of industries. The cutting and processing of timber were widespread, particularly in Munster, and large quantities were exported. Bark from oak trees was used in tanning, which had become well established by the end of the sixteenth century, and the iron industry was also beginning

[1] Ibid., p. 258. [2] *Cal. Carew MSS, 1589–1600*, p. 403.
[3] Moryson, *Itinerary*, iv, 194. [4] *Advertisements for Ire.*, p. 8.

to make inroads into the woods, though the extent of the iron industry has not been clearly established. There was some shipbuilding.

The mineral resources of the country were recognised, but little used. Moryson was of the opinion that 'the mountains would yield abundance of metals',[1] and another description refers to 'metalls whereof Ireland hath both diversity and plenty if the same might be sought for and safely wrought upon'.[2] A list of mines includes lead mines at Ardglass, Malahide, Clontarf, Lemcarrick (sixty miles north-west of Galway), and Kilmallock; silver mines near Waterford, and in Kerry, at Knockdrin; copper mines near Galway and at Bantry; and an alum mine forty miles west of Limerick.[3] Various attempts had been made to stimulate exploitation of Irish mines in the sixteenth century, including the silver mines at Clonmines in County Wexford, but they were all abortive.

Other industries included glassmaking, brewing, and a variety of craft and consumer industries.

The units of landholding and administration formed a mosaic in process of change, whose basis was a mixture of both indigenous and alien units that had evolved over long periods of time. Geographically the largest units were the provinces, Leinster, Munster, Ulster, and Connacht, based on ancient cultural regions but modified in the sixteenth century by transfers of territory: Louth and Longford from Ulster to Leinster, Cavan from Connacht to Ulster, and Clare from Connacht to Munster and back again to Connacht.[4] Connacht and Munster each had a special administration under lord presidents. The next tier in the hierarchy was the county, an alien form of administrative unit introduced at the time of the Anglo-Norman colonisation as a basis of sub-provincial administration. To the early counties were added, in the sixteenth century, Westmeath, King's and Queen's Counties, the five counties of Connacht, Clare, Antrim, Down, and Longford. The remainder of Ulster was nominally shired in 1585 as Donegal, Coleraine, Tyrone, Armagh, Fermanagh, Monaghan, and Cavan, but this shiring was not made effective until the early seventeenth century. The last Irish region to be shired was Wicklow, in 1606. The new counties, in some cases, were pre-existing territorial units (Monaghan, for example, deriving from McMahon's country), but in other cases the new shires comprised heterogeneous units that bore little resemblance to geographical regions. There were also enormous variations in size between counties. Although nominally completed by the end of the sixteenth century, the shire system as a whole did not

[1] Moryson, *Itinerary*, iv, 194.

[2] Quinn (ed.), 'A discourse of Ireland', p. 160.

[3] *Cal. S.P. Ire., 1601–3*, pp 670–71.

[4] J. H. Andrews, 'Territorial divisions' in V. Meally (ed.), *Encyclopaedia of Ireland* (Dublin, 1968), p. 143.

operate effectively until the early seventeenth century. Below the county was a vast complex of administrative divisions, rationalised in modern times and terms as the barony and the townland, the former based on an ancient Irish unit, the *tricha cét* (or the Welsh *cantref*), and the latter on such indigenous units as the 'ploughland', 'balliboe', or 'tate'. Considerable ignorance of the territorial extent of these smaller units was shown by both statesmen and land surveyors in the sixteenth century, but, this fact notwithstanding, they were used as bases for the granting of land to both native and settler alike. The Tudors tried to rationalise what appeared to them to be the irrational and untreated mosaic of administrative units, both by shiring the whole country and by introducing planned regional settlements or 'plantations', notably in Munster, but their efforts have been described as 'a series of locational exercises strung out along the borderline between theory and practice without penetrating very far on either side'.[1] In spite of the increase in surveying and cartography in the late sixteenth century, the English administrators still lacked the detailed geographical data necessary for a rational administrative framework, and thus relying on an imperfect perception of the geography of Ireland failed to achieve their objectives.

[1] J. H. Andrews, 'Geography and government in Elizabethan Ireland' in *Ir. geog. studies*, p. 190.

CHAPTER VI

The Irish economy, 1600–60

AIDAN CLARKE

IN so far as an international economy may be said to have existed in the early seventeenth century, the context it provided for economic activity was a largely unfavourable one. The prolonged inflation of the preceding century was followed by a period of stable and then falling prices, and although there seems to have been no reduction in the level of activity there was a critical decline in its rate of growth, so that the effect was one of relative stagnation and the period appears in the long term as a 'pause in the long economic development of Europe'.[1] The Irish situation, however, was exceptional in a number of respects. The contrast between the disturbances of the sixteenth century and the peace of the first decades of the seventeenth naturally created more favourable conditions for the realisation of the country's economic capacities and tended to produce a local reversal of the European trend. Moreover, the economy of England was affected later and less seriously than the economies of most European countries and it seems likely that the English connection helped to shelter Ireland in some degree from the prevailing conditions. This effect is perhaps seen most clearly in matters of money, for changing monetary conditions were a vital component of European difficulties, devaluation was a universal symptom, and England resisted more strongly than any other country.

The Irish monetary system was chaotic in 1600, largely as a result of frequent debasement of the coinage and the absence of any consistent policy in the issue of coins, but also because both English and Irish coins circulated freely and the relationship between their values was extremely unclear.[2] Early in James's reign a systematic attempt at improvement began. The inferior coins in circulation were called down, there was a substantial issue of Irish coins, and the circulation of English money was recognised at an official exchange ratio that made an Irish pound equivalent to fifteen English shillings. Shortly afterwards, Irish coins ceased to be issued. The effects of this programme were undoubtedly beneficial: although currency remained in short supply, as it did in most European countries, the lower

[1] F. C. Spooner, 'The European economy, 1609–50' in *New Camb. mod. hist.*, iv, 98.

[2] R. H. M. Dolley, 'Anglo-Irish monetary policies, 1172–1637' in *Hist. Studies*, vii, 45–64; and see below, ch. XVI.

value placed upon Irish money tended to reduce the flow of wealth from the weaker to the stronger economy, and the link with English money introduced an unprecedented element of stability.

This situation was symptomatic. The Irish economy was conditioned by the connection with England in two distinct ways: economic activity was directly affected by government policies in Ireland, and the use of Irish resources was indirectly limited and confined by government policies formulated for England without regard to their effects upon Ireland. The results were not always disadvantageous: conflicts of interest between the two economies were present, but they were restricted by the fact that in some important respects England and Ireland complemented rather than competed with one another.

Within Ireland, however, the conflict of interests was unrestrained. Land was the primary source of wealth, and the struggle for its ownership and possession dominated these sixty years. In 1600 most of it was owned by the Irish, and much of the remainder belonged to well-established colonists; by 1641 large-scale transfers from Irish to New English owners had produced a roughly balanced distribution in which the Irish, the Old English, and the New English were each in possession of about one-third of the country; by 1660 the greatly augmented New English group had acquired the greater part of Ireland. This change of ownership was, of course, the dominant trend, but two other tendencies can be discerned. First, despite the severe and widespread dislocation of the rural population, particularly in the early 1650s, the occupancy, as distinct from the ownership, of the land did not change significantly in character: almost everywhere the native Irish continued to form the majority of those who lived and worked upon it. Second, property became concentrated in fewer hands, not only as a result of colonisation but also because the replacement of Irish by English institutions changed the relationship of many people to the land. In the Gaelic polity,[1] property rights belonged to lineage groups rather than to individuals, the land belonging to each of these groups was redistributed among its members at intervals determined by custom (in some places, only when the death of a co-heir made reallocation necessary; in others, annually on Mayday), and the liability to render dues in money or kind to social superiors was not a tenurial obligation in the English sense. Anglicisation challenged these peculiarities. A system of individual ownership developed in native Irish areas and was quickly associated with a steady reduction in the number of native landholders. Public policy, which was directed towards eliminating smaller freeholders where possible, certainly contributed to this, as did expropriation arising from the resumption of church lands, but economic pressures also acted powerfully. The process was most conspicuous in Ulster,

[1] The most recent and most useful description of native Irish practices is contained in Nicholls, *Gaelic Ire.*, pp 57–67; and see above, vol. ii.

where the proportion of land that had been left in Irish possession under the plantation scheme dwindled appreciably in the decades that followed, but the trend was general. The possibility of raising cash while retaining possession seems to have tempted many freeholders, and arrangements by which property was sold or mortgaged, while occupancy was continued on the basis of tenancy, were widespread and seem to have been particularly common in places where the persistence of the native Irish system of landholding produced uneconomic holdings.[1] In Connacht and some other areas there was the added direct inducement of threatened plantation in which, according to precedent, proprietors of smaller estates might expect to lose all their land while those who aggregated larger estates might expect to retain three-quarters of them. More generally, in a situation in which holdings of less than 100 acres were at greater risk than larger ones, the tendency towards consolidation was pronounced, and the acquisition of innumerable small properties by local chiefs and gentry, and by the merchants of neighbouring towns, was continuous. The evidence suggests that by 1641 the depression of small freeholders was almost complete. Significant differences in the extent of property distribution remained, with ownership most concentrated in New English, and most dispersed in Irish areas: there were, for example, less than 100 proprietors in both Donegal and Tyrone, about 200 in both Waterford and Meath, but more than 500 in Mayo. But in all three groups the unit of ownership was normally large. The Old English third of Ireland was shared by about 2,000 owners, the New English third by considerably fewer, the Irish third by rather more: the total number of proprietors cannot have exceeded 6,000.

In legal theory, this land was feudally held: it belonged to the king and those who claimed to own it were either immediate or mediate royal tenants or intruders. The principle was simple, but unreal. Its application raised many problems in a country where the course of conquest had frequently made occupation more important than ownership and had extensively eroded royal entitlements. As a result, the related questions of the uncertainty of land titles and the true extent of the liabilities of ownership remained constantly a political issue in the early seventeenth century. Moreover, the tangled process of colonisation was not the only source of confusion in the forms and conditions of ownership. Equally important was the contrast between the English and Irish land systems, and their formal and informal assimilation. In reality, the land system outside the plantation areas was hybrid. Both traditional native and authentic feudal arrangements survived in many places in varying stages of modification. It was neither unusual for land to be held in common 'without partition' in the Irish manner, nor uncommon for it to be held according to the most elaborate stipulations of feudal overlordship. In some areas these extremes coexisted. In County

[1] J. M. Graham, 'Rural society in Connacht, 1600–1640' in *Ir. geog. studies*, pp 192–208.

Tipperary, for example, the parish of Killea was in the undifferentiated possession of a family group of thirteen, while land in the parish of Ballybecan was liable to

> rents and casualties of three shillings and ninepence, five grubbs of wheat, seven grubbs of malt, eighteen candles, one weeding hook, one reaping hook, one garron to draw corn in harvest, twenty-seven ridges to be plowed, three quarts of honey and suit of court and service to the manor of Newcastle.[1]

In the more firmly established areas of colonisation this kind of manorialism was obsolescent, and in many Irish areas a relatively stable apportionment of land was taking place, but survivals were frequent enough to defeat generalisation. And the position was complicated further by the creation of a kind of pastiche feudalism through surrender and regrant arrangements designed to replace irregular Irish exactions by fixed charges and to introduce formal manorial structures, though the effect was perhaps more often to put an English veneer on Irish arrangements than to replace them. Gaelic practices also survived in areas where the 'degenerate Englishry' had been accustomed to enjoy the advantages of both systems. On the lands of the earl of Ormond, for instance, at the beginning of the century, refection and cess of horse and horseboys were still routine impositions within a manorial structure which, however authentic, had become increasingly baroque with the overlay of Irish customary dues upon English ones. As late as 1641, indeed, Ormond held some of his lands in common with Irish proprietors in the Irish manner. Thus, for example, the first entry in the Civil Survey of County Tipperary records Ormond's partnership with three O'Meaghers in the possession of 'two-thirds of a quarter colpe', and notes that 'the said lands are not clearly divided between the said proprietors'.[2]

The explanation of this diversity is related not only to the historical circumstances of each case but also, more generally, to economic considerations. In the Gaelic and gaelicised areas, landowners might rely on labour tenancies to work the land, employ labourers who were paid in kind, or, most usually, practise a form of metayage, renting their land in return for the third or fourth sheaf (that is, one-third or one-quarter of the produce). It was this emphasis upon non-financial arrangements that distinguished relations of production in these areas from those in the originally feudal areas of early colonisation, where labour dues had been commuted and, though sharecropping was not unknown, the nexus between landlord and tenant was normally a financial one. This distinction was also reflected in the different status of the dues exacted by the landlord 'towards the provision of his house':[3] in the eastern counties these had become tokens; elsewhere they were not only systematically exacted as customary entitlements but

[1] *Civil Survey*, i, 5–6, 335.
[2] Ibid., p. 4.
[3] *Inchiquin MSS*, p. 339.

incorporated in ordinary commercial leases, in which they could constitute a substantial proportion of the rent due. It is clear that anglicised Ireland, outside the plantation areas, exhibited a contrast between areas of relatively archaic organisation, where the continuance of a subsistence economy was reflected in the survival of a form of manorialism that mingled English and Irish influences, and areas of more advanced development in which only the vestiges of economic feudalism remained. In both areas the estate was a unit of ownership rather than of production: as a rule it did not consist of a single block of land but of an aggregation of dispersed parcels of land, some of which were reserved for the direct use of the owner, either for tillage or grazing, some of which were leased, and some of which were let in small pieces to tenants. In both areas the ordinary unit of subsistence agriculture continued to be the open-field community, in which individual holdings were fragmented and interspersed with each other.

In anglicised areas these communities were organised on the familiar three-field rotation system, and it was the Pale that constituted the model that native grantees in the Ulster plantation were required to follow. The general character of settlement is suggested by the arrangements in the parish of Dromiskin, in County Louth, where the land was divided into a 400-acre demesne, leased out for £400; nineteen separate holdings, ranging from 3 to 140 acres, distributed among thirteen proprietors, of whom only one was resident; a 500-acre common, mainly pasturage; and an 80-acre plain 'fit for horse coursing'. There were ten 'towns and villages' located on the larger holdings, all with rights on the common, while the smaller properties contained tenements and messuages. The amenities included two corn mills, a salmon weir, an eel weir, a pigeon house, a rabbit 'burrough', and a twice-yearly fair. Mixed farming was normal.[1]

The native Irish areas were distinctive, most conspicuously because of the central position of livestock, which had traditionally been the chief form of wealth, and which continued to feature prominently in dowries, jointures, and even mortgages, while cattle were still occasionally used as a medium of exchange. Stock-raising remained the essential function of the native Irish production system, and its most obtrusive feature continued to be transhumance, or booleying. The evidence relating to organisational details is limited and inconclusive, but it is clear that the arrangements differed considerably according to terrain, population density, local custom, colonising influences, and other variables. Generalisation is correspondingly difficult, and the outlines of the native Irish manner of life have yet to be convincingly reconstructed. What is known of Gaelic agricultural practices suggests a considerable measure of community cooperation. That this did not necessarily involve nucleated settlement is evident, for the wattle and turf houses of the Irish were sometimes scattered and sometimes clustered like 'so

[1] *Civil Survey*, x, 101–4.

many hives of bees',[1] but it does seem to have involved the collective use of resources by communities sharing rights to both arable and pasture land.

The cultivated area was sometimes farmed in common and sometimes subdivided into separate strips and plots which were redistributed from time to time in many parts of the country. Each year, without rest, it was used to produce a crop, most commonly of spring oats. Rye, barley, and wheat were also grown where the quality of the soil made it necessary or possible, but oatcakes, griddle-baked, and milk products were the principal element in the diet of the poorer Irish, regularly supplemented with blood let from the cattle, and their ale was brewed from oat-malt. Cultivation was normally by the plough, drawn by teams of four horses, with the plough harnessed to their tails (apparently, to induce the earliest possible response to obstacles in the soil), but in mountainous country spade cultivation was usual, and the different techniques may well have been associated with differences of social organisation. Sand was often used to fertilise the soil, and lime and marl were not unknown, but the exceptional intensity of cultivation was made possible by the heavy manuring which resulted from the use of the arable land as a communal pasture from October to April. In many cases, moreover, it was customary to move the site of cultivation periodically, so that the process of intensive cultivation was actually short-term, and took place within the context of an extensive system of land use. The resources of the community were complemented by the exploitation of outlying land which was mainly used as rough pasture. They were supplemented by the use of summer pasturage, on which grazing rights were normally related to the amount of land held in the cultivated area. The celebrated seasonal migration to pastures 'upon the mountain and waste wild places'[2] took place while the crop was being produced, and it was not uncommon for a substantial part of the community to accompany their own and their landlord's cattle to the booley, which was in a sense an ancillary settlement. Although there was undoubtedly a strong pastoral bias in the Irish system, none the less in normal conditions booleying was merely one part of a complex manner of life: in abnormal conditions, however, when war or expropriation disturbed the balance of the system, many were forced to rely almost entirely upon livestock for their subsistence. In the first part of the seventeenth century two opposite tendencies may be tentatively discerned. In most places the advent of more ordered conditions tended to reinforce the element of fixity by restricting freedom of movement and interfering with customary rights and practices. In plantation areas, however, dislocation tended to remove the element of stability and to promote a dependence upon raising cattle on rented land.

[1] Luke Gernon, 'Discourse', quoted in James Carty (ed.), *Ireland, 1607–1782* (Dublin, 1949), p. 4.

[2] Spenser, *View*, ed. Renwick (1970), p. 49.

Although the possibility of attracting capital investment in the development of an unproductive region played some part in the design to plant Ulster, the considerations that prompted the experiment were not economic. None the less, plantation implied improvement, community building of its nature involved conceptualisation in social and economic terms, and it was taken for granted that the interests to be served were not only those of 'true religion, civility and justice', but also those of commerce.[1] These were, of course, interrelated: trade would produce wealth and, as a later lord deputy, Sir Oliver St John, phrased it, 'the love of [money] will sooner effect civility than any other persuasion whatsoever'.[2] Accordingly the Ulster scheme provided for towns and villages to be built, fairs and markets to be established, tillage and enclosure to be encouraged: it stipulated grant units which were neither too large to be efficient nor too small to be economic; and it visualised a carefully structured population profile based on 1,000-acre units, each containing one owner, two freeholders, three leaseholders, and four husbandmen, artificers, or cottagers. Within this framework, the success of the plantation as a whole necessarily depended to a large extent upon the success with which the economic advantage of individual participants could be reconciled with the objectives of the state. In fact, that reconciliation did not prove easy, and conflicts of interest emerged from the outset. Most of them were connected in one way or another with the remarkable discrepancies between the intended grant sizes and the amount of land actually received. Although grants nominally ranged from 1,000 to 2,000 acres, in practice a combination of crude measurement techniques and generous supplementation with bog and wasteland resulted in the creation of many estates so large as to be beyond the capacity of the grantee to develop within the terms of his grant. And this was aggravated by the fact that it rarely proved possible in the selection of grantees to adhere to the optimistic view of the plantation as 'rather an adventure for such as are full, than a setting up of those that are low of means'.[3]

The inflation of the unit of settlement naturally altered the proposed density of settlement radically, even where the quota conditions were fulfilled. In fact, in many cases they were not fulfilled. The effects were twofold: in the first place, the distances involved frequently made the notion of tenant villages impractical, and the result was a far more scattered colony than had been intended. In the second place, the fundamental principle of segregating settlers and natives on undertakers' land was undermined. Planters found it convenient and profitable to undertake the plantation of only a part of their grant, while exploiting the remainder by entering into illegal short-term arrangements with native tenants, whose interest in these circumstances was

[1] T. W. Moody and J. G. Simms (ed.), *The bishopric of Derry and the Irish Society of London* (I.M.C., Dublin, 1968), i, 164. Recent writings on Ulster are noted below, p. 197, n. 2.

[2] *Cal. S.P. Ire., 1611–14*, pp 501–2.

[3] Moody, *Londonderry plantation*, p. 32.

normally in grazing and whose fines for remaining in prohibited areas were often paid by their landlords. Both the acquisition of spare land by most undertakers and the advantages of gaining a quick return from Irish tenants as against undertaking the costly and troublesome business of importing tenants from outside Ireland ensured the continued presence of natives in large numbers in virtually all plantation areas. Their value to the new landholders did not, however, bring the Irish commensurate gains. Both native and immigrant tenants eventually found themselves in competition for land. Though the result was to force up rents for both, the Irish were at a long-term disadvantage. As time went on, the land available to them tended to shrink while prices tended to rise to virtually uneconomic levels, and their economic position steadily deteriorated.[1]

A significant number of planters certainly honoured, to a greater or lesser extent, the obligation to devote their energies and resources to the plantation and improvement of their lands: they took up residence, supported themselves on their estates, and brought in tenants from England and Scotland. None the less, the numbers involved were not great: by the early 1620s the number of British adults in the six escheated counties did not greatly exceed 13,000. Large-scale immigration was not one of the results of planting Ulster. Nor was the attempt to introduce new settlement patterns conspicuously successful. The principle of community grouping involved not only the establishment of tenant villages on each estate, but the building of more than twenty new towns: moreover, the larger grantees in the non-plantation counties of Antrim and Down were encouraged to follow suit. In the initial planning stages the special character of urban settlement was recognised, and the need to deal with it separately was acknowledged. As the scheme developed, however, the government neglected its implied undertaking to manage the establishment of towns directly and simply devolved the responsibility upon individual undertakers and servitors. In the process, the scale of operations was considerably reduced and the need for property endowments, trading privileges, and a 'levy or press' of tradesmen and artificers was overlooked.[2] In consequence the towns that were founded lacked both independence and distinctive urban identity. Typically, they were subordinate to the influence of local landlords and acted essentially as local service-centres, with a population consisting partly of shopkeepers and craftsmen but mainly of local cultivators. Apart from the special cases of Derry and Coleraine, which reached adult male populations of about 500 and 300 respectively by 1641, only Strabane attained sizeable proportions, with some 200 adult males at the same date; few of the other towns contained

[1] Moody, 'The treatment of the native population under the scheme for the plantation in Ulster' in *I.H.S.*, i, no. 1 (Mar. 1938), pp 59–63.

[2] R. J. Hunter, 'Towns in the Ulster plantation' in *Studia Hib.*, no. 11 (1971), pp 40–79; G. Camblin, *The town in Ulster* (Belfast, 1951).

as many as 100. Growth was necessarily related to need, and although the rate of building did not meet with official approval, urban development was undoubtedly taking place as quickly as rural settlement justified. Most of them probably differed little from the tenant villages except in size. Where villages were created, they were extremely small: a report from the Ironmongers' proportion in Derry, that 'there will be a town of six houses, which is a great town in this country', indicates the scale often involved.[1] And in fact the pressures towards community settlement were more often than not ignored. Outwardly, Ulster was not transformed. The norm continued to consist of small hamlets and scattered farms: the village, with its bawn, church, and mill, remained the exception.

Both church and mill were symbols, for tillage, like protestantism, was an aspect of civility. None the less, the plantation does not seem to have altered the pattern of land use in Ulster dramatically. This arose partly from the fact that arable production had in any case been a component part of the Irish system, as a proclamation of 1610 acknowledged when it postponed the removal of the natives until the following year so that the land might be prepared and sown with seed as usual; but it arose also from the fact that many settlers were slow to plough the land, the English, it was alleged, being particularly reluctant to do so. There were, naturally, local differences, the Coleraine area for instance being notably well cultivated, and wheat certainly became more common in Ulster than in most of Ireland outside Wexford, but the achievement did not match the intention. The export of grainstuffs was undoubtedly an important source of profit in the first years of the plantation, but the imposition of high rates of duty by the Scottish council after 1618, to protect local producers from Baltic competition, sharply reduced the incentive to concentrate upon arable farming in Ulster. Although oats were regularly shipped from Coleraine, Derry, and Carrickfergus to Scotland, the prominence among Ulster exports of cows, hides, sheepskins, beef, and cheese indicates that the plantation did not greatly affect the characteristically pastoral nature of economic activity in the area. Apart from oats, the only major non-pastoral product of the area was linen yarn, which was exported in significant quantities through Derry, Coleraine, Carrickfergus, Dundalk, and Drogheda to Chester and Liverpool. Its destination was Lancashire, and the Manchester area in particular, where it was mixed with cotton to produce fustian goods. Its source was very general, though there was a certain concentration in the north-east. In many places the spinning of yarn was a neatly self-contained domestic industry. The growing of flax was an economic proposition on the smallest holdings; its spinning was a task normally undertaken by women and children. For the most part, production was in Irish hands. Both the activity and the trade connection were traditional, and the planters who profited did so with minimal effort:

[1] Moody, *Londonderry plantation*, pp 298–311.

their role was not that of the entrepreneur, but that of the middleman, just as their role in the cattle trade was less often that of producer than that of middleman, for much of the stock which formed so vital a part of Ulster's wealth was owned by the Irish. In general, it seems clear that while the resources of the province were exploited more intensively in the seventeenth century than they had been in the past, the manner in which they were exploited was not markedly different. What the plantation altered in Ulster was not the economy, but control over the economy. Moreover, despite the markedly commercial attitude of the planters, none of the Ulster ports acquired a position of major importance in Irish trade.

The tendency for the production of exportable surpluses to be based on pastoral activity was common to all parts of Ireland. To a great extent, the heavy demands upon the land in the past, for the supply of basic industrial materials as well as for the satisfaction of subsistence needs, had been met by animal husbandry. Alive, cattle provided a substantial part of the ordinary diet: dead, their hides were Ireland's chief export.[1] In the seventeenth century the importance of stock-raising was augmented, and the character of the trade based upon it significantly altered, as producers in Ireland responded to developing market-opportunities in England. Though hides remained of importance, the main profit came quickly to derive from the export of cattle on the hoof, for the most part to the west and south-west of England, but in some cases further afield, as for instance to the new colony of Virginia.[2] The English market was also catered for by the growth of a trade in barrelled beef. By 1621 the scale of the traffic in store cattle was already so great that English and Welsh producers sought parliamentary aid against Irish competition, while more general fears that the trade contributed seriously to England's unfavourable trade balance were voiced. In the debate which followed in the house of commons, probability was certainly on the side of those who argued that 'though money be carried from hence, yet it comes hither again',[3] but the discussion was not an informed one and estimates by different speakers of the quantities involved ranged from 40,000 to 100,000 head of cattle annually. Though even the lower figure, which represented a cash value of about £100,000, was probably an overestimate, the extent of cattle exports gave rise to different anxieties in Ireland, where the danger that the stock would become seriously depleted led in 1625 and 1626 to measures to prevent both cattle and cattle products from being sent to 'any part beyond the seas'.[4] Though the decision was unpopular, related arrangements to allow cattle to be imported to Ireland without licence suggest that the motive was genuine. The earliest official estimates, relating

[1] O'Donovan, *Econ. hist.*, ch. 1; Longfield, *Anglo-Ir. trade*, pp 58–77.
[2] *Anal. Hib.*, no. 4 (1932), pp 161–6.
[3] H. F. Kearney, 'Mercantilism and Ireland, 1620–40' in *Hist. Studies*, i, 62.
[4] O'Donovan, *Econ. hist.*, p. 35.

to 1640, when trade was alleged to be in a depressed condition, indicate that more than 45,000 head of cattle had been exported. They also show that such cattle products as hides, beef, tallow, and butter continued to rank high on the list of exports. The cattle estimate, taken in association with the extremely limited capacity of most of the vessels involved in Irish trade, which in many cases did not exceed twenty cows, suggests an impressive density of traffic. The organisation seems to have been fairly rudimentary: though Dublin was the most important centre, little specialisation developed, and the trade was notable for the relatively large numbers of individuals who took part in it on an extremely small scale.[1]

Cromwellian settlers, even more prone to think in terms of quick return cash products than their predecessors in Ulster, found livestock the best investment in Irish conditions, and the number of cattle in Ireland actually increased between 1640 and 1660. Both the degree of dependence upon stock and the extent of success in raising it are suggested by successive government regulations which early in 1652 prohibited the export of both cattle and cattle products, in June of the same year permitted cattle to be exported 'in numbers that will not impoverish the stock',[2] in October partly lifted the restrictions on the export of cattle products, and in January 1655 removed the remaining restraints altogether. The scale of production certainly increased in the late 1650s and early 1660s, but there can be no doubt that the situation revealed by Irish export statistics of the mid-1660s, when more than half the annual value of exports was based on cattle, was not of recent development. Cattle must have had a similar prominence in Irish trade since the second decade of the century.

Stock was not, of course, confined to cattle: sheep-raising enjoyed the same advantages of minimal labour content and profitable by-products, and cattle and sheep production were usually associated activities, though there were areas in which sheep predominated, perhaps especially in Munster on the lands of colonists, but also in Monaghan and Westmeath. Exports of sheep were quite substantial, amounting to 35,000 head in 1640, but their primary value was derived from their wool. This was used in the manufacture of frieze, a loosely woven low-quality cloth made in the home. The widespread presence of tuckmills for shrinking cloth indicates that small-scale production was carried on throughout the country. In the Dublin area, local demand naturally justified more elaborate arrangements and by the 1620s 'a goodly clothing work' had been established 'where in cording, spinning, weaving, working, dressing, and dyeing cloth, many poor people are daily set on work'.[3] Bandon and, to a lesser extent, Mallow occupied special positions as outposts of the English west-country woollen industry

[1] D. M. Woodward, 'The Anglo-Irish livestock trade in the seventeenth century' in *I.H.S.*, xviii, no. 72 (Sept. 1973), pp 489–523.

[2] O'Donovan, *Econ. hist.*, p. 39.

[3] *Cal. S.P. Ire., 1615–25*, p. 361.

in which immigrant merchants, master clothiers, and craftsmen combined to create veritable industrial colonies, producing cloth for the English market. More significant, perhaps, was the existence of an export industry organised on a domestic basis in Munster, from which frieze, rugs, mantles, and caddows (rough woollen blankets) were sent to the west and south-west of England. This was a well-established trade, which seems to have declined towards the end of the sixteenth century. The absence of protest against it by English interests may indicate that the decline continued; on the other hand, a selective increase in Irish customs duties in 1632 picked out rugs as one of the nine exports with worthwhile revenue potential, and it is possible that the acceptability of Irish cloth goods on the English market was due to the fact that there was no English product of comparably low quality.

Cloth exports were, however, of little significance in comparison with the export of wool itself.[1] In the long term, the changes in the English clothing industry associated with the development of 'new draperies' towards the end of the sixteenth century were to the advantage of Irish wool producers. In the short term, however, serious disadvantages arose from a regulatory system that confined the market to England at a time when the English cloth industry was in severe difficulties. Wool was central to the English economy, and Ireland simply provided a marginal source of supply: its output was needed when English wool production was low, or when the export demand for English cloth exceeded the capacity of English producers to supply the raw material necessary. At other times, Irish wool was neither wanted in England nor legally exportable elsewhere. And until the mid-1630s favourable conditions rarely prevailed. Moreover, poor trading conditions were aggravated by the introduction of export controls based on staple towns in 1617, which created a buyers' market by confining export dealings to a small number of authorised merchants. The arrangement was particularly resented in Munster, where no doubt its effects were not adequately distinguished from the consequences of recession in England: it was alleged that the English tenants of planters were unable to continue to pay rent and were being forced either to 'bring their English sheep back again into England'[2] or to resort to smuggling. Since arable land in Munster continued to be converted to grazing, the complaint was probably overstated; but later developments suggest that the level of illegal exports was high. In the early 1630s the staple system was replaced by licensing controls, and in the years that followed, as English cloth sales expanded into new markets, Irish exports to England rose dramatically. The figures indicate a threefold rise to a peak of 160,000 great stones in 1638–9; while it is clear that the period was

[1] P. J. Bowden, *The wool trade in Tudor and Stuart England* (London, 1962); George O'Brien, 'The Irish staple organization in the reign of James I' in *Econ. Hist.*, no. 1 (1926); Kearney, *Strafford in Ire.*, pp 137–54.

[2] Bowden, *Wool trade*, p. 204.

one of considerable expansion, none the less an increase of this order is likely to have been in part the result of the diversion of exports from illegal to legal channels. The chief ports of exit for wool were Dublin and Youghal and the chief market was certainly the clothing industry in south-west England, but considerable quantities also went through Chester and Liverpool, and manufacturers of cheap cloth in Yorkshire increasingly drew their supply of the cheaper grades of wool from Ireland. As early as the end of the 1620s, indeed, it was reported that most of the 'new draperies' were made of 'a great part of Irish wool'.[1] Precise information about illegal markets is naturally lacking, but the evidence tends to confirm English fears that Irish wool was reaching competitors in France and the Netherlands. In all probability, however, the incidence of smuggling depended upon market conditions in England.

Those Irish exports that were not pastorally based consisted for the most part of marketable natural resources, especially timber and fish. Timber was available in apparent abundance, particularly in Ulster and Munster, and lent itself extremely well to short-term exploitation.[2] Local demand for building purposes in Ulster was considerable, and the woods were officially reserved for that use in the plantation counties, though a good deal was illegally exported and some was diverted to supply a modest shipbuilding enterprise in Coleraine. Shipbuilders in England, Scotland, and further afield also drew upon Ireland for some materials, and there was a steady trade in boards and planks. Tanner's bark and charcoal were produced for the Irish market, but the principal use of timber was in the production of staves, narrow pieces of wood for making barrels, casks, hogsheads, and winepipes. Since a fair proportion of Irish exports were carried in containers of this kind, home demand was substantial, but a good deal of production was for export. Staves were already being sent to England in the middle of the sixteenth century, but in the seventeenth the chief market was clearly Spain. This arose in part from the fact that it was for some time forbidden to carry wine from Spain without first importing staves; as a result, both English and Dutch ships engaged in the wine trade regularly collected consignments of staves in Ireland. The advantage of so ready a market enhanced an already attractive business, for production involved little capital and little labour skill, and profit margins were large: in Munster, staves sold at about £6 per 1,000, which was four times as much as it cost to produce them. Leading landowners were actively involved (the sale of timber was a common way of maximising the profit on a short lease), and the growth of both Killarney and Tallow was chiefly due to timber processing. Both the increasing scale of the business and the competitive advantage which it enjoyed are indicated

[1] A. P. Wadsworth and Julia de L. Mann, *The cotton trade and industrial Lancashire, 1600–1780* (Manchester, 1931), p. 13.

[2] McCracken, *Irish woods.*

by the fact that local materials were being supplemented by the importation of Norwegian timber in Dutch ships in the 1630s.

The timber trade was subjected to frequent official stoppages, both for political reasons and for fear of the destruction of the woods, which, as a contemporary protested, 'if not timely prevented, it may be conjectured that the inhabitants of this nation must with Diogenes live in tubs, for the choicest timber is employed to that use'.[1] In fact, however, large-scale production of staves was confined to three districts, south Cork and the Slaney and Bann valleys, and the aggregate value of the trade was not great: the annual export quota of half a million staves established in the 1630s, for instance, represented a market value of about £3,000. The destruction of the woodlands, which was already well advanced by the 1650s, was not confined to areas of commercial exploitation, and the traditional profligate use of timber for fuel, building, and annually renewed fencing must have contributed a good deal to the process.

As an export activity, fishing was largely centred on the ports of the south coast, to such an extent, indeed, that they were even used at times as exit ports for Derry salmon. Their connections were with both the Mediterranean and the west and south-west ports of England and Wales. They were, however, in decline. In 1614, in the peak month of November, 10,000 barrels of salted herrings were exported from Wexford: total exports from the entire country in 1640 amounted to little more than twice as much. The loss was actually twofold, for the profitable ancillary business of provisioning foreign fishing vessels also contracted. Contemporaries usually found the explanation for the evident decline in the fact that fishing 'runs for the most part into the hands of strangers',[2] and proposals to restrict access to Irish fishing waters were regularly made, but the real problem seems to have been that the shoals of herring deserted the Irish coast early in the century. 'The fish begins to wander from our shores',[3] it was noted in 1620, and Irish fishermen for the most part failed to adapt to a less advantageous situation. Where exceptional efforts were made, however, the trend was reversed. In south-west Munster, where planters both introduced inshore 'seine' netting and invested considerable sums in shore-based facilities for salting and barrelling the catch, the export of pilchards rose significantly, at least in the 1620s and early 1630s. The industry was characterised by small-scale plantation-type development, and the trade, which was based on Kinsale, Crookhaven, Baltimore, Bantry, and Berehaven, was dominated by English and continental shipping.

Irish export activity formed part of a simple colonial trading pattern in which a relatively small range of primary products was exchanged for manufactured goods, luxuries, and some essential raw materials. Demands for the

[1] *Civil Survey*, x, 12.
[2] *Cal. S.P. Ire., 1615–25*, p. 426.
[3] *Lismore papers*, 2nd series, iii, 69.

promotion of native manufactures were common, but it was both more profitable and less troublesome to export primary goods than to work them up at home. The amount of industrial activity connected with exportation was small: the making of cloth, the spinning of yarn, and the cutting of staves accounted for most of it. Tanning had received a good deal of official encouragement during the Tudor period and was of some importance at the beginning of the century, when about one-fifth of the hides exported were already processed: by 1641, however, they were invariably exported raw. This decline was typical. In theory, the possibility of developing existing resources was attractive: in practice, such schemes usually failed. The most notable failure was that of Wentworth, who used all the resources of the lord deputyship in an unsuccessful attempt to build a linen industry on the existing supply-base in the mid-thirties:[1] on a smaller scale, the East India Company's effort to develop shipbuilding in Munster came to nothing. At first sight, the failure of secondary production to develop is easily accounted for by the large-scale export of raw materials. But the extent of those exports was in part due to deficiencies in the necessary factors of production. Capital was in extremely short supply, rates of interest were almost impossibly high, and investment in industry did not compare favourably in either financial or social terms with land purchase. Significantly, much of the vitality of parts of Munster, with its timber processing, cloth manufacture, ironworks, and 'pilchard palaces', was attributable to the earl of Cork's unconventional readiness to venture his immense landed wealth in productive enterprise. There was also a shortage of skilled labour, and although the incidence of emigration at all social levels suggests a good deal of under-employment, the industrial entrepreneurs of the period commonly thought in terms of importing their work-force. From Sir Henry Sidney's settlement of Flemish tanners at Swords in the 1570s to Wentworth's introduction of Dutch linen workers in the 1630s, there was a constant tendency to visualise industrial undertakings as a form of plantation, imposed upon the local environment rather than emerging from it, and justified in part by the necessity of 'planting this idle country with industrious people'.[2]

Perhaps the chief obstacle to the development of secondary production, however, was the character of the home market. The size, low profitability, and relative self-sufficiency of the agricultural sector, combined with the concentration of real wealth in very few hands, severely restricted consumption. Moreover, the limited demand for manufactured goods was spread thinly over a widely dispersed population, and most needs were supplied at local level by craftsmen working in market conditions which offered no opportunity to increase output or to engage in specialisation. The

[1] Kearney, *Strafford in Ire.*, pp 154–9.

[2] J. H. Andrews, 'Notes on the historical geography of the Irish iron industry' in *Ir. Geography*, iii, no. 3 (1956), pp 139–49.

larger the concentration of population, the more varied and the more elaborately organised was industrial activity. Urban dwellers required the everyday services of bakers, butchers, brewers, and the like, made occasional use of the more exotic skills of such people as apothecaries, wig makers, and painter-stainers, and supported the activities of coopers, tanners, cutlers, tallowchandlers, and so on. But even in the larger towns the pattern was one of production in small units for local consumption. Only Dublin acted as more than a local service centre, and it did so because, in the nature of its function as capital, visiting customers were numerous. The exceptionally rapid growth of the city in the early seventeenth century, as a result of both its enhanced social and political prominence and its access to an unusually affluent and consumption-prone hinterland, naturally generated greater industrial diversification than elsewhere. None the less, for the most part Dublin, like the other seaports, acted as an entrepôt rather than as a production centre, and the demand for better-quality products and inessential consumer goods was met by importation rather than by manufacture. The dependence of certain social levels of demand upon English industry is vividly illustrated by the constant stream of small quantities of such articles as looking-glasses and urinals, wooden tableware and household pottery, hats and gloves, spurs and stirrups, tennis rackets and playing cards, which entered Irish ports.[1] Even the theatre company which opened the St Werburgh Street Playhouse in Dublin in 1637 was imported from England, as was its principal playwright, James Shirley.[2] More significant, however, was the trade in cloth, the most important commodity brought from England. Velvet, satin, gold lace, and other continental finery featured regularly, but the bulk of the trade was in ordinary broadcloth which, though it was not a luxury product in the normal sense, was greatly superior to anything produced in Ireland and represented the socially accepted norm of dress. England was also the main source from which Irish consumers were supplied with such aids to more comfortable living as sugar, spices, and currants. Tobacco, on the other hand, was often brought directly to Ireland, while wine, which was probably Ireland's single most important import, was usually shipped from the Continent and must have formed the basis of a substantial trade of which little trace remains.[3]

The import trade in raw materials mainly involved salt, which came from both England and continental sources, and was used to preserve meat, fish, and butter; hops, which tended to come to the more recent areas of settlement from both England and the Low Countries; coal, which came from

[1] Piecemeal information about this kind of trade can be gleaned from the port books in the P.R.O.; see W. B. Stephens, 'The overseas trade of Chester in the early seventeenth century' in *Transactions of the Historic Society of Lancashire and Cheshire*, no. 120 (1968), and D. M. Woodward, 'The port books of England and Wales' in *Maritime History*, iii, no. 2 (Sept. 1973), pp 147–65.

[2] W. S. Clark, *The early Irish stage* (Oxford, 1955).

[3] H. F. Kearney, 'The Irish wine trade, 1614–15' in *I.H.S.*, ix, no. 36 (Sept. 1955), pp 400–42.

England so cheaply as to inhibit local production almost completely, except in the most inaccessible places, and was principally for domestic use; and, in small amounts, such dyestuffs as alum and madder. Iron was also regularly imported from England, in both crude and processed form, and iron goods, especially nails and cutting tools of all kinds, were brought to Ireland in substantial amounts. But iron was also exported, to the Low Countries, and even to Madeira and the Canary Islands, as well as to England. In fact, not only was iron ore mined in Ireland, but Irish ironmasters enjoyed more favourable conditions than their English competitors in one vital respect: because wood was both plentiful and improvidently used, Irish charcoal was cheap enough to give Irish producers a distinct cost advantage.[1] On the other hand, however, the carriage of iron overland was difficult and expensive. As a result, ironworks could draw upon only very restricted local supplies of ore, supplemented in some cases by imports; moreover, it was essential that all stages of production should be grouped in the same place. In consequence, although there were ironworks in many places, their capabilities were severely limited and the scale of organisation and production was typically small. There were exceptions: a relatively elaborate industry, equipped with furnaces, forges, steelworks, and slitting mills, did develop in the Blackwater valley in County Waterford, and at Mountrath in Queen's County, based on the exploitation of local resources by imported labour, and using Youghal and Waterford as exit ports from which iron was dispatched not only overseas, but by sea to other parts of Ireland as well. Quite apart, however, from the difficulties of distribution which often made foreign markets easier of access than Irish ones, the level of production fell well short of need; and the essentially plantation character of the industry was signalised by its rapid destruction when rebellion broke out in 1641.

The rebellion worked an abrupt change in the economic condition of the country. The preceding period was one of recovery and expansion, based on a significantly more intensive exploitation of Ireland's marketable resources than in the past. The growth of prosperity was most significantly reflected in the rising value and increasing profitability of land, which stimulated both a vigorous struggle for its possession and a large-scale diversion of commercial and professional earnings into its purchase. Population increase and trade expansion were other indications of a recovery for which peace and the resilience of an unsophisticated economy were no doubt largely responsible, but which was also connected with the closer economic relationship with England that followed conquest. Political influences contributed to this latter development, as did the immigration of those colonists whose input of energy and capital not only assisted growth but inevitably had a British orientation. But such direct economic considerations as new market oppor-

[1] Andrews, 'Notes on the historical geography of the Irish iron industry', as above; H. F. Kearney, 'Richard Boyle, ironmaster' in *R.S.A.I. Jn.*, lxxxiii (1953), pp 156–62.

tunities and more convenient sources of supply also exerted their influence in the same direction, and at the centre of the process was the increased business generated by the developing cattle trade. The provision of services for a prospering Irish economy enabled both Chester and Liverpool to improve their trading position at a time when few outports were able to do so, and Chester's trade to Ireland illustrates in microcosm the stages of growth:[1] until 1620 it grew slowly and somewhat erratically; through most of the 1620s it increased steadily; in 1628, at a time of severe dearth throughout western Europe, it contracted sharply; in the early 1630s it rose again gradually, and then expanded rapidly to reach a peak in 1638–9. All the evidence suggests that this sequence accurately indicates the course of Anglo-Irish trade in general; but because Irish trade not merely increased in these years, but changed direction as well, the rate of increase in trade with England is not an entirely reliable index of the rate of Irish economic development, and perhaps tends to exaggerate the importance of the 1630s. The boom in Anglo-Irish trade in that decade certainly reflected a long-term improvement in productive capacity, and certainly resulted in part from such immediate influences as the elimination of piracy and the onset of more favourable international conditions, but it also represented the intensification of a tendency to channel Irish trade more narrowly to England, rather than broadcast to the Continent.

In the years after 1641 war brought devastation, famine, plague, and depopulation. Land values and returns slumped, trade virtually ceased, and a severe currency shortage made matters worse. In the early 1650s foodstuffs were brought from England and Wales in large amounts. So also were cattle and sheep, and this restocking, in conjunction with exceptionally favourable trade conditions, was to provide the basis for an extraordinarily rapid recovery. Low rents and high prices prevailed, and before long the resumed exchange of Irish agricultural products for English necessities had raised customs yields to an unprecedented level. In 1658 the customs farm was set at £70,000 per annum, which was £13,000 more than the highest yield returned in the 1630s. Locally, this contract was alleged to be unrealistic. Complaints may in part have reflected disappointment at the withholding of the advantages of free trade with England, which had been expected to follow the *de facto* political union of the two countries after 1653, but the evidence suggests that a downward trend was already under way towards the end of the 1650s.[2] The effects of the government's inability to control piracy and to regulate a badly debased coinage were aggravated by declining

[1] W. B. Stephens, 'The overseas trade of Chester in the early seventeenth century' in *Transactions of the Historic Society of Lancashire and Cheshire*, no. 120 (1968), pp 23–34; D. M. Woodward, 'The overseas trade of Chester, 1600–1650', ibid., no. 122 (1970), pp 25–42; D. M. Woodward, *The trade of Elizabethan Chester* (Hull, 1970).

[2] T. C. Barnard, 'Planters and policies in Cromwellian Ireland' in *Past & Present*, no. 61 (1973), pp 62–4.

prices and relatively high taxes, and in parts of Ulster and Connacht there was widespread failure to pay rents. None the less, the brief period of frenzied activity in the 1650s generated a momentum that was to make Irish trade more valuable in the mid-sixties than it had been before the rebellion.

Commercial activity was not, of course, central to Ireland's basically subsistence economy, or relevant to the lives and living standards of many. And there was certainly an economic level which prosperity never reached. Even before 1641, the kind of people whom Owen Roe O'Neill was to find 'so rough and barbarous and miserable that many of them are little better in their ways than the most remote Indians'[1] did not share the benefits of a buoyant economy; nor did those displaced Irishmen who were caricatured in a parliamentary enactment as 'walking up and down the country with one or more greyhounds, coshering or lodging or cessing themselves, their followers and greyhounds upon the inhabitants'.[2] It was not, in short, Ireland that prospered in these years, but those who controlled Ireland's resources, and this distinction was to become increasingly plain in the years that followed. The war that temporarily destroyed the economy also diverted the profits of recovery into new pockets. The trade revival that took place against a background of expropriation and deprivation in the 1650s was not the product of a healthy economy: it was a manifestation of the hectic exploitation of low-cost investments in Irish resources by men whose circumstances compelled them to capitalise their gains intensively and quickly through production for the market. The effect was to accelerate the tendency towards commercialisation which was already evident in the earlier part of the century, and which was inherent in the process of conquest. There is, of course, a crude sense in which conquest was progressive, because it loosened traditional restraints upon the use of land and allowed freer responses to market conditions; but the economic gains accrued to individuals, while the social cost was borne by the conquered community.

[1] *Wild geese in Spanish Flanders*, p. 507.
[2] O'Brien, *Econ. hist. Ire., 17th cent.*, p. 34.

CHAPTER VII

Pacification, plantation, and the catholic question, 1603–23

AIDAN CLARKE WITH R. DUDLEY EDWARDS

THE government of Jacobean Ireland was exploitative in the dual sense that it subserved both English purposes and private interests. The intention, however, was reformative. The principle that the resistance of the native Irish could best be overcome by 'civilising' them was generally accepted, though not always sincerely, and the fundamental objective of government policy was the consolidation of control through deliberate acculturation. Three related ideas about the nature and direction of the process of social change influenced this approach. The first was the belief that social systems were actually formative, so that communities whose institutional forms were systematically altered would tend to lose their distinctive characteristics and acquire those which corresponded to the imposed system. The second was the conviction that where different social systems competed directly with one another, the superior would necessarily prevail. The third was the presumption that English institutions were normative and that all others were inferior, to a degree simply measured by the extent of their difference. In the contemporary English view, an acceptable level of civilisation required an orderly social structure, related to a stable system of landownership and land use, and a governmental system characterised by effective central control. The pastorally based socio-agricultural customs and fragmented distribution of political power in Ireland were far removed from this model, and the language, religion, and laws were equally deviant. Accordingly, it was difficult neither to perceive the necessity for a general policy of anglicisation, nor to identify its essential components with precision: in the words of Sir John Davies, successively solicitor general (1603–6) and attorney general (1606–19), to make the Irish 'become English'[1] required the assertion of the primacy of central government, the establishment of a national system of jurisdiction parallel to that of England, the introduction of fixed units of landholding, the encouragement of arable farming, and the adoption of English laws of property and inheritance. Moreover, it seemed

[1] His *Discovery of the true causes why Ireland was never entirely subdued . . . until . . . his majesty's happy reign* (London, 1612) exemplified the approaches discussed here at their most coherent.

reasonable to presume that the wayward English colonists, with their greater innate propensity to conform, would assist the conditioning process considerably.

The intention of anglicising Ireland was basic to the formulation of policies, but in practice there was little consistency of approach. The influence of particular circumstances or personalities frequently dictated that general principles be modified or disregarded in response to other considerations, and this tendency was promoted not only by the insincerity of many government officials, but also by the fact that the determining assumptions of policy were legalistic rather than political in character, and their application to specific situations not always readily apparent. As a result, the systematisation which was an acknowledged condition of success was continually impaired by failure to relate short-term policies to long-term objectives. Inevitably, this failure was most pronounced where the programme of acculturation was weakest in conception—in matters of religion. The policy was actually conceived in exclusively secular terms: it was never clear whether protestantism was to be an instrument of anglicisation or a product of it, and since the government in practice regarded the promotion of religious change as an urgent priority, the absence of coordination between civil and religious objectives undermined its intentions. The effects of this confusion varied significantly. The religious factor was merely one aspect of a larger problem posed by the Gaelic Irish, and its importance was easily obscured; but religious difference was central to the relationship between the government and the colonists. Although catholicism was already a proscribed religion, and a policy of excluding catholics of all kinds from office had been followed for some time, the older settlers ignored the possibility that, as catholics, they were among the defeated rather than, as English, among the victors, and laid strenuous claim to the continuation of the privileges of colonial status. The facile official assumption that military conquest had been achieved in a purely protestant interest was challenged by the intractable reality that a substantial body of catholics in Ireland was accustomed to exercise considerable influence and power within the colonial system rather than in opposition to it. It became increasingly clear that the major political point at issue after the war was to determine how the colonial sector of Irish society had been affected by the conquest and whether the government's freedom of action was subject to limits set by catholics despite the conquest.

The ambiguities of the post-war situation, in which the government might find its friends more difficult to deal with than its enemies, were fully exposed during Mountjoy's last months in Ireland. Both the history of local religious change and the general principle of *cuius regio eius religio* supported the belief that regnal and religious change were closely connected, and naïve optimism as to the probable religious views of the son of Mary, queen of Scots, prompted general expectations of change. In those exceptional urban areas where a combination of authority and discretion had imposed restrictions in the past, particularly in the south, opportunist pre-emptive action resulted. Townsmen restored the public observance of catholicism with a defiant ostentation which extended in places to public processions, the expulsion of protestants, and the reclamation and reconsecration of churches. These displays neither shocked nor greatly disturbed Mountjoy, who saw 'no great damage in the matter'[1] in the absence of Spanish involvement, and chose at first to remonstrate with the townsmen rather than to admonish them. When they remained recalcitrant, however, he diagnosed a local hostility to outside authority, particularly in the area controlled by the presidency of Munster, which called for action. In Cork, this had been pressed to the extreme of a short-lived refusal to proclaim the succession of King James and developed into a virtual insurrection against the government's local representatives. In Waterford, when Mountjoy arrived at the head of 5,000 men early in May 1603, it took the form of refusing him entry on the basis of immunities conferred by a 400-year-old royal charter. Throughout his progress, in which he briskly disposed of municipal presumptuousness in Kilkenny, Thomastown, Clonmel, Wexford, Waterford, Cork, Limerick, and Cashel, the lord deputy was careful to concentrate upon the jurisdictional implications of the townsmen's activities, stressing his competence to prevent the unauthorised profession of catholicism and insisting upon his right to place garrisons where he wished, while undertaking to allow private worship until he received firm instructions in the matter from James. In the interests of appeasement, he condescended to engage in theological disputation with the canonically attired vicar-apostolic of Waterford and Lismore, Fr James White, but their discussion of catholic teaching on temporal obedience was not amicable and Mountjoy subsequently demanded widespread subscription to an oath of allegiance to King James.

The lord deputy was sufficiently learned to know that such an oath was of more than ceremonial importance. The issue which it raised was at the kernel of the problem that confronted the old colony and its new government. The political creed of the established catholic settlers was based upon the deceptively simple proposition that catholicism and loyalty were perfectly compatible: it followed that for catholics of English origin to enjoy property, political rights, and religious freedom was in no way contrary to the interests of the state. The difficulty of securing acceptance of this position was twofold. In the first place, it involved a fairly selective use of one element in the colonial tradition: in the aftermath of war 'loyal subjects' and 'English rebels'[2] quickly came together under the collective name of Old English. But not all the members of this emerging group could colourably lay claim to loyal records or reasonably demand a presumption of their credibility: they

[1] *Cal. S.P. Ire., 1603–6*, p. 25.
[2] *S.P. Hen. VIII*, ii, 1.

had first to acquire the attributes and appropriate the tradition of the dominant Palesmen. In the second place, the colonists' position stood in direct and unconvincing contradiction to the common assumptions of English protestants, who were brought up to believe that in the catholic church Christianity had degenerated into an erroneous and idolatrous organisation, characterised by lay ignorance and clerical power, which aimed at worldly dominion, forbade its members to give loyalty to a temporal prince, and was destined to a downfall in which England would play a leading part. The difficulties posed by this deep-set conviction that the interests of catholicism were in direct and continuously active conflict with those of England were aggravated by the fact that Rome did indeed claim authority to depose rulers for offences against religion or natural law, and reserved to itself the right to judge the lawfulness of oaths of loyalty. Thus many catholics who themselves experienced no difficulty in reconciling their spiritual allegiance to the pope with their temporal obedience to the king could be by no means certain that their position was doctrinally valid. Nor could the government meet the problem satisfactorily by exacting an oath of allegiance, for though the willingness of catholics to subscribe might attest their personal loyalty, it could not exonerate them from their spiritual obligations. The dilemma was genuine, and for a government accustomed to believe that the line between friend and enemy was a religious one, adequately familiar with the tenets of catholicism, and understandably mindful of Pius V's excommunication of Elizabeth, it was not unnatural to regard the claims of professedly loyal catholics in Ireland with puzzlement and suspicion rather than with respect and goodwill.

The task of adopting a firm policy towards catholicism in Ireland was complicated by differences of opinion and perspective. The common aim was to achieve total conformity to the religion established by law, but there was wide disagreement as to the proper means. The most influential of the Irish bishops, Jones of Meath and Loftus of Dublin, counselled absolute rigour, arguing that the catholic clergy inculcated disobedience and should be banished, and that the laity should be compelled to attend the established church. The Irish council, of which they were both prominent members, accepted their views so far as to urge repeatedly that the minimal condition upon which successful headway could be made against catholicism was the expulsion of priests. The personal inclinations of King James were towards liberty of conscience, by which he meant that, while disabilities might fittingly be imposed upon catholics, they ought not to be compelled to attend protestant worship: as he expressed it to petitioners from the Pale some years later, 'though he would much rejoice if the Irish catholics would conform themselves to his religion, yet he would not force them to forsake their own'.[1] He was confirmed and supported in these views by Mountjoy,

[1] *Cal. S.P. Ire., 1611–14*, p. 542.

who became James's chief adviser on Irish affairs upon his return to England, and shared the belief that conformity would only effectively be achieved by conversion. From this point of view, the obvious prescription was a long-term policy of evangelism, and this was, in any event, the course realistically dictated by the condition of the established church in Ireland. An investigation, undertaken at the king's direction early in 1604, made it clear that throughout most of the country the protestant presence consisted of ruined churches in which no ceremonies could or did take place. The problems of dealing with catholicism in Ireland, however, could not be approached without reference to the English situation, where James began by treating catholics leniently but found it increasingly difficult to continue doing so. His religious objectives, which involved an affirmation of mainstream anglicanism against puritan extremism, exposed him to suspicions of crypto-catholicism which he could not afford to ignore, and it was probably English rather than Irish pressures which prompted him to concede the Irish council's request for authorisation to pursue a vigorously anti-catholic policy in July 1605. In a proclamation published in October, he denounced the presumption that he was prepared to allow toleration, ordered the catholic clergy to quit the realm by 10 December, and instructed the laity to attend divine service in accordance with the law.

There followed a brisk struggle, as the catholic colonists, appearing in organised opposition for the first time, set themselves to resist the enforcement of conformity. By good fortune, they were able to make their initial stand in circumstances that made success likely, for the English government had no real intention of implementing an extreme policy, and the plan itself was obviously impractical in Irish conditions. It was accepted from the outset that the proclamation could only apply to those members of the laity for whom protestant services were actually available, and agreed early on that it would be futile to try to capture priests who ignored it, 'for every town, hamlet and house was to them a sanctuary'.[1] The result was that the government's severity was incongruously confined to members of the colonial community. Early in November a group of Pale landholders, claiming the right to 'the private use of their religion and conscience',[2] requested that action under the proclamation should be postponed until they had been allowed an opportunity to persuade the king that his views on catholic disloyalty and priestly subversion were mistaken. By ill luck, their petition reached the council on the day on which news of the gunpowder plot reached Ireland, and the council, suspecting some connection, at once committed its promoters to prison. In the course of the following week, selected citizens of Dublin who had failed to obey mandates requiring their compliance with the royal proclamation were sentenced to fines and imprisonment in the court of castle chamber. The Old English peers associated with

[1] Ibid., p. 405. [2] Ibid., p. 362.

the Pale petition complained to England of the treatment of both groups, while the Irish government requested royal approval and extended its activities to other towns, making use of both mandates and the more regular procedure of collecting the statutory fine of one shilling for each absence from divine service. James was both unwilling to endorse these proceedings and reluctant to express explicit disapproval of them, but the Irish government proved impervious to hints, and the king's hopes of being able to avoid appearing to choose between his government and its opponents were frustrated by Sir Patrick Barnewall, a Palesman who became the central figure in a direct conflict with the Irish executive which complicated the issue by dramatising it.

Barnewall argued that the council mandates were unlawful, because they rested upon prerogative power, while recusancy was a statutory offence with set procedures for its prosecution and prescribed penalties for its punishment, and he spoke slightingly of the judge whom he believed to have been the author of the policy. This indiscretion provided an opportunity for the government to withdraw without loss of face from its intemperate treatment of the petitioners: in the spring of 1606, all were released except Barnewall, who was transferred from Dublin castle to the tower of London. The plan misfired: not only was the scapegoat popularly believed to have been brought to England to negotiate over the heads of the Dublin government, but he managed to establish himself there as the spokesman of loyal catholics in Ireland and was supported by a national collection while doing so. His criticism of the mandates impressed the English privy council, and the Irish government could only counter it by resorting to the equivocal argument that since the mandates required attendance at church, not participation in the service, the issue was one of obedience, not conscience. In the event, the prisoners in the Dublin case were released and their fines reduced. But government policy in Ireland did not change: proceedings against recusants continued to be taken actively in the towns until the English privy council abandoned its vague counsels of moderation and issued a specific directive in April 1607. Underlining the absurdity of executing the law selectively against those who had proved their loyalty in the recent war, and the futility of attempting to produce religious change through the exercise of temporal authority alone, the privy council demanded that the existing policy of repression be replaced by a policy of conversion. To avoid conveying any impression that the Dublin administration had been censured, permission was granted to effect the change gradually, but that strategem was defeated by bad timing. Barnewall was allowed to return to Ireland at the same time, and the easing off of anti-catholic activity was quickly noted and readily attributed to his agency. As the priests abandoned circumspection and the government admitted failure, the developing political consciousness of the Old English responded to success, as it had already responded to danger.

While settler opposition was emerging, native Irish resistance was succumbing. Ulster, where the Gaelic polity was least disturbed, the tradition of local autonomy strongest, and the geopolitical considerations most important, was the acknowledged testing-ground for the official policy of anglicisation, and the Dublin government showed a real determination to effect genuine change rather than to be satisfied with token modifications. Support from London was less than wholehearted, for James and Mountjoy were inclined to the view that the earls should not be too closely pressed so soon after their submission, but there was no disagreement about the need to introduce the apparatus of regular civil administration to the area, and on the basis of a substantial military presence, garrisoned in the network of recent strongholds, the government made its arrangements steadily. A nine-county structure was established, sheriffs, justices of the peace, coroners, and constables were appointed, and assizes were held. Formal innovations of this kind, however, could achieve little while the old power-bases remained, and it soon became evident that Tyrone was adapting to his new situation with unwelcome efficiency.[1] Capitalising on the exceedingly generous royal terms of pardon granted in September 1603, he managed to establish rights of ownership over a far greater proportion of the lands of his earldom than he was traditionally entitled to, and held effective sway over three counties, exploiting his position to favour his immediate relatives against the collateral branches of the O'Neills. This remarkable restoration was quite unacceptable to the Devon servitor who succeeded to the lord deputyship early in 1605, Sir Arthur Chichester, who was himself a substantial landowner in Antrim and had hopes of exchanging his vice-royalty for a lord presidency to be created for Ulster. It was equally objectionable to Sir John Davies, who regarded Tyrone's clear intention of recreating an independent jurisdiction in Ulster as the supreme challenge to the state's authority. Moreover, where Tyrone led, others sought to follow. The groundwork for a constructive programme of containment was laid in a proclamation issued in March 1605, which assured all persons in the realm that they were the 'free, natural and immediate subjects'[2] of the king, wholly independent of lords and chiefs, and declared that the pre-existing rights of freeholders were unaffected by the letters patent issued in connection with the post-war settlement to Tyrone, O'Donnell, O'Doherty, O'Hanlon, and O'Neill of the Fews. It proved easier to persuade James to expound thus the principles of royal government than to induce him to authorise appropriate action, but, after Davies had travelled to England to argue the case, a commission was appointed 'for division and bounding of the lords' and gentlemen's livings',[3] which was to serve as an instrument for reconstructing Ulster.

[1] Nicholas P. Canny, 'Hugh O'Neill, earl of Tyrone, and the changing face of Gaelic Ulster' in *Studia Hib.*, no. 10 (1970), pp 7–35; 'The flight of the earls, 1607' in *I.H.S.*, xvii, no. 67 (Mar. 1971), pp 380–99.

[2] P.R.O., S.P. Ire., 63/217, 17.

[3] *Desid. cur. Hib.*, i, 453–7.

Tyrone smoothly circumvented the commissioners, but the activities of Rory O'Donnell (created earl of Tyrconnell in 1603), were investigated in 1605. Confronted with the rival claims of Sir Niall Garbh O'Donnell, Rory had failed even to gain full possession of the demesne lands of his chiefry, but he had attempted to follow Tyrone's example by dispossessing the MacSweeneys and O'Boyles in the north and west of Donegal. The commissioners forced him to restore the rights of both, allocated freeholds throughout the territory, and dealt generously with Sir Neill, to the considerable discomfiture of Tyrconnell, who suffered in both status and income. In the following year, the commissioners returned to Ulster to deal with Monaghan, Cavan, and Fermanagh. In Monaghan it proved necessary to do little more than confirm the arrangements made in 1591 for distributing the land of the MacMahons among freeholders. Cavan was adjudged crown property, so that the creation of freeholds presented no problem and was left to be undertaken at leisure. The position in Fermanagh was confused by a succession dispute, with rival Maguire chiefs laying claim to the entire county, and the commissioners decided to divide the demesne lands equally between them and distribute the remainder of the county in freeholds. The embittered Tyrconnell thereupon found a partner in Cuconnaught Maguire, and the commissioners congratulated themselves upon having cut off 'three heads of that hydra of the north, namely, MacMahon, Maguire and O'Reilly'.[1] Methodically, they were establishing central control, dismantling local power structures, and introducing stabilised landholding. Their work was consolidated by a judicial resolution that all Irish land must descend according to the common law. This ruling was not always observed, and the court of chancery continued to recognise Irish practices when equitable considerations justified it in doing so,[2] but the local effect in Ulster was to ensure that the new freeholdings could not be fragmented by subdivision in the customary Irish manner.

The activities of the commissioners were not the only sources of change in Ulster. Government action in the west and south was complemented by the enterprise of a few influential individuals in the east, where Scottish migration had already altered the traditional arrangements, and where in the first years of James's reign the lands of Clandeboye in south Antrim and north Down passed from the unsure hands of Conn O'Neill into the possession of James Hamilton, Hugh Montgomery, and Sir Arthur Chichester. All three of them proved to be able and rapid colonisers, and by 1606 immigration from both the Scottish lowlands and England was under way, with the active encouragement of the government. Throughout the province, moreover, the assertion of the state's civil power was linked with the exten-

[1] Morley, *Ire. under Eliz. & Jas I*, p. 379.

[2] Some examples of this approach are contained in K. W. Nicholls (ed.), 'Some documents on Irish law and custom in the sixteenth century' in *Anal. Hib.*, no. 26 (1970), pp 105–29.

sion of the organisation of the established church. There was a bitter and calculated symbolism in the promulgation of the royal proclamation against catholicism in Tyrone's manor of Dungannon, and there was a real threat of widespread claims for the resumption of ecclesiastical property in the appointment, for the first time, of a protestant bishop, George Montgomery, to the sees of Raphoe, Derry, and Clogher in 1605.

Despite the changes which surrounded him, Tyrone remained in control of his own situation. And despite the death of Mountjoy in April 1606, he could still rely upon the favour of James, with whom, rather than with the Dublin government, he chose to deal. His one major anxiety seems to have been that the state would complete its arrangements by appointing a lord president of Ulster: on that point he was reassured by the king in the late summer of 1606. Sir John Davies, however, remained intent upon reducing Tyrone to the level of an ordinary subject and found his opportunity in the development of a dispute between the earl and his son-in-law, Donal O'Cahan, over whose country of Coleraine the earl claimed control. Davies, now attorney general, prepared a case in which he sought to prove that O'Cahan's country was in fact legally vested in the crown. A favourable decision would provide the government with a means of reducing Tyrone to the demesne lands of the O'Neills and establishing crown tenants and freeholders upon the remainder of the earldom. O'Neill managed to have the dispute referred to London in July 1607, and prepared to attend the hearing in person, justifiably confident of a successful outcome. Events abruptly transformed his situation. The suspicions of the Dublin government had already been aroused by the fact that Tyrone's son Henry was serving with a Spanish army in the Netherlands, but the English privy council had refused to consider recalling him. It was common knowledge that Tyrconnell and Cuconnaught Maguire had resolved to try their fortunes in the Netherlands also, but again the privy council had refused to consider preventing them from doing so. Tyrone had advised Tyrconnell to request royal permission to leave Ireland, but his advice was ignored, and Maguire went to the Continent in the summer of 1607 to arrange transportation. He returned to Lough Swilly with unexpected rapidity late in August. The news of his arrival placed Tyrone in an intolerably compromising position. Tyrconnell's secret departure would undoubtedly be interpreted as conspiratorial: the presumption would be 'that Rory O'Donnell, like his brother before him, was gone to raise an army abroad while O'Neill remained at home to rouse the north again'.[1] The best that Tyrone could hope for was to end his days on dwindling estates under the unremitting scrutiny of a local lord president; the probability was that he would not be allowed to return home from England. Quickly gathering his family together, he joined Tyrconnell and Maguire and their followers at Rathmullan and sailed for the Continent on 4 September 1607.

1 Canny, 'The flight of the earls', loc. cit., p. 398.

Privately, the government was mystified by Tyrone's conduct, but the event was providential. Its effect was to enlarge the state's freedom of action dramatically and to raise the possibility, which had been inconceivable when the war ended, of extending to Ulster the standard sixteenth-century settlement-formula of confiscation and colonisation. With this in mind, it was easy to rationalise the 'flight of the earls' for public purposes, on the basis of what was known of Tyrconnell's recent activities; it was announced that having conspired against the king abroad, and oppressed his subjects at home, they had fled to escape the consequences. 'Attainted by outlawry' in the court of king's bench, the earls were adjudged in December to have forfeited their lands to the crown. The preparation of plans for a limited introduction of British colonists on the demesne lands, with the distribution of the remainder in small lots to Irish freeholders, was actively under discussion when the sudden revolt of Sir Cahir O'Doherty opened up even more extensive possibilities. O'Doherty owed his lordship of Inishowen to official support against a rival, had been rewarded for services to the crown by a knighthood and new letters patent, and had acted as foreman of the jury which indicted the earls of treason. His chief point of contact with government authority, however, was through his friend and ally Sir Henry Docwra, governor of Derry. In 1607 Docwra was replaced by Sir George Paulet, who treated O'Doherty with contempt and hostility, and this not merely alienated him personally, but made it increasingly difficult for him to sustain his authority in Inishowen. He appears to have seen his alternatives with stark melodrama. In February 1608 he requested a place at court in the retinue of the prince of Wales. In April he rose in arms, captured Culmore fort, and burned Derry. In the ensuing months, under pressure from a government army led by Marshal Wingfield, he first retreated into Donegal, then changed direction to make sorties into Tyrone and Armagh, and finally returned to Donegal, where he was killed in an engagement at Kilmacrenan in July. He had been openly supported by some of the O'Cahans, whose chief, Donal, was already in Dublin castle under suspicion of treason, and by some of the O'Hanlons, and there was reason to believe that he had been secretly encouraged by Sir Niall Garbh O'Donnell, so that his rebellion neatly demonstrated the intractability of the problem of maintaining order among the Ulster Irish despite the conquest. At the same time, it helped to create the opportunity to solve the problem, and a small hint of larger possibilities was suggested by the London government's decision to levy a Scottish force to assist in the suppression of the revolt. The news of O'Doherty's death at once prompted recommendations that the proposed British colony be extended to the entire province. Before long, the established policy of remodelling Ulster through a slow process of anglicising its native population was abandoned in favour of a thorough colonisation by Englishmen and lowland Scots, which would both instantly anglicise much of the socio-agricultural framework of the area and help to achieve the original goal more quickly, by transmitting 'civility' and 'true religion' to the natives at first hand.

The summer assizes of 1608 were combined with an official survey which judged almost all of the land in the six counties of Armagh, Cavan, Coleraine, Donegal, Fermanagh, and Tyrone to be in the king's hands. The legal grounds for these decisions were more evident in some cases than in others, but in no case were they plain. Considerations of equity were entirely absent, and the general principle, that the treason of the few justified the expropriation of all, both violated specific undertakings given after the flight of the earls and stood in direct contradiction to the government's repeatedly declared policy of sustaining the small freeholders' independence of the lords. The treatment of Donal O'Cahan and Niall O'Donnell amply illustrated the subordination of justice to policy. Though neither was convicted of any offence, both spent the remainder of their lives as prisoners in the tower of London.[1]

Late in 1608 a committee was appointed in London, with Davies and Bishop Montgomery among its members, to prepare a detailed scheme of plantation.[2] The plan which it presented in January 1609, though considerably modified in subsequent discussions, and lacking precision until the completion of a mapping survey in the summer of that year, was in essentials put into effect in five of the escheated counties in 1610. The proposals reflected the views of Davies, who believed that the 'civil' planters must outnumber the Irish, rather than those of Chichester, who had presumed that the Irish would be left in possession of most of the land; and they resembled the arrangements already taking effect in Down, where colonisation was closely concentrated, rather than in Antrim, where settlers were fairly dispersed. The basic principle of the scheme was segregation. In the greater part of the area, communities composed of English or Scottish undertakers with their imported tenants were to be settled on land completely cleared of its native inhabitants, who were to be allowed to reside only on land granted to favoured Irishmen, to the church, and to military officers who had served during the late war ('servitors'). Proportions of three sizes were designated as grant-units—a great proportion of 2,000 acres, a middle proportion of 1,500 acres, and a small proportion of 1,000 acres, each with a

[1] Seán Ó Domhnaill, 'Sir Niall Garbh O'Donnell and the rebellion of Sir Cahir O'Doherty' in *I.H.S.*, iii, no. 9 (Mar. 1942), pp 34–8. Ó Domhnaill convincingly argues that Sir Niall did not take part in the rebellion, but disregards the more likely possibility that he calculatedly encouraged Sir Cahir.

[2] Moody, *Londonderry plantation*, introduction; 'The treatment of the native population under the scheme for the plantation in Ulster' in *I.H.S.*, i, no. 1 (Mar. 1938), pp 59–63; M. Perceval-Maxwell, *The Scottish migration to Ulster in the reign of James I* (London, 1973); J. G. Simms, 'Donegal in the Ulster plantation' in *Ir. Geography*, vi, no. 4 (1972), pp 386–93; R. J. Hunter, 'Towns in the Ulster plantation' in *Studia Hib.*, no. 11 (1971), pp 40–78; 'The Ulster plantation in the counties of Armagh and Cavan, 1608–41' (M.Litt. thesis, University of Dublin, 1968).

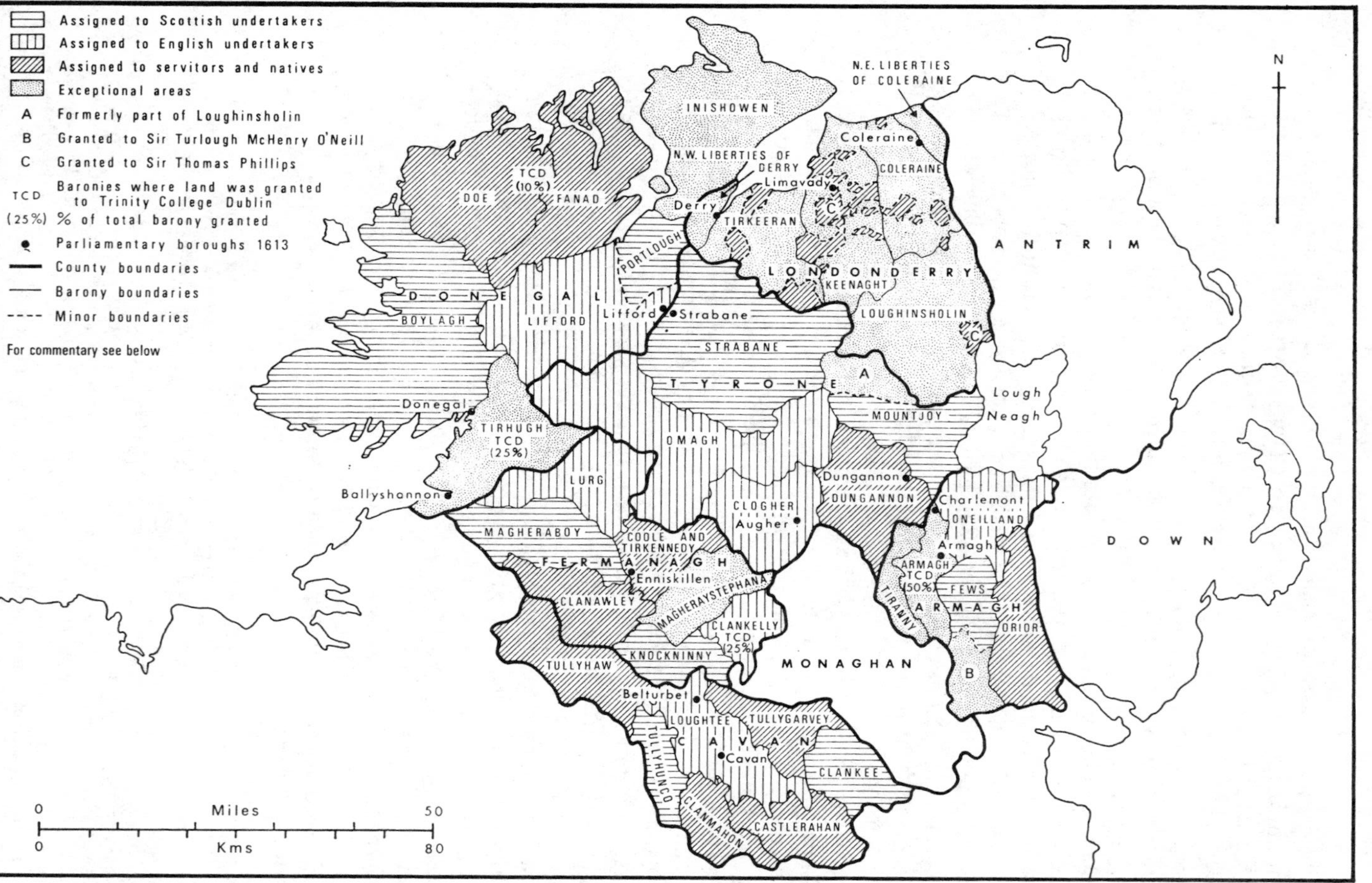

Map 5 THE ULSTER PLANTATION, 1609–13, by T. W. Moody and R. J. Hunter

The map shows the broad pattern of the plantation arrangements in the six escheated counties in terms of plantation 'precincts'. These correspond with modern baronies, or represent subdivisions of baronies (e.g. Doe + Fanad = Kilmacrenan), or combinations of baronies (e.g. Knockninny = Knockninny + Coole). Mountjoy and Dungannon represent subdivisions of the then barony of Dungannon, now represented by the three baronies, Upper, Middle, and Lower Dungannon. In general each precinct was assigned to one of the three classes of grantees specified in the key to the map. But there were important exceptions to this principle of appropriation.

(1) In each of the six counties the former 'termon and erenagh' land, which was interspersed among the lands granted to the planters, was assigned almost entirely to the bishops of the established church. In Londonderry, church land amounted to 23% of the whole area, in Armagh to 20%, and in Cavan to 10%.

(2) Certain grants made shortly before the plantation were not interfered with. These included lands granted in 1603 to Sir Turlough MacHenry O'Neill in the Fews, and in 1605 to Sir Henry Óg O'Neill in Tiranny and Dungannon; and lands of dissolved monasteries, granted for the most part to servitors, which in County Armagh amounted to almost 10% of the whole county, mainly in the baronies of Armagh, the Fews and Orior.

(3) Under the plantation scheme lands were assigned to corporate towns and a free-school in each county; and Trinity College, Dublin, received 95,000 acres in Counties Armagh, Donegal and Fermanagh.

(4) An area marked out for exceptional treatment was the county of Londonderry, formed in 1613 as a combination of (*a*) the former county of Coleraine (see map 4), (*b*) the barony of Loughinsholin, detached from Tyrone (except the south-west corner), (*c*) Derry and its north-western liberties, and (*d*) Coleraine and its north-eastern liberties. All the temporal land in this county, except an area of 4% granted to a servitor, Sir Thomas Phillips, and 10% to native Irish, went to the city of London under a special agreement of 28 January 1610.

(5) Five exceptional baronies were: (*a*) Inishowen, granted (except the church land) to Sir Arthur Chichester, the lord deputy, in February 1610; (*b*) Tirhugh, where Trinity College had 25% of the area and the rest was divided between the church, servitors, native Irish, a school, and Ballyshannon fort; (*c*) Armagh, half of which went to Trinity College and the rest to the church and to servitors; (*d*) Tiranny, mainly granted to the church and to native Irish; (*e*) Magheraystephana, where the greater part of the temporal land was granted to Conor Roe Maguire and the rest to a Scottish undertaker, Lord Burley.

(6) Two other exceptional areas were (*a*) the south-west corner of Loughinsholin, which, detached from the rest of the barony in 1613, when the county of Londonderry was formed, and added to Dungannon barony, was granted principally to the archbishop of Armagh and a native grantee, Brian Crossagh O'Neill; (*b*) the southern half of Fews barony, which went to Sir Turlough MacHenry O'Neill (see (2) above).

(7) In County Cavan native Irish grantees received 10% of the land in Loughtee (assigned to English undertakers), and Old English owners held 14% of the county, mainly in Clanmahon, Castlerahan, and Clankee.

The map and the notes are based on: *Cal. pat. rolls Ire., Jas I*; 'Ulster plantation papers, 1608–13', ed. T. W. Moody, in *Anal. Hib.*, no. 8 (1938); T. W. Moody, *Londonderry plantation* (1939); R. J. Hunter, 'The Ulster plantation in the counties of Armagh and Cavan' (M. Litt. thesis, T.C.D., 1969); J. G. Simms, 'Donegal in the Ulster plantation' in *Ir. Geography*, vi, no. 4 (1972); J. H. Andrews, 'The maps of the escheated counties of Ulster' in *R.I.A. Proc.*, lxxiv, sect. C, no. 4 (1974); P. S. Robinson, 'The plantation of County Tyrone in the seventeenth century' (Ph. D. thesis, Q.U.B., 1974). We are grateful to Dr Robinson for his cooperation.

rent-free allowance of bog and woodland. In each county, proportions were grouped together in precincts, normally corresponding to the existing barony structure, and separate precincts were reserved for English undertakers, Scottish undertakers, and for servitors and native grantees combined. Particular precincts were to be allocated by lot to chief undertakers, who were charged with certain managerial duties, including the distribution of proportions, and were rewarded with enlarged proportions of 3,000 acres. English and Scottish undertakers, who were obliged to take the oath of supremacy, were to hold their lands by the easy tenure of common socage at a yearly rent of £5 6*s.* 8*d.* for each 1,000 acres; they were required to reside on their proportions for five years, to introduce a stipulated quota (comprising twenty-four able-bodied males from at least ten families on each small proportion) of English or lowland Scottish colonists, and to provide for the defence of the settlement by building a strong place, or bawn, and maintaining a supply of arms; they were forbidden to accept Irish tenants or to alienate land to the Irish. Servitors were to receive their grants on the same terms and conditions, except for the provision that on payment of a fifty per cent surcharge they might take Irish tenants, while native grantees were excused the oath of supremacy, but obliged to build houses and bawns, 'to use tillage and husbandry after the manner of the English Pale', and to pay double rent.

A number of considerations led to the exclusion of the county of Coleraine and adjoining areas from these arrangements. Misgivings aroused by an initially disappointing public response to the scheme certainly prompted the decision to invite the city of London to undertake the corporate plantation of an entire county, in the hope of adding to the prestige of the project as well as to its practical support. The choice of the area was due in part to its obvious potential for commercial development, but also to a realisation that the settlement of O'Cahan's country was likely to be especially difficult, while the maintenance of the strategically vital towns of Coleraine and Derry would certainly require resources both greater than the state was willing to spare and greater than it could reasonably expect private individuals to provide. Negotiations opened in May 1609, and the reluctance of the Londoners to become involved enabled them to dictate their own terms. The rights, privileges, and exemptions conceded by the crown in the final agreement, reached in January 1610, were generous, and the city's grant comprised not only O'Cahan's country and the towns of Derry and Coleraine, but also the Tyrone barony of Loughinsholin to the south-east. These territories were excluded from the detailed arrangements for the plantation, but it was perfectly clear that the city was obliged to conform to the central principles of the project, and to observe the same conditions as other undertakers. The Londoners began building work in Derry and Coleraine as soon as the articles of agreement were concluded, advertised for settlers shortly afterwards, and had already made encouraging progress when they entered into formal possession in the summer of 1610.[1]

The general plantation emerged from the planning stage in May 1610, when final instructions were sent to Dublin. Undertakers had already been chosen and had been assigned in groups to particular precincts by the English and Scottish privy councils, which had each disposed of roughly one-third of the land that remained after provision had been made for the church, Trinity College, and a free-school in each county. The remainder was available for division between native and servitor grantees in the proportion of two to one. It was left to the Dublin government to select suitable recipients and to make detailed arrangements for the transfer of possession throughout the escheated territories and for the removal of the natives from the undertakers' proportions. Between July and September, commissioners, headed by the lord deputy, set to work in Ulster, in an atmosphere of antagonism and tension, and amidst rumours of the imminent return of Tyrone, which confirmed Chichester in his reservations about the scheme to which he was giving effect, and which he believed to be too generous to the undertakers and too parsimonious to the natives and to the servitors who were to supervise them.

In the light of this weakness, the small area of discretion left to the commissioners assumed major importance, and they approached the problems of allotting land to 'deserving natives' with particular care.[2] Indeed, they deliberately chose to begin their proceedings in Cavan, where the provision for the Irish seemed more generous than elsewhere, in the hope of creating a misleadingly favourable first impression of what was involved. Their guiding principles were clear-cut: the severity of the treatment of leading families must be offset by greater lenience towards others, so that 'the contentment of the greater number may outweigh the displeasure and dissatisfaction of the smaller number of better blood',[3] while at the same time the more influential of the Irish must receive sufficient land to give them a vested interest in the settlement. A few of the Irish, of course, were exempt from plantation, most notably Conor Roe Maguire in east Fermanagh, Sir Turlough MacHenry O'Neill of the Fews, and the heirs of the Armagh and Tyrone estates of Sir Henry Óg O'Neill, who had been killed in action against O'Doherty. These provided the framework within which the commissioners selected a few individuals in each county for special treatment. In Armagh, Tyrone's brother, Art MacBaron, and Henry MacShane O'Neill received great and middle proportions respectively in the east of the county. In Cavan, Mulmory Óg O'Reilly was singled out and awarded two

[1] See Moody, *Londonderry plantation*, ch. II.

[2] I am grateful to Mr R. J. Hunter for allowing me to make use of an unpublished paper, 'The native Irish and the plantation of Ulster', read to the Dublin Historical Association in 1972.

[3] *Cal. S.P. Ire., 1608–10*, p. 358.

proportions, one great and one small, while the O'Reilly chief, Mulmory MacHugh Connelagh, received a great proportion and Mulmory MacPhilip O'Reilly, Hugh O'Reilly, and Felix MacGovern were each granted small proportions. In Donegal, Turlough O'Boyle and the heads of the three branches of the MacSweeneys received great proportions in the north-west, and Hugh MacHugh Duff O'Donnell a small proportion around Ramelton. Of the Fermanagh Irish, only Bryan Maguire was selected for a great proportion, while Conn MacShane O'Neill was assigned a middle proportion around Clabby on the Tyrone border, at a safe remove from his brother in Armagh. Conor Roe Maguire's exempted portion was scaled down, for in Chichester's view the king was not 'bound in honour to make so barbarous and unworthy a man greater than his neighbours'.[1] In Tyrone, Turlough O'Neill was granted two middle proportions and Bryan Crossagh O'Neill one small one. For the rest of the 'deserving Irish' the system of plantation proportions was not used. The land available in each county was allotted to about fifty carefully chosen individuals in carefully calculated amounts, approaching 1,000 acres in a few cases, but averaging out at less than 300 acres. Few of the favoured Irish received grants of the land which they actually occupied; none received as much as they believed themselves entitled to. They had every reason to remain resentful and unreconciled, and their discontent merged with that of the majority, who had received nothing, to generate a hostility that endangered the success of the project.

The reorganisation of land ownership in the five counties was virtually complete by September 1610, but the precision of the blueprint was defeated by the inaccuracy of the surveys upon which it had been based. Without exception, the allotted proportions far exceeded their nominal acreage, by margins that varied widely. In consequence, the intended ratio between different categories of owners was not observed. The general effect seems to have been that the undertakers, who numbered about 100, with Scots in a small majority, received rather more than one-quarter of the total acreage; the fifty or so servitors who reaped their reward for services in the late war received about one-fifth; and the amount of land left in Irish possession (through exemption as well as by grant, and distributed among about 300 owners) lay somewhere in between. The remainder was accounted for by the church lands, which were principally annexed to the bishoprics, substantial grants to Trinity College in three counties, and such exceptional cases as the retention of established Old English proprietors in County Cavan and the bestowal of the entire barony of Inishowen upon the lord deputy.[2]

The plantation conditions required the undertakers to come to Ireland to receive their grants by 24 June 1610, take up residence before 29 September following, and fulfil building and settlement conditions by Easter 1613. Most of them did present themselves during the summer of 1610. A few

[1] *Cal. S.P. Ire., 1608–10*, p. 364. [2] See map 5.

came merely to complete the formalities which would enable them to sell their interest, and a few came with their possessions and followers in readiness to begin operations, but most came to secure their titles, inspect their property, and request permission to return home to complete their arrangements. Although it had originally been taken for granted that the natives must be moved before the undertakers were installed, it soon became evident that in practice the replacement of natives by settlers in the forbidden areas would have to be a phased process. In August 1610 a transitional arrangement was authorised which allowed the Irish to remain until Mayday 1611, on payment of rent to the undertakers. Ostensibly, this concession was intended to protect the interest of the undertakers by ensuring that the land was cultivated without interruption, and that rent-paying tenants and food supplies were available for incoming settlers, but it also helped to ease the general problem of transferring the Irish, whose unwillingness to leave their homes was strengthened by the practical difficulties of moving to already occupied areas where ownership was often in transition. There was no possibility that so many families could and would on their own initiative at once find alternative holdings, negotiate tenancies, and move their possessions, and the government was not anxious to test its power to compel them to do so. As a result, the undertakers took possession of tenanted estates, and the rent, food, and labour provided by the Irish reduced their costs and simplified their logistical problems. In a few cases, the needs supplied by the Irish were genuinely short-term, as in the Scottish precinct of Portlough, between the Foyle and Swilly, which was systematically colonised from Ayrshire, and in isolated proportions on other precincts. In most cases, however, the undertakers quickly discovered that the interim arrangement was actually more advantageous than the terms of plantation, and the Irish were from the beginning so closely integrated into the economy of the colony as to become indispensable to it. The government's inadvertent generosity was partly to blame: few undertakers had the resources to finance the colonisation of estates so much larger than they had expected, and even those who observed the settlement conditions in full had ample land to spare for Irish tenants. The prime reason, however, was simply that the exploitation of the native Irish offered a higher return to the undertakers for a lower investment than did the introduction of settlers. The nature of the possibilities are revealed by the accounts of Sir Claude Hamilton, the grantee of a large proportion in Strabane, who within a few years of the institution of the plantation was able to supplement his landed income of less than £300 a year in Scotland with a further £200 a year from his undeveloped Irish estate. Most settlers, however, adopted a middle course, developing part of their estates along plantation lines and renting the remainder to the Irish. The deadline for the removal of the natives was officially extended for a further year in 1611, but in practice it was still unenforced in 1618, when the government announced that the natives must either leave the undertakers' lands by the following Mayday or pay fines. The natives remained, fines were paid (often by the undertakers themselves), and ten years later the matter was settled after a fashion by a compromise under which, at the price of fines and double rents, the undertakers were permitted to have native tenants on one-quarter of their estates. This face-saving arrangement meant that the segregation principle which had been central to the plantation scheme was finally abandoned by the government.[1]

The territory assigned to the Londoners exhibited similar tendencies in an exaggerated form. Though the city took its responsibilities for the towns of Derry and Coleraine seriously enough, it made no corresponding effort in the rural areas. It was not until the summer of 1611 that a comparatively meagre allocation of land was made to the Irish. Thirteen native freeholders were chosen, of whom Captain Manus O'Cahan received a great proportion and three other O'Cahans, including Donal's wife, received small proportions. This division left about one-tenth of the land in Irish possession and almost six-tenths in the possession of the corporate undertaker: the only servitor in the area, Sir Thomas Phillips, had holdings amounting to almost four per cent of the total, and the remainder belonged to the church. In theory, this meant that almost three-fifths of the territory was forbidden to the Irish. In practice, the Londoners made no attempt to replace them, and were indeed suspected of inviting more from elsewhere to swell the rentals. It was not until late in 1613, after the charter formalities had been completed and the area renamed Londonderry, that the city authorities divided the land into twelve proportions and assigned responsibility for their development to twelve groups made up from the fifty-five companies which had contributed to the costs of the undertaking. The policies of these groups did not differ from those of the private undertakers in other counties, and the familiar pattern of native occupation interspersed with colonial settlement appeared in Londonderry also.[2]

The common interest which planters and natives discovered was not forged in amity. The ethos of the plantation areas in the early years of colonisation was a disturbed and perilous one. The hope that Tyrone would return with foreign aid soon faded, and the Irish grantees signalled their resignation by moving to their new estates. Those who had no place in the scheme, however, the dispossessed and the 'swordmen', for the most part evaded the government's efforts to transport them to Sweden or to other parts of Ireland and withdrew to the woods and bogs to 'stand upon their keeping' and prey upon the settlers. Moreover, although the undertakers needed Irish tenants, they did not need to court individual Irishmen, and a

[1] Moody, 'The treatment of the native population', loc. cit., pp 61–3; and see below, p. 223.

[2] Moody, *Londonderry plantation*, pp 110, 455, map 1, and *passim*; 'Sir Thomas Phillips of Limavady, servitor' in *I.H.S.*, i, no. 3 (Mar. 1939), pp 251–72.

system of short leases and high rents typically ensured that the Irish derived minimal benefit and little stability from the relationship, and nourished their hostility. The result was that, in the words of a Fermanagh undertaker, 'although there be no apparent enemy, nor any visible main force, yet the wood-kern and many other (who have now put on the smiling countenance of contentment) do threaten every house, if opportunity of time and place doth serve'.[1] The image of the colonist in Londonderry, at work 'as it were with the sword in one hand and the axe in the other'[2] was a universal one.

By contrast, the resettlement of the plantation lands scattered through the counties of Waterford, Cork, Limerick, and Kerry went ahead peacefully and unobtrusively, on the basis of official indulgence rather than assistance.[3] There was no question of penalising the undertakers for past defaults, and when they were ordered in 1604 to go back to their lands and to stay there they were rewarded by revised patents and reduced rents. Not all returned, and not all remained: one seignory was abandoned, six or seven were recovered by Old English claimants, five were bought by servitors, seven were amassed by the deputy escheator and clerk of the Munster council, Richard Boyle, who acquired the interests of Sir Walter Raleigh, and three came into the possession of the Limerick undertaker, George Courtney. Within twenty years, only one-third of the thirty-three seignories in Munster remained in the hands of descendants of the original grantees. In this second phase, the resumption of the plantation was neither complete nor uniform. Some of the seignories were exploited, more or less efficiently, as absentee estates; in others, an undertaker's demesne and a number of large leasehold farms were superimposed upon an Old English and Irish tenantry; in a few, fairly intensive settlement was organised, drawing largely upon the south and west of England. Inland towns of some importance were established at Tallow, Mallow, Bandonbridge, Tralee, and Killarney, timber and mineral resources were exploited, grazing became characteristic, and an active trade was carried on through the established port towns. In terms of settler population, growth seems to have compared quite favourably with that of Ulster, but property ownership was much more narrowly concentrated, the social structure differed correspondingly, and the small group of large protestant proprietors dominated regional government through their membership of the presidency council. In 1612 they emphatically signalised their ascendency by introducing the English game laws, which reserved the right to shoot deer, hare, partridge, and pheasant to landowners only. Not all their preoccupations were trivial, however, and they were both an important element

[1] Thomas Blenerhassett, *A direction for the plantation in Ulster* (London, 1610) in Gilbert, *Contemp. hist.*, i, p. 319.

[2] Moody, *Londonderry plantation*, p. 329.

[3] D. B. Quinn, 'The Munster plantation; problems and opportunities' in *Cork Hist. Soc. Jn.*, xxi (1966), pp 19–40.

in the New English colony in Ireland and a source of some anxiety to their neighbours, for among them was more than one 'private scraper after other men's lands'.[1]

In Ulster the conciliation of native landholders was abandoned in the interest of public policy: elsewhere, it was defeated by private interest. The imposition of English property law left many of the Irish with no valid title to the lands they occupied. To give them an opportunity to secure firm titles, a commission for remedying defective titles was established in 1606, authorised to compound with those whose titles were unsound and issue new patents. The incentives to conform were strong, for such patents were not merely a necessary protection, but a means of ensuring that the grantee's eldest son would succeed to the undivided property, despite customary collateral rights. The advantages of the process to the crown were also considerable, for it brought the patentees within the system of feudal tenures by which the colonists, and those Irish who had undertaken similar transactions in the sixteenth century, held their land.[2] In legal form, this system involved the presumption that, in return for an annual rent, crown tenants received a life interest in the property, which reverted to the crown on death. In practice, this technicality was used as the basis for a burdensome system of taxation upon land, the details of which varied according to the tenure involved. All tenants who wished to sell land had to pay for a licence to do so, and all heirs had to buy a symbolic regrant of the lands they inherited. Those who held by knight-service were also subject to special conditions when a minority occurred: the wardship of both the heir and the lands was assumed by the crown, and possession could only be regained by suing for livery upon coming of age, for which the charge was normally one year's income, and which nominally involved taking the oath of supremacy. The liabilities involved in gaining legal title were therefore substantial, and although the policy was conciliatory in intent it was usually exploitative in effect. The real threat to the Irish landholders, however, lay in the fact that, while the crown had abandoned its earlier policy of resuming royal lands and no longer encouraged private individuals to seek them out by promising favourable leases, private investigations did not cease. And the fact that they were conducted without official direction and control meant that in practice only catholic landholders were challenged while protestant ones enjoyed immunity. The process of 'racking for concealments' went on, in devious and sophisticated ways, and the New English consolidated their position at the expense of both the Irish and the crown.

The pivot of the complex system of exploitation that developed was the reckless and unconsidered generosity with which King James bestowed

[1] *Cal. S.P. Ire., 1598–9*, p. 220.

[2] Victor Treadwell, 'The Irish court of wards under James I' in *I.H.S.*, xii, no. 45 (Mar. 1960), pp 1–27.

grants upon his courtiers and their clients.[1] In form, these grants consisted of directions to the authorities in Ireland to convey royal land of a specified annual value to the grantees in perpetuity, sometimes at a fixed rent, sometimes rent-free. There was, in fact, no reserve of royal land from which such grants could be made. They were used to improve the terms upon which land was already held from the crown—to gain full possession of leased land, to convert fee farm (which involved paying rent) into fee simple (which did not), or to substitute a civil tenure for a military one. As such, they were in practice saleable commodities: their management was largely controlled by a small group of officials in Dublin and it was open to any landholder to benefit from royal liberality, at a price. They were extensively used to convert into holdings in fee simple or fee farm land leased at preferential undervaluations, arising from grants of 'concealed' royal lands made in the 1590s to those who had rediscovered unacknowledged crown titles, and they were also regularly used to secure illegal grants of newly discovered concealments. Official dishonesty maximised both their uses and their value. This was an ethos in which it was possible for a man to gain the fee simple of a property from the crown on the basis of an annual lease value of £3 19*s.* in the course of one year, and surrender the same property to the crown in the course of the next at an annual valuation of £100. The same willingness to sacrifice the interests of the crown characterised the practices of the commission for defective titles: for protestants, composition arrangements were no more than a formality, and it was perfectly possible to improve conditions of tenure significantly in a new patent. The New English, in short, had every opportunity to have the most doubtful titles confirmed, to minimise their feudal obligations, and to acquire land from the crown on spectacularly favourable terms: and in doing so they enjoyed the ready and well-paid cooperation of royal officials in Dublin. Thus royal resources were diverted to the entrenchment of an adventurer class which inexorably gained in wealth and influence.

As a corollary to this process, the hope of dealing fairly with the Irish was unrealised. The search for concealed royal lands was unabated and property remained in jeopardy, so that 'these people begin to think that we mean by little and little to root them out utterly'.[2] Under local control the commission for defective titles itself became an instrument of exploitation, seizing every opportunity to introduce more onerous tenures for Irishmen, and on occasions even attempting to resume a proportion of their land in exchange for a patent to the remainder. The position of older royal tenants, among them the Old English, deteriorated in similar ways as a result of the widespread business practice of 'searching and prying curiously'[3] into other men's affairs. In the recent past, disturbed conditions and official

[1] Terence O. Ranger, 'Richard Boyle and the making of an Irish fortune' in *I.H.S.*, x, no. 40 (Sept. 1957), pp 257–97. [2] Quoted ibid., p. 285 n. [3] *Cal. S.P. Ire., 1603–6*, p. 518.

inefficiency had made it easy to evade feudal obligations, altogether or in part: in particular, military tenures were often concealed and the less onerous conditions of common socage observed instead. The more settled situation in James's reign made it possible for royal tenants to be more closely supervised and for past transgressions to be investigated, lost rights recovered, and unpaid dues exacted. Before long, the practice was adopted of rewarding those who discovered concealments of this kind with a large proportion of the fines. The irregularities uncovered by the resultant scrutinies often included flaws in title, and in these cases the discoverer might expect to receive a lease of the property upon favourable terms and to collect rent from its occupiers: by buying the facilities provided by a royal grant he could convert his lease into ownership. The ways in which catholic landowners could be mulcted were as various as the ways in which protestants could enrich themselves. And although Gaelic Irish were clearly at greatest hazard, the Old English were subject to harassment as well. Their discontent, already aroused by the state's public policies, was enlarged by official connivance at the private activities of acquisitive English adventurers who busied themselves in profiting from the confusion that surrounded property rights in Ireland.

Public policy continued to vacillate disturbingly, as the London and Dublin governments continued to disagree about the treatment of catholics. In the context of the plantation in Ulster, the existing difference of opinion was compounded by divergent views as to the risk of foreign intervention. The facts were that hostility between France and Spain inclined both towards good relations with England, that Pope Paul was disposed to work for the well-being of English and Irish catholics by diplomatic means, and that no genuine welcome underlay the ceremonial receptions which greeted Tyrone and Tyrconnell in Europe. The English government, confident that there was no likelihood of intervention, took the view that the settlement of Ulster would be more easily and more peacefully managed if other provocation were avoided, and the plantation was adduced as an additional reason for restraint in religious matters. But in Dublin, where it was observed that the brief period of moderation had brought a fresh influx of priests and dissipated what gains had been made, there was a tendency, increasingly pronounced after O'Doherty's revolt, to assume that an international conspiracy was on foot and that the clergy were its agents. Insistently, permission was sought to deal severely with them, but the sole response was a grant of authority to forbid catholics to have their children educated abroad. For some years, Chichester resentfully followed the moderate course prescribed by London. The recusancy fine was still fitfully imposed and the oath of supremacy intermittently required of municipal officers, but interference with both laity and clergy was minimal. So also, in Chichester's view, was the effect of the policy: the catholics, he believed, were already so disloyal that persecution could not make them more so. Thus, when James brought to his attention a memorandum in which the recently appointed bishop of Raphoe, Andrew Knox, suggested that the episcopate should be given extraordinary powers to suppress catholicism, including the right to arrest catholic priests, the lord deputy used the king's commendation as a pretext to reissue the 1605 proclamation in July 1611. A month later, the English privy council reaffirmed its original view that the bishops could best counter catholicism by nurturing protestantism, and directed that action against priests should only be taken where there was suspicion of treason; it was conceded, however, that it might be useful to make an example of a titular bishop or two. Thereafter, though there was a marked tendency to extend recusancy proceedings from the towns into country districts where possible, the Dublin government was forced to derive what satisfaction it could from the indictment and execution of the aged bishop of Down, Cornelius O'Devany, and one of his priests, in February 1612.

O'Devany's death was an event of unexpected importance in the development of the counter-reformation in Ireland.[1] Although there had been a great deal of priestly activity in the country in recent years it had been poorly coordinated, unevenly distributed, and inadequately supervised, for the supply of clergy was chiefly governed by the haphazard evolution of the continental seminaries, the secular and regular clergy acted independently of one another, and the longstanding practice of appointing vicars apostolic in place of bishops had left the missionaries largely uncontrolled. After O'Devany's death, the Irish hierarchy consisted of four archbishops and a single bishop, and of these only Kearney of Cashel was resident in Ireland. There was, of course, justification for informal structures and loose lines of control in a situation of danger, but the results seemed objectively so unsatisfactory that it became imperative to question the assumptions upon which papal policy was founded. The aim of the counter-reformation church was to preserve the faith by improving its practice; the model it worked towards was an organisation of well-defined parish units within which the uniform observance of the tridentine decrees regulating attendance at mass and participation in the sacraments could be enforced, and catechetical instruction given. In Ireland, the parochial system was underdeveloped, and neither the standards of ordinary religious observance nor local marriage and funeral customs conformed to the rigorous tridentine

[1] John Bossy, 'The counter-reformation and the people of catholic Ireland, 1596–1641', and Helga Hammerstein, 'Aspects of the continental education of Irish students in the reign of Elizabeth I' in *Hist. Studies*, viii, 155–71, 137–54; John Brady, 'The Irish colleges in Europe and the counter-reformation', and P. J. Corish, 'The reorganisation of the Irish church, 1603–41' in *Ir. Cath. Hist. Comm. Proc.*, iii (1957), pp 1–8, 9–16; J. J. Silke, 'Later relations between Primate Peter Lombard and Hugh O'Neill', and 'Primate Lombard and James I' in *Ir. Theol. Quart.*, xxii (1955), pp 15–30, 124–50; P. J. Corish, 'An Irish counter-reformation bishop: John Roche' in *Ir. Theol. Quart.*, xxv (1958), pp 14–32, 101–23, xxvi (1959), pp 101–16, 313–30.

code of practice. No significant improvement could result from the work of individual missionaries, who might help to sustain Irish catholicism, but could do little to reform it. Indeed, the prominence of regular clergy on the Irish mission actually tended to impede change by obscuring the importance of the parish. It was evident to the absentee primate, Peter Lombard, that the exercise of authority by a resident episcopate was the most effective means of recovering the detailed control that was essential if systematic reform were to be undertaken.

There were difficulties: it would be necessary to have Ireland reclassified as a reasonably safe area in which abnormal arrangements were no longer necessary, and this would in turn require the resolution of certain contradictions in papal policy. Pope Paul, though he was inclined to be conciliatory in principle, none the less indulged Tyrone, both by granting him considerable influence in the appointment of clergy in Ulster, and by acceding to his request for the appointments of Florence Conry and Eugene MacMahon to the archdioceses of Tuam and Dublin. Lombard, who had until recently been an influential advocate on Tyrone's behalf, came to believe that aggressive gestures of this kind were no longer compatible with the best interests of the catholic church in Ireland. In a memorandum to Pope Paul, in 1612, he interpreted O'Devany's death as a direct response to the translation of MacMahon to Dublin, contrasted the treatment of O'Devany with the leniency shown towards other clergy, and concluded that the only clergy whom the government found objectionable were those associated with Tyrone. On this reasoning, he urged the pope to appoint resident bishops whose loyalty to the king was unquestionable, for if that condition were fulfilled their safety and freedom of action seemed assured. Slowly, his view prevailed, and the notion of meeting moderation with moderation won approval, but not before events in Ireland had revealed the weakness of his argument.

In its early years, James's government was without significant support in Ireland. Most of those who professed loyalty to it opposed its policies. Its power to rule was frankly derived from conquest and its authority from England. Its aim was the evolutionary transformation of the total Irish environment. The Ulster plantation changed this entire emphasis. When the undertakers and servitors were chosen and endowed, a new aristocracy was created. Its task was primarily to establish a protestant colony to counterbalance the catholic one and lend ever-growing local support to the administration, and only secondarily to accelerate the anglicisation of the Irish, as the principle of segregation frankly acknowledged. This, too, was a strategy that needed time to develop fully, but the government could no longer afford to wait.

Shortly after returning from Ulster in the autumn of 1610, the lord deputy announced that the Irish parliament would meet in the following year.[1] The immediate need was for statutory confirmation of the forfeitures, but the government had always regarded a parliament as a necessary stage in the assertion of its control. A good deal of prospective business had already accumulated, as both the experience of administering a system of national government and the experiment of enforcing religious conformity revealed the additional laws that would be required 'for the reformation and settlement of this people and country'.[2] Indeed the Dublin government had grown so accustomed to the idea of holding a parliament that its approach towards actually convening one was politically outdated. It presumed that parliament would contain a catholic majority, and its objectives were consequently limited at the outset by an inappropriate regard for the practical possibilities that had existed before the plantation began. The substantial legislative programme that was dispatched to London in rough draft in February 1611 was largely uncontroversial in character. When it was considered in England, the basic assumption that catholic political power must be deferred to was questioned, and James concluded that the matter could not be decided without detailed study. He was already troubled by Ireland: his financial position was precarious, and the possibility of increasing Ireland's contribution towards the cost of its government needed to be investigated, as did conflicting reports of the progress of the plantation. In July he sent the former lord president of Munster, Lord Carew, to Ireland to report on the situation and prepare recommendations. When Carew returned three months later, he presented a complete and convincing plan to gain governmental control over parliament. Preparations were thereupon resumed on the revised assumption that it would not be necessary to cultivate catholic support.

The delay had already generated suspicion. When Chichester once again, in the Michaelmas term of 1611, brought the nobility and gentry to the council table to invite them to submit legislative proposals for the forthcoming parliament, their reaction was hostile. Their spokesmen alleged that they were members of the 'grand council' mentioned in Poynings' act and were entitled to take part in the consideration of all legislative proposals. Chichester denied that any such right existed, and he was at least formally correct, for Poynings' act contained no such provision.[3] But the disagreement did not turn upon the matter of fact, and custom may have supported the

[1] T. W. Moody, 'The Irish parliament under Elizabeth and James I: a general survey' in *R.I.A. Proc.*, xlv, sect. c, no. 6 (1939), pp 41–81; Victor Treadwell, 'The house of lords in the Irish parliament of 1613–1615' in *E.H.R.*, lxxx (1965), pp 92–107; H. F. Kearney, 'The Irish parliament in the early seventeenth century', in *The Irish parliamentary tradition*, ed. Brian Farrell (Dublin and New York, 1973), pp 88–101.

[2] *Cal. S.P. Ire., 1611–14*, p. 154.

[3] R. Dudley Edwards and T. W. Moody, 'The history of Poynings' law: part I, 1494–1615' in *I.H.S.*, ii, no. 8 (Sept. 1941), pp 415–24.

Old English, who were acting upon the traditional assumption that meetings of parliament were essentially occasions upon which the king consulted his subjects and gave them an opportunity to influence his policies. The administration was acting within the equally valid tradition that parliament was primarily an instrument of government, and the conflict simply reflected the fact that in changing circumstances the two traditions no longer complemented one another. In fact, the government's legislative and electoral arrangements were still far from complete, and Sir John Davies was to spend seven months in England perfecting them in 1612, but the intention to seek a direct confrontation with the Old English on the religious issue was clearly signalled. The municipal officials who were elected at Michaelmas 1611 were required to take the oath of supremacy and deposed when they refused to do so. O'Devany's execution was followed by the adoption of increasingly aggressive attitudes towards lay catholics, with the extension of recusancy proceedings from the towns to the countryside and the prosecution and exemplary punishment of jurors who failed to present recusants. When the towns again failed to elect protestants in 1612, they were threatened with the revocation of their charters and the institution of royal governors. In this atmosphere, there was every reason to believe official hints that, when parliament met, members would be required to take the oath of supremacy, and good reason to fear, as Archbishop Kearney did, 'that things will take place in it such as have not been seen since the schism of Henry VIII began'.[1]

In reality, however, the legislative programme that was finally agreed upon in September 1612 was less draconic than catholics feared. It included a bill against Jesuits and seminary priests and those who received or relieved them; it made provision for applying the more severe English recusancy laws to English catholics who came to Ireland to escape them; and it proposed to enact the prohibition against foreign education which had previously been enforced by proclamation. But the opportunity to strengthen the unsatisfactory law relating to attendance at protestant services was not taken. The remainder of the programme was something of an anticlimax also. From amongst the multiple measures which had been intended to contribute a dramatic impetus to shaping the future development of the country along English lines, only a handful remained. Tyrone and Tyrconnell were to be attainted; the king's title to the Irish crown was to be formally recognised; extended powers to deal with the increasing problem of piracy were to be assumed; abuses of the outmoded plea of 'benefit of clergy' were to be regulated; and a subsidy bill which introduced the more profitable English system of taxation was to be passed. The fact was that in the course of the long-drawn-out discussions and preparations the emphasis had changed: the actual measures to be passed had gradually come to be regarded as far less important than the demonstration of the government's ability to

[1] *Spicil. Ossor.*, i, 122.

have them passed. The specific purposes for which a parliament had been deemed necessary had become secondary to the overriding need for a political victory over catholic power.

The terms of reference that James had given Carew had been to suggest how the government could gain control of a parliament in which a majority of commoners and a sizeable minority of peers were bound to be catholics. The stark kernel of Carew's recommendation was that protestant representation should be boosted to the level required for an effective majority, and the consequential detailed exercise in political arithmetic added 84 seats to the existing 148. There was good reason to update parliament's composition to match the new political unity which an effective national administration had created: although the counties, including the Cross of Tipperary, were uniformly entitled to return 2 knights, the 41 two-seat borough constituencies were ill-distributed, with only 4 situated in Ulster and 2 in Connacht. The government's plans to repair this situation, however, were governed by political and religious, not by regional, considerations, and the means adopted was the creation of new boroughs, in each of which the right of election was vested in a corporation composed of a provost and 12 burgesses, all of them named in the charter of incorporation and required to take the oath of supremacy. In many instances, the places chosen were no more than villages; in some, they were no more than the sites upon which plantation towns were to be built. In this way, 38 additional members were assigned to Ulster, 18 to Munster, 16 (including Dublin University) to Leinster, and 12 to Connacht. The implementation of the scheme was left until the last possible moment: a few of the new boroughs were incorporated late in 1612, and a larger number in the following February, but many did not receive their charters until after the writ for calling parliament had been issued on 6 March 1613. The government's intentions, however, had been known for some time. When Chichester made his third Michaelmas announcement that parliament would meet in the spring, the Old English lords of the Pale not only renewed their claim to be consulted about projected legislation, and appealed to James to recognise that his interests would be best served by 'withdrawing such laws as may tend to the forcing of your subjects' conscience', but protested vigorously against the packing of parliament through the elevation of 'beggarly cottages' to the status of corporations 'that by the votes of a few elected for that purpose, under the name of burgesses, extreme penal laws should be imposed upon your subjects'.[1]

Confident of its calculations, the government made only one direct attempt to influence the elections in catholic constituencies. Sir Patrick Barnewall was summoned to England to prevent his election. Otherwise the government was content to hope that the rumour that members would be presented with the oath of supremacy would favour moderate candidates.

[1] Moody, 'The Irish parliament under Elizabeth and James I', loc. cit., pp 53–4, 57–8, 72–6.

The results of the elections, which took place in April and early May, amply justified official confidence. The new boroughs duly returned 84 protestants, and although the returns elsewhere were two to one in favour of catholics the aggregate result was a protestant majority of 32. The protestant membership illustrated the narrowness of the government's political base: more than half were either office-holders or pensioners, and almost half sat for Ulster constituencies. Among the 100 catholic members there were some native Irish, and even a few who were unable to speak English, but the bulk of them were Old English. It was colonial Ireland that was represented in the Irish house of commons, and the new political geography of that Ireland was reflected in the conversion of Ulster from the chief area of Irish resistance to the chief area of government support: only one of the 64 seats in the province was won by a catholic. In the house of lords, the government's bloc vote was provided by the 20 members of the episcopate, who actually outnumbered the 12 catholic and 4 protestant peers who attended. This position was only marginally affected by the acceptance of proxies, and the government had a safe majority of 11 votes.

The government's intention was to obliterate the constitutionally sanctioned political influence of the Old English. The concerted purpose of the Old English was to contest the government's ability to invert the balance of power in parliament. Their chosen tactic in opposition was to sabotage official plans by refusing to work within the arbitrarily revised political conditions. The catholic peers lost no time in making their position plain: indignantly criticising the blatant presumption of their disloyalty, alleging that the elections had not been fairly conducted, and objecting to parliament sitting in Dublin castle in the presence of an armed guard, they refused to attend the opening meeting on 18 May. The catholic commoners took their seats on that day for the sole purpose of disputing the legality of the protestant majority. They could not profitably raise the political issue of the packing of parliament, because the king's power to enfranchise boroughs was unquestionable, so their approach was necessarily indirect. They claimed that fourteen sheriffs had made false returns, and that many members were ineligible because they were not resident in their constituencies, and they contended that parliament could not commence its business until the validity of the returns had been determined and the right of those elected to take their seats established. When the government supporters none the less proceeded to the election of a speaker, the catholics refused to cooperate. The official nominee, Sir John Davies, whose own election to the house was in dispute, was opposed by Sir John Everard, the last avowed catholic to hold high office, who had been forced to resign from the king's bench in 1607. When Davies's supporters, as the 'ayes' in the division, left the chamber to be counted, the opposition installed Everard in the chair and held him there while the tellers of the returning majority placed Davies in his lap.

After a scuffle, Everard was ejected, and the opposition withdrew. 'Those within the house are no house', observed Sir William Talbot as they did so, 'and Sir John Everard is our speaker, and therefore we will not join with you, but we will complain to my lord deputy and the king, and the king shall hear of this'.[1] Neither persuasion nor a peremptory summons altered this resolution. Although both houses continued to sit, the opposition remained aloof, and the outcome verified the soundness of the political judgement of the opposition leaders. In theory, it was perfectly possible for the government to proceed without the absentees: in practice, their participation was essential if parliament were to have the requisite authority to commit the community to its decisions. Parliamentary opposition in itself implied consent, and was, paradoxically, indispensable to the government's political purposes. After a series of adjournments, parliament was prorogued on 17 June to await the results of an appeal to England.

The appeal proceedings were protracted, partly because of the difficulties involved, and partly because of other demands upon the king's attention. An English parliament had been convened and dismissed in acrimony before James finally adjudicated the Irish dispute in August 1614. The first stage had been the appointment in August 1613 of a commission, unsuitably headed by Chichester, to inquire into the elections, the events of 18 May, and grievances in general. It detected three electoral irregularities and uncovered fairly widespread evidence of extortion by soldiers and officials. But, although its investigations led one of its members to the private conclusion that 'these Irish are a scurvy nation, and are as scurvily dealt with',[2] its official report dismissed the professed grievances as entirely trivial and the allegations of electoral malpractice as largely unfounded. On the basis of these findings, James dealt roughly with the opposition delegation at an audience in April 1614: 'my sentence is that you have carried yourselves tumultuously, and that your proceedings have been rude, disorderly, and worthy of severe punishment',[3] he declared, assuring them that their complaints were commonplace and would have been attended to as a matter of routine by the lord deputy on request, and that he would create boroughs and dispense with residential qualifications for election as he saw fit. When he made his final decisions three months later, however, his attitude was incongruously conciliatory, and he ignored the commission's recommendations in the interests of achieving a compromise that would bring the opposition back into parliament. Largely by disallowing returns from boroughs that had received their charters after writs of summons had been issued, he reduced the government majority to six: at the same time, he arranged for the anti-catholic bills to be withdrawn. The result, so far as the immediate issue was concerned, was an opposition victory. The

[1] *Cal. Carew MSS*, *1603–24*, p. 274.
[2] *Cal. S.P. Ire.*, *1611–14*, p. 432.
[3] *Desid. cur. Hib.*, i, 302.

shrewdness of the king's solution went unrecognised: the opposition gained nothing that they could not have gained through abstention; James yielded nothing that was not already lost. But the right of the excluded boroughs to send members to future parliaments was protected, as was the right of non-residential representation, and future protestant majorities were assured. By making it possible for opposition members to take their seats, James committed them to a political revolution which was not the less effective for being achieved in two stages rather than in one.

The presence of an opposition deputation, which expanded in time from six to twenty members, gave James a prolonged first-hand experience of Irish problems that confirmed his prejudices. His deceptive compromise, with its concession to present reality and its assurance of future protestant hegemony, was devised in a spirit of profound dissatisfaction with the old colony, whose representatives had equivocated about their own position and failed to understand his. At the outset, he had probed the attitudes of the principal members of the delegation, forcing them to face the ultimate dilemma of the loyal catholic and declare for pope or king in his presence. Sir Patrick Barnewall, fresh from the Tower, unreservedly denied that the pope could depose kings or absolve subjects from their allegiance. His fellow Palesmen, Sir William Talbot, who was regarded as the leader of the group, and Thomas Luttrell were unwilling to follow suit. Three months in the Fleet prison reduced Luttrell to submission, but Talbot, who had recently been dismissed from the recordership of Dublin for refusing to take the oath of supremacy, held fast to his contention that he was not competent to pronounce upon a matter of faith. In January 1614 he was prosecuted in the star chamber by Francis Bacon, and given an exemplary sentence.

James's efforts to convey his own attitude to the deputation yielded equally unsatisfactory results. In a valedictory speech to members who were returning to Ireland in the autumn of 1613, he asked them to let it be known that he did not intend to 'extort any man's conscience'.[1] Sir James Gough, the county member for Waterford who had proposed Everard for the speakership, busily spread the news that the king did not wish to have the laws against recusancy enforced. This was the reverse of the truth. James, who felt understandably free to prejudge the results of the commission's investigations, had already decided to punish the opposition by requiring lawyers, pensioners, municipal officers, and justices of the peace to take the oath of supremacy, and was at one with Chichester's view that if new anti-catholic laws could not be passed, then the old ones should be rigorously enforced. James was embarrassingly constrained to issue a denial of Gough's report, and Gough was obliged to confess that he was at fault. That there was no disagreement between them as to the words which James had used made

[1] *Cal. S.P. Ire., 1611–14*, p. 547.

their misunderstanding all the more significant. Gough's error in interpreting a declaration of respect for private beliefs as a promise of public toleration demonstrated to James the prevalence of assumptions and expectations that were anathema to him. A major part of the delegation's task had been to convince the king of the opposition's sincere loyalty to the crown. The members attempted to do this repeatedly, with prolix fervour, but James drew his own conclusions and stated them bluntly in the formal audience which he gave on 21 April 1614. He spoke at length on catholicism, as well as on the political quarrel, dealing with papal supremacy and the intercessory power of the saints, and 'saying many other things on this topic, in more or less disordered fashion', the Roman curia was told, before unleashing a swingeing condemnation of those who attended him:

> Surely I have good reason for saying that you are only half-subjects of mine. For you give your soul to the pope, and to me only the body and even it, your bodily strength, you divide between me and the king of Spain. . . . Strive henceforth to become good subjects, that you may have *cor unum et viam unam*, and then I shall respect you all alike.[1]

The opposition had good reason to hope that the king's policies would prove more accommodating than his opinions. James himself was aware that his political compromise would encourage expectations of similarly ungracious religious concessions, and he and Chichester were at pains to prevent that inference from being drawn. Although the extreme course of mounting exemplary proceedings against the clergy was considered only to be discarded, the level of government activity against the laity was deliberately stepped up from the summer of 1614: the disqualification of catholic lawyers was enforced, the county commissions of the peace were purged of catholics so far as was practicable, the pressure against catholic municipal officers was maintained, and recusancy proceedings continued, as did proceedings against jurors who refused to present the names of catholics. The effect was to strengthen the opposition's determination to use parliamentary influence to gain a measure of toleration. The government's parliamentary objectives correspondingly dwindled: it now sought only to procure the passage of a few useful bills, of which the subsidy bill had become the most important, and to avoid making religious concessions in order to do so.

When parliament assembled on 11 October 1614, even these aims seemed ambitious, for the more regular attendance of the opposition members gained them an unexpected majority in the commons. They used it, however, to place the king under an obligation by behaving as responsibly as he could wish, even going so far at first as to attend opening prayers each morning. The government's chief difficulty actually arose from the failure of the English privy council to return the subsidy bill in time for the session. There was some initial unpleasantness in the commons, generated by the

[1] Silke, 'Primate Lombard and James I', loc. cit., pp 131–3.

recriminations of the member for Enniskillen, Humphrey Farnham, who obliquely resumed the attack a little later by proposing that 5 November should be declared a public holiday, but the atmosphere in general was studiously polite and businesslike. The government's principal measures, concerning the king's title, the attainder of the earls, benefit of clergy, and pirates, passed without difficulty, and although other bills were amended, which involved their return to England for approval, and a few were rejected, the predominant tone was constructive rather than carping. The group of government supporters, led by the vice-treasurer, Sir Thomas Ridgeway, played along: when the house turned its attention to preparing the ground for the revision of fees, officials readily cooperated; and when Sir John Everard, who led the opposition, moved for the relaxation of measures against catholics, the privy councillors in the house undertook to convey the request to the lord deputy. By this stage, however, parliament had more time than business on its hands, and there were signs that the opposition was gaining the confidence to reconsider its policy of restraint. Accordingly, Chichester decided to await the arrival of the subsidy bill no longer, and prorogued parliament on 29 November. When the bill finally reached him two days later, he was tempted to abandon both it and the parliament, but the financial circumstances in both England and Ireland were too pressing to allow the chance to be wasted. Parliament was reconvened in April 1615 on the basis of a firm resolve to have the subsidy without conditions or not at all.

The suspicion that the opposition would try to bargain proved well founded. When the bill was first introduced, an opposition member reminded the house of an old saying:

Little said, soon amended,
A subsidy granted, the parliament ended.[1]

He went on to move that its consideration be deferred, but his proposal was lost, and attempts to attach conditions to the bill at its second reading were also unsuccessful. These tactics proved to be exceptional. In other respects, the policy of the opposition members was unaltered, and dutiful conduct and loyal words remained their principal weapons. They voted for the subsidy, supported government legislation, contributed constructively to the business of the house, and went to considerable lengths to soothe protestant fears. 'If any man here will stick to a Jesuit, he will spit in his face', declared Sir John Everard, and went on to claim, in a deliberate evocation of the king's words, that the commons were *cor unum et animus unus*.[2] If the opposition's policy was unchanged, however, its situation was very different, for it no longer possessed a majority in the house. Though demands for religious concessions were redoubled, the most that could be gained was the endorsement of a recommendation that catholic lawyers should be readmitted to the

[1] Moody, 'The Irish parliament under Elizabeth and James I', loc. cit., p. 61.
[2] Ibid., p. 62; *Commons' jn. Ire.* (2nd ed., 1796), p. 34.

bar, which had been adopted in the previous session, and the dispatch to the lord deputy of the unimpressive message 'that a great number of the house desire that his lordship would recommend to his majesty that some suspension might be had of the statute of 2 Elizabethae'.[1] It proved unnecessary to answer these demands: parliament was prorogued on 16 May and dissolved during the recess.

Before parliament ended, James had reached the obvious conclusion that control over Ireland could be securely established only by extending the area of plantation. The model he had in mind was not the major Ulster scheme, but a smaller-scale project which had evolved in Wexford and which straddled the obscure borderline between public and private interest in such a way as to suggest the possibility of using defects of title to establish limited English settlements within the broader context of a reorganisation of Irish landholding. In 1610 landholders in the area that extended roughly from the sea to the Slaney and from Wicklow to Enniscorthy had surrendered their lands to the crown but had failed to secure a regrant because a number of New English had discovered a 'long slept' royal title to much of the area and secured grants within it. Although the occupiers were mainly Gaelic Irish, of the Kinsella, Kavanagh, and MacMurrough families, a few Old English proprietors were also involved and the issue was strenuously contested. The government, fresh from its successful completion of the Ulster arrangements, had taken over the claim on the crown's behalf and instituted plantation proceedings: all those freeholders who occupied less than 100 acres had been expropriated and converted into leaseholders and this, combined with dishonest measurement, had released more than half the land for allocation to undertakers, among them the lord deputy's nephew. In 1613, however, Walter Synnott, a substantial Old English proprietor in the area, had been elected to parliament as a county member, accompanied the opposition delegation to London, and succeeded in having the treatment of the Wexford freeholders investigated by the commissioners. A great deal of discussion ensued, punctuated by command and countermand, out of which emerged a firm purpose to proceed and the two guiding principles that only one-quarter of the land should be planted, and that those with less than 100 acres should be excluded from regrant. After 1615 the scheme became a pilot experiment, and despite protests and resistance, in the course of which a group of resolute petitioners who carried their objections as far as London were summarily transported to Virginia, effect was given to it. Following a fresh survey in 1618, about 150 local occupiers were given grants, perhaps one in four of those who had participated in the original surrender, and the eighteen undertakers who were already in possession received their patents.

[1] Moody, ibid., p. 63.

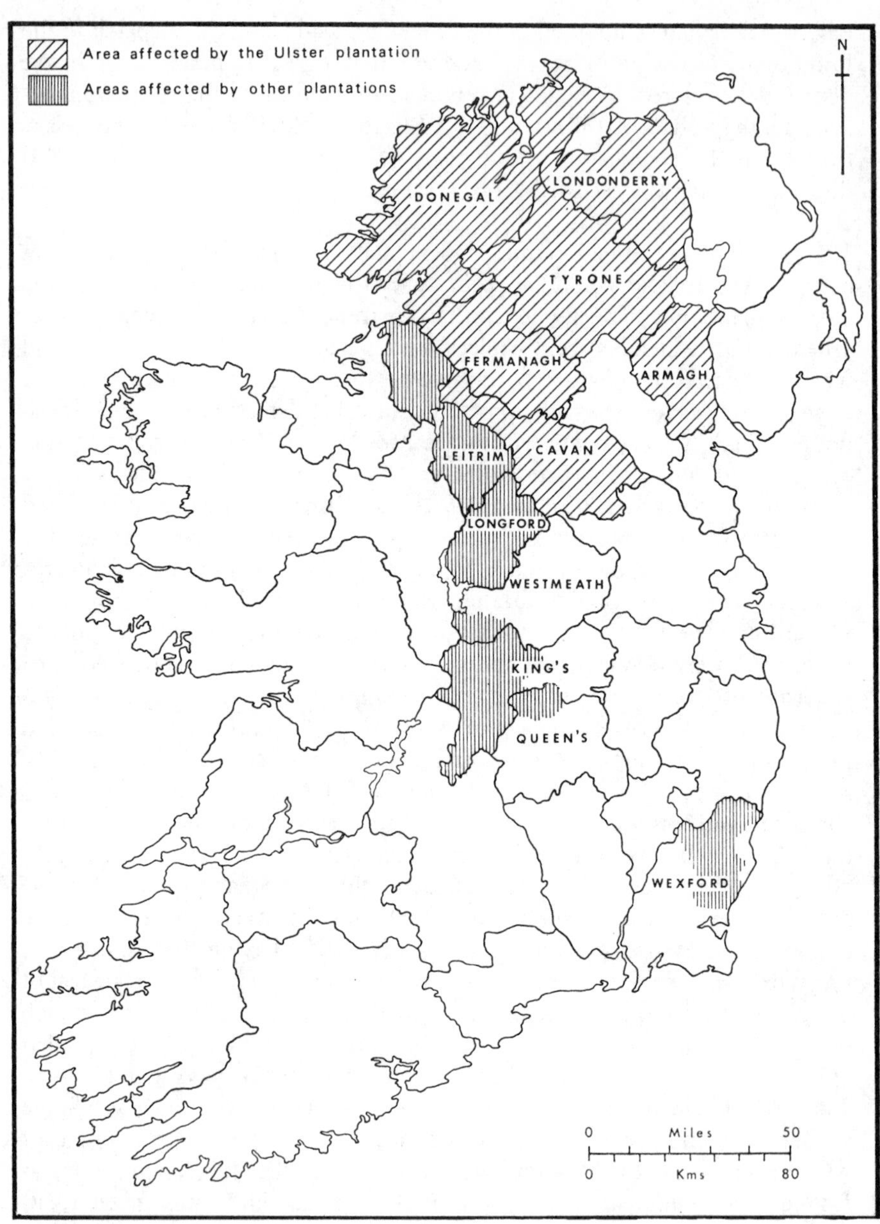

Map 6 PLANTATIONS, 1609–25, by Aidan Clarke

Over the next two years, this policy was extended to strategically situated land in Irish possession in the midlands.[1] In Leitrim, 45 undertakers received grants, as did 33 in Longford and 19 in Ely O'Carroll, while 28 more were provided for in a cluster of smaller schemes involving O'Dunne's country in Queen's County, the countries of O'Molloy, MacCoghlan, and Fox in King's County, and O'Melaghlin's country in Westmeath. In each case, the land taken for plantation was a quarter of the area to which crown title had been proved, except in Leitrim where one-half became available as a result of a special arrangement involving the compensation of Brian O'Rourke, who was under the negotiating disadvantage of being a minor at university in England. In each case, the land exempted from plantation was distributed in freeholds to occupiers who established claim to more than 100 acres, while the 'inferior natives' were converted into leaseholders. Grant-units for undertakers were small by Ulster standards, and extremely irregular in size. The upper limit was usually 1,000 acres, but few reached it, and some received less than 100 acres. Undertakers were not permitted to sell land to one another, 'lest the lands should come into the hands of a few and the plantation come to nothing'. Since similar restrictions applied to the Irish, the detailed arrangements could not be altered without government sanction, and this was central to the modified scheme of plantation that was employed. The essentials of the arrangements lay in the stabilisation of landholding and in the personal presence of the planters, for, though building conditions were stringent and residential requirements heavily stressed, the undertakers were under no obligation to introduce British tenants. Instead, the conditions imposed upon Irish tenants were designed to provide an elaborate substitute for an authentic British tenantry: they were to build their houses 'streetwise' in villages, complete with chimneys, gardens, plots, and orchards, to enclose and hedge one-sixth of their land, and to grow a set proportion of hempseed.

These plantations did not develop according to plan. The disgruntled native lessees did not show 'any desire to settle in that kind'. The local freeholders for the most part ignored the building conditions required of them, except in King's County where their fortifications were so good that the area reportedly 'seemeth rather to be displanted than planted'. Moreover, only a handful of the undertakers showed any inclination to settle upon their estates, preferring to 'receive their rents by their servants or agents'. Since they included many government officials, among them the lord deputy, and since many of them (including the lord deputy) received grants in more than one area, it was scarcely to be supposed that they had ever intended to do otherwise. The position revealed by a survey made in 1622,[2] which found that the plantations amounted to little more than the superimposition of a

[1] See map 6.

[2] B.M., Add. MS 4756. Quotations in this and the preceding paragraph are from this source, ff 123–30.

substantial number of absentee landlords upon the 'inferior Irish' of Wexford and the midlands, was an inexorable consequence of the way in which the scheme had been administered. Under local control, James's policy of interspersed planting was converted into a new, predatory form of surrender and regrant directed towards the enrichment of the New English.

The king's plans for the settlement of Connacht met with a somewhat similar fate. In July 1615, in the familiar interests of stabilising landownership and undermining the dependence of followers upon their chiefs, James ordered that the composition arrangements which had been made by Perrot and Bingham in the 1580s,[1] but never subsequently formalised, should be put into effect. Appropriate action followed: surrenders were received, fees paid, patents granted, and commissioners appointed to determine the sums due to the crown. But official opposition quickly developed in Ireland. To some extent it was based on valid equitable considerations, for the accuracy of the survey made in 1585 was open to serious question, and the indiscriminate regularisation of its findings would certainly have perpetuated injustices. More to the point, however, was the unwelcome generosity of the terms granted by James, who had chosen to confer a blanket retrospective pardon upon all previous transgressions in matters of wardship, intrusion, alienation, mean profits, and fines. The effect was to withhold the lucrative possibilities of a whole province from both the commissioners of wards and the private entrepreneurs whose self-appointed business it was to discover such defaults for personal profit. Mystery surrounds the way in which the opponents of the king's policy set to work, but the result is clear: the final stage in the process of validating the new titles, by enrolling the patents and surrenders in the court of chancery, was never completed. Responsibility was locally attributed to Sir Charles Coote, a servitor who was both provost-marshal of the province and collector of its composition rents. But Coote, who already had plantation interests in Munster and was shortly to acquire more in Leitrim, lacked the influence necessary to defeat the king's policy unaided. The means by which this limited anglicisation of landholding in Connacht was impeded, and the Old English and Irish landowners prevented from securing the firm titles that James had decided to grant them, undoubtedly involved the collusion of royal officials in Dublin.

Even in conception, however, the plantations in Leinster and Leitrim offered little substance for Francis Bacon's hope that 'the new plantations would rate the other party in time'.[2] The possibility of building up a substantial British presence to confront the catholics still depended on progress in Ulster, and James watched its development anxiously. In fact, it proceeded patchily. Absenteeism was partly to blame, but the manner in which the land had been distributed was an important contributory influence. The

[1] See above, pp 109–11.

[2] *The works of Francis Bacon*, ed. James Spedding (7 vols, London, 1857–74), v, 375.

better, more accessible land usually went to the chief undertakers and their closer associates, who had the resources to meet the costs of building, stocking the land, importing tenants, and providing for them, and these proportions developed quite quickly. The outlying areas posed greater problems, were allocated to less influential men with smaller resources, and developed more slowly. Before long, a pronounced process of consolidation began, as many of those who had been unsuccessful, or who had never intended to devote themselves to the venture, were bought out by the more competent and more resolute planters at low prices; and a related tendency appeared in the unreserved precincts, where the number of native proprietors steadily declined as enterprising servitors acquired their lands. Most of those undertakers who came to Ireland probably gained larger returns from their Ulster estates than they did from their cross-channel ones, but the initial costs of settlement were high and the margin of income over expenditure was not large. In these conditions, the planters naturally tended to cut costs and maximise revenue, neglecting the conditions upon which they had received their grants. They avoided creating freeholders, gave only short-term leases in the expectation of rising values, let lands to the Irish, charged high rents, and fell behind both on their building programmes and on the provision of arms for defence. On the other hand, although there were many defaulters, in the aggregate the undertakers fulfilled the obligation to settle the land with British. Calculations based on a survey made in 1622, and on related evidence, suggest that a minimum of about 3,700 settler families had been introduced into the six escheated counties, representing an adult population of some 13,000. English and Scots were present in about equal numbers, with Scottish majorities in Donegal and Tyrone, and though the Scottish proportions were more densely settled, both groups actually exceeded the stipulated requirement of twenty-four men to each proportion. The shortcomings of the plantation arose from two considerations: firstly, that the distribution was uneven, with areas of active settlement compensating for areas of inactivity, and secondly, that the excess acreage of the proportions made the predetermined settlement ratio quite inadequate. There were few precincts in which the settlers were not greatly outnumbered by the Irish.

Ironically, Down and Antrim, which had been settled privately and for the most part in advance of the plantation, were more extensively settled than any of the escheated counties by the early 1620s, with a combined adult British population of some 7,500. Whether measured against this unofficial achievement, or against the original plan, the plantation was far from successful, and the king's displeasure was constant. His interest certainly provided a stimulus, but it was also a growing source of apprehension. There were few planters who had not defaulted upon their terms and placed their grants in jeopardy, and it became imperative for them to guard against forfeiture or penalty by negotiating some modification of the original conditions of plantation. In 1620 they petitioned for permission to observe the stipulated requirements on only three-quarters of their estates, retaining Irish tenants on the remainder. This formula, which amounted in practice to a recognition of the failure to establish segregated British communities, was not accepted in principle until 1625, and not agreed in detail until three years later, and its promotion contributed markedly to the development of the planters as a coherent and distinctive interest-group.

The corollary of James's policy of strengthening protestant control and influence through plantation was his determination to enforce the disabilities and inconveniences that attached to catholicism. Although his long-sustained effort to arrange a Spanish marriage for his son and heir, Charles, perhaps imposed a certain restraint, at local level the laws against recusancy were executed within the limits of practicality until the negotiations with Spain rose to a pitch of urgency in 1623. There was a politic lull in anti-recusant activity in 1615, due probably to a certain wariness of Old English reaction to the abrupt termination of parliament and to a sense of the need to ease the collection of the parliamentary subsidy, but attributable in some degree to a loss of drive and purpose by Chichester. When he was honourably relieved of office at the end of the year, the appointment of the consistently hard-line Archbishop Jones to joint lord justiceship with Chief Justice Denham was followed by firmer action, and this was sustained by Sir Oliver St John, a servitor who had come to Ireland with Mountjoy, who became lord deputy in July 1616. The outstanding problem was posed by a number of towns which had stubbornly disregarded repeated instructions to stop electing recusant officials. It had already been agreed in principle that their charters should be confiscated if the offence were repeated, as it was in 1615, but the lords justices sought a less severe solution. Town officials in both Munster and Leinster were deposed and heavily fined, and a number of municipal electors were summoned to Dublin and cautioned. The elections of 1616, however, were uninfluenced by these measures: recusants were again chosen, deposed, and fined. Waterford was thereupon selected for exemplary treatment: a commission of inquiry led to a chancery order revoking its charter in March 1618 and to the installation of a governor to administer its business. There was no further municipal defiance until 1623, when most of the Munster towns again elected catholics.

The year 1618 also saw significant changes in the collection of recusancy fines. There had been no intermission in their exaction: indeed, liability had been extended from men to women, and recalcitrant juries had been dealt with in the court of castle chamber from time to time, but the results were uneven. The enforcement procedures, modelled upon those used in England, relied upon the cooperation of local government agencies drawn from the community. Where there were local protestants of standing in sufficient numbers to take office and sit on juries, cooperation was forthcoming, fines could be routinely levied, and the yield could be considerable: the fines imposed in nine Dublin parishes amounted to more than £3,000 per year. But these conditions were abnormal. As a rule, local control was in the hands of catholics and there was no means of bringing pressure to bear upon them, apart from the punishment of jurors, which was irregular, troublesome, and ineffectual. In 1618 the system was changed in an attempt to create a uniform routine procedure for all areas. It was decided to allocate the fines to the rebuilding and repair of parish churches; the primate was appointed to receive them, and the onus of collection was transferred to the ecclesiastical officials. The faults in this arrangement soon became clear: lacking both effective supervision and support, the collectors made little effort to levy the fines upon those who had the means to pay but the assurance to refuse to do so, and confined their attentions to the 'poor sort'.[1] The result, combined with extensive peculation, was greater oppression and smaller returns. Before long, the system was again modified, with the local mechanism unchanged, but the collectors made responsible to the lord deputy. As it happened, however, this arrangement never took effect. For some years James had tried desperately to offset the consequences of his son-in-law Frederick's acceptance of the Bohemian crown in 1619 by completing a marriage alliance with Spain. At the beginning of 1623, when Charles was about to travel to Spain to press his case in person, the Irish government received instructions to suspend recusancy proceedings. And though the prince's mission was unsuccessful, the new leniency generated by international considerations was to remain.

The enforcement of discriminatory legislation upon the laity after 1615 was not associated with any action against the clergy. A proclamation was issued in 1617, requiring the banishment of those priests who had been educated abroad, but no effort was made to give it effect. The assumption upon which it was based, that continentally trained clergy posed a greater threat than those educated locally, was largely a political one, and it oversimplified an extremely complex reality. Although the government was unaware of the fact, the pressures towards 'civility' in Ireland were not wholly English and protestant. In some respects, the counter-reformation involved related objectives, and the provincial synods designed to introduce the tridentine *ius novissimum*, the first of which were held in 1614, posed an insidious threat to Gaelic Ireland. The aims of Archbishop Lombard's representative in Ireland, David Rothe, who saw the catholic religion as a means to 'eliminate barbarous customs, abolish bestial rites and convert the detestable intercourse of savages into polite manners and a care for maintaining the commonwealth',[2] were not dissimilar to those of the English government, and in practice the counter-reformation thrust was tinged with

[1] *Lismore papers*, 2nd series, iii, 6.

[2] David Rothe, *Analecta*, ed. P. F. Moran (Dublin, 1884), p. 100.

Old English assumptions. The continental seminaries, which standardised the training of priests for the Irish missions, were dominated by Old English clergy, while the influence of Lombard ensured that when his request for the appointment of resident bishops was met after 1618 the dioceses were entrusted to committed reformers. The Old English influence was reinforced by the nature of the tridentine decrees, which were sharply at variance with Irish customs and social organisation. The parochial unit itself was not wholly appropriate to a community structured upon kinship and characterised by feud, and a parochial sacramental system was unfamiliar to a people who had been accustomed to associate the performance of spiritual duties with the religious orders rather than with parish priests. The Irish tendency, 'to cling tenaciously to all the old usages',[1] by which Fr John Roche, later bishop of Ferns, explained the survival of catholicism in 1613, provided a barrier to catholic, as well as to protestant, reformers, and conservatism was assisted by tensions within the church itself.

The regulars, often equipped with special missionary faculties, strongly resisted the parish-centred structure which threatened to exclude them from the administration of the pastoral sacraments. The older clergy, who lacked the rigorous formation and continental experience of the seminary priests, were content with the pre-tridentine standards with which they were familiar. Many of the Irish clergy treated local customs more indulgently than did the Old English clergy, who associated religion with 'civility', and looked upon themselves as engaged in 'this new plantation'[2] of the catholic faith. Irishmen were understandably sensitive to the implications of such phraseology, and their approach was consequently somewhat ambivalent: while they accepted the need for spiritual renewal, they had reservations about the stereotyped European norms of civilised conduct associated with it. To the extent that the counter-reformation contained anglicising tendencies, their commitment to it was incomplete. Moreover, before long this tension was reproduced at the highest level. In the mid-1620s, the papacy agreed to bring appeasement to an end and resume an aggressive policy:[3] the decision was dramatised by the conflict surrounding the appointment of a successor to Lombard in 1625, and it left a good deal of control in the hands of Irishmen whose attachment to tridentine catholicism was qualified by their commitment to the preservation of Gaelic Ireland. In practice, a rough-and-ready recognition of spheres of influence developed, with Irish bishops appointed to Irish, and Old English bishops to Old English, dioceses. As a result, the integrated impulse towards uniform change provided by Rothe and Lombard was diluted, and a form of devolution prevailed. The effect of the wide variety of approaches

[1] P. J. Corish, 'John Roche' in *Ir. Theol. Quart.*, xxv (1958), p. 31 n.

[2] *Ibernia Ignat.*, p. 161.

[3] H. F. Kearney, 'Ecclesiastical politics and the counter-reformation in Ireland' in *Jn. Ecc. Hist.*, ii (1960), pp 202–12; Aidan Clarke, 'Ireland and the general crisis' in *Past & Present*, no. 48 (1970), pp 83–4.

within the church was the more pronounced since the unbeneficed clergy lived among the people and were dependent upon their offerings, and the result was that the rigorous requirements of the counter-reformation church were greatly softened in practice. Novelty was minimised, and there developed a variegated catholicism, sensitive to the requirements of particular communities, adapting itself to its immediate local environment. Strictly speaking, such irregularities as the presence of married priests in Ulster in the 1620s, the continued imposition of money penances on those who confessed at Easter in Ulster and Connacht, the unabated popularity of wakes, the persistent casualness towards marriage regulations, and the well-attested failure to achieve a satisfactory system of catechetical instruction indicated a considerable measure of failure by tridentine standards. On the other hand, a well-supplied and active ministry provided an intricate and flexible spiritual presence, which allowed the technically proscribed church to consolidate its position among both Irish and Old English, accommodating itself to their differences, and gaining a general acceptance which made it possible for the counter-reformation to go to work more gradually in the future. Though the renewal of catholicism was very imperfectly achieved, the preliminary task of ensuring its survival was thoroughly performed.[1]

Catholic success was achieved in part by protestant default, for the Church of Ireland made no concerted effort to mount a competing apostolate, and proved incapable of softening inherent cultural antipathies in the interests of conversion. Protestantism was not only the religion of conquest, but was typically purveyed in the language of the conqueror by men who were too sure of their own superiority to excite interest or support, and too colonially minded to work wholeheartedly for the radical transformation of the church that success would accomplish. It was later alleged of the English that 'they took more pains to make the land turn protestant than the people',[2] and these were in practice opposing goals. Although a protestant Ireland was plainly desirable in the abstract, the privileges and opportunities invested in colonial status were of more immediate concern, and a sense of the practical inexpediency of widespread conversions created a private protestant colonial interest which ran counter to public objectives. It was this ambivalence which underlay the inability of the church to overcome its practical problems, the unwillingness of the laity to assist it in doing so, and the failure of the government to arrive at an unequivocal and detailed formulation of religious policy. That it was a primary objective of the state to introduce protestantism was perfectly clear; but it was not clear how responsibility in the matter was to be divided between church and state, and it was not clear whether the emphasis was to be on persuasion or compulsion. Government officials, from the king down, tended to stress the church's

[1] See below, ch. XXIII.

[2] [Hugh Reily], *Ireland's case briefly stated* ([? Louvain], 1695), preface.

obligation to evangelise the catholics; churchmen were inclined to rely upon the government to provide them with congregations by coercion. In this confusion of responsibilities, no initiative was firmly taken, despite the fact that there was no ambiguity about the basic task in hand. Both approaches clearly depended for their success upon the creation of a systematic nation-wide ecclesiastical organisation by the refurbishing of disused churches and the recruitment of a trained ministry to take charge of them. In the absence of unified and purposeful direction, the practical difficulties of doing so proved insuperable.

The principal problems were financial in form, though their sources often lay more deeply in the self-interest of both clergy and laity. In terms of nominal assets, the Church of Ireland was well endowed: it had a great deal of land and was legally entitled to the support of the laity through tithes. In reality, however, the church's income was disproportionately small, badly distributed, and to a significant extent outside ecclesiastical control. In more than half the parishes, church assets had been appropriated by laymen who paid the incumbent whatever salary they chose, while much church land had been alienated to laymen on long leases at increasingly unrealistic rents. The exaction of large entry fines in return for such leases was one of the ways in which the higher clergy endowed their families at the expense of their offices, and clerical malversation was a significant drain on the church's resources. When Christopher Hampton was appointed archbishop of Armagh in 1613, one of the telling points in his favour was the fact that he was unmarried 'and therefore more unlikely to spoil the church and impoverish his successors as most of the bishops have done and continue to do'.[1] But it was not only through deliberate misappropriation that the bishops, deans, and others tended to 'make havoc of the church's revenue':[2] because of their own relatively small provision, they also absorbed a disproportionate amount of the income available for the lower clergy. In protestant parishes, tithe income might compensate for other deficiencies, and in plantation areas fairly adequate provision was made for the lower clergy. But elsewhere, tithe payment was extremely uncertain and clergy depended upon receiving the dues for marriages, christenings, and burials which were payable to them whether or not they actually officiated at the ceremony. In many cases, it was necessary to combine the resources of a number of parishes to support a single incumbent. The aggregate result of all these difficulties was that most livings, and some bishoprics, were too poor to attract competent clergy, and neither in quality nor quantity did the ministry measure up to requirements. By the early 1620s, only one parish in six possessed a preaching minister, and this national ratio concealed wide variations between different dioceses that partly reflected the different degrees of energy and determina-

[1] *Hastings MSS*, iv, 12.

[2] George Andrews, *A quaternion of sermons* (Dublin, 1624), p. 35.

tion of individual bishops, but chiefly related to the distribution of protestant settlers. Where largish congregations and adequate arrangements for maintenance existed, the position was satisfactory: elsewhere, the clergy were thinly spread and 'as ignorant as poor'.[1]

In general, though there was no coordinated missionary effort, and though the established church lacked even a formal presence in many areas, it succeeded reasonably well in providing for the spiritual needs of its members. Its standards were certainly uneven, and often low, but they did not differ markedly from those of the established church in England, which faced similar financial problems with similar consequences. Moreover, despite the worldliness of many of its clergy, the church did possess vitality, and, despite the fact that it was fairly thoroughly staffed by Englishmen at the higher level, it did develop a distinctive sense of identity. When the convocation of the church met in association with the parliament of 1613–15, the opportunity was taken to draw up a set of articles for the Irish church. Composed by James Ussher, the professor of divinity at Trinity College, Dublin, they tended, while perfectly consistent with anglican tradition, to emphasise its more Calvinist aspects.[2] In this, they reflected local tradition, expressed the particular bias of Dublin University, and catered usefully for the doctrinal preferences of the Scots in Ulster. In practice the lack of authoritative direction that adversely affected the church's missionary activity gave it a flexible strength that enabled it to contain a wide variety of opinion, like its catholic counterpart. But the interests of its more intellectually active and committed members tended to centre upon the kind of doctrinal controversies which concerned their English equivalents,[3] rather than upon the specific challenges of evangelism in Ireland. Those who did confront those challenges were prone to misunderstand the problem: making superficial assumptions about the nature of religious devotion, and equating ignorance with lack of commitment, they proceeded as if the proscription of catholicism would eliminate it and the adoption of protestantism naturally follow. There was some attempt to appeal to Irish conservatism, particularly by James Ussher, who published a persuasively named *Discourse of the religion anciently professed by the Irish and Scottish, showing it to be for substance the same with that which at this day is by public authority established in the Church of England*.[4] But the approach was too rarefied to influence ordinary opinions, and actual missionary work was exceptional. For the most part, the established church served the protestant colony and left the remainder of the community to Rome.

[1] B.M., Add. MS 4756, f. 69v.

[2] R. Buick Knox, *James Ussher, archbishop of Armagh* (Cardiff, 1967), pp 16–23, provides the most convincing treatment of this question.

[3] Philomena Kilroy, 'Division and dissent in the Irish reformed church, 1615–34' (M.A. thesis, National University of Ireland, 1973).

[4] Dublin, 1622.

It had been recognised from the outset that the young were more likely to be susceptible to protestantism than the old, but the problems of creating a protestant monopoly of education were too large to be tackled. Schemes for the education of the sons of the nobility in England were fitfully discussed, and occasionally implemented in individual cases, but it was only in the special case of the king's wards that a systematic educational policy was feasible. These minors at law were, in effect, under the control of commissioners whose responsibility was to provide them with acceptable guardians; in doing so, they normally stipulated that wards should be brought up 'in English habit and religion'[1] in Trinity College. In practice, there was little supervision of either the spiritual or material interests of wards, and little profit to the crown, and the commissioners, being both inefficient and unpopular, excited a uniquely unanimous condemnation. Reorganisation began in 1616, with the issue of a new commission, and there followed a period of systematisation during which the appointment of specialised officers and the elaboration of standardised procedures, combined with more purposive management, resulted in a marked expansion of revenue. This was associated, too, with a distinct hardening of attitude, as subscription to the oath of supremacy began to be insisted upon as wards reached their majority: from 1617 the commissioners became involved in a new kind of business, the administration of estates remaining in the king's hands because of 'want of livery'. In 1622 the new arrangements were formalised, with the creation of a regular court of wards and liveries on the English model. This refinement owed more to the ambitions of the surveyor general, Sir William Parsons, than to genuine need: as the court's first master, Parsons gained control over the extensive patronage involved in disposing of wards and arranging leases, and under his direction the court continued to make it impossible for catholic heirs to sue their livery and secure possession of their estates,[2] so that the resources available for the court's exploitation increased continuously.

The revised arrangements for dealing with wards and liveries were characterised by a new severity towards catholics, but the primary inspiration was financial. In England, the king's financial situation had long since reached crisis point, fitful attempts to cut costs and improve revenue had become the order of the day, and there were hopes of doing likewise in Ireland and thereby relieving the English exchequer of its annual subvention of £20,000 towards the costs of governing Ireland. Already, the Irish customs system had been remodelled along unified English lines and farmed out to a London syndicate in 1613 at an annual rent of £6,000. In 1618 fresh arrangements were made: in a neat reconciliation of those conflicting claims of public

[1] Victor Treadwell, 'The Irish court of wards under James I', loc. cit., p. 8.

[2] H. F. Kearney, 'The court of wards and liveries in Ireland, 1622–1641' in *R.I.A. Proc.*, lvii, sect. C, no. 2 (1955), pp 29–68.

and private interest that made reform so difficult in England, the new royal favourite, Buckingham, took over the farm at the existing rent, but on condition of sharing the profits with the crown. Despite revenue improvements both from this source and from the more rigorous exploitation of feudal incidents by the new commissioners of wards, the deficit remained, the Irish government debt accumulated, and the army, which was the principal charge, was also the principal sufferer. Both English experience and Irish evidence suggested that the real problem was not the inadequacy of the revenue itself, but the laxity and dishonesty of the administration. When Lionel Cranfield, who had been the chief agent of reform for some years, became lord treasurer of England in 1621, one of his subsidiary interests was to extend his improvements to Ireland. By this stage, the arrears outstanding to the army alone were greater than the annual revenue, and there were innumerable indications that the state of Ireland and its government required systematic attention: the lord deputy and council were bitterly at odds with one another; a recent survey had revealed the widespread failure of the Ulster planters to observe the conditions of their grants, and their request for modification of those conditions had yet to be answered; reports of the progress of the newer plantations were not encouraging; the missionary failure of the established church was manifest; trade was alleged to be decaying; and unending complaints of petty oppression caused by official irregularities and improper judicial proceedings suggested that administrative standards needed scrutiny.

In the event, a full-scale investigation into the ecclesiastical and civil condition of Ireland was decided upon and a commission jointly composed of English and Irish officials was appointed to conduct it. The opportunity was taken to recall Sir Oliver St John, and the commissioners, who were formally appointed in March 1622, conducted the bulk of their inquiries in the interval between the lord deputy's departure in May and the arrival of his successor, Lord Falkland, an English client of Buckingham's, in September. They approached their task efficiently and systematically, and produced results with what proved to be deceptive rapidity.[1] Their investigation of complaints relating to the administration of justice generated recommendations which, in the form of forty-seven 'directions for ordering and settling the courts', were agreed in June. In July the lords justices proclaimed their intention of introducing these reforms without delay.[2] Otherwise, the work of the commissioners proved largely barren. They uncovered a great deal of inefficiency and peculation, and demonstrated that government procedures were so casual and disorganised that the exchequer had no effective control over either income or outgoings. Although it was difficult to tell where

[1] Commission and report in B.M., Add. MS 4756.

[2] Geoffrey Hand and Victor Treadwell, 'His majesty's direction for ordering and settling the courts within his kingdom of Ireland, 1622' in *Anal. Hib.*, no. 26 (1970), pp 179–212.

incompetence ended and dishonesty began, Cranfield attempted to call officials to account for the sums they had handled, while at the same time arranging for a partial bankruptcy by writing off one-third of the army arrears and one-half of the arrears on pensions. A new, ruthlessly pared establishment, with official salaries and allowances sharply reduced, was put into effect at the beginning of the financial year in 1623, and Cranfield hoped that, with related reforms of exchequer procedure, equilibrium would result. However, in 1624, before his policies could begin to produce results, Cranfield was successfully impeached in the English parliament. Ironically, the charge related to taking bribes, but the real reasons were political. Charles and Buckingham, humiliatingly rebuffed in Spain, now called for war, and thus disposed of Cranfield's opposition. Soon, a marriage was being sought for Charles with the king of France's sister.

The information collected by the commissioners in 1622 made it plain that the broad constructive hopes with which James's reign had begun had ended in comprehensive failure, characterised in every sphere by the same sacrifice of public to private interest. But, though much of the fault lay where the commissioners placed it, with the New English, none the less their perversion of public policy was a symptom of the state's inadequacy. The situation called for more than administrative reform and the curtailment of local influences through the appointment of an English lord deputy: it required a thorough reconsideration of governmental objectives and the means of achieving them. But there was no return to fundamentals: it was not the commissioners' findings that generated change, but the international situation. When policy revision began, it did so in response to immediate political pressures, and a decade of improvisation was to pass before Ireland experienced the novelty of a government that pursued coordinated policies related to clearly defined objectives.

CHAPTER VIII

Selling royal favours, 1624–32

AIDAN CLARKE

AT the end of January 1624 Falkland received permission to publish a proclamation against priests and instructions to enforce the laws against recusants: a month later he was ordered to suspend the operation of those laws: a year later he was forbidden to enforce that proclamation. This series of decisions was symptomatic of a situation in which the formulation of policy had come to depend upon international rather than local considerations. As a result, the Irish administration was virtually precluded from influence, and the effective exertion of political pressure upon government involved dealing directly with the king. The diplomacy of pacification brought incidental benefits to catholics in Ireland, but the inspiration was transient convenience, the source was royal indulgence, and the substance was elusive. The diplomacy of war seemed to offer the Old English the possibility of firmer gains, induced by necessity but founded upon interdependence, stipulated by contract but secured by goodwill. In the event, the interdependence was to prove shortlived and the goodwill unattainable, and royal favours conferred under duress of war did not outlast it. And in the meantime, the activity of the Old English had stimulated the developing political consciousness of the protestant community. When the return of peace removed external constraints, conflict within colonial Ireland was sharper.

As the effects of the abrupt reversal of English foreign policy, from friendship with Spain to war against her, worked themselves out, the initiative passed gradually from the crown to its subjects in Ireland.[1] Preparations for war, begun with the enthusiastic support of the English parliament in 1624, went steadily ahead, scarcely affected by the death of King James in the spring of 1625; a fleet was assembled and an army raised, the young King Charles was married to the sister of the king of France, and plans were made for an attack on Cadiz in the autumn. The strategic implications were familiar. Experience had shown how dangerous it was in these circumstances 'to have the pope keeper of the keys of your back door',[2] and reports that the

[1] Clarke, *Old English*, pp 28–59; *The graces, 1625–41* (Dublin Historical Association; Irish History series, no. 8, 1968); 'The army and politics in Ireland, 1625–30' in *Studia Hib.*, no. 4 (1964), pp 28–53.

[2] The image was a common one. It occurs in this form in a sermon published under the title *Ireland's advocate* (London, 1641).

accession of Charles had been greeted in parts of Ireland with prayers for 'Philippum regem nostrum'[1] served as a sinister reminder that if war were to be waged on Spain, Ireland must be secured not only against attack from without but against rebellion within. Arrangements were quickly made to send 2,250 foot-soldiers to strengthen the peacetime force of 1,350 foot and 400 horse. More were needed, and coastal fortifications required renovation. Money was promised, but when the English parliament disowned government policy and refused to subsidise it, in the early summer of 1625, it became necessary to defend Ireland at its own expense, which not only entailed raising at least £3,000 each month to support the new soldiers but also involved finding the means to finance essential improvements. For some years, the financial and political problems thus generated by an impulsive and unpopular foreign policy changed the terms of Irish politics.

For the Old English, war with Spain provided a model opportunity to consolidate their claim to the privileged status of colonists by verifying their contention that loyalty and catholicism were perfectly compatible. In the summer of 1625, in the context of proposals that the serious deficiencies in the regular military establishment should be made good by raising auxiliary local forces, they offered to play their part in the defence of Ireland, making it clear that in doing so they were deliberately testing the official attitude towards them. When the issue was thus forced in direct negotiations between the English government and Sir John Bath, acting as unofficial spokesman for his fellow Palesmen, Charles had little choice but to declare, as he did in September 1625, his willingness 'to repose himself upon the fidelity and ready affection of his natural subjects',[2] and to substantiate it by authorising the formation of militia units in the Pale and elsewhere. The officials and prominent settlers who administered Ireland were less ready to place security at risk by abandoning the principle that organised force should remain a protestant monopoly. Though they initiated a 'trained-band' system on the English model, their reluctance to 'put arms into their hands of whose hearts we rest not well assured'[3] was strengthened by the growing apprehension of Spanish counter-attack that followed the humiliating failure of the Cadiz expedition. Their sustained opposition proved decisive: by the spring of 1626 the scheme had been abandoned and the problem of defending Ireland had been reopened.

The only remaining possibility was to expand the army. The difficulty was to raise the money to do so without resorting to methods that might drive professedly loyal catholics to acquiesce in Spanish invasion. In fact, the earlier negotiations contained the elements of a solution, for Bath had made his specifically military proposals in the context of a survey of local grievances and had suggested that the community might be willing to pay for

[1] *Cal. S.P. Ire., 1625–32*, p. 15.
[2] *Acts privy council, 1625–6*, p. 15.
[3] P.R.O., S.P. Ire., 63/242, 283.

measures of reform. Already, some minor reforms had been introduced and some money had been forthcoming. During the summer of 1626, the English government explored the possibility of funding the army in this way in further discussions with Bath, the earl of Westmeath, and others, and in September firm proposals were brought forward. A list of twenty-six 'matters of grace and bounty to be rendered to Ireland' was sent to the lord deputy, together with instructions to convene a meeting of the nobility to discuss arrangements for the maintenance of an expanded army of 5,000 foot and 500 horse. The list of concessions was largely composed of useful reforms of minor importance, affecting all sections of the community, but a few were of major significance, and these were relevant only to catholics. The most striking in its implications was an offer to suspend the collection of recusancy fines; the most radical was an undertaking to abolish religious tests for inheritance, appointment to office, and admission to legal practice. Superficially, the proposals met Bath's earlier criticisms of government policy in full and seemed to open the way for a dramatic improvement in the conditions and status of catholics and catholicism in Ireland. But the form in which the concessions were offered inevitably cast doubt upon their content, for they were linked with a request for money which was only needed because the government was unwilling to trust a share in the defence of Ireland to catholics. The lords of the Pale who attended the meeting of nobles that Falkland called in November 1626 were not prepared to discuss the projected bargain until this contradiction had been resolved, and they insisted that the government should first commit itself convincingly to Old English loyalty by reintroducing trained bands. The only progress made at the meeting was an unenthusiastic agreement to the government's proposal that the matter should be referred to a delegate assembly to be dealt with 'after a parliamentary way'. When that assembly convened in Dublin in April 1627, the attitude of the Old English representatives was the same: they were not prepared to trust Charles unless he was prepared to trust them; they were not willing to pay the army to perform a task which they were anxious to undertake themselves.

The Old English were not alone in using the 'great assembly' to express their collective dissatisfaction with government attitudes. The New English did so too. Unconvincing though royal overtures might seem to the one, to the other the apparent implications were deeply disturbing. It was already evident that the degree of influence that the New English could exert in Ireland was becoming severely restricted by governmental practices that tended to concentrate effective power in England. It was also increasingly clear that their perspectives and interests as settlers were in some respects distinctive: while they might like to think of themselves as belonging to an 'English empire',[1] they did not therefore necessarily identify themselves

[1] The term was used by Sir William Parsons in 1625 (*Cal. S.P. Ire., 1625–32*, pp 56–8).

with the English government rather than with its English or Scottish critics, nor did they relinquish the right to judge the needs of their own situation. They could scarcely be expected to react favourably to proposals that would so modify established policies as to reduce their privileges and undermine their religion. Though catholics had not in practice been forced to pay recusancy fines for some years, their legal liability to do so remained as the essential outward symbol of the state's refusal to recognise catholicism, while the exaction of the oath of supremacy was the essential condition of the retention of power by the New English. That Charles was prepared to treat both fine and oath as bargaining counters suggested a willingness to compromise both the status of protestants in Ireland and the very principles of protestantism itself. And these misgivings were reinforced by the lack of attention to protestant interests in Charles's offer, which confined its major concessions to catholics but proposed to take payment from catholic and protestant alike.

Protestant opposition to government policy was fittingly initiated by the bishops of the established church. When the assembly of nobles dispersed in November 1626, the bishops met privately and prepared a statement castigating the royal proposal 'to set religion to sale'. While the 'great assembly' was in session in April 1627 their statement was made public for the first time by the bishop of Derry, who read it in the course of a sermon preached in Christ Church cathedral to a congregation who received it with thunderous approval. On the following Sunday, the lord primate of Ireland, James Ussher, and the archbishop of Cashel preached supporting sermons. Both were members of the Irish privy council. That they spoke, however unofficially, on its behalf became quickly evident. When the 'great assembly' came to a profitless conclusion at the beginning of May, the Irish government took the opportunity to recommend formally that the recusancy fine should be exacted to meet military costs. They did so in the full knowledge that the English government was preparing to wage war with France as well as Spain, and that the arguments in favour of propitiating loyal catholics were twice as strong as they had been before. In the face of so evident a divergence in the priorities of the Irish and English governments Charles had little choice but to agree to an Old English request, conveyed through the earl of Westmeath, that the negotiations should be transferred to England. In June 1627 he directed that a representative delegation should be sent to him from Ireland.

The selection of its members took place at provincial conventions, dominated outside Ulster by the Old English, and strung out in a leisurely series from mid-July to early November. By that time, an expedition which had left England in June to bring aid to disaffected French huguenots in La Rochelle had failed and returned. In Ireland, counter-attack was again imminently expected and was likely, in Falkland's opinion, to be successful, for the level at which it had proved possible to maintain the troops, through cajolement and intimidation, by borrowings, billetings, and exactions, had left the army at the mercy of an invader and at 'the courtesy of the disaffected subject'.[1] In England, where similarly irregular methods had been used to meet military expenses, extra-parliamentary taxation was under formidable political attack and was to prove one of the overriding concerns of the parliament that met in March 1628. In significant respects, therefore, the military and political context within which the agents negotiated was favourable to their enterprise.

They arrived in England in January 1628. Eight were Old English catholics and three were protestant settlers:[2] between them, they represented a very fair cross-section of colonial society in Ireland, qualified to speak for New and Old English, nobility and gentry, landowners and townsmen, soldiers and civilians, planters and officials. Their demands were correspondingly diverse, and the agreement that they finally reached with a special committee of the English privy council in May was a profuse amalgam of reform, which stretched over fifty-one separate articles and ranged from insignificant administrative improvements to fundamental policy changes. There were regulations to control the public nuisances committed by the army and to reduce the element of official discretion in ordinary legal proceedings; the working rules of the court of wards were amended and the jurisdiction of ecclesiastical courts over catholics was curtailed; a general scaling-down of official fees was initiated, licensing controls on primary exports were relaxed, and exploitative industrial and commercial monopolies were revoked. The offer to allow heirs and lawyers to qualify by taking an oath of allegiance instead of the oath of supremacy was renewed, and although no explicit statement of the right of loyal catholics to bear arms in defence of the kingdom was included, the point was separately conceded when Charles agreed to entrust some of the new companies in the expanded army to Old English commanders. By 1628, however, the Old English negotiators, though they were as concerned as ever to persuade the government to trust them, were still more concerned to protect their property against the unmistakable threat revealed by the government's inability to do so. They demanded an unequivocal guarantee of security for their lands, taking as their model an English statute of 1624 in which the crown had renounced all claims to land titles of more than sixty years' standing. When that demand was favourably reported upon by the privy council committee, and an undertaking given to permit the passage of a similar statute of limitation in the next Irish parliament, together with more specific legislation dealing with the tangled state of land titles in Connacht, the possibility of

[1] *Cal. S.P. Ire., 1625–32*, p. 295.

[2] The Old English agents were Lord Killeen, Sir Thomas Luttrell, Sir William Talbot (Leinster), Sir Lucas Dillon, Sir Henry Lynch (Connacht), Sir Edward Fitzharris, Sir John Meade and Lord Power (Munster). The protestant agents were Richard Osborne (Munster), Arthur Forbes, and Andrew Stewart (Ulster).

future expropriation seemed to have been excluded. Charles had pledged himself to uphold the existing rights of ownership and signalled a halt to the process of piecemeal confiscation and plantation.

'His majesty's instructions and graces'[1] were the apex of Old English political achievement, but they were significantly incomplete: the offer to suspend the recusancy fines had not been renewed, and proposals to secure the right of catholics to hold public office had been rebuffed. In short, though the claim of the Old English to a place in the system of colonial privilege was successful, the place assigned to them was an inferior one. The greater privileges of the protestant settlers remained intact and, over all, the advantages that the New English derived from the 'graces', though relatively unobtrusive, were of decisive importance. Most obviously, they won a significant victory for vested interest by securing concessions that in effect terminated the careful policy of segregated settlement in Ulster: undertakers' titles were to be confirmed without reference to their observance of the plantation conditions. More fundamentally, the New English protected their position against the dangers of too thorough a policy of conciliation and preserved the centrality of protestantism as a determinant of status. Moreover, in preventing the English government from formulating its Irish policies without reference to the interests and opinions of protestants in Ireland, they achieved an emergent independence of identity that was increasingly to complicate Anglo-Irish relations.

In return for the 'graces' the agents agreed that three successive annual subsidies of £40,000 (English), payable quarterly, should be raised to meet the calculated deficiency in the cost of supporting the army. The status of this agreement was less clear than its terms. The government regarded it as binding upon the Irish parliament, which was scheduled to meet on 3 November 1628 to enact consequential legislation, while the agents intended it to be subject to the approval of that parliament. The practical arrangements, however, favoured the government's interpretation: in exchange for the withdrawal of a proposal that revenue losses resulting from the 'graces' should be offset by proportionate increases in the level of the subsidies, the agents agreed that the collection of the first subsidy might begin immediately. To do so seemed doubly advantageous: it both fixed the number and value of the subsidies and made it possible to set against them the money that would in any case have to be contributed to the support of the soldiers before parliament met. In effect, however, the agents had unwittingly surrendered the initiative by giving the government all that it could hope to gain from a parliament, and had strengthened its hand against them at a time when other circumstances were weakening it.

In Ireland, the inevitably depressing effect of the negotiations upon the standing of the local administration was complicated by internal divisions,

[1] The 'graces' are printed in full in Clarke, *Old English*, pp 238–54.

and the episode seriously affected Falkland's position within his government as well as his relations with outside interests. Throughout the 1620s, the New English had shown a pronounced tendency towards faction: groups had formed in support of the lord deputy, led by Richard Boyle, earl of Cork, Lord Ranelagh, and Sir William Parsons among others, and in opposition to him, led by Lord Chancellor Loftus, Vice-Treasurer Annesley, and Lord Wilmot, who was not only joint president of Connacht but also a member of the English privy council. Both factions energetically cultivated the English influence on which power in Ireland depended, and in 1628 there were clear indications that the opposition group, which was alleged to have encouraged Old English agitation, now enjoyed greater royal favour. The assassination of Falkland's English patron, the duke of Buckingham, in August, undermined his position still further. It also threw the English government into disarray at a time when military failure abroad and parliamentary hostility at home made an urgent reconsideration of foreign policy essential. The result was that in both countries during the later part of the year government was characterised by an absence of confidence and clear purpose.

In Ireland, the fulfilment of the king's promises went ahead more slowly than was popular. The government, though resentful, was inhibited from forceful criticism of the proposals by the direct responsibility of Charles, but its single specific objection, that the army regulations interfered with the suppression of disturbances in the north, was unexpectedly rewarded with the encouraging general assurance that the 'graces' would only be observed 'provided that they bring in no dangerous consequence, whereof your lordship and the council must be judge'.[1] More publicly, the king's sincerity was thoroughly compromised by an ill-considered decision to include in the Irish military establishment a regiment which had been raised locally for service in France in 1627 and which had since become expensively redundant. The plan gave general offence: it raised the army prematurely to the agreed 5,000 foot, it abrogated the undertaking to grant companies to Old English commanders, and it introduced a substantial number of Irish catholic troops in contravention of both army regulations and common sense. Neither popular protests nor official objections were heeded, and early suspicions that a significant derogation from the 'graces' was intended had hardened into certainty by the time that parliamentary elections got under way in October 1628.

The urgent need to furnish evidence of governmental sincerity had led Falkland to issue writs of summons promptly, on the authority contained in the 'graces' themselves.[2] In August, however, the English privy council realised, somewhat hazily, that Poynings' law required 'such intimations

[1] P.R.O., S.P. Ire., 63/247, p. 87.

[2] Aidan Clarke, 'The history of Poynings' law, 1615–41' in *I.H.S.*, xviii, no. 70 (Sept. 1972), pp 207–10.

from hence, and such consultations there, and returns hither and back again before the summons are to issue out for the parliament' that it was no longer possible to hold it on schedule.[1] Despite Falkland's anxiety to honour the existing commitment, the intractable opinion of the English privy council's legal advisers forced him to announce, a fortnight before parliament was to meet, that it could not now do so until the correct procedure had been followed. Its place was taken by a protest meeting, which roundly condemned the enlargement of the army, accused the government of failing to implement one-third of the 'graces', and served clear notice that parliament would feel free to alter the financial terms of the bargain if the royal promises were not fully kept. The protest was not without effect: within a month the court of wards had dropped its insistence upon the oath of supremacy, and the backlog of catholic heirs who had been unable to take formal possession of their estates was quickly processed. But the episode worked largely to the government's advantage by revealing the ineffectuality of the opposition, for despite resentment and protest the subsidy continued to be paid. In fact, the negotiations in England had been conducted on the working assumptions that the Old English could choose whether they wished to support the army or not and that the security of the state demanded that their loyalty be assured. Falkland's blunder inadvertently disclosed that no such choice was open to them, for the deprived and mutinous soldiers held them to ransom, while England's withdrawal from continental involvement significantly reduced their political importance. In these conditions the government's inclination to temporise evolved into an unexpectedly successful policy, and did so all the more easily because the 'graces', however imperfectly carried out, did confer benefits which the Old English were reluctant to jeopardise. No preparations were made to summon parliament, the Old English could find no effective counter to procrastination, and the enactment of the more important of the 'graces' was indefinitely postponed.

As the restraints that the diplomacy of war had forced upon the government in Ireland were gradually lifted, an early opportunity was taken to meet widespread criticism in both Ireland and England by discontinuing the tacit policy of religious toleration.[2] For some time, Falkland had fitfully argued that security would be better served by countenancing only the loyal, while banishing the seditious, clergy, a division he regarded as roughly corresponding to that between the secular clergy and the regulars. It was along these lines that he was authorised to proceed in March 1629. The disquiet voiced by other protestants, however, tended to be more specifically religious: the evident vitality of catholicism and the growing absence of restraint in its practice gave rise to a degree of apprehension that made it

[1] *Acts privy council, 1628–9*, p. 107.

[2] R. Dudley Edwards, 'Church and state in the Ireland of Míchél Ó Cléirigh, 1626–41' in S. O'Brien (ed.), *Measgra i gCuimhne Mhíchíl Uí Chléirigh* (Dublin, 1944), pp 1–20.

unlikely that any change in government policy would be confined for long within the political limits indicated by the lord deputy. In the event, Falkland's initiative coincided confusingly with his recall, and the clarity of the government's anti-catholic purpose was briefly blurred.

The proclamation that Falkland issued on 1 April 1629 forbade the exercise of ecclesiastical jurisdiction derived from Rome and ordered the dissolution of religious houses on pain of confiscation. The response was circumspect, not obedient. But Falkland was in no position to admit failure: within a fortnight of the publication of the proclamation, he learned that he was to be relieved of his office in apparent disgrace as a result of allegations concerning his part in the hounding of the O'Byrnes, against whom fraudulent charges had been brought in an unusually crude attempt to dispossess them of their Wicklow lands. In fact, however, it was less the evidence of misconduct, though it was fairly clear, that achieved this final victory for the lord deputy's New English opponents in Ireland, than the combination of his querulous inability to manage Ireland and his loss of influence in England. These left him with a poor case to be retained in office and without an advocate to make the best of it. The situation was complicated by the government's reluctance to state plainly the reason for its decision, and by Falkland's angry determination to vindicate his reputation, which together constituted good grounds for leaving the deputyship in abeyance until his future had been firmly settled. The conclusion of a treaty with France in April, followed by the opening of peace negotiations with Spain in May, reduced the importance of Ireland sufficiently to make it reasonable to do so. It was in these circumstances that the English government decided to have recourse to the experiment of inviting the New English factions to join forces under the leadership of Cork and Loftus as lords justices.

The two were formally reconciled before they took up their appointment in October 1629, but the factions remained distinct. Cork and his supporters assisted Falkland in an unsuccessful attempt to redeem himself by disgracing Annesley, and both Cork and Wilmot had hopes of succeeding to the lord deputyship, but agreement on policy none the less made for cohesion. With Cork enjoying the support of a majority of the privy council, and Loftus maintaining an unfriendly cooperation, the army was halved and the subsidy correspondingly reduced, which extended its period of payment to the autumn of 1632; the budget was balanced (at the price of ignoring outstanding debts); and the government addressed itself to putting an emphatic stop to policies of appeasement in the two primary areas of protestant settler interest—religion and land.

The first priority was the enforcement of Falkland's proclamation, and notice of a new rigour was served on St Stephen's Day 1629 when the archbishop, mayor, and sheriffs of Dublin, attended by pursuivants and other officers, ceremonially interrupted mass in a chapel in Cook Street with the intention of arresting the celebrant. That they were prevented from doing so by the congregation, and chased through the city by a stone-throwing mob, merely strengthened the government's resolve. In the weeks that followed, all known religious houses in Dublin were confiscated, and the initiative was sustained throughout the country until, a year later, the lords justices were confident that the catholic religion was nowhere publicly observed and the religious orders were finding it difficult to lease property. Neither clergy nor laity suffered more than inconvenience from these measures. Their significance lay in the warning they conveyed of greater severity in the future, and the nature of the danger to be feared from a government that had resolutely evaded its obligation to confirm land titles was frighteningly obvious.

The possibility of resuming the policy of plantation was first explored in relation to the baronies of Upper and Lower Ormond in County Tipperary towards the end of 1630. The novelty of what was involved was succinctly expressed in the indignant protest of the earl of Ormond, who held close to a quarter of the land concerned, that he was the first Englishman to be treated as if he were Irish.[1] In fact, titles in the area proved to be sound, but so also did the fear that the project exemplified a renewed challenge to catholic property. In June 1631 Sir Charles Coote, vice-president of Connacht, one of Cork's closest political associates, and the man whom catholics blamed for the failure to enrol the Connacht surrenders, presented the English government with a detailed proposal for plantation in Mayo, Roscommon, and Sligo. The scheme was so carefully designed to confine the profits to its local promoters, with 'no latitude left to court wisdom or favour',[2] that it failed to find approval, but the general principle of planting parts of Connacht was accepted and remained under consideration despite the royal promise that land titles in the area would be confirmed, and demands for the meeting of parliament were rebuffed. When, in the early summer of 1632, in conjunction with the appointment of a new lord deputy, local juries were empanelled and directed to compile lists of catholics to enable recusancy fines to be levied upon them as soon as the last of the subsidies expired in the autumn, the pattern of a new oppression seemed complete. The hope that the government could be moved to a conciliatory acceptance of the pluralist character of the colony in Ireland, so recently triumphant, seemed to have fallen victim to the single-minded sectionalism of the protestant settlers.

[1] *Cal. S.P. Ire., 1625–32*, p. 597.
[2] P.R.O., S.P. Ire., 63/252, 156.

CHAPTER IX

The government of Wentworth, 1632–40

AIDAN CLARKE

PERSISTENT rumours that Thomas, Viscount Wentworth, was to become lord deputy of Ireland were officially confirmed in January 1632.[1] The reasons for which he had been chosen, some six months earlier, had much more to do with English politics than with Irish problems, and Ireland was always to remain secondary to his English interests and ambitions. At the time of his appointment he was one of a group who were loosely associated together in support of the king's aim to govern England without parliament. The success of that policy depended upon finding a solution to the problem of inadequate financial resources and, less obviously, upon the development of effective techniques of prerogative government. In Ireland, Wentworth hoped to find 'the opportunity and means to supply the king's wants'[2] and intended to rule in the manner in which he hoped eventually to govern England, absolutely, efficiently, and without regard to any interest but that of the crown; in his own word, 'thoroughly'. The practical application of the principles of government in which he believed came easily to him, for they were matched by his personal qualities. A self-contained man of marked intelligence and overbearingly forceful character, remarkable executive abilities, and natural insensitivity, he was an authoritarian by inclination as well as by conviction. As an administrator, he possessed vigour and mastery of detail, made decisions clearly and unhesitatingly, thought constructively and connectedly, and was committed to success by pride and ambition. As a politician, his tactical judgement was excellent, but his manipulative skill imperfectly concealed an inability to compromise and a total incapacity either to understand or to acknowledge the legitimacy of an opposing point of view. Both as an administrator and as a politician he was dangerously prone to simplify, because he could not objectify, the analysis of problems in the interests of preconceived solutions.

[1] Clarke, *Old English*, p. 65. On Wentworth's viceroyalty in general see H. F. Kearney, *Strafford in Ireland, 1633–41* (Manchester, 1959).

[2] Quoted in C. V. Wedgwood, *Thomas Wentworth, first earl of Strafford, 1593–1641: a revaluation* (London, 1964), p. 120.

His previous experience of public office had been limited, but relevant. He had been among the parliamentary opponents of the English government until its foreign policy changed in 1628, and had then joined its regional administration as lord president of the north. A year later, he had become a member of the privy council, and later still a member of its Irish committee. It was perhaps as one of the committee delegated to inquire into the charges against Annesley, now Lord Mountnorris, that he gained the valuable working knowledge of the Irish situation which he was to put to immediate use. It was not until March 1632 that Mountnorris was formally exonerated; by then, he was already assisting Wentworth in a preliminary examination of the problems of his new office. The most pressing problem was financial, but in the nature of the situation its solution was inseparable from political choices. The subsidies which had been granted in association with the 'graces', and which now exactly covered the difference between the government's income of £40,000 and its expenditure of £60,000, would have been collected in full by the early autumn of 1632. There was, therefore, an immediate need to find an additional £20,000 for the coming year; but there was also the more general necessity to place the revenue upon a less uncertain footing. The Irish government's solution to both problems was the same: they advised the regular exaction of recusancy fines, both as a policy desirable in itself and as a sufficiently profitable measure to meet long-term requirements as well as immediate needs. Wentworth, whose experience of collecting recusancy fines in the north of England had not been encouraging, seems quickly to have concluded that the long-term problem might best be solved, as in England, by the more efficient management of the customs system. In the spring, arrangements were made to farm the customs on greatly improved terms, with the return of peace and increases in export rates as the inducements, to a group which brought existing interests into partnership with the incoming lord deputy, Sir George Radcliffe, who had been his secretary as president of the north, and Mountnorris. For immediate purposes, Wentworth decided that the voluntary continuation of subsidy payments would be least troublesome. His decision so disappointed the New English that when he devised a simple scheme to deflect the inevitable catholic opposition, the Irish government set out to sabotage it.

On 14 April, at Wentworth's instigation, Charles wrote to the lords justices in severely critical terms, expressing surprised dissatisfaction at their professed inability to procure a renewal of the subsidy, instructing them to make preliminary arrangements to levy recusancy fines if subsidy payments 'be not freely and thankfully continued', and directing them to publish his letter. The Irish government defiantly disregarded the letter's obvious objective and suppressed it. On its authority, however, they initiated proceedings under the recusancy statute, making no effort to canvass for a new subsidy, and allowing it to be understood that they were acting on behalf of the new lord deputy. Before long, a correspondent was assuring him that 'the popish recusants are more afraid of your coming than of any of your predecessors'.[1] By their conduct, the Irish government forced Wentworth to solicit catholic aid much more directly than he had wished and challenged him to establish his authority by overcoming their intransigence. In consequence, throughout the late summer and autumn Wentworth entered into a close association with the Old English, chiefly through the agency of Mountnorris, by means of which he both gained his financial ends and publicly worsted 'the earl of Cork's party'.[2] The political price was somewhat higher than he had expected: he had not only to disavow any intention of collecting the recusancy fine, but to promise emphatically 'that they yielding to the present continuing of the contribution, I will be a means that the benefit offered them by his majesty's graces shall be honourably and justly complied with'.[3] In return, he secured the dispatch of the earl of Westmeath to England in November with the offer of a further subsidy and the cooperation of the nobility and gentry of the Pale in forcing the privy council to discredit itself by publishing the king's letter of 14 April. At a council meeting on 17 November, notwithstanding the directions in the letter itself and the lord deputy's specific order to obey them, the majority refused Westmeath's request for a copy of the letter, which was supported by Mountnorris and Lord Justice Loftus, and made on behalf of a general meeting which had just resolved upon the continuation of the subsidy. Two days later, when the request was renewed by the earl of Fingall, one of the agents of 1628, the majority had perceived the wisdom of supporting 'a rising deputy' rather than 'a setting justice',[4] and the contents of the king's letter were finally admitted. The struggle dragged briefly on: it required a royal letter to prevent Cork from continuing the recusancy proceedings, which had advanced to the point of levying fines in Wicklow, and another to force him to issue warrants for the collection of the new subsidy. But by the beginning of 1633 it was plain that the lord deputy's unlikely alliance with Mountnorris and the Old English had overwhelmed the dominant faction in the planter administration. The point was confirmed when local protestant resistance to paying the subsidy was promptly dealt with by the cashiering of those of the organisers who held commissions in the army and the imprisonment of others.

They were still in Dublin castle when Wentworth arrived in Ireland in July 1633 to confront the hostility of most of the members of his privy council. His initial concern was yet again with meeting the deficit which would arise when the subsidy expired: his proposal, which was backed by the Mountnorris–Loftus group, was that the protestant community should this

[1] Aungier to Wentworth, 28 June 1632 (Strafford MSS, i).

[2] Mountnorris to Wentworth, 21 Nov. 1632 (ibid).

[3] Wentworth to Mountnorris, 16 Oct. 1632 (ibid.).

[4] The phrasing is Wentworth's: Wentworth to Hopwood, 19 Oct. 1632 (ibid.).

time take the initiative in renewing payments for a further year. It was coolly received, and the council accepted it only after he had suggested that an offer to continue the subsidy should be linked 'with the desire of a parliament'.[1] A canvass for catholic concurrence in the offer quickly demonstrated the goodwill that the lord deputy enjoyed, and the government's solvency was ensured until the end of 1634. But Wentworth needed to do more than balance the budget: he could not hope to gain political independence of local interests unless he could make himself financially independent of them. The new customs farm was a useful move in this direction, but because Wentworth's ulterior objective was to create a surplus for the king's use in England his aim was to maximise revenue, and his approach was correspondingly comprehensive. A first-hand examination confirmed him in his belief that adequate financial resources did exist in Ireland, but it also convinced him that the assistance of a parliament was essential to their realisation, both because the most promising methods of improving revenue yield required statutory provision and because parliamentary supply was the only feasible way of securing the period of freedom from financial pressure which was needed to undertake a thorough reorganisation of the system and to await its benefits. Thus, although he allowed his willingness to consider holding a parliament to appear concessionary in his early dealings with the council, his true motives were very different, and the problem to which he addressed himself in the following months was to devise a strategy by which parliament could be denied concessions but persuaded to subsidise the government and to enact its legislative programme.

Opposition from both Old and New English was certain. The events of 1632 had already prompted Wentworth to form a low opinion of the New English: by the end of that year he was already comparing them to the frogs of the fable and had cast himself in the role of the stork.[2] His early experience in Ireland did nothing to alter his view. After two meetings, he contemptuously summed up his councillors as 'a company of men the most intent upon their own ends that ever I met with'.[3] Such men were the natural victims of a policy of 'thorough', devoted to eradicating the influence of self-interest. The probability of conflict with the New English was sufficiently indicated by the enthusiasm that the prospect of a parliament had excited in councillors who had recently been instrumental in preventing it from meeting; it was assured by Wentworth's determination to enforce plantation regulations rigidly in defiance of the 'graces'. Conflict with the Old English was assured by his resolution to take advantage of the widespread weakness of land titles, by planting in some areas and raising crown rents in others, which made it impossible for him to concede their inevitable

[1] Strafford, *Letters*, ii, 65–70.
[2] Wentworth to Portland, 6 Dec. 1632 (Strafford MSS, i).
[3] Strafford, *Letters*, i, 96.

demands for a statute of limitations and the ratification of the Connacht surrenders. It was reasonable to assume, however, that the Old and New English groups would oppose each other as well as the government, and that, if neither were dominant, it would be possible to 'bow and govern the native by the planter and the planter by the native'.[1] Accordingly, Wentworth planned to exploit their differences by using his official influence to promote the return of a third party of government supporters to hold the balance in the house of commons. It was equally reasonable to assume that the confidence with which the Old English expected the 'graces' would incline them to support the government at first. Accordingly, Wentworth decided that parliament should meet in two sessions: in the first the king's financial business would be settled, and in the second the grievances of his subjects could be considered. The possibility of parliament taking independent action on the 'graces' seemed precluded by the terms of Poynings' law, which Wentworth controversially interpreted as placing full control over parliamentary business in the hands of the Irish government.[2] The house of lords presented no problems. In the years since 1615 the Irish peerage had been enlarged from twenty-five to ninety-nine members;[3] this process had begun as a calculated policy to overcome the predominance of catholics, but under Buckingham's influence it had been so indiscriminately employed as a form of patronage that, by 1634, catholic peers were outnumbered not only by protestants but by absentees, whose only connection with Ireland was their title, and whose proxies were at the disposal of the government.

By January 1634 Wentworth was sufficiently confident of success to request the king's permission to hold a parliament. He received it in April, and the formalities of Poynings' law were cursorily concluded in time to allow writs of summons to be issued on 31 May, calling parliament to meet on 14 July. Eight new boroughs had been created since the last parliament, all of them in the protestant interest, but the Old English redressed the balance in part by returning members for four boroughs that had not received writs and that had not formerly been represented, and in essentials the political geography of Ireland remained as King James had planned it. Representation was biased in favour of areas of recent settlement, and these, together with the city and university of Dublin and a few garrison towns, returned 142 protestant members. The correlation between this distribution of seats and the political influence of local settlers, however, was not high; many of those returned were non-resident, more than one-third were office-holders (though not therefore necessarily supporters of the lord deputy), and the returns from Ulster significantly under-represented the Scots. In the catholic group, it was of course the native Irish who were under-represented: eighteen of the members bore native Irish names, but only eight of them clearly represented

[1] Ibid., i, 199. [2] Aidan Clarke, 'The history of Poynings' law', loc. cit., pp 210–14.
[3] C. R. Mayes, 'The early Stuarts and the Irish peerage' in *E.H.R.*, lxiii (1958), pp 227–51.

areas of native Irish influence, in Longford, Monaghan, Sligo, and Wicklow. The political associations of the others were with the ninety-four Old English members.

The composition of the commons was tested at once. As soon as the lengthy opening ceremonies had ended the house divided on a catholic move to unseat non-residents. The count revealed that the lord deputy's supporters held the controlling votes upon which his plans depended. For the remainder of the session, which Charles's commission had confined to twenty-one days to rule out bargaining, Wentworth's parliamentary influence was placed at the disposal of the leaders of the Old English group—the Connacht lawyers Patrick Darcy and Richard Martin, the former agents Sir Edward Fitzharris, Sir Henry Lynch, and Sir Thomas Luttrell, together with Sir Nicholas White, Nicholas Plunkett, Sir William Sarsfield, and Maurice Fitzgerald. With the full cooperation of the government, they prepared, and the commons adopted, a detailed commentary upon the 'graces' in which, though sight was not lost of the special importance of the statute of limitations and the Connacht surrenders, the lessons drawn from recent royal inconstancy were evident in an insistence upon the conversion of virtually all of them into statute law. The house of lords went so far as to order its legal officers to prepare a number of bills based upon the 'graces', including an act of limitation, for transmission to England 'according to the statute', and was indulged in this by Wentworth, whose control of the house was never in question. In return for this complaisance, Wentworth was assured of catholic support for the two pieces of government business with which he wished parliament to deal.

Certain from the outset of catholic agreement, and suspicious of the uncooperative attitude of some councillors, notably Ranelagh and Parsons, Wentworth resolved to act quickly on the government's financial plans before the protestants had time 'to frame parties, and so grow into full understanding among themselves'.[1] The council had already reluctantly agreed that six subsidies, payable over four years, should be requested. When this was conveyed to the house of commons on 18 July, both catholics and protestants acquiesced without demur, 'one watching the other lest their fellow should rob them, and apply the whole grace of his majesty's thanks to themselves from the other'.[2] One week had elapsed: it remained only to 'entertain' parliament by allowing its proceedings on the 'graces' while the subsidy bills formally passed through both houses, and to transact the second urgent item in the government's programme. This was a bill to validate letters patent issued by the commission for defective titles, within which was concealed the lord deputy's counter to the demand for a statute of limitation. For some years the commission had been haphazardly administered by the

[1] Strafford, *Letters*, i, 277. [2] Ibid., i, 274.

English privy council and had provided both a costly service for landholders who wished to have uncertain titles confirmed and, more rarely, a means by which the crown might take advantage of weak titles to impose more exacting conditions of tenure. Its activities, conducted in London, had become intermittent and largely uncontentious, and Wentworth was able to present his bill as one that attended to the interests of the subject rather than to those of the crown. In reality, however, he was carefully preparing to capitalise upon the widespread insecurity of tenure by transferring the commission to Dublin and using it to institute a systematic revision of the terms on which land was held from the crown. Unwittingly, his parliamentary allies helped him to do so. The urgency of the measure was tactical; though the bill was exploitative in intention, it did at least make secure tenure available at a price and Wentworth believed that it could be used to prove that a refusal to allow a statute of limitation to pass was not a prelude to plantation.

The session ended on 2 August. Less than three weeks later the partnership between the lord deputy and the Old English which had transformed Irish politics since 1632 was abruptly dissolved.[1] Wentworth had spent the intervening weeks in a detailed examination of the 'graces'. He had found all but seven of them acceptable in substance, but in only four unimportant instances was he prepared to permit the government's discretion to be eliminated by statute as the commons requested. Of the seven articles to which he took exception, two concerned the maintenance of discipline in the army and its use for collecting crown rents, two concerned the charges and competence of the court of wards, and three dealt with land titles, one with the Connacht surrenders, one with the statute of limitations, and one with the confirmation of undertakers' estates in Ulster. There was nothing to be gained by trying to conceal his intentions. A committee of the commons, containing most of the parliamentary leaders of the Old English group, had remained in attendance upon the council's legislative committee to scrutinise the preparation of bills for transmission to England. Its members would be quick to note the absence of activity relating to the 'graces' and it seemed advisable to counteract suspicious speculation and rumour by stating the government's case plainly. As a preliminary, the commons' committee was brought before the council on 19 August and informed that the government could not 'give way to the transmitting of this law of threescore years, or any other of the graces prejudicial to the crown'.[2] Immediately afterwards, a public statement was issued, and intensively publicised through the judges of assize and justices of the peace, in which the government explained that

[1] Aidan Clarke, '28 November 1634: a detail of Strafford's administration' in *R.S.A.I. Jn.*, xciii (1963), pp 162–7. Aidan Clarke and Dermot Fenlon, 'Two notes on the parliament of 1634', ibid., xcvii (1967), pp 85–90.

[2] Strafford, *Letters*, i, 279.

the act confirming estates passed on the commission for defective titles gave greater security than a statute of limitation could confer, and cited a five-month-old order curtailing ecclesiastical jurisdiction as evidence of its goodwill towards catholics.

The Old English were not appeased by these reassurances, as Wentworth unimaginatively expected them to be. When parliament reassembled in November they appeared in opposition, contesting the most ordinary and uncontentious legislation with what the uncomprehending lord deputy could see only as 'strange and insolent forwardness',[1] while they awaited his detailed reply to their requests on the 'graces'. Wentworth, while congratulating himself upon his discovery of their 'waywardness',[2] was compelled to think in terms of finding a new source of political support, for there was still a large programme of government legislation to be introduced. In preparing his answer on the 'graces', therefore, he recognised the tactical necessity to modify his original decisions and to adopt a more conciliatory attitude. In the event, he decided to meet the request for legislation in ten cases, rather than in four, and to withhold the benefit of only two articles, those dealing with the statute of limitations and the Connacht surrenders, instead of seven. Most significantly, he not merely decided to relinquish the king's claims against the Ulster planters, but resolved to allow their estates to be confirmed by act of parliament. A new partnership between the lord deputy's supporters and the protestants was already working in the ordinary business of the commons when Wentworth finally replied to the petition on the 'graces' in an address to both houses on 27 November; but protestant attendance was dangerously slack, and the Old English were able to vent their displeasure by rejecting a government bill on the following day. They were supported by at least one protestant, Sir Piers Crosby, a restless adventurer of native Irish stock and catholic sympathies, who had recently been appointed to the privy council and was now summarily removed from it. In fact, the opposition's brief moment of success proved useful to the government. It enabled Wentworth, who had opened parliament with the adjuration 'divide not between protestant and papist',[3] to present the issue in precisely those terms. With characteristic simplisticism he attributed the opposition of the Old English to the influence of the 'friars and Jesuits', called upon protestant members of parliament to attend diligently in order to prevent their religion from being 'insensibly supplanted', assured Charles that he was absolved from any obligation to the catholics and 'free in point of honour and state' to deal with them as he thought fit, and declared his own conviction that 'so long as this kingdom continues popish, they are not a people for the crown of England to be confident of'.[4]

There were critical differences of emphasis between Wentworth's revised

[1] Kearney, *Strafford in Ire.*, p. 60.
[2] Strafford, *Letters*, i, 351.
[3] Ibid., i, 289.
[4] Ibid., i, 350–51.

approach to Irish problems and that of the New English, but they were less apparent than the similarities, and the common ground of anti-catholicism proved an adequate basis for the conversion of the protestant party into a government party. Thereafter, until April 1635, erroneously assuming a coincidence of interests, the protestants obediently and unconditionally helped to defeat the relentless opposition of the Old English. Parliament legislated against bigamy, abduction, sodomy, blasphemy, usury, primitive farming practices, and the neglect of internal communications; it extensively modified legal processes in the interests of equity and efficiency; and it significantly amended the laws relating to land and inheritance in the interests of the crown. At Wentworth's direction, it agreed to set the first four subsidies at £41,000 each, and the last two at £45,000 each, submitted a series of recommendations which enabled outstanding debts to be settled on terms extremely favourable to the crown, and introduced a new system of subsidy collection by which the contribution from each county was fixed in advance, on a basis which placed the greatest burden upon Old English areas. In April 1635, however, protestant attendance again became unreliable, the government again ran into difficulty, and Wentworth took the opportunity to establish his complete dominance. Early in the month, the Old English contrived to defeat a bill relating to the importation of gunpowder and to block the progress of two others. The lord deputy at once converted the gunpowder bill into an act of state and issued it while parliament was still in session, to show that the king 'wants not power to conform them to such a government as in his wisdom he shall best like of'.[1] Shortly afterwards, through an aptly chosen messenger, the protestant Lord Robert Dillon, whose family connections with the Old English were very extensive, he conveyed a warning to the commons that he 'would take revenge on them for showing so little regard of all things recommended unto them by me'.[2] On 18 April, the day of parliament's dissolution, the two bills which the house had previously decided not to proceed with were reintroduced and passed: to one the commons attached an obsequious request that the lord deputy should amend its terms by an act of state. Thus, in capitulation, ended what Wentworth jubilantly described as 'the only ripe parliament that hath been gathered in my time'.[3]

It had conferred money, power, and freedom of action upon the government. It had also helped Wentworth to achieve changes in the character of that government which were essential to the full success of his administration. He had inherited a divided council, and had made good use of its enmities. But his association with a particular group among the New English was no less temporary a political convenience than his alliance with the Old English,

[1] Wentworth to Cottington, 10 Apr. 1635 (Strafford MSS, iii).
[2] Wentworth to Coke, 19 May 1635 (Strafford MSS, ix).
[3] Strafford, *Letters*, i, 420.

and his success in resisting catholic demands and in binding protestants to the government relieved him of any further need to rely upon factional support. He had brought able men with him to Ireland, Sir George Radcliffe, Christopher Wandesford, and Sir Philip Mainwaring in particular, and he found other promising associates there, among them Sir Adam Loftus, Lord Robert Dillon, Sir Gerard Lowther, Sir Richard Bolton, and the young protestant earl of Ormond. Gradually, the political structure of the council changed as the lord deputy's group gained coherence and assumed control. None the less, although the antagonisms of the New English were steadily relegated to unimportance by this new regime, the influence they derived from the offices they occupied remained, and Wentworth could not achieve absolute mastery until he had displaced them. The earl of Cork had been under unremitting attack since Wentworth's arrival; by the time parliament ended, he had already been charged with the misappropriation of church property and had suffered the humiliation of having his wife's tomb, which had been so positioned in St Patrick's cathedral that the congregation could not worship without 'crouching to an earl of Cork and his lady',[1] dismantled stone by stone and packed in boxes. Lord Wilmot, who was alleged to have alienated crown property in Athlone, was the first of the rival faction to find himself in disfavour and joined the earl of Cork on the charge-sheet of the court of castle chamber.

The most inconvenient and embarrassing of the New English survivors in the administration was the lord deputy's earliest ally, Lord Mountnorris, who was, Wentworth alleged in the spring of 1635, dishonest, incompetent, and politically unreliable. More significantly, in his dual role as vice-treasurer and member of the customs farm, Mountnorris was firmly entrenched in the vital financial sector of the administration which Wentworth was determined to control himself, for reasons of both public policy and private interest. The government's cash balances were in the vice-treasurer's keeping: Wentworth, who had frankly looked forward to 'the personal profit to be gained from the place'[2] when he became lord deputy, regarded their short-term use as one of the perquisites of his office and had decided upon Sir Adam Loftus as a suitably cooperative replacement for Mountnorris. Moreover, the new customs farm, in which the vice-treasurer held a one-eighth share, had proved an unexpectedly poor bargain for the government: the former provision for a crown share in the profits had been omitted and the astonishing rise in receipts, from £22,500 in the first year of operation to £38,000 in the year ending in the spring of 1635, benefited only the farmers. To repair this error, Wentworth proposed to liquidate the interests of all concerned, except himself and Radcliffe, and to divert their share to the government. Mountnorris had considerable influence in England, where

[1] Wentworth to Laud, 18 Mar. 1634 (Strafford MSS, vi).

[2] Quoted in Wedgwood, *Wentworth: a revaluation*, p. 120.

Wentworth's position had been weakened by the uncertainty that followed the death of Lord Treasurer Portland in April 1635, but his ability to protect his interests was badly impaired by an apparently trivial incident. At a dinner-party given by Lord Loftus in April, Mountnorris, who was prone to indiscretion on such occasions, made a number of obliquely sinister comments upon the lord deputy's treatment of the Annesley family. Wentworth at once sensed an advantage, and when he sought permission to have the recent administration of the vice-treasureship investigated he also requested authority to bring Mountnorris, in his capacity as an army captain, before a court martial if it seemed desirable to call him to account for his 'table-talk'. Both requests were granted at the end of July: the former was acted upon at once, and a commission of inquiry composed of the lord deputy's supporters was set to work; the latter was held in secret reserve. In the months that followed, Mountnorris counter-attacked, and before long his attempt to wrest control of the customs from Wentworth converged with Old English resistance to official plans for Connacht and New English objections to Wentworth's conduct of government to produce a powerful challenge to the lord deputy's authority.

A planning committee had been set up to prepare for the plantation of Connacht before parliament ended. The report that it presented in May embodied a revolutionary change of policy: in recommending that claim should be made to an estimated 4,000 quarters, of which one-fourth should be confiscated and the rest surcharged, no distinction was made in favour of the Old English county of Galway. The acceptance of this proposal extended the principle of plantation from colonisation to recolonisation and placed at hazard the privileged status upon which the entire Old English community depended for the protection of its property. The decision made it certain that the scheme would meet unprecedented opposition, for those who were now to be treated as if they were Irish, as the late earl of Ormond had expressed it, did not suffer from the political disabilities of the Irish: they were acknowledged members of the political nation, and had access to its means of protest. Among them, moreover, was Richard Burke, earl of Clanricard, lord lieutenant of the town and county of Galway, who lived in England and moved familiarly at court. His influence there was attested not merely by his being the only catholic to hold important office in Ireland but by an English viscountcy (of St Albans) and an official immunity from recusancy proceedings. It was his brother, Lord Clanmorris, and his steward, John Donnellan, who took the lead in organising the Galway landholders in defence of their estates as soon as the government's intentions were revealed by the initiation of proceedings in the court of chancery towards the end of June. On their behalf, a search for records of title was being undertaken in England while Wentworth was progressing ceremonially across Ireland to preside over a series of inquisitions, at Boyle on 9 July, Sligo on 13 July, and

Ballinrobe on 31 July, at which the king's title was found to the counties of Roscommon, Mayo, and Sligo. At none of these sessions was there any pretence at a balanced investigation of the state of titles. The official view, bullyingly presented by the lord deputy to carefully selected juries, was that the crown title was incontestable and the inquisitions unnecessary, their sole purpose being to allow local occupiers to establish a claim upon the king's gratitude by admitting his rights with a good grace; the implication, that if his title were not found all the land would be resumed by other means, was clear.

In Galway, where inquisition proceedings began in Clanricard's Portumna residence on 14 August, these tactics were unsuccessful. Outraged defiance was buttressed by the discovery of additional proofs of title in England and the jury found against the king. But the ingenuous notion that plantation could be prevented by legal process was quickly dispelled. The jurors were at once bound over to appear in the court of castle chamber. The sheriff who had chosen them was heavily fined and imprisoned, investigations were instituted to determine whether a charge of conspiracy was warranted, and resumption proceedings were begun in the court of exchequer. The Galway landholders, however, remained unitedly unrepentant. Ignoring a proclamation which called for individual voluntary acknowledgements of the king's title, they delegated Patrick Darcy, Richard Martin, and a prominent native Irish landowner, Sir Roger O'Shaughnessy, to present their case to the king. Charles's complicity in the denial of the 'graces' had been concealed by Wentworth, and the Galway approach was largely an appeal to royal honour, shrewdly supplemented by an offer to double crown rents in the county. Their prospects of success, however, rested less upon the merits of their petition than upon the influence of Clanricard, and Wentworth was convinced that he faced the most dangerous crisis of his administration, for the principle involved was fundamental. 'I take it', he wrote, 'that these agencies are a kind of treaties which have more in them of the republic than consists with the independency and prerogatives of a monarchy.'[1] A successful agency would not only frustrate the plantation of Galway, in which a punitive confiscation of half the land had been decided upon, but would also destroy the new-found authority of the Dublin government. Because it was essential 'to wean them from this unbecoming way of remonstrating and negotiating their grievances',[2] he insisted that the agents should be received as conspirators rather than as petitioners and sent back to Dublin under arrest. His point was taken in England, and if there were any doubt that the lord deputy would prevail it was removed by the death of Clanricard early in November, shortly after the arrival of the agents. They were given a formal hearing, quickly dismissed, and instructed to report to Wentworth in Dublin,

[1] Wentworth to Coke, 9 Nov. 1635 (Strafford MSS, ix).

[2] Wentworth to Coke, 13 Oct. 1635 (ibid.).

but they were slow to leave, 'whether for fear or hope I know not', the secretary of state confessed to Wentworth.[1]

That they were afraid of Wentworth's wrath is clear: Martin went into hiding in London, O'Shaughnessy 'lingered' on the road to Bristol, and Darcy requested permission to live in England 'as never daring to appear again in Ireland'.[2] But they also had some hopes of benefiting from New English moves against Wentworth's management of the customs. Both Wilmot and Mountnorris were promoting alternative schemes, Sir Piers Crosby, who had guided the Galway agents about London, was closely involved, and at least two English councillors, Holland and Hamilton, were lending support. In November Mountnorris wrote to the king offering to substantiate his criticisms of Wentworth's customs dealings and expressing a wish to come to England to present a new and better proposition. The strength of the impending challenge to his control was attested by the speed and ruthlessness of the lord deputy's response: on 12 December Mountnorris was brought before the council of war, adjudged to have traduced his commanding officer, and sentenced to death. His execution was never envisaged, but his treatment was so shocking as to give rise, even in England, to considerable ill feeling against Wentworth, who was already regarded by many at court as morally responsible for the death of Clanricard. Moreover, the sentence was so disproportionate to the alleged offence that it was easy to interpret the episode as evidence that Mountnorris's criticisms of the lord deputy were well founded. Although the king approved the court martial, and replaced Mountnorris as vice-treasurer by Sir Adam Loftus as soon as he received the commission of inquiry's report in January 1636, the campaign against Wentworth continued. Wilmot's proposals were reactivated and Patrick Darcy, who was granted permission to stay in England at the request of the earl of Holland, submitted successive proposals, at first suggesting that customs farming should be discontinued in favour of direct administration, and then offering to find new contractors who would offer better terms. It was no doubt true, as Wentworth caustically observed, that Darcy's 'knowledge of customs causes hath been gathered since his going over',[3] but he had not lost sight of his original purpose and seized the opportunity to point out that Irish revenues could be usefully and easily improved by confirming estates in Connacht at increased rents. He had no success, and political developments in England reduced the importance of his supporters. In March 1636 a long-drawn-out struggle for influence ended, to Wentworth's considerable advantage, with the appointment of Laud's nominee, Bishop Juxon, as lord treasurer of England.

In Ireland, however, the lord deputy was seriously embarrassed: the delay in the return of the Galway agents had obscured the failure of their

[1] Coke to Wentworth, 23 Dec. 1635 (ibid.).

[2] *Cal. S.P. dom., 1635–6*, p. 180.

[3] Strafford, *Letters*, i, 521.

mission and the activities of Darcy and his associates aroused hopes of Wentworth's discomfiture. By the spring he had become convinced that he needed to intervene personally in England. Though he was principally concerned with settling the customs business, a second source of anxiety was revealed in April when he abruptly revised his estimate of the profits to be expected from planting Connacht, raising his original figure of £6,000 to £20,000 and handsomely outbidding the Galway proprietors. That anxiety was quickly allayed. Prevailing east winds which prevented Wentworth from leaving Ireland carried Darcy back from England and made it possible at last to bring the Galway jurors to trial. At the end of May 1636 they were convicted of both conspiracy and wilful refusal to find the king's title, fined £4,000 each, and imprisoned. They remained defiant, however, and at once, through the young earl of Clanricard, petitioned the king against the judgement, drawing false confidence from Wentworth's departure for England early in June.

In Ireland, it was widely hoped and believed that he would not return. This was partly because he seemed so obviously to have overreached himself in his treatment of powerful individuals, and partly because his management of the customs seemed so seriously in question, but it was perhaps principally because it appeared impossible for him to continue effectively in office in the absence of any body of local support. Profound disagreement with his religious policies and a growing realisation of his extraordinary indifference to local interests had alienated the New English. It is doubtful whether the support they lent to his government after the denial of the 'graces' survived even until the end of parliament, though their disillusionment was expressed in withdrawal rather than opposition. The initial conflict over the recusancy fines proved indicative: Wentworth's objections to their reintroduction, while partly based on immediate political considerations, also reflected his attitude towards the long-term problem of catholicism. Though committed to its eradication in time, he took the view that the government was not sufficiently strong or the church sufficiently viable to enable him 'to undergo so great a business'.[1] Until he was ready to act against catholicism, he was anxious to avoid complicating his other tasks unnecessarily by engaging in measures of repression that were at once provocative and ineffectual. Though he distrusted catholics and detested their religion, he judged it expedient to allow them to practise it freely and signified his decision by restraining the ecclesiastical courts from proceeding against catholic baptisms, marriages, and burials. In this, as in the matter of recusancy fines, his policy ran counter to local protestant opinion, and as soon as he left for England the forbidden jurisdiction was reasserted in a number of dioceses. This disagreement was part of a larger, less clear-cut, conflict: attitudes towards catholicism were

[1] Archbishop Ussher's words in 'Documents concerning Ussher, 1641' (B.M., Add. MS 34253, f. 3).

fundamental to the position of the New English, and during the brief period of Wentworth's rule these attitudes had undergone so significant a change at official level as to raise the possibility that indulgence towards catholicism, though justified on political grounds, was actuated by religious motives.

The grounds for suspicion lay in the success with which Wentworth had eliminated the formal differences between the Churches of England and Ireland. In the convocation that met in association with parliament, it had been agreed, with some opposition but little difficulty, to adopt the thirty-nine articles and, in a slightly modified form, the English canons of 1604. This assimilation of the two churches ignored the fact that their differences reflected significant dissimilarities in both their traditions and their operating conditions. In England, church and state, fearful of the threat generated by the growing influence of Calvinist ideas on doctrine, discipline, and church organisation, were systematically seeking to suppress the divisions within protestantism and were aiming to enforce conformity to practices and beliefs that reaffirmed the catholic heritage of the church. In Ireland, the church had naturally tended to stress its distinctively protestant elements and a tendency towards Calvinism was unmistakable. Moreover, the need for an effective common front against catholicism took precedence over the desire for an exact conformity of belief, and Irish protestantism was tolerant of diversity, even to the point where undisguised presbyterians had little difficulty in functioning within the church in the areas of Scots settlement in Ulster. The effect of the decisions made by convocation on Wentworth's prompting was, therefore, not merely to introduce a novel and unpopular insistence upon conformity, but to require conformity to a norm that was unrepresentative of Irish protestant opinion, and was, moreover, in its apparently catholic emphases, entirely inappropriate to the Irish situation. The suspicions, which were commonplace among English puritans, that Laudian policies were directed towards a restoration of catholicism, had currency also in Ireland, where the implications were revolutionary. The general tendency of government policy was the more to be feared since the direction of church affairs, by 1636, had clearly been taken out of the control of the primate, who was perhaps glad to be relieved of the burden, and assumed by the lord deputy. Though Wentworth worked mainly through John Bramhall, who had accompanied him to Ireland as chaplain and had been appointed bishop of Derry in 1634, state control was complete. It was given institutional form by the setting up of a court of high commission, modelled on that of England, which first met in February 1636, concerned itself with the central supervision of diocesan courts and the enforcement of state policy, and was equipped with powers of amercement and imprisonment. The appointment of Bramhall to Derry was followed by that of Henry Leslie to Down and Connor in 1635, and between them they ensured that conformity was most actively demanded in the areas in which the nature of that conformity gave most offence.

These changes, in the treatment of catholicism and in the nature of official protestantism, were contentious and alarming. Their effect was compounded by the measures through which Wentworth set about making good the deficiencies of the Church of Ireland, for these were such as to excite opposition on purely secular grounds. The superficial problem that the efficiency of the church was impaired by pluralism, non-residence, and incompetence had been tackled in the 'graces', one of which required pluralists to appoint qualified curates, but the real problem remained unaffected. The large-scale impropriation of rectories, many of them formerly monastic, had placed much of the church's real property and tithe income in lay hands, principally those of the crown, which usually leased its interests to laymen; a great deal more property had been let to laymen on unduly long and undervalued leases by incumbents who either deliberately exploited their offices to endow their families and drew upon the incomes of their successors by selling leases, or who were simply unable to withstand influential demands for the use of church land on easy terms. As a result, the bishoprics were seriously impoverished; and the income attached to many livings, whether it was paid by a lay impropriator or derived from property, was no longer sufficient to meet the expectations of qualified clergy, who were forced to choose between poverty and pluralism. Wentworth was convinced that the first essential was to place the church on a sound financial basis through the restitution of its property. Legislation in the 1634 parliament removed the technical obstacle that the statute of mortmain prevented the return of impropriated property to the church; regulated the conditions of leases; and made the alienation of church assets more difficult. In 1635 Wentworth agreed to convocation's request that royal impropriations should be handed back to the church, on condition that a rent was reserved to the crown. These decisions cleared the ground for an intensive campaign in which, through both informal bargaining and formal legal proceedings, impropriators and lessees were cajoled, bullied, and bribed into returning property or surrendering their interest in leases. The policy was put into effect most systematically in the north by Bramhall and Leslie, in dioceses where its declared purpose of raising the means of 'settling a rural clergy endowed with competency'[1] was least necessary. Elsewhere its application was less thorough, except where the earl of Cork was concerned, but opportunities to recover church possessions were constantly sought and ruthlessly taken.

The threat to vested interests was great: moreover, both the means used and the implications of the principle involved were deeply disturbing to the New English. Proceedings were regularly initiated by the government

[1] Strafford, *Letters*, i, 382–3.

through the commission for defective titles, and disputes were dealt with by the court of castle chamber, both of which came fully under Wentworth's control when Mountnorris's membership ceased early in 1636. The court of castle chamber was a judicial body in name only; it had powers to fine, imprison, and inflict corporal punishment, but it was not bound by ordinary procedural rules, there was no appeal against its judgements, and it was composed of members of the executive. In practice it served as an arbitrary instrument by which sanctions were enforced against opponents of government policy, and its use released the administration from any dependence upon the ordinary courts. This preoccupation with policy rather than justice was sufficiently objectionable when the court dealt with recent transgressions: the commission for defective titles, however, increasingly concerned itself with the reclamation of former monastic lands, the alienations that it discovered were frequently of very long standing, and in dealing with these the court took no adequate account of important established practices. In view of the historic uncertainty of Irish land titles both before and after the suppression of the monasteries, the common-law courts had customarily protected purchasers against the consequences of past irregularities; and in view of the questionable nature of the transactions by which many of the New English had come into possession of their estates, convention had decreed that the circumstances of acquisition should not ordinarily be too closely examined. In short, one of the essential New English privileges was the presumption of their entitlement to the property they possessed. The court of castle chamber recognised no such immunity, and did not hesitate to dispossess bona-fide New English purchasers of former church lands by means that deprived them of the protection of the common law. In these circumstances it was not merely vested interest in church property, which was not confined to protestants, that was at issue: if neither accepted privileges nor due process of law were to be respected, the whole basis of New English property-ownership was in jeopardy. By the middle of 1636, therefore, both the policies which Wentworth was pursuing and the means by which he was enforcing them were such as to offend and threaten the religious and secular interests of the New English. Both the offence and the threat were to grow in time, but the conflict between the anglocentricity of the lord deputy and the self-interest of the settlers was already well developed.

The optimism that rumoured Wentworth's removal from office proved ill-founded. The progress report that he made to the king and council on 21 June gave complete satisfaction, his argument that where authority 'was going down the hill' it must be regained by 'vigour and force' rather than with 'gracious smiles and gentle looks' was approved, and Charles emphatically assured him that he had not been unduly severe.[1] The customs

[1] Ibid., ii, 13–23.

farm was altered as he advised, with Radcliffe and himself retaining an eighth and a quarter of the profits respectively and the crown gaining entitlement to the remainder. His stay at court and about London was triumphal and his opponents were temporarily silenced. There were disheartening features: Charles's ungracious refusal to promote him in the peerage as an unmistakable mark of favour was a bitter disappointment; the unpromising international situation gave him reason to fear that his hard-won financial gains might soon be dissipated in the expense of war; and, moreover, Charles's rule in England was disturbingly lacking, by Wentworth's standards, in firm direction and effective authority. But in Ireland, to which he returned in November after spending some months in Yorkshire, his position had become unassailable.

Ireland, however, was far from being a discrete political unit. Indeed, the most novel feature of Wentworth's rule was the integration of Anglo-Irish governmental structures which it achieved. Irish government was no longer confused and weakened by the persistent tendency of the English government to interfere in Irish affairs without adequate consultation, and opponents of the local administration could no longer work effectively against it in England. Both in formulating policy and in deciding matters of administrative detail, Wentworth could rely not merely upon the support of the English government but upon its deference to his advice and its restraint in exercising direct authority in Ireland. Superficially, his accord with King Charles created the ideal conditions for a 'thorough' administration: absolved from the need to cultivate local support, his government was able to act as an independent and uncommitted force in Ireland. But in practice the experiment in 'thorough' government was not divisible: it could not succeed in Ireland if it failed elsewhere. In the later 1630s it collapsed in Scotland, where the introduction of a new liturgy in 1637 gave general offence and many separate discontents fused into a united and resolute opposition, which bound itself by covenant to defend the reformed religion against innovation, forcibly usurped the functions of government, and brought the king 'upon his knees to a parliament'[1] in England in 1640, thereby depriving the Irish government of the support which sustained it. No premonitions of disaster, however, disturbed the later years of Wentworth's deputyship: he ruled Ireland with greater confidence, wrote of it with a new affection, and invested heavily in the future; and while he added grievance upon grievance to the account that was already waiting to be settled when the opportunity came, he developed delusions of his own popularity, misjudging attitudes towards himself as thoroughly as he misunderstood reactions to his policies.

In fact Wentworth declined steadily in the estimation of both catholic and protestant communities: to his early reputation, that where king or

[1] The phrase is Laud's: *The works of Archbishop Laud*, ed. W. Scott and J. Bliss (Oxford, 1847–60), vii, 502.

church was concerned there was no right to be expected from him, was added a reputation for personal rapacity which deprived his government of what claim to moral stature it possessed.[1] For some time before his visit to England in 1636, he had been using agents to buy property in the baronies of Naas and Clane, some twenty miles south-west of Dublin and there soon took shape a 3,500-acre estate in the midst of the Old English of the Pale. This proved to be no more than a beginning. Before long, Wentworth was speculating in Wicklow, the only undeveloped area within easy reach of Dublin, where his investment was less in the land itself than in the rents of its Irish occupiers. His attention was drawn to the county through his involvement in a lengthy and now impenetrable network of intrigue and negotiation directed towards finding an unencumbered royal title to the lands of the senior branch of the O'Byrnes, which lay along the coast between Delgany and Arklow.[2] In 1637 and 1638 he bought substantial inland interests in Cosha (the region centring round the Derry Water in the barony of Ballinacor) and Shillelagh from undertakers who had deviously acquired the territory of the junior branch of the O'Byrnes by royal grant: in 1640, when the coastal lands were at last at the crown's disposal, he received grants of the manors of Newcastle and Wicklow, for which he engaged to pay an unrealistically high rent.

These grants brought Wentworth's holdings of Irish land to 34,000 profitable and 23,000 unprofitable acres; the building of a majestic house at Jigginstown, near Naas, on his Kildare estate and a hunting-lodge near Tinahely brought his total expenditure on property to £60,000. Spending on this scale inevitably gave rise to criticism, and it was all the more bitter because the way in which the lord deputy used his office for personal profit was deeply resented and considerably exaggerated. In fact, his envied and lucrative investment in the customs farm, which returned him a clear profit of £35,250 between 1632 and 1640, was his only successful venture. He lost money in an attempt to set up an iron manufacture in 1634, and lost more in 1636 in an elaborate linen-manufacturing project. In 1637 he contracted to pay £7,000 a year to the exchequer, rising to £12,000 after five years, in return for a grant that entitled him to levy sixpence per pound weight on tobacco brought into Ireland and to import it himself at preferential rates. The prospects for this monopoly were good, for tobacco was 'universally taken in smoke, snuff and chewing',[3] but the initial stockpiling costs were high, and Wentworth, who borrowed £24,000 from government funds to finance the scheme in 1638 and repaid it in 1641, never recovered his outlay. It was normal for public officials to use their positions for private gain, but

[1] Kearney, *Strafford in Ire.*, pp 171–84; J. P. Cooper, 'The fortunes of Thomas Wentworth, earl of Strafford' in *Econ. Hist. Rev.*, xi (1958), pp 227–48.

[2] J. P. Cooper, 'Wentworth and the Byrnes' country' in *I.H.S.*, xv, no. 57 (Mar. 1966), pp 1–20.

[3] Strafford, *Letters*, i, 192.

Wentworth had raised hopes that he would not do so, 'being often heard to protest against profit, as a thing he looked not after'.[1]

In fact, Wentworth did not run true to contemporary type: each of his enterprises was intended to serve the public interest as well as his own, and he arranged both his tobacco monopoly and his grant of the O'Byrnes' country in such a way as to guarantee the crown's profit at some risk to himself. The understanding which he reached with Charles about Jigginstown house epitomised his attitude: 'that when it was built, if liked by his majesty it should be his, paying me as it cost; if disliked, *a suo damno*, I was content to keep it and smart for my folly'.[2] It was his own respect for the principle that private gain must justify itself by contributing to the public good that allowed him to berate the New English for their self-interested exploitation of office. But though he could reconcile his precepts with his practice, others could not, and detestation of his apparent hypocrisy aggravated the resentment aroused by his avarice, while the unpopularity of his policies was intensified by the disrespect that was felt for him.

The first fruits of the lord deputy's triumphant vindication of his rule in England were quickly gathered. Early in December 1636 the Galway jurors, who had steadfastly refused to 'confess themselves knaves'[3] by acknowledging the justice of the proceedings against them, admitted their fault and offered to find the king's title to the county. Their offer was ignored. Two months later their ulterior motive was made plain when the landholders of the county joined them in a request that inquisition proceedings be reinstituted, pleading 'that they of this county might be as well dealt with as those of the other three'.[4] At once, a new commission was issued, and in April 1637 the king's title to Galway was found 'very readily'.[5] This compliance went unrewarded: the confiscation of half the land in Galway remained official policy, and when this was later linked with a decision to resume properties of less than 134 acres in full, the net result was the forfeiture of some four-fifths of the land in the county. This treatment was less vindictive than exemplary. Wentworth was already planning to extend the area of plantation to County Clare, and hoped to reclaim a good deal of Munster for the king thereafter. Since the king's titles were 'but indifferent'[5] it was essential that fear should supply the defects. In Clare, it did so. When the lord deputy travelled to Castlebank (near Bunratty) in August 1637 to hold an inquisition, he was met by a petition from local landholders acknowledging the royal title, and the subsequent proceedings were a formality: 'in all my whole life did I never see, or could possibly have believed to have found, men with so much

[1] Aidan Clarke (ed.), 'A discourse between two councillors of state, the one of England and the other of Ireland' in *Anal. Hib.*, no. 26 (1970), p. 166.

[2] Strafford, *Letters*, ii, 105.

[3] Clanricard's words: *Works of Laud*, vii, 284.

[4] Wentworth to Coke, 21 Feb. 1637 (Strafford MSS, ix).

[5] Wentworth to Coke, 19 Apr. 1637 (ibid.).

alacrity divesting themselves of all propriety in their estates', he wrote, without irony.[1] Some days previously, title had been found to the Ormond baronies by agreement with the earl. Thereafter, the pace slackened, largely because the process of planting Connacht proved unexpectedly slow. This was due partly to the sheer weight of administrative detail that devolved upon already busy officials, and partly to the tenacity and success with which Clanricard defended his interests at court: his exemption from plantation in June 1639 was a serious setback. But the real problem was simply that the basic assumption that there was a ready demand for the land proved mistaken. At first, the international situation seemed responsible: France had gone to war with Spain in an improbable alliance with Sweden in 1635, the elector palatine had arrived in England in 1636 to look for aid in recovering his lost inheritance, and the prospect of war against Spain damped the enthusiasm of those who had taken an interest in the scheme of plantation. It soon became clear, however, that the problem was more fundamental. The difficulty did not lie in finding undertakers, but in recruiting settlers. Although emigration from England was high at the time, America offered religious freedom for the disaffected and abundant opportunities for the ambitious, and Ireland offered little in comparison. In consequence, at a time of 'universal running to New England'[2] and steady migration to Virginia, Connacht remained unsettled. Land had been allocated to undertakers in Mayo, Roscommon, and Sligo by 1640, but the business of planting it had scarcely begun. And until it was complete, other schemes, whether in hand, as in Ormond, or in prospect, could not proceed.

Wentworth's plans for further confiscation were never expounded in detail, but they seem mainly to have been directed against the Munster Irish. He still held to his original intention of dealing with the Old English through the commission for defective titles. The king's title to Connacht, however, was no better than his title to many other parts of the old colony and apprehension was so general that even the government's best intentions became suspect. The commission had been busily rectifying titles and revising terms of tenancy since 1634, and by the end of 1637 its activities had added more than £3,000 to the annual revenue. The readiness of many landholders to use it was expressive evidence of the anxiety that parliamentary experience had evoked, for the disadvantages of gaining a secure title in this way were considerable. In particular, the commission's increasing tendency to insist upon tenancies-in-chief brought those who compounded with it under the jurisdiction of the court of wards which, though it no longer demanded the oath of supremacy, exploited feudal incidents so intensively in the 1630s as to more than double its income. The suspicion generated by plantation, and hardened by the commission's cynical abrogation of titles conferred by similar commissions in the past, reversed the balance of advantage. Old

[1] *Cal. S.P. Ire., 1632–47*, p. 168. [2] Strafford, *Letters*, ii, 169.

English lawyers advised that the titles given, though good against other claimants, offered no security against the crown, and after 1637 a widespread reluctance to use the commission developed as catholics lost all confidence in the good faith of the government. Nor was there any real consolation to be drawn from the incongruous toleration of their religion, for freedom of worship was enjoyed by the grace of a government whose hostility was not in doubt, and the exercise of restraint did not disguise Wentworth's determination to achieve religious reformation when his preparations were complete.

Wentworth's religious plans were superficially better laid than those of his predecessors, but they suffered from exactly the same fundamental failure to oppose the catholic challenge with a matching dynamism. While the lord deputy bided his time on behalf of the Church of Ireland, the Church of Rome sustained its initiative. With religious practice unimpeded and clergy unmolested, the thrust of the counter-reformation increased in effectiveness as success generated success. Catholic bishops took up residence in most dioceses, seminary priests grew more and more numerous, religious houses proliferated, novitiates were set up locally, and the level of vocations ran satisfactorily high. The problems were those of success: regulars, supported by the holy office, and seculars, supported by the congregation *de propaganda fide* (and discreetly favoured by the Dublin government), quarrelled not merely about pastoral cares, but about the possession of former monastic churches impropriated after the reformation, and occasionally brought their disputes into the common-law courts. Among themselves, the orders divided on both national and international issues, with some, like the dominant Franciscans who outnumbered all others, being identified with Spanish and native Irish interests, and others like the Capuchins and the Jesuits, being associated with French and Old English interests. Regulars and seculars alike were closely linked with the landed families, from among whom their members were largely drawn and upon whose patronage they largely depended. This interrelationship contributed immeasurably to the local ethos, for the significance of counter-reformation activity was by no means confined to its spiritual effects. It also invested Irish political struggles with an additional dimension, creating among catholics a sense of involvement in a wider movement, which sustained native Irish in their hopes of overturning the conquest and Old English in their refusal to conform to new colonial norms.

While the alienation of the old colony grew, the new one remained unreconciled. Protestants also suffered from the attentions of the commission for defective titles, which proved as ready to find fault with plantation titles as with older ones. They were increasingly affected by the official policy of reclaiming church lands which gathered pace with the enthusiastic support of the clergy: as an embittered agent put it, 'like wolves the churchmen now look and con about where to snatch and catch a prey, not regarding either right or wrong, but where they set on they must be served and no people so ravenous as they, for they grow insatiable'.[1] The New English also found that, more and more, the centralising effects of Wentworth's restructured government reduced their customary local independence; under the supervision of the courts of castle chamber and high commission there was much less room for local influence and control in civil and religious matters. And, in some eyes at least, the summary interference of these courts was aggravated by the indifference with which they proceeded against great and small alike, often redressing the balance in favour of the weak at the cost of offending the powerful. In the administration itself, the removal of Lord Chancellor Loftus, who fought bitterly and unsuccessfully to retain the office which he had continuously misused since he had bought it from Buckingham in 1619, made Wentworth's dominance complete. In the church, the enforcement of the new canons continued, in sharp contrast to the liberal treatment of recusancy, and the tendency to confine positions of influence and responsibility to men newly brought from England became more pronounced. Beset by evidence of their unimportance to the government, the New English, however they might welcome the treatment of the Old English, had no reason to be satisfied with their own condition and every reason to fear that it would continue to deteriorate.

In Ulster, there were special discontents, and they were not solely due to the effects of an Anglo-Scottish crisis upon an Anglo-Scottish settlement. There was religious dissatisfaction in County Londonderry, where Bramhall's regimen compared unfavourably with that of George Downham, the celebrated controversialist and puritan sympathiser who had preceded him for eighteen years, but it was not complicated by national divisions: Scots were few, except on the Clothworkers' and Haberdashers' proportions farmed by Lord Kirkcudbright, and Scottish nonconformists were rare enough to allow Bramhall to joke about his occasional encounters with 'anabaptistical prophetesses'.[2] None the less, at a time when the state was becoming aware that it might need the goodwill of the English in Ireland, the settlers in Londonderry were carelessly and profitlessly alienated. Their maltreatment, as Wentworth was careful to emphasise, 'had life and motion'[3] in England where, in February 1635, the court of star chamber condemned the city of London to pay a fine of £70,000 and to surrender their patent to Londonderry.[4] Though the principal charge against them was that they had failed to replace the native population of the area with British settlers in accordance with the general conditions of plantation, the prosecution arose from the crown's need for money, not from any genuine concern with the

[1] Quoted in T. O. Ranger, 'Strafford in Ireland: a revaluation' in Trevor Aston (ed.), *Crisis in Europe, 1560–1660* (London, 1965), p. 290.

[2] Moody, *Londonderry plantation*, p. 395.

[3] Strafford, *Letters*, ii, 251.

[4] For a full account of the city's trial in the court of star chamber, the execution of the sentence, and the disposal of the forfeited property, see Moody, *Londonderry plantation*, chs XIV–XVI.

progress of the plantation. It was at first taken for granted that the city would negotiate terms of composition and continue in possession, leaving the plantation itself unaffected. Wentworth, however, strongly pressed the financial advantages of farming the property, and offered to lease it himself in December 1636. Though his offer was ignored, his advice was taken, and the city's surrender was completed in July 1637. The formal cancellation of the charter in the court of chancery seven months later transformed the situation, for its effect was to void the titles of the settlers. Already, Wentworth's own tender had been outbid by two groups who clearly contemplated the eviction of existing occupiers, and the settlers, having petitioned unsuccessfully for confirmation of their holdings, offered to assume the farm of the forfeited property themselves in July 1638. Wentworth's aim was an arrangement that would profit the crown without disturbing the settlers, and he urged that either his offer or theirs should be accepted; the object of the other interested parties, among whom the catholic earl of Antrim was prominent, was, he alleged, 'to out a company of poor planters'.[1] In fact, Antrim's principal associate was the king's trusted adviser, the marquis of Hamilton, and Charles resolved the conflict of interest by appointing a commission to manage the property directly.

The arrangement seemed unexceptionable: in fact the intervention of an independent agency, answering to London, concerned only with raising money, and oblivious of broader policy-considerations, proved disastrous. In 1639, to the accompaniment of 'a great clamour',[2] the conditions of tenancy in Londonderry were revised, and large and small tenants alike were systematically and unscrupulously rack-rented. Neither Wentworth nor Bramhall believed that the new rents could be collected, and they proved to be correct, but the real objection to the commission's proceedings was not that they were impractical but that they were impolitic. This was partly for the obvious reason that the Anglo-Scottish situation made it a wise general principle to deal gently with the English in Ulster, but it was also partly because the Londonderry issue was not as unrelated to the general predicament as it seemed. On the one hand, Wentworth was convinced that the farming tenders that had competed with his own were part of a Scottish plot to take over the area. On the other hand, the associations of the settlers' main spokesman, Sir John Clotworthy, a Devonshire settler in Antrim who farmed the Drapers' proportion, were suggestive: by his own marriage to Lord Ranelagh's sister he was connected with the leading New English opponents of the Irish administration; through his sister's marriage he was connected with John Pym and other prominent opponents of the English government; his family were patrons of presbyterianism, and he was himself reputed to have subscribed the covenant in Edinburgh.

[1] Wentworth to Conway, 31 Aug. 1638 (Strafford MSS, x).
[2] P.R.O., S.P. Ire., 63/257, p. 40.

Such interconnections were to contribute significantly to the process by which the attempt to recover royal authority in Scotland weakened it elsewhere, for the chief significance of the crisis in both England and Ireland lay in the political opportunities that it created. In Ireland, however, the position was complicated by the direct effects of Scottish resistance upon communities of Scots who were prompted by both fellow-feeling and a sense of similar grievances to bestir themselves. They were quickly emboldened by Scottish example to abandon their recent sullen compliance with the newly prescribed religious forms and to behave once more 'as if all religion consisted in the hearing of a sermon'.[1] For some time, this revival of nonconformity was relatively unimpeded, for Wentworth was under instructions to take no action that might interfere with Charles's efforts to come to terms with the Scots—or, more exactly, his efforts 'to flatter them . . . until I be ready to suppress them'.[2] Antrim and Down were chiefly affected: in Henry Leslie's diocese, the 'contagion'[3] was so widespread in 1638 that the machinery for its regulation was stultified by the nonconformity of those whose function was to enforce conformity. Almost everywhere there were Scots, there was similar defiance, partly imitative and partly the result of direct encouragement. Contacts between the north of Ireland and Scotland were close and continuous, and the pamphlet literature of Scottish protest reached Ulster as a matter of course. As the Scottish movement became increasingly organised its leaders included northern Ireland in their plans, and deliberately solicited support and cultivated unrest. In the diocese of Raphoe some Scots 'endeavoured to draw their countrymen there into the covenant',[4] but for the most part the Scots in Ulster seem to have been more concerned with worship than with politics, and to have preserved a sense of their separate local needs. Thus their reaction to Charles's conciliatory policy was distinctive. On 10 September 1638 Charles revoked the new Scottish canons and service-book, abolished the Scottish court of high commission, and authorised the convention of a general assembly. In Scotland, where the abolition of episcopacy had become the minimal objective of opposition, this 'king's covenant' was rejected. In Ulster, however, where the scale of ambition was lower, preparations were at once made to petition for similar concessions. The request was denied before it was formally made. In fact, the Scottish response had already altered the situation in Ireland, for it had removed all hope of a peaceful settlement and Charles had released Wentworth from the restraints imposed upon him. The lord deputy was now free 'to crush all their attempts in the beginning that do but look towards their covenant'.[5]

[1] Henry Leslie's words: Reid, *Presb. ch. in Ire.*, i, 229.

[2] Quoted in G. Donaldson, *Scotland: James V to James VII* (Edinburgh, 1965), p. 317.

[3] Bramhall's word: *Cal. S.P. Ire., 1633–47*, p. 182.

[4] *Works of Laud*, vii, 490.

[5] Ibid., vii, 503.

The agreed aim was to confine the covenant to Scotland. The implication, that the Scots in Ulster should be compelled to choose between conformity and expulsion, was clearly stated, and Wentworth took care to set the machinery for suppressing nonconformity to work. None the less, he hoped to simplify the problem by distinguishing between its religious and political elements. In the winter of 1638–9, when preparations for war were under way, he devised a scheme to require the Scots in Ulster to take an 'oath of abjuration of their abominable covenant'.[1] The intention was partly to disarm them morally, but the plan was principally designed to force the recalcitrant to return to Scotland and the oath was carefully confined to temporal matters to make it a specifically political test: subscribers were to bind themselves to allegiance and obedience to Charles and to renounce all contrary 'oaths, covenants and bonds'.[2] While the king moved into position, leaving London for York on 27 March 1639 and reaching Berwick with his army at the end of May, the implementation of this plan went ahead. Some three dozen northern Scots, most of whom were conforming clergy, but with some presbyterian sympathisers among them, were summoned to Dublin where they were persuaded to lodge a protest against the covenant and to request an opportunity to forswear it. In feigned response, on 16 May, the council commanded all Scots over the age of sixteen to take the oath of abjuration. At the same time, a long-standing contingency plan to station the bulk of the army in the north-east to 'amuse'[3] the Scots while Charles advanced was put into effect. Militarily, it proved unnecessary, for the inferiority of the king's forces left him with no choice but to agree on 18 June to a pacification that left the Scots in control of Scotland. But the presence of the army usefully supported the civil commissioners who systematically administered the 'black oath' to the Scots in Ulster throughout much of the summer. Some refused to subscribe, and some avoided doing so by flight, but most took the oath, and Wentworth was more than satisfied with the success of his plan and the demonstration of control that it afforded.

From the outset Wentworth had worked to create a new source of power for the crown in Ireland. In the summer of 1639, when the resources at Charles's disposal had proved insufficient to preserve his authority in Scotland, the time had come for Wentworth to fulfil the real political purpose of his deputyship by showing how Ireland could be used to redress the balance of power elsewhere in the king's favour. On 22 July he wrote to assure Charles that

> if the distempers of Scotland had either continued, or shall kindle again, I am most confident we might and shall propound a way to make this kingdom considerably

[1] *Works of Laud*, vii, 526.
[2] Strafford, *Letters*, ii, 345.
[3] Ibid., ii, 192.

active to enforce those gainsayers to due obedience, and settle the public peace of all your kingdoms.[1]

The opportunity to make good this boast was closer than he supposed. The king had already decided that, alone among his advisers, the lord deputy of Ireland seemed capable of solving his problems. On 23 July he wrote to ask Wentworth to join him in England.

[1] Ibid., ii, 371–2.

CHAPTER X

The breakdown of authority, 1640–41

AIDAN CLARKE

CHARLES had conceded nothing of substance to the Scots at Berwick. The terms of the 'pacification', which provided for the disbandment of both armies and for the king's presence at meetings of the general assembly and parliament of Scotland, did no more than refer the dispute back to political processes. And although the Scots interpreted the arrangements as a tacit admission of royal inability to resist their demands, Charles meant to imply nothing of the sort. The full extent of this misunderstanding was not apparent at once, but the absence of goodwill on both sides was unmistakable. The Scots remained in arms, and Charles did not leave England. When the general assembly reaffirmed the abolition of episcopacy on 17 August 1640, its members did not act on the available ground of compromise, that the institution was contrary to the constitution of the Church of Scotland, but on the defiant principle that it was contrary to the law of God. In Charles's continued absence, the Scottish parliament overthrew the system of control through royal appointees by reconstituting its managing committee, went on to ratify the ending of episcopacy, and formulated a series of legislative proposals which strongly suggested that its members believed that they had effectively superseded the king in the government of Scotland. Charles was slow to react. It was not until Scots commissioners arrived in London early in November, to request his approval of parliament's proceedings, that he revealed himself as unwilling to accept the plain implications of his military humiliation in the early summer. He abruptly refused to receive the commissioners and directed that parliament should be prorogued.

This unwonted firmness owed much to the influence of the lord deputy of Ireland. Wentworth had arrived in London late in September and easily gained preeminence among the king's councillors, few of whom continued to enjoy royal confidence. His passionate conviction that the authority of the crown must be recovered, and the Scots coerced rather than conciliated, reinforced the king's own inclinations and effectively determined the government's objectives. The prorogation of the Scots parliament marked the initiation of a new policy. Its more detailed development followed quickly upon the return of the king's lord high commissioner from Scotland late in November. His report both confirmed the government in its resolution and convinced it of the need to act at once. The decisions which resulted were largely dictated by Wentworth, to whom it appeared neither wise nor necessary to attempt to raise money to pay for the suppression of the Scots without first trying 'the ordinary way of parliament'.[1] His reasoning strikingly resembled his advocacy of an Irish parliament in 1634, for his case rested on the same two considerations that he had urged then: that success seemed likely, and that lack of success could be turned to advantage. He argued that if parliamentary support were not forthcoming, and Charles therefore driven to seek 'extraordinary means' to preserve 'his state and government', his right to do so would be incontestable; but he believed that it was more probable that the danger from Scotland would offset the sense of grievance in England and that a parliament could be induced to support the king, provided that it could be prevented from sensing an advantage. He stipulated that the summoning of parliament must be presented as an act of generosity and that Charles must appear as one who was following the 'old way' by giving his subjects an opportunity to express their loyalty, rather than as one who had been driven to a last resort by financial need and political pressure. Such an approach could succeed only if a convincing impression of royal sufficiency could be conveyed, and Wentworth's proposal was that temporary solvency should be created by a substantial loan raised within the privy council itself, while the king's access to ample resources outside the control of the English parliament should be made plain by a demonstration of the ease with which men and money could be obtained from Ireland. Early in December, Wentworth prevailed. The privy council agreed that the English parliament should be summoned to meet in the following April and that the Irish parliament should be convened in March to set the requisite example. Charles himself added the proviso that Wentworth 'must be at the beginning of both',[2] a severely practical condition which none the less symbolised the importance the king's Irish dominion had assumed in English politics.

In the early months of 1640, while a fresh group of Scots commissioners was held in unproductive discussion in London, the government's twin priorities were to levy a new army for summer service in Scotland and to extract the maximum advantage from Ireland. The two were linked in Wentworth's appointment as lieutenant general to the earl of Northumberland, with special responsibility for the command of a contingent of 9,000 men which was to be raised and financed in Ireland. The Irish contribution to the king's expenses was fixed at six subsidies payable over three years.

[1] Clarendon, *State letters*, ii, 81.

[2] *Life and original correspondence of Sir George Radcliffe*, ed. T. D. Whitaker (London, 1810), pp 187–8.

Men, money, and good example were all that the king needed from Ireland, but Wentworth required something more to further his own ambitions, and the subsidy bill was drafted with a lengthy preamble which eulogised his administration and represented the Irish parliament as thanking Charles 'for this your tender care over us, showed by the deputing and supporting of so good a governor'.[1]

The confidence which led Wentworth to make the Irish parliament an integral part of his plan to solve the problems of the king's other kingdoms, and which allowed him to arrange to practise this ventriloquism upon it, was based in part upon his perverse belief that opposition to his administration was self-interested and unrepresentative and in part upon the calculation that the desire to ensure the defeat of the Scots would take precedence over other considerations for most members. But the bedrock of his policy was his experience of the ease with which the Irish parliament could be controlled and his knowledge that on this second occasion the government's position would be even more firmly assured as a result of carefully considered electoral preparations. Already, the merging of the county of the Cross of Tipperary with County Tipperary and the sequestration of town charters through *quo warranto* proceedings had eliminated sixteen Old English seats. Other charters, sequestered from both catholic and protestant boroughs, had been restored 'upon agreement to send such to the parliament as those in power should name',[2] while recent changes in the pattern of influence in a number of county communities also favoured the return of government candidates. In these circumstances, Sir George Radcliffe's management of the elections, which was designed to increase the number of government supporters at the expense of both Old and New English groups, met with considerable success. In the absence of formal divisions and clear attachments it is difficult to measure official gains in protestant constituencies, but allegations of government interference gain credence from the odd discontinuity of representation from Ulster, where less than one-third of those returned in 1640 had been members of the previous parliament. Substantial inroads were certainly made upon the representation of the Old English, who lost twelve county and sixteen borough seats in the election. This was offset by gains of only three county and five borough seats and the net result was to reduce catholic representation by one-third in comparison with 1634. Ironically, this change in the balance of representation from the different communities, which had been planned in the light of the events of the previous parliament, was no longer clearly in the government's immediate interest, and its tactical approach was actually based on the assumption that it was the catholic rather than the protestant members who could be relied upon to support its policy proposals. In the first days of the new parliament

[1] *Commons' jn., Ire.*, i (1796), p. 176.
[2] *The journal of Sir Simonds D'Ewes*, ed. W. Notestein (New Haven, 1923), pp 13–14.

the earlier alliance between Old English and official members was briefly revived.

Wentworth had not yet arrived in Ireland on 16 March when parliament convened, and the houses marked time. The government's nomination to the speakership of Sir Maurice Eustace, a protestant of Old English extraction, went through without difficulty, and an unofficial understanding was reached in which the government, accepting that an exact repetition of the financial arrangements of 1634 might well establish an unwelcome precedent, agreed to a grant of four subsidies, provided that the houses would enter into a 'cheerful engagement' to give more if it were required. When Wentworth landed two days later, his prestige doubly enhanced by promotions to the earldom of Strafford and the lord lieutenancy of Ireland, he at once endorsed this agreement, which had the inestimable advantage of providing him with a promising piece of propaganda for use in England. The subsidy business was introduced on 23 March and brought smoothly, accompanied by extravagant expressions of loyalty, to its prearranged conclusion: the commons resolved to grant four subsidies and to declare their readiness to give more if more were needed. In their exuberant report of these proceedings, composed with an eye to widespread circulation in England, the Irish councillors stressed the part played by the 'natives'. No doubt the intention was to underline the extent of support for Charles in Ireland in the interests of furthering Wentworth's plans to exploit the Irish example to 'make the covenanters in Scotland and the ill-affected in your English parliament (if any such there be) less petulant and peevish than you might otherwise find them'.[1] None the less the implication, that protestant members were more reserved, is confirmed by the membership of the committee appointed to draw up an appropriate declaration, for it was composed of three prominent members of the administration and four members of the Old English group. In the few days before it reported, the subsidy bill itself was introduced, its preamble was judged objectionable, and the political climate changed. The amendment of the bill was impossible, since time was short and the statutory procedure would require its return to England for recertification. In these circumstances, objections could not be pressed, and the bill was passed on 26 March. But the resentment which had been generated was transferred to the committee's draft declaration, in which members were asked to profess

> that our zeal and duty shall not stay here at these four subsidies; but we do humbly offer and promise that we shall be ready with our persons and estates, to the uttermost of our abilities for his majesty's future supply in parliament as his great occasions, by the continuance of his forces against that distemper, shall require.[2]

Strenuous efforts were made by Old English members of both houses to introduce amendments, and it was only after prolonged debate that the declaration was adopted in its original form in the commons on 30 March

[1] Strafford, *Letters*, ii, 398–9. [2] *Commons' jn., Ire.*, i (1796), p. 141.

and in the lords on 31 March. On the following day, the Irish parliament recessed until June, and in England the king reported comprehensively to his privy council, reading both the Irish council's description of the reception of the subsidy proposals and the draft declaration. In a rare departure from his usual bleak record of the privy council's business, the clerk noted that 'their lordships were thereupon filled with joy' and both letter and declaration were entered in the register 'to remain there as a record unto posterity'.[1]

There were still further grounds for satisfaction in the progress of the king's business in Ireland. The clergy in convocation had not only accepted Strafford's original proposal and granted six subsidies over a three-year period, but had consented to a new and more onerous rate of assessment. Arrangements for the mobilisation of a new army had gone smoothly: the council had decided that the normal religious tests should not be required of its soldiers, a thousand men had been drawn from the standing army to form a nucleus, officers had been appointed, recruitment had begun promisingly, commissariat and training arrangements had been planned, and a time-table which would make the force ready for service in July had been agreed. When Strafford boarded ship, on Good Friday, 3 April, he was ill with gout and flux, but exultant with the success of his plans and exhilarated by the enthusiasm, affection, and respect with which he seemed to have been surrounded in Ireland. Several hundred printed copies of the declaration of both houses of the Irish parliament accompanied him to England on his majesty's pinnace *Confidence*.

In England, however, as parliament approached, the news from Ireland was the government's only comfort. Money had run out and borrowing proved difficult. The elections had gone decisively against the government and had generated so critical and demanding an attitude that it seemed wise to place the Scots commissioners in custody to prevent their collusion with members of parliament. The government's slender hope of winning support for its policies now rested upon the discovery that the Scots had made overtures to the king of France, which might be exploited to generalise the appeal for unity in face of national danger, for the peril of foreign invasion seemed a better basis upon which to appeal for support than the Scottish threat, which not all seemed likely to acknowledge. The responsibility for presenting the king's case to the joint meeting of both houses with which parliament commenced on 13 April fell to the lord keeper, John Finch, whose political attitudes were detested by most of those present. His task was to reveal the 'foul and horrid treasons' of the Scots and to expound the needs of the situation, and he succeeded in weaving the news from Ireland neatly into this theme: in the past, he reminded his audience, England had had two 'postern gates', but Charles's rule had wrought great changes in Ireland; it had ceased to be a disturbed and expensive charge upon the king and

[1] *Privy council registers* (facsimile edition, London, 1968), x (1 Apr.–28 June 1640), f. 421.

become instead a settled source of revenue to him; its parliament, moreover, had recently given ample proof of loyalty in both money and assurances 'so that the hopes of hurting England that way are quite extinct. Scotland then only remains.'[1] His eloquence was wasted. The evidence of the Scots' treasonable dealings with France was too slight to bear the interpretation placed upon it. Parliament paid little heed to it, and less to Ireland. Resolving that 'till the liberties of the house and kingdom be cleared, they knew not whether they had anything to give or no',[2] the commons withheld all assistance. The lords, expressly enjoined by Finch to imitate the Irish, and appealed to by the king in person, on Strafford's advice, took the opposite view to the lower house, but nothing was gained by the division, and Charles was forced to dissolve parliament on 5 May to prevent the commons from adopting a petition begging him to come to terms with the Scots.

Later on the same day the king's advisers debated what was to be done. Strafford, who was prepared for such a disappointment even if he had not expected it, and who still believed that a short campaign would suffice to defeat the Scots, argued that prerogative powers might be legitimately used to raise the means of doing so, and reminded the meeting of the availability of the Irish army in terms which implied that it might serve to suppress English as well as Scottish resistance if that unlikely need should arise. The invasion of Scotland was agreed upon, and Strafford's view that the king was absolved from ordinary restraints in financing it was accepted. In fact, however, just as Strafford had wrongly assessed the promise of parliament, so too was he mistaken about the unimportance of its failure. It did not prove easy for the king to find 'means to help himself, though it were against their wills'.[3] The serious illness which prevented Strafford from playing an active part for some weeks contributed little to the ineffectuality of the government's attempts to raise money. The fact was that the policy that Strafford had forced through was based upon assumptions far removed from the realities of the English political situation.

The assumptions which Strafford had made about Ireland proved equally false. Already, his belief in the importance of its influence upon the formation of English attitudes had been revealed as an illusion. Before long his reliance upon its contribution to the campaign against the Scots and his confidence in the obsequiousness of its parliament followed suit. The Irish government was unable to fulfil its military commitments efficiently and also unable, and to a significant extent unwilling, to perform its political obligations. It was revealing, in view of the main task that Strafford had set himself as lord deputy, that in Ireland, as in England, the central governmental deficiency was financial. The time-table for the new army had actually been based on the availability of subventions from England: when these failed to arrive, a

[1] *Lords' jn.*, iv, 46. [2] Gardiner, *Eng.*, i, 320.

[3] *The trial of Thomas, earl of Strafford*, ed. J. Rushworth (London, 1680), p. 536.

series of postponements became necessary which deferred the assembling of the soldiers from May to July, and even this was only achieved by the dangerous expedient of initiating the collection of the first Irish parliamentary subsidy without the authorisation of the house of commons. The irregularity was aggravated by the use of the new and unpopular method of assessment introduced in 1635, the council fixing upon a total sum of £45,000 and adjusting the rate of contribution accordingly. A protest from the Pale counties, which compared the council's conduct to 'the exaction by will of the council in France' and alleged that the new system had already 'drained the sponge of the commonwealth dry',[1] indicated the certainty of parliamentary objections. There seemed little reason, however, to regard the threat as important.

It was not to be expected that the alliance between government and Old English, which had arisen from the special circumstances in which parliament had been summoned, would continue in the second session, nor was it necessary, in view of their election losses, to defer to the Old English. It had not even been thought necessary to fulfil the king's original promise of legislation which would 'conduce to the happiness and prosperity of themselves and their posterities'.[2] Indeed, apart from the formal confirmation of titles granted by the defective titles commission, the only important measure proposed for the June session was an act to secure the recent plantations. The way in which the commons dealt with that bill quickly demonstrated that simple political assumptions derived from the experience of the last parliament were no longer valid. On 3 June it was referred to a committee upon which protestants outnumbered catholics by two to one; on 8 June, on that committee's recommendation, full discretion to negotiate with the council for amendments to end discrimination against Galway proprietors and to improve the treatment of smaller freeholders in all the counties was delegated to a second committee on which the ratio of membership was reversed, and to which were added the two former agents, Patrick Darcy and Richard Martin, neither of whom was a member of the house. This pattern was roughly repeated when the critical issue of the assessment of the subsidies was raised by Nicholas Plunkett on the following day. The question was first referred to a committee of largely protestant composition; on its recommendation, the commons agreed to allow the collection of the first subsidy to continue and appointed a new committee with a catholic majority to prepare a declaration of parliament's competence in the matter. The resulting statement, adopted on 13 June, not merely affirmed the general principle, but applied it, directing that future subsidies should be assessed 'after an easy and equal rate of each man his estate, without relation to any former certainty'.[3] In the meantime, on 11 June, the right of the government

[1] *Cal. S.P. Ire., 1633–47*, pp 241–2; P.R.O., S.P. Ire., 63/258/33.
[2] Strafford, *Letters*, ii, 392.
[3] *Commons' jn., Ire.*, i (1796), pp 146–7.

to control membership of the commons had been contested by the issue of writs of summons to the disfranchised boroughs. On 17 June the house turned its attention to the clergy, whose 'vexatious proceedings' were complained of in a petition demanding the immediate redress of forty-four grievances, most of them with easily traceable origins in the disgruntlement of nonconformists in the north. The house went on to take issue with the court of high commission, drawing attention sharply to a case in which it had exceeded its jurisdiction. On the same day, Christopher Wandesford, deputising for the lord lieutenant, prorogued parliament to 1 October.

Wandesford's loss of control during this brief session was even more complete than the parliamentary record suggests. Although some government supporters were absent from the commons on duties arising from the mobilisation of the new army, the success of the opposition was not due to the exploitation of a chance majority by catholic and protestant dissidents. It resulted from the diversity of the interests that came together to embarrass the administration, and Wandesford's difficulty was not the depletion of the government party, but its disintegration. The majority of the members of the committee which acted collusively in sabotaging the plantations bill were officeholders, as was a generous minority of those to whom the question of the subsidies was committed. In the discussions on the declaration, not only in the commons, but at the council table itself, the attitude of officials towards the official position was markedly reserved: in the entire episode, indeed, the lord deputy found praiseworthy the conduct of only two men, Lord Robert Dillon and the king's sergeant, William Sambach. The withdrawal of Strafford had removed the slender principle of cohesion in the government party which, though it included a few men who supported him wholeheartedly, was principally composed of men who supported him only because it was to their advantage to remain close to power and patronage. In doing so, they merely made the best of inferior opportunities until better became available. Few protestant colonists could hope to benefit in the long term from the process by which Strafford had increased the government's power, even by acquiring office, for he had succeeded in making the government independent of local influence and accentuating its English orientation. He had done so, moreover, by means that were inherently objectionable. It is significant that the area of agreement revealed by common action in parliament related to the abuse of power. The opposition was not based upon agreed objectives, but upon a shared hostility towards a governmental attitude that regarded its own convenience as sufficient reason to deprive a freeholder of his property, a burgess of his representation, a nonconformist of his freedom to refuse to act as a churchwarden, a defendant of his legal rights, or a parliament of its financial prerogatives. The motives of some of those involved ran deep: if Old English objectives were transparent, and many of the New English had obvious local axes to grind, there were also some who were committed to the cause of the Scots and some who supported the English parliament. Among the protestant settlers there were those who saw recent Irish developments in the same way as Wentworth himself, in the perspective of three kingdoms. Migration had neither broken their ties nor obliterated their interest in cross-channel affairs, and before long they were to be in active collusion with Charles's English opponents.[1]

Already, the leaders of the English opposition were in collusion with the Scots, who were in no doubt that a stable solution of their problems could only be achieved with the support of an English parliament. Encouraged by overtures from England, they determined upon an invasion, coming south in armed force in the unconvincing guise of petitioners for justice, and deliberately seeking to create a situation in which Charles could not avoid summoning an English parliament which, they had every reason to expect, would make common cause with them. Attempts to raise money in England had been uniformly unsuccessful, and although sufficient men were raised to make up a nominal army, lack of pay, training, discipline, equipment, and enthusiasm rendered them almost useless, and Charles could mount only a token resistance. When the armies met, near Newcastle-upon-Tyne on 28 August, the superiority of the Scots was manifest. With the north of England occupied, with no means of preventing the invading army from extending its control at will, Charles issued writs on 24 September for the meeting of parliament for which his opponents had schemed. By the time it met on 3 November, preliminary terms had been agreed with the Scots, which left them in occupation of two counties and obliged Charles to pay them £850 each day. The effect was to deprive him of any genuine freedom of action and to expose him to parliament's mercy.

Ireland did not play its ordained part in Charles's plans. The original intention had been to have the new army ready for service in July. In fact, it was not until mid-July that the soldiers were brought together at Carrickfergus for training, and not until the eve of the king's defeat at Newburn (28 August 1640) that the sergeant-major-general declared them ready for action. But though they were no longer relevant to their original purpose, the turn of events in England increased rather than diminished their importance. The English opposition feared Wentworth, and relied upon the Scottish army to apply the pressure that would keep the king on the defensive in England. That Strafford controlled an army in Ireland which might be used, whether in England or Scotland, to change the balance of force was a matter of vital significance, and when parliament assembled Ireland was at the centre of English politics, attracting the level of attention Wentworth had earlier hoped to achieve for it, but to very different effect. Among its

[1] New English attitudes are discussed in T. O. Ranger, 'Strafford in Ireland: a revaluation', loc. cit., pp 271–93, and Aidan Clarke, 'Ireland and the general crisis' in *Past & Present*, no. 48 (1970), pp 93–7.

members were some whose presence indicated the resourcefulness of a number of Strafford's leading New English opponents, and one whose return revealed the close interplay of English and Irish opposition activities. Cork, Ranelagh, and Wilmot were each represented by sons in the commons, and Cork himself secured a summons to the lords; but far wider significance attached to the opposition's management of the return of Sir John Clotworthy. His role was revealed on 7 November, when the whole house met in committee to hear him speak at length on the state of Ireland; his criticisms of government policy were detailed, and his somewhat tendentious emphasis upon the practice of undue toleration formed an effective background to his account of the catholicism of the new army. Although he made no direct reference to the lord lieutenant, his speech was one element in the preparations that were on foot for Strafford's impeachment, and when the opposition made its move four days later Clotworthy's contribution was to substantiate John Pym's generalised denunciation by telling of the 'black oath', describing the arbitrary nature of Strafford's government and dwelling once more upon his catholic army. He was a member of the committee of five which recommended that Strafford should be charged with high treason, and it was on his testimony that the arrest of Radcliffe was also ordered, on the basis of an alleged statement—'that this army raised in Ireland is against England and not against the Scots'[1]—which confirmed Pym's secret information as to the advice which Strafford had given at the council table on 5 May.

The singular importance of Clotworthy in the events that led to Strafford's impeachment was probably adventitious. The opposition had been forced to move more quickly than had been intended, and the evidence indicates that plans to produce compelling proofs from Ireland matured too slowly for their purposes. The Irish parliament had reassembled early in October with the antagonisms of June unabated. The commons sustained their demand for the reinstatement of the disfranchised boroughs, and worked out a new scale of assessment which reduced the value of each of the remaining subsidies to about £12,000. Wandesford savagely assured the house that if money were required it would be raised despite them, kept parliament in being only because he hoped that Strafford could suggest a way of overturning its decision on the subsidies, and resorted to a series of extraordinary adjournments in an attempt to prevent the commons from adopting a petition of remonstrance which was in substance a categorical refutation of the official claim that Ireland had recently prospered contentedly under good government. Though the petition was addressed for form's sake to the lord deputy, it was clearly designed to provide the English parliamentary opposition with an authoritative indictment of Wentworth's administration in the name of 'the loyal and dutiful people of Ireland, being now for the most part derived of British ancestors . . . .'[2] Its theme was the impoverish-

[1] *Journal of Sir Simonds D'Ewes*, p. 256. [2] *Commons' jn., Ire.*, i (1796), pp 162–3.

ment of the country by an arbitrary and predatory government. Specific reference was made to customs duties, monopolies, and fees, but the argument centred upon the comprehensive exploitation practised by an administration that respected neither the law, parliament, nor royal promises, and was concerned to enrich the king's officials rather than his treasury. The activities of the courts of castle chamber and high commission, and of the various commissioners for defective titles, plantations, and Londonderry all figured in the denunciation of a government that had brought the community 'very near to ruin and destruction'. The petition did not formally originate in parliament and was never discussed by parliament; presented to the commons without preliminaries on 7 November, it was read twice and adopted on a single division without debate. Four days later, the house decided to send a committee to England to pursue the redress of grievances: predictably, the majority of those chosen were drawn from the Old English landed interest and its lawyer spokesmen, but resentful Scots settlers, disgruntled English planters, alienated officials, New English puritans, and the special grievances of Londonderry were all represented among the committee's thirteen members.[1] Wandesford countered by proroguing parliament, forbidding the committee to leave Ireland and, on belated advice from Strafford, disallowing the subsidy order. The opposition responded by dispatching two Old English members, John Bellew and Oliver Cashell, to request the assistance of the English commons in gaining access to the king. The strategem proved unnecessary; the English commons had begun working for the removal of restrictions on passage between Ireland and England on 11 November, and John Pym was able to convey the substance of the petition of remonstrance to the house on 19 November. It had already been used to good effect in the preparation of articles of impeachment against Strafford before Clotworthy introduced the two catholic commoners from Ireland to the house, together with the letter in which those who had sent them again drew attention to the common ground that recommended both old and new colonists to an English audience, requesting the help of 'the famous people of England from whose loins they are descended . . . being therefore flesh of their flesh and bone of their bone, subjects to one gracious sovereign and bound by the same laws . . .'[2] By the end of November, a sergeant-at-arms had reached Ireland with news of Strafford's impeachment and a warrant for Radcliffe's arrest, and a proclamation removing restrictions on movement between England and Ireland had been received.

Lord Deputy Wandesford died on 3 December, and the immediate task of the committee of thirteen, which was formally received by the king on

[1] The catholic members of the committee were Nicholas Barnewall, Geoffrey Browne, Thomas Burke, Roebuck Lynch, Donough MacCarthy, Nicholas Plunkett, and John Walsh; the protestant members were William Cole, Simon Digby, Richard Fitzgerald, James Montgomery, Edward Rowley, and Hardress Waller.

[2] B.M., Eg. MS 1048.

11 December, was to make the most of the unexpected opportunity to break Strafford's control over Irish government. The appointment of the lord lieutenant's most formidable local supporters, Ormond and Dillon, was successfully prevented, and Charles compromised by naming two lords justices: Sir John Borlase, an elderly soldier whom Strafford had brought from England to become master of the ordnance, and Sir William Parsons, a former member of the earl of Cork's group, who had skilfully survived Strafford's rule and was both master of the court of wards and a member of the court of castle chamber.[1] The committee also improved their opportunity by persuading Charles to approve the revised subsidy order, but they soon became involved in a lengthy and profitless exchange of recriminations with the imprisoned Radcliffe, to whom the commons' petition had been referred for comment. To uphold the petition was a matter of common concern for the committee's members, but for different reasons. It had been conceived primarily as part of an elaborate plan to attack Strafford in the English parliament and its authenticity had to be sustained if the committee were adequately to perform its covert task of collusion with Strafford's opponents. But the committee's instructions were to deal with the king, and the petition contained, in the complaint 'that the subject is, in all the material parts thereof, denied the benefit of princely graces', a complete authorisation to pursue the redress of longstanding Old English grievances. The result was a division of purpose: the committee's New English members took an active part in the preparation of the case against Wentworth, while their Old English colleagues concentrated upon persuading the king to arrange for the enactment of the 'graces' and to agree to abandon the recent plantations.

These divisive tendencies were not in evidence in Ireland when parliament convened for its third session late in January 1641. In the lords, though Old English members were prominent, the opposition relied upon New English votes and Lord Lambert was especially active; in the commons, though the bulk of the opposition was Old English, New English representation upon important committees was disproportionately large and the most active member was Captain Audley Mervyn, a Tyrone planter who was related to Sir Piers Crosby on one side and to the Maguires of Fermanagh on the other. In both houses, though some attention was paid to exclusively local issues, the principal business of the session was to supply material for use against Strafford in England. At first, indeed, in the absence of news from England, parliament 'did but sit to adjourn',[2] and the commons confined itself to formulating demands for the acknowledgement of parliament's right to initiate legislation under Poynings' act. The return of Bellew and Cashell from England brought this desultory phase to an

[1] See above ch. VII, p. 230.

[2] Mary Hickson (ed.), *Ireland in the seventeenth century* (2 vols, London, 1884), ii, 341.

end, and a period of intensive and purposeful activity followed. A hurried inquiry was instituted into the administration of the tobacco monopoly, which was to form the substance of one article of Strafford's impeachment. A statement of grievances was compiled in the form of twenty-two 'queries' as to the legality of various administrative and judicial practices, which comprised a convenient checklist of the specific discretionary activities that had recently 'altered the face of government'. And these, although they were nominally addressed to 'the judges of the kingdom' for their comment—'not for any doubt or ambiguity that may be conceived or thought of . . . but for manifestation and declaration of a clear truth'[1]—were dispatched to England before they were submitted to the Irish judges, for they were designed to substantiate a considerable number of the charges which the managers of Strafford's trial proposed to bring against him. There remained, however, the basic weakness to be contended with in the production of such material for English use that 'all the grievances that they have voted is not to any purpose as long as the preamble of the act of subsidies remains of force';[2] and on 17 February the commons formally protested that the contents of that preamble were untrue and requested that it be revoked by act of parliament. On 23 February, after this protestation and the 'queries' had been favourably received by the lords, both were transmitted to England, together with information about the tobacco monopoly and instructions that the committee of thirteen should work for the fulfilment of the 'graces'. Four days later, in the face of impending prorogation, a commons committee containing a New English majority was instructed to initiate impeachment proceedings against four potential witnesses in Strafford's defence—Radcliffe, Bramhall, Lord Chancellor Bolton, and Lord Chief Justice Lowther.

In England, the preparation of the case against Strafford had posed intractable problems. Because no single act of treason could be imputed to him, with the doubtful exception of his alleged proposal to use the Irish army in England in the early summer of 1640, it was necessary to argue that a series of arbitrary actions, none of them treasonable in themselves, constituted cumulative proof of a general intention to subvert fundamental law and to usurp regal power. Because Strafford's chief service had been in Ireland, it was necessary to seek the main links in the chain of evidence there, and sixteen of the twenty-eight specific accusations designed to be construed together as treason related to his Irish administration. For the most part, because of the limitations imposed by prejudice and by the hope of making capital out of Strafford's army and his leniency towards catholicism, the Irish articles were based upon New English grievances, and the managers of the trial were inadequately equipped to verify the information supplied to them by such men as Cork, Ranelagh, Mountnorris, Clot-

[1] *Commons' jn., Ire.*, i (1796), pp 174–5.

[2] *Lords' jn., Ire.*, p. 155.

worthy, Crosby, and the members of the committee of thirteen. This was to prove seriously defective. In the first days, however, after the trial opened before the lords on 22 March, the prosecution's case went well. Strafford's initial reply to the charges made it clear that he did not intend to confine himself to the obvious defence, that most of his alleged offences were actions carried out in due legal form in the service of the king, but proposed to enter an indirect plea of good government, allowing what could be proved against him to appear as minor blemishes extenuated by an otherwise satisfactory administration. The production of the recent protestations in which both houses of the Irish parliament had lengthily censured his 'introducing of a new, unlawful, arbitrary and tyrannical government' proved a devastating rejoinder. But the managers were unable to retain their advantage; in the face of a virtuoso performance by Strafford, whose habitual mastery of detail and talent for lucid self-justification were perfectly suited to the occasion, the inadequacy of their preparations was plainly exposed. Some of the charges were simply misconceived, for example that which alleged that Strafford had described Ireland as a conquered nation, a sentiment much less offensive to the English lords than to the colonial Irish parliament; some of the charges were mishandled, as when the managers, accusing Strafford of equating acts of state with acts of parliament, neglected to establish the fundamental point that rejected acts of parliament had been converted into acts of state; some of the charges were ill-founded, like that alleging unlawful exactions by soldiers, which turned out to refer to the levying of the 'graces' contribution from a number of Munster towns which Cork had improperly exempted from payment; and a number of the charges, among them that which dealt with the treatment of catholicism and the new army, had to be withdrawn when the development of the trial revealed that Strafford might gain rather than lose by their presentation. Where the charges had substance, Strafford used his superior knowledge to confuse the issue or confound the prosecution, as in countering the charge that he had increased customs rates for his own profit, when he exploited his opponents' ignorance by simply denying responsibility for the revision of customs rates in 1632.

Though Strafford's government did not emerge with credit from the proceedings, it was obvious when the Irish articles concluded on 5 April that he had thrown so much doubt upon so many of them that there was no longer any possibility of demonstrating cumulative treason. In fact, his defence was doubly effective: it both exposed the tendentious nature of the charges against him and excited a respect which the ungenerous and vindictive attitude of the prosecution helped to turn into sympathy. The managers made a last bid to present his proposal to use the Irish army in England as an act of treason. When that failed for want of evidence, the English commons abandoned their pretence of justice and declared Strafford guilty of treason in a bill of attainder which passed its third reading on 21 April.

The Old English members of the committee of thirteen, and of the smaller, informally constituted committee of the Irish lords which had joined them, took only a minor part in the trial. Some appeared as witnesses in supporting roles, but an extensive use of catholic testimony was neither suitable to the political atmosphere nor necessary to the specific charges brought against Strafford. The real centre of Old English interest and activity was at court and with the assistance of Clanricard and the goodwill of such influential sympathisers as Lord Cottington dramatically successful private approaches were made to Charles, who formally agreed on 3 April 'to forgo and discharge our intended plantations',[1] to authorise the enactment of a statute of limitations, and to require the transmission from Ireland of bills incorporating the other 'graces'. This success was quickly followed by two further, predictable developments: the submission of specifically New English demands relating to the activities of the defective titles commission in Ulster, the Londonderry grievances, and the ecclesiastical abuses itemised in the commons petition of the previous June, and the presentation of comprehensive proposals for the reform of grievances which had arisen since the negotiation of the 'graces'—the dissolution of the high commission court, the voiding of the tobacco monopoly, restitution for those who had been wrongly evicted from church lands, and many other similarly obvious demands.

In Ireland, Strafford's peril and the king's concessions combined to reinforce the opposition's recent belligerence and to undermine the administration. 'Most of the councillors turn tail to us in many businesses',[2] observed Sir Adam Loftus, and the government prudently avoided practices condemned in the 'queries', conceded the opposition's interpretation of Poynings' law by transmitting the bills requested by Charles in the unsatisfactory form in which they had been prepared by the vacation committee of the commons, and tried to arrange a compromise that would allow Bolton and Lowther to carry on their official duties for the time being. But English political developments, though momentarily advantageous to the parliamentary opposition in Ireland, evoked dangerously distinctive responses within the divided community. A number of the Irish gentry, including some members of parliament, less than confident of the usefulness of parliamentary action, impressed by the success of the Scottish resort to force, and fearful of the militant protestantism which had become dominant in England and Scotland, were becoming increasingly convinced of the need to take arms and had already begun to explore the possibility of securing assistance from the Irish abroad. Among the Scots in the north, on the other hand, cross-channel events aroused hope, and a number of them entrusted to Clotworthy a petition in which they alleged that 'partly by the cruel severity and arbitrary proceedings of the civil magistrate, but princi-

[1] P.R.O., S.P. Ire., 63/258/82. [2] Ibid., 63/258/95.

pally through the unblest way of the prelacy with their faction, our souls are starved, our estates undone, our families impoverished, and many of us cut off and destroyed'.[1] Though the object of the petition was to present the English commons with grounds for the abolition of episcopacy and the chief target was the Church of Ireland, one of their criticisms of the bishops was 'their favouring popery, in this kingdom a double fault'; and the general intolerance of tone was calculated to confirm catholic fears of the dangerous tendency of English events. The undercurrents of tension were strong in Ireland in the early summer of 1641, but they were rarely reflected in parliament, where the momentum generated by the attack upon Strafford developed into a coherent assault upon the governmental system itself.

Strafford was beheaded on 12 May, 'as he well deserved' noted the implacable earl of Cork in his diary.[2] But the campaign against the viceroy had raised issues which his death could not solve, for the activities of the Irish parliament had begged the whole question of constitutional relationships in Ireland, and the new session which began on 11 May witnessed an increasingly well-defined struggle for control between the executive and the legislature. Charles would not concede that the Irish parliament could exercise the power of impeachment which would enable it to hold his ministers accountable unless it could be shown to have done so in the past: the judges were unable to see the 'clear truth' of the 'queries' in the same light as the commons, trespassing as they appeared to do upon the crown's prerogative powers; and the embattled government desperately needed to sustain Strafford's interpretation of Poynings' law if it were safely to ensure that no power claimed by parliament could be used without official cooperation. This resistance to parliamentary claims led to their systematisation into a programme of constitutional reform.[3] While the efforts of the committees in London to obtain redress of specific grievances were of undiminished importance, the fundamental need was to devise effectual means of holding the king to his word and keeping the Irish government in check, and the opposition, greatly strengthened by the return of Patrick Darcy in a by-election, devoted its principal energies to establishing the legislative initiative and judicial competence of parliament and the subordination of the executive to the law. The Irish government's hope of postponing a direct conflict over impeachment proved shortlived. As soon as the king's demand for evidence of precedent was announced, both houses busily cooperated in meeting the implicit, if unconscious, challenge to the assumptions upon which they acted. Elaborating into a systematic exposition the emotionally couched argument previously used to support the petition of remonstrance, they

[1] Reid, *Presb. ch. in Ire.*, i, 269.

[2] *Lismore papers*, 1st series, v, 176.

[3] Aidan Clarke, 'The policies of the Old English in parliament, 1640–41' in *Hist. Studies*, v, 85–102; 'The history of Poynings' law', loc. cit., pp 217–22.

claimed to share England's legal and constitutional inheritance, argued that the whole fabric of the Irish judicial system rested upon an acceptance of the validity of English precedent, and maintained that the powers and functions of the English parliament belonged as of right to the Irish parliament, which had always been the 'supreme judicature of the said realm'.[1] The issues raised by the 'queries' were closely related, for they depended for their successful resolution upon establishing a particular interpretation of the character of law in Ireland. The task of elucidating the views of the opposition was entrusted to Patrick Darcy, who rebutted the judges' answers to the 'queries' in a lengthy address to the lords early in June. His discussions of the separate points raised by each of the 'queries' cohered into an essay in the identification of the exact constituents of legal authority in Ireland, which he specified as the common law of England and the parliamentary statutes and lawful customs of Ireland. In reaching that conclusion, he firmly stripped the prerogative of its discretionary character and subordinated it to the law, excluded English parliamentary authority from Ireland, and attributed to the Irish parliament not only the power to make law but also 'the correction of all courts and ministers'.[2] Despite the historico-legal manner in which he treated his subject, the speech was actually programmatic in character, and the task of the opposition thereafter was to impose acceptance of Darcy's description of the rules by which government ought properly to be conducted.

The position, however, quickly settled into one of stalemate. The government yielded so far as to avoid using the men and the methods challenged by parliament and, as a result, the collection of customs revenue and tobacco duty was seriously impeded, the defective titles commission came to a standstill, the court of wards marked time, the ordinary courts did not sit, and the court of castle chamber became unwontedly circumspect. None the less, the government, relieved of its only pressing financial commitment by the disbandment of the new army in May, recovered confidence. 'I let them alone because I see no great danger',[3] reported Parsons, and the fact was that although the opposition made large claims for parliament, and defied both the king and the local administration by continuing the impeachment proceedings and adopting resolutions outlawing the practices complained of in the 'queries', it could do nothing decisive. The government, moreover, believed that time was on its side: the abandonment of the plantation in Connacht had already proved contentious and it seemed inconceivable that the dominant coalition, in which the catholic component was steadily increasing as a result of favourable by-election returns, could long contain

[1] *Commons' jn., Ire.*, i (1796), p. 213.

[2] Patrick Darcy, *An argument delivered . . . by the express order of the house of commons* (Waterford, 1643; Dublin, 1764).

[3] P.R.O., S.P. Ire., 63/259/33.

the disparity of interests of its members—'the endeavour of the one being to lessen the power of the government and hinder the growth of religion, the others desirous to uphold the power of the state necessary to their security and comfort'.[1] The analysis was valid—for while the New English might reasonably expect to win control of the government, the Old English could hope to do no more than limit its powers—but it proved premature. While gains remained possible, common action continued and on the level of specific grievances was attended with considerable success. On 16 July the further negotiations of the parliamentary committees in London culminated in a comprehensive series of concessions in which Charles agreed to the reduction of rates and fees, the regulation of extra-judicial conciliar proceedings and of the courts of wards and castle chamber, the suspension of the high commission court, the limitation of claims against intruders on church lands, the restoration of socage tenures in Ulster, the abolition of monopolies and the preparation of an act which would repeal the preamble to the subsidy act. Londonderry grievances were left to the consideration of the English parliament which already had them under consideration. Significantly, only one request met with an unqualified refusal: Charles was unwilling to modify Poynings' law procedures so as to allow the Irish parliament to initiate legislation.

By the end of July, the king's concessions had been converted into a set of instructions for dispatch to the Dublin government, the bills transmitted in the previous April had been processed in time to accompany them, and the London committees of the Irish parliament made ready to return home. When the news reached Ireland, the government acted quickly. The king had required compensation for revenue losses arising from his concessions in the form of two additional parliamentary subsidies, and the government, arguing that if these were not granted before concessionary legislation was passed they would not be granted at all, procured the adjournment of parliament until November.

The interaction with English and Scottish developments which had recently exercised so dominant an influence in Ireland entered a new phase in the summer of 1641. In England Charles had outwardly cooperated with parliament since Strafford's death and had acquiesced in measures which had significantly restricted his authority, but privately he sought the means of retrieving his position and came to believe that Scotland might provide them. Local divisions and, above all, the disenchantment of the covenanters with the English opposition's failure to embrace presbyterianism appeared to offer some prospect of turning the tables on parliament, and Charles made plans to travel north in August after the Scottish army had completed its withdrawal from England. At the same time, he thought in terms of making what use he could of Irish support. The secret intrigues which he instigated

[1] *Lismore papers*, 2nd series, iv, 208–9.

are the more difficult to reconstruct because they were not integral parts of a considered plan of action, but simply explorations of the possibilities from which such a plan might be improvised.[1] His sudden willingness to return the bills of grace to the Irish parliament and his generosity in meeting the demands of the London committees were designed to cultivate support, and his overtures were unwittingly timely; for the contrast between the Irish opposition's success in having grievances attended to and its failure to achieve constitutional change tended to emphasise the key position of the king in the Old English scheme of things and to remind them of the familiar reality, which had been obscured in the recent rush of events, that their position in Ireland had no more substantial basis than the royal pleasure. They must continue as before to look to the crown for protection from the avarice of protestants, for connivance at their unconcealed practice of catholicism, and for forbearance in pressing inherited claims upon their property. Their own preservation depended upon precisely those prerogative powers which the English parliament was seeking to appropriate and Charles to defend, and they were in consequence committed by circumstances to his cause. His own immediate concern, however, was with military capacity, and his undercover dealings in Ireland were principally directed towards preventing the disbanded soldiers of the new army from being dispersed and arranging for assured supporters to be ready to use them in his service if he had need of them. The accidental effect was to provide a vital stimulus to those who were already convinced of the need for armed action. The plot in which they had been fitfully engaged for some time received a new impetus and a new direction as the conspirators became aware of the king's activities, and they proceeded on the confident assumption that they were about the king's business. While the Dublin government cynically neglected the allegedly urgent need to prepare subsidy bills for November, a plan to take over the administration in October matured.

[1] The evidence is discussed in Clarke, *Old English*, pp 158–60, 227–8.

CHAPTER XI

The rising of 1641 and the catholic confederacy, 1641–5

PATRICK J. CORISH

At the end of Wentworth's administration there was almost universal discontent in Ireland. His hand had lain heavy on all groups and interests in the country, but in the nature of things the heaviest pressure had come on the catholics. By their religious profession they were marked out as 'only half subjects', as James I had earlier described them, and in consequence they were exposed to various discriminations, particularly when the executive power was strong. The Old English catholics as a body still retained their property, but they had received clear warning, especially from Wentworth's policy in Connacht, that they too might face confiscation.[1] Further fears had been raised by their steady exclusion from public office, which they had traditionally enjoyed. Yet the Old Irish, especially in Ulster, were subject to even greater pressures in the changing patterns of Irish society, and it was the leaders of this group who rose in arms on 23 October 1641.

They were not men who had lost all their property in the Ulster confiscations. Their fathers and uncles had served on the inquisition juries, and had emerged from the confiscation with properties that were in many cases still quite considerable, but though they had come to terms with the crown it was evident by the next generation that they were not able to come to terms with the new way of life imposed on Ulster. Studies of the unplanted county of Monaghan, where the Irish owned about 60 per cent of the land in 1610, indicate that they had mortgaged about half of this by 1641, for the most part to the new settlers, and that some of them were close to destitution.[2] The catholic landowners in the planted counties were in a similar position. The old Gaelic aristocracy, improvident and spendthrift, had not been able to adjust to a society where hereditary status was no longer impregnable.

It was only to be expected that in these circumstances hopes of undoing the plantation and all its consequences should have been cherished among

[1] See Clarke, *Old English*, ch. VI, especially p. 110.

[2] Pilib Ó Mórdha, 'The MacMahons of Monaghan (1603–1640)' in *Clogher Rec.*, ii, no. 1 (1957), pp 148–69; ii, no. 2 (1958), pp 311–27; Pádraig Ó Gallachair, 'The 1641 war in Clogher', ibid., iv, no. 3 (1962), pp 135–47.

the closely knit families of Gaelic Ulster. The hopes were strengthened by contacts with the Continent, through priests and soldiers, these latter for the most part in the Spanish service, where some of them developed their own version of the Spanish counter-reformation ideal. On a few occasions the hopes had strengthened into what might be almost called conspiracies. When they did at length mature into a conspiracy, it was led by Rory O'More. He was descended from a great midland family which had lost its hereditary lands, and what land he held in 1641 was almost exclusively in County Armagh. In February 1641 he met Conor, Lord Maguire, in Dublin, and proposed to him that the time was now ripe for a concerted rising to regain what they had lost. He claimed to have the support of many in Leinster and Connacht (he had family connections with many influential families of the Pale, his own wife being a Barnewall). Maguire, married to a Fleming of Slane, twenty-five years of age and deeply in debt, was ready to listen. Other Ulster leaders were contacted, notably Sir Phelim O'Neill, regarded in the province as 'chief of his name'. Since May 1640 he had been in direct contact with Owen Roe O'Neill in Flanders, and this outstanding military leader had undertaken to return to Ireland should a rising take place there.

At a further meeting of the conspirators in Dublin in May tentative plans were made for a rising in October. There were promises of support from some of the Old English families and from the Continent, but it had become evident that initially the main strength of the blow would have to come from Ulster. The administration had no suspicions, and was further encouraged by a successful adjournment of parliament until November on 7 August, even though many important issues were still pending. The Ulster plot, however, was not the only undercurrent at the time. In July Charles I, as one of a number of contingency plans to ensure that he should have an armed force at his disposal if he needed it against his parliament in England, ordered the earls of Ormond and Antrim to keep together the large part of Strafford's army not yet disbanded, and to recruit more soldiers. News of this came to the Ulster leaders through officers involved in both projects, from which they assured themselves that their plans were not in conflict with those of the king. The prospect of any such alliance, however, was quite unacceptable to Ormond, and it seems to have been at his instigation that the army officers concerned broke off their contacts with the Ulster leaders in September. At this time too Charles I had opened negotiations with the Scots.[1]

In spite of this and other difficulties, a meeting on 5 October definitely fixed 23 October as the date for a rising in Ulster. Simultaneously, Dublin castle was to be seized, thereby paralysing the administration, and securing the great quantity of arms known to be stored there. It was resolved not to

[1] See Clarke, *Old English*, p. 228.

'meddle with' the Ulster Scots, in the hope that this powerful group would not become involved, but within a few weeks they had, with a certain inevitability, been drawn into the conflict.[1] The evidence indicates that the Irish leaders had limited objectives—that they planned a tactical coup to strengthen a negotiating position.[2] Many groups in the three kingdoms were thinking in these terms in the autumn of 1641.

The attempt on Dublin castle was unsuccessful. Not all the promised contingents turned up, and in any case the plot was disclosed to the lords justices a few hours in advance by Owen O'Connolly. He had been told all the details by one of the conspirators, Hugh Óg MacMahon. O'Connolly was foster-brother to MacMahon, but he was also a servant of Sir John Clotworthy, was married to an Englishwoman, and was himself a protestant. Defences were hastily mustered from the few men available in Dublin. They were sufficient, however, to prevent the attack on the castle. Before morning two of the leaders, MacMahon and Lord Maguire, had been captured. The others escaped.

In Ulster, the rising took place as planned, and within two days much of the centre of the province, from Newry to Donegal and Cavan, was in Irish hands. On 24 October Sir Phelim O'Neill issued a proclamation from Dungannon, saying that they were not in arms against the king, but only in defence of their liberties, that they intended no injury to the king's subjects, that any injury done would be remedied, and that 'every person should make speedy repair unto their own houses under pain of death, and that no further hurt be done anyone under the like pain'.[3]

The situation, however, was already beyond stabilising. All over the north groups were spontaneously rising against the settlers, but once the initial surprise had passed walled towns and planter castles were generally held. The Erne forts were untaken, as were the forts along the Foyle and Finn, and the key city of Derry.

Subsequent research has added little of substance to Lecky's detailed and dispassionate analysis[4] of the charge that a wholesale massacre of protestants was planned as part of the rising. There was no such plan and no such massacre, but in the first months of the rising the insurgents committed many murders, often savagely. These murders were perpetrated because of lack of discipline, for private vengeance, or out of religious fanaticism. In most cases the leaders did their best to restrain the murderers, and there are many recorded instances where the catholic clergy intervened to save lives. In the territories held by the insurgents the protestant planters were turned out of their homes, and many of them died from hardship and exposure. How many in fact lost their lives can never be known precisely. Lecky surmises that in all perhaps 4,000 were murdered, possibly more, and that

[1] Lecky, *Ire.*, i, 49, with references.
[2] Clarke, *Old English*, pp 160–2.
[3] Ibid., p. 162.
[4] Lecky, *Ire.*, i, 46–89.

perhaps 8,000 refugees died from their privations. When they had recovered from the first shock the protestant forces carried out widespread retaliatory massacres of the catholics, and, in Lecky's verdict, 'it is far from clear on which side the balance of cruelty rests'.

Propaganda inflated the number of protestants killed, and it soon grew beyond all rational credibility. At this date, towards the end of the religious wars, men were ready to believe the worst; in 1644 a French traveller in Ireland, le Gouz, could accept the exaggerated numbers as in no way surprising.[1] The really vicious element in the propaganda was its motive. Both in London and in Dublin the figures were inflated in order to involve all the Irish catholics in a charge of having planned to murder all the protestants, and to use this charge as an excuse for confiscating the property of all the catholics.

On 23 October the lords justices in Dublin proclaimed a state of rebellion, which they described as 'a most disloyal and detestable conspiracy intended by some evil-affected Irish papists'. This wording could hardly reassure the catholic gentry of the Pale, who were protesting their loyalty and asking for arms to defend themselves, and the situation was not recovered when on 29 October it was amended to 'old mere Irish of the province of Ulster'. The lords justices also attempted a further prorogation of parliament, but under pressure allowed emergency sessions on 9 and 16 November, at which the catholics in attendance joined in a condemnation of the rebellion. Parliament was then prorogued until 11 January.

Catholic propaganda has accused the lords justices of deliberately attempting to extend the rising in order to have a pretext for further confiscations. Firm evidence for their motives is scanty, but their initial reaction may be explained in large measure by their state of panic and indecision. Borlase was old and tired, and much of the initiative lay with Parsons. In his case, it would seem difficult to exclude a willingness to see more catholics drawn into the rebellion, at least after the first panic had passed.

On 1 November the rising was debated in the English parliament, which voted money to send troops to Ireland. On 10 November the king appointed Ormond commander of the army, and he began to enlist men, especially from among the refugees in Dublin. A corps raised by Sir Henry Tichborne from this source had already been sent to strengthen the garrison of Drogheda on 4 November.

Meanwhile, the Ulster insurgents faced divided counsels, a lack of trained men, a lack of arms, and clear indications that the Scots would prove hostile. More by accident than design, it would appear, they turned south, captured Dundalk on 31 October, Ardee a few days later, and advanced to besiege Drogheda, though they lacked both the discipline and the equipment to invest it properly. On 4 November Sir Phelim O'Neill and Rory Maguire

[1] Cf. MacLysaght, *Ir. life after Cromwell* (2nd ed.), p. 63.

(who had taken his brother Lord Maguire's place in Ulster after the latter's capture) issued a proclamation, purporting to come from Charles I, and sealed with the great seal of Scotland, authorising them to take arms in his defence. The arguments of historians that it was a forgery[1] must be regarded as convincing, but at the time it certainly could have borne the appearance of truth.

The defeat of a force sent from Dublin to relieve Drogheda at Julianstown on 29 November, which provided the insurgents with a large quantity of captured arms, was even more decisive in psychological effect. It was followed by meetings at Knockcrofty and Tara between the Ulster leaders and representatives of the gentry of the Pale. Now finding themselves threatened by the northern army, with all kinds of stirrings within the Pale itself, and convinced of the hostility of the government, they offered to make common cause with the insurgent leaders on being assured of their loyalty to the king. 'And so', wrote Richard Bellings, who was probably present, 'distrust, aversion, force and fear united the two parties which since the conquest had always been most opposite'.[2] The Old English had joined the Old Irish in what they believed to be an essentially moderate and, for the times, constitutional movement; at the same time this momentous union of Irish catholics had been achieved less by common interests than by protestant pressure.

The agreement brought little access of military strength. On 27 October the lords justices had sent commissions to raise troops to Ulster,[3] where the Scots, many of them veterans of the continental wars, proved far superior to their untrained opponents. The west was terrorised by their Laggan corps, and in the east they defeated the Irish at Lisburn and thereafter went over to the offensive. On 15 April 1642 General Robert Monro arrived at Carrickfergus with an advance party of 2,500 men from Scotland, and on 1 May he captured Newry. Meanwhile the siege of Drogheda had been raised on 5 March, and before the end of the month Ardee and Dundalk had been retaken. After a succession of defeats for the Irish in west Ulster the Scots were by the end of June in a position to link forces. The Ulster leaders, fearing that all was lost, at a meeting in mid-July had already decided that they should flee the country, each man shifting for himself, when a messenger arrived bearing a letter from Owen Roe O'Neill with the news that he had landed with arms and men at Doe castle in Donegal in July, and that further help was on its way from Flanders to Wexford.[4]

By the summer of 1642 the revolt had spread to all Ireland and was having

[1] Summarised in Clarke, *Old English*, pp 165–8.

[2] Gilbert, *Ir. confed.*, i, 38.

[3] *L. & P. Ir. reb., 1642–6*, p. 16.

[4] Gilbert, *Contemp. hist., 1641–52*, iii, 38; *Comment. Rinucc.*, i, 331–2. For the date of O'Neill's landing see J. I. Casway, 'Owen Roe O'Neill's return to Ireland in 1642: the diplomatic background' in *Studia Hib.*, ix (1969), p. 60.

repercussions in Europe. The first reaction of the lords justices to the defection of the gentry of the Pale had been to summon them to Dublin to account for their conduct.[1] Their natural reaction was to refuse to go unless assured of their personal safety. What paper assurances they received were more than offset by the effects of the punitive expeditions from Dublin, notably the burning of Clontarf by Sir Charles Coote, and by their growing realisation that they were being summoned to Dublin, not for explanations or conferences, but simply to throw themselves on the king's mercy, in effect to put themselves into the hands of whoever was in control of the city—and they had reason to fear that effective control might in fact lie with men like Coote rather than with the lords justices, whom they had little reason to trust in any case. Their final reply to the summons was given on 19 December. They chose to maintain the position they had taken up at Knockcrofty and Tara. Though some, including the catholic bishop of Meath, Thomas Dease, had refused to join them, they began to organise an 'army of the Pale', of which Lord Gormanston was appointed commander-in-chief on 9 January 1642.

It has already been noted that even before the Knockcrofty meeting there had been popular disturbances within the Pale itself. These had occurred all over Leinster, especially among the Old Irish in the planted areas. The decisions taken at Knockcrofty had made it easier for the Old English to take arms also. By 21 December Wexford had defected. Before the end of the month Kilkenny town and county had developed the rudiments of a military organisation under the command of Ormond's grand-uncle, Lord Mountgarrett. His forces were soon assisting the movement in Munster. Here the revolt had been sparked off by the heavy-handed reactions of the lord president, Sir William St Leger. He had been nervously watching, among other things, an army raised for the Spanish service by Colonel Garrett Barry. This was quartered near Kinsale and was unwilling to disperse. St Leger led his own army into Tipperary to deal with a minor disturbance there, and his severe and indiscriminate vengeance culminated in a rejection of a protest of loyalty from the Tipperary gentry. They were all rebels, he said, and he would hang the best of them. Before long the combined Kilkenny and Tipperary forces had penetrated into Cork. Though Mountgarrett and St Leger reached an agreement based partly on mutual interests and partly on the fact that the further Mountgarrett advanced from Kilkenny the more difficult he found it to assert his authority, the insurgents in Cork found a new leader when Sir Donogh MacCarthy, Viscount Muskerry, joined them at the end of February on being assured of their loyalty to the king, after which it was agreed that Colonel Barry should command the Munster forces. By this time County Kerry was in general revolt, and by mid-April the towns of Waterford and Limerick had admitted Irish garri-

[1] The following account is based mainly on Clarke, *Old English*, pp 171–92.

sons. In Munster the government held only Cork, Tralee, Kinsale, Youghal, Bandon, and a few isolated fortresses. These, however, included Bunratty and Duncannon, which commanded the sea-approaches to Limerick and Waterford respectively.

Disorders had spread rapidly in north Connacht. In the southern portion of the province, and especially in the town and county of Galway, an important factor was the authority of the earl of Clanricard. His effective power was greater than that of the president of Connacht, Lord Ranelagh, or of the military governor of Galway, Sir Francis Willoughby, and he was determined to keep his province peaceful. In this he was not helped by the attitude of the Dublin government and the commander of Galway, whose disputes with the citizens were an important factor in the town's final decision to join the revolt, taken, however, only on 6 August 1643.

The difficulties of Clanricard's position appear from his reply to an approach made to him by Lord Gormanston about the end of January 1642. Clanricard sent his chaplain, Oliver Burke, O.P., as his personal envoy to the Pale. By the beginning of March, Burke had contacted the remaining neutrals there, and through them the leaders in arms. He produced three documents for their consideration.[1] One was an address of loyalty and another a series of demands and propositions to the king. Clanricard undertook to transmit these to Charles I, and as one of the principal grievances of the gentry of the Pale was that they had been denied access to the king Clanricard's offer must be taken as an indication of his wish to damp down the disturbances. The third document, however, was an outline plan for a provisional civil government in the areas controlled by the insurgents, and it would seem to indicate that Clanricard was at least leaving open the question of an approach to the king independently of the lords justices and council in Dublin.

There can be little doubt that at this time the Old English of the Pale would have negotiated through the government in Dublin if that had been possible. By the end of March 1642 the Dublin forces had driven the Old Irish out of the Pale, while at the same time knowledge was spreading of a proclamation signed by Charles I on 1 January and received in Dublin on 26 February, which called on all in arms in Ireland to surrender. Some of the Old English did make their way to Dublin, where they were imprisoned, and numbers of them, including the sixty-six-year-old Patrick Barnewall, were tortured. At this stage of events the desire of the government for simple vengeance and widespread confiscation can hardly be questioned. The adventurers' bill, passed by the two houses by mid-March, made it even clearer that the real enemy of the insurgents was the parliamentary faction. This made them even more determined to assert their loyalty to the king, but, since the king had on 19 March assented to this confiscatory legislation,

[1] Gilbert, *Ir. confed.*, i, 275–6.

it also forced them to face constitutional issues that could not be solved by a simple assertion of loyalty.

The military fortunes of the insurgents in Leinster deteriorated during April, though they stabilised in a situation closer to the Munster stalemate than to the threatened disaster in Ulster. The raids from Dublin penetrated more deeply, led by Coote in north Leinster and by Ormond further south. On 15 April Ormond defeated a rather disorganised insurgent army at Kilrush in County Kildare. Both Coote and Ormond, however, were hampered by supply problems at their base in Dublin, and were unable to develop their successful raids into a decisive victory.

In seeking to return to Ireland, Owen Roe O'Neill, a distinguished soldier in the Spanish army, found difficulty not only in getting material support from Spain but even in quitting the service.[1] France too was slow to give material support. The two countries were now at war, and neither wished to alienate England. The papacy was also approached. The first response was cautious, and in any case its material resources were meagre in comparison with those of France or Spain. Yet it was papal diplomatic pressure that induced the Spanish governor of the Low Countries to adopt the policy of doing nothing which eventually made it possible for O'Neill to slip away to Ireland with some officers and munitions. On 29 August 1642 an assembly at Clones accepted him as general of the Ulster army, and he began the work of organising a disciplined fighting force, though he was obviously even more dismayed by the quality of the human material than by the great shortage of equipment.

Thomas Preston, Gormanston's uncle, followed O'Neill from Flanders to Ireland in September, together with John Burke, a relative of Clanricard. Both landed in Wexford. Preston became general of the Leinster army, while Burke was accepted as military leader in Connacht, but without prejudice to the position of Clanricard, should he join the revolt. As Garrett Barry in Munster had also had considerable experience in the Spanish army each province now had a professional military commander.

These men were veteran soldiers. O'Neill and Preston had entered the Spanish service about 1605. O'Neill was now about sixty, Preston a few years younger. Both of them, O'Neill especially, had over the years assimilated Spanish views on the religious nature of the European conflict as well as learning the art of war. The same may be presumed to have been true of many of the other officers who returned with them. These continental soldiers, then, brought with them to Ireland more than their military skills. They brought a religious outlook less compromising than that of their kinsfolk who had spent the preceding generations in Ireland and who were in consequence more attuned to compromise.

Irish catholic clergy, notably the Waterford Franciscan, Luke Wadding,

[1] J. I. Casway, loc. cit., pp. 48–64.

had been prominent in the diplomatic efforts leading to the return of the soldiers. The clergy had also, of course, played a part in the outbreak in Ireland itself, and as the religious issue was so central to Irish grievances, and was destined to become even more so, their attitude was an important factor in shaping events.[1]

It would be misleading, however, to speak simply of 'the catholic clergy'. They had much in common, notably their formation in the continental seminaries, for the most part in the Spanish dominions.[2] This formation had given them a dedicated sense of mission and a very explicitly formulated sense of allegiance to the holy see. By their calling and education they were naturally inclined to emphasise the religious issue, but their work in Ireland had habituated them also to the possibilities of practical compromise in regard to the mission of the church, and when practical compromise had to be faced in the following years the clergy were divided as well as the laity, and in both groups the divisions often followed strikingly similar lines, though a basic tension remained. Among the laity, the lawyers emerged as the dominant influence in debate. They had been educated in the common law at the English inns of court, and in consequence any suggestion of two jurisdictions within the country was highly suspect to them. The clergy, on the other hand, had been educated on the Continent at a time when Roman canon law was developing rapidly, and they were therefore very conscious of papal authority.

By the spring of 1642 the insurrection was widespread, but the insurgents were beginning to have the first serious setbacks. The need for some kind of reorganisation was apparent. It was perhaps natural that the initiative should be taken by the catholic clergy, partly because the interests of religion were so deeply involved, but also because the church had a nation-wide organisation already in existence. On 22 March the bishops and vicars of the ecclesiastical province of Armagh met at Kells.[3] They declared that the war was a just one, waged against the puritans, 'who have always, but especially in recent years, plotted the destruction of the catholics, the destruction of the Irish, and the abolition of the king's prerogatives'. Catholics who supported the puritans (that is, the government in Dublin), and in effect catholics who did not join in the war, were declared excommunicated. All ecclesiastics were ordered to contribute towards the needs of the army, and all lay catholics in arms were assured that they would not be disturbed in the possession of any ecclesiastical property they held. A number of further decisions reflect an anxiety to control the disorders that had everywhere followed the rising. The most important of these was not a firm decision, which the ecclesiastics at

[1] I have discussed the position of the catholic clergy rather more fully in 'The origins of catholic nationalism' in Corish, *Ir. catholicism*, iii, ch. VIII (Dublin, 1968), pp 26–31.

[2] See below, ch. XXIII.

[3] *Comment. Rinucc.*, i, 314–19.

Kells were in no position to take, but a strongly expressed desire that a council of clergy and laity should be set up immediately as a central authority.

The deliberations at Kells could only indicate a solution of the problems of organisation, and any decisions taken there had binding force only in the province of Ulster. The necessary nation-wide authority was established by meetings of the clergy and laity in Kilkenny in May and June. This town was to remain the headquarters of the authority for nearly seven years. It was the most considerable centre now in the hands of the insurgents, and the capital of the territory of the Butlers, of whom Lord Mountgarrett, Ormond's grand-uncle, was possibly the most influential catholic nobleman now in arms. The initiative again came from the clergy, and the first meeting, held from 10 to 13 May, began as an exclusively ecclesiastical gathering. Once again they declared that the war was just, and that all catholics who did not take part in it were automatically excommunicated. A number of decisions, more explicit and far-reaching than those taken at Kells, attempted to remedy the disorders in the country. They stressed especially that there should be an end to provincial rivalries, and specifically that there should be 'no distinction whatsoever' between Old Irish and Old English. It was further decided that an oath of association should be drawn up, and that a general council and four provincial councils should be established.

At the invitation of the clergy a number of the lay leaders joined them in Kilkenny. Most of them were from Leinster and Munster, though the statement of Richard Bellings that they were 'casually met' must be regarded as a later attempt to minimise the clerical initiative, and the lay and clerical group that met in Kilkenny on 7 June certainly regarded itself as competent to take decisions on behalf of all the insurgents.

The proposed oath of association was drawn up in the following terms:

I, A.B., do promise, swear and protest before God, and his saints and angels, during my life to bear true faith and allegiance to my sovereign lord Charles by the grace of God, king of Great Britain, France and Ireland, and to his heirs and lawful successors; and that I will to my power, during life, defend, uphold, and maintain all his and their just prerogatives, estates and rights, the power and privilege of the parliament of this realm, the fundamental laws of Ireland, the free exercise of the Roman Catholic faith and religion throughout this land, and the lives, just liberties, estates and rights of all those that have taken, or shall take this oath, and perform the contents thereof; and that I will obey and ratify all the orders and decrees made, or to be made, by the supreme council of the confederate catholics of this kingdom, concerning the public cause, and that I will not seek, or receive, directly or indirectly, any pardon or protection, for any act done, or to be done touching this general cause, without the consent of the major part of the said council; and that I will not, directly or indirectly, do any act or acts that shall prejudice the said cause, but will, to the hazard of my life and estate, assist and prosecute and maintain the same. So help me God and his holy gospel.[1]

[1] *The memoirs and letters of Ulick, marquiss of Clanricarde* (London, 1757), p. 325. An additional

This oath established the 'confederate catholics of Ireland'. They were not a confederation in the sense to which the word later came to be restricted, that is, an alliance of states or politically organised groups. Though subsequent developments and the debates they gave rise to might give the impression that what happened in Kilkenny in 1642 was a confederation or alliance between two parties, the Old Irish and the Old English, what really happened was that a number of the king's subjects came together as individuals and bound themselves by oath to work together to redress certain grievances, as the Scottish covenanters had done in 1638. In Ireland, as in Scotland, the confederation had a religious basis, because it was as catholics that the Irish had been subjected to various religious and political disabilities.[1]

It remained to give this confederation the necessary political and military structures. A provisional executive council was set up, presided over by Lord Mountgarrett, and consisting of twelve members, to direct affairs until a representative assembly of the confederate catholics could be convened. Plans were made for the election of the assembly on the basis of the existing parliamentary machinery, by 'letters in the form of writs' sent from the council 'to all the lords spiritual and temporal, and all the counties, cities and corporate towns that had the right to send knights and burgesses to parliament'.[2]

Before the assembly met at the end of October 1642 the tensions between king and parliament in England had erupted into civil war on 22 August. The outbreak of the war naturally sharpened the existing divisions among the king's Irish executive in Dublin, but at Kilkenny it helped to clarify the issues and unite the confederate catholics. The activities of the provisional council at least spread the idea of a central directive authority, even though it had to act with caution and circumspection. Perhaps even more important was the landing of the officers from the Continent, for it began to give some direction to military affairs, though this in turn presented the assembly when it met with a provincial military organisation already in existence, to the exclusion of a unified command.

The assembly met on 24 October in the house of Robert Shee in Kilkenny. It resembled a parliament in many ways, though it represented the Irish catholics only, and the title of parliament had to be avoided. Indeed the first act of the assembly was to repudiate this title explicitly, for by their oath of association the confederate catholics had undertaken to defend the king's rights, and it was part of the royal prerogative to summon parliament. The

clause, swearing to repudiate any peace not approved by the general assembly, was added by the first assembly of 1647: see below, pp 322–3; Gilbert, *Ir. confed.*, ii, 210–11; *Comment. Rinucc.*, ii, 511–13.

[1] J. C. Beckett, 'The confederation of Kilkenny reviewed' in *Hist. Studies*, ii, 29–41.

[2] Gilbert, *Ir. confed.*, i, 87. The clergy were to sit as convocation while the assembly was in session.

catholics' genuine loyalty was further strengthened by considerations of self-interest. They were well aware that what toleration they had enjoyed in recent years had been because the laws against them had been suspended by the exercise of the royal prerogative. Though pressure of events was already driving them to seek for more than toleration of this kind, the assembly at Kilkenny contained too many experienced politicians to miss the point that by emphasising this aspect of the royal prerogative they were pointing the contrast between their own attitude and that of the rebellious parliament in England, were at least by implication denying the right of the English parliament to legislate for Ireland, and affirming that the only authority competent so to legislate was the king and his Irish parliament.

The independence of the Irish parliament had been a chief point of debate in the last parliamentary session of 1641. It might be noted that Patrick Darcy's *Argument*, presented in these debates in June 1641, was first printed in Waterford in 1643 by the 'printer to the confederate catholics of Ireland'. Darcy had maintained that the king's prerogative lay in upholding the law, 'to defend the people's liberty', not in altering it: the making of law was the prerogative of king, lords and commons in parliament. Ireland, because it was 'annexed to the crown of England', was governed by the laws of England, but only after they had been 'received and enacted in parliament in this kingdom'. The question had been given a new urgency by the English parliament's act of adventurers in March 1642, proposing to pay for the reconquest of Ireland from the proceeds of confiscated Irish land. So, although the confederate assembly repudiated the title of parliament, and emphasised the confederates' unqualified loyalty to the king, the scheme of provisional government adopted advanced claims uncomfortably similar to those the king had determined to oppose by force of arms in England. The scheme had been formulated by the same group of catholic lawyers, led by Patrick Darcy, who had been the spokesman for the catholic alliance with the Ulster protestants in Strafford's last parliament. The ideas that had taken shape in this earlier conflict led them, at Kilkenny, to emphasise that the representative 'parliamentary' assembly was the supreme authority of the confederate catholics, from which the executive, or supreme council, derived its mandate.

The parallel with the claims of parliament in England is obvious, but it is not complete. The Kilkenny assembly was not a parliament, nor could the executive authority required to run confederate affairs claim to derive its authority from the king, even if it wished to do so. In the climate of current political debate this executive almost inevitably had to be regarded as deriving its mandate from the representative assembly. It would be a mistake to regard Darcy and his fellow lawyers as enunciating a doctrine of executive responsibility to the legislature. The indications that there was any coherent scheme of abstract thought behind their actions are scant indeed, and the background must be seen in the traditions of the common law rather than in anything that might be regarded as a political philosophy. There are no indications of any protest when by a natural development the supreme council, a small body permanently in session, inevitably came to exercise an authority wider than its mandate, though it always did remain conscious of an obligation to justify its actions to the assembly.

The scheme of provisional government was essentially unitary, even to the extent of requiring lords and commons to debate and vote together, the lords being merely allowed to take counsel separately on individual issues, should they wish to do so. This unicameral system seems to have been designed to limit the influence of the catholic bishops, who sat as the lords spiritual. In a number of matters, however, allowance had to be made for the fact of divergent interests. These had already shown signs of taking shape on provincial lines. Though provision was made for councils at provincial and county level, there is little evidence to show how the provincial councils functioned, and almost none at all for the county councils. Separate military commands for the four provinces were also approved, with a central reserve to support each as needed. The pattern of four commands had in fact taken shape before the assembly met, and it was only good sense to adopt it in a war where each province had its own enemy and there was nothing like a front line.

In laying down the fundamental constitutional position of the confederate catholics it was stated:

> that the Roman Catholic church in Ireland shall and may have and enjoy the privileges and immunities according to the great charter, made and declared within the realm of England, in the ninth year of King Henry III, sometime king of England, and afterwards enacted and confirmed within this realm of Ireland. And that the common law of England, and all the statutes of force in this kingdom, which are not against the Roman Catholic religion, or the liberties of the natives, and other liberties of this kingdom, shall be observed throughout the whole kingdom, and that all proceedings in civil and criminal cases shall be according to the same laws.[1]

In one important respect the position here adopted is quite unambiguously unitary. In accepting English law for the whole of Ireland, even with the qualifications that (*a*) it was to be that law as received in Ireland and (*b*) in so far as it was not against the catholic religion, the Kilkenny assembly may be said to have endorsed the work of Sir John Davies in the reign of James I.[2] The qualifications, of course, raised very great issues. As regards the catholic church, it became clear that the issues were practical as well as constitutional when it was decided that the question of land-ownership was to be regarded as stabilised as it had existed on 1 October 1641. More specifically, catholic

[1] Gilbert, *Ir. confed.*, ii, 74.

[2] See above, ch. VII, pp 187–8.

owners of confiscated ecclesiastical property were confirmed in possession, provided that they joined the confederates, until the matter could be decided in parliament. While no other decision was in practice possible, it inevitably raised doubts as to how far the church was in fact to be restored. It also seemed to exclude the possibility of a review of other earlier confiscations, whose victims had little hope of restoration under English law.

Finally, a petition was drawn up to be forwarded to the king. In language clumsy from obsequiousness—'with hearts bent lower than our knees'—the confederates protested their loyalty, declared that they had banded together against the king's puritan enemies, and that their fixed and immovable purpose was to be ruled only by the common laws of England and the statutes enacted by parliament in Ireland. They asked the king—speaking in carefully vaguer terms than they had used in drawing up their own constitution—to be left free in the profession of their faith and given security for their estates and liberties: 'that hereafter your majesty will make no distinction between us and the rest of the nations subject to your empire . . . which granted, we will convert our forces upon any design your majesty may appoint'.[1]

As expressed to the king, the issues were not new, but, as the last words quoted above indicate, the time to negotiate them now seemed more propitious. The intractable problems remained, however, and were to be wrangled over for the next six years. Inevitably, most studies of the period have concentrated on these negotiations and the great constitutional issues they involved. The military history has been fairly well studied, and in any case is not of equal importance, for the confederates soon agreed on a truce with the royalist forces in Ireland. There has been one notable, though unpublished, study of the organisation and personnel of the confederation.[2] Much remains unknown concerning many points of practical administration, on the business of government, the administration of justice, the collection of taxes, and the supply of provisions and munitions to the army. On this last point alone, perhaps, more information may ultimately be extracted from the surviving records, but the administrative records of the confederation, which fell into Cromwell's hands when he captured Kilkenny in March 1650, were for the most part destroyed in a fire in the Surveyor General's Office in 1711, and what survived was lost in 1922. Most of the administrative detail they presumably contained must be regarded as having been lost with them.

The confederate catholics had at least found a basis for unity and had equipped themselves with a central government and administration in Kilkenny, even though the unity proclaimed only concealed for the moment

[1] Carte, *Ormonde*, v, 368–70.

[2] D. F. Cregan, 'The confederation of Kilkenny: its organisation, personnel and history' (Ph.D. thesis, N.U.I., 1947). I am deeply obliged to Dr Cregan for putting this work at my disposal.

the real differences between the various catholic interests; and the administrative system was better suited to a peacefully established government than to one that in every sense of the word had to fight for its existence. In contrast, however, the New English and protestant interest was deeply divided. Geographically, they held isolated outposts in the four provinces, and everywhere they were divided among themselves on the issues now driving king and parliament to civil war in England.

The English parliament had sent troops to Dublin at the end of 1641. Following on the adventurers' act[1] an expedition was fitted out under the command of Lord Forbes. It arrived in Kinsale from Dover in July 1642, and after a campaign of terror in the south-west went on by sea to Galway. Here again the lands surrounding the city were devastated, but Galway itself refused to yield, and the parliamentary forces reembarked for England on 26 September. In military terms, their campaign had decided nothing, but the fierceness with which it had been conducted had increased the bitterness of the catholics and beyond question helped the confederate cause in Galway.

The greatest concentration of protestants, refugees, and others, was at Dublin, the seat of parliament and government. While they were divided in their loyalties in the English conflict between parliament and king, they were, understandably, bitterly hostile to the Irish catholics. On 22 June 1642 forty-one catholic members of parliament were formally expelled on the ground that they were in rebellion. There were further proposals that they should be attainted, and that the full rigour of English anti-catholic legislation should be immediately introduced in Ireland, even if this entailed by-passing Poynings' law. However, these projects had come to nothing when parliament was adjourned on 16 August, to reconvene on 10 November.

The Irish parliament, then, was not in session when the civil war broke out in England, and it had not yet met when at the end of October a committee from the English parliament arrived in Dublin, where they found that a strong party in the council was prepared to support them. By the initiative of Parsons, they were from 2 November allowed to sit at council meetings, on the advice of the lord chancellor, Richard Bolton. Ostensibly, they had come to Dublin to settle army affairs, and specifically to induce the officers to accept land-debentures instead of pay. They were soon involved in political efforts to win Dublin for the parliamentary cause, and to win the army from its royalist commander, Ormond. On 13 November one of their preachers, Stephen Jerome, delivered a political sermon in Christ Church, and soon others were 'venting parliamentary politics from the pulpits in Dublin'. When parliament reassembled on 10 November its royalist members, led by Ormond and the bishops of the established church, opposed themselves to the lords justices' patronage of the parliamentary faction. After an indecisive

[1] See above, pp 295, 300.

and ineffective session, parliament was prorogued on 14 December until 20 April 1643.

An important factor restraining the Dublin parliamentarians was the success of the king's cause in the early stages of the civil war in England. The battle of Edgehill on 23 October was not very decisive militarily, but it did leave the king in a position to threaten London, and this threat remained until after the battle at Newbury on 20 September 1643. In the struggle for the command of the Dublin army neither the lords justices nor the representatives of the English parliament had anything tangible to offer, and by the end of 1642 it was fairly clear that the officers would continue loyal to Ormond and Charles I.

A royal command dated 3 February 1643 ordered the lords justices to expel the English parliamentarians from the Irish council. Parsons had little option but to obey, and they left Dublin by sea for Ulster. Here they had somewhat more success with the royalist forces, but they returned to England without getting any clear commitment. An earlier royal commission, dated 11 January 1643, was an even more striking indication that Charles was coming to realise that he could not hope to control Irish affairs through Parsons. It was addressed, not to the lords justices, but to Ormond, Clanricard, and five others, and authorised them to meet the Irish catholics and hear their grievances. As has been seen, the first confederate assembly had sent a petition to the king at the end of November, but the king's letter of 11 January seems to have been in reply to an earlier petition from the provisional supreme council sent in the previous July. The lords justices had objected to its being transmitted to England, and its progress to the king had been slow. However, when the king's commission arrived in Dublin on 30 January they and their supporters in the council were not in a position to oppose it, though the prospect of talks with the confederate catholics was highly displeasing to Irish protestants generally.

The terms of the king's commission did not in fact promise very much to the catholics. He had appointed commissioners to hear their grievances, he said, because he would not admit rebels to his presence, and his immediate aim seems to have been some agreement won as cheaply as possible which would release Ormond's Dublin army for his service in England.[1] On one point, that statutes made in the English parliament should not bind in Ireland, he showed some sympathy with the catholic demands, but otherwise he did not seem prepared to make any real concessions. He said that he could not agree to a repeal of the penal laws against the catholic religion, but only gave an assurance that they would continue to be mildly executed, so that catholics could continue to practise their religion privately by connivance. He would not consider the repeal of Poynings' law nor in any way countenance an independent parliament, nor would he accept any limitation

[1] Gilbert, *Ir. confed.*, ii, 140–43.

of the royal prerogative in nominating to public office, nor agree to any inquiries into land-titles that should go back before the beginning of his reign.

On 3 February Ormond and his fellow commissioners established contact with the confederate catholics. More precisely, they addressed themselves to a group of ten individuals from among them, and invited them to send representatives to a meeting in Drogheda on 23 February. The representatives were to be not more than thirty in number, and were to be laymen. Their mission would be covered by a safe-conduct from the lords justices.

It was clear that Ormond and his group were drawing a distinction between the Old English, who might be negotiated with, and the clergy and the Old Irish, who might not. But even if the terms they had to offer had been more attractive, any such distinction was unacceptable to the first supreme council of the confederates, where the catholic bishops and the Old Irish were well represented. The reply from Kilkenny was not enthusiastic. The confederates asked for a safer meeting-place than Drogheda, and insisted that they choose their delegates without preconditions. They took particular exception to a phrase which, they said, meant that they would have 'to come in the repute of rebels' to set down their grievances. Their first two points were met. On the third, it was made known to them that the offending phrase was taken directly from the king's commission, and a copy of this was sent to them. On 25 February the supreme council named delegates for a meeting in Trim on 17 March.

Meanwhile, the council in Dublin had been planning a major military effort to capture New Ross and Wexford. There was reason to suspect that their motives were not altogether military, though Dublin, and especially the army there, had been helping to keep itself provisioned by means of such forays, and Wexford was important because it was through this port that the confederates received most of their supplies from the Continent. On the other hand, an expedition strong enough to reduce it presented a great military risk, for it would entail so denuding Dublin of troops that the capital might fall to a confederate attack. The proposal that the expedition be commanded by Lord Lisle gave reason to fear that this was another attempt to detach the army from Ormond. Lisle was the son of the absentee lord lieutenant, the earl of Leicester. Both inclined to support the English parliament. Finally, a large-scale, and conceivably decisive, military venture at this time could be expected to prejudice gravely the conference arranged for Trim.

Ormond could not afford to allow Lisle to command the expedition, so on 1 March he himself led the army out of Dublin. Its strength was insufficient, however, and he had to raise the siege of New Ross and set out to return to Dublin (18 March). A few miles north of the town he had to fight his way through the narrow glen of Poulmounty, where he was challenged by the Leinster army under Preston. The first major military effort by Preston did him little credit, but on the other hand the only thing achieved by Ormond was to get his forces back to Dublin without severe losses. He had gained no military advantage, and his army was not even better provisioned than before.

While Ormond was besieging New Ross the meeting had taken place at Trim as arranged, four delegates from each side being present. The confederate catholics had stated their grievances.[1] They complained that the party now in arms against the king in England had openly plotted their extermination. They asked for a repeal of the penal laws, so that catholics could take their full part in public life, thereby controlling the new upstarts who had been admitted to office and who had used their authority to rob the catholics. They accused Parsons by name of continuing Strafford's policy of confiscation, and asked that he be dismissed. They asked that no English statute should bind in Ireland. Here to some extent they were on common ground with the king, and the act of adventurers was constitutionally unprecedented. Finally, they asked for redress of their grievances in a free parliament, that is, a parliament representative of the men of estate in the kingdom, and with Poynings' law suspended while it was in session.

The two sides were clearly very far apart. However, the king was already moving towards the dismissal of Parsons. From the beginning of the civil war he had continued to correspond with parliament as well as with the king, and his personal inclination was to the parliament. A royal commission dated 3 April dismissed him from the office of lord justice and appointed Sir Henry Tichborne in his place. In practice, moreover, the king was acting more and more through Ormond. A further commission of 23 April ordered Ormond to seek a truce for one year with the king's 'Roman Catholic subjects in arms'. Ormond now had firm control of the army, and the lords justices had had difficulties with parliament (one of Parsons's last acts was to prorogue it in very contentious circumstances just after it had reassembled on 20 April). Ormond's hand was further strengthened when in July, by royal command, Parsons and his principal supporters, Loftus, Meredith, and Temple, were expelled from the council. His position as representative of the king's interests in Ireland was legalised when he was appointed lord lieutenant on 13 November 1643 after he had successfully negotiated a truce with the confederate catholics.

For nearly fifty years, until his death in 1688, Ormond was the dominant figure in Irish politics. At this moment, when his dominance began, he was thirty-three years of age. To the confederates he was an unknown figure, although nearly all his relatives and friends were in their own ranks. In many ways he proved to be a limited man, with little originality or initiative, but in playing a difficult hand over the next five or six years he showed him-

[1] Gilbert, *Ir. confed.*, ii, 226–42.

self to be a patient and competent diplomat. He had been brought up a protestant under the court of wards, and had no sympathy for his ancestral religion. His stubborn refusal to make religious concessions to the catholics was, however, motivated more by a concern for the New English interest with which he had identified himself than by bigotry. The puritan strain that may be discerned in his religious outlook was not uncommon among the members of the established church in Ireland in his time. The fact that in the years ahead he sometimes resisted religious concessions that the king was prepared to make must also be explained by political, rather than by strictly religious, considerations. Although his personal loyalty was unquestioned, as the civil war in England turned against the king he had to consider the possibility of a parliamentary victory or a negotiated settlement, and no one in his position could put out of his mind the fate of Strafford.

In discharging his commission to make a truce he adopted a stiff approach to the confederates. On 16 May 1643 he sent envoys to Kilkenny informally, to ensure that the formal initiative would have to come from there, and when he learned that these envoys had led the catholics to believe that they might expect major concessions he corrected this impression brusquely. At Kilkenny the decision lay with the second general assembly, which met on 20 May. The decision to seek a temporary truce had been a shrewd move on the part of the king and Ormond. The confederates were all agreed, many of them passionately agreed, on their loyalty to the king. They could not easily refuse to agree to a truce with him, especially when it could be represented as the necessary prelude to further negotiations in which they could press their case. While it might be argued that the king's forces in Ireland were in a bad plight, during the summer of 1643 affairs were going well for him in England. The confederates had already received sufficient warning of what they might expect from the English parliament. Any arguments that they should commit themselves to nothing, until they had some further indications that the king would negotiate on their demands, had to take into account the fact that their own position was by no means free from anxiety. The first assembly had sent embassies to seek help from various foreign powers. Some help had come from Spain, and some from the papacy. Cardinal Richelieu had raised hopes of considerable French help in the early days of the war, but he had died on 4 December 1642 (N.S.). Though both France and Spain were to accredit envoys to the confederate catholics, they continued to be interested in Ireland chiefly as a potential recruiting-ground for troops for their own armies.

Help from abroad was essential in order to equip an army in Ireland. Here too the confederates had reason to be anxious, even though they controlled most of the country. Preston's defeat by Ormond, though not a catastrophe, had not been reassuring. The Scottish forces in Ulster were very strong, and O'Neill was trying to form an army from raw recruits and with inadequate supplies. His position was so difficult that he decided to retire to Connacht in the hope of finding some respite to drill his forces, and for this purpose he ordered a rendezvous at Clones, County Monaghan.[1] Here he was challenged by the Laggan forces under Robert Stewart. They outnumbered him by nearly two to one, and he was not anxious for battle, but was over-ruled by his council of war. The battle took place on 13 June 1643, and O'Neill was defeated, in consequence of a mistake made by one of his commanders, a veteran of twenty-five years of the continental wars. The loss of many of the officers who had come to Ireland with him was particularly serious. Nevertheless, he recovered the situation, retired to Connacht as planned, and by the autumn had a reasonably effective army. He proved to be by far the most capable of the confederate commanders. He never lost another battle, nor did he ever again allow his hand to be forced by a council of war.

The assembly decided to negotiate for a short truce, of a year or less, and appointed commissioners representative of the four provinces to meet Ormond. Negotiations began on 24 June, but were adjourned after an exchange of views had shown the positions of the two parties to be still far apart. About the middle of July an envoy arrived from the pope to the confederates, Pier Francesco Scarampi. Of noble Italian stock, he had been a soldier until the age of forty, when he became an Oratorian priest. He objected to the proposed truce from both the religious and military points of view, and with shrewd comment and analysis he urged the confederates to rely on building up their own strength to achieve their declared aims. What Scarampi was not so well placed to grasp was the complex political situation. In spite of his objections, the truce was signed on 15 September 1643. It was a simple armistice for one year, and no more. No points of substance were decided, but the catholics could hope that, on these, negotiations could now begin.

The truce divided the Irish protestants. Important military leaders, Inchiquin in Munster, Coote in Connacht, Esmond who held Duncannon, and Thomond who held Bunratty, had reservations serious enough to make them question the royal cause. The truce provided a marvellous opportunity for propaganda for the English parliament. With hysteria or worse 'the furious, bloodthirsty papists'[2] were denounced, in particular the soldiers sent by Ormond from Dublin to England after the truce had been made, although these were all protestants, nearly all English, and many of them defected to parliament at the first opportunity. It was above all this news of collusion between the king and the papists in Ireland that made possible the publication of the solemn league and covenant with the Scots by order of the house of commons in London on 25 September. It was a fateful

[1] For an account of the battle see Pilib Ó Mórdha, 'The battle of Clones, 1643' in *Clogher Rec.*, iv, no. 3 (1962), pp 148–54.

[2] *Journals of the house of lords*, vi, 238 (30 Sept. 1643).

step in the English civil war. In Ireland, it meant that the Ulster Scots were now fighting both Ormond and the confederates, and as most of the rank and file of the royalist forces in Ulster were Scots, Ormond had in effect lost all control in Ulster. With so many other Irish protestants deeply disturbed by the truce, it was very doubtful how much either party to it had gained.

What fighting took place in 1644 and 1645 did not break the military stalemate, though it did confirm Scots control of most of the province of Ulster. Following their truce with the royalist forces, the confederates in December 1643 planned an attack on Monro's forces there. The disadvantages of a fragmented military command now became evident, especially when it was coupled with strong personal rivalries. The decision finally taken, to entrust the over-all command to the earl of Castlehaven, was logical because he had already been appointed commander of the central reserve forces, but it had in fact been taken because O'Neill was not acceptable in Kilkenny and Preston was not acceptable in Ulster.

While the confederates were preparing this attack Monro was in April 1644 appointed by the parliament in London to lead all the English forces in Ulster. Though the colonels of the English regiments there had some misgivings, Monro's position was strengthened, and on 14 May he seized Belfast. When the confederate armies took the field in the summer of 1644 there was no coordination between the forces of O'Neill and Castlehaven, and their mutual suspicions made common action impossible. No general engagement took place during the summer, and at the beginning of October Castlehaven withdrew his army from Ulster. Mutual distrust was succeeded by mutual recrimination. O'Neill demanded an investigation but though a committee of inquiry was set up it never issued a report.

In Munster, the protestant forces had been divided on the issue of the truce between the confederates and the king. Inchiquin, who had been acting governor there since the death of Sir William St Leger early in 1642, found it difficult to hold his army together for the royalist cause. When he was passed over for the presidency of Munster in favour of the absentee Lord Portland, and when it became clear that the king was prepared to negotiate a peace with the catholics, Inchiquin abandoned him and declared for parliament on 17 July 1644. The confederates now faced military opposition in Munster as well as in Ulster. In March 1645 they captured Duncannon, the key to the ports of Waterford and New Ross. Though technically royalist, the bulk of the garrison had parliamentary sympathies, and the commander, Esmond, had ignored the truce. A campaign led by Castlehaven in Munster in the summer of 1645 had some striking successes at first, but in the end petered out indecisively. The confederates did not succeed in clearing the approaches to Limerick until 14 July 1646, when they captured the castle of Bunratty.

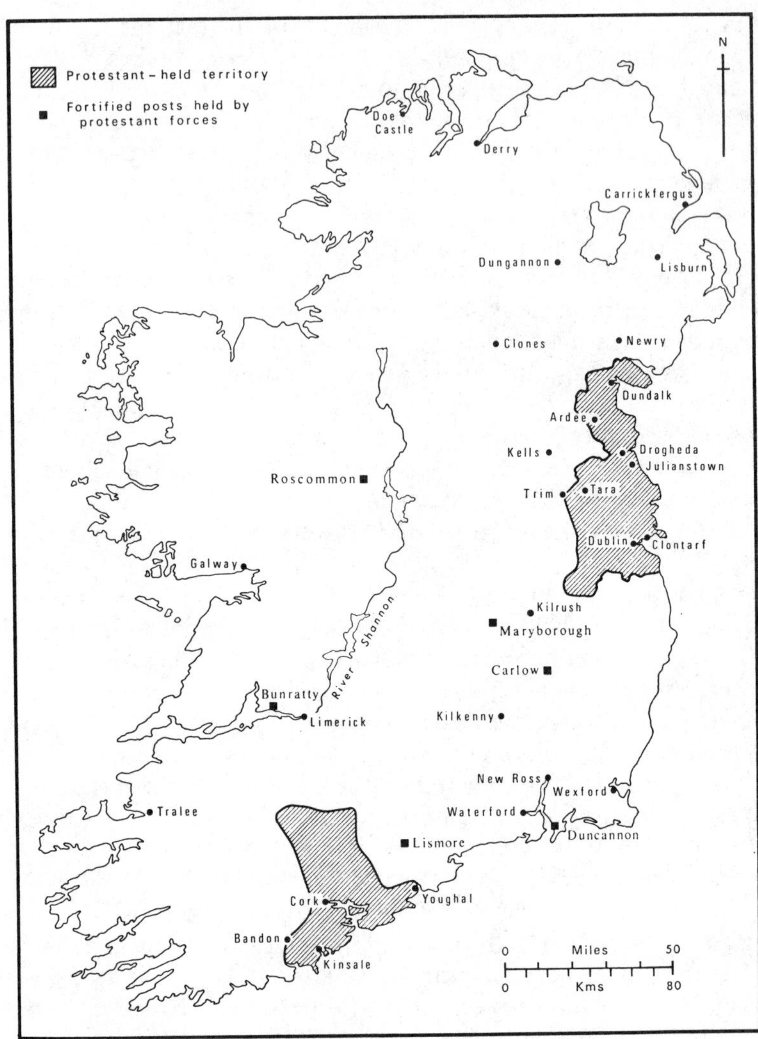

Map 7 THE ORMOND TRUCE, Sept. 1643, by Patrick J. Corish

For the lines of demarcation between protestants and catholics in Leinster and Munster see the articles of cessation in Gilbert, *Ir. confed.*, ii, 365–76. These further laid it down that each party should retain any fortified posts it actually held outside the boundaries agreed on. A few of the more important are indicated. In fact, the Dublin enclave extended rather uncertainly towards the south-west, and the Cork enclave similarly east into Waterford. The Scots were not a party to the truce and in consequence no demarcation line was drawn in Ulster. They held Down, Antrim, and much of Londonderry, while the catholics controlled Cavan, Monaghan, and parts of Fermanagh and Armagh. Connacht was recognised as catholic territory, but the position there was very uncertain because of the ambiguous stance of Clanricard.

The third general assembly in November 1643 had appointed delegates to meet Charles I at his headquarters in Oxford, not without some differences of opinion as to what exactly these delegates were to be instructed to ask for. They reached Oxford on 24 March 1644 and were received by the king four days later. On hearing of the catholics' presence in Oxford, the Irish protestants from Dublin sent a delegation to put their case. In so far as it was representative, it represented the element in Ireland that had disapproved of the truce, suspected the king for having agreed even to meet the catholics, and had already shown strong sympathies with parliament. When this protestant delegation arrived in Oxford on 17 April, the king had already sent to Ireland for members of his government there to advise him, and had referred the confederates' demands to a committee of his privy council.

Though the confederates soon scaled down their first demands, and their revised version was regarded as 'more reasonable', it still presented great problems. It was substantially the same as what they had asked for at Trim a year before. Certain points were spelled out more specifically—the annulment of all proceedings of the Irish parliament since its last meeting before the rising in August 1641, and an act of oblivion for all offences committed since that date, together with the reversal of all forfeitures to the crown since 1634, that is, since Strafford's policies had begun to impinge on the Old English catholic interest (the king's first approach in January 1643 having indicated that he might negotiate on this issue). In return, the confederates undertook to supply and equip an army of 10,000 men in the royalist cause. The catholics could scarcely have asked for less, given the position they had established for themselves. The Irish protestant delegates, however, were altogether intransigent. They demanded a rigorous implementation of the penal laws and of the policy of plantation. The king temporised by declaring that he would issue a new commission to Ormond to continue the negotiations in Ireland.

Here they went on tortuously until January 1649, and the agreement then reached did not really resolve the constitutional issues dividing the parties. It was not just because the king's English support was always seriously threatened by any suggestion that he would agree to an accommodation with a party so successfully represented by English propaganda as the murderous Irish papists. Apart from all propaganda, the question of the repeal of the penal laws was seen more clearly, as both sides considered its implications, to raise very grave constitutional problems indeed. These laws—the act of supremacy, the act of uniformity, the act of appeals, the act of faculties, to name only some of the more important—restricted the freedom of the king's catholic subjects, no doubt, but they also raised the problem of whether the king could have catholic subjects, the problem of his jurisdiction over them *vis-à-vis* a foreign power, the papacy. Charles I could afford to accept Scots presbyterianism and still remain king of Scotland, but he could not in a similar way accept Irish catholicism as posing no threat to his royal authority in Ireland. After the experience of a hundred years of religious division, monarchy and papacy could no longer succeed in tolerating one another in practice under legal systems theoretically in conflict, as they had succeeded in doing in the fifteenth century. The confederates were caught between these two intolerant systems. Their practical experience gained in trying to satisfy both had led them, particularly the Old English laity, to develop a fairly sophisticated approach towards giving spiritual allegiance to the pope and temporal allegiance to the king, but this only made them suspect to both authorities as men of divided allegiance, 'only half-subjects'.[1]

Practical difficulties further complicated this basic problem. The personal influence of Ormond on the negotiations has already been briefly noted. The king was notoriously unstable, to a large extent ignorant of Irish problems, and his intelligence service was not good.[2] His court was full of intrigue and he listened to everyone. His councillors were hesitant, and some of them were fundamentally hostile to the Irish catholics. Physical communications between Ireland and England were bad and uncertain. The confederates, for their part, were very much amateurs in matters of government, even at the level of the supreme council. They had experience of parliament, but none of administration. In the supreme council power was concentrated in a small Old English group, but they were answerable to the general assembly, and had always to take account of the latent but developing hostility of the clergy and the Old Irish to any settlement on terms Ormond was prepared to grant. The Old Irish, though increasingly conscious that their interests were being ignored, can scarcely be said to have succeeded in formulating their demands. The clergy, on the other hand, did succeed in arriving at a comprehensive programme for the future of the catholic church, and in this they could count on support from among the Old English, especially in the towns, where the new reformed catholicism had made a very effective impact.

The promised royal commission, granted to Ormond on 24 June 1644, made a number of advances. However, the king would not agree to the repeal of the penal laws, but only to their lenient execution, and while he indicated a willingness to summon a new parliament he would not consider any suspension of Poynings' law. If Ormond found it impossible to agree on a peace treaty, he was ordered to renew the truce. The commission can hardly have been in Ormond's hands when the king suffered his first decisive military setback, at the battle of Marston Moor on 2 July. Thereafter, he sought peace in Ireland with a new urgency, but the cautious Ormond held back on concessions the king in his growing desperation was prepared to make.

[1] Cf. above, ch. VII, pp 216–17.

[2] For a general survey of the problems of the negotiations see John Lowe, 'Charles I and the confederation of Kilkenny' in *I.H.S.*, xiv, no. 53 (Mar. 1964), pp 1–19.

The fourth confederate assembly met in July and August 1644. It heard their report from the seven delegates to the king at Oxford, and added six others to the delegation to continue the negotiations with Ormond. Ormond objected strenuously to the nomination of Thomas Fleming, the catholic archbishop of Dublin, and in a compromise agreement he in effect won his point. When negotiations began in Dublin on 1 September, the confederate delegation consisted of a small group of Old English laity. They immediately agreed to extend the truce to 1 December, but had to suspend discussion of the peace-terms to allow Ormond to seek further instructions from the king on what had now become the two key issues—the catholic church and the Irish parliament. Ormond had, however, succeeded in probing the weak spot in the men who faced him. They were rebels, he said, declared to be such by a legitimate parliament, and the most they could expect was the king's grace and favour. The laws they sought to have repealed were not directed against religion, but against a foreign jurisdiction. If they were prepared to assist the king as loyal subjects they might expect his protection and the measure of religious toleration by connivance that they had previously enjoyed.

The reply of the confederate envoys showed signs of indecision. They pointed out that it could only be to the king's advantage to treat all his subjects equally, and asked that he should at least commit himself publicly to the exercise of his prerogative in tempering the application of the penal laws. They were now appealing rather than demanding, and Ormond had every encouragement to stand firm. At Kilkenny, indecision grew. One group argued that the viceroy's terms should be accepted, for only by accepting them could the confederates discharge their clear duty of loyalty. Another group pinned its hopes of resistance on further help from catholic Europe.

The assembly had decided to send an envoy to the continental powers to sound out their position and ask for help. Richard Bellings left Ireland at the end of the year on this mission. When he arrived in Rome he met a new pope, Innocent X, elected on 15 September 1644 (N.S.) in succession to Urban VIII. The pope informed him that he had nominated a nuncio to Ireland and was sending further help. The news was not altogether to Bellings's satisfaction, for the help offered was small, though as much as papal resources could provide, and the fact that the nuncio was an Italian was disappointing. The confederates had earlier asked for a nuncio, but had expected that an Irishman would be named, probably Luke Wadding, who had been appointed confederate agent in Rome by the first assembly.[1] However, Bellings diplomatically put the best face on things, and his subsequent experiences in France and the Spanish Netherlands may have made him more appreciative of papal help. Spain could do nothing, and in France Cardinal Mazarin's

[1] Supreme council of the confederates to the pope, 28 Nov. 1642, in *Spicil. Ossor.*, i, 275–6

government was suspicious of the new pope, who was believed, in contrast to his predecessor, to favour the Spaniards. Mazarin told Bellings that the confederates could expect no help from France unless they repudiated all dependence on Spain. A disappointed Bellings returned to Ireland together with the nuncio, John Baptist Rinuccini, archbishop of Fermo. They landed at Kenmare on 12 October 1645.

By that time, the peace negotiations had become very involved indeed. The further instructions which Ormond had sought from the king at the end of September 1644 did not arrive in Dublin until the beginning of the following March. From them it was clear that Charles, as affairs turned against him in England, was prepared to bid higher for catholic support in Ireland, but the guidelines he gave—'conclude a peace with the Irish, whatsoever it cost; so that my protestant subjects there may be secure and my regal authority preserved'—were of little practical use to Ormond, for it was precisely on these two points that he had sought guidance in detail, though the further instruction, 'make me the best bargain you can', could be interpreted as giving him a reasonably free hand.[1]

Ormond, however, was living in the midst of the Irish protestant concentration in Dublin, and he had reason to think that further extensive concessions were impossible, and in any case probably not necessary. He divulged nothing of this latest royal commission either to his council or to the confederate negotiators. However, when he met these latter again in Dublin about the middle of April he found them slow to yield any further in what they considered their reasonable demands, especially now that the king was in even greater need of their help. Negotiations ground slowly on, to the point where the gap seemed bridgeable on every issue except the religious one. Here, Ormond continued to work on his well-founded belief that differences existed among the catholics, but the party unwilling to make further concessions was strengthened when the fifth general assembly met on 15 May. Clanricard attended at Kilkenny as Ormond's representative, and was naturally able to supply him with valuable information, as he came to know almost everything that was going on. He advised Ormond that the religious concessions sought by the catholics should be granted. That they were not prepared to yield in this matter was demonstrated by the outcome of a dispute between the clergy and an Old English group in the assembly. The viewpoint of the clergy secured the backing of the majority, and formally committed the confederates to insisting on retaining possession of all the churches they held, and to the exemption of catholics from any religious jurisdiction other than that of their own clergy.

Almost exactly at the time when these decisions were being taken in Kilkenny, the battle of Naseby was fought in England on 14 June 1645. It was a disaster for the royal cause, and left the king without any army to

[1] Gilbert, *Ir. confed.*, iv, 153–4.

continue the war. At this stage his personal envoy, the earl of Glamorgan, arrived in Dublin about the end of June. It may be taken that the main mysteries of Glamorgan's mission have now been cleared up, though on some points of detail there will continue to be room for conjecture.[1] On 11 November 1644 Ormond had offered his resignation to the king, apparently despairing of reaching an agreement with the confederates. Charles had refused to accept it, wisely judging that no one could succeed where Ormond failed. He decided, however, to send Glamorgan to Ireland, with instructions, of their nature public, to assist Ormond, and others, of their nature private, giving him wide and undefined powers to negotiate an agreement independently if this were necessary. That he did in fact receive credentials to this effect, substantially as he represented them to be, is beyond question.

Glamorgan had been for a long time a close friend of the king, and had used his great family wealth to support him during the war. As well as being a deeply committed royalist he was a devout catholic. There may have been a quixotic strain in him, but he was no man's fool. He had already shown some capacity in organising and provisioning troops, and the immediate practical purpose of his mission was to get confederate troops sent to England as quickly as possible, whatever the cost.

He had received his mandate from the king in January 1645, supplemented by another on 12 March. The reasons for his long delay in arriving in Dublin are very imperfectly documented, but the sheer physical difficulties of transport—we know that at one stage he was shipwrecked—must explain much of it. From what Ormond was told he could only have surmised that Glamorgan had a general mandate to assist him, and in this capacity he had no reason to mistrust him. To the Kilkenny peace-delegation now at Dublin he was of course welcome as a personal envoy from the king and a well-known catholic. In consequence, when he went on to Kilkenny early in August the stage was set for further negotiations.

The assembly agreed that these should begin on 14 August, as soon as they had finished discussing Ormond's latest propositions. They had reason to believe that Glamorgan might offer them further concessions, if only because a letter from the king to Ormond, printed by order of the English parliament, and authorising him to grant repeal of the penal laws, was at the time in circulation in Kilkenny. They were not deterred by Glamorgan's insistence that he would not deal directly with the assembly, but only with the delegation they had named to negotiate the peace with Ormond. Open opposition came only from the papal delegate, Scarampi. He questioned both Glamorgan's authority and the sufficiency of his offers, and said that in any case nothing should be made final until the papal nuncio, now on his way, should arrive.

[1] It is discussed in detail by John Lowe, 'The Glamorgan mission to Ireland 1645–6' in *Studia Hib.*, iv (1964), pp 155–96.

The discussions went on, however. Glamorgan was now extremely anxious to have an Irish army for the king's service, and the calamity that had overtaken the royalist forces at Naseby gave him every inducement to interpret his mandate as widely as possible. Agreement was reached on 25 August. It conceded the religious demands spelled out by the assembly the previous June, but it was to be conditional on agreement being reached with Ormond on other matters, and was to be kept secret until an Irish army should have landed in England, when the king could commit himself with more safety.

Secrecy, of course, could be only relative. Clanricard was still in Kilkenny during August, and this meant that Ormond must have had some inkling of what was going on. News of developments in Kilkenny trickled through to England, though this could be no more than rumour, without details or proof. Glamorgan returned to Dublin, as did the confederate delegates, and negotiations, still stubborn, continued with Ormond. On 12 November 1645 the papal nuncio, Rinuccini, arrived at Kilkenny.

CHAPTER XII

Ormond, Rinuccini, and the confederates, 1645–9

PATRICK J. CORISH

RINUCCINI, born in Rome of a Florentine family, had just passed his fifty-third birthday. He had been a brilliant student, and after ordination had entered the curial service. At the age of thirty-three he was appointed archbishop of Fermo in the papal states. His friendship with the Scottish Capuchin, Fr Leslie, had directed his attention to the religious affairs of the northern islands. In 1644 he had published *Il Cappuccino Scozzese*, a vivid but highly romanticised story of the life of a priest in Scotland. It quickly became popular devotional reading throughout Italy and France. He was a deeply religious man, kind and urbane in manner, shrewd and masterful in sizing up a situation. In many ways he appeared admirably qualified to discharge his overriding mandate, 'to restore and reestablish the public exercise of the catholic religion in the island of Ireland'.[1]

His weakness was that his vision of how this might be done was markedly limited by his previous administrative experience in the papal states. Nowhere does this appear more clearly than in his assessment of the Irish hierarchy as he found them—one can sense that he measures Irish problems by the standards of Bernini's Rome:

> The older bishops have grown used to carrying on a limited functioning without interference or restraint, and so do not consider the splendour and grandeur of religious ceremony to be a matter of great importance . . . They would incline to be satisfied were the king and the marquis to grant them freedom to practise their religion, even in secret, as they believe this would guarantee the faith in substance, and not bring any troubles down on themselves . . . But the younger bishops, who have begun their work in better times, show more determination and boldness.[2]

As a man detached from personal commitments in Ireland, he could see with great clarity that the king and Ormond were only trying to use the Irish catholics for their own ends; but he did have a deep personal commitment to the catholic religion as he had experienced it in the papal states, and in

[1] G. Aiazzi, *Nunziatura in Irlanda* (Florence, 1844), p. xxxv. The English translation by Annie Hutton, *The embassy in Ireland* (Dublin, 1873), is not always reliable.

[2] Aiazzi, *Nunziatura in Irlanda*, pp 110–11.

consequence his programme for Ireland contained elements that, on his own admission, were questioned by a number of the Irish hierarchy.

Glamorgan returned at once from Dublin to Kilkenny for discussions with Rinuccini. The agreement they reached on 20 December included, the nuncio reported to Rome, 'all I thought necessary for the security of religion'.[1] In several important respects it made a striking advance on anything hitherto conceded to the catholics. The next lord lieutenant was to be a catholic. The catholic bishops were to sit as lords spiritual in the Irish parliament. The agreement in civil matters, hammered out with Ormond, was to be published at the same time as this agreement on religious matters made with Glamorgan, that is, after the king had ratified the latter; and only then was the supreme council of the confederacy to be dissolved.[2]

Peace on these terms would in fact have made the catholic religion the established church of Ireland, and must have gone beyond any understanding between Glamorgan and Charles I. To some extent Glamorgan may have been won over by the charm and masterfulness of Rinuccini, but it must also be remembered that he was now desperately anxious to get the promised Irish troops to England, for the parliamentary army was closing in on Chester, the only port where they could be conveniently disembarked. An even more interesting question is why Rinuccini considered it worth his while to make an agreement with Glamorgan. The answer must revolve round two letters, now in the Vatican archives, dated 20 October 1645, from Charles I to the pope and to the cardinal secretary of state, commending Glamorgan absolutely and promising to ratify any agreement made by him. Their authenticity has been questioned, but it seems beyond doubt that they are in the king's handwriting.[3] In any case, Glamorgan was able to show to Rinuccini, though he would not let him see the contents, 'a letter from the king consisting of a quarter of a sheet, folded in the smallest possible compass and directed to his holiness'.[4] That the king should have sent a letter of this kind through Glamorgan is plausible. He should have received it about the middle of December, and it seems to have been the production of this letter that finally decided Rinuccini.

At this stage, secrecy was irretrievably lost. Archbishop O'Queely of Tuam had been killed in a skirmish near Sligo at the end of October. On his person was found a copy of the agreement reached in August between Glamorgan and the confederates.[5] It was sent to London, where it was printed by order of parliament. A copy also found its way to Ormond in Dublin. Glamorgan was arrested on 26 December on his return to the city. The following day

[1] Aiazzi, *Nunziatura in Irlanda*, p. 78.

[2] *Comment. Rinucc.*, ii, 88–9.

[3] Vatican Archives, Instrumenta Miscellanea, no. 6635. See Charles Burns, 'Sources of British and Irish history in the Instrumenta Miscellanea of the Vatican archives' in *Archivum Historiae Pontificiae*, ix (1971), p. 117; Gordon Albion, *Charles I and the court of Rome* (London, 1935), p. 423; John Lowe, 'The Glamorgan mission to Ireland 1645–6' in *Studia Hib.*, iv (1964), pp 176–7.

[4] Aiazzi, *Nunziatura in Irlanda*, p. 81.

[5] See above, p. 316.

he was brought before the council and charged with treason. In his defence, he was clearly trying to save both the king and himself, but he did not give any impression that he had acted traitorously. At Kilkenny, the supreme council summoned a general assembly, declared that it would negotiate no further until Glamorgan was released, and even threatened to resume the war.

Ormond released Glamorgan on 22 January 1646, without waiting for orders from the king. It is hard to see why he did so unless he had reason to believe that he had in substance told the truth. Glamorgan returned immediately to Kilkenny. Here he found Rinuccini less disposed to deal with him, all the more as he had received a copy of a treaty signed in Rome on 20 November 1645 (N.S.) between Pope Innocent X and Sir Kenelm Digby, on behalf of Queen Henrietta Maria. The queen had gone to France after the defeat of the royalists at Marston Moor. As the war in England went against her husband, she was prepared to make generous promises to the catholics in return for their support. Her choice of an envoy to Rome was not particularly fortunate, for Digby was temperamentally expansive and imaginative. The terms he had agreed to were even more favourable than those offered by Glamorgan, and they were now in Rinuccini's hands.[1]

The sixth assembly met on 7 February 1646, and as usual acted as a restraint on those who wished to see a peace signed with Ormond. Glamorgan was now desperate, for Chester was actually besieged. On 16 February he succeeded in having the truce prolonged until 1 May, when it was hoped the king might have ratified the Roman treaty. No treaty of any kind was to be published before this date, but the confederates were to continue their negotiations with Ormond, and Rinuccini his with Glamorgan. With Rinuccini, Glamorgan agreed to ratify the Roman treaty and to procure its ratification by the king. If this could not be achieved by 1 May, the agreement he himself had made with the nuncio might be resumed. He was allowed to begin assembling an army for the relief of Chester.

Considering his circumstances, it was a creditable achievement. But a month later all his schemes collapsed. He ran out of money, the ships to transport the army gathered for the relief of Chester failed to arrive, and, after report and counter-report, it was finally confirmed in Dublin, but only towards the end of the second week in March, that Chester had fallen to parliament.[2] At the same time it became known in Ireland that Charles had publicly disowned all that Glamorgan had done in his name there. Private letters written shortly afterwards by the king to Glamorgan confirm that he had in fact given him very wide powers in his mission, but the circumstances in which its results had become known made it politically impossible for the

[1] *Comment. Rinucc.*, ii, 118 ff. See also Vittorio Gabrieli, 'La missione di Sir Kenelm Digby alla corte di Innocenzo X, 1645–1648' in *English Miscellany*, v (Rome, 1954), pp 247–88.

[2] Gilbert, *Ir. confed.*, v, 257–320, more especially pp 261, 272–3.

king to do anything except disown him. He might conceivably have gambled on the August agreement if he had had an army of 10,000 Irish troops in England, but not without them.

Ten days later, on 28 March 1646, the confederate delegates in Dublin signed a peace with Ormond. It is a long, comprehensive, and rambling document.[1] Religious matters were dismissed with a reference to 'his majesty's gracious favour and further concessions', which the signatories must have known could not now mean what both sides might reasonably have interpreted it to mean before the king disowned Glamorgan. On certain points it was satisfactory, especially to the Old English, for it safeguarded their right to a place in public life and reversed Strafford's confiscations. It also provided for a general pardon for everything that had occurred since the outbreak of the insurrection. It was less satisfactory concerning the freedom of the Irish parliament, but it left room for hope of improvement. The treaty was not to be published as yet, but Ormond had declared that he could not wait beyond 1 May, the date already agreed between Glamorgan and Rinuccini.[2]

By this date the Roman treaty on which the nuncio now pinned his hopes had made no further progress; indeed the king's fortunes were now so low that it had lost all meaning. At the end of April he had decided to put himself in the hands of the Scots. They had become disillusioned with their alliance with parliament, but in spite of fair words they were determined to force the solemn league and covenant, with its commitment to presbyterianism, on the king, and soon he was to all intents and purposes their prisoner. This made it all the more important for Ormond to have his treaty with the confederates published, for without them his position in Dublin was untenable. The Old English confederates also wished for a union with Ormond, but they had to convince Rinuccini. He was not prepared to agree, now that he saw no hope of any formal guarantee for the catholic religion. O'Neill's decisive defeat of the Scots at Benburb on 5 June 1646 stiffened his resistance, and on 14 July the confederates captured Bunratty, commanding the approaches to Limerick. Tense confrontations between the nuncio and the supreme council at Limerick seem to have left each side convinced that it had convinced the other. The council left Limerick for Kilkenny, and Rinuccini left for Waterford, where a legatine national synod of the clergy had already been arranged. While he was on his way there, Ormond published the peace in Dublin on 30 July. On 3 August it was published by the council in Kilkenny.

It was fortunate for Rinuccini that plans had been made for the legatine synod, as it allowed him to oppose the peace, not just in his own name but in the name of the whole church. On 6 August the synod rejected the peace,

[1] Gilbert, *Ir. confed.*, v, 286–308.

[2] Ibid., v, 270–73, 282–3; and see above, pp 318–19.

and six days later declared that all who supported it must be judged to have broken the oath of association they had taken on joining the confederacy, and that if any of those who had negotiated it were to go to Dublin to assist Ormond in its implementation they were thereby excommunicated. A tense and complex battle now developed for the loyalty of the confederates. Rinuccini knew in advance that he could count on O'Neill, who moved his army south (thereby forfeiting any hope of following up his victory at Benburb and destroying Scots power in Ulster). An important factor, possibly a decisive one, was the support given to the nuncio by the Old English of the towns. The synod at Waterford stepped up its pressure. A decree of 17 August pronounced an interdict on all places and a suspension on all priests accepting the peace, and declared that the confederate catholics were no longer bound to obey the supreme council which had agreed to it. Ormond had come to Kilkenny to oversee the proclamation of the peace, but his support finally disintegrated after a decree from Waterford on 1 September excommunicating all who in any way showed themselves in favour of it. Preston, after hard struggles with conscience, coupled with uncertainty as to where his army's loyalties lay, finally declared for the nuncio. Ormond was forced to return to Dublin on 13 September. On 18 September Rinuccini returned to Kilkenny, now able to dictate his terms. The members of the council who had promulgated the peace were imprisoned, and a new council of sixteen was nominated, with the nuncio as president. Dionisio Massari, the dean of Fermo, was sent to Rome to seek new support and supplies from the pope.

Actions so essentially unconstitutional could only be made acceptable by some striking success, and the new council decided on an immediate attack on Dublin. At best, such a winter campaign was a risky undertaking. In addition, there was the problem of command. The nuncio would undoubtedly have liked to see it entrusted to O'Neill, but this was politically impossible, because Preston's officers and men simply would not serve under him. In consequence, to the hazards of a winter campaign were added the hazards of divided command, with very lukewarm enthusiasm on the part of Preston and his army.

Shortly after his return to Dublin, Ormond, seeing no alternative, had opened negotiations with representatives of the English parliament. They had made no progress, principally because parliament was unwilling that the king should be in any way a party to them. By 5 November the confederate armies were within a few miles of Dublin, Preston being camped at Lucan. Once again Ormond sent Clanricard to the nuncio, but it became clear that he would not confirm any public agreement on matters concerning religion, and still insisted that all the confederates could expect was a private assurance of the king's good intentions. This could hardly be expected to content the nuncio, but Clanricard had more success with Preston. Jealous of O'Neill, resentful of Rinuccini, Preston was finally ordered, under threat of excommunication, to withdraw his army to winter quarters, as the nuncio feared that he might reach agreement with Ormond, who for his part suspected that a proposal to bring Preston's troops into Dublin was a plot between him and the nuncio to gain control of the city.

O'Neill had retired to winter quarters shortly before this threat of excommunication against Preston. The campaign against Dublin had been a complete failure—worse than a failure, because it had exacerbated the divisions among the confederates, and further identified Rinuccini, whether he liked it or not, with O'Neill and the Old Irish.

The nuncio agreed with some reluctance to the calling of a new general assembly, and with even more reluctance to the release of the imprisoned members of the previous supreme council. Not all his advisers were of the same mind, but the two men who seem to have convinced him that these steps were necessary were Nicholas French, consecrated bishop of Ferns in November 1645, and Nicholas Plunkett, an eminent lawyer who had been deeply involved in confederate affairs from the beginning. Both had given invaluable support in the crisis of the previous August. From now on they were to be prominent in the attempts to save the confederacy from disintegration.

When the assembly met on 10 January 1647 it was clear that the Ormond peace still had supporters. They were outnumbered, however, and on 2 February it was formally rejected, though with a conciliatory clause exonerating all who had been involved in it from blame. The clergy now produced four articles, and asked that they be incorporated in a new oath of association. These were: that in any future agreement there should be provision for the free and public exercise of the catholic religion as in the time of Henry VII; that the catholic clergy should have their jurisdiction, privileges, and immunities as they had then enjoyed them; that all penal laws since 20 Henry VIII should be repealed; and that the catholic clergy should have their churches on the same terms as the protestants had held them on 1 October 1641, 'it being understood however that the rights of the laity according to the laws of the land remain unimpaired'.[1] This, the last clause, echoes the continuing controversy over the confiscated church and monastic lands. As has been seen,[2] the first assembly had confirmed catholic owners in their possession of this property. Rinuccini had come from Rome with powers to confirm them in their titles, but he several times complained that few approached him for such confirmation. To have done so, of course, would have been to admit that the titles might be suspect. The new oath of associations was adopted, with, however, two important amendments to the four points requested by the clergy: that the confederates were not to consider

[1] *Comment. Rinucc.*, ii, 512–13.
[2] See above, pp 301–2.

themselves bound to insist on catholic possession of the churches in places still to be recovered from the protestants; and that in any peace treaty the general assembly was to be the final judge of whether the confederates could insist on the four articles put forward by the clergy. There followed an attempt to impeach Preston for his conduct during the campaign against Dublin. It was ill-advised, for it only exposed again the depth of division among the confederates, and the conciliators succeeded in having it shelved. On 17 March a new council was chosen. The nuncio found most of its members satisfactory, though it contained four men whom he had to be persuaded to accept. The assembly dispersed on 4 April, having made arrangements to convene again on 12 November. The confederation was still in being, but no real union had been achieved among its members, and a testing summer lay ahead.

Ormond, as has been seen, had opened negotiations with parliament after the rejection of the peace of 1646, but had later broken them off. His hopes that they might not be necessary had been raised by fresh evidence of dissension among the confederates. However, he could now maintain his position in Dublin only because he was being supplied by parliamentary shipping, and serious negotiations between the two parties began again in February. In January the Scots had handed the king over to parliament, as part of a new agreement, and although Ormond in Ireland continued to keep his communications open with the confederates this was only to forestall any attack they might possibly make on Dublin. Events in England had overtaken Queen Henrietta Maria's attempts to bring together the royalist and catholic forces in Ireland. On 5 April, the day after the assembly had dispersed, her envoy, Fr George Leyburn, travelling under the assumed name of 'Mr Wintergrant' arrived in Kilkenny. This led to new exchanges with Dublin, but they were empty posturing, for the parliamentary takeover of the city was already under way. On 7 June 1647 an army of 2,000 men was landed under the command of Colonel Michael Jones.

Ormond, like his royal master, had placed some hopes in the possibility of a settlement with parliament from which something of substance might be rescued. Now that the war had been won, differences of interest were appearing among the victors. They came to a head in a confrontation between the parliament, committed to presbyterianism, and the army, demanding religious independency. A few days before Jones had landed in Dublin the army had forcibly seized the king in England, thus making it very uncertain to what power Ormond was preparing to hand over the city. The decision had been taken, however, and both parties moved towards the formal agreement dictated by the facts of the situation. A treaty was signed between Ormond and the parliamentary commissioners on 19 June. The same day the commissioners proscribed the liturgy of the established church. Ormond retained control of Dublin castle until 28 July, when he sailed for England, having left his insignia of office to be delivered to the parliamentary commissioners.

The surrender of Dublin to parliament had at least resolved Preston's scruples and vacillations. That summer he acted with energy and decision. On 2 June he had captured the outpost Ormond had held at Carlow since the beginning of the war, and planned the investment of Dublin. He was joined by a number of protestants, unable to accept Ormond's surrender to parliament. (Rinuccini had scruples over this, but it is interesting to note that when he consulted his superiors in Rome they did not make a great deal of them.) Then disaster struck on 8 August, when Preston attacked Jones at Dungan's Hill near Trim. He had been urged to give battle by his civilian advisers, Bishop French and Nicholas Plunkett. They had been anxious because Jones was strengthening his position, whereas they knew that the supplies available to Preston were insufficient for a long campaign. Preston gave battle in a very unfavourable tactical situation, and was completely routed. O'Neill's army had to be called in to protect Leinster, and he too was short of arms and money, while the consciousness of dependence on him further embittered the Old English.

No better news came from Munster, where Inchiquin was exploiting the confederate weakness. Dungarvan had fallen to him in May, and this had threatened Waterford. On 14 September he stormed and sacked Cashel. Agents from the queen were still active in Ireland, urging that the confederates should make a declaration of loyalty to the king, and that when this was done the prince of Wales would come over from France. It was not a very practical proposal, and reflected only the queen's desperation, but to the Old English it might seem to offer a prospect of removing the stigma of disloyalty and of curbing O'Neill's predominance. This mood of frustration and despair was well caught in the flare-up over the book by the Irish Jesuit, Conor O'Mahony, *Disputatio apologetica et manifestativa de iure regni Hiberniae pro catholicis Hibernis contra haereticos Anglos*. This was an analysis of Irish affairs in the context of Jesuit political theory by a violent partisan of the Old Irish. He savagely attacked the English in Ireland, Old and New, and urged the Irish to rebel against Charles I and elect a native king for themselves. The work was published at Lisbon in 1645, and copies had circulated in Ireland for some time. Now, in the autumn of 1647, it was burnt in Kilkenny by the public hangman, and a search for copies was ordered throughout the country. Its sentiments were too close to what men feared.

The next assembly met as arranged on 12 November, 'in the uncertainty of a realm not only divided, but full of suspicions of treachery, and with no one able to untie the knots'.[1] A few days after it opened, news came that Inchiquin had destroyed the army of Munster at the battle of Knocknanuss

[1] The comment is Rinuccini's: *Comment. Rinucc.*, ii, 773.

near Mallow on 13 November. The Old English feared O'Neill, and at the same time despised his army and his supporters. O'Neill's natural response was a haughty lack of cooperation. The news of Knocknanuss threw the assembly into panic, and the dominant Old English party there saw in the disaster the final collapse of the nuncio's policy of refusing to work with Ormond and of prosecuting the war independently. Help would have to be sought, and they proposed that a new declaration of loyalty be made and the queen invited to Ireland. Rinuccini protested that this was acceptable only if adequate guarantees for the catholic religion were first given. It was finally agreed that an attempt should be made to seek a suitable agreement with the queen; failing this, the confederates would seek the support of some foreign prince as their protector.

These debates had strained nerves and tempers in the assembly. The following debates, on the choice of envoys to be sent to Spain, France, and the papacy, strained them even further. Viscount Muskerry and Geoffrey Browne, the principal negotiators of the Ormond peace, were chosen to go to France, together with Bishop MacMahon of Clogher. It is hard to see why the bishop was chosen except in order to get him out of the way. He refused the appointment, and the assembly almost broke up in bitter recriminations. Finally the marquis of Antrim was nominated in his place. This was small comfort to Rinuccini, for Antrim was a vain man, chiefly interested in being named lord lieutenant to succeed Ormond. Bishop French and Nicholas Plunkett were chosen to go to Rome. By now Rinuccini had some reservations in regard to these two men, and although they had kept up good relations with the Ulster leaders, O'Neill and the bishop of Clogher, reservations here were even more marked. In the long debates the embassy to Spain was almost forgotten. One envoy was named, Sir Richard Blake, but in fact he never set out at all.

The election of a new supreme council also brought the assembly near to breaking-point. The Old Irish were poorly represented, so the dispute resolved itself into a tussle between the Old English and the clergy. Finally it was decided to have an election 'by compromise': two from each party were chosen to nominate the new council of twelve members. Rinuccini's inevitable suspicions were not lessened when at the end of a long session a proposal was slipped through, designed to strengthen the Old English predominance, to name forty-eight 'supernumeraries' to reside permanently in Kilkenny to take the place of any council members who might be absent. The assembly dissolved on Christmas eve, leaving the council and the clergy to work out detailed instructions for the embassies to be sent abroad.

The key point of the instructions for the envoys to Paris was that in any agreement with the queen they were to secure the terms for the catholic religion already granted by Glamorgan, and also that the viceroy should be a catholic, unless the pope waived this point (it having already been agreed, while the assembly was in session, that any agreement negotiated in Paris must await papal approval). The envoys to Rome left with two sets of instructions. Officially, they were to ask the holy see to mediate a treaty between the queen and the confederates, but they were to stress that the country was in desperate need, and to ask whether any religious concessions must be publicly agreed to, and specifically whether it were necessary to insist on a catholic viceroy. They were to ask the pope to assume the protectorate of Ireland, but only as a last resort, if no agreement with the queen were possible, and any such papal protectorate would need the queen's approval. Rinuccini's private instructions, while in the same general context, suggested different priorities. They were first to ask the pope to become protector, should the queen approve. They were to stress that no final agreement would be reached in Paris without prior Roman approval, and that while an agreement with the queen would bring no practical advantages it could do no harm if it contained adequate guarantees for religion and might lead to the confederates getting what they really needed, money and supplies.

This final point made by Rinuccini meant in effect that he believed that O'Neill still had a fighting force and that it could be made effective, either to subdue the Scots in Ulster or possibly even to join forces with them, for the Scots had been very restive since the English army had imprisoned the king. This prospect of military domination by O'Neill was precisely what the Old English could not accept. A group among them was already committed to making peace in Paris. The last squabble was over which set of envoys should leave first. Logically, it should have been the Roman mission, for Rome was so much farther away and it had been understood that any agreement in Paris depended on prior agreement in Rome. As a final compromise, they sailed together on 10 February 1648.

Meanwhile, Ormond in England had been trying to retrieve his position. After the army leaders had seized the king at the beginning of June they had stepped up their demands on parliament, seeking now not just a redress of their own grievances but a voice in settling the affairs of the nation generally. This tension between army and parliament seemed to offer Charles an opportunity to mend his own fortunes. At the end of August he received Ormond, who gave him his version of affairs in Ireland and was confirmed in the office of lord lieutenant. Early in October he began to be drawn into the king's plans to recover his position in so far as they concerned Ireland. The authority of parliament was now challenged by the army, the army was divided, the more conservative leaders being afraid of their own radicals, and there was a marked royalist reaction in the country as a whole. Charles inclined to rely on the support of this factor in England, reach a new agreement with the Scots, depend on Ormond to save the situation in Ireland, and by a combination of these forces outmanœuvre both army and parliament. On 26 December 1647 he signed an engagement with the Scots.

The English parliament, increasingly suspicious of Ormond, had forbidden him access to the king, but in letters dated 5 and 27 January 1648 Charles commissioned him to try again to reach a peace with the Irish, if it could be done 'without ruining conscience and honour'. He was to be guided by any instructions he received from the queen and the prince of Wales, and not to hesitate because of lack of any public authorisation from the king.[1] Probably after he received these letters, possibly before, Ormond sent Colonel John Barry to Ireland to sound out the well-disposed, and especially to try to win over Inchiquin to the royalist cause. He then sailed for France, where he arrived at the end of February, shortly before the confederate envoys, who had had great difficulties in making the crossing from Ireland.

In Paris, he had to make concrete plans. There were difficulties and opponents, but the king had confirmed him as lord lieutenant and he had the support of Mazarin and the French court. When the confederate envoys arrived, Muskerry and Browne made it clear they were prepared to treat their official instructions lightly, and were ready for an accommodation with Ormond. The three envoys, including Antrim, were received in formal audience by the queen on 2 April 1648 (N.S.). They had to admit that on the basis of their instructions they could reach no agreement until word arrived from Rome. Three days later Ormond submitted a memorial to the queen. He proposed that the confederates should be given fair words but only in generalities, for they could not at this time reasonably expect more; that an expedition should be fitted out to help Inchiquin and the Scots; and that only then would it be necessary to decide what terms the confederates must be offered.[2] This advice was acceptable.

About the beginning of May encouraging news arrived from Scotland and Ireland. On 10 May (N.S.) the confederate envoys were again received by the queen, and again they had to admit that they had no news from Rome. Three days later the queen told them that, notwithstanding their past ingratitude and their having broken the terms of peace agreed on, 'we shall speedily give power to such as we think fit to receive there and upon the place more particular and full propositions', and that this person would be empowered to grant 'whatever may consist with justice and with his majesty's interest and honour'.[3] Muskerry and Browne must have taken the lecture lightly, for they knew that 'the person' was Ormond. There was no more talk of awaiting word from Rome. They went back to Ireland with good news for those to whom it might be safely told.

Colonel Barry had arrived in Ireland about the middle of February 1648 to discuss Ormond's proposals with Inchiquin. He found him cautiously receptive. His relations with parliament had never been easy. Parliament had

[1] Bodl., Carte papers, xxii, no. 7. [2] Ibid., xxii, no. 37.
[3] Gilbert, *Ir. confed.*, vi, 231 ff.

made only very limited provision for his army, and the recent developments in England had left him very uncertain in his loyalty. There were problems in reversing it, however. His support from parliament had been slender, but what he might expect from the king's resources would certainly be slenderer still. A decision for the king implied an accommodation with the confederate catholics on this score alone, and the proposals Barry put before him provided for such an accommodation. His army contained a number of protestant officers who might be expected to resist. He himself did not like it either. In contrast to Ormond, who opposed the catholic claims because of political considerations, Inchiquin was at this time hostile to catholicism as a creed, perhaps all the more because of his latent uncertainties. He had a catholic brother among the confederates, and he became a catholic himself in exile in the 1650s, and remained so until his death.

Barry, however, was sufficiently encouraged to approach the council in Kilkenny, where he found cautious approval for the proposal for a truce with Inchiquin. Here too there were problems, notably the problem of getting the nuncio's consent. It was not that he opposed the idea of a truce with one or other of the enemies of the confederates, but he favoured a truce with the Scots, in order to strengthen O'Neill, rather than one with Inchiquin, that might, he already had some reason to suspect, ultimately involve the return of Ormond as lord lieutenant. O'Neill, however, was not particularly anxious for a truce with the Scots, regarding their new involvement in English affairs rather as providing an opportunity to move against them in Ireland. Negotiations with the Scots were mooted, but came to nothing.

Rinuccini's determination to oppose a truce with Inchiquin was strengthened by the return of Massari on 13 March 1648 from the mission to Rome that he had undertaken after the rejection of the Ormond peace in 1646. He brought some arms and money—as usual, not enough to be in any way decisive. He also brought papal bulls for the consecration of bishops to nine vacant sees. Their respective roles in the nomination of bishops had long been a point of contention between Rinuccini and the confederate government, and the council had objected to some of these nominations. Nevertheless, Rinuccini proceeded to consecrate the nine bishops. Some of them were later to be prominent among his supporters after an open breach had occurred, and the nuncio's insistence that they be consecrated did not improve his relations with the council. But mutual suspicions reached the point where any frank discussion became almost impossible when it became known that Massari had brought from Rome the sword of Hugh O'Neill as a gift for Owen Roe. It seems that in fact Luke Wadding personally had been responsible for sending the sword, but inevitably the rumour circulated that it was a gift from the pope, and that O'Neill might shortly expect the crown of Ireland from the same source.[1]

[1] *Comment. Rinucc.*, iii, 59–61.

Discussions between Rinuccini and the council on the proposed truce made little progress, for neither party was willing to reveal its mind fully. In the meantime, Inchiquin's hand was forced by a threatened mutiny by some of his officers. On 3 April 1648 he assembled his army and told them that he had decided to oppose the enemies of the king in England. A small number of officers resisted but they were imprisoned. By this action he had committed himself to reaching agreement with the confederates quickly.

While Rinuccini was becoming more convinced that the truce was part of a plot to recall Ormond and thereby eclipse himself and O'Neill, he had nothing approaching proof of this, and so had to base his arguments on a claim that it did not provide adequately for the interests of the catholic church. On these grounds he openly declared his opposition, but the council, though some were hesitant and uncertain, arranged to send envoys to meet Inchiquin at Dungarvan in a fortnight's time, on 22 April. They were not anxious for a direct confrontation with the nuncio, and hoped to use this delay to win his assent. They were also determined to work as hard as they could for satisfactory religious terms, and were encouraged by the knowledge that some of the bishops were at least very reserved in their support of Rinuccini. On 27 April the nuncio vetoed a draft of the proposed truce. After this suspicions and rumours tended to get completely out of hand.[1] Early in the morning of 9 May Rinuccini left Kilkenny secretly and went to O'Neill's camp near Maryborough. He had been alarmed by a story that there was a plot against his life. This story seems to have been without any real foundation, though doubtless there were plenty of hot words from which it could be concocted.

Both parties still moved carefully, even after the truce with Inchiquin had been signed on 20 May and promulgated in Kilkenny two days later. The crisis came in consequence of another unfounded rumour. On 2 May the hierarchy had set up a permanent committee, consisting of the nuncio and four bishops, to act in their name in matters concerning the truce. This committee had been given explicit power to impose censures if these were deemed necessary, and the nuncio had been authorised to name substitutes for any member who could not attend meetings. It was natural that after the promulgation of the truce he should wish to consult his committee. One member, the bishop of Clogher, was with him in Maryborough. On 25 May he wrote to the other three inviting them to a meeting at Ferbane on 30 May. The letter gave no indication that when writing it he was contemplating recourse to ecclesiastical censure. On 27 May, while he was still with O'Neill, news was brought that Preston was marching to attack the Ulster army. The news was not true, but Rinuccini panicked. Hastily, he called on three other

[1] For these events, see P. J. Corish, 'Rinuccini's censure of 27 May 1648' in *Ir. Theol. Quart.*, xviii, no. 4 (Oct. 1951), pp 322–37.

bishops present—the bishop of Ross, always his faithful supporter, and two recently consecrated, the bishops of Down and of Cork and Cloyne, the former being O'Neill's nephew—and with himself and the bishop of Clogher they jointly pronounced excommunication against all who should support the truce with Inchiquin, hoping thereby to check the attack by Preston.[1]

Debate was to rage for years on the legality of his action. Its legal validity, however, must be considered beyond doubt,[2] but it was a political disaster, for it was an irrevocable declaration of war on the supreme council, made in circumstances much less favourable than in 1646; and though Rinuccini had been successful on that occasion, he had since been repeatedly warned by his superiors in Rome that he should never so act again.

The excommunication was published in Kilkenny on 29 May, and two days later the supreme council decided to lodge an appeal to Rome against it. Rinuccini acquiesced in the appeal, but declared that its effect was not suspensive, that is, that the censure remained in force until the appeal should have been decided. This reaction had not been expected in Kilkenny, where it had been accepted that an appeal would automatically suspend the censure. The claim that it did not was disturbing, for it naturally told against the council in the battle with the nuncio for the allegiance of the Irish catholics. At the end of July they decided to draw up a defence of their position, entitled *Queries concerning the lawfulnesse of the present cessation*. Its principal author, Peter Walsh, O.F.M., was a man of some learning in canon law, but the legal sources he drew on were almost all medieval, and took no account of post-tridentine developments, notably the growth of the papal diplomatic service and of the influence of the curial congregations since the pontificates of Gregory XIII (1572–85) and Sixtus V (1585–90). His final conclusion, insinuated rather than expressed, was that the excommunication might be 'against the law of the land as in catholic times it was practised', pointing to the possibility that Rinuccini's programme might involve not merely the repeal of legislation passed since 20 Henry VIII but also of the statutes of provisors and praemunire.[3]

The Old English and Rinuccini had reached the stage of mutual incomprehension. His final verdict on them was that they were not catholics in any sense he could understand: 'these people are catholics only in name; the ideas they hold are almost the same as those of Henry VIII and Elizabeth'.[4] The Old Irish, as already noted, have left little concrete indication of their

[1] *Comment. Rinucc.*, iii, 205–10.

[2] This is the conclusion reached by Kevin Mullen, after an exhaustive examination of the legal aspects of the question, in 'The ecclesiastical censures of the Irish confederacy' (D.C.L. thesis, Angelicum University, Rome, 1970), which he has kindly put at my disposal.

[3] P. J. Corish, 'The crisis in Ireland in 1648: the nuncio and the supreme council: conclusions' in *Ir. Theol. Quart.*, xxii, no. 3 (July 1955), pp 245–55.

[4] Aiazzi, *Nunziatura in Irlanda*, pp 350, 362.

political stand, but a verdict, close to that of Rinuccini, on the religion of the Old English, in contrast with Owen Roe O'Neill and the Old Irish, may be quoted from one of their poets:

> Ní mar sin don chloinn chuilsi
> ghonus corp na heagluisi;
> madh clann do Phádraig an fhian
> meallta an Pápa 's a naoimhchliar.
> Do shénsat Pádraig ar mhír,
> ní feas dáibh an leo Cailbhín,
> ní caraid dóibh cliara Gall,
> fala leo ag fianuibh Éireann.

(Not so with the spurious children who wound the body of the church: if that crew be Patrick's children then the pope and the holy clergy have been deceived. They have denied Patrick for the sake of a trifle; they do not know whether they agree with Calvin or not; the clergy [even] of the Goill do not like them while the troops of Éire hate them.)[1]

The confederacy fell apart on what seemed inevitable lines of division. O'Neill and the Old Irish in general supported Rinuccini. Among the bishops, eight opposed him, though, as the lines quoted above indicate, the Old Irish could not understand why. The Old English, with varying degrees of hesitation, came to support the truce, when not moved by clear conviction urged by weariness of war and the misery of the country, where the spread of disease was now adding to the ravages of battle and the strain of supporting so many armies. The nuncio was forced to retire to Galway. In Kilkenny a general assembly was called for 4 September. Meanwhile, Ormond in France was preparing to return.

Rinuccini's supporters did not attend the assembly. Those who came were nearly all from Leinster and Munster. The attendance from Connacht seems to have been thin, and there were only three from Ulster among the elected commoners, Sir Phelim O'Neill, Antrim's brother Alexander MacDonnell, and Henry O'Neill. Rinuccini had forbidden the bishops to attend, but eight of them disobeyed his order. The assembly sent an envoy to Rome to follow up the council's appeal against the excommunication, made various efforts to win further support, especially from the clergy, and proclaimed O'Neill a traitor to the confederate cause. But there was a general understanding that its real business would begin only when Ormond returned.

He landed on 30 September 1648, at Cork, for his first preoccupation was to make certain of Inchiquin and his army. His plans and those of the king his master had not gone well since the confederate envoys had left Paris in May. He brought with him to Ireland little more than the prestige of his

1 Lambert MacKenna (ed.), 'Some Irish bardic poems: xci' in *Studies*, xxxviii, no. 151 (Sept. 1949), pp 342, 344.

name. In England, the invading army of the Scots had been routed by Cromwell at Preston on 17 August, and thereafter the king's support fell to pieces. He still had some prospect of playing army and parliament against one another, but he failed to reach agreement with either of them.

Having assured himself of Inchiquin, Ormond turned to the confederates and moved to his own house at Carrick-on-Suir to negotiate with them. It was clear from the beginning that the only points really at issue between the parties were those concerning religion. In civil matters, the confederates would content themselves with minor improvements on what had been agreed between them and Ormond in 1646. As the basis of a religious settlement they presented the four points drawn up by the clergy and incorporated by the assembly in the new oath of association in February 1647: that there be free and public exercise of the catholic religion; that their traditional jurisdiction, privileges, and immunities be restored to the catholic clergy; that the penal laws be repealed; and that the catholics retain the churches in the territories they held. These were far in advance of anything Ormond had hitherto expressed himself willing to grant, and though he came to Kilkenny to speed the negotiations little progress was made. On 21 November he had to leave for Cork, where Inchiquin was again threatened by an army mutiny.

The same day the envoys from Rome landed at Waterford. They had arrived in Rome on 23 April (N.S.).[1] They found the pope very reluctant to commit himself to a formal approval of terms for peace between catholics and their protestant ruler. Throughout May and June his hesitancy was reinforced by disquieting rumours trickling through from Ireland and Paris. Though the French nuncio found solid information hard to come by, he was able to write on 15 June that in Paris it was no longer a secret that Ormond was planning to return to Ireland. This letter arrived in Rome on 12 July, and the envoys now pressed for a definite decision as to what the Irish catholics should do if it came to making peace with Ormond. It was five weeks before they got any reply, and it gave them little practical guidance. The pope told them merely 'that when there was question of a peace between catholics and heretics it was not the custom of the holy see to approve positively, but that he had good hopes that in all their actions the envoys and all the Irish catholics would strive for the greater advancement and advantage of the catholic religion'.[2] As regards the money and supplies asked for, he said that a great deal had been given already and now there was no more to give. A few days later news arrived from Ireland of Rinuccini's excommunication and of the supreme council's defiance and appeal to Rome.

The envoys took desperate council with Luke Wadding. All three were

[1] I have given a fuller account of the mission to Rome in 'The origins of catholic nationalism' in Corish, *Ir. catholicism*, iii, ch. VIII (Dublin, 1968), pp 48–50.

[2] *Comment. Rinucc.*, iii, 409.

agreed that Rinuccini had made a bad mistake. They asked for an audience with the pope to urge this view, but were refused. Their only hope now was to return to Ireland and possibly persuade Rinuccini to change his mind. For this purpose they succeeded in getting a cardinal friendly to Wadding to write him a letter, saying that there were divided opinions in Rome on the prudence of his actions. They left Rome on 28 August (N.S.). One can perhaps understand why they made the return journey slowly. When they landed at Waterford and learned exactly how matters stood in Ireland they decided that priority must be given to the negotiations at Kilkenny and not to convincing Rinuccini.[1] On 24 November Bishop French addressed the assembly. He at least allowed it to be inferred that the religious terms that had been put to Ormond would not meet with papal disapproval, and—here he was certainly making the most of the Roman cardinal's letter he had brought with him—that in Rome minds were divided over Rinuccini's excommunication. His speech did much to lessen what influence the nuncio still retained; a short time afterwards the eight bishops in Kilkenny were joined by the archbishop of Cashel and the bishop of Waterford.[2]

Ormond, of course, had not yet accepted the confederates' proposals. He made his own offer on 19 December, after his return from Cork. The catholics would be free to practise their religion, but he had no authority to settle the question of ecclesiastical jurisdiction. In regard to churches and livings, he could assure them that they would not be disturbed in the possession of those they held until the king should declare his pleasure after hearing their views expressed in a free parliament. This marked little advance on the position he had taken in 1646, and it was rejected. The next day, however, the assembly asked him if he could give an assurance that they would not be disturbed in the churches, livings, and jurisdictions they held until the king's pleasure was known. Ormond sensed their weakening, and replied that he had no authority to settle anything concerning livings and jurisdictions, but that catholics would not be molested in the churches they possessed or in the exercise of their functions in them. This neutral word did not satisfy the confederates. They insisted on a recognition of ecclesiastical jurisdiction, and the deadlock seemed complete.

At this stage, on 28 December 1648, the dramatic news arrived from England of the remonstrance of the army, demanding that the king be put on trial for his life. In a surge of loyalty the assembly indicated its willingness to accept Ormond's offer. The bishops were thrown into confusion. Some felt that they had no option but to leave Kilkenny and join the nuncio. Again it seems to have been Bishop French who persuaded them to stay, reminding

[1] For a detailed account of the negotiations, see P. J. Corish, 'Bishop Nicholas French and the second Ormond peace, 1648–9' in *I.H.S.*, vi, no. 22 (Sept. 1948), pp 83–100.

[2] Ultimately, twelve bishops in all opposed Rinuccini. See Corish, 'The origins of catholic nationalism', loc. cit., p. 52, n. 23.

them of the recently signed treaties of Westphalia, where catholic and protestant had reached agreement in spite of opposition from a papal nuncio. The bishops at Kilkenny still had bargaining power, for if they refused to accept the treaty it might be very ineffective. Finally Ormond agreed to 'give unto the Roman Catholics full assurance that they shall not be molested in the possession of the churches and church livings, or of the exercise of their respective jurisdictions as they now exercise the same' until the king should declare his pleasure after hearing them in a free parliament.[1] Agreement on these terms was reached on 17 January 1649. It was still only a promise, but it promised the catholics the king's constitutional consideration for what they sought, legal recognition of their church organisation, and not mere toleration by connivance. Whether it would have survived the king's consideration was never put to the test, for his trial began two days later and he was executed on 30 January. Charles would almost certainly have refused the catholics what they sought for their church, for in his negotiations with the army and parliament he had shown no consideration for his catholic subjects in Ireland, and the negotiations had finally broken on his stubborn defence of the position of the established church.

By the treaty the confederate government was dissolved, and in its place twelve 'commissioners of trust' were appointed to manage affairs in the areas held by the catholics under Ormond as lord lieutenant of the new king, proclaimed as Charles II after his father's execution. The Ulster Scots also agreed to put themselves at Ormond's disposal. The catholic clergy were still to some extent divided, and O'Neill had made his position clear before the treaty was signed. He would accept any agreement that provided for the interests of the country and of religion, but the papal nuncio would have to be a party to it. Ormond, however, did not want to have any dealings with Rinuccini—'no subject of his majesty's'—nor did Rinuccini wish for dealings with Ormond. He sailed from Galway on 23 February 1649.

Inevitably, he was to be accused of dividing the Irish catholics by his intransigence, but if he left them divided he also found them divided, and divided on an intractable issue with no precedents to point to its solution, namely the legal basis for the existence of the catholic church under a protestant ruler. Shortly after his arrival he faced a crisis in which he could not follow his instructions to secure the position of the church while at the same time keeping himself clear of political issues. He decided not to allow the essential interests of religion, as he saw them, to be put at risk, and it is hard to see how he could have decided otherwise. He might be criticised for not having a clearer or more flexible view of what was really essential, but in the last resort this is to fault him for not being greatly in advance of his time, for not having found the answer to a problem to which there was no contemporary solution. He might perhaps with more reason be faulted for

[1] Gilbert, *Ir. confed.*, vii, 186.

the inflexibility of his tactics, especially in the excommunication of 1648, but excommunication had been successful in 1646, and, if at that time he had not taken the course he did, would he have had any alternative to leaving the country and confessing his mission a failure, as he had to do three years later in 1649?

CHAPTER XIII

The Cromwellian conquest, 1649–53

PATRICK J. CORISH

THE forces of parliament under George Monck, commander-in-chief in Ulster, held small enclaves in the north, but their main strength was with Jones in Dublin and the surrounding territory. Ormond concentrated his efforts on recovering this key area which he had surrendered in 1647. By mid-June 1649 he was advancing on Dublin, with armies led by Inchiquin, Preston, and Castlehaven.[1] In July Inchiquin captured Drogheda, Dundalk, Newry, and Trim, and the armies closed in on Dublin, but the investment of the city by this heterogeneous force of very uneven fighting capacity was a slow process. On 26 July the garrison was reinforced by the arrival of 2,600 troops from England. This brought Jones's strength almost up to Ormond's. A rumour was spread by the parliamentarians that Cromwell with the main English army planned to land in Munster. Ormond had to send strong forces south under Inchiquin to counter this threat. A general engagement took place at Rathmines on 2 August, and Ormond's army was routed by Jones. In consequence of this victory, 'an astonishing mercy, so great and seasonable that we are like them that dreamed', Oliver Cromwell was able to land unopposed at Ringsend on 15 August with the main army of 12,000 men for the conquest of Ireland.

'Crumwell came over', wrote Bishop Nicholas French years later in exile, 'and like a lightning passed through the land'.[2] Any account of Irish history over the next few years must concentrate on military affairs, even though these have been so often told in detail that there can be little new to add.[3] The difficulty is rather to do justice to all the complications within a brief account. As one fortified post after another fell to the armies of parliament, the conflict took on more and more the character of a guerrilla war. Bands of soldiers from a defeated army could still be a serious military threat, and an

[1] The account of military affairs in the summer of 1649 is taken from Hayes-McCoy, *Ir. battles*, pp 200–13.

[2] Nicholas French, *The unkinde desertor of loyall men and true frinds* (1846 ed.), p. 13.

[3] The most detailed account is by Denis Murphy, *Cromwell in Ireland* (Dublin, 1892). For Cromwell personally see Cromwell, *Writings*, ed. Abbott. In addition to general histories of the period and biographies of Cromwell a number of specialised articles on the war have appeared over the past generation, especially in *Ir. Sword*.

army could even re-form quickly after a defeat. The divisions between the royalist groups had only been papered over by the peace of January 1649, and they reappeared as soon as Cromwell's campaign began. This led to a series of very complex political conflicts, waged with great bitterness while the country was being overrun.

The luxury of such conflicts could be afforded while England was distracted by civil war with neither party there able to devote its attentions to the affairs of Ireland. Some account has already been given of the tortuous negotiations between the king and the Irish confederates. Parliamentary thinking was not complicated by any consideration other than that of simple reconquest, but until the English wars had been won an army sufficient for this purpose could not be sent to Ireland, nor could the forces loyal to parliament there be adequately supplied. The 'sea adventure' led by Lord Forbes against the southern and western coasts in 1643 was no more than an ineffective raid and brought no relief to Inchiquin. In consequence, he had had little choice but to accept the 1643 cessation, and although in the following year he changed sides again he was nearly overrun by the confederates in 1645. In January 1646 parliament had appointed Lord Lisle as its lord lieutenant in Ireland. He arrived early in February 1647 with some troops but very little money, and his presence did little except to alienate Inchiquin, and sow dissension between him and a group of influential New English protestants, the most prominent being Lord Broghill, son of the earl of Cork, who had returned from England with the expedition. On Lisle's departure the military reinforcements he had brought came under Inchiquin's control, but they served him uneasily, especially after his truce with the confederates in the spring of 1648 and the Ormond peace at the beginning of the following year.

After the execution of the king and the establishment of the commonwealth, it was necessary to secure the new English state from royalist dangers from Ireland and Scotland. Ireland was given priority. The enclaves held by parliament there were threatened by the royalist forces now united under Ormond; satisfaction was due to the adventurers, who had invested money in the reconquest of Ireland on the strength of acts of the English parliament since 1642; and vengeance had to be exacted for what was now unquestionably accepted as the planned general massacre of 1641. Cromwell prepared his army carefully, ensuring that it would be adequately paid and supplied from the public revenue. On 10 July he left London for Milford Haven, as Munster seemed the most promising landing-point because of the very divided loyalties of Inchiquin's army. It was the news of the victory at Rathmines that decided him to set sail for Dublin. He brought with him 12,000 men, 8,000 foot and 4,000 horse, to add to the 8,000 already in Dublin under the command of Jones. More decisive, perhaps, in view of the way the war was to develop, he had a train of modern artillery.

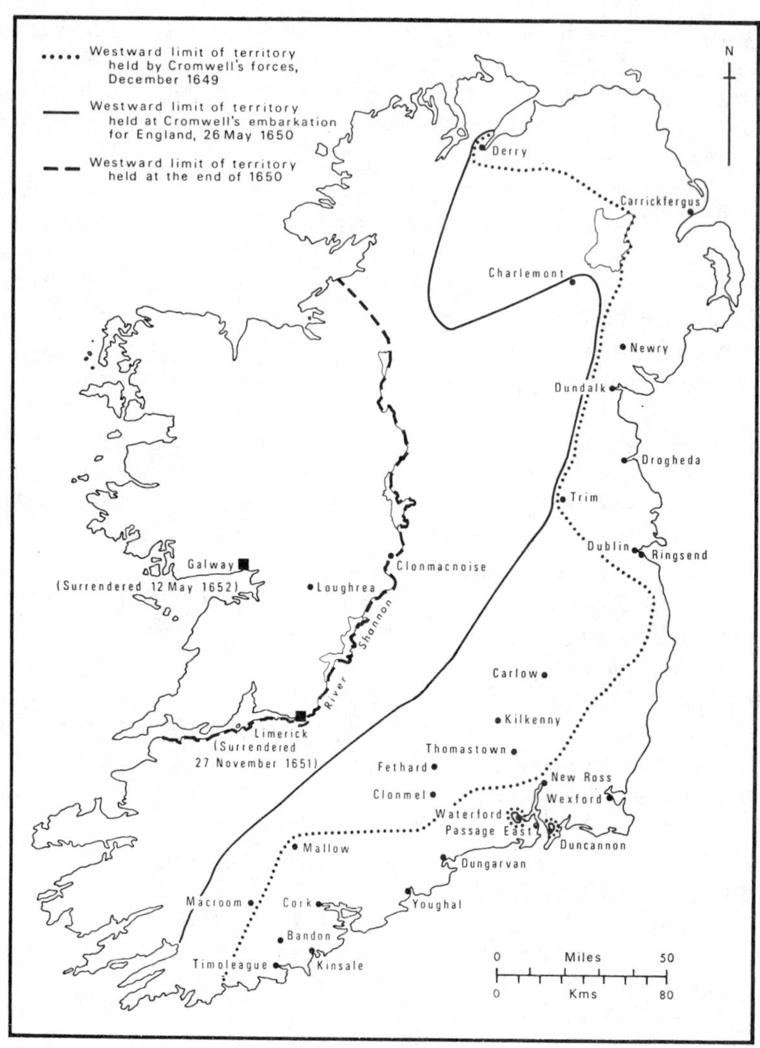

Map 8 THE CROMWELLIAN CONQUEST, by Patrick J. Corish

It may be well to recall that the New Model army was not now, or indeed at any time, an egalitarian group bound together by a religious ideology, though once in the ranks the soldiers were subjected to continuous indoctrination for which most of them were prepared.[1] The level of education among the infantry was low, and most of them were pressed men, not volunteers. In the more élite cavalry, men of education and strong religious conviction, and even of some little property, could be found among the rank and file. Although promotion from the ranks was not uncommon most of the officers were propertied gentlemen. There was a great disparity in rates of pay, the private infantry soldier receiving eightpence to tenpence a day, probably less than the wages of an agricultural labourer, while his captain had eight shillings and his colonel one pound. Pay had been in arrears since the early days of the civil war, and the private soldiers' best hope lay in the 'lawful plunder' allowed when a town or fortress was taken by assault. Even when terms were made, they often demanded a payment in compensation for the loss of plunder. At Kilkenny, for example, the citizens had to agree to pay £2,000 to the army.[2]

It is not so easy to estimate the strength of the forces opposing Cromwell, because they were so fragmented and so variably equipped. The defeat at Rathmines had been a severe blow to morale, and mistrust was everywhere. Nevertheless, if one counts all the forces theoretically available to Ormond, including those of Owen Roe O'Neill, who was to reach an agreement with him on 20 October, they outnumbered those under Cromwell's command in Dublin, though militarily they were far less effective. This military disparity was increased by the strategy forced on Ormond. He was unable to venture a pitched battle, for which he could not assemble an army. He could not waste the country, for he depended on it for his supplies to a far greater extent than did Cromwell, whose communications with England were open. He had little choice but to garrison the fortified towns and castles, himself retaining a small army in reserve. The towns were particularly suspicious of Ormond, for they had consistently been among Rinuccini's strongest supporters. Their fortifications might appear impressive, but they were for the most part simple medieval curtain walls, quite unable to resist Cromwell's modern artillery.

Cromwell's first objective was to enlarge his bridgehead by the capture of Drogheda. This town had always been part of the Dublin enclave until it had been taken by Inchiquin in July 1649. It now had a garrison of about 2,600 men, badly provisioned and with little ammunition. How many of them were English and how many Irish seems beyond establishing, but the senior officers were chiefly English, as was the commander, Sir Arthur

[1] The standard study is still C. H. Firth, *Cromwell's army* (London, 1902). The introduction by P. H. Hardacre to the latest (1962) edition lists later writings.

[2] See below, p. 345–6.

Aston, a catholic royalist. Cromwell's army of 10,000 men arrived before the town on 3 September. A week later, with the investment completed and his batteries in position, a summons to surrender was rejected. An entry was forced the following day, about 5 o'clock in the afternoon. On Cromwell's orders, no quarter was given to the garrison, and those who did not manage to escape were killed almost to a man. The few prisoners taken were shipped to the Barbados.[1]

By the strict rules of war, Cromwell had the right to refuse quarter to a town carried by storm after rejecting a call to surrender. This was a right sparingly invoked, however, and in his justification of the slaughter at Drogheda it does not appear as the dominant motive. By his own testimony, supported by that of many others, the massacre was not confined to the garrison, but became quite indiscriminate. For this he offers two lines of justification. One was policy, and as policy it proved only partly effective: that such ruthless severity would 'tend to prevent the effusion of blood for the future'. The second, ominously, was revenge: this 'marvellous great mercy' was 'a righteous judgement of God upon these barbarous wretches who have imbrued their hands with so much innocent blood'.[2] That this justification could be advanced for the massacre of the inhabitants of a town that had never at any time been in the hands of the confederate catholics was a sombre indication of how far the guilt for 'innocent blood' was now presumed to extend.

Cromwell now detached a force under Colonel Robert Venables to penetrate Ulster, with such success that by the end of November Carrickfergus was the only coastal town in royalist hands. On 20 October Owen Roe O'Neill reached an agreement with Ormond. A major obstacle, that O'Neill believed Ormond's catholic followers to be excommunicated, while they insisted that they were not, was overcome when they gave O'Neill an undertaking to petition the pope to grant absolution from Rinuccini's censures, without prejudice to the question of their validity or invalidity, and to write to the nuncio asking for his personal forgiveness and future goodwill. In return O'Neill agreed to serve under Ormond as general of the Ulster army, and in case of his death or removal the nobility and gentry of Ulster were to nominate his successor. O'Neill was in fact dying, and his death came on 6 November at Cloughoughter, in Cavan, as he moved slowly south with his army.

Cromwell's main effort, however, was directed towards exploiting the disaffection in the Munster garrisons nominally commanded by Inchiquin. About 23 September he left Dublin and marched along the coast towards Wexford. The town had been the centre of the confederates' naval strength and their principal supply-port. Its people had been strong supporters of

[1] Presumably as indentured servants; see below, p. 363.

[2] Cromwell, *Writings*, ed. Abbott, ii, 127.

Rinuccini, and now refused to admit an Ormond garrison. The small garrison in the town, commanded by David Synnott, an officer of Preston's army, had rather uneasy relations with the townsmen. On 3 October Cromwell issued his summons to surrender. After some initial parleying, the citizens agreed with Castlehaven, Ormond's representative, to accept a garrison of 1,500 Ulster troops who had been maintaining themselves in Wicklow, and the negotiations with Cromwell were dropped. On 6 October his artillery arrived by sea, though because of rough weather it was possibly some days later before the guns could be landed and the bombardment begun. Within the town counsels were divided. On 11 October Synnott sent envoys to Cromwell with a set of propositions demanding the continuation of catholic worship as it had been during the years of the confederacy, leave for the garrison to withdraw, and full legal protection for the lives and property of the inhabitants. Cromwell described these proposals as 'abominable', and the men who made them as 'impudent'. He would give quarter to the garrison, the private soldiers to go free, but the officers to be taken prisoner, and he would protect the town from plunder, but no more. Meanwhile, as one party inside was actually admitting reinforcements from Ormond, one of Synnott's envoys, Captain James Stafford, in Cromwell's cryptic words, 'being fairly treated, yielded up the castle'. The indications are that he represented a group—how large it is impossible to say—who believed more might be hoped for from Cromwell than from Ormond. In the confusion, the besieging army scaled the walls and fought their way through the streets. Cromwell's own account makes it clear that the killing was indiscriminate, and that about 2,000 people were killed. He speaks of a 'stiff resistance', but this is hard to reconcile with his claim that his own losses were 'not twenty'. He also makes it clear that what resistance there was ended in the market-place. Within a few years of the restoration the story of 200 women massacred there had found its way into print.[1] This may mean that the full truth could now be openly told, or it may mark the beginning of a legend. Truth or legend, it came to be accepted as truth: MacGeoghegan's *History of Ireland*, published in 1758–63, usually cited as the first written evidence of the event, obviously gleans it from the traditions of Irish soldiers in the French service. At Drogheda, the massacre had broken out because Cromwell, 'in the heat of action', had ordered that all the garrison be killed; at Wexford, the army had no such order, but ran amok once inside the town, and the killing took place when negotiations for surrender had been initiated and not yet broken off. Here there could be no appeal to the recognised laws of war. Cromwell described the massacre at Wexford in the same terms as he had described that at Drogheda, as a just judgement of

[1] James Heath, *Flagellum or the life and death, birth and burial of Oliver Cromwell, the late usurper* (2nd ed. enlarged, 1663), p. 83, cited in Antonia Fraser, *Cromwell our chief of men* (London, 1973), pp 345–6.

God, and he seemed more concerned with the damage done to the town than with the fate of its inhabitants.

The decision to surrender New Ross without resistance might seem to indicate that Cromwell's policy of terror had begun to bite, but it was in fact dictated by tactical considerations. The town had admitted an Ormond garrison of 2,500 men. Inchiquin's soldiers formed a substantial part of this, and many of them were unreliable (500 or 600 joined Cromwell's army after the surrender of the town). Ormond was on the Kilkenny bank of the Barrow in some force, but the town was on the east or Wexford bank. In these circumstances, Cromwell had little choice but to allow the garrison to withdraw with its arms. The inhabitants were guaranteed protection from plunder, but the answer to a demand for liberty of conscience was: 'I meddle not with any man's conscience. But if by liberty of conscience you mean a liberty to exercise the mass, I judge it best to use plain dealing, and to let you know, where the parliament of England have power, that will not be allowed of.'[1]

New Ross surrendered on 19 October. Cromwell remained there for a month. There was sickness among his soldiers and he wished to build a bridge across the Barrow before venturing into Munster. His attempt to capture the great fortress of Duncannon had to be abandoned on 5 November in the face of a spirited defence, and the parliamentary troops seem to have withdrawn in some disorder. Before he was ready to leave New Ross he had the good news that Lord Broghill, his emissary to the disaffected officers in Munster, had succeeded. Broghill had gone to England after Inchiquin's truce with the confederate catholics. After the king's execution he was preparing to go to the Continent when he was visited by Cromwell and they agreed to work together. He joined Cromwell shortly after he had come to Ireland and had been his principal contact with the Munster army officers. By the beginning of November it was clear that he had succeeded, and by the middle of the month officers pledged to him had seized control of Cork, Youghal, Kinsale, Bandon, and Timoleague. As well as securing these important garrisons for parliament, the officers' coup had neutralised Prince Rupert's royalist fleet, which had been based on Kinsale.

Cromwell, however, still had to link up with the Munster garrisons. It was late in the season, and there were mutinous mutterings among his troops. Ormond's army had been strengthened by forces sent south by Owen Roe O'Neill in advance of his own slow progress. Their commanders, General Richard O'Farrell and Colonel Hugh O'Neill, both seasoned veterans in the Spanish service, had brought with them Owen Roe's advice to Ormond: to avoid a pitched battle. Ormond did little as Cromwell, encouraged by the unusually mild weather, advanced through County Kilkenny to cross the Suir at Carrick on 20 November. The following day an advance party summoned Waterford to surrender.

[1] Cromwell, *Writings*, ed. Abbott, ii, 146.

Waterford, then the second city of Ireland, had been markedly loyal to Rinuccini, and at this juncture was very unwilling to accept an English or protestant commander. The defender of Duncannon, Edward Wogan, though of an Old English family, was a protestant. Castlehaven was a catholic, but he was English. The mayor, John Lyvett, finally agreed to accept General Richard O'Farrell and the troops he could muster, approximately 2,000.

This arrangement had been made but O'Farrell's troops had not yet arrived when Cromwell's main forces came up to Waterford on 24 November. When the promised garrison arrived Lyvett broke off the negotiations he had begun in order to gain time. Though Cromwell captured the fortifications at Passage East to the south, he was unable to reduce Waterford. It was very late in the season, the weather had at last broken, and his army was suffering from dysentery and reduced to about 3,000 effectives. On 2 December he marched west from Waterford, receiving at Kilmacthomas the welcome news that Dungarvan had surrendered to Broghill. A more forceful commander than Ormond might well have penned his opponent into a very unpleasant corner, but Cromwell was now assured of comfortable winter quarters. What further news arrived was good. Wogan and O'Farrell were heavily defeated in an attempt to recapture Passage East. From the north news came that Carrickfergus had been captured. The autumn campaign had yielded, in Cromwell's own words, 'a great tract in longitude along the shore, yet it hath but little depth into the country'. It stretched from Derry round to west Cork, with the enclave of resistance at Waterford harbour.

The conquest had been made easier by the divisions among the royalist forces: divisions between English and Irish, between catholic and protestant, and internal divisions between catholics. O'Neill's agreement with Ormond had been based on the understanding that a new petition be sent to the pope to grant absolution from Rinuccini's censures, thereby reviving an issue which had seriously divided the catholic hierarchy. The main initiative in a decision to convoke a bishops' meeting seems to have come from Heber MacMahon, the heir to much of O'Neill's influence among the Ulstermen. Ormond had no very happy memories of bishops' meetings, but he was quite prepared to let this one go ahead in the hope that it would do something to remedy the crippling disunity. The bishops met at Clonmacnoise from 4 to 13 December 1649.

To avoid raising contentious political issues, the bishops declared that they were meeting *motu proprio*, that is, purely as an ecclesiastical congregation. Their discussions led to agreement to issue a declaration, to be printed and posted in every parish, proclaiming their unity in the cause of their religion and their king, and calling on all for an end to dissensions. Two further declarations went into more detail. They warned that nothing was to be expected of Cromwell, though some people nourished empty delusions on this point. It was clear, they said, that he planned to extirpate the catholic religion in all the king's dominions, as was proved by his declaration at New Ross. It was further clear that he planned the extirpation of the Irish, as well as the confiscation of their property. In proof, they appealed to the fact that he had already deported many to the 'tobacco islands', and said that if for the moment there might seem to be indications that he was treating the common people with some consideration this was only a deceit. They appealed to people not to allow themselves to be deceived, but to contribute generously to the war in loyalty to the king and Ormond.[1]

The bishop of Clogher appears to have been the principal architect of the unity displayed in these declarations. In reality the bishops were still deeply divided, each party anxious to justify the stand it had taken twelve months before. This call for loyalty to Ormond had been a difficult decision for some bishops. The division became open when they took up the question of what was to be done in regard to the nuncio's censures. The group who had supported Rinuccini sent a letter of apology to him, and to the pope they sent a petition seeking absolution. The others insisted that the censures were invalid, and would agree only to a petition for conditional absolution, to quiet scruples of conscience, and without prejudice to the appeal already lodged against Rinuccini.

This meeting at Clonmacnoise, then, had only a very qualified success, but its printed declarations moved Cromwell to a long and impassioned reply, drawn up at Youghal in the second half of January 1650, and printed at Cork before the end of the month.[2] It deserves study, for it reveals in some detail his future plans for Ireland and his reasons for them. Historians of the English liberal tradition have seen in it 'God's Englishman' at his most bullheaded—'it combines in a unique degree profound ignorance of the Irish past with a profound miscalculation of the Irish future' is the verdict of John Morley[3]—and it is hard to dissent.

'I will give you some wormwood to bite on', he retorted to the bishops: the facts of the case, in reply to their deceptions. These facts were that Englishmen bought their interests in Ireland, that Irishmen had equal justice with them before the law, and yet they rose in rebellion and massacre. Making all allowance for what must have gone on in Cromwell's mind as a result of a decade of intensive propaganda against everything Irish and catholic, it remains an almost inexplicable statement from a man who had stood beside John Pym when he had built up the elaborate web of charges against Strafford's maladministration in Ireland. He goes on to say that the bishops cannot call on people to fight for anything lawful. Even their professions of loyalty to the king are false. As for their people, the 'laity', their 'flocks' as

[1] *Comment. Rinucc.*, iv, 318–40.
[2] Cromwell, *Writings*, ed. Abbott, ii, 196–205.
[3] *Oliver Cromwell* (2nd ed., London, 1908), p. 318.

they call them, the difference this suggests between Christians arouses Cromwell's religious convictions to fury, but he promises deliverance. He does not plan to 'extirpate' the catholic religion, for it is impossible to extirpate what the law does not recognise to exist. He repeats that he will not allow the mass, but that he will not interfere with the conscience of those who keep the law. Neither will any man not in arms suffer in his person except by due process of law, nor, he claims, has any man so suffered with his consent. 'Give us an instance', he asked, 'of one man since my coming into Ireland, not in arms, massacred, destroyed or banished; concerning the first two of which justice hath not been done or endeavoured to be done'. Confiscation of property there will be, in accordance with laws already passed, and justly framed 'to raise money by escheating the lands of those who had a hand in the rebellion'. There will be no mercy for rebel leaders. Those innocent of rebellion may expect the protection of the law, 'testifying their good affections, upon all occasions, to the service of the state of England'. Those who had been or now are in arms 'may, submitting themselves, have their cases presented to the state of England'; private soldiers may expect to be permitted to 'live peaceably and honourably at their several homes'. 'We came, by the assistance of God, to hold forth and maintain the lustre and glory of English liberty in a nation where we have an undoubted right to do it.' Irishmen, as Gardiner comments, were to be what Englishmen were, or to bear the penalty.[1] It was not an original solution for the 'Irish question', but it was seldom stated so bluntly. Not even Cromwell could make it work.

It was a mild winter, and Cromwell was able to begin his campaign early. The mild weather may also have helped the rapid spread of another misery, the bubonic plague, starting in Galway, brought there, it was said, by a Spanish ship.[2] On 29 January 1650 Cromwell marched from Youghal, through Mallow and into Tipperary, his ultimate objective being Kilkenny. He easily overcame what resistance he met. The private soldiers got the quarter he had promised them in his January declaration, but the officers were taken prisoner. The town of Fethard, County Tipperary, received exceptionally favourable terms. The documentation does not make the reason for this absolutely clear, but indicates that Cromwell may have particularly needed a rapid surrender and that he got it.[3] Under their terms the townspeople successfully resisted the Cromwellian transplantations as 'a people to be differenced from the rest of the whole nation'.

Simultaneously, John Hewson had begun his campaign from Dublin, advancing southwards to link up with Cromwell. Their armies met at Gowran on 19 March. Three days later they were before Kilkenny and

[1] S. R. Gardiner, *Oliver Cromwell* (London, 1901), p. 179.

[2] It is called 'bubonis pestis' in the case-book of Dr Thomas Arthur, B.M., Add. MS 31885: see J. G. Simms, 'Hugh O'Neill's defence of Limerick 1650–51' in *Ir. Sword*, iii (1957–8), pp 115–23.

[3] Murphy, *Cromwell in Ireland*, pp 254–60, especially p. 258.

the city was summoned to surrender. The commander of the garrison was Sir Walter Butler, one of Ormond's many cousins, and inevitably there were tensions between him and the citizens. Though the plague had broken out in the city, it nevertheless put up a stiff resistance, so stiff that at one stage Cromwell's forces became mutinous. However, the Irish town was captured on 25 March, and three days later the city surrendered. The garrison was allowed to march out under arms, but had to surrender them two miles outside the town. The citizens were secured against violence to their lives, estates, and goods on paying a fine of £2,000. Although the city was not plundered, the churches were pillaged, especially the Ormond family tombs in St Canice's cathedral. The clergy were included in the general protection, on condition that they left the city. David Rothe, the aged catholic bishop, was among those who went away, but he was brought back by a party of soldiers. One of two irreconcilable accounts says that he was imprisoned, the other says that Cromwell allowed him to live with his family. He had not long to live in any case, for he died on 20 April. He was seventy-eight, and for the thirty-two years of his episcopate had been the leading architect of that catholic reorganisation now under threat of destruction.

While Cromwell's forces were driving inland, the opposition was still trying to remedy its disunity. On 8 March 1650 Ormond and the commissioners of trust[1] met the bishops and other notables at Limerick. Ormond threatened to abandon the country unless he got the obedience due to him as viceroy: in particular, he demanded that Limerick admit a garrison under his command. In reply he received a long list of complaints of administrative, military, judicial, and financial mismanagement. There was some substance to the complaints, though in the state of the country it was hardly realistic to demand redress as the price of cooperation. Ormond promised to do what he could, but Limerick refused to admit his garrison, and he retired to Clanricard's headquarters at Loughrea. On 28 March the catholic bishops wrote to Ormond protesting their sincere loyalty, despite, they said, all that had been rumoured to the contrary. It was the day Kilkenny surrendered to Cromwell.

In the same month of March the Ulster leaders met to choose a successor to Owen Roe O'Neill. There were many candidates, and much intrigue and jealousy. Finally, Bishop MacMahon of Clogher was chosen. He had many statesmanlike qualities, and was highly esteemed by the Ulstermen, but he was quite unfitted for military command. Shortly afterwards the Ulster Scots threw in their lot with Coote and Venables, the parliamentary commanders. On 21 June the bishop committed his army to battle against Coote at Scarrifhollis near Letterkenny, very rashly, for his forces were inferior and his commanders had urged him not to take the risk. The Ulster army was routed. A number of officers were executed by Coote after quarter had

[1] See above, p. 334.

been given. The bishop escaped from the field, but was captured near Enniskillen and hanged.

The forces of parliament now held a commanding position in every province except Connacht. Broghill put an end to organised resistance in Munster when he wiped out an army assembled by Lord Roche and Boetius MacEgan, the catholic bishop of Ross, near Macroom on 10 April. The bishop was captured and executed. During April many protestant royalists surrendered all over the country. Cromwell was prepared to accept them into his army, but very few seem to have joined him. He put no obstacles in the way of their leaving the country, and Ormond made no difficulties—indeed it is hard to see how he could have done so. Cromwell even sent passes to leave the country to Ormond and Inchiquin. (Inchiquin's army had disintegrated in consequence of the large-scale surrenders by protestant royalists.) Cromwell's offered passes were rejected, but it became known that the offer had been made, and this further weakened Ormond's authority.

His following was now almost exclusively catholic. At a meeting in Loughrea on 27 April further attempts were made to restore mutual confidence. Ormond made fairly open threats to abandon the country. The meeting asked him to stay, but Limerick still refused to admit his troops, though only after a long haggle had made clear how deep the divisions were within the city. Neither would Galway admit a royalist garrison. In spite of these rebuffs, Ormond decided to stay. The king's affairs were not yet hopeless. They were, indeed, beginning to take a promising turn in Scotland, and Ormond with dogged loyalty determined to keep up the fight in Ireland.

Meanwhile, Cromwell's conquest ground on. On 27 April he surrounded Clonmel, defended by Hugh O'Neill. Though O'Neill was short of provisions and ammunition, and could not be supplied, when the parliamentary army breached the walls and stormed the town they met a check described by Ireton as 'the heaviest we ever endured, either in England or here', losing about 2,000 men. O'Neill's ammunition was gone, however, and under cover of night he slipped out to Waterford with his men. They were refused admission to the plague-stricken town, and his army had to break up. The citizens of Clonmel, on O'Neill's advice, made terms with Cromwell, securing the now normal guarantee of protection for their lives and property (10 May). Cromwell was very angry when, on entering the town, he found that the garrison had escaped, but he honoured the terms he had given.

On 26 May he left for England in face of the threat of a Scottish invasion. The command in Ireland passed to his son-in-law, Henry Ireton. This slowed the pace of military operations. Ireton was more plodding and cautious, and the very disintegration of Irish resistance made it harder to strike a decisive blow. That summer was spent in trying to clear up the region east of the Shannon. The most notable strong-points to fall were Carlow on 24 July and Waterford on 6 August. Duncannon fort surrendered a week after the fall of Waterford. In all cases the garrison was allowed the honours of war, the lives of civilians were guaranteed, as was their property from plunder by the army. On 14 August Charlemont fort, the last surviving stronghold in the north, surrendered to Coote and Venables on the same terms. Sir Phelim O'Neill received 'leave to go beyond the sea'. Unfortunately for himself, he did not take advantage of it.

It had not been a dramatic campaign. Nevertheless, all strong-points in Ulster, Leinster, and Munster had now been occupied, and Ormond and Castlehaven failed in their attempts to assemble various isolated bands into an army. Ireton's policy was to make surrender attractive, and in particular to offer every inducement to the soldiers who surrendered to go into foreign service. The only resistance left consisted of 'the several commanders forming so many independent parties, living like freebooters, making a sort of war of tories',[1] too disorganised even to attempt to sue for collective terms of peace. Everywhere there was fear and despair.

The soldiers in arms against parliament were now all catholic. The tensions between Ormond and the confederate catholics had not been really resolved by the peace of 1649, and the sequence of military defeats had only increased them. The catholic bishops had several times declared their continuing loyalty to Ormond as the king's representative, in spite of the growing evidence that he did not in fact command enough confidence to unite the Irish in their resistance. By midsummer 1650 there were indications that some of the bishops who had supported him against the nuncio were no longer willing to back him. On 29 July the bishops as a body informed Ormond of their plans to meet at Jamestown, County Leitrim, to review the situation. The meeting began on 6 August, and six days later issued a public declaration.[2] This began by listing alleged violations by Ormond of the peace of 1649, what was claimed to be his consistent ignoring of the catholic interest, despite the bishops' repeated protestations of loyalty, and his disastrous conduct of the war. They now declared that catholics could no longer accept him as their leader. The people were released from all duty of obedience to him, and the ecclesiastical congregation proposed to take over the direction of affairs until a general assembly could be called to revive the confederacy.

This desperate expedient was in many ways reminiscent of what had happened at Waterford in 1646. On one point the bishops drew back, taught by past experience and possibly wearied by it. A proposal that there should be a formal excommunication of all who supported Ormond was met by a compromise. It was decided first to write to him at Loughrea, suggesting that it might be better if he were to delegate his authority to some acceptable person and himself go to France to seek help. The bearers of this letter

[1] Carte, *Ormond*, iii, 543–4. See below, p. 375, n. 1.

[2] Gilbert, *Contemp. hist., 1641–52*, ii, 100; see also *Comment. Rinucc.*, iv, 417–25.

received no reply. When they returned to Jamestown the episcopal meeting had broken up, leaving there, however, a representative committee consisting of the bishops of Raphoe, Clonfert, Cloyne, and Ferns. The first three had supported the nuncio eighteen months before, whereas the bishop of Ferns had taken a decisive part in bringing about the Ormond peace. It seems that it was he who now persuaded the others to defer publishing the excommunication authorised by the synod should Ormond not accept their proposal. The bishops, however, appealed to the commissioners of trust to depose the viceroy. Under this mounting pressure he agreed to negotiate, and asked for a full episcopal meeting at Loughrea. The bishops replied that this was impossible, but agreed to send two representatives. Ormond, assured of the support of his commissioners, took a stiff line. He said that he had no intention of leaving, and told the bishops sharply to give up their bickering and do what they could to carry on the war. The bishops were equally inflexible, and their excommunication was made public on 15 September, French of Ferns having withdrawn his objections. Shortly afterwards their worst fears seemed confirmed when news arrived of Charles II's declaration at Dunfermline on 16 August.

This represented what the king had to pay for the support of the Scots. As part of the price he denied all terms to the 'Irish rebels' and revoked the 1649 peace. Even the Jacobite historian Carte described it as a base betrayal.[1] It betrayed Ormond equally with the Irish catholics: he now had no authority to appeal to. Yet the commissioners of trust could argue that unless some royal representative remained—on the tacit assumption that the declaration of Dunfermline had been forced from an unwilling king—most of the Irish laity would seek what terms they could from parliament. The name of Clanricard had already emerged as an alternative to Ormond acceptable to the bishops. Yet the laity were slow to desert Ormond. An assembly met at Loughrea on 26 November, and this ghost of confederate assemblies of the past kept up their traditions of mutual recriminations and threatened deadlock. It was finally agreed, however, that Ormond be asked to leave and delegate his authority to Clanricard—not altogether logically, for Charles II at Dunfermline had revoked the authority he was now to delegate. The laity may have come to accept this compromise because of fears that he might well depart without naming any heir to his authority. He had in fact embarked several days before he actually left, and it was while he was on board ship that he agreed to nominate Clanricard. He finally sailed from Galway on 11 December 1650. With him went Inchiquin, Bellings, Daniel O'Neill, and many others. The aim of the clergy was the restoration of the confederacy, and so their acceptance of Clanricard as lord deputy could be only very lukewarm, for, though a catholic, he had consistently refused to join it in the 1640s. What nerved their opposition to Ormond was a growing

[1] Carte, *Ormond*, iii, 569–72.

hope of powerful subvention from the Continent, from Charles, duke of Lorraine.

The negotiations with Lorraine are another tangle of complexities, and their disentangling is not made easier because most of the evidence is embedded in memoirs written primarily to justify their authors.[1] Lorraine had been expelled from his duchy by the French in 1633. He entered the imperial service as a mercenary commander, but his claim to his duchy had not been admitted at the peace of Westphalia. He still had considerable resources, and raided across France during the Fronde troubles from his headquarters in the Spanish Netherlands. Irish catholic writers later portrayed him as a kind of knight errant thirsting to come to their rescue. Their opponents found a simple motive for his interest. He had contracted a second marriage while his first wife was still alive. He wanted a papal annulment of the first marriage, and hoped to secure this by making a grand gesture to show his devotion to the cause of catholicism when the pro-Spanish pope, Innocent X, succeeded the pro-French Urban VIII in 1644. This may have been one of his motives, but it is likely that as a whole they were more complex. It is not likely that as a whole they were altruistic.

As early as 1645 Lorraine had tentatively considered the possibility of military intervention in Ireland, but the project came to nothing. In the spring of 1650 a Waterford lawyer, Hugh Rochford, with the approval of Charles II, or so he claimed, was in Brussels sounding out possible help from Lorraine (the internuncio was very sceptical, feeling that neither Spain nor the papacy would approve). However, Lorraine sent one of his mercenaries, Oliver Synnott, to Ireland to discuss the subject with Ormond. At the end of the summer Ormond sent Lord Taaffe to Brussels to continue the negotiations. Lorraine was willing to help, but on condition he was accepted as 'protector royal' of Ireland. The queen-mother and the duke of York (the king had gone to Scotland in June) favoured the scheme, but Taaffe was doubtful. It was finally agreed that Lorraine would send an envoy to Ireland to conclude the negotiations there.

The envoy arrived at the end of February 1651. He must have been a little disconcerted to find that Ormond had left. A few days before he arrived two Irish envoys, Hugh Rochford and Bishop French of Ferns, had sailed to the Low Countries to negotiate with Lorraine. They had credentials, issued in the light of the declaration of Dunfermline, from the catholic bishops and the mayors of Limerick and Galway, but Clanricard had refused to be a party to the mission. In his negotiations with Lorraine's representative, he was perhaps fortunate to secure £15,000 by pledging Limerick

[1] The material published from the despatches of the internuncio in Flanders (Cathaldus Giblin, 'Catalogue of material of Irish interest in the collection Nunziatura di Fiandra, Vatican Archives' in *Collect. Hib.*, i (1958)) still leaves a number of problems unresolved.

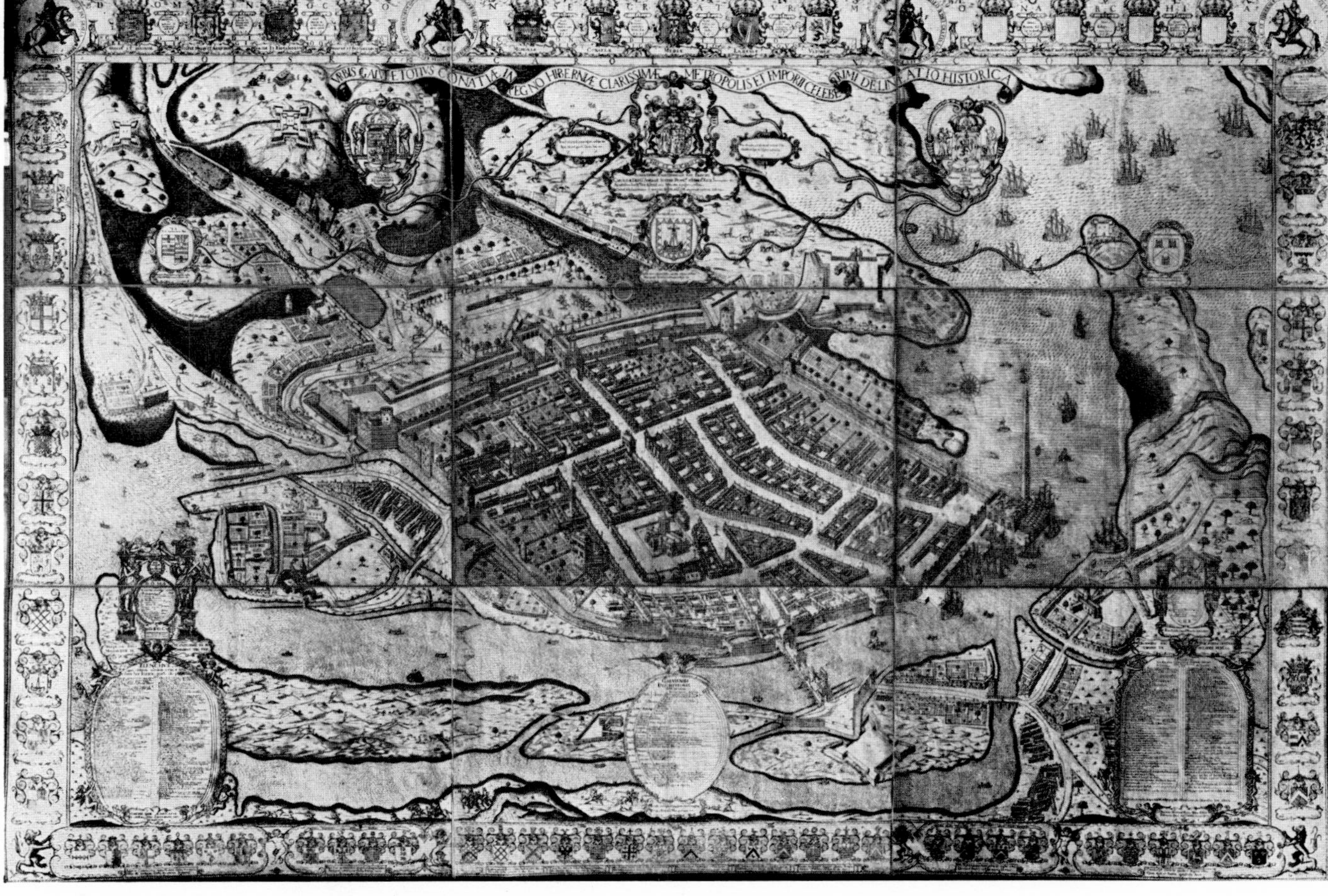

Plate 7. GALWAY 1651 (T.C.D., MS 1209, no. 73); size of original 79″ × 54″

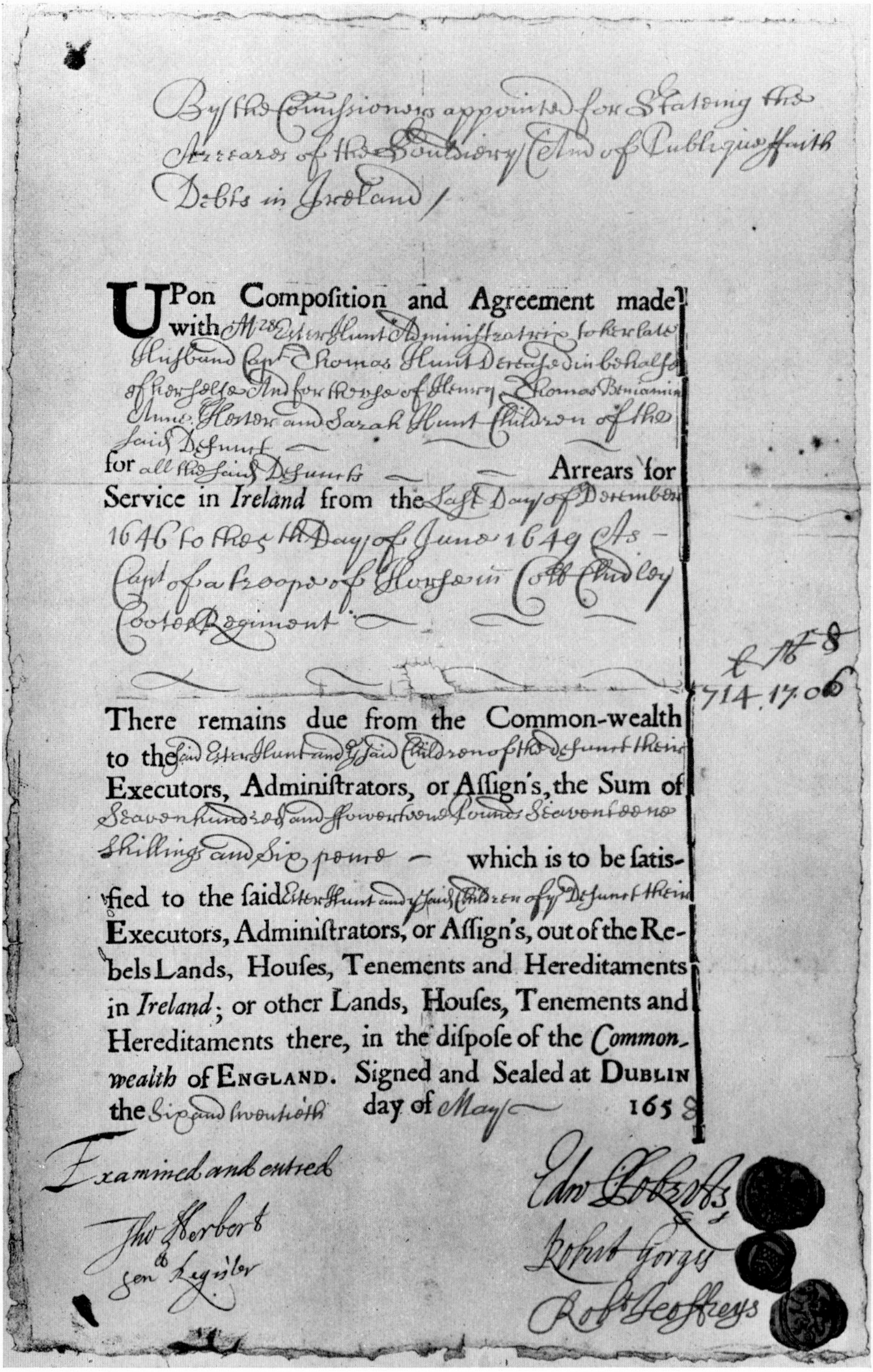

By the Commissioners appointed for Stating the Arrears of the Souldiery And of Publique ffaith Debts in Ireland.

UPon Composition and Agreement made with Mrs Ester Hunt Administratrix to her late Husband Capt Thomas Hunt Deceased in behalfe of her selfe And for the use of Henry Thomas Beniamin Anne Hester and Sarah Hunt Children of the said Deceased
for all the said Deceaseds Arrears for Service in *Ireland* from the Last Day of December 1646 to the 5th Day of June 1649 As Capt of a troope of Horse in Coll Chidley Cootes Regiment

£ No 8
714.17.06

There remains due from the Common-wealth to the said Ester Hunt and ye said Children of the deceased their Executors, Administrators, or Assign's, the Sum of Seaven hundred and ffowerteene pounds Seaventeene shillings and Six pence which is to be satisfied to the said Ester Hunt and ye said Children of ye Deceased their Executors, Administrators, or Assign's, out of the Rebels Lands, Houses, Tenements and Hereditaments in *Ireland*; or other Lands, Houses, Tenements and Hereditaments there, in the dispose of the *Common-wealth* of ENGLAND. Signed and Sealed at DUBLIN the Six and twentieth day of May 1658

Examined and entred
Tho Herbert
gen. Register

Edw Roberts
Robert Gorges
Robt Jeoffreys

Plate 8. LAND-DEBENTURE, 1658; from facsimile in J. P. Prendergast, *The Cromwellian settlement of Ireland* (2nd ed., London, 1870); size of original 12″ × 7½″

and Galway (their very qualified obedience to him was not strengthened by this undertaking), and by agreeing to send envoys to Brussels for further negotiations, on instructions to be received from the queen, the duke of York, and Ormond.

Lorraine was now dealing with two sets of envoys from Ireland, one insisting on terms acceptable to the papacy, the other on terms acceptable to the king. No such terms were possible, and it may have been only the increasing desperation of Lorraine's own affairs that kept life in the project until the end of fighting in Ireland (Lorraine was finally arrested by the Spaniards in March 1654). The glimmer of false hopes that it continued to raise helped to keep the fighting going in Ireland, where Clanricard continued Ormond's policy of resistance to the end in the interests of the king, though this policy had lost all meaning after Cromwell had destroyed Charles's Scottish army at Worcester on 3 September 1651.

Ireton, moving cautiously, had consolidated his control east of the Shannon by the end of the 1650 campaign. That autumn a governing body was appointed, with Ireton as lord deputy and commander of the army, and parliamentary commissioners consisting of Edmund Ludlow, Miles Corbet, John Jones, and John Weaver. During the winter unsuccessful attempts were made to negotiate a general surrender. In the spring Coote thrust deep into Connacht from the north, and Ireton moved on Limerick. It was the end of the summer before he had completed his investment of the city. Stricken by plague, famine, and divided counsels, it surrendered on 27 October. Twenty-two persons were excepted by name from the usual protection for life and estate. Many escaped but the bishop of Emly was among those executed. Hugh O'Neill was sent a prisoner to London, but after a few months Spanish diplomatic intervention secured his release. In November Ireton and Ludlow overran Clare. The weather was very bad and Ireton caught a cold which led to his death on 26 November. Ludlow succeeded him as commander of the army with the title of lieutenant general.

Galway was the only fortified town remaining.[1] There again counsels were divided, some hoping to make the best terms they could, some still pinning their hopes on Lorraine, and Clanricard determined to fight to the last. The terms of surrender were negotiated without his consent on 12 April 1652. In some respects they were very favourable. They guaranteed the property of the citizens beyond protection from immediate plunder, and extended protection to the clergy. However, the Irish council of state refused to accept these provisions, but their demand that they be amended arrived in Galway only after the town had been surrendered on articles which the council then refused to ratify.

Meanwhile, what remained of organised resistance was surrendering. In Leinster, John Fitzpatrick made his terms on 7 March. This led to the

[1] See plate 7.

surrender of what still called itself 'the Leinster army' at Kilkenny on 12 May, though a band under Richard Grace held out until 14 August.[1] Those who submitted on 12 May were promised that every effort would be made to allow them to enjoy 'such a remnant of their lands as might make their lives comfortable', should they choose to stay in Ireland.[2] In Munster, Muskerry finally yielded at Ross castle on 22 June, and Clanricard, after a campaign which brought some initial success, surrendered six days later. The last formal capitulation was by Philip O'Reilly at Cloghoughter on 27 April 1653. By now nothing was left except small bands of 'tories'[3] to be hunted.

The conquest was complete. No general terms of surrender had been negotiated, and with few exceptions nothing had been guaranteed in the surrenders except freedom from immediate pillage. Cromwell's reply to the bishops' declaration at Clonmacnoise had made it clear that a vast confiscation of property was to be part of any final settlement.

[1] Dan Bryan, 'Colonel Richard Grace 1651–1652' in *Ir. Sword*, iv (1959–60), pp 43–51.

[2] Prendergast, *Cromwellian settlement*, p. 81.

[3] See below, p. 375, n. 1.

CHAPTER XIV

The Cromwellian regime, 1650–60

PATRICK J. CORISH

IN England, Cromwell made repeated and varied but unsuccessful attempts to reconcile his commitment to the 'rule of the saints' with his hankering after a return to a constitutional regime acceptable to the 'political nation'. He was forced from one expedient to another, and when he died he was worn out and prematurely aged. His government was a dictatorship depending ultimately on military force, and there was no one fit to succeed him. The Irish executive was influenced by the problems and factions of both England and Ireland, but the manner in which the war had been fought and won had made it certain that far-reaching changes would be harshly and rigorously imposed on the country.

Cromwell had come to Ireland as lord lieutenant and commander-in-chief. When he left on 26 May 1650 his power was delegated to Ireton as lord deputy and army commander. The first step towards setting up a civil administration was taken on 4 October 1650, with the appointment of four 'commissioners of parliament', Edmund Ludlow, Miles Corbet, and John Jones, all three of them regicides, and John Weaver, who had been appointed a judge for the king's trial, but had not acted.[1] Ludlow was a difficult, unbending character, with political views that became much more radical than Cromwell's, and there was a suggestion that he had been sent to Ireland to have him out of the way. After the death of Ireton, he was provisionally appointed commander-in-chief by his fellow commissioners on 2 December 1651, being the only one of the four with the requisite military experience, and he commanded the army until the war ended the following year. While it continued, the commissioners could only take preliminary steps towards a system of civil government. They divided the country into six precincts, later increased to fifteen, and finally stabilised at twelve. Each was under a military governor, and for some time officials called 'commissioners of revenue' performed all the civil functions.

Cromwell's commission as commander-in-chief expired in July 1652, and

[1] Administrative documents may be found under their respective dates in *Acts & ordinances, interregnum* and Dunlop, *Commonwealth*. Specific references to these will be given only for a few documents of outstanding importance, and for direct citations. Some further material of this nature is in *Cal. S.P. Ire., 1647–60*.

Charles Fleetwood was appointed acting commander-in-chief and a parliamentary principal commissioner of government on 9 July. He had married Ireton's widow, Cromwell's daughter Bridget. Ludlow resented the appointment and was not mollified when Fleetwood, a man of flexible and accommodating temperament, not merely tolerated but encouraged the baptists and other sectaries, though he himself was an independent.[1] He arrived in Ireland about 10 September, with a daunting set of instructions directing him to settle the country in accordance with the recent enactment, to raise a monthly revenue of £40,000, to promulgate 'the gospel and the power of true religion and holiness', and to see that the laws of England be put into execution in Ireland, 'as near as the present affairs will permit'.[2]

A union of the two kingdoms was signalised on 2 March 1653, when the 'Rump parliament' voted that henceforth Ireland be represented by thirty members in the new house of 460. The Rump was dissolved on 20 April, but six Irish members sat in the nominated or 'Barebones' parliament when it opened on 4 July. When this in turn was forced by the army to surrender its powers to Cromwell, and he was named lord protector on 16 December 1653, the 'instrument of government' confirmed the Irish representation of thirty members in parliament, which was to sit for at least five months every third year. Ireland was represented in this way in the British parliaments of 1654, 1656, and 1659. Elections were held, but government influence normally succeeded in securing the returns required. Parliament, of course, was only one of several factors the lord protector had to keep in balance in order to maintain the state: in particular, the factor of military intervention had always to be considered. The demand that Ireland should have a separate parliament began to revive, principally because legislation was not enacted to bring about the free trade that should have resulted from the parliamentary union.[3] In consequence, it was easy to revert to the old state of affairs after the restoration, all the more as Ireland had kept its separate executive, and this soon settled into a form scarcely distinguishable from the traditional one.

The proclamation of Oliver Cromwell as lord protector was made in Dublin on 30 January 1654. It led to much dissatisfaction among the more radical element in the army. Fleetwood shared their misgivings at what seemed a strange ending to demands for popular sovereignty, but in July he was appointed lord deputy and in August a council of state of six was appointed to assist and advise him: Miles Corbet (one of the original 1650 commissioners), Robert Goodwin, Robert Hammond, Richard Pepys, William Steele, and Matthew Tomlinson. All in all, they had a much less radical complexion than the commissioners originally named in 1650.

[1] See below, p. 380.

[2] Dunlop, *Commonwealth*, pp 263–8.

[3] T. C. Barnard, 'Planters and policies in Cromwellian Ireland' in *Past & Present*, no. 61 (Nov. 1973), pp 60–5. A full-length study by the same author, *Cromwellian Ireland: English government and reform in Ireland, 1640–1660*, has just appeared (May 1975).

Cromwell for his part had his own misgivings that Fleetwood might be too accommodating towards the army radicals. His own son, Henry, had been named to the Irish council of state in August, but the protector did not acquiesce in this appointment, being for a complexity of reasons reluctant to countenance the emergence of what could be objected to as dynastic power. Before the end of the year, however, he had changed his mind. On 25 December Henry Cromwell was nominated to the Irish council. The other members now were Corbet, Goodwin, Pepys, and Tomlinson. Steele did not act as a member of the council till he came to Ireland in September 1656 on being appointed lord chancellor, and Hammond had died in October 1654. Henry Cromwell did not arrive in Ireland until July 1655, but he achieved effective even if limited control when Fleetwood, though remaining lord deputy, was forced to return to England on 6 September.

This was a further step towards reducing the influence of the more radical faction. Ludlow, displaced as lieutenant general in August 1652, had steadily refused to acknowledge the legitimacy of the protectorate, and to the best of his ability had worked actively against it. One of Fleetwood's last acts had been to give him leave to go to England to argue his case with the protector. Henry Cromwell would have preferred to keep him in Ireland, but he was insistent, and after the indignity of a six weeks' detention at Beaumaris he and the lord protector did have some frank exchanges. They produced no effect, but he was allowed to live in England quietly, though unrepentant, and powerless until the downfall of the protectorate.

When Henry Cromwell arrived in Ireland the baptist sectaries were in control of the administration. By 1659 he had displaced not merely these but also the independents, and had instead forged a *politique* alliance with the 'old protestants', as the protestant planters who had settled in Ireland before 1641 came to be known after the restoration. These had succeeded, after some anxieties and uncertainties, in retaining their property and even in adding to it.[1] Indications multiplied that 'revolutionary government' was being displaced by a closer association between economic strength and political power. In 1655 and 1656 the local government and judicial systems were restored. In this process, the 'old protestants' emerged in some strength. The 1656 parliamentary elections returned such members as Lord Broghill, Sir Charles Coote, and Vincent Gookin. Many government officials, including more than half the twenty-one sheriffs appointed in 1656, had been in Ireland before 1641. The somewhat puzzling and ineffective act for convicting popish recusants, imposing an oath of abjuration of the distinctive tenets of popery, passed in this parliament, may be an indication of fears that the 'protestant interest', in seeking to define itself, might have to take some cognisance of the existence of the papists.[2]

[1] Barnard, 'Planters and policies in Cromwellian Ireland,' loc. cit., pp 31–49.
[2] See also below, p. 384.

On 4 August 1656 William Bury was nominated to the council of state. The appointment of this 'religious and prudent gentleman', a strong presbyterian, was certainly intended to strengthen Henry Cromwell's position against the radical faction. Though he was removed from office when the Irish administration was once again transferred to commissioners of parliament in May 1659, he remained in the country and worked actively with Coote and Broghill in preparing for the restoration.

Fleetwood was succeeded as lord deputy by Henry Cromwell on 17 November 1657. The lord protector died on 3 September 1658. His ineffective son Richard was named his successor, and the protectorate began to disintegrate. Even under Oliver, its structure had become increasingly rickety, due primarily, it must be noted with some irony, to chronic financial difficulties that could be remedied only by a vote of supplies that parliament was unwilling to give. Although Henry Cromwell was named lord lieutenant of Ireland on 6 October 1658, this had little significance as power slipped from his brother's hands in England. On 6 May 1659 the army forced Richard to recall the Rump parliament and on 24 May he formally resigned the protectorate. A demand for the recall of the excluded members—they finally returned on 21 February 1660—made the restoration of Charles II inevitable. On 7 May 1659 parliament once again named five commissioners for Ireland (Ludlow now being commander-in-chief): Corbet, Goodwin, Jones, Steele, and Tomlinson. Henry Cromwell left on 27 June. Over this period, however, the forms of government mattered less than the struggle for position and power, of necessity tortuous as long as the restoration remained a great imponderable.

In England, the question whether the country should recall the king or have a successor to Oliver Cromwell in the person of General John Lambert, representing the independent faction of the army, was resolved by the decision of General George Monck not to support Lambert but to call for a free parliament. Indeed, Monck did not so much take the initiative as allow public opinion to express itself. In Ireland, Monck's party staged a *coup d'état* in December that gave them control of the army. The leading figures were of 'old protestant' stock—Broghill, Coote, Theophilus Jones, and Hardress Waller. A convention, controlled by the *politiques*, among whom the 'old protestants' were dominant, opened in Dublin on 7 February 1660. In defence of their interests, now threatened by loyalists, catholic as well as protestant, returning with the king from exile, they asserted Irish legislative independence in terms that recalled the arguments of the catholic lawyers in the 1641 parliament and during the confederacy. They had no guarantee of their position when Charles II was proclaimed king in Dublin on 14 May, but their fears proved to be unfounded, because he was no more able to rule Ireland without their support and cooperation than Henry Cromwell had been.[1]

[1] Barnard, loc. cit., pp 65–7.

Contemporary catholic writers described the state of the country after the Cromwellian conquest in apocalyptic terms: in the succinct phrase of one of the poets, it had been *an cogadh do chríochnaigh Éire* (the war that finished Ireland).[1] This was not too far from the truth. Especially in the later stages of the war, the armies of parliament had deliberately laid waste the land as a military tactic. Already in November 1650 Ireton reported that in stretches of thirty miles he had seen no life but only ruin and desolation. By the end of the war tillage had almost ceased and even livestock had to be imported. In June 1653 'the small number of inhabitants now remaining in County Clare' told the commissioners that of its nine baronies containing 1,300 ploughlands only thirty ploughlands in the barony of Bunratty were inhabited, 'except some few persons who for their own safety live in garrisons'.[2] Some modern critics would suggest that Petty's estimate of the population in 1652—a total of 850,000, of whom 160,000 were protestants—may be too low, perhaps by a factor of 40 per cent. His further estimate that 616,000 had perished since 1641 is reached by an even more oblique calculation, but it is the best we have.[3]

Inevitably, it was the poor who suffered most from the hunger, disease, and widespread misery: 'some found feeding on carrion and weeds, some starved in the highways, and many times poor children, who have lost their parents or deserted by them, are found exposed to, and some of them fed upon by ravening wolves and other beasts of prey'. The country was 'almost a blank sheet on which the English commonwealth could write what it wished'.[4] The commonwealth's wishes appeared in the act for the settling of Ireland of 12 August 1652.[5]

The preamble of the act stated that it was not the intention of parliament to extirpate 'the entire nation', but that pardon as to life and estate would be granted to 'the inferior sort', and that those of rank and quality would be treated according to their 'respective demerits'. Five groups were exempted from pardon for life or estate: all who before the first general assembly at Kilkenny had abetted the 'rebellion, murders or massacres'; all Jesuits and priests involved in any way in the rebellion; 105 named magnates, headed by the earl of Ormond; all who had been guilty of the murder of civilians; and all who refused to lay down their arms within twenty-eight days. All officers

[1] Seán Ó Conaill, 'Tuireamh na hÉireann' in Cecile O'Rahilly (ed.), *Five seventeenth-century political poems* (Dublin, 1952), p. 75.

[2] Dunlop, *Commonwealth*, i, 343–4.

[3] 'Political anatomy of Ire.', ed. Hull, i, 146–50. The '1659 census' (*Census Ire., 1659*, ed. Séamus Pender) raises still unsolved problems. It is incomplete, lacking returns for five whole counties and thirteen baronies in two others, but for the rest of the country it gives detailed numbers, townland by townland. On a generous extrapolation, it would indicate a population of no more than 500,000 for the whole country. The suggestion that it was made in connection with the poll-tax, and therefore listed only those over fifteen years old, would bring it at least roughly into line with Petty's figures, but this suggestion in turn is not altogether free from difficulties.

[4] Dunlop, *Commonwealth*, i, 340; Curtis, *Ire.*, p. 251.

[5] *Acts & ordinances, interregnum*, ii, 598–603.

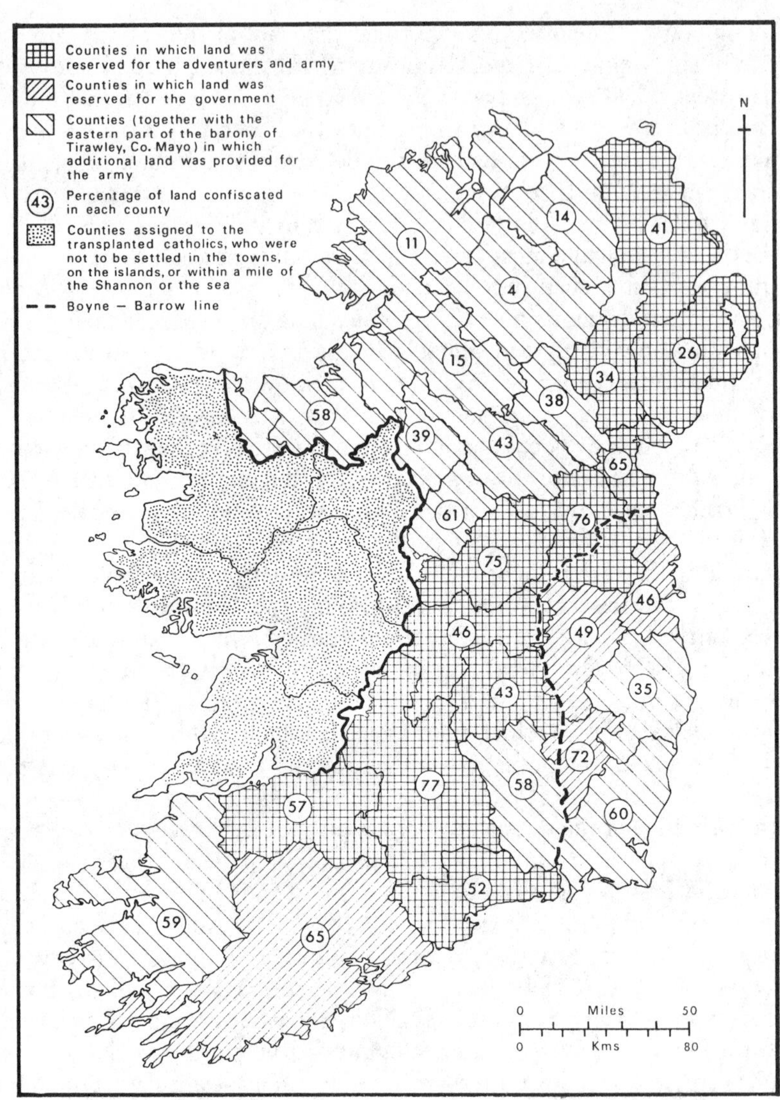

Map 9 THE CROMWELLIAN LAND-CONFISCATION
by Patrick J. Corish

who had fought against parliament were to be banished, but their wives and children were to be assigned the equivalent of one-third of their forfeited estates wherever parliament might decide. All others who had fought in the war were to forfeit their estates in return for the same compensation. All papists who had not shown 'constant good affection' to parliament were to be compensated by the equivalent of two-thirds of their estates, to be allotted where parliament might decide. All others who had not manifested 'good affection' were to surrender one-fifth, but to retain possession of the remainder (by an ordinance of 2 September 1654 these were allowed to compound for a fine, which, except for a few Ulster Scots, they never paid). As promised in the preamble the 'inferior sort' were granted full pardon on submission.

This draconian legislation thus came to be directed almost exclusively against catholics, and was so framed that no person of any property could hope to escape.[1] Under the first clause alone it has been estimated that 80,000 people were liable to the death penalty—probably half the adult males.[2] This was the retribution planned for 'blood-guilt'. The fact that no serious attempt was made to give effect to it confirms the conviction that while the emotional drive behind the land confiscation was a device to punish a people believed to be collectively guilty, there was a hard economic motive making it necessary to confiscate most of Ireland, and it can be stated quite simply: nothing less would satisfy the debts parliament had pledged against Irish land.

To try those guilty of murder, a high court of justice was established in October 1652. The partial records of its proceedings available in print indicate that the court's sessions, held in a number of provincial centres as well as Dublin, were designed rather as an instrument of political intimidation rather than as a serious attempt to deal judicially with the vast numbers who might have been charged.[3] Two cases might be singled out. One was that of the 'arch-rebel', Sir Phelim O'Neill, captured on 4 February 1653. He was tried, found guilty, and executed, but he might well have saved his life had he not continued to deny that he had received a commission to take arms from Charles I. The other is that of Edmund O'Reilly, catholic vicar general of Dublin. He was condemned to death, on not very satisfactory evidence, but after twenty-one months in prison he was banished to the Continent. One can only speculate why, but there are indications that his commitment to the cause of Owen Roe O'Neill had led him to do some service for Colonel Michael Jones at the time of the battle of Rathmines, and

[1] The act emerged after 'months of struggle over the severity or lenity of the settlement'. The action of Henry Jones in producing to the commissioners lengthy abstracts (later printed) of the depositions he had taken in 1642 'revived, and, to a probably extensive degree, invented a moral vindication for the expropriation of property' (K. S. Bottigheimer, *English money and Irish land* (Oxford, 1971), pp 127–8).

[2] S. R. Gardiner, 'The transplantation to Connaught' in *E.H.R.*, xiv (1899), pp 702–4.

[3] Mary Hickson, *Ireland in the seventeenth century* (London, 1884), ii, 171–235.

it is possible that he was protected by one of the colonel's two surviving brothers.[1]

How many were executed we do not know, but they were at most hundreds, not thousands, and by the end of 1654 the court's activities seem to have come to an end. This failure to carry out the most draconian provision of the act of 1652 complicated the land settlement, in that many persons exempted from all pardon, even some of those exempted by name, received lands in Connacht, and the land available could not meet the demands on it.

The demands on the land of Ireland had begun with the adventurers' act of March 1642.[2] This had allotted 2,500,000 acres in return for subscriptions of £1,000,000; the fact that the land was to be allotted in the four provinces indicates that already by February 1642 parliament had accepted, on what must then have been slender evidence, that all the Irish were guilty. The response was not up to expectations, even though further ordinances provided for a double allotment in 'Irish' acres measured at 21 feet to the perch in return for an addition of a quarter to the original subscription. Nevertheless, 1,533 in all subscribed £306,718, a sum exceeded among contemporary joint-stock ventures only by the East India company. The 'adventurers' had a strong urban and merchant element, especially from London, and many sold their bonds as the years went by, being very conscious that their money was earning no interest and having little personal inclination to become landlords in Ireland.

In 1643 one of these additional ordinances had allowed soldiers serving parliament in Ireland to receive their pay in Irish lands at the 'act rates', that is to say on the same terms as the adventurers. It is uncertain how and when this option became an obligation, as it is uncertain how and when it was extended to cover other arrears of pay.[3] Between 1642 and 1649 very little money had been sent to Ireland to pay the parliamentary armies, and arrears had soared. When it came to a settlement, about 35,000 men had claims, first for service in Ireland since Cromwell's appointment as commander-in-chief on 30 March 1649, second for previous service in England (the 'English arrears'), and third, for previous service in Ireland (the '1649 arrears'). Finally, by an act of 18 October 1644, parliament had accepted responsibility for the Irish war as a charge on the English public finances. It was assumed that this would be discharged from Irish land, 'the great capital out of which all debts were paid, all services rewarded, and all acts of bounty performed'.[4]

[1] Tomás Ó Fiaich, 'Edmund O'Reilly, archbishop of Armagh 1657–1669' in *Father Luke Wadding*, pp 183–4.

[2] See especially Bottigheimer, *Eng. money & Ir. land*; also Hugh Hazlett, 'The financing of the British armies in Ireland, 1641–9' in *I.H.S.*, i, no. 1 (Mar. 1938), pp 21–41, and J. R. MacCormack, 'The Irish adventurers and the English civil war', ibid., x, no. 37 (Mar. 1956), pp 21–58.

[3] Bottigheimer (p. 119) suggests that such proposals may have taken final shape as late as 1651.

[4] *The life of Edward, earl of Clarendon* (Oxford, 1888), ii, 218. See plate 8.

What was clear was that an immense amount of land would be required, though how much could only be conjectured. The adventurers had the prior claim, and the sum they subscribed was known exactly, as was the quantity of land required to discharge it. How much money was due to the soldiers could to some degree be only conjectured. The estimate adopted, £1,750,000, was possibly on the low side, but to discharge it at 'act rates' would clearly demand very widespread confiscation indeed. The claims of the state were even harder to determine exactly. Between 1642 and 1649 at least £500,000 had been sent sporadically from England to Ireland. The Cromwellian conquest had cost about £3,500,000. Of this, over £2,000,000 had been raised in England, the remainder coming from Irish taxation, leaving a debt of over £2,500,000 to be discharged.

The act of settlement of 1652, as has been seen, envisaged an almost universal confiscation of land held by catholics. It was clear that nothing less would meet the debt. The confiscation was confined to catholics: proposals in 1653 to transplant the Ulster Scots to allotments in Munster petered out as an accommodation was gradually reached between the Scots and parliament.[1]

As soon as the conquest was effectively over in 1652 pressure mounted to carry out this vast social upheaval quickly. It became possible to disband some of the army and the state's financial position urged that this be done as quickly as was compatible with safety. But the army could not be allotted land without settling the prior claims of the adventurers. Yet no one knew how much land was available for confiscation, or indeed how much land Ireland contained, for the only reliable survey hitherto attempted was that made by Strafford for Connacht and some adjoining areas. Rapid and accurate surveys were required. They could not be easily drawn up in a country so wasted as Ireland.

On 22 June 1653 an order authorised the taking of three surveys: a survey by inquisition from juries; a survey by measurement and mapping; and a 'gross survey'. This last, which could be little more than a survey by guesswork, was to be attempted first. It began with the counties at that time allotted to the soldiers and adventurers,[2] and was completed for these by the end of the year. It was then extended to other confiscated lands. Only a fragment of this survey has come to light,[3] but there were complaints of serious inaccuracies, as was indeed only to be expected. On 14 April 1654 orders were given for a 'civil survey' to be made by inquisitions taken from

[1] See below, p. 379. [2] See above, map 9 and p. 370.

[3] Among the French (of Monivea) papers, an unsorted collection in N.L.I., is a certified copy, dated 19 March 1708, of the Gross Survey of part of Moylough parish, Tiaquin barony, County Galway. It names the proprietors actually in possession at the time the survey was made, in addition to the proprietors as of 23 October 1641, and gives particulars of changes of ownership in the intervening period. It also gives details of such matters as jointures and mortgages to a much greater extent than does the Civil Survey. I owe this information to Mr K. W. Nicholls.

juries of 'the most ancient and able inhabitants'. It was carried through quickly, and provided a much more reliable estimate, but still in the nature of things only an estimate, and in fact a serious underestimate, of the land available.[1] At the end of 1654 William Petty signed an agreement to begin the survey by measurement and mapping, the 'down survey'.[2] His first contract was for the soldiers' lands, where the problem was most urgent. Two years later his contract was extended, this time in conjunction with the surveyor general, to all confiscated lands. This portion went more slowly, partly because of bad relations between Petty and the surveyor general, partly because the adventurers did not welcome the survey, and it was not completed until 1659. While Petty's remarkable work was in advance of anything hitherto done in surveying and map-making, even he underestimated by between 10 and 15 per cent.

The history of these three surveys will give some idea of the basic confusion made inevitable in the Cromwellian settlement by the fact that land had to be allotted before it had been surveyed. To keep some path through this confusion, and to try to decide, in the light of the surviving records, what actually happened, it is proposed to deal first with the clearance of the Irish catholics and their settlement in Connacht, and then with the plantation of the confiscated lands.

On surrender, the Irish soldiers were normally allowed to go abroad. As war was to continue between France and Spain until 1659, these countries were willing to absorb the many Irish 'swordmen' who chose to follow the now long-established practice of enlisting in continental armies. Almost all of them did so choose, to a total of 34,000.[3]

Others left less willingly, being transported to the English plantations in America. Contemporary accounts would claim that vast numbers were rounded up in organised slave-hunts, and this version of events has become part of the Irish legend, being repeated, for example, by Prendergast when he wrote a hundred years ago.[4] The hard facts are not easy to come by with certainty, because of serious gaps in the surviving evidence.[5] The English West Indian plantations originated with the occupation of St Kitts in 1624, and quite a number of Irish were among the original settlers, especially in the island of Montserrat. At first, their main crop was tobacco grown on small-

[1] See the introduction by R. C. Simington to each volume of the *Civil Survey*.

[2] T. A. Larcom (ed.), *The history of the survey of Ireland commonly called the Down Survey, by Doctor William Petty* A.D. *1655–6* (Dublin, 1851); Seán Ó Domhnaill, 'The maps of the down survey' in *I.H.S.*, iii, no. 12 (Sept. 1943), pp 381–92. See also the introduction by R. C. Simington to the published volumes of *Bks survey & dist.*

[3] Again the figure is from Petty, 'Political anatomy of Ire.', ed. Hull, i, 151.

[4] *Cromwellian settlement*, pp 85 ff, 145 ff.

[5] Aubrey Gwynn, 'Documents relating to the Irish in the West Indies' in *Anal. Hib.*, no. 4 (1932), pp 139–286; 'Cromwell's policy of transportation' in *Studies*, xix (1930), pp 607–23; xx (1931), pp 291–305; J. W. Blake, 'Transportation from Ireland to America, 1653–60' in *I.H.S.*, iii, no. 11 (Mar. 1943), pp 267–81.

holdings, but this gave way to sugar-cane, introduced in 1642 and grown on large plantations. Both crops demanded a good deal of labour, supplied either by slaves from Africa or by indentured servants from the home islands. These latter might either go freely or be transported as convicts. The crime of many of the convicts was that, in the language of the time, they were 'sturdy beggars', or, as a possibly more humane age would put it, they were poor and unemployed.

Prisoners of war were first transported by the English parliament in 1648, Scots after the battle of Preston and English after the capture of Colchester. It came quite naturally to Cromwell, then, to set aside those who had survived at Drogheda to be 'shipped to the Barbadoes'. It was only with the completion of the conquest, however, that a government policy emerged. It is clear that between 1652 and 1655 many orders for transportation were issued, sometimes for great numbers of people. These fell into two broad classes: first, persons dangerous to the state (we sometimes find transportation ordered for extreme recalcitrance as shown by refusal to transplant to Connacht, or by support for tories); and second, the poor and vagabonds.[1] Persons in these categories were liable to the same penalty in England, but the circumstances of Ireland made the categories much more extensive there. It is clear also that during these years the government tried and ultimately succeeded in controlling ruthless speculators, inured to the methods of the African slave trade, and not given to interpreting government orders too nicely. We have no direct indication of the numbers of those transported. That many in fact were transported is only an inference, but it would seem a reasonable one.

The national legend of the man-hunts is therefore founded on fact, although it exaggerates their scale and it errs in so far as it attributes them to government policy. They arose from commercial greed. This seems further proved by the fact that the scale of transportation slackened off after 1655, though it was in this year that the English occupied Jamaica. At the end of 1655 there was a proposal to transport 2,000 Irish boys and girls to that island; it may be taken as certain that they were not in fact transported. More revealingly, it would also seem certain that this scheme collapsed because the merchants did not find it profitable. Because the West Indies were now developing an economy based on large plantations, the African slave yielded better returns than the indentured servant. Irish bondsmen were particularly unprofitable, for the planters regarded them as a turbulent and politically unreliable element. Transported priests were especially unwelcome, for they gave cohesion to the catholic Irish community. One thoroughly documented case shows four transported priests being ordered to leave Barbados immediately on their arrival.

Transportation took place to Virginia as well as to the West Indies, but

[1] For the transportation of priests, see below, pp 383–4

the colonists in New England refused to accept Irish catholics. For the West Indies, we have some figures for the late 1660s which may give some idea of the scale of the transportation, making allowance for the fact that they include the original Irish settlers or their descendants and also for an undoubtedly high death-rate. These figures indicate a total of about 8,000 Irish in Barbados, 'derided by the negroes and branded with the epithet of white slaves',[1] and 12,000 in the West Indies as a whole. Since sugar had been introduced in 1642 the number of African slaves had risen from 6,400 to 50,000.

Transportation and the exile of 'swordmen', however, only touched the fringes of the problem of clearance. Parliament was still preparing a bill when it was disbanded by Cromwell on 20 April 1653. The actual decision on what form the clearance should take was made by Cromwell and the council of state in an instruction to the Irish commissioners on 2 July, confirmed by the act for satisfaction of adventurers and soldiers passed by the nominated parliament on 26 September.[2] All forfeiting proprietors were to be settled in Connacht and Clare, but not in any port town or garrison. The act of 26 September added the further restriction that none was to be settled within four miles of the Shannon or the sea. This indicates the basic reason for the choice of Connacht, that its natural boundaries set it off from the rest of Ireland. The rates set out in the act of adventurers show that Ulster was then regarded as a poorer province.

Though an adequate survey of Connacht was available, immense practical problems faced the committee set up on 1 August to consider them. At this stage settlement was a secondary consideration. While the assumption was that only those qualified under the act of settlement were entitled to land in Connacht, the problem of clearance came first, as is indicated by a proclamation dated 14 October, which ordered to Connacht, before the appointed date of 1 May 1654, even those exempted from pardon for life or estate by the act of settlement.[3] It was for a long time undecided whether there should be a total clearance, or a clearance of landowners only. The 1652 act of settlement had granted pardon to 'the inferior sort', but the army radicals pressed for a total clearance as retribution for collective guilt. It became evident, however, that there would be no mass settlement of protestant yeomen colonists: even the army rank and file were reluctant to settle. The 'old protestants' too were gradually consolidating their position. Their propaganda of the 1640s was now an embarrassment, but they urged the hard economic consideration that if the land was to be worked at all it must be worked by a catholic tenantry. The controversy came to a head in 1655, with a series of pamphlets exchanged between Vincent Gookin, an

[1] Aubrey Gwynn, 'Documents relating to the Irish in the West Indies', loc. cit., p. 250.

[2] Dunlop, *Commonwealth*, pp 355 ff; *Acts & ordinances, interregnum*, ii, 722 ff.

[3] Published from a contemporary printed copy in *Ormonde MSS*, ii, 400–05.

'old protestant', and Richard Lawrence, a baptist army officer. This was the year in which Henry Cromwell arrived. The final decision was that only landowners should be transplanted, together with those dependants who should choose to go with them.

Among the landowners, there were some who claimed that they had surrendered on articles entitling them to at least a portion of their estates. Very few established this claim. The 'articles of Galway' and the 'articles of Kilkenny' were declared to have been abrogated by the acts of settlement and satisfaction. The 'ancient inhabitants' of the Munster ports believed they had shown 'constant good affection' to parliament. It is perhaps an indication of how absolutely impossible it was for any catholic to sustain such a claim that they failed to prove it to the satisfaction of a court. In what must be accepted as a sincere expression of final despair they said they would rather be transported to the Barbados than face the intimidation they might expect if transplanted to Connacht. Finally, they were assigned land in the Cork baronies of Barrymore and Muskerry. In this dispensation from the obligation to transplant they were almost unique.[1]

For those who had to go, courts of delinquency were set up in each military precinct, to decide their 'qualifications' according to the act of settlement. The revenue commissioners in each precinct were to issue passports with certificates giving particulars of each party, so that in every case an allotment of land in Connacht might be made by a group of five commissioners sitting in Loughrea, of necessity as yet provisionally, for no man could be allotted lands equivalent to one-third or two-thirds of his estate, as the case might be, while this was as yet unsurveyed. The wording of these certificates brings out with vivid pathos a shattered people on the move:

Sir Nicholas Comyn, numb at one side of his body of a dead palsy, accompanied only by his lady, Catherine Comyn, aged thirty-five years, middle stature; and one maidservant, Honor ny McNamara, aged twenty years, brown hair, middle stature; having no substance, but expecting the benefit of his qualification. . . .

Pierce, Viscount Ikerrin, going with seventeen persons, four cows, five garrans, twenty-four sheep and two swine, and claiming against sixteen acres of winter corn. . . .

Ignatius Stacpole of Limerick, orphant, aged eleven years, flaxen haire, full face, low stature; Katherine Stacpoole, orphant, sister to the said Ignatius, aged eight years, flaxen haire, full face; having no substance to relieve themselves, but desireth the benefit of his claim before the commissioners of the revenue.[2]

There was a flood of petitions from people seeking to delay transplantation, and the evidence is that many of these were granted, at first for one month to certain tightly defined categories only, but later more freely, while the very flood of petitions forced the postponement of the final date for departure

[1] For the special terms granted to the town of Fethard see above, p. 345.

[2] Prendergast, *Cromwellian settlement*, pp 104–5; see also pp 363–76.

to 1 May 1655.[1] As the months passed, an even more basic consideration began to obtrude: it was necessary to plant a crop and in turn reap the harvest. But in the summer of 1654 very many crossed into Connacht, to present themselves before the Loughrea commissioners or at least spy out the land. Though the evidence suggests that this occurred on a scale that can only indicate widespread panic, and that all who presented themselves were given every facility that circumstances allowed, things were still going too slowly for the government, and an order of 30 November 1654 ordered all 'transplantable persons' to be gone by 1 March following.

That they did not in fact go is indicated by the setting-up of courts martial on 19 March, with power to inflict sentence of death for refusal to transplant, though this was with few exceptions reserved as an ultimate threat, and the penalties normally imposed for recalcitrance were banishment, transportation, or enforced transplantation. One factor favouring the government's plans was that the Civil Survey was taking shape, making possible a definitive settlement in Connacht. Much confusion had arisen from the desire to transplant as many as possible without enquiring too nicely into their qualification, and some of the Loughrea commissioners, without surveys or records to control their decisions, had used the opportunity to enrich themselves, either by seizing lands or by accepting bribes, for which two of them were later dismissed. They were comparatively small fry, and unlucky to be caught.[2] At the end of 1654, a 'court of claims and qualifications' where all must present themselves was set up in Athlone. This court was provided with the Civil Survey and what were officially known as the 'books of discrimination' but were soon popularly called 'the black books of Athlone', notably the depositions compiled in 1642 and the records of the Kilkenny confederates. On the other hand, the task of settling Connacht was made more difficult because enough land was not available in the rest of Ireland to satisfy the soldiers, and by this date Sligo, Leitrim, and the barony of Tirawley in County Mayo had been taken for this purpose from the lands allotted to the Irish catholics, and people already settled there had to transplant again. Up to 1656 the final fate of Clare was quite uncertain, though in the end most of it was available to the Irish. The important decisions on those affected by the articles of Kilkenny and Galway were not taken until April and July 1655 respectively. In consequence, notwithstanding the progress of the Civil Survey and the establishment of the Athlone commissioners, the work of settlement still went slowly, and now with fears that there might not be enough land in Connacht to satisfy those entitled to it.

Various attempts were made to sort out the confusion. Detailed 'additional instructions' of 16 June 1655 ordered the Loughrea commissioners to set out the lands in order within each county, taking the baronies one after the other

[1] Prendergast, loc. cit., pp 377–85. [2] Dunlop, *Commonwealth*, pp 569–70.

and filling each before proceeding to the next. They were further urged to speed things up, even with rough justice (with an implication that this had already been meted out fairly frequently). If possible, they were not to disturb further those already settled, unless they agreed to move, though the reference to provision for forfeiting proprietors who already held lands in Connacht could be read as indicating that this was the first time the administration had seriously adverted to the fact that Connacht as well as the other three provinces had papist inhabitants for whom it was necessary to provide.

The pressure to transplant was maintained, and if anything stepped up. The news that Irish troops in the French service had taken part in the massacre of the Vaudois in April 1655 prompted a letter from Ireland to the lord protector in May urging 'let the blood of Ireland be fresh in your view, and their treachery cry aloud in your ears . . . and let not such be left untransplanted here, or unminded in England';[1] and Milton's blazing sonnet calling for vengeance, while it omits mention of the Irish, closes with almost predictable reference to 'the triple tyrant' and 'the Babylonian woe'. Nevertheless, the sheer shortage of land was giving rise to serious problems. A further attempt to impose some kind of order on the settlement came in February 1656, in the form of proposals that all those transplanted from named counties should be assigned lands in named baronies in the four counties of Clare, Galway, Mayo, and Roscommon. This was only partially achieved, though perhaps to a surprising extent in view of the numbers already settled under totally different instructions or no specific instructions at all, and in view of the reports of the Loughrea commissioners that certain baronies were 'totally exhausted' or that they could not find any land to satisfy decrees already given. At this stage one gets the impression of the growth of a mood of indifference and irresponsibility, of land being broken up and people moved around indiscriminately. This impression is particularly strong if one considers the records of the Connacht proprietors transplanted within the province.

Attempts were made to make more land available, especially by reducing to one mile the exempted line along the Shannon and the sea, but the pressure on land could not be met. At the end of 1656 it was admitted that many who fell under 'the first qualifications', that is, those entitled neither to life nor land, were in fact in possession of lands in Connacht, while at the same time there was no land to give to those who were entitled to it, that indeed there had been 'great stopes [*sic*] of land' set out to the former, 'either through inadvertency or supposing that there would be forfeited lands to spare'.[2] This tongue-in-cheek statement obviously does not fully explain why during 1656 persons exempted by name from pardon for life or estate had received considerable estates in Connacht—for example, 11,574 acres

[1] Thurloe, *S.P.*, iii, 467.
[2] Dunlop, *Commonwealth*, p. 648.

were granted to William Nugent, earl of Westmeath, 3,427 acres to Sir Thomas Esmond, and 2,852 acres to Sir Richard Barnewall.

Dr R. C. Simington speculates on 'a secret compromise, this being the repeal of the death sentences, coming within the first qualifications, for the territorial reductions in the province and county [Clare] in the interests of the commonwealth armies'.[1] Some understanding there must have been, though one might question if it was in these terms (for in this context the commonwealth had no need to bargain), or if indeed it was expressed in any explicit terms at all. The situation must have arisen from the concurrence of a number of decisions: the decision not to press ahead with the workings of the high court of justice; the decision to allow, indeed to command, those not entitled to land or life to betake themselves to Connacht; and the fact that the Loughrea commissioners granted them land there, not always perhaps 'through inadvertence'. As already suggested, the two commissioners dismissed for corrupt practices were probably small fry sacrificed as a covering gesture. In circumstances like this, wealth and connection could sometimes help catholics too. Cromwell himself occasionally intervened in favour of individuals, usually unsuccessfully. Not always, however: on 2 June 1654 Fleetwood wrote to John Thurloe, the secretary of state, asking him to ensure that Sir Richard Barnewall and other Irish magnates then in London were not allowed access to the lord protector,[2] but Barnewall's extensive grant of land in Connacht indicates that he not merely gained access to Cromwell but successfully pleaded his case with him.

By the end of 1656, then, the situation may be summarised somewhat as follows. There was no more land left for catholics. Some legally liable to execution, even some named as such, had received lands. Some who had been allotted land, and who were legally entitled to it, had to be told that no land was available. Some had not transplanted, either in continuing defiance or because there was nothing to transplant to, 'living only and coshering on the common sort of people who were tenants',[3] and shading imperceptibly into those in active defiance, the 'tories'.

An 'act for the attainder of the rebels in Ireland' was passed on 26 June 1657 in an attempt to make good the legal uncertainty and subsequent administrative confusion.[4] In effect, it declared that the transplantation was over, that the instructions of 2 July 1653 had been 'duly executed and performed'. It set this in the context of a declaration that all 'rebels' and 'papists'—the terms were now synonymous—had been guilty of high treason, but that this was pardoned to those who had transplanted. Those not transplanted by 24 September would forfeit all claim to benefit, and no claim

[1] *The transplantation to Connacht, 1654–58* (Dublin, 1970), p. xxiv.

[2] Thurloe, *S.P.*, ii, 343.

[3] Prendergast, *Cromwellian settlement*, p. 326, n. 1.

[4] *Acts & ordinances, interregnum*, ii, 1250–62.

could be prosecuted after 1 June 1658. Prosecution and punishment of those not transplanting continued, though what claim they could advance if there was no more land to allot was a question discreetly ignored. The transplantation was over. While a survey of the country as a whole must be deferred until we have seen what happened in the other three provinces, at this stage a brief summary may be given of the effects of the transplantation on the catholic landowners.

The work of Dr Simington has provided the materials for assessment,[1] but it still awaits detailed analysis. However, even at this stage some general conclusions may be drawn. It has already been noted that, with very rare exceptions, all catholic landowners were transplanted. Dr Simington has given preliminary estimates of the effects of the whole transplantation. To these I would add equally preliminary estimates of the impact on one county, Wexford.[2] They fit fairly well into his general pattern.

On Petty's estimate—and so far we have nothing really better—there were about 3,000 'landed Irish papists' in Ireland in 1641.[3] Approximately 1,900 transplanters received decrees for about 700,000 acres, plantation measure, in Connacht, but of these only about 770 came from the other three provinces. Between them these received 420,576 acres. Sixty-five received allotments of more than 2,000 acres, but, as must be obvious, many got very small holdings indeed. The experience of the Connacht proprietors transplanted within Connacht was similar.[4]

The case of Sir Thomas Esmond is excluded from the Wexford figures, partly because he also held land in Wicklow, for which the Civil Survey is not extant, and partly because his exclusion may help to give a better picture of what happened to those who could bring no particular influence to bear. Again, the figures must be approximations, taking into account the imperfections of the Civil Survey and the fact that a complete cross-check of homonyms among proprietors' names would demand immensely detailed local research, with final accuracy perhaps impossible. Nor is this the only complication. For example, 'Nicholas Devereux esq. and Richard Devereux his son gent.' are named as 'tituladoes' in Kilmore parish, Bargy barony, in the '1659 census'. A check of those of their family name in the transplantation lists and Civil Survey—almost all of them here listed as 'Irish papists' but with the occasional 'English protestant' to complicate matters—can do no more than suggest ramifications of family relationships, now beyond recovery, that even before 1641 may have transcended differences of religious allegiance in the interests of family property and position, and possibly continued to exercise an influence through the 1650s.

[1] In *Civil Survey* (10 vols, Dublin, 1931–61); *Bks survey & dist.* (4 vols, Dublin, 1949–67); *The transplantation to Connacht, 1654–58* (Dublin, 1970).

[2] Based, of course, primarily on Dr Simington's publications.

[3] 'Political anatomy of Ire.', ed. Hull, i, 153. Petty's estimate must be assumed to have been based on his survey.

[4] Cf. above, p. 367.

In 1641 catholics still held almost 60 per cent of the land in County Wexford, approximately 210,000 profitable acres, divided among about 380 proprietors, many of them with comparatively modest holdings. Of these, 86, that is 23 per cent, had lands set out to them in Connacht, to a total of something over 20,000 acres, almost exactly 10 per cent of the land in catholic hands in Wexford in 1641. This gives each Wexford proprietor in Connacht an average of 43 per cent of his former holding. Most of them, therefore, may be presumed to have fallen under the seventh qualification of the act of settlement, that is, they had taken part in the war and were entitled to one-third of their estates. A total of almost 300, or 77 per cent, disappeared as landed proprietors, some no doubt dead, some having emigrated, some banished or transported, some still unsatisfied when the act of 1657 declared the transplantation finished. This rough-and-ready survey for one county can of course be offered only as an example, and it would be foolhardy to propose it as a pattern for the country as a whole. It might be noted, for example, that relatively few Ulster names turn up among those assigned lands in Connacht, and it seems certain that migrants from Ulster settled in the inhospitable lands of Leitrim, though this had been assigned to the army. All in all, however, the figures I have tried to establish for Wexford may not be an inaccurate indication of the general pattern of what took place in Leinster and Munster.

To turn now to the adventurers and soldiers. When it came to a settlement, the adventurers as a group had changed considerably, many of the original investors having sold their interests. The original number, 1,533, had shrunk to 1,043, of whom 664 had invested at the beginning and 379 had subsequently bought their way in. On 6 April 1652 they put in their claims for 1,038,202 acres of profitable land.[1] They were, however, not anxious to plant while the country was still so disturbed, and meanwhile the army officers began to press for a general settlement which would not have to await the satisfaction of the adventurers. A plan emerged, ultimately to be embodied in the act of satisfaction, to settle, by equal divisions between the adventurers and soldiers, ten contiguous counties—Antrim, Down, Armagh, Meath, Westmeath, King's, Queen's, Tipperary, Limerick, and Waterford, with Louth held as additional security for the adventurers, should it be needed. The act reserved four counties for the government, Dublin, Kildare, Carlow, and Cork, and assured the army that all arrears would be met, and that if possible even the rank and file would receive land at the 'act rates'. From the beginning, the soldiers had justified fears that this would not in fact be possible even though their satisfaction was made the first charge on all remaining confiscated land, except in Connacht.

The act of adventurers had stipulated that the land was to be distributed

[1] For the complexities in calculating the acreage due to them, see Bottigheimer, *Eng. money & Ir. land*, pp 121–2.

by lot, and this was confirmed in the act of satisfaction. For security reasons, soldiers and adventurers were to be mixed in the plantation, the baronies of each county being divided into two equal parts, to be drawn for by lot between them. In the subsequent division, also by lot, the adventurers had certain advantages, because it was fairly certain that there would be enough land to satisfy them and because, being a comparatively small number, they could draw their lots directly as individuals. However, the gross survey was so imperfect that even the adventurers were groping in the dark. It did not indicate exactly how much land a barony contained, nor how much was profitable and how much unprofitable, and there was no clear knowledge of how much was to be confiscated and how much was not. Further, the flat rates at which the land had been valued in 1642 bore little relation to the varying value of the land now to be actually distributed. Yet the adventurers as a body clung to the 'gross survey' and the 'act rates', fearing that any revision must work to their disadvantage in favour of the soldiers. Some baronies might turn out in fact to have too much land, others too little, so that a man drawing in one of the latter might find that there was no land to satisfy him, while no one was willing to admit to a surplus. The way was open for greed, scramble, and bribery. Inevitably, it was the small investor who suffered.[1]

Three separate surviving sources list the adventurers and the land they actually drew.[2] Many drew large estates that established them as landlords, such as Sir William Brereton with 6,700 acres in Tipperary and Armagh, William Hawkins with 32,395 acres in Down, and Thomas Vincent with 19,044 acres in Meath, King's, and Queen's Counties. But many drew very small areas; up to 20 per cent had credits of less than £50. These small investors are the most intriguing element in the mass of information recently assembled by computer[3]—men like John Winkfield, a London haberdasher, a married man, who invested £40 under the original act for adventurers, made no further investment, but did not sell, and drew 66 acres in the barony of Stradbally in Queen's County. Unfortunately, the one question the computer has not answered is what he did with it. Did he settle, did he sell it, or did he lose it in the scramble? The first would seem by far the least likely. The Books of Survey and Distribution have been published for three of the planted counties only: Cork, Kilkenny, and Westmeath.[4] While the evidence of these books needs much further sifting and collation with the lists in the

[1] For some of the problems that arose, see the document in Dunlop, *Commonwealth*, ii, 509–13.

[2] Bottigheimer, *Eng. money & Ir. land*, pp 143–63.

[3] Ibid., pp 164–213.

[4] Anne Waters, 'Distribution of forfeited estates in county of Corke returned by the Downe survey' in *Cork Hist. Soc. Jn.*, xxxvii (1932), pp 83–9, xxxviii (1933), pp 39–45, 72–9, xxxix (1934), pp 33–7, 79–84, xl (1935), pp 43–8, 91–4, xli (1936), pp 37–41, 97–104; William Healy, *History and antiquities of Kilkenny* (Dublin, 1893), i, appendix i; John Charles Lyons, *The book of survey and distribution of the estates in the county of Westmeath forfeited in the year MDCLII* (Ledestown, 1852). For the Books of Survey and Distribution generally, see below, ch. XVII, p. 426.

1659 'census' before any firm conclusions can be drawn it does seem clear that many adventurers who drew small lots did not in fact plant, and that numerous speculators were profitably active. Of the 1,043 adventurers who drew land, about 500 had it confirmed to them by the restoration acts of settlement. Almost certainly they formed the great majority of those who actually planted, and most of them drew sufficient land to establish them as landlords.

In their allotment of land the army faced all the adventurers' problems, and others as well. First, the sum due to each soldier had to be established. He was then issued with a debenture. This was not in itself a title to land, nor could it be, for the army continued to press for a more realistic valuation of the land available, convinced that this could only work in its favour. What was clear was that there simply would not be enough land, even though most of Ireland, excluding what was reserved to the government and the adventurers, but including Sligo, Leitrim, and the barony of Tirawley in County Mayo from the catholics' share, was quickly made available. When Petty was commissioned to survey the soldiers' lands he made a preliminary estimate that they could be satisfied at the rate of 12*s*. 6*d*. in the pound. The army was not inclined to regard this as satisfaction, but it became the rate generally adopted.

In spite of the progress of the Down Survey, the great numbers of the soldier-claimants made definitive allotment difficult. The general plan was that they should draw for their lots regiment by regiment as they were disbanded, and that within the regiments each troop or company should make the final division among themselves by lot or agreement. The private soldiers could expect only very small allotments, because their pay was so small in comparison with that of the officers. Most of them were not anxious to settle. For some, soldiering had become a way of life: in 1656, 1,500 enlisted for service in Jamaica. Many just wanted to get back to England and the simple necessities of life, like good beer and cheese. It was the officers who conducted the long and involved negotiations with the government, and in the outcome they more and more came to dictate the pattern of the settlement of the army.

Of the land drawn by individual soldiers we have no detailed records such as exist for the adventurers. In all 33,419 debentures were issued, but only 11,804 were returned for certificates of possession. The number who actually settled may have been slightly greater, for there are instances of soldiers who held on to their debentures even after being put in possession, because they still hoped that they might be awarded land at better rates. The explanation for the missing 21,615 lies in the fact that most of the soldiers disposed of their debentures, normally by sale to their officers. In these circumstances, the debentures naturally depreciated. The government, seeing the threat to its plan to establish a protestant yeoman class, at first tried to stop the sales. Then it tried to hold the debentures at a rate of 8*s*. in the pound, but, on Petty's evidence, as early as 1653 they regularly changed hands at 4*s*. or 5*s*.[1] Nor was all the dealing honest. The way was open for all kinds of chicanery and again we may reasonably suspect it was the small men who suffered.

Petty was reluctantly allowed to survey the adventurers' lands only in 1658. The survey disclosed a surplus, but a small one. The settlement was still unfinished at the restoration. It seems certain that some soldiers and even some adventurers received nothing. This is beyond doubt as regards the Munster garrisons who had defected to Cromwell in 1649. No provision had been made for them in the act of satisfaction, but their claims were recognised in an ordinance of 27 June 1654. This, however, still left them at the end of the list, and the restoration act of settlement makes it clear that at least some of them got nothing.

It may be taken as certain that about 12,000 soldiers actually settled. Of these, about 7,500 had their lands confirmed to them after the restoration. The officers of the Cromwellian army became a prominent element in the new landlord class.[2] The yeoman element was sizeable, but thinly spread over the country as a whole, and, as continuing complaints were to make clear, they were dangerously prone to intermarry and go native.

The failure of the catholic inhabitants of the Munster port towns to prove 'constant good affection' may be taken as indicating that it was almost impossible for any catholic to do so, and that in consequence, under the commonwealth, catholics almost without exception ceased to be property-holders east of the Shannon. That this loss of property in no way involved a clearance of all catholics will be apparent from a consideration of the towns and the 'five counties' bounded by the Boyne and the Barrow, where it was most explicit policy that no papist should remain.

The towns had suffered heavily in a war that had been a succession of sieges. Protestant colonists did not come to them from England in sufficient numbers, and efforts to attract protestants from the Continent or the New England colonies came to little or nothing, so that the towns did not recover their prosperity during the commonwealth regime. Their fortunes varied, of course, from Dublin, which had never suffered siege or capture, and was predominantly protestant, to Galway at the other end of the scale, where civic life to all intents and purposes broke down. Under the commonwealth the catholics lost control of the town corporations and were not permitted to engage in trade, though before this the bulk of overseas trade had been in catholic hands, Dublin alone having a sizeable protestant mercantile community. These two developments represented an erosion of catholic political and economic power comparable to what had been lost in the land-confiscations.

[1] 'Political anatomy of Ire.', ed. Hull, i, 152.
[2] See the examples in D. F. Gleeson, *The last lords of Ormond* (London, 1938).

Yet the towns could not continue to function at all if catholics were altogether excluded. In March 1654 the military governor of Wexford was asking the commissioners in Dublin whether any Irish papist could be permitted to live in the town, and in particular how many seamen, boatmen, and fishermen, how many packers and gillers of herrings, how many coopers, how many masons and carpenters, how many labourers and porters? He was told that none might remain without special licence after 1 May, and that he was to give the Dublin authorities a list of the tradesmen and labourers that he and the commissioners of revenue in Wexford thought it absolutely necessary to retain.[1] If there was further correspondence on the point it has not survived, but it is not hard to decide what happened. Continuing proclamations ordering the towns to be cleared of papists indicate only that they were ineffective.

It was planned also to clear entirely of papists the lands between the Barrow, the Boyne, and the sea, but the absence of yeoman protestant planters made it in the interest of the new landowners to press for the retention of a catholic working class. By the spring of 1655 the proposal to clear the whole area had diminished into an attempt to decide what part of it might be totally cleared, in what part Irish labour might be allowed to remain, and how for security the rest might be temporarily laid waste. The grim reality of this last proposal is confirmed by a report in the summer of the following year that the Irish were returning in such numbers to Wicklow that 'that fast county is in short time likely to become a nest and sheltering place of loose and dangerous persons'. By now one can almost predict the reaction: an order to remove 'all such Irish papists out of the said county of Wicklow . . . it being hoped and intended the same should be thoroughly and seasonably planted and inhabited by protestants of this and the English nation'.[2] One can also be certain that this order was not effectively carried out.

The Irish remained, then, as tenants, some of these being the old proprietors. Tenants to work the land were indeed in such demand that they were in a very strong position. John Lynch, an aristocratic ecclesiastic from a Galway that had vanished, noted from his exile in St Malo reports of their growing 'insolence'.[3] They remained as labourers and tradesmen in the towns. There is one class that history is inclined to forget, because it has left such scanty traces, the landless labourers, the 'pedees and garcones' whom an order of 1655 still judged to be 'transplantable persons'.[4] They possibly made up three-quarters of the population, and were scarcely affected at all. The hearth-money rolls and the census of 1659 show that they remained in large numbers, even in the northern counties of Ulster. The tempest that

[1] Hore, *Wexford town*, pp 311–12.

[2] Dunlop, *Commonwealth*, pp 602–3.

[3] *Alithinologia* (St Malo, 1664), p. 136.

[4] Glossed by Dunlop, *Commonwealth*, p. 530, as 'paddies and gossoons'. See also MacLysaght, *Ir. life after Cromwell* (2nd ed., 1950), pp 124–5.

had passed over the country had left those who had survived it in a condition possibly not markedly more wretched than it had been before.

The Irish also remained as 'tories' who 'went on their keeping' and defied the government. In the later days of the confederate wars the opposing armies had to some extent lived by raiding one another's quarters. The English adopted the abusive word 'tory' to describe those who raided them.[1] After the surrender of the Irish armies in 1652, resistance continued from many small bands of 'tories'. The government hunted them down for execution—the tory with the wolf and the priest were the 'three beasts that lay burthens upon us', as they were described by Major Anthony Morgan, and they were dealt with by putting a price on their heads. They were killed in great numbers, and the government encouraged the formation of bands of Irish to hunt them, being prepared even to dispense proprietors from transplantation in return for this service.[2] The 'tories' could count on the support of the local Irish population, though these were exposed to fine, imprisonment, transplantation, or transportation as deterrents, but in spite of all repressive measures toryism was to survive as a problem after the restoration.

In some respects the economy improved. There was little else for it to do. The new planters did bring greater efficiency in the long run, but in the short run there was a temptation to take a quick profit. The indications are that by 1660 the over-all situation had not recovered the level of 1640. Again, much detailed research in what documents are extant is still required to get an accurate picture of the land and towns of Ireland at the end of the commonwealth, but a note in the particulars accompanying the parish maps of the Down Survey for the barony of Gorey may not be untypical: 'the soil is generally arable, meadow and pasture, but of late years grown much over with shrubs, heath and furze'.[3]

The second great impact of the Cromwellian settlement was in matters of religion. 'I meddle not with any man's conscience', Cromwell had declared at New Ross on 19 October 1649. There can be no real questioning of his sincere attachment to this difficult principle, but even before his Irish campaign events had already forced him to some modifications in his attempts to define how it might be applied in practice. His concept of religious liberty sprang from a root of congregationalism. Of long standing within the Christian tradition as a whole, its influence has been seen in pre-reformation England with Wyclif and the Lollards. After the reformation, it drew strength from the opposition to the Elizabethan state-church and

[1] The first use of the word 'tory' (Irish *toraidhe* 'raider') seems to be in a document dated 22 Jan. 1646 (*Ormonde MSS*, new series, i, 105), where it is clearly equated with 'highwayman'.

[2] Prendergast, *Cromwellian settlement*, p. 343, indicates that public accounts show that a 'vast number' were killed.

[3] Cited by M. Tóibín, 'The population of County Wexford in the seventeenth century' in *Past*, vi (1950), p. 130.

especially the interpretation given to this by Archbishop Laud. Its basic tenets were that all Christians shared a common priesthood, and that each local church should be independent (this word, indeed, being normally used at the time rather than congregational) as to its discipline and worship. However, what independency was to mean in practice had been decided in the great debates of 1647 within the council of the New Model army. Cromwell's victory over the 'levellers' had led to the acceptance of what might be described as 'independency for men of property'. An essential element was that public order would be guaranteed by public authority. There was to be no absolute freedom in the propagation or open profession of opinion.

The basic confession of faith, drawn up by the Westminster assembly and approved by parliament in 1648, was something of an embarrassment, because it was essentially a presbyterian document (it has remained a basic confession of that faith), and presbyterianism was radically incompatible with congregationalism, because of its rigid insistence on a uniform and detailed church-order. The directory for public worship approved by parliament in 1645 was more to the point. While it excluded the Book of Common Prayer, it did not prescribe a set form of worship but contented itself with giving general directions.

Under the commonwealth, then, the state kept a strict watch over religion. The act of uniformity was repealed, and men were not compelled to attend services repugnant to their consciences. But not all forms of service were allowed. Specifically 'popery' and 'prelacy' were excluded because they were 'idolatry' and were therefore forbidden by scripture.

The trouble in Ireland was that none of the denominations there, presbyterian, Church of Ireland, or catholic, could agree in conscience with the congregational principle. However, the first two managed to reach a practical accommodation with it. Having first outlined the system as established in Ireland, we can then turn to the question of how various shades of protestantism fared under it. Finally, there is the position of the catholic church, to which no toleration was extended.

In 1649 the presbyterians were solidly established in the north-east, where they had tenaciously defended themselves through the 1640s. With scattered exceptions, members of the Church of Ireland were concentrated in the enclaves round Dublin and Cork. The 1649 peace with Ormond had recognised the claims of the confederate catholics and the Church of Ireland in the areas they respectively held, though there were soon disputes about churches, church-livings, and ecclesiastical finances generally, especially in Munster where the border of each confession was by no means clearly defined.

When Ormond had handed Dublin over to parliament in 1647 the new authorities immediately notified the clergy that they must cease using the

Book of Common Prayer.[1] Protests only led to an order imposing the directory for public worship. It seems fairly certain, however, that there was some clandestine use of the prayer-book at least over the next few years, if only because the parliamentary authorities had too much else on hand to have time to track down every instance of religious nonconformity.

The commissioners appointed in October 1650 had as part of their instructions an order to impose the English pattern of religion, to encourage qualified ministers and schoolmasters, and to pay them from the public funds. Church property was to be confiscated and let out to rent to produce the required revenue.

Schoolmasters were appointed only in very inadequate numbers. Neither was it easy to get ministers: even the Cromwellian army was quite short of them. Attempts were constantly made to attract ministers from England and the New England colonies, but there was no widespread enthusiasm for a call to Ireland, and some of those who came held views that imperilled the public-order aspect of the religious settlement. Under various pressures, a practical toleration of all protestant denominations began to emerge, always however with the proviso that the Book of Common Prayer would not be tolerated in divine service.

In England, an ordinance of 1654 had set up a committee of 'triers', composed of twenty-five ministers and nine laymen, to examine the qualifications of prospective ministers. The principle was followed in Ireland, but the pattern was less rigid. What happened was that prominent ministers, for the most part living in or near Dublin, were invited to serve on committees as occasion arose. Samuel Winter seems to have acted as unofficial chairman. Himself an independent, but of eirenic temperament, his basic puritanism approximated closely to that of the average Church of Ireland minister. In consequence, Winter's influence made it possible to smooth over many problems in appointing a ministry. He also showed himself a capable administrator of Trinity College, of which he had been appointed provost on 3 June 1652.

When the committee approved a candidate, the government appointed him on salary. These salaries were generous. Some received £200 a year, and the sum aimed at seems to have been about £100, though many received less. Every effort was made to provide the minister with a suitable house. On every Lord's Day he was to conduct the approved service at the meeting-house. This was to be maintained by local contribution; in almost every case it was in fact the old parish church.

Between 1651 and 1659 there are records of the appointment of 376

[1] The standard work is still St John D. Seymour, *The puritans in Ireland 1647–1661* (Oxford, 1921, reprinted Oxford, 1969). As it draws extensively on documents since lost it must remain in many respects irreplaceable. The same author's treatment of the subject in Phillips, *Ch. of. Ire.*, iii. 59–116, is, as he himself indicates, based on his earlier work.

state-salaried ministers. Of these, at least sixty-five can be identified as former ministers of the Church of Ireland (an enumeration made in 1647, certainly incomplete, lists ninety-one in the country at the time). Sixty-seven were presbyterians. A few can be identified as baptists, and almost all the remainder may be classed as independents. There were also quite a number of ministers not on salary. Some presbyterians, many baptists and other sectaries,[1] and doubtless some of the Church of Ireland ministers, refused a state salary for reasons of conscience.

Further developments, especially after the arrival of Henry Cromwell, made it easier for the conscience of presbyterian and Church of Ireland ministers. In 1656 and 1657 attempts were made to restructure the parish system (hitherto ministers had been appointed to specified localities, principally towns and garrisons). The plan adopted aimed at producing reasonably compact units, capable of yielding a salary of about £80 a year. This proved practicable only where there was a sizeable protestant population, and it seems to have been put into effect mainly in the presbyterian areas of Ulster.

In April 1658 Henry Cromwell summoned an assembly of ministers in Dublin. At this it became clear that many ministers of presbyterian or Church of Ireland convictions desired a restoration of payment by tithe. No record of its decisions is extant, but by the end of 1658 eighty ministers (fifty-nine of them, nearly all presbyterians, in the precincts of Belfast and Derry) were receiving their tithes directly, and it seems a reasonable inference that where these eighty ministers had been appointed the traditional parish system had been fully restored.

The question of ministerial ordination also moved towards a settlement in favour of the presbyterians and, in some measure, of the Church of Ireland, and away from the congregational position that ordination was only 'an act of conveniency in respect to [public] order'. After 1655 the formation of associations of ministers was encouraged, and they began to give expression to the view that it was necessary that a minister be ordained by a minister. The Cork association, where episcopacy was strong, even admitted the validity of episcopal ordination. However, the times were not in favour of anything beyond the presbyterian point of view, though it is clear that on this central issue opinion had turned against the more radical sectaries.

To all intents and purposes the Church of Ireland clergy accepted the congregational structure. Their basically puritan religious outlook was in many cases strengthened by a political inclination to parliament. The most practical point of conscience at issue was the ban on the prayer-book, and this, by and large, they accepted. Four of their bishops lived in Ireland during the decade. One, Henry Jones of Clogher, made for himself a civil

[1] See below, pp 379–80.

and military career. The other three accepted government pensions. The personnel of the church, then, was not seriously disrupted.

The presbyterians formed a more compact community, with a stronger political position and, one might venture to say, tougher convictions.[1] One strong conviction was a commitment to monarchy with the covenant, and the execution of Charles I had led to a protest made famous by Milton's attack on the 'blockish presbyters . . . set so haughtily in the pontifical see of Belfast'.[2] As the Cromwellian conquest proceeded and as Scottish support rallied to Charles II, pressure on the Irish presbyterians grew. Some of the ministers had to flee to Scotland or go into hiding, while others were imprisoned.

In January 1651 Charles II, having accepted the covenant, was crowned in Scotland. The Irish government stepped up its persecution of the presbyterians, and attempted to impose on them the oath of 'engagement' to be loyal to the commonwealth. Government and presbyterian accounts differ as to whether any ministers took it, but it seems a fair inference that a few did. At the worst period only five or six ministers in all remained at liberty. In May 1653 an order was made for the transplantation of about 260 leading presbyterians to Kilkenny, Tipperary, and Waterford. It came to nothing, and indeed the presbyterians may have been more willing to go than the government was to transplant them.

In any case, by now the situation in Scotland was being brought under control, and a few months later a change of policy became apparent when the government announced its willingness to pay salaries to presbyterian ministers. They for their part were slow to accept, but from now on they were in practice free to function, their main problem arising from the fact that those returning from Scotland brought with them the involved disputes that had broken out there between 'resolutioners', who supported Charles II, and 'remonstrants', prepared to work with the commonwealth. While the majority of Irish presbyterians came to accept the 'remonstrant' position, a minority remained hostile 'resolutioners'. By the end of 1655 a number of ministers had accepted salaries, and an uneasy agreement was gradually reached with Henry Cromwell's administration. It was uneasy because on certain points the presbyterians as a body did not really yield, notably in their insistence that a minister needed presbyterial ordination and a call from his congregation. The tensions remained even though on this point events turned in their favour, and possibly only the death of Oliver Cromwell prevented a new confrontation.

The sects did not proliferate in Ireland to anything like the same extent as in England, but two at least call for some notice, the baptists and the quakers.

[1] The contemporary account by Patrick Adair, *A true narrative of the rise and progress of the presbyterian church in Ireland*, ed. W. D. Killen (Dublin, 1866), provides useful detail.

[2] *Observations on the articles of peace . . . and a representation of the Scots presbytery at Belfast in Ireland* (1649).

Both may be regarded as essentially 'congregational', but each because of special tenets had problems in fitting into the qualified independency of the state religion. The baptists did not fit into the pattern of independency because they absolutely refused to accept that infant baptism was true baptism. For this reason their opponents frequently called them 'anabaptists'. Though they tended to reject the name as abusive, it implied a radical political and spiritual outlook that many of them did in fact accept. They found Cromwell's acceptance of the protectorate very hard to stomach, and on this point they made common ground with Charles Fleetwood, though he himself was an independent. In 1653 baptist congregations had been established in Dublin, Wexford, Waterford, Clonmel, Kilkenny, Cork, Kerry, Limerick, Galway, and Carrickfergus. Less than a dozen of their ministers are to be found in the lists of those salaried, but they were reluctant to accept salaries and many were unlicensed. They were especially strong in the army. Henry Cromwell clearly regarded them as a threat to civil order as well as to military discipline, but at the beginning of 1658 he could report to Thurloe that they had become very quiet and that if they were content to accept equal treatment he was prepared to give it to them.

He adopted the same attitude to the quakers, though these, with their central tenet of the 'inner light', were less tractable. Before their organisation by George Fox in 1669 their undoubtedly sincere witness could pose problems for those responsible for public order (in 1658 two quakers arrived in Rome to convert the pope). Many of their practices, notably their refusal to pay tithes or to contribute to the upkeep of 'steeple-houses', as they disparagingly called the churches, or their insistence on entering the 'steeple-houses' to dispute with the 'hireling' minister, drew persecution on them. At the end of 1655 an order was made for the arrest of all quakers, and ninety-two were imprisoned and six banished. Though in the last three years of the commonwealth there is record of only nine quakers being imprisoned, they continued to be a strain on the official policy of toleration.

No toleration could be extended to the papists.[1] Many plans were proposed for their conversion, and a number of ministers deputed to preach in Irish, though converts were few and their motives nearly always suspect. The assembly of ministers in 1658 discussed the topic, though by this time it seems to have been accepted that in fact there would not be large-scale conversions.

At the outbreak of the war there were fifteen catholic bishops in Ireland, all of them appointed between 1618 and 1630. Three further provisions had been made on 16 September 1641 (N.S.), though that of Louis Dillon to

[1] Two useful recent studies are R. D. Edwards, 'Irish catholics and the puritan revolution' in *Father Luke Wadding*, pp 93–118, and Benignus Millett, 'Survival and reorganization 1650–95' in Corish, *Ir. catholicism*, iii, ch. VII, pp 1–12. For state documents concerning the catholic church see [James MacCaffrey], 'Commonwealth records' in *Archiv. Hib.*, vi (1917), pp 175–202; vii (1918–21), pp 20–66.

Achonry did not take effect, so that at the beginning of the confederacy there were seventeen bishops. At its end there were twenty-seven, only three sees being vacant, Derry, Kildare, and Achonry. Ten of these bishops were survivors of the original eighteen, and most of them were now old men. Seventeen had been provided during the confederate period, ten in 1647.

It is possible to give a rough estimate of the numbers of the regular clergy. There were about 1,600 friars, of whom 1,000 were Franciscans and 400 Dominicans. In addition there were about sixty monks, nearly all of them Cistercians. Even a rough estimate of the numbers of the diocesan clergy is not possible, but it may be said with certainty that there were not enough to man all the parishes. For this and other reasons only a very untidy parish-system had developed before 1641. Further complications were the claims of the friars to minister independently of the bishops in virtue of faculties from Rome, monastic claims based on extensive impropriations of parishes in pre-reformation times, and the dependence of all the clergy on the more wealthy catholic laity, which introduced an unofficial but very real element of lay patronage. Between 1642 and 1649 little was done to resolve the problems or to tidy up the system, but in the areas held by the confederates catholic priests ministered freely and in sufficient numbers, and the peace of 1649 had granted them the churches and church-livings in these areas.

When he broke with the Kilkenny confederates, Rinuccini and his party had come to place some hopes in the commitment of the English independents to religious toleration, and these hopes were certainly a factor in Owen Roe O'Neill's agreement with parliament in 1649. But Cromwell's declaration at New Ross in October, confirmed the following January in his reply to the prelates at Clonmacnoise, made it unequivocally clear that for him liberty of conscience did not extend to tolerating the mass or the catholic church.[1] Cromwell—it was part of his almost tortured commitment to freedom of conscience—was concerned over the position of catholics in England, and his relations with them present problems as yet only partially explored. But whatever may have lain deep in his conscience—and theologically he was far removed from catholicism—toleration of popery in Ireland was an emotional, political—and economic—impossibility.

Catholic priests had inevitably been among those killed at Drogheda and Wexford. Cromwell recounts that at Drogheda all except two 'were knocked on the head promiscuously'. These two were later captured and executed. One of them, having tried to pass as a lieutenant, confessed that he was a friar when he learned that there was no quarter for officers, but, Cromwell adds grimly, 'that did not save him'.[2] Cromwell's reply to the declaration of the bishops at Clonmacnoise, issued at the end of January 1650, had

[1] See above, pp 342, 344–5.
[2] Cromwell, *Writings*, ed. Abbott, ii, 128.

attacked the clergy as leaders of the rebellion and responsible for the massacres of 1641, and had threatened blood for blood. Yet the practice varied during the campaign of 1650. There are instances of priests being treated more or less as officers in a hostile army, and put to death in circumstances in which officers were executed, but there are also instances of their lives being spared, and Cromwell was more merciful than 'old protestants' such as Broghill and Coote.

The act of settlement of 12 August 1652 seemed to introduce a distinction among the clergy, for it laid down that all 'priests and Jesuits' involved in any way in the rebellion were to forfeit their lives. This too was not applied with full rigour, for the high court of justice did not seriously attempt to deal with all the cases it should in theory have dealt with.[1] How many priests were killed or executed cannot be known with certainty. Some accounts do not name the victims, and it is a not unreasonable assumption that during the war some deaths went unrecorded. In regard to those recorded, mainly by refugees in Europe, it is likewise a not unreasonable assumption that in this emotional context there was the possibility of legendary development, at least in regard to details, and in some cases possibly in regard to the very substance of the story. A total of ninety-two names based on the evidence of contemporaries has been submitted in the cause for the beatification of the Irish martyrs.[2]

1649	1650	1651	1652	1653	1654	1655
19	7	37 (15)	15 (7)	9	2	3

Questions have been raised in a number of these cases. It has been urged that some, including the three bishops executed (Boetius MacEgan of Ross, Heber MacMahon of Clogher, and Terence Albert O'Brien of Emly) were put to death on primarily political charges, though in the circumstances the distinction between politics and religion is not easily drawn, while other cases have been questioned because the evidence comes from one source only, recognised as untrustworthy at least in regard to detail.[3]

By the middle of 1651 it is clear that many priests were being held in prison. As the Irish field armies surrendered in 1652 a new policy began to take shape. These soldiers were allowed, even encouraged, to go into exile, and were given time to arrange their transport. In some instances the articles of surrender allowed the same terms to their chaplains. Further ordinances promised passes to migrate from Ireland to all priests not facing capital charges, and with the suspension of the activities of the high court of justice in 1654 it became more or less settled policy that catholic priests should be

[1] See above, pp 359–60.

[2] *Positio super introductione causae* (Rome, 1914), pt 1, pp 229–32; *I.E.R.*, series 5, xi (Apr. 1918), pp 311–21. The figures in brackets under the years 1651 and 1652 indicate the number of laymen included.

[3] Anthony Bruodin, *Propugnaculum catholicae veritatis* (Prague, 1669).

exiled.[1] The priests do not appear to have gone as readily as the soldiers, although on 6 January 1653 the commissioners of parliament ordered that any priest who had agreed to go but had delayed his departure for more than twenty days, or who had gone but had returned from exile, was to be subject to the penalties of the English statute of 1585 (27 Eliz., c. 2), which had made a catholic priest guilty of treason by the very fact of his presence in the country, and made it a felony to harbour or assist him. There were several petitions against the extension to Ireland of this harsh English legislation, but the commissioners, while insisting that no one would be compelled to attend worship or divine service contrary to his conscience, were equally insistent that the order banishing the priests must be strictly executed.[2]

Very many priests did go into exile. Again we can have no certain figures, but 1,000 may be a conservative estimate. Many found succour in one measure or another in catholic Europe, and in exile continued even more bitterly the recriminations that had rent the confederacy.[3] In practice, a month's protection, or even more, was regularly extended to priests who undertook to leave. To bring in those who would not, the government offered a reward for their capture, fixed at £5 in 1653. Attempts were made to levy this 'head-money' on the barony in which the priest was captured, while those who sheltered him, legally guilty of felony, were imprisoned. Occasionally priests were allowed to remain because of age or ill-health, if they gave an undertaking not to exercise their ministry, to live in a designated place, and to do nothing prejudicial to the commonwealth. One bishop, Eugene Sweeney of Kilmore, remained in Ireland on these terms for the whole of the 1650s.

While one can at times see shafts of human concern lighting up this unremitting persecution, it was dominated by a hatred of popery and the conviction that the success of the Cromwellian settlement depended on its eradication. At the beginning of 1655 it was ordered that those who refused to go into voluntary exile should be transported to Barbados. They were to be concentrated in prison to await shipment, first at Carrickfergus and later in the western islands of Aran and Inisbofin as well, where 'popish priests and other dangerous persons' could, at 'sixpence daily allowance' be employed in the 'building of cabins and making of prisons'.[4] The problem remained that the transporting of an indentured servant had to show a

[1] R. D. Edwards, 'Irish catholics and the puritan revolution' in *Father Luke Wadding*, pp 101–2.

[2] Dunlop, *Commonwealth*, pp 309, 318; [James MacCaffrey], 'Commonwealth records' in *Archiv. Hib.*, vii (1918–21), pp 41, 55; *Comment. Rinucc.*, v, 85–90. The text of the order does not seem to have survived in the administrative records of the commonwealth, but Latin translations, clearly made from copies in circulation among the Irish catholic exiles, are to be found, for example, in *Comment. Rinucc.*, v, 85–7; Dominic O'Daly, O.P., *Initium, incrementa, et exitus familiae Geraldinorum . . . ac persecutionis haereticorum descriptio* (Lisbon, 1655), pp 375–82.

[3] See below, pp 570–74, 614–15.

[4] [James MacCaffrey], 'Commonwealth records' in *Archiv. Hib.*, vi (1917), pp 179–81.

profit, and the priests were not attractive merchandise, either because of age or ill-health, or because no one in the plantations wanted them even if they were young and healthy.[1]

Under this pressure a few—the surviving records suggest very few—abandoned their religion. Far more, but still a small minority of those active in 1649, tried to continue their ministry. After 1656 it is clear that priests were returning from Europe. They had to walk very warily. It would have been too dangerous, both for themselves and for their hosts, to have tried to depend on the laity. Some sought safety in the fastnesses of bogs or mountains, others moved around in disguise, or settled down as farmers or labourers. The tradition of a local 'mass-rock' is very widespread in Ireland, and in many places it may more probably be traced to this period than to the opening decades of the eighteenth century. The priestly ministry was reduced to a minimum, and its organisation to even less. Yet a Jesuit was able to teach school in the neighbourhood of New Ross, and in 1657 mass was being said in the Marshalsea prison in Dublin.

Among the laity, only the schoolmasters were singled out for direct persecution similar to that of the clergy. There were constant orders for their arrest and transportation, as they could not be moved to Connacht because, like the clergy, they were regarded as corrupting the people. Even less documented than the clergy, they seem like them to have been able to continue their work to some extent, but with great stealth, in constant danger, and drastically reduced numbers.

The trial, though sharp, was short. Not many defected. Lack of religious instruction was a more serious problem, as was the deprivation of sacramental life in a church where it was so central. The laity suffered if they harboured priests or schoolmasters, but in principle no one was compelled to attend religious worship contrary to his conscience. The upper classes suffered heavy loss of property and were excluded from all public office, though in the later years of the commonwealth it is clear that Henry Cromwell's administration was beginning to face the problem of what provision might be made for a whole population without any civil status at all, and how Irish papists might be distinguished from papists in England in 'what privileges they may be deemed capable of'.[2] Two years later it had reached the wholly negative conclusion that the imposition of an oath of abjuration of the Stuarts, in terms involving the abjuration of popery as well, was not the answer.[3] It does not seem to have got any further with the problem when the regime began to crumble.

On 16 April 1657 (N.S.) Edmund O'Reilly, the exiled vicar general of

[1] See above, p. 363.

[2] The chief baron of the exchequer was asked to deal with this on 21 Mar. 1656 ([J. MacCaffrey], 'Commonwealth records' in *Archiv. Hib.*, vi (1917), p. 187).

[3] See above, p. 355.

Dublin, was nominated archbishop of Armagh.[1] The same day Bishop Anthony MacGeoghegan of Clonmacnoise was appointed to Meath, and shortly afterwards thirteen vicars apostolic were named in other sees. Less than three years before. O'Reilly had been sentenced to death by the high court of justice in Dublin. It has already been suggested that he may possibly have owed his life and subsequent release to connections he had with people in power.[2] When after his consecration in Brussels in May 1658 he arrived in London in August with commendatory letters from Cardinal Mazarin he was able to make contact with Thurloe. Indeed in the uncertainty following the death of the lord protector, his chief difficulties seem to have arisen from other Irish catholic ecclesiastics in London who did not like him because they suspected that he was not loyal to the Stuarts. At any rate, he was deported to France in the spring of 1659, but the following autumn he sailed directly to Ireland, arriving at Passage, County Waterford, in October. Bishop MacGeoghegan had arrived a few months before him.

Archbishop O'Reilly's reports provide some definite information on the state of the catholic church in Ireland when he arrived. The five dioceses of the Dublin province had an average of seven priests apiece: the province of Armagh was better supplied, with an average of twenty-two. In some dioceses he found a number of regular clergy as well. They all lived, he wrote, 'in much endurance and misery as to worldly things; they visit the sick by night; they celebrate mass before and round about dawn, and that in hiding places and recesses, having appointed scouts to look around and with eyes and ears agog to keep watch lest the soldiers come by surprise'. The archbishop himself had to be especially careful: 'I did not enter the house of any catholic', he wrote; 'I had made for myself a small hut in a mountainous district, one here, another there, so that no one else should suffer for my sake'.[3]

His mission in Ireland was short. Charges of disloyalty made by fellow catholics grew in intensity, as the restoration of Charles II took shape, and in July 1660 he was summoned to Rome to explain himself. The letter may not have arrived in Ireland until near the end of the year. He sailed from Dublin on 25 April 1661, five weeks after the government had ordered his arrest. It was clear that the catholic church in Ireland was still dogged by the disputes and recriminations of the 1640s.

Even 300 years later, any Irish historian indulging in general reflections on Irish history in the troubled years between 1641 and 1660 puts himself to some extent at risk, for the cry of its ghosts still troubles our own days.

[1] Tomás Ó Fiaich, 'Edmund O'Reilly, archbishop of Armagh 1657–1669' in *Father Luke Wadding*, pp 171–228.

[2] See above, pp 359–60.

[3] Cited by Ó Fiaich, loc. cit., pp 203–4.

It is clear who the winners were in the great upheaval. They were now established as the landed class, with, as Petty put it, 'a gamester's right at least to their estates', and in the years ahead would come to define themselves as 'the protestant interest'. Political and economic considerations would ensure that the interest of the adventurers and army officers who had become landlords would be assimilated to that of the 'old protestants'. 'As for the bloodshed in the contest', Petty continues, 'God best knows who did occasion it'.[1] One might venture to add, trusting not to disturb too many ghosts, that the working up of the propaganda about the 'guilty nation' of papists was a deliberate appeal to religious passion made by a group grown rich on confiscated lands, in the interests of still more confiscation. By and large, the soldiers of the Cromwellian army were not the winners. In 1660 Ireland had more protestants than in 1641, but the broad pattern of their distribution was not greatly changed, the only heavy concentration being in north-east Ulster.

The catholics were clearly the losers. Here again one might recall how much suffering there was in Christian Europe at the time, as the religious wars drew to an end and a recognisably modern world began. One might recall in particular the hardships of the settlement of Bohemia after 1620 or the expulsion of the Moriscos from Spain at about the same time. But one can hardly parallel the ruin that fell on the Irish catholics. For the Old Irish it was the last of a series of blows: the Old English lost almost everything in one catastrophe. Both retained their catholic religion, but history can scarcely assess what scarring it may have suffered. Both lost their property and in consequence lost political influence, and their basic culture was gravely at risk. The Old Irish culture, with incredible toughness, managed to survive, but the Old English found it much more difficult to retain their distinctive cultural qualities. That this was so must be only matter for regret. They may have been conservative to a fault, and ill equipped to meet much lesser developments than the catastrophe which struck them, but their political thinking, though it drew heavily on the past, did make an appeal to principles of lasting value. By 1660 these principles were stirring in a new context as 'the protestant interest' began to take shape, and the line of descent from Patrick Darcy continues in the catholic 'patriot parliament' of 1689 and with William Molyneux in 1698.[2]

[1] 'Political anatomy of Ire.', ed. Hull, i, 154.

[2] Cf. T. C. Barnard, 'Planters and policies in Cromwellian Ireland' in *Past & present*, no. 61 (Nov. 1973), p. 66.

CHAPTER XV

Economic trends, 1660–91

L. M. CULLEN

WITH the restoration we approach a period when the course of Irish economic and social history becomes easier to chart. Economic commentary in one form or other becomes continuous, and the statistical materials for trade, output, and population, though imperfect, are numerous. However, it is difficult to put the post-restoration decades in perspective against any established trends for preceding decades. The economic and social history of Ireland before 1660 is obscure: for Ireland even more than for England the period constitutes, to employ Professor Fisher's term, the 'dark ages' of modern economic and social history.[1] Understanding of the seventeenth-century economic and social history becomes all the more unsettled once we accept the argument that the malevolent intent claimed for English policy towards Ireland has been greatly overstated. The pursuit of a mercantilist policy by England at Ireland's expense provided a convenient framework, in the absence of more detailed research, for the study of the economic and social background. Dr Ada Longfield's book on Anglo-Irish trade was informed by mercantilist assumptions about policy,[2] and similar assumptions were presented even more centrally by the late George O'Brien.[3] Professor Hugh Kearney has, however, persuasively questioned these assumptions.[4] The fact of confiscation of course remains in the policy of plantation, but fundamentally plantation rests on benevolent economic intentions because it implies the attraction of external man-power and capital and the pursuit of economic policies consonant with these aims.

One of the hypotheses which helped to hold together a bare fabric of fact has therefore to be left aside. The resulting uncertainty of conclusion about the economic and social character of the period is heightened if the belief in the cataclysmic nature of the late 1640s and early 1650s has to be substantially qualified. Belief in a cataclysm, together with a political orientation in historical writing, brought events in the mid-century into a sharp focus:

[1] F. J. Fisher, 'The sixteenth and seventeenth centuries: the dark ages in English economic history?' in *Economica*, N.S., xxiv (1951), pp 2–18.

[2] Longfield, *Anglo-Ir. trade.*

[3] O'Brien, *Econ. hist. Ire., 17th cent.*

[4] H. F. Kearney, 'Mercantilism and Ireland' in *Hist. Studies*, i, pp 59–68; Kearney, *Strafford in Ire.*, ch. II and bibliographical note, sect. 3.

destruction was followed, as in George O'Brien's model, by impressive recovery, and concern with succeeding waves of destruction and recovery lessened the need to identify or assess the character or force of long-term economic and social trends. What may be regarded as the cataclysmic view was itself reflected in contemporary writing. As early as 1672 Sir William Petty made a point of correcting or modifying, in the light of his own demographic calculations, its magnitude. Referring to the native population, he wrote: 'wherefore those who say, that not one-eighth of them remained at the end of the wars, must also review their opinion, there being by this computation now two-thirds of them'.[1] Prendergast, on slender evidence, believed that five-sixths of the population had perished.[2] His case rests on a few graphic but impressionistic comments and on a statement by Gookin in 1655 that scarce one-sixth of the population survived.[3]

The first figure for Irish population which may be regarded as reasonably reliable is the figure, based on the hearth money tax adjusted by the late Kenneth Connell to allow for fiscal evasion, of 2,791,000 in 1712.[4] One of the reasons for its acceptability is the fact that, compared with the census data for 1821–41, it yields a population growth-rate in line with that of other countries. Connell's figure of 2,167,000 for 1687[4] was calculated on similar adjustment procedures but it is less easy to accept with confidence. It allows for a substantial increase in population in Ireland in a period when change was limited elsewhere, and when some countries such as Scotland and France experienced a demographic crisis. Growth in Ireland is, of course, possible, a plausible reason for the apparent contrast being more benign climatic and harvest conditions in Ireland than elsewhere in this period. The large influx of Scots in the 1690s is in part a reflection of the exceptionally favourable conditions in Ireland. It is, however, unlikely that the immigration, which was concentrated in the 1690s, would have been large enough to be responsible for a rise of 27 per cent in the Irish population between 1687 and 1712. This consideration either throws us back to possible demographic trends reflecting conditions in Ireland, or suggests that Connell's figure for 1687 may understate the population at that date, and hence may exaggerate the rate of growth of population between 1687 and 1712. Connell himself makes this point about his adjusted figures generally: 'the indications are that the error in these figures, which may well be substantial, is one of deficiency'.[5] However, within limits, the estimate for 1687 is likely to be a useful one.

Suggestions of a rapid growth of population are either implicit or explicit in all accounts of seventeenth-century Ireland. Where population figures for 1600 have been suggested, a figure of about half a million has been mentioned.

[1] Petty, 'Political anatomy', ed. Hull, i, 150–51.

[2] Prendergast, *Cromwellian settlement*, p. 307.

[3] Ibid., p. 139.

[4] Connell, *Population*, p. 25.

[5] Ibid., p. 24.

Professor Beckett, for instance, states that the population in 1603 'cannot greatly have exceeded half' the figure of 1·1 million suggested by Petty for 1672.[1] Froude indicates a figure of half a million, a figure based apparently on a 1580 estimate of that magnitude.[2] This, however, would imply a fourfold increase in population between 1600 and 1687, and an almost sixfold increase between 1600 and 1712. The rate of increase is all the greater, if the demographic disaster of the early 1650s is allowed for. This has been overstated, but if plague experience elsewhere offers a parallel, up to a third of the population at the outside could have been wiped out. It is likely that the incidence was less severe than this, but the fact of a demographic setback in the early 1650s makes a remarkably rapid growth of population in the seventeenth century inherently improbable. In England and Wales with relatively favourable demographic conditions, population may have increased by only 25 per cent in the seventeenth century; in many other parts of Europe, it rose even less. It would in these circumstances be hard to hypothesise a rapid growth of population in Ireland. The only factor likely to contribute to a different demographic outcome in Ireland was immigration. But it could have altered the situation radically only if it was massive. And there is no evidence to suggest that it was, except in the 1690s. Even at the end of the 1630s, Ulster towns were very small; in the 1640s land values in the north were lower than elsewhere, not excluding those in Connacht, and the ports of the north compared unfavourably in revenue with those elsewhere as late as the 1660s. The slowness of recovery in the 1650s suggests that immigration at that time was limited, as does undoubted economic stagnation in the 1660s and early 1670s. There is a likelihood for several reasons of greater immigration subsequently, but sustained immigration in the late 1670s and early 1680s is hardly likely to have contributed to a dramatic rise in population. A doubling of population at the outside seems the most likely demographic development for Ireland in the seventeenth century. This would of course have as a corollary a much larger population in 1600 than has commonly been assumed.[3] The following would seem to be possible population figures for the sixteenth and seventeenth centuries:

year	millions	year	millions
1500	1·0	1672	1·7
1600	1·4	1687	2·2
1641	2·1	1712	2·8

Study of demographic trends qualifies some aspects of seventeenth-century history. At the same time, even if the rate of growth of population is reduced, it still remains high by seventeenth-century standards, a fact

[1] Beckett, *Mod. Ire.*, p. 25.

[2] Froude, *Ire.* (1881 ed.), i, 33, 78.

[3] L. M. Cullen, 'Population trends in seventeenth-century Ireland' in *Economic and Social Review*, vi, no. 2 (Jan. 1975), pp 149–65.

consistent with the rapid expansion of Irish trade in the same century. The growth in trade, as much as or perhaps even more than general population growth, has implications for urban development and population size. Where trade is relatively static, town hinterlands are stable, and towns themselves change slowly. In a dynamic situation, however, towns were likely to change, and success was reflected in the emergence of significant variations in town growth and size. This can be seen in the growing prominence of Dublin in the economy. In this respect, Dublin reflected the growth of London. Dublin in the 1680s probably held about one-fortieth of the population of Ireland: London one-tenth that of England and Wales. Dublin's smaller relative importance reflected in part comparatively belated economic development; in part simply the absence of organs of power, legislation, and justice as powerful as those of London. Confining comparison to foreign trade, Dublin's role must have been less unfavourable. In the 1660s 40 per cent of Ireland's foreign trade revenue derived from Dublin. The fact that the proportion was so high in the 1660s and increased only by a further 10 per cent subsequently is a reminder that much of Dublin's advance relative to other Irish ports must have occurred in the first half of the century. A dynamic urban situation meant that the relative position of towns changed rapidly. In 1600 Dublin was not much larger than Galway, and possibly Limerick, only double the size of Cork and Waterford, and less than three times the size of Kilmallock. Dublin in 1600 had a population of not less than 5,000, Galway of less than 4,200, Limerick of between 2,400 and 3,600, Waterford and Cork of about 2,400. These calculations are based on the study of contemporary maps, and assume an average household size of six persons. The fact that within their walls Irish towns tended to have about 300 houses suggests that medieval towns are likely to have had a population of about 2,000, on the assumption that suburbs outside the walls were, without exception, small, and seems to corroborate the suggestion that towns originally varied little in size. This was still broadly true in 1600. Suburbs at that date seem to have been small. The fact that only Galway and Dublin had very large suburbs seems to suggest that they were the two cities which had grown most rapidly in the preceding centuries.

The outstanding feature of urban development in the seventeenth century was the emerging predominance of Dublin. This feature is, however, in the main a development of the first half of the century and the emphasis on the city's post-restoration expansion may be in part, though by no means wholly, misplaced. Dublin's population may have risen at the outside fivefold in 1600–60, doubled between 1660 and 1682, and stagnated for the remainder of the century.[1] Cork on the other hand grew relatively slowly by about 50

[1] This view, necessarily conjectural, is supported by the evidence of trade trends and by general evidence indicating rapid growth. For a different view of the increase in Dublin's population see below, ch. XVII, p. 448.

per cent in the first half of the century, but grew rapidly subsequently: if its expansion followed its fortunes in trade, the city possibly doubled in size by the 1680s and doubled again by 1706. Galway expanded in the first half of the century, when it was reputed the second town of Ireland, and stagnated thereafter. Limerick and Waterford at least doubled in size in the seventeenth century. Town life was backward in the north; even in the 1680s neither Derry nor Belfast probably greatly exceeded 2,000 in population.

Whatever the interpretation, even one of deflating the more general assumptions, Irish population by European—and English—standards grew rapidly in the seventeenth century. In addition the growth of certain towns relative to others reflects the introduction of a novel dynamic consequent on the expansion of trade. The wool trade grew rapidly in the first half of the century, a fact underlined by its modest role in the sixteenth century and substantial exports of 160,000 stone a year by the end of the 1630s. The expansion of the wool trade is associated with the growing prominence of the new draperies in international trade and in English textile output. The coarse, long-stapled Irish wool was suitable for the new draperies and hence was in demand. Exports were lower in 1665 than in the late 1630s, but the fall was compensated by a rise in young sheep exported. It has been suggested that the increased production of long-stapled wool in Ireland for the woollen industry of the English south-west owed something to the importation of sheep from England.[1] Some imports of livestock to Ireland to make good the destruction during the Cromwellian campaigns in the early 1650s did take place. But, as far as long-term trends are concerned, the substantial proportions of the export trade in sheep would suggest that sheep from Ireland were helping to expand production of long-staple wool, especially in the south-west, to which as the restoration port-books for Minehead, and more particularly Barnstaple and Bideford, show,[2] the trade was mainly directed.

Even more striking was the growth of the export trade in live cattle which, unlike wool, was negligible in 1600 but was the main item in Irish export trade by 1665. The London food market was the motor behind the expansion of this trade. Young Irish cattle were imported to stock the grazing lands in counties which supplied the capital. Suggestions of 100,000 Irish cattle being imported yearly at the outset of the 1620s are misleading, but the rapid growth of the trade is undoubted. As early as 1634, according to Professor Kearney, the port books of Chester show that between June and October 'almost every ship . . . carried live cattle, especially from Dublin'.[3] By the restoration a brisk trade in cattle existed from Dublin to Chester, Youghal

[1] P. J. Bowden, 'Wool supply and the woollen industry' in *Econ. Hist. Rev.*, 2nd series, ix, no. 1 (1956), pp 44–58.

[2] See, for examples, P.R.O., E.190/955/5/6/7, E.190/961/7/1, E.190/1090/3, E.190/1090/5.

[3] Kearney, *Strafford in Ire.*, p. 135. See also Donald Woodward, 'The Anglo-Irish livestock trade in the seventeenth century' in *I.H.S.*, xviii, no. 72 (Sept. 1973), pp 489–523.

to Somerset, and Donaghadee to the north-west of England. The growth of a substantial population engaged in textiles in both the north-west and south-west of England in creating larger local markets for agricultural produce helped to sustain the demand for Irish cattle.

The outstanding feature of Irish trade in 1660 was its dependence on the English market. Of exports valued at £402,389 in 1665, £295,833—some 75 per cent—were consigned to England.[1] By 1683, exports to England and Wales had fallen to £171,191. The decline was, however, solely attributable to the closure of the trade in cattle and sheep[2] which had been worth £125,594 in 1665. In other respects Anglo-Irish trade remained no less active than in the past. The brunt of the effect of the cattle acts was borne by a few ports actively engaged in the trade while it lasted. Dublin's trade, however, was too large and varied for the cattle acts to have any major effect; Youghal was more than compensated for the loss of its cattle trade by the growth of its traffic in butter; east-coast ports generally suffered as a result but only Donaghadee was eclipsed. The invoice book of the Bristol merchant James Twyford[3] affords a glimpse of Anglo-Irish trade from 1673 to 1678: tallow, skins, wool, timber in the form of scantlings and barrel-staves, frieze, and candles feature regularly in imports. Little Irish butter was imported, although butter was not excluded until 1681. Small quantities of beef and pork were purchased by Twyford, some for direct shipment to the colonies but some also for Bristol, apparently in disregard of the cattle acts. Despite the growth in wool exports, wool was not prominent in Twyford's purchases: the wool trade was increasingly dominated by the merchants of the port towns of Devon and Cornwall, who employed their own factors in Ireland.

Despite the contraction in livestock, the value of exports rose from £402,389 in 1665 to £570,343 in 1683. As the valuation of the main commodities fell somewhat in this period, the actual volume of exports must have risen rather more sharply than their value. In gross terms the shortfall in cattle and sheep exports was £125,594; allowing for compensating increases in exports of beef, tallow, and wool, the net shortfall attributable to the cattle act of 1667 was £54,703. This suggests an increase of £222,657 in exports between 1665 and 1683, excluding those commodities affected by the cattle acts, i.e. a rise in the value of exports other than cattle, sheep, beef, tallow, and wool of 64 per cent or even more in volume terms as valuations fell somewhat. This would suggest at first sight a remarkably buoyant foreign market for Irish products, a factor which would merit special comment because slow population growth, agricultural surplus, and low prices were general in Europe in the second half of the century. In reality, the appearance

[1] For export figures for 1665 and 1685 and sources, see Cullen, *Anglo-Ir. trade*, pp 30–31, 36–7.

[2] See below, ch. XVII, pp 443–4.

[3] Memoranda book of James Twyford, merchant, Bristol, 1674–81 (in the possession of Lord Hylton, Ammerdown Park, Radstock, Somerset).

of buoyancy suggested by the statistics was highly deceptive. Of the £222,657 rise in export values, 54 per cent—or £121,078—was caused by the striking expansion in butter exports. The rise in butter exports was remarkable. But the butter market was volatile, its prosperity depending on the somewhat erratic relationship between Irish supply and continental market demand. Emphasising this was the dependence on the French market, largely the custom of north-east France. France in 1683 took 99,122 of the 136,972 cwt of butter shipped from Ireland. Markets existed in other centres as well, the Dutch market on occasion absorbing Irish butter at high prices, but the uncertain demand from these markets added to the volatile character of the butter trade. Petty and Temple thought that the English in Ireland produced the only butter fit for foreign markets. This may exaggerate somewhat but the opinion is at least partly vindicated by the fact that Belfast (33,880 cwt) and Youghal (31,055) together, both with hinterlands densely settled by English or Scots, accounted for 47 per cent of exports in 1683.

The butter trade was thus the main factor contributing to the buoyancy of Ireland's external trade. In 1683 it accounted for just over a quarter of the total value of exports, and a government proclamation in 1685 recognised butter as the commodity that made 'the greatest return in moneys'.[1] The rapid growth of the butter trade, and the high prices often commanded by butter, were an important factor in the enhanced prosperity of Cork and Youghal and of Belfast in the 1670s and 1680s. The export business of George Macartney, the most substantial merchant in Belfast, largely revolved around butter.[2] The importance of butter in sustaining the economy was made all the more decisive by the poor foreign market for beef. The total export of beef in 1683 was only half the corresponding total for beef and cattle combined in 1665. The price was low, too, conspicuously so in wartime, but even in peacetime it was not reassuring. The beef trade of this period has, of course, been frequently represented as being large and profitable. This view, however, involves an uncritical acceptance of opinions expressed in 1679–80 when the renewal of the prohibition on cattle and sheep was being debated in the English parliament. Opponents of the prohibition argued that Ireland had built up an extensive trade in beef.[3] But the argument itself was an admission of the lowness of Irish prices: part of the argument lay in the emphasis on the advantage which foreigners enjoyed as a result of the cheapness of Irish beef. In fact, in volume and price the beef trade was a disappointing one which failed to live up to the high hopes of those who saw in the relative firmness of prices of beef compared with

[1] B.M., G 6022(5), dated 12 June 1685.

[2] Letter book of George Macartney, merchant, Belfast, 1678–81 (in Linenhall Library, Belfast). An unidentified Dublin merchant whose letter book for 1684 and early 1685 survives (T.C.D., MS 3961) made some of his butter purchases in the north, employing Macartney as his factor or correspondent.

[3] For sources, see p. 400, n. 2.

cattle in the sixties an augury of bright prospects for themselves and the economy.[1] Modern accounts of the beef trade by combining the arguments of 1678–80 with the undoubtedly buoyant prices of the trade from the 1740s have often exaggerated its extent and profitability, overlooking in the process the low prices and uncertain trend in volume from the 1660s to the 1720s at least.[2]

The other main support of the economy after the passing of the cattle acts was the export trade in wool, after butter the country's main export. Unlike beef, the underlying price-trend was firm. In fact the proceeds from wool more than compensated for the termination of sheep exports, and must have greatly exceeded them in the dramatic upsurge in wool exports in the late 1660s and early 1670s. Wool prices bore up better than other prices in the early 1670s. From the evidence of actual quotations wool prices did not fall as sharply as several contemporary polemical accounts suggested, and in particular they held ground better than other agricultural commodities during the Dutch war from early 1672 to early 1674 which disrupted contact with the Continent. Temple in 1673, for instance, wrote 'there is in a manner no vent for any commodity but of woole'.[3] A continued rise in wool output in the absence of clear alternatives was hardly surprising. Wool exports were of record proportions in 1671, and the upsurge probably continued for several years. In December 1675 a warrant was issued from the treasury to increase the salary of the collector of Minehead, one of the main ports for Irish wool, on account of the great imports from Ireland.[4] The stability of the trade at such a high level depended on the state of English demand. Difficulties became evident in the English industry in the mid-1670s, and the 'ruinated and undone' clothiers in 1677 blamed their plight on the export of Irish and English wool to foreign manufacturers.[5] They may well have believed that proof of the diversion of Irish wool lay in a decline in exports to England, which presumptively began in the mid-1670s, and which had certainly worked itself out by the early 1680s. At the reduced level—still far above the volume of exports in 1665—wool prices remained remunerative. Even in 1677 prices had recovered. In that year the patentees of the office for registering wool bonds claimed that wool had sold at 8*s.* a stone during the Dutch war and that prices were now not above 9*s.*[6] A circumstance helping to secure this underlying firmness of wool prices, outside the years of recession

[1] *Hastings MSS*, ii, 374–5; *Cal. S.P. Ire.*, *1663–5*, p. 658; *Ormonde MSS.*, N.S., iii, 64, 72.

[2] The most recent instances are R. D. Crotty, *Irish agricultural production: its volume and structure* (Cork, 1966), and C. A. Edie, 'The Irish cattle bills: a study in restoration politics' in *Amer. Phil. Soc. Trans.*, N.S., lx, pt 2 (1970), pp 5–66.

[3] William Temple, 'Essay upon the advancement of trade in Ireland' in *Miscellanea* (London, 1697), pt 1, p. 107.

[4] *Cal. treas. bks.*, *1672–5*, p. 866.

[5] P.R.O.I., Wyche documents, series 1, 1/15.

[6] Charles McNeill, 'Reports on the Rawlinson collection of manuscripts preserved in the Bodleian Library, Oxford, class D' in *Anal. Hib.*, no. 2 (1931), pp 68–70.

in the textile industry, was the fact that the exclusion of Irish sheep had handicapped the stocking of sheep lands and slowed down the response of English farmers to the sustained demand for wool from the expanding textile industry. As late as 1687 it was reported from Somerset that 'the people here are in great hopes of being allowed to import both black cattle and sheep from Ireland which they very much desire'.[1]

A further factor helping to sustain the price of wool was the existence of a foreign market for it. Contemporaries were prone, because of mercantilist obsessions, to exaggerate this traffic. But, this tendency allowed for, the fact was that a steady continental demand existed, at least in St Malo which seems to have attracted most of the Irish supply sent to the Continent. The patentees for registering wool bonds, whose interest it was of course to minimise the traffic, claimed in their defence that the fraudulent consignment of cargoes nominally directed under bond to England had never exceeded one-quarter of the total shipments.[2] Euclid Speidel, the official responsible on the English side for registering these bonds, was quoted in 1680 as stating that 'in the year 1678 there were forty ships' lading of wool shipp'd off from Ireland, that according to the dockets ought to be unladen in England, but none of it arrived here'.[3] The quantity of wool shipped from Ireland was in the region of 200,000 stone a year at the outset of the eighties. As one-quarter of this would amount to 50,000 stone and as, from the evidence of the English port-books, wool ships at this time had typically a cargo of around 1,000 stone of wool,[4] there is some crude corroboration both for the patentees' statements and for Speidel's figure. The fact that an average of fifty-two ships a year entered St Malo from Ireland[5] in the 1680s and that wool was frequently the cargo, lends some further support to this estimate of the trade.

Wool and butter both in global value and in price were the mainstay of the economy. Combined, in 1683 they made up 40 per cent of exports. Of the effective net increase of £222,657 in exports between 1665 and 1683 butter accounted for £121,078. Of the balance of the increase in exports—£101,579—corn (rising from £6,285 to £20,545) and frieze and drapery (rising from £19,348 to £49,201) made up half. These increases are modest enough, but they constitute evidence none the less of significant underlying features in the economy. Grain exports were held down by surpluses elsewhere. But in years when demand and supply conditions were both appropriate, exports could rise sharply; for instance from 54,787 barrels in 1683 and 46,936 barrels in 1684 to 148,715 barrels in 1685. In May 1687 the export

[1] *Orrery papers*, p. 330.

[2] McNeill, as above, in *Anal. Hib.*, no. 2, p. 69.

[3] John Collins, *A plea for the bringing of Irish cattel* . . . (London, 1680), p. 5.

[4] e.g. P.R.O., E.190/955/5/6/7; E.190/961/7/1.

[5] J. Delumeau, *Le mouvement du port de Saint-Malo: la fin du xviie siècle (1681–1710)* (Rennes, n.d.)

of grain was prohibited until Michaelmas on account of high prices 'from the great quantities of corn which have of late been carried out of this to foreign ports'.[1] Grain cultivation was extensive, a fact reflected in the widespread place of grain in the diet. The problem for the farmer was one of low prices. Before 1672 corn prices had been below 12*s.* a barrel.[2] In May 1668 wheat was valued at 7*s.* to 8*s.* a barrel.[3] In May 1684 wheat prices rose from 15*s.* to 22*s.* a barrel but slumped again after the harvest to 11*s.* 6*d.* by the end of the year.[4] Low prices may have been a disadvantage to the farmer, but they implied abundant harvests, and this, in view of the importance of bread in the diet, benefited the consumer.

As to textiles, the smallness of the export figures reflects the under-development of the industry, and hence the limited prospects for men and women to supplement agricultural earnings or employment by spinning and weaving. Both Temple and Petty recognised the scope for such supplementary income that the idle hands of women seemed to offer. Exports of woollens in 1683 (at £49,201) very substantially exceeded those of linen and linen yarn combined (£12,188). Moreover, the upward trend in the woollen industry was sharper than in linen. Petty in 1672 had thought that the woollen industry had not recovered its 1641 level of activity.[5] But exports rose very definitely between 1665 and 1683, and again almost as sharply in the four years from 1683 to 1687. By contrast, the linen industry seemed faltering until the 1680s. Exports of linen were lower in 1683 than in 1669; exports of yarn were not much larger than in 1641. The rapid advance of linen exports in the 1680s seems a distinctly novel feature, perhaps not to be dissociated from the fact that Armagh, the centre of new initiative in the linen industry, was the only Ulster county where hearth-money returns seemed to rise rapidly in the early 1680s. The woollen industry was both larger and geographically more widespread. The output was sizeable—Petty thought in 1672 that three times as much wool was worked up as was exported.[6] He estimated 30,000 workers of wool and their wives. The main centres of the industry were Dublin, Carrick-on-Suir and Bandon, where Cox in 1684 reported 500 families 'almost all mechanics that live by their industry'.[7] Cloth was made in the countryside, too, Dineley reported the making of good quality frieze between Kilkenny and Carlow.[8] But much of Irish cloth-making was primitive: cloth was still manually tucked, at least in some districts, as late as the 1680s.[9]

[1] Proclamation of 4 Apr. 1687 (B.M., C.21, F.12).

[2] Petty, 'Political anatomy', ed. Hull, i, 152.

[3] *Orrery papers*, p. 62.

[4] T.C.D. MS 3961, *passim*.

[5] Petty, 'Political anatomy', ed. Hull, i, 209.

[6] Ibid., p. 281.

[7] T.C.D., MS 883/1, p. 253.

[8] Thomas Dineley, 'Observations on a voyage through the kingdom of Ireland [*c.* 1680]', p. 79 (N.L.I., MS 392).

[9] Ibid., p. 267.

The growth of Ireland's external trade must be seen against the background of limited outlets for the agricultural produce of the economy. Restrictions on Irish trade are of course relevant, although they have frequently been given too decisive a role in determining the course of events. In consequence, insufficient attention has been focused on the economic background itself and on institutional barriers in other countries which would impede access for Irish exports. Paradoxically, the adverse effects of the cattle acts have been frequently underestimated by the acceptance of the argument that they were on balance beneficial by diverting exports from the livestock trade into more remunerative dead-meat exports. In fact, this assessment is seriously misleading. Beef proved neither a remunerative nor a profitable export. There is, however, real difficulty in disentangling the effects of the cattle acts on the economy from more transient events, such as bad seasons and war years when access to external outlets became especially hazardous. A close succession of these factors—a bad season followed early in 1672 by war—was responsible for a dramatic deterioration in the exchange rate of the Irish pound in 1671, 1672, and 1673. Before and after these years, exchange rates were less adverse, suggesting a definite but modest devaluation of the Irish pound. In the early 1660s £100 sterling purchased £103 or £104 Irish; over the 1670s and 1680s the rate averaged roughly £107 Irish. In 1689 with war breaking out again, an exodus of capital from Ireland and the effect of rampant livestock disease in the previous year, the rate of exchange was settled by proclamation at £108⅓ Irish to £100 sterling. This reflected in effect a further devaluation of the Irish currency. The adverse drift in the exchange rates between the 1660s and the 1680s is the only approximate measure available for quantifying in any coherent sense the impact of the cattle acts.[1] It is true of course that this drift reflects the general weakening in agricultural prices in the period, and not simply the direct and indirect effects of the cattle acts. On the other hand, but for the firmness of wool prices and the buoyant though volatile market for butter, the deterioration in the exchange would have been more decisive.

The philosophy behind English economic policy towards Ireland was perfectly clear: 'you shall in all things endeavour to advance and improve the trade of that our kingdom so far as it shall not be a prejudice to this our kingdom of England, which we mean shall not be wronged how much soever the benefit of that our other kingdom might be concerned in it'.[2] As far as actually restricting Irish trade was concerned, these instructions were specific only in relation to wool, the raw material of England's main textile industry: 'you must be most careful more particularly to renew a strict and severe prohibition against the transportation of wool to any parts beyond the seas, causing very sufficient security to be taken that whatsoever quantities

[1] Cullen, *Econ. hist. Ire. since 1660*, pp 15–16.

[2] *Cal. S.P. Ire., 1660–62*, p. 16. For a later statement see *Cal. S.P. dom., 1685*, pp 110–14.

shall be at any time shipped for England be indeed and truly brought and landed there'.[1] The acts of 1569 and 1571[2] imposing high duties on wool exports had been intended to keep wool in Ireland. In practice, a procedure for licensing, doubly welcome because it was a source of revenue, had developed, to offset effects 'very prejudicial not only to us in our customs and to our subjects in Ireland, [they] wanting . . . sufficient means to manufacture all their wool and commodities in that our kingdom, but also to our subjects in England'.[3] Licences had been granted for export to countries other than England on occasion, and even when bonds had been given to land the wool in England, the undertaking was frequently evaded.[4] At the restoration, instructions were given for the vigorous prosecution of forfeited bonds. But despite the well-defined policy which had now emerged, licences were granted to Major Henry O'Neill and Sir Francis Hamilton to export wool to the Continent.[5] In July 1661 it was decided to grant no further licences to foreign ports, and to stay Hamilton's licence.[6] In September 1663 it was decided to renew O'Neill's licence which he had not exercised,[7] but in October orders were made in council to stop both Hamilton's and O'Neill's licences.[8]

From this time onwards, there was no wavering from the policy defined at the restoration of confining wool exports to the English market only. An office for registering wool bonds, ensuring that they were properly executed and that forfeitures were prosecuted, had already been established in 1662. The patentees, Sir Nicholas Armorer and Gabriel Silvius, had power to compound for the penalties, and because lenient compositions were held to have undermined the prohibitive purpose of the office, it was determined in 1677 to buy the patentees out before the expiry of their patent. In the characteristically venal fashion of the seventeenth century a new patent was issued in 1684, experience again leading to a decision in 1688 to cancel this patent as well.[9] Abuses remained rife in the wool trade, fraudulent and insolvent sureties were often entered for bonds, and ships detected in the practice were sold in France or Holland. A contemporary pamphleteer, writing in 1698, described the practice at some length, adding: 'this appears from wool bonds taken in Ireland for several years before the war, for some thousands of pounds . . . with names as fictitious as those of John a Nokes or John a Styles'.[10] The government's concern with the problem was intermittent, being especially evident in 1662–3, between 1669 and 1674, in 1678,

[1] *Cal. S.P. Ire., 1660–62*, p. 16.
[2] 11 Eliz., sess. 3, c. 10; 13 Eliz., c. 2.
[3] *Cal. S.P. Ire., 1669–70*, p. 104.
[4] B.M., Harl. MS 4706, ff 21–2, 29; *Cal. S.P. Ire., 1660–62*, p. 575.
[5] *Cal. S.P. Ire., 1660–62*, p. 305; *1663–65*, p. 230; B.M. Harl. MS 4706, f. 29.
[6] *Cal. S.P. Ire., 1660–62*, p. 385.
[7] Ibid., *1663–5*, p. 230; *1669–70*, p. 659.
[8] Ibid., p. 476.
[9] Cullen, *Anglo-Ir. trade*, pp 141–2.
[10] *A discourse concerning Ireland and the different interests thereof in answer to the Exon and Barnstable petitions . . .* (London, 1698), pp 54–5.

again in 1683–4 when the port of Galway was specified as a centre of fraud,[1] and finally in 1687–8 when the deputy controller of the port of Exeter was sent to Ireland to expose the practice of returning fraudulent certificates of the wool actually having been landed in England and when John Kirwan, the largest merchant in Galway, forfeited wool bonds.[2]

Control of the wool trade in so far as the prohibition of continental markets was concerned was, however, on the mercantilist principle of discouraging exports of vital raw materials, to Ireland's advantage as well as being in England's interest. In any event evasion was rife, the penalties through easy composition for the bonds forfeited were very light and enforcement measures before 1689 were clearly ineffectual. Only in and after 1689 did enforcement acquire real teeth.[3]

The navigation acts[4] were in effect somewhat similar in their impact and enforcement. The act of 1663 had confined direct exports from Ireland to the colonies to provisions, horses, and servants. The measure had been intended to prohibit direct importation to Ireland also but the relevant clauses proved legally inoperable. At length, in 1671, the importation of statutorily enumerated goods was prohibited in a measure which lapsed in 1681 and was reimposed in 1685. The negative impact of this legislation may have been very limited. First, evasion was rife, its extent testified to by the constant preoccupation on this score expressed in the administrative correspondence of the period.[5] Secondly, the measure had no clear adverse effect on the consumption of colonial goods in Ireland. The upward trend in tobacco consumption was impressive; it was likely that by the 1680s *per capita* tobacco consumption had attained a level which was not surpassed until the nineteenth century. Thirdly, while the measure may have affected the profits of individual merchants by restricting their range of trading operations, a very high proportion of Irish trade was conducted on the account of British merchants. Merchants acting as factors in this fashion would not have been seriously affected by the operation of the navigation acts. It is possible, however, that the act may have had a more perceptible impact on the merchants of smaller ports such as Galway and Belfast where a significant proportion of the port activity seems to have been conducted on the account of local merchants. Galway and Belfast, whose prominence was striking in tobacco importation from the plantations in 1683 and which held their place in tobacco imports in 1686, the first year of the reimposition of the colonial ban, lost heavily in subsequent decades. The navigation acts undoubtedly may have reinforced the centralising tendencies evident in the economy

[1] *Cal. treas. bks, 1681–5*, p. 1418; *Ormonde MSS*, N.S., vii, 142.

[2] Cullen, *Anglo-Ir. trade*, p. 141; B.M., Add. MS 18022, f. 75; *Cal. treas. bks, 1685–9* pp 1786, 1806, 1910, 1997, 2049; Cullen 'Tráchtáil is bainceáracht i nGaillimh san 18ú céad' in *Galvia*, v (1958), p. 60 n.

[3] Cullen, *Anglo-Ir. trade*, pp 54, 143.

[4] See below, p. 444.

[5] Notably documents listed in *Cal. treas. bks*.

between 1680 and 1700, Dublin gaining, Belfast and Galway more particularly losing, among other ports. Taking the economy as a whole, the navigation acts do not seem to emerge as of crucial importance. Evasion softened their impact; the shift of the tobacco trade to east-coast ports generally reflects deeper centralising influences as well as the navigation acts.

The cattle acts[1] remain the only legislative measure of serious consequence. Yet the cattle acts were not part of an economic policy directed towards Ireland. The 1667 act was passed against the wishes of the executive. Parliament had so little confidence in the royal will to enforce the act that cattle imports were declared a 'nuisance' in the act to prevent the king from exercising his prerogative to dispense with the prohibition. The English government, in an effort to alleviate distress in Ireland consequent on the act, accorded the quite exceptional permission of trading with the king's enemies in war time. A proclamation to give effect to this was issued on 1 April 1667 and passes were provided for Irish or neutral ships engaged in this trade to protect them from interference by privateers or the king's navy. The act, which was temporary—to last from enactment for seven years and until the end of the next following session of parliament—, had its critics even while it was in force. With its expiry in prospect in the spring of 1679, the debate was joined in parliament on the question of renewing the prohibition. Progress of the bill was held up by prorogation of parliament and it was only in November 1680 that a measure coming into effect in February 1681 at last was adopted by parliament. Discussion was vigorous, the division being largely between the fattening interests and the breeding interests, which were opposed to admission, and within the western counties between the rural population and urban centres such as Bristol and Chester engaged in the Irish trade.[2] As long as the prohibition lapsed, the revival of the trade seems to have been significant. In August 1680 an officer was stationed in Holyhead because of the great numbers of Irish cattle imported there.[3] The preceding January an extra waiter had been stationed in Liverpool because of 'trouble of the officers there by the importation of Irish cattle'.[4] Youghal was undoubtedly one of the focal points of the trade on the Irish side. In 1681 there was complaint of a great decay of trade in Youghal, because of the prohibition of the cattle trade, 'the chief support of their town'.[5] There must, however, have been some exaggeration in this statement, because Youghal's trade was wide-based and other sources suggest that its vigour in no way depended on the cattle trade.

[1] See below, ch. XVII, pp 443–4.

[2] On the arguments employed in the debate, see 'Reasons for taking off the prohibition . . . of Irish cattel' (B.M., Harl. MS 4706, f. 39; B.M., Add. MS 4761, f. 210); also Collins, op. cit.

[3] *Cal. treas. bks, 1679–80*, pp 658–9. For the suppression of the post, see ibid., *1681–5*, p. 105.

[4] Ibid., *1679–80*, p. 403.

[5] *Ormonde MSS*, N.S., vi, 206. See Thomas Dineley, 'Observations on a voyage through the kingdom of Ireland [1675–80],' pp 218–19 (N.L.I., MS 392), for an account of Youghal's trade.

Living standards had undoubtedly been relatively high in the 1650s. The population through plague, famine, and war in that order had been diminished; on the other hand, agricultural prices were higher than in subsequent decades. The Cromwellian settlement affected only a small portion of the population—between 1,000 and 2,000 families plus such retainers as wished to follow them to the new lands allotted to them. With its low rents and high wages, both consequent on depopulation, and high prices, the 1650s must have been a prosperous decade for the ordinary people, whether tenant farmers or labourers. This was Petty's view of the decade in retrospect,

> nine parts of ten of that nation, who lived as labourers and tenants, did live more plentifully and freely . . . between 1653 and 1660 than they had done in the seven years next before the wars. For they had lands at small rents even at one-fifth of the present, and yet sold their commodities at greater rates than now and, paying their rents, were as free as their landlords.[1]

Even an Irish source,[2] no friend of the Cromwellians, thought the ordinary people never more wanton or insolent.

The living standards of the ordinary people are likely to have deteriorated subsequently. There is little doubt about the likelihood of a downward trend from a peak in the 1650s; whether the downward trend was sharp enough to cancel out all the benefits of the 1650s is, however, another question to which no firm answer can be hazarded. Whatever the trend, there are some aspects worth bearing in mind, although they do not in themselves support either an optimistic or pessimistic view of trends. Tobacco consumption, for instance, rose sharply and fairly continuously from the 1660s to the early 1680s. Imports doubled between 1665 and 1683 and *per capita* consumption in the 1680s was probably at a level not exceeded until the second half of the nineteenth century. The ownership of a horse—some criterion of property—was quite extensive. Petty commented that 'the poorest now in Ireland ride on horse-back who heretofore but ran on foot like animals';[3] elsewhere he thought that one-third of Irish cabins possessed a small horse.[4] He remarked as well that the Irish countryman was better clothed than his French counterpart.[5] Sir Henry Piers's account of Westmeath in 1682 shows that the practice of dowries was prevalent among farmers, a circumstance pointing to some degree of wealth and family continuity.[6] Diet, too, was far from being impoverished. The references in Petty's writings to potatoes are at first sight ambiguous, and they have frequently been quoted in support of the case for the early diffusion of a general potato diet. Kenneth Connell has, however, pointed out that Petty's

1 Petty, 'Treatise of Ire.', ed. Hull, ii, 617, 620.

2 John Lynch, *Alithinologia* . . ., quoted in Prendergast, *Cromwellian settlement*, p. 347.

3 Petty, 'Political anatomy', ed. Hull, i, 203.

4 Ibid., p. 175.

5 Ibid., p. 191.

6 T.C.D., MS 883/2, p. 26.

authority is of questionable use in showing that the potato was in any sense the Irishman's staple foodstuff, and that Petty, if anything, simply shows the potato to have been a supplement to the staple diet.[1] Petty stated in fact that 'their food is bread in cakes, whereof a penny serves a week for each; potatoes from August till May . . . '[2] Dineley was even more explicit on the nature and variety of the diet and on the 'bread in cakes' or 'oatcakes' sometimes referred to in contemporary accounts:

Dyet generally of the vulgar Irish are potatoes, milk, new milk which they call sweet milk, bonnyclobber, mallabaune, whey, curds, large brown oatcakes of a foot and a half broad bak't before the fire, bread made of bare, a sort of barley, peas, beans and oatmeale, wheat and rye for great days.[3]

An account of County Kildare in 1683 writes of the people's diet being generally 'very mean and sparing, consisting of milk, roots and coarse unsavoury bread'.[4]

The ordinary people, even if their condition was above bare subsistence level, were hardly well-off. Prices were low, and low prices for much of the produce of their farms helped to ensure that their incomes changed little. Their expectations were low; conservatism coloured both their outlook and their farming methods. Sir Henry Piers noted in 1682 of County Westmeath that

gentlemen proprietors set out their estates at the highest rents to the poor farmer so that from him little is to be expected, for if he be able to pay his rent and live he thinks himself happy and rich nor indeed doth the genius of the Irish farmers incline them to be at any present expense or labour in expectation of a future greater benefit.[5]

The poor economic condition of the ordinary people and the lack of expectations of better things were contributed to not only by the weak price trends but by the underlying instability both of prices and of weather and farming conditions. The savings of good years were swept away by the disasters of intervening years. After a season of abnormal livestock mortality, much of a farmer's subsequent earnings went into restocking his land; in a few years' time he was certain to face loss again. Gain over several years depended more on fortuitous circumstances than on the farmer's management. In such conditions there was no prospect of general economic improvement; certainly no expectation of one. There had been heavy livestock losses in 1660; again in 1665 when, for instance, it was reported from Castleisland in County Kerry that 'the tenants have had

[1] Connell, *Population*, pp 127–8.

[2] Petty, 'Political anatomy', ed. Hull, i, 191.

[3] Thomas Dineley, 'Observations', as above, p. 268 (N.L.I., MS 392). Dunton describes the baking of these cakes in his account of Iar-Connacht in MacLysaght, *Ir. life after Cromwell* (2nd ed., 1950), p. 331. He refers elsewhere to 'a heap of oaten cakes about a foot high' on the table (p. 338).

[4] Quoted in MacLysaght, op. cit., p. 315.

[5] T.C.D., MS 883/2, p. 24.

great losses this winter. Lord Kerry's tenants ran away by droves leaving nothing but the cabins, so that he has above [£]400 per annum upon his hands unset'.[1] There was, judging by the customs revenue, little uplift in conditions in the course of the 1660s, and a definite worsening at the outset of the new decade. In the spring of 1671, report had it that 'milch cows are dear because of a great mortality of cattle last winter and spring, and many tenants much prejudiced thereby'.[2] Reflecting the harsh spring, exchange rates rose sharply to 8–10 per cent in 1671. War early in 1672 along with scorching weather made the already bad economic conditions worse: Rawdon wrote to Conway in May 1672 that 'you will find a strange alternation here of scarcity of money, all Spanish and other carried away daily, no trading of merchants abroad or buying anything, and want of rain and burning weather beyond example here'.[3] The year 1672 was not apparently the only one of scorching weather in the early 1670s; dearth in the summer of 1674, recorded by the Gaelic poet Ó Bruadair, may reflect the consequence of a further year's drought.[4]

With peace in 1674, conditions began to look up: 'the price of country commodities begins to rise already', wrote a correspondent in February 1674,[5] and the outlook was distinctly promising in November 1675.[6] Customs revenue had stagnated or fallen slightly between 1664 and 1670. But by 1675/6[7] a distinct rise took place: customs revenue in 1675/6 was 16 per cent above the level of 1669/70; in 1677/8 it was 42 per cent above the level of 1669/70. The year 1678 was not a good year, the revenue plunging from £115,155 in 1677/8 to £100,894 in 1678/9. A harsh winter and spring created problems for the farmer: in March 'there's hardly grass to preserve cattle alive' and even at the end of May 'grazing is very dear, and the grass bad'.[8] Rumour of war darkened the prospects further, and in the autumn the outbreak of the popish plot created a domestic political crisis, 'which startles and amazes the English in this kingdom and trade is worse than before though then bad'.[9] Foreign trade soared in 1679/80 in part because of the buoyancy of the butter trade. Revenue in 1679/80 reached a total of £121,391, a level not surpassed until 1684, a year characterised by high prosperity in the butter trade and high grain prices when it reached £124,746. The revenue fell in 1685, almost exclusively because of a fall in customs on exports. Livestock disease appeared early in 1684 and farmers' losses were said to be great in County Cork 'because of the very great loss of all sort of cattle to that degree that many farmers are quite ruined and their lands wholly waste'.[10]

[1] *Herbert corresp.*, p. 188.

[2] Ibid., p. 198.

[3] *Cal. S.P. dom., 1672*, p. 90.

[4] Ó Bruadair, *Poems*, i, p. xxix.

[5] *Orrery papers*, p. 124.

[6] *Cal. S.P. dom., 1675*, p. 397.

[7] The use of a solidus here and later indicates a fiscal year, as distinct from a year ending in December. On the other hand, 1675–6 would mean a period including all or part of 1675 and 1676.

[8] *Herbert corresp.*, p. 240.

[9] Ibid., pp 251–2.

[10] *Orrery papers*, p. 296.

Captain Henry Boyle observed that 'it may very well be said to be a just judgement of God's upon us, who but very few months since complained of too great plenty and cheapness of all sorts of commodities in this nation'.[1] These views seem, however, to have been somewhat alarmist; disease must have been confined largely to sheep as in wool alone did exports fall sharply in 1685. The fall was, however, extremely severe in wool exports, and in so far as sheep were concerned alarm in 1684 was fully borne out by subsequent events. A high price for wool—12*s*. 6*d*. a stone—in the Clonmel market in 1684 may have reflected the onset of disease.[2] The year 1685 was not a prosperous one; rents were unpaid.[3] In the following year, however, customs revenue soared to the record level of the entire period from 1662 to 1687—£138,880. The rise in exports in 1686 and in 1687 from the low level of 1685 was especially remarkable.

Abundance had its problems no less than dearth. Little less than two years after the livestock disease of the spring of 1684, the complaint in July 1686 was of 'the great plenty of country commodities and the great scarcity of money to be had for them. A continuation of this state of affairs will mean little or no rent from the tenants.'[4] With such abundance and low prices exports soared in 1686 and 1687. But the two years of low prices sapped the basis of general prosperity.[5] Despite the record level of exports in 1686 and more particularly in 1687—the greatest of the entire period—revenue on imports sagged sharply in 1687. Political difficulties leading to the emigration of some protestants or protestant capital may have contributed to this outcome, but the major factor was purely economic. Good farming conditions abroad contributed to a downturn in the demand for Irish exports in 1687–8. Ormond in July 1687 noted that 'the complaints of want of money in Ireland continue, and the only commodity that yields any reasonable rate is wool'.[6] Seven months later, there had been no change. In February 1688 'nothing now bears a price but wool, cattle being extremely cheap'.[7] Low prices thus perpetuated poor economic conditions, which became even worse with the appearance of an alarming cattle distemper in the spring of 1688: 'there was never such a loss of cattle for many years, many dying fat and no one knowing their distemper'.[8] By June in Castleisland 'the tenants' hope is that one cow will give [as] much this year as two last; and that they all [will be] bought [*sic*] into County Cork to repair the dairies there'. But high prices were poor compensation for the decimation of cattle stock: 'above a hundred families are gone a begging out of the seigniory and as many more are starving; abundance are turning to thieving'.[9]

[1] *Orrery papers*, p. 296.

[2] C. L. Vaughan-Arbuckle, 'A Tipperary farmer and Waterford tradesman of two centuries ago' in *Waterford Arch. Soc. Jn.*, viii (1902), p. 84.

[3] *Egmont MSS*, ii, 158.

[4] *Orrery papers*, p. 316.

[5] See e.g. *Cal. S.P. dom., 1686–7*, p. 205.

[6] *Ormonde MSS*, ii, 307.

[7] *Orrery papers*, p. 353.

[8] *Herbert corresp.*, p. 335.

[9] Ibid., p. 337.

Exports, measured by revenue collected on them, fell dramatically in 1688, but even so were larger than they had been in any of the years 1683–5. The trend in revenue from imports, except in 1686, did not parallel that on exports. The inference must be that prices realised by the swollen volume of exports were falling and that the uncertain export income prevented a continuous rise in prosperity. The year 1686 was the peak year of prosperity—with total revenue at £138,880 well above the level of other years. The valuations of exports for fiscal purposes in 1662 approximated to the then current prices, and duties were as a rule 5 per cent of the official valuations. This would, by multiplying the yield of the outwards customs yield by a factor of twenty, afford an estimate of the actual value of exports.[1] Applied to the 1687 data this would produce an export value of £825,720 (£41,286×20). A rise in the volume of exports of these proportions, if the price level had been maintained, would have guaranteed prosperity in 1687. In fact, a fall in prices suggests that this must have cancelled out the benefit of a dramatic rise in the volume of exports. A declining intake of dutiable goods in 1687, the effect of diminished purchasing power, seems to have been one of the consequences. The sharpness of the fall in prices is mirrored in Petty's drastic revision of the value of the cattle stocks in Ireland in 1687: their value at market, estimated at £5 million in 1683, Petty thought to have fallen to £3 million in 1687.[2] Total customs revenue fell sharply in 1687: in both 1687 and 1688 it was below the level of 1684. In fact, excepting the year 1686, the picture the revenue data affords is one of a stagnant economy. Prices, as one can see from other data, fell, and a rise in the volume of exports was unable to generate sufficient income to boost the intake of taxed consumer goods from abroad. The 1684 revenue level of £124,746 was itself only slightly above the 1679/80 level of £121,391. The corollary of this is that the general increase in customs revenue standing at £81,000 in 1669/70 must have been confined to the 1670s, and more definitely to the second half of the seventies. Duties on imports were far and away the major component of the customs revenue, and trends in their collection offer inferences about levels of consumption and living standards. If so, one of the inferences must be that from the outset of the restoration the only period characterised by a rapid increase in consumption standards was the second half of the 1670s. If this conclusion is correct, the low expectations of the ordinary people were fully justified by the general economic situation. Improvement came not from personal effort but from fortuitous or external forces. The drastic decline in population in the 1650s was one; the coincidence after 1674 of virtually a decade uninterrupted except in 1678 by the prospect of involvement in war and in the same year by abnormal weather conditions was another.

Of course, the economic and social environment itself did change

[1] B.M., Harl. MS 4706, ff 5–8.

[2] Petty, 'Treatise of Ire.', ed. Hull, ii, 591.

considerably. Immigration was substantial; population rose by a sizeable proportion. Rents rose from the abnormally low level of the 1650s. Increased rents, while they pressed on the uncertain incomes of the ordinary rural inhabitant, appeared to hold out improved prospects for the landowning class. Historians have tended to equate the evidence of growing trade and rising rentals with rising incomes in the economy. This was, moreover, the view of contemporaries, the earl of Clarendon for instance writing in March 1686 that 'trading flourisheth and daily increaseth; land riseth in its value, which is a sign the people grow rich'.[1] The sanguine expectations of the beneficiaries of this situation can be seen also in the building of substantial houses and in the extensive investment by many individuals in settling and building villages beside their demesnes.[2] The dependence of the farmer on purely fortuitous events bringing either disaster or good fortune in their wake, justifies a wariness about accepting readily conclusions about equally bright prospects for the population at large. The uneven growth in the intake of consumer goods seems to confirm this. General improvement came erratically in only two periods, the 1650s and the late 1670s. In the intervals, much of the gain must have been eroded. Rises in rent pressed on income in the short term, while on the other hand the long term offered no consolation in the form of an upward trend in prices. In the short term, the farmer, even the substantial one, was haunted by the fear of cattle disease, and there must have been many like the unfortunate Captain Nicholl 'every yeare havinge the murraine amongste his blacke or white cattell or in his own braines'.[3]

The changes in the Irish economy in the second half of the century were of permanent significance. Growth in the volume of trade, a change in its structure with Dublin's preeminence becoming more marked, and late in the century a significant advance in the formerly backward north-east. Low prices, however, lay like a shadow across the economy. Prices fell decisively in the second half of the 1680s, and the advance of the economy was halted. The only off-setting advantage was the fact that low costs benefited the manufacturer, both the native and the immigrant. Just as the low price of land in the north, lower than elsewhere in Ireland, attracted Scottish or English immigrants, low costs gave a competitive edge to exports of linen and woollens. Industrial advance, at any rate in textiles, was more considerable in the 1680s than in any other comparable time-span in the seventeenth century. Agricultural prices, however, effectively determined living standards in Ireland. Prosperity was determined, too, by peace, and war loomed again on the horizon in 1689.[4]

[1] *Downshire MSS*, i, pt 1, p. 134.

[2] The reports compiled in the 1680s have some interesting concrete illustrations of this development (T.C.D., MSS 883/1, 883/2).

[3] Edward MacLysaght, 'Interim reports: Doneraile papers' in *Anal. Hib.*, no. 15 (1944), p. 348.

[4] This paragraph, with some changes, is taken from Cullen, *Econ. hist. Ire. since 1660*, p. 25.

The war that broke out in 1689 did not produce economic dislocation in any way comparable with that of the 1640s and early 1650s. The campaigns were short-lived; after July 1690 the northern half of the country was free from conflict between full armies, and by the autumn of the same year the Irish had been pushed back to the line of the Shannon. In contrast with the 1650s there was no plague; population losses were minimal (although while the campaigns lasted there were some population movements—notably, before the battle of the Boyne, the temporary return of many Scots to their mother country). Economic destruction, apart from livestock losses, was limited, and even livestock losses must be assessed in the context of the alarming distemper appearing in 1688. In consequence of reduced livestock numbers the recovery of the export trade was slow when peace returned in 1691. However, the impact of a reduced export trade was greatly mitigated by a substantial capital inflow (including the return of capital diverted to Britain in and after 1687) and extended immigration.[1] Many significant developments were to take place in the 1690s, which were to prove one of the three decisive threshold periods—the others being the 1650s and the late 1670s—in the economic history of Ireland in the second half of the century.

[1] See volume IV.

CHAPTER XVI

The Irish coinage, 1534–1691

MICHAEL DOLLEY

THE striking of coin in Ireland appears to have petered out, rather than to have been formally discontinued, quite late in the reign of Henry VII, and over the next thirty years or so the colony's further requirements for specie seem to have been met by selective import of certain English denominations on a scale unprecedented since the middle of the fourteenth century.[1] Significantly the preferred coins continued to be silver and not gold. The existing Anglo-Irish issues of Edward IV, Richard III, and Henry VII remained current, though their marked inferiority of weight, and even of alloy, led to the heavier sterling groats and half-groats of Henry VII and Henry VIII from London, Canterbury, and York being clipped in a manner that recalls vividly the systematic shearing of their precursors in the first half of the fifteenth century. A developing crisis was brought to a head by the Geraldine revolt of 1534. Even in England the economy was under pressure as a result of unsound fiscal policy aggravated by royal extravagance, and we do well to remember that western Europe as a whole was experiencing inflationary tendencies not altogether attributable to Spain's still embryonic exploitation of the precious metal resources of the New World. The urgent need that now arose to pay the troops sent into Ireland under Skeffington was a charge on the English treasury that would have been unwelcome at the best of times, but the tottering Anglo-Irish administration was in its wonted state of bankruptcy, while the new Tudor style of monarchy had begun to exhibit a pronounced reluctance to devolve or to delegate what were seen as critical royal prerogatives.

It was against this background that the decision was taken to break with tradition and to strike in London a separate and distinct coinage for Ireland. The new coins, first struck in 1534, had as their obverse type a crowned shield with the arms of England and France, and for reverse the badge of a crowned harp, the novel Irish armorial recently assumed by Henry VIII for reasons that remain to this day obscure but may well have something to do with an earlier exchange of musical instruments between music-loving king

[1] As this chapter is drawn almost entirely from research published, or in process of publication, by the writer, footnote references have not generally been given. All the relevant material is listed in the bibliography to this volume, § IV D, 7.

and pope in happier days when the first 'defender of the faith' still courted the approbation of Rome. 'Coin of the harp' was the official name, soon shortened to 'harp', of the larger denomination, which superficially corresponded to the English groat but was promptly tariffed as a sixpence Irish in order to discourage export from the lordship. There was good reason for this royal fear of the new coins' introduction into England, though the subsequent proclamation of a formal ban was very careful to maintain a discreet silence. Totally unbeknown to the world at large, the new coins were being struck in silver of less than sterling fineness, and over the next few years the so-called 'Irish mint', designedly set up as a distinct establishment behind the walls of the Tower of London, carried out a progressive debasement of the coins for Ireland which by 1546 had brought the standard down to as little as 3 oz fine. Only recently, too, has it begun to be realised that it was in this mint that Thomas Cromwell's administration carried out what amounted to a 'dummy run' of the policies of debasement which would be applied to the English coinage after 1544, and it is fascinating to note how closely the later and far more extensive operation followed *pari passu* the Irish model, even if in England the 1546 nadir did not fall below 4 oz fine.

The earliest 'harps' and their halves, those struck between 1534 and 1540, were of silver no more than 10 oz fine, what we would term 833 as against the 925 of sterling. The initial mark at the head of the legends was an open crown, and flanking the harp of the reverse type were the crowned initials of Henry and of the second, third, and fifth of his queens, Anne (Boleyn), Jane (Seymour), and Katherine (Howard). There is a certain amount of evidence, too, that what we would term 'stock-piling' may have taken place, with the mint now anticipating and now perhaps falling behind the king's matrimonial vagaries; by 1540 the 'half-harp' had been discontinued, while on the 'harp' the initial of the consort had been replaced by a discreet 'R' (for *Rex*). In 1540 the initial mark was changed to an elaborate leaf, an indication to those in the secret that the silver content had been reduced to 9 oz fine (modern 750), and in the following year Henry's assumption of the crown, as opposed to the lordship, of Ireland[1] led to the substitution of REX for DOMINUS in the Irish titulature which concluded the reverse legend. By the time of this change relatively few of the new 9 oz coins appear to have been struck, so that a whole century later the 'dominick grote', i.e. the 'harp' with the reverse legend reading DOMINUS, would be a preferred denomination when obsolescent coin was given a new lease of life by the exigencies of the wars of the 1640s. Just as proportionately rare, too, were some more 'harps' put out in 1543, where the initial mark was a rose and the silver content ephemerally reverted to the 10 oz standard of a decade earlier. No sooner, however, was public confidence won than debasement was resumed, a trick likewise employed in the English series, and it is revealing of English

[1] See above, ch. II, pp 46–8.

attitudes to the Irish 'guinea-pig' that the 'harps' were always baser by an ounce than their English counterparts. Early in 1544 the issues for Ireland were still 8 oz fine (667), but when Henry died in January 1547 the Irish standard had fallen to 3 oz (250). Innovations in the intervening period had included the addition to the reverse legends of the arabic numerals 37 and 38 to indicate the regnal years, and in 1546 the 'Irish mint' was removed from London to Bristol. The new master was the nefarious William Sharington, whose initials were added to the coins. After the king's death he continued to strike without proper authority, though it is not clear to what extent he was doing this for private gain or to build up a reserve of coin to be deployed for political advantage in the ensuing manœuvrings for the regency. These last of the 'harps' properly so called were ultimately unloaded on Ireland, and can be distinguished from their immediate predecessors only by their omission of the indication of the regnal year.

Paradoxically enough these London- and Bristol-struck base issues of Henry VIII seem to have achieved within Ireland a currency far wider than that of the Irish-minted issues of the preceding three-and-a-half centuries. The new policy of 'surrender and regrant'[1] was bringing the native Irish aristocracy into an entirely new relationship with the English crown, and the newly belted earls were far from slow to realise the financial benefits that might accrue from systematic exploitation of former 'freeholder' subjects, now 'tenants' of very precarious status. Almost overnight the native Irish came to exhibit an interest in, and taste for, coinage as such. The debasement of 1546 figures in the Annals of the Four Masters, with the justified implication that the principal sufferers would be the Anglo-Irish,[2] and we begin to find in the Irish records carefully drawn distinctions between payments made in *salfás* and in *croise caoile* money, that is, between the sterling English groats of Henry VII and Henry VIII, so very conveniently differentiated by a profile ('half-face') bust, and the old Anglo-Irish pieces from the later 1480s and early 1490s where the cross of the obverse type was of exceptional thinness. The impression given for the first time is that coin at last was really current among the Irish: earlier references in fourteenth(?)-century glosses on the law-tracts would seem to have been occasioned by a desire to render intelligible to Anglo-Irish lords customary payments made in kind. We cannot but be struck, too, by the facility with which the Irish appear to have mastered the niceties of debasement, and the very name *boṇn geal* (white groat), later anglicised 'bungal(l)', accorded to the base issues of Henry VIII and his progeny, very probably reflects an appreciation of the irreproducible sheen of high-grade silver among a people with a tradition of craftmanship in the precious metals extending back over many centuries.

Henry VIII, then, had deprived the Anglo-Irish of the possibility of producing their own money, and it was to be typical of Tudor monetary

[1] See above, ch. II, pp 48–51.

[2] *A.F.M.*, v, 1498–9.

policies that the decision was as abruptly reversed under his successor. An instruction dated 10 February 1548 authorised one Thomas Agard to strike at Dublin sixpences Irish with their halves, quarters, and eighths in silver 4 oz (333) fine. The new coins, however, were to be of purely English type, only the mint-signature constituting the reverse legend serving to distinguish them from contemporary English groats; and like the latter they bore the name and portrait of the dead Henry. Clearly Edward VI was reserving his own likeness for the day when it should be possible for him to restore the coinage to something like the old sterling standard that had obtained in England since Anglo-Saxon times, a day that in the event never would dawn where Ireland was concerned. The mint-signature apart, the Anglo-Irish nominal sixpences were indistinguishable from English groats, and the hope was that their tariffing at the higher figure would prevent their being siphoned out of the Irish economy. It was not only the public, however, that found the virtual identity of fabric and type confusing, and the sixpences Irish were actually termed groats when their manufacture was resumed under Martin Pirry, who succeeded Agard in 1550. The minor denominations, with the smallest tariffed as three-halfpence and three-farthings Irish, were also continued, though the mint was naturally reluctant to produce such fiddling pieces in any quantity.

Under Pirry as under Agard the principal preoccupation of the Dublin authorities was the search for bullion, and the dearth of precious metal was reflected in their failure even to attempt to implement in Ireland Edward VI's design to restore sterling standard where the English coinage was concerned. In England the expedient was attempted of issuing coin simultaneously to two different standards, the one 11 oz (917) and the other 3 oz (250), the latter pieces being light into the bargain. In 1552 Pirry appears to have concluded production at Dublin by the striking of a number of these base shillings with the initial mark of a harp, which are not uncommon but sedulously ignored by English proclamations that eventually demonetised their English counterparts. Needless to say there was no attempt in Ireland to produce analogues of the 11 oz fine shillings and sixpences, which did succeed in establishing themselves as an integral part of the English currency; and a final humiliation for the colony was the unloading in the same year on Ireland of a large consignment of base pennies of English type, which had been struck at York and originally intended to form part of the English series. The precedent was one that would be followed on more than one occasion during the next two reigns.

The accession of Mary in 1553 witnessed more vacillations of policy. The new queen was very much her father's daughter, and at once the Dublin mint was dismantled. It may not have helped matters that the assayer had been intimate with Bishop Bale,[1] but Mary's prime concern must have been

[1] See above, ch. III, pp 74, 75.

to ensure that the crown enjoyed a monopoly of access to the sinews of war. It was typical of the queen's pragmatism that she instinctively endorsed her father's assumption of the theory as well as the reality of sovereign authority in Ireland: within months of her accession the revived 'Irish mint' in the Tower of London was turning out shillings, groats, half-groats, and pennies Irish with legends proclaiming her Irish queenship. The new coins were relatively fine, the standard being 7 oz (583), though still 4 oz (333) worse than the corresponding standard for England, and the emission was not very substantial before it was discontinued in 1554. The Spanish marriage might have given Mary access to new sources of bullion, but the decision now was taken to give absolute priority to the schemes for the restoration of sterling standard in England. A continuing need for coin in Ireland was to be met by a new flood of base money, and as a first instalment there was struck with the London mint-signature a massive run of English-type pennies in silver that again was no more than 3 oz (250) fine. The analogy is with the York pennies of a couple of years earlier, but this time it was always the intention that the coins should be dispatched to Ireland. In 1555 there followed shillings with an English-type obverse but a reverse incorporating the crowned harp so characteristic of the Anglo-Irish issues of Henry VIII. Again the standard was the execrable 3 oz fine one, and in 1556 and 1557 the shillings were accompanied by groats. Such was the scale of production that over large parts of Ireland surviving pre-debasement issues, English as well as Anglo-Irish, were driven underground, so that for all practical purposes 'white money' was the basis of the island's economy, the principal sufferers being as usual the Anglo-Irish mercantile class and the salaried officials of the Dublin administration.

It was this system that was inherited by Elizabeth in 1558, and for the first two years of her reign base shillings and groats continued to be poured into Ireland. In time, too, the frugal and practical queen realised that there was little point in recoining the base issues of her father and half-brother, which flooded into the English exchanges as restoration of sterling standard became a reality where England was concerned; and as an act of deliberate policy they were sent over to Ireland and tariffed according to their precious metal content. Groats predominated, and were valued at three to the new groat sterling, so that $1\frac{1}{3}$*d.* is a sum frequently met with in the surviving fiscal accounts of the reign. It was these coins *par excellence* that were termed 'bungal(l)s' by the Anglo-Irish, but the evidence of coin-hoards is that the problem they presented was at once exaggerated and of relatively brief duration. To her credit, too, Elizabeth contemplated a restoration of sterling standard in Ireland as well as England, and in 1561 there was a relatively small emission of 11 oz (916) shillings and groats Irish with the novel reverse type of a crowned shilling displaying three harps disposed two and one like the crowns on the earlier Irish armorial. The coins were too distinctive, and this, added to their meagre quantity, meant that they failed to make any real impact upon the currency. Only one or two have been recorded in Irish hoards, and one has turned up in an English context. It is at this juncture, too, that the pattern of reported coin-hoards from Ireland begins once again to reflect with fair accuracy the course of events this side of the Irish Sea. Characteristic of the early part of the reign is a significant concentration of hoards from Ulster, a reminder of the threat to English authority posed not just by Shane O'Neill but by the 'red-shanks', Scottish colonists from the Isles. The finds of this period still are dominated by the base issues of the previous decade, and in this contrast sharply with the notably fewer finds from the 1570s and 1580s which exhibit a much wider geographical distribution, and which are composed of a mixture of the old 'white money' and of fine silver brought in from England. What is very clear is that Elizabeth's advisers had come to the conclusion that there was little point in continuing to attempt a separate coinage for Ireland. Capital investment in Ireland, the colony's most urgent need, could be secured, and the insular economy protected, by the simple expedient of according English sterling money a premium of a third. In Ireland, then, the English shilling was in practice tariffed at and passed for sixteen pence, and the evidence of a whole crop of hoards associated with the outbreak of O'Neill's rebellion is that in a matter of two decades the island had been flooded with English sterling. Find after find from the Ulster mearing contains only the English shillings and sixpences of Elizabeth, while 'white money' appears to have lingered on only in the more remote and less anglicised areas. After 1588, however, one novel factor did begin to make itself felt as a limited amount of Spanish coin, much of it in fact obsolete where Spain itself was concerned, competed with sterling in the south and west, but it is clear that its introduction was intermittent and never on anything like the same scale.

Unfortunately for Ireland, and more especially for the predominantly Old English mercantile class, the ascendancy of sterling was to falter seriously at the very end of the reign. Just to find the pay for the troops sent over under Essex[1] in unprecedented numbers proved an intolerable strain on Elizabeth's severely limited financial resources, and one at least of her advisers was only too aware of the extent to which Hugh O'Neill was using English sterling to purchase the sinews of war, most notably gunpowder. In 1601, then, there was struck in London and put in issue in Ireland a new coinage for Ireland which reverted to the old 3 oz (250) standard abandoned forty years before. To their ruin the queen's most loyal subjects were forbidden to discriminate against the new coins, and within a matter of months there were unloaded on Ireland shillings, sixpences, and threepences Irish with a face value in excess of a quarter of a million pounds sterling. The Irish council itself had to hear an appeal from a trader seeking to avoid their acceptance in settlement of a

[1] See above, ch. IV, pp 127–9.

debt due to be paid in good and lawful coin, and the incomplete record of the pleadings shows the lawyers seeking precedents going back for centuries in what was clearly a *cause célèbre*. The queen herself is supposed to have disliked the project, and it could be significant that her likeness did not figure on the coins. Curiously there is no certain record of a hoard containing them, and even as single finds they are rare. Clearly they were not worth hoarding, and the unlucky holders sought the first opportunity of getting rid of them when the issue was formally demonetised early in the next reign. The contretemps was the more deplorable because it prejudiced another innovation as financially sound as socially laudable. For generations Ireland had been bedevilled by a shortage of small change. To meet this want, which bore most heavily upon the poor, the administration authorised the striking in quantity of copper pence and halfpence. Technically they were tokens in that the copper was not worth anything like the face value, but stringent control of their emission, coupled with safeguards to prevent their use outside petty transactions, conferred on them acceptability if not popularity. A comparable coinage for England was very much in the air at the time of the queen's death, and in fact was very soon to be implemented there under her successor.

Where Ireland was concerned, then, James I can be said to have inherited something approaching fiscal chaos. One consequence of the volte-face of 1601–2 had been to give a new and unlooked-for lease of life to the old 'white money', which until then had been falling back on virtually every front before the impact of sterling; and for the next half-century the Irish currency would remain an astonishing amalgam of the latest fine silver issues from England and of Anglo-Irish pieces going back as far as Edward IV. A Stuart king, however, was well enough qualified by his Scottish experiences of debasement and its evils to take firm but sensible action to restore public confidence in coin as a medium of exchange. The first problem was to rid the system of the scandalous 'mixt money' of 1601–2 which called into question the integrity of the crown. As a first step the 'mixt money' was formally 'cried down', i.e. tariffed at a figure approximating to its precious metal content, the shilling as a groat and the lower denominations in proportion. The copper tokens, on the other hand, were to retain their face value, and continued to enjoy popularity as a consequence of checks on their possible abuse. English sterling would continue to pass as bullion, and would still be encouraged to remain in the island by the premium of a third which it attracted. In addition a special coinage was struck for Ireland with denominations of a shilling and a sixpence. The new pieces were repeatedly proclaimed as being no more than 9 oz (750) fine, but recently it has been established that they were in fact of sterling (925) standard.[1] The thinking behind the

[1] I am grateful to Fr G. Rice, of Navan, for allowing me to see his paper on this series, in advance of publication.

ploy appears to have been a typically shrewd appreciation of the need to ensure a wide circulation of acceptable coin before the next development, the revaluation of the 'mixt' shilling at twopence Irish, a figure slightly below its precious metal content. Possessors of the 'mixt money' now had a positive inducement to turn it in at the exchanges for its bullion value, but the new shillings and sixpences meant that there would be a sufficient reservoir of money of fair quality to prevent the scarcity of ready money that could have led to hoarding of coin and a consequent set-back to the whole economy. If, however, the new coins had been proclaimed as fine silver, they might well have been culled from currency and stored away as a hedge against further debasements. By 1607 the time was thought ripe to 'cry down' the 'mixt money' below its precious metal content, and the opportunity was also taken to proclaim English sterling legal tender at the accepted premium of one-third. With the 'mixt money' of 1601–2 finding its way to the crucible, the door would be left open for a clearly defined 'two-tier' currency, the upper composed of recent fine-silver issues in the names of Elizabeth and James, and the lower of obsolete English and Anglo-Irish coin, much of it base and all very obviously differentiated by its types and quality.

Separate Anglo-Irish coins ceased to be struck in 1607, and this in itself ensured that English sterling would play an increasing role in the expanding monetary economy of Ireland. In 1613 English farthing tokens were proclaimed current in both kingdoms, and Stuart policy appears to have been to allow the two coinages to grow together. The problem was to prevent a flow of money out of Ireland, and it is noticeable that when in the next reign proposals were entertained for the reopening of a mint in Dublin the coins contemplated, gold for the first time as well as silver, were to have distinctively Irish types though struck to the English standard. As it happens the project came to nothing, but in 1637 another proposal was implemented ordaining the quotation and rendering of all prices, rents, and official payments of every description in sterling instead of the traditional money Irish. It was a check on administrative malpractice, and no longer could royal officials line their pockets and discredit the crown by demanding payment in sterling or its equivalent but settling in base money at sterling rates. Clearly the day was envisaged as not far distant when general convenience would dictate universal employment of sterling, with the last of the inferior issues of the previous two centuries finding their way as bullion to the royal exchanges.

The wars of the 1640s[1] gave a new lease of life to the old monetary chaos. The English parliament controlled the London mint, and in Ireland the different interests were thrown back on such resources as might be improvised on the spot. The confederate catholics were early off the mark when in November 1642 the Kilkenny assembly tariffed and declared legal tender a wide spectrum of foreign, notably Spanish and French, and of obsolescent

[1] See above, ch. XI–XIII.

Anglo-Irish and English, money. Authority was also given for the striking of new silver and copper coins. These included a number of half-crowns on the English model, the so-called 'blacksmith's half-crowns', and more doubtfully a number of crowns and half-crowns in imitation of certain Dublin issues of 1643–4, though the latter pieces, which are virtually anepigraphic, have been associated with 1648 and with the English parliamentary commander Michael Jones. The copper pence and halfpence were struck in quantity and nearly as extensively forged, which may explain a series of official-looking countermarks, notably a 'K' and castle and a rose, perhaps intended to authenticate controversial pieces of low weight.

In Dublin the lords justices representing the protestant royalist interest showed themselves no less energetic. In 1642 they first coined six denominations in silver which ranged from a crown down to a groat, the design on both sides being the weight expressed in arabic numerals and pennyweights and grains; and later in the year there was put out a further emission of the ninepence, sixpence, and groat with the addition of a threepence, the reverse type now taking the form of a symbol indicative of the value in pence. In 1643 a third issue of silver consisted of crowns and half-crowns with the value expressed on both sides in shillings and pence and roman numerals. Later the same year and extending into 1644 came another extensive series of more overtly royalist and even nummiform pieces where the obverse type consisted of a crowned royal cipher while the reverse continued to spell out the monetary value. The seven denominations ranged from a crown down to a half-groat, the novel ninepence being discarded.

In 1646 the continuing need for coin was met by a remarkable issue of gold, the only time apparently when this metal has ever been coined in Ireland. Under Ormond's crumbling authority the Dublin goldsmiths supervised the production of two small issues of base gold, the bullion derived from melted-down plate. The weight standard adopted for the two denominations was a continental one, that of the French and Spanish pistole, and as on the silver of 1642 the troy weight was stamped on both sides. There was an element of cheat, however, as the alloy was appreciably worse than the insular norm, and the legal status of the pieces as coin of the realm was and remains dubious. From 1645, too, and continuing into 1647, the embattled protestants along the south coast at Bandon, Cork, Kinsale, and Youghal were improvising their own shillings and sixpences in silver, threepences in pewter, half-groats in brass, and halfpence and farthings in what passed for copper. Finally in 1649 Ormond marked his definitive break with the regicide parliament by a small issue of silver crowns and half-crowns in the name of Charles II. It is only natural that all these diverse issues from the 1640s should have exercised the student and collector over the past three centuries, but it is still not sufficiently appreciated that all these issues added up to a very small proportion of the money circulating in Ireland during the decade in question. This continued to be dominated by English sterling, though the absence of a strong central authority meant increasingly its dilution with foreign coin, and we now begin to find in the coin-hoards a significant proportion of silver from Spain and the Low Countries.

The recrudescence of minting at Dublin and Kilkenny was brought abruptly to an end by the Cromwellian intervention in Ireland, and the very completeness of the English victory meant that the monetary position was rapidly stabilised. It was in the 1650s in fact that the last of the 'white money' quietly faded away, the need for a petty currency now being met, as in England, by copper and brass tokens put out privately by individual tradesmen. The earliest belong to around 1653, and by 1658 the initial trickle had become a flood. The issuers behaved generally with responsibility and restraint, and in most cases the dies and even the blanks were ordered from a tight little circle of established manufacturers in London. Complaints of abuse were few, but technically such pieces could be thought an infringement of sovereign prerogative, so that it is possibly no coincidence that in 1660 Charles II essayed a reversion to earlier Stuart practice by granting to Sir Thomas Armstrong an exclusive patent to strike and issue farthings for Ireland. The new pieces were odious on principle, and more practically fitted ill into an economy where coins no larger or heavier passed freely as pence and halfpence, so that the opposition of the Dublin administration proved decisive. Since there was, however, a continuing need for small change, the later 1660s witnessed a second burgeoning of the private token, the issuers once again being local merchants and tradesmen. Curiously it was only around Athlone that any significant proportion of the names relate to catholics, and the series as a whole affords a neat illustration of the extent to which commerce in Ireland had passed into protestant hands. The principal objection to the token, of course, was the technical problem of its redemption, and in the 1670s there was a move towards a larger coin with the metal content approximating to the face value. Most notable was a large issue of halfpence and farthings from Dublin, where the obverse type was King David and the reverse the national apostle, who is shown on the halfpenny holding aloft the shamrock, perhaps the earliest pictorial representation of the national emblem in its Patrician context.

As in England, what finally killed the private token was an adequate coinage of regal copper. A mint was established under licence at Capel Street, Dublin, and between 1680 and 1686 there was a steady flow of copper halfpence. The new coins were struck in theory at twelve-thirteenths of the English standard to reflect the premium of one-twelfth which English money was to enjoy in Ireland for the next century and a half. It was hoped, by this expedient, if not to encourage English investment in Ireland at least to discourage the export of money from the island, and the policy was more or less successful. The mint in Dublin, however, was not allowed to strike in the precious metals, and there was a continuing shortage of gold and more especially of silver coin in the country. One consequence was the toleration in practice of large quantities of foreign coin, and particularly of the so-called ducatoon from the Netherlands. The position was further complicated by the introduction of inferior imitations, and had not been resolved when the crisis of 1688 broke.

The decision of James II to use Ireland as a base for the recovery of his English throne[1] was accompanied by coinage on a quite unprecedented scale. Unfortunately there was no ready source of bullion, and hence the decision to coin what were in effect monetary pledges in base metal. The main series began in June 1689 with the striking of sixpences in a nominal brass, and in July shillings and half-crowns were added. Dublin was the chosen mint, but it was planned to open a second at Limerick as soon as conditions allowed. The personnel worked in shifts around the clock, and, the metal apart, the coins were of high quality. Each bore the name of the month as well as the year, in order to facilitate orderly redemption when the king should come into his own, and the surviving accounts bear out contemporary suggestions that the whole coinage amounted to £1,100,000 or a little more. Output on this scale posed one unlooked-for problem when it proved difficult to find sufficient base metal to keep the press in full production, and the surviving coins are struck in a wide range of bronze and brass alloys. By December 1689 Limerick was being instructed to cut up and melt down unserviceable cannon and to send the resulting ingots to Dublin, a hint that the Limerick mint had still to begin striking on its own account, and royal agents were scouring the island for suitable scrap metal. In Ireland the coins were and are generally known as 'brass money', but in England 'gun-money' is the preferred designation even though it is likely that domestic utensils rather than cannon provided the bulk of the 'bullion'.

In the spring of 1690 the decision was made to step up still further the production of the coin so urgently needed to put the Jacobite army into the field. The production of sixpences was effectively discontinued, and instead a coinage of crowns initiated. The original design was to produce these in a white metal, tin, or pewter, these last being alloys the Dublin mint was learning to handle as a consequence of a small issue of pence and halfpence in March and April. By May the Limerick mint appears to have been coming haltingly into production, but this only served to accentuate the shortage of suitable 'bullion', and the decision had already been taken to abandon coinage in white metal and pewter, to reduce the size and weight of the half-crown and shilling, and to restrike as crowns existing stocks of the large half-crowns. Before, however, the new policies could become fully effective, the Williamite army had broken out of Ulster, and the fate of the Dublin mint was settled at the Boyne. No attempt appears to have been

[1] See below, ch. XIX.

made to evacuate or even to destroy the Capel Street establishment, which in 1692 resumed the striking of copper halfpence in the names of William and Mary. In the meantime the new mint at Limerick had continued to coin 'brass' crowns, half-crowns, and shillings, but recent research has established that the scale of their production was exiguous in the extreme, and by October 1690 the press was idle.

The failure of the Limerick mint to come into full operation when the 'James' press at Dublin fell into the hands of the enemy need not be laid at the door of the staff, who appear to have been competent, nor of continuing shortages of suitable metal. The whole concept of the 'brass money' depended for its success on complete control of the economy, and even then could hope to command acceptance only if there was public confidence in an early victory. From the first the new issues were vulnerable to a propaganda campaign mounted with considerable astuteness by the Williamite interest in Ireland, and the military reverses of 1690 destroyed the last chance of widespread acquiescence in the expedient. Repeated proclamations had laid down penalties for refusal of the new coin, and attempts had been made to cajole the public by offers of discounts. Even before the Boyne campaign, however, resistance to the new medium of exchange was rife, and by no means confined to the mercantile community which was strongly Williamite in its sympathies and traditions. The fall of the capital in July was the new money's death-knell, and recognised as such by all the protagonists. From his camp at Finglas William III 'cried down' the emergency issues to something like their value as scrap metal, the crown and large half-crown to pass for a penny, and the smaller 'brass' pieces in proportion, while the tin pence and halfpence were now tariffed as halfpence and farthings respectively. No more than months later the Jacobite authorities in beleaguered Limerick recognised reality when a need for an acceptable petty currency was met by recoining stocks of large shillings as halfpence and small shillings as farthings. These coins, known as 'Hibernias' from their reverse type, were dated 1691, and brought to a close a phase of Anglo-Irish monetary history of unparalleled interest for the economist. The issues were fiduciary, but no more so than most modern currencies, and, for all the barrage of propaganda mounted against them at the time and surviving even to this day as part of the Orange myth, there seems no good reason to think that they would not have been redeemed in gold and silver had James II been restored to his English throne. Inevitably, however, military defeat brought about their final discredit, and their formal demonetisation by a proclamation of February 1692 occasioned neither surprise nor any new resentment. 'Unmourned' could be thought the best epitaph for the 'brass money' and for its author, and this was a verdict which provided common ground for virtually every interest in the last of James II's kingdoms to pass into the control of his enemies.

CHAPTER XVII

The restoration, 1660–85

J. G. SIMMS

IN the course of 1659 there were signs that the commonwealth regime in Ireland, as in England, was collapsing. The recall of Henry Cromwell in June led to a power struggle among the army officers in Ireland parallel to that which developed in England. By the end of the year it became clear that the section of the army that supported Monck had gained the upper hand. In Ireland it was represented by Sir Theophilus Jones, who seized Dublin castle, and by Sir Charles Coote and Lord Broghill, who secured the garrisons in Connacht and Munster. In February 1660 Coote sent an emissary to offer his services to Charles II. Broghill at the same time sent his brother to invite Charles to Cork, where the Munster army would be ready to declare for him. A council of officers summoned a convention, which was primarily designed to raise funds to pay the army, but also prepared the way for the restoration of the monarchy. The convention, which contained some royalist members, met on 7 February[1] under the chairmanship of Sir James Barry, who had a royalist background. In March a document, 'signed by thousands of good people and soldiers of the kingdom', was published in Dublin. It asked Charles to return, begged for his forgiveness, but stipulated for a general indemnity and the payment of army arrears.[2]

On 14 May the king was proclaimed in Dublin, and soon afterwards the convention sent a delegation to him, which presented a series of requests. The king was asked to appoint royal courts and to call a parliament consisting of protestant peers and commons. It was also requested that the Church of Ireland should again be established as it had been in the reign of Charles I and, according to the law of Ireland, still was. In September Coote and Broghill became, respectively, earls of Mountrath and Orrery. At the end of 1660 they, together with Sir Maurice Eustace, the lord chancellor, were appointed lords justices to conduct the administration in the place of Monck, who was appointed lord lieutenant but did not come to assume the office.

With the restoration of Charles II catholics looked forward to toleration

[1] This is the date usually accepted. According to Samuel Coxe, *Two sermons* . . . (Dublin, 1660), the first meeting was 2 Mar.

[2] *Ireland's declaration* (Dublin, 1660). For this and the preceding reference I am indebted to the M.A. thesis of Fergus O'Donoghue, 'The Irish parliament of Charles II' (N.U.I., 1970).

for their faith and recovery of their land. The confederate catholics had continually protested their loyalty to the king. The peace they had made with Ormond in 1649 had guaranteed religious toleration and security of property. Many of them had shared the exile of Charles II, had fought under his standard on the Continent, and now expected the rewards of loyalty. But the protestant army officers, who had served the commonwealth and had then joined Monck in calling for the king's return, were determined to keep the estates they had acquired and to ensure that the country should remain under protestant management. The claims of returning catholics and entrenched protestants were incompatible. Successive governors of Ireland were to be baffled by them throughout the twenty-five years of Charles II's reign.

Of the viceroys the outstanding figure was Ormond, who had been made a duke in 1661 and whose two terms of office, 1662–9 and 1677–85, lasted for most of the reign. He had an unmatched record of loyalty to the crown and had helped significantly in securing the king's restoration. The protestant head of a famous Old English family, most of whose members were catholics, he seemed admirably placed to effect a compromise that would maintain the protestant interest and at the same time go far to meet the claims of the catholics who had shown themselves ready to come to terms with him. It says something for his moderation that he satisfied neither side. The intractable problems that confronted him were made more difficult by the intrigues of Whitehall courtiers who looked on Ireland as a land of golden opportunity and took advantage of an extravagant and easy-going king. Ormond had sufficient standing at the English court to attract the enmity of politicians such as Buckingham, Danby, and Shaftesbury; their attitude to Irish questions was influenced by their desire to damage him. He had also to face criticism from the English parliament, which was concerned that English interests should not be endangered by concessions to catholics or the development of Irish commerce. Ormond had not the skill to outwit those who regarded him as an obstacle to their schemes. There is an evident connection between changes in the Irish administration and the vicissitudes of English politics, but its exact nature has not been fully established. Ormond's recall in 1669 followed on the fall of Clarendon and the rise of Buckingham. But it has also been suggested that Charles wished to prepare for his policy of religious toleration by replacing Ormond with a less inflexibly anglican successor. However, the morose, pro-presbyterian Robartes (1669–70) and the easy-going, pro-catholic Berkeley (1670–2) had short and troubled terms of office.

The earl of Essex, who came next, lasted from 1672 to 1677. He had no previous experience of Ireland, but he took pains to grasp its problems, and we are indebted to him for the compilation of several economic and statistical statements of value. His correspondence shows that he was subjected to continual interference from English ministers and from men, and women, of ambition who were adept at securing support from London for schemes to profit from Irish revenues and land-grants. Essex appears to have tried to govern Ireland honestly and impartially. The effort created for him a host of enemies, particularly among the financiers who had undertaken to manage the revenue and expenditure for the king's advantage and their own.

Ormond owed his second period of office partly to the tactics of Danby and partly to the determination of James, duke of York, that the post should not go to his nephew, the duke of Monmouth. Ormond's second administration was soon exposed to the problems created by the popish plot and the exclusion crisis. His position was continually threatened, and shortly before the end of the reign Charles had decided to recall him.

The land question was a major preoccupation throughout the reign, and no satisfactory solution to it was found. Even before Charles's return to England, Cromwellians and catholics had begun to press their respective claims. All through the summer and autumn of 1660 rival agents were busy in the corridors of Whitehall. The chief spokesman of the protestants was Orrery, and he was a formidable opponent of catholic claims. He and his clients could rely on the prevailing anti-Irish sentiment in England, and they made the most of reports that catholics were trying to recover their estates by force. They succeeded in getting a provision in the English act of indemnity and oblivion[1] for the exclusion of all concerned in the 'rebellion of Ireland'; these were to be left to future legislation. The catholics, led by Sir Nicholas Plunkett, pleaded loyalty to the crown and the terms of the Ormond peace of 1649. Great numbers of individuals petitioned for the recovery of their estates. Royal letters in their favour were issued in profusion, few of which had any effect.

A specious solution, which Charles was glad to accept, was devised by Orrery. He furnished statistics which seemed to show that the titles of soldiers and adventurers could be confirmed and enough land remain to meet the claims of catholics. In November 1660 Charles issued a long and elaborate declaration for the settlement of the Irish land question. Soldiers and adventurers, other than those to whom pardon had been refused, were to keep what they already held on 7 May 1659, with certain exceptions such as the lands of 'innocent papists'. If they had to give up any of their holdings they were to be 'reprised' with lands elsewhere. Provision was also made for the '49 officers—protestants who had served in the royal forces in Ireland before 5 June 1649.[2] They were to get whatever lands had not been disposed

[1] 12 Chas II, c. 11.

[2] 7 May 1659 was the date on which the rump of the long parliament reassembled. 5 June 1649 was the date on which Cromwell's army was ordered to proceed to Ireland. For an account of the '49 officers see Prendergast, *Cromwellian settlement*, pp 187–95.

of in the 'mile-line' along the coasts of Connacht and Clare; in the counties of Donegal, Leitrim, Longford, and Wicklow; and in corporate towns—provisions that seriously reduced the land available for other claimants. The king acknowledged his obligation to those who had been faithful to the Ormond peace of 1649, but better terms were offered to those who had followed the king into exile than to those who had accepted lands in Connacht. A number of named individuals were singled out for preferential treatment, either on account of special merit or because they had served faithfully under the king's ensigns.

The king's declaration made no mention of the Londonderry plantation, which had been forfeited to the crown as a result of the star chamber sentence passed in 1635. In November 1641 Charles I had offered to restore the forfeited property, saying that he hoped to recover it first and then to give it to the city. He took no further action, but, with the suppression of the rebellion, the London companies resumed possession. The Civil Survey of 1655 lists them as the holders in 1641, ignoring the sequestration. In 1657 Cromwell gave a fresh charter to the Londoners. This was unacceptable to the restoration government, and on 10 April 1662 Charles II issued his own charter, granting all the rights that had been forfeited in his father's time.

A commission was appointed to carry out the king's declaration. It comprised thirty-six members, all protestants and most of them concerned in claims to Irish land. Prominent among them was Orrery, who was also a lord justice. The commissioners had little incentive to change the *status quo*, and their indifference was fortified by a ruling of the judges that an act of parliament was necessary to give effect to the king's declaration. A parliament was accordingly summoned, which met for the first time on 8 May 1661. There was no legal bar to the election of catholics. The Irish government's proposal to make the oath of supremacy a statutory requirement for membership was not accepted in England. A subsequent resolution of the commons asking the lords justices to authorise the administration of the oath to all members of the house was not complied with. However, protestants were in a dominant position, and only one catholic was returned. This was Geoffrey Browne, whose name was on one of two conflicting returns sent in from the borough of Tuam. The debate on the conflict was inconclusive, but it appears that Browne never took his seat and that the house of commons was, in fact, an all-protestant body, in which Cromwellians and those 'old protestants' who had cooperated with the commonwealth regime were strongly represented. Several catholics sat in the house of lords, but they were in a powerless minority. A number of catholic peerages had been affected by outlawry proceedings following on the rising of 1641, but peers who had been declared 'innocent' were allowed to take their seats.

The main business of the first session was discussion of the form to be taken by the land-settlement bill. When the draft bill was transmitted to

England for approval both catholics and protestants sent representatives to urge their case, and once again the protestants were more than a match for their opponents. Contributions from soldiers and adventurers were alleged to have been used to win the support of influential courtiers. The catholics seem to have made a tactical error in ignoring Ormond, who was the king's chief adviser on Irish affairs and was about to become lord lieutenant. They relied instead on Richard Talbot, a member of an Old English family who was high in the favour of the king's brother, the duke of York, and was to play an important, and controversial, part in Irish politics for the next thirty years. Neither Ormond nor Clarendon, the English chancellor, had any liking for Talbot, with whom they had both been in conflict. Catholics felt that these two influential statesmen had tilted the balance in favour of the protestants.

The bill, with a strongly anti-catholic preamble, was finally returned to Ireland and passed during the summer of 1662. The act of settlement, as it is usually called, vested in the crown all the lands involved in the Cromwellian confiscation, with the exception of church and college lands and the lands of 'innocents', whether catholic or protestant. The exclusion of innocents from the scope of the act was intended to ensure that they should recover their lands immediately without waiting until the Cromwellian occupants had first been reprised with lands elsewhere. This gave innocents an advantage over other claimants such as 'nominees' or 'ensignmen', who were to wait for reinstatement until lands elsewhere had been found for the Cromwellians. If, however, the property claimed was in a corporate town, the 'innocent papist' was not to recover it but to get equivalent land in the neighbourhood. The king's declaration and a set of instructions were incorporated in the act. One of the instructions made over to the duke of York the lands that had been given to the regicides—those who had signed Charles I's death-warrant. This provision made it harder than ever to find enough land to satisfy the king's promises to the rival sets of claimants.

The execution of the act was entrusted to seven commissioners, one of whom was Winston Churchill, father of the future duke of Marlborough. This body is usually referred to as the 'court of claims'. By another act the period for hearing claims was limited to twelve months. In fact, the court sat for less than eight months and confined its hearings to claims of innocence. Preference was given to those claimants who had not received lands in Connacht from the commonwealth. The majority of claims heard were admitted in spite of the restrictive interpretation that the instructions put on the term 'innocent papist'. Widows and orphans found it easiest to meet the severe conditions laid down, but decrees of innocence were often issued to persons who appear to have taken an active part in the confederation. Influence was brought to bear in a number of cases, the most notorious being that of the marquis of Antrim, for whom both Charles II and Henrietta Maria intervened. In all the court issued 566 decrees of innocence to catholics and 141 to protestants: 113 catholics were declared 'nocent'. Several thousand claims remained unheard at the expiry of the time allowed for hearing cases, and this became a major grievance for catholics. Protestants, on the other hand, were highly dissatisfied with the court's liberality to catholics. The house of commons protested strongly, and the court's proceedings were among the factors that led to a protestant conspiracy—Blood's plot—to seize Dublin castle and kidnap Ormond, the lord lieutenant.

Difficulties soon arose over the execution of the court's decrees and of the king's orders in favour of particular individuals. It became evident that there was not going to be enough land for 'reprisals', and that further legislation would be necessary. After much negotiation this took the form of the act of explanation, passed in 1665. It is a lengthy document, complicated by the number of private interests taken into account in the drafting. It broke the deadlock by providing that most soldiers and adventurers should surrender one-third of their holdings and that the land thus freed should be used to reprise those protestants who had to make way for catholics. The decrees of innocence granted by the court of claims were, with a few exceptions, confirmed, but no fresh hearings were allowed. Lord Antrim's decree of innocence was set aside, but it was provided that he should be restored to his estates. The quit-rents imposed on them were granted to Jermyn, the courtier who had been the intermediary. The act specified a number of other catholics who were to be restored, and in particular named fifty-four who were each to get back their principal residence and 2,000 acres.

This was far from meeting the demands of catholics. But it was a severe blow to those protestants who were called on to give up a third of their holdings. To ease its passage into law extensive grants were provided in favour of persons of influence. Notable among them was Arlington, the English secretary of state, who was awarded the Clanmaliere estates in Leix and Offaly. Arlington, whose name was commemorated in the town of Portarlington, had long coveted the property of Lord Clanmaliere, whose claim of innocency remained unheard. Orrery and a number of prominent Cromwellians were exempted from having to surrender a third of their property, and this helped to secure their support for the passage of the act. A year's rent was levied on all estates that had belonged to catholics in 1641. From the proceeds £50,000 was allotted to Charles, and £50,000 to Ormond. £10,000 went to Arlington.

A second court of claims was appointed to administer the act of explanation. It consisted of five members of the first court, Churchill among them. It sat from 1666 to the beginning of 1669. Its decrees led to a large-scale exchange of lands, chiefly in Leinster and Munster, in the course of which a number of catholics recovered portions of their former property, but protestants were still left in a dominant position. The process by which the surrender of part of their lands by Cromwellians made room for some of the catholic claimants remains obscure. The proceedings were long-drawn-out and in many cases catholic holders of decrees were obstructed by those in possession.

In 1671 a petition on behalf of the catholic nobility and gentry was presented to the king by Richard Talbot in his capacity as 'agent general of the Roman Catholics of Ireland'. The petitioners protested their loyalty and complained that they had not been able to recover their lands. Though the English attorney general, Sir Heneage Finch, reported against it, a committee was appointed to examine the entire settlement. This was followed by the appointment of a commission of inspection, headed by Prince Rupert. These measures produced a strong reaction from protestants, who denounced what they called an attack on the acts of settlement and explanation, and seem to have decided that it would pay them best to take their stand on the acts. Their protest was supported by the English house of commons, which by 1673 was acutely dissatisfied with the pro-catholic policy of the court. The commons demanded that the king should recall Prince Rupert's commission and should dismiss Talbot from his military command and refuse him access to court. Charles yielded to the storm and recalled the commission; Talbot went into exile.

The next move in the Irish land question was made in 1675, when commissioners were appointed to determine the cases of the Connacht 'transplanters' who had so far been left out of consideration. A large number of decrees were issued both to Connacht families and to those from other provinces who had not recovered their original estates. The final stage of the land-settlement was the appointment, at the end of the reign, of a commission or 'court of grace', which for a money payment confirmed defective titles, of which there were many.

Particulars of these complex transactions are contained in the 'books of survey and distribution', of which several sets have survived. The most complete of the sets records, parish by parish, on facing pages the pre-Cromwellian and the post-restoration holders of all the lands confiscated by the commonwealth and of much of the adjacent unforfeited land.[1] They show that at the concluding stage of the restoration settlement the catholic share of the land had been reduced from three-fifths in 1641 to little more than one-fifth.[2] Most of those who had received decrees for the restoration of lands as innocents had recovered at least part of their claim. The fate of others was diverse. Some recovered large estates, many got nothing at all. Some of the latter turned 'tory', took to the woods and hills, and harassed the settlers; others lived on the charity of their more fortunate kinsmen. Some of those who eventually got their land back did so only after a rancorous and expensive contest with the Cromwellian occupants. Essex summed

[1] The 'quit-rent office set' in P.R.O.I.; see *Bks survey & dist., Roscommon* [etc.].

[2] For territorial changes between 1641 and 1688 see map 10.

it up well: 'the truth is the lands of Ireland have been a mere scramble and the least done by way of orderly distribution of them as perhaps hath ever been known'.[1]

Many catholics owed the recovery of their estates to Richard Talbot, who was well rewarded for his efforts on behalf of his co-religionists. A number of other catholics—lawyers and men of affairs—made good use of an unsettled market to acquire land. This 'new interest', as it was called, was later on to be significant. Influence was often the deciding factor in the recovery of land, and the official correspondence of the period has many references to pressure being exerted on behalf of individuals. The earl of Clancarty (the former Lord Muskerry, who was married to Ormond's sister) got an enormous estate in County Cork. Most of the Old English nobility recovered a good proportion of their former property. The Ulster Gaels—who had mostly supported the nuncio—fared badly, though Lord Antrim was a notable exception. In Leinster and Munster catholics, who had held two-thirds of the land before Cromwell, were now reduced to about one-fifth. In Connacht, where catholics had held over four-fifths of the land in 1641, they still held about half. They were particularly strong in County Galway, where the earl of Clanricard had a great estate and the merchants of Galway town were landowners on a large scale. Though catholics were the weaker side, they had a strong enough nucleus of great proprietors to enable them to take advantage of the political situation created by the accession of James II.

Catholics felt that they had got the worse of the bargain and they refused to accept the settlement as final. Their point of view was vigorously expressed in *A narrative of the settlement and sale of Ireland* (1668), written by a catholic bishop in the character of a protestant gentleman.[2] He made Clarendon the villain of the piece, but also criticised Ormond; the acts of settlement and explanation were condemned as repugnant to the laws of God and nature, sound policy, and reasons of state. He returned to the attack in *The bleeding Iphigeneia* (1675) and *The unkinde desertor of loyall men and true frinds* (1676), the deserter being Ormond. The poet Ó Bruadair attacked the settlement in a poem entitled 'The sum of the purgatory of the men of Ireland'. He deplored the ill-breeding of the Cromwellians—'roughs formed from the dregs of each base trade, [who] range themselves snugly in the homesteads of the noblest chiefs . . . as if sons of gentlemen'.[3]

Protestants regarded the settlement as unduly favourable to those whom they continued to regard as conquered rebels. Petty refers to 'some furious spirits' who would like the Irish to rebel again 'that they might be put to the sword'. His own view was that protestants had got the better of the bargain:

[1] *Essex papers*, ed. Osmund Airy, i (London, 1890), p. 201.

[2] Published under a Louvain imprint, and attributed to Nicholas French, bishop of Ferns.

[3] Ó Bruadair, *Poems*, iii, 15.

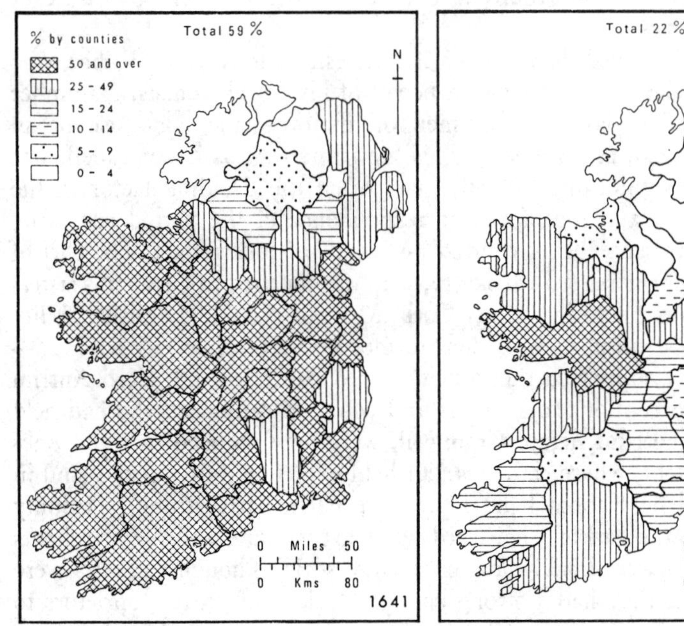

Map 10 LAND OWNED BY CATHOLICS IN 1641 AND 1688,
by J. G. Simms

'upon the playing of this game or match . . . the English won and have . . . a gamester's right at least to their estates'.[1]

Catholic hopes for religious toleration were to be disappointed. In the peace of 1649 Ormond had agreed that the next parliament should free them from all penalties that hindered the practice of their religion. But there was no prospect of such legislation getting through the restoration parliament. On the contrary, in November 1661 the commons asked for a bill for the suppression of the catholic hierarchy, though the government blocked the proposal. It was unfortunate for the catholic church that the primate, Edmund O'Reilly, had supported the nuncio against Ormond. O'Reilly, who had returned to Ireland in the autumn of 1659, was the subject of bitter attack and it was thought advisable to recall him to Rome in 1660. Peter Walsh, the Franciscan who had taken Ormond's side, had great hopes of getting support, both lay and clerical, for a 'loyal formulary or Irish remonstrance', which would make it clear that the attachment of catholics to their faith did not detract from their loyalty to the king. The remonstrance was signed by a number of the catholic laity and by a few of the clergy, but the attempt to get it generally accepted by the church led to a prolonged controversy in which Walsh was opposed both by the majority of the Irish clergy and by the Vatican. Ormond welcomed the remonstrance as a means of distinguishing between loyal and disloyal catholics, and he strongly encouraged Walsh in his efforts to collect signatures from the clergy. The formulary represented an attempt to show that the loyalty of catholics in temporal matters was in no way qualified by their spiritual allegiance to Rome, 'notwithstanding any power or pretension of the pope . . . or of any authority, spiritual or temporal, proceeding or derived from him or his see against your majesty'. The pope's power to absolve catholics from the king's authority was disclaimed; kings of whatever religion were declared to be God's lieutenants on earth and the doctrine that any private subject might kill his prince was abhorred. These terms were condemned by Rome and opposed by many of the Irish clergy. But Walsh continued his efforts to get them accepted and persuaded Ormond to summon the catholic clergy to a meeting in Dublin and to allow O'Reilly to return and take part in the proceedings.

The meeting, which was attended by about a hundred of the clergy, took place in June 1666, when the remonstrance was openly debated. The opposition was too strong for Walsh, and his formulary was rejected. What was more remarkable was that the assembled clergy agreed to an alternative, proposed by O'Reilly himself, which gave the substance of Walsh's demands in more guarded language. They disclaimed the doctrine that subjects could be absolved from allegiance to their prince, as well as any notion that a

[1] Petty, *Econ. writings*, i, 154.

subject might kill 'the anointed of God, his prince'. They subscribed to the first three of the Sorbonne propositions—drawn up in 1663 by the Gallican church—as modified to suit subjects of Charles II. They declared that the pope had no authority in temporal matters over the king, and that no power on earth could dispense subjects from their duty of obedience. Short of adopting a form of words that had been specifically condemned by Rome, the Irish clergy were evidently eager to meet protestant objections and to come to terms with the government. But this was not enough for Walsh, who wanted the whole formulary and nothing but the formulary. On his advice the alternative was rejected by Ormond, who seems to have preferred a clear-cut division between remonstrants and anti-remonstrants rather than a compromise acceptable to O'Reilly. Negotiations were broken off, the primate was deported, and there was some harrying of anti-remonstrants.[1]

At Rome the proceedings were looked on with a disfavour that was natural. The Vatican had not wished O'Reilly to return to Ireland for the meeting nor for any of the bishops to attend it. The document signed by O'Reilly and the others 'caused indescribable sorrow at Rome, because it contains atrocious errors which are contrary to the truth of catholic teaching . . . fortunately by the infinite mercy of God the duke of Ormond refused to accept it'.[2] To impress on the Irish clergy the gravity of their error a special envoy was sent to Ireland, a Franciscan named James Taaffe, who was so imprudent as to forge a document purporting to show that he had been appointed apostolic visitor and commissary of the Irish church. His deceit was detected and he was recalled. The episode was highly unfortunate, but seems to have aroused the authorities at Rome to the necessity of providing Ireland with an adequate hierarchy.

Ormond's recall and the replacement of Clarendon by the cabal led to a period of increased toleration for the catholic church, marked by cooperation between the government and the hierarchy. The Vatican, which had appointed no bishops since the restoration, made a number of fresh appointments in 1669, and the views of Charles II and his ministers were taken into account in making the selection. Peter Talbot's nomination to the archbishopric of Dublin was influenced by the fact that he was *persona grata* to the court, as well as being Richard's brother. O'Reilly had died and Oliver Plunkett, a Meathman of a well-known Old English family, was appointed to Armagh instead of the Gaelic Ulsterman whom most of the clergy of the province would have preferred. Plunkett was a zealous and devoted prelate, but autocratic and unbending. He met with opposition from his own clergy, and his decision in a controversy between Dominicans and Franciscans was not acceptable to the latter.

[1] Peter Walsh, *History and vindication of the loyal formulary or Irish remonstrance* (1674).

[2] Cathaldus Giblin (ed.), 'Catalogue of material of Irish interest in the collection *Nunziatura di Fiandra*, Vatican archives: part 8, vols 137A–147C' in *Collect. Hib.*, xii (1969), p. 82.

Several of the bishops appointed at this time were men of outstanding ability. John O'Molony, who became bishop of Killaloe in 1672, was regarded by the government as its most formidable opponent. Essex considered him as 'the most dangerous (because the wisest) of all'. John Brenan, who became bishop of Waterford in 1671 and archbishop of Cashel in 1677, was an able and courageous administrator who remained at his post in bad times and good until his death in 1693. His reports to the Vatican are a valuable source for the problems and opportunities of the catholic church at this period.[1] An attractive figure was Luke Wadding (to be distinguished from his celebrated Franciscan namesake), who was nominated coadjutor bishop of Ferns in 1672 and succeeded to the bishopric in 1683. Wadding expressed the teaching of the church in simple verses which, collected under the title of 'A small garland', became a catholic classic of the penal days.

In the middle of the reign there were said to be 1,000 seculars and 600 regulars in the country. During Berkeley's short period of office they came out into the open in a way that stirred up protestant hostility. Plunkett regarded Berkeley as a man of great moderation and equity, and even discerned in him 'some spark of religion'. Berkeley for his part appreciated Plunkett's zeal in rounding up Ulster 'tories'. The political climate was sufficiently favourable to allow a general synod of the Irish bishops to be held in Dublin in 1670. This was marked by a rancorous dispute between Talbot and Plunkett about the relative precedence of Dublin and Armagh—one of a series of internal disputes that proved a greater disturbance in the life of the church than were its relations with successive viceroys.

Some of these disputes arose from the deterioration of church order that had set in during the commonwealth and the first years of the restoration. Central control had been minimal and local factions had developed which resented the discipline that the new arrivals from the Continent sought to impose upon them. There were disputes in many dioceses—between individuals, between regulars and seculars, between Gaels and Old English—and the Vatican was bombarded with charges and counter-charges.

Much use was made of diocesan synods to bring uniformity into pastoral work and to remedy abuses. A pressing problem was the training of priests, many of whom had little education. Archbishop Plunkett tried to find a solution by setting up Jesuit schools in Drogheda, but they were forcibly closed at the end of 1673. Bishop Brenan complained of the difficulty of maintaining schools under the threat of legal penalties and without skilled teachers. A school of philosophy, conducted by the dean of Clonfert, who had been trained in Spain, had an exceptional power of survival. In the main the church depended for its higher education on the continental colleges, and the result was a cultural division between a trained élite and an ill-educated body of lower clergy.

[1] See Patrick Power, *A bishop of the penal times* (Cork, 1932).

Berkeley's administration coincided with the pro-French policy associated with the treaty of Dover, and it aroused similar hostility in the English parliament. In 1671 both houses presented an address to the king, in which they referred to the 'great insolencies of the papists in Ireland'. Charles was asked to expel priests in general and to order the arrest of Plunkett and Talbot. Nothing came of this, but a subsequent address in 1673 resulted in a proclamation expelling bishops and regulars. It was only partially effective. Talbot and a number of regulars left the country, but Plunkett and most of the other bishops went into hiding, under conditions of extreme hardship, and after the initial hue and cry were able to resume their ministry. In 1675 Bishop Brenan reported from Waterford diocese that the persecution was very moderate, that bishops could tour inconspicuously, and that priests were performing their parochial duties. Two years later he reported even more optimistically.

The catholic church ran into much more serious trouble when the 'popish plot' agitation began in England in 1678. Peter Talbot who had returned, a very sick man, was alleged to be concerned in a plot to assassinate Ormond. He was arrested and lodged in Dublin castle, where he died not long afterwards. Evidence of a conspiracy in Ireland was slow to appear, and Ormond maintained that there was no cause for alarm. This did not suit the needs of English politicians: a popish plot that left out Ireland lacked credibility. Shaftesbury was determined to have an Irish plot and took active steps to find witnesses in Ireland. He had a useful ally in Orrery who was assiduous in looking for plots and came up with a story of an impending French invasion of Ireland. Statements were taken from sea-captains and a shipload of arms was said to be on the way to enable Irish catholics to collaborate with the invaders. The ship's cargo turned out to be salt and other allegations proved no more substantial.

There does not in fact seem to have been any French design on Ireland at the time. However, sufficient witnesses were available to convince a large body of opinion that there really was an 'Irish plot'. A lengthy inquiry was held by the English house of lords into accusations made against Richard Power, earl of Tyrone, and a number of other prominent Irishmen to the effect that they had accepted commissions from the French king with a view to collaborating when the invasion should occur. After hearing a number of witnesses the house of lords passed a resolution in January 1681 that there was a 'horrid and treasonable plot and conspiracy contrived and carried on by those of the papist religion in Ireland for massacring the English and subverting the protestant religion'. The English commons agreed to the resolution, adding that 'the duke of York's being a papist and the expectation of his coming to the crown hath given the greatest countenance and encouragement thereto'. The commons resolved to impeach Tyrone of high treason and pressed the lords to commit him to safe custody.

That parliament came to an end before the impeachment was further pursued, but Tyrone was held a prisoner for over three years before being released on bail. Another of those accused was Sir John Fitzgerald of County Limerick, the patron of the poet Ó Bruadair. He was summoned to England, fortified by a poem which declared that when the king saw the noble countenance of Sir John he would refuse to believe him capable of treason. The poet's optimism was justified when the grand jury at Westminster returned a verdict of *ignoramus* and the case against Fitzgerald was dropped. One of those alleged to be implicated in the plot was Bishop O'Molony, whose French contacts made him a particular object of suspicion. He had been educated in Paris, and before his elevation to the episcopate had been a canon of Rouen. A reward of £150 was offered for his apprehension, but he managed to escape to France and remained there until the hue and cry died down.

The most notable victim of Shaftesbury's activities was Oliver Plunkett, who was accused, on the evidence of dissident priests, of abetting a scheme for a French landing in Carlingford Lough. Ormond did what he could for him and allowed the trial to be held in Dundalk, in Armagh diocese, where a protestant jury threw out the case. But orders followed that he should be tried again in London where, at the second attempt, he was found guilty of treason. It is generally accepted that he was the victim of political intrigue and that his trial was a travesty of justice. With his execution in 1681[1] the troubles of the catholic church in Ireland had reached their height. In the remaining years of the reign Charles was his own master and life was easier for Irish catholics. Mass-houses reopened and in many places the religious orders reappeared. Repression had not altogether ceased, but there was general toleration for the unobtrusive practice of catholicism.

Twelve years of war, followed by the commonwealth regime, had left the Church of Ireland in a sorry state, with churches in ruins, clergy and congregations scattered. With the restoration of the monarchy, bishops and clergy returned and the slow process of reconstruction began. Eight bishops had outlasted the commonwealth and twelve more were consecrated at the beginning of 1661. The church was fortunate in the first primate of the restoration. John Bramhall was a man of considerable intellectual and administrative ability who had, as bishop of Derry, been Wentworth's right-hand man in church affairs. In his short reign at Armagh—from 1661 to his death in 1663—he did much to provide new foundations for the church. James Margetson, his successor and also one of Wentworth's men, was less forceful, but much admired for piety and charity. He rebuilt Armagh cathedral, which had been burned by Sir Phelim O'Neill in 1642.

The primate presided over the convocation, which sat from 1661 to 1666, contemporaneously with the parliament. In addition to regulating the affairs

[1] Oliver Plunkett was canonised on 12 Oct. 1975.

of the church, convocation provided the clergy with an opportunity to tax themselves. The subsidies to be paid by the prelates and clergy were not included in those levied on the temporality, but were the subject of a separate act (1662) which embodied the decision taken by convocation. This was the last occasion on which this procedure was followed. The archbishops and bishops made a joint protest against a proposal to include the clergy in a levy to raise £30,000 for Ormond's benefit. They claimed that it was the inalienable right of the church to be taxed only by itself in convocation. After a lengthy argument it was decided to exempt the tithes and glebes of the lower clergy from the levy on the ground of 'their present poverty through the distractions and unsettlement of these late times'. The principle that the clergy had the exclusive right to tax themselves was not conceded. The bishops, who had to pay the levy, yielded, but they demanded that the case should not be treated as a precedent.

Patronage and family influence weighed heavily in the selection of bishops, but a number of them (such as Ezekiel Hopkins of Derry and Narcissus Marsh of Ferns) were men of some intellectual capacity, who compared favourably with their eighteenth-century successors. Ormond prided himself on the care he took over church patronage, and claimed that he had had no reason to repent of any of his recommendations. His practice was not to make any proposal until he had consulted the archbishop of Canterbury. It was Berkeley who recommended Thomas Hackett for the bishopric of Down. He turned out to be the most notorious of the Church of Ireland bishops, a constant absentee who bore an unsavoury reputation and was finally deprived. The most distinguished of the new bishops was Jeremy Taylor, whose *Holy living* and *Holy dying* had gained a high reputation. He had taken shelter in the north of Ireland towards the end of the commonwealth regime, and at the restoration he became bishop of Down and Connor, where he found himself in constant conflict with the presbyterians.

The dilemma of the church was that its claims to be the church of the country were at variance with the predominance of presbyterians in many parts of the north and of catholics in most of the rest of Ireland. Dublin and such towns as Cork and Limerick provided the chief congregations. In Dublin both cathedrals were restored after the years of war and puritanism. St Patrick's was re-roofed and provided with a new altar, resplendent in paint and gilt. Christ Church repaired its choir and installed a four-faced chiming clock. Both cathedrals got new sets of bells. Over much of the country churches were few and dilapidated. There was a certain amount of rebuilding during the reign, but the most evident result of the alliance between church and state was in the revenues of church dignitaries. The restoration land-settlement was favourable to the church and in particular to the bishops. By 1668 the archbishopric of Armagh was worth more than £3,500 a year and the see of Derry £1,800. Several other bishops had incomes of £1,000 and upwards. Impropriation of tithes (alienation to laymen) left little for the lower clergy. In country parishes absenteeism and pluralism were the general rule. An act of 1666 attempted to prevent cross-channel pluralism by prohibiting the holding of benefices in both England and Ireland. Even in the diocese of Derry, where conditions were comparatively favourable, the bishop reported in 1670 that the churches were in ruins and the congregations too poor to repair them; worship was often conducted 'either in a dirty cabin or in a common alehouse'.[1] Derry was a particularly troublesome diocese on account of the large number of militant presbyterians that lived within its boundaries. Ormond referred to it as a see 'where a bishop is more necessary than he will be welcome, and though it be one of the best bishoprics in the kingdom yet most of our clergy here had rather have a worse with more quiet than that with the trouble that will attend it'.[2]

The least satisfactory province of the Church of Ireland was Tuam, where protestants were fewest and lay impropriations had reduced the income to a miserable fraction of its original value. William King, the future archbishop of Dublin, started his clerical career in Tuam and has given a depressing account of the situation. He became domestic chaplain to Parker, the archbishop, who bestowed on him seven parishes, a large stretch of wild Connemara country with a total income of less than £60. However, he shared in the good things of the archiepiscopal table—'sixteen dishes for dinner and twelve for supper, with a very large variety of wines and a profusion of other generous liquors'.[3]

There was little in the way of missionary effort, though sporadic publications drew attention to the shortcomings of rival beliefs. Jeremy Taylor wrote a *Dissuasive from popery, to the people of Ireland*, in which he accused priests of preserving the Irish language so that the people should have no opportunity of benefiting from English-speaking instructors. Some polemical writing came from Andrew Sall, an ex-Jesuit who had been head of the Irish College in Salamanca; he entered the Church of Ireland in 1674 and became prebendary of Cashel. A revision of Bedell's Irish bible was sponsored by Robert Boyle, but as there was no Gaelic type in Ireland it had to be printed in London.

At first the establishment relied on the Elizabethan act of uniformity in proceeding against nonconformists. But the bishops' powers were strengthened by the act of uniformity of 1666, modelled on the English act of 1662, which prescribed a revised Book of Common Prayer and declared that episcopal ordination was a *sine qua non* for clergy. The act laid down that all persons in holy orders and also schoolmasters and private tutors should declare that they were under 'no obligation from the oath commonly called

[1] Richard Mant, *History of the Church of Ireland* (London, 1840), i, 667.

[2] *Cal. S.P. Ire., 1666–9*, p. 1.

[3] C. S. King, *A great archbishop* (London, 1906), p. 14.

the solemn league and covenant to endeavour any change or alteration of government'.

There was a provision in the act of uniformity requiring schoolmasters to be licensed by the bishop, but this merely strengthened the control of education that was already exercised by the bishops, as for example in the schools of the Ulster plantation where the right to nominate teachers rested in the bishop and the school lands were vested in the archbishop of Armagh as trustee. An example of episcopal interference in school affairs is to be found in the acrimonious correspondence between the bishop of Derry and the parishioners of Lifford, County Donegal, who had selected a Scottish schoolmaster in 1664.[1]

An important contribution to education during this period was made by Erasmus Smith, a successful speculator in land-debentures, who had acquired a large estate during the commonwealth regime. Whether—as has been suggested—he wished to bolster up a weak title by public benefaction or for some other reason, he had entered into an undertaking in 1657 to found schools so that 'the poor children inhabiting any part of his lands in Ireland should be brought up in the fear of God and good literature and to speak the English tongue'. The lands earmarked for the purpose were confirmed to him by the act of explanation, and in 1669 a royal charter was given for a corporation (which included the archbishops of Armagh and Dublin and the provost of Trinity College) to be known as 'Governors of the schools founded by Erasmus Smith Esq.' with power to establish free grammar schools in Drogheda, Galway, and Tipperary, in each of which twenty poor children in addition to the children of Smith's tenants were to be placed under a schoolmaster and usher who were to teach writing and accounting, the Latin, Greek, and Hebrew tongues, and to fit the scholars for the university if required. The first headmaster of the Galway school, Elisha Coles, was a man of some distinction, who has earned a place in the *Dictionary of national biography* as a 'lexicographer and stenographer'. He did not long survive the rigours of Galway, but under his successors the school appears to have flourished.

The best known of the Irish schools at this period was Kilkenny College, which was given a new lease of life about 1667 by Ormond who provided a building and the salaries of the master and usher. Swift, who was at the school between the ages of six and fourteen, was to be the most distinguished of the pupils of the time. Congreve entered the school shortly before Swift left. In Swift's recollection his schooling was arduous and tough: he remembered 'the confinement ten hours a day to nouns and verbs, the terror of the rod, the bloody noses and broken shins'; but there were compensations in 'the delicious holidays, the Saturday afternoon, and the charming custards

[1] T. W. Moody and J. G. Simms (ed.), *The bishopric of Derry and the Irish Society of London*, i Dublin, 1968), pp 380 ff.

in a blind alley'.[1] He had two able masters in Jones and Ryder, both of whom were Cambridge men and were subsequently rewarded with bishoprics. Another foundation of note was the King's Hospital, Dublin—the Blue-coat School—which received its charter in 1671.

At the restoration most of the protestant ministers were presbyterians or independents, and those who refused to accept the Book of Common Prayer were ejected by the bishops. In Ulster alone over sixty ministers were deprived. They formed the strongest centre of opposition to the established church, but there were also non-conforming ministers and congregations in Dublin and other parts of Ireland. In his statistical account of Ireland in 1672 Petty put the number of protestants at 300,000, of which 100,000 were Scots presbyterians. Of the remainder he estimated that rather more than half belonged to the established church, which would leave a large number of non-conforming protestants outside Ulster.

The close links between Scotland and Ulster were alarming to the establishment, and the friction between Scottish bishops and covenanters had its immediate reactions in the north of Ireland. The Scottish turmoil in the latter part of Charles II's reign led to a marked increase in the number of Scots settling in Ulster, and at the close of the reign Petty's estimate must have been much exceeded. The treatment of presbyterian ministers varied with the political climate. Some of them were implicated in Blood's plot (1663) and a number were arrested. From time to time there were other outbreaks of unrest in the north, leading to further arrests, notably after the Scottish troubles of 1679. In its dealings with the Ulster Scots the government's 'trouble-shooter' was Sir Arthur Forbes, who became marshal of the army in 1670 and was later made earl of Granard. He was a Scot with estates in Longford and elsewhere and had supported the royalist cause in Scotland under Montrose. He understood the Ulster Scots and was respected by them. On a number of occasions he was sent north to deal with impending trouble, and the comparative peace of Ulster at a time when Scotland was in an uproar was largely due to him. In 1672 he was the intermediary in the grant of the *regium donum* of £600 per annum to presbyterian ministers. The grant corresponded to that offered to, but scornfully declined by, Scottish ministers in 1669. In Ulster it was accepted as a gesture of goodwill. There is some doubt as to the regularity of the payment, but it served as a precedent for later payments on an increased scale.

It is hard to say how much protestant dissent there was outside Ulster. Some of the commonwealth ministers conformed, but there continued to be independent and presbyterian meeting-houses in Dublin and elsewhere. Samuel Mather, who had been a commonwealth fellow of Trinity College, had a congregation at New Street, Dublin. Dr Daniel Williams had twenty years of ministry in Drogheda and Dublin before he made his name in

[1] Swift, *Corr.*, i, 105.

Edinburgh and London. The Ulster presbyterians sent help to their brethren in places as far afield as Wexford and Roscommon. When Ormond took up his second viceroyalty he noted the great increase in the dissenting congregations of Dublin. 'Fanatics' were looked on with great suspicion, particularly after the Rye House plot of 1683. We hear of conventicles being suppressed in Cork, Limerick, and other places.

Quakers were an important addition to the religious spectrum. Their teaching was introduced into Ireland by William Edmundson, who had been a commonwealth soldier, and spread rapidly among the new settlers. George Fox spent some months in Ireland in 1669, contending with catholics and organising meetings. Dublin, Cork, and Waterford were thriving centres of quakerism and many of the community prospered as traders. But they were also to be found in the countryside, notably in Mountmellick, to which Edmundson moved with the deliberate intention of challenging the tithe claims of the established clergy. William Penn, whose father had estates in County Cork, was a conspicuous convert, and his influence was to be of use to Irish quakers in the following reign. Most of the troubles endured by quakers came from refusal to pay tithes, but we also hear of a number being punished for interruptions in 'steeple-houses'—the churches of the establishment. A more unusual 'suffering' was that of Solomon Eccles who was arrested in Galway after he had entered a catholic chapel, stripped to the waist, carrying a dish of burning brimstone and denouncing the congregation as idolaters.

Even before the revocation of the edict of Nantes in 1685 huguenots had begun to come to Ireland. Most of those who came in Charles II's reign, encouraged by an act for the settlement of protestant strangers (1662), settled in Dublin, though there were also some in Cork. In Dublin they were given permission for a French church in a chapel of St Patrick's cathedral, with their own minister and services conducted in a French version of the Book of Common Prayer. The records of the church show that there was a colony of several hundred in Dublin by the end of Charles II's reign.

The Irish budget had a political, as well as a monetary significance. Both Ormond and Essex were attacked for their financial policy. The king was always ready to listen to those who would promise an Irish surplus that might help to meet his financial needs and the demands of his favourites. The English commons was critical whether there was a deficit or a surplus. A deficit laid a burden on the English taxpayer, a surplus helped to free the king from parliamentary control. The management of Irish revenues was a political prize to be ruthlessly fought for.

The financial framework was laid in the parliamentary session of 1662, when the revenue provisions were enacted that were to be in force throughout the reign. To begin with, these provisions were inadequate to meet expenditure, but their yield grew with the expansion of the economy, and by the end of the reign there was a substantial annual surplus. But for many years after the restoration the administration was in trouble as a result of the failure of the revenue to come up to expectations, with the result that payments to the establishment fell heavily into arrears. There was severe criticism of the way in which the finances were handled by Lord Anglesey, who was vice-treasurer up to 1667, and subsequently by Lord Ranelagh, whose 'undertaking' to meet the expenses of government provided a major scandal.

The new structure of Irish finances followed closely that adopted by the cavalier parliament in England. In both countries the court of wards and feudal land-tenures were abolished, and in their place an internal excise revenue was granted in perpetuity to the king and his successors. The main differences in the two taxation systems was that in Ireland the customs and external excise were granted in perpetuity and not merely for the king's life, and that quit-rents on estates affected by the land-settlement provided an additional source of revenue. The English government attempted to maintain a strict control of Irish finances; it approved tax-farm contracts and scrutinised the accounts. Within Whitehall there was a contest between the secretary of state and the treasury as to which should have the control. From the middle of the reign the treasury established its right. Most of the tax-bills were framed by the Irish and English privy councils without preliminary discussion in the commons. But the hearth-tax of 1662 took its rise in the commons where 'heads of a bill'—a device designed to mitigate the effects of Poynings' law—were drawn up and presented to the lord lieutenant for further action. This was a foretaste of the claim later advanced by the commons to have the 'sole right' of initiating money-bills. However, in this case an independent line was not adopted: 'the late precedent in England was worthy the imitation of his house', and the Irish act, which granted the tax in perpetuity, was the counterpart of an act passed earlier that year in England. In both countries the rate was two shillings per hearth, and there were broad provisions for exemption. The proceeds in Ireland were disappointing, and an amending act of 1666 limited exemptions to widows and prescribed that each house without a chimney should be charged for two hearths. It was said that this would bring the people 'to the decorum of the English', but that 'some rather pay double than by having a chimney to lose the benefit of so much good smoke'.[1] A contemporary versifier satirised the Irishman who was so fond of smoke that he would not have a chimney:

And thus for smoke, although 'twas dear,
He paid four shillings every year.[2]

[1] E. P. Shirley, 'Extracts from the journal of Thomas Dineley' in *R.S.A.I. Jn.*, iv (1856), p. 181. Dineley's MS is N.L.I., MS 392.

[2] Quoted in MacLysaght, *Ir. life after Cromwell* (1950), p. 104.

The tax returns provided Petty and others with a convenient, but inexact, basis for population statistics.

During the first half of the reign the unsettled state of land-ownership, the Dutch wars, and English commercial policy had an adverse effect on the revenue. The collection of revenue from excise and hearth tax was 'farmed' or leased to contractors for lump sums. The first farms came to £124,000 which, with quit-rents and miscellaneous income, was inadequate to meet the civil and military establishment of approximately £180,000. Even this revenue was not received in full as rebates had to be made to the tax-farmers on account of wars and trade restrictions. To make up the deficiency of the regular taxes the Irish parliament voted a number of subsidies. These expired in 1670, and as parliament did not meet after 1666 no further taxation was voted. Proposals made by Essex and Ormond to call another parliament proved abortive. However, the improvement of trade in the latter part of the reign resulted in a buoyancy of revenue that more than made up for the absence of subsidies. By 1683 the figures for customs, for excise, and for hearth-tax were more than double the corresponding figures for 1665—an indication of the remarkable expansion of the Irish economy during the reign.[1]

Even with the subsidies, Ormond's first administration was constantly in financial trouble and required substantial aid from England. In 1662 £100,000 was sent over, and £60,000 in 1663. Smaller sums, including amounts to strengthen the defences against the Dutch, were received in later years. Even so, the pay of the army was badly in arrears. In 1670 the backlog was £142,000, representing twelve months' arrears for a large part of the force. The military list accounted for the greater part of the establishment. In 1666 the respective civil and military charges were £25,601 and £163,810. At this date the army consisted of thirty troops of horse and sixty companies of foot, making a total of over 5,000 men. The regimental system, adopted by the newly established standing army in England, was not fully adopted in Ireland till later in the reign. At the end of 1684 there were three regiments of horse and seven of foot. The standing army had long been part of the establishment in Ireland and in the early part of the reign its numbers were greater than those of the embryo force established in England at the restoration. Its primary object was internal security, to prevent trouble from Gaelic Irish, Ulster Scots, or sectarian 'fanatics'. But it might also be needed to prevent invasion by a continental army. At times of crisis contingents were sent to serve in England (still on the Irish payroll); in 1672 eight companies were ordered to serve with the fleet. When Tangier was besieged by the Moors in 1679 troops were sent from Ireland to relieve the garrison, and subsequently the Tangier establishment was made a charge on the Irish revenue—an annual expenditure of over £40,000. Fortunately for the Irish

[1] See the figures in *Eng. hist. docs, 1660–1714*, viii, 744–5.

taxpayer Tangier was abandoned in 1684, but in that year the sum of £30,000 per annum was ordered to be paid from Irish revenues for the upkeep of the army in England, and this was continued by James II. It has been pointed out that the army in Ireland was treated as a local organisation of the land forces of the crown and did not constitute a specifically Irish army.[1]

The army in Ireland was, with rare and short-lived exceptions, an all-protestant force. Before Ormond assumed the vice-royalty in 1662 he was commissioned to raise a regiment of foot-guards in England for the Irish establishment. Towards the end of the reign protestant dissenters were excluded and all ranks were required to take the sacrament according to the Book of Common Prayer. However, catholics had some opportunity of military service abroad. There was an Irish regiment at Tangier in which several of the officers appear to have been catholics. In 1671 George Hamilton, a catholic nephew of Ormond, was authorised to raise a regiment of 1,500 catholics for service under the king of France. This force, which was in the French service until 1678, gave military experience to Patrick Sarsfield and a number of others who were to take a prominent part in the war between James II and William III. On its return from France the regiment was for a short time put on the Irish establishment under the command of Justin MacCarthy, another of Ormond's catholic nephews. But the popish plot crisis made this a short-lived experiment. Other Irishmen got military experience in the Spanish forces serving in the Low Countries, where there was an Irish regiment throughout Charles II's reign; many of its officers are mentioned in the Brussels archives.[2]

Apart from the regular army there was a protestant militia, which in 1672 consisted of 10,000 horse and 14,000 foot. A major item of military expenditure during the reign was the building of a large modern fort—Charles Fort—on the shore of Kinsale harbour. The security of Irish ports was a source of anxiety. Surveys were made by military engineers who recommended extensive protective works in Dublin, Limerick, and elsewhere, but these were never carried out.

The unsatisfactory state of Irish finances was made the ground of an attack on Ormond and on Anglesey, the vice-treasurer. A commission, which included Buckingham and other prominent English politicians, examined as much of the accounts as they could find, and commented severely on the state of both accounts and finances. In 1669 the whole revenue was farmed to a London syndicate at a rate that was eventually to rise to £204,500 a year. This should have yielded a modest surplus, but a more attractive proposition was advanced by Lord Ranelagh, a plausible rogue who was Orrery's nephew. He offered to manage the finances in such

[1] G. J. Hand, 'The constitutional position of the Irish military establishment from the restoration to the union' in *Ir. Jurist*, iii (1968), pp 330–35.

[2] *Wild geese in Spanish Flanders.*

a way as to pay off the debts, meet current expenditure, and provide a substantial sum for the king. In 1671 Charles entered into an extraordinary agreement with Ranelagh, by which he resigned all right to his own exchequer for five years and left the entire disposal of the revenue to Ranelagh and his partners. The tax-farmers were to transfer their remittances to Ranelagh, whose 'undertaking' was to be responsible for all government expenditure. The contract provided that Ranelagh should pay the king £80,000 within two years of the expiry of its term. But by an unpublished addition to the agreement it was arranged that Ranelagh should make secret payments of £10,000 a year to Charles's privy purse in return for a promise that he should not suffer for any failure to meet his obligations. The principal beneficiary of this arrangement was the reigning mistress, the duchess of Portsmouth, who in return gave whole-hearted support to Ranelagh.

The undertaking was hopelessly mismanaged. There were constant complaints from Essex, who found Ranelagh 'very backward and shuffling in all his payments', and was particularly concerned that the army was not being paid. Permission had to be given for outside employment 'so as the soldiers by their work can help themselves to bread'. At the end of the contract period Ranelagh was far short of meeting his obligations, but a prolonged wrangle over his accounts ended in the king remitting the balance due from Ranelagh himself, though his partners were forced to pay up most of their liabilities.[1] Ranelagh in return conducted an intrigue that resulted in the removal of Essex, though he did not succeed in getting his friend Lord Conway appointed deputy, with the duke of Monmouth as a figure-head lord lieutenant. The Irish government resumed control of its own expenditure, and a new revenue farm was made for £240,000, which in 1678 was increased to £300,000. The farm provided for the annual payment of £20,000 (increased to £27,000) to the king, part of which was used for rebuilding Windsor castle.

Courtiers were constantly on the watch for what they could pick up in Ireland. Pensions on the Irish establishment were paid to Buckingham, Rochester, Sunderland, and others. Nell Gwyn had expectations (unfulfilled) from the Irish land-settlement. Essex succeeded with difficulty in blocking a gift of the Phoenix Park to another royal mistress, the duchess of Cleveland. He also frustrated an attempt on the part of her rival, the duchess of Portsmouth, to get £4,000 to buy jewellery. But the Irish estimates for 1676 contained an item of £7,600 to enable her to redeem jewels that she had pawned. Essex compared the treatment of Ireland to 'nothing better than the flinging the reward, upon the death of a deer, among a pack of hounds where everyone pulls and tears what he can for himself'.[2]

[1] Maurice Twomey, 'Charles II, Lord Ranelagh and the Irish finances' in *I.C.H.S. Bull.*, no. 89 (1960), pp 1–2.

[2] Arthur Capel, earl of Essex, *Letters written in the year 1675* (Dublin, 1773), p. 334.

There were several reasons for the expansion of the economy during the reign. It was a period of unusual peace; the natural increase of the population was added to by immigration from England and Scotland and, on a much smaller scale, from the Continent; once their titles appeared secure the new landowners set about exploiting their acquisitions; labour was cheap and plentiful, prices were sensationally low; the new trading communities in the seaport towns were energetic in promoting business. By the end of the reign there was a brisk overseas trade, shared not only by Dublin and Cork but by a number of other ports.

The chief source of Ireland's wealth was in her livestock, cattle, and sheep. The way in which this source could be exploited was to a great extent dependent on the limitations imposed by English laws. During the early years of the reign there was an active trade in exporting live cattle to England —mostly young grass-fed bullocks, which were fattened in England. The trade was objected to by English cattle-breeders who campaigned against exports from Ireland. The first restriction, that of 1663, barred such imports from 1 July to 20 December, the period in which grass-fed cattle were in good condition. It was to remain in force until the end of the first session of the next parliament, but before that another act, passed in 1667, prohibited all imports of cattle, sheep, swine, beef, pork, and bacon. This prohibition, combined with the effect of the Dutch wars, reacted severely on the Irish economy, and this was reflected in the customs returns. There was some smuggling, but it was not an adequate substitute for the regular cattle trade. However, with the return of peace the situation improved. Cattle-farmers were able to take advantage of a growing trade in salt beef and butter, which were in demand by shipowners and in continental markets. Soon there were complaints that the restriction on imports had done more harm than good to the English economy. English dealers found that they had lost the benefit of hides and tallow from Irish animals. The Irish export trade to foreign countries was believed to encourage a return trade in foreign imports.

The life of the act of 1667 was due to expire after the parliamentary session of 1679. In that session a bill for its renewal ran into opposition and had not been completed when the session ended. Imports of Irish cattle were quickly resumed and we hear of shipments to Liverpool and Holyhead. In the next parliament the ban was made permanent and extended to mutton, butter, and cheese (1681). But by this time the Irish provision trade to the colonies and the Continent was well established, and the act does not seem to have seriously affected the economy, to which butter exports in particular were of growing importance. A proclamation of 1685 referred to the great quantities of butter sent overseas, and made regulations to correct such abuses as packing in unseasoned barrels, which affected both the weight and the quality of the butter.

One consequence of the cattle acts was a shift to sheep-breeding. Landlords imported English stock, and the wool thus produced was reckoned as good as that of Northampton or Leicester. Export of Irish wool to foreign countries had long been prohibited. In 1662 an English act made such export a felony: English clothiers did not wish continental rivals to have the benefit of Irish wool. Exports of wool to England were under licence, and the fees were a valuable addition to the lord lieutenant's income. The cheapness of Irish wool created a demand for it in the English west country. It also encouraged a trade in friezes both in England and on the Continent, to which Irish cloth exports were permitted until the end of the century. The manufacture of friezes attracted immigrant weavers from England, many of whom settled in the Dublin liberties. Ormond tried to encourage the linen industry; he imported workers from the Continent and set up manufactures at Chapelizod and Carrick-on-Suir. In Ulster flax-spinning became a common domestic industry, though its economic importance was still of a minor order.

The English navigation acts had a variable influence on Irish trade. The first of the restoration acts (1660) treated England and Ireland as an economic unit, which excluded Scotland. English-built shipping was defined as including ships built in Ireland; vessels going to the plantations had to give a bond to bring back their return cargoes to England or Ireland. There was a change of policy in 1663 when exports to the plantations were confined to goods shipped in England, though an exception was made for provisions exported from Ireland and Scotland, a concession which was to be important for the Irish economy. It was apparently intended to confine direct shipments from the colonies to English ports, but as the 1660 act had not been repealed such shipments continued to be made to Ireland until 1671. Ireland was then specifically prevented from receiving direct shipments. The bill as passed by the commons would have prohibited the export of provisions from Ireland to the plantations, but the clause was rejected by the lords. The life of that act expired in January 1681, and direct shipments to Ireland from the plantations were then resumed on a large scale until the ban was renewed in 1685. The chief Irish import from the plantations was tobacco, for which there was a growing demand. Petty remarked that for the peasantry 'tobacco taken in short pipes . . . seems the pleasure of their lives, together with sneezing'.[1] During the years that direct imports were allowed Cork had the largest share of the trade, though considerable consignments also came to Dublin, Kinsale, Belfast, and Galway.

Irish trade with the plantations was facilitated by the number of Irish settled in the West Indies. Many of them had been indentured labourers, transported by the commonwealth regime. But there were also traders and planters. During the latter part of Charles II's reign the governor of the

[1] Petty, *Econ. writings*, i, 191.

Leeward Islands was William Stapleton, a Tipperaryman who is referred to as an 'Irish papist'. His two brothers were in turn governors of Montserrat, where the great majority of the white population was Irish. Stapleton's son-in-law, James Cotter, became deputy governor of Montserrat and later played a prominent part in Ireland under the Jacobite regime. Two brothers Blake who had settled in Trinidad and Montserrat were substantial traders who maintained links with Galway.

The best-known account of Ireland in the reign of Charles II was written by Petty in 1672 as a report commissioned by Whitehall; after his death it was published as *The political anatomy of Ireland.* Petty knew Ireland well—as map-maker, landowner, litigant, and industrialist; and he had a passion for statistics. He saw Ireland through the eyes of a colonist. According to him three-quarters of the natives lived in a 'nasty, brutish condition' in cabins that had neither chimney nor windows; their staple diet was milk and potatoes; however, their clothing, made from narrow strips of frieze, was far better than that of the French peasantry. Their economy, apart from tobacco, was self-sufficient, and they had little incentive to exert themselves. It would clearly be of advantage for them to be assimilated to English ways, adopt the English language, and 'qualify their houses so that English women may be content to be their wives'. He considered the poorer Irish to be completely under the power of their priests, whose influence was derived from family status, fluency in Latin, and alarming sermons. He thought, however, that there was little to be feared from the Irish masses, who had no cause to be grateful to their traditional masters and had benefited from the introduction of English standards.

A major problem, in Petty's opinion, was the conflict between the old and the new landowners. He realised that the former owners resented the loss of their lands and still hoped to get them back. Common suffering had united Gaels and Old English. The division between them was 'asleep now, because they have a common enemy'. But he thought that the protestants were too strong for their rivals. They had three-quarters of the land, control of the walled towns, and a monopoly of the civil and military organisation. He considered that there were good prospects for the development of the economy and that increasing prosperity would reconcile catholics and protestants. There were, in fact, indications that the gap between protestant and catholic was often bridged. Families were divided in religious allegiance. O'Briens, Fitzgeralds, and many others were to be found in both camps; mixed marriages were frequent. Protestants often employed catholic agents, and many landlords prided themselves on their treatment of catholic tenants, asserting that the rents they levied were less oppressive than the traditional demands of old-style Irish landlords. However, differences of language, religion, and custom were barriers between Irish tenants and the newly established landlords; the near-reverence that was given to the Gaelic aristocracy was not offered to less highly-bred newcomers.

Petty's air of confident optimism was shared by many of his contemporaries. The apparent stability that the land settlement had acquired after the passing of the act of explanation encouraged the new owners to build houses, plant trees, and develop their property. Little of what they built remains. Many of the houses were too modest for the even greater affluence of eighteenth-century landlords. The attractive red-brick of Beaulieu, County Louth, built by Sir Henry Tichborne about 1665, is an exceptional survival from the reign of Charles II. The most magnificent of the restoration houses was Charleville, County Cork, which Orrery built in 1667 and surrounded with gardens and a large park. It was burned by the Jacobites in 1690. Thomas Dineley, who travelled through Ireland in 1680 (getting as far west as Clare), wrote a detailed account of his journey, with attractive illustrations. He gives the impression of rapid development by energetic immigrants, mentioning tradesmen who had prospered and converted themselves into country gentlemen. One of his illustrations is of the fine house and gardens of Mount Ievers in County Clare; its owner had come to Ireland after the restoration as a lawyer's clerk and had secured a lucrative post in the quit-rent office. Dineley found clean market-towns and well-managed inns in many places—the product of English enterprise. He shared Petty's view of the poorer Irish: they had the concomitant qualities of 'nastiness and laziness'.[1]

Other accounts stress the fertility of the country, the remarkable cheapness of provisions, and the opportunity for leading the life of a gentleman on a much smaller income than would be needed in England: an ordinary farmer could keep a better house in Ireland than those of four or five hundred a year in England. Jouvin de Rochefort, a Frenchman who visited Ireland in 1668, found it a land of plenty, 'the richest of all Europe in things necessary for human life, but the poorest in money': butter, cheese, veal, and mutton were sold for a penny a pound, and for the price of two-pennyworth of beer you could eat your fill without further charge.[2]

A number of landowners were concerned to exploit the resources of their estates, notably by the establishment of iron-works, some of them using Irish ore and some of them ore imported from Britain or the Continent. The chief advantage that Ireland enjoyed was its timber, which ensured a supply of charcoal at a time when charcoal was getting scarce in England. One of the best-known of the restoration iron-works was that established by Petty in 1670 at Kenmare to exploit the local ore. The iron was of poor quality. Petty had difficulty in selling it and lamented his ill fortune: 'the iron-works in Kerry, invented in hell, which they much resemble, have

[1] Shirley, loc. cit., p. 180.
[2] Falkiner, *Illustrations*, p. 415.

wiped me cruelly, and the misery is I must go on'.[1] Petty brought over a colony of workers from England who remained until the revolution of 1688 made Kerry too hot for them. Another Kerry landowner, Sir Francis Brewster, had iron-works at Brewsterfield near Killarney.[2] The company established under the commonwealth to conduct the iron-works at Enniscorthy, County Wexford, brought over several hundred English workmen and their families. Their title was contested by the former owner, Dudley Colclough, who had obtained a decree of innocency. The company got a clause in its favour inserted in the act of explanation, but a few years later, when the local woods were exhausted, the works closed down.

Petty also exploited the fishing off the Kerry coast, introducing seine nets to catch pilchards in the Kenmare River. He refers in his *Political anatomy* to twenty gentlemen in the west of Ireland who engaged in pilchard fishing. Among them were his friend Sir Robert Southwell, who had a fishing at Kinsale, and Brewster, who fished in Dingle Bay. There was a ready market for pilchard and herring in France and Spain. In 1668 it was estimated that the Munster fisheries yielded £20,000, though it was feared that the income would drop unless French poachers were checked. In Ulster the chief fishing was that of the Irish Society on the Foyle and Bann. Salmon were salted and exported as far as Bilbao, Leghorn, and Venice. In 1684 1,885 barrels of salmon were sent from Derry to Spain.

Much information about the Irish countryside is to be found in the reports collected by William Molyneux, a gifted member of a distinguished Dublin family.[3] They were designed for use in the Irish section of Moses Pitt's *English atlas*, but the project was still-born. The contributors included Roderick O'Flaherty, whose 'chorographical description' of West Connacht is the most famous of them. O'Flaherty had a high reputation as an expert on the Irish past and was held in much esteem by the Molyneux family and other members of the intelligentsia, though he had fallen on evil days and had recovered only a fraction of his ancestral property in Connemara.

Molyneux's papers contain descriptions of a number of other areas by writers whose names suggest Gaelic or Old English as well as New English origin. Local patriotism may be detected in the glowing descriptions of fertile lands and fishy rivers, the houses and parks of the gentry, the cheerfulness and good-nature of the peasantry. The main complaint is that the few remaining woods are being destroyed by the 'devouring iron-works'. Sir Henry Piers in his report on Westmeath noted that 'the people are become more polite and civil and of their own accord are very ready to accommodate themselves in many things to English modes as particularly in their habit, language, names and surnames'. He remarked that 'all the youths of this age learn English in their Irish schools', and that English words were infiltrating

[1] Marquis of Lansdowne, *Glanerought and the Petty-Fitzmaurices* (London, 1937), p. 20.
[2] *Cal. S.P. dom., 1693*, pp 221–2.
[3] T.C.D., MSS 888–9.

into the Irish language. He regretted that the people clung so obstinately to their religion 'in all its gaiety and superstitious forms'. The report on Leitrim noted that it was well planted with protestants: the 'native or Irish inhabitants' were 'civil, hospitable and ingenious, very fond of their ancient chronicles and pedigrees and as much abhorring theft; they are great lovers of music and fond of news'. The Kerry report described the people as addicted to 'gaming, speaking of Latin, and inclined to philosophy'. The Kildare report remarked on the size of the sheep, the long-stapled wool, and the improved breed of cattle; the farmers were praised for their skill in ploughing. In Longford Lord Granard was commended for draining bogs and planting trees, including the first plane tree to appear in Ireland. In Cork there is mention of Lord Orrery's magnificent house of Charleville and its fine park. There is a vivid description of the Irish Society's salmon-fishery on the Bann. The general, and rather misleading, impression is of a progressive and stable countryside, in which the relations between landlord and tenant were harmonious and agriculture was thriving.

A less peaceful side of rural life is alluded to in the Kildare report, which says that the country people gave shelter to 'tories and wood-kernes, who are usually the offspring of gentlemen that have either mis-spent or forfeited their estates'. The years following the restoration have been called the 'classic period of the Irish tories'. They derived a natural satisfaction from harassing the landowners who had taken their place, and they were regarded as a major threat to law and order. One of the most famous was Redmond O'Hanlon—referred to as Count Hanlon—who terrorised the Armagh countryside until his foster-brother was induced to assassinate him. His name passed into legend as an Irish Robin Hood who robbed the rich and helped the poor.[1] Dudley Costello, the most celebrated of the Connacht tories, was an 'ensignman' whose estate was held by Lord Dillon, against whom he conducted a vigorous private war. Eventually Costello was killed and his head sent to Dublin where it was put up on St James's Gate, pointing towards Connacht. The 'three Brennans' were dispossessed gentry of Kilkenny who terrorised the county; on one occasion two of them broke into Ormond's castle and stole some of the plate.

The growth of Dublin was the outstanding example of economic expansion during Charles II's reign. In twenty-five years its population trebled, and at the end of the period it was between 50,000 and 60,000.[2] It was the second city in the British dominions and much the largest in Ireland. The expansion burst the bounds of the medieval city and by the end of the reign more of Dublin was outside the walls than within them. Quays were made

[1] T. W. Moody, 'Redmond O'Hanlon' in *Belfast Natur. Hist. Soc. Proc.*, 2nd series, i (1937), pp 17–33.

[2] J. G. Simms, 'Dublin in 1685' in *I.H.S.*, xiv, no. 55 (Mar. 1965), p. 212. For a different view of Dublin's population during the later seventeenth century see above, ch. xv, p. 390.

along both banks of the Liffey and extensive tracts of the foreshore were reclaimed. Four new bridges were built in addition to the single bridge that had previously joined the city to the growing suburb of Oxmantown. Within the walls the streets were narrow and badly paved, but some of the new developments were on a grander scale. St Stephen's Green was a fine square laid out with walks and trees. To the north of the river Capel Street (called after Essex) and its neighbours formed a rectangular grid which stood the test of time. Dublin castle was dilapidated, particularly after a fire that broke out in 1684. But the new Kilmainham hospital for retired soldiers was a masterpiece which satisfied Ormond's taste for public splendour. The municipal tholsel, embellished with grotesque statues of Charles I and Charles II, was a less happy architectural achievement.

Immigration from England and the Irish countryside was responsible for much of the growth of population. Dublin offered many opportunities as the capital of a rapidly developing kingdom. Viceroys were in residence for most of the time, and Ormond in particular kept a brilliant court, which must have been good for trade. The city was the administrative and legal focus of a great deal of activity at a time when the ownership of most of Ireland was at stake, and courts and offices were busy with the rival claims of catholics and protestants. The abolition of the presidencies of Munster and Connacht and their attendant courts in 1672 added to the importance of Dublin. A new and socially-ambitious class of rising gentry looked to the capital for skilled craftsmanship and imported consumer goods. Dublin's harbour was bad, but its position in the middle of the east coast gave the city an advantage over the southern ports as a distributing centre for the country. Petty estimated that in 1685 Dublin was responsible for nearly 40 per cent of the total customs revenue.

Most of the trade was in the hands of protestants. Full membership of the guilds was restricted to them, but catholics could become quarter-brothers, and this gave them some of the advantages of membership. A catholic merchant who prospered in restoration Dublin was Thomas Hackett, who acted as banker and money-lender in addition to trading overseas; under the Jacobite regime he became lord mayor.[1] New rules, prescribed by the viceroy in 1672 for Dublin and other towns in accordance with a section of the act of explanation, required members of the corporation to take the oath of supremacy, though the viceroy could grant exemption in individual cases. Dublin's first citizen was given the title of lord mayor by Charles II, a sign of the city's status. The lord mayor, sheriffs, recorder, and town clerk had to be approved by the lord lieutenant and the privy council. This followed on a violent dispute during Berkeley's viceroyalty, in which there were warring factions in the corporation. Most of the common council were elected by the guilds. The new rules prescribed that all foreigners, 'as

[1] Mark Tierney, *Murroe and Boher* (Dublin, 1966), p. 32.

well others as protestants', who were merchants, skilled artisans, or seamen should be admitted to guild privileges on taking the customary oaths.

Trinity College had suffered severely from the troubles that followed the rising of 1641, and by 1649 it was almost deserted. The commonwealth administration showed an immediate concern for its revival. An act of the Rump parliament (8 March 1650) applied the revenues of the archbishop of Dublin and of St Patrick's cathedral to educational purposes. Most of the money went to the college, which enjoyed a period of academic distinction under Provost Samuel Winter and a number of able fellows. A scheme for establishing a second college in the university was projected, but it had not been put into effect by the end of the commonwealth regime. At the restoration there was a purge of most of the commonwealth fellows, and it was some time before the college recovered from the transition. The act of settlement (1662) made provision for the college revenues, and also gave power for the creation of a second college in the university, to be known as King's College, but the power was left unused.

By the latter part of the reign Trinity College had developed both academically and materially. The number of students steadily increased and by 1683 it had reached 340. Most of them were the sons of recent arrivals, but there are a number of Gaelic names in the lists. All had to conform to the established church. The teaching was old-fashioned, and Aristotle dominated the curriculum. Molyneux, who entered in 1671, 'conceived a great dislike to the scholastic learning then taught in that place'.[1] John Stearne, who was appointed professor of medicine in 1662, attempted to organise a medical school, but it made little progress during the remainder of the century. However, many of the fellows were able men and the college had a good reputation for sound learning. The library was extended to accommodate Ussher's books and a large residential block was built with the bequest of Sir Jerome Alexander. The appearance of the college as it was in 1680 is well shown in one of Dineley's sketches.[2] Two of the provosts, Narcissus Marsh and Robert Huntingdon, were distinguished orientalists, imported from Oxford. Marsh was the author of *Institutiones logicae, in usum iuventutis Academiae Dublinensis*, familiarly known as 'the provost's logic', which remained on the course for a century. He encouraged the teaching of Irish and allowed the public to attend Irish services in the college chapel. Irish was taught by Paul O'Higgins, a former catholic priest who had been vicar general of Killala. Huntingdon invited the newly formed Philosophical Society to meet in his lodgings.

The society, which included several fellows of the college, owed its existence to William Molyneux, who had met members of the Royal Society in London. Petty was the first president, and for several years the society

[1] Cited in K. T. Hoppen, 'The Royal Society and Ireland' in *R. Soc. Notes & Records*, xviii (1963), p. 125.

[2] See plate 9.

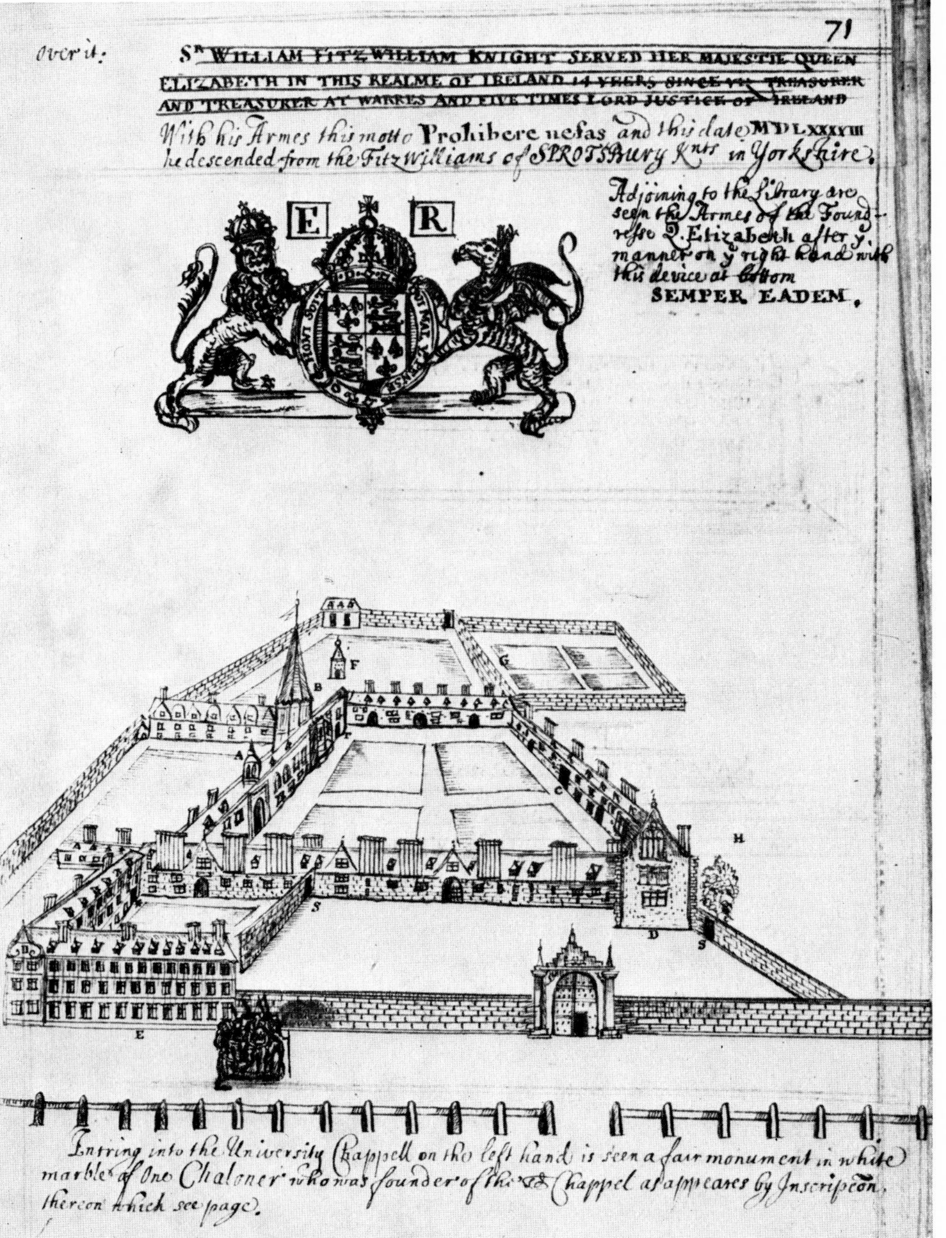

Plate 9. TRINITY COLLEGE, DUBLIN, 1680, by Thomas Dineley (N.L.I., MS 392); size of original 8″ × 5″

Plate 10. LIMERICK 1680, by Thomas Dineley (N.L.I., MS 392); size of original 7″×6″

was actively engaged in a variety of studies, many being of Irish interest. A number of its papers were published in the transactions of the Royal Society, with which the Dublin society corresponded. The society fostered the study of the Irish landscape and of Irish antiquities. One of its published papers was by William King, the future archbishop, on the bogs and loughs of Ireland. Most of the members were protestants, but several of them had names that were racy of the soil and at least one was a catholic. Some were doctors, who read papers on such subjects as 'a monstrous double cat' and the anatomy of a circus elephant which had been accidentally burned.[1]

Soon after the restoration a College of Physicians was established in Dublin, which chiefly owed its origin to Dr Stearne, professor of medicine in the university. The charter imposed no religious bar, and several catholics were fellows during Charles II's reign. The college controlled practice within seven miles of Dublin, and those who practised without its licence in that area were liable to fine. In the closing years of the reign the president was a well-known Scots doctor, Patrick Dun. Outside the seven-mile radius practice was open and largely in the hands of traditional medical families, such as the O'Mearas, who were hereditary physicians to the Ormond family, and the Hickeys, who were hereditary physicians to the O'Briens. The most distinguished doctor of the period was Thomas Arthur of Limerick. He was a devout catholic, but was often asked to treat Cromwellians.

The theatre was a conspicuous feature of the Dublin life of the time. In 1661 John Ogilby, whose actors had diverted Wentworth's Dublin, was reappointed master of the revels in Ireland with licence to build a new playhouse. Smock Alley, the site selected, was a dingy lane behind the south-bank quays, but the building was a fine one with three tiers of galleries above the pit and a music loft above the stage. The outstanding production of Smock Alley's first season was Corneille's *Pompey*, translated by Katherine Philips, 'the matchless Orinda', who had become a colourful figure in Dublin society. Orrery sponsored the production, which was soon followed by his *Altemera*, a dramatic allegory of his own career. A disaster occurred in 1670, when the galleries collapsed at a performance of Ben Jonson's *Bartholomew fair*, attended by Berkeley, the viceroy. The viceregal box withstood the shock, but there were four deaths and many injuries among the packed audience. Puritans regarded the event as the judgement of God on restoration frivolity. The damage was repaired and the theatre continued to put on plays during the remainder of the reign. The reputation of the company was high enough to lead Ormond to bring it over to Oxford, of which he was chancellor.

The second city in Ireland was Cork, which also expanded remarkably during Charles II's reign. In the earlier part of the century it had ranked

[1] For a recent account of the society see K. T. Hoppen, *The common scientist in the seventeenth century* (London, 1970).

fifth among the Irish towns. By 1675 it had reached second place. Essex described it as 'now wholly inhabited by protestants, and the ancient natives or freemen are either dispersed in the country abroad or do only inhabit in the suburbs without the walls, but the trade is almost wholly carried on by the protestants'.[1] Richard Cox observed that the suburbs had grown twice as big as the city; he estimated that the whole amounted to 20,000 souls. The original city was on an island in the Lee; the suburbs spread over the hilly ground to north and south. Quays were made along the river so that merchants could ship and unship their goods at their own doors, which made it difficult to prevent evasion of duty. The prosperity of Cork owed much to the provision trade. There was substantial export of salt beef to the American colonies, and ships called in to Cork harbour to take on provisions. It was estimated that 10,000 bullocks a year were slaughtered in Cork.

Limerick and Waterford were about the same size, with a population estimated at 5,000 each. Limerick was regarded as of the greater strategic significance. Much of it had been awarded to the '49 officers in the act of settlement,[2] and their interest was acquired by Orrery who devoted a good deal of attention to the development of Limerick's trade. The minutes of Limerick corporation show that in 1672 and the following years a number of the former catholic inhabitants were admitted to be freemen. This was in accordance with Charles II's desire, to which effect had been given by a viceregal proclamation of 1672. Dineley was favourably impressed by Limerick and its walls, 'fair and strong with a paved walk thereon'. He noted that there were 'houses of black unpolished marble with partition walls some five feet thick which have battlements on the top and the best cellars for so many of any city in England or Ireland'. The council books of Waterford show an active community controlled by the protestant section. There was also a considerable catholic population, as we learn from several letters of John Brenan, catholic bishop of the diocese from 1671 to 1677, who retained the administration after his translation to the archbishopric of Cashel.[3] In 1678 there were four parishes in the city, each under its priest. There were houses of Dominicans, Franciscans, and Jesuits. In a later letter, dated 1687, he estimated the population at 5,000, of whom at least half were catholics, a proportion that may have increased during the early part of James II's reign.

Galway was the most catholic of the Irish towns. The traditional merchant families had succeeded in retaining much of their wealth, and their old stone houses lent dignity to the streets. But the trade of the port declined during the reign of Charles II. The protestants who took over the corporation were less interested in commerce than those in the Munster towns. Catholics

[1] Essex, *Letters written in 1675*, p. 187.
[2] See above, p. 422, and plate 10.
[3] Published in Power, *A bishop of the penal times*, pp 21–52.

continued to conduct the greater part of the trade, but were operating under difficulties; disputes with the corporation, wrangles over property, temporary expulsion from the town. The Blake family had trading links with the West Indies, and there was some, but not very much, trade with France and Spain.

Of the Ulster towns Derry was the largest and, with its walls and regular streets, the most impressive, though its population can hardly have exceeded 2,000. Belfast was still a small town, with a population of perhaps between one and two thousand, but it was growing in importance as a centre of overseas trade. In the early 1660s there were twenty-nine Belfast-owned ships, fourteen of them built locally. By 1682 the number of ships had risen to sixty-seven. The greatest Belfast merchant of the day was George Macartney, a Scot who had arrived during the period of the confederate war. His letter-books show that he traded to the West Indies as well as to France and Spain. He introduced sugar-refining to Belfast and set up the first sugar-house in the town in 1666. The early inhabitants of Belfast had been mostly of English stock, but during the confederate war and the Scottish occupation of north-east Ireland there were many immigrants from Scotland and the presbyterians became predominant.

By the end of Charles II's reign the country had made a remarkable recovery from the devastation caused by war and civil strife. Many protestants and a considerable number of catholics had benefited from stable conditions and an expanding economy. William King, the future archbishop, summed it up with substantial accuracy, in spite of his partisan phraseology:

> Ireland was in a most flourishing condition. Lands were everywhere improved, and rents advanced to near double what they had been in a few years before. The kingdom abounded with money, trade flourished, even to the envy of our neighbours. Cities, especially Dublin, increased exceedingly. Gentlemen's seats were built or building everywhere, and parks, enclosures, and other ornaments were carefully promoted, insomuch that many places of the kingdom equalled the improvements of England. The papists themselves, where rancour, pride, or laziness did not hinder them, lived happily, and a great many of them got considerable estates, either by traffic, by the law, or by other arts and industry.[1]

The prosperity in which some catholics shared rested on a narrow base of protestant privilege, secured by the land settlement, the legal system, a monopoly of political and administrative power, and the support of the English government. But the structure was subject to stresses caused by the discontent of those who had been deprived of land, office, and political influence, and who resented the treatment of the catholic church. The weaknesses of the established order were soon to be revealed in the following reign.

[1] William King, *The state of the protestants* (London, 1691), p. 42.

CHAPTER XVIII

Land and people, *c.* 1685

J. H. ANDREWS

TWO different Irelands appear in seventeenth-century writings. To the observer who remembered Cromwell, the country at the death of Charles II looked peaceful and prosperous, a world away from the horrors of forty years before. Seen for the first time through eyes adjusted to life and landscape across the channel, however, its aspect was strange and wild, evocative of ancient perils as well as offering opportunities for a better future. Each of these contrary impressions was capable of statistical verification. The demographic trend seemed favourable enough: in 1672 William Petty had put the population of Ireland at 1,100,000, an advance of 250,000 over twenty years earlier,[1] and in 1687 he registered a further increase to 1,300,000.[2] Petty was a ready source of statistical estimates on almost every subject, and his first-hand knowledge of Ireland went back to the 1650s when he had organised the 'down survey' in which most of its estates had been measured and mapped. If he made the rather elementary mistakes attributed to him by some modern writers, his absolute figures were too small, perhaps by about 40 per cent;[3] but they were good enough for most contemporary opinion, and he seems at any rate to have been right about the upward trend. In the early 1680s the country had been attracting immigrants at the rate of several thousands every year; and if some of its recent prosperity appeared to have been won at the expense of native Irishmen, at least they were getting enough food to maintain a higher rate of natural increase than their oppressors. Yet whatever its exact size, the population was still generally agreed to be too small either for economic health or for military efficiency. 'Scarcity of people', the lord lieutenant declared in 1686, 'is the greatest want this kingdom at present has'.[4]

The reasons for the scarcity were less obvious than its existence. Physical geography seemed to favour Ireland. The progress of European settlements across the Atlantic had placed it 'commodiously for the trade of the new American world',[5] and there were plenty of good harbours, some communi-

1 Petty, 'Political anatomy', ed. Hull, i, 149.
2 *Petty papers*, i, 265; Petty, *Econ. writings*, ii, 555.
3 Connell, *Population*, pp 22–5, 259–60.
4 *Clarendon corr.*, ii, 13.
5 Petty, 'Political anatomy', ed. Hull, i, 190.

cating by navigable rivers with the interior, that seemed ready to take advantage of this situation. Fertile land abounded, and the east-central lowland in particular was held to challenge comparison with any area of similar size in England.[1] It was true that in a climate both wetter and milder than England's the soil was more suited to grass than corn, and that much of it could not be tilled for long without losing heart. Even in the south-east, climatically more fit for grain than any other part of the country, land prepared for crops by burning would need a twelve- to fifteen-year rest after only two or three harvests.[2] But rapid exhaustibility was mainly an affliction of non-calcareous soils. On the lime-rich lowlands of much of the interior, there were places where corn could be raised for twenty years without a break;[3] and near the coast a soil deficient in lime could sometimes be improved by applications of local seasand, seaweed, or shells.

It was also true that much Irish land lay outside the categories of 'meadow, arable and profitable pasture' that had been defined as profitable for the purpose of the Cromwellian settlement. Upland masses were widely scattered through the country (a fact that Rev. William King proposed to turn to advantage in his scheme for a scientific triangulation of the whole kingdom),[4] and though most of them were less rugged and extensive than the notorious mountains of Kerry, they were all a source of danger for the authorities, offering shelter to tories and rapparees within their own limits and interdigitating with their surroundings in a way that left many peaceful lowland communities too small to be easily organised or defended. Similar problems might well have to be faced at lower altitudes, as King remarked in his essay on the Irish bogs,[5] but lowland and upland waste differed significantly in the relative ease with which the former could be improved: if trenches were cut as tributaries to the natural river system, the extraction of turf for fuel could be made to serve a double purpose by helping to drain the surface of the bog and so perhaps to render it fit for cultivation. The later seventeenth century was a time of hopeful if sporadic experiment along these lines, and a number of improvers were encouraged by the tokens of past fertility—in the form of buried tree-stumps, field fences, and cultivation ridges—that were brought to light by turf-cutters from under the peat.

It was archaeological evidence of this kind that led King to place the formation of the bogs among the consequences rather than the causes of poverty and underpopulation in Ireland. Similar evidence of land abandonment

[1] *The interest of England in the preservation of Ireland* (London, 1689), p. 10.

[2] H. F. Hore (ed.), 'A chorographic account of the southern part of County Wexford, written *anno* 1684 by Robert Leigh, Esq., of Rosegarland, in that county' in *R.S.A.I. Jn.*, new series, v (1858–9), p. 466.

[3] Daniel Hignet's description of Limerick, n.d. (*c.* 1682–3), T.C.D., MS 883/1, 244.

[4] T.C.D., MS I 4, 19, 8.

[5] William King, 'On the bogs and loughs of Ireland' in *R. Soc. Phil. Trans.*, xv (1685), pp 948–60.

Map 11 THE MOLYNEUX SURVEY, 1682–5, by J. H. Andrews

Authorship and territorial coverage of the regional descriptions collected by William Molyneux, in T.C.D., MS 883.

could be found on dry hillsides and under mature oakwood; and at least one traveller came to the conclusion that 'considerable ruins that are about small places' were a characteristic feature of the Irish scene.[1] Not all these phenomena were proof of general depopulation, for some of them, as the naturalist Gerard Boate pointed out, might simply mark a shift of settlement from poorer to better soils.[2] But the balance of opinion probably favoured the Roscommon writer who argued that local variations in the man–land ratio were not so much a mark of regional identity in Ireland as a comparatively recent product of the changing incidence of famine, plague, and war.[3] On this view it was man himself and not nature that had opened the demographic gap which, in spite of thirty years of progress, still separated Ireland from other countries in western Europe. Evidently a long period of calm would be needed before numbers approached the five million or so that Petty considered the country as capable of supporting.[4]

As far as the recent past and the immediate future were concerned, it was the economic aspect of population geography that received most notice from contemporaries. Whatever yardstick was applied the Irish economy was overwhelmingly pastoral. Fourteen out of fifteen acres of profitable land were supposed by Petty to be under grass and in the (rather more circumstantially based) trade figures for 1682–6 compiled from official sources by Sylvanus Stirrup,[5] livestock products accounted for almost 80 per cent by value of all outgoing trade. The ban on cattle exports to England in 1667 had changed the character and direction of the livestock trade without diminishing its total importance. Instead of selling his cattle as stores to be fattened on English pastures, the Irish farmer was now finishing them for slaughter at home. He was also paying more attention to dairy products: in 1683 butter made up 27 per cent of all exports, considerably more than either hides (14½ per cent), beef and mutton (9½ per cent), or tallow (8½ per cent). Sir William Temple had predicted ten years earlier that the trend from live to dead meat would quicken the pace of improvement by encouraging farmers to build more fences and make more hay.[6] The result should have been a strengthening of the demand for labour; but the ban of 1667 had also helped to bring about an increase in sheep farming: wool and lambskins accounted for 12½ per cent of all exports in 1683, and Petty estimated that for every three sheep that clothed the home population there was a fourth contributing to the export trade. Since sheep needed fewer hands than cattle, the over-all difference in labour requirements between tillage and livestock

[1] *The journal of John Stevens, 1689–91*, ed. R. H. Murray (Oxford, 1912), p. 116.

[2] Gerard Boate, *Ireland's naturall history* (London, 1652), p. 83.

[3] John Keogh's description of Roscommon, 1684 (T.C.D., MS 883/1, 168).

[4] *Petty papers*, ii, 51.

[5] B.M., Add. MS 4759.

[6] 'An essay upon the advancement of trade in Ireland, 1673' in William Temple, *Miscellanea* (5th ed., London, 1697), p. 124.

husbandry was probably little less in the middle 1680s than when Petty had first discussed the subject more than ten years earlier: his figures then had been 120,000 men and women at work on 7,000,000 acres of grass, as opposed to the 100,000 that were employed by a mere 500,000 acres of arable. Nor is there much sign of any substantial expansion of tillage during this period: twice in the eighties corn was so scarce in Ireland that exports had to be prohibited,[1] and even in 1683, a good year, grain and other crops contributed less than 4 per cent of the total export trade.

Useful descriptions of certain Irish counties and baronies survive from the early 1680s (map 11), and by comparing these essays with contemporary and near-contemporary trade and taxation figures the interplay of physiography, political history, and land use may be treated with more regard for geographical differences than was attempted by those writers, like Temple and Petty, whose interests were national rather than regional. These figures present their own problems. Tax returns are notoriously inadequate as aids to population study, and trade statistics can cause trouble by combining widely separate harbours in a composite figure for a single 'port'. In the case of fiscal data some at least of these difficulties can be avoided by ignoring absolute totals and confining the inquiry to a series of inter-regional comparisons, and in the present instance it is reassuring to find that unit-area values calculated from the hearth and poll taxes (the former available by counties for 1682–5, the latter by baronies for 1696) yield results that are broadly consistent with other, more fragmentary, evidence.

The sparseness of settlement in all the major hill masses in Ireland emerges clearly and unsurprisingly from the last-mentioned figures, but at lower altitudes there are some interesting and less easily predictable variations (map 14). In general, the regions with the highest poll-tax values per unit area show two features in common: on the one hand, a history of inward migration by non-Irish peoples at one or more periods since the twelfth century; on the other, a tradition of arable farming nourished by favourable conditions of soil and climate and stimulated by proximity to urban markets. The largest of these regions was the area still sometimes known as the English Pale. Since it occupied several counties, the Pale was never treated as a unit in contemporary descriptions; but its regional character may be inferred from such facts as that Kildare was described as an important source of grain for Dublin,[2] that half of Meath was judged capable of supplying an army with bread,[3] and that disproportionately large shipments of corn were recorded from the otherwise minor east-coast ports of Drogheda and Dundalk. Less extensive and less continuous, but apparently just as densely

[1] *P.R.I. rep. D.K. 23*, app., p. 41.

[2] 'Co. Kildare in 1683' (T.C.D. MS 883/1, 290) in MacLysaght, *Ir. life after Cromwell* (2nd ed., Cork, 1950), p. 313.

[3] Gilbert, *Jacobite narr.*, p. 48.

populated, were certain lowland areas further south where there was also a close coincidence between grain production in the present and Anglo-Norman influence in the past. Strongbow's colony in south-east Wexford was still famous as 'the granary of the county and parts adjacent'[1] and the origins of its farming community were said to be attested by a local preference for English barley over the bere (or Irish barley) more common elsewhere. Population densities were also high in the other 'English baronies' of south Wexford as well as in the lowlands of south Kilkenny, east Waterford, and southernmost Tipperary. To the west, the cities of Cork and Limerick each stood among well-inhabited arable lands, County Limerick being especially noted as 'the garden of the kingdom . . . , producing great crops of all kinds of grain'.[2]

In Cork also, and particularly in the north and east of the county, more recent colonisation and recolonisation had left their mark on the pattern of population and settlement. The same was true of the lowlands east of the Leinster chain, where County Wicklow, dismissed as 'restless and unquiet' in an early translation of Camden's *Britannia*, was reassessed in the 1695 edition of the same work as 'so well inhabited with English and by them improved to that degree, as to make it inferior to few counties in this kingdom'.[3] In fact, the Wicklow tax returns for the following year do not quite match up to this description, and on the whole, other things being equal, areas of mainly seventeenth-century immigration show lower densities than those that had been given more time for colonisation to take effect.

The chief exception to this statement was in the north. Ulster had long been placed well below the national average in both economic promise and performance, but by the 1680s it was reputed the most populous of all the provinces, much of its recent progress being ascribed to the many Scotsmen—'lusty, able-bodied, hardy, and stout'[4]—who had settled alongside the English in this area. Petty calculated that there were half as many Scotsmen in Ireland (most of them, it went without saying, in Ulster) as Englishmen, and that was before the arrival of a new wave of immigration, in the early 1680s, that brought another thousand of them every summer to the ports of Donaghadee and Glenarm and the coast in between.[5] In this as in other areas of plantation there were sharp local differences in the ratio of British to Irish. 'Mountainous and boggy and coarse lands inhabited only by natives', noted in 1667 as part of the Ulster scene,[6] were still present nearly twenty

[1] H. F. Hore (ed.), 'Particulars relative to Wexford and the barony of Forth, by Colonel Solomon Richards, 1682' in *R.S.A.I. Jn.*, vii (1862–3), p. 86.

[2] Daniel Hignet's description of Limerick, T.C.D., MS 883/1, 244.

[3] Edmund Gibson (ed.), *Camden's Britannia, newly translated into English, with large additions and improvements* (London, 1695), p. 991.

[4] *Ormonde MSS*, new series, v, 576.

[5] Richard Dobbs's description of Antrim, 1683, in Hill, *MacDonnells of Antrim*, p. 381.

[6] Bodl., Carte MS xlv, 309, quoted by J. P. Prendergast, *Ireland from the restoration to the revolution, 1660–1690* (London, 1887), p. 99.

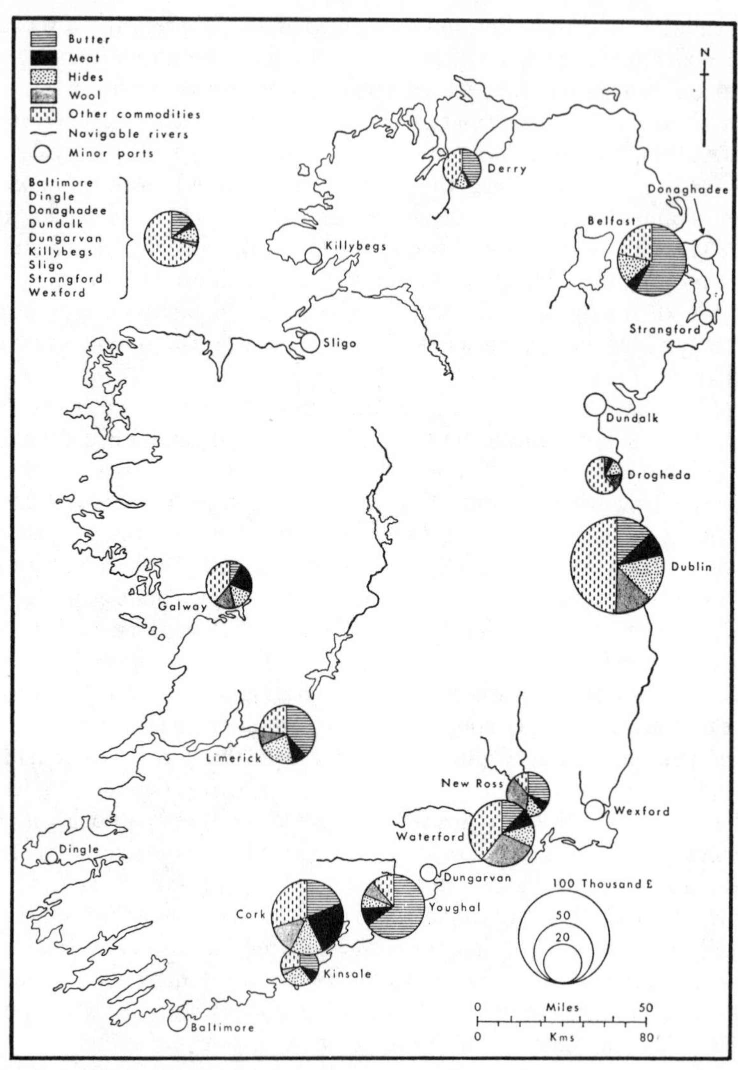

Map 12 EXPORTS AND MAJOR NAVIGABLE WATERWAYS, 1683, by J. H. Andrews

Exports—B.M., Add. MS 4759; navigable waterways—from various sources and partly conjectural.

years later, even in the districts most accessible to Scotsmen: thus behind the Antrim coastal fringe (where whole parishes were presbyterian almost to a man) the people 'above in the glens' remained for the most part Irish and catholic.[1] In general, 'Nova Scotia', to use Sir George Rawdon's not very friendly nickname,[2] could be defined as the lowlands that adjoined the principal northern harbours from Strangford Lough round to the head of Lough Swilly, whereas Englishmen predominated in the Lagan valley and in north Armagh. In their different ways both immigrant communities were devoted to tillage. The Scottish cropping pattern resembled the Irish, with farmers on both sides of Lough Foyle showing little knowledge of wheat cultivation while producing a good surplus of oats and barley. The barony of Oneilland in Armagh by contrast had a 'vast quantity' of wheat to spare for the neighbouring county of Antrim even after supplying bread to some two thousand (mainly English) families of its own.[3] To judge from the poll-tax returns, the wheat economy was the more productive: densities in north Armagh, south Antrim, and north Down were similar to those in the best parts of the English Pale, with the lowlands west of the Bann rather lightly peopled by comparison.

East–west population gradients of a similar kind can also be traced in the centre and south of Ireland. In the 1690s as in earlier periods, there was a sharp contrast where the rich plains of Louth and Meath gave way to the drumlin counties of Cavan and Monaghan. Elsewhere the changes were more gradual and less uniform. Longford was described in 1682 as very populous and abounding in corn, but at the same time two of its six baronies were classed as more fitted for livestock than for tillage, and the only exports recorded from the county at large were wool and cattle. In Westmeath a traveller could pass through sheepwalks for ten miles at a time. Across the Shannon he could go for more than twenty, between Roscommon and Boyle, and still see few inhabitants but sheep. Nor was the pastoral character of these middle-western lowlands regarded at the time as wholly explicable in terms of soil and climate. Some of the Roscommon grasslands, according to one local writer, would have done excellently for corn.[4] Another observer, in Tipperary, while finding very little arable land 'and consequently not much people', nevertheless pronounced the county in general to be 'very fruitful and rich'.[5] In fact the poll-tax figures for the Suir valley suggest a comparatively dense population, but Tipperary as a whole was sharply distinguished in this respect by Cox from his own barony of Carbery in County Cork, the county being reckoned forty times as valuable as the barony but not more than twice as populous.[6]

[1] Dobbs in Hill, *MacDonnells of Antrim*, p. 382.

[2] *Cal. S.P. dom., 1677–8*, p. 398.

[3] William Brooke's description of Oneilland, 1682 (T.C.D. MS 883/1, 223).

[4] John Keogh's description of Roscommon, (T.C.D., MS 883/1, 162).

[5] Clarendon, *State letters*, ii, 9.

[6] Petty, *Econ. writings*, i, 180, n. 2.

Outside the counties for which topographical notices have been preserved it is more difficult to provide an economic background for the regional variations in tax-paying capacity, depicted in map 14. The value of trade statistics by themselves (map 12) is limited by the fact that, with 92 per cent of all Irish exports consigned to Britain and western Europe, much traffic originating in the west of Ireland inevitably found its outlet in the east and not through local harbours. The best wool, for example, came from the counties of Clare, Limerick, Tipperary, and Cork,[1] but wool exports from the port of Limerick were smaller in 1683 than those from Dublin. One significant regional difference seems to emerge from the export figures, however. Temple had remarked that Irish butter had come mainly from animals unfit for the English meat market,[2] and since Dublin had been the principal outlet for live cattle and was still the principal outlet for meat, tallow, and hides, it is not surprising that it was outside the central lowland, in Munster and Ulster, that specialised dairying regions had begun to develop. In the south, their centre of gravity lay somewhere east of Cork city: among all the ports of Ireland, Youghal yielded only to Belfast in quantity of butter exported while in quality it ranked second to none, as a leading Belfast merchant, George Macartney, seems to have been ready to admit. Most of Macartney's own butter probably came from south Antrim and north Down, but he was well informed about conditions further west and in 1679 he warned a correspondent of the difference between 'English' butter, available in the Enniskillen district at twenty-four shillings a hundredweight, and the inferior Irish butter, eight shillings cheaper, that came from 'Sligo and all along the coast'.[3] Here was a hint that the west of Ireland, except in areas of recent plantation, had not yet received much benefit from the intensification of farming predicted by Temple. In livestock husbandry, as with corn, productivity fell off from east to west.

Dimly and patchily, then, broad regional patterns may be discerned in the geography of trade and population in restoration Ireland, some of them not very different from the patterns familiar in modern times. Then, as now, the landscape and its inhabitants would have repaid a closer examination from the geographer than contemporary accounts of whole counties or whole baronies were able to accommodate. The materials for such a scrutiny are scarce. Even Petty's Down Survey, which had provided a cartographic foundation for the Cromwellian and restoration land-settlements, is disappointing in this respect, for like the earlier Strafford survey of the western counties it took more notice of territorial boundaries than of the topographical features that lay inside them. The small territories or 'denomina-

1 *Cal. S.P. dom., 1673–5*, p. 171.
2 Temple, 'Advancement of trade in Ireland', pp 120–21.
3 Belfast, Linen Hall Lib., Macartney letter books, ii, 25 Oct. 1679.

tions' marked on Petty's maps deserve attention in their own right, however, as some of the most deeply-rooted entities in the human geography of Ireland and as the matrix within which the detail of much modern landscape change has been worked out. Petty's historically neutral word 'denomination', embracing townlands, balliboes, ploughlands, and other local divisions of roughly comparable size, underlined the practical importance of Ireland's huge store of minor place-names, which however 'uncouth and unintelligible' (an Englishman's judgement of them embodied in the act of explanation) had provided an essential aid to the granting, holding, and transferring of landed property since the earliest years of the English settlement. These denominations were generally known by 'ancient meares and bounds' as well as by name. Some of the boundaries were water partings, where in Petty's words 'if the rain fell one way then the land whereon it fell did belong to A, if the other way to B';[1] others followed streams or roads; and most could be recognised on the ground, to judge from the relative ease with which the Down Survey was carried out. Besides noting names and boundaries, the surveyors had computed the acreage of each denomination or small block of denominations. The results, even when corrected by reference to modern maps, varied more than would have been expected from such contemporary equations as 60 acres to the ballibo or 120 acres to the ploughland. Nevertheless most denominations were of a size that suited the government's land policy: they could be granted as single farms, combined to form estates, or partitioned without difficulty by running a straight line across the middle.

The main interest of the Down Survey lies in its local detail, but explicit or implicit in many of Petty's subsequent writings is the idea that his maps would help in distributing the catholic and protestant landowners of Ireland to the best political advantage. On a small-scale map, simplistic solutions to this problem were quick to offer themselves. The Cromwellian settlement had itself been simple enough in overall conception, and some of its features survived in the actual pattern of post-restoration landownership: one was the appreciable proportion of land permitted to remain catholic in certain traditionally peaceful areas near Dublin; another, differently motivated, was the much more notable concentration of catholic ownership in the western counties of Galway, Mayo, and Clare, safe behind the natural barrier of the Shannon. On closer inspection, however, this regularity soon becomes blurred. When land passed from catholic to protestant under the act of satisfaction, the acreage of the new estates necessarily depended on the amount of money invested by each adventurer or the amount of arrears due to each ex-serviceman. And the method of distributing land by lot, which the new settlers themselves had considered preferable to a planned allocation, introduced a random element into the pattern of large and small estates. By arranging forfeited land into continuous blocks or 'strings', each

[1] Petty, 'Political anatomy', ed. Hull, i, 206.

holding could be brought within a single boundary, but the existence of predetermined size-limits made it impossible to harmonise the new property boundaries with those of the historic parishes and baronies. In any case, the limited amount of order achieved by these means in the 1650s had subsequently been much disturbed by the 'retrenchments' made by protestant owners under the acts of settlement and explanation, as well as by the cumulative effects of normal private transactions in land. As matters turned out, then, the new proprietorial geography was not demonstrably simpler or more rational than the old; and whatever the shape of their possessions on the map, the juxtaposition of owners of different cultural backgrounds meant that tenurial structures, and indeed the whole texture of the landscape, were liable to rapid variations from one estate to the next. No short essay could encompass all these variations; in any case a mixture of general impressions and arbitrarily chosen samples, in the manner of the following paragraphs, is the best that the surviving source materials allow.

Perhaps the best example of an essentially Irish form of land use, noticed in contemporary accounts of Kerry and Connemara and certainly widespread elsewhere, was the ancient practice of booleying, whereby both men and cattle spent the summer months on upland pastures at some distance from their winter habitations. These movements cut across denomination boundaries to embrace lands that were still undivided (like the 'mountain in common 12,600 acres' that appears on Petty's map of County Galway), but they are not to be confused with the apparently aimless wanderings of the 'creaghts'[1] which are mentioned as a by-product of wartime and post-war disturbances in many early-seventeenth-century writings and again after 1689. On the contrary, the booleys among the mountains of Connemara were complementary to crop production from the adjoining lowlands, which were ploughed, dug, weeded, and manured with an intensity that was the reverse of nomadic, leaving a surplus of wheat, barley, oats, and rye for both local landlord and city merchant. Roderick O'Flaherty, who in 1684 described this dual system in the area of which his own family had long been chiefs,[2] could be taken to stand for Gaelic society at its purest. His visitors, once they got west of Galway city, felt as modern tourists feel that here at last was the real Ireland, an impression that was strengthened when they found the eminent latinist and historian sharing a booley house with his cattle.

Meanwhile in Westmeath, traditional centre of Ireland, Sir Henry Piers had been observing a group of small tenant farmers or 'scullogues', for whom the local equivalent of the O'Flahertys had been replaced by landlords of an alien breed—in the area under observation presumably by the family of Piers himself. To judge from the state of quarrelsome disorganisation in which he claimed to have found them, such truncated communities had

[1] See above, ch. 1, p. 35.

[2] O'Flaherty, *West Connaught*.

begun to suffer from a lack of sympathetic leadership. But from the confusion Piers unearthed several features of agrarian life which modern folklorists have agreed with him in regarding as very old. 'It is usual with them', he wrote in 1682,

to have ten or twelve ploughs at once going in one small field; nevertheless everyone here hath tillage distinct, though all appear fenced up in one mear or ditch. They commonly divide one field by acres, half-acres, stangs, i.e. roods, into so many lots, as there are ploughs in the town; so as a man whose fallow may come to three acres, will not have perhaps half an acre together but scattered up adown as his lot shall fall in all quarters of the field.[1]

Unfortunately he says little about the number or layout of these settlements, except that most people lived 'scattered in rural villages and mostly in poor small cottages'. But to judge from the amount of space he gives them, such communities were far from uncommon in the Westmeath of Piers's day, and in another passage he describes the manners and customs of this county as typical of Ireland as a whole. Perhaps in this respect they could also be taken to represent at least a proportion of the Ulster Scots, whose own homeland remained under the influence of putatively Celtic agrarian traditions throughout the period of their emigration, but this is a matter on which there appears to be no positive local evidence.

Piers places his scullogues in the context of a 'town' or townland. Elsewhere, social fragmentation had gone a stage further and the native Irishman survived only as a cottier or day labourer, with no agricultural resources to his name beyond half an acre or so of potatoes (already recognised as a poor man's diet) and the privilege of pasturing a cow on someone else's farm. If Petty's figures were correct, about half the population of Ireland belonged to this landless category. 'There are above 100,000 houses in Ireland which are not worth ten shillings each, one with another', he wrote in 1686, 'whereof the dwellers have no pretence to land; whose stocks in cattle are not worth [ ] one with another; who live upon milk, potatoes and weeds, and in which no English is spoken—all catholics.'[2]

Among the various class-indicators listed in the foregoing catalogue, it was the houses that attracted most attention. 'Lamentable sties' was what Petty called them on another occasion,[3] and several other writers professed to be shocked by their lack of proper doors, windows, and chimneys. In fact the cabins depicted in contemporary drawings do not look very different, externally, from the kind of thatch-roofed house which one observer of the present-day Irish landscape has described as a dwelling of comfort, character, and beauty.[4] But the hostile reaction of the seventeenth-century

[1] T.C.D., MS 883/1, 339. Neither the first sentence nor the last six words of this quotation occur in the Trinity College manuscripts of Piers's description. They are taken from the printed version edited by Charles Vallancey (*Collectanea de rebus Hibernicis*, i [Dublin, 1770], pp 116–17).

[2] *Petty papers*, i, 58.

[3] Petty, 'Political anatomy', ed. Hull, i, 147.

[4] Evans, *Ir. folkways*, pp 39–40.

Englishman may have sprung from more complex causes than a sympathetic concern for the cabin-dweller's comfort: a house that could be built in three or four days was in itself an affront to a work-loving nation; it also threatened to perpetuate the instability of rural settlement-patterns that had made the Irish a hard people to conquer and was still making them a hard people to govern. It is certain at least that poverty, as defined by quantity of land or quality of housing, extended beyond the cottier class to embrace a large number of tenant farmers. Petty, while putting the number of landless men's houses at something more (but not much more, his context suggests) than 100,000, had already stated the number of houses without chimneys to be 60,000 more than this. With seven out of eight Irishmen living in wretched cabins, to quote yet another of his estimates, it was natural for contemporaries to equate Irishness with poverty.[1] No doubt the relative affluence of the remaining eighth was sometimes evident in landscapes like the well-farmed and well-enclosed barony of Oneilland, where the local Irish farmers were accounted almost as good as the English. In general, however, 'Englishlike' retained its meaning as a term of praise applicable not only to houses but also to fields, roads, and methods of land management.

If what was most Irish in the Irish landscape had apparently to be sought among the scullogues and labourers, it was at the other end of the social scale that the champions of the Englishlike were most obtrusive. Protestants, though only 300,000 in an estimated total population of 1,100,000, owned four-fifths of the country's profitable land. The absolute number of landowners was relatively small, it is true, and not all of them lived among their Irish possessions: Petty's guess was that a quarter of the country's real and personal wealth belonged to men whose homes were still in England. The well-appointed gentleman's house was still comparatively rare: Nicholas Dowdall, who seemed to enjoy describing them, mentioned no more than twelve in his account of County Longford dated 1682.[2] But with the eclipse of the Irish monasteries—half tolerated, at best, under Charles II and in many cases more than half ruined—the gentleman's seat had become the most conspicuous feature of the Irish rural scene and its occupant the mc effective agent of rural change. And it was in counties like Longford, where much land had recently changed hands, that new kinds of architecture and gardening were most noticeable. By comparison some parts of the Pale, Kildare for instance, were dominated by the earlier styles, whether tower house or thatched farmstead, that still satisfied many of the Old English gentry at this period. As Thomas Dineley's drawings show, tower houses were now being improved by the enlargement of windows and the addition of uncastellated wings,[3] but the new fashion, surviving today in no more

[1] Petty, 'Political anatomy', ed. Hull, i, 142, 164. [2] T.C.D., MS 883/2, 254–67.
[3] See e.g. E. P. Shirley (ed.), 'Extracts from the journal of Thomas Dineley' in *R.S.A.I. Jn.*, vii (1862–3), p. 47.

than a handful of examples such as Shannongrove, County Limerick, was for a symmetrical façade, commonly of red brick, with wide eaves, dormer windows, and tall chimneys, alongside a rectangle of garden in which paths and flower beds were lined up geometrically in the continental manner. Some seats were embellished with groves and avenues of beech, lime, or fir; but the park proper, a walled enclosure of perhaps four or five miles in circumference, still served mainly as a repository for deer and was often situated at a considerable distance from its owner's house.

While the houses and gardens of noblemen and gentlemen were being remodelled to suit the trend of taste, landholding arrangements of varying age and origin continued to subsist among the tenantry in areas of English as well as Irish influence. In the Pale there were still traces of large nucleated villages with complex field-systems of the type presumably imported in the middle ages: an eighty-acre tenement near Kilcullen, County Kildare, leased in 1688, included fifteen small patches of land 'in the open fields', as well as a number of other scattered parcels, not much larger in size, that were now separately fenced under their own names.[1] It would be easy to exaggerate the area occupied by these supposedly Anglo-Norman landscapes, however. In other areas where the English imprint was considered to be strong, such as the barony of Forth in County Wexford, open fields, if they had ever existed, had given way to 'lands well fenced in small enclosures'.[2] In any case the denominations mapped by the Down Survey of south Wexford, and for that matter of most of Ireland, were too small to accommodate the fields and houses of a nucleated village in the midland English sense.

In estate administration, as in the government's land programme, it was the townland or its local equivalent that provided the most convenient unit; and though many townlands were sublet in small parcels, the resident leaseholder of a single denomination may be regarded as one of the most important channels of English rural influence at this period. It would not be difficult to compile a manual of seventeenth-century improvements from the covenants agreed between these men and their landlords. Some of them were remarkably specific, as where land was required to be ploughed with 'three or four of the ordinary or usual ridges laid into one ridge and then smoothly harrowed after the English manner'.[3] Elsewhere orchards and gardens were to be laid out, houses built of specified materials and to specified dimensions, turf to be cut trenchwise as an aid to drainage, and underwoods preserved 'after the English fashion'. Most often of all, land was to be fenced, an essential process when old denominations were being carved into new farms. Thus at Lismore, County Galway, a tenant was given

[1] *Inchiquin MSS*, p. 394.

[2] H. F. Hore (ed.), 'A chorographic account of the southern part of the county of Wexford' in *R.S.A.I. Jn.*, v (1858–9), p. 467.

[3] *Inchiquin MSS*, p. 365.

two years in 1680 to dig a ditch five feet deep and four feet broad and plant a double row of quicksets, in the meantime preserving the boundary with 'notable marks wherever the surveyor made crosses or holes in the mearings'.[1] This kind of quickset bank and ditch was soon to receive parliamentary recognition as the standard Irish fence (9 William III, sess. 1, c. 37), except where the soil was too thin for a bank and a drystone wall took its place. In many areas, no doubt, the only fences as good as this were the ones that separated different properties or leaseholds. In a grazier's farm internal divisions would be less useful—he might even remove those put up by his predecessors—and in mixed farming districts the partitions between arable and pasture were often no more than flimsy brushwood screens unlikely to outlast the corn they were made to protect. On the whole it is clear that the evolution of the Irish fieldscape, like the progress of Irish agricultural improvement in general, was still in a comparatively early stage. The Ards of County Down, where William Montgomery's description of 1683 singled out enclosures only in the immediate vicinity of gentlemen's houses,[2] was more typical in this respect than showplaces like Forth and Oneilland. And in 1692 the whole country could be dismissed with the comment that 'enclosures are very rare among them, and those no better fenced than an old midwife's toothless gums'.[3]

Nowhere in rural Ireland were there non-agricultural resources sufficient to support the economy of a whole region. The herring harvest, though widely distributed around the coast, was liable to unexpected fluctuation; the same was true of pilchards, which in any case were mainly confined to the south-west; and there were occasional bad years even where output was as sharply concentrated as at the famous salmon 'cuts' near Coleraine. In these circumstances the capitalistic approach to fishing attempted by Petty and other large landowners in Kerry was perhaps less appropriate than the more characteristically Irish practice of treating land and sea as complementary sources of family income; the latter system is inevitably less well documented, but we catch a glimpse of it in Cork, where Cox told how employment in fishing enabled a multitude of poor people to pay high rents for the coarse land near the coast.[4]

Fish could return another year. Timber, unless managed 'after the English fashion', was a rapidly wasting asset, its cheapness partly dependent on a nation-wide lack of interest in replacing it. Large parts of Ireland, notably the English Pale, had been short of wood for many centuries, but up to the

[1] Dunsandle papers, 25 May 1680, in *Anal. Hib.*, no. 15 (1944), p. 396.

[2] D. B. Quinn, 'William Montgomery and the description of the Ards, 1683' in *Irish Booklore*, ii (1972), pp 34–43.

[3] *A brief character of Ireland* (London, 1692), p. 5.

[4] S. P. Johnston, 'On a manuscript description of the city and county of Cork, *c.* 1685, written by Sir Richard Cox' in *R.S.A.I. Jn.*, xxxii (1902), p. 355.

Cromwellian period a good deal of forest had survived, some of it in glens and foothills, some on intractable drumlin soils, and some on land that had been shielded from earlier development by natural barriers of bog or lake. By the 1680s little of this reserve was left. Much had been cut for building, for tanners' bark, and for export in the round or as pipe-staves. During the same period, low charcoal prices had helped to establish a considerable iron-smelting industry, and at some furnaces near navigable water it was even found economical, where local ores were deficient in quality or quantity, to bring extra supplies from the mines of Cumberland or Gloucestershire. But the 'devouring ironworks',[1] though technologically a form of manufacturing, were as short-lived as any extractive industry. They were also just as barren of industrial progeny, for both furnaces and forges were too scattered and inaccessible to generate new ancillary enterprises with better long-term prospects than their own. As a domestic fuel, wood could be replaced to a large extent by turf, as had already happened, especially among the poor. For many industrial purposes there was no comparable indigenous substitute. British coal, though imported in considerable amounts (42,727 tons in 1683), was little used outside the seaport towns. Irish coal production was almost confined to the Castlecomer plateau, and Kilkenny city was the only important population centre with easy access to it.

Bulky commodities like coal, iron, and timber presented special problems of transport in a country where roads were badly maintained and where both vehicles and horses were smaller than the west European average. More valuable goods—fish sent from Galway to Athlone for instance, or linen from Ulster to Dublin—travelled with less difficulty. And there was certainly little impediment to the coming and going of men and animals. Irishmen were already noted for their mobility, and information, true and false, could radiate from the towns with a speed that would have seemed impossible in England. Watering places, like the one visited by Dineley at Drumkitt, County Carlow, were much frequented in the season by people of all classes. Horse races were run on the Curragh of Kildare and many lesser-known tracks, while holy wells and sacred relics could draw pilgrims from half-way across the country. Livestock trading fitted easily into these patterns of seasonal movement, and fairs, like pilgrimages, were often held in places that had few other claims to importance.

Assemblies of this kind, which left no hostage to authority after the last ale-seller's booth had been demolished, could easily be represented as a danger to the public peace. They certainly did nothing to foster the kind of orderly circulation of people and goods, from farm to village and back again, whose virtues had been preached by many would-be reformers of

[1] William O'Sullivan, 'William Molyneux's geographical collections for Kerry' in *Kerry Arch. Soc. Jn.*, iv (1971), p. 44; cf. above, pp. 446–7.

Map 13 TOWNS AND PRINCIPAL ROADS, *c.* 1692, by J. H. Andrews

Parliamentary boroughs from *Commons' jn. Ire.* Separate parliamentary representation is the only test of urban status that can be uniformly applied to the whole country at this period, though the parliamentary boroughs included a number of places that were too small to be classed as towns in a socio-economic sense. The main roads are those shown by Christopher Browne, *A new mapp of the kingdome of Ireland* (London, 1691).

Irish society. In fact the framework for any kind of regular centre-and-hinterland relationship was still imperfectly developed. Some of the country's 252 baronies and 2,278 parishes (the figures once again are Petty's)[1] had emerged as genuine units of regional consciousness with parish and barony teams competing in local sports and games. But the barony suffered from the lack of an administrative establishment, apart from its high constable, and consequently from the lack of a definite geographical focus. And no amount of rationalisation of parish boundaries (of the kind proposed by the Cromwellian government and carried out in more modest and piecemeal fashion under legislation of 1662)[2] could obscure the fact that the parish had lost a good deal of its social significance in Ireland as a result of the failure of the reformation. In any case the scarcity of large agricultural villages had left most parishes without an obvious centre; and the disharmony between proprietorial and parochial geography, noticed above as one of the consequences of the new land-settlement, meant that the manor court, where it existed, did not necessarily serve the same area as the local parish church.

Meanwhile further complications were threatened by recent improvements in the country's road system. Hitherto Irish trunk roads had been for the most part consequences rather than determinants of the pattern of rural and urban settlement. Though it was only now that they were beginning to appear on published maps (map 13), they give the impression of having been slowly evolved, without centralised planning or supervision, by generations of travellers between one population focus and the next. Yet there are also several references to the making of new roads across the bogs, and although little is known about the precise location of these improvements they may be supposed to have created new route intersections favourable to settlement. There were certainly a number of new bridges, some of them spanning major rivers at hitherto undeveloped or unimportant sites such as Lanesborough and Portumna on the Shannon, Cappoquin on the Blackwater, Enniscorthy on the Slaney, and Portglenone on the Bann.

Whether the totality of nodal sites is regarded in all these circumstances as inadequately small or as confusingly numerous, the times were favourable in other respects to the growth of some kind of minor service centre. In Ireland as in England the word village could carry more than one meaning. It could refer to a hamlet-like community of farmers, like the villages, 'near one another and of narrow extent', that figure in a contemporary description of County Wexford.[3] Or it could be something larger, as was presumably intended by the proclamation of 1677 that sought to establish nightwatches in Irish towns and villages. A village in the latter sense might be pictured as

[1] 'Political anatomy', ed. Hull, i, 117.

[2] 14 & 15 Chas II, c. 10.

[3] H. F. Hore (ed.), 'An account of the barony of Forth, in the county of Wexford, written at the close of the seventeenth century' in *R.S.A.I. Jn.*, iv (1862), p. 69.

a group of fifty or so small houses, its people practising a few basic rural crafts and dealing in commodities like tobacco (the one import from overseas that could be found in almost every Irish home), hops, iron, salt, and of course ale; in the town of Mullingar there was said to be no house at which ale could not be bought. Many of these settlements were of post-medieval origin, if one can judge by comparing village geography with parish geography: of twenty-eight places described as villages in Cox's essays on County Cork, not more than fifteen had given their names to parishes.[1]

Apart from legal and administrative differences, the best criterion for distinguishing urban from rural settlement in Ireland was probably still the town wall. As recently as the early seventeenth century, impressive stone-built fortifications had been provided for places which in other respects aspired to Englishness and modernity, like Londonderry, Coleraine, Bandon, and Jamestown. An earthen rampart had been thrown up round Belfast in 1642; some forty years later another was planned if not actually executed at the new town of Portarlington. And in 1682 Richard Lawrence was still recommending the 'well planting our wall towns and erecting them where they are wanting'[2] as essential to the security of the realm. It was true that the latest fashion in military science favoured a large star-shaped citadel detached from the built-up area of the town, as proposed in Thomas Phillips's beautifully illustrated survey of the principal towns of Ireland made for James II in 1685.[3] But at the same time Phillips was also careful to map the medieval walls with great exactitude and to complain that the allowances intended by the government for their upkeep had often been diverted to other uses. So town walls had a part to play: their gates were locked every night at places as large as Limerick and as small as Trim; and however badly maintained they might appear to the expert eye of the military surveyor, they still did much to help in the collection of tolls, the regulation of livestock movements, and the apprehension of law-breakers.

In fact there was nothing remarkable about Lawrence's views on the subject of walled towns except that they had never been acted upon in any comprehensive manner. Only the shire towns, with their gaols and sessions houses, could be regarded as part of a national system, and much of that system was now more than a century old, dating from an era when geographical values had been different and, in particular, when rivers could be seen as doing more to divide their banks than unite them. Not every Irish county was still administered from the place that had originally supplied the county name—there were some half-dozen contrary examples—but changing

[1] Richard Cox, 'Regnum Corcagiense' in *Cork Hist. Soc. Jn.*, viii (1902), pp 65–83, 156–79; S. P. Johnston, as above, pp 353–76.

[2] Richard Lawrence, *The interest of Ireland in its trade and wealth stated* (London, 1682), ch. II, pt 2.

[3] Copies in N.L.I., MSS 2557, 3137.

the shire town without changing the boundary was not enough to cure the system of its faults: this much was implicitly recognised in the interesting pattern of revenue districts adopted in 1692, several of which cut across the old counties and had their headquarters in border towns like Strabane, Lisburn, Drogheda, Athlone, and New Ross.[1] But this experiment was not repeated: in their treatment of administrative divisions, as in other fields, restoration governments dealt tolerantly with geographical untidiness, perhaps in reaction to the territorial radicalism that had been fashionable in Cromwell's time. The result was that corporations were constituted, market rights granted, and parliamentary boroughs created at individual places on their individual merits, and not necessarily all at the same place at the same time. Despite the absence of a national plan, however, *ad hoc* town foundation by both government and private enterprises had been making good progress, and of the more than 100 corporations existing in 1685, the great majority had been constituted in the course of the seventeenth century. Connacht was the only one of the four provinces that could still be regarded as under-urbanised (map 13).

There was of course no guarantee that any town created by a process of plantation would acquire enough economic momentum to justify its socio-political promise. Some medieval centres such as Athenry and Kilmallock had long been sunk in lethargy, and not all the seventeenth-century foundations had proved lastingly successful: the borough of St Johnstown in Longford was no more than a village, and the same was true of its namesake and coeval in Donegal. It could still be said, as Orrery had said in 1667, that the good towns of Ireland were on navigable rivers.[2] This was a category that included Athlone, Kilkenny, Clonmel, Carlow, Carrick-on-Suir, and New Ross, as well as the estuarine cities whose supremacy dated from the beginnings of Ireland's urban history. More recently, Orrery's principle had found further expression in the prominence given in the Ulster plantation project, and justified by subsequent events, to the sites of Londonderry and Coleraine, as well as in the rapid growth of Belfast. At the same time the ports were in competition among themselves and some harbours were already becoming inadequate. In the Shannon the largest ships had to unload near Bunratty; in the Liffey they could get no higher than Ringsend. But the greater part of Ireland's maritime trade was carried in ships small enough to reach the quays built in the middle ages; and a good harbour was certainly no defence against the increasing concentration of traffic in the largest ports, as the merchants of Kinsale could see by comparing their progress with that of Cork. By 1683, about two-thirds of the country's export trade was handled by the five largest ports. The concentration of imports, though

[1] A list of the revenue districts is to be found in *Commons' jn. Ire.*, ii, II (1796), app., pp xxii–xxviii.

[2] *Orrery state letters*, ii, 186.

impossible to estimate in the same terms, is likely to have been even more pronounced. Urban population showed a similar tendency to inequality. Dublin had about 60,000 people, Cork about 20,000; the next largest towns, Limerick and Waterford, about 5,000 each.

Livestock-based industries like slaughtering, tanning, and soap-making were probably shared among the seaport towns in much the same proportions as the export trade in livestock products. The textile manufactures, apart from home spinning and weaving for family use, were less evenly distributed. Labour and wool were cheap in all parts of Ireland, but the entrepreneurs who brought them together were most active in a belt of strong New English influence that stretched from Dublin across to south County Cork and included the towns of Kilkenny, Carlow, Callan, Clonmel, and Bandon. The pattern of cloth exports reflects this distribution: the leading ports in this field were Dublin, Cork, and Waterford; those of the second rank included Kinsale, Youghal, and New Ross. The linen industry was already well established in Ulster, where Lawrence claimed that more linen was made than 'in the like circuit' in Europe,[1] but it had made relatively little impression as yet on the development of towns and trade.

The leading branches of the Irish textile industry were still in protestant hands. So too were almost all the other key positions in the towns—not surprisingly, if Petty was correct in stating that half the protestants of Ireland were townsfolk. But not many places could echo Bandon's claim to have no catholic inhabitants at all. Elsewhere, in addition to the Old English catholics who were still prominent in towns like Wexford and Galway that had stood apart from the main stream of recent immigration, there was a considerable 'new Irish' element of traders and urban working men. As late arrivals on a scene created by the planter races, these people were most numerous on the outskirts of the built-up area. The centre of Cork city, for example, was still inhabited by 'rich and industrious Englishmen',[2] the suburbs 'stuffed' with dangerous Irish papists.[3] In fact it was the policy of the government, restated in a proclamation of 1678, to exclude the Irish, along with the markets and mass houses that they patronised, from the walled centres of at least the more important towns.

In these circumstances the typical suburb was both poor and planless, with cabins grouped in irregular clusters around the outer periphery of the town wall or lining the approach roads in untidy ribbons that were sometimes longer than the principal streets of the urban core. Inside the wall, buildings were strong and substantial, and contemporary authors, by ignoring the suburbs, were able to describe the larger provincial towns of Ireland in surprisingly favourable terms. But there was still little to suggest

[1] Lawrence, *Interest of Ireland*, pt 2, p. 190.
[2] Richard Cox, 'Regnum Corcagiense' in *Cork Hist. Soc. Jn.*, viii (1902), p. 161.
[3] *Ormonde MSS*, new series, iv, 336.

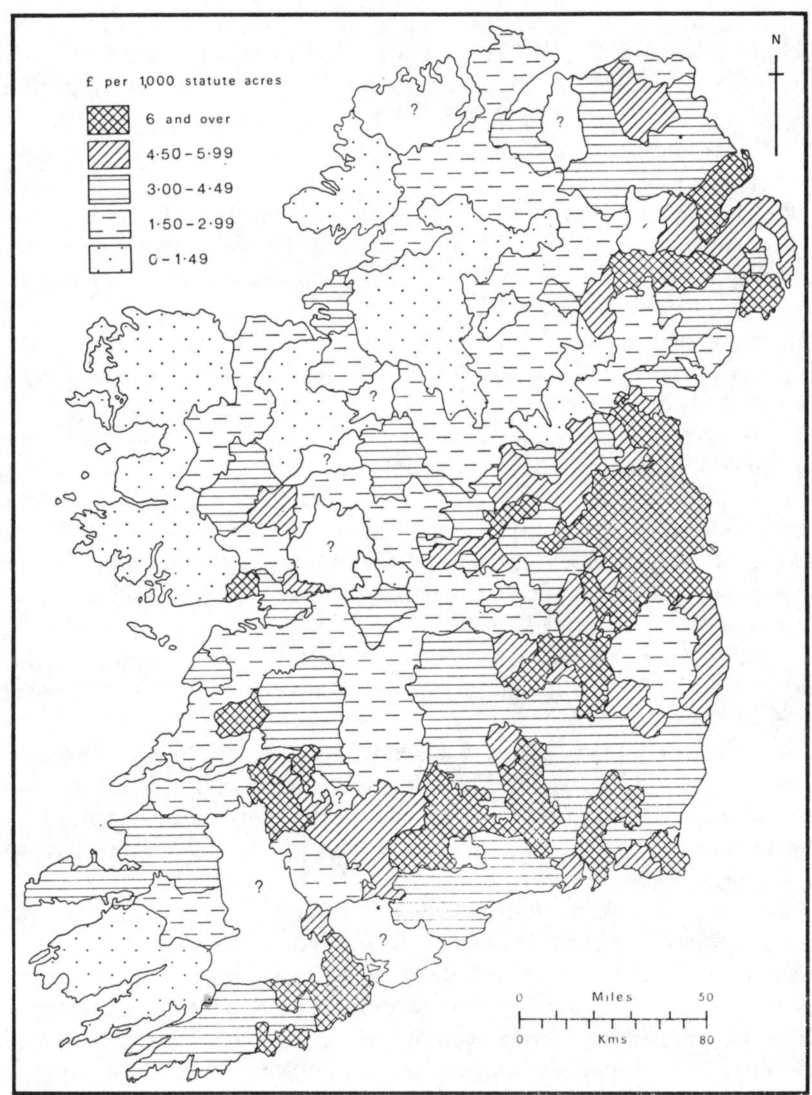

Map 14 POLL-TAX RECEIPTS ACCORDING TO BARONIES, 1696, by J. H. Andrews

Commons' jn. Ire., ii, II (1796), pp xxxv–xxxix

that residential, commercial, and industrial uses were clearly differentiated within their central areas, and at Cork the main slaughtering place for livestock stood at the very heart of the city. Except at Cork and Waterford, quays in the outports were still of small extent, not so much a distinctive urban zone, in some cases, as an adaptation for shipping of the concept of the fortified town gate.

Apart from the difference between centre and suburb, the chief morphological contrasts of this period were between the old towns and the new. In historic foundations such as Waterford the streets already appeared to seventeenth-century eyes as 'narrow, thrust close, and pent together',[1] and not only churches and abbeys but also ordinary dwelling-houses preserved an air of the antique: in Limerick for instance the ancient lanes and streets were described as 'castle building, each inhabitant having been so afraid of his neighbour that many partition walls are six foot thick'.[2] Such impressions were probably exaggerated, for Phillips's drawings of these places suggest that the piecemeal advance of urban renewal had left a mixture of styles in which stepped gables and medieval battlements rubbed shoulders with the steeply pitching wide-eaved roofs of the latest phase. The new towns of the seventeenth century were altogether more regular and uniform. Their streets were wider, straighter, and more rationally grouped, with public buildings sited in conspicuous positions; their over-all population density was lower than that of the old towns, and their suburbs were comparatively small.

So far it was only in Dublin that the new kind of street network could be inspected side by side with the old. Though now only a fraction of the total metropolitan built-up area, the old city (as the area inside the walls had already come to be called) still had more than its share of large buildings—26 per cent of all the city's hearths, in 1682, as against 19 per cent of the houses. But there was nothing of the cabin suburb about the handsome new quays, bridges, and residential quarters that had been rapidly developing to the east of the medieval kernel. With about two-thirds of its people protestant, Dublin functioned especially as the capital of the new immigrant class whose growth and prosperity it had shared and whose efforts had made it comparable to London in range of services and amenities, if not in population. 'Men live alike in these two cities',[3] was one contemporary verdict, 'though very different in the rest of the kingdom'. Even in population, Dublin ranked second among the cities of the British Isles; and like London it flourished equally as seaport, industrial centre, and seat of national government, its supremacy in the last respect having been underlined in 1672 by the abolition of the separate provincial administrations for Connacht and

[1] Laurence Eachard, *An exact description of Ireland* (London, 1691), p. 98.
[2] E. P. Shirley, as above, in *R.S.A.I. Jn.*, viii (1864–6), p. 444.
[3] *Cal. S.P. dom.*, *1686–7*, p. 93.

Munster. Its attractions included a university, a second cathedral, a college of physicians, a theatre, a flourishing book-trade, and a philosophical society. No other Irish town had any of these things.

Nor could any other Irish town claim a position in the world of geographical scholarship. Dublin and London had been brought into direct association in this field when William Molyneux, secretary to the Dublin Philosophical Society, had agreed to compile a section on Ireland for the *New English atlas* projected by the London bookseller Moses Pitt. Molyneux's queries, printed in 1682 and circulated throughout the country, dealt with several aspects of physical and social geography as well as with local history and antiquities. They drew replies from twenty-two counties (map 11), including the essays by O'Flaherty, Piers, Cox, and others quoted in the preceding pages. Though this section of the *Atlas* was never published, Molyneux's collections marked the first time that Ireland had been described in detail for its own sake, and in a more or less scientific spirit, rather than simply as a source of plunder or a theatre of war. Dublin also possessed a number of land surveyors and at least one map engraver, and there were several projects for new maps of both the city and the country. In the event, however, it was Petty, publishing in London, who caught the market with his *Hiberniae delineatio* (1685), the first printed atlas of the Irish counties, based mainly on his own surveys of forfeited land. More than any of their predecessors, Petty's maps are recognisably modern; they also present many difficulties of interpretation; and they are marred by empty spaces and loose ends, as well as by crudities of design and execution. In 1685 the same sort of thing might have been said of the Irish landscape itself.

CHAPTER XIX

The war of the two kings, 1685–91

J. G. SIMMS

THE prospect for catholics became brighter in the closing years of Charles II's reign, when the king had dispensed with parliament and was relying on subsidies from France. The influence of the duke of York was in the ascendant, many of those who had been arrested in connection with the popish plot were released, and there were reports that catholics were to receive commissions in the Irish army. In the autumn of 1684 Charles warned Ormond of impending changes and told him that he was to be recalled to save him the embarrassment of putting them into effect. Ormond, however, was still in Ireland when Charles died on 6 February 1685 and was succeeded by his brother James. The news was received with joy by Irish catholics, and with corresponding gloom by protestants. The accession of a catholic king was of particular significance for Ireland, where protestants were in a minority and had depended on the active support of the English government to maintain their monopoly of power and privilege. Protestants feared, and catholics hoped for, a reversal of government policy that would affect civil and military employment, religion, and the ownership of land. It was known that James was a devout catholic and it was presumed that he would do his best to meet the wishes of his co-religionists in Ireland.

But James was king of England, shared many of the prejudices of his English subjects, and was aware that he would have to take account of English opinion. For over a century the protestant colonists had been regarded as the guarantors of English power in Ireland. In particular, the maintenance of the successive settlements that had put protestants in possession of four-fifths of the land was regarded as a cardinal English interest. The recall of Ormond was confirmed, but no immediate decision was taken on who was to succeed him. The lords justices who were appointed to fill the gap, Archbishop Boyle of Armagh and the earl of Granard, were eminently reassuring to protestants. Less reassuring were the advance of Richard Talbot to be earl of Tyrconnell and the grant of commissions in the Irish army to a number of catholics. Regimental commands were given to Tyrconnell and to Justin MacCarthy; the new officers were exempted from taking the oath of supremacy.

Tyrconnell's ambition was to be the next viceroy, but English catholics regarded him as too violent and too unpopular. The post, after being rejected by Rochester, the lord treasurer, and Sunderland, the secretary of state, was given to Rochester's brother, the second earl of Clarendon. He was a high-church tory, well-meaning, conscientious, and cultured—he was the owner of a fine library—but lacking in toughness and political sense. His appointment was taken in Ireland as a sign that no major reversal of policy was imminent. Protestants welcomed it; catholics, and in particular Tyrconnell himself, were disappointed.

Clarendon reached Dublin on 9 January 1686, and remained in office for little more than a year. It was an unhappy time. His position was continually being undermined by Tyrconnell, who found an invaluable ally in Sunderland, while Rochester, whose influence was declining, was unable to protect his brother. Clarendon's correspondence, particularly with Rochester, is an excellent account of Irish administration in 1686, and shows how ill-suited the viceroy was to handle the situation in which he found himself.[1] His temperament was invincibly English, and he had little understanding of Irish catholics. To him they were a conquered people to whom it would not be safe to give military or judicial power. If such powers were to be exercised by catholics, let them be English catholics. He believed that James shared his views and was mortified to find that his advice was continually ignored by James.

For the first few months of Clarendon's viceroyalty Tyrconnell was in London, from which there came constant reports of impending changes in the army and the civil administration. Soon the rumours were confirmed. Tyrconnell was to be a lieutenant general and take command of the army; three catholic judges were to take the place of protestants. Archbishop Boyle was removed from the chancellorship, but for the time being his successor was to be an English protestant, Sir Charles Porter. In June Tyrconnell returned to Dublin and Clarendon found his presence even more trying than his absence had been. He was worn out by Tyrconnell's ranting and swearing; he was disturbed by the drastic reorganisation of the army, for which a convenient cover was found in the need to remove Cromwellians and other disloyal elements. Four hundred men were turned out of a single regiment in one day, and it was not long before two-thirds of the rank and file were catholic. There was a similar, but more gradual, change-over of officers. Clarendon reported that protestants were alarmed at the changes and that many were preparing to leave the country. There was great anxiety for the land-settlement and much talk of its alteration.

Tyrconnell's primary aim was to replace Clarendon, whom he had no difficulty in representing as a half-hearted instrument of royal policy,

[1] *The correspondence of Henry Hyde, earl of Clarendon, and of his brother, Laurence Hyde, earl of Rochester*, . . . ed. S. W. Singer (2 vols, London, 1828).

completely unacceptable to catholics. It was harder to get approval for his own appointment. The English catholic nobility regarded him as dangerously extreme and were well aware what effect his appointment would have on protestant opinion in both countries. However, Sunderland's support and James's long-standing friendship carried the day. Tyrconnell was appointed, but with the title of lord deputy, not lord lieutenant. Clarendon was abruptly recalled (January 1687) and instructed to hand over to Tyrconnell within a week of the latter's arrival.

Tyrconnell reached Dublin early in February 1687, to the joy of catholics. Signs of protestant discontent included defiant sermons, and it was reported that Trinity College students were plotting to assassinate the deputy. Tyrconnell declared his intention of governing impartially and seems to have been anxious not to drive protestants into open opposition. But the policy of catholicisation was pushed forward, and soon the majority of judges and privy councillors were catholics. Porter was replaced as chancellor by the catholic Fitton. Richard Nagle, the ablest of the catholic barristers, became attorney general and could expect to be speaker of the commons in the forthcoming parliament. These developments gave natural satisfaction to catholics, and Ó Bruadair gave expression to the prevailing sentiment:

> On the bench now are seated the Dalys and Rices,
> And a sage of the Nagles is urging them
> To listen to the plea of the man who cannot speak
> The lip-dry and simpering English tongue.[1]

All the counties—with one unintended exception—were provided with catholic sheriffs, who would be returning officers in an election. Corporation charters were called in by *quo warranto* proceedings, and new charters were issued which gave substantial majorities to catholics everywhere except in Belfast, where the sovereign and half the membership were assigned to presbyterians in an attempt to gain their support. Protestants were given representation in many boroughs, notably in Dublin, but the reconstitution made it certain that a future house of commons would be overwhelmingly catholic. The administrative changes and the fear of what parliament might do made protestants apprehensive. A number of dismissed officers left the country, some of whom went to Holland and took service under William of Orange. But up to the autumn of 1688 there was no large-scale migration and no evidence that conditions for protestants had become impossible.

The land settlement was to be the most important question of the new reign. While it remained intact protestants could count on preserving the influence that was traditionally associated with the possession of land. They welcomed the assurance brought by Clarendon that James had no intention of altering the acts of settlement. But the matter could not rest there.

[1] Ó Bruadair, *Poems*, iii, 89.

Catholics were determined to get relief and they had the support of Tyrconnell. James had told Clarendon that he would like to find some way of relieving hard cases, and Clarendon's answer was to propose another commission of grace: holders of land would have their titles confirmed in return for a payment that could be used to relieve those who had come badly out of the settlement. But catholics wanted land, not money, and protestants feared that there was to be a 'new scramble'. James rejected the proposed commission and preferred to have the question raised in parliament. When Tyrconnell left for England in August 1686 he took Nagle with him, an indication that the settlement was to be discussed.

The English government was well aware of protestant feeling on the land question, and Sunderland proposed that to offset the shock of Tyrconnell's appointment as viceroy there should be a proclamation guaranteeing the settlement—something worth more than Clarendon's verbal assurance. It was to counter this proposal that the 'Coventry letter', from Nagle to Tyrconnell, was written. It argued that any such guarantee would be a severe blow to the hopes of catholics. All that they had gained in the army and the judiciary could be taken from them if James should die and be succeeded by his protestant daughter Mary of Orange. It was only by giving catholics a substantial share of the land that their future could be secured. In Nagle's view James should declare that the acts of settlement had not fulfilled the intentions of Charles II and that a fresh act should be passed to give redress to those who had been unjustly treated, in particular the 'innocents' whose claims had been left unheard.[1] News of the letter soon spread, to the alarm of protestants. Petty sent a copy to his friend Southwell, who replied that 'the settlement like St Sebastian is stuck full of arrows'.[2] But no immediate action was taken to interfere with the settlement. In August 1687 James, who was on a tour, summoned Tyrconnell to meet him at Chester and there was much speculation about their deliberations. The French ambassador reported that the act of settlement was to be repealed and that this would effectively undermine English control of Ireland. But things had not gone so far. Tyrconnell's proposals, which were brought by two judges to London in the spring of 1688, were for a compromise that would leave the Cromwellians in possession of half their holdings, the other half going to the former proprietors. James accepted the scheme, and it was proposed to hold a parliament later in the year to give effect to it. But political developments in England made it advisable to postpone the holding of an Irish parliament.

The resurgence of the catholic church was gradual. In the middle of 1685 the primate, Dominick Maguire, and the bishop of Clogher, Patrick Tyrrell, went to England to negotiate the future treatment of the church. They

1 The text of the letter is in *Ormonde MSS*, N.S., vii, 464–7.

2 *Petty–Southwell corr., 1676–87*, ed. marquis of Lansdowne (London, 1928), p. 264.

returned in the following spring, when Clarendon was asked to see that protestant authorities did not molest catholic clergy. The bishops were permitted to appear in public in clerical dress, but without pectoral crosses. Modest salaries—£300 to £150—were to be paid to them. Diocesan synods were held in many places, and the work of reorganising the church was entered upon with vigour. There was much activity on the part of the religious orders, and a number of schools and convents were established. James authorised a subsidy of £30 a year for Capuchins. Benedictine nuns came from Ypres and set up a house in Sheep Street, Dublin. In 1687 the archbishop of Cashel, John Brenan, referred to schools kept by Franciscans, Jesuits, and Dominicans. He had about thirty priests in his diocese, ministering in mud-walled, thatched chapels. The 'long tempest of persecution' had ended, but priests still suffered from poverty, having no tithes or church lands.[1]

James took a 'Gallican' view of his authority over the catholic church. He expressed his strong disapproval of provisions made by the pope without prior consultation. He told the pope that no person whatsoever should be promoted to any benefice in his dominions except on his nomination. He nominated Gregory Fallon to be bishop of Ardagh and Clonmacnoise, and Bishops Tyrrell and O'Molony for translation to Meath and Limerick. The papal briefs mention the royal nominations, and it is clear that James's stand was successful.

The Church of Ireland had a solicitous, but critical, advocate in Clarendon, who was shocked at its neglected condition: absentee clergy, 'pitiful curates', and ruinous buildings. He was anxious to improve matters and devoted much thought to proposals for vacancies in the gift of the crown. But it was James's policy to leave vacancies unfilled, and to use the revenue for other purposes, among them the subsidy to catholic bishops. When the reign began, the archbishopric of Cashel had already become vacant, and by 1688 three more bishops had died and their places remained unfilled. Otherwise the church's position was not officially assailed, though there were many complaints that priests were encouraging the people to withhold tithes. The arrival of Tyrconnell as viceroy did not change the policy, and in the main the structure of the Church of Ireland remained intact. Two buildings were turned over to catholic worship, but they were special cases: the chapel of the Royal Hospital, Kilmainham, which had been hurriedly consecrated to Church of Ireland use just before Clarendon's departure, and the chapel of Dublin castle, which was taken over for the viceroy's own devotions.

In contrast to his policy in England James made no appointments to benefices in the Church of Ireland up to the revolution. After his arrival in Ireland he appointed a catholic priest, Alexius Stafford, to be dean of Christ Church, Dublin. In 1687 James entered into the controversy that arose

[1] Patrick Power, *A bishop of the penal times* (Cork, 1932), pp 84–8.

when the dean of Derry, Peter Manby, became a catholic. He ordered a dispensation to be issued to allow Manby to hold the deanery 'any law, statute or custom to the contrary notwithstanding'.[1] Two Trinity College graduates who had become catholics obtained royal orders for appointment as Irish lecturer and as fellow respectively, but the college made a successful resistance, and up to the end of 1688 the chief disadvantages that it suffered under the Jacobite government were the refusal of permission to export its plate and the withholding of the annual subsidy of £388. What must have been a shock to protestant opinion were orders empowering the catholic primate to appoint a master for the free school of Enniskillen and directing vacancies in other schools to be filled by Jesuits.[2]

For the first three years of James II's reign protestants were comforted, and catholics made uneasy, by the thought that James would sooner or later be succeeded by his protestant daughter, Mary of Orange. In that case the trend that had set in since 1685 would be reversed and protestant ascendancy reestablished. It seemed that this situation was altered by the birth, in June 1688, of a son to James's second wife, Mary of Modena. The apparent prospect was now that a catholic dynasty would continue and that catholics in Ireland would strengthen their hold over the administration. In fact, the birth was one of the factors that led to the English revolution. It also contributed to the growing estrangement between James and William of Orange, and there were strong rumours that the latter was preparing a *coup d'état*. James had for some time planned to strengthen his position in England by bringing over regiments from Ireland. In October three infantry regiments and a regiment of dragoons made the crossing, and were dispatched to quarters in the neighbourhood of London. The move proved to be highly unpopular, both with the English army and with the population in general. There was strong prejudice against the Irish, based on anti-catholic sentiment and on traditions of 1641. There were a number of incidents in which Irish troops were involved, and they lost nothing in the telling. The importation of Irish regiments was regarded as an affront to the English army and contributed to its abandonment of James. After the collapse of James's cause the Irish regiments were ordered to be disbanded. Some units were interned in the Isle of Wight preparatory to being sent to serve William's ally, the emperor, but most of the men succeeded in getting away, either to Ireland or to France.

The replacement of James by William in England created a crisis in Ireland. Protestants did not conceal their support for the revolution. In Dublin and the north it appeared that they might be strong enough to challenge the Jacobite government and render effective aid to the Williamite expedition that was expected to arrive in the near future. Tyrconnell was in a

[1] *Cal. S.P. dom.*, *1686–7*, p. 415. [2] Ibid., p. 353; ibid., *1687–9*, p. 217.

dilemma. A large part of his army was in England, his treasury was empty, he was the representative of a fallen king. For a time he appeared uncertain whether to make a stand for James or come to terms with William. Protestants in Dublin kept armed guard in Trinity College and elsewhere. Extremists among them plotted the seizure of Dublin castle and the arrest of Tyrconnell, but were dissuaded by more moderate advice. In the north the walled city of Derry was a danger spot for the Jacobite government as Tyrconnell had imprudently garrisoned it with the regiment of Lord Mountjoy, which contained a strong protestant element. He ordered this regiment to withdraw and be replaced by a regiment to be raised by the catholic earl of Antrim. This led to a celebrated episode—still commemorated annually—when on 7 December 1688 thirteen apprentice boys closed the gate against Lord Antrim. But this was not the beginning of the siege. Tyrconnell compromised and the protestants of Mountjoy's regiment were sent back to Derry. At the same time Tyrconnell tried to strengthen his position by issuing commissions for raising 20,000 men, a figure that was to be greatly exceeded in the following months. There was no money to pay the men, so colonels' commissions were given to those who undertook to support regiments in the meantime. Soon the men were living off the country. The new levies were entirely catholic, and priests were the most effective recruiting agents.

There was a general feeling of tension, built up by rumours of invasion and massacre. Many protestants fled either to England or to the north. In the rural areas an excited population was seizing cattle and taking over land, and there was a general breakdown of law and order. Protestants formed associations for self-defence at various centres, some of which took an aggressively Williamite attitude. In Bandon, County Cork, they turned out the catholics and maintained an independent enclave until Justin MacCarthy forced them to submit. In Sligo the association declared that it would 'unite with England and hold to the lawful government thereof'.[1] It held control of an extensive region until the end of March 1689, when it was decided to join the protestants of Ulster, where pro-Williamite associations were in considerable strength.

The refugee protestants in England pressed William to follow up his English success with an immediate invasion of Ireland. They were disappointed at his indifference to their advice. William was preoccupied with other problems: the uncertain state of English opinion, Jacobite strength in Scotland, the problems of the Dutch republic. He put his trust in negotiation. Tyrconnell had given strong hints that he was ready to disband his army and hand over the government if he could be assured that catholics would be no worse off under William than they had been at the end of Charles II's reign. William sent over an emissary, Richard Hamilton, who

[1] Simms, *Jacobite Ireland* (London, 1969), p. 50.

was a catholic nephew of the first duke of Ormond and a brother of Lady Tyrconnell's first husband. But by that time Tyrconnell had assurance of French help, Hamilton abandoned his mission and joined Tyrconnell, and the negotiations came to nothing. Tyrconnell steadily established his authority and by the end of February 1689 he had succeeded in disarming the protestants in Dublin and the south of the country.

The English revolution and the flight of James to France were to bring Ireland into European strategy. William of Orange was a key figure in the resistance to the aggressive designs of Louis XIV, which threatened the empire and Spain as well as the Dutch republic. In the formation of the anti-French front that culminated in the grand alliance—cemented in May 1689 by the treaty of Vienna—Pope Innocent XI played an active part, giving financial aid and diplomatic support. When the fugitive James applied for help to Rome he was given the chilly reply that his troubles sprang from his subservience to France. For Louis XIV, who had declared war on the Dutch in November 1688, support for the Jacobite regime in Ireland offered a cheap means of exerting pressure on William. This was a policy favoured more by Seignelay, the French minister of marine, than by his rival, Louvois, the minister for war. A French naval officer was sent to Ireland in January 1689 to report on Tyrconnell's position and the extent of French aid that would enable him to maintain James's cause. The officer's report was favourable: the catholic population was enthusiastic, and with French help in arms and money it would get the better of the protestants, repel a Williamite invasion, and even carry the fight into England. The report was accepted and it was decided to send James to Ireland, where it was calculated that his presence would inspire the catholics with added enthusiasm for his cause. James was reluctant to go. The revolution had shattered his nerve and he had sunk into a state of dazed apathy. However, under strong French pressure he agreed to make the attempt, attracted by the thought that Ireland would be the first step on the way back to England and the recovery of his throne.

On 12 March 1689 James landed at Kinsale, County Cork, accompanied by a lieutenant general of the French army, Conrad von Rosen, a number of French officers, and an assortment of Irish, English, and Scottish supporters. The most important of the Scots was John Drummond, earl of Melfort, who was, to begin with, James's most trusted adviser and highly unpopular with everyone else. A notable member of the party was the French ambassador, the comte d'Avaux, whose correspondence is a valuable source of Irish history for the next twelve months.[1] He was more of a commissar than an ambassador. He played an active part in the administration and was severely critical of both James and Melfort. The English navy had been ordered to prevent the French from sending help to Ireland, but it failed to intercept James's convoy. A second expedition, which followed at the end of

[1] *Négoc. d'Avaux en Irl.*, and supp.

Map 15 IRELAND, 1689–91, by J. G. Simms

April with a further supply of arms and a number of Jacobite troops, got safely in to Bantry Bay in west Cork. An English fleet then caught up with it and fought an inconclusive battle, which failed to prevent the French from landing their cargo and returning to Brest. At this time the French navy was the stronger of the two, though it never ventured into the Irish Sea. A feature of the war was the failure of either side to interfere with the sea communications of the other.

The war that followed was a major crisis in Irish history. In the long struggle for power between catholics and protestants it offered to catholics an unusually favourable prospect of establishing their predominance. They were supporting the legitimate claimant to the throne and were in control of the army and the administrative system. Their cause was backed by France, the most powerful state in Europe. William, the rival claimant, was handicapped by having to fight on two fronts, in continental Europe as well as in Ireland. His position in England and Scotland was by no means assured. The protestant settlers were well aware of what was at stake. The English revolution had temporarily worsened their position in Ireland, but it gave them the opportunity of reversing the catholic revival that had taken place since James's accession. In their view, as William was lawful king of England, he was automatically king of Ireland, which was 'united and knit to the imperial crown of the realm of England'.[1] They were confident that William's government would not abandon the English stake in Ireland and that William could not afford to allow Ireland to provide a base for his rival. A series of pamphlets, published in 1689, described the horrors of the popish regime in Ireland and impressed on the English public the advantages to be gained from a reconquest of the country.

The two sides were more evenly matched than in any other Irish war. Both were able to raise large armies with regular formations and professional leadership. The quality varied on both sides, but Jacobites as well as Williamites were capable of good performances. The protestant defence of Derry was matched by the catholic defence of Limerick. At Aughrim, in the initial stages of the battle, the Irish army came near to making up for their defeat at the Boyne. Protestants made a hero of William: catholics, in a minor key, made one of Sarsfield.

The war decided the balance of power in Ireland for over two centuries, and its effect is still to be seen in the six counties of the north-east. The annual celebrations of the Boyne and of the opening and closing of the gates of Derry are a reminder to both communities of the historic foundations of the prevailing power-structure. For catholic Ireland the walls of Limerick and the siege of Athlone have given their names to traditional dances that commemorate a brave, but unavailing, defence.

[1] 33 Hen. VIII, c. 1.

The course of the war is well documented and, because of its international character, sources in English are supplemented by material in French, Dutch, German, and Danish. Accounts published at the time are mostly on the Williamite side. English readers were provided with a regular flow of information, and misinformation, in the form of broadsheets, which often reproduced letters from the scenes of action in Ireland or the stories of eye-witnesses. The siege of Derry was graphically described by a leading defender, the Rev. George Walker; his account was challenged and supplemented from the presbyterian side. Similarly, but less acrimoniously, the defence of Enniskillen was described from two points of view. The main Williamite account of the war is the *Impartial history* of George Story, a regimental chaplain, who tried to live up to his title, though his own sympathies are not in doubt. In addition to the English sources there are a number of letters and memoirs written by foreigners who took part in the war on the Williamite side. Particular mention may be made of the correspondence of the officers of the contingent hired by William from the king of Denmark.[1] Their observations are often more objective than those of writers more closely committed to either side.

There are two Irish Jacobite histories of the war, both of which were written by contemporaries but not published till the nineteenth century. They are interesting because of the strongly contrasting views of their writers. Charles O'Kelly, who gave to his account the title 'The destruction of Cyprus' and disguised the names of persons and places in classical forms, was a Gaelic Irishman from County Galway. He was violently hostile to Tyrconnell and accused him of betraying the Irish cause in the interests of England. The other account, which in its manuscript form is called 'A light to the blind', champions Tyrconnell and severely criticises his opponents.[2] Both accounts are subjective and more important as evidence of conflicting opinions than as exact narrative. The opinions of James himself are incorporated in his *Life*, edited by J. S. Clarke (1816), which is valuable not only for the point of view that it expresses but for the remarkable amount of detailed information that it contains. The journal of John Stevens is an illuminating account of wartime Ireland as seen by an English catholic who fought in the Jacobite army. A mass of information about military problems is to be found in the French dispatches, a number of which have been published by the Irish Manuscripts Commission. They are designed to show their writers in the best possible light and to place the blame for shortcomings on the Irish. But they are a valuable corrective and supplement to the Irish accounts and contain much detail not to be found elsewhere.

Of more modern histories the most graphic is that of Macaulay, who has covered the war in Ireland in four chapters of his history. He is, of course, strongly Williamite in his prejudices, but he has made use of an extraordinary

[1] *Danish force in Ire.* [2] Gilbert, *Jacobite narr.*

range of sources, including both the Irish accounts. His is the version that has impressed itself on the English-speaking world. It has clearly influenced a succession of English historians and it has helped to mould the protestant Ulster view of events.

After landing James proceeded to Cork where he was met by Tyrconnell, who presented a report of his achievements and was rewarded with a dukedom. The prospect in Ireland appeared highly favourable. A large army had been raised: it was unpaid and virtually unarmed, but French aid would remedy these deficiencies and there was no doubt about the enthusiasm of the men. Protestant resistance had been overcome except in the north, and it was expected that Richard Hamilton, who had been sent north with an army, would have little difficulty in bringing Ulster under James's control. The Jacobite position in Ireland appeared strong enough to justify James in making an early crossing to Scotland, where Viscount Dundee had raised the Highlanders in his cause. James, encouraged by Melfort, was strongly in favour of the plan. D'Avaux urged caution until the protestants in Derry and elsewhere had been suppressed.

James's journey to Dublin was a triumphal progress; enthusiastic crowds welcomed him 'as if he had been an angel from heaven'.[1] His Irish supporters regarded his arrival as an opportunity for reversing the land-settlement and restoring the position of the catholic church. In response to the general demand James summoned a parliament which, after an uncontentious election, met on 7 May. It was overwhelmingly catholic in composition. There were six protestants in the commons, two of them representing the University of Dublin. But more than two-thirds of the commons bore English names, and the house was much more representative of the Old English than of the Gaelic Irish. Two members each were returned from 115 constituencies. There were no returns from those parts of Ulster where protestants were in control. There were also some boroughs which had not had their charters restored to them by Tyrconnell.[2] In the house of lords there were five lay peers who were protestant. There was astonishment that James had summoned the bishops, not of the catholic church, but of the Church of Ireland. Four of them attended, among them Anthony Dopping, bishop of Meath, who was in effect leader of the opposition.

The parliament passed a declaratory act asserting that the parliament of England could not legislate for Ireland: a forerunner of what was to be a constitutional argument that did not end till the time of Grattan. James agreed to this, with no very good grace; but he succeeded in blocking a bill for the repeal of Poynings' law. He had no mind to remove the subordination of Ireland to the English crown. He was also reluctant to allow the repeal of

[1] Ibid., p. 46.

[2] See vol. viii, map 50.

the acts of settlement and explanation, and was well aware of the effect that such a measure would have on English opinion. D'Avaux protested strongly at James's attitude and urged the importance of granting what the majority of catholics wanted. He accused James of holding up the proceedings by encouraging the complaints of a few catholics who had bought land since the restoration. Eventually James had to give way before the threat that his Irish subjects would withdraw their support. But his reluctance did much to damp the enthusiasm with which he had at first been greeted. The act of repeal prepared the way for the restoration of lands to the families which had held them in 1641. It also cancelled the city of London's plantation in Ulster, but did not restore the land to the former Gaelic proprietors. Much land was temporarily taken over, but there was little formal transfer, as James decided that no court of claims should sit for the time being for fear that investigations of title might distract attention from the prosecution of the war. Within a year the battle of the Boyne had been lost and there was little prospect of giving reality to the repeal legislation. An act of attainder, which rendered some thousands of protestants liable to the penalties of treason, threatened to confiscate most of the land owned by protestants before the Cromwellian settlement. Both acts aroused indignation in England, and helped to harden Williamite feeling against the Jacobites. But it does not appear that they were the primary cause of the policy of outlawry and confiscation adopted by the Williamite government. The forfeiture of rebels' lands was a commonplace of Irish history. Who were rebels and who loyalists would depend on the outcome of the war.

Catholics were disappointed that the parliament did so little to establish their church. James would go no further than offering 'liberty of conscience', which put all varieties of Christian worship on a level. Another act provided that catholics should pay tithes to their own clergy instead of to the protestant ministers.

From the point of view of the government the chief advantage gained from the parliament was the grant of a subsidy of £20,000 a month for thirteen months, which was agreed to as the price of the act of repeal. How much of the subsidy was realised is not known, but it was not nearly enough to meet James's needs. A desperate remedy for the deficit was found in 'gun-money'—coins of brass, copper, and gunmetal which took the place of silver coinage to the value of £1,000,000. This experiment in managed currency was long regarded as one of the horrors of the Jacobite regime from which, along with popery and wooden shoes, William delivered the country. The brass money led to inflation, but retained nearly half its value up to the battle of the Boyne, after which it was drastically devalued by the Williamite government in the areas it took over. The economic legislation of the parliament set aside the restrictions imposed by the English navigation laws and made provision for direct trading with the colonies. The import of coal from Britain was forbidden, but a proposal to transfer to France the English monopoly in Irish wool was blocked by James's opposition.

The parliament sat for ten weeks and was prorogued on 18 July. It was severely criticised by both Williamites and Jacobites. Williamites condemned it as a 'pretended parliament', summoned by an ex-king, and disfigured by unjust and discriminatory legislation. Jacobites condemned it for failing to do full justice to the demands of catholics and for diverting to parliamentary wrangles the energies that were urgently needed for the war. James himself regretted that he had summoned an assembly that paid such scant regard to his prerogative and to his need to conciliate English opinion.

The chief interest of the parliament is the indication it gives of what its members wanted and of how far they were able to press a reluctant king. As with the Kilkenny assembly of the 1640s it was the Old English who set the tone. What was contemplated was self-government under the crown with laws and institutions modelled on those of England. There would be no return to the Gaelic system. The later reputation of the parliament was mainly based on the fact that in the declaratory act it gave formal expression to a demand for independence from the English parliament and courts. Its most effective historical champion was Thomas Davis, the Young Irelander, who praised it highly: 'the king, lords and commons of 1689, when looked at honestly, present a sight to make us proud and hopeful for Ireland'.[1]

Throughout the parliamentary session the Jacobites were engaged in a frustrating and ultimately unsuccessful attempt to besiege Derry. The city had become the main centre of protestant resistance after Richard Hamilton had won a victory on 14 March at the 'break of Dromore' which enabled him to become master of the whole of eastern Ulster. The protestants in Derry received arms and money from William and proclaimed William and Mary as sovereigns. Lieutenant-colonel Lundy, who commanded the garrison, reluctantly accepted a Williamite commission and two regiments were dispatched from Liverpool to assist him. It was clearly of importance to the Jacobites to secure Derry without delay. James decided to go there himself in the belief that his presence would be enough to bring the city under his control. He had some grounds for his belief. Hamilton's advance was marked by further successes at Coleraine and at Cladyford on the Finn, and many of the Ulster protestants thought that Derry, crowded as it was with refugees, would be indefensible. Lundy expressed the same view and persuaded the two English regiments to go back to Liverpool. Negotiations were opened in which a leading part was taken by an archdeacon of the Church of Ireland. The bishop had already left after declaring against resistance to King James.

When James reached Derry on 18 April he was sanguine of success. But

[1] Thomas Davis, *The patriot parliament*, ed. C. Gavan Duffy (London, 1893), p. xcii.

the peace party was overborne by a militant section in which George Walker, a Church of Ireland rector, and Adam Murray, a colonist of Scottish stock, were conspicuous. James was refused admittance and was actually fired on. The defenders created an improvised organisation and assisted Lundy to leave. His reputation lives on as that of a traitor and his effigy is annually burned; but he did not join James, and it is probable that he was moved by pessimism rather than by treachery.

James returned to Dublin and the siege of Derry began. In the protestant tradition, which has its finest expression in the pages of Macaulay, it was a heroic ordeal in which the defenders, inspired by religious faith and pride of race, held out against overwhelming odds. In contrast, Jacobite accounts have stressed the inadequacy of the besieging army and its lack of equipment. There is some truth in both versions.

The city and its walls had been built some seventy years before by the city of London, to which it had been given in the Ulster plantation.[1] Individual London companies had furnished it with guns. It was a fortress intended to protect a colony from the original inhabitants and was not up to recent European standards. It was on a steep hill and almost surrounded by river and marsh, which gave protection but restricted the movement of the defenders.[2] Their chief problem was to be the feeding of an inflated population, which Walker estimated as originally 30,000, though 10,000 of them were allowed out as a result of James's misguided policy of granting protection to those who would acknowledge his authority. The garrison was thus able to rid itself of many 'useless mouths'.

The chief problems of the besiegers were to be lack of equipment—particularly siege guns and engineers' tools—a raw and undisciplined army, and an unenterprising command. The conduct of operations was to begin with in the hands of Maumont, a French lieutenant general, who was soon killed in a skirmish. The command then devolved on Richard Hamilton, who had little experience of siege warfare and was on bad terms with the French officers. The dispatches of the latter are full of complaints of Hamilton's inefficiency and of Melfort's failure as an administrator.

The Jacobites did little more than establish a blockade and demolish a number of houses with mortar fire from across the water. News that William was sending a relief force to Lough Foyle led to the hurried construction of a boom across the river. The Williamite force—three regiments under Major-general Kirk—arrived in the lough on 13 June, but brought no early relief to the city. Kirk regarded the boom as an insuperable obstacle. For over six weeks he refused to tackle it, while the plight of the defenders from hunger and fever grew more and more acute. They despaired of relief and began negotiations with Hamilton, who offered them security of property and religious toleration. But the talks were broken off when news came of

[1] See above, p. 200.

[2] For the topography, see plate 11.

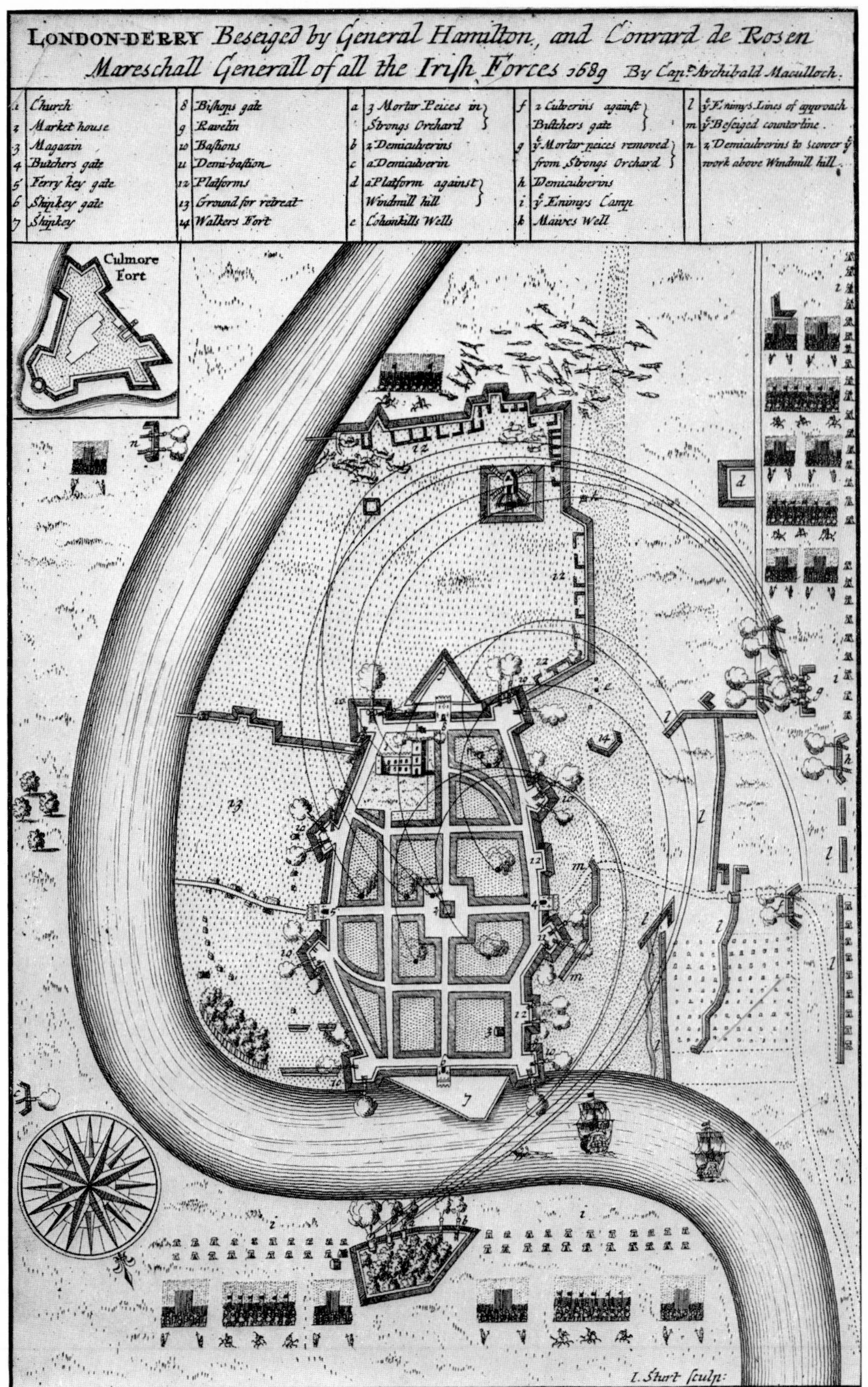

Plate 11. SIEGE OF DERRY, 1689, by Capt. Archibald Macculloch (London, 1689)

Plate 12. BATTLE OF THE BOYNE, 1690; from engraving in N.L.I. of contemporary painting by the Dutch artist, Theodore Maas; size of engraving 32″ × 17″

renewed activity on Kirk's part and the defenders, though very near starvation, determined to hold out. At last, on 28 July, under strong pressure from William, Kirk made his attempt on the boom, which soon collapsed under the impact of two merchantmen, the *Mountjoy* and the *Phoenix*. The ships, undeterred by erratic firing from the Jacobite guns, came up to the quay. Their cargoes removed any prospect that Derry would be starved into surrender. Three days later, after an investment which had lasted 105 days, the Jacobites raised the siege. The resistance of Derry was a severe blow to them and a corresponding gain for the Williamites: their first success in Ireland, but one that owed more to the endurance of the Ulster colonists and to Jacobite mismanagement than to the enterprise of the relief expedition.

Walker's *Account*, with its story of heroic resistance and its grim descriptions of hunger kept at bay by a diet of dogs, rats, and tallow, was excellent propaganda and did much to raise Williamite morale. Walker himself was lionised in England, handsomely rewarded, and promised the bishopric of Derry. His book, which did full justice to his own achievements, was challenged by a presbyterian minister, John Mackenzie, who thought that enough credit had not been given to his community. A war of words followed, which revealed the ill-feeling between presbyterians and episcopalians, even at a time when they had so recently been sufferers in common.

Less was heard of Enniskillen, the second centre of resistance, where protestants from southern Ulster and northern Connacht conducted an aggressive defence, which hampered the Jacobite operations against Derry and culminated in a sensational victory over Justin MacCarthy at Newtownbutler on 31 July, the same day that the Jacobites abandoned Derry. MacCarthy himself was taken prisoner and his army routed with heavy losses.

James's prospects, which had seemed so bright in March, were now almost desperate. His troops had withdrawn from most of the north in great disorder; there was widespread desertion, and regiments were only a fraction of their normal strength. News of an impending invasion was received with panic by catholics and with ill-concealed satisfaction by the Dublin protestants. The French advised that Dublin was indefensible and should be burned, and that James should retire to the line of the Shannon. James reacted sharply: 'he was resolved not to be tamely walked out of Ireland, but to have one blow for it at least'.[1] A scapegoat was found in Melfort, who was advised for his own safety to go back to France. Tyrconnell now came to the fore again and showed remarkable energy in rebuilding the army and organising the country to resist invasion. Strict precautions were taken against fifth-columnists. Trinity College was seized and occupied by troops. Its library was fortunately saved from their depredations by the intervention of Michael Moore, the learned priest whom James appointed provost of the

[1] J. S. Clarke, *James II* (London, 1816), ii, 373.

college. Protestants, including William King, dean of St Patrick's, were imprisoned in Dublin castle and in the college. Christ Church and some other Dublin churches were seized, and mass was celebrated in them.

William's early hopes of getting the Irish Jacobites to surrender without a fight had soon faded. Sending Richard Hamilton to Tyrconnell had proved worse than useless. A proclamation, dated 22 February 1689, calling for surrender with promises of security of property and toleration for religion—and threats to confiscate the estates of those who did not obey—had met with no response. It became clear that military force was needed to establish William's authority in Ireland. Apart from the limited assistance sent to Derry, preparations for the expeditionary force proceeded slowly. William was not prepared to trust the regular army in Ireland; instead, he sent it to Holland under Marlborough. The plan for Ireland was to raise a number of new regiments to be commanded in the main by Irish protestants, nobles and gentlemen who had taken refuge in England. They would be supported by a stiffening of Dutch and huguenot regiments. The commander was to be the duke of Schomberg, who had won a reputation in the French army, but had left it on the revocation of the edict of Nantes and had subsequently entered William's service. Schomberg had a great name, but he was now in his seventy-fourth year; he was also of a professional cast of mind, cautious and opposed to improvisation. He took up his command at Chester in the middle of July, but was delayed there for several weeks waiting for troops, equipment, and shipping. He complained bitterly of the delay, for which he chiefly blamed Shales, the supply officer. The interval gave a much-needed breathing-space to James's army to recover from its disastrous experiences at Derry and Enniskillen. Schomberg finally sailed on 12 August, landed in Bangor Bay in Belfast Lough the next day, and occupied Belfast without opposition. The main centre of Jacobite resistance in the north was the Norman fortress of Carrickfergus which, after a vigorous defence, surrendered a week later.

Schomberg now prepared to march south, but most of his provisions and transport wagons had not yet arrived from England. He ordered the supply ships to put in to Carlingford Lough, some forty miles south of Belfast. When he reached Dundalk the ships had not arrived and the army was already suffering for want of provisions. Schomberg therefore took the disastrous decision to camp just north of Dundalk, where he was to remain for the next two months. At the end of September a review of his army showed a total of almost 19,000 men.[1] The camp site was on marshy ground at the foot of the hills and subject to heavy rainfall, an extraordinary choice for a commander of Schomberg's experience. The raw troops levied in England had no idea of sanitation, and the result was that the army was devastated by sickness.

[1] *Cal. S.P. dom., 1689–90*, p. 273.

One of the regimental chaplains was George Story, whose *Impartial history* gives a grim picture of conditions in the camp, where fever and flux accounted for several thousand deaths.

James had summoned up courage to lead a small force as far as Drogheda, thirty miles north of Dublin. He hoped to add sufficiently to his forces to challenge Schomberg there on the river Boyne. Schomberg's failure to advance was both puzzling and encouraging. Reports came in that the Williamite army was short of provisions and riddled with sickness. Deserters brought news that Schomberg was digging in at Dundalk and seemed to be preparing for a siege rather than a battle.

Emboldened by Schomberg's inertia, James decided to advance and challenge his opponent at Dundalk. The challenge was declined and the Jacobites were able to claim a moral victory. They also suffered from sickness, but not to the same extent as Schomberg's men. Eventually both sides withdrew to winter quarters, but the advantage lay with the Jacobites. Schomberg's mission had been to bring Ireland under Williamite control. James was well satisfied that his opponent had failed in his objective. In England there were loud complaints that the expedition had been mismanaged. Shales, the supply officer, was made the chief scapegoat, but Schomberg's reputation was also damaged. William came to the reluctant conclusion that, unless he went to Ireland himself, nothing worth while would be done. It was a great disappointment to him that the Irish problem was not solved in 1689, and that during the summer of 1690 he would be unable to take part in the continental fighting against Louis XIV. He wrote to his ally, the elector of Bavaria, that it was a 'terrible mortification' to him to be able to do so little for the common cause and to have to go to Ireland, where he would be 'as it were out of knowledge of the world'.[1]

During the early months of 1690 both sides prepared for the coming conflict. William was determined not to repeat his mistake of the previous year, when he had seriously underestimated the effort required for an Irish expedition. A major addition to his forces in Ireland was a contingent of 6,000 infantry and 1,000 cavalry hired from the king of Denmark, which arrived in March 1690, awakening memories of the old Norse invasions.[2] In April and May, English, German, and Dutch troops were sent over and the supply position was built up. One of the supply officers who replaced Shales was Bartholomew van Homrigh, a Dutch merchant who had settled in Dublin: the father of Swift's Vanessa. The bread contract was given to Isaac Pereira, a member of a well-known Jewish firm in Holland. William's supply convoys regularly crossed the Irish Sea without interference, and Tyrconnell lamented the lack of a few French frigates to cut off the enemy's supplies.

[1] Nicolaas Japikse (ed.), *Correspondentie van Willem en Bentinck*, iii (Hague, 1927), p. 158.

[2] *Danish force in Ire.*, pp 11, 18.

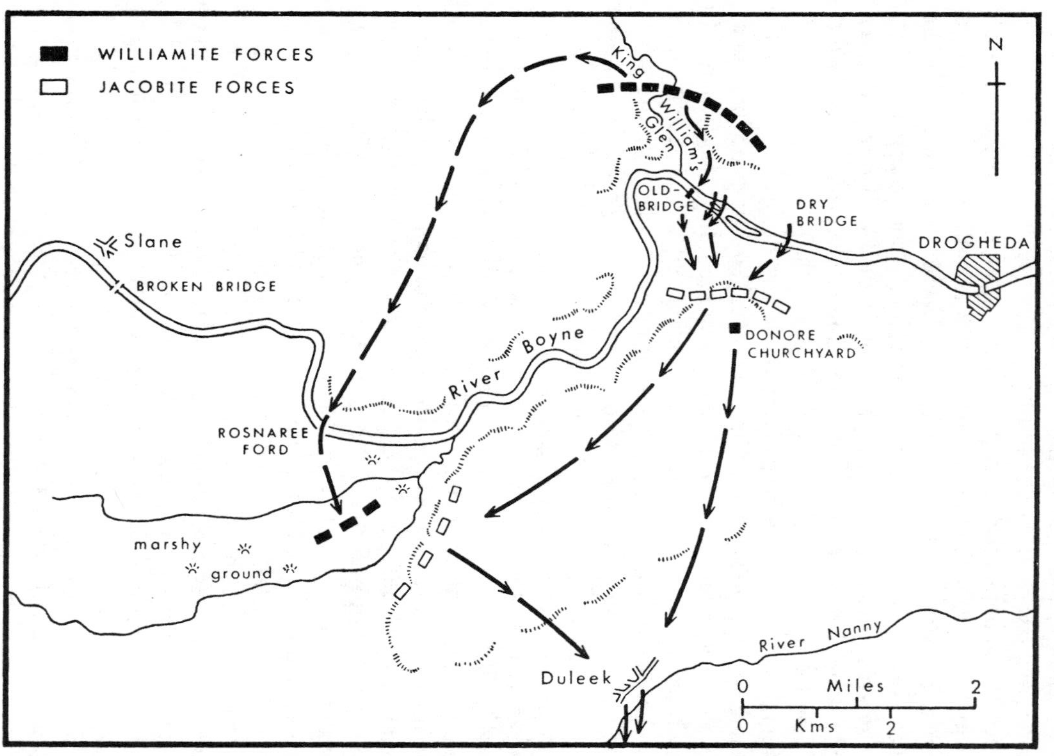

Map 16. BATTLE OF THE BOYNE, 1 July 1690, by J. G. Simms

William himself arrived on 14 June with a fleet of about 300 ships, bringing 15,000 troops and a train of artillery. According to a contemporary broadsheet Belfast Lough was like a wood, with hundreds of ships laden with provisions and ammunition: 'so that now we fear no Dundalk wants'. William's arrival created much excitement. Presbyterians were particularly gratified with his reception of their address of welcome and his promise to increase the *regium donum* to their ministers from £600 to £1,200 a year.

On the Jacobite side some preparations had been made, but there were complaints that the winter had been wasted in revelry and dissipation. James had relapsed into pious apathy and did little to get ready for the coming campaign. But Tyrconnell showed considerable energy in equipping the army, getting uniforms made and organising the local manufacture of muskets. His letters to Mary of Modena, enlisting her support in extracting aid from France, give a picture of strenuous effort under difficulties.[1] The French, whose help in 1689 had been limited to officers, arms, and money, now sent six regiments, in all about 7,000 strong. They arrived at Cork in March 1690, but Louis demanded that an equivalent number of Irish troops should be sent to France in their place. The Irish regiments that were sent under Justin MacCarthy, now Viscount Mountcashel, served with distinction in Savoy and Catalonia and the good impression they created encouraged the French to ask for more. MacCarthy's men paved the way for the subsequent transfer of the thousands of Irish soldiers who served in the French armies from the treaty of Limerick to the French revolution.

The French troops were under the command of the comte de Lauzun, who replaced Rosen as James's principal commander. D'Avaux had also returned to France, to the relief of James, who was tired of the ambassador's criticisms. Lauzun was an unfortunate choice. He was a courtier with little military experience. He owed his appointment to Mary of Modena, who was grateful for his service in escorting her and her infant to France in 1688. He was on bad terms with Louvois, who was less inclined than ever to support the Jacobite cause in Ireland.[2] French policy was to avoid committing the troops to action, and their part in the subsequent campaign was purely defensive.

William announced that he had not come to let the grass grow under his feet, and he lost no time in moving south. James, rejecting French advice to move westwards, marched north to meet him and got as far as Dundalk. He then thought discretion the better part and retreated back to the Boyne, followed at a day's interval by William. On 30 June William reached the north bank to find his adversary on the southern slopes beyond the river. The stage was set for the most celebrated of Irish battles. William had the larger army, 36,000 strong: Dutch, huguenots, Germans, Danes, English, and

[1] *Anal. Hib.*, no. 4 (1952), pp 99–133.
[2] See above, p. 485.

the Inniskilling and Derry regiments of Ulster colonists. James had 25,000 Irish and French.

That day was spent in bombardment and a reconnaissance in the course of which William was slightly wounded; the rumour that he had been killed spread as far as Paris and Rome. The French thought the Boyne an indefensible position, fordable at many points. William was impressed with the difficulty of a frontal assault. His tactic was to send his right wing to cross the river upstream early next morning (1 July) and so draw enemy strength away from the fords at Oldbridge where his centre was.[1] The tactic was even more successful than might have been expected. James and the French presumed that the main battle was to be upstream, and the bulk of the Jacobite army, including all the French regiments, moved in that direction. There they found the Williamite right wing on the other side of an impassable marsh. Neither force could reach the other. Tyrconnell, who refused to move upstream, was left with a third of the army to meet the main Williamite attack at Oldbridge. To begin with, Tyrconnell's cavalry fought magnificently and the Williamites were hard pressed. Schomberg and George Walker—militant to the last—were killed in the mêlée. Then a flanking movement by William and the Inniskillings broke the Irish resistance. Horse and foot fled southwards in disorder, guns and baggage were abandoned, small arms were thrown away.

As soon as they heard the news the Jacobites upstream also retreated beyond the next river-crossing, where the French held up the Williamite pursuit. James himself was first into Dublin; the next morning he left for the coast and on 4 July sailed from Kinsale to France. His precipitate flight fatally damaged his reputation, and the Irish had bitter memories of his stay among them:

> It is the coming of King James that took Ireland from us,
> With his one shoe English and his one shoe Irish,
> He would neither strike a blow nor would he come to terms,
> And that has left, so long as they shall exist, misfortune upon the Gaels.[2]

William, on the other hand, had won a victory to which his own courage and energy had markedly contributed. The victory gave him possession of Dublin and the greater part of eastern Ireland. It was acclaimed in much of Europe as a triumph over France. *Te deums* were sung in the cathedrals of catholic Austria for the success of the emperor's ally. In Ireland the battle has ever since been commemorated as a decisive blow for the protestant cause. But it was the psychological, more than the military, effect of the battle that was important. The French played it down as an insignificant skirmish: a scuffle followed by a stampede. Losses were not heavy on either side, the Jacobite

[1] For the topography of the battle, see map 16 and plate 12.

[2] Quoted in Hyde, *Lit. hist. Ire.* (1967 ed.), p. 594.

army was scattered but not destroyed, and the war was to go on for more than a year longer.

The Williamite take-over of Dublin raised difficulties for those protestants who had remained under the Jacobite regime, and in particular for those who had retained public office. They were accused of collaboration, it was proposed to prosecute some of them for treason, and it was strongly suggested that they were less loyal to William than were those protestants who had taken refuge in England. Churchmen who had remained in Jacobite Ireland, and had prayed for King James after he had fled from England, were subjected to criticism. The bishops who had sat in the Jacobite parliament were specially open to attack. There was a distinct risk that the Church of Ireland, with its devotion to the divine right of kings, might lose ground to the presbyterians, whose attachment to the revolution was unqualified and whose church in Scotland had already, with the abolition of episcopacy, become the establishment.

Bishop Dopping led a deputation of clergy to William's camp outside Dublin, and was at pains to defend himself and his brethren from the charge of being 'trimmers or favourers of popery': he maintained that they had collaborated with James no further than was demanded by prudence or the needs of self-preservation, and claimed credit for those who had stuck to their flocks in adverse circumstances. William's reply was short and brusque; he promised protection to the protestant religion rather than to the established church.[1] The conduct of the protestants who had endured the Jacobite regime to the end was vigorously vindicated by William King. His book, *The state of the protestants of Ireland under the late King James's government*, was a skilful piece of dialectic which reconciled good conscience with change of allegiance and provided excellent propaganda against the Jacobite regime. It was too severe on James and many of its assertions were rightly criticised by Charles Leslie, the non-juror; but King's book, which went through many editions, became the accepted version for historians of the protestant school. By the latter part of 1690 advance portions of the book were being circulated in England and helped to gain the bishopric of Derry for King himself and a reappraisal of the part played by those protestants who had stood their ground in Ireland.

After what appeared to be the crushing defeat of the Boyne Tyrconnell and the French were in favour of making terms with William. They were opposed by an army group led by Patrick Sarsfield, who had already won a reputation as a dashing cavalry commander and was to be the Irish hero of the war, 'the darling of the army'. On his father's side he belonged to a well-known Old English family. His mother was a daughter of Rory O'More, the 1641 leader, which gave him a special standing with the Gaelic Irish. He

[1] [Charles Leslie], *Answer to a book intituled The state of the protestants* (London, 1692), app., pp 29–31.

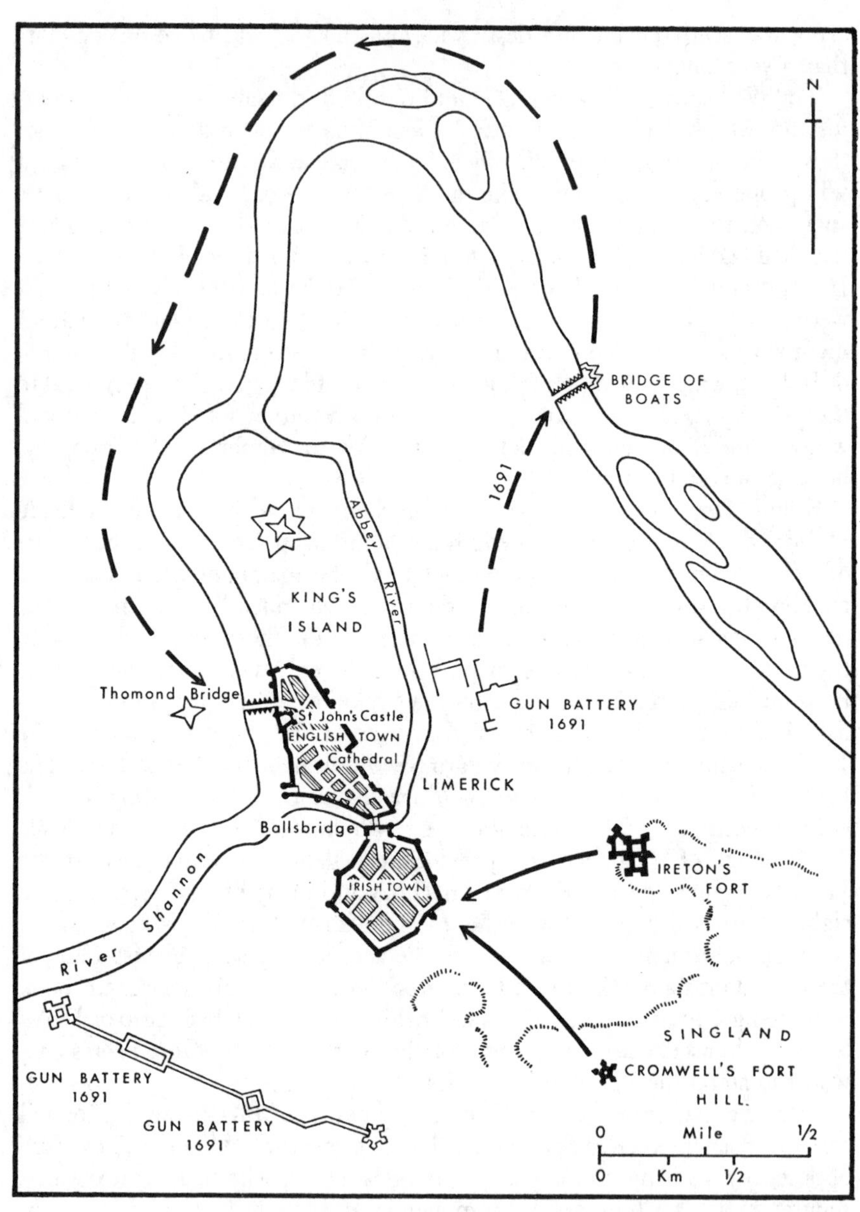

Map 17. SIEGES OF LIMERICK, 1690–91, by J. G. Simms

had a fine physique, an attractive manner, great courage—everything, some people thought, but brains. The resistance group were helped by the news that the French had won a naval victory off Beachy Head in the English Channel and that England was threatened with invasion. This kept William near the east coast of Ireland for a month, in doubt whether to return to England or continue his Irish campaign. The delay gave the Irish time to rally at Limerick. They held the line of the Shannon with strong points there and at Athlone, which resisted a Williamite attack. Another factor that helped resistance was William's overestimate of his victory. He issued a declaration calling on the leaders to surrender unconditionally and this stiffened their determination to fight on for better terms.

William reached the neighbourhood of Limerick in the second week of August. The fortifications were not formidable but it was a place of great natural strength, as the main, or English, town was on an island in the Shannon. Linked to it by a bridge was the Irish town on the eastern side of the river and it was against this that William directed his operations.[1] His heavy guns were still on the way from Dublin, and a major set-back occurred when Sarsfield fell on the convoy, burst some of the guns, and destroyed a string of ammunition wagons. This delayed operations and, though more guns were brought up, little progress had been made when the weather broke and threatened to turn the area into a morass. A breach was made in the Irish-town wall, but it was courageously held by the Irish. William's ammunition ran out and he decided to raise the siege and return to England at the end of August. Limerick was a severe set-back for William and an encouragement to the Irish resistance party. Remarkably, the French army maintained its decision to leave Ireland and Tyrconnell went with it, leaving the young duke of Berwick, James's illegitimate son, in charge of an army torn with dissension.

Shortly after William's departure Marlborough arrived at the mouth of Cork harbour with a well-equipped force. With the help of Danish and Dutch troops it succeeded in taking the important seaports of Cork and Kinsale, which had been the main links with France. After completing his mission Marlborough left Ireland, and for the remainder of the war the Williamite commander was the Dutch general, Ginkel, a cautious soldier who took the view that the war in Ireland was an undesirable side-show, which diverted strength from the main theatre of war in the Netherlands.

Ginkel was convinced that generous terms ought to be offered to the Irish Jacobites in return for the speedy settlement that the European situation required. Accordingly he opened negotiations with an Irish peace party, with land and religion as the chief bargaining points. His efforts were frustrated by William's reluctance to grant a general pardon, and by Sarsfield's success in

[1] For the topography, see map 17.

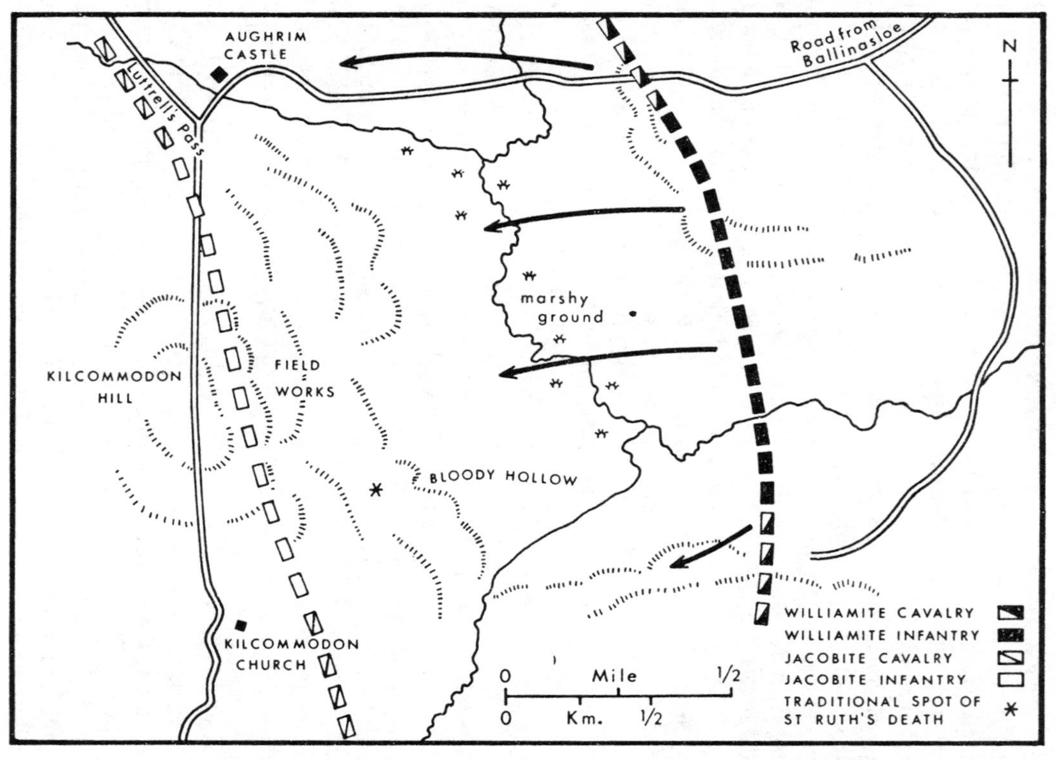

Map 18 BATTLE OF AUGHRIM, 12 July 1691, by J. G. Simms

suppressing the peace party. Sarsfield kept up Irish morale during the winter by a series of raids across the Shannon into the Williamite quarters. The regular Irish army received effective cooperation from the rapparees, guerrillas who stole the Williamites' horses, intercepted their dispatches, and did enormous damage to the persons and property of both soldiers and civilians. Hopes of further French aid also helped the resistance movement An army deputation to France combined complaints against Tyrconnell with a request for a French general, and received a favourable hearing. Tyrconnell, who had changed his mind about Irish prospects, also urged the French to give help. He returned to Ireland in January 1691, bringing with him an earldom for Sarsfield, though this did not put an end to friction among the Jacobites. The French general, who arrived in May, was St Ruth, who had earned a favourable reputation as commander of MacCarthy's Irishmen in Savoy.

The Williamite campaign of 1691 opened with an attack on Athlone, which commanded the middle stretch of the Shannon. The main resistance was centred on the Irish town on the Connacht side of the river. The garrison was commanded by the French lieutenant general, d'Usson, while St Ruth himself brought up an army to within two miles of the town. There was heavy bombardment from Ginkel's guns and hot fighting at the bridge, where the Irish had broken down arches that the Williamites vainly attempted to plank over. Eventually, on 30 June, the river was forded and the town stormed, while St Ruth and his army remained inactive outside. The line of the Shannon was breached and Ginkel had scored a notable success.

St Ruth was determined to redeem his reputation and prepared for battle on the slopes of Aughrim hill, sixteen miles south-west of Athlone. His position was well chosen, with a marsh to his front crossed by narrow passes at its northern and southern ends.[1] The two armies were about equal in number, each approximately 20,000 strong. Ginkel opened his attack on the afternoon of 12 July in the face of strong resistance from an enemy fighting with the courage of desperation, aided by the exhortations of the church and the vigorous leadership of St Ruth. The ground favoured the Irish, who drove the Williamites back across the marsh and came near to capturing their guns. An Irish victory seemed in sight when a dramatic reversal of fortune occurred. A cannon-ball carried away St Ruth's head, and after that all was confusion. The Irish cavalry at the northern causeway rode off the field and allowed a Williamite force to cross unopposed. De Tessé, St Ruth's second-in-command, was wounded and went off, apparently without making any arrangements for a successor. The main Irish army, left without a leader, broke and ran, ruthlessly pursued by the Williamite cavalry. Sarsfield, who seems to have been put in reserve, did what he could to cover the retreat. The death roll was estimated at 7,000, and those who fell included

[1] See map 18.

members of many of the leading catholic families. In a military sense Aughrim, rather than the Boyne, was the major battle of the war. It left the Irish army broken and disheartened, and it prepared the way for the final surrender.

Before the campaign of 1691 began, Ginkel had obtained authority to offer security of estates to those officers who surrendered a town or garrison or brought over a body of troops. Similar terms were offered to citizens who procured the surrender of Limerick or Galway. A proclamation to this effect had been published in the name of the lords justices shortly before Aughrim. At the time it had little effect on the Irish, though protestants maintained that the terms were far too generous. But after Aughrim there was a growing desire to make peace, and this was particularly noticeable in Galway which was Ginkel's next objective. The Galway merchants had large holdings of land throughout Connacht, and most of their title-deeds depended on the act of settlement. They had strongly opposed the Jacobite repeal of the act and were ready to reach a settlement that would guarantee their estates. As Ginkel advanced towards Galway he was approached by leading townsmen who told him of the general desire to capitulate. The protests of d'Usson, the French commander, were brushed aside, and terms of surrender were agreed to on 21 July. Pardon and security of property were promised to the inhabitants. Officers of the garrison were offered the choice of submitting on similar terms or of joining the main Jacobite army at Limerick. Ginkel went beyond the terms of the lords justices' proclamation on several points. The catholic clergy and laity were promised the private practice of their religion; the clergy were to have protection for themselves and their property. Lawyers were to have freedom to practise and gentlemen were allowed to carry arms. Ginkel was severely criticised in England, but he pointed out the military advantage gained by the prompt surrender of the town.

Limerick was now the focus of Jacobite resistance, which was strongly encouraged by the French, who saw real advantage in keeping a Williamite army engaged in Ireland into the following year and promised to send assistance. Tyrconnell supported the French policy, but there was growing pressure for a settlement. In August Tyrconnell died, and Williamites thought this removed one of the obstacles to a settlement: it was he who kept the French and Irish together. In the last week of August Ginkel began his investment of Limerick from the eastern side of the Shannon. He saw little prospect of taking the town by storm and pinned his hope on negotiations. But it was not till he crossed the river and cut off the English town on its island from County Clare that the Irish were prepared to talk. Ginkel had hemmed them in, there was no news of the French convoy, supplies were running short, and there was a general war-weariness. Sarsfield, who had been the leader of resistance in the previous year, decided that it was now time to give up the struggle. He had obtained the reluctant consent of the

French officers on terms that had much attraction for him: Ginkel should be asked to let the Irish army go to France.

On 23 September Sarsfield asked for a cease-fire preparatory to arriving at a settlement on this basis. It was a great relief to Ginkel that the Irish had at last decided to negotiate. His own position was not easy. Although he had hemmed Limerick in on both sides of the Shannon he had still made no progress towards taking the place, and the English town on King's Island was a formidable obstacle. It was getting late in the season—nearly a month after the previous year's siege had been raised—and he was running short of ammunition. He had not expected Sarsfield to be associated with a peace-move. It had seemed possible that even if Limerick surrendered he would have to face a further period of guerrilla warfare in which Sarsfield would take the leading part. He concluded that Sarsfield's primary interest was to have a military career in charge of a body of his countrymen in France, and he decided that it was worth while to grant Sarsfield's request at the price of presenting an army to William's enemy. He therefore agreed to the proposal and a series of talks followed, in which the military and civil articles of surrender were hammered out. The talks were conducted with cordiality on both sides. Ginkel recognised Sarsfield's Jacobite title; Sarsfield brought a boat-load of claret across the river. Ginkel's dinner-parties included not only the leading Jacobite soldiers but also lawyers and the catholic archbishops of Armagh and Cashel.

The military articles gave little trouble. They provided that all who wished to go to France should be allowed to do so, and that Ginkel should give them transport. He seems to have considered that this remarkable arrangement came within his discretion as commander on the spot, although it went much further than the terms of an ordinary capitulation. The real bargaining took place over the civil articles, the terms that were to apply to those who stayed in Ireland. To begin with, the Irish asked for very liberal terms: a complete indemnity with no confiscation of estates; liberty of worship; the right of catholics to follow all professions, trade freely, and hold military and civil appointments. An interesting proposal was that the Irish army should be transferred to William's service on condition that it should be prepared to fight against France: a symptom of the strained relations that had developed between French and Irish officers. These demands, which would have put catholics in a more favourable position than they had held in Charles II's reign, were far too sweeping to be acceptable to Ginkel. His hands were tied by previous instructions which precluded a general pardon or more than bare toleration for the catholic church.

Ginkel rejected the Irish proposals out of hand, and substituted twelve propositions which formed the basis of the civil articles. They represented the utmost that he could give in the light of his instructions and of what he knew of protestant opinion. The first article promised catholics such freedom of worship as was 'consistent with the laws of Ireland or as they did enjoy in the reign of King Charles II'—an ambiguous offer which was not made much better by an undertaking that the Irish parliament would be recommended to give catholics even greater security.

In the second article pardon and property-rights were offered to those still holding out in Limerick or any other Irish garrison, provided that they stayed in Ireland and took an oath of allegiance to William. Those who went to France and those who had died or surrendered before the end of the war did not get the benefit of these terms and their property was liable to confiscation. The second article also provided that those admitted to its benefits could carry on their professions or trades as freely as they had done in Charles II's reign. Noblemen or gentlemen admitted to the second article were by another provision permitted to carry arms. In the course of the negotiations Sarsfield demanded that the terms should cover those under the protection of the Irish army in certain counties. This was agreed to, but in the final version of the agreement which was signed and taken to London the clause was later found to be missing, whether by accident or by design on the part of the huguenot who prepared the document. The 'missing clause' was debated in the English privy council, where its inclusion in the treaty was strongly opposed. William, however, followed Ginkel's advice and, in his ratification of the civil articles, reinserted the words on the ground that they had been 'casually omitted' by the writer and that the omission had been discovered before the surrender of the English town, the surrender having followed an assurance that the defect would be remedied. The 'missing clause' continued to be the subject of controversy, and it was left out when the Irish parliament gave partial confirmation to the articles.

Both sets of articles were signed on 3 October 1691 in what is commonly called the treaty of Limerick, which brought the war in Ireland to an end. The Irish town was at once handed over to Ginkel, but the Irish army was to remain in control of the English town till Ginkel provided transport to France. Individual soldiers were to choose whether to go to France or to remain behind. Sarsfield made a speech in which he held out hopes that those who went would soon be invading England or Ireland with a powerful army. Ginkel countered with offers of employment in William's service. The catholic clergy took Sarsfield's side with sermons on the religious advantage of helping France and the danger to the souls of those who joined the heretics. The majority opted for France. Only 1,000 declared themselves ready to enter William's service at the time, and 2,000 others went home. Later on there were some changes of mind and William was able to send 2,000 men to his ally the emperor. It was estimated that 12,000 men went with Sarsfield to France, where they were formed into a corps under James's control, but paid for by Louis. They formed the nucleus of the celebrated Irish regiments—the 'wild geese' who distinguished themselves in the French service during the eighteenth century. Sarsfield himself did not long survive; he was mortally wounded at the battle of Landen (1693). The men were accompanied by a number of women and children. Many of them went on the French fleet, which reached the Shannon on 20 October.[1] The gross delay in the dispatch of the French fleet from Brest was caused by administrative blunders which undermined the French policy of helping the Irish to hold out over the winter.

The terms of the treaty were severely criticised by both Jacobites and Williamites. Jacobite critics argued that the negotiators had been too weak and should have exacted much better terms from Ginkel. O'Kelly regretted that the articles 'were not so warily drawn but room was left for captious exceptions, neither was there any article made for assuring the true worship . . . and no condition had for prisoners of war nor the orphans of those who were slain in the service of their prince'. Williamites, on the other hand, thought that the terms were too favourable. 'A smart poem on the generous articles of Limerick and Galway' expressed the view that Ginkel had been outwitted:

> Hard fate that still attends our Irish war,
> The conquerors lose, the conquered gainers are;
> Their pen's the symbol of our sword's defeat,
> We fight like heroes but like fools we treat.[2]

Bishop Dopping preached a sermon against the treaty, in which he said that no reliance should be placed on the treacherous promises or submissions of the Irish.

Catholics regarded the penal laws of William and Anne as a breach of faith, and Limerick is traditionally referred to as the city of the 'broken treaty'. Protestants argued that the imposition of new laws was not in conflict with the treaty and that such laws were necessary for the security of the regime. The wording of the first article was certainly ambiguous, but there is no doubt that the penal code was in conflict with the spirit (and in respect of certain property-rights with the letter) of the treaty. It was unfortunate for catholics that peace in Ireland did not mean peace in Europe, and that Irish catholics as soldiers and clerics continued to be associated with attempts to restore the Stuart dynasty. The military articles, which gave James an Irish army, were not easy to reconcile with the civil articles, which offered toleration in return for allegiance to William. But the surrender of Limerick had given a real advantage to William and his allies by enabling them to devote all their resources to the continental war. Story summed it up well: 'since the Irish had it still in their power to give us the town or keep it

[1] Not, as often stated, two days after the treaty was signed.

[2] *The British muse* (London, 1700).

to themselves, I see no reason why they ought not to make a bargain for it and expect the performance of their contract'.[1]

The treaty of Limerick was nominally a compromise. In fact, it represented a Williamite victory and prepared the way for the protestant ascendancy that followed. The protestant colonists had much at stake and they were duly grateful to William for restoring their ascendancy. For many years they kept his birthday and, after his death, drank toasts to his 'glorious, pious, and immortal memory'. Those catholics who remained in Ireland were politically helpless and for many years made no attempt to resist the severe conditions imposed on them. They were under no illusions about the bleak prospect that lay before them.

The accession of James, which had given such hopes to Irish catholics, in the end left them worse off than ever. Tyrconnell's policy of establishing a catholic ascendancy had humiliated and frightened the protestants, and they were determined that such a situation should not recur. After the revolution, the Jacobite regime in Ireland depended on French help, which proved to be half-hearted and inadequate. Even if that help had been greater it is not likely that the result would have been different. Lack of unity and inability to keep up a sustained resistance were serious disadvantages on the Irish side. The securing of Ireland was a more important objective for William and his supporters than the buttressing of the Jacobite regime was for Louis. James turned out to be an uninspiring leader, out of sympathy with Irish aspirations, given to spasmodic bouts of energy followed by periods of indecision, gloom, and apathy. William, though slow to grapple with the Irish problem, showed energy and leadership when he did so. His armies and their equipment, after a poor beginning in 1689, were stronger than those of his opponent, and it was to the credit of the Irish army that it resisted as long as it did.

[1] George Story, *Continuation of the impartial history* (London, 1693), p. 279.

CHAPTER XX

The Irish language in the early modern period

BRIAN Ó CUÍV

THREE and a half centuries after the Anglo-Norman invasion of Ireland, Irish was still the dominant language throughout the country. The efforts, by the enactment of statutes and by other means, to promote the English language and to prevent the spread of Irish speech and habits to the non-Irish parts of the population had on the whole been unsuccessful, with the result that, outside the towns and parts of Leinster, the people were almost exclusively Irish-speaking, and Irish-speaking only. In an act passed in 1495 confirming the statutes of Kilkenny the provisions relating to the Irish language were excepted.[1] Twenty years later the complaint was made—in a well-known account of the state of Ireland about 1515—that, in addition to the Irish chiefs who were not subject to the king's rule, there were 'more then 30 greate captaines of thEnglyshe noble folke, that folowyth the same Iryshe ordre'.[2] These included the earl of Desmond, Lord Barry, Lord Roche, the Powers of Waterford, Sir Piers Butler, and all the captains of the Butlers of the county of Kilkenny and of the county of Fethard, the two Burke lords in Connacht, and many others. There were large areas of the country 'that obey not the kinges lawes, and have neyther justyce, neyther shyryffs, under the king', and 'all thEnglyshe folke of the said countyes ben of Iryshe habyt, of Iryshe langage, and of Iryshe condytions, except the cyties and the wallyd tounes'. Of the very limited areas described as being 'subjett unto the kinges lawes', 'all the comyn people of the said halff countyes, that obeyeth the kinges lawes, for the more parte ben of Iryshe byrthe, of Iryshe habyte, and of Iryshe langage'. While there may be exaggeration and inaccuracy in this account, the state papers for the rest of Henry VIII's reign indicate firstly, that the extirpation of the Irish language continued to be state policy, and secondly, that Irish continued to be generally the language of the country.

'An act for the English order, habite, and language', passed in 1537 in the Dublin parliament, planned to use various instruments, including education and religion, to propagate the English language. It ordered, for instance, not

[1] 10 Hen. VII, c. 8. [2] *S.P. Hen. VIII*, ii, 6–8.

only that the word of God should be preached in English, but even that priests should 'bid the beades' in that language.[1] Yet it seems likely that at least some members of the parliament which enacted that measure were themselves Irish speakers. It is revealed in reports of the passing, five years later, of the act whereby Henry VIII was acknowledged as king of Ireland, that Irish was used in presenting the bill in both houses of parliament, the interpreter for the lords being the earl of Ormond.[2]

It is probably this parliament of Henry VIII's that is referred to in a contemporary Irish poem that is an interesting comment on some recent events.[3] The poet, whose name has not come down to us, made no attempt to hide his feelings of shame and contempt for the Irish chiefs who had abandoned their heritage and submitted to the king of England. He mentions several families and names specifically Murchadh Ó Briain who accepted the title of earl of Thomond some time after he succeeded to the headship of the O'Briens in 1539, and Maghnus Ó Domhnaill whose submission was received by the lord deputy in 1541. He concludes:

Fúbún fán ngunna ngallghlas,
fúbún fán slabhra mbuidhe,
fúbún fán gcúirt gan bhéarla,
fúbún séanadh Mhic Mhuire.

A uaisle Inse seanAirt,
neamhmaith bhur gcéim ar gclaochlúdh;
a shluagh míthreórach meata,
ná habraidh feasta acht 'faobún' !

(Shame for the grey foreign gun, shame for the golden chain, shame for the court without [? English] speech, shameful the denial of Mary's son.

O nobles of the island of Art of old, ill is the change in your dignity; O weak cowardly lot, henceforth say nothing but 'shame'!)[4]

De-gaelicising was part of the process designed to produce the centralised state aimed at by the Tudors, but its achievement seemed remote in the first half of the sixteenth century. A necessary element in this process was the transfer of the ownership and control of much of the land of Ireland to the crown or to persons who would be amenable to state policy—*Goill ag comhroinn bhur gcríche* (foreigners sharing out your land), in the words of

[1] 28 Hen. VIII, c. 15, sect. 9; cf. above, p. 51.

[2] *S.P. Hen. VIII*, ii, 304.

[3] See Aodh de Blacam, *Gaelic literature surveyed* (Dublin, 1929), pp 125–7, for the text of this poem; for another edition see *Éigse*, xv (1974), pp 267 ff. Editorial note: it is possible that the word *béarla* here retains its older meaning—not 'English' but 'technical language', as *bérla filed* 'obscure poetical language', or *bérla Féne* 'legal language'; the latter seems most suitable here. If we were to read *gúna* 'gown' rather than *gunna* 'gun' the metre would not be affected and the quatrain would gain in consistency.

[4] For a modern view on the comment of the Four Masters on the submissions, see above, ch. II, p. 50.

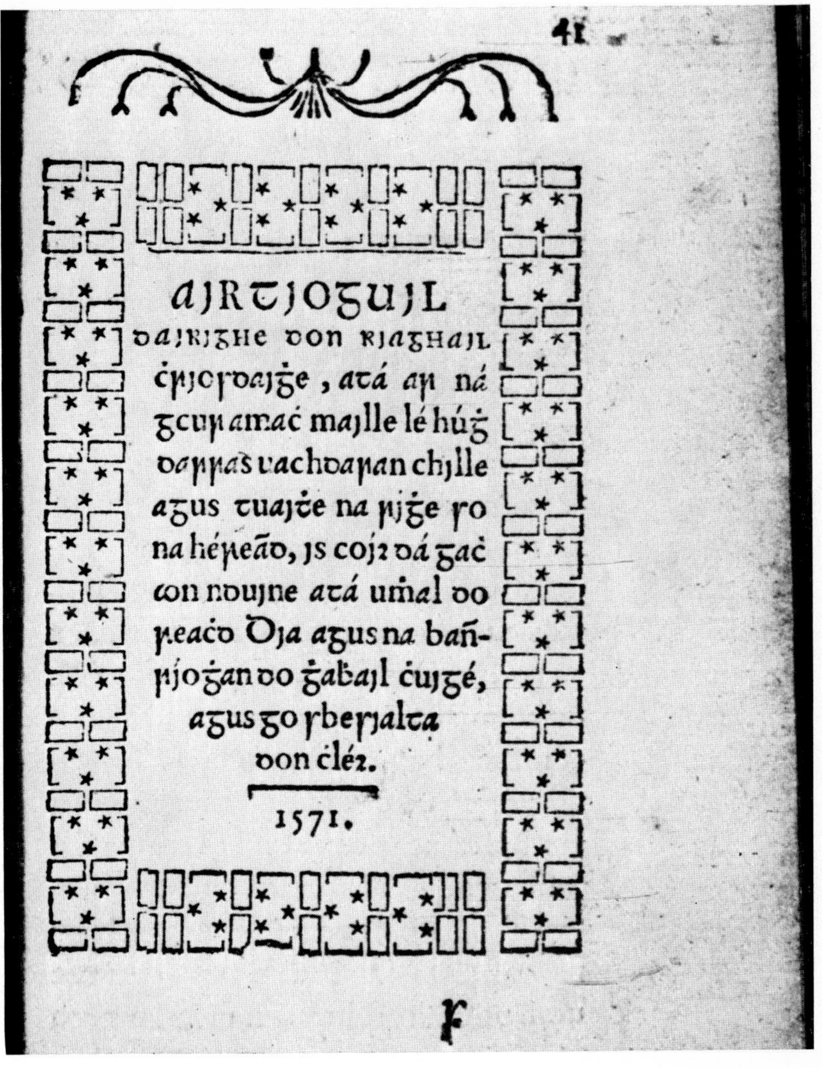
41

AIRTIOGUIL
DAIRIGHE DON RIAGHAIL
ċriosdaiġe, atá ar ná
gcur amaċ maille le húġ
darras uachdaran chille
agus tuaiṫe na ríġe so
na hÉreann, is coir dá gaċ
aon nduine atá umal do
reaċt Dé agus na ban-
ríoġan do ġabail ċuigé,
agus go sbesialta
don ċléir.

1571.

F

Plate 13. PAGE FROM JOHN KEARNEY (Seaan O'Kearnaigh), *Aibidil Gaoidheilge & caiticiosma* (Dublin, 1571): 'Irish alphabet and catechism'—the first Irish book printed in Ireland

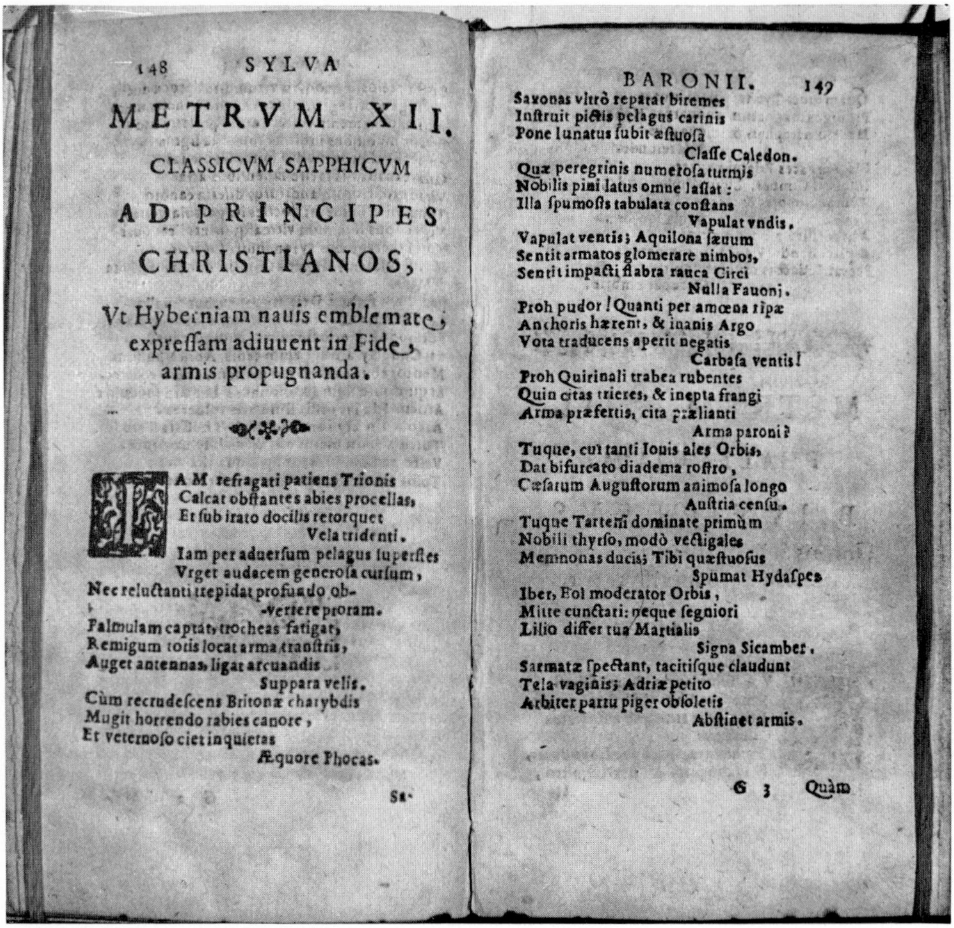

148 SYLVA

METRVM XII.

CLASSICVM SAPPHICVM

AD PRINCIPES CHRISTIANOS,

Vt Hyberniam nauis emblemate, expressam adiuuent in Fide, armis propugnanda.

IAM refragati patiens Trionis
Calcat obstantes abies procellas,
Et sub irato docilis retorquet
Vela tridenti.
Iam per aduersum pelagus superstes
Vrget audacem generosa cursum,
Nec reluctanti trepidat profundo ob-
-vertere proram.
Palmulam captat, trocheas fatigat,
Remigum totis locat arma transtris,
Auget antennas, ligat arcuandis
Suppara velis.
Cùm recrudescens Britonæ charybdis
Mugit horrendo rabies canore,
Et veternoso ciet inquietas
Æquore Phocas.

Sa-

BARONII. 149

Saxonas vltrò reparat biremes
Instruit pictis pelagus carinis
Pone lunatus subit æstuosâ
Classe Caledon.
Quæ peregrinis numerosa turmis
Nobilis pini latus omne lassat:
Illa spumosis tabulata constans
Vapulat vndis.
Vapulat ventis; Aquilona sæuum
Sentit armatos glomerare nimbos,
Sentit impacti flabra rauca Circi
Nulla Fauoni.
Proh pudor! Quanti per amœna ripæ
Anchoris hærent, & inanis Argo
Vota traducens aperit negatis
Carbasa ventis!
Proh Quirinali trabea rubentes
Quin citas trieres, & inepta frangi
Arma præfertis, cita prælianti
Arma paroni?
Tuque, cui tanti Iouis ales Orbis,
Dat bifurcato diadema rostro,
Cæsarum Augustorum animosa longo
Austria censu.
Tuque Tartesi dominate primùm
Nobili thyrso, modò vectigales
Memnonas ducis; Tibi quæstuosus
Spumat Hydaspes
Iber, Eoi moderator Orbis,
Mitte cunctari: neque segniori
Lilio differ tua Martialis
Signa Sicamber.
Sarmatæ spectant, tacitisque claudunt
Tela vaginis; Adriæ petito
Arbiter partu piger obsoletis
Abstinet armis.

G 3 Quàm

Plate 14. POEM XII, from Bonaventure Baron, *Metra miscellanea* (Rome, 1645); size of original $5\frac{5}{16}'' \times 3''$

the poet referred to above. Various stages in the implementation of this policy, whether by military or quasi-legal methods, are reflected in the Irish literature of the following centuries. So, too, is the religious struggle which stemmed from the tenacity of the majority of the people of Ireland in remaining true to the catholic faith and the Church of Rome after Henry VIII's rejection of papal authority—*séanadh Mhic Mhuire* as the poet described it.

The policy of the crown in promoting the reformed religion involved, in the second half of the sixteenth century, a change of policy towards the Irish language, resulting in the encouragement by Queen Elizabeth and her officials of the use of that language even in the heart of the Pale. Indeed, Elizabeth herself is reported to have expressed a desire to understand Irish, and Sir Christopher Nugent, ninth baron of Delvin, compiled a little primer of Irish designed to enable her to learn it.[1] Early in her reign she decided that the Bible should be translated into Irish, and she provided type and a press to print it. In 1564 we find her recommending a certain Robert Daly to the vacant see of Kildare 'the rather because he is well able (as we heare saye) to preache in the Irish tongue'.[2] Before long she was showing her impatience over the delay in preparing the translation of the Bible, for in 1567 we find the bishops being threatened that, if they did not presently print the New Testament, the queen should be repaid the money she had advanced for making the type.[3] In that same year the first book to be printed in Gaelic was published—not in Ireland, however, but in Edinburgh. This was a translation of John Knox's 'Liturgy'[4] by John Carswell, bishop of the Hebrides, who used for his work a slightly modified form of the literary language which was common to Ireland and Scotland at that time, and who used the 'roman' type-characters which henceforth remained in favour in Scotland. Four years later the first Irish book to be printed in Ireland was published in Dublin. It was a protestant 'catechism' and contained a brief introduction on the spelling and sounds of the Irish language.[5] Its author was John Kearney, treasurer of St Patrick's cathedral, and the cost of printing was borne by John Ussher, a Dublin alderman. The type used was that supplied earlier by Queen Elizabeth, which was also used in 1571 to print a religious poem in classical Irish by a fifteenth-century Franciscan. This was possibly a trial piece for the printer, and may well have been provided by Kearney who showed in the introductory part of his book that he had a great respect for the learning of the Irish poets. The type, which had

[1] *Facs. nat. MSS Ire.*, pt IV, 1, no. XXII.

[2] *Cal. S.P. Ire., 1509–73*, p. 234; quoted from Shirley, *Ch. in Ire., 1547–57*, pp 149–50.

[3] *Cal. S.P., Ire., 1509–73*, p. 356; Shirley, p. 317.

[4] *Foirm na nvrrnvidheadh . . . ar na dtarraing as Laidin, & as Gaillbherla in Gaoidheilg . . .* Dobuaileadh so agcló indún Edin . . . 1567, le Roibeard Lekprevik.

[5] *Aibidil Gaoidheilge & caiticiosma . . .* Do buaileadh so agcló Ghaoidheilge, amBaile Athaclíath . . . 1571. See plate 13.

features common in Irish manuscripts, was the forerunner of all those which were later classed as 'gaelic' type.

More than thirty years passed before work on the translation of the New Testament was brought to a conclusion with its publication by the Dublin printer Francke in 1602–3.[1] Those responsible for the preparation of the translation showed commendable discernment in finding scholars capable of doing this literary work in Irish. It need not surprise us that such were to be found in Dublin, for among the clergy attached to St Patrick's cathedral were Irish speakers who had the advantage of a university education, some in Cambridge, some in the new college in Dublin itself. What is more significant is that the help of a professional Irish poet, Maoilín Óg Mac Bruaideadha of Thomond, was enlisted, which suggests that Dublin was becoming a centre to which people from beyond the Pale were being attracted.[2] The extension of royal control—reflected in the entry for 1584 in the Annals of Loch Cé: *Éire uile ar na gabháil le Gallaibh* (all Ireland was taken over by the foreigners)—led to the attendance of Irish and Old English lords from various parts of the country at the parliament held in Dublin under Sir John Perrot in 1585.[3] The Four Masters list over fifty lords or their representatives who attended. So many Irish-speakers, accompanied by Irish-speaking followers and servants, must have attracted attention in Dublin.[4] We have another instance of Irish speakers being in Dublin—though unwillingly—about that time in the case of Aodh Ruadh Ó Domhnaill (Hugh Roe O'Donnell) and his companions who were kept in captivity in Dublin castle. Lughaidh Ó Cléirigh says that there were at that time numbers of Irish nobles and some Old English in captivity.[5] We should not suppose that either those attending the parliament or those in captivity would have had any language difficulties during their stay, for a short while earlier Lord Chancellor Gerrard had stated (1578) that 'all English, and for the most part with delight, even in Dublin, speak Irish'.[6]

There is ample evidence of the ambivalent attitude towards Irish on the part of those in government circles. Hostility is shown in Richard Stanihurst's comment:

Now put the case that the Irishe tongue were as sacred as the Hebrewe, as

[1] *Tiomna Nuadh ár Dtighearna* . . . Ar na chur a gcló a mBaile Athá Cliath . . . ré Seón Francke, 1602 [1603]. The translation of the Old Testament was made many years after this; see below, p. 534. Francke's patron was William Ussher, clerk of the council and son of John Ussher.

[2] An anecdote dating from about the end of Queen Elizabeth's reign, found in a praise composition (of the type known as *crosántacht*) made for an Ó Broin (O'Byrne) chief, tells of a Dublin merchant buying an Irish poem from some poets who had come to the city to buy arms and clothes from him. See *Leabhar Branach*, ed. Seán Mac Airt (Dublin, 1944), pp 215–16.

[3] *A.L.C.*, ii, 466; *A.F.M.*, v, 1826–40.

[4] It is even conceivable that Mac Bruaideadha was in the retinue of one of the O'Briens on that occasion.

[5] *Beatha Aodha Ruaidh Uí Dhomhnaill* (Dublin, 1948), pp 10–12; see also *A.F.M.* v, 1864. According to a later entry in *A.F.M.* vi, 2012, there were in Dublin city in 1597 children of gentlemen from every part of Ireland who had come there to be educated.

[6] *Cal. S.P. Ire., 1574–85*, p. 130.

learned as the Greeke, as fluent as the Latin, as amarous as the Italian, as courtious as the Hispanish, as courtelike as the French, yet truely (I know not which way it falleth out) I see not but it may be very well spared in the English Pale.[1]

This comment was made at about the same time as Lord Deputy Sidney suggested to Elizabeth that Gaelic-speaking ministers of religion should be brought from Scotland.[2] In 1587 and again in 1588 Sir William Herbert in Munster was expressing satisfaction at having had the Lord's Prayer and other religious matter translated into Irish,[3] while at the same time the lord deputy and council in Dublin were ordering that the laws made at Kilkenny be put 'with all severity in due execution in the province of Connacht and the country of Thomond'.[4] A few years later Edmund Spenser set down in very vivid form a philosophy applicable to the whole island: 'it hath been ever the use of the conqueror to despise the language of the conquered, and to force him by all means to learn his. . . . The speech being Irish, the heart must needs be Irish.'[5] The following century, which saw the extension of English power over the whole of Ireland and the dispossession of most of the Irish lords, also saw the beginning of the real decline of the Irish language.

The decades that saw the foregoing changes in policy also saw some decline in the fortunes of the Irish professional learned classes—poets, chroniclers, brehons, scribes, and so on. The destruction of manuscripts during the sixteenth century and also in later times has, of course, deprived us of much of the evidence of scholarly activity, including much of the literary production of that period. Nevertheless what remains is considerable, and indeed not all of it has yet been classified and studied. Though our knowledge is far from complete, we may assume that the organisation of learning in Gaelic Ireland of this period was much as it had been in the fourteenth and fifteenth centuries. As well as activity associated with the monasteries, there were secular schools of poetry, history, medicine, and law, and the leaders in the various professions were men of great social importance. What follows is intended to show the continuity of the learned tradition established earlier, together with elements that are particular to the circumstances of the period under review.

No detailed study of manuscripts of the sixteenth century has been published, but an examination of existing catalogues indicates that about a hundred items have survived, some on paper but the majority on vellum. The identity of the scribe and the date and place of writing are not known for all of these, but there are certain facts about the extant material which are worth noting. The long-standing antiquarian tendency to recopy older material was maintained; so tales, glossaries, and other texts from the

[1] Stanihurst, 'Description of Ire.' in Holinshed, ii, 11.
[2] *Cal. S.P. Ire., 1574–85*, p. 93. [3] Ibid., *1586–8*, pp 331, 533.
[4] Ibid., p. 564. [5] Spenser, *View*, ed. Renwick (1970), pp 67–8.

Middle and Old Irish periods, as well as genealogical and historical matter, feature in sixteenth-century manuscripts. About a score of manuscripts contain religious texts in prose and verse, saints' lives, devotional works, and so on. Some important law-texts transcribed in this period by members of professional families, such as Mac Aodhagáin, Mac Flannchadha, Ó Deóradháin, Ó Duibh dhá Bhoireann, and Ó Luinín, have survived,[1] and in addition there are contemporary legal documents—decisions,[2] agreements, deeds, wills[3]—which throw light on the practice of law in Gaelic areas,[4] as well as being of interest to linguistic scholars.[5] Two surviving items (T.C.D., MS H 2. 12, no. 8 III, and B.M., Eg. MS 90, f. 8.) relate to pleadings in court and may date from the sixteenth century. Neither has been published, but Professor D. A. Binchy has discussed the first of them at some length and has shown that it is largely an exercise in antiquarianism.[6] Among other survivals are letters in Irish, from such persons as Seaán Ó Néill, An Calbhach Ó Domhnaill, and James Fitzmaurice Fitzgerald. From these we see that Irish was used in correspondence not only between Irishmen but also between Irishmen and English officials, including the lord deputy. One such letter, which is of some importance in connection with Irish professional learning, is discussed later.[7]

Since the Irish annals are the most copious and reliable native sources for the history of Ireland and as such are without parallel elsewhere, it is appropriate that the annalistic compilations of the sixteenth century should be dealt with at this point. Originally the annals were records kept in

[1] See e.g. B.M., Eg. MSS 88, 90; Harl. MS 432; Cott. MS, Nero A VII; R.I.A. 23 Q 6; T.C.D. H 3. 17; H 4. 22.

[2] Among the brehons named in connection with extant decisions are members of the families of Mac Aodhagáin, Mac Flannchadha, and Ó Maoil Chonaire.

[3] Many of them were published by James Hardiman as 'Ancient Irish deeds' in *R.I.A. Trans.*, xv (1826). A very large proportion relate to lands and persons in Thomond. Seven documents from the Inchiquin archives, dating from 1576 to 1621, have been published by Gearóid Mac Niocaill in *Anal. Hib.*, no. 26 (1970), pp 45–70. Of special interest is an agreement dated 1539 between Ó Domhnaill and Tadhg Ó Conchubhair setting out the conditions upon which the latter held Sligo castle, for in it we find pledges being given for its observance by the poets of Ireland (in the persons of Ruaidhrí Mac an Bhaird, Ó Cléirigh and Fearghal Mac an Bhaird) as well as the church (in the person of the archbishop of Tuam). Note that it provided that the poets would use their powers of satire if required. See Maura Carney (ed.), 'Agreement between Ó Domhnaill and Tadhg Ó Conchubhair concerning Sligo castle (23 June 1539)' in *I.H.S.*, iii, no. 11 (Mar. 1944), pp 288–9.

[4] The annals do not give much information about lawyers. I have noted no references in them in this period to lawyer members of the Ó Breisléin, Ó Deóradháin, or Ó Duibh dhá Bhoireann families. Tadhg Mac Aodhagáin (d. 1584) is described in *A.L.C.* as *ollamh* in law to the family of Riocard Óg a Búrc. Three members of the Mic Fhlannchadha are recorded in A.F.M.: Aodh (mac Baothghalaigh) (d. 1575), Baothghalach Óg (d. 1576), both of Thomond, and Seaán (mac Domhnaill) (d. 1578), *ollamh* to the earl of Desmond. Marginal notes and colophons in extant manuscripts record many more names and throw light on the collaboration in learning and scribal activity between members of different families and schools.

[5] Not surprisingly several of the documents show evidence of word-borrowing from English.

[6] 'Distraint in Irish law' in *Celtica*, x (1973), pp 67–70.

[7] See below, p. 521.

monasteries, but by the sixteenth century lay scholars were engaged in their transmission and compilation. The Annals of Ulster, which had been compiled from earlier materials by Cathal (mac Maghnais) Mág Uidhir who died in 1498, were continued for some time after his death, but the entries that lie within the period from 1534 on are very few, extending from 1534 to 1541, when Ruaidhrí Ó Caiside, the continuator scribe, died, with, in addition, brief entries for eight further years between 1542 and 1586. Such entries as there are have particular reference to Ulster and the midlands. For events in the west the Annals of Connacht and the Annals of Loch Cé, both of which, apparently, derive from an Ó Duibhgeannáin school,[1] continue to be our major sources. The Annals of Connacht extend to 1544 with one further item, a eulogy on Brian Ó Ruairc on the occasion of his death in 1562. The Annals of Loch Cé, which have a special connection with the family of Mac Diarmada of Loch Cé, near Boyle, are the major sixteenth-century source still extant, for they record events of the century continuously down to 1590. Again there are a few isolated entries for later years, the longest being a eulogy on Brian Óg Mac Diarmada, lord of Magh Luirg, who died in 1636. The best known of the annalistic compilations, *Annála ríoghachta Éireann*, commonly known as the Annals of the Four Masters, belongs to the seventeenth century and will be discussed later.

In matter, language, and style the sixteenth-century annals are in the same mould as those of the previous period. The Irish is basically the current literary language without undue archaism but with an occasional flowery passage or learned allusion.[2] As in earlier annals there are some graphic and detailed descriptions which would appear to derive from on-the-spot reporting. The annals contain many items of local significance, some on a broader, even national, level,[3] and occasionally a record of some foreign event.[4] Apart from their importance as a record of events they are useful as a source of information on other matters, such as family relationships, men of learning, and even social and material culture.[5]

Although no other major sixteenth-century collection of annals has come down to us, we may assume that records similar to those mentioned above were compiled in other areas. From one of the prefatory documents prefixed to the text of *Annála ríoghachta Éireann* we know of several historical collections which were used in the seventeenth century but are no longer extant.

[1] See Aubrey Gwynn, 'The Annals of Connacht and the abbey of Cong' in *Galway Arch. Soc. Jn.*, xxvii (1956–7), pp 1–9.

[2] E.g. the onomastic reference to the prehistoric battle of Magh Tuireadh in *A.L.C.*, ii, 296.

[3] E.g. the destruction of statues and relics throughout the area controlled by the English in 1538 (*Ann. Conn.*; *A.L.C.*; *A.U.*), or the attendance of Irish and Anglo-Irish at the council of Ireland in 1543 (*A.L.C.*, ii, 338).

[4] E.g. the execution of Anne Boleyn (*A.U.*, 1536), or—further from home—the war between the Persians and the Turks over the killing of the king of Portugal (*A.L.C.*, ii, 428–30 (1579)).

[5] In the field of entertainment we may note the description of Niall Ó Néill as *fer lán . . . do cheól beóil agus láime* 'a man full . . . of music, both of voice and hand' (*Ann. Conn.*, p. 734 (1544)).

Of these special mention may be made of 'The book of Maoilín Óg Mac Bruaideadha' which is said to have covered the years from 1588 to 1603. In view of what has been said already about Mac Bruaideadha's connection with the work on the New Testament it may well be that some of the details of events in Dublin between 1588 and 1603 given in *Annála ríoghachta Éireann* derive from this 'book'. Another compilation covering about the same period is named the 'Book of Lughaidh Ó Cléirigh'. This is clearly the work known now as *Beatha Aodha Ruaidh Uí Dhomhnaill*, a detailed account of the career of Aodh Ruadh from the time of his capture and imprisonment in Dublin in 1587 to his death in Simancas in 1602.[1] Aodh Ruadh was a hero to his biographer, and this has led to inaccuracies and defects in the 'Life', which nevertheless remains an interesting and useful document of the period. From a literary point of view it is disappointing, for Ó Cléirigh chose to write in an extravagantly archaic and artificial Irish which his most recent editor, Paul Walsh, has, with justice, termed 'repulsive'.

Members of the learned families of Ó Duibhgeannáin, Ó Cléirigh, and Mac Bruaideadha, mentioned above in connection with the annalistic compilations of the sixteenth and seventeenth centuries, had for a long time been associated with the profession of *senchas* or history; and, together with the families of Mac Fir Bhisigh, Ó Cianáin, Ó Luinín, Ó Maoil Chonaire, and others, they continued in the sixteenth century to provide historiographers and chroniclers for the great ruling families. They also maintained schools of history, wrote manuscripts, and in many cases, like other men of substance, acted as hosts to travellers by maintaining *tighe aoigheadh* or 'guest-houses'. References to a *teach aoigheadh* maintained by a well-off professional man are frequent enough in the annals, and, together with accounts from other sources, indicate that hospitality towards strangers was without question a feature of Irish life. An anecdote in Séathrún Céitinn's *Trí biorghaoithe an bháis*,[2] written in 1631, emphasises the amazement of an Irishman travelling in England at being asked to pay for the hospitality he had enjoyed.

The extant annals for the period after 1533 contain references to only eighteen members of these families who followed the profession of history. Of the Ó Duibhgeannáin family, who were historians to the MacDermots and other chiefs of Clann Mhaoil Ruanaidh, they record Maghnas Buidhe (d. 1534, *A.U.*), Duibhgeann (d. 1542, *Ann. Conn.*), Fearghal (d. 1542, *A.L.C.*), Dolb (d. 1578, *A.F.M.*), and Maol Mhuire (who succeeded Dolb as *ollamh* in 1578, *A.F.M.*). Of the Ó Maoil Chonaire family, who were historians to the O'Connors and other branches of Síol Muireadhaigh, they record Muirgheas (d. 1543, *Ann. Conn.*; *A.L.C.*), Lochlainn (d. 1551, *A.L.C.*), Fiontan (d. 1585, *A.L.C.*), Seaán Ruadh (d. 1589, *A.L.C.*). One

[1] Ir. Texts Soc., xlii (1948), xlv (1957). Walsh's valuable introduction is in vol. xlv.
[2] *Ed.* Osborn Bergin (Dublin, 1931), pp 117–18.

Ó Luinín is mentioned, Matha Ruadh (d. 1588, *A.L.C.*). The Four Masters record four members of the O'Clerys who were historians to the O'Donnells: Tadhg Cam (d. 1565), Muiris Ballach (d. 1572), Muiris mac an Ghiolla Riabhaigh (d. 1573), and Mac Con (d. 1595), and four members of the Mac Bruaideadha family, who were historians to the O'Briens and other Dál gCais families: Diarmaid (d. 1563), Maoilín (d. 1582), Giolla Brighde (who succeeded Maoilín as *ollamh*), and Maoilín Óg (d. 1602).

Apart from the annals our sources of information about the professional historians—also about the Irish poets, doctors, and lawyers[1]—include manuscripts written by or for them, works composed by them and not infrequently surviving only in later copies, official documents of the English government and of municipal administrations in Ireland,[2] and the works of Old English writers such as Richard Stanihurst.[3] So extensive was the destruction of manuscripts that very little of the work of the historians named in the annals or of their contemporaries has come down to us, and hence we are not in a position to judge how effectively they performed their official duties to the great families. The few compositions still extant that are attributed to them consist for the most part of poems.[4] Some of these reflect their authors' family background, but others are hardly distinguishable from the work of the regular praise-poets. Exceptionally Muirgheas Ó Maoil Chonaire is known as scribe of a version of *Lebor gabála Érenn*, as compiler of the Book of Fenagh, an antiquarian hagiographical work about St Caillín which is based on earlier poems and which he wrote in 1516, and as author of an Irish translation of the twelfth-century Latin text known as *Visio Tundali*.[5] For this work he used an archaic Irish which is very different from the Irish seen in the early-sixteenth-century annals. A poem of the *dinnshenchas* (or placelore) type is also attributed to Muirgheas, but no historical work by him of immediate relevance to his times has been preserved.

One noteworthy manuscript of family history dating from the second half of the sixteenth century was begun for Seaán (mac Oilbhéarais) Búrc who became Mac Uilliam Íochtair in 1571, was appointed seneschal of Connacht by the English government in 1575, and died in 1580. It seems to have been intended to combine in it a history of the Burkes and poems composed in

[1] For some of these see Walsh, *Ir. men of learning*.

[2] See e.g. T. F. O'Rahilly's 'Irish poets, historians, and judges in English documents, 1538–1615' in *R.I.A. Proc.*, xxxvi, sect. C (1922), pp 86–120.

[3] Stanihurst's 'Description of Ireland' in Holinshed, ii, 39–44, gives the names of 'the learned men and authors of Ireland'.

[4] They include two poems by Dubhthach Ó Duibhgeannáin, one to Hugh O'Neill *c.* 1598 (beginning *Cumam croinic do chloinn Néill*), the other to Red Hugh O'Donnell *c.* 1600 (beginning *Leanam croinic chlann nDálaigh*). The first of these was composed to commemorate the battle of the Yellow Ford (1598; see above, pp. 124–5), in which, according to the poet, 1,800 English soldiers were killed as well as twenty-three 'captains' and the chief-marshal of Ireland.

[5] *Bk Fen.* and *Bk Fen.*, *supp.* For criticism of Macalister's disparaging criticism of Muirgheas in the latter volume see Paul Walsh, *The book of Fenagh* (Dublin, 1940); for *Visio Tundali* see V. H. Friedel and Kuno Meyer, *La vision de Tondale* (*Tnudgal*) (Paris, 1907), pp 89–155.

their honour, but two-thirds of the leaves have been left blank, possibly owing to the death of the patron who is the subject of the only two poems which were transcribed in the book. Apart from the poems the main contents, which are partly in Irish and partly in Latin, are an account of the territories supposed to have been held by the Burkes, and of rents and other rights due to them, and the history of the Burkes in the centuries following the Anglo-Norman invasion. This book[1] is most unusual among Irish manuscripts in that it has a series of fourteen illuminated pictures. Four of them are of religious subjects, one shows the Burke arms, and nine are portraits of various Burkes including Seaán mac Oilbhéarais.

Of medical manuscripts, more have survived from the sixteenth century than any other category—there are over thirty of them. One important factor in this survival is that members of medical families were given to compiling books for their own use and for fellow doctors, and that such books were commonly retained within the family circle of the owner. An indication of the value placed on such manuscripts is the fact that in 1500 the earl of Kildare gave twenty cows for the manuscript of a medical textbook.[2] There is also the fact that Irish medical men do not seem to have been subjected to the same criticism and harsh treatment as members of the other hereditary professions, possibly because their services were useful to members of the English colony,[3] and also because of the European element in their educational background which they shared with English and continental doctors. Hence in the sixteenth century we find Irish leeches active throughout the four provinces and even practising in Dublin.[4] Of the families known to have practised medicine as a hereditary profession there is evidence of one sort or another—in annals, official documents, and manuscripts—of over twenty in the sixteenth century. In the north and west the most renowned families were Ó Siadhail (who were leeches to the O'Dohertys of Inishowen but were also found in many other places in the northern half of the country), Ó Caiside (leeches to the Maguires of Fermanagh, but also found as far south as the midlands), Ó (or Mac) Duinnshléibhe (leeches to the O'Donnells, but also found in Leitrim, Sligo, and Meath), Ó (or Mac) Maoil Tuile (leeches to the O'Connors of Connacht), Ó Fearghusa (leeches to the O'Malleys

[1] T.C.D. MS F 4. 13; see Tomás Ó Raghallaigh, 'Seanchus na mBúrcach' in *Galway Arch. Soc. Jn.*, xiii (1924–7), pp 50–60, 101–38; xiv (1928–9), pp 30–51, 142–67.

[2] See *B.M. cat. Ir. MSS*, i, 220–21.

[3] Cf. for instance, the protection granted by the government to James Nealan, physician, in 1560 (*Fiants, Ire., Eliz.*, no. 215) and the reward made to him in 1585 (ibid., no. 4761).

[4] See *Anc. rec. Dublin*, ii, 146–7, for a record concerning a Nicholas Hykie, doctor of physic, who was the subject of an ordinance (dated 1580) regulating his practice of medicine in Dublin. Some years earlier, in 1572 and again in 1578, an Ó Maoil Tuile was arrested for practising as a surgeon in Dublin (*R.S.A.I. Jn.*, xxxiii (1903), pp. 225–6). When Brian Óg Mac Giolla Pádraig, lord of Upper Ossory, was released from prison in Dublin in 1581 he was brought to the house of William Kelly, surgeon, in an ailing condition. His own physician, Donnchadh Óg Mac Caisín of Ossory was sent for but was unable to save his patron's life. See William Carrigan, *History and antiquities of the diocese of Ossory*, introd., p. 84.

of Mayo), Ó Ceannabháin (leeches to the O'Flahertys); Mac an Leagha (in Sligo), Ó Cearnaigh and Mac Beatha (both in Mayo). In Munster there were Ó Troighthigh (Tipperary), Ó Callanáin (Tipperary, Cork, and Kerry), Ó hÍceadha (Tipperary, Clare, and Cork), and Ó Nialláin (Clare). In Leinster there were the Mac Caisín (leeches to the Fitzpatricks of Ossory), Ó Conchubhair (also in Ossory), Ó Bolgaoi, Ó Cadhla, and Ó Cuileamhain.[1] Although the hereditary nature of their profession and their patronage by Irish and Anglo-Irish chieftains were maintained, Irish medical men travelled around a great deal, partly to exercise their skills, but also, no doubt, to extend their knowledge. It must be remembered that in the fourteenth and fifteenth centuries some of their predecessors had gone to European centres for training and had brought back medical texts which continued to be in vogue centuries later. In the sixteenth century, too, there is an occasional record of an Irishman studying medicine outside Ireland. Thus a James Neylon, who graduated in arts and medicine in Oxford in 1545 and 1549, was probably one of the Clare family who were leeches to the O'Briens of Thomond. Mostly, however, their studies were carried on in their own schools in Ireland and Scotland, and in these schools textbooks were compiled and copied. To what extent the contents of these books were used in practice is, however, not clear.

Manuscripts written wholly or in part by members of more than half of the families listed above have survived, and a notable feature in them is the evidence, seen in colophons and marginalia, of collaboration between different families. There are, naturally, many instances of medical scribes copying far away from their native districts. Thus Cairpre Ó Ceannabháin of Connacht finished his work on a manuscript (R.I.A., MS 24 P 15) in Ros Broin in Cork,[2] and Maoil Sheachlainn Mac an Leagha, who was *ollamh* in medicine to Mac Donnchadha in Sligo, wrote part of a manuscript (King's Inns, Dublin, MS 15) in Kildare, from an exemplar lent to him by a Conaire Ó Maoil Chonaire, at a time when Mac an Leagha's own father was in Munster.[3] In the Advocates' Library, Edinburgh, there is a manuscript written in 1596 in Donnchadh Óg Ó Conchubhair's medical school in Aghamacart, Ossory, by a Donnchadh Albanach, who seems to have been leech to a Mac Dougall of Dunolly in Scotland.[4] An earlier extant manuscript from this school (N.L.I., MS G 12) was written mainly by Giolla Pádraig Ó Conchubhair, grandfather of the Donnchadh Óg mentioned above, and

[1] Many of these continued to be associated with medicine after the downfall of the Gaelic order. They will be more easily recognised now as Sheil, Cassidy, Donlevy or Downley, Tully or Flood, Fergus, Canavan, MacKinley, Carney, MacVeigh (the Scottish equivalent is Beaton), Troy, Callanan, Hickey, Nealon, Cashin, Connor, Bolger, Keily, and Culhoun.

[2] See *R.I.A. cat. Ir. MSS*, pp 1181–2.

[3] See *King's Inns cat. Ir. MSS*, pp 37–8.

[4] See Donald Mackinnon, *Descriptive catalogue of Gaelic manuscripts* (Edinburgh, 1912), pp 273–7; see also ibid., pp 63–71, for another important manuscript which can be connected with this.

another (R.I.A. MS 3 C 19) was written in 1590 in the house of Finghín Mac Giolla Pádraig—an Irish lord 'loyal' to the government—by a kinsman and pupil of Donnchadh Óg named Risteard Ó Conchubhair.[1] This latter manuscript contains a well-known translation of Bernard of Gordon's *Lilium medicinae* by Conchubhar Mac Duinnshléibhe as well as other works copied from exemplars written by Donnchadh Óg and a Fearghus Mac Beatha. Another school was that of Ó Bolgaidhir, in south Leinster where a manuscript in the National Library (G 8) was written in 1548 with the collaboration of members of the Ó Cléirigh and Ó Cuileamhain families. This manuscript has been described as 'a pocket-size medical encyclopaedia, containing texts, in a digested form, on almost every branch of medicine and medico-philosophy. It was perhaps intended as a teacher's note-book written with the collaboration of a whole medical school.'[2]

The activity of the sixteenth-century medical scribes and translators and of their successors in later times has left us many thousands of pages of scientific matter in Irish. Only a part of this has been published, for its interest is now mainly linguistic. The doctors, unlike the lawyers, were outward-looking scholars and instead of preserving old native texts and loading them with learned commentaries, they took textbooks of medicine and philosophy that were familiar elsewhere and translated them,[3] using the ordinary language of their day. The Irish in these works is generally unencumbered by archaism or undue stylism, and the translators handled the problem of technical terminology with a considerable measure of success.

While the doctors seem to have escaped the full hostility of the English government in Ireland, other professional men, and especially the poets, were not so fortunate. Thus an ordinance made in 1534 decreed that 'no Yryshe mynstrels, rymours, shannaghes (*seanchaidhes*), ne bardes, unchaghes (*óinseachs*), nor messangers, come to desire any goodes of any man dwellinge within the Inglyshrie, uppon peyne of forfayture of all theyr goodes, and theyr bodyes to prison'.[4] This was in line with government policy towards the Irish language already referred to, but there were special reasons for hostility to poets as is clear from a complaint made in 1537 to Lord Chancellor Thomas Cromwell by a Robert Cowley who wrote:

Harpers, rymours, Irishe cronyclers, bardes, and isshallyn [*aois ealadhan*], comonly goo with praisses to gentilmen in the Englishe Pale, praysing in rymes, otherwise callid danes, their extorcioners, robories, and abuses, as valiauntnes, whiche rejoysith theim in that their evell doinges; and procure a talent of Irishe

[1] See *R.I.A. cat. Ir. MSS*, pp 1167–73, for colophons and marginalia which contain interesting comments on contemporary events and on the scribe's travels in Leinster. Note his description of Donnchadh Óg Ó Conchubhair as 'chief physician of Ossory and best of the doctors of Ireland—and that without leaving Ireland to study'.

[2] *N.L.I. cat. Ir. MSS*, p. 42.

[3] For a list of medico-philosophical texts see *Féilsgríbhinn Eóin Mhic Néill*, pp 144–57.

[4] *S.P. Henry VIII*, ii, 215.

disposicion and conversacion in theme, whiche is likewyse convenient to bee expellid.[1]

A further effort to curb the activities of the poets was made in a statute of 1549 which ordered that 'no poet or any other person hereafter shall make or compose any poems or anything which is called "auran" to any person, except to the king, on pain of forfeiting all his goods, and imprisonment'.[2] Evidence of the continuation of the campaign against the poets is seen in a document compiled by a Dublin apothecary named Thomas Smyth in 1561[3] and is reflected in accounts of the Irish poets by later writers such as Spenser[4] and Fynes Moryson.[5]

While poetry was used by lawyers and historians, it was in the field of encomium that the poetic art was most used at professional level. It has been shown that in the centuries after the Anglo-Norman invasion certain families came to be associated with the practice of praise-poetry and that they succeeded in gaining extensive patronage from both Irish and Anglo-Irish chieftains. It seems likely that although 'shannaghes' and 'cronyclers' are listed as well as 'rymours' and 'bardes' in sixteenth-century English documents, it was against the professional praise-poets that official hostility was especially directed. This is indicated in a letter written in 1589 to the earl of Thomond, Donnchadh Ó Briain, by Conaire Ó Maoil Chonaire who complained that he had been seized by two officers and held for execution merely for composing, as they alleged, a poem for Ó Ruairc. Ó Maoil Chonaire asserted that the allegation was false and added that his family had never adopted the profession of poetry (*dán*) but rather 'that which is approved by both Irish and English, namely chronicling'.[6] However, the contemporary evidence on the subject in state papers is far from conclusive,[7] and despite Ó Maoil Chonaire's statement there is no doubt that some members of families who were primarily associated with the profession of history, including Ó Maoil Chonaire, Ó Cléirigh, and Mac Bruaideadha, composed encomiastic

[1] Ibid., p. 450.

[2] *Cal Carew MSS., 1515–74*, pp 214–15. While no Irish poem is known to have been composed in honour of Edward VI, during whose reign this law was made, there is still extant a poem which ostensibly at any rate was made in praise of Queen Elizabeth. Irish manuscript tradition is such that this poem has come down to us solely because a seventeenth-century poet, Dáibhidh Ó Bruadair, composed a vigorous answer to it (see J. C. Mac Erlean (ed.), *Duanaire Dháibhidh Uí Bhruadair*, iii (1917), p. 64). It has been dated to about 1588 or 1589 and it is believed that its author, who is not named in the extant manuscripts, is to be identified with a poet who composed panegyrics for members of the Butler family of Ormond (see James Carney (ed.), *Poems on the Butlers . . . 1450–1650* (Dublin, 1945), p. 137).

[3] This document was preserved in the S.P.O. and was published with annotations in *U.J.A.*, series i, vi (1858), pp 165–7, 202–12.

[4] *View*, ed. Renwick (1970), pp 72–5, 117–18.

[5] 'Itinerary', ed. Falkiner, p. 311.

[6] *Ir. texts*, iv, 27–9; see also Walsh, *Irish chiefs*, pp 285–97.

[7] See T. F. O'Rahilly, 'Irish poets, historians, and judges in English documents, 1538–1615' in *R.I.A. Proc.*, xxxvi, sect. C (1922), pp 86–120.

verse and might have been regarded as following the profession of praise-poet.

What is certain is that despite the expansion of the area affected by English rule the poets maintained their profession, with its elaborate system of training and its conventions and privileges, until the seventeenth century. Since the thirteenth century they had counted among their patrons Anglo-Norman lords such as the Burkes, and no amount of legislation could deprive them of the patronage of either Gall or Gaedheal. Indeed one of the most important sixteenth-century manuscript collections of verse that has survived was handed down in the Nugent family of Delvin and it contains a collection of poems for members of that family, one of whom was himself the author of poems in Irish.[1] Even Sir George Carew, the president of Munster under Elizabeth, was happy to be the subject of a typical praise-poem by a member of the Ó Dálaigh family of south-west Munster who had held lands under the Carews for centuries.[2] The panegyrics and other poems composed for members of Anglo-Irish families did not differ to any great extent from those composed for Gaelic lords.

Much of the poetry composed in the sixteenth century has come down to us in manuscripts of the seventeenth century or later, but there are some earlier manuscripts, including a number belonging to the class of *duanaire* or poem-book, of which the fourteenth-century *Leabhar Mhéig Shamhradháin* is the earliest extant example. The most noteworthy of the poem-books are those of the MacSweeneys,[3] O'Donnells,[4] Burkes,[5] Butlers,[6] Maguires,[7] O'Reillys,[8] and O'Haras.[9] Some other *duanaireadha*, such as those of the O'Byrnes of Wicklow, are known to us only from late copies. For the most part the remainder of the encomiastic verse from the sixteenth century is in manuscripts of the miscellany type.[10]

The annals of the sixteenth century record the names of only a small number of the poets of that period. Between 1534 and 1600 there are about a dozen entries concerning members of the families of Mac an Bhaird, Mac Con Midhe, Mac Eochadha, Ó Cobhthaigh, Ó Domhnalláin, and Ó hUiginn, but we know of at least six times as many poets for the period in question. Other families following the profession included those of Mac Céibhfhinn,

[1] N.L.I., MS G 992.

[2] See Anne O'Sullivan, 'Tadhg O'Daly and Sir George Carew' in *Éigse*, xiv (1971), pp 27–38.

[3] R.I.A., MS 24 P 25.

[4] Bodl., MS Rawl. F 514; compiled for Maghnus Ó Domhnaill in 1534.

[5] T.C.D., MS F 4. 13; begun, apparently, for Seaán Búrc, but not continued after his death in 1580.

[6] R.I.A., MS 23 F 21; compiled for Tiobóid Buitléir about 1576.

[7] Copenhagen, Ny Kgl. Saml. 268^{b}; compiled for Cú Chonnacht Мág Uidhir about 1590.

[8] Camb. Univ. Lib., MS 3082; written at various times between 1596 and 1639.

[9] Still in the possession of the O'Hara family of County Sligo; written mainly for Cormac Ó hEadhra in 1597.

[10] See Brian Ó Cuív, *The Irish bardic duanaire or 'poem-book'* (Dublin, 1974).

Mac Craith, Ó'n Cháinte, Ó Cionga, Ó Dálaigh, Ó hEodhasa, Ó Gnímh, and Ó Ruanadha. Many of the annalistic entries are obits, and we find in them terms such as *ollamh Connacht* (chief poet of Connacht), *ollamh Laighean* (chief poet of Leinster), *oide scol Éireann le dán* (teacher in poetry of the schools of Ireland), *oide fear nÉireann agus Alban le dán* (teacher in poetry of the men of Ireland and Scotland), which indicate that those whose names are recorded were men of standing. The position of *ollamh taoisigh* was firmly maintained down to the seventeenth century with, for example, the Mac an Bhaird family providing poets for the O'Donnells, the Ó hEodhasa for the Maguires, the Ó Gnímh for the O'Neills, the Ó Dálaigh for the MacCarthys, the Fitzgeralds, and the O'Keeffes. No more than in earlier times were poets restricted to composing for one chief and in fact they tended to compose for a wide range of patrons.[1] Thus among the extant work of Tadhg Dall Ó hUiginn (1551–91) are poems to members of the following families in Ulster, Connacht, and Leinster: Ó Domhnaill, Ó Néill, Mág Uidhir, Mac Suibhne, Mac Domhnaill, Ó Conchubhair, Ó Ruairc, Búrc, Ó hEadhra, and Ó Broin. We also have from him a poem in which he recalls a group of notable persons for whom he had great affection and who were in London at the time that he was writing. These included Donnchadh Ó Briain of Thomond, Donnchadh Ó Conchubhair of Sligo, Pádraig Pluingcéad of Dunsany, Irial Ó Fearghail, and Brian Mag Eochagáin. The poem serves to remind us of a plan proposed in 1562 by William Cecil for putting 'gentlemen's sons to school in England',[2] for at least some of those mentioned are known to have been brought up or educated in England.[3]

Sixteenth-century annalistic entries record a custom of which there is evidence from earlier times, that of the issuing by a chief of a general invitation (*gairm scoile*) to poets and other men of learning to visit him. Thus at Christmas 1540 Ruaidhrí Mac Diarmada and his wife, the daughter of Riocard Búrc, entertained a large number of chiefs along with a company of professional scholars from various parts of Ireland.[4] A similar event is recorded for 1549. In their obit of Toirdhealbhach Luineach Ó Néill in 1595 the Four Masters describe his generosity to poets, and they mention in particular the many invitations he issued to them to visit him at Christmas.[5] One of these occasions is described in a poem by Tadhg Dall Ó hUiginn in which he tells how Toirdhealbhach Luineach entertained him and his fellow poets at Christmas 1577.[6] He recalls that the poets caused Ó Néill great displeasure by refusing to provide him with panegyrics to his liking.

[1] The term *ollamh cuarta* (travelling *ollamh*) is used in a poem addressed to Cú Chonnacht Mág Uidhir by Conchubhar Crón Ó Dálaigh, a Munster poet who had lost three patrons in quick succession and who sought the post of *ollamh* to Mág Uidhir. See David Greene (ed.), *Duanaire Mhéig Uidhir* (Dublin, 1972), poem xix.

[2] *Cal. S.P. Ire., 1509–74*, p. 188.

[3] See Ó Huiginn, *Poems*, ii, 279–80.

[4] *A.L.C.*, ii, 326.

[5] *A.F.M.*, vi, 1984.

[6] Ó Huiginn, *Poems*, i, 50–56.

In spite of this Ó Néill insisted on paying them their due for the poems which they had composed. Not all poets were so fortunate, for we learn from the Annals of the Four Masters that in 1572 Conchubhar Ó Briain, earl of Thomond, had two poets hanged for some reason which is not specified. Not surprisingly this outrage earned the earl satires by many poets of the Northern Half. Among these is one by Uilliam Óg Mac an Bhaird in which he denounces Ó Briain for his deed and declares that henceforth Aodh Ó Domhnaill will be the protector of the poets.[1]

Two poems composed for this Conchubhar Ó Briain by hereditary Thomond poets reflect in different ways the history of their times. The first, by Domhnall Mac Bruaideadha, describes the ceremonial procession on the occasion of the installation of Conchubhar as earl of Thomond at Magh Áine in 1558.[2] Those attending included the lord deputy, who had overthrown the ruling Ó Briain in order to set up Conchubhar in the earldom, and the earls of Ormond, Clanricard, and Desmond. The second poem, written some sixteen years later by Maoilín Óg Mac Bruaideadha, is very different from the conventional panegyric.[3] It is a complaint about the poverty that has beset the poet following his abandonment by his patron. The poet threatens to avenge himself on Ó Briain by reporting that he is given to various practices which are disapproved by the authorities, including the levying of Irish dues, idolatry, and the encouragement of poetry.[4] Such a threat might seem foolhardy in view of Conchubhar Ó Briain's treatment of Irish poets a few years earlier, but Mac Bruaideadha appears to have been confident of sympathetic consideration. It is probably a fair indication of the esteem in which the professional poet was held that, though Conchubhar's successor as earl, his son Donnchadh, had been reared in the English court, the Mac Bruaideadha poets were maintained by him as professional poets until his death in 1624.

The traditional conservatism of the Irish professional poet is seen to a high degree in sixteenth-century verse where the literary motifs and concepts associated with the Ireland of the past are strongly represented both in panegyrics and in poems composed as comments on current situations. Nevertheless the reality of contemporary events, including the continuing expansion of English power, is reflected in such themes as the adoption of English habits and dress,[5] the introduction of English law,[6] the necessity to oppose the English in arms and hence to negotiate with them from a position of strength,[7] the abandonment of a friary because of confiscation or

[1] This poem, which is still unpublished, begins *Biaidh athroinn ar Inis Fáil.*

[2] Lambert McKenna (ed.), *Aithdioghluim dána* (Dublin, 1939), poem 27.

[3] T. F. O'Rahilly (ed.), *Measgra dánta* (Dublin and Cork, 1927), poem 26.

[4] Though Conchubhar Ó Briain was a catholic, his son, who is the earl referred to on p. 521, was brought up a protestant.

[5] Osborn Bergin, *Irish bardic poetry*, ed. David Greene and Fergus Kelly (Dublin, 1970), poem 9.

[6] Ibid., poem 19; also Ó Huiginn, *Poems*, poem 30.

[7] Ibid., poem 16.

persecution,[1] the destruction of a castle to prevent its being used by the English,[2] a victory over the English in an important battle,[3] the rigours of a military campaign in winter.[4] In theory, at any rate, the poets had not abandoned the idea of the possibility of Ireland being united under a rightful ruler, and so Ireland might be represented as a woman waiting for her rightful spouse.[5] A variant of this motif which became increasingly popular after the end of the sixteenth century shows her as a harlot ready to accept any newcomer.[6]

Of the surviving body of professional poetry a considerable amount belongs to the last decades of the sixteenth century and the first decades of the seventeenth, and much of it is still unpublished. Most numerous are the compositions of Tadhg Dall Ó hUiginn, Eochaidh Ó hEodhasa, Fearghal Óg Mac an Bhaird, Eóghan Ruadh Mac an Bhaird, and Tadhg Mac Bruaideadha, but there are many other poets whose extant work marks them as men of distinction in their profession. Ample illustration of the main characteristics and qualities of the work of the professional poets will be found in the known extant poems of Ó hUiginn, numbering forty-seven, all of which have been published.[7] More than three-quarters of them belong to the panegyric type, but they display an impressive variety of themes and treatment. An interesting feature is the use by Ó hUiginn of a relatively large number of literary allusions and apologues derived from external sources. This doubtless reflects a growing acquaintance in Gaelic Ireland with English and continental literature since the introduction of printing. This extension of literary experience is, naturally, also seen in the work of later poets such as Eochaidh Ó hEodhasa. Atypical of the rest of Ó hUiginn's extant work is a small number of poems which includes an amusing description of some poor-quality butter which was given to him, a satire on a mendicant friar, and another satire on a group of six men to whose behaviour in his house on one occasion he took exception.[8] According to a scribal note those satirised in this last poem were O'Haras and as a revenge they cut out the poet's tongue. We also have two poems[9] by Ó hUiginn on St Patrick's Purgatory in Lough Derg, composed, it seems, on the occasion of a visit to this holy place by himself and some other poets. Most unusual of all in content are two poems[10] which combine certain characteristics of the *amour courtois* genre of literature with elements of the 'vision' literature of early

[1] Cuthbert Mág Craith (ed.), *Dán na mBráthar Mionúr* (Dublin, 1967), poem 21.

[2] O'Rahilly, *Measgra dánta*, poem 56.

[3] A poem to Aodh Ó Néill, as yet unpublished, was composed on the occasion of the battle of the Yellow Ford.

[4] Bergin, op. cit., poem 29.

[5] Ó Huiginn, *Poems*, poem 1.

[6] Lambert McKenna, *Aonghus Fionn Ó Dálaigh* (Dublin, 1919), poem 53.

[7] Ó Huiginn, *Poems*; two additional poems in Lambert McKenna, *The Book of O'Hara* (Dublin, 1951), pp 290–312.

[8] Ó Huiginn, *Poems*, poems 37, 38, 44.

[9] Ibid., poems 45, 46.

[10] Ibid., poems 39, 40.

Irish tradition.[1] One of Ó hUiginn's poems[2] shows him as an innovator in form, for it is in *amhrán* metre and is the earliest specimen of its type.

Tadhg Dall died in 1591 while there was still hope of an Irish victory in the struggle against the English, but the other poets named above lived on to see the defeat at Kinsale and the subsequent confiscations and the exodus of Irish to the Continent. A lament for Aodh Ruadh Ó Domhnaill by Fearghal Óg Mac an Bhaird is one of the earliest extant poems dealing with the period after the battle of Kinsale.[3] The prospect of a Stuart king in place of the Tudors on the thrones of England and Ireland may have given a brief period of hope, for in a poem beginning *Trí coróna i gcairt Shéamais* (Three crowns in James's charter) Fearghal Óg eulogised James VI of Scotland in the familiar terms of traditional encomium.[4] But for the most part Mac an Bhaird and his fellow poets saw little to raise their spirits. They continued to perform their professional duties as praise-poets as long as there was a demand for them, but more and more their poems carry a message of impending doom for the Irish way of life and consequently for their profession. Fear Flatha Ó Gnímh, who composed several fine poems lamenting the downfall of the O'Neills for whom his family had provided hereditary poets, set down his view of the plight of Ireland as a whole in a national lament beginning *Mo thruaighe mar táid Gaoidhil* (Pitiful are the Gaeil).[5] He sees the Irish weakened and dispossessed, no longer practising their time-honoured customs and pastimes and with no prospect of relief from the conqueror. We find the note of despair very clear in some verses where the poet anticipates the thought underlying the later term 'West Briton':

Má thug an Deónaghadh dhi,
Sacsa nua dan hainm Éire
  bheith re a linn-se i lá imh bhiodhbhadh,
  don innse is cáir ceileabhradh.

(If providence has ordained that Ireland—a new England in all but name—should be in the hands of enemies in their time it is fitting to bid farewell to the isle.)[6]

In this poem Ó Gnímh refers to the lands being tilled in the English style. In another poem composed about the same time the author (possibly Lochlainn Ó Dálaigh) is even more specific about the new methods of fortification, enclosure, and cultivation that followed the displacement of the native Irish by English and Scottish planters.[7] While poems such as these

[1] For courtly love poetry see below, p. 528. [2] Ó Huiginn, *Poems*, poem 35.

[3] P. A. Breatnach, 'Marbhna Aodha Ruaidh Uí Domhnaill' in *Éigse*, xv (1973), pp 31–50.

[4] *Aithdioghluim dána*, poem 44. [5] *Measgra dánta*, poem 54.

[6] Ibid., lines 89–93. Cf. *Narab tusa Saxa óg, / a Bhanbha mhór, is fearr ainm* (May you not be a junior England, O great Ireland whose name is better), in another poem of this period (*Dán na mBráthar Mionúr*, poem 28, quat. 3).

[7] See Bagwell, *Stuarts*, i, ch. v. For this poem see William Gillies, 'A poem on the downfall of the Gaoidhil' in *Éigse*, xiii (1969–70), pp 203–10.

have no special literary merit, they contain matter which has not been adequately considered by social and political historians.

Even in the seventeenth century much of Scotland was still at one with Gaelic Ireland culturally. But it was alien in another way, as we see from a poem written in Scotland by Fearghal Óg Mac an Bhaird, in which he says that he had left Ireland in the hope of gaining wealth through his profession and that he now finds himself in a country where he cannot practise his religion:

Dámadh liom a hór bog,
dá bhfaghainn a bhfuil d'argad
i gcrích bhraonuair na mbeann bhfionn
dob fhearr aonuair an tAifreann.

(Were all its generously-given gold mine and were I to get all the silver in the cool fresh land of the fair peaks, better than these would it be to hear mass once.)[1]

The poet speaks of the real presence of God in the host and he prays to God and Mary that he may return to Ireland. Here, in the studied form of professional poetry, we come up against the reality of the reformation and we get a glimpse of the steadfast faith which was the mainstay of many an Irishman in the following centuries.

At the same time there is abundance of moral and religious verse from these centuries that gives little or no hint of religious change. Some of the poems are anonymous, others are attributed to well-known professional poets such as Diarmaid Ó Cobhthaigh, Gofraidh Mac an Bhaird, Mathghamhain Ó hUiginn, Giolla Brighde Ó hEodhasa, and Eochaidh Ó hEodhasa. The best known of those who composed religious poetry is Aonghus Fionn Ó Dálaigh, who lived in the latter part of the sixteenth century and the beginning of the seventeenth.[2] Over fifty such poems are attributed to him, many of them having the Virgin Mary as their subject. These are in the same mould as other religious verse of the Early Modern Irish period, being characterised by excellent technique and felicity of language but lacking the freshness and charm of the best of the Middle Irish religious lyrics. The qualities of simplicity and fervour, though without the perfection of technique, are seen in a Christmas hymn by the somewhat later Aodh Mac Aingil, a Franciscan who became archbishop of Armagh.[3] Very different in character is a long poem by another Franciscan, Eoghan Ó Dubhthaigh, who addressed it to the famous Maol Mhuire Mág Craith (Miler Magrath), the apostate bishop who turned protestant and ended his days as archbishop of Cashel, and to some other clerics.[4] This consists to a large extent of a diatribe against protestant clerics who had made little of the Virgin Mary, the mother of God. It is in syllabic verse with comparatively little use of

[1] *Aithdioghluim dána*, poem 53.
[2] See McKenna, *Aonghus Ó Dálaigh.*
[3] Mág Craith, *Dán na mBráthar Mionúr*, poem 30.
[4] Ibid., poem 27.

metrical ornaments, and in style is not unlike some of the later ballads of the Fenian cycle. A remarkable feature is the number of late borrowed words as well as Latin and English phrases which it contains. Another but gentler reproach to a 'heretic' is Giolla Brighde Ó hEodhasa's *Truagh liom, a chompáin, do chor.*[1] These two poems are part of the religious literature which sprang from the counter-reformation movement and which included a considerable number of interesting prose works referred to later.

While panegyric was a fundamental activity of the professional poet he also, of course, was capable of satire and the role of the Irish poet as satirist can be seen from early times. Mention has been made of satires on Conchubhar Ó Briain and on Maol Mhuire Mág Craith. There are others extant from this period, but the best known, which belongs to the seventeenth century, is not a satire on an individual but on the most important Irish families of the time.[2] It is attributed to Aonghus Ó Dálaigh, nicknamed An Bard Ruadh, and it is an extraordinarily vituperative work for a member of a profession that received so much from Gaelic rulers. It has been said in explanation of it that this satire on the Irish families was commissioned by Sir George Carew in order to belittle them in the eyes of their contemporaries, and while there is little evidence to support this theory it may not be without foundation.

This description of poetic activity would not be complete without some reference to the poetry of courtly love of which over a hundred specimens survive, most of them dating from the sixteenth and seventeenth centuries.[3] This poetry owes a great deal to external sources, but its form is essentially the syllabic verse used in the schools. Most of the poems are anonymous, but among the few named authors are noblemen such as Maghnus Ó Domhnaill, lord of Tír Chonaill, and Domhnall Mac Carthaigh, earl of Clanna Carthaigh, and professional poets such as Domhnall Mac Bruaideadha, Laoiseach Mac an Bhaird, and Eochaidh Ó hEodhasa. In this body of poetry we find a combination of lyrical and epigrammatic qualities which will be looked for in vain in the professional panegyrics of the time and which earn it a place beside the lyric poetry of the Old and Middle Irish period.

Syllabic verse, in a variety of categories and metres, had been cultivated now for the best part of a thousand years by Irish poets. In that period certain trends of fashions can be seen from time to time. For instance, in the sixteenth and seventeenth centuries, we find a metre called *droighneach* achieving a temporary popularity. Another form of composition called *crosántacht*, in which prose and syllabic verse are combined, also appears to have been especially cultivated at that time. Probably one reason for its

[1] Mág Craith, *Dán na mBráthar Mionúr*, poem 9.

[2] Aenghus O'Daly, *The tribes of Ireland*, ed. John O'Donovan (Dublin, 1852).

[3] See T. F. O'Rahilly, *Dánta grádha* (Dublin and Cork, 1926), which contains a long intro duction in which Robin Flower has discussed the origin and qualities of this genre of poetry.

popularity is that it was used as a vehicle for humorous anecdotes which must have provided audiences with a welcome change from the more serious side of professional poetry. The most significant metrical innovation of all, however, is the use by professional poets in the latter half of the sixteenth century of the non-syllabic type of metre known as *amhrán*. Within fifty or sixty years of the earliest datable extant example of this metre (composed prior to 1579) *amhrán* was on its way to ousting the syllabic metres which had held the field for so long. Its adoption as the common verse form is symptomatic of the upheaval that was taking place in the Gaelic world and which presaged the real decline of the Irish language.

Although at the beginning of the seventeenth century Irish had not lost its dominant position, there is no doubt that the confiscations and plantations that accompanied and followed the Elizabethan conquest left the way open for the spread of English. Before long many of the lords had fled abroad, and those who remained were not in a position to withstand the pressure of English rule. It was the upheaval among the landholders rather than any official measures against the Irish language that gained for English a foothold in the Irish countryside. Thus began the era when English would be learned for utilitarian reasons. This is indicated in a comment of Sir John Davies on the extension of the assizes to all parts of the country:

> Because they find a great inconvenience in moving their suits by an interpreter, they do for the most part send their children to schools, especially to learn the English language. . . . We may conceive an hope that the next generation will in tongue and heart and every way else become English, so as there will be no difference or distinction but the Irish sea betwixt us.[1]

A mere fifteen years later Conell Ma Geoghagan, an Irish historian, wrote of his fellow chroniclers.

> Because they cannot enjoy that respect and gain by their said profession as heretofore they and their ancestors received they set naught by the said knowledge, neglect their books, and choose rather to put their children to learn English than their own native language.[2]

There is no doubt that as the century proceeded more and more people learned English and this fact is reflected in many regretful comments in texts in prose and verse by authors who were seemingly very conscious of the significance for the Irish people of the linguistic change that was taking place.

When we consider Irish learning in the early seventeenth century we are immediately struck by the immense amount of literary and scribal activity that continued despite the unsettled state of the times. The old patterns of life were upset but the strong links with the Continent, which are discussed elsewhere in this history,[3] broadened the education of many Irishmen and

[1] *Discovery*, in Morley, *Ire. under Eliz. & Jas I*, pp 335–6.

[2] *Ann. Clon.*, p. 8.

[3] See below, ch. XXII, XXIII.

equipped them for what must be counted as one of the great rescue operations of a country's traditions. Conscious of the danger of the loss of their nation's literary heritage, devoted workers, who included members of the old professional classes and members of religious orders, set about collecting and recopying old manuscripts and utilising their contents for fresh compilations. A new element in the situation was the interest now being shown in Irish history and antiquities by members of the English official class in Ireland and of the reformed church, a fact amply demonstrated by the history of Irish manuscript collections from that time on.

About 200 seventeenth-century Irish manuscripts have been noted in the major libraries in Ireland and abroad. Some of these are of contemporary or near-contemporary works, but many of them contain Old and Middle Irish texts which are otherwise unknown. These texts do not concern us here but the part played by seventeenth-century scholars in their preservation is significant. Among the known scribes we find members of the old professional families such as Ó Maoil Chonaire, Ó Duibhgeannáin, Ó Cléirigh, Ó Duinnín, and Mac Fir Bhisigh, but there are also names not previously recorded in this field of activity. An interesting feature is the carrying on of scribal work among the Irish emigrants in European countries. Thus between 1626 and 1631 an Irishman named Aodh Ó Dochartaigh, working in the Netherlands under the patronage of Captain Somhairle Mac Domhnaill, wrote two collections of poetry, one of them consisting of Fenian ballads, the other being an anthology of some 340 pieces, comprising praise-poems, historical poems, love-poems, and many on religious and didactic themes.[1] Another manuscript anthology of poetry compiled in the Netherlands is that made by Fearghal Ó Gadhra, O.S.A., between 1655 and 1659.[2] Among the seventeenth-century family poem-books is one which is known as 'The book of O'Donnell's daughter' which contains a large number of poems to contemporary and earlier members of the Ó Domhnaill family of Donegal and which is believed to have been written in Flanders for Nuala, daughter of Aodh (mac Maghnuis) Ó Domhnaill, who is known to have been living in Louvain from about 1613.[3] It need hardly be said that this scribal activity was only one of the ways in which the Irish language and Irish literature and learned traditions were cultivated on the Continent in the seventeenth century. Through the foundation of the various colleges, and in particular the Franciscan College in Louvain, the work of Irish men of learning at home was supported and supplemented. Continental education introduced a new element which is reflected most conspicuously, perhaps, in the catholic religious prose works that were produced from the end of the sixteenth century on and which are dealt with later on in this chapter.

[1] Now MS A 20 in the Franciscan Library, Killiney, and 'The book of O'Conor Don', respectively.

[2] Now R.I.A. MS 23 F 16.

[3] Now MS 6131–3 in the Bibliothèque Royale in Brussels.

The link between the Irish abroad and those at home is probably most clearly seen in the work of Míchéal Ó Cléirigh and his associates—the 'Four Masters'. Encouraged and supported by his Franciscan superiors and aided by the patronage of Fearghal Ó Gadhra of Sligo, Ó Cléirigh travelled around Ireland collecting materials for research on history, hagiography, and other subjects. He and his fellow workers ensured the preservation of many old texts by recopying them, but they are remembered especially for their work *Annála ríoghachta Éireann* which recorded events in the history of Ireland from early times down to 1616. As has been noted already, this work incorporated materials found in earlier collections of annals, but for later events it is an important independent historical source. It is fitting that the names of Míchéal Ó Cléirigh's main associates in this work should be recorded here: Cú Choigcríche Ó Cléirigh, Fear Feasa Ó Maoil Chonaire, and Cú Choigcríche Ó Duibhgeannáin. Mention may also be made of two further works for whose compilation Míchéal Ó Cléirigh was largely responsible: a revised version of *Lebor gabála Érenn* and a new Irish martyrology which is now known as *The martyrology of Donegal.*

A historical work of a totally different character was composed by Ó Cléirigh's contemporary Séathrún Céitinn (Geoffrey Keating) who is also well known as a poet and as a writer of religious works. Born in Tipperary, he had attended one or more of the native secular schools before going to France to be educated for the priesthood. Like Ó Cléirigh, he collected a vast amount of material, but instead of presenting it in annalistic form he used as a framework the list of kings of Ireland found in manuscripts such as the Book of Leinster. Into this framework he wove materials from disparate sources—stories, semi-historical tracts, historical poems and so on—to produce a most readable narrative on Ireland down to the end of the twelfth century. This he called *Foras feasa ar Éirinn* (a basis of knowledge about Ireland), and in a long preface he criticised other writers who had, he claimed, put out false accounts of Ireland. In particular he took issue with Giraldus Cambrensis, Spenser, Camden, Stanihurst, Hanmer, Fynes Moryson, and others. Céitinn is remarkable on the one hand for his familiarity with, and handling of, earlier source material, and on the other for his knowledge of the works of foreign authors. His achievement doubtless reflects a training of some sort in the native learned tradition, followed by the very different sort of education he acquired as a clerical student in France. His monumental historical work, which was written in a pleasant style, proved immensely popular and it circulated widely in manuscript form in the following centuries. It was not printed in full until the present century.[1]

Céitinn seems to have had some special relationship with Seaán mac Torna Ó Maoil Chonaire of Thomond and other members of that family

[1] Geoffrey Keating, *Foras feasa ar Éirinn; the history of Ireland*, ed. David Comyn and P. S. Dinneen (Ir. Texts Soc., 4 vols, London, 1902–14).

who made transcripts of his major prose works during his lifetime and later. Indeed it seems likely that they were responsible in no small measure for the early circulation of his work. Outstanding members of two other families of hereditary scribes and scholars may also be mentioned. The last representative of the Mac Fir Bhisigh family was An Dubhaltach, who was murdered in 1671 after a long life spent in scholarly pursuits, during which he assisted Sir James Ware in his historical researches.[1] To him we owe the survival of the annalistic text known as *Chronicum Scotorum*,[2] and a historical narrative published by John O'Donovan under the title *Annals of Ireland; three fragments*.[3] Mac Fir Bhisigh also compiled a list of Irish writers[4] and a 'Book of Genealogies'[5] which is a remarkable repository of information on Irish families. Contemporary with Mac Fir Bhisigh was Dáibhídh Ó Duibhgeannáin whose scribal labours in Sligo, Leitrim, Mayo, and Galway ensured the preservation of such texts as *Buile Shuibhne*, *Cath Muighe Rath*, and *Cath Muighe Tuireadh*. He seems to have died in 1696, almost at the end of a century which saw the final stages in the disruption of the hereditary professional system to which he belonged.

The earliest printed books in Irish were doctrinal works produced for members of the reformed church. The first of these had been printed in Dublin as early as 1571 but it was not until forty years later that the first of the catholic works was published, and even then it was not in Ireland but on the Continent that they were printed.[6] But at least one important work designed for the instruction of the catholic Irish had been compiled before the end of the sixteenth century. This was a short doctrinal catechism which had been translated from Spanish in 1593 by Flaithrí Ó Maoil Chonaire, a member of the Connacht family of hereditary historians who became a Franciscan and like other Irishmen of his day went to the Continent for his religious training. Ó Maoil Chonaire sent his text to Ireland in 1598 but it remained in manuscript form until recently.[7] The course of events in Ireland in the first decade of the seventeenth century increased the need for catholic books. The protestants' translation of the New Testament (1603) had been followed up with *Leabhar na nUrnaightheadh gComhchoidchiond* (Dublin, 1608), a translation of the Book of Common Prayer by Uilliam Ó Domhnaill who soon after was rewarded by being appointed archbishop of Tuam. Here, as in the earlier work with which Ó Domhnaill was associated, we find a slightly modified form of the literary language of the poets used to produce a very readable prose text. The Franciscans now took the matter in

[1] Among his work for Ware was a translation of fifteenth-century annals (published by John O'Donovan in *Ir. Arch. Soc. misc.*, pp 198–302).

[2] Printed in the Rolls Series, ed. W. M. Hennessy, 1866.

[3] Dublin, 1860.

[4] Printed in *Celtica*, i (1946–50), pp 86–110.

[5] The original manuscript is in University College, Dublin.

[6] Below, pp 582, 632.

[7] Printed in *Celtica*, i, 161–206.

hand. The result was the publication of a number of works within a decade: Giolla Brighde Ó hEodhasa's *An teagasg Criosdaidhe* (Antwerp, 1611), *Suim Riaghlachas Phroinsiais* (no date but probably printed in Louvain between 1610 and 1614), Flaithrí Ó Maoil Chonaire's *Sgáthán an chrábhaidh* (Louvain, 1616), and Aodh Mac Aingil's *Scáthán shacramuinte na h-aithridhe* (Louvain, 1618).[1] The importance of Ó hEodhasa in this endeavour of the Franciscans is emphasised by Mac Aingil who also refers to the need for books 'since, because of the violence of the persecution, we are not allowed to engage in oral instruction'.[2] Most interesting to the historian is the work of Ó Maoil Chonaire who had been confessor to Aodh Ruadh Ó Domhnaill and who was active in political matters for many years. It is an adaptation of an early sixteenth-century Spanish work on the Christian endeavour to achieve the love of God but Ó Maoil Chonaire worked into his version a great deal of additional matter intended to guide and support Irish catholics in the difficulties in which they found themselves. Among the topics discussed are the banishment of the catholic clergy, attempts to persuade catholics to abandon their clergy, the legitimacy of catholic laymen sitting in judgement on clerics, the supposed authority of the protestant bishops, the authority of temporal powers, the oath of supremacy, and recusancy fines. It is noteworthy that Ó Maoil Chonaire puts forward the view that civil government derives its authority from the governed. In this he was probably following the teaching of his contemporary, the Spanish Jesuit Francisco Suarez, who had already written to this effect in two important treatises, the second largely directed against the oath of allegiance to the English king, and forbidden by James I to be read, under the severest penalties.

After the publication of Mac Aingil's work there was a gap of twenty years during which the need for books of instruction became all the greater as the number of Irish speakers who emigrated increased. Then came Teabóid Gállduf's *Catechismus* (Brussels, 1639), a catechism in Irish and Latin, Bernard Conny's *Riaghuil Threas Uird S. Froinsias* (Louvain, 1641), and Antoin Gearnon's *Parrthas an Anma* (Louvain, 1645). Gállduf, who was very conscious of the difference between the current spoken language and the literary language, modified the traditional spelling to make his text easier to read and he also used the conventional roman and italic types instead of the 'gaelic' type which was used in other works. No further catholic book was published until after the restoration of Charles II and then came John Dowley's *Suim bhunudhasach an teaguisg Chriosdaidhe* (Louvain, 1663), and Proinsias Ó Maoil Mhuaidh's *Lóchrann na gcreidmheach* (Rome, 1676). On the protestant side one other major work published

[1] An effort was made by an English agent in 1614 to prevent the publication of such works. See *Downshire MSS*, iv, 443.

[2] *Scáthán shacramuinte na h-aithridhe* (2nd ed., Dublin, 1952), ll 3086–8.

in the seventeenth century was the translation of the Old Testament. This had been made in the first half of the century under the direction of William Bedell, one-time provost of Trinity College in Dublin and later protestant bishop of Kilmore, but it was not published until 1685 when it was printed in London. Bedell stands out among his contemporaries in the reformed church for his efforts to make the Bible available in Irish, and it is clear that catholics saw him as being very different from those protestant clergymen and government officials from whom they had suffered so much.

Apart from books published, many other religious works were composed, both in Ireland and on the Continent. Some of these became very popular and circulated widely in manuscript copies. Others remained almost unknown. To the first category belong two works by Séathrún Céitinn: *Eochairsgiath an aifrinn*, a work on the mass, and *Trí biorghaoithe an bháis*, on moral and philosophical topics, completed in 1631. Like other similar works of their time these reflect the continental training of their author, who drew heavily on contemporary works in other languages. Among the less well known works are a version of the Rule of St Clare and associated texts[1] made in 1636 and the following years by three authors, one of whom was the historian An Dubhaltach Mac Fir Bhisigh, for the Franciscan nuns who eventually settled in Galway, and *Buaidh na naomhchroiche*,[2] a translation of Savonarola's *Triumphus crucis* made in 1650 by a Franciscan named Bonaventúr Ó Conchubhair. While some of the authors of such religious texts may have looked forward to seeing their work in print the majority must have known that their writings would, at most, achieve the limited circulation that was possible for manuscript works. For twentieth-century scholars they have special interest as specimens of Irish prose composed by authors close to the classical tradition.

There are several prose works of this period that are important as historical records. Firstly there is a long account of the travels of the earl of Tyrone and others of the Ulster fugitives after they sailed from Lough Swilly in 1607. Like most of the writings of the time the work remained in manuscript form until the present century.[3] Its author was Tadhg Ó Cianáin, a member of a family of professional scholars who in the past had provided historians to the Maguires. He accompanied the emigrants abroad and his autograph record, which is in diary form, covers their journey from Ireland to Normandy and thence through north-eastern France to Flanders and then southwards to Switzerland and on to Rome, which the remnant of the original party (numbering ninety-nine) reached in April 1608. This part amounts to about two-thirds of the text; the remainder contains an account of the doings

[1] *Ed.* Eleanor Knott in *Ériu*, xv (1948), pp 1–187.

[2] *Ed.* Pádraig Ó Súilleabháin (Dublin, 1972). Nothing is known of the history of this work between 1650 and the present century, when the author's manuscript turned up in Rome in a dentist's premises.

[3] *The flight of the earls*, ed. Paul Walsh (Dublin, 1916).

of those who reached Rome and covers the period from May to the end of November 1608. Many Irish pilgrims made the journey from Ireland to Rome between the ninth century and the seventeenth, but none of them left such a detailed record as this. In abandoning Ireland with Ó Néill, Tadhg Ó Cianáin had left his wife behind, and there is nothing to show that they were ever reunited. His account does not disclose this personal tragedy, however, but rather the tribulations suffered by the company as a whole during their travels, as well as the many kindnesses and honours they received. As a professional historian Ó Cianáin was familiar with the linguistic archaisms that were part of the inheritance of the learned classes and he chose to use many of these in his narrative. The result is that his work, though highly interesting in its content, is not as attractive stylistically as some other contemporary prose writings such as the religious works already dealt with. In this it resembles somewhat the 'Life' of Aodh Ruadh Ó Domhnaill by Lughaidh Ó Cléirigh, though Ó Cianáin's Irish is far from being as artificial as that of Ó Cléirigh.

Another historical work to be noted is an account of the wars in Ulster and Leinster under Sir Féilim Ó Néill and Eoghan Ruadh Ó Néill between 1641 and 1647. This is of little literary merit, but it is of considerable interest for its detailed information about persons and events as well as for the light it throws on the process of word-borrowing from English in the seventeenth century. Its author was probably Toirdhealbhach Ó Mealláin, a Franciscan priest, who was chaplain to Féilim Ó Néill.[1]

A work of a totally different kind is *Páirlimint Cloinne Tomáis*. This, like several verse compositions of the seventeenth century, reflects the feelings of members of the professional learned classes who saw their position and privileges being swept away in the unsettled times in which they lived. The poets and others had seen the lords on whom they depended for patronage deprived of their wealth and in many cases forced to leave the country. One of the dominant notes in the literature of the seventeenth century is the plight to which poetry and music have been reduced. But the *Páirlimint Cloinne Tomáis* also presents a picture of a social revolution for which it is itself the chief evidence. It is a satirical attack on the *Clann Tomáis* or *Clann Orlaithe* who are apparently families that have come up in the world and become tenants of the English planters who were engaged in developing their newly acquired estates. The author describes the Clann Tomáis as 'coarse and brutish peasants, gluttonous and quarrelsome, aping the gentry, trying to dress fashionably, too low to understand the meaning of refinement, but lost in admiration of a man who could talk broken English'.[2] This work purports to describe, among other things, the assembly of the peasantry in the form of a 'parliament' on a number of occasions in the seventeenth

[1] 'Cín lae Ó Mealláin' in *Anal. Hib.*, no. 3 (1931), pp 1–61.

[2] Osborn J. Bergin's comment in the preface to his edition in *Gadelica*, i (1912–13), pp 35–6.

century. The dates 1632 and 1645 are mentioned, as is Cromwell who is described as 'Protector'. Neither the author nor the date of composition is known, and indeed it may not all have been composed at one time, for it is in two 'books'. Though clearly composed by a professional scholar it is full of slang, supposedly the normal speech of the churls and rabble being satirised. Later in the century the poet Ó Bruadair used the same device to point his sarcasm and invective. In this way some of the normal vocabulary of later Munster Irish appears for the first time in Irish literature. It was in part the conventionalism of the schools that had excluded such words from literary use for hundreds of years. Their use now on a literary level reflects the changing conditions among the learned classes, just as the use of English words and phrases reflects the changing linguistic situation during the seventeenth century.

A noticeable feature about *Páirlimint Cloinne Tomáis* is the occurrence in it of stylistic features that were part of the stock-in-trade of the storytellers of the sixteenth and seventeenth centuries, and were to some extent a continuation of earlier narrative methods. It seems likely that the author of the *Páirlimint* felt that his satire would be made more effective by a sort of burlesque of what was still a very real element in the entertainment of people of all classes. For there can be no doubt that storytelling flourished during the sixteenth and seventeenth centuries. There were many changes in style and themes between the ninth century and the sixteenth, even apart from changes in the form of the language in which the stories were composed or narrated, but manuscripts reflect only some of these changes. Thus manuscripts of the sixteenth and seventeenth centuries contain versions of tales which belong to the Old or Middle Irish periods, such as early stories belonging to the mythological cycle, to the heroic cycle, or to the king cycles. We also find later versions or adaptations of early tales, such as the Early Modern Irish version of *Táin bó Cuailnge* of the Ulster cycle. However, there are few new tales from this period about persons who feature in the heroic or king cycles, and those that exist show the influence of other categories of contemporary storytelling. In fact storytelling in the heroic and kingly traditions seems for the most part to have passed out of fashion during the twelfth century, and at the same time tales about Fionn mac Cumhaill (Finn MacCool), which had been popular at lower levels of society, came into vogue.

The available evidence suggests that after the Anglo-Norman invasion Irish storytellers favoured tales in which marvellous and romantic themes were dominant. Such themes were characteristic of contemporary continental tales, but in Ireland the matter of the stories remained almost completely native for a considerable time. It was in this period that the Fionn cycle achieved its greatest development at a literary level, both in tales and ballad form. Following the consolidation of the power of the Anglo-Norman lords and their adoption of Gaelic ways the continental culture with which they were familiar exercised an even greater influence on Irish literature. Already in the fifteenth century Irish storytelling was enriched by continental fictional matter and the process continued in the sixteenth. Some of these later Irish tales are adaptations of stories popular in France and England in which chivalry, wizardry and magic, romantic love, and overseas adventures feature prominently. Others are native compositions woven about Irish characters but featuring many of the characteristics of the borrowed tales. To the latter category belong many of the extant tales of the Fionn cycle, such as *An bhruidhean chaorthainn* and *Bás an mhacaoimh mhóir*, as well as some late tales of the Ulster cycle, notably *Tóruigheacht Gruaidhe Griansholas*, *Eachtra na gcuradh*, and *Coimheascar na gcuradh*. To it also belong tales woven about historic Irish persons from the remote past, such as *Eachtra Chonaill Ghulban* which recounts supposed adventures of the fifth-century eponymous ancestor of Ceinél Conaill, and others about more recent persons, such as *Eachtra cheithearnaigh Uí Dhomhnaill* whose plot is laid in the time of Aodh Dubh Ó Domhnaill. It is believed that at least some of these stories were composed by professional men of learning but nearly all of them have come down to us without any information about their authors. An exception is *Eachtra mhacaoimh an iolair*, a typical adventure romance of the continental kind, which, according to the earliest extant copy, written in 1651 by Dáibhídh Ó Duibhgeannáin, was based on a French original by a Brian Ó Corcráin. Ó Corcráin is almost certainly to be identified with a poet of that name who composed encomiastic verse for Cú Chonnacht Mág Uidhir of Fermanagh about 1608.[1]

One aspect of Irish storytelling about which there is considerable doubt is the interrelationship between the oral and literary traditions. Many of the folktales recorded from oral narration in the twentieth century, both in Ireland and Scotland, are versions of tales that are extant in manuscripts from the sixteenth and seventeenth centuries, and it is clear that many of the features that characterise the modern folktale go back to that time. It is possible, though not certain, that a large number of these tales began as literary tales and that they passed into the oral stream in the fifteenth and following centuries, thus enriching that part of Irish tradition. What seems beyond doubt is that, whether their characters were Irish in origin or were of the class familiar from international folktales, the romantic and adventure tales appealed to a very wide public and that, whether oral or literary in their origin, they were being told at most levels of society when the author of *Páirlimint Cloinne Tomáis* parodied their style.

It is clear from what has been said already that the events of the seventeenth century left the poets in no doubt about the decline of their profession

[1] See Gerard Murphy, *The Ossianic lore and romantic tales of medieval Ireland* (Dublin, 1955); Alan Bruford, *Gaelic folktales and mediaeval romances* (Dublin, 1969).

for which liberal patronage was essential. So we find Mathghamhain Ó hIfearnáin posing the question:

Ceist, cia do cheinneóchadh dán?
  a chiall is ceirteólas suadh,
an ngéabha nó an ál le haon
  dán saor do-bhéara go buan?

(Question! who would buy a poem? Its meaning is genuine learning of scholars. Will anyone accept or does anyone wish for a noble poem which will make him immortal?)

And he comments:

Ceard mar so ní sochar dhún
  gé dochar a dol fá lár,
uaisle dul ré déineamh cíor
  gá bríogh d'éinfhior dul ré dán?

(Such an art is profitless to me, though it were a pity that it should decline; it were nobler to become a maker of combs—what use is it for anyone to make poetry?)[1]

In another poem he counselled his son *A mheic, ná meabhraigh éigse* (My son, do not cultivate the poetic art)[2]—advice that reminds us of the comment of the historian Conell Ma Geoghagan quoted earlier.

However, since professional poets did not suddenly cease to exist we find evidence of their craft throughout the seventeenth century—poems to members of the families of Ó Briain, Ó Broin, Ó Domhnaill, Ó hEadhra, Ó Néill, Ó Raghallaigh, and so on. Some of these are found in manuscript miscellanies, others are in family collections. An interesting manuscript, which was written in 1680 for Cormac Ó Néill, contains historical texts relating to the O'Neills and also a collection of poems on members of the Clann Aodha Buidhe (Clandeboye) branch from the fifteenth century to the end of the seventeenth.[3] Another, slightly later, manuscript contains a collection of poems for the O'Donnells which covers an even wider span—from the thirteenth century to the beginning of the eighteenth.[4] One item in this manuscript deserves special mention. It is an introductory note to an early-seventeenth-century poem which Eoghan Ruadh Mac an Bhaird addressed to a book that he had dedicated to Aodh Ó Domhnaill, son of the exiled earl, Ruaidhrí. In view of the strong call for national unity that the poem contains the scribal note is of considerable importance, for according to it the book was a translation of a work on the rules and art of war. Apparently Mac an Bhaird had made his translation on the Continent and was sending it to Ireland. Unfortunately the translation itself does not seem to

[1] See *Seven centuries of Irish learning, 1000–1700*, ed. Brian Ó Cuív (second ed., Cork, 1971), pp 122–3; also Bergin, *Irish bardic poetry*, poem no. 37.

[2] See *B.M. cat. Ir. MSS*, i, 392–3.

[3] *Leabhar Cloinne Aodha Buidhe*, ed. Tadhg Ó Donnchadha (Dublin, 1931).

[4] N.L.I., MS G 167.

have been preserved. Among a number of collections of family poems still unpublished is a group of thirty-eight poems composed for four generations of the Dillon family from about 1620 to 1690.[1] A statement by one of the authors, Doighre Ó Dálaigh, that he was an *ollamh* to the Dillons shows that this material belongs to the bardic tradition.

Apart from the more conventional type of bardic poetry which the panegyric represents the first half of the seventeenth century is marked by a number of poetical arguments or disputations. A minor example deals with rival claims to the Shannon by northern and southern poets. Better known is a collection of thirty poems that features frequently in later Irish manuscripts under the general title *Iomarbhágh na bhfileadh* (The contention of the poets), and reflects the same age-old rivalry between Leath Cuinn and Leath Mogha.[2] It seems to date from the latter half of the reign of James I when the country had settled down somewhat after the recent wars and confiscations. The occasion of the 'contention' is not clear, but it was initiated by a Munster poet, Tadhg Mac Bruaideadha, who had the fourth earl of Thomond, Donnchadh Ó Briain, as patron. The main defender of the northern claims was Lughaidh Ó Cléirigh and on both sides there was a great display of the type of learning in which the *seanchaidh* poets had specialised in earlier times. About a dozen poets took part but not all of them were professionals; indeed one of them, Aodh Ó Domhnaill, has been identified as a grand-uncle of Aodh Ruadh. In the 'contention', as in so much of their compositions, the poets looked to the past and their work had little relevance to the Ireland in which they were living, as was pointed out by one of those who contributed to it, Mathghamhain Ó hIfearnáin. However, it is to Flaithrí Ó Maoil Chonaire, the exiled catholic archbishop of Tuam, that the most succinct comment on the *Iomarbhágh* is attributed:

Lughaidh, Tadhg agus Torna,
  filidh eólcha bhur dtalaimh,
coin iad go n-iomad bhfeasa
  ag gleic fán easair fhalaimh,

(Lughaidh, Tadhg and Torna, the learned poets of your land, are hounds of great knowledge wrangling over an empty dish).[3]

A characteristic feature of Ireland in the sixteenth and seventeenth centuries reflected in Irish literature is the concern Irish exiles had for their homeland. They grieved over the plight of their fellow Irishmen and sought ways to ameliorate it. One of the most moving expressions of Ireland's woes from the early years of the seventeenth century is Séathrún Céitinn's poem beginning:

Óm sceól ar Árdmhagh Fáil ní chollaim oíche
'S do bhreóidh go bráth mé dála a pobail dílis;

[1] R.I.A., MS A v 2. [2] *Ed.* Lambert McKenna (2 vols; London, 1918).
[3] *Dánfhocail*, ed. T. F. O'Rahilly (Dublin, 1921), p. 31.

gí ró-fhada 'táid 'na bhfál ré broscar bíobha
fá dheóidh gur fhás a lán den chogal tríothu,

(At night I sleep not with the tidings from Ireland, and the plight of her dear people has crushed me; though long they have been as a hedge against the host of enemies, latterly much cockle has sprung up among them.)

Such a poem,[1] though in accentual metre, is in its own way as literary a production as any *dán*. It is a by-product of the bardic schools and in a sense vindicates their existence for five centuries. Though they were to disappear within a generation or two their effect on the literature was to endure.

Céitinn's poetry marks him as a transitional figure in Irish literature for he seems to have been equally at home in syllabic and accentual metres. Thus he used accentual metres for elegies on a member of the Butler family of Knocktopher and on John Fitzgerald, Lord Decies, but he chose syllabic metre for an elegy on the two sons of Lord Dunboyne who were killed in the fighting in 1642. He also used syllabic metre for a poem beginning *Mo thruaighe mar tá Éire*,[2] which is a comment on the distressed state of Ireland after 1641, as well as for a fine poem beginning *A bhean lán de stuaim*, a moving renunciation of physical love.[3]

A poem attributed to Céitinn is also, probably correctly, attributed to his contemporary, Pádraigín Haicéad. It is not surprising that these two authors should be the subject of confusion, for they had much in common. They were both of Old English Tipperary stock; they were both fervently attached to the Irish language and to the catholic faith; both were educated for the priesthood on the Continent and both wrote Irish poems during their exile; both ministered in north Munster about the same time; and they both supported the Old Irish party after 1641. Some fifty poems are attributed to Haicéad, the majority of them being in accentual metres. Nevertheless he used syllabic metres expertly on occasions, for instance in the poem *Éirghe mo dhúithche le Dia*,[4] which reflects the hopes of the Irish on the outbreak of the war in 1641, and in *Muscail do mhisneach, a Bhanbha*,[5] the poem which is also attributed to Céitinn and which is a call made to the Irish people to stand firm in support of the confederate cause in 1646. Haicéad also composed love-poems, elegies, and a variety of occasional poems.

Two other members of Old English families deserve special mention here. Thomas Dease (d. 1651), a Palesman who was catholic bishop of Meath, was a vigorous opponent of the nuncio during the confederate wars. Nevertheless he was given to composing poems in Irish and a number of these are still extant, though unpublished. Very different was Piaras Feiritéir of west

[1] Published in full in *Dánta amhráin is caointe Sheathrúin Céitinn*, ed. E. C. Mac Giolla Eáin (Dublin, 1900), no. III.

[2] Ibid., no. XV; a better edition is in *Éigse*, viii (1956–7), pp 302–8.

[3] *Dánta amhráin is caointe Sheathrúin Céitinn*, no. XIII.

[4] *Filíocht Phádraigín Haicéad*, ed. Máire Ní Cheallacháin (Dublin, 1962), no. 32.

[5] Ibid., no. 36.

Kerry who took the confederate side in 1641 and maintained the struggle until 1652 when Ross castle in Killarney fell and he was treacherously seized and hanged. Feiritéir, who is remembered in local Irish tradition to the present day, exemplified the cultured Anglo-Irishman with an interest in music and literature who could be a brave and gallant soldier when the occasion required it. He was an accomplished poet, the best known of his compositions being some love-poems which are in the *amour courtois* tradition. One of Feiritéir's poems is especially interesting, for it shows the close link which still existed in the middle of the seventeenth century between the literary classes of Gaelic-speaking Scotland and their Irish counterparts. This is an encomium in syllabic verse composed for Maol Domhnaigh Ó Muirgheasáin, a renowned Scottish poet who is described as having visited the centres of poetic learning in Ireland 'like a bee stealing honey from every flower'.[1] Feiritéir mentions over a dozen places in all the four provinces of Ireland which Ó Muirgheasáin visited. Among Ó Muirgheasáin's extant work is an elegy on Cú Chonnacht Ó Dálaigh (d. 1642) who conducted a poetic school in County Limerick, and an encomium composed for Séafraidh Ó Donnchadha who was head of the Glenflesk branch of his family and who was himself an eminent poet.

A number of long political poems, which date from between 1630 and 1660, express in the popular accentual verse-form the feelings of their little-known authors at the unprecedented sufferings of their fellow Irishmen.[2] They are in places vague, rhetorical, and figurative, and the authors are inclined to hark back to the glories of the past and to attribute Ireland's misfortunes to the sins of her people. But they contain a considerable amount of detailed reference and comment from the Old Irish side on such things as the operation of the court of wards, the star chamber, and the king's bench to the detriment of Old Irish interests, the confiscations and transplantations, the transportation of the Irish to the West Indies, the confederate wars, the exploits of Eoghan Ruadh Ó Néill who more than any man of his time was celebrated in Irish poetry, the savagery of Cromwell's campaign, and the religious disabilities imposed on the catholics. The use in these poems of a variety of English words, many of them technical terms connected with the processes of government, is a reminder of the spread of the English language which was partly due to the need for a knowledge of that language among Irishmen who would be otherwise at a disadvantage where legal processes were concerned,[3] and partly a result of the influx of planters which is reflected in the poems in such phrases as *bodaigh an Bhéarla* (the English-speaking churls) and *bruscar an Bhéarla* (the English-speaking rabble). Referring to the policy of Charles I one poet said:

[1] *Ériu*, xiii (1940–2), pp 113–18.
[2] See Cecile O'Rahilly (ed.), *Five seventeenth-century political poems* (Dublin, 1952).
[3] Cf. Davies as quoted above, p. 529.

Leis do hiarradh Dia do thréigean
's gan labhairt i dteanga na Gaeilge
's gan 'na háit ag cách acht Béarla,

(By him it was required that God should be abandoned and that people should not speak Irish but that in its place all should have English.)

His religion and the Irish language were important to this poet and in a note of hope towards the end of his poem he wrote *Is treise Dia ná fian an Bhéarla* (God is more powerful than the English-speaking crowd).[1] This particular poem is an early example of the political *aisling* or 'vision-poem' that attained its full development in the eighteenth century, for it describes a vision which the poet had as he lamented on the tombs of the Irish lords in Rome. There a maiden of great beauty came to him and told of past and recent events in Ireland. Unlike the outlook in later poems of this type her hope for Ireland's future rests on the efforts of the Irish leaders and it is on this note that the vision ends. This poem was composed in 1650, but before the end of the decade another poet, Éamann an Dúna, was looking forward to the Irish having Charles II as their 'leader'.[2]

What has been referred to represents only a small proportion of extant seventeenth-century poetry. Indeed it seems that the decline of the schools was more than compensated for by a blossoming of non-professional poetry at many levels of society. This was a factor in the maintenance of a literary tradition in the following century, as was the fact that manuscript-writing became a more widespread accomplishment. Many of the seventeenth-century poems are anonymous; others are ascribed to authors about whom little is known; and not infrequently such an author is the first person of his family-name to appear as a poet. To this century, it appears, belong the earliest of the extant Irish songs—poems such as *Eibhilín a rúin* and *Seán Ó Duibhir an Ghleanna* which were set to music and survived because of the popularity they achieved. Some of the tunes were to be used over and over again by later poets. So it was that the seventeenth century saw the tastes of the ordinary people prevailing to a large extent in the field of poetry. Yet, paradoxically, it was towards the second half of that century that there emerged a poet whom some critics would regard as the finest Irish poet of all time, Dáibhídh Ó Bruadair.

Very little is known about Ó Bruadair's background and it is still a matter of doubt whether it was in Cork or in Limerick that he was born. What is certain is that he received a good education, that he knew Latin and English, and that his knowledge of Irish literature, history, and genealogical lore was worthy of a professional scholar. One feature of his work raises a question

[1] O'Rahilly (ed.), as above, poem II. Whereas the other four poems were written by Munster poets this one was written by someone from the northern half of Ireland or from the midlands.

[2] Ibid., poem V. The surname of the author is not given in the manuscripts but he may have been a MacCarthy from west Cork.

about the training he is likely to have had as a professional poet. In the schools in earlier centuries great attention was paid to the details of syllabic metre in its various forms, whereas Ó Bruadair's use of syllabic metre is quite limited. On the other hand his use of accentual metre is varied and skilful and at a far higher level artistically than, for example, in Seán Ó Conaill's *Tuireamh na hÉireann*. In the light of this it may be suggested that by his day the potential of the song-metres had been irrevocably recognised in the schools of poetry—at least in Munster—and that metrical and linguistic teaching was directed towards an understanding and appreciation of current speech-forms and their coordination with metrical patterns and, most probably, the relation of the whole to music. A poetic school that was to be a focus for learning in the following century was already in existence in Blarney in County Cork during Ó Bruadair's lifetime, and he had contacts with it.

Ó Bruadair was born about the beginning of the reign of Charles I and died in January 1698, so that he experienced the sufferings and joys of Irishmen for nearly seventy years, and he has left a unique commentary on what he saw and felt. Throughout his life his main interest was Ireland and the catholic religion, and like others in his time he expressed the view that some, at least, of Ireland's ills were the result of the past sins of Irishmen. Thus in the poem entitled 'The summary of the purgatory of the men of Ireland' he held that the defeat of the Irish in the Cromwellian wars was a punishment for the indiscipline of the Irish troops in the first year of the war, and for the murders and plunderings then committed by them. He linked the men of those times with the following generation, and in twenty-four stanzas he reviewed the tyranny of the Cromwellians which created Ireland's purgatory that still existed long after the restoration of Charles II.[1]

His comments were not always direct and this is one of the features which set him above other poets of his time. For instance some poet whose name is not known had composed a poem of praise for the duke of Ormond in which he said:

Is fearra fá sheacht don talamh a theacht, dá chasnamh ar neart aineólach,
ná Conn is Niall, Goll is Brian, is Fionn na bhFiann bhflaith-ólach,

(Better seven times over for this land is his coming, to protect it from oppression of strangers, than Conn and Niall, Goll and Brian, and Fionn of the princely-drinking Fianna.)[2]

Ó Bruadair would have been satisfied had the duke, under whose rule Ireland was not notably discontented, been praised in a reasonable way, but his sense of justice was offended by the other poet's unjust comparison of the duke with five great heroes of the past. And so he composed a rejoinder beginning with the phrase *A shaoi re gliogar*,[3] which has been translated

[1] *Duanaire Dháibhídh Uí Bhruadair* (London, 1910–17), iii (1917), pp 12–22.

[2] Ibid., i (1910), p. 194.

[3] Ibid., pp 196–206.

'thou sage of inanity', in which he demonstrated his own superiority in handling the same metrical form, at the same time leaving his hearers in no doubt as to his real opinion of Ormond. This capacity for taking the work of another poet as a prelude to a work of his own is seen again in a poem[1] to James II, which he linked to a poem supposedly composed about a century earlier in praise of Queen Elizabeth.

In 1652 Ó Bruadair had depicted the Ireland he saw after the Cromwellian wars and confiscations in a poem beginning *Créacht do dháil mé im arthrach galair* (A wound has made of me an ailing vessel).[2] Down the years he continued to raise his voice against the injustices done to Irish catholics, but when the occasion called for it he was ready to pay a tribute to a protestant. Such an occasion arose in 1682 when the chief justice, John Keating, a protestant, acquitted some catholic gentlemen of Munster who had been accused by false witnesses of complicity in the Titus Oates plot. Keating was an Irish speaker and Ó Bruadair wrote a long poem[3] praising in alternate stanzas Séathrun Céitinn, the scholar priest who half a century earlier had defended Ireland from detractors, and Keating who defended her gentry from their present calumniators.

The crowning of James II gave Ó Bruadair great hope for a happier Ireland, and some of his best poems belong to these last years of his life. The admission of Irish catholics to the army and a comment on it by his friend and fellow poet, Diarmaid Mac Carthaigh, led him to write *Caithréim Thaidhg* (The triumph of Tadhg) which is full of hope.[4] Irish hopes and disappointments in the brief reign of James II are mirrored in further poems, one of the best of which is *An longbhriseadh* (The shipwreck) which was written in 1691.[5] This ends with two fine stanzas in the first of which he has a moving prayer to God for his country while in the second there is a humorous consideration of his own poverty in the light of the new oppression suffered by 'the men of Fodla':

> Gé shaoileas dá saoirse bheith seasgair sódhail
> im stíobhard ag saoi acu, nó im ghearra-phróvost,
> ós críoch di mo stríocadh go sean-bhrógaibh
> *finis* dom sgríbhinn ar fhearaibh Fódla.

(Though I had hoped as a result of their freedom to be snug and comfortable as steward to some good man among them, or as a petty provost, since it has ended by reducing me to old shoes here's *finis* to my writing about the men of Fódla.)

The very large number of Ó Bruadair's poems that have survived is partly due to his own scribal activity and partly to that of his friends and admirers who recognised the qualities of his work and copied and recopied

[1] *Duanaire Dháibhídh Uí Bhruadair* (London, 1910–17), iii (1917), pp 76–92.
[2] Ibid., i, iii (1910), pp 26–50.
[3] Ibid., ii (1913), pp 264–86.
[4] Ibid., iii, 126–40.
[5] Ibid., iii, 164–80.

much of it. Included are an exceptionally fine religious poem and praise-poems for members of Cork and Limerick families—Barrys, Burkes, Fitzgeralds, Mac Carthys, and others—and two epithalamia or wedding-songs which are in the mixed form of poetry and prose known as *crosántacht* and which must have caused great mirth on their recitation. Ó Bruadair was clearly a welcome guest in the houses of the Irish gentry of Munster as long as they were in a position to give him hospitality. But the day came when his poverty was such that he complained:

> Teastuighim na bealaighe go minic dom chois
> is tathuighim bheith tearc mí gan pinginn im purs.

(Frequently I test the roads on foot and I am used to being hard up without a penny in my purse for a month.)

When he died the Gaelic order he valued so much had received its death-blow.

CHAPTER XXI

The English language in early modern Ireland

ALAN BLISS

DURING the latter part of the middle ages in Ireland the use of Latin and French for official records gradually gave way to the use of English, and from the sixteenth century onwards English was freely written, not only by the new administrators but also by the Old English and even by the native Irish: in 1627, for instance, the Annals of Clonmacnoise were translated into English by Conell Mageoghagan.[1] With the spoken language the case was different: by the middle of the sixteenth century spoken English was in a state of almost total eclipse. The reformation had brought about a unity of purpose between the Irish and the Old English, and the Irish language became a symbol of the catholic religion; the English settlers, who for a long time had been bilingual, now began consciously to reject the English language in favour of Irish. In 1577 Richard Stanihurst lamented the displacement of English by Irish in highly rhetorical terms:

Now whereas Irelande hath beene, by lawfull conquest, brought vnder the subiection of Englande, not onelye in king Henry the second his reigne, but also as well before as after (as by the course of the Irish hystorye shal euidently be deciphered), & the conquest hath béene so absolute and perfect, that all Leinster, Méeth, Ulster, the more parte of Connaght and Mounster, all the ciuities & burroughes in Irelande, haue béene wholly Englished, and with Englishe conquerours inhabited, is it decent, thinke you, that theyr owne auncient natiue tongue shal be shrowded in obliuion, and suffer the enemies language, as it were a tettarre, or ring woorme, to herborow it self within the iawes of Englishe conquerours? no truely.[2]

Before 1600 Fynes Moryson noted that

at this tyme wherof I write, the meere Irish disdayned to learne or speake the English tounge, yea the English Irish and the very cittizens (excepting those of Dublin where the lord deputy resides) though they could speake English as well as wee, yet commonly speake Irish among themselues, and were hardly induced by

[1] *The Annals of Clonmacnoise . . . translated into English, A.D. 1627, by Conell Mageoghagan*, ed. Denis Murphy (Royal Society of Antiquaries of Ireland, Dublin, 1896).

[2] Stanihurst, 'Description of Ire.', in Holinshed (1577 ed.), i, f. 3, cols 2–3.

our familiar conversation to speake English with vs, yea common experience shewed, and my selfe and others often obserued, the cittizens of Watterford and Corcke hauing wyues that could speake English as well as wee, bitterly to chyde them when they speake English with vs.[1]

By 1600 the use of the English language was confined to a small number of places. No doubt it was still extensively used in Dublin and other towns, though the evidence for this is scanty and indirect. It was certainly used in two rural areas: the so-called 'English baronies' of Forth and Bargy in County Wexford, and the district north of Dublin known as Fingall. This latter district is described by Moryson as 'Fengall, a little territory, as it were the garner of the kingdome, which is environed by the sea and great rivers, and this situation hath defended it from the incursion of rebels in former civill warres'.[2] In these two districts a distinctive form of English survived until about the end of the eighteenth century.

Before the middle of the sixteenth century, written documents had ceased to display any of the features characteristic of medieval Hiberno-English; the written language conformed entirely to the official standard English used in England. This does not necessarily mean, of course, that the spoken language also conformed to English usage, and there is in fact ample evidence that it did not. In a well-known passage Stanihurst described some of the main characteristics of the dialect of the Wexford baronies, and implied that the Fingall dialect was similar:

But of all other places, Weiseforde with the territorye bayed, and perclosed within the riuer called the Pill, was so quite estranged from Irishry, as if a traualler of the Irish (which was rare in those dayes) had picht his foote within the pile and spoken Irishe, the Weisefordians would commaunde hym forthwith to turne the other ende of his tongue, and speake Englishe, or else bring his trouchman with him. But in our dayes they haue so aquainted themselues with the Irishe, as they haue made a mingle mangle, or gallamaulfrey of both the languages, and haue in such medley or checkerwyse so crabbedly iumbled them both togyther, as commonly the inhabitants of the meaner sort speake neyther good English nor good Irishe.

There was of late dayes one of the péeres of England sent to Weiseford as commissioner, to decide the controuersies of that countrey, and hearing in affable wise the rude complaintes of the countrey clownes, he conceyued here and there, sometyme a worde, other whyles a sentence. The noble man beyng very glad that vpon his first commyng to Ireland, he vnderstood so many wordes, told one of hys familiar frends, that he stoode in very great hope, to become shortly a well spoken man in the Irishe, supposing that the blunte people had pratled Irishe, all the while they iangled Englishe. Howbeit to this day, the dregs of the olde auncient Chaucer English are kept as well there as in Fingall. As they terme a spider, an

[1] Charles Hughes (ed.), *Shakespeare's Europe: unpublished chapters of Fynes Moryson's itinerary* (London, 1903), p. 213.

[2] *Itinerary*, iv, 189.

attercop; a wispe, a wad; a lumpe of bread, a pocket or a pucket; a sillibuck, a copprouse; a faggot, a blease, or a blaze, for the short burning of it, as I iudge; a phisition, a leache; a gappe, a sharde; a base court or quadrangle, a bawen, or rather, as I suppose, a barton; the household or folkes, meany; sharppe, kéene; estraunge, vncouth; easie, éeth or éefe; a dunghill, a mizen; as for the worde bater, that in English purporteth a lane, bearing to an high way, I take it for a méere Irishe worde, that crepte vnawares into the English, thorough the daily entercourse of the English and Irish inhabitants. . . .

And most commonly in wordes of two sillables, they giue the last the accent. As they say, markeate, baskeate, gossoupe, pussoate, Robart, Niclase, &c. which doubtlesse doth disbeautifie their Englishe aboue measure. And if they could be weaned from that corrupt custom, there is none that could dislyke of their English.[1]

The comparison of the dialect of the Wexford baronies to the language of Chaucer recurs again and again. A hundred years after Stanihurst, it was made by Colonel Solomon Richards:

Shilburne, Bargye, and Forth are the English baronies, but Forth chiefly retains the name, and justlie. Its idiom of speech, tho its not Irish, nor seems English as English is now refined, yett is it more easy to be understood by an Englishman that never heard Irish spoken than by any Irishman that lives remote. Itt's notorious that itt's the very language brought over by Fitzstephen, and retained by them to this day. Whoever hath read old Chaucer, and is at all acquainted therewith, will better understand the barony of Forth dialect than either an English or Irishman, that never read him, though otherwise a good linguist. Itt was an observation of the inhabitants of this barony of Forth, before the last rebellion, that they had kept their language, lands, and loyaltie.[2]

In 1672 Sir William Petty described the dialects of Wexford and of Fingall, pointing out that, though similar, they were not identical:

The language of Ireland is like that of the north of Scotland, in many things like the Welch and Manques; but in Ireland the Fingallians speak neither English, Irish nor Welch; and the people about Wexford, tho they agree in a language differing from English, Welch, and Irish, yet 'tis not the same with that of the Fingalians near Dublin.[3]

A hundred years later still Arthur Young reported on the two dialects in terms not unlike Petty's. In Wexford, he says, 'they all speak a broken Saxon language, and not one in an hundred knows any thing of Irish';[4] the Fingalians are 'an English colony planted here many years ago, speaking nearly the same language as the barony of Forth, but more intermixed with Irish

[1] Stanihurst, f. 2., col. 4; f. 3, col. 1.

[2] Herbert F. Hore, 'Particulars relative to Wexford and the barony of Forth: by Colonel Solomon Richards, 1682' in *R.S.A.I. Jn.*, iv (1862–3), p. 86.

[3] Petty, 'Political anatomy of Ire.', ed. Hull, i, 106.

[4] Arthur Young, *A tour in Ireland: with general observations on the present state of the kingdom* (1780), p. 81.

in language, &c., from vicinity to the capital'.[1] The comparison of the Wexford dialect with the language of Chaucer recurs at a date not specified, but presumably about 1800, in an anonymous report on the 'English' baronies:

It may be related, as a singular fact, that the Rev. William Eastwood, rector of Tacumshane, barony of Forth, while amusing himself one day in his field with a volume of Chaucer, fancied some of the obsolete words which met his eye resembled those which also met his ear, as his workmen conversed together; he accordingly called them around him, and commenced reading a page or two of old Geoffrey aloud, to their great delight, as they well understood the most obscure expressions, and often explained them better than the glossarial aids of Dryden and Johnson.[2]

In 1836 the Wexford dialect was used for a congratulatory address to Earl Mulgrave, lord lieutenant of Ireland;[3] but this seems to have represented an artificial revival of a form of speech already obsolescent if not quite obsolete. The date at which the Fingall dialect became extinct is not known.

For the nature of the dialect of Fingall the only evidence is an anonymous satirical work published in 1689, *The Irish Hudibras, or Fingallian prince*; it has been attributed, but without much plausibility, to the Englishman James Farewell. The dialect of Forth and Bargy is much better documented. The first printed account of it, prepared by the indefatigable Major-general Charles Vallancey, gives a seven-page glossary and the text of a song.[4] In August 1857 Dr C. W. Russell, president of St Patrick's College, Maynooth, read a paper on the dialect to a meeting of the British Association in Dublin; this paper, which was subsequently published, includes a useful analysis of the main features of the dialect.[5] By far the most important contribution to the study of the dialect was made by William Barnes, the Dorset poet, who in 1867 published an extensive glossary accompanied by a number of verse texts;[6] the bulk of the glossary was prepared by a Wexford man, Jacob Poole, who died in 1827, but Barnes incorporated the additional words mentioned by Stanihurst and Vallancey, and reprinted all the earlier sources. The most striking characteristic of the Forth and Fingall dialects is their extreme conservatism, both in vocabulary and in pronunciation—hence the repeated comparisons with the language of Chaucer. Irish influence is discernible, but it is not very strong. A striking feature, not, apparently, paralleled in any other form of English, was singled out by

[1] Ibid., p. 95.

[2] 'Observations on the social habits and dialect of the baronies of Forth and Bargy, by an officer of the line' in *The graphic and historical illustrator*, ed. E. W. Brayley (1834), p. 246.

[3] William Barnes, *A glossary of the old dialect of the English colony in the baronies of Forth and Bargy* (1867), pp 113–17.

[4] Charles Vallancey, 'Memoir of the language, manners and customs of an Anglo-Saxon colony settled in the baronies of Forth and Bargie' in *R.I.A. Trans.*, ii (1788), pp 19–41.

[5] C. W. Russell, 'On the inhabitants and dialect of the barony of Forth in the county of Wexford' in *Atlantis*, i (1858).

[6] As above, n. 3.

Stanihurst for special comment: the tendency to stress the final syllable in disyllabic words. This tendency was associated by T. F. O'Rahilly with the similar tendency in the Munster dialect (and perhaps in the lost Leinster dialect) of Irish; he suggested that in both cases the aberrant accentuation might be due to the influence of Norman French, in which the final syllable was regularly stressed.[1]

Evidence about the kind of English used in the towns is to be found mainly in the non-standard spellings used to represent the speech of Irish characters in Elizabethan and Jacobean plays. This evidence must be treated with considerable reserve, for a number of reasons: the significance of the spellings is often doubtful; in the earlier period none, and in the later period few, of the dramatists were Irish; it appears that in the early seventeenth century a conventional 'stage Irish' had already been established. However, the earliest of these plays seems to be much more authoritative than the others, and the evidence it offers is of very great interest: this is *The famous historye of the life and death of Captaine Thomas Stukeley*. This is probably identical with a play, *Stewtley*, mentioned by Philip Henslowe as a new play acted by the Admiral's Men on 11 December 1596;[2] at all events, it was entered in the Stationers' registers on 11 August 1600,[3] and printed in 1605. Thomas Stukeley was not a fictional character but an English adventurer who engaged in military exploits in various parts of the world. According to the play he took part in the defence of Dundalk when it was besieged by Shane O'Neill in May 1566. By some strange chance the seventh scene, which deals with the siege of Dundalk, has survived in two different versions, printed consecutively in the sole edition of 1605: the first (like the rest of the play) is in blank verse, and in standard English; the second is in prose, and in broad Anglo-Irish dialect.[4] The relative priority of the two versions of the scene has been much discussed, but it is not relevant to our purpose; what is important is the probability that the unknown author had some knowledge of Ireland and of the languages in use there. There is no direct evidence that the author was an Irishman; but, if he was not, his knowledge of the Anglo-Irish dialect and of the Irish language is such that he must have spent some considerable time in Ireland.

The scene is fairly liberally sprinkled with Irish words and phrases correctly used. The presence of Irish words and phrases is not in itself any proof of special knowledge, since they also occur in the work of English dramatists who had no connection with Ireland, and evidently formed part of conventional 'stage Irish'. Three of the phrases used in *Stukeley*, for instance, occur together in Dekker's *The honest whore* (part II, 1603): 'slawne loot,

[1] T. F. O'Rahilly, *Irish dialects past and present* (Dublin, 1972), pp 94–8.

[2] *Henslowe's diary*, ed. W. W. Greg (1904).

[3] *Transcript of the registers of the company of Stationers, 1554–1640*, ed. Edward Arber (5 vols, 1875–94).

[4] This scene is reprinted with a commentary in vol. ix, appendix.

fare de well, fare de well. Ah marragh frofat boddah breen.' However, in *Stukeley* the Irish phrases are used with remarkable correctness: the distinction between *slán agat* and *slán leat*, for instance, is accurately made, whereas *slán leat* is misused by Dekker in the line quoted above. Moreover, it is a remarkable fact that the word *buidheach* (if the 'booygh' of the play has been correctly identified) is used only in Oriel Irish; that is, though it might indeed have been used in Dundalk, it would be unfamiliar in other parts of Ireland. The English used in *Stukeley* bears a close resemblance to that recorded 200 years later in Forth and Bargy. It is markedly conservative; if it is less conservative in appearance than the Wexford dialect, this is because some of the features retained in Wexford had not yet become obsolete in standard English, and therefore did not call for special representation in the spelling. It is subject to Irish influence, rather more strongly than the Wexford dialect. Both these features can be observed in such a form as *féete*, 'white': the spelling of the vowel-sound shows that it had retained the Middle English sound unchanged, without the diphthongisation characteristic of modern English; the spelling of the initial consonant suggests the substitution of the Irish 'broad' *f*-sound for the English *wh*-sound which it somewhat resembles. A further feature shared by *Stukeley* and the Wexford dialect is the tendency to stress the final syllable in words of two syllables: such spellings as *blankead*, 'blanket', and *ovare*, 'over', closely resemble those used by Stanihurst, as well as those used by Vallancey and others much later.[1]

A similar type of English was used as late as 1663 in an indecent play entitled *Hic et ubique: or, the humors of Dublin*; but this was written by a Richard Head, who spent much of his life in England, and it is possible that the dialect was imitated from *Stukeley*, or from some other play now lost. The rest of the drama gives evidence of a somewhat different type of English, evidently accepted in England as characteristic of Irishmen. It is likely enough that this language was conventional, and was imitated by one dramatist from another: yet it is reasonably self-consistent, and the possibility that it represents some real variety of the Anglo-Irish dialect cannot be wholly excluded. Perhaps the most probable explanation is that it represents some variety of urban Anglo-Irish—possibly the same as that represented in *Stukeley*, possibly different—conventionalised and elaborated so that it ceased to reflect any real type of pronunciation; something similar can be observed in the conventional representation of English rural dialect in Elizabethan and Jacobean drama, where the individual dialect features are genuine enough, but the totality does not correspond to any real dialect. An extreme example of conventional Anglo-Irish is to be found in a book called *Bog-witticisms*; the date of publication is uncertain, but since it is referred

[1] For a more detailed comparison of the phonology of *Stukeley* with that of the Wexford dialect, see vol. ix, appendix.

to in *The Irish Hudibras* in 1689, it was probably published not long before that year. It is a jest-book, obviously aimed at the English market, which presents the Irish in a very unfavourable light. Its general tone, as well as the type of language it uses, can be illustrated by the title-page:

Bogg-VVitticisms:

OR

Dear Joy's

Common-Places

BEING

A Compleat Collection of the most Profound *Punns*, Learned *Bulls*, Elaborate *Quibbles*, and Wise *Sayings* of some of the Natives of *Teague-Land*

Shet fourd vor Generaul Nouddificaushion: And Coullected bee de grete Caare and Painsh-Tauking of oour Laurned Countree-maun

Mac O Bonniclabbero of *Drogheda*
Knight of the *Mendicant* Order

PRINTED

For Evidansh *Swear-all*
in *Lack-Plaush* Lane
Price Bound Two Shilling Sixpence

It must have proved very popular, since it went through at least seven editions, the last in 1750.

Neither the dialect of *Stukeley*, nor that represented in the other plays can possibly be the ancestor of present-day Anglo-Irish. One of the most characteristic features of this earlier Anglo-Irish was its extreme conservatism, which preserved unchanged many of the pronunciations of the Middle English period. Though present-day Anglo-Irish is also conservative, its conservatism does not reach nearly so far back in the history of English. Both the older and the newer dialects have been subjected to the influence of the Irish language, but that influence shows itself in different ways. There can be no doubt that the present-day Anglo-Irish dialect represents a fresh introduction of English into Ireland; and, indeed, it is historically plausible enough that this should be so. The older language had become restricted to the towns and to two limited rural areas, so that there was no likelihood that it would undergo expansion over all the rest of the country. On the other hand, the extensive plantations of the sixteenth and seventeenth centuries provided plenty of opportunities for the spread of new kinds of English introduced by the planters. In northern and eastern Ulster they came mainly from Scotland, in the rest of Ulster and in the other three provinces mainly from England.

There is no direct historical evidence to determine the date at which the Anglo-Irish dialect ceased to be substantially influenced by fresh immigration from England. The origin of the present dialect can only be determined with certainty by the use of linguistic evidence, and fortunately the pronunciation of the Anglo-Irish dialect, which can be observed directly and is not a matter of inference, provides sufficient evidence. Though the actual sounds now used have been extensively influenced by the sounds of Irish, the pattern of the sounds used has not been liable to much change; it is therefore possible to compare the sound-pattern of Anglo-Irish with the sound-pattern of English as it existed at various periods during the sixteenth and seventeenth centuries. It is fortunate that from the sixteenth century onwards the pronunciation of English is well documented in the works of the so-called 'orthoepists', writers who discussed pronunciation either in strict theory or in connection with the reform of English spelling. The result of this comparison is clear: the dialects of northern and eastern Ulster are derived from Lowland Scots; the dialects of the rest of Ulster and of the other three provinces are derived from English as it was spoken about 1650, and their ancestor was a sub-standard, probably dialectal, form of English. Presumably until about 1650 the English introduced into Ireland by the plantations developed *pari passu* with the English of England; after that it went its own way. This conclusion fits in very well with historical considerations which would not in themselves be decisive. About the middle of the seventeenth century several factors combined to bring about both the diffusion and the isolation of the English language in Ireland. No doubt the wars of the 1640s brought English into places where it had seldom been heard before. Under the Cromwellian settlement of the 1650s the catholic, mainly Irish-speaking, landowners of Leinster and Munster were removed to Connacht, and their places were taken by English owners. From this time onward, therefore, there was in every province but Connacht a substantial body of English-speakers far removed from contact with the English of England. It is easy, too, to understand why the type of English which took root in Ireland was sub-standard and probably dialectal. The type of standard English described by the seventeenth-century orthoepists had a very limited currency: it was restricted mainly to court and university circles. Much less social stigma was attached then than now to the use of dialectal forms of English, and outside London the well-to-do and the well educated tended to use a regional rather than a standard dialect. In the circumstances of the seventeenth-century plantations it seems improbable that many Irishmen would come into contact with the more important of the planters, those who might perhaps be expected to speak standard English; the contacts of most of them would be with soldiers, merchants, and the tenants of the great lords, all of whom might be expected to speak the type of English represented in present-day Anglo-Irish. A study of the distinctive vocabulary of Anglo-Irish leads to similar conclusions: if we leave aside Irish loan-words and words used in a way dictated by Irish influence, the non-standard element in the vocabulary is partly archaic—that is to say, words long obsolete in England may survive in Ireland—but also very largely dialectal, with a preponderance of words characteristic of the northern dialects of English.[1]

As time went on, the mid-seventeenth-century English which had taken root in Ireland became more and more conservative, and more and more subject to the influence of Irish. The increasing conservatism was not, of course, an active process; the dialect did not, as it were, go back on its tracks. What happened was that continuing developments in the speech of England left a wider and wider gap between the two types of language. Before the act of union there was relatively little traffic between Ireland and England; many landowners remained on their remote estates, rarely meeting anyone but their landowning neighbours and their Irish servants and tenants. Thus the changes which affected the English language in its homeland passed Ireland by; as often happens, a language divorced from its cultural roots stagnated. The increasing influence of Irish, on the other hand, was not only active but cumulative. At first the influence of Irish was mainly selective and preservative: where there was a choice available of English words and idioms, one would be preferred to another because it had some support in Irish usage. Later the influence became more direct, and Irish words and idioms were introduced which had no analogy at all in English usage. In the course of time the sounds of seventeenth-century English were replaced by the sounds of Irish. At the present day, it is a matter of observation that, in districts where Irish is still spoken, bilingual speakers use no sound in speaking English which they do not also use in speaking Irish; in neighbouring districts where Irish is no longer spoken, the same sounds are used. Where Irish has been so long extinct that there is no reliable evidence of its pronunciation, as (for instance) in Leinster, it cannot be proved that the sounds used are the sounds of the lost Irish of the same district; but it is noteworthy that many of the sounds used in Leinster are rare or unknown in dialects of English spoken outside Ireland, but are common enough in various dialects of Irish.

The extent of the influence of Irish on the Anglo-Irish dialect presupposes some considerable degree of contact between Irish-speakers and English-speakers, and a fair amount of bilingualism. At first glance it is not easy to

[1] For a more detailed study of the origin of the present-day Anglo-Irish dialect, see vol. ix, appendix.

see how this could have come about under the social system prevailing in Ireland during the seventeenth and eighteenth centuries. A vivid picture of the Irishman's experience of the English language is given by the political poems of the mid-seventeenth century; English words are either superficially gaelicised, or included in their English form. The general impression given is, on the one hand, of abuse and violence, and on the other hand of legalised extortion. Thus, in the poem *Mo lá leóin go deó go n-éagad*, Éamann an Dúna gives his impression of the English language:

> Transport, transplant, *mo mheabhair ar Bhéarla.*
> Shoot him, kill him, strip him, tear him.
> A tory, hack him, hang him, rebel,
> a rogue, a thief, a priest, a papist.[1]

In the poem *Tuireamh na hÉireann*, Seán Ó Conaill describes the legal severities imposed on the Irish:

> *Siosóin cúirte is téarmai daora,*
> wardship livery *is cúirt* exchequer
> *cíos coláisde* in nomine poenae;
> greenwax, capias, writ, replevin,
> *bannaí, fíneáil, díotáil éigcirt,*
> provost, *soffré*, *portré*, *méara*,
> *sirriaim*, *sionascáil*, *marascáil chlaona.*

(Court sessions and expensive law-terms, wardship livery and exchequer court, college tax *in nomine poenae*; greenwax, capias, writ, replevin, bonds, fining, unjust indictment, provost, sovereign, portreeve, mayor, sheriffs, seneschals, prejudiced marshals.)[2]

Only the wealthy would be subjected to extortion, legal or illegal. The contact of the peasant classes with the English language is amusingly portrayed in a work called *Páirlimint Cloinne Tomáis*, written about 1650. This is a ruthless satire on the Irish peasantry, and describes a series of peasants' parliaments held in Munster. At one point the proceedings are interrupted by the arrival of an itinerant tobacco-seller. In the following translation of the Irish text the words that are in English in the original are italicised.

It wasn't long before they saw a young Englishman approaching.

'Who's that young man who's coming?', said one of them.

'I know him', said another, 'he's Robin the Tobacco, and he usually has good tobacco'.

'I'll buy some', said Bernard Ó Bruic, 'but which of us will speak English to him?'

'I will', said Tomás.

[1] Cecile O'Rahilly, *Five seventeenth-century political poems* (Dublin, 1952), p. 90.

[2] Ibid., pp 73–4.

The young Englishman came up, and greeted them politely, and said: '*God bless you, Thomas, and all your company*'.

Tomás answered him urbanely, and this is what he said: '*Pleshy for you, pleshy, good man, Robin*'.

'By my mother's soul', said Bernard Ó Bruic, 'you swallowed down a fine lot of English'.

They all clustered round, wondering at Tomás's English.

'Ask the price of the tobacco', said Bernard.

Tomás spoke, and this is what he said: '*What the bigg greate órdlach for the what so penny, for is the la yourselfe for me?*'

Said Robin: '*I know, Thomas, you aske how many enches is worth the penny!*', and he raised two fingers as a sign, and said, '*two penny an ench*'.

'By my godfather's hand, that's a good price', said Tomás.

'What's that?', said Diarmuid Dúr.

'An inch for two pennies', said Tomás.

'Make an agreement for us', said everyone.

'I will', said Tomás, and said: '*Is ta for meselfe the mony for fart you all my brothers here*'.

Said Robin: '*I thanke you, honest Thomas, you shall command all my tobacco*'.

'*Begog, I thanke you*', said Tomás.

At that word Tomás took the tobacco and gave it out to everyone.[1]

It is obvious that the situations described in these mid-seventeenth-century Irish texts could not have promoted the extensive Irish influence revealed by the present-day Anglo-Irish dialect. However, an Irish story written about 1715 is more enlightening. This is Seán Ó Neachtain's *Stair Éamuinn Uí Chléire*, the light-hearted biography of an Irish schoolmaster.[2] Several pages of it are devoted to an elaborate linguistic joke at the expense of the English spoken by ignorant Irishmen, who take an Irish sentence and translate it word by word into English, often using the wrong English equivalent of an Irish word. There are whole paragraphs of English which are totally unintelligible until they are translated literally into Irish and then back into English: the word *cheap*, for instance, is regularly replaced by *carpenter*, because both words correspond to Irish *saor*. This story is important in two ways. First, the mistranslation of Irish words is a fruitful source of non-standard uses of standard English words in Anglo-Irish—though not to such an extreme and ludicrous extent as in the story. Secondly, the fact that any writer thought it worth while to concoct so elaborate a linguistic joke presupposes the existence of a bilingual audience: a monoglot Irishman, or even an Irishman whose English was less than good, would miss the point of the joke completely.

The extent of the influence of the Irish language on the language of the

[1] Text edited by Osborn Bergin in *Gadelica*, i (1912–13), pp 35–50, 127–31, 137–50, 220–36. Passage translated on pp 148–9.

[2] *Stair Éamuinn Uí Chléire*, do réir Sheáin Uí Neachtain, i n-eagar ag Eoghan Ó Neachtain (Dublin, 1918).

planters can be proved by the evidence of no less an authority than Jonathan Swift. Swift's concern with the niceties of language is well known, and is fully illustrated in his *Polite conversation* (1738), in which he recorded with devastating accuracy the inanity and conventionality of the language of the English upper classes. About the time when he was preparing *Polite conversation* for the press, he was also engaged in noting down some of the peculiarities of the English language as spoken in Ireland. He arranged the material he had collected into two different forms: into a conversational exchange (as in *Polite conversation*) under the title *A dialogue in Hybernian stile between A. and B.*; and into the form of a letter, under the title *Irish eloquence.*[1] These two pieces record the same hibernicisms so consistently that they can conveniently be treated as one. There is no doubt that Swift is satirising the English, not of the native Irish, but of the planters, as a characteristic passage in the *Dialogue* reveals:

A You have a country-house, are you [a] planter?
B Yes, I have planted a great many oak trees, and ash trees, and some elm trees round a lough.

Yet, though the speakers are landowners, their language (some two generations after the Cromwellian settlement) is already very strongly influenced by the Irish language. In some fifty lines there are no less than seventeen Irish words. This is not, perhaps in itself very significant, since certain types of word, particularly topographical terms like *loch* in the quotation above, could have been picked up casually. Much more significant is the fact that there are at least three sentences more or less literally translated from Irish idiom: 'Pray how does he get his health?', reproducing Irish *cé'n chaoi a bhfaghann sé a shláinte?*; 'it is kind father for you', reproducing Irish *is dual athar duit*; 'I wonder what is gone with them?', reproducing Irish *céard atá imithe orrtha*. These sentences reflect the usage of someone who is thinking in Irish but speaking in English. It is no doubt possible that some of the planters had learned some Irish (though Swift advises against it), but they could scarcely have been so deeply versed in Irish as to think in Irish when they were speaking English; they could only have picked up these idioms through daily intercourse with bilingual Irishmen.

The existence of bilingual Irishmen in the time of Swift is attested by *Stair Éamuinn Uí Chléire*; but it is far from clear they could have been in daily contact with the planters. No doubt most of the planters must as babies have been cared for by Irish nurses, and in their childhood they would no doubt have fraternised with the children of their servants; but this seems hardly enough to account for the extent of the Irish influence on their speech—children quickly lose their peculiarities of speech once they begin

[1] Swift, *Prose works*, iv, 277–9.

to mix with adults. A clue to the solution of this problem is given by Maria Edgeworth's *Castle Rackrent* (1800). The title-page of this novel states that it describes 'the manners of the Irish squires, before the year 1782', and in her preface Maria Edgeworth assures us again that 'the manners depicted in the following pages are not those of the present age'; it is not unfair, therefore, to assume that these 'manners' prevailed in the age of Swift. In *Castle Rackrent* the narrator is the steward, Thady Quirk; his family has lived rent-free on the estate 'time out of mind'; he is familiar with all the financial and legal entanglements of his successive masters; and he even receives confidences about their matrimonial intentions. In a significant passage Thady refers to his master, Sir Condy Rackrent, and describes how he made bold 'to speak to him one night when he was a little cheerful, and standing in the servants' hall all alone with me, as was often his custom'. If, as seems likely, the landlords had little opportunity of talking to speakers of standard English, then the kind of daily confidential intercourse described by Thady Quirk would no doubt be sufficient to explain the degree of Irish influence illustrated by Swift.

The hibernicisms singled out by Swift are peculiarities either of vocabulary or of idiom; it may perhaps seem strange that he does not satirise other aspects of the Anglo-Irish dialect, such as the non-standard tense formations so characteristic of 'stage Irish' at a later date. However, it seems that these tense-formations, closely based on the usage of the Irish language, were a relatively late development in Anglo-Irish. One of them, the equivalent of the English perfect, illustrated in such a sentence as 'he is after writing', was first used in 1690, and did not become common until the early part of the eighteenth century, so that it was still new in Swift's time. Another, the reproduction of the Irish consuetudinal present in such a sentence as 'he does be writing', seems not to have been used until as late as 1815, so that Swift could not possibly have known of it.

What is much more surprising is the fact that Swift makes no attempt whatever to indicate any of the non-standard pronunciations used in Ireland, though he was certainly very conscious of them, as the following quotation reveals:

What we call the Irish brogue is no sooner discovered, than it makes the deliverer in the last degree, ridiculous and despised; and, from such a mouth, an Englishman expects nothing but bulls, blunders, and follies. . . . It is too well known that the bad consequences of this opinion affects those among us who are not the least liable to such reproaches, further than the misfortune of being born in Ireland, though of English parents, and whose education hath been chiefly in that kingdom.

I have heard many gentlemen among us talk much of the great convenience to those who live in the country, that they should speak Irish. It may possibly be so. But, I think, they should be such who never intend to visit England, upon pain of being ridiculous. For I do not remember to have heard of any one man that spoke

Irish, who had not the accent upon his tongue, easily discernible to any English ear.[1]

For details of eighteenth-century Anglo-Irish pronunciation we must turn to the work of Thomas Sheridan, the son of Swift's friend of the same name, who prefixed to his *Dictionary* a set of 'Rules to be observed by the natives of Ireland in order to attain a just pronunciation of English'. Sheridan's comment at the end of his 'Rules' makes it clear that he is thinking not of the lower but of the upper classes in Ireland:

> A strict observance of these few rules, with a due attention to the very few exceptions enumerated above, will enable the well-educated natives of Ireland to pronounce their words exactly in the same way as the more polished part of the inhabitants of England do.[2]

Some of the pronunciations against which Sheridan warns his readers may still be heard in Ireland, though hardly in the mouths of 'well-educated natives'; others seem to have become obsolete. Similarly, in the list of specific words appended to the general rules, only about half are still to be heard with the pronunciation indicated. Few of the pronunciations reprehended can be attributed to Irish influence; they seem to be due either to archaism, or (in a few cases) to false analogy.

The fate of spoken English in Ireland after the end of the middle ages can be summarised as follows. In most parts of rural Ireland English had been displaced by Irish before 1500. Medieval Hiberno-English survived in only two rural areas, the remote baronies of Forth and Bargy in County Wexford, and the district known as Fingall north of Dublin; in these districts it survived with relatively little change until about 1800. The English of the towns was related to these two rural dialects but distinct from them; both forms of speech had been influenced by the Irish language. From the sixteenth century onwards new forms of English were being introduced into Ireland: in northern and eastern Ulster, Lowland Scots; in the rest of the country, the English of England—not the rather academic standard English of the period, but a type of speech displaying certain sub-standard and dialectal features, related in some way to the dialects of the north of England. By the middle of the seventeenth century English had been spread rather widely through all the provinces of Ireland except Connacht, and from then on it was not affected by changes occurring in England, but developed in its own way. This new English did not at first displace either Irish or the older English of the towns, but remained the perquisite of the planters; since developments in the language of England were not reflected in Ireland, the

[1] 'On barbarous denominations in Ireland' in Swift, *Prose works*, iv, 280–84; quotation on p. 281.

[2] Thomas Sheridan, *A general dictionary of the English language, to which is prefixed a rhetorical grammar* (Dublin, 1780), p. lxvi.

dialect of the planters became more and more distinctively archaic. At a surprisingly early date, certainly by about 1700, the planters' English had been influenced by Irish, as a result of daily intercourse with their Irish servants and tenants. The ultimate fate of the language of the towns is not known; it does not survive in any recognisable form, but it is possible that some varieties of present-day urban Anglo-Irish may show its influence.

CHAPTER XXII

Irish literature in Latin, 1550–1700

BENIGNUS MILLETT

IN 1516 Desiderius Erasmus made a very uncomplimentary reference to the Irish in the preface to his edition of the New Testament.[1] For him the Irish, like the Scots, Turks, and Saracens whom he also names, were barbarians in 'ultima Thule', living in remote regions beyond the fringe of what he regarded as civilisation. He obviously believed that the Irish were untouched by the refining influences of the renaissance and as a consequence deficient in Latin learning. This accusation could not be made against his contemporary, Maurice O'Fihilly, known in the European schools as 'flos mundi', but there were very few, if any, other scholars from Ireland who attained his eminence. Forty-eight years later Pius IV issued a papal bull to facilitate the erection in Ireland of tridentine seminaries and of a university on the lines of those at Paris and Louvain. But the unsettled religious and political situation prevented any such development, and David Wolfe had to be content with some form of grammar school.[2] Latin indeed was being taught and studied in Ireland, but the great flowering of Latin learning among the catholic Irish did not appear until the counter-reformation had become established. Almost incredible progress was made in just over half a century. This can be assessed to some extent by a study of two books written in the 1620s, both products of a literary battle between the Irish and the Scots which we will have occasion to discuss later. The first was published at Antwerp in 1621.[3] Its unidentified author, whose initials are given as G. F., sets out to refute a current libel that there were very few Irishmen who had received a university training. He does this by listing distinguished Irishmen abroad: three prelates, twelve Jesuits, ten Franciscans, two Dominicans, three Augustinians, together with four scholars at Paris and five others, including four Capuchins, elsewhere in

[1] 'I would have the weakest woman read the Gospels and the Epistles of Saint Paul . . . I would have those words translated into all languages, so that not only Scots and Irishmen, but Turks and Saracens might read them.'

[2] *Spicil. Ossor.*, i, 32–8; Hogan, *Ibernia Ignat.*, i, 15. The bull has been wrongly attributed by Moran to Pius V.

[3] G. F., *Hiberniae sive antiquioris Scotiae vindiciae adversus immodestam parecbasim Thomae Dempsteri moderni Scoti nuper editam* . . . (Antwerp, 1621), pp 30–36.

France. He says that he refrains from naming the very many in Spain and other countries who were not known to him personally. Next he names fifteen clerics who had become doctors of theology at Bordeaux, Toulouse, Florence, Salamanca, and other university centres. The second work, the Zoilomastix of Philip O'Sullivan Beare, is even more informative. With a welcome richness of biographical detail it lists eighty-six Irish catholic clerics of the late sixteenth and early seventeenth century, with their academic qualifications, and then gives twenty-nine others who at the time of writing were professors abroad.[1] Though defective these lists clearly demonstrate that at least among the catholics Latin learning had made a remarkable recovery.[2]

In the sixteenth century Latin was the language used by the Irish in correspondence and conversation with foreigners. Its use as such was not restricted to clergy and scholars. The well-educated among the nobility, both Gaelic Irish and Old English, had Latin as well as Irish and English, and some of them also spoke French. In the Gaelic districts some of the common folk also spoke Latin. In reference to the 'mere Irish' Edmund Campion said (1571) that 'they speake Latine like a vulgar language, learned in their common schools of leach-craft and law . . . ' In 1588 a Spaniard, shipwrecked from the Armada on the north-west coast of Ireland, found that the local people could converse with him in Latin. And a century later, about 1683, it is recorded that the inhabitants of the Gaelic districts of County Kerry spoke Latin, described as 'bald and barbarous and very often not grammatical'.[3]

The evidence is by no means complete. There were whole classes that never attained to literary expression. Between 1540 and 1600 much that must have once existed perished. But enough remains of the Latin literature, especially from the Irish abroad, to help us to appreciate the multiplicity of intellectual strands that were woven into the pattern of Irish culture. After Henry VIII's break with Rome the Gaelic tradition attached itself intensively to the pope and the old religious loyalties, and was influenced by the theology and polemics of the counter-reformation. The Old English either took a similar stand or, in many instances, became protestant and more pronouncedly English in outlook. Neither rejected the renaissance; they were by no means unwilling to accept the classical tradition as an instrument of Christian education and Irish culture.

[1] O'Sullivan Beare, *Zoilomastix*, ed. O'Donnell, pp 16–27. Of the 86 clerics 14 were Franciscans, 6 Dominicans, 4 Augustinians, 6 Jesuits, 4 Cistercians, the remaining 52 being bishops and secular priests. At least 21 had the doctorate in theology. Of the 29 professors named there were 2 Augustinians, 3 Dominicans, 7 Franciscans, 14 Jesuits, and 3 laymen.

[2] To avoid burdening the text with too many Latin titles and an unnecessary wealth of detail, a select list of first editions is printed in vol. ix, appendix.

[3] Cited in W. B. Stanford, 'Towards a history of classical influences in Ireland' in *R.I.A. Proc.*, lxx (1970), sect. C, pp 45–6.

For the rest of the sixteenth century, in those Irish districts where the royal power did not extend, the traditional schools of Gaelic culture continued and in some places flourished. We find them in many places, even in Leinster, but especially in Ulster. A typical product was the Gaelic poet Aodh Mac Aingil (Hugh MacCaghwell), who was better known, later as a Friar Minor, by his Latinised name 'Hugo Cavellus' throughout Europe, where his theological writings brought him a high reputation which still survives. He was the young, unnamed scholar who, with Friar Nangle, was acting as tutor to the sons of the earl of Tyrone when Sir John Harington paid them a visit in 1599.[1]

Most towns had a school. In some places there were Jesuit schools for catholics, in others English parish schools and then grammar schools for protestants; in these, 'Greek and Latin dominated all teaching in the humanities, as in other countries'. Towards the end of the century the city of Dublin was given a university. Here and there we find an urban school run by a competent and zealous schoolmaster, which did not fit into any of the above categories. The flourishing of Latin among catholic scholars in the seventeenth century is due in no small measure to the solid foundations laid in these various schools. The Jesuits were specialists in teaching Latin by the direct method. One of them, the Dublin-born William Bathe, published at Salamanca in 1611 a book that offered a new approach to the study of Latin and was acclaimed by educationalists throughout Europe.[2]

The grammar school opened in Dublin in 1562 had a succession of excellent teachers. One such was the Oxford-educated Patrick Cusack, who compiled Latin epigrams, probably for the use of his pupils. Another was Michael Fitzsimon, who published three minor Latin works. In Kilkenny the grammar school, established by Piers Butler, was conducted about 1565 by 'the happy schoolmaster of Munster', Peter White, one-time fellow of Oriel College, Oxford. This very competent teacher, who was himself the author of five small Latin works, attracted to his school many promising scholars, including two who were later to distinguish themselves as latinists —Richard Stanihurst and Peter Lombard. The school founded in Galway early in Elizabeth's reign by Dominic Lynch was attended by a great number of pupils, not all from Connacht, in the second decade of the seventeenth century. There John Lynch, the future historian, Duald MacFirbis, the antiquarian, Roderick O'Flaherty, and many catholic priests first imbibed their love of Latin and history. In Munster Waterford became a Mecca for brilliant pupils at the beginning of the seventeenth century because of the reputation of its professor of classics, John Flahy. Between 1603 and 1617 he

[1] See Maxwell, *Sources, 1509–1610*, p. 338.

[2] Stanford, as above, pp 74–5. See also Timothy Corcoran, 'Early Irish Jesuit educators' in *Studies*, xxix (1940), pp 545–60; xxx (1941), pp 59–74; John Kingston, 'William Bathe, S.J., 1564–1614' in *I.E.R.*, 5th series, lxxxii (1954), pp 179–82.

Map 19 LITERARY ACTIVITY IN LATIN BY IRISHMEN, *c.* 1550–*c* 1700, by Benignus Millett

taught many young men who then set out to enter the Irish college at Salamanca. His most distinguished pupil was the Clonmel youth Bartholomew (Bonaventure) Baron, whose many tomes provide ample evidence of the excellence of the latinity which he had acquired in Ireland.[1]

The post-tridentine seminaries and colleges, founded overseas for the education of Irish secular and regular clergy, opened up in the seventeenth century avenues of university training to counter-reformation priests from Ireland. In his chapter on the Irish abroad,[2] Dr Silke gives the geographical location of various groupings of Irish exiles. A statistical survey of the Irish writers overseas with reference to the places where they studied, taught, and worked will put Louvain and Rome easily at the head of the list. In reasonably large numbers they were also attracted to such university centres as Paris, Oxford, Salamanca, and Prague. Men like Augustine Gibbon Burke, Stephen White, and Francis Molloy, without the support or companionship of their fellow countrymen, carried Irish learning to various university centres in the German empire. But to a large extent the siting of the various Irish colleges decided their place of work for the majority of these Irish writers and teachers. Accordingly, we find not a few at Douai and Antwerp in the Low Countries.

Most of these seminary-trained clerics appear to have spoken and written Latin with ease, as the wealth of extant letters and documents shows. The Latin writings of Irishmen, in particular their books, reflect the tension and struggle so evident in seventeenth-century Europe. Resurgent catholicism, ardent, devout, and at times fanatical, and stalwart protestantism, convinced, ruthless, and frequently self-righteous, engaged each other in a long-drawn-out struggle which ended in stalemate. But Irish writers, especially clerics, who mirrored this contest as faithfully as their French, Italian, or Spanish counterparts, were to a less extent influenced by the contemporary struggle between monarchical absolutism and representative constitutionalism.

The Latin literature[3] of the period under review was not exclusively ecclesiastical. It was also a literature of medical doctors, lawyers, university fellows, schoolmasters, poets, and lexicographers.

Until the foundation of a formal school of medicine at Dublin in the seventeenth century, medicine in Ireland was practised, for the most part,

[1] Holinshed, *Chronicles* (ed. 1808), vi, 34, 59, 61, 64, 65; A. S. Green, *The making of Ireland and its undoing* (London, 1908), pp 367–71, 393–4; James Ware, *The history of the writers of Ireland*, ed. W. Harris (Dublin, 1764), pp 95, 100; J. Rabbitte, 'Alexander Lynch, schoolmaster' in *Galway Arch. Soc. Jn.*, xvi (1936), pp 34–42; Thomas Wall, 'Parnassus in Waterford' in *I.E.R.*, 5th series, lxix (1947), pp 708–21.

[2] Below, ch. XXIII.

[3] Besides Harris's enlarged edition of Ware's bibliography (see above), some well-known bibliographies have been consulted, including those by Quétif and Echard, Sommervogel, Wadding, and H. Hurter, *Nomenclator literarius theologiae catholicae*, facsimile ed. (New York, 1962), iii and iv. See also E. R. McC. Dix, *Catalogue of early Dublin-printed books 1601–1700* (Dublin, 1898–1905); Michael Walsh, 'Irish books printed abroad, 1475–1700' in *The Irish book*, ii (1963), pp 1–36.

by hereditary physicians. Some few, especially the Old English, went abroad for training. O'Sullivan Beare, who defends their training and professional skill against the calumnies of Stanihurst, gives an incomplete list of Irish doctors practising abroad.[1] Dermot O'Meara, M.D., of Tipperary, who was educated at Oxford, published a Latin text on pathology at Dublin in 1619. It was well received and within the next fifty years was reprinted twice. His son Edmund also became a doctor, graduating at Rheims. In 1665 he published at London a Latin volume attacking a work on fevers by the Oxford professor Thomas Willis. Two years later another Irish doctor, Conly Cashin, replied with a Latin vindication of Willis. A more interesting and colourful character was Niall Ó Glacan of Tyrconnell, who was first trained by one of the hereditary physicians, possibly a Dunleavy, and later abroad. He became physician to the king of France and occupied chairs of physic at Toulouse and Bologna. Among his Latin writings were a treatise on pestilence and a three-volume course of medicine.

The founder of the Irish College of Physicians, John Stearne (1624–69), studied medicine at Cambridge and Oxford. But his six Latin works, all of them Dublin printings, were more theological than medical. The literary contributions of some other members of the medical profession were equally dull. In 1686 a Dutch doctor practising in Dublin, Jacobus Sylvius, published a tract on fevers, and a work on the state and problems of medical practice, by John O'Dwyer, appeared at Mons. At Limerick, there was a very cultured doctor, Thomas Arthur, whose classical education stayed with him. Educated at Bordeaux, he studied medicine at Paris and Rheims, and acquired a library of some 275 works, all but seven of them in Latin. In his free moments he composed some Latin verses, mostly hexameters, on his career, his family, and the public men of his day.[2] On the whole the Latin writings of these medical men, despite the educational advantages of the authors, were uninspired.[3]

The historical writings in Latin were much more remarkable, and not a few are of enduring value. The traditional Gaelic schools had fostered among the Irish a love of history, as had also, in a more limited way, the various church schools, which had been centres of a reasonably developed literary culture. The interest in history continued, and the Latin literature of the period is rich in historical material. The increasing threat to catholicism in Ireland gave a strong incentive to catholics to develop a new sense of history. Richard Creagh, the catholic archbishop of Armagh who died in the tower of London in 1585, produced a Latin work on the Irish language,[4]

[1] *Zoilomastix*, ed. O'Donnell, p. 91.

[2] See Edward MacLysaght, 'The Arthur manuscript' in *N. Munster Antiq. Jn.*, viii (1958–9), pp 2–19, 79–87; ix (1962–5), pp 51–9, 113–16, 155–64.

[3] The writings of the highly distinguished and skilled Bernard Connor of Kerry (1666?–98) belong to the closing decade of the century.

[4] *De lingua Hibernica*: T.C.D., MS F 4. 30.

a history of Ireland, and some Latin lives of Irish saints. The chancellor of Leighlin, Thady Dowling, continued the annals of Duiske to 1593[1] and compiled a Latin chronicle. Cornelius O'Devany, bishop of Down and Connor, wrote an account of contemporary Irish martyrs, the manuscript of which was used by the historian David Rothe. The catholic theologian Peter Lombard, soon to become archbishop of Armagh, was opposed to Elizabeth, though he later came to accept James I. He was author of the historical commentary on the kingdom of Ireland, written in 1600 to win the support of Clement VIII for Hugh O'Neill's war and published posthumously.

On the English side a flood of propaganda supported the Elizabethan wars, much of it crude defamation of all things Irish; but by the early Stuart period the propaganda designed to justify a war of conquest had been replaced by genuine historical scholarship, with a recognisably Irish flavour, in such writers as Ussher and Ware. The noted pupil of Peter White, Richard Stanihurst (1547–1618), son of the speaker of the Irish house of commons, besides writing a Latin life of St Patrick compiled a history of Ireland, which carried in an appendix his annotations on Gerald of Wales. The obvious propaganda value for the English cause of such writers as Stanihurst and John Hooker inspired a burst of literary and scholarly activity on the part of Irish exiles on the Continent.[2] The only non-cleric who took up his pen to defend the ancient glories of his native land was Philip O'Sullivan Beare, a soldier educated at Compostella. With the help of some Irish friends in Spain he began to assemble material. He is best known for his compendious history of Ireland, which despite its partisanship and occasional inaccuracies has useful information for the period of the Elizabethan wars. We have already referred to his Zoilomastix, which, though a tedious polemic against Gerald of Wales and Richard Stanihurst, does contain valuable material.[3] Other Irish exiles who entered the fray included the Jesuit, Stephen White, and the cultured archdeacon of Tuam, John Lynch, both of whom composed refutations of Gerald of Wales.

The scholarship and classical culture of Stanihurst's nephew, James Ussher, primate of the established church, were esteemed by academic contemporaries of all persuasions. The Latin learning of this biblical and patristic scholar and church historian is clearly in evidence in his writings. The earliest was a historical treatise on the descent of the churches of the west from apostolic times (1613). Then came his history of Gotteschalk and his predestination controversy. The year 1632 saw the publication of two important works, one dealing with early Irish letters, the other on the antiquities of the churches of Britain. Then came a celebrated edition of the

[1] T.C.D., MS E 3. 10.

[2] P. J. Corish, 'The origins of catholic nationalism' in Corish, *Ir. catholicism*, iii (1968), ch. VIII, pp 27–31.

[3] Among his other works are a Latin life of St Patrick, some unpublished lives of saints, and a severe criticism of Archbishop Ussher.

letters of SS Ignatius and Polycarp in 1644, a treatise on credal development in 1647, a Latin work on the solar year of the Macedonians and Asians, and a lengthy study of biblical history. His posthumous Latin publications include one on chronology, a treatise on the history of doctrine, and a reply to the teaching of St Robert Bellarmine. It was not unnatural that his background, training, and position orientated him towards England. This and a famous sermon he preached in 1622 against the papists made him suspect to many catholic Irishmen at home and abroad, though they respected his scholarship. By temperament a lone worker, he established contact with several catholic scholars, chiefly for the purpose of setting up a two-way traffic of documents and information on matters historical. For ten or twelve years he had friendly relations with some of the Irish Franciscans. Fr Thomas Strange was allowed to use Ussher's valuable library, to copy documents, and send the copies to Rome to Luke Wadding for a projected ecclesiastical history of Ireland, which in fact never materialised. There was some reciprocation, though for a variety of reasons Wadding seems to have been slow in responding to repeated messages for help. Ussher was also on friendly terms with at least one of Colgan's collaborators in the Louvain school, Fr Brendan O'Conor.[1] It has not been established that he had any contact with two contemporary priests, Donagh Mooney and Francis O'Mahony, who compiled in Latin two valuable histories of the Franciscan province of Ireland.[2]

Sir James Ware (1594–1666), son of the auditor general, had an excellent classical education and was encouraged by Ussher in his antiquarian pursuits. His first work, a collection of Latin biographies of the archbishops of Cashel and Tuam, was soon followed by a similar study of the bishops of Leinster. Both were expanded into a larger work in 1665. A by-product of this historical research was Ware's *De scriptoribus Hiberniae* (1639), the beginning of scientific bibliography in Ireland. Among his other works[3] were a Latin annals of Ireland for the years 1485–1558 and his well-known treatise on Irish antiquities, which appeared in 1654, with a second edition in 1658.

Among the catholic scholars with whom Ussher corresponded was David Rothe (1573–1650), catholic bishop of Ossory, who had been educated at Douai. Rothe's first work was his significant account of the sufferings of the Irish catholics for their religion, the three-part *Analecta sacra* (1616–19) which, despite the Old English background of the author, rejected the plantations as a national calamity. This was followed by a Latin life of St

[1] See Aubrey Gwynn, 'Archbishop Ussher and Father Brendan O'Conor' in *Father Luke Wadding* (Dublin, 1957), pp 263–83.

[2] *Anal. Hib.*, no. 6 (1934), pp 12–191.

[3] Including an unpublished account of his sojourn in France during the commonwealth, editions of works ascribed to St Patrick and of two letters of St Bede, lives of the abbots of Wearmouth and Jarrow, and a dialogue of St Egbert of York.

Brigid of Kildare (1620) and the *Hibernia resurgens* (1621), a defence of Ireland and its saints against the Scot, Thomas Dempster. With this publication Rothe joined forces with other Irish scholars abroad, in particular the Franciscans, who also had decided that it was high time to put an end to the wholesale appropriation of their ancient Irish heritage by Scottish polemical writers.

One incentive to these patriotic Franciscans in exile to press forward with their plans for an ecclesiastical history of Ireland was the existence of unreliable histories of Ireland by pro-English catholics such as Campion and Stanihurst and the re-publication of two works of Gerald of Wales. Moreover, the appearance of historical works by learned protestant scholars —Camden, Ussher, and others—impressed upon them what could and should be done. But the immediate motivation was to refute the claim by Scottish scholars that in medieval terminology *Scotia* meant Scotland and *Scotus*, a Scotsman. This gave unity to two seemingly disparate and unconnected activities at St Anthony's College, Louvain, the one concerned with the lives of the early Irish saints, the other with the place of origin, the life and works of the medieval Franciscan, John Duns Scotus. The latter enterprise forged an even closer link with St Isidore's, Rome, where, under the guidance of Luke Wadding, their brethren were making a strong case for claiming Duns Scotus as an Irishman. Between the Irish Franciscans at Louvain and those in Rome there was a two-way traffic in the field of church history. Each could appeal to the other for copies of texts and for help in the solution of points of detail. While Rome was concentrating on Franciscan history, Louvain was specialising in Irish history.

The chief spokesman on the Scottish side was Thomas Dempster, a learned but erratic Scot, who claimed for his country, among other things, all the medieval Scottic monasteries of Europe, all the Scottic missionaries from the seventh to the twelfth century, and a large number of the early Irish saints. He propounded his theories in four works written in the 1620s. The first two appeared in 1620 and sparked off an immediate reaction in David Rothe. Some few other Irishmen also responded, with works in a minor key. The most formidable reply came from the friars at Louvain. Though various plans formulated by the Franciscans at Louvain and Rome, under the influence of Baronius's work, for the publication of the ecclesiastical history of Ireland, never reached full fruition, at Louvain they did bring forth important by-products. Hagiography was in favour in Europe, especially in Flanders, and the Irish Franciscans overseas played a major role in this hagiographical movement, under the initial prompting of Thomas Messingham, rector of the Irish college in Paris, who published an important study of the Irish saints in 1624. The extraordinary fertility of historical talent and industry among the Irish friars at Louvain bore some fruit despite the unsettled conditions in Ireland. The first volume of John

Colgan's *Acta sanctorum Hiberniae* was issued in 1645 and his more valuable *Trias thaumaturga* in 1647. Thomas O'Sheerin, his successor, revised and published Hugh Ward's life of St Rumold and Patrick Fleming's *Collectanea sacra*. In November 1671 he had another volume of the lives of the Irish saints almost ready and had made considerable progress on a third. His death in 1673 marks the demise of the Louvain historical scheme.[1] Though there was a fairly regular correspondence between the Bollandists and the Irish Franciscans, especially those at Rome,[2] there is no evidence of any connection between the plans of the friars at St Anthony's, Louvain, and the Bollandists' famous *Acta sanctorum*.

Among the catholic exiles from Cromwellian persecution there were some writers of distinction. William St Leger produced a Latin biography of Archbishop Thomas Walsh of Cashel, the Dominican Dominic O'Daly a history of the Munster Geraldines, and Maurice Conry a study of the sufferings of the Irish catholics under the puritans. All these appeared in the 1650s. In the same decade a battle of pamphlets was waged by the Irish in Paris over the question of Rinuccini's censures. The Franciscan Paul King, on his way to Rome from Ireland, sparked off the row with a small pamphlet. Its very one-sided views of recent developments in Ireland invited a reply, which came from a Cork priest, John Callaghan (or MacCallaghan). The authorship of this small book was hidden under the pseudonym *Philopater Irenaeus*, and almost from its publication down to recent times it has been wrongly ascribed to Richard Bellings, the secretary of the catholic confederation, under whose name it found its way into the Vatican index of forbidden books. A defence of the Irish bishops and their stand, prepared for the archbishop of Paris by Nicholas French, bishop of Ferns, appeared in print in 1651. Bellings, finding himself black-listed by French, published a booklet to vindicate himself. In 1653 John Punch, then living in Paris, entered the fray with a pamphlet that was primarily a reply to Bellings but also a castigation of Callaghan. Bellings then responded with a new pamphlet in 1654, and the Franciscan, realising that he had got the worst of the battle, retired to his Scotist studies.[3]

One of the most outstanding contributions to Irish history by the exiles was compiled in the next decade. This was the monumental *Commentarius Rinuccinianus*. Archbishop Giovanni Battista Rinuccini, the nuncio accredited by Innocent X to the government of the catholic confederates at Kilkenny in 1645, left among his papers not merely his reports and official records but also a great body of controversial material which had accumulated

[1] See Canice Mooney, 'Father John Colgan, O.F.M., his work and times and literary milieu' in T. J. O'Donnell (ed.), *Father John Colgan, O.F.M.* (Dublin, 1959), pp 7–40.

[2] See Fergal Grannell, 'Letters of Daniel Papebroch, S.J., to Francis Harold, O.F.M. (1665–1690)' in *Archivum Franciscanum Historicum*, lix (1966), pp 385–455.

[3] The above account is based mainly on P. J. Corish, 'John Callaghan and the controversies among the Irish in Paris, 1648–54' in *Ir. Theol. Quart.*, xxi (1954), pp 32–50.

when, as a result of his excommunication of the supporters of the cessation with Inchiquin, Rinuccini himself became a cause. In November 1648 he sent to Rome two of his supporters, Giuseppe Arcamoni and Richard O'Ferrall, to counter an appeal. O'Ferrall, educated at Lille and then at Douai, had entered the Capuchins at Charleville, on the confines of Champagne, in 1634. Though associated with the French diplomatic machine when he returned to Ireland in 1644, he quickly became a loyal supporter of Rinuccini. Through Irish contacts in Europe the issues at stake were brought by interested parties to Paris, Rome, and elsewhere, and O'Ferrall, whose literary services had been enlisted by the nuncio, identified himself completely with Rinuccini's cause. The former nuncio died on 15 December 1653. From 1648, for almost thirteen years, O'Ferrall was his most active defender, but his efforts, especially at the Roman court, were not successful, owing in no small way to political complications.

When his advocacy was almost at an end, he had an opportunity to examine the nuncio's papers and, out of the atmosphere of the appeal, to see the problem more clearly. The register of the nuncio's letters was certainly used by him, and possibly Rinuccini's diary and his report on the mission, completed on his return to Italy, both of which were used by O'Connell, his co-author. A useful parallel source is the memoirs of Rinuccini's auditor, Dionisio Massari. From August 1649 to April 1657, when he was secretary of the sacred congregation *de propaganda fide*, Massari had free access to all letters and reports on Irish affairs. He apparently allowed O'Ferrall every facility to examine many of them, and then asked for his help in compiling an account of his own part in Rinuccini's embassy. But it is not clear that he ever showed the completed work to the friar.

Before leaving Rome for Florence in failing health, O'Ferrall was fortunate in getting his superiors to assign to him as collaborator Robert O'Connell. This confrère, who had compiled in Latin an excellent history of the Capuchin mission in Ireland, was a man with both literary experience and a sense of history. Between them they completed an extensive history of Rinuccini's mission to Ireland. The work of compilation began in 1661 and was finished in 1666, three years after O'Ferrall's death. The family background and loyalties of the two authors were pronouncedly Old Irish and catholic. The O'Ferralls of Annaly and the O'Connells, the hereditary wardens of the MacCarthy Mór at Ballycarbery, had few doubts about the real crisis through which Ireland had passed in the reign of James I. It was, it seems, Robert O'Connell who elaborated in the *Commentarius* the patriotic catholic interpretation of Irish history already begun by Lombard, Rothe, and Keating. The work that these two Capuchins produced, which runs to six large volumes in the published edition, is one of the principal sources for the history of the catholic confederates. It is not, however, an unprejudiced account.

'It is fair to say that, while the faith was his motive in supporting the nuncio, he was also concerned with the interests of the O'Ferralls and of the Old Irish.'[1] This candid admission was made by Robert O'Connell in reference to his collaborator. His passionate temperament, his attachment to his family, his growing conviction that the disaster which had so recently taken place was due to the faint catholicism and worldly interests and innate prejudices of the Old English, all guided O'Ferrall's pen in the *Commentarius*. The citation of contemporary documents and the interpretation of events can to some extent be controlled with the aid of the originals and of other contemporary sources and writings.

The *Commentarius*, when it comes to treat of the split of the Irish catholic confederacy over the Ormond peace and the Inchiquin truce, frequently injects current Old Irish arguments and interpretations, and sometimes treats mere rumour as fact. For example, despite the mass of documents of the period now available to us, there is no concrete evidence to support the case that the *Commentarius* makes against Fr Luke Wadding and its interpretation of his letter of 2 September 1646 to Rinuccini. It casts further suspicion on Richard Bellings and Wadding when it deals with Bellings's statement to the general assembly in February 1647 about his audience with Innocent X (27 February 1645). It blames Bellings for concealing from the nuncio a letter of corroboration from Wadding which in fact never existed. This pronounced partiality to the Old Irish cause so clouded O'Ferrall's judgement that he claimed that Wadding had not only used his position of influence at Rome to secure the promotion of Old English candidates to church benefices, but, in his monumental history of the Franciscans, had slanted his treatment of Irish affairs in favour of the Old English. These and many other accusations and innuendoes have been examined and challenged by a modern scholar.[2]

A further example may serve to illustrate the point. The writers of the *Commentarius* have left their readers in no doubt about what they thought of Archbishop John Burke of Tuam, especially because of his attitude to Rinuccini's censures of 1648. But this prelate also suffered from the pen of another writer of the Old Irish and pro-nuncio camp, the unknown author of the contemporary 'Aphorismical discovery', who has a scathing attack on Burke and his brother Hugh.[3] The authors of the *Commentarius* could not easily escape from the influences of their Old Irish heritage and, unconsciously perhaps, were also affected by the bitterness in the ranks of the Old Irish exiles in Europe which became so notable after the collapse in ignominy of the Irish catholic confederacy. The modern historian, aware of such

[1] *Comment. Rinucc.*, v, 420.

[2] See Canice Mooney, 'Was Wadding a patriotic Irishman?' in *Father Luke Wadding*, pp 15–92.

[3] *Comment. Rinucc.*, iii, 340–42, 594, 599; v, 478. For other references, see Millett, *Ir. Franciscans*, pp 312–13.

prejudices, will approach certain comments and opinions of the Capuchin authors with suitable caution. They have given to posterity the greatest and probably the most valuable collection of source material for the history of Irish affairs in the period in question. There are contemporary reports, letters, petitions, and memoirs which are not available elsewhere in print. Not a few of these can now be checked against the originals or copies preserved in the archives of the Propaganda in Rome. Any such comparison will show that the compilers of the *Commentarius* accurately reproduced the texts in question.

Robert O'Connell, who had been detached for more than twenty years from the minutiae of Irish political life, was less passionate than his collaborator and more prudent. He was also more concerned about giving his readers an impartial verdict. For example, he tells us that he urged O'Ferrall to give him the sources for his charge that the bishops of Ferns, Ardagh, and Dromore, together with Robert Nugent, S.J., and Nicholas Plunkett, had betrayed secrets entrusted to them by the nuncio, and that he did not get satisfaction.[1] There is an attractive gentleness about O'Connell. He reveals this in the brief but vivid pen-picture he gives of the Franciscan missioner and future bishop, Boetius MacEgan, to whose preaching he had listened.[2] Another example of his tendency to insert into a narrative some personal experience is his description of the position of the catholics of Cork in the years 1637–40, during which, as a youth before entering the Capuchins, he had studied in that city. He could remember only about four protestant families in all within the city walls.[3] Besides the insertion of the occasional autobiographical element and also of some corrections to the text written by his colleague, O'Connell wrote more than two-thirds of the text, though the preparation and planning of the work as a whole have rightly been attributed to O'Ferrall. Between them they produced a lengthy and complex history of about 1,200,000 words, which is something more than a pious literary monument to Rinuccini. It is an attempt at a contemporary official statement of the nuncio's part in Irish affairs set in its historical perspective.

Richard O'Ferrall's devastating condemnation of the Old English was also expressed in a celebrated memorandum submitted to Propaganda in 1658. Its text was leaked to the opposition parties among the Irish exiles and brought a lengthy reply in two volumes, *Alithinologia* (1664, 1667), from John Lynch, then at St Malo.[4] Lynch, whose polished and pure Latin is the best witness to the renaissance learning imparted to him at Galway, was also the author of a Latin life of Bishop Francis Kirwan and of an excellent history of the Irish episcopate. If Lynch was on the Old English side in this controversy, his patriotism was broadly enough based for him to rise to the

[1] *Comment. Rinucc.*, v, 429. [2] Ibid., iv, 392. [3] Ibid., i, 307–8.

[4] See Patrick J. Corish, 'Two contemporary historians of the confederation of Kilkenny: John Lynch and Richard O'Ferrall' in *I.H.S.*, viii, no. 31 (Mar. 1953), pp 219–20.

defence of the native Irish against their traducers in his well-known work *Cambrensis eversus* (1662). He agreed with that other Anglo-Irishman, Geoffrey Keating, in singling out Giraldus Cambrensis as 'the leader of the herd', though he displayed greater historical exactitude and knowledge of chronology than the literary Keating.[1] To Lynch, Roderick O'Flaherty wrote the prologue to his *Ogygia seu rerum Hibernicarum chronologia*, published in London in 1685 and dedicated to James, duke of York, who that year was to become king. O'Flaherty was a pupil of An Dubhaltach Mac Fir Bhisigh, last of the professional genealogists and collaborator of Sir James Ware.[2] O'Flaherty possessed a large number of valuable Irish manuscripts and contributed much that is still of value to the establishment of true chronological criteria for the Irish annals. The extension of pseudo-scientific exactitude to the fabulous prehistory of Ireland renders the *Ogygia* a bizarre work to modern readers, but O'Flaherty was in the tradition of his time (it was Ussher who established the true date of the creation as 4004 B.C., and Newton devoted much energy to a study of the Book of Daniel). O'Flaherty's work received the approbation of the distinguished orientalist Dudley Loftus, and he himself has some interesting remarks on Chinese and Japanese script in his discussion of the ogham alphabet. The *Ogygia* is the most learned exposition of Gaelic loyalty to the Stuart dynasty and to the concept of the kingdom of Ireland (a feeling expressed earlier by the Four Masters in the title of their annals).[3] Its main object is to assert the superior antiquity of that kingdom as a political entity over the sister kingdoms of England and Scotland (interestingly, O'Flaherty does not hesitate to use the term 'the British Isles'), and to vindicate the claims of the Stuart dynasty to the crown of Ireland, not merely by virtue of inherited claims and by conquest, but because of their genealogical descent from Gaelic kings of Munster. O'Flaherty's patriotism is all-embracing and unsectarian, though his family had lost much in the confiscations of the century: he is proud to count the protestant primate Ussher 'one of us' (*Usserius noster*). He wrote also in English a 'chorographical description' of his native Iar-Chonnacht,[4] a contribution to a project of William Molyneux's in 1684.

During this period Irish scholars, especially the friars at St Isidore's, Rome, made many useful literary contributions to the study of the history of the catholic church. The more important were from the pen of Luke Wadding. His critical edition of the writings of St Francis (1623) was soon followed by his great annals of the Franciscan order in eight folio volumes, and then by a defence of the real St Francis, a biographical study of Blessed Peter Thomas of Aquitaine, a bio-bibliography of Franciscans, a life of St Anselm

[1] See above, ch. XX, p. 531.
[2] See above, ch. XX, p. 532.
[3] See above, ch. XX, p. 531.
[4] *Ed.* James Hardiman, for the Irish Archaeological Society, 1846.

of Lucca, and several other useful works. His humanist nephew, Bonaventure Baron, also ventured into history with a study of three distinguished Tuscans and his annals of the Trinitarians. Francis Harold, another nephew, compiled a two-volume epitome of his uncle's annals, prepared a ninth volume and also a life and critical edition of some letters and discourses of Albert of Sartiano. Works of lesser moment were written by Anthony Bruodin, Bonaventure Delahoid, and others.[1]

Biblical scholarship received little impetus from the Latin writings of Irishmen, with the exception of James Ussher. Overseas, Luke Wadding and the two Jesuits, Paul Sherlock and Peter Reade, contributed some commentaries. At home the jurist and orientalist, Dudley Loftus, issued a Latin version of the psalms translated from the Armenian.

An examination of the long list of Latin writings produced by Irishmen shows that works in theology easily predominate. This, of course, is not surprising, for the majority of those writing in Latin were clerics. And they covered a wide field. In this brief survey mention is made of but a few of the more noteworthy. The well-known Richard Stanihurst and his son William published a number of pious books on a variety of religious topics—christology, the eucharist, eschatology, mariology—and some of them ran into many editions. William, who had a fluency in Latin, was an eclectic and a populariser, with little originality of thought. Another literary Jesuit was Peter Wadding, cousin of the famous Luke. The classical education he had received in boyhood at Waterford or Kilkenny was an appropriate foundation for the classical and philosophical studies he pursued for four years at Douai. His busy teaching life, at Utrecht, Antwerp, Louvain, Prague, and Gratz, did not allow him the necessary leisure to see through the press more than two of his many theological writings—a treatise on the incarnation and a large tome on the morality of contracts. He left some thirty-six treatises in manuscript, which are preserved in the Bodleian Library, Oxford, besides a half-dozen minor publications in Latin.[2] A seventeenth-century best-seller in theology was written by a third learned Jesuit, Richard Archdekin of Kilkenny, who also lectured at Louvain and Antwerp.[3]

The remarkable development and popularity of Scotism in the seventeenth century was due in no small measure to the writings and teaching of certain Irish Franciscans.[4] This was one of the outstanding contributions to religious culture in that age. It may be said to have begun with the erudite Ulster

[1] Millett, *Ir. Franciscans*, pp 464–70, 487–95.

[2] Paul O'Dea, 'Father Peter Wadding, S.J.: chancellor of the university of Prague, 1629–1641' in *Studies*, xxx (1941), pp 337–48.

[3] Originally called *Praecipuae controversiae fidei*, the work is better known by the title of the Antwerp edition of 1678, *Theologia tripartita*. See Thomas Wall, 'Richard Archdekin's catechetical hour' in *I.E.R.*, 5th series, lxx (1948), pp 305–15.

[4] D. de Caylus, 'Merveilleux épanouissement de l'école scotiste au XVIIe siècle' in *Études franciscaines*, xxiv (1910), pp 5–21, 492–502; xxv (1911), pp 35–47, 306–17, 627–45; xxvi (1912), pp 276–88.

poet-friar Aodh Mac Aingil or Hugh MacCaghwell, who later became archbishop of Armagh. MacCaghwell was the first really bright star shining in the Irish theological sky for more than a hundred years, since the death of Maurice O'Fihilly in 1513. He provided scholars with satisfactory editions of some of the works of John Duns Scotus, and these were used by Luke Wadding and his collaborators who prepared and published in 1639 the first critical edition of the *opera omnia* of the 'subtle doctor'. This edition initiated a new epoch in the history of Scotism. The story of the part played by the Irish in this development has been told elsewhere, with a wealth of historical and bibliographical detail.[1] The motivation behind this scholarly and literary project was a twofold one. These friars, operating principally from their colleges at Louvain, Rome, and Prague, had an ardent desire to vindicate the honour of their order's favourite theologian, and the added stimulus of patriotism to rescue Scotus, whom they claimed as an Irishman, from the clutches of the Scots.

During the greater part of the period under review Thomism, the coherent and intellectually satisfying system evolved by Aquinas, was not, as is commonly believed, the most influential. Until the counter-reformation was well established it was but a unit in the European intellectual pattern. It was only with the nineteenth century that Thomism came to be regarded as in some respects synonymous with catholic thought. In fact, from 1350 to 1650 Scotism claimed more followers in the schools than Thomism.[2] Among Irish catholic clerics, when the issues created by the break with Rome had become clearer and positions had hardened, trends were not dissimilar. In truth, however, the share taken by Ireland in the intellectual life of the sixteenth century was meagre. But as the seventeenth century advanced, Irish clerics, with the exception of the Franciscans, drifted more and more towards Thomism. And in an age when some of the best minds turned to positive theology, a theology more and more allied to apologetics and geared to refuting the assertions of the protestants, controversial theology attracted many an Irish pen.

Beginning with Thomism, we find in the sixteenth century a doctor of theology named Edmund Tanner, who compiled lectures on Aquinas's *Summa*. An inspection of Sommervogel's bibliography shows what devoted Thomists some of the Irish Jesuits were. Among them were Stephen White of Clonmel (1574–1648) and Richard Lynch of Galway (1610–76). But contrary to what might be expected, Thomism received at this stage little enrichment from the Irish Dominicans. One of them, the Limerick-born

[1] See Charles M. Balic, 'Wadding, the Scotist' in *Father Luke Wadding*, pp 463–507; Millett, *Ir. Franciscans*, pp 464–95; Cathaldus Giblin, 'Hugh MacCaghwell O.F.M. and Scotism at St Anthony's College, Louvain' in *De doctrina Ioannis Duns Scoti*, iv (Rome, 1968), pp 375–97; Benignus Millett, 'Irish Scotists at St Isidore's College, Rome, in the seventeenth century', ibid., pp 399–419.

[2] See David Knowles, *The evolution of medieval thought* (London, 1962), pp 266–7, 309.

Didacus Arthur, did contribute a series of commentaries on almost the entire *Summa* of the Angelic Doctor, and John Baptist Hacket another series on the *Prima secundae*.

A scholar who was undoubtedly influenced by Thomism, and yet in a very real sense was the last representative of the old Augustinian school, was Augustine Gibbon Burke. Though not one of the most original of Irish theologians he was one of the most influential, especially in the field of controversial theology. Born in 1613, he probably received his early classical education at Galway, and after becoming an Augustinian friar he studied at Salamanca and Valladolid. His labours on the Irish mission were interrupted by the puritan persecution. In 1656 he became a doctor of theology at Würzburg, published his thesis, and then was appointed professor at Erfurt. There in 1663 he had printed his remarkable *De Luthero-Calvinismo, schismatico quidem sed reconciliabili*, a work which displays how well acquainted he was with the works of Luther, Melanchthon, Gerhard, Beza, and Brenz, with Calvin's *Institutions*, the various Confessions of the reformers, the Geneva catechism, and the controversies of the reformers among themselves. Within six years it was followed by a two-volume work of scholastic theology, later incorporated at the beginning of a multi-volume work on speculative theology which became a recognised textbook. He was also the author of a volume of moral theology based on St Thomas, and of treatises on three of the sacraments, published posthumously in 1687 under the title *Probatica piscina*, a work that clearly shows his extensive knowledge of contemporary theology.[1]

Controversial theology may be said to begin in Ireland with John Travers, who was punished severely for writing a book in defence of the pope's supremacy in the reign of Henry VIII. John Ussher, the mayor of Dublin in 1574, revealed his attitude to the changing world around him in a tract called *De reformatione Hiberniae*. The papal archbishop of Armagh, Richard Creagh, entered the field with a work on controversies of the catholic faith. A more decisive intervention was made by Richard Stanihurst, who took issue with his nephew James Ussher, the future protestant primate, in a small book first published at Antwerp in 1584. The next on the controversial scene were two Jesuits, Christopher Holywood and Henry Fitzsimon. The most important of Holywood's writings was his volume in defence of the council of Trent and of Robert Bellarmine's views on the authority of the Vulgate. Fitzsimon, one of the ablest controversialists in Ireland from his return from Louvain in 1597 until 1604, when he was deported, wrote a defence of catholic doctrine and a refutation of theories propounded by the reformers, which appeared at Douai in 1614. Protestant theology too had its champions in Ireland. One such was Rudolph Hollingworth, whose work

[1] John Hennig, 'Augustine Gibbon de Burgo; a study in early Irish reaction to Luther' in *I.E.R.*, 5th series, lxix (1947), pp 135–51.

supporting the reformers' thesis of justification through faith alone was printed in Dublin in 1640.

There were Irishmen in many camps. John Sinnich of Cork, who was semestral rector of Louvain University in 1643 and several times dean of the faculty of theology, took part in the Jansenist controversy through books and pamphlets, often published under a pseudonym, and his name occurs several times in the Vatican index of forbidden books. His erudition is visible on every page of his best-known work, the *Sanctorum patrum trias* (1648). He also wrote, among other treatises, a kind of manual for catholic princes and the *Goliathismus profligatus*, in which he revealed himself as an apologist against protestantism.

The principal advocate of the Irish remonstrance of the years 1661–6, Peter Walsh, a stormy petrel but a very able controversialist, published only one of his many pamphlets and books in Latin, the *Causa Valesiana*. His friend and erudite supporter, Raymund (or Redmond) Caron, issued a theological defence of the remonstrance, which he dedicated to Charles II. Posterity has not been kind or always fair to Caron, who has been remembered principally for his association with Walsh. What has been frequently overlooked is his valuable contribution to theology, especially in the field of missiology. His four other Latin publications include a manual of apologetics, two works on missiology, and a volume of controversial theology.[1]

It was probably in 1673–4 that Peter Talbot, the catholic archbishop of Dublin, found leisure, during his forced retirement to France, to resume his literary pursuits. Four of his five works published between 1674 and 1678 were explicitly controversial and three of them were in Latin. Two of these Latin writings were an examination and refutation of the opinions of Thomas White, *alias* Blacklow, the friend of Hobbes. The third dealt with the primacy of the see of Dublin, the subject of a bitter dispute for two and a half years between Talbot and Archbishop Plunkett of Armagh. On the protestant side Roger Boyle, dean of Cork and afterwards bishop of Clogher, was the author of an inquiry into Christian belief, which appeared at Dublin in 1665, and of a theological *summa* (1681). In the period under review stoicism, which in ancient times had been presented as a model of life for the sage, was revived, but it attracted the attention of very few Irishmen. One such was Henry Dodwell the elder, scholar and fellow of Trinity College, Dublin. He compiled a Latin treatise, printed at Dublin in 1672, in which he discussed the use of philosophical principles, especially those of the stoics, in theology.

Francis Porter was another Irishman whose interest was engaged by controversial theology during this century. His bulky *Securis evangelica*, which appeared in 1674 and was twice reedited, is a fine piece of controversial reasoning. It follows the apologetic method of François Véron and borrows

[1] Millett, *Ir. Franciscans*, pp 498–502.

much from Bossuet's *Exposition de la doctrine de l'église catholique*. Five years later he brought out the *Palinodia*, using especially the reformers' principles to refute their teaching. Meanwhile Porter became gradually enmeshed in the current anti-Jansenist intrigues and campaigns. His *Syntagma*, a useful ready-reckoner of church definitions which in its choice of documents and its presentation leaves much to be desired, was partially forbidden by the holy office at the instigation of his enemies. He was also the author of a small laxist treatise on equivocation.[1]

One of the sharpest Irish controversialists of the period, and with an international reputation, was Francis Martin, an Augustinian canon regular. Born at Galway, and a graduate of Louvain, he was appointed professor of Greek in the Collège des Trois Langues in 1683. Three years later, he published a thesis defending the infallibility of the pope and attacking the claims of the Gallican church. There was an organised protest by fifty-three graduates in theology of the university to prevent his gaining the doctorate in 1688, but their efforts were defeated by the influence of the papal nuncio, Tanara. Shortly afterwards, he was appointed professor of theology in the diocesan seminary at Malines and published a thesis on Genesis, in which he attacked some of the views attributed to St Augustine, then the inspiration of so many theologians at Louvain and Paris. Martin courted still more disfavour by publishing a further thesis reflecting on the University of Louvain. For one six-months he was banned in 1690 from teaching in the university, but he revelled in controversy and in 1694 was appointed regius professor of holy scripture and one of the eight regents of the faculty of theology in the university. His chief controversial work was *Scutum fidei contra haereses hodiernas*, published at Louvain in 1714, and three more notable books appeared between 1719 and 1721. He died in October 1722. His main controversies concerned Jansenism, papal infallibility, and the Gallican church. For most of his life he was a vehement advocate of the ultramontane party in the catholic church, but in his later years he modified his views in advising the English catholics to accept the new regime in England. He also corresponded with Edward Synge, anglican archbishop of Tuam, even advocating in 1719 a union of catholics and protestants.[2]

In the vast field of theology there were many other areas into which Irishmen ventured. Sermons as a matter of course were the preserve of clerics, some of whom published them in Latin. Mention may be made of Nicholas Walsh, protestant bishop of Ossory, the Jesuit Barnabas Kearney, and Francis Burke, who produced a preacher's vade-mecum. Theobald Stapleton and James Miles were attracted to catechetics. The versatile Miles also wrote, among other things, a small volume on music.

[1] Lucien Ceyssens, 'François Porter, franciscain irlandais à Rome (1632–1702)' in *Miscellanea Melchor de Pobladura* (Rome, 1964), i, 387–419.

[2] See *Collect. Hib.*, iii. 113, 134; iv–v, *passim*; xii, 100; xiii, xv, *passim*.

Between 1550 and 1700 few Irishmen made any worthwhile contribution to philosophical thinking, though we find at least sixteen authors who published volumes on various philosophical topics. The distinguished MacCaghwell put his philosophical learning at the service of theology, as indeed did most catholic clerics. The most significant contribution was made by the Cork friar, John Punch, with his large and impressive course of Scotist philosophy, which went into five editions between 1642 and 1672. He receives the credit for breaking away from the classical commentaries and being the first to give a complete course in philosophy and theology, distinct from the traditional commentary on the *Sentences*.

The troubled Ireland of the seventeenth century, in the context of a Europe seething with vitality with which it was in regular contact, saw from time to time disputes and controversies, rows and bickerings, among its sons, some of whom indulged in literary polemics. *Arktomastix*, meaning 'one who castigates a bear', is apposite as a title for an essay against an author using the pseudonym *Ursulanus*. It was the title given in 1633 by Paul Harris, an English priest working in Dublin, to his small quarto volume attacking the famous *Examen iuridicum* and its author Francis O'Mahony. It is also a vicious literary onslaught on the Irish regular clergy and especially on Archbishop Fleming of Dublin.

A sorry literary controversy, turbulent and not a little vulgar, between the Franciscan Anthony Bruodin and Thomas Carew regaled educated readers of Latin in central Europe in the years 1669–72. The main bone of contention was a defamatory statement about Ireland in Carew's *Itinerarium* which gave great offence to Irishmen abroad, particularly the Old Irish, who assailed him with lampoons and satires. But the chief attack came from the ready pen of the Scotist theologian Bruodin, the grand-nephew of Tadhg mac Dáire Mac Bruaideadha, *ollamh* to the O'Briens and the poet who had opened the 'contention of the bards'.[1] The resulting literary battle, which produced four interesting books, has been investigated with satisfying thoroughness in recent times. These vituperative, forceful writings also contain some valuable fragments of information about Irish institutions in the seventeenth century. Moreover, some of Bruodin's works are among our few sources of knowledge of the fate of Irish catholic victims of religious persecution, but are not always reliable.[2]

Among the educated Irish in the sixteenth and seventeenth centuries, even the medical men and clerics, the imbibing of Latin learning frequently led to further cultivation of the humanities, and with some to the production of Latin poetry and prose. For the period 1550–1650 there are extant many tastefully written monographs, laudatory addresses, epigrams, letters, and verses not merely from some of the teachers, such as Patrick Cusack and

[1] See above, ch. XX, p. 539.

[2] Thomas Wall, 'Bards and Bruodins' in *Father Luke Wadding*, pp 438–62.

Peter White, but also from not a few of their pupils. Latin poets were not in short supply, but not all their poetry has survived. Worthy of mention are the poem of welcome published by Fr Martin Walsh when the prince of Wales, the future Charles I, arrived in Madrid in 1624 to court the Infanta, and the eulogistic verses composed in 1633 by the Dominican, Henry O'Ryan, to mark the arrival of the duc de Créqui in Rome as ambassador to Urban VIII. The publication of specially composed verses, sometimes in highly stylised form, on broadsheets and in booklets was an accepted usage in academic and court circles for important occasions. Irish clerical professors and students in various European centres of learning frequently contributed. Perhaps the best example is the skilfully wrought *Coronatae virtuti* composed by the Irish in Rome in 1629 on the occasion of the episcopal ordination of the Augustinian Patrick Comerford, of Waterford. In the ranks of the priest-exiles there were at least a dozen minor poets whose elegies, acrostic poems, and religious verses still survive.

On the home front the muse was not entirely asleep, even during the disturbed decade of the catholic confederacy. *Musarum lachrymae* (1630) carries short elegies, mostly in Latin and Greek, by twenty-four members of Trinity College, Dublin, on the occasion of the death of Catherine, wife of Richard Boyle, earl of Cork. Dermot O'Meara, M.D., wrote verses in honour of Ormond, and the *Commentarius Rinuccinianus* has the text of two poems by his son Edmund.

But Ireland's leading humanist and eminent Latin versifier and prose writer was overseas. He was Bonaventure Baron of Clonmel, who in excellent Latin traversed the entire range of Latin composition—not merely verses but panegyrics, eulogies, prolusions, portents, epistles, and quodlibets.[1] Readers of his many Latin volumes are arrested by the generous sprinkling of Greek in their pages and by their author's familiarity with the writings of the more prominent humanists.

Finally, brief mention must be made of three lexicographers—Richard Plunkett, who in 1662 completed an Irish–Latin dictionary,[2] the Jesuit, Balthazar Fitzhenry, who published a Hispano–Latin dictionary, and Elisha Coles, headmaster of Galway grammar school, who was the author of popular Latin–English and English–Latin lexicons.[3]

A chronological survey of this extensive output of Latin literature shows that, throughout the seventeenth century, there were few years in which no Latin volume by an Irishman was published. Often in one year as many as five or six works were printed. What inspired these Irish scholars to publish? A combination of leisure, training, intellectual gifts, and the desire to write stimulated such men as Ussher, Ware, Loftus, and William Stanihurst. This and an awareness of recent pastoral problems may explain why Peter

[1] See, for example, plate 14.
[2] Marsh's Library, Dublin, MS Z4. 2. 5.
[3] Stanford, 'Towards a history of classical influences', loc. cit., p. 52.

Talbot had the urge to publish when enjoying a forced exile in 1674. An academic milieu undoubtedly spurred on Peter Wadding, Augustine Gibbon Burke, John Sinnich, Baron and his confrères at St Isidore's College, and many others. The early classical training imparted in Waterford, Kilkenny, and Galway inspired the humanist effusions of Bonaventure Baron, Peter Wadding, and John Lynch. Luke Wadding and James Ussher belonged to that category of men who revel in pure scholarship, and they aimed at an academic public. Membership of a religious order also helped. Peter Lombard, who had no such inspiration or backing, was content to circulate his writings in manuscript. For a small number—men such as John Callaghan, Anthony Bruodin, and Peter Walsh—an innate desire to indulge in polemics seems to have been the main incentive. A burning wish to vindicate St Francis and his religious family was the motive behind Wadding's critical edition of the saint's writings. The great majority of his publications, which between compilations and editions averaged out at well over a volume a year, were about Franciscans or Franciscan subjects. For Wadding, Rothe, Colgan, and others there was the additional stimulus of patriotism, as we have already explained earlier.

It is an error to think that these Latin writers were paid by their publishers. Until the middle of the eighteenth century it was considered bad manners to write for money instead of for reputation.[1] The poverty, at times near-destitution, of many of the Irish writers was such that the historian cannot but wonder how some of their books were published at all. This is especially true of the Irish abroad, who were responsible for the greater part of this literary output in the seventeenth century. With few exceptions—for example, James Ussher in his more fortunate days—they could not afford personally to pay the expenses involved. Most of them depended on a form of patronage. Luke Wadding, for example, dedicated his edition of the writings of St Francis to two influential friends, the brothers Trejo, who were reasonably well-to-do and almost certainly gave a generous donation towards the printing costs. Theobald Stapleton dedicated his catechism to Prince Ferdinand, cardinal and governor of Belgium and Burgundy, from whom he probably received money gifts. It would seem from the dedications of his three philosophical works that John Baptist Hackett was indebted to the Pamfili family.

Royalty, nobility and gentry, Irish soldiers abroad, these and many others were approached for financial assistance. It might be thought that a writer who was a member of a religious order would have had few worries about the cost of printing his books. But this was not the case, except when a work was of major import to the religious institute itself. With the aid of some manuscript sources we can give rather detailed information on the production of four works.

[1] See S. H. Steinberg, *Five hundred years of printing* (2nd ed., Penguin Books, 1961), p. 220.

The first is Luke Wadding's *Annales Minorum*, on which he laboured for thirty years. In a very busy life, amid many non-literary and at times exhausting preoccupations, he snatched every free moment to continue and complete this large history in eight folio volumes, which are so bulky that in all subsequent editions each has been divided into two. This would not have been possible without help. The Franciscan order sponsored the work and paid the costs. The enthusiastic aid and cooperation went much further. In 1619 the minister general ordered that in each province suitable friars should transcribe and forward to Rome all relevant documents. Among Wadding's immediate collaborators were Bartolomeo Cimarelli, who worked in the archives and libraries of northern and central Italy, and Jacobus Polius who worked in those of Germany. From Ireland, through the assistance of Thomas Strange, he obtained copies of manuscripts from James Ussher and David Rothe. MS D 14 in the Franciscan library at Killiney contains the text of the contract, dated 4 July 1653, between Wadding and Jean Baptiste Devenet, the Lyons publisher, for the printing of volume VIII of the annals. Wadding bound himself to hand to a Signor Pizzenti, the publisher's agent at Rome, a clearly copied manuscript and at the same time to make an advance payment of 200 Roman scudi. He further contracted to take 200 copies of the volume, paying the remaining costs on receipt of them, to defray all customs expenses at Civitavecchia and Rome and the cost of carriage from Civitavecchia to Rome. Devenet was obliged to complete the printing within eighteen months, with the same paper, type, and format as in the sixth and seventh volume, to pay for carriage to Civitavecchia, to send forty extra copies as a gift to the author, and during the course of printing to send Wadding proofs for correction either by packet or by courier.[1]

Wadding's edition, in sixteen large folio volumes, of the works of John Duns Scotus was financed and produced in much the same manner. At one stage of the printing the expenses had come to 1,803 scudi and 65 baiochi. This work was a joint Franciscan undertaking. At Rome Wadding was assisted in the preparation of the text by Hickey, Punch, and other qualified friars, while others, including Cavalli and Tyrrell, attended to the proof-reading and the checking of the packaging. Paid copyists were also used for transcribing some of the manuscripts. A series of receipts, all dated April 1636, reveals the names of some of these: John of Paderborn, John of Münster, Titus of Maastricht, and Herman Rulle from Münster. Finally, in 1639, the edition was published. At this stage Wadding himself dealt with the minutiae of expenses, to be reimbursed later from headquarters. He paid, among other moneys, 38 scudi for costs at Marseilles, Genoa, and

[1] See also Mooney, 'The writings of Father Luke Wadding, O.F.M.' in *Franciscan Studies*, xviii (1958), pp 227–31.

Leghorn, and customs duties at Rome, and 120 scudi for carriage on seventeen packages and three large cases.[1]

It was then up to Wadding to keep an accurate account of the sale and distribution of the copies he received. This he and his assistant and successor, Francis Harold, attended to most carefully. Because they were not in the publishing business to make financial profits, they had an arrangement with intending purchasers from among the religious orders, especially their own confrères, whereby no money was actually forwarded to them but a specified number of masses was celebrated by the purchasers, who stipulated that the offerings should remain with Wadding. This acceptable method of payment eliminated the very real danger of money being stolen in the post. However, not all religious accepted this arrangement. Some, especially those living in or near Rome, preferred to send payment directly to Wadding or his agent.[2]

MS D 18 in the Franciscan library at Killiney contains a ledger with detailed accounts of receipts and expenses for the printing and sale of the large epitome of Wadding's annals compiled by Francis Harold, and also a large mass of papers dealing with the same transactions. To defray the initial cost of paper and printing Ercole Roncone gave 1,115 scudi and James Dooley, the future bishop of Limerick, 100 scudi. The syndic of St Isidore's College, Pietro Bellori, repaid this bill. From time to time Harold received various small money gifts from friends, including Virgilio Spada, Andrew White, Dooley, and Roncone. The work was printed with a type described as *silvio*,[3] on paper called *mezzana grande*. This paper was purchased directly by the printer, Nicola Angelo Tinassi, from a merchant named Giuseppe Gallione, and two agents and friends of the order, Francesco Nunez and Ercole Roncone, repaid him the sum of 448 scudi for twenty-eight packages of paper.

There is more interesting information available on the economic and other circumstances surrounding the printing of the critical edition of the works of Albert of Sartiano, which was prepared by Harold but seen through the press after his death by Patrick Duffy. The printer, Giovanni Battista Bussotti, signed a contract obliging him to print the text in *soprasilvio* type and the notes in *silvio*. The format was to be folio, the paper *mezzarella*. The text was to be printed in two columns, with marginal notes arranged as in the sample submitted, and the agreement was for 500 copies. There was to be no special charge for the small amount of Greek type needed. Bussotti further agreed to procure the paper at his own expense, to present the bill to Bellori, the college syndic, when the printing was completed, and to wait

[1] Expense sheets, receipts, and lists in Franciscan Library, Killiney, MS D 14.

[2] See Franciscan Library, Killiney, MS D 3, p. 35; MS D 5, pp 23, 60, 131, 171, 173; and MS D 17. These contain many receipts.

[3] For this type, invented at Amsterdam by G. Silvius, see D. B. Updike, *Printing types, their history, forms, and use* (3rd ed., Cambridge, Mass., 1962), ii, 28.

for one year after publication for final payment. So that printing could begin, Bellori paid him 100 scudi, and as it progressed he was to give a further sum, not exceeding 150 scudi. The services of a competent *scriptor*, Famiano Bravi, were engaged by the friars. Technically he was employed in the archives of the college and was paid by Bellori. The entire printing bill, including small accounts for special plates and for packaging, came to 254 scudi and 40 giulii.[1]

Between 1550 and 1700, as this survey has attempted to show, Latin learning and literature not only survived but indeed flourished among the Irish, particularly among the Irish abroad. However, this literary vitality was restricted, as before the reformation, to a fortunate, privileged minority, though the number of catholic clerics who had opportunities for university studies in the seventeenth century was far greater than in pre-reformation days. The bulk of the population in Ireland, as elsewhere in Europe, had small interest in the professions of the humanist educator. The clergy of Ireland, though by no means the sole focus of Latin literary culture in the days before Henry VIII broke with Rome, were undoubtedly its mainstay. But the religious, political, and social upheavals and the entrenched positions taken up by protagonists during the first hundred years or so after the reformation entailed the eventual transference, in the eighteenth century, of cultural leadership from the catholic clergy and their institutions to Trinity College and the established church. In the seventeenth century, however, classical culture was by no means a preserve of the establishment.

The extensive spiritual movement of the counter-reformation, gathering momentum during the sixteenth and into the seventeenth century, revitalised studies, and especially theology, in many catholic centres of western Europe. More remarkable even than the great influx of Irish pupils and teachers to continental universities and colleges was the flowering of scholarship among them at a high level of literary productivity, and also the large proportion of such men who were of a high intellectual calibre, as witnessed by their writings, mostly in Latin, and their contemporary reputation. The protestant Irish, on the other hand, produced relatively few serious scholars writing in Latin. James Ussher and James Ware are distinguished examples of these few.

Outside the traditional schools of Gaelic culture the pattern of classical education was more or less uniform; grammar—in the much expanded sense of that era—rhetoric, and the study of Latin authors were all part of the curriculum. Lily's grammar and Melanchthon's *Grammatica Latina* had the same repute among protestant schoolteachers as had later the *De institutione grammatica* of the Portuguese Jesuit, Emmanuel Alvarez, among catholics. Alvarez, who eventually enjoyed a high reputation throughout the schools of Germany, is better known in the English-speaking world as the

[1] The contract and accounts, all in Italian, are in Franciscan Library, Killiney, MS D 18.

author of a succinct treatise on Latin prosody, which was reprinted in Dublin in 1671. The student of those days, unlike his modern counterpart who reads in order to know, read in order to write and speak with freshness, forcefulness, and suitability of phrase.[1] Contemporary sources occasionally make reference to unusual displays of Latin oratory by proficient young scholars such as Bonaventure Baron and to the successful participation in scholastic disputations by Irish students in the higher grades.

[1] See *New Camb. mod. hist.*, ii, 422–6; Timothy Corcoran, *Studies in the history of classical teaching* (Dublin, 1911), pp 133–97.

CHAPTER XXIII

The Irish abroad, 1534–1691

JOHN J. SILKE

CERTAIN forces, propulsive at home and attractive abroad, created an unprecedented exodus of Irish after 1534, and the emigration thus begun continued unabated until the end of the Stuart monarchy, and after. The exiles fled from religious and political oppression and the havoc caused by wars, depressions, and economic dislocation; abroad they found asylum, spiritual and material aid in the war against the reformation, opportunities for education and livelihood, and, as the American colonies opened up, the prospect of a better life in the New World.

These motives for emigration to Europe and America and their consequences will be examined in the following pages. After an outline of the European setting of the Irish exodus, the various elements that left the country, their reasons for doing so, and their destinations abroad will be analysed. The occupations and organisation of the Irish abroad will then be examined, and the last section will deal with their religious and intellectual activities.

The period 1534–1691 was one of intense turmoil in Europe, a period of profound change in political, economic, and social (including religious) institutions. Within the Continent, the states of the Atlantic seaboard developed new patterns of political, economic, and artistic expression which gave them preeminence; without, these same states, however torn by rivalry, were fast establishing their political, economic, and intellectual hegemony over the globe.

The struggle between the 'new' renaissance monarchies and the upholders of feudal and civil liberties resulted by the sixteenth century in a great measure of success for the absolutist territorial states of northern and western Europe. The newly powerful monarchies of France, England, and Spain became models for a great many lesser principalities, in Germany and elsewhere. The era of the sovereign, if not yet the national, state had arrived. At the same time there developed a militant nationalist rivalry between the ascendant house of Habsburg, France, and the Ottoman empire. This threefold struggle, in which were adumbrated the principles later reduced to a science in the age of the balance of power, was fought out between the years 1519 and 1555. Lesser powers, such as England, anxious to maintain its political independence, and the papacy, fearful of imperial domination, were drawn into the conflict, which, so far as the Valois–Habsburg struggle was concerned, resulted in compromise (treaty of Câteau-Cambrésis, 1559). The Habsburg possessions were now partitioned: Spain, Naples, the Netherlands, and New Spain were given to the emperor Charles V's son, Philip II (1556–98), while Bohemia, Austria, and western Hungary passed to Charles's brother, Ferdinand, who was also recognised as emperor (1558–64). In northern Italy, a particular battleground, Spanish dominion over the duchy of Milan was recognised, and thus only the republics of Venice and Florence and the papal states maintained a quasi-independence. The French kingdom, the strongest political unit in Europe, remained intact.

But with political fires quenched, credal differences burst into flame. The religious wars had begun in Germany and had raged there until the peace of Augsburg (1555) brought a truce to central Europe that lasted into the seventeenth century. Elsewhere, between 1517 and 1560, protestant and catholic rulers had been able to damp the fires of the religious crisis. While some of them established national protestant churches, in England, Sweden, and Denmark, others, no less Erastian, remained catholic, but at the price of exacting the maximum political concessions from the papacy. France was the most notable example of a country that maintained its sovereign authority against a reforming papacy, but in Spain (despite its zeal for the counter-reformation), in Milan, Naples, and certain German principalities the position was broadly similar.

After 1560 the religious conflict moved into western Europe with totally unexpected force. The Calvinists, whom a recent writer has labelled the first modern radical political party, and militant catholics both organised effective opposition to the *status quo*.[1] The catholic reform movement, begun in the 1530s, and the counter-reformation (in origin rather different) had culminated in the council of Trent, which, in clarity of doctrinal statement, was the catholic counterpart of Calvin's *Institutes of the Christian religion* (1536). Now matching each other in grasp of purpose and in strictness of discipline, Geneva and Rome were locked in combat. By the 1570s Calvinists, influenced by both the teaching of Knox and the ambitions of noble and middle-class adherents, were teaching resistance to tyrants. The Jesuits, devoted to papal supremacy, taught with Bellarmine the right to depose heretical kings and a return to papal overlordship.[2] Against both, monarchists developed a doctrine of absolutism as of divine right, and this was upheld by James I, the French kings from Henry IV to Louis XIV, and others. But the Calvinists in Scotland overthrew Mary (1568) and in the Netherlands staged a successful rebellion against Philip II's efforts at

[1] See Michael Walzer, *The revolution of the saints* (Cambridge, Mass., 1965; London, 1966).

[2] Peter Lombard, archbishop of Armagh, was to make a significant attack upon this position; see below, pp 597–8, 629–30.

centralisation. Catherine de Medici failed to suppress the huguenots and the ultra-catholic crusaders. In Ireland Elizabeth was faced by James Fitzmaurice Fitzgerald, who sought to rally the forces of the counter-reformation and to restore catholicism in its integrity.[1]

At first the protestant thrust gained much ground. At the time of the closing of Trent (1564) much of Germany and all of Scandinavia had been won by the Lutherans. England and Ireland were experiencing an anglican revival, while Calvinism had gained Switzerland, Scotland, the northern provinces of the Low Countries, and the Palatinate, and threatened to gain France, Poland, Hungary, the southern Netherlands, and Bohemia. But in Europe this was to be the limit of the protestant advance. An extraordinary succession of saintly men and women, such as Peter Canisius in Bavaria, the Habsburg lands, and Poland, and Francis de Sales in Savoy, took in hand the tridentine programme of reform. Irish names are not wanting in this roll of missioners. Catholic rulers, while determined to maintain their control over the church, gave warm support to these apostolic spirits, both in the old world and in the new. De Sales, for example, had a remarkable influence on Henry IV. The Jesuits were foremost in evangelisation by word and by example.

In the latter part of the reign of Philip II, Spanish imperialism and the militant counter-reformation were both strongly on the offensive. Annexing Portugal and its empire (1580), Philip set out to crush the Netherlands revolt, conquer England, and end the French religious wars, making France a satellite of Spain. Henry IV saved France by his conversion to catholicism, made peace with Philip and the catholic nobility, and conciliated the huguenots. In the Netherlands Philip secured Belgium for Spain and for catholicism, but under William the Silent and his son Maurice of Nassau the seven Calvinist United Provinces of the north fought the Spaniards to a standstill (1609), as had the French in 1598 and the English in 1604. In Poland, as in France, protestantism had to be content with toleration, and in Hungary, by the end of the century, catholicism was gaining the upper hand. In Germany Lutheranism no longer threatened the existence of catholicism, but was itself threatened by Calvinism. In Ireland the oppressed majority was firmly catholic. In Austria, in the Tyrol, and in Bohemia protestantism was on the defensive, while in the New World Rome had more than made up for its losses in Europe. Thus threatened, the protestants were 'almost everywhere in a state of almost hysterical alarm' about the future,[2] and this alarm was a main cause of the terrible sequence of conflicts that is remembered as the thirty years' war.

That war (1618–48) brought little change in the religious map, though in

[1] Memorandum by Dr Nicholas Sanders, 1578 (*Archiv. Hib.*, vii (1918–21), pp 156–8).

[2] T. M. Parker, 'The papacy, catholic reform and Christian missions' in *New Camb. mod. hist.*, iii, 60.

France, Flanders, Austria, and Bohemia protestantism was suppressed. On the political front the thirty years' war was the occasion for renewing the dynastic struggle between the Habsburgs and France. The threat of Habsburg encirclement, with Spain, by its acquisition of the Palatinate, now bordering France all the way from Flanders to Milan, and with Ferdinand II (1619–37) strengthening the monarchy's position in the empire, alarmed the French. Gustavus Adolphus of Sweden saved German protestantism and earned Richelieu's subsidy by defeating the Habsburg effort to establish absolutism in the empire before the Swedes were overthrown at Nördlingen (1634). Now, with unfortunate Germany as theatre, France renewed again her old fight with Spain, and so successfully that by 1659 the Bourbon power outmatched that of the Habsburgs. Meanwhile Spain, despite the efforts of Olivares, Philip IV's intelligent chief minister (1621–43), to overcome Spanish particularism and the country's essential lack of resources, was beginning to go into slow decline. The Dutch renewed the war in 1621, and in 1648 Spain at last recognised the independence of the United Provinces. Internal revolts in Portugal, Catalonia, Naples, and Sicily and the burden of the thirty years' war forced Spain to recognise the independence of Portugal (1668) and to cede territory to France in the regions of the Rhine and the Pyrenees.

After Louis XIV personally took over as ruler (1661), he set out to establish French domination in Europe, and in further wars with the Habsburgs he continued the French advance towards the Rhine. His challenge to the liberties of Europe was taken up by Prince William III of Orange, *stadholder* of the Dutch republic, who sought by a system of alliances to stem the French tide. He organised the league of Augsburg, into which England, after many years of peace with France, was drawn after the revolution of 1688 had placed William on the English throne. This was the situation at the end of the period under review.

With the beginning of the Tudor conquest of Ireland, the European politico-religious ferment began also to work within the western island. As the impact of the viking invasions and the attractions of the Carolingian court had driven Sedulius Scottus and so many of his contemporaries abroad, so now the Tudor and Stuart attacks on the political and religious liberties of the Irish, together with the hospitality offered to them in Rome, Nantes, Corunna, and Brussels, brought about another exodus. For the next two and a half centuries Ireland continued to send her sons and daughters abroad, until the great convulsions of the French revolution and the Napoleonic wars made the Continent again inhospitable at a time when toleration for catholicism by the administration in Ireland was increasing. Meanwhile the Irish also shared in the European expansion that followed the age of discovery.

In the sixteenth and seventeenth centuries the Continent received wave upon wave of Irish catholic immigrants. Rome provided refuge and aid, material as well as spiritual, for the Irish. Spain gave them upon arrival all the rights of citizenship. In the Lowlands they had the protection of the Spanish governors and the support of the Irish regiments generally quartered there. The French monarchs also gave them asylum. At Rome and such centres of the northern renaissance as Louvain, Douai, and Paris, priests received the spiritual and intellectual training that fitted them to return home to fight the reformation. The mendicant orders found help among their continental brethren; while friars and priests became active promoters of a politico-religious war, travelling to and from Scotland, mainland Europe, and especially Rome. Refugees, both lay and clerical, lent their support to the pleas of those leaders at home who sought political and military aid from the catholic powers. Before many years had passed, Irishmen were repaying, as professors, scholars, missioners, and even reformers of the religious life, their country's debt to Europe.

In the seventeenth century emigration across the Atlantic began, the majority of the emigrants being catholics, the rest mainly presbyterians. The catholics were chiefly indentured servants and went to both mainland America and the West Indies, even before the commonwealth period. Bridenbaugh has suggested that already in the 1630s emigration was in progress from Ireland no less than from England; young women and men, driven by hardships at home and hope of a better life in America, went off willingly, if not wisely.[1] Presbyterians, denied liberty of conscience by the Stuarts, found new opportunities in Virginia and Massachusetts. But before the eighteenth century, presbyterians who emigrated were few by comparison with catholics.

First among the groups of emigrants were those who went into exile on grounds of conscience. Bishops and priests who remained faithful to the old religion fled abroad to alert Rome to the perils facing catholicism in Ireland, to forge weapons (such as an educated clergy) for the struggle with the protestants, or simply to seek shelter. In Elizabeth's reign there was always a war upon the clergy, against whom government agents regularly resorted to prerogative acts and to martial law, and who might, if caught, face a capital charge of treason or at least sentence of expulsion. Under James I repeated royal proclamations ordered priests to leave Ireland; and in the commonwealth period a determined effort to remove the catholic clergy reached its peak in 1653 when, in accordance with an order to go abroad on penalty of death, over a thousand bishops, priests, and nuns fled to the Continent or were shipped abroad by the government. Stepping up its

[1] Carl Bridenbaugh, *Vexed and troubled Englishmen, 1590–1624* (New York, 1968), p. 411; Carl and Roberta Bridenbaugh, *No peace beyond the line: the English in the Caribbean, 1624–40* (New York, 1972), p. 14.

campaign, between 1655 and 1657 the government dispatched priests, friars, and schoolteachers to the distant Barbados. Priests, however, were generally too old to be suitable material for indentured service. In desperation the government sought to confine the clergy to the Aran Islands and Inishbofin. Then in the last year of the commonwealth there was a return to the policy of allowing them to go to the Continent.

From early in Elizabeth's reign the papacy was beginning to reconcile itself to the loss of temporalities, and was coming to rely upon a succession of bishops whose contacts with Rome were personal and who were reinforced by a parish clergy trained abroad and dedicated to the cause of the counter-reformation. William Walsh, appointed bishop of Meath in 1554, had lived at Rome some years previously, in Cardinal Pole's entourage. Early in the 1560s, David Wolfe, S.J., the apostolic commissary, dispatched a number of clerics to Rome, to be confirmed in personal loyalty to the holy see and to be made bishops: Thomas O'Herlihy (Ross), Donald MacCongail (Raphoe), Andrew O'Crean, O.P. (Elphin), Eugene O'Hart, O.P. (Achonry), Donat O'Taig (Armagh, 1560), and Richard Creagh (Armagh, 1564). O'Herlihy, MacCongail, and O'Hart went on from Rome in 1562 to attend the closing sessions of the council of Trent, and thus gained first-hand knowledge of the papal programme of reform. Redmund O'Gallagher, bishop of Derry, is mentioned in 1571 as lately come from Rome well armed with faculties—*qui nuper venit ex Roma cum multis mandatis.*[1] Patrick O'Hely, O.F.M., finding himself in Rome in 1576, was appointed by Gregory XIII to Mayo, and Dermot O'Hurley five years later was similarly provided to Cashel. By now a significant proportion of the clergy received training abroad, and if already in the 1570s the state church was fighting a losing battle with the forces of reinvigorated catholicism these bishops and priests were mainly the cause.

So the religious links between Ireland and the Continent, especially Rome, were strengthened. Early in the seventeenth century the Irish church was sufficiently reconstituted under the Roman congregation *de propaganda fide* (established in 1622), with an episcopate, clergy, and, as auxiliary force, religious, to take in hand the work of enforcing the tridentine legislation at parochial level. Whatever the strains within this structure, and they were many, it was held together by the cement of loyalty to Rome.

Another class of refugees was composed of those driven abroad for political and economic reasons. The earliest fairly considerable group of this class went as a result of the failure of the Munster Geraldine revolt. Many went as soldiers in Leicester's service to Flanders, while some members of the Geraldine gentry went to reside in Lisbon, under the protection of Archduke Albert, then governor of Portugal. The repressive policy of the government, after the gunpowder plot, drove hundreds of refugees to France, to Brittany,

[1] 'A note of the confederates in Ireland, 1571' in P.R.O., S.P. 63, f. 67^v.

up the Seine to Rouen and Paris, where they swelled the ranks of *les bélîtres*, the ragamuffin Irish colony already settled on the Ile de la Cité, up the Loire to Nantes and Angers, or to Bordeaux, to increase the colony there. Such numbers, without means of support and living in squalor that brought threat of plague, presented problems to the authorities. Rouen ordered the Irish away; the Bretons dispersed the 'invaders' throughout western France; and the French government in 1606 returned two boatloads of the settlers in Paris to Ireland. After Kinsale the Irish colony in Galicia was strongly augmented, mostly by those Old Irish of Munster who had thrown in their lot with the combined Hispano-Irish forces, the O'Sullivans, the MacCarthys, and the O'Driscolls.

Ireland was now losing her old aristocracy, Gaelic and Anglo-Irish. Among the 'noble shipload' that sailed down Lough Swilly on an autumn day in 1607 were the leading representatives of the great Ulster families. The motives underlying Hugh O'Neill's flight[1] remain obscure, and probably there was something of a snap decision about it. But his independence and perhaps even his life were being threatened, others had gone and were leaving and his son's regiment in the Low Countries offered a last possible hope of renewing the challenge in arms to the crown. His going marked the end of an era. Within a generation or two the direct issue of Hugh O'Neill, Rory O'Donnell, and Daniel O'Sullivan Beare came to an end on foreign soil. Other lines of these families, however, and of others, Desmond, Maguire, and O'Doherty, continued, generation after generation, to win honour in their adopted countries, in church, court, and camp.

Lord Deputy Mountjoy, who knew Ireland well, said that three out of four Irishmen did not return from foreign service. It therefore became government's general policy between Mountjoy's day and the 1641 rebellion to encourage the departure of able-bodied men from the country. Recruiting in Ireland by the armies of the protestant powers, Denmark and Sweden, was actively encouraged. Chichester claimed that during his tenure of office (1605–16) he had been instrumental in sending 6,000 swordmen to serve in the armies of Sweden. It would appear that many of them never arrived—about a thousand men, led by Oghy Óg O'Hanlon (Tyrone's nephew) and Art Óg O'Neill, during transit to Sweden in 1609 were driven by storms into English harbours, whereupon a number escaped—and some who did arrive went over to the Poles or made their way to the Spanish and imperial armies.[2] Recruiting by the catholic powers was generally tolerated, particularly at times of peace between England and these countries.

Irish exiles tended, or at times were obliged, to form colonies in particular places. They naturally settled down in European ports with Irish trading

[1] See above, ch. VII, p. 195.

[2] E. Burke, 'Irish levies for the army of Sweden, 1609–10' in *Ir. Monthly*, xlvi (1918), pp 396–404; Hill, *Plantation*, pp 189, 205.

links, such as Rouen, St Malo, 'or in other places where Irish merchants are established in trade'.[1] To such places, for example, as Lisbon, Nantes, Bordeaux, and the ports of the Netherlands and even of the West Indies the members of the old Galway families, Blake, Martin, Joyce, French, and the rest of the 'fourteen tribes' betook themselves after their ruthless expulsion from Galway city in the 1650s. The same names are to be found figuring prominently in the university records at Louvain and elsewhere, for university towns also attracted large numbers of Irish exiles.[2] Rome of course had its colony. In the Iberian peninsula Madrid, Compostela—where two Irish bishops, Thomas Strong of Ossory (1602) and Thomas Walsh of Cashel (1654), ended their days—and Lisbon were all notable centres, and groups were to be found, among other places, at Valladolid, Salamanca, Seville, and Oporto. In Flanders, Brussels, the headquarters of the Irish regiment, had the chief Irish colony; while in France there were settlements at Paris, Nantes, Rheims, and Bordeaux, to name the chief towns.

A distinct group among the emigrants were those who sought help from foreign catholic rulers in the struggle against the English crown. They based their appeals upon two grounds, the political advantages to be gained by these rulers from coming to the aid of the hard-pressed Irish nobility, and (especially as the century wore on) the danger that Ireland would become protestant. On this latter ground they turned ever more to the holy see, imploring it to use its good offices with catholic rulers. Irish leaders, like their English and Scottish co-religionists, thus appealed to both the piety and the self-interest of the powers. They sought to exploit to their own advantage the international situation in which Henry VIII, and after him Elizabeth, tried to maintain a balance between warring continental powers. It was generally understood that a foreign army of 6,000 men would be sufficient, when combined with the native forces, to drive out the English. A lesser force would be better than nothing, as it would serve to keep the war alive in Ireland. It was also generally understood that the necessary price for effective help would be the bestowal of the lordship of Ireland upon a foreign prince. There existed therefore throughout the sixteenth century a recurrent danger to England of an attack through her back-door, from either the French or the Habsburgs. Continually throughout Hugh O'Neill's war the Irish urged the Spanish to take a leaf out of Elizabeth's book and cause a diversion in Ireland which would be as advantageous to Spain as was Elizabeth's support of the Dutch to England. A century later Louis XIV would seek to distract the attention of the English government from the Low Countries by sending troops to Ireland in 1690.

[1] *Ovvero in altro luogo dove sogliono capitar mercanti Ibernesi*: Nuncio Bentivoglio to cardinal secretary of state, Brussels, 28 Sept. 1613 (*Archiv. Hib.*, iv (1915), p. 283).

[2] J. P. Spelman, 'The tribes at Louvain: Francis Martin, S.T.D.' in *I.E.R.*, series 3, vii (1886), pp 1100–06.

And so, between the time (1523) when James Fitzgerald, the tenth earl of Desmond, sent Anthony Daly as his emissary to the king of France, and the death of Shane O'Neill (1567), a succession of leaders dispatched emissaries to the courts of the king of France, the emperor, and the king of Scotland. At first, in the cases of Desmond and Silken Thomas, dynastic rather than national, their aims broadened as time went on. The Geraldine League could claim to be a country-wide association of nobility. But it is doubtful if the league which one Alexander Lynch claimed to represent before Quadra, Spanish ambassador in London, in 1559, existed outside the imagination of James Fitzmaurice Fitzgerald; and Shane O'Neill's designs, in spite of certain claims he made, were provincial rather than national. From another viewpoint, it was significant that, from the time (1534) that Lord Offaly dispatched the archdeacon of Kells to Pope Paul III to seek absolution from excommunication, the Irish began regularly to turn to the holy see for aid and comfort. The Geraldine League besought the holy father to intercede with the emperor Charles, and both Alexander Lynch and Shane O'Neill strongly maintained that among their chiefest aims was the restoration of catholicism. Given the appeal to religion, and given of course the standard practice, it is no surprise to find that Irish emissaries to European courts were for the most part clerics. Charles Reynolds, archdeacon of Kells, County Meath, was the first of a long line of these clerical diplomats.

With the appearance of James Fitzmaurice Fitzgerald in France in 1575, the call for a religious war in Ireland grew louder. The time, during the pontificate of Gregory XIII (1572–85), was becoming more favourable. Until now, the popes, in the interest of the counter-reformation, had sought to maintain the precarious peace between the Habsburgs and France. The pope was concerned about the fate of catholics in England, Ireland, and Scotland; Philip II was worried about the international complications presented by the 'British question'; Catherine de Medici and the Guise leaders, the duke and the cardinal of Lorraine, had a special interest in the fate of Scotland and of its queen, Mary.

In 1576 the leading English and Irish exiles in Rome and Spain began to take concerted action. The English included Dr William Allen (then president of the English college, Rheims), Sir Francis Englefield, and Robert Persons, S.J., while Scotland was represented by Archbishop Beaton of Glasgow, ambassador to Mary, queen of Scots. The Irish, supporting first Fitzmaurice, then after Fitzmaurice's death James Eustace, Viscount Baltinglass, included in their number some half-dozen bishops, as well as other ecclesiastics.

The Friars Minor were especially active in seeking to arouse the sympathy of catholic Europe in Ireland's cause. Amongst those who worked most vigorously abroad in the interests of James Fitzmaurice Fitzgerald in the late seventies were three Observant bishops, Patrick O'Hely of Mayo, Cornelius O'Mulryan (or Ryan) of Killaloe, and Donat Óg O'Gallagher of Killala (1570–80) and later of Down and Connor (1580–1). Together with Archbishop Fitzgibbon of Cashel, Bishops Thomas O'Herlihy of Ross, Maurice O'Brien of Emly, Edmund Tanner of Cork,[1] and William Walsh of Meath, who died at Alcalá in 1577, they pleaded Fitzmaurice's cause at the catholic courts. These bishops could fairly claim to be the representative voice of the Irish catholic church, or at least of a very considerable part of it. Their acquaintance with the militant spirit of the counter-reformation, which was so powerful at this time on the Continent, especially in Spain, made them all the more ready to seek a military solution for Ireland's troubles. It is noteworthy that Wolfe, papal commissary to Ireland for about fifteen years prior to his escape to Spain in 1572 or 1573, worked hand in glove with Fitzmaurice and O'Hely to concert a plan of action acceptable to Spain and to the pope. The activities of these men on behalf of Fitzmaurice are worthy of more detailed study than they have yet received, and the survivors among them, together with some other clerics, kept counter-reformation militancy alive after the failure of the Desmond rebellion.

Thus Ryan, who died in Lisbon in 1616, was a living link between the Desmond wars and the nine years war.[2] Edmund MacGauran, archbishop of Armagh (1587–93), was also busy on the Continent from 1585 until 1592 seeking support for an Irish uprising, especially from the king of Spain and the Irish captains in Flanders. He got sufficient encouragement to join with Hugh O'Donnell and Archbishop James O'Hely of Tuam (1591–5) in forming a confederacy which was led by the bishops and chiefs of the north-west. Archbishop O'Hely went to Spain in 1593, but Philip II, with his troops engaged in France and in the Netherlands, made little response to his appeals.

When in 1595 Tyrone took over the leadership of the war in the north, he set about creating a 'diplomatic service' in Europe to bring what pressure he could to bear upon Spain and upon Clement VIII. Tyrone had as permanent agents in Spain Dean Edmund MacDonnell of Armagh and Matthew de Oviedo, a Spanish Franciscan. About 1598 Fr Peter Lombard of Waterford, professor at Louvain, was sent by his university to Rome to act as its agent; very soon he became O'Neill's representative as well. In spite of his Old English background, he threw himself enthusiastically into the cause, and his diplomacy was seen to effect when he gained the support of both Robert Persons, of the 'Spanish' party among the exiles, and the Spanish ambas-

[1] W. M. Brady, *Episcopal succession* (3 vols, Rome, 1876), ii, 87, says that in May 1575 'he set out from Rome on his return to Ireland'. But he was in Madrid in November (*Archiv. Hib.*, vii (1921), 80).

[2] It is perhaps worthy of note that Archbishop Dermot O'Hurley of Cashel, who received the pallium in Rome on 27 Nov. 1581 and returned to Ireland in September 1583, was not apparently involved in any of the plots.

sador, the duke of Sessa. Persons was convinced that there was a party of 'politiques' in England who would support the succession of Philip's daughter, Isabel, to the English throne after Elizabeth, and he and Sessa urged Philip to invade Ireland now, in order to rally those wavering politiques and to have a main base for the attack upon England when Elizabeth died.

But, against Lombard, other representatives of the Old English in Rome maintained that there were no just grounds for rebellion against the queen, who (they said) did not disturb the consciences of catholics. Lombard, therefore, in a document of considerable power, *De regno Hiberniae sanctorum insula commentarius* (1600),[1] sought to show Clement VIII that O'Neill was wholly dedicated to the cause of the church. His diplomacy had some results: O'Neill's appointment as captain general of the catholic army in Ireland and Oviedo's appointment to the archbishopric of Dublin, both in 1599, and Lombard's own appointment to Armagh, in 1601. But Clement VIII, and this was vital, refused to judge between the two catholic parties in Ireland and would not make it a matter of conscience for catholics to support Tyrone.

Archbishop MacGauran had made the Irish regiment in Flanders a key-point in his planning. After the battle of the Yellow Ford, Tyrone pressed Archduke Albert, now governor of the Netherlands, to send over the Irish veterans, but Albert had his hands full with the Dutch and ignored the Irish leader's requests. Some few officers came home to give a leaven of professionalism to the forces that O'Neill was trying to fashion into a modern army. But that was all. At the battle of the Dunes (2 July 1600) the Irish regiment, fighting in Albert's rearguard, suffered severe losses, in company with the rest of the army. It will be clear from all this why Águila's expedition in 1601 to Ireland had no Irish strength in it.

After 1607 the O'Neill family on the Continent remained the centre of Old Irish hopes for renewing the war and restoring the old order. Not that the powers—with Spain (from 1604) as well as France at peace with England—gave any encouragement to these hopes. In 1611 Spain and England began negotiations for a marriage alliance. A temporary rupture in the negotiations (1612–13) made Hugh O'Neill, for the last time, think that he might yet go home at the head of an army, in which his son's regiment would play a foremost part. But in 1613 the negotiations were reopened, and while they remained in train for the next ten years neither Rome nor Madrid entertained any idea of an attack on Ireland.

Lombard had taken no part in the invasion projects of 1612. Kinsale, the peace of London, the refusal of the powers and of the papacy to restore O'Neill, the Spanish marriage projects, and the plantation in Ulster, all combined to teach him that the only policy now was to make the best accommodation possible with James I. Thus he sought to bargain for some

[1] Published Louvain, 1632; ed. P. F. Moran, Dublin, 1868.

measure of toleration in return for a guarantee of catholic loyalty. If the government, he felt, could be convinced of the political inoffensiveness of the catholics, more bishops might be appointed who would at last implement the decrees of Trent.

The grant of a dispensation for the Spanish match was something that met with Lombard's approval. The catholic church in granting the dispensation demanded a complete cessation of persecution. The negotiations of course fell through in the end, but when Charles married a French princess the papacy, in granting a dispensation, gained freedom for catholics secretly to practise their religion. John O'Neill, the new titular earl of Tyrone, sought more than once to get Philip IV to influence James I to restore him to his ancestral estates, but Philip was not in a position to press James to do this, even before the Anglo-Spanish negotiations failed.

The O'Neill family were again central to the plans for the rising of 1641. With the death of John, Hugh's last surviving son, leadership devolved upon Owen Roe, Hugh's nephew. The planners of the rising placed great hopes in the Irish soldiers in Flanders, but in the end O'Neill and Thomas Preston were each able to bring over only a token force, O'Neill from Flanders, and Preston from France. Owen Roe, aware that the power of France was in the ascendant and that of Spain in decline, sought help from Richelieu, but with very limited results. Yet during the period of the confederation, Irish diplomatic activity abroad was intense. But those charged with missions were very much at loggerheads with one another. The general assembly in 1642 appointed agents to foreign courts, Wadding to the holy see, Matthew O'Hartegan, S.J., to the French court and to Henrietta Maria, and others. The various crises in the history of the confederation were reflected in the rival missions sent by contending parties to Rome and Paris. So at Paris Geoffrey Baron (who succeeded O'Hartegan in 1645) and Dr Edward Tyrrell waged a diplomatic campaign against the royalist agents, Castlehaven, Richard Butler, and Thomas Talbot, O.F.M.; while in 1646 the congregation of the clergy found it necessary to send Dionisio Massari, Rinuccini's auditor, to Rome, to counteract the diplomacy of the royalist Digby.

The treaty with Inchiquin sent more rival agents abroad. Muskerry went to join Geoffrey Baron in acting for the now dominant Leinster party in the assembly, which sought the return of Ormond, while Lord Antrim brought Rinuccini's case to Paris and Nicholas French, bishop of Ferns, and Nicholas Plunkett—who were later joined by Joseph Arcamoni, the Theatine, and Richard O'Ferrall, O.F.M.Cap.—brought it to Rome. Later the Carmelite John Rowe and John Callaghan sought a condemnation of Rinuccini's censures from the Sorbonne faculty of theology. Rinuccini's case was made by John Punch, O.F.M., and by John O'Molony and Richard Nugent; and the faculty refused to condemn.

These various missions produced mixed results. Rome sent Scarampi and later Rinuccini, appointed the bishops of Rinuccini's choice, and in 1648 sent, by Massari, 50,000 crowns from the pope and another 10,000 collected by Wadding. But both Urban VIII and Innocent X, who were anxious about the welfare of the English catholics, tried to avoid an open break with the anti-Rinuccini forces in the confederation, and each of the opposing sides was able to interpret Rome's position in 1648 as favourable to itself. Richelieu's renewal of the Franco-Habsburg rivalry, domestic turmoil in France, the presence of Henrietta Maria and her advisers in Paris, and later Mazarin's alliance with Cromwell, all combined to operate against any substantial French—or Spanish—aid to Ireland in the period of the confederate wars and of the commonwealth.

But with France's star rising, Irish hopes of French aid were rising too. In 1666 Louis XIV, in accordance with his treaty of 1662 with the Dutch, declared war on England. A group of Irish exiles in France sought to take advantage of this situation by persuading Louis to invade Ireland. The influential Bishop John O'Molony II, of Killaloe, a good friend of Colbert, was the most active member of this group, which had been in communication with the king since 1662. Louis's enmity towards England was, however, half-hearted at best. At the death of Philip IV (1665) he had begun to plan an invasion of the Spanish Netherlands. To further this scheme, he sought to gain English neutrality, while, as part insurance, part prod to Charles, giving some encouragement to Irish hopes. When Colonel Byrne, who went to Ireland in 1667 to arouse the country, was captured and disclosed the plot, Louis put the blame on his cousin Admiral de Beaufort for supporting the Irish invasion scheme.[1] He now made the first of his secret agreements with Charles, and until 1688 there was no real danger of a French invasion of Ireland, in spite of the government's obsession with fears of such an invasion. But when in 1688 Louis took into his pay three foot regiments in England, including one composed of Irish catholics under Colonel Roger MacElligott, and William of Orange was invited over to England, it was clear that a new page was to be written in the relations between England, Ireland, and France.

Irishmen were involved in Raleigh's short-lived colonies in Virginia in the 1580s, and another colony of Irish adventurers, established at the mouth of the Amazon by Sir Thomas Roe in 1612, had a brief existence until its final suppression by the Portuguese in 1629. Now, however, the demand for white labour in the plantations of North America and the West Indies really began to arouse interest in Ireland, as elsewhere. This demand for farmers, labourers, and artisans grew ever more insatiable. Thousands of English,

[1] The matter of the Franco-Irish plot is discussed, not altogether satisfactorily, in James Hogan, 'John O'Molony (II), 1617–1702' in *Studies*, ix (1920), pp 213–31, 421–37.

Welsh, and Irish and hundreds of Scots, Dutch, and French were propelled abroad by such forces as wars, depressions, religious oppression, and the desire of authorities to rid themselves of vagrants and military opponents, at the same time as they were attracted by success stories from the colonies and promotion literature spread by agents of the emigration trade. Both peasants and townsmen were lured overseas. A minority were 'gentlemen emigrants' who paid their own passage and became planters, but the vast majority, men, women, and children, indentured themselves to enterprising traders, who then transported them to the Chesapeake, to the Virginia rivers, or to the Caribbean and sold them into service to the planters. The period of service ran from three to seven years, after which the servant, if he survived, gained his freedom or redemption, and might become a paid labourer or even a small planter himself. Many indeed did not survive. White servants were not well endowed to endure the rigours of tropical field-labour, and masters were notoriously more careful of their slaves than of their servants.[1]

Bristol merchants were foremost in the business of transporting indentured servants. The Bristol men had brought hundreds of Irish peasants to England in the early years of the seventeenth century, and Bristol had established commercial relations with Londonderry and Coleraine. Bristol and other traders, English, Irish, and Flemish, now called at Irish ports to fill out their human cargoes.

These cargoes were mostly made up of catholics. In 1636 the ship *Eagle wing*, carrying 140 Ulster presbyterians fleeing from Wentworth's rule, was forced by storms to return when already half-way across the Atlantic, and it was not until the restoration that presbyterian emigration began in earnest. In the 1680s, with ministers in the lead, it became a steady trickle, principally from the Lagan and Foyle valleys and chiefly to the Chesapeake Bay area. Prior to 1689 the quakers from Ireland who settled in the New World—Robert Turner, of Dublin, and Nicholas Newlin, of Mountmellick, for example—were either originally English or of English descent. One of their settlements became known as the Irish Tenth (Camden county, West Jersey).

Catholics then made up the main bulk of the early Irish emigrants. The Massachusetts Bay Company, which controlled emigration to New England from 1629, remained selective in its admittance policy, strongly favouring puritans. But elsewhere the case was different. By the head-right system, established in Virginia in 1625, in Maryland by Lord Baltimore in the 1630s, and in the Carolinas in the 1680s, planters who settled servants received fifty acres of tobacco land. This, together with the 'tobacco boom', favoured rapid colonisation, and England alone could not supply the demand, so that there was opportunity for Irish catholics. In the 1620s a traffic in Irish peasants, vagrants, and convicts to Virginia was becoming regular; in

[1] Richard Ligon, *A true and exact history of the island of Barbados* (1657; 2nd ed., 1673), p. 44.

1622, for instance, Daniel Gookin, then of Carrigaline, brought about forty settlers to Newport News. St John proposed to transport a number of dispossessed Waterford landlords to Virginia in 1620. It is possible that therc were soms Irish catholics in the region of the Chesapeake (Maryland) in the time of the second Lord Baltimore in the 1630s. Thereafter Maryland, with its policy of toleration, attracted bond servants away from Virginia. But even the Massachusetts Bay Company recruited some Irish servants.

Between 1624 and the middle of the century a great attempt was made to turn the Leeward Islands[1] and Barbados into white English-speaking colonies, with a diversified rural economy. Here the growth of the catholic Irish population was remarkable. Two factors in particular facilitated emigration of Irish to the Caribbean: the establishing of an export trade in grain and pork from Ireland to the West Indies; and the promise of £10, payable on redemption to the servant who had worked out his indentures. There is ground for supposing that merchants from Kinsale, Cork, and Youghal took a lead in developing the Irish connection with the Leeward Islands. In any case, at Kinsale in the 1630s the 'Blewe Anker' tavern became a centre to which people from Youghal to Bandon repaired on hearing the recruiting drum beaten, to drink their glass of beer and to settle for a four years' indenture. In 1636, for example, Matthew Cradock, puritan governor of the Bay Company, took off fifty-six willing men and women, to be landed and sold in Barbados. These young people preferred the West Indies to Virginia, and the twenty women among them were 'very lustye and strong boddied', and 'reddear to go then men'.[2]

With the commonwealth, emigration took a new turn. In 1651 the council of state decided to deport the Scots taken prisoner at Worcester to America, and the principle of transporting unwelcome elements was soon extended to other classes than soldiers. There was sure to be room somewhere in the colonies for them all. From Ireland between 1652 and 1656, and in compliance with a series of orders issued in 1652 and 1653 to the Irish commissioners, many soldiers, their wives and children, together with widows and orphans of those who had fallen in the war, were shipped away.[3] These unfortunates had no indentures, but had to serve at the discretion of their masters. They were given little welcome in New England, and the majority ended up in Virginia, Barbados, and the Leeward Islands.

In 1657 the council of state repealed the instructions of 1652–3, but even after 1657 there were many instances of people regarded as rebels receiving a pardon and being shipped into service in the Caribbean. Perhaps the experience of these years turned the people against emigration for some

[1] Nevis, Antigua, Montserrat, St Christopher (today St Kitts).

[2] A. E. Smith, *Colonists in bondage: white servitude and convict labor in America, 1607–1776* (Chapel Hill, N.C., 1947), p. 65, quoted in Bridenbaugh, *Vexed and troubled Englishmen*, p. 413.

[3] The numbers involved are considered on pp 602–03; see also P. J. Corish, above, ch. XIV.

time; at any rate the agents of the plantation-owners of Carolina (a place admittedly unattractive for other reasons) found in 1667 that the Irish were 'loth to leave the smoke of their cabins'.[1]

In Virginia, Maryland, and even the Carolinas there was a growing number of Irish catholics by the end of the century, sufficient to make the legislatures enact laws against imporing more. In 1674 Cecilius Calvert, second Lord Baltimore, designated part of Cecil county as 'the county of New Ireland'. In the middle colonies Irish redemptioners were also in request, and in 1688 Thomas Dongan of Kildare, governor of New York province, settled a number of his countrymen on Long Island and along the Hudson River, in Dutchess and Columbia counties. In New England there remained but cold welcome for the Irish. In 1680 the governor of Massachusetts reported to the board of trade that there were about fifty or sixty Irish servants in his jurisdiction, 'brought hither at severall times'.[2] But while opportunity was less and intolerance greater in New England, there can be no doubt that the Irish, catholic as well as protestant, contributed towards the foundation of 'old New England stock', even before the commonwealth.

While the majority of Irish began life in America as redemptioners, a number of them were or became labourers, artisans, farmers or even merchants and businessmen. Already in the seventeenth century there were MacCarthys, Fennings, Butlers, and O'Kellys prominent in New England. Darby Field, who discovered the White Mountains in New Hampshire in 1642, was an extensive landowner. Memorable for the pathos of her fate was a Mrs Glover, an Irish-speaking widow, who was executed as a witch in 1688. James Moore, son of Rory O'More, who came out to Charleston in 1655, later became governor of South Carolina, as did his son, also James, after him. Charles O'Carroll, from Tipperary, attorney general of Maryland in 1688, was grandfather of Charles Carroll of Carrollton.

On the Leeward Islands and Barbados the growth of the catholic Irish labour force after 1624 was remarkable, and there were also some Irish catholic planters. Nevis was first settled with Irish, and Montserrat was an 'Irish' island, its first governor being Anthony Briskett from County Wexford. Although Briskett was probably protestant, by 1634 there was in Montserrat 'a noble plantation of Irish catholiques, whom the Virginians would not suffer to live with them because of their religion'.[3] Until 1666 the English and French divided St Christopher between them, but now with the outbreak of war between the two countries, the French gained control of all St Christopher, winning the support of the Irish. The victors

[1] *Cal. S.P. colonial, 1669–74*, p. 40.

[2] Mass. Hist. Soc. Gay Transcripts, quoted in R. H. Lord, J. E. Sexton, and E. T. Harrington, *History of the archdiocese of Boston, 1604–1943* (3 vols; New York, 1944), i, 32.

[3] Narration of Andrew White, S.J., 1634, quoted in T. Hughes, *The history of the Society of Jesus in North America: colonial and federal*, text I: *From the first colonization till 1645* (Cleveland, Ohio, 1907), p. 279.

then took in the French inhabitants from St Martin's and St Bartholomew, replacing those on St Bartholomew with the Irish from St Christopher. France held St Christopher for nearly two years, until the signing of the peace of Breda.

France also took Antigua and Montserrat in 1667, but England soon won back both islands. After the armistice Lieutenant-colonel Sir William Stapleton, an Irish officer in the English service, was appointed deputy-governor of Montserrat, which was now 'very well resettled, most of the inhabitants Irish'.[1] He became governor of the Leeward Islands, and under his efficient administration (1672–85) both the separate government and the prosperity of the islands were established firmly and lastingly.

Commonwealth anxiety to develop Jamaica, won from Spain by Venables in 1655, as part of Cromwell's ill-considered 'western design' to gain the West Indies, meant that considerable numbers of Irish were allowed in, together with the English and Scots. These included troops from Venables's army, time-expired servants from Barbados and other Caribbean islands, and convicts and indentured servants from England, Scotland, and Ireland. In 1655 Henry Cromwell was making plans to transport 1,000 Irish boys and 1,000 Irish girls from the ports of Galway and Kinsale to Jamaica, but so far as is known this scheme fell through. In the beginning the bulk of the Irish were, as might be expected, redemptioners, but in course of time some became property-owners, and by 1670 out of 717 property-owners listed by Sir Thomas Modyford some 10 per cent or more were apparently of Irish extraction. The English revolution of 1688 struck a deadly blow at the flourishing catholic church on Jamaica. Left with only the occasional services of a bondsman priest, ministering secretly, the catholic population began to dwindle, and within a generation or two the bulk of the Irish must have lost their faith. (The records of the catholic church for the century after the revolution have disappeared.) Eventually, swallowed up by the African, the Irish population lost its identity, but the names of the 'black Irish' of Jamaica still bear witness to its former strength.

In 1669 it was reported that there were some 12,000 Irish in the West Indies. Barbados had 8,000, Montserrat 2,000, Nevis and St Christopher 600, Antigua 400, and Guadeloupe 800.[2] Stapleton, in a census return to the lords of trade in 1678, gives the following figures: St Christopher, 187 Irish; Nevis, 800; Montserrat, 1,869; and Antigua 610. The Irish had something of a reputation for instability as contrasted with the English, Welsh, and Scots, who whatever their unpromising beginnings—broken traders, spendthrifts, and so on—were more willing to settle down and make a success of the plantations. The Irish of course had more reason to be discontented with

[1] Joseph J. Williams, *Whence the 'black Irish' of Jamaica?* (New York, 1932), pp 54–5.

[2] Relation by Fr John Grace, of Cashel diocese, Paris, 5 July 1669 (Moran, *Spicil. Ossor.*, i, 486–7).

their lot, and in 1689 they again joined the French in a short-lived rising against the English settlements in the Leeward Islands. But whites of whatever origin were now greatly outnumbered by the African slaves, as a result of the change-over to a sugar economy that was taking place in Barbados and the Leeward Islands from the mid-century. By 1690 the 'most thoroughgoing social revolution in the history of the New World'[1] was nearly complete, the servile population of whites driven away to America by the incoming blacks.

To a large extent, the Irish found abroad opportunities denied them at home. While priests generally returned home on completion of their studies, a considerable number remained on as professors, as chaplains to the Irish regiments, or as pastors. The laity found employment as soldiers, or in the professions and trades. Of necessity they had many difficulties, linguistic, climatic, financial—*gan spré ghlan*, *gan éadach*, *gan déagh-tháinte* (bereft of fortune, clothing, wealth of flocks). The Irish colleges in general were poorly funded and were often reduced to begging, in spite of which they could not maintain their houses in repair. Those of the nobility who lived on pensions from Spain, the pope, or the archdukes often found that these pensions were not paid. On the other hand Spain was able to provide for Hugh O'Neill and his companions-in-exile quietly, although officially and for reasons of state denying them hospitality. Occasionally—in France, as noted already, and also in Spanish territories—the Irish found themselves unwelcome. In 1610, for instance, there was talk of clearing the Spanish court of Irish civilians and soldiers. But, as the English court was informed in 1614, 300 Irish students in Flanders and Spain, and over 3,000 Irish soldiers (including 1,000 nobles) in the same countries, were in the service of the Spanish king.[2] Irish merchants enjoyed the privileges of trading freely with Spain—a privilege of which they might be deprived for a time, when Spain was at war with England, as in 1627.[3] In France too the Irish benefited from the generosity of the monarchy, the parliament, bishops, and others, and in that country too they might become citizens. But problems were never far away. The exigencies of the clash between reform and counter-reform in Europe meant that missionary-minded priests, like the Capuchin Nugent, at times found their designs for the Irish mission-field thwarted by their continental brethren. For many the worst pain was that of exile. Homesickness found temporary relief in dreams:

[1] Carl and Roberta Bridenbaugh, *No peace beyond the line*, p. 9; see also Marcus Lee Hansen, *The Atlantic migration, 1607–1860: a history of the continuing settlement of the United States*, ed. A. M. Schlesinger (Cambridge, Mass., 1941), pp 41–3.

[2] Report by Spanish council of state, 1610 (Archivo General de Simancas (hereafter referred to as A.G.S.), Estado 4126); report of speech by James I, 1614 (*Archiv. Hib.*, iii (1914), p. 315).

[3] *Wadding papers*, p. 244.

Insan bhFrangc im dhúiseacht damh,
In Éirinn Chuinn im chodhladh.

(While awake I am in France; in Ireland when I'm sleeping.)[1]

Morning brought something akin to despair:

Mar éirighim gach aon mhaidin moch-thrátha,
Dhul d'fhéachaim sean-mhacha mong-Mháine;
's do laedughadh mo chéime 's mo chónaigh-se;
Ní léir dhamh Rí Éirne san chómhdháilse.

(For daily at the dawn I rise up sadly, look forth in hope to see grass-grown Hy Maine; but now my course is curbed, my fortune waning; no more I see Erne's king among his people.)[1]

Still the Irish came to feel more and more at home on the Continent. By the middle of the seventeenth century the Continent, in turn, had again become accustomed to the sight—and sound—of the learned, disputatious Irish. Le Sage amusingly depicts Gil Blas as perfecting his dialectic on Irishmen, 'who asked for no better. You should have seen us argue! Such gestures! Such grimaces! Such contortions!'[2] An observer at the university of Paris put it thus:

Vidi avidos vultus et mentem pasta chimaeris
Spectra Hibernorum turmatim invadere portas.

(With hungry looks and minds on whimsies nursed, gaunt troops of Irish through the doorways burst.)[3]

Their reputation for chop-logic the Irish priests and students maintained; Montesquieu was later to write of their *rédoubtable talent pour la dispute*.[4]

Europeans, although at times they might be bemused, at times dismayed by the 'gaunt troops of Irish', generally made them welcome. A number of exiles, such as Tyrone and Tyrconnell, whose Irish titles continued to be recognised in Spain, and others as well, were admitted into the Spanish military orders of Santiago, Alcántara, and Calatrava. The first of these was Daniel O'Sullivan Beare (1561–1618), already acknowledged as *conde de Birhaven*, who became a knight of Santiago in 1607. Dr Micheline Walsh estimates that the Spanish knights of Santiago who were Irish or of Irish extraction numbered in all nearly 200.[5] John O'Neill succeeded to his father's title, *conde de Tirón*, in 1616 and was made a knight commander of Calatrava in 1632. His natural son, Hugo Eugenio (1633–60), became knight of Calatrava in 1644. Thereafter until the end of the seventeenth century

[1] A. de Blacam, *Gaelic literature surveyed* (Dublin, 1929), p. 274.

[2] Alain René Lesage, *The adventures of Gil Blas of Santillana*, trans. Henri Van Laun (3 vols, Edinburgh, 1886), i, 5.

[3] In Charles McNeill's translation.

[4] Montesquieu, *Lettres persanes*, ed. Paul Vernière (Paris, 1960), p. 79.

[5] *Spanish knights*, i, introduction, p. vi.

the title *conde de Tirón* was maintained by collateral branches of the family. In Portugal the Counts O'Neill of Lisbon were descended from Brian Ballach, one of the Lower Clandeboye family. In 1629 Hugh Albert O'Donnell, who had succeeded his father Rory as *conde de Tirconel*, was made knight of Alcántara. He married a kinswoman of the last duke of Guise, and died without issue in 1642. The Irish of highest rank, generation after generation, occupied foremost places in the service, military and diplomatic, of their adopted countries. Those of gentle birth, but of less princely rank, might still expect to be commissioned as officers. Philip O'Sullivan, the historian, received a commission in the navy from Philip II. He would have preferred a life of study, but had his living to make.

The Irish brought with them overseas their pride of race, their strong feeling of kinship, and their consciousness of class. The nobility continued to set great store by their ancient lineage and sought to maintain their hereditary chroniclers, physicians, and other clients. Such a savant as Tuileagna mac Torna Ó Maoil Chonaire, O.F.M., who was a sort of official custodian of genealogical records—'chosen', he said himself, 'by the nobility of Ireland, clerical and lay, as general custodian of the antiquities of the country'[1]—was an honoured figure among the Irish on the Continent in the seventeenth century. His claim was not all bombast indeed. Philip O'Sullivan as late as the 1620s records the names of O'Sullivan Beare's physician and judge and of MacCarthy More's judge. These latter-day brehons were continental-trained.[2]

For the most part Irish continued to marry Irish. Hugh Albert O'Donnell, Dermot O'Mallun, and Thomas Preston all found brides among the Netherlands nobility, and Dermot O'Sullivan Beare's first wife was Doña Mariana de Córdoba y Aragón, a descendant of the Gran Capitán (Gonzalo de Córdoba). The Irish nobility were received on terms of equality by the continental. Bishops continued to be chosen from among the gentry, as also army officers. Even a large proportion of the clergy was of gentle birth—although O'Sullivan Beare in 1613 complained of the new type of plebeian clerical student being received at Santiago. Francis Nugent was a firm believer in educating gentry as priests, so that they would influence their own class.

In the field of diplomacy a number of Irish, both clerical and lay, made their mark during the seventeenth and eighteenth centuries. One of them, Peter Lombard, whose diplomatic efforts at Rome on behalf of Hugh O'Neill have already been noticed,[3] sought also to further the effort (which in the end proved vain) to prevent the Jesuits from breaking the university's monopoly of higher education in Louvain city. While showing a zealous interest for his alma mater, Lombard's letters from Rome urged moderation

[1] *Spanish knights*, ii, 111.
[2] O'Sullivan Beare, *Zoilomastix*, ed. O'Donnell, pp 85, 91.
[3] Above, pp 596–8.

on his colleagues. In Madrid, the interests of Louvain were defended by the Franciscans Archbishop Florence Conry and Hugh Burke. Conry was one of those who negotiated, though unsuccessfully, for a marriage between Doña Maria, daughter of Philip III, and Charles, prince of Wales. This was a notable change for Hugh O'Donnell's former chaplain. Luke Wadding's diplomatic career began early, when in 1618 he went to Rome as theologian to the extraordinary Spanish legation which sought to have the immaculate conception made defined doctrine.

Lombard, Wadding, and Conry all showed an ability to grapple realistically with a developing political situation. The case of another friar, Dominic O'Daly, O.P., a Kerryman (Frei Domingo de Rosario), is illustrative of the change which a life spent in high diplomacy could work in Irish loyalties. During the 1650s he was among the diplomats employed by King John of Braganza to seek recognition abroad of the newly independent kingdom of Portugal, and served at Rome and at the court of Louis XIV. He also acted as Portuguese agent of the Stuarts and worked hard to protect their interests. Frei Domingo, like a lesser Richelieu, accepted without qualm the new secular diplomacy that was in vogue after Westphalia. His aim was that Portugal should hold the balance of power between France and England. Like Peter Lombard before him O'Daly believed that the interests of Ireland would best be served by a catholic marriage for the English king. His further aim was that Ireland should become an independent kingdom under its ruler, Charles Stuart. Another Irishman, Cornelius Mahoney (Conor O'Mahony), was impressed differently by the independence of Portugal. This Jesuit professor at Évora caused a famous stir in the ranks of the confederation of Kilkenny by demanding complete independence for Ireland in his work, *Disputatio apologetica* (1645).

Another faithful servant of the Stuarts was Ignatius White of Ballyneety, whose father, Sir Dominic, had been mayor of Limerick in 1636. Charles II employed him at the court of Vienna and made him a baronet. Not to be outdone, Leopold I made him marquis d'Albeville (*Baile an Fhaoite*, White's town) and a count of the holy Roman empire.[1] An interesting figure who awaits a biographer was Sir Patrick Moledi (or O'Mulledy), a native of County Wexford, who in 1650 acted at Brussels for the Irish bishops and was at a later date Spanish ambassador to England and member of the council of Flanders.

Finally, among Charles Stuart's closest intimates was Theobald, second Viscount Taaffe (d. 1667). This confederate general and Ormondist was chief of those who represented Ormond in the negotiations conducted between 1649 and 1652 in which nuncioists and royalists vied for the support of Duke Charles IV of Lorraine. Later he was attached to Charles's court

[1] *Spanish knights*, iii, 13; *Wild geese in Spanish Flanders*, pp 384, 456; *Comment. Rinucc.*, iv, 411–13; Gilbert, *Ir. confed.*, iv, 189–210.

on the Continent, leader among the 'good fellows'[1] and in fact one of the king's closest confidants and agent in amatory as well as in diplomatic affairs. Taaffe's loyalty earned him the title of earl of Carlingford at the restoration. His last mission for his king was in 1665–6 to seek the help of the emperor Leopold and the prince-bishop of Münster in the war against the Dutch.

For every Irishman at home in the courts of Europe there were thousands whose only home was the camp. All over Europe, in Spain, the Low Countries, France, the Empire, Sweden, and Denmark, they followed the soldier's trade. The first Irish regiment serving under the Spanish flag was originally recruited for Leicester in Ireland by Colonel William Stanley, after the Desmond wars, and brought to the Low Countries to fight against the Spaniards. Stanley defected to the Spanish service in 1587; in 1605 his regiment was reconstituted under Colonel Henry O'Neill (1587–1610), as the first 'regiment of Tyrone'. When Henry died, his half-brother John was appointed colonel. Other Irish regiments formed in the Low Countries were those of Colonels O'Donnell, Owen Roe O'Neill, and Preston. The Irish saw much service and suffered many casualties. John O'Neill and Hugh O'Donnell were both competent officers, who died soldiers' deaths. Preston, about whose sobriety there is some question, was precipitate and erratic. On occasion he could fight, although his sterling defence of Louvain against a combined Franco-Dutch army in 1635 was overshadowed by Owen Roe's exceptional defence of Arras five years later.

France, from the time of its entry into the thirty years' war, came to rely heavily upon Irish mercenaries, and Michael Wall, of Coolnamuck, County Waterford, was made general of 'the entire foreign army' in France during the war. Several regiments of infantry were raised in Ireland; in 1639–40 alone perhaps 5,000 soldiers came over. Then for various reasons recruiting slackened: the war against Spain was going better for France, there was often poor provision made for arriving Irish contingents, and many of the soldiers in both France and Spain were eager to answer the call of arms at home. Richelieu before his death in 1642 allowed a number of officers and men home in French ships, with supplies of arms. In June 1645 the two remaining Irish regiments in the French army were amalgamated under Edmond Robert du Wall, brother of Michael.

At the same time, right through the confederate war, recruiting for France and Spain was encouraged both by the confederation, in hopes of money, arms, and ammunition, and by Ormond, in order to keep troops from the confederation. Viscount Muskerry and Colonel Preston brought men to France, and Dermot O'Sullivan Beare, *conde de Birhaven*, to Spain.[2] In

[1] Eva Scott, *The travels of the king* (1907), p. 140.

[2] Dermot stood high in the councils of Philip IV, being chamberlain, chancellor of the exchequer, and member of both the council of state (privy council) and royal council of the galleys.

1652 the movement abroad again began in earnest. The commonwealth government allowed troops to leave for Spain, Flanders, and France, on condition of surrendering. In the next two years perhaps 25,000 men were shipped to Spain and 10,000 or 15,000 to France, these latter comprising eight regiments. Little provision was made for the men arriving in Spain, so that they endured great hardship and loss of life. Only half of them (says Clarendon) were able to take the field, and very few of them returned at the restoration.

But France, the new great power, was attracting more and more Irish allegiance from Spain. The Irish garrison holding Bordeaux under its *condottiere* Condé in the Fronde wars went over to France at the peace, and Inchiquin, holding a French command in Catalonia, persuaded other Irish soldiers to change sides. A number of Old English clustered around Charles II's court in exile, and when Cromwell formed a political alliance with France in 1655 this increased Old English hopes of using French influence to gain religious tolerance in Ireland. When the regular French army was reorganised, an Irish regiment was formed in 1653, under its *maréchal de camp*, or major general, James, son of Theobald, first Viscount Dillon. Others followed, but Dillon's remained outstanding. It gave distinguished service in Flanders, especially at the battle of Dunkirk, and retained its identity, under successive Viscounts Dillon, down to 1793. When in 1656 the duke of York left for Flanders, many Irish officers (including Richard Talbot, his lieutenant colonel) followed him, and the Irish regiments were re-formed. With the end of the war and the restoration, further regiments were disbanded.

After the restoration recruiting of Irish for foreign service continued. Louis XIV took into his service the English, Scots, and Irish guards whom Charles had to dismiss in 1667, and in 1671 Sir George Hamilton recruited an infantry regiment of 1,500 men for France. Mountcashel and Sarsfield began their military apprenticeship in the *régiment d'Hamilton*. Clare's Irish regiment in the Dutch service was originally formed in 1675 to fight under Spanish colours, still, as Oliver Plunkett testified, the most favoured by the Irish.[1] Colonel Denis O'Byrne was allowed in 1681 to recruit 500 Irish to go to the Netherlands, on condition that he clothe them in red coats with blue lining. The following year Sir Thomas Nugent raised 400 men, also for Flanders. But at this time there was also a homeward movement of those who had gone abroad towards the end of the commonwealth period; by 1672 almost half had returned.

The Austrian service also attracted hundreds of Irishmen, and such families as Taaffe, Brown, Butler, and Wallis (Walsh) had already gained fame along the Danube well before the eighteenth century. Irishmen fought in the imperial armies from the early stages of the thirty years war. It is

[1] P. F. Moran, *Memoir of Oliver Plunket* (2nd ed., Dublin, 1895), p. 125.

probable that the first contingents came from Flanders to serve under Tilly; with them was Henry Fitzsimon, S.J., whose diary of the Bohemian war[1] is a valuable historical source. Somewhat later Thomas Carew (Carve) another Irish priest, made an equally important contribution to the historiography of these wars.[2] Irish officers were in demand in Austria, for not only were they catholics but their knowledge of Latin was a useful asset. As the war went on and losses occurred, their companies probably became more international in character.

No fewer than six officers of the name Butler distinguished themselves in the thirty years war. The famous Walter, who played a prominent part in the murder of Wallenstein (25 February 1634 N.S.), was born at Roscrea and was colonel-proprietor of a regiment of dragoons. When the Swedes stormed Frankfurt-on-Oder in 1631, Butler and his Irish stood well in the defence, according to Robert Monroe, who was on the winning side that day. Walter was given the estate of Friedberg, which had belonged to Wallenstein. Associated with him in the murder was Captain Walter Devereux, who, before dealing the fatal blow, gave Wallenstein time to say an act of contrition.

Colonel William Count Gall von Bourckh or Burke (d. 1655) of Gallstown, County Kilkenny, fought in both the imperial and Polish services. Richard Walsh, whose family owned Carrickmines castle, commanded a regiment of infantry and received his death-wound on the day of Lützen. Related to him was Oliver Wallis or Walsh, who also fought in the thirty years war and was made first Graf Carrighmain and imperial chamberlain by Ferdinand III in 1642, became major general in 1666 and died the following year. The Carrighmain house was destined to provide many loyal officers to the Habsburg service. Another distinguished Austro-Irish family, the Counts Taaffe, was founded by Francis, third earl of Carlingford (1639–1704) and second son of Theobald, first earl. As colonel proprietor of a cuirassier regiment, Graf Franz helped in the relief of Vienna. He became lieutenant general of cavalry in 1687 and was given command of an Irish regiment.

Thus, whether as regular officers or simply as soldiers of fortune, the flower of Ireland's nobility was to be found fighting all over Europe, from Nieuport to Vienna, for a century and more before the 'wild geese' took flight after Limerick. Ordinary Irishmen served in the ranks on soldier's pay (when they got it), and sometimes this was supplemented by a monthly allowance (*ventaja*) or by a grant-in-aid (*ayuda da costa*). They supplied the manpower for the Irish regiments; a few of them were little better than vagabonds, moving from camp to camp.

It would seem that on the whole the Irish deserved whatever pay they

[1] 'Father Fitzsimon's diary of the Bohemian war of 1620', edited from two anonymous Latin works of Fitzsimon, *Pugna Pragensis* (Brünn, 1620) and *Buquoi quadrimestre iter* (Brünn, 1621), in Henry Fitzsimon, *Words of comfort . . . , letters from a cell . . . , and diary of the Bohemian war of 1620*, ed. Edmund Hogan (Dublin, 1881), pp 83–108.

[2] Thomas Carve, *Itinerarium* (Mayence, 1639).

earned. The kern displayed the same qualities of agility, endurance, and ferocity in battle abroad as at home. Of the 700 Irish who fought at the siege of Boulogne in 1544 it was said, if Stanihurst can be believed, that they were such savage fighters as to appear devils to the French. Stanley's kern struck an observer as belonging 'not to Christendom but to Brazil'.[1] Montrose's Irish, led by Colkitto MacDonnell, struck home with the effect of charging cavalry, and their winter march of forty miles over the mountains from Blair Athol into Argyle's Inverlochy was a feat to match Red Hugh's passage over the heights of Slieve Felim. But these men, it seems, had known Owen Roe as drill-sergeant.

The character of the confederate wars in Ireland was affected by the fact that generals on both sides had fought in the Low Countries. Here was the great military training-ground of the period, where for the previous half-century Irish regiments had been fighting in the Spanish service and English in that of the Dutch. The war in the Netherlands had seen notable developments in both fortifications, whether of earth or of stone, and in siege warfare, and the confederate wars were notable for sieges of castles, forts, towns, and even villages. Owen Roe, Preston, Garret Barry, John Burke, Monck, Castlehaven, and Pierce Fitzgerald or MacThomas were among the commanders who had learned their trade of fighting in the Low Countries. Others had gained experience in the thirty years war, a conflict also noted for its sieges.

To turn from the trade of killing to that of healing, not a few Irish abroad followed the profession of medicine. Ireland had a few university-trained doctors, men who had studied at Oxford, Paris, or the southern medical schools. With the reformation, would-be Irish medical students seem to have turned more to Spain. John Nynan was a graduate of Lérida; he became Red Hugh's physician and about 1625 was doctor to the Irish regiment in Belgium. About the same time Christopher Humphreys was lecturing at Salamanca. Others served in the medical corps of the Spanish army, and a number of these returned home during the confederate wars, including Owen Magrath and Owen O'Shiel of County Westmeath, 'the eagle of doctors'. O'Shiel had studied at Douai, Paris, Louvain, and Padua. In Flanders he had been chief doctor of the catholic king's army and had served as surgeon to Owen Roe's regiment. Both he and Magrath had been attached to the medical faculty of the famous Royal Military Hospital at Mechlin, and O'Shiel had been its chief. Bishop Nicholas French and Nicholas Plunkett were entertained at Bologna by Niall O'Glacan, professor of medicine, when on their way to Rome in 1648.

Irish graduates of Paris included Donough Ultach or Dunlevy,[2] hereditary physician to O'Donnell; Niall O'Glacan; Bernard Connor, John

[1] See Charles Wilson, *Queen Elizabeth and the revolt of the Netherlands* (Berkeley and Los Angeles, 1970), p. 99.

[2] Both Stanihurst and *A.F.M.* remark on the medical skill of his son Owen.

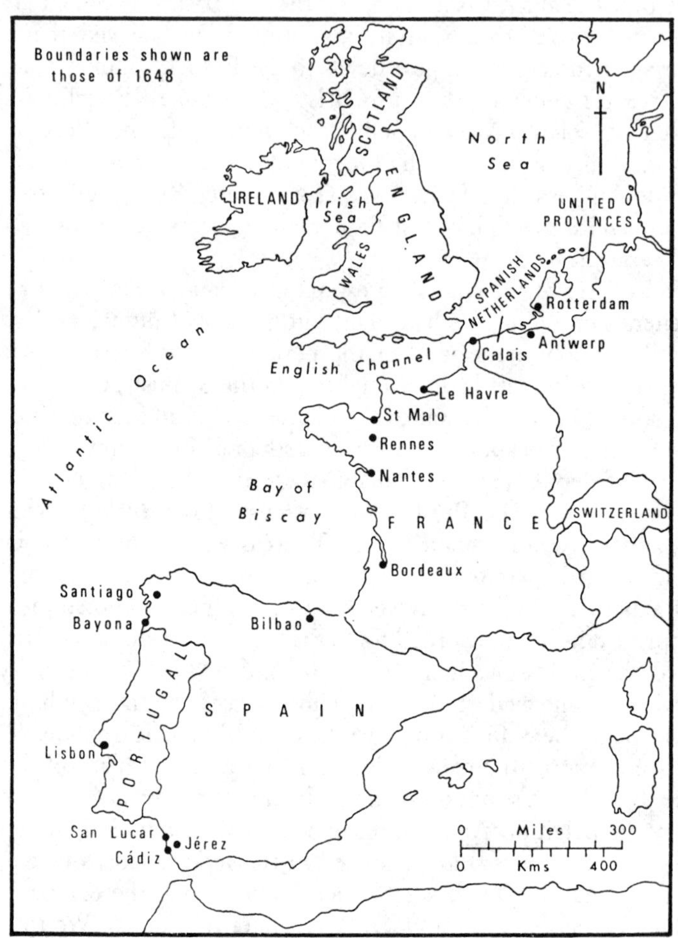

Map 20 CONTINENTAL PORTS TRADING WITH IRELAND, by John J. Silke

Sobieski's doctor; Callaghan Garvan (1644–1735), physician to the Old Pretender. 'Monsieur Maurice de la Roche, docteur en médicine, Waterfordiensis',[1] appears among the Irish ecclesiastical exiles maintained by Archbishop de Sourdis at Bordeaux between 1605 and 1621.

Under Elizabeth and James I youths from the Pale continued to frequent the Inns of Court in London, and during James's reign were increasingly joined by young men from the towns of the south-east. Although these lawyers maintained a stout tradition of recusancy, the evidence suggests that would-be lawyers from the rest of the country preferred or were obliged to go abroad for studies. Philip O'Sullivan gives the names of some of his fellow students of law at Compostela: Edward Sweetman, Moling O'Canty, and Edmond O'Hosey, the famous Oliver's son.[2] About the same time Dermot O'Sullivan, Owen O'Finnilly, and Walter O'Kearney gained their doctorates in law in France. Maurice O'Connor, who studied in Portugal, was skilled in both civil and canon law, and received an appointment from Philip III to examine petitions from Irishmen, a post he held until misfortune befell him. Thady O'Brenan was attached to the Irish regiment as judge. Dermot O'Mallun or O'Mallum (d. 1637) of County Clare was learned in law and poetry, and served Archdukes Albert and Isabella as lawyer. Knight of Calatrava (1616), he was created Baron Glean O'Mallun and Courchy, County Clare, in the Irish peerage by James I, in 1622.

Because of their trading links with the Continent, it was natural to find Irish merchants who found conditions at home unendurable setting up as merchants abroad. In the Low Countries they could turn for assistance or advice to the *hôtel* or consulate of the Irish nation which had stood at Bruges between 1383 and 1590, and was then, consequent upon the decay of Bruges and the rise of Antwerp, removed to the latter city.[3] Diego Geraldino appears as consul general of the Irish nation for the coast of Andalusia in 1620.[4] Even before that, Thomas White, S.J., in 1596 collected money for his college at Salamanca from the Irish merchants of Bayona (in Galicia) and in 1598 received 200 *reales* from the Irish merchants in Bilbao. Army veterans too sometimes set up in trade. One Marshall set up as an innkeeper at Calais after Rocroy. His son, Georges Maréchal (1658–1736), became a famous surgeon and founder of the Royal Academy of Surgery at Paris.

A number of merchants from the south and east, fleeing from the Cromwellian persecution, settled in Nantes, St Malo, and other French ports and engaged in the business of importing raw materials—beef, hides, and

[1] *Cal. S.P. Ire.*, *1615–25*, p. 319.

[2] O'Sullivan Beare, *Zoilomastix*, ed. O'Donnell, p. 85.

[3] Charles Terlinden, 'L'Irlande et la Belgique dans le passé: extrait de *Revue Générale de Bruxelles*' (Bruges, 1928).

[4] Memorials of the year 1620, Estado 2646.

tallow—from Ireland. Such names as Lee, Lincoln, Everard, Hore, and Lombard indicate their origin. A number of them founded families later prominent in French life. For example, the various branches of the well-known Giraldin family had their origin in the union of Raymond Giraldin (Redmond Geraldine) and Helène Lincoln, both of Waterford, who married and settled down in St Malo.

Old English formed colonies in Brittany and Old Irish clung together in Galicia: even in exile, it was clear, differences remained keen. The Jesuits, who staffed a number of colleges, were in conflict now with the Irish laity, for turning the colleges exclusively into seminaries, now with the secular clergy, who like Lombard accused them of inveigling candidates for the priesthood into the society. Men like Lombard, Archer, and Wadding, through their experience of the wider world and their association abroad with the Old Irish, found themselves losing their anti-Gaelic prejudices—if only temporarily in the case of Lombard. Military camaraderie too acted as a solvent of old prejudices. Old English as well as Old Irish officers served under Colonel Henry O'Neill. To some degree the old rivalries continued even in the camp, however, the young Tyrconnell (Hugh Albert) demanding a regiment when his cousin Tyrone had been given one, and Colonels Preston and Owen O'Neill competing for recruits in Ireland.

All of the old ideological bitterness flared up again among the exiles after the puritan conquest. All over the Continent, in Irish circles, controversy raged over who was to blame, Old Irish or Old English, for the defeat. In Rome, over the period of a decade (1648–59), each party sought to gain the approval of the pope, with the nuncioists, led by Rinuccini himself and the Capuchin Richard O'Ferrall, of Annaly, outmatching their opponents in the ability to present a case. While the chief reply to O'Ferrall came from John Lynch, in exile at St Malo, the pope himself, Alexander VII, was displeased with the Capuchin. Alexander indeed disapproved of Rinuccini's extreme action in 1648. In that very year as nuncio at Cologne the future pope had refrained from invoking censures against those who accepted the peace of Westphalia.

The Irish in Paris, like those in Rome, were deeply involved in the acrimonious debate over the censure; in Paris, however, the debate was complicated by the fact that the protagonists were engaged in other controversies, especially the Jansenist, as well. The Franciscan Paul King, for the nuncioists, and the controversial and none too scrupulous Cork priest, John Callaghan, for the Ormondists, were the leading figures in the Paris debate. Callaghan's powerful defence of the Inchiquin truce, *Vindiciarum catholicorum Hiberniae* (1650), which was wrongly ascribed to Bellings and placed on the Index in 1654, was considered to be very damaging to the nuncioist position and besides drawing a reply from Punch (1653) was also a main target for *Commentarius Rinuccinianus*. That these controversies were not conducted on strict Old English–Old Irish lines is again indicated by the respective positions of Punch and Callaghan.

Generally speaking however the nuncioists were Gaelic and the Ormondists Old English. Thus among the Friars Minor, at home and in exile, the majority party looked upon the Old English as traitors both to land and religion. The fair-minded Luke Wadding in particular came in for bitter attack. He was Old English and had a position of great influence at Rome upon the direction of Irish affairs, and those who were overcome and in some cases even distraught—as was perhaps Father Francis Magruairk—by Ireland's woes, now saw Wadding's influence in the most baleful light. The result was that the latter's final years—he died in 1657—were clouded by the fact that his advice was no longer asked on Irish affairs (although it was on other matters) and above all by thought of the sorrows that had overcome his native land.

A minority view among the Franciscans, that of Peter Walsh, which found expression in the *Remonstrance*, reopened the old quarrel in the 1660s. Most of the Irish priests on the Continent (even John Sinnich), backed by Rome and the internuncio, were strongly against Walsh, and only a small minority (mainly Old English) supported him. The air of Europe resounded with the cries of the warring Irish, the most wordy and most vituperative battle of all being that between the Franciscan Anthony Bruodin and Thomas Carew. Bruodin like Carew was a man of some note; as a member of the Czech province of his order (1651–75), he was a leader in the successful struggle of that province to resist absorption by the Austrian province. Unfortunately in the abuse which this learned but undignified pair hurled at each other, the Irish tragedy was indeed repeating itself as farce.

Violence in debate came all too readily to religious-minded men of this age, dedicated as they were to a war, fought with weapons spiritual and intellectual—but not always with those weapons alone—for the minds and hearts of men. Both reformers and counter-reformers saw the value of education in this war, and the reply to Calvin's seminary at Geneva was the decree of Trent establishing seminaries.[1] In Italy and Spain the work of foundation went ahead fairly rapidly, in Germany and France more slowly. Cardinal Allen's seminary, founded at Douai (1568) for English students, became, as is well known,[2] the model for many later seminaries, including the Irish colleges on the Continent. It welcomed lay as well as clerical students and sought to fashion a clergy learned as well as zealous. In the result it had a very strong formative influence upon the counter-reformation in England, Scotland, and Ireland.

[1] Sessio XXIII, cap. 18, *De reform.* (15 July 1563).

[2] See Peter Guilday, *The English catholic refugees on the Continent, 1558–1795* (London, 1914), i, 63–120.

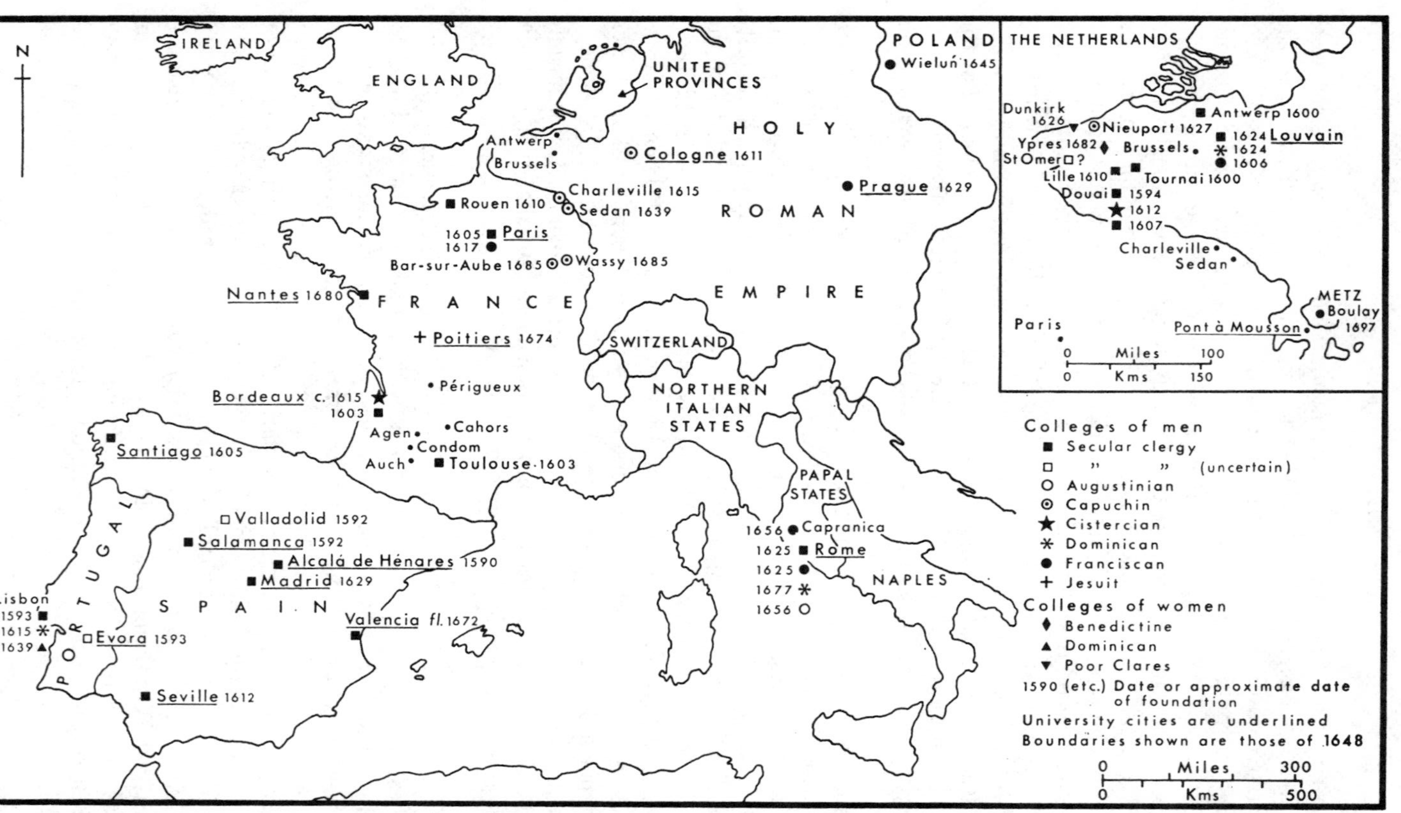

Map 21 IRISH COLLEGES ABROAD, by John J. Silke

The Jesuits were commonly entrusted with the guidance of the seminaries. Imbued with the ideals of the catholic reform and wholehearted in their acceptance of the new learning, they revolutionised the whole structure of catholic education. The *ratio studiorum*, fashioned according to humanist principles at the end of the sixteenth century, had as its aim the moral as well as intellectual formation of students on the best liberal lines. While the Jesuit seminaries concentrated on giving a solid grounding in scholastic theology and in the pastoral ministry, the *ratio studiorum* governed the instruction imparted by the society in both lower and higher branches of education and gave catholicism a philosophy and methodology of education that were unsurpassed. Jesuit colleges, higher and lower, providing both secular and clerical education, spread throughout Europe in hundreds, and beyond Europe as far as India and the New World. Other orders were prominent in the work of catholic education, the French Oratorians, and the Barnabites for instance, but the Jesuits were by far the most important.

Of the catholic universities, Louvain, amid the upheavals of the late sixteenth century, was still a centre of learning and even of piety. Teaching of arts, following upon the establishing of the Collegium Trilingue (*c.* 1517), was remodelled according to the new learning and, although philosophy and theology remained true to the scholastic traditions, they too were affected by the transformation in the arts. Above all Louvain was proud of the leading role its theologians had taken at Trent. At Douai, English humanism imported by the Oxford divines, Allen, Campion, and others, blended with that of the Netherlands. The new Jesuit college at Pont-à-Mousson played a great part in the development of the counter-reformation in Lorraine and Alsace. Long before the end of the sixteenth century, the effect of the counter-reformation was being felt in the Netherlands. Spain, which had put through its own reform before Luther, saw a remarkable late flowering of scholasticism, especially of Scotism, in the sixteenth century, and theology now attracted the liveliest minds. At Paris too the methods of the scholastics still prevailed in philosophy and theology, but here also, as in the Spanish universities and Louvain, humanism took over the arts, particularly at Sainte-Barbe, the college whose system became the basis of Jesuit pedagogy.

This was the background against which the story of the Irish colleges on the Continent unfolded. In this unfolding three stages may be distinguished. At first, from even before the middle of the sixteenth century, Irish youths sought education at catholic universities and upon receiving ordination returned home. Next, they repaired in numbers to the English and Scottish centres in the Low Countries, to Douai, Pont-à-Mousson, and elsewhere. Finally, and largely through the efforts of individual priests, the Irish seculars and regulars succeeded, from about 1590 onwards, in founding colleges. Between then and 1681 some twenty in all were established.

Early in the reign of Elizabeth, and particularly within the Pale, where the effect of the royal ecclesiastical policies was most strongly felt, the need for a new policy in education was becoming apparent. In 1564 Archbishop Creagh sought an annual grant from Pius IV to provide for the education of Irish priests. To Creagh, David Wolfe and like-minded priests such as Edmund Tanner, later bishop of Cork, if not to the Marian bishops, the need for a pious and learned clergy was apparent, to instruct a people ignorant of the elements of their religion and to combat the reformation doctrines. So zealous young Irishmen now followed the example of the Oxford recusants who fled abroad to Douai or Pont-à-Mousson. The first Jesuit chancellor (1584–90) of Pont-à-Mousson was Richard Fleming of Dublin. A list, drawn up in 1580, possibly by O'Hurley, gives the names of thirty-seven priests and students at Louvain, Douai, Paris, Rome, and elsewhere, and claims that there were many others studying in Spain, Portugal, and France.[1] Besides priests there were laymen, doctors, lawyers, and other professional men. Sir Patrick Barnewall, a leader of the Irish recusants in the reign of James I, 'was the first gentleman's son of quality that was ever put out of Ireland to be brought up in learning beyond the seas'.[2]

The grounding that these students, clerical and lay, had received in their Irish schools was developed abroad. Gregory XIII intended to found an Irish college in Rome, but the funds earmarked for the purpose were diverted towards the expenses of Fitzmaurice's expedition. Another alternative offered, and the Scottish Jesuit seminary at Pont-à-Mousson was supported by Gregory as a 'Scots and Irish college'. Thus Creagh's plea of twenty years previously bore some fruit, and this Limerick merchant who left his wares in Spain for the priesthood and long suffering in prison may perhaps be regarded as the father of the Irish colleges abroad. In 1593 the Scots college moved to Douai, still attended by some Irish. But by this time purely Irish colleges were in being. To compare the rise of the Irish colleges on the Continent with that of the European universities is to compare small things with great, but the historically minded Irish scholars who made this comparison remembered with pride that Irish monks had helped to preserve European culture fighting for survival during the dark ages.

The first seminaries were located in Spanish territories, established, it is worthy of note, at a time when Spain, under Philip II, had not only assumed the leadership of the counter-reformation but was also moving in the direction of rigid orthodoxy. Much of the history of the colleges remains to be investigated. Salamanca, Lisbon, Santiago, and Madrid colleges were founded by priests, and Seville was set on its feet by a priest. But Alcalá, it seems, was founded by a Portuguese nobleman, whose mother was a MacDonnell from Antrim. Évora was founded by Cardinal Henry; it later became a house for training Jesuit missionaries for Japan. Santiago was set

[1] *Archiv. Hib.*, vi (1916), pp 161–3.

[2] *Cal. S.P. Ire., 1611–14*, p. 394. See also above, p. 192.

up for the education of the sons of the Irish nobility, especially those from south-west Ireland in exile after Kinsale. All the others, it seems, were founded as seminaries for diocesan priests. Even Santiago in 1613 became an exclusively clerical seminary.

Generally, as at Salamanca, the Jesuits also conducted the local seminary and sent the students to classes there and not to the university. From Lisbon, Santiago, Seville, and probably elsewhere, students after completing philosophy regularly passed on to Salamanca for theology. After about 1650 this arrangement between Lisbon and Salamanca ceased, perhaps because the Portuguese Jesuits took over control of Lisbon from their Irish brethren. Salamanca was the most outstanding of the Iberian colleges. Nurse of bishops, provincials, theologians, martyrs, and in great number missioners, it sent home in the space of a hundred years some 500 priests to Ireland, England, and Scotland.

The Jesuits' monopoly of control of the Irish seminaries in the Peninsula caused criticism. Archbishop Peter Lombard, for instance, complained strongly to the pope about the number of students the Jesuits were recruiting for themselves;[1] and there were other critics. To put the matter in perspective, the English colleges at Douai and Rome, the Scots college at Douai, and the German college at Rome also experienced friction because students passed to the Jesuits and other religious orders. White and his colleagues may have done some recruiting, but they were sincere in their efforts to ensure a regular supply of priests for Ireland. The various colleges were small, together providing no great total of places, and therefore the Jesuits sought to eliminate lay students. The Scots college at Rome, which was founded in 1600 expressly for both clerical and lay students, was also turned into an exclusively clerical college under Jesuit supervision. Archbishop David Kearney of Cashel (1603–24) supported, if he did not indeed inspire, the securing of control of the Iberian colleges by the Jesuits. Official court circles in Spain agreed with Kearney that control by the Jesuits would ensure stability and eliminate unhealthy contests for control in Santiago.[2] Kearney and the Society probably also feared that Santiago, like Bordeaux, would be reserved completely for Munstermen.

Peter Lombard's complaint of Jesuit control of the colleges was upheld by Oliver Plunkett three-quarters of a century later. He feared that the Jesuit superior in Ireland was inclined to nominate only those students he saw disposed to become regulars. He therefore urged Propaganda to place the nomination of students in the hands of the archbishops and to ensure that the provinces be represented equally. The father general, Oliva, fell in readily

[1] Fr Thomas White to Fray Gaspar de Córdoba, O.P., 7 Feb. 1606 (Dominican General Archives, Santa Sabina, Rome, sect. XIV, MS 165).

[2] See memorandum by Gaspar de Córdoba, O.P., on representations by Kearney, Madrid, 4 Feb. 1611 (A.G.S., Estado 840, f. 58).

with this suggestion. Oliva claimed—and this was the other side of the picture—that many of the dissensions within the colleges, particularly in Rome, arose from the fact that candidates unsuitable for the priesthood were being forced upon the colleges by influential relatives on the Continent.

Several factors made the Low Countries even more attractive to Irish students than Portugal and Spain: their proximity, the regular presence there of the Irish regiment, and not least—as Bishop Roche pointed out in 1625—the fact that the climate was congenial. As distinct from the Peninsula the secular colleges in the Netherlands educated students destined for both clerical and lay states. Foremost was Douai College, established (1594) by a Meath Cusack, Fr Christopher. As numbers grew, Douai became the mother house of a group which included colleges at Antwerp (*c.* 1629), Tournai, and (in a certain sense) the seminary founded by Cusack's cousin, the Capuchin Fr Francis Lavalin Nugent, at Lille. Less permanent than Cusack's was the work of Fr Gelasius Lorcan, who maintained a seminary at Douai between 1607 and 1614, and sought in 1609 to set up another at Rouen. Archbishop Matthews of Dublin is regarded as the founder of the Irish Pastoral College at Louvain (1625); like the others, it had to struggle with poverty. If, as Harris was informed, there was for a period an Irish seminary at St Omer, it must have had an evanescent existence. Perhaps the fact was that Irish students attended the English school, forerunner of Stonyhurst, that was founded by Father Persons in 1593.

In the course of the seventeenth century France began to replace the Spanish dominions as the main supporter of the Irish colleges abroad, and the Lombard College, in Paris, eventually became the largest of all the Irish colleges. Founded in 1605 by Fr John Lee, of the Waterford merchant family, it secured seminary status from the university, during the rectorship of Thomas Messingham of Meath, in 1624. About half a century later two Irish priests prominent in court circles, Drs Patrick Maginn and Matthew Kelly,[1] established a new college on the ruins of the old Italian Collège des Lombards. The college was open to students from all the Irish dioceses, who read philosophy (two years) and theology (three years) at the university, a sixth year being given to pastoral studies.

The college at Bordeaux (1603–1793) was founded by Fr Dermot MacCallaghan MacCarthy of Muskerry with the help of Cardinal de Sourdis. The benevolence of de Sourdis and the people of the Gironde attracted so many young Irish priests and students that numbers of them had to be educated at other centres—Toulouse, Auch, Agen, Cahors, Condom, and Périgueux—all subject to the rector of Bordeaux. The college at Nantes

[1] Called Malachy in the index to Ruth Clark, *Strangers and sojourners at Port-Royal* (Cambridge, 1932). He was apparently something of a Jansenist, and prior to the restoration he had acted as intermediary between the Stuarts in exile and Port-Royal.

(*c.* 1680) was subject to Nantes university and catered for students from all over Ireland. In time it became the next largest college after Paris, with eighty students and (unusually) its own professorial staff.

Finally, a college was founded in Rome through the generosity of Cardinal Ludovico Ludovisi.[1] At first attached to St Isidore's, the college was in 1635 turned over to the Jesuits, who remained in charge until 1687. The students, who generally numbered only seven or eight, went for classes to the Jesuit Collegio Romano.

To the secular colleges there were soon joined regular houses of study. Franciscans, Capuchins, and Dominicans established firm bases from which to launch their missionary offensives, but Cistercians, Augustinians, and Carmelites all failed to found permanent houses abroad and were forced to send their young men to the houses of their continental brethren. The Jesuits, drawing a continuous supply of recruits from the secular colleges, found it unnecessary to establish a college of their own, which in any case they were convinced would only encourage Irishmen to stay abroad. Over a period of about a hundred years Lisbon, for example, supplied about fifty Jesuits, Santiago ninety. Eventually the Jesuits did set up a grammar school, an Irish St Omer, at Poitiers: the Collège Petit (1674–1762). When increased persecution brought a greater exodus, new houses were acquired: Capranica (Franciscan), San Clemente (Dominican), San Mateo in Merulana (1656–61), the house which Alexander VII gave for some years to the Irish Augustinians; and the Cistercian monastery at Bonlieu, near Bordeaux.

The Franciscans opened most houses: St Anthony's, Louvain (founded in 1606 by Florence Conry); St Isidore's, Rome (founded in 1625 by Luke Wadding), a novitiate at Capranica near Sutri (1656), a refuge at Boulay near Metz (1697), as well as shorter-lived foundations at Prague, Wielun (Poland), and Paris. St Anthony's generally housed thirty to forty friars. It gave ardent missionaries to Ireland and Scotland, and such distinguished scholars to Europe as Hugh MacCaghwell (Cavellus), the Scotist, and was indeed the chief factor in the making of that 'golden age' (1616–50) of the Irish Franciscans when they outshone all other provinces in zeal and learning. St Isidore's played a prominent part in the Scotist revival of the seventeenth century, attracting students from other colleges to its lecture halls to hear, besides Wadding himself, Anthony Hickey, the fertile-minded Clare giant, John Punch of Cork, who reduced Scotism to a system, Bonaventure Baron, theologian and poet, and others. In the comparatively settled period 1625–41, some of the orders trained their young men initially in Ireland, but from the outbreak of the 1641 rising preparation in Ireland became ever more difficult, and the orders, Franciscans and others, showed a decline in recruits. In the second half of the century most Franciscans seem to have been

[1] Archbishop Lombard may have left some money for the purpose. See L. F. Renehan, *Collections on Irish church history*, ed. D. MacCarthy, i (Dublin, 1861), p. 25.

ordained and educated abroad, and the novitiate at Capranica was thus of great importance.

The Dominican foundations were Holy Cross, Louvain (1624, reorganised in the troubled fifties by Canon Gregory Joyce), Corpo Santo, Lisbon (organised by Daniel O'Daly in 1634) and San Clemente, Rome (acquired in 1667). Holy Cross, like St Anthony's, was a college of Louvain university. Corpo Santo, a *studium generale*, sent many missionaries to Ireland and was proud of its reputation as a 'seminary of martyrs'. At Bilbao the Dominicans maintained a lodging for friars *en route* to and from Ireland.

The founder of the Irish Capuchin mission was Francis Lavalin Nugent (1569–1635),[1] son of Sir Thomas Nugent of Moyrath castle, and cousin of Christopher Cusack. Fr Francis at first relied upon Cusack's colleges in the Netherlands for recruits; he then (1610) established a secular college at Lille, coming to an agreement with Cusack that the Capuchins should have control and that men from Meath and Leinster only should be admitted. In spite of Augustinian attempts to gain control and of other attempts to change the constitution of the college, these conditions were maintained until its suppression in 1793. Lille accommodated thirty students during its peak in the 1630s, the boys going for classes in the humanities to the local Jesuit college. Many went on to the friary of Charleville, in the Ardennes, which Nugent with the help of noble patrons established in 1615 for clerical studies. The Irish Capuchins thus grew in number: in 1640 there were fifty-eight, of whom at least twenty-six were Lille men.

In 1639 Nugent founded a friary at Sedan, under Propaganda, part mission-centre among the Calvinists, part training-ground for the Irish friars. He also founded a very successful Capuchin mission at Cologne for the Rhineland, but he failed in his other object of setting up another training-centre there for the Irish Capuchin mission. In 1685, Louis XIV gave the friaries at Sedan and Charleville, which were located in strategically important areas, to the French Capuchins, and gave the Irish in exchange the friaries of Bar-sur-Aube and Wassy, in Champagne.

Not a few regular houses failed, but whether able to establish houses of their own or not, the Irish religious were revitalised by the reform movement common to a number of orders in the late sixteenth and early seventeenth centuries. This movement was particularly strong in Spain, producing the Cistercian reformed congregation of Castile, the Discalced (Teresian) Carmelite reform and the Dominican renewal, and giving impetus to the later Strict Observance (which began in Clairvaux in 1615). Irish Cistercians were trained in the reformed monasteries in Castile (Salamanca, Matallana, and Palazuelos) and León (Nogales or Nucale); others went to Paris or Louvain. The Teresian reform trained Irishmen too, and the Teresians

[1] See F. X. Martin, *Friar Nugent: a study of Francis Lavalin Nugent (1569–1635), agent of the counter-reformation* (London and Rome, 1962).

founded a college at Louvain for the missions to England, Scotland, Ireland, and Holland. The Cistercians, like the Jesuits, remained few in number; the order sought mature candidates and recruited a high proportion of secular priests. Early in the seventeenth century men like Candidus Furlong, O. Cist., of Wexford, and Stephen Browne, O. Carm., of Dublin, were leading pioneer groups of missioners home. The Canons Regular of St Augustine were able to form a new congregation in the confederate period.

If the story of Irish priests abroad in the sixteenth and seventeenth centuries contains many gaps, that of nuns has hardly been investigated at all. One catches glimpses of individuals, such as those in Spanish convents whose names O'Sullivan records, or even of groups, such as the one which Fr Henry Fitzsimon was planning to take abroad in 1598. There must have been many others, whose names may never be traced. The first Irish foundation was probably at Dunkirk (1626); this Colettine Poor Clare group moved to Dublin a few years later, with Cicely Dillon as prioress. In 1639 Dominic O'Daly founded the Irish Dominican convent of Bom Successo at Belém, in Portugal. The convent, which soon housed forty sisters, was well provided for by Doña Irene de Britto, countess de Atalaya. In the beginning it was contemplative and extremely rigorous, but in time the rigour was modified and the convent adopted the active life.

Nuns too were victims of the Cromwellian persecution. The majority of the Poor Clares went into exile, most of them to be maintained in Spanish convents by Philip IV. Mother Catherine Bernard Browne, of Galway, who died in the Poor Clare convent, Cavallero de Garcia, Madrid, in 1654, was reputedly a saint. A group of six Irish Poor Clares, after many travels, were able, with the assistance of Father Raymond Caron, to make a foundation at Dieppe. There five of them ended their days. In 1652 the sisters of the Dominican convent at Galway, founded in 1644, were also forced into exile in Spain. Most of the thirty or forty Tertiary Sisters of Saint Francis, distributed in five houses in Ireland in 1644, also probably fled abroad. We hear of two of these nuns, from Kilkenny, whose death sentence was commuted to exile, and of eight nuns from one house, led by their superioress, Sister Marie-Baptiste, who were driven into exile in Nantes, in 1650. The likelihood is that they had originally come from Nantes to Ireland.

The Irish Dames of Ypres were an offshoot of the English Benedictines. A house founded at Ypres from Ghent about 1665 had a difficult start, but two Irish nuns, Dames Alexia Mary Legge and Mary Joseph Ryan, went to Ireland in 1681 and gathered postulants and financial aid. The convent then in 1682 became an Irish one, with Dame Flavia Cary as first abbess.[1] Among others associated with the foundation were Dame Mary Christina White, only daughter of Sir Andrew White, Count d'Albie, and niece of Sir Ignatius

[1] Was she one of the four daughters of Viscount Falkland who became Benedictine nuns at Cambrai? See G. C. Fullerton, *The life of Elizabeth, Lady Falkland, 1585–1639* (1883).

White, marquis d'Albeville,[1] and Dame Mary Joseph Butler of Callan (1641–1723), Ormond's cousin.

The return of the foreign-trained priests was causing concern to the government by the last quarter of the sixteenth century; and from about 1590 the seminaries were providing a steady supply. During the quarter-century 1590–1615, we have the names of over 500 priests trained in four of the seminaries, and perhaps the total number of those ordained abroad, secular and regular, in the period would amount to double that figure. This gives an average of forty priests at most returning home each year in this vital period. Numbers varied a great deal, but of the secular colleges it can be said that Alcalá, Lisbon, Santiago, Seville, Antwerp, Tournai, Louvain, and Rome were small institutions, each sending home perhaps two to five priests a year. Salamanca, Douai, Bordeaux, and Toulouse were rather larger. Of the priests trained at Salamanca, 68 seculars were at work in Ireland in 1611, while 80 had joined the religious orders. Douai by 1613 had sent home 149 priests. Larger again were Paris, which in the 1670s housed perhaps 100 students and in 1689 had 180, and Nantes, which began with 30 or 40. The regular colleges were also generally small, but St Anthony's had 43 students in 1681 and Holy Cross 40.

All in all, these foreign-trained priests—'seminary priests' or 'Jesuits', as they were indiscriminately called by the Elizabethans and early Stuart officials[2]—formed an extremely important proportion of the total in sixteenth- and seventeenth-century Ireland. The proportion probably lessened as time went on. In 1612 there were 800 diocesan priests, most of them trained in the Irish colleges.[3] But of the 1,088 (or 1,089) registered priests in 1704, only 253 had been educated on the Continent. Doubtless—as Archbishop Brenan noted more than once—some preferred the comfort of the Continent to the trials of the home mission. But the evidence that the majority did in fact return home and that their labour was decisive in checking the reformation in Ireland is compelling. Receiving from the universities of Spain and the Low Countries and from the Jesuit colleges a formation that made them clearly aware (as training at home could not have done) of the issues raised by the reform, inspired by the chivalric and crusading ideals of Spain, vigorously tridentine in spirit—John Lynch recalled vividly, sixty years after, the sermons which Father Eugene MacDermot, home from Spain, had preached in Galway, urging frequent confession and communion—and encouraged by the fortitude of those of their number who had gained a martyr's crown, these priests stood in marked contrast to the preachers of reform, so that, as Spenser noted in a famous passage, it was

[1] See above, p. 607.

[2] In the Irish (as distinct from the English) context, 'seminary priests' and 'Jesuits' were convenient labels to distinguish seculars and regulars ordained abroad from 'massing-priests'.

[3] Bentivoglio to Paul V, 6 Apr. 1613 (*Archiv. Hib.*, xxiii (1960), pp 29–30).

great wonder to see the odds which is between the zeal of popish priests and the ministers of the gospel; for they spare not to come out of Spain, from Rome, from Rheims, by long toil and dangerous travel hither, where they know peril of death awaiteth them and no reward nor riches. . . .[1]

In the latter part of Elizabeth's reign the 'seminary priests', braving prerogative acts and martial law and providing in their colleges an alternative to the new challenge at Trinity College, Dublin, stiffened the resistance of the Irish to reform; and in the following generation they confirmed their people in the Roman obedience.

Adventure, hardship, and danger were the common lot of those students who took the road to the Continent. Catholic gentry, townspeople, and merchants all cooperated in conveying the young men to France, Flanders, Spain, Italy, and elsewhere, and home again, in defiance of the law. If his way was not paid, the student might ship as a merchant's clerk or work his way as a sailor; or he might take ship in a smuggler or fishing craft. In 1624 Father John de la Roche, O.P., borrowed 100 ducats from Father Conway, S.J., and set out from Cadiz four times for Ireland, but each time was forced back by storm. Overcome no doubt by hardship, the young priest died in Cadiz.[2] Following a general custom, young Thomas Mulcloye of Meath went north in 1599 to seek aid to go abroad. Eventually Hugh O'Neill gave him letters to get shipping from Scotland to France. After all this he was captured, but in the end he did get to Douai and then to Salamanca. Showing if possible even more resolution, Christopher Roche of Wexford wandered eight years (1583–91) through France, Flanders, and Lorraine, supporting himself by such jobs as that of porter in a college and tutoring, and acquiring what education he could in a number of colleges.[3]

Once admitted to a college, the student generally took three oaths: (1) to take holy orders and return to the mission whenever the superior of the college ordered; (2) to recoup the college in the event of his not doing so; (3) to observe the rules. In Seville, he swore as well, if a priest, to say his masses while a student for the intention of the rector and to defend to the death the doctrine of the immaculate conception. The students might be ordained in virtue of their acceptance for the Irish mission, on the nomination of the rector of their college, without the need of a recommendation from any bishop in Ireland. This was a privilege granted to the colleges by a brief of Paul V, secured in 1614 by Archbishop Lombard,[4] and confirmed

1 Spenser, *View*, ed. W. L. Renwick (Oxford, 1970), p. 162.

2 Memorial by Fr Richard Conway, S.J., to council of state, Madrid, 12 Jan. 1628 (A.G.S., Estado 2752).

3 *Cal. S.P. Ire., 1588–92*, pp 455–6, quoted in John Brady, 'Father Christopher Cusack and the Irish College of Douai, 1594–1623' in Sylvester O'Brien, ed., *Measgra i gcuimhne Mhichíl Uí Chléirigh* (Dublin, 1944), p. 98. See also A. S. Green, *The making of Ireland and its undoing, 1200–1600* (1908), pp 442–3.

4 Peter Lombard. *De regno Hiberniae . . . commentarius*, ed. P. F. Moran (Dublin, 1868), pp xlii–xliii.

by a bull of Urban VIII, *Piis Christifidelium* (15 July 1626 N.S.). While this arrangement emphasised the missionary character of Ireland in the sixteenth and seventeenth centuries, it added to the difficulty of implementing the tridentine legislation. Gradually a system evolved whereby students were divided in financial terms into three classes: pensioners, who paid their own way or were maintained by their friends; recipients of burses; and students maintained at the expense of their colleges.[1] John Lynch of Galway, when a pensioner at Douai, studying humanities in 1620, found his allowance from home delayed, and was tided over his period of difficulty by Fr William Tyrrey, of Cork, professor of theology, who remembered the old friendship between Cork and Galway.[2]

Until 1641 the catholic gentry sent their sons to the catholic universities or to the less expensive Irish colleges. As a result of the mid-century confiscations, they found it more difficult to do so, especially in Ulster, where very few of the catholic gentry recovered anything of their estates. In 1660 a provincial synod of Armagh decreed that financial aid should be given for the education of students in the colleges abroad from the province,[3] but with an impoverished laity the money could not be found. Higher education was now more difficult for both clergy and laity. A number of priests had always been ordained on the understanding that they should go abroad for education. This served three purposes: it enabled the priest-students to maintain themselves by fees received for performing clerical functions; it saved them from being penalised under an English statute of 1585 against supporting foreign seminaries and a proclamation of 1605, repeated in 1611, expelling Jesuits and seminary priests from Ireland; and it avoided the danger that the young man would enter one of the professions abroad. Now ordinations at home became more common, but, as Archbishop Brenan observed, the priests did not always fulfil the obligation of going abroad, and when they went they did not always return home.

The students were supported in various ways. But if sources of revenue were numerous, they were also uncertain, and financial embarrassment was the usual lot of the colleges. Many Irishmen were exempted from matriculation fees and other expenses at the universities, enjoying the privileges of *pauperes*. In Spanish territories royal assistance was by way of endowments, annual grants (when paid), and from the time of Philip III a travelling-allowance of 100 ducats (about £20) to each student returning home upon completion of his studies. This 'viaticum', covering the costs of a disguise of Irish secular dress and passage home, was already customary by 1621.[4] The

[1] C. Giblin, 'Irish exiles in catholic Europe' in Corish, *Ir. catholicism*, iv, ch. 3, p. 11.

[2] John Lynch, *De praesulibus Hib.*, ii, 148.

[3] Moran, *Spicil. Ossor*, ii, 200.

[4] See, for example, Council of state, *consulta de parte*, 9 June 1621, concerning requests for viaticum by Father Conway, S.J., rector of Irish College, Seville, for three priests, William Supple, Thomas French, and Daniel Bruodin (A.G.S., Estado 2751). A *consulta de parte* of 5 Mar. 1630

Spanish kings also gave extraordinary grants to students of gentle birth. Father Philip O'Sullivan More, of Dunkerron, enjoyed a grant of 100 ducats a year from 1620 until his death in Seville College in 1625, and in 1628 Father Thady Conway, also at Seville, successfully petitioned that this grant be paid to him.[1]

The Irish College at Paris was granted the right to hold property rights by both Louis XIII and Louis XIV, and Anne of Austria endowed the colleges at Bordeaux and Toulouse each with 1,200 livres a year and also granted their students naturalisation privileges, so that they could receive gifts and possess benefices. As one result of these privileges, many Irish priests stayed on in the Gironde after 1685, at first temporarily, then permanently.

The holy see from its own resources was able at times to give financial assistance to the colleges. Ireland came under the Congregation of Propaganda, founded in January 1622 (N.S), and thereafter papal help became more regular.[2] Many European nobles, bishops, clergy, and laity of means were benefactors of the colleges. Alcalá owed its foundation to Count Jorge de Paz y Sylveira, and the Irish College, Rome, to Cardinal Ludovisi, protector of Ireland. Cardinal Sourdis assisted in the foundation of the Bordeaux college, and Saint-Just, president of the *parlement* of Paris, in that of the Paris college. The duke of Nevers built Nugent's friary and church at Charleville at very substantial cost. Benefactions took many forms, donations, grants of bonds or property which provided for rents and burses, offerings of their catch by fishermen, allowed by indult to go fishing on Sundays for the purpose, or travelling allowances. The cathedral chapter in Seville regularly gave a grant of 100 ducats each to priests, secular and regular, returning home from that city, besides giving an annual grant of 100 ducats each to the English and Irish colleges. Benefactors generally stipulated that masses be said for their intentions.

The original purpose of the colleges was to provide diocesan clergy, together with an educated laity, but from the very beginning the various religious orders used them as recruiting-grounds. Because of the lack of novitiates in England and Germany, the Jesuits and others made similar use of the English and German colleges in Rome. Originally too there was a preponderance of Old English students. Then the presence in the Spanish dominions, after Kinsale and the flight of the earls, of so many Old Irish,

grants to Nicholas Devereux the 100 ducats which it is customary to give to the priests returning home to Ireland *que los abran menester para su viaje y mudar de hauito, a viso de su Patria por no ser conocido* (A.G.S., Estado 2757).

[1] Memorial by Don Tadeo Combeo to council of state, Madrid, 12 Jan. 1628 (A.G.S., Estado 2755).

[2] Apportionment of papal grants often caused dissension between college and college, and between Irish and English colleges; see Guilday, *English catholic refugees on the Continent*, p. 33.

their patronage by the Spanish crown and the archdukes, their contact with the counter-reformation as exemplified by Spain—Oliver Plunkett said later of the Irish students returning from Spain, 'they could speak of nothing but Spain, *totam spirabant Hispaniam*'—all combined to make the Old Irish demand a greater share of the places in the colleges, as of patronage over episcopal appointments. A meeting of the Irish clergy in Tournai in 1607 agreed that Douai and Antwerp would grant eight or nine places, normally occupied by students from Leinster to natives of other provinces.

The regulars vied with each other for recruits from the colleges. The Irish Franciscans, much to their annoyance, lost control of the Ludovisian College at Rome a few years after its foundation; many of the students here, said Archbishop Plunkett, became Jesuits and never returned to Ireland. It was borne in upon Rome that secular control of the colleges made for both lack of stability and racial disputes—for example, the election of rectors at Bordeaux, Toulouse, and Alcalá by the students led to intermittent provincial rivalry—but both Lombard and Plunkett objected to Jesuit control. The Observants, particularly Franciscans, looked with disfavour upon the new orders, Jesuits, Capuchins, and Discalced Carmelites, as journeymen come late to the harvest. Where Jesuit control meant that the superiors were not Irish, there was often an added cause for friction. At Seville, for instance, when a Spanish rector succeeded an Irishman, the students in 1630 complained to Cardinal Ludovisi that he provided for only a dozen students, whereas a few years previously an Irish Jesuit rector had maintained twice that number.[1]

Meanwhile provincialism was everywhere apparent. Alcalá was founded for Ulstermen alone; Bordeaux and Toulouse were preponderantly associated with Munster dioceses. Fr Nugent founded Lille college in 1610 exclusively for students from the dioceses of Meath and Leinster and succeeded in maintaining this college's exclusive character against all opposition. Laurence Sedgrave gave preference to Leinstermen at Antwerp.[2] In 1625 the rector of the Sorbonne had to complain that Thomas Messingham maintained only Meath men, except three, at Paris. Within the Franciscan order there was a struggle for control of colleges, almost from the time of foundation of their first college at Louvain. Meath Franciscans tried hard, but without success, to gain control of this college. The Old English were more successful in the case of Prague; Father Patrick Fleming, the first superior there, and most of his associates, were Leinstermen. A group, mainly Old Irish, the Aracoelitani,[3] at Rome, fought a long and not too principled battle to oust Wadding from control of St Isidore's. The Dominicans also had to yield to provincial feeling in the rotation of offices. The colleges

[1] *Wadding papers*, p. 353.

[2] *Archiv. Hib.*, xvi (1951), p. 15.

[3] So called, because they lived at the Franciscan mother-house, S. Maria d'Aracoeli.

generally sought to make students proficient in English, Irish, Latin, and one or more of the continental languages, and in 1650 Propaganda made a knowledge of Irish mandatory for all students for the Irish priesthood except for those of the English-speaking areas of Leinster.[1]

The problem of provincialism was never resolved in the seventeenth and eighteenth centuries. During the seventeenth century generally in the colleges, both secular and regular, the system was evolved whereby offices were alternated between the provinces and a fixed number of student places was allocated to each province. This system, and the bitterness it engendered whenever one group was thought to be getting more than its fair share, persisted.

Provincial these priests in exile might at times be. But in the religious struggle they generally rose above provincialism, as they did too in their literary activity. Exiles played a considerable part in Ireland's literary renaissance of the sixteenth and seventeenth centuries. Influenced by the twin forces of counter-reformation and renaissance (especially in its more religious form) a considerable number of Irishmen displayed remarkable and many-sided aptitude for doctrinal, spiritual, and even mystical writing, historical, catechetical and even humanistic studies.

One of these was Archbishop Lombard, who for quarter of a century combined the roles of diplomat and leading theologian at the papal court. From 1602 until 1607 he was chief episcopal theologian in the congregation *de auxiliis*, which sought to judge between the Molinist and Thomist views of the action of grace. For that most important period, the first quarter of the seventeenth century, he was leading adviser at the Roman court on Irish affairs. His pastoral interest in Ireland made him devote himself to enforcing the tridentine legislation there, to securing the appointment of bishops both worthy and acceptable to the crown and to ensuring the success of the seminaries. Called into consultation by the holy office, about 1615, on the Wisbeach 'stirs' in England, he seized the opportunity to elaborate a theological formula whereby catholics could accept a heretical monarch (James I) as their lawful sovereign. He thus broke through the barrier of a juridical tradition that had defeated the Jesuit 'hard-liners', Bellarmine, Suarez, and Persons. He contributed towards a changing climate in church–state relations, his work having, for example, some bearing on Rome's willingness to accept first the anticipated Anglo-Spanish match and later the union between Charles I and Henrietta Maria. As chief consultor to the holy office he was mainly responsible for the adverse opinion on the heliocentric theory (1616). In this action, so unfortunate in its consequences, Lombard was unable to give the matter in question due consideration. He later made amends by a closely reasoned opinion in favour of Roberto

[1] Archiv. Propaganda Fide, Atti, 1648–50, x, no. 23.

de Nobili, which, as incorporated in Gregory XV's epoch-making bull, *Romanae sedis antistes* (1623), still stands as an authoritative expression of Rome's respect for non-Christian culture.

The talented Franciscans, Conry and Wadding, were, like Lombard, men of far-ranging interests and activities. Theologian, poet, historian, and linguist, Wadding was one of Europe's leading scholars. He was a member of various Roman congregations, holy office, index, and others, and while it may be too much to say with Renehan that 'the Irish bishops from 1624 to 1646 were nominated by Wadding',[1] he did have great influence upon the whole field of Irish politico-religious affairs between 1625 and 1652.

Somewhat like Lombard and Wadding, Francis Nugent[2] found that he could be of greatest service to the Irish church by working on the Continent; like them too he played a significant part, although of a different kind, in European religious affairs. Not only in the Rhineland and in his order's Belgic province, but also in Germany and Switzerland he played a very effective missionary role. He was a man of mystical experience, in the tradition of the Low Countries, like Benet of Canfield, and he and his companions brought to the Rhineland a revival of mysticism.

Other prominent Franciscans were Denis O'Driscoll of Castlehaven, archbishop of Brindisi (1640–50), and Raymond Caron, a pioneer in missiology. MacCaghwell reanimated the Franciscan intellectual life in Paris, and Hugh Burke revised studies in the Franciscan province of Aquitaine and later reorganised the Germanic provinces of his order after the disasters of the thirty years war. Two Augustinians who performed similar services for the Austrian provinces of their order were Nicholas Donnellan (*c.* 1610–79), who became vicar general there, and Mark Forstall, who was provincial before Leopold I secured for him the bishopric of Kildare in 1676. Augustine Gibbon Burke (1613–76) was a celebrated professor at Luther's old university of Erfurt. The contribution to contemporary theology of this last of the 'old Augustinian school', soon to give way to that established by Noris, is discussed elsewhere.[3] Conscious of his position as vicar-general of Luther's province, his position was clear but eirenic.

Prominent Dominican theologians were James Arthur of Limerick (d. 1670?), who professed at Coimbra; John Baptist Hackett; Peter Garravan, in Bohemia; and Dominic Lynch of County Galway (d. 1697?), who became rector of the University of Paris. Among Jesuit scholars, Stephen White, professor of theology at Dillingen, was much admired by Ussher for his knowledge of Irish and other antiquities. He collaborated with his confrere, William Bathe, in *Janua linguarum* (Salamanca, 1611), a pioneer work in the scientific

[1] L. F. Renehan, *Collections on Irish church history* (Dublin, 1874), ii, 8, quoted in G. Cleary, *Father Luke Wadding and St Isidore's College, Rome* (Rome, 1925), p. 49; see *Father Luke Wadding*, p. 32.

[2] See above, p. 622.

[3] See above, ch. XXII.

teaching of languages.[1] Richard Archdekin of Kilkenny wrote a treatise on miracles (1667), 'said to be the first book printed in English and Irish conjointly';[2] his *Theologia tripartita* (Antwerp, 1671, etc.), devoted to controversy, was widely used in the schools and ran to many editions. An older Jesuit, Peter Wadding, was successively chancellor of the universities of Prague and Gratz.

During the seventeenth century Irish secular priests commonly held professorships of theology in the constituent colleges of the Sorbonne and at least one of the regius chairs of theology. They also generally held the procuratorship of the German nation, one of the four sections into which the faculty of arts in Paris was divided. Malachy O'Queely, for instance, held this office in 1618, 1620, and 1621. Hugh Brady was (semestral) 'rector magnificus' of Louvain in 1661, and was succeeded by Thomas Stapleton of Fethard, an alumnus of the Pastoral College of Louvain, who held the office ten times between 1661 and his death in 1694. John O'Sullivan of Dunkerron was 'rector magnificus' in 1690. An influential, if very controversial, professor at Louvain was Dr Francis Martin of Galway (1652–1722).

Irish members of several religious orders trained on the Continent engaged in mission work in Scotland. The Franciscans conducted from Louvain a very successful mission between 1619 and 1650; the Vincentians, who came to Ireland about 1640, undertook a mission to Scotland ten years later. Irish Dominicans were involved not only in Scotland but also in England, Germany, Bohemia, and Tangier, where they had charge of the house of their order between 1666 and 1681. Father Peter French, O.P., spent thirty years on the mission in Mexico and elsewhere in the New World and wrote a catechism for the Indians in their own tongue.

The first Irish priest in the New World was perhaps Fr Achilles Holden, who was teaching in the cathedral school of Santo Domingo, in the West Indies, at the early date of 1525. Thomas Field (Fihilly), S.J., of Limerick (1542–1626), spent many years in the vast mission-field of Paraguay. The first Irish priest to serve in what is now the United States was Richard Arthur, who came as pastor to St Augustine in 1597 and was appointed by the bishop of Santiago de Cuba as vicar-general for the whole province of Florida. Father Michael Wadding (Godínez), who was related to Luke Wadding, spent the years from 1610 until his death (1644) in Mexico and earned a great reputation for missionary zeal, learning, and mysticism. In 1637 Archbishop O'Queely, of Tuam, sent two priests to the West Indies. Father John Stritch, S.J., conducted a successful mission to the Leeward Islands (1650–60); he was followed there by Father John Grace, of the

[1] Bathe's interesting theories are commented upon in Silke, 'Irish scholarship and the renaissance, 1580–1673' in *Studies in the renaissance*, xx (1973), 203–5.

[2] Webb, *Ir. biog.*, p. 5. The Irish version was really the Franciscan John Dowley's *Suim bhunadhasach an teagaisc críosdaidhe* (Louvain, 1663).

diocese of Cashel.[1] Christopher Bathe, S.J., went from Liège to St Christopher in 1652.

The Irish priests and friars on the Continent were foremost in preserving the national literature and antiquities and in defending Irish culture. Stephen White, S.J., Peter Lombard, and the layman Philip O'Sullivan Beare were among those who wrote in defence of Ireland. From the Irish fount cut at St Anthony's, Louvain, in 1611 came devotional works such as MacCaghwell's treatise on penance (1619), catechisms such as O'Hosey's pioneer *Teagasc críosdaidhe*, and grammars. But the great work associated with St Anthony's was that in Irish history and hagiography. It took the lead here, as did St Isidore's in philosophy and theology, the two between them forming the counterpart of the English College, Douai, in scholarship.

Among other exiles writing historical works, John Lynch's *De praesulibus Hiberniae* (1672) remained in manuscript, but his elegant life of his uncle, Bishop Kirwan, was published at St Malo in 1669. Francis Nugent's influence can be seen in the work on Capuchin historiography of Nicholas Archbold (1589–1650), Robert O'Connell (*c.* 1623–78), and Bonaventure Donnelly (1661–1775). O'Connell's Latin manuscript history of the Irish Capuchin mission between 1591 and 1653 has been described as a landmark in Irish historiography for its critical acumen and skill in interpretation.[2] O'Connell was co-author with Richard O'Ferrall of another monumental and critical work, though exhibiting its own particular bias, *Commentarius Rinuccinianus*.

Lombard, Conry, and Wadding were all immersed in the bitter controversies of the day over the doctrine of grace. Conry, who during sixteen years' study read Augustine's whole works ten times, was, perhaps without exaggeration, called by Peter Walsh 'the greatest Augustinian of the age'.[3] For Pascal he was foremost among the forerunners of the seventeenth-century defenders of Augustine. Lombard, in the Roman congregation *de auxiliis*, consistently opposed the propositions of the Jesuit Molina.[4] Lombard, Conry, and Wadding, together with John Barnewall, O.F.M., a disciple of Conry, and Hugh Burke, all favoured the stricter Augustinian-Thomistic interpretation of the action of grace against the more lenient Jesuit view, which to them was a recrudescence of semi-Pelagianism. They held to the traditions of Louvain university, but also felt that Ireland was endangered unless a strict orthodoxy was maintained. Conry and Jansen took opposite sides, but Jansen's denial of free will was not apparent at once even

[1] The writer was informed by P. José Castro Seoane, O. de M., in 1957, that he had seen records of Irish priests going from Seville to the mission in the New World, in the Archivo General de Indias, in Seville, but to date this source has not been investigated.

[2] F. X. Martin, 'Sources for the history of the Irish Capuchins' in *Collectanea Franciscana*, xxvi (1956), p. 73.

[3] Peter Walsh, *The history and vindication of the loyal formulary or Irish remonstrance* (1674), quoted in *Father Luke Wadding*, p. 312.

[4] Augustine Leblanc (pseud. of J. H. Serry, O.P.), *Historia congregationum de auxiliis . . . libri quatuor* (Antwerp, 1709), cols 291–506.

to such a sharp critic as Wadding. However, both Wadding and Burke accepted without qualification Urban VIII's condemnation of Jansen's *Augustinus*.

The Jansenists were now forced to declare themselves. John Sinnich (1603–66), a Cork priest, had, like Lombard before him, a brilliant career at Louvain, becoming semestral rector in 1643, and again in 1660. He compiled the index to *Augustinus*, and his *Augustini Hipponensis et Augustini Iprensis . . . homologia* (Louvain, 1641) tried to establish that there was total conformity between Jansen and the 'doctor of grace'. Jansen's *Augustinus* was, however, condemned at Rome. As delegate of the University of Louvain at Rome (1643–5), Sinnich sought to have this work, in defence of which he wrote several books, cleared from censure. Though his writings leave him open to suspicion of Jansenism, he died at peace with the church. In 1652 the Jansenists reprinted Conry's *De statu parvulorum*,[1] as an appendix to the new edition of the *Augustinus*, in an effort to show identity of doctrine between him and Jansen.

When the controversy spread to Paris, the university, and especially its Irishmen, divided sharply. John Callaghan's defence of Jansenism provoked an Irish answer: in February 1651 twenty-seven young Irish priests led by Father Richard Nugent, of Cloyne, published the 'Declaration of the Irish against Jansenism', condemning the five propositions. They were perhaps inspired by M. Vincent himself, who hoped to flush out the Jansenists. If so, he succeeded. In the ensuing storm, the Irish were supported by the faculty of theology, especially by the syndic, François Hallier, but were opposed by the rector, Jean Courtin, a Jansenist, and his supporters in the assembly of the university. They were also opposed by some of their Jansenist compatriots, notably Dr Philip O'Lonergan, of the faculty of theology, who claimed Lombard for the Jansenist cause; Dr Clonsinnil, in his *Défense des Hibernois* (Paris, 1651); and the turbulent Callaghan, who was lionised by Port-Royal and who for some years carried on a controversy with Père Jean Brisacier, S.J., the vehement anti-Jansenist from Blois, at the same time that he was vigorously defending the Ormondist position against Punch. It was as a contemporary wrote, *une dispute en règle*, *un choc opiniâtre*,[2] an Irish broil. Calm came at last, and in the 1680s a turn in the tide of Irish opinion was apparent, when two Franciscans, Patrick Duffy, professor at St Anthony's, and Francis Porter, at St Isidore's, distinguished themselves as anti-Jansenists, working for a condemnation of Jansenist propositions at Rome.

[1] Lucien Ceyssens, 'Florence Conry, Hugh de Burgo, Luke Wadding, and Jansenism' in *Father Luke Wadding*, pp 329–30, 351–2.

[2] Quoted in P. Boyle, *The Irish college in Paris, 1578–1901* (1901), p. xi.

BIBLIOGRAPHY

J. G. SIMMS

INTRODUCTION

HITHERTO the only extended treatment of early modern Ireland has been the work of Richard Bagwell (*Ireland under the Tudors*, 3 vols, 1885–90; *Ireland under the Stuarts*, 3 vols, 1909–16). Bagwell was a careful and conscientious writer who made thorough use of the printed sources available to him for the production of a narrative that leaned heavily towards the political, administrative, and military aspects of history. His use of manuscript sources was very limited, but he consulted the state papers in the London Public Record Office, particularly for the middle years of the sixteenth century, for which the printed calendars are seriously inadequate; he also made some use of the Carte manuscripts in the Bodleian Library at Oxford for his treatment of Ormond's administration.

Even at the start of Bagwell's work, and still more so at its conclusion, there was a very considerable body of printed sources on which he could draw. The largest single source was the calendars of English state papers, which covered almost the whole period; their value was greatly increased by the much fuller scale of treatment given to the seventeenth century. Contemporary histories, from the Irish as well as from the English side, were available for parts of the period. Richard Stanihurst represented the Anglo-Irish viewpoint; the Four Masters, whose work Bagwell could consult in John O'Donovan's translation, were passing from bare chronicle to narrative history as they approached their own day. Apart from translations of Annals Bagwell made no use of sources in Irish. Several English Elizabethans, among them Edmund Campion, wrote histories of which editions were subsequently printed. In the seventeenth century the periods of the civil and confederate wars and of the Williamite revolution were the subject of much writing, narrative and polemical, in both England and Ireland. A feature of the Irish writing on these periods was that rival versions were available from the Old English and Gaelic Irish sides. For the confederate war Bagwell could make use of the two multi-volume editions by J. T. Gilbert; for the revolution there were Gilbert's and O'Callaghan's respective editions of the manuscripts known as 'A light to the blind' and 'The destruction of Cyprus'. Eighteenth-century works such as Knowler's edition of Strafford's letters and Carte's life of Ormond made available much material for important periods of seventeenth-century history. The work of antiquaries such as Walter Harris and the members of the Irish Archaeological Society resulted in the publication of many tracts, mostly on the Anglo-Irish or English side.

Robert Dunlop was a Scot who worked for many years in England on Irish history of the sixteenth and seventeenth centuries. His study of the plantation in Munster was published in the *English Historical Review* in 1888; and his *Ireland under the commonwealth*, a valuable collection of documents, many of them transcribed from manuscripts since destroyed, appeared in 1913, accompanied by a masterly introduction. Dunlop's skill and judgement in the interpretation of the period were displayed in the narrative chapters that he contributed to the third, fourth, and fifth volumes of the *Cambridge modern history* (1905–8). He was also the compiler of the bibliographies for Irish history in those volumes. They show that he cast his net wider than did Bagwell; he gives some account of manuscript sources, and he lists books and tracts published on the Continent.

During the sixty years that followed the completion of Bagwell's work there have been great changes in the range of sources available for Irish historiography of the sixteenth and seventeenth centuries. The first change was, unfortunately, the disastrous destruction of the Public Record Office in Dublin in 1922, which obliterated a great mass of political, administrative, and personal records. These documents had not, except to a very limited degree, been made use of by previous historians, although successive deputy keepers of the records had summarised many of them in their reports.

The formation of the Irish Manuscripts Commission in 1928 has led to the publication of a large body of important source-material for the period. For the sixteenth century they include such publications as *Sidney state papers, 1565–70*, *The Walsingham letter-book*, and *The compossicion booke of Conought*. Among seventeenth-century sources may be mentioned the six-volume edition of the *Commentarius Rinuccinianus*, which is a major source for the confederate war; Dr R. C. Simington's editions of the Civil Survey and of four of the Books of Survey and Distribution, which are invaluable for the study of the land and its settlement; numerous reports of family documents, such as the *Orrery papers* and *Inchiquin manuscripts*. The Public Record Office of Northern Ireland has also rendered exemplary service in preserving and cataloguing many documents in private custody.

The establishment of the School of Celtic Studies as part of the Institute for Advanced Studies in Dublin has led to the editing of many works in Irish, which have proved to be important sources for the Gaelic aspects of the history of the period. This field has also been greatly enlarged by the work of the Irish Texts Society, notably by the publication of such works as *The bardic poems of Tadhg Dall Ó Huiginn* and *The poems of David Ó Bruadair*.

A marked feature of the sixteenth and seventeenth centuries was the creation of links between Ireland and the continent of Europe. These links—ecclesiastical, military, and commercial—produced a large mass of manuscript records and correspondence which have been preserved in repositories in various countries of western Europe. A great deal of work has been done in the last half-century to examine and record such material, particularly by Franciscans and members of other religious orders. Much of this material has been microfilmed for the National Library of Ireland: a magnificent guide to it is *The manuscript sources of Irish civilisation*, the work of the former director of the library, R. J. Hayes. Much of the ecclesiastical material has been edited in such publications as *Collectanea Hibernica*, published by the Franciscans of Killiney, County Dublin, and *Archivium Hibernicum*, a publication of the Catholic Record Society of Ireland. For the political and military activities of Irishmen abroad in the sixteenth and seventeenth centuries, Paris, Brussels, and Simancas are the richest sources.

The advance achieved in making sources known and available for research has been matched by a greatly increased production of learned articles and books. Many new societies, both national and local, have been established, with journals carrying a wide variety of articles, some of them of high quality. In particular, the Irish Historical Society and the Ulster Society for Irish Historical Studies, with their joint journal *Irish Historical Studies* (1938–), have promoted the development of a school of historians committed to the study of Irish history in a broader and less nationalistic spirit than was common among their predecessors, and in accordance with professional standards previously lacking. Most of the new work has been published in article form, but while substantial books on the period have been comparatively few, some of them have been of very high quality.

The bibliography of early modern Ireland has been well served by the Oxford bibliographies of British history for the Tudor and Stuart periods (edited by Conyers Read and Godfrey Davies), each of which has gone into a second edition with a greatly expanded Irish section that owes much to the zeal of R. Dudley Edwards. Books and articles published since 1936 have been systematically recorded by *Irish Historical Studies* in the series 'Writings on Irish history'. The most significant developments in the historiography of the sixteenth and seventeenth centuries in the years 1936–70 have been examined in chapters iii and iv of *Irish historiography, 1936–70*, edited by T. W. Moody (Dublin, 1971).

This bibliography is organised in accordance with a plan laid down by the editors, and has been executed in consultation with them. Dr R. F. Foster gave valuable help in the initial assembling of material, much of which is derived from 'Writings on Irish history', mentioned above. The contributors also supplied lists, which have been indispensable.

The bibliography is designed to include not only the materials used in the writing of this volume but also the principal sources and works available for further study of, and research on, early modern Ireland. Individual manuscripts and collections are not listed, but the major repositories of relevant manuscript material are specified. Material on the visual arts and on music will be included in the bibliographies to volumes II and IV, where the treatment of these topics covers the early modern period.

CONTENTS

Except for special reasons, items that relate to more than two of the seven volumes comprising the text of this history are not included in the period bibliographies, but will be incorporated in the general bibliography in volume IX. For example, Edmund Curtis's *History of Ireland* will appear only in the general bibliography.

Periodicals as such are not listed, but relevant items published in periodical form are treated in the same way as separate publications. A comprehensive list of all periodicals used in this history will be included in the general bibliography. The full titles of periodicals cited in a contracted form in this bibliography are included in the key to abbreviations at the beginning of the volume; and the same applies to most other contractions used below.

The following abbreviations are also used:

ed. edited by; or, edition.
[N.D.] no date of publication given, and date not ascertained.
[N.P.] no place of publication given, and place not ascertained.
N.S. new series.

I BIBLIOGRAPHIES AND GUIDES

A BIBLIOGRAPHIES

Backer, Augustin de, Backer, Aloys de, Sommervogel, Carlos, and others. *Bibliothèque de la Compagnie de Jésus.* 12 vols. Facsimile ed., Héverlé–Louvain, 1960.

Bibliographie de la réforme, 1450–1648, ouvrages parus de 1940 à 1955. Pt ii: Belgique, Suède, Norvège, Danemark, Irlande, États-Unis d'Amérique. *Ed.* L-E. Malkin. Comité International des Sciences Historiques, Commission Internationale d'Histoire Ecclésiastique Comparée, Leiden, 1960.

Items on Ireland supplied by Aubrey Gwynn (fasc. 2, pp 51–61).

Bibliotheca catholica Neerlandica impressa, 1500–1727. The Hague, 1954.

Cambridge modern history. Vols. iii–v. Cambridge, 1905–8. Bibliographies to chapters by Robert Dunlop (see below, pp 672–3): iii (1905), pp 852–9; iv (1906), pp 913–18; v (1908), pp 829–37.

Davies, Godfrey. *Bibliography of British history: Stuart period, 1603–1714.* Royal Historical Society and American Historical Association, Oxford, 1928; 2nd ed., by M. F. Keeler, 1970.

Section XV: Ireland.

Dix, E. R. McC., and Dugan, C. W. (ed.). *Books printed in Dublin in the 17th century.* 4 parts and supplement. Dublin, 1898–1912.

Dix, E. R. McC. *The earliest Dublin printing, with lists of books, proclamations, etc., printed in Dublin prior to 1601.* Dublin, 1901; 2nd ed., retitled *Printing in Dublin prior to 1601*, Dublin, 1932.

Grose, C. L. *A select bibliography of British history, 1660–1760.* Chicago, 1939; reprinted N.Y., 1966.

Pollard, A. W., and Redgrave, G. R., and others. *A short-title catalogue of books printed in England, Scotland and Ireland, and of English books printed abroad, 1475–1640.* London, 1926; reprinted 1946.

Read, Conyers. *Bibliography of British history, Tudor period, 1485–1603.* Royal

Historical Society and American Historical Association, Oxford, 1922; 2nd ed., 1959.

Section XIII: Ireland.

Silke, J. J. Spanish intervention in Ireland, 1601–2: Spanish bibliography. In *Studia Hib.*, iii (1963), pp 179–90.

See also Silke, *Kinsale* (Liverpool, 1970), below, p. 681.

Walsh, M. O'N. Irish books printed abroad, 1475–1700. In *The Irish Book*, ii, no. 1 (1963), pp [i–viii], 1–36.

Wing, D. G. *Short-title catalogue of books printed in England, Scotland, Ireland, Wales, and British America, and of English books printed in other countries, 1641–1700*. 3 vols. N.Y., 1945–51.

Supplement on Ireland by J. E. Alden, 1955.

B GUIDES

Guides to individual collections of manuscripts are listed under their respective repositories in § II below.

Aalen, F. H. A., and Hunter, R. J. The estate maps of Trinity College: an introduction and annotated catalogue. In *Hermathena*, xcviii (1964), pp 85–96.

Andrews, J. H. *Ireland in maps*. Dublin, 1961.

—— Ireland in maps: a bibliographical postscript. In *Ir. Geography*, iv, no. 4 (1962), pp 234–43.

Burke, Bernard. The Commonwealth records. In *P.R.I. rep. D.K. 14*, pp 14–52.

Corish, P. J. Irish history and the papal archives. In *Ir. Theol. Quart.*, xxi (1954), pp 375–81.

De Brún, Pádraig. Cnuasaigh de lámhscríbhinní Gaeilge: treoirliosta. In *Studia Hib.*, vii (1967), pp 146–81.

Falley, M. D. *Irish and Scotch-Irish ancestral research: a guide to the genealogical records, methods and sources in Ireland*. 2 vols. Evanston (Ill.), 1961.

Gleeson, D. F. Sources for local history in the period 1200 to 1700. In *Cork Hist. Soc. Jn.*, xlvi (1941), pp 123–9.

Grosjean, Paul. Sur quelques pièces imprimées et manuscrits de la controverse entre Écossais et Irlandais au début du XVIIe siècle. In *Anal. Bolland.*, lxxxi (1965), pp 436–46.

Hanley, John. Sources for the history of the Irish College, Rome. In *I.E.R.*, series 5, cii (1964), pp 28–34.

Hardy, T. D., and Brewer, J. S. *Report . . . upon the Carte and Carew papers in the Bodleian and Lambeth libraries*. London, 1864.

McNeill, Charles. Copies of Down Survey maps in private keeping. In *Anal. Hib.*, no. 8 (1938), pp 419–27.

—— Publications of Irish interest . . . by Irish authors on the Continent . . . prior to the eighteenth century. In *Bibliog. Soc. Ire. Pub.*, iv (1930), pp 3–48.

Martin, F. X., and de Meijer, A. Sources for the history of the Irish Capuchins, 1591–1791. In *Collectanea Franciscana*, xxvi ([Rome], 1956), pp 67–79.

Millett, Benignus. Guide to material for a biography of Father Luke Wadding. In *Father Luke Wadding* (Dublin, 1957), pp 229–62.

Murray, R. H. *Ireland, 1603–1714*. London, 1920 (Helps for Students of History).

Ó Domhnaill, Seán. The maps of the Down Survey. In *I.H.S.*, iii, no. 12 (Sept. 1943), pp 381–92.

Povey, Kenneth. The sources for a bibliography of Irish history, 1500–1700. In *I.H.S.*, i, no. 4 (Sept. 1939), pp 393–403.

Quinn, D. B. Guide to English financial records for Irish history, 1461–1558, with illustrative extracts, 1461–1509. In *Anal. Hib.*, no. 10 (1941), pp 1–69.

—— Information about Dublin printers 1556–73 in English financial records. In *I.B.L.*, xxviii (1942), pp 112–15.

Shaw, Francis. Medieval medico-philosophical treatises in the Irish language. In *Féil-sgríbhinn Eóin Mhic Néill*, pp 144–57.

Woodward, D. M. Sources of maritime history: (iii) the port books of England and Wales. In *Maritime History*, iii, no. 2 (Sept. 1973), pp 147–65.

II MANUSCRIPT SOURCES

The following is a list of the principal repositories of manuscript material relating to the period covered by the volume.

A IRELAND

Armagh

Public Library

See James Dean, *Catalogue of manuscripts in the public library of Armagh* (Dundalk, [1928]).

Belfast

Public Record Office of Northern Ireland

See *Report of the deputy keeper of the records* [*of Northern Ireland*] *for the year 1924* [etc.] (Belfast, 1925–).

Cork

Corporation archives

University College Library

See Pádraig de Brún, *Clár lámhscríbhinní Gaeilge Ollscoile Chorcaí: cnuasach Thorna* (Dublin, 1967).

Dublin

Archbishop Marsh's Library

See J. R. Scott and N. J. D. White, *Catalogue of the manuscripts remaining in Marsh's Library, Dublin* (Dublin, [1913]).

Christ Church Cathedral

Corporation archives, City Hall

See *Calendar of ancient records of Dublin . . .*, ed. J. T. Gilbert (19 vols, Dublin, 1889–1944).

Genealogical Office, Dublin Castle

King's Inns Library, Henrietta Street

See Pádraig de Brún, *Catalogue of Irish manuscripts in King's Inns Library, Dublin* (Dublin, 1972).

National Library of Ireland

See R. J. Hayes, *Manuscript sources of Irish civilisation* (11 vols, Boston, Mass., 1965); Nessa Ní Shéaghdha, *Catalogue of Irish manuscripts in the National Library of Ireland* (2 fasc., Dublin, 1961–7).

Public Library, Pearse Street

See Douglas Hyde and D. J. O'Donoghue, *Catalogue of the books and manuscripts comprising the library of the late Sir John Gilbert* (Dublin, 1918).

Public Record Office of Ireland

The bulk of the records was destroyed in 1922. For the records previous to 1922 see Herbert Wood, *A guide to the records deposited in the Public Record Office of Ireland* (Dublin, 1919); for surviving material see *Fifty-fifth* [etc.] *report of the deputy keeper of the public records in Ireland* (Dublin, 1928–).

Representative Church Body of the Church of Ireland Library, Braemor Park

See J. B. Leslie, *Catalogue of the manuscripts in possession of the Representative Church Body . . .* (Dublin, 1933).

Royal Irish Academy

See T. F. O'Rahilly and others, *Catalogue of Irish manuscripts in the Royal Irish Academy*. 28 fasc., and 2 index vols, ed. Kathleen Mulchrone (Dublin, 1926–70).

St Patrick's Cathedral

Society of Friends in Ireland; Historical Library, Eustace Street

See O. M. Goodbody, *Guide to Irish quaker records, 1654–1860* (I.M.C., Dublin, 1967).

Trinity College Library

See T. K. Abbott, *Catalogue of the manuscripts in the library of Trinity College,*

Dublin (Dublin, 1900), and T. K. Abbott and E. J. Gwynn, *Catalogue of the Irish manuscripts in the library of Trinity College, Dublin* (Dublin, 1921).

University College Library

Galway

Diocesan archives

See Edward MacLysaght, 'Report on documents relating to the wardenship of Galway' in *Anal. Hib.*, no. 14 (1944).

University College Library

See 'Archives of the town of Galway', ed. J. T. Gilbert, in *H.M.C. rep. 10*, app. v (1885), pp 380–520.

Killiney, County Dublin

Franciscan Library, Dún Mhuire

See Canice Mooney, 'Franciscan Library, Killiney: a short guide' in *Archiv. Hib.*, xviii (1955), pp 150–56; Myles Dillon, Canice Mooney, and Pádraig de Brún, *Catalogue of Irish manuscripts in the Franciscan Library, Killiney* (Dublin, 1969).

Maynooth, County Kildare

Royal College of St Patrick Library

See Paul Walsh, *Catalogue of Irish manuscripts in Maynooth College Library* (Maynooth, 1943); Pádraig Ó Fiannachta, *Lámhscríbhinní Gaeilge Choláiste Phádraig, Má Nuad*, fasc. II–VIII (Maynooth, 1965–73).

B GREAT BRITAIN

See *Bulletin of the National Register of Archives* (H.M.C., London, 1948–); *Record repositories in Great Britain* (H.M.C., London, 1973). Irish material is to be found in many county record offices.

Aberystwyth

National Library of Wales

See W. J. Smith (ed.), *Herbert correspondence* (Cardiff and Dublin, 1965).

Cambridge

University Library

Chatsworth, Derbyshire

Duke of Devonshire's manuscripts.

Edinburgh

General Register House

See Matthew Livingstone, *A guide to the public records of Scotland deposited in H.M. General Register House, Edinburgh* (Edinburgh, 1905).

National Library of Scotland

See Donald Mackinnon, *A descriptive catalogue of Gaelic manuscripts in the Advocates' Library, Edinburgh* . . . (Edinburgh, 1912).

Greenwich

National Maritime Museum

Dartmouth collection.

Hatfield House, Herts

Cecil MSS

See *Calendar of the manuscripts of the . . . marquess of Salisbury* . . . (H.M.C., London, 1883–).

Leeds

Central Library

Papers of Sir Arthur Ingram from the collection at Temple-Newsam (see *H.M.C., Various collections*, viii (1913), pp 3–195).

London

British Museum (now British Library)

See catalogues of all the major collections, and *B.M. cat. Ir. MSS.*

Guildhall Library

Irish Society and city company records. See Moody, *Londonderry plantation*, pp 422–4. Some companies have retained their records in their halls.

House of Lords Record Office

See *House of Lords MSS*, i (*H.M.C. rep. 11*, app. ii, 1887) [etc.].

Lambeth Palace Library

Carew Papers. See T. D. Hardy and J. S. Brewer, *Report . . . upon the Carte and Carew papers in the Bodleian and Lambeth libraries* (London, 1864).

Public Record Office

See *Guide to the contents of the Public Record Office* (3 vols, London, 1963–8).

Manchester

John Rylands Library

See *John Rylands Library (Manchester) Bulletin*

Oxford

Bodleian Library

See T. D. Hardy and J. S. Brewer, *Report . . . upon the Carte and Carew papers . . .*; Charles McNeill, 'Report on recent acquisitions in the Bodleian Library, Oxford' in *Anal. Hib.*, no. 1 (1930), pp 1–78; no. 2 (1931), pp 1–291.

Sheffield

City Libraries

Strafford papers. See *Guide to the manuscript collections in the Sheffield City Libraries* (Sheffield, 1956).

C THE CONTINENT

For microfilms of material of Irish interest see *Reports of the council of trustees, National Library of Ireland, 1949–50* [etc.].

AUSTRIA

Vienna

Gräflich Harrach'sches Familienarchiv

Papers relating to Irish Franciscans at Prague.

Kriegsarchiv

Oesterreichische Nationalbibliothek

Oesterreichishes Staatsarchiv

BELGIUM

Brussels

Archives générales du royaume

Bibliothèque Royale

Malines

Archives de l'archevéché de Malines

See Brendan Jennings (ed.), 'Irish preachers and confessors in the archdiocese of Malines, 1607–1794' in *Archiv. Hib.*, xxiii (1960), pp 148–66.

Sint-Truiden

Minderbroedersklooster

See Brendan Jennings (ed.), 'Sint-Truiden: Irish Franciscan documents' in *Archiv. Hib.*, xxiv (1961), pp 148–98; xxv (1962), pp 1–74; xxvi (1963), pp 1–39.

CZECHOSLOVAKIA

Prague

Universitni Knihovna [Karlova University Library]
Archives of Irish Franciscans.

DENMARK

Copenhagen

Kongelige Bibliotek

Rigsarkivet
See *Danish force in Ire.*

FRANCE

Bordeaux

Archives départementales de la Gironde
Archives municipales

Nantes

Archives départementales de la Loire atlantique
See Richard Hayes, 'Irish associations with Nantes' in *Studies*, xxviii (1939), pp 115–26.

Paris

Archives de la guerre, Vincennes

Archives du ministère des affaires étrangères

Archives nationales

Bibliothèque Nationale

Rennes

Archives départementales d'Ille-et-Vilaine
Records of Irish at St Malo.

Troyes

Archives départementales de l'Aube

Bibliothèque municipale
Material relating to Irish Capuchins.

ITALY

Rome

Archivum Generale Ordinis Fratrum Minorum Capuccinorum
Irish Capuchin documents of the seventeenth century.

Archivum Romanum Societatis Jesu

Material on Irish Jesuits.

Archivum Generale Augustinianorum

See F. X. Martin and A. de Meijer, 'Irish material in the Augustinian archives, Rome, 1354–1624' in *Archiv. Hib.*, xix (1956), pp 61–134.

Biblioteca Casanatense

See P. J. Corish, 'Two reports on the catholic church in Ireland in the early seventeenth century' in *Archiv. Hib.*, xxii (1959), pp 140–62.

Collegio di San Clemente

See Conleth Kearns, 'Archives of the Irish Dominican College, San Clemente, Rome' in *Archiv. Hib.*, xviii (1955), pp 145–9.

Collegio di Sant' Isidoro

Material on Irish Franciscans.

Collegio San Patrizio

See F. X. Martin, 'Archives of St Patrick's College, Rome: a summary report' in *Archiv. Hib.*, xviii (1955), pp 157–63.

Curia generalizia dei Frati Minori

Material on Irish Franciscans.

Pontificio Collegio Irlandese

S. Congregazione de Propaganda Fide

See Benignus Millett, 'The archives of the Congregation de Propaganda Fide' in *Ir. Cath. Hist. Comm. Proc.*, 1956, pp 20–27; 'Catalogue of Irish material in fourteen volumes of *Scritture originali riferite nelle congregazioni generali* in Propaganda archives' in *Collect. Hib.*, x–xii (1967–9).

Santa Sabina

See Hugh Fenning, 'Irish material in the registers of the Dominican masters general, 1390–1649' in *Archivum Fratrum Praedicatorum*, xxxix (1969), pp 249–336.

Vatican City

Archivio Segreto Vaticano

See Leonard Boyle, *Survey of the Vatican archives and its medieval holdings* (Toronto, 1972); Charles Burns, 'Sources of British and Irish history in the Instrumenta Miscellanea of the Vatican archives' in *Archivum Historiae Pontificiae*, ix (1971), pp 7–141; Cathaldus Giblin, 'Catalogue of material of Irish interest in the collection Nunziatura di Fiandra, Vatican archives' in *Collect. Hib.*, i (1958), pp 7–134; iii (1960), pp 7–144; iv (1961), pp 7–137;

v (1962), pp 7–130; ix (1966), pp 7–70; x (1967), pp 72–138; xi (1968), pp 53–90; xii (1969), pp 62–101; xiii (1970), pp 61–99.

Biblioteca Apostolica Vaticana

NETHERLANDS

Amerongen Castle, Utrecht

Huisarchief

Ginkel papers

The Hague

Algemeen Rijksarchief

SPAIN

Madrid

Archivo Historico Nacional

See J. J. Silke, 'Spanish intervention in Ireland: Spanish bibliography' in *Studia Hib.*, iii (1963), pp 179–90.

Ministerio de Asuntos Exteriores, Fondo Santa Sede

See Benvenuta Curtin [MacCurtain], 'Irish material in Fondo Santa Sede, Madrid' in *Archiv. Hib.*, xxvi (1963), pp 40–49.

Seville

Archives of Archbishop's Palace

Archives of cathedral

See J. J. Silke, 'The Irish College, Seville' in *Archiv. Hib.*, xxiv (1961), pp 103–47.

Simancas

Archivo General

See J. J. Silke, 'Spanish intervention' in *Studia Hib.*, iii (1963), pp 179–90.

SWEDEN

Stockholm

Krigsarkivet

D THE U.S.A.

Cambridge, Massachusetts

Harvard University Library

See *Harvard Library Bulletin.*

San Marino, California

Huntington Library

See *Huntington Library Quarterly.*

III PRINTED SOURCES

A RECORDS

1 Records of central administration

Book of Survey and Distribution, Cork: a distribution of forfeited land in the county of Corke, returned by the Downe Survey. Transcribed by Anne Waters from R.I.A. MS. In *Cork Hist. Soc. Jn.*, xxxvii (1932), pp 83–9; xxxviii (1933), pp 39–45, 72–9; xxxix (1934), pp 33–7, 79–84; xl (1935), pp 43–8, 91–4; xli (1936), pp 37–41, 97–104.

Book of Survey and Distribution, Kilkenny. Copied from original MS in P.R.O.I. In William Healy, *History and antiquities of Kilkenny* (Dublin, 1893), i, app. i.

The Book of Survey and Distribution of the estates in the county of Westmeath forfeited in the year MDCLII. *Ed.* J. C. Lyons. Ledestown, 1852.

Books of survey and distribution. Ed. R. C. Simington. 4 vols. Dublin, 1944–67 (I.M.C.).

Roscommon, Mayo, Galway, Clare.

CAREW. *Calendar of the Carew manuscripts preserved in the archiepiscopal library at Lambeth, 1515–1624.* 6 vols. London, 1867–73.

CASTLE CHAMBER. Court of Castle Chamber records. In Egmont MSS, *H.M.C. rep. 17*, app. i (1905), pp 1–60.

A census of Ireland circa 1659, with supplementary material from the poll money ordinances (1660–1661). Ed. Seamus Pender. I.M.C., Dublin, 1939.

Chester customs accounts, 1301–1566. Ed. K. P. Wilson. Liverpool, 1969.

CHICHESTER. Seventeen letters from James I and council of England to the lord deputy and council of Ireland, 1605–7. In *Desid. cur. Hib.*, i, 441–513.

—— Letter-book of Sir Arthur Chichester, 1612–14. *Ed.* R. D. Edwards. In *Anal. Hib.*, no. 8 (1938), pp 3–177.

The Civil Survey, A.D. 1654–56. Ed. R. C. Simington. 10 vols. I.M.C., Dublin, 1931–61.

i, Tipperary (E. & S. baronies), 1931; ii, Tipperary (N. & W. baronies), 1934; iii, Donegal, Londonderry, Tyrone, 1937; iv, Limerick (with part of Clanmaurice barony, County Kerry), 1938; v, Meath, 1940; vi, Waterford (with Muskerry barony, County Cork, Kilkenny city and liberties (part), and valuations, *c.* 1663–4, for Waterford and Cork cities), 1942; vii, Dublin, 1945; viii, Kildare, 1952; ix, Wexford, 1953; x, Miscellanea, 1961.

CLARENDON. *Calendar of the Clarendon state papers preserved in the Bodleian Library.* 5 vols. Oxford, 1872–1970.

—— *The correspondence of Henry Hyde, earl of Clarendon, and of his brother, Laurence Hyde, earl of Rochester, with the diary of Lord Clarendon from 1687 to 1690. . . . Ed.* S. W. Singer. 2 vols. London, 1828.

—— *The state letters of Henry, earl of Clarendon, lord lieutenant of Ireland . . . and his lordship's diary for the years 1687, 1688, 1689, and 1690.* 2 vols. Oxford, 1765.

CLARKE. George Clarke's Irish war correspondence, 1690–91. *Ed.* N. B. White. In *Anal. Hib.*, no. 10 (1941), pp 245–9.

COMMONWEALTH. *Ireland under the commonwealth: being a selection of documents relating to the government of Ireland, 1651–9. Ed.* Robert Dunlop. 2 vols. Manchester, 1913.

Commonwealth records. [*Ed.* James MacCaffrey.] In *Archiv. Hib.*, vi (1917), pp 175–202; vii (1918–21), pp 20–66.

Commonwealth state accounts, 1650–56. *Ed.* Edward MacLysaght. In *Anal. Hib.*, no. 15 (1944), pp 227–321.

The compossicion booke of Conought. Ed. A. M. Freeman. I.M.C., Dublin, 1936. *Index to*, by G. A. Hayes-McCoy. I.M.C., Dublin, 1942.

CROMWELL. *The writings and speeches of Oliver Cromwell. Ed.* W. C. Abbott. 4 vols. Cambridge, Mass., 1937–47.

—— *The letters and speeches of Oliver Cromwell, with elucidations by Thomas Carlyle* (1845). *Ed.* S. C. Lomas. 3 vols. London, 1904.

The Desmond survey of County Kerry. Ed. S. M. Hussey. Tralee, 1923 (privately printed); reprinted in *Kerryman*, Aug.–Oct. 1927.

Docwra, Henry. A narration of the services done by the army ymployed to Lough-Foyle. . . . In *Miscellany of the Celtic Society*, ed. John O'Donovan (Dublin, 1849).

ESSEX. *Letters written by Arthur Capel, earl of Essex, lord lieutenant of Ireland, in . . . 1675.* London, 1770.

Essex papers. Vol. i, ed. Osmund Airy; vol. ii, ed. C. E. Pike. London, 1890, 1913.

FIANTS. Calendar of fiants, Henry VIII to Elizabeth. In *P.R.I. rep. D.K.7–22.* Dublin, 1875–90.

FINCH. *Report on the manuscripts of the late Allen George Finch, Esq., of Burley-on-the-Hill, Rutland.* Vol. ii, 1922; vol. iii, 1957 (H.M.C.).

Fitzwilliam accounts, 1560–65 (Annesley collection). Ed. A. K. Longfield (Mrs H. G. Leask). I.M.C., Dublin, 1960.

GERRARD PAPERS. Lord Chancellor Gerrard's notes of his report on Ireland, 1577–8. *Ed.* Charles McNeill. In *Anal. Hib.*, no. 2 (1931), pp 93–291.

HEARTH-MONEY. Seventeenth-century hearth-money rolls with full transcript relating to Co. Sligo. *Ed.* Edward MacLysaght. In *Anal. Hib.*, no. 24 (1967), pp 1–89.

Letters and papers relating to the Irish rebellion, 1642–6. Ed. James Hogan. I.M.C., Dublin, 1936.

MONASTIC POSSESSIONS. Accounts of sums realised by sales of chattels of some suppressed Irish monasteries. *Ed.* Charles McNeill. In *R.S.A.I. Jn.*, lii (1922), pp 11–37.

—— *Extents of Irish monastic possessions, 1540–1541, from manuscripts in the Public Record Office, London. Ed.* N. B. White. I.M.C., Dublin, 1943.

PATENT ROLLS. *Calendar of the patent and close rolls of chancery in Ireland. Ed.* James Morrin. Vol. i (1514–75); vol. ii (1576–1603); vol. iii (1625–33). Dublin, 1861–3.

—— *A repertory of the inrolments on the patent rolls of chancery in Ireland, commencing with the reign of James I. Ed.* J. C. Erck. Vol. i, pts 1, 2. Dublin, 1846, 1852.

—— *Irish patent rolls of James I: facsimile of the Irish record commission's calendar prepared prior to 1830.* Foreword by M. C. Griffith. I.M.C., Dublin, 1966.

—— *Calendar of the patent rolls preserved in the Public Record Office, Edward VI to Elizabeth, 1547–75.* 16 vols. London, 1924–73.

PERROT. *The government of Ireland under Sir John Perrot, 1584–8.* By E.C.S. London, 1626.

PRIVY COUNCIL. Acts of the privy council in Ireland, 1556–71. *Ed.* J. T. Gilbert. In *H.M.C. rep. 15*, app. iii (1897), pp 1–256.

—— Calendar of the Irish council book, 1 March 1581 to 1 July 1586, made by John P. Prendergast between 1867 and 1869. *Ed.* D. B. Quinn. In *Anal. Hib.*, no. 24 (1967), pp 91–180.

—— *Acts of the privy council of England, 1542–1631.* 46 vols. London, 1890–1964.

—— *Privy council registers preserved in the Public Record Office, 1637–45, reproduced in facsimile.* 12 vols. [London], 1967–8.

—— *Register of the privy council of Scotland*, vols viii–xiii (1607–25). *Ed.* David Masson. Edinburgh, 1887–96.

PROCLAMATIONS. *A bibliography of royal proclamations of the Tudor and Stuart sovereigns and of others published under their royal authority, 1485–1714. Ed.* R. R. Steele. 2 vols. Oxford, 1910.

SALISBURY. *Calendar of the manuscripts of the . . . marquess of Salisbury . . ., preserved at Hatfield House.* 23 vols. H.M.C., London, 1883–1973.

SIDNEY. *Letters and memorials of state . . . written and collected by Sir Henry Sidney . . ., Sir Philip Sidney and his brother, Sir Robert Sidney. . . . Ed.* Arthur Collins. 2 vols. London, 1746.

Sidney, Henry. Memoir of government in Ireland. In *U.J.A.*, series 1, iii (1855), pp 33–44, 85–90, 336–57; v (1857), pp 299–315; viii (1860), pp 179–95.

Sidney state papers, 1565–70. Ed. Tomás Ó Laidhin. I.M.C., Dublin, 1962.

SIDNEY. Additional Sidney state papers, 1566–70. *Ed.* D. B. Quinn. In *Anal. Hib.*, no. 26 (1970), pp 89–102.

STATE PAPERS. *Calendar of the state papers relating to Ireland, 1509–1670.* 24 vols. London, 1860–1912.

—— *State papers, Henry VIII.* 11 vols. London, 1830–52.

—— *Letters and papers, foreign and domestic, Henry VIII.* 21 vols. London, 1862–1932.

—— *Calendar of state papers preserved in the Public Record Office, domestic series, 1547–1695.* 81 vols. London, 1856–1972.

After 1670, when the State Papers, Ireland, series ends, the domestic series has many more papers relating to Ireland.

—— *Calendar of state papers preserved in the Public Record Office, foreign series, 1547–89.* 23 vols. London, 1861–1950. Continued for 1590 as *List and analysis of state papers, foreign.* 2 vols. 1964, 1969.

STRAFFORD. *The earl of Strafforde's letters and despatches. Ed.* William Knowler. 2 vols. London, 1799.

Strafford inquisition of County Mayo (R.I.A., MS 24 E 15). Ed. William O'Sullivan. I.M.C., Dublin, 1958.

Talbot, Richard. Letter-book of Richard Talbot. *Ed.* Lilian Tate. In *Anal. Hib.*, no. 4 (1932), pp 99–133.

Thurloe, John. *A collection of state papers of John Thurloe, esq., secretary first to the council of state and afterwards to the two protectorates. Ed.* Thomas Birch. 7 vols. London, 1742.

TREASURY BOOKS. *Calendar of treasury books, 1660–92.* Vols i–ix. London, 1904–31.

Ulster plantation papers, 1608–13. *Ed.* T. W. Moody. In *Anal. Hib.*, no. 8 (1938), pp 179–298.

The Ulster state papers. *Ed.* H. F. Hore. In *U.J.A.*, series 1, vii (1859), pp 45–65.

The Walsingham letter-book or register of Ireland, May 1578 to December 1579. Ed. James Hogan and N. McNeill O'Farrell. I.M.C., Dublin, 1959.

WILLIAM III. *Correspondentie van Willem en van Hans Willem Bentinck, eersten Graf van Portland. Ed.* Nicholas Japikse. Vol. iii. The Hague, 1927.

WINE-TRADE. The Irish wine-trade, 1614–15. *Ed.* H. F. Kearney. In *I.H.S.*, ix, no. 36 (Sept. 1955), pp 400–42.

2 *Records of local administration*

BELFAST. *The town book of the corporation of Belfast, 1613–1816 . . . Ed.* R. M. Young. Belfast and London, 1892.

CORK. *The council book of Cork. Ed.* Richard Caulfield. Guildford, 1876.

—— Original documents relating to the county and city of Cork. *Ed.* Richard Caulfield. In *Gent. Mag.*, 1862, Nov., pp 559–62; 1865, Mar., pp 316–28; Apr., pp 449–52; June, pp 719–22; Aug. pp 176–80.

DUBLIN. *Calendar of ancient records of Dublin, in the possession of the municipal corporation.* Vols i–v (1172–1692). *Ed.* J. T. Gilbert. Dublin, 1889–95.

GALWAY. Archives of the town of Galway. *Ed.* J. T. Gilbert. In *H.M.C. rep. 10*, app. v (1885), pp 380–520.

Kilkenny city records: Liber primus Kilkenniensis. Ed. Charles McNeill. Dublin, 1931; trans. by A. J. Otway-Ruthven, Kilkenny, [1961].

KINSALE. *The council book of Kinsale. Ed.* Richard Caulfield. Guildford, 1879.

LONDON. *The bishopric of Derry and the Irish Society of London, 1602–1705. Ed.* T. W. Moody and J. G. Simms. Vol. i (1602–70). I.M.C., Dublin, 1968.

—— Schedules of the lands in Ulster allocated to the London livery companies, 1613. *Ed.* T. W. Moody. In *Anal. Hib.*, no. 8 (1938), pp 299–311.

Londonderry. See London.

WATERFORD. Archives of the municipal corporation of Waterford. *Ed.* J. T. Gilbert. In *H.M.C. rep. 10*, app. v (1885), pp 265–339.

—— *Council books of the corporation of Waterford, 1662–1700 . . . Ed.* Séamus Pender. I.M.C., Dublin, 1964.

—— Report by J. T. Gilbert on corporation records of Waterford. In *H.M.C. rep. 1*, app., pp 131–2 (1874).

YOUGHAL. *The council book of Youghal. Ed.* Richard Caulfield. Guildford, 1878.

3 Parliamentary records

(*a*) Statutes

The statutes at large passed in the parliaments held in Ireland . . . Vols i–iii (1310–1698). Dublin, 1786.

The bills and statutes of the Irish parliaments of Henry VII and Henry VIII. *Ed.* D. B. Quinn. In *Anal. Hib.*, no. 10 (1941), pp 71–169.

Statutes 10 Henry VI to 14 Elizabeth established in Ireland. London, 1572.

The statutes of Ireland . . . newly perused and examined. [*Ed.* Richard Bolton.] Dublin, 1621.

The statutes at large of England and Great Britain. Vols ii, iii (1509–1708). London, 1811.

Acts and ordinances of the interregnum, 1642–1660. Ed. C. H. Firth and R. S. Rait. 3 vols. London, 1911.

(*b*) Journals

John Hooker's journal of the Irish parliament, 17 Jan.–23 Feb. 1569. *Ed.* C. L. Falkiner. In *R.I.A. Proc.*, xxv, sect. C (1904–5), pp 563–6.

Journal of the Irish house of lords in Sir John Perrot's parliament (1585–6). *Ed.* F. J. Routledge. In *E.H.R.*, xxix (1914), pp 104–17.

Journals of the house of lords [*of Ireland*]. Vol. i (1634–99). Dublin, 1779.

Journals of the house of lords [*of England*]. Vols i–xiv (1510–1691).

Journals of the house of commons of the kingdom of Ireland. Vol. i, 2 pts (1613–66). Dublin, 1796.

Journals of the house of commons [*of England*]. Vols i–x (1547–1693).

Commons debates, 1621. Ed. Wallace Notestein and others. 7 vols. New Haven, 1935.

The commons debates for 1629. Ed. Wallace Notestein and F. H. Relf. Minneapolis, 1921.

The journal of Sir Simonds D'Ewes. Ed. Wallace Notestein. New Haven, 1923.

4 Legal records

Agreement between Ó Domhnaill and Tadhg Ó Conchobhair concerning Sligo Castle (23 June 1539). *Ed.* Maura Carney. In *I.H.S.*, iii, no. 11 (Mar. 1944), pp 282–96.

Ceart Uí Néill (R.I.A., MS 24 P 33). In *Lr Cl. Aodha Buidhe*, pp 41–7; English translation by Myles Dillon in *Studia Celt.*, i (1966), pp 1–18.

COURTS. *His majesties directions for the ordering and settling of the courts, and course of justice, within his kingdom of Ireland.* Dublin, 1622.

Reprinted with introduction by G. J. Hand and V. W. Treadwell, in *Anal. Hib.*, no. 26 (1970), pp 179–212.

Davies, John. *Le primer report des cases et matters en ley resolues et adiudges en les court del roy en Ireland: collect et digest per Sir John Davys.* Dublin, 1615. Translated as *A report of cases and matters in laws, resolved and adjudged in the king's courts in Ireland.* Dublin, 1762.

DEPOSITIONS. *Ireland in the seventeenth century, or the Irish massacres of 1641–2....* *Ed.* Mary Hickson. 2 vols. London, 1884.

Depositions transcribed from T.C.D., MSS 809–41.

Inquisitionum in officio rotulorum cancellariae Hiberniae asservatarum repertorium. 2 vols. Dublin, 1826–9.

IRISH LAW. Ancient Irish deeds and writings, chiefly relating to landed property from the twelfth to the seventeenth century. *Ed.* James Hardiman. In *R.I.A. Trans.*, xv (1826), pt 2, pp 3–95.

—— Some documents on Irish law and custom in the sixteenth century. *Ed.* K. W. Nicholls. In *Anal. Hib.*, no. 26 (1970), pp 105–29.

OUTLAWRIES. Oireachtas library, list of outlaws, 1641–7. *Ed.* R. C. Simington and John MacLellan. In *Anal. Hib.*, no. 23 (1966), pp 317–67.

—— Irish Jacobites: lists from T.C.D., MS N.1.3. *Ed.* J. G. Simms. In *Anal. Hib.*, no. 22 (1960), pp 11–230.

PRESENTMENTS. *The social state of the southern and eastern counties of Ireland in the sixteenth century . . .* *Ed.* H. F. Hore and James Graves. Royal Historical and Archaeological Association of Ireland, Dublin, 1870.

Jury presentments.

STRAFFORD. *The trial of Thomas, earl of Strafford.* *Ed.* John Rushworth. London, 1680.

5 Ecclesiastical records

ALEN. *Calendar of Archbishop Alen's register, c. 1172–1534; prepared and edited from the original in the registry of the united dioceses of Dublin and Glendalough and Kildare.* *Ed.* Charles McNeill. Dublin, 1949.

BRENAN. *A bishop of the penal times* [John Brenan, bishop of Waterford and Lismore, 1671–7, archbishop of Cashel, 1677–93]. *Ed.* Patrick Power, Cork, 1932.

CHRIST CHURCH, DUBLIN. Calendar to Christ Church deeds, 1174–1684. *Ed.*

M. J. McEnery. In *P.R.I. rep. D.K. 20* (1888), app., pp 36–122; *23* (1891), app., pp 75–152; *24* (1892), app., pp 100–94; *27* (1895), app., pp 3–101 (index).

CISTERCIANS. Three unpublished Cistercian documents. *Ed.* Colmcille [Ó Conbhuí]. In *Louth Arch. Soc. Jn.*, xiii, no. 3 (1955), pp 252–78.

The court book of the liberty of St Sepulchre. Ed. Herbert Wood. Dublin, 1930.

DERRY. *The bishopric of Derry and the Irish Society of London, 1602–1705. Ed.* T. W. Moody and J. G. Simms. Vol. i, 1602–70. I.M.C., Dublin, 1968.

DUBLIN. Archbishop Bulkeley's visitation of Dublin, 1630. *Ed.* M. V. Ronan. In *Archiv. Hib.*, viii (1941), pp 56–98.

—— The royal visitation of Dublin, 1615. *Ed.* M. V. Ronan. In *Archiv. Hib.*, viii (1941), pp 1–55.

FLANDERS. Catalogue of material of Irish interest in the collection Nunziatura di Fiandra. *Ed.* Cathaldus Giblin. In *Collect. Hib.*, i (1958), pp 7–134; iii (1960), pp 7–144; iv (1961), pp 7–137; v (1962), pp 7–130; ix (1966), pp 7–70; x (1967), pp 72–138; xi (1968), pp 53–90; xii (1969), pp 62–101; xiii (1970), pp 61–99.

FRANCISCANS. The Irish Franciscans in Poland. *Ed.* Brendan Jennings. In *Archiv. Hib.*, xx (1957), pp 37–56.

—— Documents of the Irish Franciscan college at Prague. *Ed.* Brendan Jennings. In *Archiv. Hib.*, ix (1942), pp 173–294.

—— *The Irish Franciscan mission to Scotland, 1619–46: documents from Roman archives. Ed.* Cathaldus Giblin. Dublin, 1964.

—— *Liber Lovaniensis: a collection of Irish Franciscan documents, 1629–1717. Ed.* Cathaldus Giblin. Dublin, 1956.

JESUITS. *Ibernia Ignatiana: seu Ibernorum Societatis Jesu patrum monumenta collecta. . . . Ed.* Edmund Hogan. Vol. i (1540–1607). Dublin, 1880.
No further vol. published.

LOUVAIN. *Facultates Lovanienses, 1426–1797, praecipue quae nomen Hibernicum spectant. Ed.* Timothy Corcoran. Dublin, 1939.

Miscellaneous documents, 1588–1715. *Ed.* Brendan Jennings. In *Archiv. Hib.*, xii (1946), pp 70–200; xiv (1949), pp 1–49; xv (1950), pp 1–73.

Plunkett, Oliver. *Memoir of the Most Rev. Oliver Plunkett, archbishop of Armagh.* By P. F. Moran. Dublin, 1861; 2nd ed., 1895.

SALAMANCA. Students of the Irish College, Salamanca. *Ed.* D. J. O'Doherty. In *Archiv. Hib.*, ii (1913), pp 1–36; iii (1914), pp 87–112.

Shirley, E. P. (ed.). *Original letters and papers in illustration of the history of the church in Ireland during the reigns of Edward VI, Mary and Elizabeth.* London, 1851.

Spicilegium Ossoriense, being a collection of original letters and papers illustrative of the history of the Irish church from the reformation to the year 1800. Ed. P. F. Moran. 3 vols. Dublin, 1874–84.

Theiner, Augustine (ed.). *Vetera monumenta Hibernorum et Scotorum.* Rome, 1864.

VATICAN. Miscellanea Vaticano-Hibernica. *Ed.* John Hagan. In *Archiv. Hib.*, iii (1914), pp 227–365; iv (1915), pp 215–318; v (1916), pp 74–185; vi (1917), pp 94–155; vii (1918–21), pp 67–356.

6 Family and personal letters and papers

The Arthur manuscripts. *Ed.* Edward MacLysaght and John Ainsworth. In *N. Munster Antiq. Jn.*, vi (1949–52), pp 29–49; vii, no. 1 (1953), pp. 168–82; no. 4 (1957), pp 4–10; viii (1958–9), pp 2–19, 79–87; ix (1962–3), pp 51–9, 113–16, 153–64.

Blake family records, 1300–1600. Ed. M. J. Blake. London, 1902.

—— *1600–1700. Ed.* M. J. Blake. London, 1905.

Boyle, Richard, earl of Cork. *Lismore papers. Ed.* A. B. Grosart. 10 vols. London, 1886–8.

BUTLER. *Poems on the Butlers. Ed.* James Carney. Dublin, 1945.

CHAMBERLAIN. *The letters of John Chamberlain. Ed.* N. E. McClure. 2 vols. Philadelphia, 1939 (Amer. Phil. Soc. Memoirs, xii).

CORK. Caulfield, Richard (ed.). Wills and inventories, Cork. In *Gent. Mag.*, 1861, May, pp 530–2; July, pp 33–7; Sept., pp 257–62; Nov., pp 501–5; 1862, Jan., pp 28–31; Feb., pp 165–8; Apr., pp 439–44; June, pp 710–14; Sept., pp 299–302.

DE L'ISLE AND DUDLEY. *Report on the manuscripts of Lord de L'Isle and Dudley.* 6 vols. H.M.C., London, 1925–66.

Doneraile papers: interim report by Edward MacLysaght. In *Anal. Hib.*, no. 15 (1944), pp 335–62.

Dowdall deeds. Ed. Charles McNeill and A. J. Otway-Ruthven. I.M.C., Dublin, 1960.

DOWNSHIRE. *Report on the manuscripts of the marquess of Downshire preserved at Easthampstead Park, Berks.*, vols i–iv. H.M.C., London, 1924–40.

Dunsandle papers. Interim report by Edward MacLysaght. In *Anal. Hib.*, no. 15 (1944), pp 392–405.

EGMONT. *Report on the manuscripts of the earl of Egmont.* 2 vols. H.M.C., London, 1905, 1909.

FITZGERALD. *The Red Book of the earls of Kildare. Ed.* Gearóid Mac Niocaill. I.M.C., Dublin, 1964.

—— The rental book of Gerald Fitzgerald, ninth earl of Kildare, begun in the year 1518. *Ed.* H. F. Hore. In *R.S.A.I. Jn.*, v (1858–9), pp 266–80, 301–10; vii (1862–3), pp 110–37; viii (1864–6), pp 501–18, 525–46.

—— Rental of Gerald, earl of Kildare, A.D. 1518. *Ed.* J. T. Gilbert. In *H.M.C. rep 9*, app. pt 2 (1884), pp 274–89.

—— Unpublished Geraldine documents. *Ed.* Samuel Hayman. 4 pts. Dublin, 1870–81.

Gearnon, Anthony. Papers of Anthony Gearnon, O.F.M. *Ed.* Anselm Faulkner. In *Collect. Hib.*, vi (1964), pp 212–24.

HACKET. *The letters of Sir John Hacket. Ed.* E. F. Rogers. Morganstown, West Virginia, 1971.

The Hamilton manuscripts: containing some account of the settlements . . . in the county of Down . . . in the reigns of James I and Charles I . . . by Sir James Hamilton, Viscount Clandeboye. Ed. T. K. Lowry. Belfast, 1867.

HASTINGS. *Report on the manuscripts of the late Reginald Rawdon Hastings, Esq., of the Manor House, Ashby de la Zouch*, vols ii–iv. *Ed.* Francis Bickley. H.M.C., London, 1930–47.

Henslowe's diary. Ed. W. W. Greg. 2 vols. London, 1904, 1908.

Herbert correspondence: the sixteenth and seventeenth century letters of the Herberts of Chirbury, Powis Castle and Delguog, formerly at Powis Castle in Montgomeryshire. Ed. W. J. Smith. Univ. of Wales Press, Cardiff, and I.M.C., Dublin, 1965.

INCHIQUIN. Seven Irish documents from the Inchiquin archives. *Ed.* Gearóid Mac Niocaill. In *Anal. Hib.*, no. 26 (1970), pp 45–70.

The Inchiquin manuscripts. Ed. John Ainsworth. I.M.C., Dublin, 1961.

MAC CARTHY. *The life and letters of Florence MacCarthy Reagh.* By Daniel MacCarthy. London, 1867.

MAC SWEENY. *Leabhar Chloinne Suibhne. Ed.* Paul Walsh. Dublin, 1920.

MAGUIRE. *Duanaire Mhéig Uidhir. Ed.* David Greene. Dublin, 1972.

The Montgomery manuscripts. Ed. George Hill. Belfast, 1869.

O'BYRNE. *Leabhar Branach. Ed.* Seán Mac Airt. Dublin, 1944.
The book of O'Byrne.

O'HARA. *The book of O'Hara. Ed.* Lambert McKenna. Dublin, 1951.

O'HARTEGAN. The strange letters of Matthew O'Hartegan, S.J., 1644–5. *Ed.* Thomas Morrissey. In *Ir. Theol. Quart.*, xxxvii (1970), pp 159–72.

O'REILLY. *Poems on the O'Reillys. Ed.* James Carney. Dublin, 1950.

ORMOND. *Calendar of the manuscripts of the marquess of Ormonde, preserved at Kilkenny Castle.* 11 vols. H.M.C., London, 1895–1920.

—— *Calendar of Ormond deeds*, vols iii–vi (1413–1603). *Ed.* Edmund Curtis. I.M.C., Dublin, 1935–43.

ORRERY. *Calendar of the Orrery papers. Ed.* Edward Mac Lysaght. I.M.C., Dublin, 1941.

—— *A collection of the state letters of the . . . first earl of Orrery. Ed.* Thomas Morrice. 2 vols. Dublin, 1743.

OVIEDO. Some unpublished letters of Mateo de Oviedo, archbishop of Dublin. *Ed.* P. P. McBride. In *Reportorium Novum*, i (1955–6), pp 91–116, 351–68.

PAPEBROCH. Letters of Daniel Papebroch, S.J., to Francis Harold, O.F.M. (1665–90). *Ed.* Fergal Grannell. In *Archivum Franciscanum Historicum*, lix (1966), pp 385–455.

Petty–Southwell correspondence, 1676–87. Ed. marquess of Lansdowne. London, 1928.

RADCLIFFE. *The life and correspondence of Sir George Radcliffe. Ed.* T. D. Whitaker. London, 1810.

Rawdon papers. Ed. Edward Berwick. London, 1819.

WADDING. Some correspondence of Father Luke Wadding, O.F.M. *Ed.* Brendan Jennings. In *Collect. Hib.*, ii (1959), pp 66–94.

—— Le lettre inedite di Luca Wadding ad Antonio Caracciolo e la riforma liturgica di Urbano VIII. *Ed.* Severino Govi. In *Archivum Franciscanum Historicum*, lxvi (1973), pp 110–41.

Wadding papers, 1614–38. Ed. Brendan Jennings. I.M.C., Dublin, 1953.

7 *Other records*

AVAUX. *Négociations de M. le comte d'Avaux en Irlande, 1689–90.* Introduction by James Hogan. I.M.C., Dublin, 1934. *Index to*, by Lilian Tate. I.M.C., Dublin, 1956.

The Danish force in Ireland, 1690–1691. Ed. Kevin Danaher and J. G. Simms. I.M.C., Dublin, 1962.

FLANDERS. *Wild geese in Spanish Flanders. Ed.* Brendan Jennings. I.M.C., Dublin, 1964.

Franco-Irish correspondence, 1688–91. Ed. Lilian Tate. In *Anal. Hib.*, no. 21 (1959), pp 1–240.

GINKEL. Correspondence of General Ginkel (de Ros MSS). In *H.M.C. rep. 4* (1874), app., pp 317–25.

JAMES V. Unpublished letters of James V of Scotland relating to Ireland. *Ed.* G. A. Hayes-McCoy. In *Anal. Hib.*, no. 12 (1943), pp 179–81.

Macpherson, James (ed.) *Original papers.* 2 vols. London, 1775.

MILAN. *Calendar of state papers and manuscripts existing in the archives and collections of Milan, 1385–1618.* London, 1913.

O'NEILL. The last years of Hugh O'Neill. *Ed.* Micheline Walsh. In *Ir. Sword*, iii (1957–8), pp 234–44; v (1961–2), pp 223–35; vii (1965–6), pp 5–14, 136–46, 327–37; viii (1967–8), pp 120–29, 230–41, 299–303; ix (1969–70), pp 59–68, 135–46.

ROME. *Calendar of state papers relating to English affairs, preserved principally at Rome, in the Vatican archives and library, 1558–78.* 2 vols. London, 1917, 1926.

SPAIN. *Calendar of letters, despatches, and state papers relating to the negotiations between England and Spain, preserved in the archives at Simancas and elsewhere, 1485–1558.* 13 vols. London, 1862–1954.

—— *Calendar of letters and state papers relating to English affairs, preserved principally in the archives of Simancas: 1558–1603.* 4 vols. London, 1892–9.

STATIONERS COMPANY. *Transcript of the registers of the company of Stationers, 1554–1640. Ed.* Edward Arber. 5 vols. London, 1875–94.

VENICE. *Calendar of state papers and manuscripts, relating to English affairs, existing in the archives and collections of Venice, and in other libraries of Northern Italy, 1534–1674*, vols v–xxxviii. London, 1873–1947.

B CONTEMPORARY WORKS

1 Contemporary histories and descriptions

Adair, Patrick. *A true narrative of the rise and progress of the presbyterian church in Ireland (1623–70)*. *Ed.* W. D. Killen. Belfast, 1866.

Advertisements for Ireland. *Ed.* George O'Brien. Dublin, 1923.

Annála Connacht: the Annals of Connacht, A.D. *1224–1544*. *Ed.* A. M. Freeman. Dublin, 1944.

Annala rioghachta Eireann: Annals of the kingdom of Ireland by the Four Masters from the earliest period to the year 1616. Ed. and trans. John O'Donovan. Vols v–vii (1501–1616). Dublin, 1851; reprint, New York, 1966.

Annála Uladh, Annals of Ulster . . .: a chronicle of Irish affairs, 431–1131, 1155–1541. *Ed.* W. M. Hennessy and Bartholomew MacCarthy. 4 vols. Dublin, 1887–1901.

Annals of Ireland from 1443 to 1465. In *Ir. Arch. Soc. Misc.*, i (1846), pp 258–9.

The Annals of Loch Cé: a chronicle of Irish affairs, 1014–1590. *Ed.* W. M. Hennessy. 2 vols. London, 1871; reflex facsimile, I.M.C., Dublin, 1939.

Aphorismical discovery. See Gilbert, *Contemporary history*.

Beacon, Richard. *Solon his follie*. Oxford, 1594.

BEDELL. *Two biographies of William Bedell, bishop of Kilmore*. *Ed.* E. S. Shuckburgh. Cambridge, 1902.

Bellings, Richard. See Gilbert, *Irish confederation*.

Berwick, James FitzJames, duke of. *Memoirs of the marshal duke of Berwick*. 2 vols. London, 1779.

Boate, Gerard. *Ireland's naturall history. . . .* London, 1652.

[Borlase, Edmund]. *The history of the execrable Irish rebellion traced from many preceding acts to the grand eruption the 23 of October 1641, and thence pursued to the act of settlement, 1662*. Dublin, 1680; 2nd ed., Dublin, 1743.

Burnet, Gilbert. *Bishop Burnet's history of his own time*. 2 vols, London, 1724; 6 vols, Oxford, 1823.

Camden, William. *Britannia sive . . . Angliae, Scotiae, Hiberniae chorographica descriptio*. London, 1586; trans. Philemon Holland, 1610; newly translated into English with large additions and improvements, ed. Edmund Gibson, 1695; trans. Richard Gough, 3 vols, 1789.

Campion, Edmund. Campion's historie of Ireland (1571). In *The historie of Ireland collected by three learned authors, viz Meredith Hanmer . . ., Edmund Campion . . ., and Edmund Spenser . . .*, ed. James Ware (Dublin, 1633);

reprinted as *Ancient Irish histories: the works of Spencer, Campion, Hanmer, and Marleburrough* (2 vols, Dublin, 1809).
See also Holinshed, below, p. 660.

—— *Two bokes of the histories of Ireland compiled by Edmund Campion . . . (1571). Ed.* A. F. Vossen from MS Jones 6, Bodleian Library, Oxford. Assen, Netherlands, 1963.

Carve [Carew], Thomas. *Itinerarium . . . cum historia facti Butleri, Gordon, Leslie et aliorum.* Mayence, 1639.

Clanricard, Ulick de Burgh, marquis of. *The memoirs and letters of Ulick, marquis of Clanricarde . . . printed from an authentic manuscript and now first published by the present earl of Clanricarde.* London, 1757.

Clarendon, Edward Hyde, earl of. *The history of the rebellion and civil wars in Ireland.* London, 1720.

Cox, Richard. *Hibernia Anglicana, or the history of Ireland from the conquest thereof by the English to this present time . . .* 2 pts. London, 1689–90.

—— On a manuscript description of the city and county of Cork, *circa* 1685, written by Sir Richard Cox. *Ed.* S. P. Johnston, with notes by T. A. Lunham. In *R.S.A.I. Jn.*, xxxii (1902), pp 353–76.

—— Regnum Corcagiense. *Ed.* Robert Day. In *Cork Hist. Soc. Jn.*, viii (1902), pp 65–83, 156–79.

Dalrymple, John. *Memoirs of Great Britain and Ireland.* 3 vols. Edinburgh, 1771–88.

Davies, John. *The complete prose works of Sir John Davies. Ed.* A. B. Grosart. 3 vols. London, 1869–76.
See also Henry Morley (ed.), *Ireland under Elizabeth and James I* (London, 1890).

—— *A discovery of the true causes why Ireland was never entirely subdued . . . until . . . his majesty's happy reign.* London, 1612; facsimile reprint, Shannon, 1969.

Davies, Rowland. *Journal of the Very Rev. Rowland Davies. . . . Ed.* Richard Caulfield. London, 1857.

Derricke, John. *The image of Irelande.* London, 1581; another edition, with the notes of Walter Scott, ed. John Small, Edinburgh, 1883.
See plate 2.

The description of Ireland . . . in anno 1598. Ed. Edmund Hogan. London, 1878.

Dineley, Thomas. Extracts from the journal of Thomas Dineley [1681]. *Ed.* E. P. Shirley. In *R.S.A.I. Jn.*, iv (1856–7), pp 143–6, 170–88; v (1858), pp 22–32, 55–6; vii (1862–3), pp 38–52, 103–9, 320–38; viii (1864–6), pp 40–48, 268–90, 425–46; ix (1867), pp 73–91, 176–202. *Ed.* F. E. Ball, ibid., xliii (1913), pp 275–309.
See plates 9–10.

—— *Observations in a voyage through the kingdom of Ireland . . . in the year 1681.* [*Ed.* James Graves.] Dublin, 1870.
Shirley's extracts: only 50 copies printed.

Dymmok, John. A treatice of Ireland. *Ed.* Richard Butler. In *Tracts relating to Ireland*, ii (1843), pp 1–90.

Eachard, Lawrence. *An exact description of Ireland.* London, 1691.

Edmundson, William. *A journal of the life, travels, sufferings, and labour of love in the work of the ministry of . . . W. E.* Dublin, 1715.

Gainsford, Thomas. *The true, exemplary and remarkable history of the earl of Tyrone.* London, 1619.

Gernon, Luke. A discourse of Ireland [*c.* 1620]. In Falkiner, *Illustrations*, pp 345–64.

Gilbert, J. T. (ed.). *A contemporary history of affairs in Ireland from* A.D. *1641 to 1652. . . .* 3 vols. Dublin, 1879.

From the manuscript, 'An aphorismical discovery of treasonable faction' (T.C.D., MS 846).

—— *The history of the Irish confederation and the war in Ireland (1641–9).* 7 vols. Dublin, 1882–91.

Richard Bellings's account (T.C.D., MS 747(2); B.M., Add. MS 4763).

—— *A Jacobite narrative of the war in Ireland, 1688–1691.* Dublin, 1892; reprint, with introduction by J. G. Simms, Shannon, 1971.

Parts of the Fingall MS 'A light to the blind'. See introduction to 1971 ed.

Hamilton, Andrew. *A true relation of the actions of the Inniskilling men.* London, 1690.

Holinshed, Raphael. *The . . . chronicles of England, Scotlande and Irelande. . . .* London, 1577; ed. John Hooker and others, 3 vols, 1587; ed. Henry Ellis, 6 vols, 1807–8.

Includes contributions on the history of Ireland by Campion, Stanihurst, and Hooker.

Hooker, John, *alias* Vowell. The description, conquest, inhabitation, and troublesome estate of Ireland . . . continued from the death of King Henrie the eight untill this present time [1586]. In Holinshed, *Chronicles* (1587 edn.), ii.

Hughes. See Moryson.

KERRY. William Molyneux's geographical collections for Kerry. *Ed.* William O'Sullivan. In *Kerry Arch. Soc. Jn.*, iv (1971), pp. 28–47.

King, William. On the bogs and loughs of Ireland. In *R. Soc. Phil. Trans.*, xv (1685), pp 948–60.

—— *The state of the protestants of Ireland under the late King James's government.* . . . London, 1691.

LEIGH. A chorographic account of the southern part of County Wexford, written *anno* 1684, by Robert Leigh, esq., of Rosegarland in that county. *Ed.* H. F. Hore. In *R.S.A.I. Jn.*, v (1858–9), pp 17–21, 451–67.

A light to the blind. See Gilbert, *Jacobite narrative.*

Ligon, Richard. *A true and exact history of the island of Barbados.* London, 1657; 2nd ed., 1673.

Lombard, Peter. *De regno Hiberniae sanctorum insula commentarius.* Louvain, 1632; ed. P. F. Moran, Dublin, 1868.

See M. J. Byrne (ed.), *The Irish war of defence, 1598–1600: extracts from the De Hibernia insula commentarius of Peter Lombard....* (Cork, 1930).

[Lynch, John]. *Alithinologia* ... St Malo], 1664; ... *supplementum*, 1667.

—— *Cambrensis eversus* ... [?St Malo], 1662. Trans. Matthew Kelly, 3 vols. Dublin, 1848–52.

—— *De praesulibus Hiberniae potissimis catholicae religionis in Hibernia serendae, & propagandae, et conservandae authoribus. Ed.* J. F. O'Doherty. 2 vols. I.M.C., Dublin, 1944.

McCarmick, William. *A further impartial account of the actions of the Inniskilling men.* London, 1691.

Mackenzie, John. *A narrative of the siege of Londonderry.* London, 1690.

Moryson, Fynes. *An itinerary....* 3 pts. London, 1617; new ed. in 4 vols, Glasgow, 1907–8; extracts from 4th pt, published from Moryson's MS, in *Shakespeare's Europe* (ed. Charles Hughes, London, 1903), include 'Of the commonwealth of Ireland' (pp 185–260) and 'Of Ireland, touching nature, manners etc.' (pp 481–6).

See also Falkiner, *Illustrations*; Morley, *Ireland under Elizabeth and James I* (London, 1890).

—— *An history of Ireland, from the year 1599 to 1603: with a short narration of the state of the kingdom from the year 1169: to which is added a description of Ireland.* 2 vols. Dublin, 1735.

A reprint of pt ii and pt iii, bk 3, ch. v, of Moryson's *Itinerary.*

Mullenaux, Samuel. *Journal of the three months' royal campaign of his majesty in Ireland.* London, 1690.

Ó Cianáin, Tadhg. *The flight of the earls. Ed.* Paul Walsh. Dublin, 1916.

—— *Imeacht na nIarlaí. Ed.* Pádraig de Barra. Dublin, 1972.

Ó CLÉIRIGH. *The life of Aodh Ruadh O Domhnaill, transcribed from the book of Lughaidh Ó Cléirigh. Ed.* Paul Walsh. 2 pts. Dublin, 1948, 1957.

O'Connell, Robert. See O'Ferrall, Richard.

O'Ferrall, Richard, and O'Connell, Robert. *Commentarius Rinuccinianus, de sedis apostolicae legatione ad foederatos Hiberniae catholicos per annos 1645–9. Ed.* Stanislaus Kavanagh. 6 vols. I.M.C., Dublin, 1932–49.

O'Flaherty, Roderick. *A chorographical description of West or h-Iar Connaught, written A.D. 1684. Ed.* James Hardiman. Dublin, 1846.

—— *Ogygia, seu rerum Hibernicarum chronologia....* London, 1685; trans. James Hely, 2 vols, Dublin, 1793.

—— *The Ogygia vindicated* ... *Ed.* Charles O'Conor. Dublin, 1775.

O'Kelly, Charles. *Macariae excidium, or the destruction of Cyprus. Ed.* J. C. O'Callaghan. Dublin, 1850.

O'MELLAN. Cín lae Ó Mealláin. *Ed.* Tadhg Ó Donnchadha. In *Anal. Hib.*, no. 3 (1931), pp 1–61.

O'Sullivan Beare, Philip. *Historiae catholicae Iberniae compendium.* Lisbon, 1621; ed. Matthew Kelly, Dublin, 1850.

—— *Ireland under Elizabeth . . . being a portion of The history of catholic Ireland by Don Philip O'Sullivan Bear.* Trans. M. J. Byrne. Dublin, 1903.

Perrot, James. *The chronicle of Ireland, 1584–1608. Ed.* Herbert Wood. I.M.C., Dublin, 1933.

Petty, William. *The history of the survey of Ireland commonly called the Down Survey, by Doctor William Petty, A.D. 1655–6. Ed.* T. A. Larcom. Dublin, 1851.

—— *The political anatomy of Ireland* [1672]. Dublin, 1691.

Piers, Henry. A chorographical description of the county of West-Meath, written A.D. 1682. In Charles Vallancey (ed.), *Collectanea de rebus Hibernicis*, i (Dublin, 1770), pp 1–126.

Porter, Francis. *Compendium annalium ecclesiasticorum regni Hiberniae.* Rome, 1690.

Rich, Barnaby. *A new description of Ireland.* London, 1610; ed. Edmund Hogan, London, 1878.

RICHARDS. Particulars relative to Wexford and the barony of Forth, by Colonel Solomon Richards, 1682. *Ed.* H. F. Hore. In *R.S.A.I. Jn.*, vii (1862–3), pp 84–92.

[Rothe, David]. *Analecta sacra, nova, et mira de rebus catholicorum in Hibernia . . . gestis* . . . [N.P.] 1616. 2nd ed., 2 vols, Cologne, 1617, 1619; ed. P. F. Moran. Dublin, 1884.

Sidney, Henry. *Diary of the times of Charles II. Ed.* R. W. Blencowe. 2 vols. London, 1843.

Spenser, Edmund. A view of the state of Ireland [1596]. In *The historie of Ireland collected by three learned authors, viz Meredith Hanmer . . ., Edmund Campion . . ., and Edmund Spenser . . .*, ed. James Ware (Dublin, 1633); reprinted as *Ancient Irish histories: the works of Spencer, Campion, Hanmer, and Marleburrough* (2 vols, Dublin, 1809).

Later editions: Henry Morley (ed.), *Ireland under Elizabeth and James I*; ed. W. L. Renwick, London, 1934, reprinted Oxford, 1970.

[Stafford, Thomas]. *Pacata Hibernia: Ireland appeased and reduced, or a historie of the late warres of Ireland, especially in the province of Munster under the command of Sir George Carew.* London, 1633; 2 vols, Dublin, 1690; 2 vols, ed. S. H. O'Grady, London, 1896.

Stanihurst, Richard. The thirde booke of the historie of Ireland, comprising the raigne of Henry the eight. In Holinshed, *Chronicles* (1577 ed.).

—— A treatise containing a plain and perfect description of Ireland. . . . In Raphael Holinshed, *Chronicles* (1577 ed.).

See above, p. 660

STEVENS. *The journal of John Stevens. Ed.* R. H. Murray. Oxford, 1912.

[Story, George]. *A true and impartial history of the most material occurrences in the kingdom of Ireland during the last two years.* London, 1691.

Story, George. *A continuation of the impartial history of the wars of Ireland.* London, 1693.

Temple, John. *The Irish rebellion: or the history of the beginning and first progress of the general rebellion raised within the kingdom of Ireland, upon the three and twentieth day of October, 1641.* London, 1646; later editions, 1674, 1679.

Walker, George. *A true account of the siege of Londonderry.* London, 1689.

Ware, James. *De scriptoribus Hiberniae libri duo. . . .* Dublin, 1639; facsimile reprint, Farnborough, Hants, 1966.

—— *De Hibernia et antiquitatibus eius disquisitiones . . .* London, 1654; 2nd ed., 1658.

—— *Rerum Hibernicarum annales . . ., 1485–1558.* Dublin, 1664.

—— *De praesulibus Hiberniae commentarius . . .* Dublin, 1665.

For translations see below, p. 672.

2 *Pamphlets and newspapers*

A brief character of Ireland. London, 1692.

The British muse, or tyranny exposed . . . To which is added A short poem on the generous articles of Limerick and Galway. London [1701].

Blenerhassett, Thomas. *A direction for the plantation in Ulster.* London, 1610.

Bog-witticisms, or Dear Joy's commonplaces. . . . [London, *c.* 1683].

[Callaghan, John]. *Vindiciarum catholicorum Hiberniae . . . libri duo.* Paris, 1650.

Caron, Raymond. *Remonstria Hibernorum contra Lovanienses ultramontanasque censuras. . . .* London, 1665.

Collins, John. *A plea for the bringing of Irish cattel. . . .* London, 1680.

Darcy, Patrick. *An argument delivered . . . by the express order of the house of commons.* Waterford, 1643; reprinted, Dublin, 1764.

A discourse concerning Ireland and the different interests thereof in answer to the Exon and Barnstable petitions . . . London, 1698.

Dublin intelligence, 1690–91.

[? Farwell, James]. *The Irish Hudibras, or Fingallian prince.* London, 1689.

[French, Nicholas]. *The bleeding Iphigeneia.* [Paris], 1675.

—— *A narrative of the settlement and sale of Ireland.* Louvain, 1668.

—— *The unkinde desertor of loyall men and true frinds.* [N.P.], 1676.

Gookin, Vincent. *The author and case of transplanting the Irish into Connaught vindicated from the unjust aspersions of Col. R. Laurence.* London, 1655.

—— *The great case of transplantation in Ireland discussed.* London, 1655.

Harris, Paul. *Arktomastix*. Dublin, 1633.

Heath, James. *Flagellum, or the life and death, birth and burial of Oliver Cromwell, the late usurper*. London, 1663.

Hiberniae sive antiquioris Scotiae vindiciae adversus immodestam parecbasim Thomae Dempsteri moderni Scoti nuper editam. . . . [By G. F.] Antwerp, 1621.

Ireland's advocate. London, 1641.

Ireland's declaration, being a remonstrance. Dublin, 1649.

[Leslie, Charles] *An answer to a book intituled The state of the protestants in Ireland under the late King James's government*. London, 1692.

Lawrence, Richard. *The interest of England in the Irish transplantation stated . . . an answer to a scandalous seditious pamphlet, entituled The great case of transplantation in Ireland discussed*. London, 1655.

The London Gazette, 1665–91.

Mackenzie, John. *A narrative of the siege of Londonderry*. See above, p. 661.

Milton, John. *Observations on the articles of peace . . . and a representation of the Scots presbytery at Belfast in Ireland*. London, 1649.

The News-Letter. Dublin, 1685.

O'Mahony, Conor. *Disputatio apologetica et manifestativa de iure regni Hiberniae pro catholicis Hibernis contra haereticos Anglos*. Lisbon, 1645.

Philips, George. *The interest of England in the preservation of Ireland*. London, 1689.

Porter, Francis. *Palinodia religionis praetensae reformatae*. Rome, 1679.

—— *Securis evangelica ad haeresis radices posita*. Rome, 1674.

Punch, John. *D. Richardi Bellingi vindiciae eversae*. Paris, 1653.

[Reily, Hugh]. *Ireland's case briefly stated*. [Louvain], 1695.

Sinnich, John. *Confessionistarum Goliathismus profligatus*. Louvain, 1657.

Walsh, Peter. *The history and vindication of the loyal formulary of Irish remonstrance*. [N.P.], 1674.

—— *Causa Valesiana. . . .* London, 1684.

—— *Queries concerning the lawfulnesse of the present cessation*. Kilkenny, 1648.

Walwin's wiles. London, 1649; reprinted in William Haller and Godfrey Davies (ed.), *The leveller tracts* (Gloucester, Mass., 1964).

White, Stephen. *Apologia pro Hibernia adversus Cambri calumnias. . . . Ed.* Matthew Kelly. Dublin, 1849.

3 Other contemporary writing

Historical writing on pre-1534 subjects is included here.

Andrews, George. *A quaternion of sermons*. Dublin, 1624.

The Annals of Clonmacnoise from the earliest period to A.D. 1408, translated into English by Conell Mageoghagan, A.D. 1627. Ed. Denis Murphy. Dublin, 1896.

Annals of Ireland from 1443 to 1465. Trans. Dubhaltach Mac Fir Bhisigh. In *Ir. Arch. Soc. Misc.*, i (1846), pp 258–9.

Archdekin, Richard. *Praecipuae controversiae fidei ad facilem methodum redactae.* Louvain, 1671; reissued, with the title *Theologia tripartita*, Antwerp, 1678.

BACON. *The works of Francis Bacon. Ed.* James Spedding. 7 vols. London, 1857–74.

BALE. The vocacyon of John Bale to the bishoprick of Ossorie in Ireland. . . . In *Harleian Miscellany*, vi (1734), pp 402–28.

Baron, Bonaventure. *Metra miscellanea.* Rome, 1645.
See plate 14.

Bergin, Osborn (ed.). *Irish bardic poetry. Ed.* David Greene and Fergus Kelly. Dublin, 1970.

BOYLE. *Musarum lachrymae.* Dublin, 1630.
Verses on the death of the countess of Cork.

Boyle, Robert. *The sceptical chymist.* London, 1661.

Boyle, Roger (bishop of Clogher). *Inquisitio in fidem Christianorum hujus saeculi.* Dublin, 1665.

Bruodin, Anthony. *Propugnaculum catholicae veritatis.* Prague, 1669.

Burke, Augustine Gibbon. *Probatica piscina naturae per peccatum lapsae morbos sanans. . . .* Würzburg, 1687.

—— *De Luthero-Calvinismo, schismatico quidem, sed reconciliabili.* Erfurt, 1663.

Camden, William. *Anglica, Hibernica, Normannica, Cambrica, a veteribus scripta* . . . Frankfurt, 1602.
Includes Giraldus Cambrensis, 'Topographica Hibernica' and 'Expugnatio Hibernica'.

Céitinn, Séathrún. See Keating, Geoffrey.

Churchyard, Thomas. *A generall rehearsal of warres. . . .* London, 1579.

Clonsinnil, Dr. *Défense des Hibernois.* Paris, 1651.

Colgan, John. *Acta sanctorum veteris et maioris Scotiae, seu Hiberniae sanctorum insulae. . . .* 2 vols, Louvain, 1645; facsimile reprint, with foreword by Brendan Jennings, I.M.C., Dublin, 1948.

—— *Triadis thaumaturgae, seu divorum Patricii, Columbae, et Brigidae . . . acta.* Louvain, 1647.

COMERFORD. *Coronatae virtuti.* Rome, 1629.
Verses on the episcopal ordination of Patrick Comerford.

Conny, Bernard. *Riaghuil Threas Uird S. Froinsias.* Louvain, 1641.

Coxe, Samuel. *Two sermons . . . preached March 2 and 9, 1659* [1660]. Dublin, 1660.

Dekker, Thomas. *The honest whore.* London, 1604.

A discourse of Ireland (*circa* 1599): a sidelight on English colonial policy. *Ed.* D. B. Quinn. In *R.I.A. Proc.*, xlvii, C, no. 3 (Feb. 1942), pp 151–66.

A discourse between two councillors of state, the one of England and the other of Ireland. *Ed.* Aidan Clarke. In *Anal. Hib.*, no. 26 (1970), pp 159–75.

Dodwell, Henry. *Prolegomena apologetica de usu dogmatum philosophicorum, praecipue Stoicorum, in theologia.* Dublin, 1672.

Dowley, John. *Suim bhunudhasach an teaguisg Chriosdaithe.* Louvain, 1663.

Exhibitio consolatoria tabulae emblematicae serenissimae principi Isabellae . . . Douai, 1622.

See Brady, Irish colleges (below, p. 671).

Farquhar, George. *The twin rivals.* London, 1703.

FENAGH. *The Book of Fenagh. Ed.* W. M. Hennessy and D. H. Kelly. Dublin, 1875; reflex facsimile, I.M.C., Dublin, 1939.

Transcribed by Muirghas Ó Maoil Chonaire.

—— *Book of Fenagh, supplementary volume. Ed.* R. A. S. Macalister. I.M.C., Dublin, 1939.

Fitzsimon, Henry. *Words of comfort . . . letters from a cell . . . and diary of the Bohemian war of 1620. Ed.* Edmund Hogan. Dublin, 1881.

With a sketch of Fitzsimon's life by Hogan.

—— *The justification and exposition of the divine sacrifice of the mass.* Douai, 1611.

Gállduff, Teabóid (Theobald Stapleton). *Catechismus . . . an teagasc Chriostui. . . .* Brussels, 1639.

Gearnon, Antoin. *Parrthas an anma.* Louvain, 1645.

Gillies, William (ed.). A poem on the downfall of the Gaoidhil. In *Éigse*, xiii (1969–70), pp 203–10.

Giraldus Cambrensis. See Camden, above, p. 665.

HACKET. *Filíocht Phádraigín Haicéad. Ed.* Máire Ní Cheallacháin. Dublin, 1962.

Harold, Francis. *B. Alberti a Santhiano . . . vita et opera. . . .* Rome, 1688.

—— *Epitome annalium ordinis minorum. . . .* Rome, 1662.

Jonson, Ben. *The Irish masque.* London, 1613.

Kearney, John. *Aibidil Gaoidheilge & caiticiosma. . . .* Dublin, 1571.

See plate 13.

Keating, Geoffrey. *Eochair-sgiath an aifrinn . . .; an explanatory defence of the mass . . . Ed.* Patrick O'Brien. Dublin, 1898.

—— *Foras feasa ar Éirinn: the history of Ireland. Ed.* David Comyn and P. S. Dinneen. 4 vols. Irish Texts Society, London, 1902–14.

—— *Trí biorghaoithe an bháis* (1631). *Ed.* Osborn Bergin. Dublin, 1931.

Laud, William. *The works of Archbishop Laud. Ed.* William Scott and James Bliss. 7 vols. Oxford, 1847–60.

Mac Aingil, Aodh. *Scáthán shacramuinte na h-aithridhe.* Louvain, 1618; ed. Canice Mooney, Dublin, 1952.

Mac Fir Bhisigh, Dubhaltach. Introduction to his book of genealogies (U.C.D.

MS). *Ed.*, with translation, by Toirdhealbhach Ó Raithbheartaigh in *Genealogical tracts*, i (I.M.C., Dublin, 1932), pp 1–106.

See also Annals of Ireland from 1443 to 1465, above, p. 665.

McKenna, Lambert (Láimhbheartach Mac Cionnaith) (ed.). *Aithdioghluim dána.* Dublin, 1939.

—— *Dioghluim dána.* Dublin, 1938.

—— *Iomarbhágh na bhfileadh.* 2 vols. London, 1918.

—— Some Irish bardic poems: XCI. In *Studies*, xxxviii (1949), pp 57–62; 183–8, 338–44.

Mageoghagan, Connell. See *The Annals of Clonmacnoise . . .*

[Marsh, Narcissus]. *Institutiones logicae, in usum inventutis Academiae Dublinensis.* Dublin, 1679.

[Matthews, *alias* O'Mahony, Francis]. Brevis synopsis provinciae Hiberniae fratrum minorum. *Ed.* Brendan Jennings. In *Anal. Hib.*, no. 6 (1934), pp 139–91.

Messingham, Thomas. *Florilegium sanctorum, seu vitae et acta sanctorum Hiberniae . . .* Paris, 1624.

Mhág Craith, Cuthbert (ed.). *Dán na mBráthar Mionúr.* Dublin, 1967.

Michelburne, John. *Ireland preserved, or the siege of Londonderry.* London, 1705.

Mooney, Donagh. De provincia Hiberniae S. Francisci. *Ed.* Brendan Jennings. In *Anal. Hib.*, no. 6 (1934), pp 12–138.

Ó BRUADAIR. *Duanaire Dháibhidh Uí Bhruadair; the poems of David Ó Bruadair. Ed.* J. C. MacErlean. 3 pts. London, 1910–17.

O'Clery, Michael (Mícheál Ó Cléirigh). *Genealogiae regum et sanctorum Hiberniae. Ed.* Paul Walsh. Maynooth, 1918.

—— *The martyrology of Donegal. Ed.* J. H. Todd and William Reeves. Dublin, 1864.

—— The O'Clery book of genealogies. *Ed.* Séamus Pender. In *Anal. Hib.*, no. 18 (1951).

Ó Conaill, Seán. Tuireamh na hÉireann. In Cecile O'Rahilly (ed.), *Five seventeenth-century political poems* (Dublin, 1952), pp 50–82.

O'DALY. *Dánta do chum Aonghus Fionn Ó Dálaigh. Ed.* Lambert McKenna. Dublin, 1919.

O'Daly, Dominic. *Initium, incrementa, et exitus familiae Geraldinorum . . . ac persecutionis haereticorum descriptio.* Lisbon, 1655.

O'DONNELL. Marbhna Aodha Ruaidh Uí Domhnaill. *Ed.* P. A. Breatnach. In *Éigse*, xv (1973), pp 31–50.

Ó Glacan, Niall. *Cursus medicus.* 2 vols. Bologna, 1655.

—— *Tractatus de peste. . . .* Toulouse, 1629.

Ó HUIGINN. *The bardic poems of Tadhg Dall Ó Huiginn. Ed.* Eleanor Knott. 2 pts. London, 1922, 1926.

O'Hussey, Bonaventure (Giolla Brighde Ó hEodhusa). *An teagasc Criosdaithe.* Antwerp, 1611.

[O'Mahony, Francis]. *Examen iuridicum censurae facultatis theologiae Parisiensis.* [? Frankfurt], 1631.

—— See also Matthews.

O'Mahony, James. Sanguinea eremus martyrum Hiberniae ord. Eremit. S. P. Augustini (1655). *Ed.* F. X. Martin. In *Archiv. Hib.*, xv (1950), pp 74–91.

Ó Maoil Chonaire, Flaithrí (Florence Conry). *Desiderius, otherwise called Sgáthán an chrábaidh.* Louvain, 1616; ed. T. F. O'Rahilly, Dublin, 1941.

Ó Maoil Chonaire, Muirghes. Aisling Tundail, ed. Kuno Meyer, in V. H. Friedel and Kuno Meyer, *La vision de Tondale* (*Tnudgal*) (Paris, 1907), pp 87–155.

See also *Fenagh*, above.

Ó Maolmhuaidh, Froinsias. *Lucerna fidelium ... Lochrann na gcreidmheach.* Rome, 1676.

O'Meara, Dermot. *Pathologia haereditaria generalis. ...* Dublin, 1619.

O'Meara, Edmund. *Examen diatribae Thomae Willisii ... de febribus.* London, 1665.

O'Rahilly, Cecile (ed.). *Five seventeenth-century political poems.* Dublin, 1952.

O'Rahilly, T. F. (ed.). *Dánfhocail.* Dublin, 1921.

—— *Dánta grádha.* Dublin and Cork, 1926.

—— *Measgra dánta.* Dublin and Cork, 1927.

Ó Súilleabháin, Pádraig (ed.). *Buaidh na naomh croiche.* Dublin, 1972.

O'Sullivan Beare, Philip. *Selections from the Zoilomastix of O'Sullivan Beare. Ed.* T. J. O'Donnell. I.M.C., Dublin, 1960.

Párliament na mBan. *Ed.* Brian Ó Cuív. Dublin, 1952.

Pairlement Chloinne Tomáis. *Ed.* Osborn Bergin. In *Gadelica*, i (1912–13), pp 35–50, 127–31, 137–50, 220–36.

The Petty papers: some unpublished writings of Sir William Petty. Ed. Marquess of Lansdowne. 2 vols. London, 1927.

Porter, Francis. *Syntagma variarum ecclesiae definitionum.* Rome, 1681.

PRAYER-BOOK. *Foirm na nurrnuidheadh ... ar na dtarraing as Laidin agus as Gaill-bherla in Gaoidheilg. ...* Edinburgh, 1567.

—— *Leabhar na nVrnaightheadh gComhchoidchiond* [Book of Common Prayer]. Trans. Uilliam Ó Domhnaill. Dublin, 1608.

Price, Liam (ed.). Armed forces of the Irish chiefs in the early sixteenth century (list from B.M. Cott. MS, Dom. A, xviii). In *R.S.A.I. Jn.*, lxii (1932), pp 201–7.

[Serry, J. H.]. *Historiae congregationum de auxiliis ... libri quatuor.* Antwerp, 1709. Under pseudonym of Augustine Leblanc.

Shadwell, Thomas. *The Lancashire witches and Tegue O Divelly.* London, 1682.

Sinnich, John. *Sanctorum patrum ... trias.* Louvain, 1648.

Spenser, Edmund. *The faerie queene.* 2 vols. London, 1590–96.

Stanihurst, Richard. *De rebus in Hibernia gestis....* Antwerp, 1584.

—— *De vita S. Patricii....* Antwerp, 1587.

STUKELEY. *The famous historye of the life and death of Captaine Thomas Stukeley.* London, 1605.

Suim Riaghlachas Phroinsiais. [? Louvain], 1610–14.

SWIFT. *The prose works of Jonathan Swift. Ed.* Herbert Davis. 14 vols. Oxford, 1939–68.

Taylor, Jeremy. *A dissuasive from popery, to the people of Ireland.* Dublin, 1667.

—— *The rule and exercises of holy dying.* London, 1651.

—— *The rule and exercises of holy living.* London, 1650.

Temple, William. Essay upon the advancement of trade in Ireland [1673]. In *Miscellanea* (London, 1697), pt. 1, pp 97–145.

Testament, New. *Tiomna Nuadh ár dTighearna.* Trans. Uilliam Ó Domhnaill. Dublin, 1602 [1603].

Testament, Old. *Leabhuir na Sein-Tiomna ... tre chúram ... Uilliam Bedel....* London, 1685.

TUNDAL. See Ó Maoil Chonaire, Muirghes.

USSHER. *The whole works of ... James Ussher.... Ed.* C. R. Elrington and J. H. Todd. 17 vols. Dublin, 1847–64.

—— Of the original and first institution of corbes, herenaghs and termon lands (1609), ed. Charles Vallancey, in *Collectanea de rebus Hibernicis*, i (Dublin, 1770).

—— *Discourse of the religion anciently professed by the Irish and Scottish, showing it to be for substance the same with that which at this day is by public authority established in the Church of England.* Dublin, 1622.

—— *A discourse of the religion anciently professed by the Irish and British.* Dublin, 1631.

—— (ed.). *Veterum epistolarum Hibernicarum sylloge.* Dublin, 1632.

—— *Britannicarum ecclesiarum antiquitates ...* Dublin, 1639.

Wadding, Luke. *Annales minorum.* 8 vols. Lyons, 1625–54.

—— (ed.). *Francisci Assisiati opuscula nunc primum collecta....* Antwerp, 1623.

—— (ed.). *Joannis Duns Scoti ... opera omnia.* 16 vols. Lyons, 1639.

4 *Contemporary maps*

Andrews, J. H. Baptista Boazio's map of Ireland. In *Long Room* (Bulletin of the Friends of the Library of Trinity College, Dublin), no. 1 (1970), pp 29–36.

—— An early map of Inishowen. In *Long Room* (Bulletin of the Friends of the Library of Trinity College, Dublin), no. 7 (Spring, 1973), pp 19–25.

Boazio, Baptista. *Map of Ireland, c. 1600.* London, 1938. Facsimile issued by B.M.

DERRY. *Londonderry beseiged* [sic] *by General Hamilton and Conrard* [sic] *de Rosen, Mareschall Generall of all the Irish forces, 1689.* By Capt. Archibald Maculloch. London, 1689.

See plate 11.

—— *A new map of the city of Londonderry . . . as it was besieged by the Irish army in the year 1689: exactly surveyed by Capt. Francis Nevill.* Dublin [*c.* 1693].

Maps of the escheated counties in Ireland, 1609. Ordnance Survey, Southampton, 1861.

Mercator, Gerard. Map of Ireland. In *Atlas*, iii (Dusseldorf, 1595).

Ortelius, Abraham. Map of Ireland. In *Theatrum orbis terrarum* (Antwerp, 1572).

Petty, William. *Barony maps of the Down Survey.* 2 vols. Ordnance Survey, Southampton, 1908.

—— *A geographicall description of the kingdom of Ireland: collected from the actual survey made by Sir William Petty, corrected and amended. . . .* London, 1685.

—— *Hiberniae delineatio.* [London, 1685.]

Facsimile reprint of *Hiberniae delineatio* and *A geographicall description*, with introduction by J. H. Andrews, Shannon, 1969.

—— *A new mapp of the kingdome of Ireland done from Sir William Petty's survey. . . .* Printed and sold by Christopher Browne. . . . London, 1691 (copy in R.I.A.).

Pitt, Moses. *The English atlas.* 4 vols. London, 1680–2.

Speed, John. *The theatre of the empire of Great Britain.* London, 1611.

See plate 5.

Ulster and other Irish maps, c. 1600. Ed. G. A. Hayes-McCoy. I.M.C., Dublin, 1964.

See plates 3–4.

ULSTER. A plot of the six escheated counties of Ulster [*c.* 1610] (facsimile of B.M. Cotton MS, Augustus I, ii, 44). In *Anal. Hib.*, no. 8 (1938), facing p. 298.

C *SOURCE COMPILATIONS*

Analecta Hibernica, including the reports of the Irish Manuscripts Commission. Dublin, 1930– .

Ancient Irish histories: the works of Spencer, Campion, Hanmer, and Marleburrough. Ed. James Ware. Dublin, 1633; reprint, 2 vols, Dublin, 1809.

Archivium Hibernicum: or Irish historical records. Catholic Record Society, Maynooth, 1912– .

Brady, John (ed.). The Irish colleges in the Low Countries. In *Archiv. Hib.*, xiv (1949), pp 66–91.

Documentary collection, including *Exhibitio consolatoria* . . . (above, p. 666), and list of students at Douai.

Burke, W. P. (ed.). *The Irish priests in the penal times (1660–1760).* Waterford, 1914; reprint, Shannon, 1969.

Carty, James (ed.). *Ireland from the flight of the earls to Grattan's parliament (1607–1782): a documentary record.* Dublin, 1949.

Collectanea Hibernica: sources for Irish history. Dublin, 1958–

Desiderata curiosa Hibernica, or a select collection of state papers. Ed. [John Lodge]. 2 vols. Dublin, 1772.

See Chichester, above, p. 648.

English historical documents. General editor D. C. Douglas. Vol. viii (1660–1714), ed. Andrew Browning. London, 1953.

Facsimiles of the national manuscripts of Ireland. Ed. J. T. Gilbert. 4 vols. Dublin, 1874–84.

Falkiner, C. L. *Illustrations of Irish history and topography, mainly of the seventeenth century.* London, 1904.

Itinerary of Fynes Moryson; Sir Josias Bodley's Visit to Lecale, 1602; Luke Gernon's Discourse of Ireland, *c.* 1620; Sir William Brereton's Travels in Ireland, 1635; M. Jorevin de Rocheford's Description, 1688.

Gwynn, Aubrey (ed.). Documents relating to the Irish in the West Indies. In *Anal. Hib.*, no. 4 (1932), pp 139–286.

Harris, Walter (ed.). *Hibernica. . . .* 2 vols. Dublin, 1747, 1750.

McNeill, Charles (ed.). Reports on the Rawlinson collection of manuscripts preserved in the Bodleian Library, Oxford, classes A–D. In *Anal. Hib.*, no. 1 (1930), pp 12–178; no. 2 (1931), pp. 1–92.

Maxwell, Constantia. *Irish history from contemporary sources, 1509–1610.* London, 1923.

Miscellany of the Celtic Society. Ed. John O'Donovan. Dublin, 1849.

Moody, T. W., and Simms, J. G. (ed.). *The bishopric of Derry and the Irish Society of London, 1602–1705.* Vol. i (1602–70). I.M.C., Dublin, 1968.

Morley, Henry (ed.). *Ireland under Elizabeth and James I.* London, 1890.

Spenser, View of the state of Ireland; Davies, Discovery of the true causes, and other items; Moryson, Description of Ireland.

Nugae antiquae, . . . original papers . . . written [Henry VIII to James I] by Sir John Harrington and others. . . . Ed. Thomas Park. 2 vols. London, 1804.

O'Rahilly, T. F. (ed.). Irish poets, historians, and judges in English documents, 1538–1615. In *R.I.A. Proc.*, xxxvi, sect. C (1921–4), pp 86–120.

PETTY. *The economic writings of Sir William Petty. Ed.* C. H. Hull. 2 vols. Cambridge, 1899.

Ronan, M. V. *The reformation in Dublin, 1536–1668: from original sources.* London, 1925.

—— *The reformation in Ireland under Elizabeth, 1558–1580: from original sources.* London, 1930.

Simington, R. C. (ed.). *The transplantation to Connacht, 1654–58.* I.M.C., Dublin, 1970.

The Tanner letters. Ed. Charles McNeill. I.M.C., Dublin, 1943.

Tracts relating to Ireland. 2 vols. Ir. Arch. Soc., Dublin 1841, 1843.

Vallancey, Charles (ed.). *Collectanea de rebus Hibernicis.* 6 vols. Dublin, 1770–1804.

Walsh, Micheline (ed.). *Spanish knights of Irish origin: documents from continental archives.* 3 vols. I.M.C., Dublin, 1960–70.

WARE. *The whole works of Sir James Ware concerning Ireland, revised and improved. Ed.* Walter Harris. 3 vols in 2. Dublin, 1739, 1746. 2nd ed., 1764.

Vol. i contains a translation of *De praesulibus*, continued by Harris; vol. ii contains a translation of *De Hibernia* with omissions and additions by Harris; vol. iii contains a translation of *De scriptoribus*, continued by Harris. See above, p. 663.

Ware, James (ed.). *The historie of Ireland collected by three learned authors, viz Meredith Hanmer . . ., Edmund Campion . . ., and Edmund Spenser . . .* Dublin, 1633; reprinted as *Ancient Irish histories: the workes of Spencer, Campion, Hanmer, and Marleburrough*, 2 vols, Dublin, 1809.

IV SECONDARY WORKS

A GENERAL HISTORY

Bagwell, Richard. *Ireland under the Tudors: with a succinct account of the earlier history.* 3 vols. London, 1885–90; reprint, 1963.

—— *Ireland under the Stuarts and during the interregnum.* 3 vols. London, 1909–16; reprint, 1963.

Beckett, J. C. *The making of modern Ireland, 1603–1923.* London, 1966; reprint, 1969.

Black, J. B. *The reign of Elizabeth, 1558–1603.* Oxford, 1936; 2nd ed., 1959.

Clark, G. N. *The later Stuarts, 1660–1714.* Oxford, 1934; 2nd ed., 1955.

Clarke, Aidan. The colonisation of Ulster and the rebellion of 1641 (1603–60). In Moody & Martin, *Ir. hist.*, pp 189–203.

Davies, Godfrey. *The early Stuarts, 1603–1660.* Oxford, 1937; 2nd ed., 1959.

—— *The restoration of Charles II, 1658–1660.* San Marino and London, 1955.

Dunlop, Robert. Ireland to the settlement of Ulster. In *Camb. mod. hist.*, iii (1905), ch. XVIII, pp 579–616.

—— Ireland from the plantation of Ulster to the Cromwellian settlement (1611–59). In *Camb. mod. hist.*, iv (1906), ch. XVIII, pp 513–38.

—— Ireland from the restoration to the act of resumption (1660–1700). In *Camb. mod. hist.*, v (1908), ch. x (3), pp 301–23.

—— (ed.). *Ireland under the commonwealth.* Introduction, pp i–clxii. Manchester, 1913.

Firth, C. H. *The last years of the protectorate, 1656–1658.* 2 vols. London, 1909.

Froude, J. A. *History of England, from the fall of Wolsey to the defeat of the Spanish armada.* 12 vols. London, 1856–70; new ed., 12 vols. 1870; later eds.

—— *The English in Ireland in the eighteenth century.* 3 vols. London, 1872–4 2nd ed., 1881.

Gardiner, S. R. *History of England from the accession of James I to the outbreak of the civil war, 1603–42.* 10 vols. London, 1863–81; 2nd ed., 1883–4.

—— *History of the great civil war, 1642–9.* 3 vols. London, 1886–91. Revised ed., 4 vols, 1893.

—— *History of the commonwealth and protectorate, 1649–56.* 3 vols. London, 1894–1901; 2nd ed., revised by C. H. Firth, 4 vols, 1903.

Green, A. S. *The making of Ireland and its undoing.* London, 1908.

Hayes-McCoy, G. A. The Tudor conquest (1534–1603). In Moody & Martin, *Ir. hist.*, pp 174–88.

Klopp, Onno. *Der Fall des Hauses Stuart.* 14 vols. Vienna, 1875–88.

Lecky, W. E. H. *History of Ireland in the eighteenth century.* 5 vols. London, 1892.

Macaulay, T. B. *History of England from the accession of James II.* 5 vols. London, 1849–61.

MacCurtain, Margaret. *Tudor and Stuart Ireland.* Dublin and London, 1972.

MacGeoghegan, James. *Histoire d'Irlande ancienne et moderne.* 3 vols. Paris and Amsterdam, 1758–63; English translation, Dublin, 1831–2.

Murray, R. H. *Revolutionary Ireland and its settlement.* London, 1911.

Ogg, David. *England in the reign of Charles II.* 2 vols. Oxford, 1934.

—— *England in the reign of James II and William III.* Oxford, 1955.

Otway-Ruthven, A. J. *A history of medieval Ireland.* London and New York, 1968.

Petrie, C. A. *The Jacobite movement.* London, 1932; 2nd ed., 2 vols, 1948–50; 3rd ed., 1959.

Prendergast, J. P. *Ireland from the restoration to the revolution, 1660–1690.* London, 1887.

Ranke, Leopold von. *History of England, principally in the seventeenth century.* 6 vols. Oxford, 1875.

Silke, J. J. *Ireland and Europe, 1559–1607.* Dundalk, 1966 (Dublin Historical Association, Irish History Series, no. 7).

Simms, J. G. *Jacobite Ireland, 1685–91.* London, 1969.

—— The restoration and the Jacobite war (1660–91). In Moody & Martin, *Ir. hist.* pp 204–16.

Wilson, Philip. *The making of modern Ireland.* Dublin and London, 1912.

B HISTORICAL GEOGRAPHY AND CARTOGRAPHY

Andrews, J. H. Geography and government in Elizabethan Ireland. In *Ir. geog. studies*, pp 178–91.

—— The Irish surveys of Robert Lythe. In *Imago Mundi*, xix (1965), pp 22–31.

—— The maps of the escheated counties of Ulster, 1609–10. In *R.I.A. Proc.*, lxxiv, sect. C (1974), pp 133–70.

—— Notes on the historical geography of the Irish iron industry. In *Ir. Geography*, iii, no. 3 (1956), pp 139–49.

—— Territorial divisions. In Victor Meally (ed.), *Encyclopaedia of Ireland* (Dublin, 1968), pp 142–50.

Goblet, Y. M. *La transformation de la géographie politique de l'Irlande au XVIIe siècle.* 2 vols. Paris, 1930.

Lynam, Edward. *The mapmaker's art.* London, 1953.

Map of monastic Ireland. Compiled by R. N. Hadcock. Ordnance Survey, Dublin, 1959; 2nd ed., 1969.

Meinig, D. W. A macrogeography of western imperialism: some morphologies of moving frontiers of political control. In Fay Gale and Graham H. Lawton (ed.), *Settlement and encounter* (Melbourne, 1969), pp 213–40.

Ó Danachair, Caoimhín. Representation of houses on some Irish maps. In Geraint Jenkins (ed.), *Studies in folk life* (London, 1969), pp. 91–103.

Ó Domhnaill, Seán. The maps of the Down Survey. In *I.H.S.*, iii, no. 12 (Sept. 1943), pp 381–92.

Ulster and other Irish maps, c. 1600. See above, p. 670.

C TOPOGRAPHY AND PLACE-NAMES

Power, Patrick. *The place names of Decies.* London, 1907.

Price, Liam. The place-names of the books of survey and distribution and other records of the Cromwellian settlement. In *R.S.A.I. Jn.*, lxxxi (1951), pp 89–106.

—— *The place-names of County Wicklow.* 7 pts. Dublin, 1945–67.

Walsh, Paul. *The place-names of Westmeath.* Dublin, 1957.

D SPECIAL FIELDS AND TOPICS

1 Political history

Barnard, T. C. Social policy of the commonwealth and protectorate in Ireland (D.Phil. thesis, University of Oxford, 1972).

—— *Cromwellian Ireland: English government and reform in Ireland, 1649–1660.* Oxford, 1975.

Beckett, J. C. The confederation of Kilkenny reviewed. In *Hist. Studies*, ii (1959), pp 29–41.

Canny, N. P. Glory and profit: Sir Henry Sidney and the government of Ireland, 1558–78 (Ph.D. thesis, University of Pennsylvania, 1972).

—— The flight of the earls, 1607. In *I.H.S.*, xvii, no. 67 (Mar. 1971), pp 380–99.

Clarke, Aidan. The Old English in Ireland, 1625–42 (Ph.D. thesis, University of Dublin, 1959).

—— The army and politics in Ireland, 1625–30. In *Studia Hib.*, no. 4 (1964), pp 28–53.

—— *The graces, 1625–41.* Dundalk, 1968 (Dublin Historical Association, Irish History Series, no. 8).

—— Ireland and the general crisis. In *Past & Present*, no. 48 (1970), pp 79–99.

—— *The Old English in Ireland, 1625–42.* London, 1966.

—— The policies of the Old English in parliament, 1640–41. In *Hist. Studies*, v (1965), pp 85–102.

Corish, P. J. The crisis in Ireland in 1648: the nuncio and the supreme council: conclusions. In *Ir. Theol. Quart.*, xxii, no. 3 (July, 1955), pp 231–57.

—— The origins of catholic nationalism. In Corish, *Ir. catholicism*, iii, ch. 8 (1968).

Cregan, D. F. The confederation of Kilkenny: its organisation, personnel and history (Ph.D. thesis, N.U.I. (U.C.D.), 1947).

See also D. F. Cregan, 'The confederation of Kilkenny' in Brian Farrell (ed.), *The Irish parliamentary tradition* (Dublin and New York, 1973), pp 102–15.

—— Irish recusant lawyers in politics in the reign of James I. In *Ir. Jurist*, N.S., v (1970), pp 306–20.

Edie, C. A. The Irish cattle bills: a study in restoration politics. In *Amer. Phil. Soc. Trans.*, new series, lx, pt 2 (1970), pp 5–66.

Henry, L. W. The earl of Essex and Ireland, 1599. In *I.H.R. Bull.*, xxxii (1959), pp 1–23.

Hogan, James. *Ireland in the European system.* Vol. i (1500–1557). London, 1920.

No further vol. published.

Kearney, H. F. *Strafford in Ireland, 1633–41: a study in absolutism.* Manchester, 1959; reprint, 1961.

Lindley, K. J. The impact of the 1641 rebellion on England and Wales, 1641–5. In *I.H.S.*, xviii, no. 70 (Sept. 1972), pp 143–76.

Lowe, John. Charles I and the confederation of Kilkenny. In *I.H.S.*, xiv, no. 53 (Mar. 1954), pp 1–19.

—— The Glamorgan mission to Ireland, 1645–6. In *Studia Hib.*, iv (1964), pp 155–96.

McGuire, J. I. Politics, opinion, and the Irish constitution, 1688–1707 (M.A. thesis, N.U.I. (U.C.D.), 1968).

McGuire, J. I. Why was Ormond dismissed in 1669? In *I.H.S.*, xviii, no. 71 (Mar. 1973), pp 295–312.

Mooney, Canice. Was Wadding a patriotic Irishman? In *Father Luke Wadding*, pp 15–92.

Ó Domhnaill, Seán. Sir Niall Garbh O'Donnell and the rebellion of Sir Cahir O'Doherty. In *I.H.S.*, iii, no. 9 (Mar. 1942), pp. 34–8.

Perceval-Maxwell, Michael. Strafford, the Ulster Scots, and the covenanters. In *I.H.S.*, xviii, no. 72 (Sept. 1973), pp 524–51.

Ranger, T. O. Strafford in Ireland: a revaluation. In Trevor Aston (ed.), *Crisis in Europe, 1560–1660* (London, 1965), pp 271–93.

Walsh, Paul. *Irish chiefs and leaders. Ed.* Colm Ó Lochlainn. Dublin, 1960.

White, D. G. The reign of Edward VI in Ireland: some political, social, and economic aspects. In *I.H.S.*, xiv, no. 55 (Mar. 1965), pp 197–211.

2 *Constitutional and administrative history*

Bradshaw, Brendan. The opposition to the ecclesiastical legislation in the Irish reformation parliament. In *I.H.S.*, xvi, no. 63 (Mar. 1969), pp 285–303.

Canny, N. P. The treaty of Mellifont and the reorganisation of Ulster, 1603. In *Ir. Sword*, ix (1969–70), pp 249–62.

Clarke, Aidan. The history of Poynings' law, 1615–41. In *I.H.S.*, xviii, no. 70 (Sept. 1972), pp 207–22.

See also Edwards, R. D., and Moody, T. W.

—— 28 November 1634: a detail of Strafford's administration. In *R.S.A.I. Jn.*, xciiii (1963), pp. 161–7.

—— and Fenlon, Dermot. Two notes on the parliament of 1634. In *R.S.A.I. Jn.*, xcvii (1967), pp 85–90.

Davis, Thomas. *The patriot parliament of 1689. Ed.* Charles Gavan Duffy. London, 1893.

An abridgement of Davis's articles in *The Dublin Magazine and Citizen*, Jan.–Apr. 1843, entitled 'Irish state papers, no. 1, statutes of 1689'. See Brian Farrell, 'The patriot parliament of 1689' in *The Irish parliamentary tradition* (ed. Brian Farrell, Dublin and New York, 1973), pp 116–27, 272–3.

Edwards, R. Dudley, and Moody, T. W. The history of Poynings' law: part I, 1494–1615. In *I.H.S.*, ii, no. 8 (Sept. 1941), pp 415–24.

For part II, see Clarke.

Edwards, R. Dudley. The Irish reformation parliament of Henry VIII, 1536–7. In *Hist. Studies*, vi (1968), pp 59–84.

Fenlon, Dermot. See Clarke.

Kearney, H. F. The court of wards and liveries in Ireland, 1622–1641. In *R.I.A. Proc.*, lvii, sect. C, no. 2 (1955), pp 29–68.

Mayes, C. R. The early Stuarts and the Irish peerage. In *E.H.R.*, lxxiii (1958), pp 227–51.

Moody, T. W. The Irish parliament under Elizabeth and James I. In *R.I.A. Proc.*, xlv, sect. C, no. 6 (1939), pp 41–81.

O'Donoghue, Fergus. The Irish parliament of Charles II (M.A. thesis, N.U.I. (U.C.D.), 1970).

Quinn, D. B. Tudor rule in Ireland in the reigns of Henry VII and Henry VIII, with special reference to the Anglo-Irish financial administration (Ph.D. thesis, University of London, 1934).

—— Anglo-Irish local government, 1485–1534. In *I.H.S.*, i, no. 4 (Sept. 1939), pp 354–81.

—— Government printing and the publication of the Irish statutes in the sixteenth century. In *R.I.A. Proc.*, xlix, sect. C, no. 2 (1943), pp 415–24.

Richardson, H. G. and Sayles, G. O. *The Irish parliament in the middle ages.* Philadelphia, 1952; reissue, 1964.

Simington, R. C. A 'census' of Ireland, *c.* 1659. In *Anal. Hib.*, no. 12 (1943), pp 177–8.

Treadwell, V. W. Irish financial and administrative reform under James I: the customs and state regulation of Irish trade (Ph.D. thesis, Queen's University, Belfast, 1960).

—— The house of lords in the Irish parliament of 1613–1615. In *E.H.R.*, lxxx (1965), pp 92–107.

—— The Irish court of wards under James I. In *I.H.S.*, xii, no. 45 (Mar. 1960), pp 1–27.

—— The Irish parliament of 1569–71. In *R.I.A. Proc.*, lxv, sect. C (1966–7), pp 55–89.

3 *Diplomatic history*

Albion, Gordon. *Charles I and the court of Rome.* London, 1935.

Casway, J. I. Owen Roe O'Neill's return to Ireland in 1642: the diplomatic background. In *Studia Hib.*, ix (1969), pp 48–64.

Gabrieli, V. La missione di Sir Kenelm Digby alla corte di Innocenze X, 1645–1648. In *English Miscellany*, v (Rome, 1954), pp. 247–88.

4 *Ecclesiastical history*

Aiazzi, Giuseppe. *Nunziatura in Irlanda.* Florence, 1844. Trans. Annie Hutton with title *The embassy in Ireland* (Dublin, 1873).

Bellesheim, Alphons. *Geschichte der katholischen Kirche in Irland von der Einführung des Christentums bis auf die Gegenwart.* 3 vols. Mainz, 1890–91.
Vol. ii: 1509–1690.

Bolton, F. R. *The Caroline tradition in the Church of Ireland.* London, 1958.

Balic, Charles. Wadding, the Scotist. In *Father Luke Wadding*, pp 463–507.

Beckett, J. C. *Protestant dissent in Ireland, 1687–1784.* London, 1948.

Bossy, John. The counter-reformation and the people of catholic Ireland, 1596–1641. In *Hist. Studies*, viii (1971), pp 155–69.

Bradshaw, Brendan. *The dissolution of the religious orders in Ireland under Henry VIII*. Cambridge, 1974.

—— The opposition to the ecclesiastical legislation in the Irish reformation parliament. See above, p. 676.

—— George Browne, first reformation archbishop of Dublin, 1536–1554. In *Jn. Ecc. Hist.*, xxi (1970), pp 301–26.

Brady, John. Oliver Plunket and the popish plot. In *I.E.R.*, 5th series, lxxxix (Jan.–June 1958), pp 1–13, 340–54; xc (July–Dec. 1958), pp 12–27.

Carrigan, William. *History and antiquities of the diocese of Ossory*. 4 vols. Dublin, 1905.

Ceyssens, Lucien. Florence Conry, Hugh de Burgo, Luke Wadding, and Jansenism. In *Father Luke Wadding*, pp 295–404.

Corish, P. J. Bishop Nicholas French and the second Ormond peace, 1648–9. In *I.H.S.*, vi, no. 22 (Sept. 1948), pp 83–100.

—— An Irish counter-reformation bishop: John Roche. In *Ir. Theol. Quart.*, xxv (1958), pp 14–32, 101–23; xxvi (1959), pp 101–16, 313–30.

—— The reorganisation of the Irish church, 1603–41. In *Ir. Cath. Hist. Comm. Proc.*, iii (1957), pp 1–14.

—— Rinuccini's censure of 27 May 1648. In *Ir. Theol. Quart.*, xviii, no. 4 (Oct. 1951), pp 322–37.

De Caylus, D. Merveilleux épanouissement de l'école scotiste au XVIIe siècle. In *Études franciscaines*, xxiv (1910), pp 5–21, 493–502; xxv (1911), pp 35–47, 306–17, 627–45; xxvi (1912), pp 276–88.

Edwards, R. Dudley. The history of penal laws against catholics in Ireland from 1534 to the treaty of Limerick (1691) (Ph.D. thesis, University of London, 1933).

—— Church and state in the Ireland of Míchél Ó Cléirigh, 1626–41. In Sylvester O'Brien (ed.), *Measgra i gcuimhne Mhichíl Uí Chléirigh* (Dublin, 1944), pp 1–20.

—— *Church and state in Tudor Ireland*. Dublin, 1935.

—— Ireland, Elizabeth I, and the counter-reformation. In *Elizabethan government and society*, ed. S. T. Bindoff, Joel Hurstfield, and C. H. Williams (London, 1961), pp 315–39.

—— The Irish catholics and the puritan revolution. In *Father Luke Wadding*, pp 93–118.

Grubb, Isabel. *Quakers in Ireland, 1654–1700*. London, 1927.

Gwynn, Aubrey. *The medieval province of Armagh, 1470–1545*. Dundalk, 1946.

Hennig, John. Augustine Gibbon de Burgo: a study in early Irish reaction to Luther. In *I.E.R.*, 5th series, lxix (1947), pp 135–51.

Jones, F. M. The counter-reformation. In Corish, *Ir. catholicism*, iii, ch. 3 (1967).

Kearney, H. F. Ecclesiastical politics and the counter-reformation in Ireland, 1618–1648. In *Jn. Ecc. Hist.*, ii (1960), pp 202–12.

Kilroy, Philomena. Division and dissent in the Irish reformed church, 1615–34 (M.A. thesis, N.U.I. (U.C.D.), 1973).

Kingston, John. William Bathe, S.J., In *I.E.R.*, 5th ser., lxxxii (July–Dec. 1954), pp 179–82.

Mant, Richard. *History of the Church of Ireland.* Vol. i: from the reformation to the revolution; vol. ii: from the revolution to the union of the churches of England and Ireland, January 1, 1801. London, 1840.

Martin, F. X. *Friar Nugent, agent of the counter-reformation.* See below, p. 693.

—— The Irish friars and the Observant movement in the fifteenth century. In *Ir. Cath. Hist. Comm. Proc. 1960* (1961), pp 10–16.

—— Ireland, the renaissance and the counter-reformation. In *Topic: a journal of the liberal arts*, no. 13 (Washington, Pa, 1967), pp 23–33.

Millett, Benignus. *The Irish Franciscans, 1651–1665.* Rome, 1964.

—— Survival and reorganisation, 1650–95. In Corish, *Ir. catholicism*, iii, ch. 7 (1968).

Mooney, Canice. Accusations against Oliver Plunkett. In *Seanchas Ardmhacha*, ii (1956), pp 119–40.

—— The church in Gaelic Ireland. In Corish, *Ir. catholicism*, iii, ch. 2 (1967).

—— The first impact of the reformation. In Corish, *Ir. catholicism*, iii, ch. 2 (1967).

Mullen, Kevin. The ecclesiastical censures of the Irish confederacy (D.C.L. dissertation, Angelicum University, Rome, 1970).

Ó Conbhuí, Colmcille. The lands of St Mary's abbey, Dublin. In *R.I.A. Proc.*, lxii, sect. C (1962), pp 21–84.

Ó Fiaich, Tomás. The appointment of Blessed Oliver Plunkett to Armagh. In *Ir. Theol. Quart.*, xxv (1958), pp 144–53.

—— Edmund O'Reilly, archbishop of Armagh, 1657–1669. In *Father Luke Wadding*, pp 171–228.

—— The fall and return of John MacMoyer. In *Seanchas Ardmhacha*, iii (1958), pp 51–86.

Otway-Ruthven, A. J. The medieval church lands in County Dublin. In *Med. studies presented to A. Gwynn*, pp 54–73.

Parker, T. M. The papacy, catholic reform and Christian missions. In *New Camb. mod. hist.*, iii (1968), pp 44–71.

Phillips, W. A. (ed.). *History of the Church of Ireland.* 3 vols. London, 1933–4.

Positio super introductione causae. Rome, 1914.
Cause for the beatification of the Irish catholic martyrs.

Reid, J. S. *History of the presbyterian church in Ireland. Ed.* W. D. Killen. 3 vols. Belfast, 1867.

Renehan, L. F. *Collections on Irish church history. Ed.* Daniel MacCarthy. Vol. i, Dublin, 1861; vol. ii, 1874.

Rutty, John. See Wight.

Seymour, St J. D. *The puritans in Ireland, 1647–1661.* Oxford, 1921; reprinted, 1969.

Silke, J. J. Later relations between Primate Peter Lombard and Hugh O'Neill. In *Ir. Theol. Quart.*, xxii (1955), pp 15–30.

—— Primate Lombard and James I. In *Ir. Theol. Quart.*, xxii (1955), pp 124–50.

—— Hugh O'Neill, the catholic question, and the papacy. In *I.E.R.*, 5th series, civ (July–Dec. 1965), pp 65–79.

Simms, Katharine. The archbishops of Armagh and the O'Neills, 1347–1471. In *I.H.S.*, xix, no. 73 (Mar. 1974), pp 38–55.

Walzer, Michael. *The revolution of the saints.* Cambridge, Mass., 1965; London, 1966.

Wight, Thomas, and Rutty, John. *A history of the rise and progress of the people called quakers in Ireland, from the year 1653 to 1700.* Dublin, 1751.

5 *Military history*

Bryan, Dan. Colonel Richard Grace, 1651–1652. In *Ir. Sword*, iv (1959–60), pp 43–51.

Butler, George. The battle of Affane. In *Ir. Sword*, viii (1967–8), pp 43–51.

Ehrman, John. *The navy in the war of William III, 1689–97: its state and direction.* Cambridge, 1953.

Falls, Cyril. *Elizabeth's Irish wars.* London, 1950.

—— *Mountjoy: Elizabethan general.* See below, p. 693.

Firth, C. H. *Cromwell's army.* London, 1902.

Hayes-McCoy, G. A. The army of Ulster, 1593–1601. In *Ir. Sword*, i (1949–53), pp 105–17.

—— The early history of guns in Ireland. In *Galway Arch. Soc. Jn.*, xviii (1938–9), pp 43–65.

—— *Irish battles.* London, 1969.

—— *Scots mercenary forces in Ireland, 1565–1603. . . .* Dublin and London, 1937.

Hazlett, Hugh. The financing of the British armies in Ireland, 1641–9. In *I.H.S.*, i, no. 1 (Mar. 1938), pp 21–41.

—— A history of the military forces operating in Ireland, 1641–9 (Ph.D. thesis, Queen's University, Belfast, 1938).

McKerral, Andrew. West Highland mercenaries in Ireland. In *Scot. Hist. Rev.*, xxx (1951), pp 1–14.

Mangan, Henry. Sarsfield's defence of the Shannon, 1690–91. In *Ir. Sword*, i (1949–53), pp 24–32.

Milligan, C. D. *History of the siege of Londonderry, 1689*. Belfast, 1951.

Murphy, Denis. *Cromwell in Ireland*. Dublin, 1892.

Ó Danachair, Caoimhín. Armada losses on the Irish coast. In *Ir. Sword*, ii (1954–6), pp 321–31.

—— Montrose's Irish regiments. In *Ir. Sword*, iv (1959–60), pp 61–7.

Ó Domhnaill, Seán. Warfare in sixteenth-century Ireland. In *I.H.S.*, v, no. 17 (Mar. 1946), pp 29–54.

Ó Gallachair, Pádraig. The 1641 war in Clogher. In *Clogher Rec.*, iv, no. 3 (1962), pp 135–47.

Ó Lochlainn, Colm. Ó Domhnaill's claims for military service. In *Ir. Sword*, v (1961–2), pp 117–18.

Ó Mórdha, Pilib. The battle of Clones, 1643. In *Clogher Rec.*, iv, no. 3 (1962), pp 148–54.

O'Rahilly, Alfred. *The massacre at Smerwick, 1580*. Cork, 1938.

Petrie, Charles. The Hispano-papal landing at Smerwick. In *Ir. Sword*, ix (1969–70), pp 82–94.

Silke, J. J. *Kinsale*. Liverpool, 1970.

Simms, J. G. Cromwell at Drogheda, 1649. In *Ir. Sword*, xi (1973–4), pp 212–21.

—— Cromwell's siege of Waterford, 1649. In *Ir. Sword*, iv (1959–60), pp 171–9.

—— Hugh Dubh O'Neill's defence of Limerick, 1650–51. In *Ir. Sword*, iii (1957–8), pp 115–23.

White, D. G. Henry VIII's Irish kerne in France and Scotland. In *Ir. Sword*, iii (1957–8), pp 213–25.

Wilson, Charles. *Queen Elizabeth and the revolt of the Netherlands*. Berkeley and Los Angeles, 1970.

6 *Economic and social history*

Aalen, F. H. A. Enclosures in eastern Ireland. In *Ir. Geography*, v, no. 2 (1965), pp 30–34.

Bernard, Jacques. *Navires & gens de mer à Bordeaux vers 1400–vers 1500*. 3 vols. Paris, 1968.

Bowden, P. J. Wool supply and the woollen industry. In *Econ. Hist. Rev.*, 2nd series, ix, no. 1 (1956), pp 44–58.

—— *The wool trade in Tudor and Stuart England*. London, 1962.

Carus-Wilson, E. M. *Medieval merchant venturers*. London, 1967.

—— *The overseas trade of Bristol in the later middle ages*. Bristol, 1937.

Clark, W. S. *The early Irish stage*. Oxford, 1955.

Connell, K. H. *The population of Ireland, 1750–1845*. Oxford, 1950.

Crotty, R. D. *Irish agricultural production: its volume and structure*. Cork, 1966.

Cullen, L. M. *Anglo-Irish trade, 1660–1800.* Manchester, 1968.

—— *An economic history of Ireland since 1660.* London, 1972.

—— Tráchtáil is baincearacht i nGaillimh san 18ú céad. In *Galvia*, v (1958), pp 43–[78].

—— Population trends in seventeenth-century Ireland. In *Economic and Social Review*, vi, no. 2 (Jan. 1975), pp 149–65.

Delumeau, J. *Le mouvement du port du Saint-Malo: la fin du XVIIe siècle (1681–1700).* Rennes, [N.D.]

Evans, E. Estyn. *Irish folkways.* London, 1957.

Fisher, F. J. The sixteenth and seventeenth centuries: the dark ages in English economic history? In *Economica*, new series, xxiv (1951), pp 2–18.

Graham, J. M. Rural society in Connacht, 1600–1640. In *Ir. geog. studies*, pp 192–208.

Kearney, H. F. Mercantilism and Ireland, 1620–40. In *Hist. Studies*, i (1958), pp 59–68.

—— Richard Boyle, ironmaster. In *R.S.A.I. Jn.*, lxxxiii (1953), pp 156–62.

Leister, Ingeborg. *Das Werden der Agrarlandschaft in der Grafschaft Tipperary (Irland).* Marburg, 1963.

Longfield, A. K. Anglo-Irish trade in the sixteenth century as illustrated by the English customs accounts and port books. In *R.I.A. Proc.*, xxxvi, sect. C (1924), pp 317–32.

—— *Anglo-Irish trade in the sixteenth century.* London, 1929.

Lucas, A. T. Cattle in ancient and medieval Irish society. In *O'Connell School Union Record, 1937–58* (1958), pp 75–85.

McCracken, Eileen. *The Irish woods since Tudor times.* Newton Abbot, 1971.

MacLysaght, Edward. *Irish life in the seventeenth century: after Cromwell.* Dublin and London, 1939; 2nd ed., Cork, 1950.

Nicholls, K. W. *Gaelic and gaelicised Ireland in the middle ages.* Dublin and London, 1972.

Ó Bric, Breandán. Galway townsmen as the owners of land in Connacht, 1585–1641 (M.A. thesis, N.U.I. (U.C.G.), 1974).

O'Brien, George. *The economic history of Ireland in the seventeenth century.* Dublin, 1919.

—— The Irish staple organisation in the reign of James I. In *Econ. Hist.*, no. 1 (1926), pp 42–56.

O'Donovan, John. *The economic history of livestock in Ireland.* Cork, 1940.

O'Sullivan, William. *The economic history of Cork city from the earliest times to the act of union.* Cork, 1937.

Quinn, D. B. *The Elizabethans and the Irish.* Ithaca, N.Y., 1966.

—— *England and the discovery of America, 1481–1620.* London, 1974.

Spooner, F. C. The European economy, 1609–50. In *New Camb. mod. hist.*, iv, 67–102.

Stephens, W. B. The overseas trade of Chester in the early seventeenth century. In *Transactions of the Historic Society of Lancashire and Cheshire*, no. 120 (1968), pp 23–34.

Vaughan-Arbuckle, C. L. A Tipperary farmer and Waterford tradesman of two centuries ago. In *Waterford Arch. Soc. Jn.*, viii (1902), pp 80–92.

Wadsworth, A. P., and Mann, J. de L. *The cotton trade and industrial Lancashire, 1600–1780*. Manchester, 1931.

Went, A. E. J. Historical notes on the oyster fisheries of Ireland. In *R.I.A. Proc.*, lxii, sect. C, no. 7 (1962), pp 195–223.

Woodward, D. M. The Anglo-Irish livestock trade of the seventeenth century. In *I.H.S.*, xviii, no. 72 (Sept. 1973), pp 489–523.

—— *The trade of Elizabethan Chester*. Hull, 1970.

Young, Arthur. *A tour in Ireland: with general observations on the present state of the kingdom: made in the years 1776, 1777, and 1778, and brought down to the end of 1779*. London, 1780.

7 *The coinage*

Batty, David. *Batty's catalogue of the copper coinage of Great Britain, Ireland, British Isles and colonies, local and private tokens, jettons etc.* 4 vols. Manchester, 1868–98.

Brady, Gerard, and Dolley, Michael. A parcel of 'white money' from (?) County Tipperary. In *Numismatic Society of Ireland Occasional Papers*, nos 10–14 (1970), pp 15–19.

Dolley, Michael. Anglo-Irish monetary policies, 1172–1637. In *Hist. Studies*, vii (1969), pp 45–64.

—— Elizabethan bungal(l)—a contribution to Anglo-Irish lexicography. In *British Numismatic Journal*, xxxvi (1967), pp 118–21.

—— George Petrie and a century of Irish numismatics. In *R.I.A. Proc.*, lxxii, sect. C (1972), pp 165–93.

—— The pattern of Elizabethan coin-hoards from Ireland. In *U.J.A.*, xxxiii (1970), pp 77–88.

—— Was there an Irish coinage in the name of Edward VI? *Spink's Numismatic Circular*, 1969, pp 274–5.

—— and Hackman, W. D. The coinages for Ireland of Henry VIII. In *British Numismatic Journal*, xxxviii (1971), pp 84–108.

Dowle, Anthony, and Finn, Patrick. *The guide book to the coinage of Ireland: from 995 A.D. to the present day*. London, 1969.

Fitzgerald, E. Early references to Irish brass money. In *Seaby's Coin and Medal Bulletin* (1966), pp 282–5.

Frazer, William. On the Irish 'St Patrick' or 'floreat rex' coinage, subsequently circulated in New Jersey by Mark Newbie: with reasons for connecting it with Lord Glamorgan's attempts to levy troops in Ireland for Charles I. In *R.S.A.I. Jn.*, xxv (1895), pp 338–47.

Lane, S. N. A late seventeenth-century bronze hoard from County Kerry. In *British Numismatic Journal*, xxxiv (1965), pp 126–31.

Nelson, Philip. *The coinage of Ireland in copper, tin, and pewter, 1460–1826.* London, 1905.

—— The obsidional money of the great rebellion (1642–9). In *British Numismatic Journal*, ii (1905), pp 291–357.

O'Sullivan, William. The only gold coins issued in Ireland (1646). In *British Numismatic Journal*, xxxiii (1964), pp 141–50.

Seaby's standard catalogue, pt. 3: coins and tokens of Ireland. Compiled by Peter Seaby. London, 1970.

Simon, James. *Essay on Irish coins, and of the currency of foreign monies in Ireland: with Mr Snelling's supplement.* Dublin, 1810.

Smith, Aquilla. On the coin commonly called St Patrick's. In *R.S.A.I. Jn.*, iii (1854–5), pp 67–76.

—— On the Irish coins of Mary. In *R.S.A.I. Jn.*, iii (1854–5), pp 357–68.

—— Money of necessity issued in Ireland in the reign of Charles I. In *R.S.A.I. Jn.*, vi (1860–61), pp 11–20, 134–44.

—— Money of necessity issued in Ireland in the reign of James II. In *Numismatic Chronicle*, 1870, pp 244–66.

—— Notes on the Irish coins of James I. In *Numismatic Chronicle*, 1879, pp 185–90.

Stevenson, David. The Irish emergency coinage of James II, 1689–91. In *British Numismatic Journal*, xxxvi (1967), pp 169–75.

Symonds, Henry. The coinage of Queen Mary Tudor, 1553–8. In *British Numismatic Journal*, viii (1911), pp. 195–201.

—— The Elizabethan coinages for Ireland. In *Numismatic Chronicle*, 1917, pp 97–125.

—— The Irish coinages of Henry VIII and Edward VI. In *Numismatic Chronicle*, 1915, pp 192–229.

Williamson, G. C. *Trade tokens issued in the seventeenth century in England, Wales, and Ireland by corporations, merchants, tradesmen, etc.: a new and revised edition of William Boyne's work.* London, 1889–91.

Yeates, F. W. The coinage of Ireland during the rebellion, 1642–52. In *British Numismatic Journal*, xv (1919–20), pp 185–223; xvi (1921–2), pp 189–93.

8 Literature and language

Adams, G. B. An introduction to the study of Ulster dialects. In *R.I.A. Proc.*, lii, sect. C (1948), pp 1–26.

Barnes, William. *A glossary of the old dialect of the English colony in the baronies of Forth and Bargy*. London, 1867.

Bartley, J. O. *Teague, Shenkin and Sawney*. Cork, 1954.

Braidwood, John. Ulster and Elizabethan English. In [G. B. Adams] (ed.), *Ulster dialects* (Ulster Folk Museum, Cultra, Co. Down, 1964), pp 5–109.

—— *The Ulster dialects lexicon*. Belfast, [1969].

Brayley, E. W. (ed.). Observations on the social habits and dialect of the baronies of Forth and Bargy. By 'an officer of the line'. In *The Graphic and Historical Illustrator*, 1834.

Bruford, Alan. *Gaelic folktales and mediaeval romances*. Dublin, 1969.

Carney, James. *The Irish bardic poet*. Dublin, 1967.

De Blacam, Aodh. *Gaelic literature surveyed*. Dublin, 1929.

Gwynn, Aubrey. Archbishop Ussher and Father Brendan O'Conor. In *Father Luke Wadding*, pp 263–83.

Hyde, Douglas. *A literary history of Ireland from the earliest times to the present day*. London, 1899; reissue, with introduction by Brian Ó Cuív, London, 1967.

Lesage, Alain René. *Gil Blas de Santillane*. 4 vols. Paris, 1715–35. Trans. Henry Van Laun, 3 vols, Edinburgh, 1886.

McIntosh, Angus, and Samuels, M. L. Prolegomena to a study of medieval Anglo-Irish. In *Medium Aevum*, xxxvii (1968), pp 1–11.

Marshall, J. J. The dialect of Ulster. In *U.J.A.*, series 2, x (1904), pp 121–30; xi (1905), pp 64–70, 122–5, 175–9; xii (1906), pp 18–22.

Montesquieu, Charles Louis, baron de. *Lettres persanes*. Cologne, 1721.

Mooney, Canice. Father John Colgan, O.F.M., his work and times and literary milieu. In *Father John Colgan*, O.F.M., ed. Terence O'Donnell (Dublin, 1959), pp 7–40.

—— The writings of Father Luke Wadding, O.F.M. In *Franciscan Studies*, xviii (1958), pp 227–31.

Murphy, Gerard. *The Ossianic lore and tales of medieval Ireland*. Dublin, 1955.

Ó Cuív, Brian. *The Irish bardic duanaire or 'poem-book'*. Dublin, 1974.

—— (ed.). *Seven centuries of Irish learning, 1000–1700*. [Dublin], 1961; reprint, 1971.

O'Rahilly, T. F. *Irish dialects past and present*. Dublin, 1972.

O'Sullivan, Anne. Tadhg O'Daly and Sir George Carew. In *Éigse*, xiv (1971), pp 27–38.

Russell, C. W. On the inhabitants and dialect of the barony of Forth in the county of Wexford. In *Atlantis*, i (1858).

Sheridan, Thomas. *A general dictionary of the English language, to which is prefixed a rhetorical grammar*. Dublin, 1780.

Stanford, W. B. Towards a history of classical influences in Ireland. In *R.I.A. Proc.*, lxx, sect C (1970), pp 13–91.

Steinberg, S. H. *Five hundred years of printing*. London, 1955.

Updike, D. B. *Printing types, their history, forms, and use*. Cambridge, Mass., 1922; 3rd ed., 1962.

Vallancey, Charles. Memoir of the language, manners, and customs of an Anglo-Saxon colony settled in the baronies of Forth and Bargie. In *R.I.A. Trans.*, ii (1788), pp 19–41.

Wall, Thomas. Bards and Bruodins. In *Father Luke Wadding*, pp 438–62.

Walsh, Paul, *Irish men of learning*. *Ed.* Colm Ó Lochlainn. Dublin, 1947.

9 Historiography

Carty, James. Contemporary accounts of the battle of Kinsale (1601). In *I.C.H.S. Bull.*, no. 6 (1940).

Corish, P. J. Two contemporary historians of the confederation of Kilkenny: John Lynch and Richard O'Ferrall. In *I.H.S.*, viii, no. 31 (Mar. 1953), pp 217–36.

Edwards, R. Dudley, and Quinn, D. B. Sixteenth-century Ireland, 1485–1603. In T. W. Moody (ed.), *Irish historiography, 1936–70* (Dublin, 1971), pp 23–42.

Revised version of 'Thirty years' work in Irish history: (II) sixteenth-century Ireland, 1485–1603' in *I.H.S.*, xvi, no. 61 (Mar. 1968), pp 15–32.

Gwynn, Aubrey. The *Annals of Connacht* and the abbey of Cong. In *Galway Arch. Soc. Jn.*, xxvii (1956–7), pp 1–9.

Henry, L. W. Contemporary sources for Essex's lieutenancy in Ireland, 1599. In *I.H.S.*, xi, no. 41 (Mar. 1958), pp 8–17.

Jordan, John. The Jacobite wars: some Danish sources. In *Studies*, xliii (1954), pp 431–40.

Kenney, J. F. *The sources for the early history of Ireland, an introduction and guide*. Vol. i, ecclesiastical. New York, 1929.

Ch. I: History of Ireland.

Ó CLÉIRIGH. *Michael Ó Cléirigh, chief of the Four Masters, and his associates*. By Brendan Jennings. Dublin, 1936.

Quinn, D. B. See Edwards, above.

Simms, J. G. Report on the compilation of a bibliography of source material for the history of Ireland, 1685–1702. In *Anal. Hib.*, no. 22 (1960), pp 1–10.

—— Seventeenth-century Ireland, 1603–1702. In T. W. Moody (ed.), *Irish historiography, 1936–70*. (Dublin, 1971), pp 43–54.

Revised version of 'Thirty years' work in Irish history: (I) seventeenth-century Ireland (1603–1702)' in *I.H.S.*, xv, no. 60 (Sept. 1967), pp 366–75.

Walsh, Paul. Historical criticism of the life of Hugh Roe O'Donnell. In *I.H.S.*, i, no. 3 (Mar. 1939), pp 229–50.

Wormald, Brian. The historiography of the English reformation. In *Hist. Studies*, i (1958), pp 50–58.

10 Education

Corcoran, Timothy. Early Irish Jesuit educators. In *Studies*, xxix (1940), pp 545–60.

—— *Studies in the history of classical teaching*. Dublin, 1911.

Cregan, D. F. Irish catholic admissions to the English inns of court, 1558–1625. In *Ir. Jurist*, N.S., v (1970), pp 95–114.

Hammerstein, Helga. Aspects of the continental education of Irish students in the reign of Queen Elizabeth I. In *Hist. Studies*, viii (1971), pp 137–54.

Hay, Denys. Schools and universities. In *New Camb. mod. hist.*, ii (1958), pp 414–37.

Kearney, H. F. *Scholars and gentlemen*. London, 1970.

Mahaffy, J. P. *An epoch in Irish history: Trinity College, Dublin, 1591–1660*. London, 1903.

Maxwell, Constantia. *History of Trinity College, Dublin, 1591–1892*. Dublin, 1946.

O'Boyle, James. *The Irish colleges on the Continent*. Dublin, 1935.

Rabbitte, James. Alexander Lynch, schoolmaster. In *Galway Arch Soc. Jn.*, xvii (1936), pp 34–42.

Silke, J. J. Irish scholarship and the renaissance, 1580–1673. In *Studies in the Renaissance*, xx (1973), pp 169–206.

Stubbs, J. W. *History of the University of Dublin*. Dublin, 1889.

Urwick, William. *The early history of Trinity College, Dublin, 1591–1660*. London, 1891.

Wall, Thomas. Parnassus in Waterford. In *I.E.R.*, 5th series, lxix (1947), pp 708–21.

11 Science and medicine

Barnard, T. C. The Hartlib circle and the origins of the Dublin Philosophical Society. In *I.H.S.*, xix, no. 74 (Mar. 1974), pp 56–71.

—— Myles Symner and the new learning in seventeenth-century Ireland. In *R.S.A.I. Jn.*, cii (1972), pp 129–42.

Boas, Marie. *Robert Boyle and seventeenth-century chemistry*. Cambridge, 1958.

Hoppen, K. T. *The common scientist in the seventeenth century*. London, 1970.

Knowles, David. *The evolution of medieval thought*. London, 1962.

Logan, Patrick. Medical services in the armies of the confederate wars (1641–52). In *Ir. Sword*, iv (1959–60), pp 217–27.

12 Local and family history

Butler, W. F. T. *Gleanings from Irish history.* London, 1925.

The Butler lordship. By C. A. Empey. In *Butler Soc. Jn.*, 3 (1970–1), pp 174–87.

CLONMEL. *History of Clonmel.* By W. P. Burke. Waterford, 1907.

CORK. *Antient and present state of the city and county of Cork.* By Charles Smith. Dublin, 1750.

DARTAS. The descendants of Margaret Dartas. By K. W. Nicholls. In *Ir. Geneal.*, iv (1968–72), pp 392–6.

Devereux, W. B. *Lives and letters of the Devereux, earls of Essex. . . .* 2 vols. London, 1853.

DONAGHMORE. *Domhnach Mór.* By Éamon Ó Doibhlin. Omagh, 1969.

FITZMAURICE. The Fitzmaurices of Kerry. By K. W. Nicholls. In *Kerry Arch. Soc. Jn.*, iii (1970), pp 23–42.

GALWAY. *History of the town and county of the town of Galway.* By James Hardiman. Dublin, 1820; reprint, Galway, 1926, 1958.

MACDONNELL. *An historical account of the MacDonnells of Antrim.* By George Hill. Belfast, 1873.

MACMAHON. Cios Mhic Mhathghamhna. By Seosamh Ó Dufaigh. In *Clogher Rec.*, iv (1960–62), pp 125–33.

The MacMahons of Monaghan. By Pilib Ó Mórdha. In *Clogher Rec.*, ii, no. 1 (1957), pp 148–69.

MONTGOMERY. William Montgomery and the description of the Ards, 1683. By D. B. Quinn. In *Irish Booklore*, ii (1972), pp 29–43.

Ó Ceallaigh, Séamus. *Gleanings from Ulster history.* Cork, 1951.

O'NEILL. Hugh O'Neill, earl of Tyrone, and the changing face of Gaelic Ulster. By N. P. Canny. In *Studia Hib.*, no. 10 (1970), pp 7–35.

—— The making of an O'Neill. By G. A. Hayes-McCoy. In *U.J.A.*, series 3, xxxiii (1970), pp 89–94.

O'REILLY. *A genealogical history of the O'Reillys. Ed.* James Carney. Cavan, 1959.

Otway-Ruthven, A. J. Ireland in the 1350s: Sir Thomas de Rokeby and his successors. In *R.S.A.I. Jn.*, xcvii (1967), pp 47–59.

POWERSCOURT. The manor and castle of Powerscourt . . . in the sixteenth century. By Walter Fitzgerald. In *Kildare Arch. Soc. Jn.*, vi (1909–11), pp 127–39.

Ulster, 1460–1550. By D. B. Quinn. [Belfast], 1935 (reprinted from *Belfast Natur. Hist. Soc. Proc.*, 1933–4, pp 56–78).

ULSTER. *The town in Ulster.* By Gilbert Camblin. Belfast, 1951.

The Wall family in Ireland, 1170–1970. By Hubert Gallwey. Naas, 1970.

WATERFORD. *Antient and present state of the city and county of Waterford. . . .* By Charles Smith. Dublin, 1746; 2nd ed., 1774.

—— *History of Waterford.* By R. H. Ryland. London, 1824.

WEXFORD. *History of the town and county of Wexford.* By P. H. Hore. 6 vols. London, 1900–11.

—— The population of County Wexford in the seventeenth century. By Micheál Toibín. In *Past*, vi (1960), pp 118–37.

Youghal, County Cork—growth, decay, resurgence. By A. R. Orme. In *Ir. Geography*, v, no. 3 (1966), pp 121–49.

13 Confiscation and colonisation

Arnold, L. J. The restoration land settlement in the counties of Dublin and Wicklow, 1660–88 (Ph.D. thesis, University of Dublin, 1967).

Atkinson, N. D. The plantation of Ely O'Carroll, 1619–93 (M.Litt. thesis, University of Dublin, 1958).

Barnard, T. C. Planters and policies in Cromwellian Ireland. In *Past and Present*, no. 61 (1973), pp 31–69.

Bonn, M. J. *Die englische Kolonisation in Irland.* 2 vols in 1. Stuttgart and Berlin, 1906.

Bottigheimer, Karl. *English money and Irish land: the 'adventurers' in the Cromwellian settlement of Ireland.* Oxford, 1971.

—— The restoration land settlement in Ireland: a structural view. In *I.H.S.*, xviii, no. 69 (Mar. 1972), pp 1–21.

Butler, W. F. T. *Confiscation in Irish history.* Dublin, 1917.

Canny, N. P. The ideology of English colonization: from Ireland to America. In *William and Mary Quarterly*, series 3, xxx (1973), pp 575–98.

Carré, Albert. *L'influence des huguenots français en Irlande aux XVIIe et XVIIIe siècles.* Paris, 1937.

Cooper, J. P. Strafford and the Byrnes' country. In *I.H.S.*, xv, no. 57 (Mar. 1966), pp 1–20.

Dunlop, Robert. The plantation of Leix and Offaly, 1556–1622. In *E.H.R.*, vi (1891), pp 61–96.

—— The plantation of Munster, 1584–1589. In *E.H.R.*, iii (1888), pp 250–69.

Edwards, R. Dudley. Chichester letter-book, introd. See above, p. 648.

Gallagher, D. A. The plantation of Longford, 1619–41 (M.A. thesis, N.U.I. (U.C.D.), 1968).

Gardiner, S. R. The transplantation to Connaught. In *E.H.R.*, xiv (1899), pp 700–34.

Gleeson, D. F. *The last lords of Ormond.* London, 1938.

Hill, George. *An historical account of the plantation in Ulster . . . 1608–20.* Belfast, 1877; reprint, Shannon, 1970.

Hunter, R. J. The Ulster plantation in the counties of Armagh and Cavan, 1608–41 (M.Litt. thesis, University of Dublin, 1969).

—— Towns in the Ulster plantation. In *Studia Hib.*, no. 11 (1971), pp 40–79.

Lee, G. L. *The huguenot settlements in Ireland*, London, 1936.

MacCormack, J. R. The Irish adventurers and the English civil war. In *I.H.S.*, x, no. 37 (Mar. 1956), pp 21–58.

MacLysaght, Edward. *Short study of a transplanted family in the seventeenth century*. Dublin, 1935.

Moody, T. W. The Londonderry plantation, with special reference to the resulting relations between the crown and the city, 1609–41 (Ph.D. thesis, University of London, 1934).

—— *The Londonderry plantation, 1609–41: the city of London and the plantation in Ulster*. Belfast, 1939.

—— Sir Thomas Phillips of Limavady, servitor. In *I.H.S.*, i, no. 3 (Mar. 1939), pp 251–72.

—— The treatment of the native population under the scheme for the plantation in Ulster. In *I.H.S.*, i, no. 1 (Mar. 1938), pp 59–63.

—— Ulster plantation papers, introd. See above, p. 651.

Perceval-Maxwell, Michael. *The Scottish migration to Ulster in the reign of James I*. London, 1973.

Prendergast, J. P. *The Cromwellian settlement of Ireland*. London, 1865; revised ed., 1870; 3rd ed., Dublin, 1922.

Quinn, D. B. Ireland and sixteenth-century European expansion. In *Hist. Studies*, i (1958), pp 20–32.

—— The Munster plantation: problems and opportunities. In *Cork Hist. Soc. Jn.*, lxxi (1966), pp 19–40.

—— *Raleigh and the British empire*. London, 1947.

—— Sir Thomas Smith (1513–77) and the beginnings of English colonial theory. In *Amer. Phil. Soc. Proc.*, lxxxix, no. 4 (1945), pp 543–60.

Ranger, T. O. The career of Richard Boyle, first earl of Cork, in Ireland, 1588–1643 (D.Phil. thesis, University of Oxford, 1959).

—— Richard Boyle and the making of an Irish fortune. In *I.H.S.*, x, no. 40 (Sept. 1957), pp 257–97.

Robinson, P. S. The plantation of County Tyrone in the seventeenth century (Ph.D. thesis, Queen's University, Belfast, 1974).

Rowse, A. L. *The expansion of Elizabethan England*. London, 1955.

J. G. Simms. The Williamite land-confiscation (Ph.D. thesis, University of Dublin, 1952).

—— The Civil Survey, 1654–6. In *I.H.S.*, ix, no. 35 (Mar. 1955), pp 253–63.

—— *The Williamite confiscation in Ireland, 1690–1703*. London, 1956.

White, D. G. The Tudor plantations in Ireland before 1571 (Ph.D. thesis, University of Dublin, 1968).

14 The Irish abroad

Binchy, D. A. An Irish ambassador at the Spanish court, 1569–74. In *Studies*, x (1921), pp 353–74, 573–84.

Blake, J. W. Transportation from Ireland to America, 1653–60. In *I.H.S.*, iii, no. 11 (Mar. 1943), pp 267–81.

Bourke, E. Irish levies for the army of Sweden, 1609–10. In *Ir. Monthly*, xlvi (1918), pp 396–404.

Boyle, Patrick. *The Irish college in Paris, 1578–1901.* London, 1901.

Bridenbaugh, Carl. *Vexed and troubled Englishmen, 1590–1624.* New York, 1968.

—— and Roberta. *No peace beyond the line: the English in the Caribbean, 1624–40.* New York, 1972.

Ceyssens, Lucien. François Porter, franciscain irlandais à Rome (1632–1702). In *Miscellanea Melchor de Pobladura*, i (Rome, 1964), pp 387–419.

Clark, Ruth. *Strangers and sojourners at Port-Royal.* Cambridge, 1932.

Cleary, Gregory. *Father Luke Wadding and St Isidore's College, Rome.* Rome, 1925.

Corish, P. J. John Callaghan and the controversies among the Irish in Paris, 1648–54. In *Ir. Theol. Quart.*, xxi (1954), pp 32–50.

—— The beginnings of the Irish College, Rome. In *Father Luke Wadding*, pp 284–94.

Finegan, Francis. Irish rectors at Seville, 1619–1687. In *I.E.R.*, series 5, cvi (July–Dec. 1966), pp 45–63.

Giblin, Cathaldus. Hugh MacCaghwell, O.F.M., and Scotism at St Anthony's College, Louvain. In *De doctrina Ioannis Duns Scoti*, iv (Rome, 1968), pp 375–97.

—— Irish exiles in catholic Europe. In Corish, *Ir. catholicism*, iv, ch. 3 (1971).

Guilday, Peter. *The English catholic refugees on the Continent, 1558–1795.* Vol. i. London, 1914.
No more volumes published.

Gwynn, Aubrey. An Irish settlement on the Amazon (1612–29). In *R.I.A. Proc.*, xli, sect. C (1931–2), pp. 1–54.

—— Early Irish emigration to the West Indies (1612–1643). In *Studies*, xviii (1929), pp 377–93, 648–63.

—— Indentured servants and negro slaves in Barbados (1642–1650). In *Studies*, xix (1930), pp 279–94.

—— Cromwell's policy of transportation. In *Studies*, xix (1930), pp 607–23.

—— The first Irish priests in the New World. In *Studies*, xxi (1932), pp 213–28.

Hansen, Marcus Lee. *The Atlantic migration, 1607–1860: a history of the continuing settlement of the United States. Ed.* A. M. Schlesinger. Cambridge, Mass., 1941.

Hayes, Richard. Irish associations with Nantes. In *Studies*, xxxvii (1948), pp 115–26.

—— *Old Irish links with France*. Dublin, 1940.

Hughes, Thomas. *The history of the Society of Jesus in North America: colonial and federal*. Cleveland, Ohio, 1907.

Jennings, Brendan. Irish students in the university of Louvain. In Sylvester O'Brien (ed.), *Measgra i gcuimhne Mhichíl Uí Chléirigh* (Dublin, 1944), pp 74–97.

—— Irish swordsmen in Flanders, 1586–1610. In *Studies*, xxxvi (1947), pp 402–10; xxxvii (1948), pp 189–202.

Lord, R. H., Sexton, J. E., and Harrington, E. T. *History of the archdiocese of Boston, 1604–1943*. 3 vols. New York, 1944.

Martin, F. X. The Irish Augustinians in Rome, 1656–1956. In J. F. Madden (ed.), *The Irish Augustinians in Rome, 1656–1956* (Rome, 1956), pp 16–74.

Millett, Benignus. Irish Scotists at St Isidore's College, Rome, in the seventeenth century. In *De doctrina Ioannis Duns Scoti*, iv (Rome, 1968), pp 399–419.

O'Boyle, James. *The Irish colleges on the Continent*. Dublin, 1935.

O'Dea, Paul. Father Peter Wadding, S.J.: chancellor of the University of Prague, 1629–41. In *Studies*, xxx (1941), pp 337–48.

Scott, Eva. *The travels of the king*. London, 1907.

Silke, J. J. The Irish appeal of 1593 to Spain. In *I.E.R.*, series 5, xcii (July–Dec. 1959), pp 279–90, 362–71.

Smith, A. E. *Colonists in bondage: white servitude and convict labour in America, 1607–1776*. Chapel Hill, N.C., 1947.

Spelman, J. P. The tribes at Louvain: Francis Martin, S.T.D. In *I.E.R.*, series 3, vii (1886), pp 1100–06.

Terlinden, Charles. L'Irlande et la Belgique dans le passé. In *Revue générale de Bruxelles*, 1928.

Walsh, Micheline. Some notes towards a history of the womenfolk of the wild geese. In *Ir. Sword*, v (1961–2), pp 98–106.

—— Further notes towards a history of the womenfolk of the wild geese. In *Ir. Sword*, v (1961–2), pp 133–45.

Williams, Joseph J. *Whence the 'black Irish' of Jamaica?* New York, 1932.

15 Biography

CLARENDON. *The life of Edward, earl of Clarendon*. By T. H. Lister. 3 vols. Oxford, 1888.

COTTER, James Cotter, a seventeenth-century agent of the crown. By Brian Ó Cuív. In *R.S.A.I. Jn.*, lxxxix (1959), pp 139–59.

CROMWELL. *Oliver Cromwell and the rule of the puritans in England*. By C. H. Firth. London and New York, 1900.

—— *Oliver Cromwell.* By John Morley. London, 1900; 2nd ed., 1904.

—— *Oliver Cromwell.* By S. R. Gardiner. London, 1901.

—— *God's Englishman: Oliver Cromwell and the English revolution.* By Christopher Hill. London, 1970.

—— *Cromwell, our chief of men.* By Antonia Fraser. London, 1973.

FALKLAND. *The life of Elizabeth, Lady Falkland, 1585–1639.* By G. C. Fullerton. London, 1883.

Irish chiefs and leaders. By Paul Walsh; ed. Colm Ó Lochlainn. Dublin, 1960.

JAMES II. *The life of James the second.* By J. S. Clarke. 2 vols. London, 1816.

MACCARTHY. *Justin MacCarthy, Lord Mountcashel.* By J. A. Murphy. Cork, 1959 (The O'Donnell Lectures, N.U.I.).

Marlborough, his life and times. By Winston Churchill. 4 vols. London, 1933–8.

Mountjoy, Elizabethan general. By Cyril Falls. London, 1955.

Mountjoy, 1563–1606: the last Elizabethan deputy. By F. M. Jones. Dublin, 1958.

NUGENT. *Friar Nugent, agent of the counter-reformation.* By F. X. Martin. Rome and London, 1962.

O'DALY. An Irish agent of the counter-reformation: Dominic O'Daly. By Benvenuta MacCurtain. In *I.H.S.*, xv, no. 60 (Sept. 1967), pp 391–406.

O'DONNELL. The career of Hugh, son of Rory O'Donnell, earl of Tyrconnell, in the Low Countries, 1607–42. By Brendan Jennings. In *Studies*, xxx (1941), pp 219–34.

O'HANLON. Redmond O'Hanlon. By T. W. Moody. In *Belfast Natur. Hist. Soc. Proc.*, 2nd series, i (1937), pp 17–33.

O'MOLONY. Two bishops of Killaloe and Irish freedom. By James Hogan. In *Studies*, ix (1920), pp 70–93, 213–31, 421–37.
Bishops John O'Molony I (1630–51) and John O'Molony II (1671–1702).

Ó NEACHTAIN. *Stair Éamuinn Uí Chléire, do réir Sheáin Uí Neachtain, i n-eagar ag Eoghan Ó Neachtain.* Dublin, 1918.

O'NEILL. An historical study of the career of Hugh O'Neill, second earl of Tyrone, *c.* 1550–1616. By J. K. Graham (M.A. thesis, Queen's University, Belfast, 1938).

—— The birth-date of Hugh O'Neill, second earl of Tyrone. By J. K. Graham. In *I.H.S.*, i, no. 1 (Mar. 1938), pp 58–9.

—— *The great O'Neill.* By Sean O' Faolain. London, 1942.

—— Daniel O'Neill, a royalist agent in Ireland, 1644–50. By D. F. Cregan. In *I.H.S.*, ii, no. 8 (Sept. 1941), pp 398–414.

—— *Owen Roe O'Neill.* By J. F. Taylor. London and Dublin, 1896.

—— Shane O'Neill comes to the court of Elizabeth. By James Hogan. In Séamus Pender (ed.), *Féilscríbhinn Torna . . .: essays and studies presented to Professor Tadhg Ua Donnchadha* (*Torna*) (Cork, 1947), pp 154–70.

ORMOND. *An history of the life of James, first duke of Ormonde.* By Thomas Carte. 3 vols, London, 1735–6; 6 vols, Oxford, 1851.

PETTY. *Sir William Petty: portrait of a genius.* By Emil Strauss. London, 1954.

PHILLIPS. Sir Thomas Phillips of Limavady, servitor. By T. W. Moody. In *I.H.S.*, i, no. 3 (Mar. 1939), pp 251–72.

SARSFIELD. *The life of Patrick Sarsfield.* By J. H. Todhunter. London, 1895.

Shakespeare and the earl of Southampton. By G. P. V. Akrigg. London, 1968.

STRAFFORD. The fortune of Thomas Wentworth, earl of Strafford. By J. P. Cooper. In *Econ. Hist. Rev.*, xi (1958), pp 227–48.

—— *Thomas Wentworth, first earl of Strafford, 1593–1641: a revaluation.* By C. V. Wedgwood. London, 1964.

TALBOT. *Little Jennings and fighting Dick Talbot.* By P. W. Sergeant. 2 vols. London, 1913.

—— *The great Tyrconnell: a chapter in Anglo-Irish relations.* By Charles Petrie. Cork and Dublin, 1972.

USSHER. *James Ussher, archbishop of Armagh.* By R. Buick Knox. Cardiff, 1967.

Walker of Derry. By W. S. Kerr. Londonderry, 1938.

WILLIAM III. *The history of the life and reign of William Henry . . . king of England, Scotland, France and Ireland.* By Walter Harris. Dublin, 1749.

William III. By S. B. Baxter. London, 1966.

E BIOGRAPHICAL AND OTHER WORKS OF REFERENCE

Dictionary of national biography. Ed. Leslie Stephen and Sidney Lee. 66 vols. London, 1885–1901.

Reprinted with corrections, 22 vols, London, 1908–9.

Hayes, Richard. *Biographical dictionary of Irishmen in France.* Dublin, 1949.

MacLysaght, Edward. *Irish families: their names, arms and origins.* Dublin, 1957.

—— *More Irish families.* Galway and Dublin, 1960.

—— *Supplement to Irish families.* Dublin, 1969.

—— *The surnames of Ireland.* Shannon, 1969.

Walsh, Micheline. Notes towards a biographical dictionary of the Irish in Spain: some O'Neills. In *Ir. Sword*, iv (1959–60), pp 5–15.

Webb, Alfred. *A compendium of Irish biography.* Dublin, 1878.

F COMPOSITE WORKS

Cambridge modern history. Vols ii–v. Cambridge, 1903–8.

Vol. ii (1903): The reformation; iii (1905): The wars of religion; iv (1906): The thirty years' war; v (1908): The age of Louis XIV.

COLGAN. *Father John Colgan, O.F.M. Ed.* Terence O'Donnell. Dublin, 1959.

DUNS SCOTUS. *De doctrina Ioannis Duns Scoti* (Acts of the International Scotist Congress held at Oxford and Edinburgh, 11–17 Sept. 1966). 4 vols. Rome, 1968.

Encyclopaedia of Ireland. Ed. Victor Meally. Dublin, 1968.

Father Luke Wadding. See Wadding.

NEALE. *Elizabethan government and society: essays presented to Sir John Neale. Ed.* S. T. Bindoff, Joel Hurstfield and C. H. Williams. London, 1961.

New Cambridge modern history. Vols ii–vi. Cambridge, 1958–70.

Vol. ii (1958): The reformation; iii (1968): The counter-reformation and the price revolution; iv (1970): The decline of Spain and the thirty years' war; v (1961): The ascendancy of France, 1648–1688; vi (1970): The rise of Great Britain and Russia, 1688–1715/25.

O'CLERY. *Measgra i gcuimhne Mhichíl Uí Chléirigh. Ed.* Sylvester O'Brien. Dublin, 1944.

Ó DONNCHADHA. *Féilscríbhinn Torna . . .: essays and studies presented to Professor Tadhg Ua Donnachadha* (*Torna*). *Ed.* Séamus Pender. Cork, 1947.

POBLADURA. *Miscellanea Melchor de Pobladura. Ed.* Isidorus a Villapadierna. 2 vols. Rome, 1964 (Biblioteca Seraphico-Capuccina, 23–4).

Torna. See Ó Donnchadha.

WADDING. *Father Luke Wadding: commemorative volume. Ed.* Franciscan Fathers, Dún Mhuire, Killiney. Dublin, 1957.

For composite works cited in abbreviated form, and not included in this section, see list of abbreviations at the beginning of the volume.

INDEX

All persons of rank are indexed primarily under the family name, cross references being given from the title. An exception is made for the holders of seven earldoms—Clanricard, Desmond, Kildare, Ormond, Thomond, Tyrconnell, Tyrone. These are listed under the names of their earldoms in chronological order and numbered to correspond with the succession tables given in volume VIII.

The following abbreviations are used:

abp	archbishop	L.J.	lord justice
bp	bishop	L.L.	lord lieutenant
d.	died	n.	note
dau.	daughter	pl.	plate
fl.	*floruit*	P	protestant (established church)
L.D.	lord deputy	R.C.	Roman Catholic